THE CHURCH IN THE
MODERN WORLD

CONTRIBUTORS

Volume 1

Karl Baus • Hans-Georg Beck • Eugen Ewig • Josef Andreas Jungmann • Friedrich Kempf • Hermann Josef Vogt

Volume 2

Quintín Aldea Vaquero • Hans-Georg Beck • Johannes Beckmann • Louis Cognet • Patrick J. Corish • Karl August Fink • Josef Glazik • Erwin Iserloh • Hubert Jedin • Oskar Köhler • Wolfgang Müller • Heribert Raab • Burkhart Schneider • Bernhard Stasiewski • Hans Wolter

Volume 3

Gabriel Adriányi • Quentín Aldea Vaquero • Roger Aubert • Günter Bandmann • Jakob Baumgartner • Johannes Beckmann • Mario Bendiscioli • Pierre Blet • Johannes Bots • Patrick J. Corish • Viktor Dammertz • Jacques Gadille • Erwin Gatz • Erwin Iserloh • Hubert Jedin • Oskar Köhler • Rudolph Lill • Georg May • Joseph Metzler • Luigi Mezzardi • Franco Molinari • Konrad Repgen • Leo Scheffczyk • Michael Schmolke • Antonio da Silva • Bernhard Stasiewski • André Tihon • Norbert Trippen • Robert Trisco • Ludwig Volk • Wilhelm Weber • Erika Weinzierl • Paul-Ludwig Weinacht • Félix Zubillaga

Translators

Peter W. Becker (Books 7, 8, and portions of 5) • Anselm Biggs (Books 2, 3, 4, 10, and portions of 5) • Gunther J. Holst (Book 6) • Margit Resch (Book 9)

THE CHURCH IN THE MODERN WORLD

An Abridgment of
HISTORY
OF THE CHURCH
Volumes 7 to 10

Edited by Hubert Jedin

English Translation edited by John Dolan
Abridged by D. Larrimore Holland

CROSSROAD • NEW YORK

1993

The Crossroad Publishing Company
370 Lexington Avenue, New York, NY 10017

Printed in the United States of America

Library of Congress Cataloging-in-Publication Data

The Church in the modern world : an abridgment of History of the
    church, volumes 7 to 10 / edited by Hubert Jedin ; abridged by D.
    Larrimore Holland. — Abridged ed.
        p.   cm. — (History of the church ; v. 3)
    Contents: Bk. 7. The church between revolution and restoration —
Bk. 8. The church in the age of liberalism — Bk. 9. The church in
the Industrial Age — Bk. 10. The church in the modern age.
    ISBN 0-8245-1255-3
    1. Catholic Church—History—18th century.   2. Catholic Church—
History—19th century.   3. Catholic Church—History—20th century.
I. Jedin, Hubert, 1900–   . II. Holland, David Larrimore.
    III. Series: Handbuch der Kirchengeschichte. English (Crossroad
(New York, N.Y. : Firm : 1992)) ; v. 3.
BR141.H35132   1992 vol. 3
[BX1365]
270 s—dc20
[282'.09'03]   93-28763
                                                          CIP

Contents

Section Two
The Ascension of Pius IX and the Crisis of 1848

Book Eight / Part Two
The Catholic Reaction to Liberalism

Section One
The Temporary Improvement in the Situation of the Church

Section Two
The Missions between 1840 and 1870

Section Three
Light and Shadows of Catholic Vitality

Section Four
The Altercation between Catholicism and Liberalism

BOOK NINE
THE CHURCH IN THE INDUSTRIAL AGE

Book Nine / Part One
The Problem of Adapting to the Modern World

Section Two
The Development of Catholicism in Modern Society

Section Three
Forms of Piety

Section Four
Teaching and Theology

Book Nine / Part Two
Defensive Concentration of Forces

Section One
The Reform Work of Pius X

BOOK TEN
THE CHURCH IN THE MODERN AGE

Section One
The Institutional Unity of the Universal Church

Section Two
The Diversity of the Inner Life of the Universal Church

Book Seven

THE CHURCH BETWEEN REVOLUTION AND RESTORATION

Translated by Peter W. Becker

Part One

The Catholic Church and the Revolution

Roger Aubert

The Catholic Church at the End
of the Eighteenth Century

The Crisis of the Church during the Old Regime

Today it is increasingly recognized that the "crisis of the European spirit, between 1680 and 1715," of which the French literary historian Paul Hazard wrote in 1935, was in reality a crisis of growth during which many positive elements which were important for the future attempted to find cautious expression and form on the level of thought and institutions. On the other hand, it cannot be ignored that the eighteenth century was an exceedingly difficult period for all Christian Churches and that the Roman Church especially displayed the appearance more of decadence than of renewal. While on the surface the Church still possessed the power of immeasurable riches, countless privileges, and state support, its authority was shaken. Each year there were further discords. Finally, the disparity became evident between a world which was in the process of full economic, social, and cultural development and that of a clerical hierarchy which was simply incapable of differentiating between the real requirements of faith and the nonessential accessories with which the Church and religion had surrounded themselves in the course of centuries. The Church clung tenaciously to completely obsolete positions.

This was especially evident in the case of the Holy See. Gallicanism and Febronianism were not limited to the theses of a certain school of thought. Both were more accurately the doctrinaire expression of a sentiment hostile to Rome which became more widely accepted throughout Catholic Europe. Many members of the clergy, of the higher civil service, and of the judiciary came to accept the notion that the spiritual supremacy of the Pope was nothing more than an honorary privilege. The devaluation of the authority of the Pope was strengthened by the ambiguity of his position as a small Italian territorial ruler. Under Europe's enlightened despotism, governments attempted to improve the economic conditions of their states, and to reform governmental institutions so as to provide a more rational direction, and to promote general education. In light of such circumstances, the backward administration of the Papal States generated widespread sarcastic and critical commentary. This vulnerable state was also in a rather difficult position internationally. It was the object of rivalry between Vienna, Paris, and Madrid, and thus forced its ruler constantly into accommodations and compromises. It was impossible for the Father of all the faithful to rise above party factions and to exercise his really supranational authority. Temporal power, which was demanded from the world as an irreducible prerequisite for the independence of the papacy, had in reality become an additional cause of the weakness of this institution. Other matters were becoming of even graver consequence.

With the exception of the pontificate of Benedict XIV, one must agree with Professor Rogier's assessment of the papacy in the eighteenth century. "In general, the actual influence of Rome on international happenings was extremely small; its contributions to the development of thought exhausted themselves in stereotype and sterile protest. Surveying the cultural history of the eighteenth century, one repeatedly misses the participation of the Church and its supreme leadership in the discussions of the burning issues of the period. If Rome contributed at all, it did so only negatively: with an admonition, an anathema, or an exhortation to silence. Regrettably, Rome not only failed to join in dialogue with a generation as strongly affected by the currents of the age as that of the eighteenth century, it systematically avoided it." On the eve of the upheavals of 1789, the 1740 formulation of Charles de Brosses was still valid: "If in Europe the credit of the Holy See is shrinking daily, this loss stems from an unawareness by the papacy of its antiquated modes of expression."

The broad masses of the population continued to perform their religious duties. The performance of these duties, however, was frequently more an accommodation to the structure of social tradition than a matter of conviction. In particular, the nobility and the educated bourgeoisie, under the influence of the Enlightenment, adopted an increasingly emancipated stance. Philosophy, influenced positively by the progress of the empirical sciences, and negatively by the endless and fruitless Jansenist controversies, gradually came to provide the intellectual constructs which formerly had their origins in theology. This shift was promoted by the insistence of the official Church that it was the champion of a global concept of the world, science, society, and education which was immutably fixed. Consequently, in the area of thought or of practical implementation, there was no room left for progress. The reaction against these increasingly anachronistic pretensions was unavoidable in a world obsessed by modernity. The tendency grew stronger to reorder social life on a secular basis, to glorify the autonomy of the individual against all political and clerical authorities, and to demand a "natural religion" corresponding to what man had determined. Religion was to tolerate all opinions and to replace not only ridiculous exercises of piety, regarded as revelations of superstition, but also dogmas, sacraments and the entire clerical organization.

The movement began in England and rapidly spread first to France and then to Germany. In Germany, the Protestant north quickly caught up with the Catholic south, whose urban areas after the Thirty Years War were the cultural centers of the country. After the middle of the century, the Protestant north actually became the carrier of future values, in contrast to the stagnation of the important Catholic centers of learning, for which the old Jesuitic *ratio studiorum* was in the process of becoming an antiquated iron collar. The "Catholic Enlightenment" attempted to marshal all its vital forces to defeat the Protestant challenge, to prevent the spread of religious indifference and unbelief, to fight the sclerosis of the Church of the Counter Reformation, and to bring about the victory of the mysticism of salvation parallel to the development of the profane sciences and the striving of mankind for an improvement of its earthly condition. The number of its followers, however, was relatively small. In addition, the Catholic Enlightenment was frequently compromised in France and Italy because of its relationship to the Jansenists. Above all, its searching attempts, although intuitively auguring well for the future, were for the time being a rather shy groping, which among many — similar to the fermentation following the Second Vatican Council — awakened an impression of doctrinal confusion and disintegration of traditional Catholicism. All of this could only strengthen the impression among contemporaries that Catholicism was dealing with a double crisis, because to the attacks from the outside had been added a profound internal discontent.

The responsible leaders of the Catholic Church lacked the acuity necessary to develop a new religious anthropology to respond to the message of revelation as well as the spiritual reorientation of the age. They were equally incapable of clearing away the confusion which stemmed from the Middle Ages with respect to the difference between real clerical structures based on the gospel and the aristocratic structure of the Church of the Old Regime.

Toward the end of the Old Regime many ecclesiastical institutions were failing to function well. One of the chief sources of dissatisfaction was the system of benefices. Noteworthy also were the problems within the monastic systems. It would be an inaccurate generalization to say there were not large numbers of zealous monks. But in the eyes of the world the monastery had for some time ceased to be a place to exercise the virtues of the Gospel. To be sure, monasteries were not the dens of iniquity painted in certain types of literature, but it must be admitted that the religious atmosphere within their walls was in general rather mediocre. Aside from some particularly strict orders such as the Carthusians, the Trappists, and the Carmelites, the world often regarded monasticism as an easy life which provided good incomes to the monks who administered extensive pieces of real estate and undertook expensive construction projects. The mendicant orders provoked less criticism with their lack of riches, but their members suffered from a crisis of belief to which was added, especially in the southern countries, a crisis of discipline. The opponents of monastic life criticized not only the frequent enervation of these institutions, but also asserted that the orders were totally useless to society. In their eyes only those orders were acceptable which devoted themselves exclusively to education and the care of the sick. Consequently, in the second half of the eighteenth century, it was not surprising to see governments, encouraged by public opinion, secularize a part of the monasteries. In this sense, the radical measures ultimately taken during the French Revolution were only the culmination of a policy which had been developing for a quarter of a century in all Catholic countries and against which the ecclesiastical authorities, although fully aware of the unhealthy conditions, had protested only feebly.

While the crisis was particularly painful for the monasteries, it was also felt among the secular clergy with major differences from country to country. In the Belgian provinces and in the Rhineland, for example, the situation was relatively satisfactory, but lamentable in the kingdom of Naples and in some areas of Spain. One could in fact notice during the course of the eighteenth century an attempt in many areas to upgrade the intellectual and spiritual education of the lower clergy, and, by the end of the century, educated priests and self-sacrificing pastors were more numerous than a century earlier. This did not alter, however, the existence of many abuses which an enlightened public opinion was no longer willing to countenance. In this context, as in so many others, factual determinations must not allow the historian to forget that psychological reactions also played a considerable role. A striving for an improved education did indeed exist among the lower clergy, but many became interested in Richeristic doctrines whose goal it was to reduce the authority of the Pope and the bishops and which prepared the way for the democratic notions which found a reflection in the Civil Constitution of the Clergy. The acceptance of Richeristic doctrine was facilitated by the desire of many pastors to reduce episcopal "despotism" and an unjust distribution of the income from the estates of the Church. To this must be added that in the rural areas of such countries as France the dissatisfaction created by unpopular tithing was aggravated by a feudal reaction of the landlords. Further friction arose from the attitude, taken by many civil servants, that the clergy was merely a depository of immense land wealth and that its prerogatives were dependent upon the decisions of the sovereign. This view won increasing acceptance among the circles concerned with the modernization of religious and secular institutions.

The various foundations of the power of the Church in the Old Regime, its wealth, its prestige, and its moral authority were questioned systematically. In spite of sporadic and embryonic attempts to reach a highly necessary adjustment, the Catholic Church on the eve of the revolution made a weakened impression, and the still remaining spiritual forces, whose strength became evident in the course of affliction and which were to explain why the Church was able to regenerate itself so quickly, proved ineffective. Catholic resistance was made more difficult because not only did it lack a cohesive leadership but also because of the prevailing confusion of concept and opinion regarding the role of the Church. The situation was aggravated by the fact that the upper clergy and the secular leadership were accustomed to intervention by the government in ecclesiastic affairs. Missing at the head of the Church was a highly gifted man with extraordinary energy. When the storm of revolution broke loose in France, the greater part of Catholic Europe eventually became involved. At that moment, there sat on Peter's chair a Pope who was conscientious but who lacked precisely those characteristics which were needed under such trying circumstances.

Pius VI

After the death of Clement XIV, the more than four-month-long conclave between October 1774 and February 1775 faced the nightmare question to what extent the Society of Jesus was to be dissolved. The cardinals representing the chief powers could not agree among themselves. Representatives from Austria and France desired a moderate interpretation, while those from Spain and Portugal were in favor of a radical implementation. Although both factions faced opposition from the group of so-called "zealots" who regretted Clement XIV's capitulation to the great powers, they were undecided among the several candidates. After numerous vain attempts, Zelada, who functioned as mediator, succeeded in getting all zealots to unite behind Braschi, who, although he was regarded as a partisan of the Jesuits, had kept away from political and religious controversies under the two previous pontificates. The candidacy of Braschi was supported emphatically by Cardinal de Bernis, the French legate, who skillfully managed to remove the remaining doubts of the Austrians and Spaniards. The result was Braschi's unanimous election.

Gianangelo Braschi, who adopted the name of Pius VI because of his high esteem for Pius V, was born on 25 December 1717 at Cesena in the northern region of the Papal States. He studied law and only became a priest in 1758. The protection of Cardinal Ruffo, legate at Ferrara, and his personal characteristics assured him of a quick rise in the Curia. In 1766, Clement XIII appointed him treasurer of the apostolic chamber, i.e., as secretary of the treasury, and he succeeded in improving somewhat the strongly shaken economic and financial position of the Papal States. The new Pope was indeed pious and honest, and he demonstrated irreproachable and genuine courage in the face of adversity. But Pius VI was not a prepossessing personality. He was vain, worldly, and proud of his handsome appearance. Moreover, he was determined to imitate Leo X as promoter of art and architecture. Pius VI spent large amounts of money for the beautification of the Eternal City, encouraged archeological digs, and surrounded himself with such scholars as Cardinal Garampi and Cardinal Gerdil. He also revived nepotism once more and practiced it to a greater degree than any other Pope during the eighteenth century. During the course of his quarter of a century pontificate he repeatedly showed that he lacked both energy and acuity. Pius VI was reluctant to make decisions and was totally absorbed by secondary problems of prestige. Yet Pius VI was also able to act independently. In the conclave he had been the candidate of the zealots, but he immediately disassociated himself from their position and pursued a flexible and moderate policy which did not offend the European courts. In pursuing this policy, however, he ignored his secretary of state, Cardinal Pallavicino, who had been pressed on him by the powers, and allowed the Cardinal little initiative. Concerned with both the welfare of his subjects and the defense of the rights of the Church, Pius VI conscientiously pursued the double task of secular ruler and Pontiff.

Still relatively young at the time of his election, Pius VI nurtured a number of major plans. With regard to the administration of the Papal States, he introduced reforms which were in part inspired by mercantilistic theories. These undertakings were frequently badly planned or badly implemented, but some of them are of interest. Public works projects required financial means which Pius VI did not have at his disposal and, in combination with the huge expenditures which he committed toward immortalizing his memory in Rome, led to a tremendous rise in the public debt. Pius constantly wavered between a policy of improving conditions in the Roman Campagna and a protectionist policy in the area of manufacture and trade.

From the beginning, Pius VI met with difficulty in maintaining the traditional position of the Pope. The Holy See encountered increasingly hostile public opinion toward the Curia, and governments became more determined to exact from the Pope one concession after another, with the goal of strengthening their influence over the national clergy. The situation was not altered by the fact that in France and Portugal a certain improvement of the general situation was recorded. The new French King, Louis XIV, showed himself to be favorably inclined toward the position of the Pope, and in Portugal Pombal fell into disgrace and was dismissed after the coronation of the pious queen, Mary I, in 1777. Aware of his weakness, Pius VI tried within reason to gain time. The Pope was more forceful in counteracting attempts at Jansenist reform in Rome. After hesitating for eight years, Pius VI, with the Bull *Auctorem fidei* of 28 August 1794, finally condemned the main decrees of the Synod of Pistoia. With regard to the Jesuits, he maneuvered exceedingly carefully so as not to offend the Bourbon courts, and finally tacitly allowed the Jesuits to secretly regroup themselves around the nucleus which continued to exist in the western part of the Russian Empire.

The outbreak and the subsequent effects of the French Revolution in 1789 introduced a much more threatening period for the Catholic Church in general and for the Holy See in particular. But during his last years Pius VI increasingly failed to supply a much needed decisive stance and became torn by the opposing factions of his entourage.

CHAPTER 1

The French Revolution and Pius VI

For a number of years following the French Revolution, the concept grew not only in France but also in the United States that the revolution and the period beginning around 1770 was not merely a remarkable national event, but one which comprised a part of a larger "Atlantic Revolution," which had transformed the entire western world. This interpretation is certainly justified from a social and political point of view; yet it does not change the fact that from the point of view of the Catholic Church the events which occurred specifically in France between 1789 and 1801 were totally predominant. France was not only the country with the largest Catholic population, it also was the country in which the monastic orders had their largest number of houses; the country whose theological and spiritual influence was particularly strong both for all of Europe and America. It was incontestably the epicenter of the earthquake which within a few years caused the fall of the antiquated structures of the Catholic Church in a large part of Europe and profoundly transformed the position of the Catholic Church, especially in Germany and the Netherlands, relative to the Protestant Churches. Beyond this, the policy of revolutionary France in Italy considerably affected the situation of the papacy. After a decade of conflict, the new solutions worked out by Napoleon and Pius VII influenced and lastingly determined the relationship between Church and state in the course of the nineteenth century.

The Gallican Church on the Eve of the Revolution

A first view of the Church in France in 1789 gives a solid impression of strength and power. In reality, though, its standing among the educated had been weakened. Debilitated by internal wrangles and new ideas which had found fertile soil, the level of institutions showed indications of arteriosclerosis that became ever more noticeable.

The Catholic Church in France, as in other Catholic European countries, was an official institution linked to the state and one which enjoyed significant political, juridical, and financial privileges. Roman Catholicism was the established religion in France, and as such it was supported by the secular power. The concept of religious tolerance, which increasingly had gained ground during the past several decades in the Anglo-Saxon and German states, found hardly an echo among the bourgeois institutions of France. Public divine services for non-Catholic denominations remained outlawed. Although the Protestants had succeeded by the edict of 1787 in gaining recognition for marriages performed without the services of a Catholic priest, this regulation was opposed by clergy and laymen alike. The principle of unity of faith in the kingdom thrived and toleration continued to be equated with atheism. In spite of the concessions of 1784, which were limited to Alsace, the position of Jews also remained a delicate one.

The relationship between the Church in France and the Holy See continued to be governed by the concordat of 1516, whose implementation gave rise to no major complaints. The concordat conceded important rights to the King. Among these were the right to distribute benefices. Even though in the case of bishoprics and abbeys the King was required to seek the consent of the Pope, his selection always was the decisive one. Thereby the King assured himself the loyalty of the clergy. To these rights were added the traditional esteem in which the monarch always had been held. Coexistent was the equally traditional distrust toward all ultramontane demands and the frequent differences of opinion between Rome and Versailles in the arena of international politics. The combination of these factors explains the widespread popularity of the Gallican doctrines. During this time a balance had been reached between the rights of the Holy See and the rights of the crown, and both the clergy and the faithful felt more commitment to the Pope than might be gathered at first sight.

The clergy enjoyed a predominant position in every respect. It constituted an estate equal to those of the nobility and the commoners and was in fact the only estate with an organization which acted increasingly like a pressure group of nobles. The delegates of this estate met every five years in general convention. In Paris, its representative was the *Agence Générale*. Talleyrand had succeeded between 1780 and 1785 in changing this agency into a type of permanent ministry of the clergy. The clergy retained the right to its own system of justice, although interventions by the fiscal solicitor as representative of the state became more frequent and occasionally extended even to religious matters. The French Church was divided into 135 remarkably unequal dioceses with antiquated and inexpedient districts. The clergy consisted of approximately fifty thousand priests laboring in the parishes and between fifteen thousand and eighteen thousand canons who served virtually no function. There were also twenty thousand to twenty-five thousand monks and thirty thousand to forty thousand nuns. The French clergy thus comprised approximately one hundred twenty thousand persons. Additionally, there were a large number of sacristans and chorists, as well as businessmen and staff who took care of worldly concerns. This secular and regular clergy possessed impressive economic power. It owned numerous urban buildings and, more importantly, ecclesiastical real estate in the countryside in amounts which fluctuated from region to region. In the whole country, the Church owned about 10 percent of the land and received an annual income of more than 100 million livres. The tithe, which also fluctuated from region to region and which, after 1770, led to actual peasant uprisings, produced an equal amount.

The influence of the Church was especially strong in the countryside. While the monks and cathedral canons were often regarded as burdensome landlords, the parish clergy were held in esteem, because they provided education, maintained the register, and supported the poor. In some areas, however, the peasants gradually dissociated themselves from the Church. Among many segments of society, above all among the landed bourgeoisie, local civil servants, innkeepers, and retired soldiers, free spirits abounded. The concepts of the philosophes touched not only the educated circles, but other population groups as well. This condition should not be generalized too much, however, as foreign travelers were particularly impressed by the seriousness and the piety which people displayed during services, even in such urban centers as Paris. The success of the Freemasons should not lead to erroneous conclusions about a general lack of piety. While it is true that Freemasonry created a suitable climate for the idea of a "natural religion," one which frees man from submission to a Church, no respectable historian will defend the assertion that in the lodges of the eighteenth century there existed a systematic conspiracy against the Church. This reservation must be made, because it makes comprehensible the resilience of the old religion during the storms of the revolution. On the other hand, it must be admitted that, aside from the older anticlericalism of the trade guilds, the influence of the philosophes increasingly constituted the major competition to the influence of the Church among the rising bourgeoisie.

The situation was especially apparent among the orders in France as well as elsewhere. The contemporary literature illustrates a fashionable trend toward denouncing the sloth, greed, and immorality of the monks. Countless abuses and grievances, therefore, called urgently for reforms; reforms which needed to go deeper than the rather inept efforts which had been considered by the Commission of Regulars between 1766 and 1768. It would be too simplistic to assert that on the eve of 1789 a general decadence prevailed. Spiritual laxity was the exception rather than the rule in the convents. The contemplative female orders recorded a constant stream of admissions in spite of the spirit of the time. Public opinion, formed in the light of Diderot's novel *La religieuse*, viewed the solemn vows of the old orders with hostility, but valued the services of the numerous new congregations with their simple, or total lack of, vows. With respect to the monasteries, historians note the reduction in the number of monks between 1768 and 1789. The depopulation differed among orders and between regions. The palpable existence of abuses and grievances all too easily permitted the assumption of a general decay, and one cannot overemphasize the fact of crisis within the monasteries. This condition, however, should not be equated with general decadence. It can be interpreted as a crisis of adaptation which in actuality was a sign of vitality.

Even the upper clergy, who occupied a position of major responsibility, cannot be condemned out of hand. Neither scandal, skepticism, or unbelief associated with some of the bishops, nor the worldly conduct of others, who preferred to live at court and left the administration of their dioceses to subordinates, should make one forget that the overwhelming majority of the French bishops in the second half of the eighteenth century led a life of dignity and conscientiously attempted to fulfill the duties of office. There was no lack of such genuinely pious and virtuous pastors as Lefranc de Pompignan. Members of the episcopate for some years had been recruited from the nobility and the aristocracy and therefore demonstrated the bad as well as the good characteristics of this social class. Their social background provided them with a broad education, magnanimity, and a sense of honor; but these aristocratic bishops, who owed their appointments more to their birth and their connections than to their personal qualifications, had only a superficial theological knowledge, a deficiency which was particularly alarming at the moment when the French Church required an extraordinarily strong and firm spiritual leadership. Privileges were jealousy defended and benefices were regarded as the quite natural accumulation necessary for the kind of life which these aristocratic bishops expected to be accorded their position. Moreover, bishops of this type moved almost exclusively within circles of clerics and laity from their own background. They appeared as nothing more than part of a caste system to the middle clergy of canons, seminary professors, and scholarly priests who came from the upper middle class and whose spiritual role and influence at the local level was considerable. The parish clergy, which was drawn also from the middle class, resented the arrogance of the aristocratic bishops and angrily compared the ostentatious life style of these bishops with their own often meager incomes.

There were some isolated cases, as in the Dauphiné and in Provence in 1779, where, in defiance of the law, parish priests formed a kind of labor union to effect an improvement of their situation. However, on the eve of the events of 1789, the complaints of the lower clergy were primarily concerned with the social, pastoral, and theological situation, rather than with their economic status. These sons of the middle class utilized their strength to defend an elitist position which they saw as threatened and were angered by the aristocratic pretensions displayed toward them by the bishops. They demanded from the bishops, who never bothered to consult them, the reintroduction of diocesan synods in order to discuss with them the means for a reform of the Church to achieve greater equality and spiritualization. The indifference with which the Church hierarchy responded to a movement which was agitating the lower clergy from one end of France to the other contributed to the deepening division between the bishops and the priests. Even if it did not result in actual class warfare, as it did in Nancy, there is no doubt that many priests were prepared to accept radical changes in the position of the oligarchy; an oligarchy which had established a leadership monopoly within the Gallican Church. One has to agree with A. Latreille when he writes: "The resentment of a bourgeoisie, which was aware of its economic and social importance, and enraged that the privileged classes continued to oppress them, has often been mentioned among the causes of the revolution; analogously, one must realize that a sizable portion of the clergy was convinced of the injustice of its established order and was driven spontaneously to rise against it." The meeting of the Estates General left no doubt that the Church in France constituted its own estate within the state, but one which was severely lacking in homogeneous social unity.

The Constituent Assembly and the Church

Nothing in the summer of 1789 signaled that the incipient revolution was to develop into the most dramatic period in the history of the French Church. In the grievances prepared for the Estates General, there were rather frequent complaints about the privileges and the abuses of the Church, and about the tithe and the degeneration of monasticism, but only rarely was a dissolution of the orders mentioned and even less often was the official position of the Church and its leading role in the fields of education and charity called into question. Generally, there was a desire that necessary reforms be effected with the advice and cooperation of concerned circles. Under pressure from the priests, those groups concerned with reform made a number of suggestions and supported various political, legal, and fiscal demands of the Third Estate. During the period in which the Estates General transformed themselves into the Constituent Assembly, it became clear that the clergy, after an initial hesitation, was again willing to be cooperative. On 23 June the King attempted to save the situation by closing the meeting hall. About eighty priests joined with the members of the Third Estate in refusing to disperse and, by remaining, contributed to the success of the revolution.

A few weeks later, on the famous night of 4 August, the clergy accepted almost unanimously the abolition of feudalism, the discarding of the tithe, and all of the consequences for the Church resulting from this action.

A much more radical measure was to be considered on 2 November. The increasing gravity of the financial situation made it obligatory to discuss once again the confiscation by the state of Church lands. This time, many members of the Church, who normally were favorably inclined toward reforms, resisted such a proposal. They considered it dangerous to change the clergy into salaried officials of the state. Many of the secular delegates also hesitated to break with the tradition of centuries. The Assembly's final decision was influenced more by the specter of bankruptcy than by the ideal of secularization. The Church lands were nationalized under the conditions that priests were to be paid a minimum salary of 1,200 livres, more than double the amount which many had received, and that the state would assume the care of the poor. The sale of Church lands began in the following month.

At the same time in which the Constituent Assembly dealt with the problem of Church property, it also took up the question of the monasteries, as the nationalization of Church lands implied their secularization. Many of the regular clergy were convinced in any event that monastic vows were incompatible with the Rights of Man. A decree of 13 February 1790 forbade such vows for the future and, simultaneously, dissolved all orders and congregations with solemn vows which were not active in education or the care of the sick. Monks and nuns had two alternatives: they could return to public life and draw a pension from the state or they could gather in a number of houses which would remain at their disposal until they died. The nuns were permitted to remain in their houses, which were then merely sequestered. Only in August 1792 did the Legislative Assembly dissolve all congregations, including those in the service of the poor, and complete the dispersal of the monastic orders.

Many members of the Church noted with concern the progressive destruction of the traditional structures of the Gallican Church. In Paris, several anticlerical demonstrations by the excited masses had been staged. Initially, most of the clergy, some with resignation and some with enthusiasm, accepted the religious policy of the National Assembly. The Assembly, far from having decreed the separation of Church and state, attempted to connect the Church intimately with the revolution. Subsequent developments demonstrated, however, that the general acceptance of the alliance between the Church and Third Estate had come about on the basis of mutual misconceptions. The problem of the legal status of non-Catholics caused the first major rift in April 1790. In August of the previous year, a small group of Protestant delegates, supported by liberal nobles, had demanded complete equality of religion during the vote on the Declaration of Rights of Man and the Citizen, a vote against which no objection had been raised from the Catholic side. The Assembly failed to grant the equality to Protestants, and instead limited itself to a negative formulation which provided that no one could be molested because of his convictions, including his religious beliefs. This situation subsequently was to be exploited by the forces of counterrevolution. The Catholics of the south demanded recognition of Catholicism as the established religion in the constitution. When a motion to this effect was introduced on 12 April and voted down, many Catholics saw in this rejection a national apostasy. Although this rejection had in truth a political rationale, many priests overreacted and dissociated themselves from the progressive wing of the revolution. A more serious result, was that the unrest among many Catholics was capitalized upon by several bishops in organizing resistance in the provinces against the whole religious policy of the National Assembly. Consequently, the Left became convinced of an aristocratic and clerical conspiracy. It was in this aggravated political and religious atmosphere that the debates on the new status of the French Church took place; debates which were to lead to an open break between Church and state.

The reform of the ecclesiastical organization appeared to the Constituent Assembly as a natural consequence of the general transformation of all institutions and of the radical change of the economic foundations of the French Church. The legal experts adopted the eighteenth-century principle that the Church stood within the state, and joined with numerous priests in accepting the difference in canon law between dogma and discipline. They, therefore, asserted that the Constituent Assembly had the right, as long as it did not touch doctrine, to reform ecclesiastical institutions along with all others. This was held to be doubly true as the state had agreed to pay the salaries of clergymen and thus needed to be able to control their number and recruitment. The idea of a Civil Constitution of the Clergy was born.

After two months of sometimes heated debate, the Constituent Assembly, on 12 July 1790, passed the Civil Constitution of the Clergy. It produced three substantive changes. First, dioceses were to be redivided and reduced to eighty-three and their boundaries were to be made the same as those of the Departments. Secondly, bishops, priests, and vicars were to be paid salaries by the state with the condition of performing all religious services free of charge. Thirdly, there was to be election of bishops and priests by electoral colleges on the level of Department and districts, and the canonical investment of the bishops by the metropolitan without prior confirmation by the Pope. Bishops only were to be entitled to inform the Pope of their election. Allied with this regulation was to be a severe reduction of episcopal authority through a council of priests, which was to participate in the administration of the diocese.

In spite of their appearance, these decrees had no specifically revolutionary-content. They were simply an inheritance of the past and belonged more to the Old Regime than to the new. They owed very little to a philosophy of laicistic inspiration and instead were designed to underline the intimate connection of Church and state. In their essential part, the decrees were the expression of the Gallicanism of the eighteenth century. The Constitution raised the claim to have the right to make changes in the area of religion without the participation of the Church, however, and the error of this position was stated firmly by thirty dissenting bishops (not including Talleyrand and Gobel) who were still members of the Constituent Assembly.

In Rome, even before the arrival of the first emigrants, who formed themselves into a powerful group and exerted strong antirevolutionary pressure, the reaction to the events of the summer of 1789 in France had been negative. Without focusing upon the depressing turn of events at Avignon, one discovers objections being raised to the abolition of the annates, the confiscation of Church property, and the destruction of the monasteries, as well as to the declaration of political and religious freedom which was seen as incompatible with the God-given social order. Pius VI, determined not to aggravate the position of Louis XVI, whom he trusted, decided to adopt a reserved attitude and to limit himself secretly to condemning the Rights of Man in an address to the consistory. He stuck to this cautious conduct even when he was asked to comment on the Civil Constitution of the Clergy.

On the political level, a confrontation with the French Assembly was to be avoided so as not to cause the sudden annexation of the county of Avignon, whose inhabitants were demanding union with France. On the religious level, irritation of the sensitive Gallicans was to be avoided, as well as the temptation to dictate the conduct of the French episcopate which jealously guarded its prerogatives. Finally, the view prevailed everywhere that the revolution was a fever attack which would pass quickly, and that it was better to leave things alone and not compromise oneself. The result was an eight-month irreparable delay, during the course of which in an unforeseen way a concatenation of circumstances caused the very schism which it had been hoped would be avoided.

The French bishops demanded to await the papal agreement and to put the constitution into effect only after its arrival. The death on 30 September of the bishop of Quimper forced the Constituent Assembly to a decision. It ordered the election of a successor according to the procedures laid down in the Constitution. Expilly, priest, delegate, and chairman of the religious committee, was designated by the electoral college of Finistere to fill the vacancy. This action signaled the intention systematically to ignore the Pope and to introduce without delay innovations which would make clergymen who were in no way allied with the aristocratic opposition into enemies. Demanded from all clergymen in a public function, i.e., from all bishops, priests, and vicars, the same oath as from all other civil servants, clergymen were to swear to be loyal to state, to the laws, and to the King and to protect the constitution with all of their power. Refusal to swear the oath was tantamount to resignation from office, and agitators were to be tried in court.

The Two Churches: Constituent and Refractory Priests

Much to the surprise of everyone, two thirds of the clerical representatives and all but seven bishops, four of whom were already discredited because of their unbelief or their scandalous lives, refused to take the oath. Almost half of the parish clergy refused as well. In some areas in the north and in Alsace, between 80 to 90 percent of the lower clergy refused to swear the oath. Even though in Paris and its environs and in the southeast of France a large, and sometimes very large, majority took the oath, it frequently was with reservations which the local authorities silently accepted. Moreover, recantations followed soon afterward. The National Assembly refused to rescind its decisions in spite of the disappointing vote. Although it was driven by its old longing for political unity based on religion and by an increasing desire to extirpate any and all opposition, it removed the refractory priests from their offices and substituted for them priests who had taken the oath.

The situation was different wherever massive refusals occurred. In spite of the reduction of the number of parishes, hundreds of positions needed to be filled and the number of applicants was small. Consequently, some refractory priests had to be left in office for a time. The reconstruction of the dioceses posed other problems as well, because there were virtually no metropolitans who could ordain new bishops. The newly elected clergy were to address themselves to the departmental authorities, who would nominate French bishops who would ordain them. But six of the seven prelates who had taken the oath refused to perform this function. Finally Talleyrand agreed to ordain two bishops. During the subsequent two months, Gobel, who had meanwhile advanced to the position of archbishop of Paris, ordained another twenty-six bishops.

The Pope was compelled to react. On 10 March 1791, in his Brief *Quot aliquantum,* he condemned the Civil Constitution of the Clergy because it had mortally wounded the divine constitution of the Church with its canonical investment of bishops, the election of priests, and the creation of episcopal councils. In the following Brief, *Caritas,* he declared the ordinations of the new bishops sacrilegious, prohibited them from performing their offices, and threatened with suspension all priests who refused to recant their oaths. On the same occasion, the Pope strongly condemned the declaration of the Rights of Man as contradictory to Catholic doctrine regarding the origin of the authority of the state, freedom of religion, and social inequality.

The Constituent Assembly was disappointed and fought back by expanding the required oath to still other groups of clergymen. While on the one hand the Constituent bishops denied the authenticity of the papal briefs and relied on the Gallican liberties to assert that the Pope had no authority to punish the French Church, during the summer other priests, who had honestly believed that they were permitted to take the oath, began to recant in substantial numbers. The Church, which eighteen months earlier had been so united, was now deeply cleft, and the rift increased for religious, social, cultural, and political reasons. The controversy between the two ecclesiologies, which disagreed about the rights of the Pope and of the state to intervene in the affairs of the Church, was complicated further by a far-reaching difference of opinion that the rights of man could be deduced from the Christian principle that Christianity is a religion of freedom and fraternity, and that the revolution would bring about a Christian renewal. Another part of the Church was convinced that the principle of equality necessarily had to lead to the republicanization of the Church and that the principle of liberty left the common man no opportunity to defend himself against religious error. For these clerics, the political and social principles of the Old Regime constituted the necessary prerequisites for the defense of Catholicism. For this reason, any other social philosophy which might have been able to reconcile the Catholic faith with the democratic movement was ruled out. Opposition to the Assembly grew more fierce also because the dissatisfaction of many of the faithful, who were encouraged by the priests loyal to Rome to reject the priests not recognized by Rome, was exploited by the royalist forces for the benefit of their counterrevolutionary plans.

Both hostile parties were convinced of the rightness of their positions and fought one another with passion. If, for religious reasons, most of the former bishops preferred to vacate their sees in favor of their Constituent competitors and to join the emigrants outside of France, the same was not true of all parish clergy. Frequently the non-juring priests stayed, celebrated the Mass, and contested the church-building with the new priest. In many areas the only important matter was that somehow the parish be administered, and it did not matter whether the priest had taken the loyalty oath or not, as the parishioners could not understand why an oath of a political nature should make a priest a schismatic. However, the liberality of the Constituent priests, some of whom even demanded the right to marry, together with the accusations of the non-juring priests, led many of the faithful to doubt the validity of the sacraments dispensed to them. Conflict broke out between priest and parishioners, with the faithful demanding to have "good" priests again. In the cities, where the issues were better understood, the competition between the two Churches was particularly sharp.

Persecutions and Dechristianization

The Legislative Assembly which followed the Constituent Assembly on 1 October 1791 was composed of people who were farther to the left both politically and religiously. Their major faction and driving force, the Girondists, were members of the bourgeoisie who, completely absorbed by the contemporary philosophy, had dissociated themselves from the Church and were occasionally irreligious. The Constituent Assembly had recognized that the religious unrest which spread in many areas of France, chiefly in the West, was a warning sign which threatened national unity. The Legislative Assembly, however, under pressure from the press and the political clubs in the larger cities which continued to characterize the non-jurors as bad citizens and agents of the counterrevolution, made a complete turnabout. In spite of protests from many representatives, who on the basis of the Rights of Man demanded freedom of conscience, it began to persecute its opponents. A decree of 29 November 1791 ordered that clergymen, regardless of whether they ministered to parishes or not, who did not take the oath within eight days would be regarded as rebelling against the law and as having evil intentions against the country. The veto which Louis XVI cast against the measure, as well as against the measures taken against the emigrants, compromised the priests loyal to Rome by lumping together their religious cause with the political reaction of the aristocrats.

In May 1792, France went to war with Austria and Prussia. When the Pope subsequently appointed Abbé Maury, who was known for his antirevolutionary stance, as legate to the Emperor in Germany, his action was seen as a direct challenge to the Legislative Assembly. The result was that clergymen who had refused to swear the oath because of their loyalty to the Pope now began to be regarded not merely as accomplices of the reactionaries but also as a "fifth column" prepared to assist the invaders. The "second revolution" on 10 August 1792, and the seizure of power by the radicals hastened the process. A new oath, the so-called Liberty-Equality Oath, was instituted. The oath was visibly without religious significance, and as such explains why Jacques-André Émery, a highly respected theologian and general superior of the Congregation of Saint-Sulpice, declared it as permissible. This action was followed a few days later by the September Massacres of 300 clergymen and three bishops who had been jailed in Paris prisons.

In the following months, more than thirty thousand clergymen fled the country. The lower clergy were being exiled by legal means. On 7 July 1793 two additional decrees of the National Assembly further aggravated the situation: these provided for the death penalty within twenty-four hours for all priests who had not obeyed the decree of 26 August and left France, and the deportation to Guyana of all non-officiating priests who had refused to take the Liberty-Equality Oath. In spite of this, several thousand priests endangered their lives by remaining in France and going into hiding in order to continue to dispense the sacraments to their flocks.

By the end of 1792, the situation was desperate for the clerics who had remained loyal to Rome. They were under persecution and bereft of all structural support. The Constituent Church, which had succeeded in taking hold in most of France and which occasionally had gloated over the measures taken against its rivals, soon found itself in the same unenviable situation. At first, Constituent clergy had to suffer the step-by-step deprivation of their official status. Thus began the process of separating Church and state. Then legal permission for divorces and priests to marry was decreed, and the Constituent Church found itself undermined and confronting the same stricture of conscience as the non-jurors of 1791. Torn between compliance with the law and adherence to its theological principles, the Constituent Church split into two camps. Much to the great consternation of their confreres for whom the intervention of the state in ecclesiastical matters had gone much too far, a number of priests and a few bishops pushed revolutionary logic so far as to marry. The second camp of the Constituent Church sincerely deplored the political development which had led from a limited monarchy to a republic. Now the Constituent Church also began to be called an enemy of the people. The enormous wave of dechristianization which swept over the country between the summer of 1793 and the summer of 1794 completed the ruin of the Constituent Church and drove it underground.

Often, what was seen in the course of the revolutionary changes was a more or less vehement reaction against the excessive interference of the Church in the everyday life of the population. This effect was aggravated by the fact that the entire Church, Constituent as well as Roman, was regarded as a social class politically hostile to the Jacobin ideology.

Although it is known now that the National Convention and the majority of the Committee of Public Safety were opposed to exaggerated hostility toward religion, extremists succeeded in pushing through a number of radical measures designed to extirpate any and all of the country's memories of the Christian legacy. The old calendar was replaced by a republican calendar; Sundays were eliminated in favor of the tenth day of the three decades into which each month was divided; purely secular feast days were organized; and a revolutionary cult of the Goddess of Reason was introduced, although its ridiculousness was soon recognized and countered by Robespierre's own spiritualistic cult of the Supreme Being. The persecution of suspected clergymen was stepped up and pressure was exerted to effect the apostasy of priests. Most of the churches were closed or torn down, and their liturgical equipment was looted. Even the lodges of the Freemasons were not spared, an act which confirms the predominant political motivation of the measures. It should be noted, however, that radicalism was implemented with little overall planning and frequently was of temporary duration. Its effect was minimized wherever the faith was still strong, ecclesiastics could organize effective resistance, and in areas where religious conformism was shaken by the excesses of the reign of terror and genuine revivals were taking place. However, enormous dislocations, whose traces were visible for a long time, occurred in those areas which had been undermined by skepticism or, as was the case around Paris and Vendée, had experienced the systematic extremism of nearby large urban areas.

The Separation of Church and State

Confronted by the growing dissatisfaction of the population, the National Convention was forced to reverse its course. At first it attempted to stop the attempts to finish off Catholicism. When this met with qualified success, the Convention moved in the direction of separation of Church and state, a move more motivated by the pressure of events than by philosophical preference. In April 1794, the payment of salaries to the Constituent priests was stopped, and on 18 September the budget item for public religious exercises was officially removed. In France itself freedom of religion was demanded and was granted by the decree of 21 February 1795, although with some important reservations. Catholics, for example, were prohibited from using churches. However, the fall of Robespierre was erroneously interpreted in many of the provinces as the end of the system of oppression, and many churches reopened spontaneously and many priests, resumed their priestly functions. The Convention had no choice but to accept these changes as accomplished facts, and a new decree of 30 May 1795 liberalized the previous one.

The Church, however, was split over the permissibility of the oath. Some were of the opinion that this oath had a purely political meaning, while others regarded it as a global submission to legislation, totally in opposition to the principles of the Church. Dissension increased with regard to the reconciliation of Constituent priests, priests who had resigned from their offices, and repentant married priests. Some churchmen, led by Émery and the eleven bishops who had remained in France, were in favor of leniency, which they felt was justified by the extraordinary circumstances; while others, on the advice of the emigrated bishops, demanded humiliating recantations and long atonements. An additional confrontation arose between the followers of the Jesuits and the Jansenists over the question of what attitude should be taken toward the faithful. Here it was a conflict between the active priests, who were of the opinion that the salvation of souls could compensate for many arrangements with regard to doctrinal strictness, and the purists, who placed above purity even evangelization.

These controversies made the restoration of the Catholic religion immensely more difficult. In many cases extraordinarily confused situations arose because most of the legitimate bishops remained outside of France. However, until 1797, the reorganization of the Church was largely successful, and many emigrated priests returned, even though it was difficult for them to adapt to radically altered conditions.

Paralleling these attempts, the Constituent Church, which now presented itself as the Gallican Church, also tried to attain a renewal. In August 1797, they succeeded in bringing about a National Council, the ground for which had been prepared by consulting the diocesan presbyteries. More interested in giving preference to quality than quantity and in planting in France a Church true to Catholic tradition, these men jointly worked out a rechristianization program. The program had the merit of making allowances for the psychological and structural shifts and for the universal longing and changes in mentality which were the constant preoccupation of the priests who had remained in France. This attempted reform met with many obstacles. Foremost was a shortage of qualified people, because both episcopate and Church had been decimated by resignations, marriages, deaths, and still increasing recantations. Added to these problems were the internal struggles between episcopalists and presbyterians, and between adherents and opponents of the use of the native language in worship.

At the beginning of the Directory, Catholics of both persuasions enjoyed relative freedom. They were permitted to distribute their own publications; the *Annales de la religion* by the Constituents, and the *Annales religieuses, politiques et littéraires* by the Romans. At the end of the summer of 1797, however, the political crisis which led to the coup d'état of 18 Fructidor again endangered the precarious improvement of the preceding two years. Not without reason, the Directory accused the Catholic clergy of continuing to support the royalist opposition and decided to return to a sharply anticlerical policy.

Much more important were the measures taken against the priests. All priests were required to swear a new oath of "royal hatred." A number of bishops and casuists considered it acceptable, while all of the emigrated bishops and many theologians declared publicly that it was insupportable, especially for a priest, to make God witness to a vow of hatred. Pius VI again declined to publicize this hostile decision officially. A strong minority of the priests swore the oath in the conviction that its formulation made it the lesser of two evils and that to take it would be better than to leave their flocks again without worship or religious instruction. Many priests refused to take this oath, however, and became subject to legal punishments which, while no longer as bloody as during the reign of terror, were of a more calculated cruelty. These priests were either incarcerated in prison ships or deported to Guyana.

Certain positive facets of this situation must not be overlooked. Many of the faithful, who earlier had practiced a largely passive conformism, now became aware of their responsibility to the Church. In areas where there were no longer any priests, prayer meetings were organized, children were given religious instruction, and Mass was celebrated. Former nuns took advantage of the article of the Constitution of the Year III which permitted private instruction and formed new groups, thus preparing during this chaotic time for the resumption of monastic life. Another indication of the surviving vitality of the French Church during these harsh times were the Daughters of the Heart of Mary, whose congregation was founded in 1791 in the search for a modern form of life devoted to God and adjusted to the new conditions. By 1799 there were 267 Daughters of the Heart of Mary in ten dioceses from Brittany to the Jura. The members of this new congregation wore no external sign, retained their occupations, and continued to live with their families.

Effects in Neighboring Countries

By the end of 1792, the French Republic was bent on conquest. In November 1792, it annexed Savoy and shortly afterward Nice, both belonging to the Kingdom of Sardinia, and in March 1793, the region of Pruntrut in the Jura, from which the Department of Mont-Terrible was formed. Belgium, at that time comprised of the Austrian Netherlands and the Ecclesiastical Principality of Liège, was first occupied in the winter of 1792–93, reoccupied after the victory of Fleurus in June 1794, and annexed on 1 October 1795. The left bank of the Rhine, which had been occupied temporarily in the fall of 1792, was again occupied in the summer of 1794. French institutions were introduced, but the Rhine territory was not officially incorporated into France until the time of Napoleon. The Greek islands won from Venice were annexed in October 1797, and French authorities were brought in contact with the Orthodox Church. Geneva became a French Department in April 1798, and Piedmont was annexed in February 1799. With the aid of the army of the Directory six satellite republics were created on the borders of France, whose institutions corresponded to those of the *Grande Nation.* These were the Batavian Republic (1795), the Cisalpine Republic and the Ligurian Republic (1797), the Roman Republic and the Helvetic Republic (1798), and the Parthenopean Republic (1799). Together with the principles of 1789 and the institutions which embodied them, France also exported its religious policy to these countries, aided by the French army. The army was not interested in providing those populations which clung firmly to their belief with additional reasons for resistance. It was eager to prevent brutal conduct and local traditions survived best in the religious sphere.

Belgium was a country strongly rooted in the Catholic religion. Its reaction to the reform attempts of Joseph II had proven clearly how ultramontane it was. Therefore, the occupation troops at first were considerate of the "prejudices" of the population. The Convention ordered the confiscation of Church property, but delayed its sale for months. Only in the summer of 1796 did the Directory dare to transfer civil registers to the authorities of the state and to close the monasteries. Even then, the orders devoted to education and the care of the sick were not touched. The Cult of Reason destroyed monasteries and profaned churches.

Aside from the short and bloody persecution of the summer of 1794, however, the exercise of religion was little affected until 1797.

The Belgian Church rejected the oath much more completely than in France, even though several vicars general considered it permissible. Conditions worsened with the arrival of Fructidor. The congregations which had been spared so far were dispersed, the University of Louvain and the seminaries were closed, the wearing of clerical garb was prohibited, and each priest was obligated to take the oath of hate against royalty as a precondition for conducting religious ceremonies. The majority of the clergy refused to take the oath. Shortly thereafter the priests were unjustly made responsible for the peasant revolts in Kempenland and the Ardennes, and the government ordered all non-jurors to be deported. Only about 10 percent of the priests actually were arrested, however, because the almost unanimous help of the population enabled them to hide themselves and to exercise their pastoral tasks in secrecy.

In the Rhineland, the French occupation did not affect the structure of the Church. Initially the troops, who did not molest the Protestants, adopted a hostile stance toward the Catholic clergy because of its resistance to the propaganda for unification with France. The commander of the Army of the Rhine, introduced a much more moderate religious policy. He granted favorable treatment to the lower clergy and allowed the orders to continue, and his successor continued this policy after his death. No restrictions were placed on the continued exercise of religion within the churches, and clergymen continued to receive their salaries from the sequestered Church lands. But the bishops who had emigrated to the right bank of the Rhine incited the priests and monks against the French, which resulted in a stiffer attitude toward the monasteries in particular, even though they were not closed. As in Belgium, the Rhineland population also helped those priests to go underground who had run into difficulties with the occupation forces. The local authorities also frequently sabotaged the measures against the Church.

In the former United Netherlands, in contrast to Belgium and the Rhineland, Protestantism was the privileged religion, and Catholics were oppressed by the ruling oligarchy. Therefore, they generally acclaimed the French revolutionaries as liberators, much to the dismay of Nuncio Brancadoro, who headed the Dutch mission. Only the southern provinces, which initially had witnessed the hostility of the French troops toward the Belgian Church, remained rather reserved. The majority of the Catholic clergy, on the other hand, under the leadership of a group of Amsterdam priests supported the Patriot Party, which early in 1795 overthrew the Old Regime with the aid of the French. The constitution of the new Batavian Republic granted Catholics full civil rights and complete freedom of religion, and most of the priests at once took the oath of "eternal hate" against the Old Regime.

The time of the Batavian Republic was for the Catholics in the United Netherlands a period of emancipation and progress, without dissonances and persecutions. Inasmuch as the University of Louvain had been closed by the French, three seminaries were opened in the Batavian Republic in 1799. Beyond this, a few Catholic notables and a number of priests drew the logical consequence from the new liberal regime which resulted from the separation of Church and state.

In Switzerland, as well, the Catholics were less numerous than the Protestants. Until the end of the eighteenth century they had been grouped in homogeneous masses in the nearly sovereign cantons. On the basis of the constitution of the Helvetic Republic created in 1798, they suddenly found themselves as a minority in a Protestant state, a circumstance which led to great discontent and to armed revolts in Wallis and the small original cantons. While the constitution granted freedom of religion and conscience, it contained some limitations directed at the Catholics and their relationship to the papacy. With respect to the practical implementation of these ordinances, the Roman Church suffered additional limitations. The Helvetic government prohibited those bishops who resided outside of Switzerland, and this was true in most cases, from exercising their jurisdiction in Switzerland. The right to assign benefices, the tithe, and the separate judicial system of canon law were abolished. Although not all orders were dissolved, they were forbidden to recruit novices, their lands were sequestered, and some monasteries were closed immediately. In contrast to Holland, Jews were not granted legal equality. Thus the religious policy of the Helvetic Republic differed fundamentally from the liberal religious policy of the Batavian Republic.

In Italy, the religious policy had a much more conservative character. The understanding with the French occupation forces was facilitated by the fact that numerous Italian priests and officials, who earlier had been won to Josephinist policies, were inclined to regard positively any reform measures directed against ultramontane practices. At the same time, the leaders of the French military and many Italian patriots who wanted to introduce a republican form of government strove not to alienate the broad mass of the people, which was strongly Catholic. Bonaparte, the commander of the Army of Italy, because he was both a realist and of Mediterranean background, understood the situation much better than the Directory. He made a few concessions to the hardline Italian Jacobins, and depended chiefly on moderate Catholics.

The Zispadanic Republic was comprised of the Duchy of Modena and the provinces of Romagna and Emilia which had been taken from the Pope. During the sessions devoted to the writing of the constitution for the new republic, the problem of the position of the Church in the state had led to passionate discussion. Catholicism became the established religion of the republic (the Jewish religion was tolerated but did not receive equality) because religion "constrains the masses." After brief hesitation, Bonaparte concurred with this article even though it completely deviated from the principles of the Directory, because he realized that this would win him the sympathy of the people and the clergy. But a few months later, in 1797, when he himself wrote the constitution of the Cisalpine Republic, he returned to the principle of complete equality of religions and the religious neutrality of the state. Consequently, many clergymen, although they favored the republican system, felt that their consciences did not permit them to take the oath under these circumstances. In the process of the practical application of the constitution local influences became noticeable. Concrete reality resulted in the following: while separation of Church and state had been nearly accomplished in France, the Catholic Church in the Cisalpine Republic depended strongly upon the state and was subjected to a renewed Josephinism. The only really new aspect was religious equality, although civil equality of Jews was not implemented without resistance by the population.

The constitution of Rome in 1798 and that of the Parthenopean Republic in 1799 adopted the principle of separation of Church and state from the constitution of the year III and the constitution of the Cisalpine Republic. In contrast, the constitution of the Ligurian Republic appears as the most Catholic of all of the constitutions adopted on the Italian peninsula. The majority of the clergy protested against this intention, and Bonaparte, eager to avoid conflict, urged a change in the draft in order to accommodate the priests and monks. The Jansenists immediately availed themselves of freedom of the press, revived Degola's *Annali politico-ecclesiastici,* and continued to plead their case after the ratification of the constitution. Their harsh criticism of the wealth of the monasteries, together with the criticism of the writers of the Enlightenment, who also were interested in a thorough ecclesiastical reform, led to the law of 4 October 1798, which permitted the dissolution of certain monasteries if this were deemed of value to the state.

Although the revolutionary period in Italy from 1796 to 1799 changed the institutional situation of the Catholic Church in Italy much less than elsewhere, one cannot conclude that this brief period was without significance.

The attitude of the Italian clergymen was differentiated. Many priests, chiefly from the upper clergy, faced the new regime with distrust, but only a few resisted from the beginning. Most of them considered it wise in view of the conciliatory stance of the French to go along with them and to attempt to save as many rights of the Church as possible. They promoted reconciliation with the new governments by pointing to the indifference of the Church toward matters of civil authority. Many of the clergy, including some bishops, emphasized the Christian character of the principles of equality and fraternity. Others went further and openly welcomed the French republicans. While constituting only a small minority, they had a large influence because they included monks who had been absolved of their vows, as well as many intellectuals and honorable priests. It is better to speak with V. Giuntella of "Catholic democrats" if one wishes to characterize priests and laymen who endeavored to return to the sources of Holy Scripture and patristics and to separate the essence of the Christian faith from the contingent aspects which it had assumed in the course of centuries. The Catholic democrats thought they could demonstrate the complete harmony of genuine Catholicism with democracy by separating the spiritual area from the secular.

Today the profound differences between these groups are more easily recognizable. Most of the Jansenists cooperated with the Jacobins in order to obtain a new religious policy, but this was only a tactical alliance. After the Jansenists failed to obtain backing for their program from the princes, they saw in the structural reforms which the Jacobins urged out of hostility toward the Church the prerequisite for a return to the Church in its original purity. This was the intention of Degola, who devised a plan for the civil organization of the Ligurian Church. The aim of the plan was to free this Church from the authority of Rome and to rejuvenate it according to the example which the French Constituent Church had provided in keeping with the guidelines worked out by Grégoire at the national council of 1797. Such sympathies with the Civil Constitution of the Clergy should not be misunderstood, however. There were, after all, fundamental differences between the Jacobins who wanted to destroy the Church and the Jansenists who wanted to reform it. Most of the Jacobins were Deists and put their trust in human nature; the Jansenists, disciples of Augustine, regarded the principles of

1789 with distrust and interpreted the enthusiasm of the Jacobins for liberty and progress as Pelagianism. Thus the Jansenists and the democratic Catholics, regardless of their frequent cooperation in the area of practical implementation, adopted fundamentally different points of view on an ideological level.

The common efforts of the Catholics and Jansenists favorably inclined toward the French Revolution formed a significant connection between the writers of the Enlightenment of the 1770s and the reformers at the Synod of Pistoia, on the one hand, and liberal Catholics and reformers of the 1830s, on the other, a connection which deserves the special attention of the historian. At that time, however, their expectations were quickly disappointed. The resumption of persecutions in France after Fructidor, the looting of Church treasures and monasteries, and finally the expulsion of the Pope from Rome awakened in many the fear of a return to the antireligious excesses of the years 1793–94. Such apprehensions together with other social and political stresses resulted in 1799 in several popular revolts. These revolts, frequently led by priests or monks, appeared as a defense of the faith against those who cooperated with the occupation forces. The democratic Catholics, never more than a minority, lost all credibility among the broad masses, and the political developments after 18 Brumaire completed their total defeat. The concordat concluded between Bonaparte and Pius VII destroyed the plans of the Jansenists to establish in Italy a rejuvenated Church according to the example set by the French Constituent Church.

The Destruction of the Holy See

The revolutionary wave which swept over Italy did not spare the Papal States. The central administration of the Church was damaged to such a degree that many came to the conclusion that they were witnessing the end of the papacy as an institution.

The events in France left Pius VI in a particularly difficult position. He felt lonely after the departure of his secretary of state, Boncompagni, and was informed rather tendentiously. The émigrés who flooded Rome during the first two years saw the events through the distorted lens of their own political prejudices. After the termination of diplomatic relations between Paris and Rome in May 1791 there remained only one official envoy in France, who combined much naivety and vacillation with exaggerated obstinacy.

At the beginning of 1791, Pius VI had missed the opportunity clearly to define the true significance of his condemnations of the revolution. In spite of suggestions by several French bishops and representatives of the Constituent Assembly, he refused to deal with the difference between the necessarily immutable principles of religious order and acceptable transactions in the civil sphere.

This situation changed drastically, however, in the spring of 1796 after the lightning strikes of General Bonaparte and the occupation of Milan. In the preceding year, Pius VI had contemptuously rejected an offer of the Spanish ambassador, Azara, to mediate between France and Rome with a view toward resuming full relations. Confronted with the new dangers, the Pope was now prepared to avail himself of such mediation services, but initial talks foundered on the French con-

ditions. The French demanded heavy reparations, and above all the renunciation
of all condemnations which the Pope had uttered against the Civil Constitution
of the Clergy and the revolutionary principles since 1790. After the French conditions were rejected by Rome, Bonaparte occupied the northern portion of the
Papal States. A march on Rome was threatened when negotiations continued to
stall. Now the Pope, who feared a revolt of his subjects if the French advanced,
decided to submit in order to save the essentials. On 20 June an armistice was
signed which contained only territorial and financial clauses; the problem of his
renunciation of his condemnations was postponed until a treaty of peace.

The negotiations for a peace treaty began in Paris during the summer. Following Azara's advice, the Curia composed a memorandum which reminded French
Catholics that the true faith was not created to overturn civil laws and which recommended their submission to the government. This action implicitly recognized
the legality of the government's existence. The Directory, however, was not satisfied with the concession of the Brief *Pastoralis sollicitudo,* although it was so
significant that Royalists and Romans alike thought it incredible. Upon the urg-
ings of Grégoire, who at all costs wanted to prove that the Constituent Church
had never ceased its ties to Rome, the Directory continued to demand from the
Pope the renunciation of the condemnations of the Constituent Church. Pius VI
refused, of course. In the meantime, the military situation in Italy appeared to
develop favorably for Austria, and Secretary of State Zelada, who favored a conciliatory approach, was replaced by Cardinal Busca. Busca called off the armistice
and attempted in vain to persuade the kings of Spain and Naples as well as the
Emperor to resume armed resistance. As soon as Bonaparte had solved his problems in northern Italy, he began preparations to march on Rome and forced the
Pope, on 16 February 1797, to accept the treaty of Tolentino. By agreeing to additional heavy reparations and ceding to France the wealthiest part of his states,
the Pope saved his secular position which, in view of the current conditions, he
regarded as the indispensable foundation for the functioning of the government
of the Church. Bonaparte, who now felt strong enough to ignore the orders of the
Directory, also no longer spoke of a renunciation of earlier papal documents, and
thereby laid the groundwork for the future religious pacification of France.

After the bellicose Cardinal Busca had been replaced by the moderate fran-
cophile Cardinal Doria, and after France had appointed as its emissary in Rome
Joseph Bonaparte, the brother of the general who had refused to destroy the
Holy See, the Pope could rest in the conviction that the essence of his power
had been saved. However, the situation deteriorated again. In France the coup
d'état of Fructidor restored the old virulence of Jacobin anticlericalism. In this
tense atmosphere, General Duphot was assassinated on 27 December 1797. The
Directory, dominated by La Révellière-Lépeaux, a sworn enemy of Catholicism
and apostle of the new religious movement of Theophilanthropy, ordered the immediate occupation of the Papal States. On 15 February 1798 Roman Jacobins,
covertly led by French agents, proclaimed the Roman Republic.

The Pope, now eighty-one years old, pleaded to be allowed to die in peace in
Rome. Instead, he was forced to flee to the still-independent Duchy of Tuscany.
Thus, to some degree the Pope promoted the formation of the second coalition
against France. Its successes induced the French, who had occupied Tuscany, to

deport Pius VI to France. The dying Pope was transported first to Grenoble, and then to Valence, where he died on 29 August.

At this point little remained of the former machinery of the Holy See. The work of the Curia was totally disorganized, the Sacred College was dispersed, and several cardinals had been imprisoned. It was not surprising that many people thought, some with joy and others with apprehension, that with the death of Pius VI, the papacy as the coping stone of the Catholic Church was disappearing under the hammer blows of the French Jacobins.

CHAPTER 2

Napoleon and Pius VII

The Election of Pius VII and the
First Restoration of the Papal States

Pius VI realized that the next conclave would take place under quite extraordinary circumstances. For this reason he decreed even before his death that it should be convoked by the most senior cardinal at a place in the territory of any Catholic sovereign. For this reason Cardinal Albani, the senior cardinal of the Sacred College who, with many other cardinals had fled to Venice (Austrian territory since 1797), preferred to place the conclave under the protection of Emperor Francis II. Two parties quickly opposed one another. The first was composed of the "politicals," whose concern was to adapt themselves to the new European situation and to maintain the bridges with France; they were discreetly supported by Spain. The other consisted of the "zealots," whose primary interest was to retain the heritage of the past undiminished and to maintain good relations with Austria. Good relations with this state seemed important to them because of Austria's hostility toward France and because they considered it the best means to regain from the Emperor the largest portion of the Papal States, which he had meanwhile conquered. The "politicals" were led by Cardinal Braschi and agreed on Cardinal Bellisomi, who quickly was able to obtain two-thirds of the votes. The "zealots" were led by the authoritarian Cardinal Antonelli, who was moved by the consequences resulting from an objective analysis of the situation. They were supported by Maury, the only French cardinal present who acted under power of attorney from Louis XVIII (whom the Sacred College had officially recognized as King of France, after Pius VI had steadfastly refused to do so) and by the Austrian cardinal Herzan, who was ordered to express the imperial veto against any candidate suspected of not being fully behind Vienna. The candidate of this party was Mattei, moderately opposed to the French. The bumbling manner with which the Emperor's plenipotentiary opposed the almost certain election of Bellisomi and pushed that of Mattei irritated the majority, and Mattei's last chances were gone when the cardinals learned that Spain would in no way recognize him. Spain was being directed by Bonaparte, who meanwhile had become France's virtual master. For three months a stalemate existed. By 12 March there was the outline of a solution: Antonelli was to get the support of the zealots — who would thus have the honor of having cast the decisive votes — for Cardinal Chiaramonti. A moderate and intelligent man, he had consistently voted with the "politicals," but had not made enemies of the opposition. Be that as it may, Antonelli agreed to this compromise solution and so did Herzan after a discussion with the new candidate. Within forty-eight hours everything was settled and on 4 March 1800, Chiaramonti, in spite of the unconcealed displeasure of Maury was elected with only one negative vote. For reasons of devotion to his predecessor, who had also been his protector, he assumed the name of Pius VII.

Barnaba Chiaramonti came from a noble family. In mature age he displayed energy tempered by friendliness, an untiring patience, and realism fed by acuity and a sense of proportion. In contrast to his predecessors in the eighteenth century, who chiefly had been administrators or politicians, he turned out to be a man of doctrine and a shepherd of souls, always interested in distinguishing between the spiritual and the secular concerns of the Church and always giving pronounced preference to the religious goals. He had the courage of his convictions, but always had great tolerance for opinions which differed from his own. His earlier experiences prepared him well for the serious problems which a world in full transition posed for the Holy See. During the conflict which in the eighteenth century confronted the supporters of the Jesuits with those who were vaguely called "Jansenists," the young Chiaramonti did not fight on the side of the Jesuits. Later, during the three years of revolution, he did not regard the undifferentiated condemnation of the principles of 1789 as the best method for defending religious interests.

The catalogue of his library at that time reveals that his mind was open to the modern ferment of thought; his library held few works of Scholastic theology, but many critical editions of the Church Fathers, works by Muratori, Mabillon, Martène, and Tillemont, and the *Encyclopedia* of d'Alembert and Diderot. As a diplomatic mediator he had an outstanding ability to hold without breaking and to reconcile without bending. Shortly after the French invasion took place, he preached a sensational homily on Church and democracy at Christmas 1797. He declared that the democratic form of government was not in opposition to the Gospel, and that religion was even more important in a democracy than in any other form of government. During the three-year existence of the republic he constantly attempted to separate the political and religious aspects of problems, tried not to identify the clergy with the opposition to the democratic regime, and demonstrated his ability to compromise in trivial matters in order to preserve the essentials.

Immediately after his election, the new Pope demonstrated that he had insight, was independent, and decisive. He refused Herzan's recommendation to appoint as his secretary of state a cardinal who was obligated to Austria. Instead his choice was Consalvi, the young prelate to whom he owed his tiara. Consalvi was a conservative reformer, in keeping with the enlightened spirit of the eighteenth century, possessing both energy and flexibility. Consalvi had no experience in diplomacy but assisted the Pope, who concentrated on the religious aspects of problems, with his strong talent for an intelligent and cautious policy. He remained his right-hand man until the end of his pontificate.

Consalvi began his diplomatic and administrative tasks without delay. One was the restitution of the papal territories occupied by Austrians, Neapolitans, and Frenchmen. Although the French maintained their position, the others eventually gave in and gradually the powers restored their representations at the Holy See. Another problem was a papal administration completely disorganized. Consalvi was fully aware of these matters, which were aggravated by numerous abuses, and was prepared to introduce a number of innovations, but encountered the reactionary opposition of the majority of the Curia. For this reason the papal Bull *Post diuturnas* of 30 October 1800, provided only for a rather modest reform of institutions. It removed a number of evident abuses and added a few noble laymen to an administration which heretofore was completely reserved for clergymen. Economically, a number of useful steps were taken. These were chiefly freedom of trade (11 March 1801); a limited land reform (15 September 1802); a compromise solution with respect to the secularized estates of the Church; a partial solution for the catastrophic financial condition; and a simplification of the fiscal system. Thus the Papal States, undermined by passive resistance of opponents from right to left, in spite of some incontestable improvements remained in an extraordinarily precarious administrative and economic situation until its annexation by Napoleon.

The Concordat of 1801

Shortly after the return of Pius VII to Rome, at the very time when the renewed arrival of French troops for the purpose of restoring the republic was feared, the Bishop of Vercelli arrived with a suggestion by the First Consul to begin negotiations with the aim of settling the religious affairs of France.

Immediately after the elimination of the Directory by the coup d'état of 18 Brumaire (9 November 1799), a reduction of tension on the religious level had set in. The persecution of the non-oath takers was suspended, many churches reopened again, and adherence to the "decades" was no longer obligatory. All of this indicated that the policy of systematic dechristianization was being abandoned. This development, regretted by many republicans in leading positions, was the direct result of a decision by the First Consul. It was not made for religious reasons but for political ones. He had become convinced that France, especially rural France, wished to remain Catholic, and his experiences in Italy had taught him that in a Catholic country the influence of priests constitutes a power which it is better to use than to fight. He also sensed that an agreement with the papacy would redound to his prestige among Italians, Spaniards, and the great powers of the Old Regime. The victory of Marengo (14 June 1800) enabled him to negotiate with Rome from a position of strength. He hurried to exploit his opportunity without worrying too much about the discontent of the numerous opponents of the Church among political and administrative officials, in the army and among the buyers of Church lands. Pius VII on his part knew well that a better understanding with revolutionary France would be protested strongly by a large segment of the Curia and the majority of the émigrés. He was irritated when he realized that Napoleon wanted to bargain for an agreement, but also immediately recognized the tremendous advantage which he could gain. He understood completely what the restoration of peace and religious unity in the most important Catholic country of Europe would mean for the Holy See and for a French Church shaken to its foundations. Besides, a ceremonious act of international law would also acknowledge the superior position of the *pontifex maximus* at the head of the Catholic hierarchy.

Negotiations were begun, proved to be extraordinarily protracted, and were concluded successfully only after a year. After four drafts a fifth one was finally sent to Rome, where the second phase of negotiations took place between March and May. Angered by the Roman delays, Bonaparte transmitted an ultimatum and Pius VII decided to send Consalvi with power of attorney to Paris. In the time from 20 June to 15 July frequently stormy discussions took place at the highest level. Until the last minute there was the danger of a termination of the negotiations, for Bonaparte absolutely refused to yield in several points, as he had to reckon with the stiff-necked opposition of a large part of his entourage, among whom Jacobin anticlericalism remained virulent. But Consalvi used all of the abilities of his flexible genius in order to achieve the acceptance of conciliatory formulations, and an agreement was finally reached at midnight on 15 July.

The relatively brief text, including the recognition by the Pope of the republic as the rightful government of France, was preceded by a preamble in which the Catholic religion was acknowledged as "the religion of a large majority of Frenchmen." This was a compromise wording, for the Curia had insisted that the Catholic religion be acknowledged as the dominant religion among all religions whose equality before the law was tacitly affirmed by Rome. Article 1 declared the Catholic religion to be public and free, but with the limitation that "it must agree with police regulations which the government might pass in the interest of maintaining public peace." Consalvi had vainly tried to exclude this clause, as it seemed to open the door to all kinds of chicanery, but had to be satisfied with the addition of the last part of the sentence which at least put a limit on capricious acts. After this basic declaration, which carried with it the renunciation of all earlier laws of restrictive character, the subsequent articles had a double objective.

The difficulties which had arisen between Church and state since 1790 were to be removed and the French Church was to be reorganized on new foundations. Two problems created difficulties. One was the sale of nationalized Church lands, with which the Holy See agreed after it had vainly attempted to achieve at least the restitution of those lands which had not yet been sold. The second was the existence of a dual episcopate. Bonaparte quietly left the Constituent Church to its own devices, and the Pope agreed in embarrassed language (Article 3) to ask all surviving bishops of the Old Regime for their resignation in order to clear the way for the creation of a totally new episcopate. With respect to the future organization of the Church of France, only general principles were stated. These included the right of the Holy See to a reorganization of the dioceses, and the right of bishops to a reorganization of the parishes, but in both cases only with the prior agreement of the government; the appointment of bishops as under the Old

Regime by the head of state, their canonical investment by the Pope; appointment of parish priests by the bishops after agreement by the government; the right of bishops to a cathedral chapter and a seminary, but without any obligation of the government to pay for their maintenance; the obligation of the government to pay appropriate salaries to bishops and parish priests as compensation for the nationalization of Church lands; and finally, in spite of initially brusk rejection, the right of the faithful to make gifts to the Church. Nothing was said in the concordat about religious congregations.

Now the compromise had to be ratified. Without a doubt it was of considerable benefit for both sides. It strengthened Bonaparte's prestige, confirmed several important accomplishments of the revolution, and conceded to the French government the right to control the Church in several significant areas. On the other hand it was the Holy See which had granted these privileges to the state on the basis of its own authority and not on the basis of a right of the state. This afforded the Church a good deal of satisfaction, as it was a matter of principle. Furthermore, the schism which had split the Church for more than ten years was healed and the foundation had been laid for a modernized restoration of the old ideal of a Christian Church based on the state. Finally, last but not least, the right of the Pope to intervene in the affairs of national Churches was strengthened. To be sure, every or almost every article contained as many intended or inadvertent ambiguities as it resolved. Pius, however, ignored the vote, publicly declared the Holy See's acceptance on 15 August 1801, and asked the legitimate bishops to submit their resignations. In Paris, strangely enough, Bonaparte hesitated to confront the hostility of the deliberative assemblies. In order at least partially to counter their objections, which were supported by the determined resistance of Talleyrand and Fouché, he resorted to a subterfuge: the text of the "Convention de Messidor," as the concordat was officially called in France, was submitted for approval with two other bills. One regulated the Protestant religion, attesting the willingness to be totally nonpartisan in religious questions, and the other placed Catholics under a comprehensive church regulation, consisting of seventy-seven "Organic Articles."

They in part retracted what had been conceded, as the Church was now being subordinated to the state in the old royal fashion. The clergy required the permission of the government before it could publish papal documents, convoke a provincial or national council, create new parishes, and even establish private chapels. Seminarians had to be taught about the Declaration of 1682; the old diocesan catechisms had to be replaced by a uniform catechism; priests were forbidden to perform church weddings before the civil ceremony; the confirmation of nuncios and other papal legates was strongly limited; each infraction of rules by priests or even bishops was to be treated like a felony and to be dealt with by the Council of State.

From now on there was no longer a French episcopate, but only bishops strictly controlled by the Ministry of Religion, permitting the bishops no organic connection and prohibiting any collective action. In their turn, the bishops were virtually given the rights of prefects in their dioceses, with a discretionary power over their parish priests, which exceeded what had been known under the Old Regime. Napoleon granted the bishops virtually unlimited power because he wanted to utilize the concordat to assure the cohesion of a nation rent by the existence of two Churches, and because he realized that this extremely difficult fusion could only be accomplished by imperial means. This strengthening of episcopal authority, dictated by the moment, was to have lasting consequences. Among the priests the parallel between the ecclesiastical organization and the civil service and the fact that they received their salaries from the state also augmented their view of themselves as regular officials. They increasingly adopted the mentality of officials, with increased respectability and punctuality and decreased initiative and sense of responsibility. The institution thereby won cohesion and functioned better, but lost freedom and innovative spirit. Aside from all this, Napoleon, by authoritatively substituting his ideal of administrative centralism for the old Gallican and presbyterian traditions of the old Church of France, unwittingly helped to prepare the triumph of ultramontanism. It would raise its head again as soon as the government was no longer sufficiently despotic to pose a counterweight to papal power.

But these future consequences could not be foreseen at that time. More immediately, Rome was worried about the unilateral changes, and therefore falsification, of the concordat by means of a strong state control over the life of the Church. Pius VII protested vigorously. In Paris, where Bonaparte's maneuver had succeeded in disarming the opposition so that the new laws on religion were passed on 8 April 1802, the government pretended amazement and replied that the Organic Articles did not introduce new law, but were merely a renewed sanction of old principles of the Gallican Church. Pius VII and Consalvi once again proved their realism. They knew that the reconciliation of the Church with the new society created by the revolution was possible only by paying this price. They did not pursue the matter further, inspired by the hope that the future would permit them to improve a situation which they were helpless to change unless they wished to jeopardize what had been gained.

The Reorganization of the Church of France

The concordat and the Organic Articles established the principles for the reorganization of the Church of France. They needed to be implemented on both national and local levels. On the national level the work was done jointly by three men. One was Cardinal Caprara, whose age, physical constitution and character disposed to a willingness to compromise bordering on weakness. Another man was Jean Portalis, in charge of religious affairs, one of the few Catholics among the leading politicals, and a conscientious lawyer. Finally and foremost there was the inconstant Bernier. He provided undeniable services in sometimes questionable fashion, especially by lending his skillful and subtle pen to both sides in an attempt to formulate the questions as well as the answers, which to him seemed the best means to reconcile both.

On the whole, Bonaparte succeeded in gaining most of his objectives with the concordat. He saw in it an essential element of his policy of pacification and wanted to fashion the Church into one of his most useful tools.

The first problem was the adjustment of the dioceses to the administrative organization of France. The French government envisioned ten archbishoprics, to correspond to the area of jurisdiction of the appellate courts, and forty bishoprics for the 102 Departments of which France was then composed. At the last minute Bonaparte raised the figure to sixty. He did this not for pastoral reasons, but with the intention to strengthen the ecclesiastical organization of the conquered areas.

Before appointments could be made to the new sees, the resignation of the old office holders had to be effected. Reluctantly, fifty-nine Constituent bishops went along with the wishes of the government. After some disputes with respect to the eventual formulation, they directed a common letter to the Pope in which they accepted the concordat and the principles which the French government and His Holiness confirmed in it. Of the ninety-two surviving bishops of the Old Regime, all those who had returned to France and those who had fled to Italy submitted their resignations without creating any difficulties. Not so with some others. An opposition group formed in England and a considerable number of the prelates as well who had fled to Germany and Spain, and among this group loyalty to the King assumed precedence over loyalty to the Pope, the more so as their Gallican theology convinced them that the Pope had exceeded his constitutional authority. Most of the others were at least prudent enough no longer to intervene in their old dioceses and to go so far as to advise their clergy and their laity to subordinate themselves to their new bishops. Two of them, however, Thémines and Coucy, organized an open resistance to the concordat and thus created a new schism.

The designation of the new bishops raised a sticky problem. Bonaparte insisted that as with his appointments to prefectures, so also with the appointment of bishops, his principle of integration be applied. The new episcopate was to consist simultaneously of bishops of the Old Regime, of Constituent bishops, and of new men. The Holy See, which regarded the Constituent bishops as schismatics, demanded from them an official recantation. Most of the government nominees from this group refused, however, to declare themselves as schismatics. Caprara, on whom Bernier worked skillfully, eventually had to be satisfied with a compromise.

Delicate negotiations took place in which Bernier and Émery played an eminent role; they went on from October 1801 to October 1802. Eventually the new episcopate consisted of sixteen, in some cases rather aged, bishops of the Old Regime; twelve former Constituent bishops, among them many vicars general, most of them relatively young. To this group also belonged an uncle of Bonaparte, Fesch, who was named Archbishop of Lyon. Although political considerations played a role, the nominations generally turned out to be good.

Everything had to be reconstructed and newly created. The new diocesan administrations not only needed to be put in place, but also had to adjust to the meager means available. The parish boundaries had to be arranged according to the directives of the government, and in them economic considerations also had to be taken into account. Church buildings which during the revolution were alienated from worship and employed for profane purposes had to be reconsecrated for divine services. A new parish clergy had to be created and this point raised complex problems. At first sight there seemed to be no lack of qualified personnel. But aside from those who for political or theological reasons declined to enter the concordat Church, many were actually unsuited for a parish position. Consequently quite a number of posts could not immediately be filled and this situation did not change for years.

Another problem was that this numerically inadequate clergy was also quite disparate in other respects. It consisted of persons who came from different dioceses with different traditions; of monks alien to their new areas who brought with them new aspects of spirituality; of émigrés who for ten years had virtually lived a life of idleness; and of former Constituents, who were regarded suspiciously by their confreres and their parishioners, and whose reconciliation posed a number of delicate problems. According to Bonaparte's plans one-third of the clergy was to come from the former Constituents. In reality this proportion was not reached, unless a bishop happened to be a former Constituent himself. State officials closed their eyes to this fact, knowing fully well that the rural population did not care for priests who had sworn the oath.

The absolutely essential personnel were placed quickly, sometimes too quickly. Thought also had to be given to replacements, for in contrast to the bishops, the clergy had reached advanced middle age.

The reopening of the seminaries was a troublesome and protracted project. Money was lacking, as the government initially had not budgeted any sums for this purpose. Many bishops had to wait five or ten years for the return of the former seminary buildings. There was also a lack of competent teachers. It was necessary to fall back on prerevolutionary teachers, who in no way were able to cope with the temper of the times. Finally, there was also an initial lack of students for the seminaries, because the small parochial schools in which they received their first training had disappeared ten years earlier, and the high officials of the public education system were eager to preserve their monopoly and reluctant to see them reintroduced. Ordinations increased from year to year, especially after seminarians had been exempted from military service and the government provided stipends for them. Besides, the material condition of the rural clergy during the first few years was anything but attractive; only district pastors were paid by the state, the other nine-tenths received room and board from their communities which were not always generous. Under such conditions, the reorganization of ecclesiastical administrations could be completed only after 1809. Gradually the general situation improved, for the government was eager to retain the good will of the clergy.

Cooperation between state and Church took place not only in the financial sphere. Several measures strengthened the prestige of the Catholic Church. Of course, the Church in turn had the obligation to cooperate with the state in maintaining order and the strict control to which all of its activities were subjected by the ministry of religion. After all, it was created by Bonaparte for the purpose of supervising the Church in the same way in which other ministries supervised other state agencies. The rigidity and strictness of this centralization should not be overestimated, however. All told, the situation differed from region to region, sometimes from one diocese to a neighboring one, depending on local circumstances as well as on the personality of the bishop or the prefect.

Although the concordat was silent on them, a limited official restoration of religious congregations took place. Napoleon and most of his advisers were quite hostile toward male orders; not only did they consider them useless, but even dangerous, as they were not under the control of the bishops. When it was noted that the Fathers of the Faith, who correctly were suspected of preparing the way for the resurrection of the Society of Jesus, had opened a number of schools thanks to the protection of Cardinal Fesch, a decree on 22 June 1804 ordered the immediate dissolution of all congregations not officially sanctioned. Government permission was granted only to mission congregations (priests of foreign missions, Fathers of the Holy Spirit, and the Lazarists) who were considered useful for the dissemination of the French spirit abroad, to the friars in the parochial schools on the basis of the irreplaceable and practically free services which they rendered for the education of the people, and to some monasteries which were used as way stations at Alpine passes. The "useful" female congregations, on the other hand, i.e., congregations which devoted themselves to education and the care of the sick, not only were not molested in any way, but were in fact often encouraged officially. A breach in the revolutionary laws was made in December 1800, with the permission for the Daughters of Charity of Saint Vincent de Paul. They also received permission to train pupils for service in hospitals and eight years later there were 1653 Daughters of Charity in 274 houses. In the course of the first decade of the new century a thoroughgoing revival took place. There were several new creations, some of which were to have a great future. Following the example of the Fathers of the Faith, Madeleine Barat in 1800 founded the Sacred Heart Society in Paris for women who devoted themselves to the education of girls. In 1803, the Belgian Pierre-Joseph Triest founded in Ghent the Sisters of Charity of Jesus and Mary, who in 1806 were officially acknowledged as the first new congregation. In 1804, Marie-Rose-Julie Billiart founded the Sisters of Notre Dame in Amiens for the education and training of girls; in 1809 the order was transferred to Namur. In 1807, Jeanne-Elisabeth Bichier des Ages founded the Daughters of the Holy Cross of Saint Andrew in Poitiers for the purpose of educating children, nursing the sick, and taking care of the poor.

A decree of the Emperor of 23 March 1805 made his mother the protector of the Sisters of Mercy in the entire Empire. In 1807, Napoleon convoked in Paris a meeting of all congregations devoted to the care of the sick. He limited himself to decreeing on 18 February 1809 common guidelines defining the age of novices, the duration of their vows and similar matters, and ordered the congregations to have their statutes approved by the government before the end of the year.

Religious Revival

The aim of rechristianizing France, which was not shared by Napoleon, was pursued by a considerable number of the concordat clergy, assisted by the reviving religious congregations and an elite of laymen. They were able to record a limited but undeniable success. These forces were aided by the ministry of religion, at least in the first few years after the signing of the concordat, a support which was due to the circle of clergymen from Provence who gathered around Portalis and Cardinal Fesch.

There were, of course, many priests among the randomly collected clergy who were totally lacking in apostolic spirit and who had no difficulty performing their office of "pious administration" to which the government wished to limit them. But many others and numerous bishops, among them many former Constituents who stood out by their special zeal (regardless of what may have been said about them before), were firmly convinced that reintroduction of religion and worship was not enough. It must be noted, though, that the reopening of the churches almost everywhere was greeted joyfully, that the faithful set about putting up the torn-down crosses, and that the jubilee pronounced at the end of 1803 was a great success. But despite all external devotion to old customs, festivities, and forms, religious indifference prevailed quite frequently in the cities. It was encountered even in the rural regions, where for a decade the population had not observed religious customs, where many abnormal conditions, especially in the area of marriages, had to be cleared up, and where most of the young people had had no exposure to a catechism and lived in deep religious ignorance.

The number of confirmations attests the seriousness with which the bishops undertook the systematic visitation of their dioceses.

The lower clergy was not idle either. Many priests organized retreats in order to encourage the zeal of their brethren. As early as 1799, still under the Directory, Abbé Allemand founded the first youth center in Marseille, an institution which was to have a great future in the nineteenth century. Others wanted to lead the intellectuals back to the Church and concentrated on a renewal of apologetic sermons. Some, rejecting the compromise of the eighteenth century, preached an open return to the great religious century of Malebranche and Bossuet, while others tried to see the future of the Church in light of the undeniable facts of the revolution. Others again, more concerned with the salvation of the masses, organized missions in the parishes, which assumed large proportions after the jubilee of 1803. While these missions were sharply watched by the police, they also frequently were aided and occasionally subsidized by the civil authorities. Through measures of this nature, which during the last years of the Empire followed one another in rapid succession and which impeded the traditional priestly apostolate, several initiatives of a more modest scope were of great value. Among others there were the Marian Congregations for students, founded in 1801 in Paris by the former Jesuit P. Delpuits. After their elimination in 1809, they played an active role in the religious resistance; the congregations of young men and young women from all walks of life which after 1806 were founded in Bordeaux by Abbé J. Chaminade; secular institutions with the aim of forming religious nuclei on the level of different social classes; and the Congregation of Lyon with an even more pronounced lay character.

The various evangelization attempts bore fruit only slowly. There were indeed baptisms and first communions of adults, and the prominent people in communities once again attended Mass, but until the end of the Empire there was little call, especially among men, for the Sacraments. But in one area an encouraging development had begun: in the world of the intellectuals.

Revolutionary excesses and the failure of an ethical philosophy without God had caused many heads to turn away from the rationalistic philosophy of the eighteenth century. They began to see again in a religion of revelation the irrevocable basis for all of social life, and inextricably tied together the ideas of truth, tradition, and authority, applying the concept of authority to the authority of the monarch in a state as well as to the authority of God and the Church. At the very moment when Napoleon reopened the churches, the great writer Chateaubriand contributed much to making Catholicism acceptable again in the eyes of the intellectuals. On 4 April 1802, he published *Le Génie du christianisme,* a radical "No" to Voltairean enlightenment. The book was a tremendous and lasting success, proving that it appeared at just the right time. In admirable language and with original force he orchestrated themes touched upon by many apologetic writers of the eighteenth century and directed the religious yearning of his contemporaries no longer to the vague Christianity of a Rousseau but directly to the Catholic Church, its dogmas, its sacraments, its rites. To Chateaubriand it was the source of poetic inspiration, equally as fruitful as heathen antiquity.

Chateaubriand continued the success of *Le Génie du christianisme* in 1809 with his novel *Les martyrs ou le triomphe de la religion,* a Christian epic. In the meantime other writers, mostly émigrés, had also taken up the battle against the philosophy of the eighteenth century as the source of atheism. After 1803 they were also supported by Fontanes, the chancellor of the university, a personally rather skeptical epicurean, who was convinced of the social utility of religion. He appointed Émery and Bonald to his General Council, and sent many members of the old congregations with teaching experience into the high schools so that they could attack the dangerous philosophy of the eighteenth century.

To be sure, as Fontanes shows exemplarily, many of these Neo-Christians, as they were then called, were only sympathizers on the surface. They also consti-tuted only a minority, for the ideologues, the heirs of the atheistic encyclopedists, still occupied strong positions in the important areas of the press, the literary salons, the scientific societies, and the humanities at universities.

In summary it can be said that by 1810 the concordat Church had justified reasons to be proud of the regained territory, but that in spite of everything its strength was weak and its successes mere seeds, to bear fruit only during the time of restoration. Before it, another storm had to be weathered.

The Pope and the Emperor

In May 1804, Bonaparte was proclaimed as Emperor of the French. To a high degree the leaders of the Church of France had fostered this development with the extravagant praises in their pastoral letters of the "modern Cyrus," the "new Constantine," and the "restorer of altars." Against the advice of the Curia, Pius VII decided to travel to Paris in order to anoint the new Emperor (2 December 1804). Fesch, appointed ambassador to Rome in April 1803, convinced the Pope that direct contact with Napoleon could effect a change in the Organic Articles and the legislation on marriage and at the same time regulate the worrisome problems which the development of the situation in Germany and Italy posed for the Church. It had useful effects for the Holy See insofar as the former Constituent bishops were finally forced to clear up their situation, a result which in France and Italy was seen as a victory of papal authority. It also gave numerous priests and the faithful, for whom the papacy in the past had been nothing more than an abstract concept, an opportunity to laud a man whose spiritual aura made such a deep impression that this journey saw the beginning of that devotion to the Pope which was to play such a large role in the church history of France during the nineteenth century. The anointment of the Emperor officially confirmed the rejection of the revolutionary ideology; it proclaimed the new alliance between throne and altar, which at that time appeared to most observers as the essential prerequisite for a religious restoration. For this reason the episcopate, followed by a large portion of the clergy, during the next three years increasingly lent the government a hand. Eventually this went so far as to include in the uniform catechism in use in all churches of the French Empire a passage which, under threat of eternal perdition, required from all the faithful "love, respect, obedience, loyalty toward Napoleon, our Emperor, service in the army, and payment of the taxes necessary for the maintenance and defense of the fatherland and its throne."

The loyalty of the French clergy toward the Emperor, which only too frequently degenerated into servility, was shaken after 1808 by the conflict between Napoleon and Pius VII.

The conflict broke out when war with Europe was renewed. Napoleon, expanding his religious policy to continental dimensions, wanted to use the Pope in western Europe as he used his bishops in France, and wanted to force Pius VII to join him politically and morally. This pretension met categorical rejection because the Pope, as head of the universal Church, wished to maintain a strict neutrality. But Consalvi's resignation (17 June 1806) only strengthened the influence of the reactionaries. In 1807 a number of peremptory demands reached the Pope: Napoleon insisted not only on the Pope's joining an Italian league against "heretical England," but also made unacceptable demands with respect to church policy in Italy, and demanded the inclusion of additional French cardinals into the Sacred College until their number had reached a third of the total. Pius VII, accusing himself of having been too weak in the question of the Organic Articles, the equality of religions, and the imperial catechism, this time did not give in and rejected Napoleon's demands.

The Emperor now ordered general Miollis to occupy Rome (2 February 1808), but left the Pontiff a faint degree of sovereignty in the hope that he would give in. Pius VII was not intimidated by this massive pressure. Quite the contrary: When fifteen papal officials were deported from Rome, he publicly accused the emperor of enchaining the government of the Church, and replied with the recall of ambassador Caprara from Paris and the refusal to perform the investment of bishops according to the concordat, i.e., by mentioning their nomination by the Emperor. After his secretary of state had also been exiled, he appointed Cardinal Pacca, the best head among the zealots, as his successor. Napoleon did not react immediately. On 17 May 1809, he annexed the Papal States to France in order to put an end to the "improper combination of secular and spiritual power." On 10 June, as the papal flag was taken down and replaced by the French tricolor, Pius VII answered with the excommunication of all "robbers of Peter's patrimony," without mentioning Napoleon by name. When the occupation forces feared a rebellion of the Roman population, they exceeded the directives of the Emperor and placed the Pope and Cardinal Pacca in a carriage going north. After a hard journey of longer than a month, the Pope was given Savona on the Italian Riviera as residence. There he remained until the beginning of 1812, separated from all advisers and — in spite of the official respect which he was shown — increasingly cut off from contact with the outside world. It was impossible for him to act as Pope, i.e., to concern himself with the affairs of the universal Church.

The French administration concerned itself with the modernization of the Papal States, dividing it into three departments, and closed the foreign colleges, such as the German, the Spanish, and the Irish college. A number of the papal offices were transferred to Paris, where Napoleon intended to move the seat of the papacy as well. In the meantime, the Curia cardinals and the head of orders had to move to the French capital. They were treated at first with respect, but this changed rapidly when, upon the advice of Consalvi, thirteen of them refused to attend the wedding of Napoleon and Marie-Louise, the daughter of the Emperor of Austria. They refused to recognize the nullification of his first marriage, issued by the Paris office. Napoleon at first prohibited them from wearing their insignias (resulting in the nickname "black cardinals"), then sequestered their possessions, and finally exiled them to the provinces.

But after the autumn of 1809, as a result of the activity of clandestine groups of laymen and clergymen, a number of documents found their way into circulation, among them the papal bull of excommunication. Additionally, reports spoke of the inability of the imprisoned Pope to exercise his duties as the head of the Church. The people hostile to the Emperor, especially the members of the royalist opposition, were only too pleased to exploit his break with the papacy, a break which the sanctions against the "black cardinals" made completely evident.

The bishops were afraid that the French Church, so recently recovered, would be drawn into a new conflict with the state, a state which now was much more powerful than at the time of the Directory. At first there was therefore the attempt to still the increasing discontent with the expectation that soon a satisfactory solution would be achieved. But the tactic of Pius VII to deny the canonical investiture to the bishops nominated by the Emperor eventually forced them to assume a less complacent attitude. By the summer of 1810 there were twenty-seven vacant dioceses and the flocks began to get worried. When the Chapter of Paris under the influence of Vicar General d'Astros refused to reassign the administration of the diocese to Cardinal Maury, popular opinion was strongly impressed. When several probes elicited no response from the Pope, Napoleon had no choice but to follow the advice of the committee of theologians, which he consulted in the matter. Their advice was to convoke a national council, which in view of the special circumstances was to decide to return to the "earlier custom" of investment of bishops by the metropolitan bishop. When the council opened on 17 June 1811, in Paris, although a good number of the participants regarded the tactics of Pius VII as exaggerated, the council proved itself much more recalcitrant than had been expected. It stated that a council decree would not be possible without the agreement of the Pope. Napoleon was angry and imprisoned the three bishops leading the opposition.

After this attempt had failed, Napoleon tried to master the situation through political chicanery against the priests and against the Sulpicians, who were made responsible for the ultramontane behavior of the young clergy. After his return from Russia, he tried to force the Pope to give in. The Pope meanwhile had been brought to Fontainebleau and, after several days of angry negotiations, completely weakened by illness, agreed on 25 January 1813 to sign the draft of a convention which in essential points corresponded to the demands of the Emperor. Although the agreement was to remain secret and to serve merely as the basis for a final settlement, the Emperor published it immediately under the name of Concordat of Fontainebleau. But three days later the Pope decided to recant his act of weakness and on 25 March wrote a long letter to the Emperor. Napoleon pretended that he was unaware of the letter and celebrated the reconciliation between Church and state with religious services of praise and thanksgiving.

Catholics became increasingly excited and agitated, especially by an extraordinarily active secret society, the "Chevaliers de la foi," recruited from the ranks of congregations. This secret society was founded in May 1810, with the double objective of returning to the Pope his freedom and secular power and restoring the monarchy. These "Knights of the Faith" accepted the views of Abbé Barruel on the freemasonic origins of the revolution, and were largely responsible for convincing French Catholics that their faith was severely endangered as long as they had a government inspired by the principles of the Revolution. This secret propaganda actively prepared the Catholics to connect the cause of religion with the restoration of the Bourbons. The anticlericalism that quickly flared up during Napoleon's Hundred Days completely stiffened the attitude of those who, after the disappointments of the final years of Napoleon's domination, saw the salvation of the Church solely in the triumph of counterrevolution. This was the negative aspect of this collision between worldly and spiritual power, and for several generations was to be a heavy burden for French Catholics. For the papacy it had a double advantage. For one, the problem of the freedom of the Church and the neutrality of the Holy See was posed for the whole world as a problem of international policy. For another, the fact that the papacy had had the courage to defy the tyrant when all other governments bowed before him, lent the papacy a moral prestige of which the governments of the subsequent generation had to take account.

Southern Europe

A large part of Italy did not belong to the French state, even though it was under the control of French armies. In this part the concordat of 1801 was, of course, not applied.

In the north, the former Cisalpine Republic was reorganized as the Italian Republic. Napoleon, aware that its population was even fonder of its religion than the French, in Article 1 of the new constitution recognized Catholicism as the established religion. Allowing for the influence which the clergy had retained for itself, he appointed a committee of clerics — and not lay jurists as in France under the leadership of Cardinal Bellisomi for the purpose of preparing the "Organic Law for the Clergy of the Italian Republic" (27 January 1802). In part, this law was modeled on the French concordat, but, in a whole series of points, was more favorable to the Church. It maintained the jurisdiction of the clergy in marriages, cathedral chapters and seminaries received subsidies, and Church lands not yet employed for other purposes were restored. Napoleon desired the confirmation of this law through a concordat with the Holy See. The concordat was signed on 16 September 1803. It was even more favorable for the Church than the Organic Law of 1802.

A severe disappointment was in store, though. On 24 January 1804, Melzi published an implementation order, which put in question several important gains. In practical terms this amounted to the reintroduction of the Josephine laws in effect before the revolution. Strong protests of the Holy See had no immediate effect. But when in 1805 the republic, through the inclusion of Venetia, was changed into the Kingdom of Italy, Napoleon with his decree of 22 May 1805 lifted the Melzi order of 1804. In the following month several steps were taken, which on a disciplinary and financial level regulated the clergy, dissolved a number of monasteries, and reduced the number of parishes in order to increase the subsidies for the remaining ones. These steps on the whole were sensible and were received well by the clergy. But their unilateral character caused new Roman protests. The extension of the concordat of 1803 and the laws resulting from it to Venetia without prior consultation also were protested, because these laws introduced the secularization of institutions to another area of the Italian peninsula. The introduction of the French civil code, and therefore of divorce, also raised objections from the Holy See. In the following years tensions between Rome and Milan increased. In October 1806 Pius VII began to deny investment to the bishops nominated by Napoleon for Italy, justifying it with the violation of the concordat. The introduction of the imperial catechism in Italy during 1807 occasioned additional polemics, just as did the inclusion of the Papal States in the Kingdom. But the heightening tensions between Pope and Emperor soon moved the focus of conflict to France.

The situation in the other Italian states was hardly more satisfying for the Roman Curia. The only exception was Tuscany which had become the Kingdom of Etruria. Bishop Scipione de' Ricci completely subordinated himself to the Pope and the new King, Louis of Parma, in a way which was particularly favorable to Rome, thereby restoring almost total freedom to the Church. In 1802 the first Catholic journal in the nineteenth century was founded in Florence as the organ of the militant Catholic group of the "Amicizie." Yet the objections of the French embassy and the incorporation of the Etrurian Kingdom in the French Empire after the battle of Austerlitz put a quick stop to the hopes of the Holy See, which after 1808 also had to suffer the dissolution of all monasteries.

In the Kingdom of Naples, the negotiations toward a concordat foundered, in part because of Acton's refusal to give up the old Josephinistic laws, and in part because of the refusal of Pius VII to reduce the number of dioceses from 131 (in a population of five million!) to 50. When Napoleon's brother Joseph succeeded King Ferdinand in 1805, he at once began a radical reform of the Church, which until then had retained its Old Regime character. For ideological and primarily financial reasons, all abbeys and priories as well as a large portion of the houses of the mendicant orders were dissolved between August 1806 and August 1809, beginning with the wealthiest. The secular clergy also were the objective of several steps designed to reduce the excessively high number of clergymen (there was one priest for every eight hundred inhabitants, and many priests lived in degrading circumstances). A considerable reduction of the number of dioceses was also planned, but diplomatic and military events as well as internal disturbances kept Joseph's successor, King Murat, so busy that he had no time left to pursue the plan. Additionally, Napoleon's violent conduct toward the Pope and other reform measures so alienated the clergy that now its secret opposition, just as effective as hard to defeat, stirred up the latent hostility of the population against the French.

Revolutionary ideas had not nearly the same success in Spain as in Italy. The reason was in part the strength of the political unity of the country at this time, in part the still strong influence of the Church and the power of the Inquisition. Yet Spain was the only Catholic state which throughout the storms maintained cordial relations with revolutionary France. Godoy, King Charles IV's favorite, even based his foreign policy on the alliance with France.

Thus the last years of the eighteenth century did not mean for Spain, as they did for France, Italy, and Germany, the end of the Church of the Old Regime. Nevertheless, the church policy of the Spanish government created some concern for the Holy See. On one hand Madrid had the not unjustified impression that secular interests, especially Avignon and the Papal States, occupied the Pope and his advisers more than religious problems. On the other hand, the old claims of the government to deal with ecclesiastical matters independently from Rome, and the episcopal leanings of a part of the clergy, freshly fueled by the recent influence of Italian Jansenism, were strengthened by the political developments after 1797 in Italy. After all, it was not at all clear how the centralized system was to continue to function in the area of ecclesiastical appointments to benefices and the granting of dispensations, once Rome had come under French control and the Roman Curia was completely disorganized. For this reason M. L. de Urquijo with the support of the Jansenists started campaigning for a return to the old church discipline. He utilized the vacancy of Saint Peter's after the death of Pius VI to publish a decree by J. Espiga, a member of the Spanish Rota, on 5 September 1799, which transferred the right of dispensation of marriages from the Roman congregation to the Spanish bishops.

This decree was declared void immediately after the elevation of Pius VII because of the resistance of the majority of the Spanish clergy and the pangs of conscience of the King, and Urquijo was pushed aside. But in the following years Godoy wrested from the King a number of measures which limited the influence of the nuncio and the Inquisition and obtained from Rome the authorization to dispose of certain Church lands and to subordinate the orders more to the King. Godoy succeeded in having the young Cardinal Luis de Borbon, who was sympathetic to his plans, put in charge of visiting all of the more than two thousand Spanish monasteries. After a rather superficial inquiry he had the King submit plans to the Pope on 30 May 1803, with the purpose of strengthening the supervision of the monasteries by the bishops and of obtaining for the mendicant orders, which constituted 84 percent of all monasteries, virtual independence from their superiors in Rome. After more than one year of negotiations the Spanish government was ready to reduce some of its demands, but the papal Bull *Inter graviores* of 15 May 1804 was still a satisfactory arrangement.

After Napoleon had substituted his brother Joseph as King of Spain for the dynasty of the Bourbons in 1808, the French administration backed the interests of the old Spanish royal prerogatives. They were represented at court by the expert in canon law, J. A. Llorente, and by Urquijo, who again had become Minister. Consequently the interventions of the government in the ecclesiastical sphere multiplied. The court of the Inquisition was immediately dissolved and the estates of the confraternities were put up for sale. The decree of 1799 on the granting of dispensations from marriages was immediately reinstituted on 16 November 1809, even though this measure could be implemented only partially, owing to the revolt which, depending on the region, lasted until the return of King Ferdinand VII in December 1813. Napoleon contemptuously called it a monkish rebellion, but in actuality it was the consequence of the tremendous dissatisfaction which the French occupation caused in the economic, social, and political areas. Undeniably it was the religious factor which gave the resistance its special flavor. Only a few prelates such as Cardinal de Borbon, archbishop of Toledo, and the archbishop of Saragossa initially supported Joseph Bonaparte in the hope that the French administration would at long last modernize the worm-eaten structures of Church and state. The majority of the episcopate, which since 1790 had castigated the revolution as the work of Satan, played a significant role in the rebellious juntas, which called upon the very religious people to rise simultaneously for the liberation of the country and the preservation of the orthodoxy and purity of their religion. The papal bull of excommunication of July 1809 strengthened the campaign against "atheistic France." Many monasteries became centers of resistance, and numerous priests and monks, not satisfied with stoking the religious fanaticism of their flocks, frequently fought together with the guerrillas.

In liberated Spain the central junta, residing at first in Seville, cancelled the measures for the confiscation of Church lands and reintroduced the Inquisition on 28 December 1808. Even the old Jesuits were permitted to return. But during the work on the constitution by the Cortes of Cádiz in March 1812, the enlightened minority, which in no way should be identified with the adherents of French revolutionary ideas, carried the day over the traditionalist majority. They did not dare go so far as a civil constitution of the clergy, but fell back on a strengthened version of Godoy's policy. In the face of financial difficulties, the bishops did not dare protest against the economic measures, such as the collection of certain taxes and confiscation of certain church lands by the state, or the decision to close about one thousand monasteries with too few members. Although the occupation of a part of the area made collective action impossible, the bishops, especially those of the north, reacted sharply against the introduction of freedom of the press and against the declaration of the incompatibility of the court of the Inquisition with the liberal principles of the constitution. It must also be noted, however, that a portion of the episcopate reacted less hostilely to the demands of the civil power for independence from the Holy See, and that about one-half of the bishops sided with Cardinal de Borbon in the jurisdictional struggles which he carried on with Nuncio Gravina after 1809. The opposition reached its peak when the Primate and the government demanded the right to fill seats made vacant by death as long as the Pope was Napoleon's prisoner. Ultimately, the nuncio was expelled in April 1813 and resided in Portugal until the restoration of Ferdinand VII.

Part Two

The Catholic Church and the Restoration

To a much more marked degree than at the election of Pius VII, the Church, now faced with a new Europe erected by the counterrevolutionary movement upon the ruins of the Napoleonic Empire and still deeply marked by the modern ideas which contemporaries termed "liberalism," had to begin a reconstruction. Pius VII concerned himself with this task immediately after his return to Rome in May 1814. With the increasing assistance of the brilliant Consalvi, whom he reappointed as secretary of state, and supported by a religious renascence which had grown spontaneously in various countries, the Pope devoted the final nine years of his pontificate to laying a solid foundation for the rapid rise of the Church. His activity, on the spiritual level more than in the political sphere, determined the history of the Church in the first half of the nineteenth century.

The effort of Pius VII and his successor Leo XII toward the reorganization of the Church was the prerequisite for the revival of Catholic vitality.

Only Austria, Spain, and Portugal had not been affected by the French Revolution and therefore experienced no essential alterations of their ecclesiastical structures. In all other countries it was necessary to adjust dioceses to the new political boundaries, to rebuild ecclesiastical institutions, and to restore the almost extinct orders and patrimony of the Church. The conditions for this restoration differed in the individual countries. In France, the basic structure of the Church was already in line with the new conditions, even though religious policy had a changed orientation after the return of the Bourbons. In Germany, the Netherlands, and Italy, the spread of French ideas and secularizations had resulted in a profound shock, and for the Church there were also important territorial changes to which it had to adjust. In Great Britain, the growth of liberal ideas was used for the liberation of the Irish Catholics from their oppressed condition. In Russia, the new situation, created at the end of the eighteenth century by the inclusion of several million Polish Catholics into an Orthodox state, had to be negotiated with an autocratic ruler. Overseas there were serious problems as well. The declarations of independence in Spanish America required a new approach to the status of the Church, which heretofore had been dependent on Spanish patronage. With respect to the Near East, which had come much closer to the Occident psychologically in the course of the Napoleonic wars, the Holy See desired to establish closer ties with the Uniate patriarchs. Even the missionary apostolate had been compelled to acknowledge the result of the changes in Europe and was in need of a reconstruction.

Consalvi deplored the fact that an overwhelming number of cardinals in Rome were engaged in the restoration of the Papal States and the German ecclesiastical states and, therefore, must neglect the regulation of religious problems. During the Congress of Vienna he negotiated future concordats with the representatives of Austria, Bavaria, Prussia, Württemberg, Switzerland, Russia, and France, and had discussions with Lord Castlereagh about the situation of the English Catholics. These were among the first achievements of an ecclesiastical restoration for which he labored untiringly until his death. It was a huge and difficult task, aggravated by the previous isolation in captivity of Pope and Curia. Thus, the major task was to regain firm control of the administration of the Church and to reconfirm papal authority.

The Reorganization of the Churches

Roger Aubert
Chap. 7; Rudolf Lill
Chap. 11: Johannes Beckmann

C H A P T E R　3

The Catholic Church after the Congress of Vienna

The *orbis catholicus* in 1815

Until the end of the Napoleonic era, the Catholic Church, in spite of earlier missionary successes, remained in essence a European church, defined by the urban areas of Vienna-Naples-Cádiz-Brussels.

In Africa only a few missionary settlements were left in Senegal and Angola, and the number of Uniate Copts in the Nile valley had sunk to a few thousand. The number of believers in other Uniate patriarchates in the Near East was hardly higher, the only exception being the approximately two hundred thousand Maronites in Lebanon. India numbered about one hundred thousand Catholics of the Eastern rite and fifty thousand of the Latin rite. In East Asia there were, aside from the Philippines, where a majority of the 1.5 million inhabitants were Catholic, and Annam with four hundred thousand Christians and 180 priests, only a few tens of thousands of Christians in China and Japan, who were virtually cut off from contact with Rome because of persecution.

Even the American churches constituted only a relatively small contingent in numerical terms. In North America there were barely two hundred thousand Catholics among the French-Canadians and in the United States only one hundred fifty thousand. Among the 15 to 18 million inhabitants of Latin America, most of whom were concentrated around the Antilles, many Indians and Mestizos had become Christian in name only.

In Europe in 1815 there were about 100 million Catholics, compared to 40 million Orthodox, 30 million Protestants, 9 million Anglicans, and a few million

Mohammedans and Jews. Of the 100 million Catholics, more than 60 percent lived in three countries relatively untouched by the Industrial Revolution and in which the clergy, in spite of the increasing importance of urbanization, continued to reflect mainly the values of their agrarian congregations. France numbered 28.5 million Catholics and seven hundred thousand Protestants; Spain had 10 million, and in the Habsburg Empire there were 24 million Catholics (about 80 percent of the population). The distribution of influence among these three Catholic states had changed since 1789. For a time, defeated France was forced to lay aside its claim to hegemony in Europe. Austria became the leading power and, of particular importance for Roman policy, gained a strong influence over Italy. In fact, for the immediate future, only Austria and France remained great Catholic powers, and they were engaged primarily in rivalries with one another.

The new distribution of Catholics which resulted from the changes in borders after the Congress of Vienna was not a satisfactory situation for the Holy See. The papacy noted with great sadness the dissolution of the ecclesiastical principalities in Germany, a dissolution which it had not been able to prevent. The shift in Catholic population centers resulted in the subordination of several million Catholics to Protestant princes and, compared with the Old Regime, resulted in a marked increase in the number of states with mixed religions.

Problems and Alternatives for the Catholic Church

The problems of adjusting the ecclesiastical geography following the shifts in state boundaries were neither the only nor the most difficult ones facing the Church. At the conclusion of a crisis which had lasted a quarter of a century, a new beginning had to be made in almost every area. For a certain group, called "ultras" in France, but with adherents to be found everywhere, the solution to the problem of reconstruction consisted simply of the destruction of the revolution and its results and the restoration of the order of yesterday.

It is surprising to see that the so-called new institutions of administration, justice, finances, economics, and the military, encompassing more nominal than real changes, retained those forms which the French had given them. Where this form was destroyed, it was often restored a few years later as a result of revolutionary risings. In many instances, these new institutions were copied by countries which had not experienced a French occupation. These institutions were the juridical realization of an economic and social development which was unavoidable and irreversible. The development occurred in the individual countries rather quickly, and brought with it the destruction of the Old Regime and the creation of a new society of the bourgeoisie, which embodied the new tendencies and which was to play the predominant role for the next century.

Parallel to the social changes, there also took place a transformation of ideas, a development of far greater significance from the religious viewpoint. Was it intelligent to try to reverse the wheel of history? Were these new tendencies wrong, or were there not beyond all the errors and excesses some basic values to be fostered? Pius VII had discussed this concept in his Christmas homily of 1797 on Christianity and democracy while he was still bishop of Imola. But only few of the men of 1815, having been victims of the painful experiences of the past, were prepared to pursue such a path. They preferred to long for what they called the golden days of Christianity in the past; an attitude which for decades was to support the reactionary stance of a majority of the Catholic clergy. Many a time it was acknowledged that the Old Regime had not been only good for the Church. In the Catholic countries it meant Gallicanism and Josephinism, among other evils, and such principles remained vital even in the Austria of Metternich, the France of the Bourbons, in Spain, and in the Kingdom of Naples in which the reaction triumphed.

Thus it became clear very quickly that the religious counterrevolution, in spite of the theses proclaimed by such lay theoreticians as Haller and Bonald, was, in fact, not identical with the political counterrevolution. This discrepancy became visible when Pius VII restored the Society of Jesus despite the disapproving attitude of most of the governments and rejected a proposal to join the Holy Alliance. Even if the Holy Alliance were undoubtedly inspired by a greater religiosity than historians have been willing to admit, it nevertheless stemmed from an understanding of Christianity which was too little oriented toward the institutional not to cause the Roman authorities grave concern. The Holy See could not conceive of states in which the Church did not occupy a central position.

The most fervent propagandists for revolutionary ideas were and remained the adherents of the philosophers of the eighteenth century, and as such declared enemies of the Church. Wherever the revolution had been successful, the Church had had to suffer. Was not, therefore, the expectation of advantages from a compromise with the revolution a game of self-deception? The dilemma which was to come into focus more dramatically during the nineteenth century was sketched only in vague outlines in 1815, and even circles advocating concessions limited to secondary aspects of the liberal demands saw in them merely a policy of the lesser evil. The rancor of the many victims of revolutionary unrest combined with the conviction that there existed a fundamental contradiction between the two dominant ideologies. Initially this led Catholic laymen and clergy almost without exception to the side of counterrevolution. Their only uncertainty was whether the counterrevolution was to be conducted implacably or with a limited tactical flexibility.

Aside from this fundamental ideological decision, there also remained problems of a practical nature. In numerous countries the Church had lost the majority of its property. While the impoverishment was advantageous as a kind of purification, it created the problem of how to finance seminaries, schools, charitable institutions, and apostolic organizations. In Rome as almost everywhere, the ecclesiastical administration was in shambles, archives dispersed, and communications disrupted. Furthermore, the clergy in many countries had not only lost its privileged position, but in many areas had suffered also from a diminished interest among young people. The problem of successors became acute. The religious orders, always a valuable apostolic tool, also suffered acutely.

Far-reaching regeneration was imperative. But the Revolution had disturbed minds even more than administrations. Spread by officials of the French Empire and its military throughout Europe, the new ideas had shaken the foundations of the traditional social and political order and had intensified a crisis of European conscience which had been developing for a century. The Church through its clergy still had a firm grip on the rural populations, as had been demonstrated by the revolts in the Vendée, the peasants' war in Belgium, the rising of the Neapolitan Sanfedists, the Spanish resistance, and the Tirolean rebellion. However, the young intellectuals had been awakened. Liberated suddenly from the strict control which the Inquisition and the censorship of books had exercised over them, many intellectuals had gone to the opposite extreme. Many crises of conscience were helped along also by the general laxity of morals. The task, therefore, consisted not merely of reopening monasteries and churches, but of healing souls.

Fortunately, the Church possessed several means with which to accomplish its enormous task. In addition to the spiritual advantage which the Church had gained through the secularization of its property, Catholicism could now count on the active support of the public purse. In addition, sovereigns as well as governments were one in believing that the altar provided the best protection for a throne and that the Church ought to have a place of priority among the institutions to be restored. Inasmuch as the institutions which served to maintain religion for the masses were of the utmost importance, the Church, at least for the moment, experienced enormous gain from the benevolent attitude of the state. A dangerous aspect for the Church of this common cause with the reactionary elements was that the young and dynamic elements among Catholics might be irretrievably driven to the ideas of the revolution. In the atmosphere of the moment, however, when upper and lower classes were still under the impact of the terrors of the revolutionary time, it was not easy to take account of the influence which these young elements would have in the future. The clergy's ability to look into the future was dimmed by the deceptive expectation of creating a new Christian society with the aid of counterrevolutionary governments and by the immediate advantage which this help constituted in the area of pastoral care and the rapid restoration of ecclesiastical foundations.

The signs of religious revival, evident in France after the end of Napoleon's reign, now became visible in all countries. This was a universal phenomenon; reversions to the faith on the Catholic side were mirrored in the Protestant world by revival movements. From both directions voices were raised calling for an alliance of all Christians against the propagators of the Enlightenment. The disorder of the past twenty years had made many people look toward religion for consolation and to doubt the validity of the rationalistic ideology which they held responsible for past catastrophes. Everywhere people turned away from the modern ideas of progress and back toward a tradition rooted in the Catholic Middle Ages. The influence of this return to tradition was felt even in Protestant circles, where a series of spectacular conversions to Roman Catholicism took place.

The shift in the intellectual climate, caused by the French counter-revolutionary thinkers, was intensified by the spreading of romanticism. The most deadly weapon against the Church had been its derogation by the aesthetes, who presented religion and especially Catholicism as marks of intellectual mediocrity and of obscurantism. But now, artists and writers, led by Chateaubriand in France, Stolberg in Germany, Schlegel in Austria, and Manzoni in Italy, praised Christianity as guarantor of high culture and Catholic rites as the fertile source of artistic inspiration. The romantic movement was not free of religious imperfections. It fostered immorality and uncritical raptures and thus was distrusted by many clergymen. Furthermore, even in the guise of Catholic romanticism, it frequently exchanged the Christian faith for pseudomysticism and a vague religiosity determined more by feeling than intellect. Romanticism was also ill-suited to deal with the problems of positivism which soon were to characterize the nineteenth century. But for the moment the Church had found powerful support in the change of mentality which led spirits from the progressive rationalism of the Enlightenment to mysticism and the heritage of medieval traditions.

These problems faced the entire Church, but especially Rome where the principles had to be determined which would govern not only the conduct of the Church in general, but the restoration of secular conditions in the Papal States in particular. In 1825 the Roman Curia was of divided mind in this matter.

One group, led by Consalvi, who were called "liberals" in a denigrating fashion by their opponents, wished to use chiefly political means to achieve the desired Catholic restoration. Its members possessed that awareness of realities which is needed for effective political action. The group considered it advantageous to keep an open mind toward some of the modern tendencies or at least not to oppose them too openly as long as the faith was not affected. Aware of the benefits which the Church could derive from the benevolent attitude of officials, these politically oriented men also exercised moderation in their relations with governments, preferring a cautious stance or even partial concession in the questions of juridical claims, if this price would assure good relations.

They encountered the determined opposition of the large majority of cardinals and prelates who were absolutely hostile to modern philosophy and all modern institutions. These churchmen favored political absolutism and return to an established religion. Simultaneously, they also wanted to see a Church free from any influence of the government and without any interference in the exercise of its doctrine and its apostolic mission.

This group of zealots, led by the aged Cardinal Pacca, consisted of conservatives who psychologically and sociologically were tied to the old customs and privileges and who placed their trust more in power and force than in admonitions and the peaceful power of clemency and tolerance. Many historians have made the mistake of seeing them only in this light. In actuality, they were driven much more by religious considerations than by reactionary attitudes; unpretentious men whose piety sometimes turned into bigotry, their chief interest was pastoral care, and they were uncompromising in moral matters and unshakeable in questions of faith. The group believed that the modern spirit of the liberals was basically nothing more than a continuation of the principles of the Protestant Reformation and that any, even the smallest, concession would invite heresy. In their attempt to shape society according to the dictates of religion, they were convinced that ecclesiastical power which represented God on earth stood above that of the princes, the servants of God and his Church. They also firmly believed that the victory of the true religion, if it was to be brought about by men of weak faith using diplomacy, would require the aid of providence. Therefore they preferred to look to the religious orders for assistance rather than to those clerics who had too much contact with the world. Finally, they saw no benefits arising from the compromises which the Church had made with the new ideas of the eighteenth century and thought an uncompromising attitude more appropriate. With the superior assurance of those who tend to see in human affairs merely the supernatural in action, they assumed an unyielding stance to all who did not think as they did. These zealots regarded the modernists as traitors to their religion and some went so far as to call them Freemasons.

With the passing of the years, two subgroups formed within the camp of these uncompromising opponents to liberalism and religious Gallicanism. The proponents of one position remained essentially persons of the eighteenth century. Fixed in their fearful rejection of Jansenism and democratic Jacobinism and defenders of a total return to an idealized past, they saw a solution in a closer cooperation between princes and ecclesiastical authorities, with the princes absolutely subordinate to the Church. The adherents of the second position, involved as they were with the beginnings of the new ultramontane movement, did not hesitate to recommend the employment of some modern methods for the realization of their ideal. Their plan would include a popular base and would make more use of the press and of lay organizations than of the powers of the police in addressing consciences directly and inculcating true principles as a foundation for the restoration of a society in the Christian spirit.

The Three Restoration Popes

Pius VII was a religious person with a spiritual power which reached far beyond the limits of the Church. In the performance of his apostolic duties he was extremely conscientious. He showed an understanding for the concerns of the zealots and did not hesitate to hurl new condemnations against the Freemasons, who in his eyes personified the incarnation of antichristian philosophy. The Pope also warned of the Bible societies, whose Protestant origins made them suspect of spreading indifferentism. Cleverly and tactfully he tried to reestablish close relations between Rome and the clergy of the different countries. He was also concerned with reviving expressions of religious life. Where he could, Pius VII fostered the organization of parish missions and looked into the devotions of the clergy. Through the granting of indulgences, he encouraged the formation of confraternities and called for processions and pilgrimages. He increased the number of Marian feasts and began new sanctification processes in the conviction that the heroic virtues of the saints would inspire the simple believer to imitation. The Pope's abilities were evident from the beginning of his pontificate. Among his many strengths were his comprehensive education and alert intelligence, combined with a conciliatory spirit; his mistrust of systematicians; his sense for appropriate judgments, which enabled him to recognize essential points and to champion them while neglecting inconsequential details; and his realism which enabled him in spite of his respect for tradition to accept the good aspects of modern institutions. With respect to the administration of the Papal States and the orientation of religious policy in different countries, Pius VII agreed with the direction favored by Consalvi, and after Pius had reached the age of seventy he left these matters frequently to this cardinal.

Supported by the confidence of his sovereign and enjoying the high reputation which his wide and moderate opinions had won him even among non-Catholic politicians, between 1815 and 1823 Consalvi guided the fortunes of the Papal States virtually by himself and with remarkable skill. Faithful to his training in the tradition of the great Roman canonists of the preceding century, he held to his belief in the irreducibility of papal sovereignty on earth and in the connection of throne and altar in individual countries. At the same time he was free of any prejudice, open to the currents of the time, and convinced that the majority of the changes during the past quarter century in Europe were irreversible. Consalvi was prepared to accept the loss of many concrete forms of the Old Regime and to acknowledge the utility of a clear separation of the ecclesiastical and secular spheres of interest. With this perspective, and almost alone in the Roman world of that period, he worked out a new method, better adapted to the circumstances of the nineteenth century, which would assure the Church a maximum of freedom of action in the political Europe of the restoration.

While Consalvi supported the work of the counterrevolution in countries such as France, Spain, and Portugal, where he hoped to gain advantages, in the interest of the Church he did not hesitate to emphasize the new ideals of liberty in the face of various forms of regalism or to improve the legal condition of Catholics in those countries in which they constituted a minority. Consalvi also recognized that the policy of the Popes of the seventeenth and eighteenth centuries to seek the support of Catholic monarchs was no longer appropriate for the new Europe. He attempted, with success, an improvement of the relations between the Holy See and the two great victorious powers of the Napoleonic wars, England and Russia. In particular, he sought the support of Russia in order to diminish Austria's influence in Italy. In spite of his basically antiliberal attitude, Consalvi recognized the danger of an uncritical acceptance of Metternich's system. Ever since the Congress of Vienna, it was clear to Consalvi that, regardless of all attempts to stifle it, the spirit of revolution was alive. It seemed to him the better course to guide this new spirit and to channel it in order to avoid being swamped by it again.

But Consalvi was becoming increasingly more isolated within the Sacred College. It was the zealots in particular who raised fundamental objections to his policy. They criticized his orientation toward reform of the administration of the Papal States and the continuation of some measures which had been introduced by French revolutionaries. They found fault in his weakness toward those governments who refused to countenance fully the demands of the Church. They disapproved of the signing of concordats, which served only to confirm government usurpations and which, actually encouraged new demands. But the fundamental objection, hitherto overlooked by many historians, was to the apparent preference which the secretary of state accorded to diplomacy over the religious concerns. Indeed, Consalvi wished to improve relations with the non-Catholic powers, especially England and Russia, in order to strengthen the position of the papacy within the European context, and to assure institutionally the effective representation of the Holy See to these governments; more so, in fact, to maintain strict orthodoxy in doctrinal questions and to exercise a direct apostolate among the Christian masses.

Pius VII died on 20 August 1823. Della Genga was elected on 28 September 1823, and as Leo XII governed the Church until the beginning of 1829.

Leo XII, relatively young but mature in outlook, was a strict and pious, simple and good man, who possessed extraordinary moral strength. He devoted a great deal of time to his pastoral tasks in the diocese of Rome. Motivated by a rigorous and active spirit of reform, he wanted to give Church and Curia a less political and more religious orientation, and soon aroused the ire of all those whose habits he disturbed. In addition, the Pope planned a necessary raising of standards in religious studies. Unfortunately, there existed a tremendous discrepancy between the leadership and administrative qualities of this former diplomat, and the degree of his personal ardor and virtue. Without the necessary skill, and always hesitant and too easily influenced by advisers who did not deserve his trust, Leo XII was not the man to master the delicate situation within the Church at that time.

The first actions of the new Pope indeed seem to indicate a clear break with the policy of the preceding administration. Merciless disfavor was shown to Consalvi, and a Congregation of State was created which, according to the wishes of the Pope's electors, consisted of declared enemies of Consalvi. The Congregation was to advise the Pope in all political and religious questions. Yet the appointment of the aged Cardinal della Somaglia (1744–1830) as secretary of state indicated an attempt by Leo not to be beholden to the group of intransigents who severely disapproved of his choice. Della Somaglia was a man without vision and his opinions placed him on the far left fringes of the zealots. After less than three months the Pope caused raised eyebrows by calling on Consalvi for advice. After the meeting he appointed him prefect of the Congregation for the Propagation of the Faith, a position to which the Pope attributed special importance in light of his apostolic zeal and his concern over the maintenance of communications with the non-Catholic countries. The sensational rehabilitation of Consalvi occurred at almost the same time that the newly created Congregation of State diminished in influence. To be sure, measures such as the Pope's first encyclical in which indifferentism and tolerance received his condemnation, his strengthening of vigilance by the Index and the Holy Officiate, his favors granted to the Jesuits, his more religiously motivated selection of new cardinals, and his decision to celebrate the Holy Year of 1825 despite the general resistance of the state chancellory, all indicated that the Pope had not changed sides to the "politicals." The Pope's attitude became even clearer with his decision once again to levy a small tribute on commuters as a symbol of the vassal status of the King of Naples to the Holy See. In an astonishing letter to King Louis XVIII of France, on 4 June 1824, Leo accused him of failing to support the clergy sufficiently and of having failed to change laws inspired by revolutionary maxims. At the same time, however, and particularly after the death of Severoli on 8 September 1824, Leo XII tended to become more independent and to exercise a moderate policy. Matters were arranged with the aid of his former secretary Consalvi and without the knowledge of his secretary of state. Of his own accord, Leo resumed Consalvi's concordat policy and adopted an understanding policy toward Latin America.

Was Leo XII, then, a genuine zealot? The answer is yes. Among the zealots there were many gradations from the strict severity of Severoli to the eighteenth-century empiricism of della Somaglia. Della Genga, like Pacca, stood in the center between these two extremes. He combined rigorism in religious matters with moderation in his relations to governments. His religious achievements consisted of strengthening the clerical influence in the administration of the Papal States, a closer alignment of the monasteries with the apostolic efforts of the Church; the introduction of a stricter way of life and an improved education for the clergy; the promotion of all initiatives designed to awaken the religious spirit of the masses and to facilitate Christian knowledge in society; resistance in word and deed against liberal indifferentism; and the attempt to remind Catholic sovereigns of their calling with respect to God and Church. At the time he was mindful of the fact that the religious division of Europe and its post-revolutionary conditions no longer permitted the traditional solutions which might have been appropriate for medieval Christianity. He was aware of the dangers inherent in antagonizing the possessors of power, and he had enough experience to realize that in his relationships with them moderation generally was more rewarding than inflexibility.

Yet to understand the policy of Leo XII in all of its variations, another aspect needs to be considered. While the Pope as Cardinal della Genga had shared the restrained views of Pacca, during the first years of his pontificate he came under the strong influence of the young ultramontane generation and especially that of Father Ventura. This new type of zealot was convinced that after the irrevocable decay of the political and social structures of the Old Regime, the great chance for the Church consisted in using its intellectual and spiritual prestige to influence the new leading classes instead of putting all its hopes in the support of Catholic princes. They were also convinced that the papacy and not, as Metternich believed, the governments had to bring about the religious and social restoration of Europe by presenting itself as the spiritual leader of humanity and by no longer relying on political action but on what later was called "Catholic Action." For a short time, Leo XII was swayed by these ideas, and they explain his first Encyclicals *Ubi primum* and *Quo graviora,* and the declaration of 1825 as a Holy Year in order to afford an opportunity for restored contact between the Pope and the Christian people. It was during the time of this persuasion as well that Leo convoked a council of the Italian bishops in Rome in order to lend more weight to the apostolic initiatives of the Pope and gave such a cordial reception to Lamennais when he visited Rome. Leo XII even seriously considered inviting Lamennais to be an expert to the council.

But Leo XII did not wish to commit himself fully to this direction which, although it held possibilities for the future, was also fraught with danger. Would it not promote the growth of revolution if one placed his confidence in peoples rather than in kings? There was also the danger that the Holy See might become too isolated during such a process, the more so as the European episcopates were very reserved toward the ultramontane movements. After 1826, the removal of Ventura from his chair; the rise of Cappellari; the appointment of Lambruschini as nuncio in Paris; and Bernetti's mission to the Tsar, who was regarded as the real foundation of the established order, demonstrated that the Pope had given up the course charted by Lamennais and his admirers and returned to the policy of collaboration by the Holy See with the conservative powers to fashion a common front against the rise of liberalism, a policy desired by Metternich, Villèle, and Nesselrode. This increasingly defensive and political orientation of Leo's pontificate, a pontificate which had begun under the sign of religious renewal and apostolic reconquest, intensified when della Somaglia was replaced by Bernetti, whom Consalvi had once regarded highly. But little time was left for Leo XII to profit from the new appointment. Continually ill, the Pope died on 10 February 1829, at a peak of unpopularity, despised by the Roman people, who did not think highly of his attempts at moral reform, looked down upon by the liberals who called him a tyrant beholden to the Holy Alliance, and unforgiven by the disappointed zealots for his turning away from their party.

In the conclave of 1829, lasting from 13 February to 31 March, politicals and zealots opposed one another as they had in 1823. Even though they were in the majority, the zealots were weakened in their prestige by the unpopularity of Leo XII. The zealots also lacked the unity of purpose which their common enmity to Consalvi had given them during the last conclave. The politicals, under the clever direction of Cardinal Albani, now had the support of the ambassadors of the Catholic powers and managed to form a sufficiently large block to eliminate de Gregorio, the candidate of the zealots, and to force them to accept the election of Francesco Saverio Castiglioni, a candidate who had been rejected in 1823.

Choosing the name Pius VIII, Castiglioni indicated his intention to resume the tradition of Pius VII, who had wished to see him as his successor. But he was not given time to prove himself. Upon his election at the age of sixty-seven, he was seriously ill and died on 30 November 1830, after only twenty months in office. As an individual primarily interested in pastorate and orthodoxy, he was more concerned with the aftershocks of Jansenism than with the new problems which occupied the attention of the younger generation. He was little interested in political questions, and his training placed Castiglioni near the zealots, but he tended more toward the smooth policy which Consalvi had conducted within the Papal States as well as in his relations to foreign governments. Yet Pius VIII remained faithful to his office as Pope. He stood unflinchingly by his principles and the defense of the rights of the Church. He knew how to deal with contingencies and was prepared to make concessions in subordinate matters and to be conciliatory in exclusively political areas. He demonstrated the latter ability in his position toward mixed marriages and "ecclesiastical pragmatism," problems which had arisen in Germany, as well as in his decision, made without hesitation and against the advice of the majority of his Curia, to recognize Louis-Philippe as King of the French after the revolution of 1830.

But in other areas Pius VIII proved to be less open. In the matter of the former dioceses of Spanish America he remained closer to the legitimist view than either Leo XII or Cappellari. He also did not disguise his hostile attitude to the national emancipation movements which broke out in Belgium, Poland, and Ireland during the last months of 1830. Toward these movements, the influence of his most important elector, Cardinal Albani, who was totally in agreement with the Austria of the Holy Alliance, was noticeable. Pius VIII named Albani as his secretary of state and left the larger part of political matters to him, while the Pope devoted himself to religious problems. It is also partly as a result of Albani's influence that the policy which Pius VIII pursued during his pontificate was no longer the policy of the Church which Consalvi, the model of so many churchmen of the nineteenth century, had perfected. Instead it was the same policy as that of the dynasties in Vienna, Paris, and Madrid. This places Pius VIII politically as well as theologically among the stragglers of the eighteenth century, who were still so numerous in the period of restoration.

The Restoration of the Papal States

The Papal States were the only ones of the former ecclesiastical states which were restored by the Congress of Vienna and were placed under the international protection of Europe. At the time of Napoleon's fall, the allied sovereigns, who from their recent experiences had gained the conviction that a totality of spiritual power in the person of a sovereign Pope would be a valuable guarantee for them, were most willing to acknowledge him. But the state chancellories at first understood this restoration to be limited in area. They stated that the papal provinces, which the Pope had renounced in the treaty of Tolentino, were French areas of conquest of which they could dispose freely. It required all of Consalvi's skill and months of negotiations to obtain the almost total restoration of the old territories.

Even this success was to be the source of a number of problems for the Popes. The most developed areas of the states, with about 2.5 million inhabitants, particularly in the districts of the Romagna, which for more than fifteen years had been separate from Rome, had enjoyed modern methods of administration and feared even a partial return to the archaic prerevolutionary system. It would be easier, it was said, to transform the goddesses, whom Napoleon had painted in the papal palaces, into madonnas than to change the minds of the young, who had known only the French regime. The difficulties which continued to surface during the course of the subsequent half century were to become an increasing source of worries to the Popes and one which would divert them from important religious problems.

While Consalvi was still negotiating in Vienna, the reorganization of the nucleus of the state, in which the Pope already exercised his rule, was begun immediately. In May 1814 Pius VII turned the reorganization over to a kind of provisional government under the chairmanship of Cardinal Rivarola. Rivarola was not satisfied to proceed against the collaborators of the destroyed Empire, but managed to do away with all French governmental offices. In their place he restored the old terribly complicated administration together with the feudal law of the barons, a unique occurrence in western Europe.

On 6 July 1816, a rescript gave final shape to the Papal States and thereby ended the governmental dualism. It introduced a number of desirable administrative and judicial reforms, inspired by the Napoleonic system, which were designed to centralize and simplify institutions and which involved a more equitable tax system. But the significance of the reform should not be overestimated. While Consalvi was a moderate with an open mind, he was not a liberal reformer. He was a representative of enlightened despotism and convinced that the independence of a Holy See which had to be assured by temporal power was incompatible with a constitutional government in which the Pope had to share responsibility with his subjects. Thus not only did the political leadership remain unchanged in spite of the suggestions made by Austria and Russia at the congress of Laibach, but even in the sphere of administration Consalvi, in spite of his serious concern with an improvement of administrative methods, was unable to disregard a number of aspects which were incompatible with the spirit of modern institutions. In particular, the laicization of personnel remained strictly limited to subordinate functions.

The reform of 1816, limited as it was, nonetheless could have been the starting point for further improvements.

Consalvi remained isolated and often had to do with mediocre subordinates. Not only in the Sacred College and among the higher prelates did he encounter men who did not share his views and therefore whom he could not place at the head of provinces, but even among the Roman laity there was no segment which afforded him support. The opposition developed in the climate of general discontent. This opposition found expression in the revolutionary secret societies, harking back to the French era, and of which the "Carbonari" and the "Gulfi" were the most important. Pressured by Metternich, the Pope vainly renewed his condemnations of them because of their revolutionary character and their connections to the Freemasons. Because of their more political than religious nature, these condemnations hardly made a dent in minds agitated by the liberal mystique, and contributed to making the Church appear in the eyes of all of Europe as an enemy of modern institutions and national movements alike.

In short, the restoration in the Papal States brought about less of a synthesis of traditions and new tendencies than in the neighboring states, and the deficiencies of the Consalvic reforms were magnified by the unwise opposition of conservatives and zealots.

After the death of Pius VII, the zealots took over the management of internal affairs and began to oppose previous policies directly. In retrospect it is clear that, just as the modern nature of Consalvi's work has often been exaggerated, the regressive character of Leo's XII government has been overemphasized. One should not overlook the administrative and judicial reforms of Pius VII. But the most important change which also took place in the neighboring states, with the exception of Tuscany, was not a legal one, but one of attitude. It was manifested as a narrow-minded puritanism which had the aim of governing daily life; in systematic attempts to extinguish all memories of the atmosphere of the "Italian rule" in clerical circles; in having only bishops appointed who were either very old or too young to have occupied important positions during the Napoleonic time; in arrogant indifference toward the constantly increasing stagnation of the political, economic, and social life; and finally in replacement of the spirit of self-possessed moderation prevailing under Consalvi by a police state.

This change in attitude engendered a spy system which embittered moderates, and the brutal methods of repression could not stop the increasing activity of the Carbonari. The policy of the zealots, embodied in the Congregation of Vigilance, became increasingly illiberal in the hope of gaining the confidence of the conservative courts, and only led to the strengthening of the revolutionary movement which Consalvi had hoped to dampen. Even when Pius VIII softened the police state with his return to the policies of Consalvi and effected some sensible changes in the economic and social sphere, the gap between the papal government and the rising classes, especially in the Romagna, was too wide to hope for a peaceful development within the heated atmosphere of 1830.

CHAPTER 4

The Rejuvenated Position of the Holy See within the Church

Rome, the Center of the Universal Church

At the beginning of the nineteenth century, the position of a sovereign Pope in the Church seemed to be endangered by the confluence of two streams of thought: the Febronianist canonists and theoreticians of Josephinism and the Gallican jurists of the French Revolution and the Empire. However, the brutal conduct of Napoleon, who intended to limit the role of the Pope to that of a high ecclesiastical functionary in the Empire, had two results. First, it earned his intended victim the respectful adoration of the faithful, especially those north of the Alps, who in the past centuries had been rather indifferent toward a Pope who never left Rome, and secondly, it called the Pope to the attention of European state governments. The restoration of the Pope's earlier prestige received another support through the recognition by the governments and leading elements that it would be useful to anchor the work of counterrevolutionary restoration on the moral authority of the Pope, who suddenly appeared in the eyes of all of Europe as the symbol of the principle of order and authority. A twofold sign of this recognition were the decisions of the Congress of Vienna to acknowledge the nuncios as doyens of the diplomatic corps and to increase the number of accredited diplomats in Rome.

Rome managed to exploit the new situation not only to the advantage of the secular interests of the Holy See, but also with respect to purely ecclesiastical concerns. At the very time that the principle of nationalism had come to the fore, a restoration of Roman authority in a supranational sense occurred; one which seemed to usher in a return to traditional Christianity.

The policy of concordats jointly carried out by Pius VII and Consalvi was one of the most important means toward this end. At the same time, as his predecessors after the great schism had done, Pius VII attempted to make Rome once again into a center of art and culture. This policy had the disadvantage that monies were diverted for purposes which lacked economic usefulness; monies which could have been employed to finance the public works of which the Papal States were in such need. This was only one example of the antinomy which existed within the two-fold tasks of the Pope as both head of the universal Church and sovereign of an Italian state.

Leo XII not only continued this patronage, which contributed to directing the eyes of the Christian world to Rome, but also, in keeping with his personal predilections, directed activities of a more religious nature. Contrary to the advice of the political party of the Curia and in the face of the disapproval of most of the European Catholic and non-Catholic governments, the Pope decided to celebrate 1825 as a Holy Year.

In his effort to portray the papacy as the spiritual leader of the Christian world, Leo XII renewed the tradition of the great magisterial messages. On 3 May 1824, the Pope addressed the programmatic Encyclical *Ubi primum* to the world. The encyclical condemned Gallicanism and Josephinism together with indifferentism and its two consequences: tolerance and liberalism. Pius VIII continued this tradition by beginning his pontificate with the Encyclical *Traditi humilitati nostrae,* a renewed affirmation of Rome's supreme magisterial office. While in the preceding century it had met stiff resistance, the claim to the spiritual leadership of mankind was now well received among the younger clergymen.

Concordat Policy

Pius VII had begun his pontificate with the signing of a concordat with Napoleon which enabled the Pope to demonstrate the full extent of his powers through the recognition of the right to remove bishops on his authority alone. The mere fact that a concordat had been concluded which reorganized completely all aspects of the Church in a country was, by itself, a moral victory for the papacy. Now the Pope no longer was regarded as he had been during the preceding centuries, as a force to be ignored or, far worse, as a foreign power against which the governments might mobilize the national episcopate. On the contrary, he was viewed as an ally, whose supreme authority over the local clergy was acknowledged and whose cooperation was sought as a desirable alternative to regulating religious questions unilaterally.

That Pius VII once again had the opportunity actually to guide the fortunes of the Church makes understandable the path which he followed. In a situation which was more diplomatically favorable than in 1801, the Pope could make higher demands and protect the interests of the Church more effectively. The result was an even more pronounced and fundamental recognition of the rights of the Holy See. Actually, though, Consalvi, the intelligent negotiator of the concordats, had a clear understanding of reality and the possible. In addition to the creation of solid foundations for the rebuilding of the Church shaken by revolution (even at the price of concessions in some secondary matters), he recognized how important it was to induce numerous governments, among them Protestant and Orthodox ones, through these diplomatic instruments to agree to a recognition of the Church as an independent society and to an acknowledgment of the leading position of Rome within the structure of the Catholic Church.

In order to guide the reconstruction of Churches from Rome, Pius VII created a new Congregation for Extraordinary Ecclesiastical Affairs. Because Consalvi was in Vienna at the time of its founding in 1814, Pacca implemented the new Congregation. Thus its membership, drawn from cardinals and theologians, consisted almost exclusively of zealots, a condition which was to complicate life for the secretary of state upon more than one occasion. Consalvi's intention to improve the mobility of the Curia caused him to concentrate in the secretariat of the state not only the leadership of the Papal States, but also of the universal Church. In order to put life into his plans, he created organizations outside of the institutional framework of the Curia. He appointed special ad hoc commissions and staffed them with prelates rather than with cardinals. In addition to Consalvi, these prelates were the real authors of the policy of restoration. Hence in the history of the Roman Curia, the pontificate of Pius VII occupies a remarkable place in that it attempted to improve the functioning of the Curia not through a reform of already existing institutions, but by creating new ones.

The Ultramontane Offensive in France

At the same time that Rome attempted to gain firm control of the central leadership of the Church, the countries in which Gallicanism and Febronianism had grown underwent a similar and parallel development in their own awareness.

Robbed of its privileges and the support of the monarchy during the years of the revolution and the French Empire, the French clergy had come to acknowledge that its best policy would consist of closer relations with the head of the Church. The attempt to subdue the clergy through the civil constitution and Napoleon's efforts at the time of the council of 1811 to erect an established church had opened the eyes of many to the dangers of the principles of Gallicanism.

Even though the development did not stop, at first it seemed to slow down with the restoration of the Bourbons The apparatus of this government remained wedded to the parliamentary Gallicanism of Pithou, which represented not only the independence of the state from the Church, but also the dependence of the Church upon the state in all matters which were not purely spiritual.

While the opposition of the clergy to the Organic Articles and to the submission of the Church to royal power was unanimous, a clear shift took place in favor of the articles of 1682, which now were interpreted very moderately. The Congregation of Saint Sulpice, which was in charge of many seminaries, remained faithful to Bossuet's tradition, and many clerics, who out of opposition to the Napoleonic despotism were open to ultramontanism and who had defended the rights of the Pope even while they were in jail, now tended to give another chance to a traditionally moderate Gallicanism.

Many individuals, especially the young, did not follow this line of thought, and soon ultramontanism became increasingly strong. Following the distribution of a Jesuit translation in French of the works of Italian ultramontanes, the first manifestation of the reawakening occurred in 1819 with the publication of the book *Du Pape* by Joseph de Maistre, a Savoyard layman. In a simplified manner, Maistre defends the most extreme positions of the papalists by relying less on biblical or patristic witnesses than on analogies with political society as seen from the perspective of an absolute monarchy.

But it was to be Abbé de Lamennais who was to achieve the conversion of the French clergy to ultramontanism. Lamennais had become a follower of a moderate ultramontane position after 1810 and upon reading Maistre's book he was confirmed in his views. Without advocating a return to theocracy (on the contrary, he depicted the Holy See as an arbiter who protects right against might), he now accused Gallicanism at every opportunity of introducing democratic principles into the Church. Lamennais accused Gallicanism of making attacks upon the divine constitution of the Church, which if successful would lead to the dependence of the spiritual power upon the political power and, in this case, upon a government corrupted by liberal ideas.

The author of the *Essai sur l'indifférence* had already gained a reputation as an apologist, and his ultramontane partisanship, or opposition to Gallicanism, to be more precise, quickly drew the attention of several young priests. With their help Lamennais was able within a few years to spread "Roman views" among the young clergy, in spite of the resistance of the hierarchy and the reserve of many older priests, who were alienated by the impetuous nature of these innovators and their lack of the sense of proportion so dear to their Sulpician teachers.

The bishops were not only angry at the disrespect with which the young clerics treated them; they also were concerned with justification about the development of a movement in which they saw the expression of a clerical anarchy; an anarchy which elevated a distantly residing sovereign in order to ignore an immediate superior.

Because Rome was aware of the inner logic of this development, it preferred to let it mature without hasty intervention which might lead to a more rigid attitude on the part of the bishops. The Holy See maintained a diplomatic silence because it did not wish to offend the pious King Charles X, and refused to lend open support to those who defended the ultramontane cause in France. This lack of support was a bitter disappointment to Lamennais. Rome avoided open approbation and confined itself to receiving with satisfaction the reports of success from the nuncio in Paris; reports which recounted the steady progress of the ultramontane movement among the clergy and the pious laity.

The Beginnings of the Development in Germany

The rebirth of ultramontanism in the German areas proceeded more modestly and at a slower pace. That it occurred, however, was an undeniable fact and the more remarkable because the way there was a more difficult one. The generally very moderate views of the school of Saint Sulpice had to be overcome as well as the much more radical and clearly episcopal outlook of Febronius and of the Josephinist canonists. Furthermore, the German bishops had for a long time shown themselves much more independent toward the Curia than was the case in France.

Secularization had reduced the power of the Rhenish archbishops. Once so proud in their relations to the Holy See, after twenty years of war and the numerous and long-lasting vacancies of episcopal sees which resulted from the many territorial redistributions, they now were forced to ask Rome for dispensations which heretofore they had reserved to themselves. This development led to a rediscovery of the thesis of the universal episcopate of the Pope. At the same time, several of the governments wished to avoid the creation of an adversary in the form of a strong and unified Church. After the Congress of Vienna, they thought it better not to foster the reorganization of the German established Church. The governments merely wanted to regulate the condition of their Catholic subjects through an agreement with the Holy See, which at this time still appeared weak and distant.

Conditions, therefore, became more favorable for the awakening of ultramontanism in Germany. Among the influential circles were the Vienna circle of Clemens Maria Hofbauer and the convert Friedrich Schlegel; those of Münster and Munich in which the friends of Princess Gallitzin and of Görres placed the accent on unity with Rome as a factor of Catholic regeneration in Germany; and finally and chiefly the Mainz circle formed around a group from Alsace: the bishop of Colmar, the seminary director Liebermann, and Professor Räss, all of whom had received their training from Strasbourg Jesuits outside of the Gallican and Febronian tradition. All of them wanted to train the clergy in a Roman and very anti-Protestant spirit and for this purpose spread the ultramontane views of Bellarmine through their seminaries and their journal *Der Katholik*.

Gradually, ultramontane views entered theological education. Even Möhler, who had little interest in the hierarchical aspects of the Church, depicted the Pope as the vital center of the unity of the Church. Ultramontanism also became visible in the teaching of many canonists who broke with the Josephinist tradition and polemicized against the idea of a German established Church. The movement was encouraged by the bold gesture of Pius VII, who, after long hesitation in 1820, finally dared to place the textbooks of canon law and church history by G. Reichsberger and R. Dannenmayer, which had been in use for the past thirty years in all Austrian universities, on the Index of Forbidden Books.

During the first decades of the nineteenth century this German ultramontanism was a very moderate one. It was much more a reaction against the extreme positions of Febronius and of Josephinism than a general reconciliation with Roman theologians and canonists on the question of the privileges of the Pope. Although many bishops spurned the doctrine of the superiority of a general council over the Pope, they thought themselves entitled to guide their dioceses without recourse to the Curia and, especially in the case of mixed marriages, to do so without heed to Rome's specific directives. Similarly, the majority of theologians rejected the interpretation of papal primacy which would have concentrated virtually all ecclesiastical authority in the offices of the Roman Curia. Gradually, however, the thesis of the personal infallibility of the Pope gained ground. The German translation of de Maistre's *Du Pape* in 1822 influenced a few laymen who sympathized with the new movement from France. Terrified by the spiritual anarchy which had sprung from the rationalism of the eighteenth century, they now willingly emphasized the necessity for a magisterial office which expressed itself with absolute authority. From a base within the laity, these ideas gradually reached the clergy.

Roman Catholics and Separated Christians

As a consequence of ultramontane enthusiasm, which brought with it a denominational hardening and a virtual expulsion of the Christians separated from Rome, the nineteenth century was to produce the peak of ghetto mentality within Catholic Church history. In spite of this, the Catholic Church, as well as other Christian denominations, experienced a revival of unifying tendencies during the first quarter of the nineteenth century; a revival generated by a variety of motives. In some cases, as in Germany and in Holland, unification was a manifestation of a dogmatic interconfessionalism which had developed in the course of the preceding century within circles which had been in contact with the Enlightenment or pietism. It was fed by a romantic tendency to prefer religious subjectiveness to precisely defined aspects of dogma and church discipline. In other cases, there was no other aim than to gather all of the disciples of Christ in order better to counter the dangers of secularism and rationalism. Still others propagated the religious unity of Europe as the best means against the progress of revolutionary ideologies. Many thought of this unity as following the precepts of the Holy Alliance and as a gathering in of all Christians regardless of frontiers and denominational boundaries. Finally, for such as Bonald, de Maistre, and Lamennais in France, it was a question of speeding up the "return" of the separated "sects" into an all-embracing Catholic unity. In the view of these men the Roman Church, based on the principles of authority, was the only useful bulwark against atheism in religion and individualism in politics.

Considerations of this nature were in fact the cause for a number of conversions to the Roman Church; especially among the Russian aristocracy and in Germany, where enthusiasm for the Middle Ages was a contributing factor. Some people believed that these were the first signs of a movement which would spread in coming years.

With respect to the Protestants in France, where even during the Empire rumors of a fusion or absorption abounded, it was hardly possible to escape triumphalistic apologetics. Without a doubt the work of J. A. Möhler at the beginning of the nineteenth century was the most fruitful contribution of Catholic Germany toward Christian unity, even though the majority of his ideas were to mature only at a later time. Study of the Church Fathers had enabled Möhler to regain a concept of the Church which had been lost to theology for a long time. He presented the Church as a dynamic unit encompassing all differences and possessing an inner affinity for all of them.

Rome, on the other hand, was receptive primarily to the conversion movement which characterized the first decades of the century and to the fact that a growing number of non-Catholic visitors were converging on Rome. These two occurrences were seen as an indication of diminishing antipapal prejudices. Although the Apostolic See would have liked to see itself again as the center of Christian unity, it hesitated to take steps which might cause consternation in London or Saint Petersburg. When in 1829 Chateaubriand invited Leo XII to place himself at the head of a comprehensive movement for Christian unity at the expense of a few concessions in the area of discipline, the Pope replied: "Matters must first mature and God himself must complete his work. Popes can only wait." On the other hand, the Popes of this period did not hesitate to obstruct everything that might promote pan-christian mixing, and this, above all else, was the reason for the negative attitude of the Holy See toward the Bible societies. It was quite evident that the papacy of this time did not wish to bring about the restoration of the Catholic Church by way of a genuine ecumenism.

CHAPTER 5

The Alliance of Throne and Altar in France

The church history of the restoration period in France, long viewed only through the distorting prism of ideological passions, gradually has become the object of genuine scientific attention. It illuminates the naivety of a clergy believing it possible to regain the preeminent position it had occupied before 1789 through the support of the reigning nobility and compromising itself in the eyes of the rising classes by its agreement with the political and social forces of reaction. It also depicts the ecclesiastical and spiritual rebuilding of these fifteen years and its lasting effect.

The Restoration of the Catholic State

"The throne of Saint Louis without the religion of Saint Louis is an absurd concept." Chateaubriand's statement, which breaks with the ideal of those in the eighteenth century who wanted to revive the old monarchical institution by transforming it according to the precepts of the encyclopedists, corresponds to an attitude which reached far beyond the group of émigrés. During the trials of the revolution many people returned to religion; some of them came to believe that it was the first duty of a ruler to lead his subjects to God; others, more concerned with political reality, concluded that the best protection for the throne lay in the social power which Catholicism represented. Integrating their social and political philosophies of counterrevolution into a religious perspective, they united in the common task of restoring the traditional church system and a powerful and respected Church in a Christian state. This goal was pursued by the ultras to its extreme, but they had to take into consideration liberal opinion which, while only weakly represented in parliament, held strong positions in society. Hence, the individualistic and liberal civil code remained untouched. For a century it governed the religious and moral life of the country, in part through an increase in birth control, which had been introduced in the preceding century. In many areas a policy of compromise was mandatory. For this reason numerous prelates and especially Catholic journalists complained bitterly about the "weakness" of the government with respect to the support which the government afforded the Church. The majority of the episcopate exercised moderation, as factually and legally there was no doubt that the Church profited considerably from the favorable attitude of the government.

Immediately after his return in 1814, Louis XVIII established "Catholicism" as the official religion of the state and required the honoring of the sabbath. There were also movements for the abolition of freedom of religion and the restitution of Church lands. In the following year the Chamber outlawed divorce and attempted to return to the clergy all functions of the civil registry and education. At the same time, secret negotiations were undertaken at the behest of the representatives of the *Petite Église* who were behind the religious policy of the first restoration. This aim was to annul the concordat of 1801, return to the concordat of 1516, restore the old dissolved dioceses, and replace the Napoleonic episcopate. Pius VII and the zealots around him were indeed interested in negotiating a new treaty which would cancel the Organic Articles and be more favorable for the Church. But the Holy See did not wish to create the impression that it had erred and now disapproved of its negotiations with the "usurper." After three years of difficult negotiations a compromise was finally reached on 11 June 1817. In spite of the intentional vagueness of many of its clauses, it was a success for Rome and restored forty-two of the old dioceses. But the reaction of Gallican jurists and of liberal opinion was such that the government did not dare submit the treaty to the ratification of both Chambers. This placed it in a quandary, but the skillful mediation of Portalis' son and the King's promise gradually to increase the number of dioceses from fifty to eighty (effected by October 1822), persuaded Pius VII to discard the idea of a new concordat. The concordat of 1801 remained in effect, paradoxically saved by the extreme demands of the ultras.

Basically prepared to improve the material and legal position of the Catholic Church, Louis above all tried to keep the state independent from the clergy, thus preventing the complete realization of the program of the ultras. But the assassination of the heir to the throne on 13 February 1820 fueled the resistance of clergy and nobility anew. The reaction deepened with the accession of Charles X in September 1824. He was the prototype of an émigré who, converted to piety, "atoned for the thoughtless sins of his youth through equally thoughtless exercises of devotion in his old age" (Dansette). His coronation at Reims appeared to be both symbol and program.

This clerical policy was supported by the even more extremist religious press, as well as by the secret ultra royalist and religious society known as Knights of the Faith, a kind of Catholic counterfreemasonry.

The rebuilding was done by an episcopate which on the basis of vacancies, of attrition, and the creation of thirty new sees was quickly "purified" (of ninety bishops appointed between 1815 and 1830, seventy were noblemen). But on the whole, the bishops of the restoration, selected by the Grand Almonry chiefly from émigrés and priests who had resisted Napoleon, were noticeably different from those of the Old Regime. Similar to the Napoleonic bishops, they were conscientious administrators, were too old, and had too little contact with the faithful and their priests. Yet they fulfilled their obligations eagerly if not always intelligently, and were irreproachable in their personal conduct. In the face of a society incapable of admitting that the past quarter century was not merely an episode, this episcopate certainly was the wrong one for the times.

One of the most important tasks was to recruit enough priests, and the results were good. With the aid of the government, which provided considerable sums for stipends, seminarists, and higher salaries for the clergy, the bishops succeeded in overcoming the critical situation within a few years. Many priests came from families with strong religious traditions, had gone through the trials of the revolution, and received their calling in contact with uncompromising and strict priests of the "resistance." In newly organized seminaries in which the influence of Saint Sulpice predominated, they received a solid ascetic training which, compared to the neighboring states, gave the French clergy a relatively high standard. Some bishops attempted to uphold these standards with the help of retreats and priests' conferences. But with respect to humanistic and even theological knowledge, this clergy, even in the cities, was only half educated. The reason for this was the low standard of education in the seminaries and the total destruction of higher ecclesiastical education during the revolution.

The regular clergy was not able to make up for the failure of the secular clergy in this respect, for of the old "intellectual" orders only the Jesuits played a role in the France of the restoration. Still small in numbers, they were absorbed with the reintroduction of their colleges and the missions to the people. Congregations engaged in ministering to the sick or teaching elementary school, however, were in full bloom, especially in the east, the southeast, and the west of France. The rapid increase of local congregations, resulting from the isolation of some of the provinces, the attempts of some bishops to remain masters of their territory, and the narrowness of some founders, unfortunately were a waste of strength. Among the school brothers, there were local groups as well, but with much greater unity.

The Attempt to Regain Society and Anticlerical Reactions

Administrative and legal advantages for the clergy, one-sided selection of civil servants, and reordering of ecclesiastical structures, all were in part designed to strengthen the monarchy; but for the Church the supreme goal was the rechristianization of society. The actual degree of dechristianization in the France of 1815 is difficult to ascertain. But in general the following can be said: The constant wars, the mutual recriminations after Napoleon's rupture with the Pope, and the discontent growing out of the tactlessness of the first restoration and its unrestrained exploitation during the Hundred Days, placed the Church in a very difficult situation, in spite of the religious renewal associated with the concordat of 1801. Of course, the conditions were different in different parts of the country. Generally it can be said that the old aristocracy as well as a few intellectuals returned to the old faith, professionals and notables of the provinces continued to be openly hostile to the clergy, and religious indifference was widespread in the world of commerce and industry. The mass of the people, on the other hand, in the rural areas as well as in some provincial towns, continued to adhere to Christian practices. But religious ignorance was profound, morals clearly had sunk lower, and the reception of Sacraments, especially among the men, had virtually disappeared. The masses were influenced by the freethinking press, which was read aloud in drinking halls, and by the dime novels sold by street vendors. In short, even though not quite as catastrophic as depicted in some pastoral letters, the situation was worrisome. The Church of France could look toward two significant means to regain its hold on the society which seemed to be slipping from its grip: the Christian education of the young and people's missions for adults.

The awareness that the rechristianization of the people would have to begin in elementary school explains both the hostility of the clergy to an education which was not single-minded and the flourishing of the teaching congregations. Their work was facilitated by several legislative measures assigning the clergy an important role in the elementary schools. The Church was chiefly interested in secondary schools which were educating the future leaders. It would have liked the restoration to return to it the monopoly of education which, after it had been lost to the revolution, was turned over by Napoleon to the *"Université."* But the change could not occur from one day to the next. At the same time, the state schools were given a more religious character. In addition to the catechism, daily Mass and weekly confession became obligatory. Then Monsignor Frayssinous, after 1822 in charge of education, purged the universities and replaced important professors, whose religious or monarchical sentiments were suspect, by clerics. The purge seems to have had some positive results in a few small towns, but in many places, especially Paris, it was a dismal failure. This partial failure of the protectionist system also explains the success of Lamennais' work toward a liberal education, in spite of the mistrust of most of the bishops, who suspected anything that had any connection with liberalism.

With respect to the missions to the people, the method employed reached back to the seventeenth century and was employed under Napoleon until he abolished it. In 1816 it was resumed with a hitherto unknown intensity. Several societies of diocesan missionaries were founded the most successful of which was the congregation of the Priests of Mercy of Abbé Jean-Baptiste Rauzan of Bordeaux. Some religious orders, Jesuits, Lazarists and Monfortians participated in this apostolate, supported by the majority of the bishops and the parish clergy as well as occasionally by the civil and military authorities. At the same time, they urged them to be loyal to the Bourbons, as they were convinced of the solidarity between monarchy and religion. The frequent mixing of politics and religion was a severe mistake in an ideologically divided country, and the missionaries often emphasized the existing divergences instead of bringing people closer together. They were ultimately the reason for the rejection of these missions as well as for the stormy reaction directed toward the "mission crosses," whose theatrical erection usually concluded ceremonies. An objective examination of the missionary activity must admit, though, that it was relatively successful.

The outbreak of hate and violence against the Church accompanying the fall of the Bourbons in 1830 was the result of a steadily growing opposition. The provocative and tactless policy of the ultras, who identified religion with the counterrevolution and wanted to subordinate the state to the Church, produced hostility in France. The liberals constituted only a small but very dynamic minority; out of an enlightened hostility against religion and with the intention of taking a slap at the throne, which was in solidarity with the clerical reaction, they used all possible means to undermine the activity of the clergy. Inexpensive editions of the encyclopedists were distributed among the lower middle class and in most villages: 2,740,000 copies between 1817 and 1824, i.e., more than in the entire eighteenth century. The liberal papers daily informed their readers of cases of intolerance or scandals among the clergy. A widespread concern with maintaining the predominating position of the state over the Church gained them the support of the moderate wing of the constitutional monarchists, who were very influential in the Chamber of Peers, in the academy, in the courts, and in the university.

The disappearance of the ultraroyalist majority after the elections of 1827 and the replacement of Martignac's ministry by Villèle assured the ordinance of 21 April 1828, withdrawing from the bishops a portion of their authority with respect to elementary schools, and the ordinance of 16 June, which removed members of nonauthorized orders from the educational system and which regulated the small seminaries in such a way that they could not be transformed into secondary schools. These were limited measures, but the Left was jubilant. Leo XII, however, skillfully influenced by the emissaries of Charles X, did not wish to add to the problems of such a devout ruler and, happy to be able to exercise his pontifical authority over the French upper clergy, advised the bishops to give in. The government also showed itself tolerant in the application of the laws. This first defeat of the priestly party far from pacified the liberal opposition, however; on the contrary it incited it more.

Balance Sheet of the Restoration

At the level of institutions, the zeal of the ultras and of the pious, ill-advised by the nunciature, brought the Church no gains. The intensity of the anticlerical reaction which became stronger in the fifteen years of the restoration, and the deplorable attitude of the students, educated in the royal secondary schools under strong ecclesiastical influence, sufficed to make evident the futility of a policy designed to change the religious thinking of Frenchmen by placing at the disposal of the Church the centralized administrative machinery created by Napoleon. To the thoughtless demands of a clergy incapable of analyzing the sociological causes of the religious indifference of the people or the true motives for the irreligiosity of the intellectuals was added the stupid resort to the secular power. It compromised the clergy with the reactionary party and damaged the Church permanently.

But, as we have seen, the balance sheet of the restoration with respect to religion is not entirely negative. A tremendous spiritual rebuilding was effected, to which the rapid increase in ordinations, the continuing renewal of the traditional life in the parishes, the flourishing of charities, an apostolate served by an elite of laymen, and the numerous cases of a return to the faith and to religious practice were eloquent testimony. But it must not be forgotten that it was the aid and protection of the government which made possible the rebuilding of the Church in France and, at least in the provinces, a genuine and permanent change of the spiritual climate. One can therefore justifiably ask with G. de Bertier: "Would the Church of France have been able, without these fifteen years of reconstruction and reconquest, to maintain and develop its enthusiasm for charity and the apostolate to the degree to which this was the case in the nineteenth century?"

C H A P T E R   6

The Continuation of the Old Regime
in Southern Europe

The Italian States

After the end of the Napoleonic interlude, Italy had once again become a "geographic expression." It consisted of eight individual states: the Kingdom of
Piedmont-Sardinia, enlarged by the former Republic of Genoa; the "Kingdom"
of Lombardy-Venetia, which was a part of the Habsburg possessions; the Duchies
of Parma, Modena, and Lucca, and the Grand Duchy of Tuscany, which were nominally independent but in reality were Austrian protectorates; the Papal States; and
the Kingdom of the Two Sicilies.

The shortage of priests which France experienced did not exist in Italy, where
the superabundance of clergy continued. But its quality often left much to be
desired. In central Italy, the landed nobility often used priests with a small living
as administrators of their estates. In the northern part of the country, though,
where the bishops were interested in an improvement of the seminaries and
began to organize exercises and retreats for the priests, the clergy definitely had
higher standards.

But there were other urgent problems: determination of the relations between
the Holy See and the new governments; adjustment of the diocesan borders
(which received the form they have retained to this day) in keeping with the territorial changes; regulation of the problems caused by the nationalization of Church
lands and the suppression of the monasteries during the French period; and regaining of the minds influenced by the anti-Roman Jansenism of the eighteenth
century and the liberal ideas spread by the French.

The institutional reorganization was completed within a few years through a
series of agreements, not all of which were easily reached. While the government
counted on the assistance of the clergy in its counterrevolutionary undertakings, it
was not at all prepared to give up old regalistic laws. In fact, the caesaro-papism of
the eighteenth century developed into a kind of modern secular jurisdictionalism
of Napoleonic character. Despite objections by the zealots, Consalvi ultimately
accepted a number of concessions to this mentality. Besides, seen as a whole,
this agreeable policy resulted in genuine benefits.

Immediately after his return to Naples, King Ferdinand I requested negotiations
for a concordat. They proved particularly difficult, because the Roman zealots in
their anachronistic pretensions wanted to see the feudal dependence of Naples
on the Holy See confirmed. But under the pressure exerted on the court by the
pro-Jesuit party and by the flexible position of Consalvi, the negotiations were successfully concluded on 13 February 1818. Like the concordat of 1801 with France,
this one made concessions to modern ideas (ending the privileged position of
the estates of the Church; limitation of ecclesiastical courts; reform of the dioceses which were too small; and reduction of feast days) as well as to regalistic
concepts (the right of the King to appoint bishops; the right of the government
to intervene in the administration of estates of the Church). These concessions

were compensated, however, by far greater advantages than the French concordat had permitted. Catholicism was recognized as the only religion, with all of the rights in the field of education and censorship of publications resulting from the privileged position; royal permission for administrative acts of the Church was abolished, and the right to appeal to Rome was authorized; the bishops received the exclusive right of jurisdiction over clerics; and the state granted far-reaching guarantees for the material support of the Church by providing the clergy with fixed incomes, restoring unsold Church estates, and providing the monasteries with land. A bilateral commission was entrusted with the implementation, and in 1819 it began to reintroduce religious orders.

The agreement appeared to the inflexible as too advantageous for the state, and it caused the strong opposition of the upper classes because of the economic clauses. The government, counting on the customary docility of the southern episcopate, tried to expand the rights left to it and to maintain as much as possible the old privileges of the monarchy. The zealots, on the other hand, had a certain satisfaction in a policy which was decidedly opposed to any softening toward the liberals.

But the intransigents were not very numerous in the Kingdom of the Two Sicilies. They found no support among the educated classes, which lived under the influence of the enlightened reformism of the eighteenth century, and among whom the Freemasons of the Scottish Rite had numerous followers, nor among the people whose superstitious religiosity had nothing clerical about it. They found no echo even among the clergy itself, for in the south the clergy more often than not were liberally oriented.

In the states to the north of the Papal States, the Jansenist clergy, which frequently had concluded compromises with the French government, lost part of its influence. While this did away with one cause of opposition to the Roman Curia, Josephinist tendencies remained alive.

In Tuscany, Grand Duke Ferdinand III demonstrated a certain degree of flexibility after the brief interlude of Prince Rospigliosi, who had annulled all French ordinances which seemed to conflict with the Catholic religion. Although Ferdinand III refused the recision of the laws of mortmain desired by Pius VII as compensation for yielding a portion of the church lands, and equally was not prepared to readmit the Jesuits to his territories, a convention was relatively easily reached on 4 December 1815. It permitted the continuation of the orders which still existed at the time of the conquest, but reduced the monasteries numerically, in view of the diminished patrimony of the Church. A compromise was also found with respect to the jurisdiction of canon law. But the jurisdictionalistic tradition which had come down from Grand Duke Leopold soon proved so strong that a regression took place, and as early as 1819 the situation at the close of the eighteenth century had been reached again, namely, a privileged but strictly controlled established religion. The accession of Leopold II in 1824 led to a reduction in the tensions with the Roman Curia, finding its expression in 1828 in the reestablishment of the nunciature at Florence, which had ceased to exist in 1788.

The situation was very similar in the duchies. The authorities counted on the favorable cooperation of the clergy in their consolidation of absolutist governments and were therefore willing to restore the external power of the Church, which in turn was agreeable with respect to the secularized Church lands. But the governments were not prepared to renounce the Josephinist habits of the eighteenth century.

In the Kingdom of Sardinia, where the French concordat remained in force, King Victor Emmanuel I and his ministers, considering the Church as the best support for the throne, were well-disposed toward the Holy See. One of the first actions of the restoration rescinded the Napoleonic laws which had emancipated the Waldensians. The bishop of Pinerolo started a conversion campaign, supported by means of coercion, heralding a return to the persecutions of the preceding centuries. The Jesuits, who in the eighteenth century had not experienced the same hostility as in the Bourbon states, quickly regained their dominant position, especially in the field of education. But it must be admitted that the conduct of many monks and nuns gave rise to complaints and after 1825 Rome had to send out apostolic visitors in order to restore discipline and to eliminate sometimes scandalous abuses. On the other hand, the secular clergy was of higher quality than in the rest of the peninsula and succeeded in forming small militant groups which, in a very reactionary spirit, became the forerunners of the future Catholic Action.

But it proved to be more difficult to shape minds than to change institutions. Tridentine Catholicism without a doubt governed the conduct of the people. Its faith generally was viable, but lacked enlightenment. Even the elite uncritically accepted the slanderous pamphlets of the Jesuits and Redemptorists against modern ideas, which were represented as derived from Protestantism. For this reason the counter-revolution in Italy more than in other countries occurred in the spirit of the Counter-Reformation. In defiance of official coercion the students of Turin, Padua, Pavia, Pisa, and even of Bologna and the Papal States, evinced an anticlericalism which rarely went so far as unbelief, but which differentiated between Church and state. They complained loudly about the growing influence of the Jesuits and, particularly after the intensification of Roman antiliberalism occasioned by the election of Leo XII, turned more and more away from the papacy. Limited as the movement was to the intellectuals, it made visible, in spite of officially shown optimism, the growing rift between the Church and the "young Italy" of the Risorgimento.

The Iberian Peninsula

In Spain as well as in Portugal the French occupation had been too short and too violent to cause a profound change in thinking. Thus the restoration of the Old Regime was total. It was undertaken by an altogether too eager political party, which more than elsewhere equated religious with political restoration.

This was no real advantage for the Church. After having been under the influence of the encyclopedists, the clergy looked with envy toward England.

Yet the organization of the Spanish Church demanded far-reaching reforms. It suffered from unsuitable diocesan and parish boundaries and excessive wealth; ignorance and sometimes lack of morality among the lower clergy; an unusually high number of people in orders (forty thousand monks and twenty-two thousand nuns in a population of 10 million) and forty-six thousand diocesan priests (proportionately twice as many as the considerable number of priests in Italy). The otherwise qualified episcopate lacked clearsighted men.

Consequently the interference of the Cortes of Cádiz in purely ecclesiastical affairs, together with certain forms of conduct engendering a revolutionary demagogy according to the French model, brought into discredit any type of liberalism, even the most moderate kind derived from Suárez and Thomas Aquinas. For this reason the clergy passionately supported the violent absolutist reaction accompanying the return of King Ferdinand VII to Madrid in 1814. During the following years "Black Spain," supported by the masses of the people loyal to the Church, triumphed over an "enlightened" minority. The Inquisition was immediately restored and turned against all who between 1808 and 1814 had toyed with the "revolution," closed monasteries were reopened, and the Jesuits were permitted to settle again, but only on condition that they respect the rights of the crown. Pius VII, with his acute sense for reality, gave in to several royal demands.

Between 1820 and 1823 the liberals succeeded in gaining power and exacted heavy punishment from the Church for its concession to the reaction. Clerics who resisted the immediately restored constitution of 1812 were incarcerated or deported; half of all monasteries were closed; the Jesuits were expelled; many Church lands were expropriated; and the Inquisition and episcopal censorship were outlawed. Finally, the appointment of Canon Villanueva, a highly anti-Curial Jansenist, who had been the soul of all ecclesiastical reform projects, as ambassador to the Holy See led to a break with Rome and the expulsion of the nuncio.

Under these circumstances it was not surprising that bishops, priests, and members of orders fervently assisted the counterrevolution, and that numerous monasteries became bulwarks in the service of the traditionalist party and the so-called *Junta apostólica*. With the restoration of the absolutist government for another ten years (1823–33) by the "one hundred thousand sons of Saint Louis," the Church was again placed in its former position. Buyers of Church property were not compensated. Nuncio Giustiniani was a representative of the Roman zealots and wanted to make of Spain an object lesson for a Catholic reconstruction of Europe on an antiliberal basis. In spite of the firm trust of the people in the traditional religious customs, the clergy was incapable of understanding that the anachronistic attitude of the Church of the Old Regime could not but jeopardize it.

The restoration of the Church in Portugal was hardly more satisfying. Even more than in Spain, the entire Church needed to be cleansed, for the decadence of the orders and the low morals of the clergy were even more pronounced. In its relationship to the Holy See the episcopate was much more emancipated, and the ideas of the French philosophes and of Freemasonry had developed deeper roots. The government wanted to reform religious orders without Rome's involvement and experienced constant difficulties with the Pope over the appointment of bishops and their jurisdiction. But this did not protect the Church from the hostility of the liberals. Consequently, the seizure of power by the Freemasons after the revolution of 1821 was accompanied not only by the abolition of a series of ecclesiastical privileges and the closing of several monasteries, but also by violence against the clergy, including bishops. In order to find protection, they were compelled to seek it from Rome. The accession of Don Miguel in 1829 reintroduced absolutism as well as the privileged position of the Church. But the removal of the fetters from the anticlerical press during the liberal administration had made evident the deep rift between the clergy and the intellectuals.

CHAPTER 7

Ecclesiastical Reorganization and Established Church in the German Confederation and Switzerland

As a consequence of secularization the Catholic Church of Germany was bereft of its material foundations, its political backing, and its educational institutions, and was dependent on the states. It also needed to be adjusted to the new conditions and reorganized from the bottom up.

Several medium-sized states, especially Bavaria and Württemberg, opposed any national or federal solution. They insisted on preserving their recently gained sovereignty, and for the first time in German history ecclesiastical particularism prevailed. It was combined with a blunt application of absolutist ecclesiastical sovereignty; in the medium-sized states whose borders had just been redefined, the established Church, bereft of its independence, was intended to be an instrument of the states' integration policies.

Only the collapse of the insecure and unstable Napoleonic system and the political reorganization by the Congress of Vienna (September 1814 to June 1815) created the prerequisites for an ecclesiastical reorganization. An all-German solution was in the realm of the possible at Vienna and was promoted by the wise and tireless Coadjutor Ignaz Heinrich von Wessenberg. Adhering to a Febronian concept, Wessenberg strove for the creation of a national Church under the prince-bishop, virtually independent from Rome and secured by a federal concordat, and the inclusion in the constitution of the new German Confederation of the right to a state Church. Consalvi, successful in Vienna with the restoration of the Papal States and of the Pope as a European sovereign, had to fight on two fronts with respect to the problems of the German Church. He opposed Wessenberg's episcopalism as well as the demands of the individual states. Wessenberg's as well as Consalvi's plans were defeated in Vienna primarily by Bavaria and Württemberg, which rejected any infringement of their ecclesiastical sovereignty. A single religious reference (Art. 16) was ultimately included in the Federal Act. It stated that the differences among the Christian denominations in the states of the confederation were not to be the basis for civil and political discrimination. Thus the denominations were not granted any corporative privileges but only equality of civil rights for their adherents.

This left the regulation of ecclesiastical problems to the individual states. While still in Vienna, Consalvi started negotiations with several state governments and continued them from Rome. The cardinal succeeded in including in his system of concordats the German states with large Catholic populations, even though a formal concordat was signed only with Bavaria. For the Protestant states, there were bulls of circumscription and annotated briefs, i.e., papal decrees in form but genuine treaties with respect to their content. They fixed the results of bilateral negotiations, and the participating states gave them the force of law without establishing precedents for the sovereign powers.

After the mediation of the bishops had removed the chief obstacle to the achievement of old Febronian demands, Bavaria between 1806 and 1809 had negotiated a concordat, but then decreed parity, toleration, and extensive state supervision of the Church with the religious decree of 24 March 1809. The negotiations, resumed again in 1815 and conducted on the Bavarian side by titular bishop (after 1818 cardinal) von Haeffelin, led to the concordat of 5 June 1817, giving in to the demand of the Church for independence from the state. The Catholic Church was guaranteed the undiminished preservation of its privileges based on the "divine order and on canon law" (Art. 1). The bishops were assured of the right to administer their dioceses according to canon law, to communicate unhindered with Rome, and the unrestricted right to train their clergy (Art. 12). They were permitted to inform the state of books in conflict with faith and Church regulations, and the state promised their suppression (Art. 13). Insults to the Catholic religion were forbidden (Art. 14), and the reestablishment of monasteries was permitted (Art. 7). Conflicting state laws were to be repealed (Art. 16), and ecclesiastical matters not specifically mentioned in the concordat were to be settled only according to the doctrines and regulations of the Church (Art. 17). The state was divided into two Church provinces; Munich-Freising encompassed Augsburg, Passau, and Regensburg, and Bamberg consisted of Würzburg, Eichstätt, and Speyer (Art. 2). The state promised adequate landed property for the bishoprics, cathedral chapters, and seminaries (Art. 4 and 5), amounting to a partial reversal of secularization.

In turn, the King and his Catholic successor were granted the right to appoint bishops, who had to swear an oath of loyalty and obedience (Art. 9, 15). The state also gained significant influence on the composition of cathedral chapters (priors, deacons, ten or eight canons). The appointment of priors was left to the Pope, but shortly afterward he agreed to the right of the King to submit nominations; the King appointed the deacons and also the canons during the six "papal" (uneven) months (Art. 10). The patronage of the sovereign was confirmed and extended to all parishes which previously had belonged to secularized monasteries and cathedrals (Art. 11).

Appointments, patronage, and the bishop's oath involved a degree of participation in the filling of Church offices that no other German state outside of Austria enjoyed in the nineteenth century. Yet the concordat encountered lasting resistance among the enlightened civil servants, the Protestants, and the liberal Catholics. The monopoly granted the Catholic Church was incompatible with the modern concept of state, the edict of 1809, and the existence of a substantial

Protestant minority in Franconia, Swabia, and the Palatinate. The concordat was published in conjunction with the new constitution and as a supplement to the religious edict of 26 May 1818, which imitated Napoleon's Organic Articles. The edict guaranteed religious freedom and equality of the three main Christian denominations, and the state's supervision of the Church was reinstated (such as royal consent and appeal of abuses). The state ultimately agreed nominally: In the Tegernsee Declaration of 15 September 1821, King Max I Joseph declared that the oath referred only to civil matters. The contradictions between edict and concordat were papered over but not removed, and during the subsequent century numerous misunderstandings resulted from them.

Prussia's population, traditionally intimately connected with Protestantism, had become two-fifths Catholic as a consequence of the Polish partitions, secularization, and the territorial shifts after the Congress of Vienna. About half of Prussia's Catholics were Poles. The result was a blending of denominational and national contrasts, as well as a fusion of German and Polish Catholics. Prussian law (1793) had granted freedom of religion and conscience to all subjects, but simultaneously it had strengthened the state's supervision of the Churches. Its application to the territories gained in the West complicated their already difficult integration. The Rhineland and Westphalia socially and politically had developed quite differently from Prussia, and the inclusion of the left bank of the Rhine in Napoleon's progressive legal system had amplified the differences. Both government and papacy were interested in at least a formal regulation of the situation of the Catholic Church. Thanks to Prussian generosity in financial questions and to the skill of Niebuhr, after 1816 Prussian envoy to the Holy See, a partial agreement was reached relatively quickly; the Bull *De salute animarum* and the Brief *Quod de fidelium* (both of 16 July 1821) summarized the content.

The bull founded the Church provinces of Cologne (with Münster, Paderborn, and Trier) and Gnesen-Posen (with Kulm); the bishoprics of Breslau and Ermland remained separate. In the cathedral chapters (priors, deacons, ten or eight canons, and four voting honorific canons), the appointment of priors was always based on royal nominations and that of canons only during the "papal" months. This, for a Protestant sovereign, unusual concession was the more important for the state, as the bull confirmed the right of cathedral chapters to elect bishops. The Brief *Quod de fidelium* exhorted the chapters to select only candidates acceptable to the King. It did not establish the positive right of nomination demanded by Prussia and always denied to non-Catholic sovereigns, but only a negative right of exclusion. An ambiguous formulation in the bull also enabled the government to continue the right of nominations.

The agreed-upon financial settlement after 1833 was to be based on real estate and property taxes, but, as in Bavaria, the implementation of this promise, which would have given the Church more independence, did not take place. Annual payments from the state were the rule.

The Bull *De salute animarum* was essentially implemented in the decade after 1821 by its executor, Bishop Joseph von Hohenzollern of Ermland, and the first bishops for the largely vacant dioceses were appointed by the Pope upon suggestions of the government. The bull regulated primarily organizational problems.

Negotiations were also started with the Kingdom of Hanover which since the secularization also comprised appreciable numbers of Catholics. Begun in 1817, they continued until 1824 because of the large demands of the state, especially in the right of nominating bishops. The Bull *Impensa Romanorum Pontificum,* on 26 March 1824, confirmed the continued existence of the bishoprics of Hildesheim and Osnabrück which were adjusted to the state's borders. The cathedral chapters received the right to elect bishops based on the so-called Irish election system. Before the election the chapters had to submit to the government a list of candidates from which it could strike the less acceptable ones, although it was expected to leave an adequate number. The real-estate transfers agreed to by the state in Hanover also were replaced by monetary payments, and even these were made to the full extent initially only for the bishopric of Hildesheim.

The Catholics of the other north and central German states were subordinated to neighboring bishops or vicars apostolic.

The reorganization was protracted and problematical in southwestern Germany, where established Church and Enlightenment were not deeply rooted. The problems were aggravated by the dispute over Wessenberg; because of his reforms in Constance (revival of social structures, introduction of the native language into the liturgy) as well as because of his religious policy after 1815, when he favored a common religious policy of at least the southwest German states, he was in full disgrace in Rome. After the Pope had rejected his election as chapter vicar (after Dalberg's death in 1817), he could remain in office, in spite of his following, only as long as the government of Baden supported him. He thus suffered the fate which many reformers experienced in the nineteenth century: in order to realize at least a part of their anti-Curial plans, they were compelled to ally themselves with established church governments and therefore were doubly suspect to the Church.

But the Febronian concept won a partial victory, in that the governments of Baden, Württemberg, Hesse-Darmstadt, Electoral Hesse, and Nassau banded together for common action against Rome. At the Frankfurt Conferences they agreed in 1818 on a declaration designed for Rome based on Josephinistic principles. It was to be kept secret for the moment and later to be decreed as the law for an established Church. In the form of an ultimatum, the declaration demanded the establishment of state bishoprics and state governmental appointment of bishops from a list of three submitted by the chapters and the deacons.

When Consalvi rejected such a right of appointment, the governments at first pretended to act as defenders of the freedom of the Church; they knew they had the support of their own clergymen. But under the impact of the restoration after 1820 they became more conciliatory, as an understanding with the ecclesiastical authority appeared more important to them than the realization of the liberalizing ideas of Wessenberg and his friends. On 16 August 1821, Pius VII published the Bull of Circumscription *Provida sollersque.* It provided for the establishment of the archbishopric of Freiburg (for Baden, instead of Constance) and the bishoprics of Rottenburg (for Württemberg), Mainz (for Hesse-Darmstadt), Fulda (for Electoral Hesse), and Limburg (for Nassau and Frankfurt), and determined the composition of the cathedral chapters (deacons, and between four and six canons) and their endowment. Only Mainz and Fulda had been bishoprics before.

The governments made the implementation of the bull dependent on a compromise in the question of filling episcopal sees, and in tough negotiations achieved an effective combination of the Prussian and Hanoverian veto rights. Leo's XII's Bull *Ad Dominici gregis custodiam,* of 11 April 1827, decreed the right to election by the cathedral chapters according to the listing procedure and equal participation by the states in the appointment of cathedral canons; the Brief *Re sacra,* of 28 May 1827, obliged the chapters to confine themselves to nominating only candidates who were acceptable to the sovereigns. Both bulls were implemented and the first bishops appointed.

The reservation of sovereign privileges had particularly grave consequences in southwestern Germany. On 30 January 1830, the five governments published identical ordinances, imposing on the Church a uniform system of state control as secretly agreed to in 1818. These involved assent, *recursus ab abusu* with simultaneous exclusion of Roman tribunals, loyalty oath of bishops and clergymen, participation of the state in ecclesiastical education and administration of property, adaptation of the ecclesiastical administrative structure to that of the state, state service instructions for deans, and sovereign patronage for most parishes. Synods also had to have governmental permission. In addition to pushing back Rome's participation, the ordinances also agreed with some of the other demands of Wessenberg. Education of clergymen was to take place in the theological departments of state universities, and an excellent theological knowledge and pastoral experience, an academic position, or a public office were to be prerequisites for the appointment as bishop or cathedral canon. The ordinances by the sovereigns were accepted by the bishops and firmly applied by state agencies in which clergymen also were active. Papal protests were successful only in Electoral Hesse, where the regulations were applied less stringently.

The ecclesiastical reorganization of Germany, which in its basic forms has continued into the present, largely followed the example of the French concordat. It also corresponded far more to the schema of a universal Church than the arrangement ending in 1803, whose complex legal titles and traditions had fostered autonomy and self-assurance. In contrast, the new arrangement rested solely on legal actions of the papacy and on its agreements with the governments; it practiced visibly and efficiently a combination of Roman jurisdictional primacy and ecclesiastical sovereignty of the state.

The division of the Church of Germany into small, weak, and isolated territorial Churches corresponded exactly to the wishes of the states and of the Curia. From now on, no priors and archdeacons stood between pastors and bishops, no powerful metropolitans between bishops and Pope, and for political reasons the rights of archbishops were reduced and several bishoprics were exempt. The new, more "Roman," church organization afforded the Curia numerous opportunities for intervention. The system of established Churches served to stimulate this movement, and fostered the development of an alliance between papacy and people's Church. As dependent minorities, the German Catholics had no recourse but to affiliate more with the Roman central office. Initiatives for the expansion of ecclesiastical freedom generally could not be expected by the cathedral chapters and diocesan curias staffed with people trusted by the state, but only from the secular clergy and laity. Appeals against abusive extensions of governmental privileges could only be made to the Pope, who alone was entitled to negotiate with the governments on the level of international law and diplomacy.

Austria was relatively little affected by the secularization. The bishoprics, whose incumbents had to renounce their sovereign rights (Salzburg, Brixen, Trent), continued to exist with adequate financial means, just as much as the monasteries permitted by Joseph II. But the government utilized the secularization in order to implement in Salzburg, Tirol, and Vorarlberg the new alignment of diocesan borders, which in the other Habsburg possessions had been undertaken between 1782 and 1788. Since then, the dioceses of the monarchy were almost exclusively limited to Austrian territory, approximately equally large, and corresponded to the political and administrative organization of the state. The emperor nominated almost all bishops. Only in Olmütz and Salzburg was the election privilege of the cathedral chapters unchanged, and the archbishop of Salzburg retained the singular privilege of appointing bishops in three of his auxiliary bishoprics.

In general, Austrian religious policy during the long reign (1792–1835) of Emperor Francis II (I), was conducted under the precepts of moderate Josephinism, and not without difficulties it was extended to the newly won and regained territories after 1815. Its principles also initially guided Metternich, who after 1809 was in charge of foreign policy. Peace between Church and state occupied an eminent position in Metternich's conservative concept of society. Earlier than others he recognized the utility of close cooperation between a restored papacy and a restored Empire, and he did not ignore suggestions from Hofbauer's circle with respect to ecclesiastical policy. After the foundering of the plans for a federal concordat, he weighed the possibility of mitigating Josephinist laws and concluding a concordat between Austria and the Holy See. But the Emperor and the highest officials, led by Count Wallis, insisted on preserving the state's sovereignty over the Church, achieved under Maria Theresa and Joseph II, which, of course, also meant protection for the Church and its activities within the limits drawn by the state. Only in the last years of his reign did Emperor Francis adopt Metternich's suggestions and start the alliance of throne and altar.

The French occupation of Switzerland (Helvetic Republic 1798–1803) had resulted in the dissolution of the monasteries and the expulsion of the nuncio, but the mediation constitution written in 1803 under Napoleon's influence improved the situation.

The federal treaty of 1815, reconstituting Switzerland as a federal state with twenty-two cantons under guarantee of the Congress of Vienna, essentially reintroduced an established Church and contained a guarantee for monasteries. Similar to the constitution of 1803, the federal treaty adjusted several borders, creating religiously heterogeneous cantons and sowing the seed for many future discords. The reorganization also made evident the main cause for the conflicts beginning in the 1830s, namely, the radicalism of many liberals and the continuing contrast between Febronian and ultramontane Catholics.

The Church in Switzerland also needed to be reorganized. The creation of a new structure for the entire country required the constant efforts of ten years, mediated by the nunciature in Lucerne. Only the bishopric of Sitten remained unchanged. The area of Constance and the Swiss portion of the prince-bishopric of Basel in 1828 were combined in the bishopric of Basel, with its seat in Solothurn.

It comprised seven cantons, whose governments had the right to influence the composition of the cathedral chapters electing the bishop. Only candidates could be chosen who were acceptable to the governments. Chur, reduced by the loss of its Austrian territory, was united in 1823 with Sankt Gallen (until 1836). In western Switzerland, enlarged by a few Catholic strips of land, the old bishopric of Geneva was reconstituted in 1821 and combined with Lausanne. The four bishoprics remained exempt, allowing the Holy See a direct influence. Tessin remained a part of the Italian dioceses of Milan and Como until 1859.

C H A P T E R   8

The Other European Churches

The Catholics in the Kingdom of the Netherlands

As an artificial creation of the Congress of Vienna, comprising the former, mainly Calvinistic, United Provinces and the nine Catholic Belgian departments and ruled by a Protestant monarch, William I of Orange, the new Kingdom of the Netherlands ecclesiastically presented a most disparate view.

In this denominationally divided state the only sensible solution was the principle of religious freedom, which was in fact imposed by the powers in July 1814 and anchored in the constitution. But while the Dutch Catholics, long treated like second-class citizens, regarded the new system as progressive in spite of the limitations imposed by the Organic Articles, the Belgian and above all the Flemish clergy, whose reactionary position had been strengthened by Napoleon's religious policy, would have preferred a restoration of the Church in the southern provinces to the privileged position it had occupied before the French occupation. This was especially true for the field of education. Consequently, the diocesan authorities under the leadership of the energetic bishop of Ghent, by their doctrinal judgment of September 1815 condemned the indifferentism of the new constitution and forbade Catholics to take the oath on it. Incited by the *Spectateur catholique* founded in 1815 in the service of counterrevolutionary traditionalism, many bowed to this exhortation. On the other hand, the former prince-bishop of Liège, François-Antoine de Méan, a member of the Estates General and raised in a less strict theological tradition than the clergy of the former Austrian Netherlands, was prepared to swear the oath. Shortly afterward he was appointed by the King as archbishop of Mechelen. In Rome, where a commission of cardinals had approved the doctrinal judgment, there was initial reluctance to confirm the appointment. But under pressure from Metternich and thanks to the flexibility of Consalvi, ultimately a compromise formula was adopted, which stated that the oath applied only to civil matters and had no dogmatic significance. In 1817 the archbishop received his bull of appointment, and in 1821 after months of protracted negotiations the King finally agreed that Catholics could take the oath "with the understanding of de Méan." This calmed the emotions for the time being.

In the meantime new difficulties had arisen. The government, brooked no interference in its sphere of competence. In order to counter the resistance of a portion of the clergy, it reinstated in 1816 the Napoleonic Organic Articles, which became a source of many administrative and police chicaneries. Likewise in 1818, Napoleonic laws concerning orders were reinstated in order to limit the reestablishment of orders to those which were devoted to works of charity. Even if the laws were applied only very cautiously in the beginning, obstacles increased noticeably after 1822. At the same time, these steps led to the laicization of education, an area in which the Belgian clergy were particularly sensitive. Between 1822 and 1824 numerous Catholic schools were closed, especially those of the Christian Brothers, who were accused of being French agents. In June 1825, two royal ordinances dissolved all free secondary schools, including the boys' seminaries. Simultaneously, there was established at Louvain a College of Philosophy, attendance at which was to be obligatory for all young men interested in becoming clergymen. Its entire faculty was to be appointed by the King independently from the bishops.

These measures, hardly touching the Catholics in the north, were joyously greeted by the Catholic middle class of the south, which had absorbed the ideas of the eighteenth century and viewed as an anachronism the intention of the clergy to resume control over public life. They were also accorded a friendly reception by some priests, influenced by the Enlightenment and German Febronianism, especially in the north and in the province of Luxemburg, which before the revolution had belonged to the diocese of Trier. But the majority of the clergy as well as some militant Catholics reacted vociferously, and opened a vehement campaign against the educational policy of the government.

Belgians especially were convinced that the King secretly aimed at Protestantizing the country, but actually the King was only interested in raising the cultural standards of the southern provinces, which were far inferior to the United Provinces. In the tradition of enlightened despotism and based on his *ius circa sacra,* the King wished to exercise strict control over the Church, which was regarded as the chief educational institution.

Under the influence of his minister Van Maanen, a good legal mind but bare of all psychological sensitivity, and surrounded by advisers, who for the most part were Catholic but motivated by Febronianism, Josephinism, and Napoleonic Gallicanism and prepared to smash clerical power, William I, after the foundering of the concordat negotiations in 1822 and 1824 and in order to settle the problem of nominating bishops, adopted the idea of a national Church guided by the state and only tenuously connected with the Holy See.

But the objections to the College of Philosophy touched on the training of the clergy, and the diocesan curias considered this as the limit of possible concessions. The resumption of negotiations with Rome for a new concordat became unavoidable. These led to an agreement for the entire country on 18 June 1827. It extended the conditions of the 1801 concordat to the northern provinces, where two new bishoprics were to be created (Amsterdam and 's-Hertogenbosch), and compromised on the nomination of bishops: the Protestant monarch was not to nominate the bishops who would be elected by cathedral chapters, but he had the right of veto.

Calm returned for only a few months, however. Giving in to the complaints of the Dutch Calvinists and Belgian liberals, the government let it be known that it intended to defer the application of the concordat, viewing it as too favorable to the Catholics. While de facto religious instruction in the schools was continued, the government persevered in its intentions to laicize education and thereby drove Catholics to increasingly bitter resistance.

In this situation, the Belgian clergy was almost exclusively occupied with institutional problems and the rebuilding of a Catholic society which was supposed to resemble the prerevolutionary one. Severely handicapped by the rudimentary training which the clergy received in the seminaries, staffed by professors who were self-taught themselves, and paralyzed by the largely unfounded fears of a Protestantization of the country, the clergy was little concerned with adapting the Gospel to the antireligious ideas imported from France and Germany. The only positive note was that the clergy, supported by some active laymen, were quick to recognize the importance of the press.

Briefly, the developments after 1815 were disappointing from the institutional point of view. But they served to strengthen Catholicism in the north, and allowed to grow a new attitude in the south, which soon would seize Europe under the name of Catholic liberalism.

The Political Emancipation of Catholics in the British Isles

After the Act of Union by which Ireland in 1800 became a part of the United Kingdom, Catholics constituted a quarter of the population. Except for the community of faith and the common loss of many civil and political rights, there hardly existed anywhere else larger differences than those between the handful of English Catholics, with their status of a missionary society, and the Church of Ireland. Through all persecutions it had preserved its episcopal hierarchy and its hold on 4 million faithful, and since the middle of the eighteenth century had seen increasing normalization.

Unaffected by any establishment tradition, the Irish Church drew its strength from the people. They had the status of semi-serfs, as the English conquerors had taken approximately 95 percent of all land, but for centuries they had been accustomed to defend with equal passion their religious faith and their national traditions. French revolutionary ideas encouraged them in vigorously demanding their religious, social, and political independence, three aspects closely intertwined in their eyes. In this atmosphere, a new generation of priests, not trained abroad but in the national seminary of Maynooth and unfamiliar with the punitive laws directed against Catholics, turned uninhibitedly to a reorganization of pastoral life and promoted the development of expressions of faith. The clergy, which maintained close contact with the people in spite of an improved material condition, continued to be assisted by the religious congregations, which after a downturn in the eighteenth century experienced a rapid growth in the first decades of the nineteenth century. The old orders, again able to function more freely, were joined by native foundings such as the Christian Brothers, who were an Irish imitation of the French Christian Brothers.

In England, on the other hand, the members of the Roman Church constituted only 2 percent of the total population. Theirs was a preference for a Catholicism of stark sobriety. The Roman Church was divided into four vicariates apostolic, whose geographical extension made an effective guidance of pastoral care difficult. Even in 1815, most of the Catholics lived isolated lives in the rural areas in the vicinity of manor houses, whose owners maintained an chaplain more because of tradition than because of religious convictions. With the beginning of the nineteenth century and Irish immigration to London and the industrial cities of the north, the Catholic community began to orient itself to them. The number of the faithful doubled within one generation, and in 1814 surpassed the two hundred thousand mark. Catholicism began to develop an urban character, while the landed gentry gradually lost its monopoly on the Church to the enterprising middle class.

Simultaneously, there occurred in the leading segments of England a transformation in the attitude toward Catholicism. The decadence in the Anglican Church and the growth of indifferentism among the upper class favored a tolerant attitude. Contact with French émigrés, together with the romantic rediscovery of the Middle Ages by Walter Scott, removed some deep prejudices against "papism." They even effected some conversions. The attitudinal change was fostered by the firm position assumed by Pius VII toward Napoleon and promoted the resumption of official contacts between the Holy See and the British government after two hundred years of nearly complete interruption.

The confluence of these diverse elements contributed to an easier resolution of the problem of the emancipation of Catholics, i.e., the lifting of the legal restrictions under which they had been forced to live since the Reformation. In 1813 a solution was close, even at the price of numerous concessions which the Catholic nobles as well as the Congregation for the Propagation of the Faith were willing to make. But the Irish were supported in their opinion by John Milner (1752–1826), the fervent vicar apostolic of the Midlands. He was an Englishman, but a decided opponent of Anglo-Gallicanism, and regarded such a solution as an attempt to subordinate the Church to a Protestant state. The efforts for a resumption of negotiations by Consalvi, who had no objections to a limited control of the clergy by the government and by Castlereagh, who viewed the British arrangement as anachronistic, foundered on the uncompromising stance of the Irish, who under no circumstances were willing to diverge from their demand for the freedom of the Church. They also failed because the Irish did not believe they had to take account of the Roman viewpoint or of the Tories in the House of Lords. The latter's demand to have veto power over the appointment of bishops was not merely a sign of antipapism, but also, in view of the situation in Canada, a security measure.

In spite of growing sympathy by the Liberals, negotiations for years remained at dead center. Regularly introduced petitions in Parliament produced virtually no result, the only exception being a bill in 1817 facilitating the appointment of Catholic officers to the army. The English Catholics were willing to wait patiently for better times, but not the Irish Catholics, whose national concerns fueled their religious demands. The press campaign started in *The Chronicle* by John England, the director of the seminary of Cork, and the thirty-two letters published by Hierophilus between 1820 and 1823 against the preferential rights of the Anglican Church in Ireland, were the first signs of a new tactic. Hierophilus was the pseudonym of John McHale, a professor of dogmatics at Maynooth who, like John England, was typical of the new generation of the clergy. A mass action was started in Ireland with the intention to ease up on the pressure only after victory had been achieved. A first decisive step was taken by Daniel O'Connell, a popular speaker and eminent organizer, who for twenty years had headed the struggle for national and religious freedom. In 1823 he transformed the old Catholic Association, heretofore confined to bourgeois circles, into a mass movement by decreasing the annual contribution of twenty shillings to one penny a month. With the aid of voluntary propagandists, who undertook the political indoctrination of the uneducated peasants even in the smallest of villages, the association organized peaceful agitation within the law.

Many priests at first hesitated to join a movement which clearly had political objectives, but following the example of some bishops and under the influence of the seminary of Maynooth, the clergy gradually joined and supported the Catholic rent by making their churches available for election meetings. Soon the entire firmly united Catholic population of the island joined the man who was called the uncrowned King of Ireland in the spirit of a crusade. The British government, vainly having attempted to stop O'Connell's campaign, felt overwhelmed. The triumphant election of the Irishman in 1828 as the Member of Parliament for Clare, even though legally he did not qualify, made the more clearsighted Tories understand that concessions had to be made if civil war were to be avoided. In the face of resistance by the royal family, the Anglican bishops, numerous peers, and the majority of the population, Wellington, who by no means was the blind enemy of Catholics as he was often depicted, threw his reputation as the victor of Waterloo behind the Catholics. Supported by Robert Peel, he managed to curtail drastically the political activities in Ireland; in return, he received the King's approval in April 1829 for a bill which with few exceptions granted Catholics, equality in civil and personal rights without compelling them to concede to the government the right to veto in the election of bishops. This victory, gained through Irish agitation, was beneficial for all Catholics under the British crown, in England and Scotland as well as in Canada and the other colonies.

The undeniable significance of the legal restructuring for the future of Catholicism in the British Empire does not alone account for the changes which the Catholic community underwent. In Ireland, Protestant propaganda during the 1820s grew more intensive and was able to record some successes. On the other hand, the work of ecclesiastical renewal begun since the end of the eighteenth century began to quicken, especially under the favorable leadership of a number of capable prelates. The development in England was slower, but no less effective. To be sure, the weight of the few hundreds of landed gentry around whom the Catholic population had centered for two hundred years remained noticeable until the 1820s; their social and economic influence and the Gallican and Jansenist education given to the French-educated clergy was the explanation for the continuing existence of the "Cisalpine" spirit. It insisted strongly not only on independence from Rome but also from the hierarchical authorities in England,

and was hostile to any Catholic initiative which might offend the Protestants. The new mentality was best represented by John Milner, from 1803 until 1826 the pugnacious vicar apostolic of the Midlands. He was the dominating figure during the first quarter of the century not only because of his uncompromising support of emancipation for the Irish, but equally because of the strength of his ultramontanism and his innovative pastoral methods. He was vehemently polemical and narrow-minded in his view of Protestants, but he was one of the first to grasp the significance of Irish immigration to England and to recognize that the future of English Catholicism was in the cities.

Intellectual life also showed some tentative signs of renewal. Without a doubt, seminary training generally remained highly superficial and was limited to morals and practice, but progress could be noted in Ushaw College. Even if the works of Poynter and Milner betrayed a very one-sided anti-Protestantism, they nevertheless pointed to the desire of Catholics to be heard again. But above all it was John Lingard's *History of England,* appearing between 1819 and 1830, which impressed everyone by its scholarly character and objectivity and persuaded many Englishmen to throw their antipapal and outdated prejudices overboard.

The Difficult Situation of Catholics in the Russian Empire

While the condition of the Catholics dependent on the British crown appreciably improved between 1815 and 1830, a worsening of the situation occurred in the Russian Empire, which with the annexation of a large part of Poland numbered several million Catholics of both rites. After the 1830 Polish revolution, the situation grew worse yet.

But immediately after 1815 hope did not appear unfounded. At the Congress of Vienna, Tsar Alexander I in the name of conservative principles actively contributed to the restoration of the Papal States, and Consalvi after an interruption of ten years succeeded in reestablishing diplomatic relations. The Tsar desired direct contacts with the Holy See in order better to counter Austrian influence in the Balkan states and to gain the support of the Roman Church in the political restoration of Europe. Italinski, Alexander's emissary to Rome from 1817 to 1823, brought some positive results, which were enhanced by Alexander's visit to Pius VII in 1822. Yet while the Tsar and his advisers were willing to regard the Pope as an ally in their common resistance to the rise of revolutionary forces, they wanted the Catholic Church in the Empire to remain under the strict control of the government and contacts with Rome were to be held to a minimum. Besides, the Church could hardly be called independent from the state in the neighboring Habsburg Empire in which Josephinist laws were still in effect. To this initial material for conflict between the two great powers, which started from two incompatible totalitarian principles, another one was added. After being open to western influences during the Enlightenment, explaining the success of the Jesuits and the forming of a group of "papalists" around the ambassador from Savoy, Joseph de Maistre, the campaign of 1812 had awakened the patriotic spirit in Russia and caused a movement of national reaction. Considering revolutionary Europe on the way to dechristianization, it insisted on bringing back the virtues of Slavism as embodied by the Orthodox Church. Fed by romanticism and the success of ideal-ist philosophy, the slavophile movement came into its own with the ascendancy of Nicholas I in 1825. He was determined to proceed even more determinedly than his brother and without paying any attention to Roman complaints. Until the eventual realization of his ideal, a Russia united by the single faith of Orthodoxy, the Catholic clergy of the Empire was to be increasingly isolated from Rome and subjected to the sole jurisdiction of the Russian state. He systematically avoided all discussions with the Holy See on the grounds of religious freedom of his subjects and denied the justification of the concerns presented to him.

In this continuingly worsening atmosphere there were repeated discussions between Rome and Petersburg which hoped to find a mode for coexistence, even though the fundamental differences made this virtually impossible. Three prob-lems were in the center of these negotiations: the condition of the Catholic Church in the autonomous Kingdom of Poland, the condition of Roman Catholicism in Russia proper, and finally the condition of the Uniates.

The blows of fate which the last ones had been forced to endure in 1839 led to a forced incorporation into the Orthodox Church. Until his death in 1826 the very controversial Monsignor Siestrzencewicz, archbishop of Mogilev, was the leading figure of Latin Catholicism in Russia. He emerges as a zealous defender of the Church, even though he liked worldly honors and power. Like many other bishops, he did not appreciate the exemption of regular clergy, but his skillful and sometimes unpredictable actions on the whole produced positive results. Through his persistent efforts to remain *persona grata* at the court, a matter of outstanding importance in an autocratic regime, he left at his death a blossoming diocese with dozens of new parishes, an almost adequate secular and regular clergy, and active charitable works.

Between 1815 and 1820 he was severely reproached by the Jesuit-influenced Catholic circles of Russia and by Rome for his membership in the Russian Bible Association, which was of Protestant origin and counted several Orthodox bishops among the members of its general council. In part his position was doubtless determined by an enlightened interdenominationalism, but he also took care that the translation for the Catholics was done according to the Vulgata.

This is not to say that the situation was ideal. While the diocese of Mogilev was in a relatively good position, this was not the case in the other dioceses in which most of the Catholics lived. The material and moral condition of the priests was often inadequate, inasmuch as the authorities disagreed with the bishops over the training of the clergy. Several dioceses were without leadership for long years (Vilna from 1815 to 1830, Minsk from 1816 to 1831), or the Tsar assigned them unqualified and unsuitable bishops. Siestrzencewicz's successor as archbishop of Mogilev, Monsignor G. Cieciszewski, also appointed without prior consultation with Rome, was an energetic and learned prelate, but he was a frail old man of eighty years of age no longer able to oppose the Russification policies of the authorities in Petersburg and Moscow. When he died in April 1831, the government, planning a reorganization of the dioceses in Russia, delayed the appointment of a successor until 1839. In 1832 Catholic institutions were hard hit by a series of ukases.

In Poland the situation was hardly better, in spite of its relative autonomy and the fact that by the constitution of 1815 Catholicism had been declared the established religion. The rationalistic tendencies of the eighteenth century had resulted in decreasing religious interest among the upper class. The Latin clergy, especially in the rural areas, were accused, often with reason, of ignorance and immorality, and the orders, although they still possessed many houses, suffered heavily from the various partitions of the country. Only in the second third of the century did Poland experience the religious revival which the other European Churches had seen since the beginning of the nineteenth century.

Without consulting the Holy See, Tsar Alexander I in 1817 had changed the Organic Fundamental Law of the Church in the direction of larger royal influence. A further step on the path toward regalism was taken in 1825 when the Diet, ignoring objections from the episcopate, placed marriage under the jurisdiction of the civil courts and thereby made divorce possible even for Catholics.

A further worsening of the situation occurred after the failed Polish revolution of 1830, in which the clergy and several bishops had actively participated. After the constitution of 1817 was repealed and Poland became an integral part of the Russian Empire, the Catholic Church was subjected to increasing control by the authorities and Russification of its leading personnel. The mobility of the clergy was limited in 1834, and the faithful were pressured to convert to Eastern Orthodoxy. Gregory XVI, very disconcerted by the wave of revolutions shaking Europe, regarded the Polish uprising not as a crusade against a schismatic oppressor, but as a subversive movement instigated by radicals and Freemasons. Following the suggestions of Metternich and some reactionary cardinals, he twice condemned the rising against the "legitimate power of the sovereigns," which he ascribed to "a few cunning and treacherous agitators." To the utter horror of western Europe's liberal Catholics, he advised the bishops to heed Saint Paul and preach submission and recommended to the Polish Catholics loyalty "to their powerful sovereign, who would show himself gracious to them." The position of the Pope originated from a feeling of mutual interest of the conservative powers. In return for his intervention, which gravely offended many Polish Catholics and led to their apostasy, he also expected the Tsar to alter his religious policy. For this reason he sent a confidential memorandum to Prince Gagarin, in which, citing precise cases, he denounced "the malice and chicanery of the government in Poland which had caused the decline of the Church." The document remained unanswered, as did a complementary note by Secretary of State Bernetti. When Gregory XVI a while later was about to protest even more vehemently against the closing of two-thirds of Russia's monasteries, Metternich persuaded him not to do so.

The Latin Catholics in the Ottoman Empire

For the first three decades of the nineteenth century all Balkan and Danube states, with the exception of the Ionian Islands, which passed from the Venetian sphere of influence under British protection, remained with the Ottoman Empire. In spite of the Muslim preponderance in this enormous Empire, about one-third of the population was Christian and almost 10 percent were Roman Catholics.

Since their conquest, the Christians enjoyed a limited freedom in the exercise of their religion and the organization of their communities. Nevertheless, their situation was not an easy one. Christians were exposed to constant injustices at the hand of the local authorities. The first interventions of the Christian powers — France, Austria, Russia, and England — in the Ottoman Empire produced political spoils which they hungrily wished to divide among themselves. Similarly, the successful Greek revolt of 1829 produced only greater Turkish suspicions of the Christians, who were thought to be receiving their orders from foreign countries and awaiting an opportunity to revolt also.

The Catholic group, imbedded in the mass of the Orthodox Christians among whom the Greek element attempted to gain dominance over the Slavs and Arabs, did not constitute a homogeneous bloc. More than half of them, especially in Syria and Egypt, belonged to other rites and had their own hierarchy. But there was also an appreciable number of Latin Catholics spread over the entire Empire. They numbered about two hundred thousand in 1815 and steadily increased in the course of the century. The growth was caused in part by conversions, in part by high birth rates in the rural and mountainous areas, and in part by Italian, French, and Austrian immigration to the centers of commerce.

The majority of the Latin communities were in a very bad position. The interruption of normal communications with Rome and the chaos following the Austrian-Turkish and Napoleonic wars had produced frequent vacancies in the episcopal sees, a reduction of missionaries, and a lack of discipline among the lower clergy. The delegates of the Congregation for the Propagation of the Faith systematically devoted themselves to an alleviation of these conditions as soon as they had reorganized themselves after the return of Pius VII to Rome, but often lacked the necessary tact.

The densest Latin center, even then accounting for only 20 percent of the population, was Albania (seventy-five thousand Catholics), where six bishoprics existed from the time of the Middle Ages, and Bosnia-Herzegovina (one hundred thousand Catholics), where in contrast to Albania virtually no secular clergy were left and where the parishes were administered by Franciscans, whose three authorized monasteries were the centers of Catholic education.

Another relatively important center was the Rumanian principality of Moldavia, which during the first half of the century experienced a particularly rapid growth of Catholics (from sixteen thousand to sixty thousand). But the apostolate in this area, entrusted to Italian and Hungarian conventuals, encountered great difficulties because of the wide dispersion of the believers and the ethnic hatreds between Rumanians and Magyars.

In the south of Bulgaria, where the few surviving Catholics lived without resident clergy, Austrian Redemptorists settled in 1830 in Philippopel, and from there began to spread over the country. The situation in Serbia was hardly better, although the Orthodox clergy there were more tolerant than in other areas.

Before 1830, Roman Catholicism was hardly represented on the Greek peninsula, and on the islands, where for a long time Latin groups of Venetian and Genoan origin had resided, the Catholic presence had been reduced to scant remains by the exodus of Italian settlers as well as by mixed marriages. The center of Catholicism was on the island of Syros. The arrival of numerous Orthodox refugees during the course of the wars of independence caused this "Island of the

Pope" to lose its long preserved exclusively Latin character. On the other hand, the recognition of independence by the London Protocol of 1830, which guaranteed complete freedom to the Catholic religion, and the subsequent installation of a Catholic sovereign, Otto von Wittelsbach, in Athens, allowed Catholicism to take hold in continental Greece. But Gregory XVI was looking farther into the future. As former prefect of the Congregation for the Propagation of the Faith he was fully informed of the problems of the Christian East. He knew that the Latin rite had no future among the Greek population, and in 1836 offered to send young Greeks to the reopened Greek College in Rome, there to train them in the Eastern rite. But this was a false hope. There was no doubt that the new Greece wished to remain faithful to its national Church.

In Constantinople and even more in the other port cities of the Levant, the Catholic missions were in full decay after the suppression of the Society of Jesus. In 1800, they had fewer than six thousand members. They were mainly foreigners and barely held together by a few Italian Lazarists and Capuchins.

Around 1830, new prospects developed for the Christians in the wake of the growing interest of the European chancelleries in the eastern problems and the shift in the balance of power occasioned by the temporary occupation of Syria and Palestine by Egyptian pasha Mohammed Ali. But the denominational map quickly changed with the acceleration of Anglo-Saxon missionary penetration, begun in 1825. The establishment of an Anglo-Prussian episcopal see in Jerusalem in 1841 was symbolic of the new interplay of political and ecclesiastical forces at work in the Middle East.

The Roman authorities observed with concern this growing influence of Protestant England and Orthodox Russia in areas in which heretofore Rome had enjoyed the nearly total support of French and Austrian diplomats. Nevertheless, they tried to gain the greatest possible benefit from the settlement of a growing number of Europeans in the Levant. The growth of the Catholic population, largely of European origin, justified the establishment of new Latin missionary stations. They were expected, more than the still insignificant numbers of the Uniates, to become centers of attraction for schismatic easterners, thanks to the prestige of western schools and in recognition of the services performed by hospitals and dispensaries for the poor. The revival of the orders in the European countries, especially France, favored this policy. The numbers of Franciscans, Capuchins, and Lazarists, pitifully small at the beginning of the nineteenth century, underwent a steady growth, and the entire movement grew until the end of the nineteenth century.

The vast majority of the members of these orders, whose cultural and spiritual influence was without a doubt beneficial for the moment, unfortunately had received no introduction to the specific problems of the Christian East. Therefore only a systematic Latinization appeared to them as an effective guarantee of Catholic unity. They refused to consider the objections which their blind zeal caused among the Uniate hierarchy already established in the area. They also ignored exhortations to be prudent by the Congregation for the Propagation of the Faith, which with its historical experience had a deeper insight. They were only interested in increasing the conversions of Uniates to the Latin rite and gradually were able to win to their view the responsible people in Rome. It was in this connection that the thought of a reestablishment of the Latin Patriarchate in Jerusalem arose.

But it was effected only ten years later, during the first months of the pontificate of Pius IX, as Rome feared offending the Uniate hierarchy. It constituted a landmark in the Latinization process of the Christian East, and was to have its effects in the second half of the century.

C H A P T E R   9

The Churches of America

Schmidlin described well the paradoxical situation of Catholicism in America at the beginning of the nineteenth century in this fashion: "In Latin, Central and South America, the Church, although overtly both Christian and Catholic, was internally deteriorating and close to dissolution; in Anglo-Saxon and French North America, Catholicism was only in its infancy and still partially in the phase of persecution, but everywhere nascent and spreading its wings."

Spanish America

When the Napoleonic interlude came to an end in 1814, and the Roman Curia was again free to make contact with the Churches of the world, there were forty bishoprics in Spanish America serving a population of about 15 million, which was centered largely in the Caribbean area. In spite of the continuing attachment of the population to the Catholic faith, an attachment which was especially concerned with external manifestations and a clear tendency toward religious syncretism among the American Indians in Mexico, Peru, and Bolivia, the Church was confronted with some extraordinarily difficult problems after the revolt of the old colonies against Spain. The revolutions, which had begun toward the end of the eighteenth century, by 1810 had led to the actual independence of most of the colonies.

Among these were financial problems. The substantial ecclesiastical property had been used by the two contending parties to cover their expenditures, and the Church, although formerly too wealthy, now was compelled to cancel some of its charities and even to close seminaries due to a lack of funds.

There were also problems of internal discipline. To the quantitative as well as qualitative regression and the turmoil produced by years of civil and military unrest for both the secular and the regular clergy there often was added a kind of ecclesiastical anarchy.

Finally, the relationship between Church and state and the consequences of this relationship carried with them extremely delicate problems. Without his permission, he did not allow the Pope to install new bishops in the area in which revolts had broken out but which he still considered as part of his Empire. The new republican governments, however, considered themselves heirs to that same patronage, and wanted to have direct influence not merely upon the administration of Church lands but also upon such internal affairs of the Church as the election of the chapter vicars in vacant dioceses and the decisions of the provincial chapters of the orders. This made the jurisdiction of those who had been placed in positions of authority through violations of canon law questionable, if not invalid. In many places situations were created which, strictly speaking, were "schismatic."

With the exception of some politicals, whose regalism exceeded even that of the radical Gallicanists of Europe, the majority of the leading laymen as well as the entire clergy were soon convinced that the only possible solution was contact with the Holy See, which, because of its universal significance, alone could correct this fundamentally irregular situation. However, the developments in both America and Europe delayed the continuation of such efforts by several years. Between 1814 and 1817, the significant military successes of Spain made possible the provisional restoration of its authority over the area except for the provinces of La Plata, and Rome, under the influence of the spirit of restoration, saw in the nationalistic American movements only a delayed effect of the French Revolution, which it hoped could be assigned to the past. In these circumstances, Pius VII, who until 1819 received inadequate information about America solely by way of Madrid, tacitly accepted the measures of the Spanish King against the patriotic bishops. Without the slightest pressure from the Spanish King, on 13 January 1816, the Pope, in his Encyclical *Etsi longissimo,* exhorted the bishops of the New World to aid the reinstallation of the legitimate authorities. Vehement polemics by the republican press against Rome and the loyalist bishops followed, and the Church in America became the victim of the same principle of legitimacy which was beneficial for the Church in Europe.

Soon the encyclical itself was to be overtaken by events, and Consalvi was astute enough to recognize this fact quickly. Between 1818 and 1820, as a result of Bolivar's victories, Latin America regained its independence. Then, when between 1820 and 1823 a liberal regime came to power in Spain and followed a pronounced anticlerical policy, the pro-Spanish sympathies still harbored by many South American clergymen disappeared quickly. The condition of the Church constantly worsened, and Rome began to eye a new, more realistic stance. A first public echo of this was a letter of 7 September 1822, from Pius VII to Bishop Lasso, who, after having been a glowing defender of legitimism until 1820, had taken Bolivar's side. In the letter, which was widely publicized by the South American press, the Pope affirmed the neutrality of the Holy See with respect to the political changes in America, an affirmation which was tantamount to an actual desertion of the Spanish cause, and was an implicit renunciation of the unfortunate "legitimist encyclical" of 1816.

The new papal position coincided with the arrival in Rome of the first official emissary from a South American republic, Canon Cienfuegos. Cienfuegos had been delegated by the Chilean government to ask the Pope to fill the vacant dioceses, if only with titular bishops, and to transfer the right of patronage, once held by the King of Spain, to the new government. In the spring of 1823, Pius VII sent Monsignor Muzi as vicar apostolic to Chile. The vicar apostolic arrived with extensive authorization to deal with the ecclesiastical situation in Chile. Before his departure, Monsignor Muzi was given jurisdiction over all areas of America no longer administered by Spain. Unfortunately, Muzi's mission ended in failure. While Muzi received a friendlier reception in the provinces of La Plata, his lack of tact and political sensibility poisoned the situation in Chile.

The new head of government, General Freire, and his foreign minister, Pinto, posed unacceptable conditions for the consecration of two new titular bishops, whose appointment was one of the most important objectives of the mission, and were equally unwilling to negotiate with respect to the orders. Muzi also encountered the intrigues of chapter dean Cienfuegos, who wanted to become bishop and did not hesitate to accept his appointment from the government as administrator of the diocese of Santiago. Thus Muzi, who had come to Chile to stabilize the hierarchy, through his ineptitude deprived the country of its only remaining bishop and thus the source of priests for years to come.

In the meantime, Leo XII had become Pius VII's successor, and with the end of the liberal regime in Madrid, the Spanish ambassador Vargas Laguna, then at the height of his prestige, reappeared in Rome. Laguna was a bitter defender of the principle of legitimacy and for this reason was hostile to any contacts between the Holy See and the insurgents even for the settlement of purely spiritual problems. Supported by the ambassadors of Austria and Russia, Laguna succeeded on 24 September 1824 in wringing from the new Pope the legitimist Encyclical *Etsi iam diu.* This document was to constitute no more than an interlude. After Varga's sudden death, the opposite opinion gained ground, and the Holy See was convinced that it should not become involved in the political struggle between Spain and its former colonies, but should confine itself to safeguarding the spiritual interests of America's dioceses. A first important step in this direction was taken in the summer of 1825. In agreement with Fra Mauro Cappellari, the future Pope Gregory XVI, who soon was to grow into an expert on Latin American affairs, Leo XII decided to follow the advice of the cardinals of the Congregation for the Propagation of the Faith to comply with the request of the episcopate of Greater Colombia. He appointed a bishop *in partibus* without informing the government in Madrid.

This was only a provisional step. In order not to provoke the radical elements and to have to face the equivalent of a Civil Constitution of the Clergy, direct negotiations with the government with respect to the entire situation of the Church were imperative. The Spanish King agreed to have J. Sánchez de Tejada, one of Bolívar's delegates, approved as a simple emissary of the bishops and the chapter of Greater Colombia. Tejada, who as a good Catholic desired a positive conclusion, exercised great diplomacy and managed to reduce the demands of his superiors without losing patience in the face of Rome's hesitation. Additionally, Bolívar himself, regardless of his own religious attitude, realized that a policy favorable to Catholic interests, symbolized by an agreement with Rome, would make it easier to tie the clergy, which still exercised a considerable influence on the masses, to the new government. Such circumstances and Cappellari's bold vision introduced a new phase in 1827. Without regard to the prerogatives once accorded the Spanish King, the Pope appointed resident bishops rather than titular ones to the vacant sees of Greater Colombia. In order to avoid the appearance of a political arrangement, the appointments were made *motu proprio* and not officially in response to the suggestions of the government.

Hardly had Leo XII made this gesture, which raised great hopes in all of Spanish America, than he appeared to reverse his position. Having always had legitimist tendencies, the Pope bowed to Ferdinand's furious objections and, in spite of the advice of Cappellari, who meanwhile had become prefect of the Congregation for the Propagation of the Faith, promised to appoint only vicars apostolic in the future. In line with this decision, the Pope suggested to the Consistory the appointment of two vicars apostolic for Chile. The Argentine crisis, particularly serious because the provinces of La Plata had not had a single bishop for years and because the government with its unilateral interference in ecclesiastical matters had gone very far, was handled by Pius VIII in similar manner in the following year when political forces propelled men into power who were less hostile to Rome.

A parallel development in Mexico, where almost half of the Catholics of Spanish America resided, also raised hopes for an arrangement before too long. But the government's emissary, Canon Vázquez, was uncompromising in one point. He considered it humiliating for his country to have to be satisfied with vicars apostolic, while Greater Colombia had been assigned resident bishops. The election of Cappellari, who in 1831 became Gregory XVI, put an end to the problem. Within three weeks, the new Pope appointed six resident bishops in Mexico and published his reasons in the Bull *Sollicitudo Ecclesiarum*. In the following year, the vicars apostolic of Argentina and Chile received the status of resident bishops and shortly afterward (1834–35) moved to reorganize the Peruvian hierarchy, to end the schism in San Salvador (1839–42), and to settle the ambiguous situation of Paraguay (1844).

After the official recognition of New Granada (Colombia) by the Holy See in 1836, an internuncio was sent to Bogota. His jurisdiction was to encompass all of Spanish America, and his appointment signalled a new phase in the normalization of the relations between Holy See and the new South American republics.

Frictions between Church and state in the La Plata states were particularly vehement, and the episcopate soon took the side of the national revolution. Difficulties from other basic causes did continue, however. These problems were primarily of a social nature, because the Church was often allied with the large land owners, while the new government officials came from the intellectuals of the cities. There were also ideological causes. The majority of the clergy wished to retain as much as possible the former control of the Church over the press, education, and society in general. The class now in power, which had been strongly affected by Freemasonry, was not yet ready for a rationalistic laicism — most of the constitutions still embodied Catholicism as the state religion — but was in favor of the main principles of the Enlightenment, the independence of the civil power, and a control of the Church by the government. The orders became the first victims of this attitude. The secular clergy was concerned when its traditional privileges were limited by an appeal to the principles of 1789. This concern was indeed justified, as the politically liberal governments still laden with the regalistic heritage of the Bourbon era rarely were able to reconcile themselves to liberty for the Church. The result was that the lower clergy, which at the beginning of the independence movements often had sympathized with the liberal constitutions, after 1830 tended to become more conservative.

Brazil

The political development of Brazil was far less problematical for the Holy See than that of the former Spanish colonies; in spite of some republican riots in which a number of clergy also participated, it did not lead to the same clear break with the Old Regime. In 1808, the Portuguese King João VI had settled in Rio de Janeiro after fleeing Napoleon's invasion. He was followed by the nuncio of Lisbon, Caleppi, who handled the sale of Church lands well and was able to prevent the appointment of bishops by the archbishops without the participation of Rome. In 1822, after João VI's return to his capital, the large Brazilian landowners persuaded Don Pedro, the hereditary prince, to declare himself as the ruler of an independent Empire which was officially recognized by Portugal. Leo XII received the ambassador of the new state in 1826.

With the continuation of the monarchial organization and the common dynasty assured, Rome did not hesitate to transfer to the Emperor the rights of patronage. It was possible to establish in Rio de Janeiro the first nunciature on the American continent; a symbol of the cooperation between Church and state.

But the cooperation was not entirely untroubled; it also produced difficult moments for the Holy See. These problems were occasioned principally by the Gallican and Febronianist attitudes of the clergy.

The United States

At the time of the Declaration of Independence of the thirteen American states, the Catholic population was very small: only twenty-five thousand in a population of 4 million in 1785. Catholics were chiefly concentrated in the two states with more tolerant legislation: sixteen thousand in Maryland, and seven thousand in Pennsylvania. There were nineteen priests in Maryland and five in Pennsylvania, principally members of the Jesuit Order. The remainder of the faithful was spread among the other states and had no native priests. In the course of the last twenty years of the eighteenth century, however, a rapid change came about. Under the influence of democratic ideals, the principle of religious freedom and the equality of all faiths was recognized. At the same time, a native Catholic hierarchy developed. After the vicar apostolic of London was no longer able to exercise his authority in the former colonies, the Holy See decided, after contemplating placing the territories under the jurisdiction of the bishop of Quebec, to succumb to the insistence of the Jesuits and to appoint one of them as head of the missions, although directly subordinated to the Congregation for the Propagation of the Faith. The choice was John Carroll (1735–1815), brother of one of the authors of the Declaration of Independence of 1776. Carroll, an experienced priest, although a man of the world, was both deeply Roman Catholic and fully American and completely convinced of the principles of separation of Church and state and of tolerance toward other religions. In the course of the years, he came to believe that only someone with episcopal authority could lead the diverse flock which posed so many problems for him. The Holy See concurred with his assessment and on 6 November 1789 established the diocese of Baltimore. After Carroll's consecration in England on 15 August 1790, he successfully continued the difficult work of organizing the new diocese. He made use of a few French priests whom the revolution had driven from France, and, with the help of four Sulpicians, in 1792 opened the first seminary in the United States in Baltimore. In the preceding year he had founded a boys college at Georgetown, under the direction of the Jesuits, who again were given regular status as an order in 1806. A good number of settlers moved to the Middle West, and a few Irish Dominicans followed them. It was much more difficult, however, to find nuns in Europe willing to take care of parish schools. In 1809, a young widow, the convert Elizabeth Bayley Seton (1774–1821), founded the first native congregation, the Sisters of Charity. It developed rapidly and acted as model for other similar congregations.

The growth of the young Church soon required the division of the huge diocese of Baltimore, which comprised the entire United States with the exception of Louisiana, which, as a French colony, had its own bishops residing in New Orleans since 1793 and was annexed in 1803. On 8 April 1808, Pius VII established four new dioceses: Boston, Philadelphia, and New York (vacant until 1814) on the East coast and Bardstown (renamed Louisville in 1841) in Kentucky. When Archbishop Carroll died in 1815, the number of Catholics had grown to one hundred fifty thousand, ministered to by one hundred priests. This figure corresponded to only a small diocese in western Europe, but the progress was to continue unabated. A quarter of a century later, shortly before the huge wave of immigrants began in the 1840s, the number of Catholics had quadrupled. This was a consequence both of the general increase in population as well as the steady immigration, particularly from Catholic Ireland. Success occurred in spite of the problems posed by the Protestant environment and the vast geographical distances. To be sure, the six hundred sixty-three thousand Catholics in the United States in 1840 were less than the Catholic population of Cuba and only 4 percent of the total population of the United States, but the percent-age had doubled since 1815. The fact that the Holy See founded twenty new dioceses between 1820 and 1837 demonstrated its prompt efforts to provide this new, growing Church with ecclesiastical administration. In Rome, the United States was still viewed as a missionary area, but in spite of many obstacles the North American Church quickly developed its own character and orientation.

The first of these difficulties was the shortage of priests. In order to provide the huge areas coming under settlement with a minimum of service, it was necessary to use European priests even at the risk that Catholicism might be viewed as an alien religion.

The national rivalries of this heterogeneous clergy further complicated the situation. The priests who had left France in order not to expose themselves to the iniquities of the revolution were without a doubt the best educated and almost always irreproachable in their conduct. Many of the new bishops and their assistants were selected from their ranks and from the persons recommended by them. Unfortunately this was sometimes a course of action fraught with disadvantages. These pastors had mastered the English language only imperfectly. The increasing number of Irish priests, full of enterprise and often boisterous, suffered under the moderation of the French prelates educated in the Sulpician spirit, a moderation which appeared to the Irish as lack of ability. In the 1840s, the American episcopate began to take on the Irish character which was to remain for almost a century. The Irish characteristics were not without disadvantages, but at least they had the advantage that they provided American Catholicism with pastors who did not expect state subsidies or who were able to exercise their apostolate in a society dominated by Protestant leaders.

After 1825, the Catholic Church was confronted with another problem, this time coming from outside the Church. A wave of hostility toward aliens, which gave the name of nativism to the movement, caused an aggressive revival of anti-Catholic sentiments. An objection by the Catholic hierarchy to the obligation of Catholic students in the public schools to attend Protestant Bible classes was presented at the very moment when there was a general renewed interest in the Bible. The objection was interpreted as proof of Catholic disregard of Holy Scripture, and a ferocious campaign began in the press, and meetings, backed by the Protestant Association, were held against the "godlessness and the corruption of papism." The growing number of Catholic immigrants from Ireland and Germany buoyed the agitation. A part of the population saw its standard of living threatened by cheap immigrant labor, and others saw in it a plot by the Holy See and the Holy Alliance to smother political and religious freedom in the United States with a flood of Catholic immigrants who would blindly obey a reactionary clergy. The result was a number of assaults on churches and monasteries between 1834 and 1836 which, after a brief phase of quietude, erupted again with renewed virulence after 1840.

The "nativist" campaign had at least the one positive result that it impelled Catholics to leave their ghettos and to defend their cause in word and print. Thus it brought about the rise of the Catholic press.

Publication was not the only area in which the influence of John England (1786–1842), Charleston's dynamic bishop, became known. It was because of his persistence that the first council of the Church province of Baltimore, which had been scheduled to convene in 1812, was finally convoked in October 1829. The immediate results were a series of decrees regarding the rights of the bishops as opposed to the clergy and the trustees, the construction and maintenance of churches; catechisms and schools; clothing of the clergy; sports; the Catholic press; and the living conditions of orders. At the conclusion of the session the archbishop and his six auxiliaries composed two pastoral letters. One was directed to the clergy with the admonition to study the Scriptures and not to become too involved in earthly matters, and the other exhorted the laity to contribute to education and the press and to beware of religious indifferentism under the guise of liberalism. The second council, meeting in 1833, urged Rome to consider the advice of the bishops when appointing new ones. Reserving the principle of freedom of action to the Holy See, the Congregation for the Propagation of the Faith accepted an arrangement according to which the names of candidates should be suggested by the American episcopate in the future. This system was retained until 1866. A third provincial council took place in 1837, and subsequently the bishops met regularly every three years.

One of the problems dealt with by the first provincial council of Baltimore concerned the orders. To alleviate the shortage of secular clergy, the bishops had sent a plea for help to the European orders and congregations. The Jesuits, Sulpicians, Augustinians, and Dominicans already present at the time of Monsignor Carroll were joined by the Lazarists (1816); the Redemptorists (1832), chiefly active in the Middle West among the people of German descent; the Holy Cross Fathers (1841); and the Franciscans (1844). Among the convents of such European congregations as the Sisters of the Sacred Heart (1818), the Sisters of Saint Joseph of Cluny (1831), and the Sisters of Our Lady of Namur (1840), there very soon were native congregations to testify to the vitality of the young American Church. To the first native congregation of Elizabeth Seton's Sisters of Charity were added, in 1812, the Sisters of Charity of Nazareth and the Sisters of Loreto in Kentucky, and shortly afterward the black congregations of the Sisters of Providence (1829) and the Sisters of the Holy Family (1842).

The sisters were engaged chiefly in the parish schools and charitable efforts. The Church hierarchy was also involved with the creation of reception stations for Catholic immigrants through the generous help of European mission organizations such as the French Society for the Spreading of the Faith, Austria's Leopoldine Foundation, and the Bavarian Mission Society. The Church administration in the United States had no experience in the area of Catholic education, but the necessity to acquire such experience very quickly became evident. In 1840, there were two hundred parish schools, half of them west of the Alleghenies. With respect to charitable works, the first Catholic orphan home was opened in Philadelphia in 1814 by the Sisters of Charity, who because of the generosity of a layman from St. Louis also were able to open the first Catholic hospital there. Thus the tight network of institutions independent from the government, which is so characteristic of present-day Catholicism in the United States, had its roots in the first decades of the nineteenth century. They were generated by the immediate needs of a Church which constituted a minority in a Protestant country, but which because of a constitutionally guaranteed separation of Church and state could develop unhindered and in complete freedom.

The young American Church was firmly determined to turn away from French and Spanish traditions which might have expanded from the mission stations of the Great Lakes or the eighteenth century Churches of Louisiana and Florida. The atmosphere of Catholic romanticism and the longing for medieval Christianity was alien to this new Church, and it developed its strength by concentrating increasingly upon the urban centers of the East Coast.

Forty years later, the most important Church leader of the next generation, John England, sounded the same note with increased optimism in a letter to O'Connell: "I am convinced that a total separation from the temporal government is the most natural and safest state for the Church in any place where it is not, as in papal territory, a complete government of churchmen." These and similar concepts appeared in the Roman Curia as dangerous paradoxes, and Rome was frequently concerned about the happenings in a Church about which it knew so little.

Canada

While only a few tens of thousands of Catholics lived in the United States at the beginning of the nineteenth century, there were one hundred fifty thousand of them in Canada, and this number grew to four hundred sixty-five thousand by 1831. Under the aegis of Bishop John Octave Plessis (1806–25) the Canadian Church, which since the conquest by England had to suffer under administrative chicaneries, experienced a period of prosperity. The Quebec Act of 22 June 1774, guaranteed the Canadian Catholics "the free exercise of the faith of the Church of Rome" and the retention of its traditional institutions. After some hesitation, the British government also granted permission for the establishment of a bishopric in Quebec. The head of the bishopric was only to employ the title of "Superintendent of the Romish Church," but was to have the privilege of appointing parish priests without the approval of the governor. The rebellion in the colonies of the United States had a positive effect upon the Canadian Church, because the Catholics constituted a rather significant element in the portion of the British colonies which survived the War of Independence. The government in turn was prepared to augment the loyalty of the Catholics with new concessions.

New vexations began, however, with the new Anglican Bishop Mountain, whom George III in 1794 appointed as "Lord Bishop of Quebec." Mountain had the backing of Governor Craig and especially of the secretary for South Canada, Ryland, both of whom held that the best means of Anglicizing the new colony was the promotion of the development of the Anglican Church. The Catholics, among others, were compelled to accept the control of the government over ecclesiastical appointments and the income of the Church.

It was under these conditions that Monsignor Plessis, coadjutor since 1800, became bishop of Quebec in 1806. This prelate, combining strength of character with an enterprising spirit, became the backbone of resistance to the anti-Catholic attacks of British local governments. At the same time, he was clever enough to remain loyal to London and gained the appreciation of the British during the War of 1812 with the United States. Bishop Plessis was rewarded with membership in the Legislative Council, where he became rather influential, as well as with the official recognition of his title as bishop of Quebec (1817); a title which initially had been rejected. Now thought could be given to dividing the Quebec diocese, which hitherto had stretched from the Atlantic to the Pacific. In spite of some obstacles posed by London, five vicariates apostolic were established between 1817 and 1820. Two of these were in the maritime provinces, where many Irish and Scottish immigrants had joined the descendants of the original Nova Scotians. One of the new vicariates, that in Montreal, even began to overtake Quebec in importance, and in the one in Kingston on Lake Ontario after 1817 an English-speaking Catholic community grew up. After Kingston (1826) and Charlottetown (1829), Montreal received in 1836 the rank of an independent diocese.

The Catholic schools were severely threatened by the founding, at the urging of the Anglican bishop, of the *Institution royale,* but were saved by the *Société d'éducation* of Quebec. With the backing of Protestant dissenters, who also fought against Anglican confiscation, a pluralistic school regulation was ultimately agreed upon, which allowed the parochial schools to develop without hindrance.

Monsignor Plessis always took a legal approach in his actions and thus incurred the displeasure of some fanatics who envisioned a rapid increase in the number of French Canadians. After Plessis' death, against the will of the bishops, an autonomist agitation developed under the pretext of religious demands, which between 1837 and 1838 led to armed riots that could have created an uncomfortable situation for the Church. But the government was understanding, and the act of union between Quebec and Ontario in 1840, which initially was viewed with suspicion by the Catholics, eventually proved to be very advantageous because it extended to the entire country the religious guarantees which in 1791 had only been granted to Lower Canada.

Yet while the legal position of Catholicism improved, its religious condition seemed to be rather mediocre, at least in Quebec, where the majority of the Catholics were located. The number of priests was far too small, and the ban on recruiting priests in France led to a Canadianization of the clergy. In spite of the founding of seminary colleges in several small towns such as Nicolet in 1807 and Saint Hyacinthe in 1811, the first part of the nineteenth century was a poor time for recruiting priests. The shortage of priests, the vast distances, the long winters, and the open way of settling made already difficult working conditions even more difficult.

C H A P T E R   1 0

The Churches of the Eastern Rite

The Uniates of the Near East

In the West, ecclesiastical reorganization began as early as 1815, but the efforts to regain the Christian communities in the Ottoman Empire met great obstacles. This is particularly true for the religious minorities which, with the exception of the Maronite Patriarchate, had just begun to mature by the beginning of the nineteenth century. In order to bring the work of renewal to fruition it was necessary, even more than in the European provinces of Turkey, to effect those structural changes which after 1830 were to change the civil and religious physiognomy of the Near East. But this change also had its dark side. The liberal attitude of the Ottoman government favored the Uniates, but at the same time facilitated missionary penetration from the West, exposing the still-weak Uniate communities to Protestant, Anglican, and Russian-Orthodox competition. It also promoted the Latinizing infiltration and the Roman process of centralization, which was to become characteristic for the history of the unity movement of the entire nineteenth century.

The Maronite Patriarchate was by far the most important group of Uniate Christians in the Near East. The crisis of authority which it underwent in the second half of the eighteenth century was resolved under the leadership of the patriarchs Yohanna Al-Halu (1809–23) and Yussef Hobeich (1823–45). Hobeich was a man of energy and vision, who based his work of ecclesiastical reconstruction on full cooperation with the apostolic delegates and a political and religious France.

After his reconciliation with Monsignor Gandolfi, the representative of the Holy See, Yohanna Al-Halu in 1818 convoked a council at Lowaizeh. It decided at last to implement the decisions of the council of Lebanon, made a century earlier in 1736. But the most important objectives were implemented only under Hobeich. In 1826 he dissolved the double or mixed monastic institutions and established an episcopal residence in each diocese. He also founded several new seminaries and thereby assured the training of a relatively well educated clergy and of many school principals. But the support of his work by the French resulted in a strengthening of Latinizing tendencies, to which the publication of the ritual (1839–40) attests. With its close to two hundred thousand faithful, the Maronite Church numerically far surpassed all other Eastern Uniate communities, many of which were still at a very low stage of development in 1815.

This was especially true for the Copts, who were still dependent on the Franciscan mission in Egypt and received an autonomous ecclesiastical organization only under the pontificate of Leo XIII. The letter with which in 1822 Pius VII asked the Monophysite patriarch of Alexandria to profess the Catholic faith and to send young Copts to Rome for study remained unanswered, and until 1831 the number of the Uniates was only 2,624 with fourteen priests, dispersed over the entire country. Nevertheless, trusting in forged letters from Mohammed Ali, Leo XII in 1824 decided to reestablish a Coptic patriarchate.

The Uniate Chaldean Church, developed as a consequence of the Roman adherence by several Nestorian prelates in the seventeenth and eighteenth centuries, was buffeted by a number of vicissitudes at the beginning of the nineteenth century. Its hierarchy was firmly established by this time, though, and the Church numbered twenty thousand faithful. In addition to being isolated in Upper Mesopotamia under extremely poor living conditions, the Uniate Chaldeans were also split by the rivalry of the two candidates for the patriarchal position. The Congregation for the Propagation of the Faith appointed as "Patriarch of Babylonia" John Hormez, who until this time had been viewed by Rome with mistrust. More important than institutional changes was the adherence to Rome in 1828 of the influential monastery Rabban Hurmuz. With this monastic center as focal point, the Chaldean union movement was immensely strengthened spiritually. In 1845, Gregory XVI recognized the rules of the monastery, which were based on the ideas of Saint Anthony.

The small Syrian community, newly organized in 1782, underwent a fairly parallel development during the first half of the nineteenth century. Here also the fights of rivaling parties delayed a reorganization until 1830. Devoting himself to a restructuring of his Church more in keeping with the demands of modern times. Pierre Jarweh changed the monastery of Scharfeh, in which he lived, into a seminary and replaced the monastic vows by the simple acceptance of celibacy, a vow of obedience, and some testamentary obligations of the former students. The Congregation for the Propagation of the Faith in 1828 at first rejected the proposal, but accepted it in 1841. Between 1827 and 1836 the Syrian community became known as the Syrian Church in order to distinguish it from the Jacobite-Monophysites and so that it would profit from the traditional reputation of the Christian community of Antioch. The Church experienced a very fortunate development in that several Jacobite bishops declared their loyalty to Rome and thereby added about twenty thousand believers to the Church.

The return of Jacobite prelates to Roman Catholicism was due to the new Melkite Patriarch Maximos III Mazlum (1833–55). Through his diverse and persistent activities he transformed his languishing community into a flourishing Church, yet was determined to defend the autonomy of the Byzantine tradition within the framework of the Roman Church. Until 1830, the Melkite Church suffered from the consequences of the council of Karkafeh (1806) to which some bishops, headed by Germanos Adam, had given a definitely Gallican orientation because they were tired of the interference of Latin missionaries and were disadvantaged by their theological inferiority. The joint reaction of the Maronite patriarch and all of the missionaries placed the Melkite Church in dependence on the apostolic delegate, Monsignor Gandolfi, who intended to master the situation by "breaking the back of the eminent personalities, weakening the hierarchy, and forcing upon it the awareness of defeat" (Hajjar). Fearing Gallican indoctrination, he demanded that the seminary of Ain-Traz, founded in 1811, remain closed. As the Melkite clergy had no other educational institutions available, and since the best educated among the laity demanded a schooled clergy, they preferred to confess to the Latin missionaries and listen to their sermons. A first step toward the reopening of Ain-Traz in 1831 was taken when Mazlum, who since 1814 had lived in exile in Rome where he had earned the respect of the future Gregory XVI, returned and brought with him a few Jesuits for the seminary. Two years later he was elected patriarch and with determination devoted himself to a general reform of the ecclesiastical institutions. He raised the religious standards of his flock, encouraged the training of an educated and pious clergy, and adjusted the legislation and the structure of the diocesan organization, which stretched across the entire Near East, to the new political and social realities of his country. As defender of patriarchal privileges against the missionaries, the apostolic delegates, and the Roman congregations, this "indefatigable fighter," very suspect in ultramontane circles succeeded in freeing his Church from the oppressive monopoly of official orthodoxy. He did so with great persistence by emancipating his national Church, a process which was started in 1831 by an ordinance of the Sultan in favor of Catholic Armenians.

As trading people, the Armenians were spread across the entire Near East and some of them had entered a union with the Roman Catholic Church. A few thousand lived dispersed in the Russian Empire, and after 1635 a Uniate Armenian archbishop resided in Lemberg in Poland, while in Venice, and after 1811 also in Vienna, two communities of learned monks, the Mechitharists, contributed to acquainting the West with some traditions of the Christian East. Within the Ottoman Empire they were found especially in Cilicia and Syria — headed by a *Katholikos,* who after 1750 resided in Bzommar in Lebanon — and in Constantinople, where in spite of the impressive number of fifteen thousand members they did not have their own prelate but were dependent on the Latin vicar apostolic. In 1830 they received an archbishop of their rite, who was independent of the patriarch. In keeping with the secular legislation of the Ottoman Empire, the Uniate Armenians were dependent on the schismatic Armenian patriarch for all civil needs, just as the other Uniate Churches were subordinated to the Orthodox patriarch. The Turkish government did not distinguish between Catholic and non-Catholic Christians as long as they belonged to the Eastern rite. In connection with the Greek rebellion in 1827, the Gregorian (i.e., non-Uniate Armenian) patriarch denounced Constantinople's Catholics as accomplices of the rebels and caused them to be persecuted. Leo XII, deeply shocked by such conduct, intervened together with France and Austria and in 1830 obtained from the Sultan, in addition to a limit to the expulsions, the emancipation of the Catholic Armenian communities. From now on they were free to build new churches and received their own civil *patrik*. As a consequence of the liberal development after Mohammed Ali's victories, the jurisdiction of this priest by the decree of 3 June 1834 was expanded to all Uniates, Maronites, Melkites, Syrians, and Chaldeans. The government at Constantinople thereby acknowledged their legal existence for the first time.

The next step was the recognition of the autonomy of each of these communities. The Melkite Patriarch Mazlum played an eminent role in the process. He succeeded in 1837, with the backing of French diplomacy and despite Russian objections, in obtaining from the Sultan recognition as the civil head of the Catholic Melkites. He remained subordinate to the Armenian *patrik* only formally. A further step was taken in 1844 when, again under the protection of the French ambassador, the Uniate patriarchs of the Syrians and Chaldeans were given an analogous position. But they lived rather reclusive lives and thought it advisable to reach an agreement with the Armenian *patrik*. Mazlum, however, continued his fight and finally on 7 January 1848 obtained a decree which freed his Church community even from any nominal tutelage.

The emancipation of the Uniate groups from the corresponding Eastern Churches, resulting from the political developments in the Near East, constituted an important turning point in the history of the unification movement. The Uniate Churches from now on were able to develop and organize freely and unhindered. But the consolidation at the same time led to a deepening of the rift which separated the Uniate Churches from those from which they had sprung. Thus they could no longer function as bridges between them and Rome. Their growth and the cultural and apostolic rejuvenation of which they had urgent need could only be effected with aid from the West; by the same token, the West's juridical, theological, and spiritual impact could be nothing but disastrous for communities which tended to have feelings of inferiority. The spontaneous and often unintentional development which increasingly estranged the Uniate Churches from the unadulterated Eastern tradition was amplified by the policy of the apostolic delegates. Sometimes with good intentions and often with tactless intransigence, which in some cases exceeded their instruction, they attempted to subordinate the Uniate patriarchates to Rome's central control. To be sure, the efforts of the Holy See to establish closer bonds between these Churches and Rome were understandable. But the almost total ignorance of the Eastern institutions and the general opinion that true unity could only be achieved through uniformity had the consequence of removing, even though done in good faith, the substance of the institution of the patriarchate and the synodal organization of the Church. This Roman policy, which aimed at a redefinition of the authority of the patriarchs in keeping with the purely nominal prerogatives of the Latin archbishops, was pursued with utmost determination only by Pius IX, but its beginnings could be noted during the pontificate of Gregory XVI. An important way station was the decision of the Congregation for the Propagation of the Faith of 23 May 1837. It decreed that the Uniate patriarchs had to ask the Roman Pope for a confirmation of their election and the investiture with the pallium, and were entitled to assume the other aspects of their jurisdiction only after receiving it. Furthermore, it demanded the approval of the Holy See for decisions of councils before they were published, and forbade the patriarch and his synod to publish decrees which deviated, even if only implicitly, from the discipline approved by the Roman authority. This decree, hardly noticed at the time, introduced a veritable revolution in Eastern law, signifying the distance which within a few decades had been traversed concerning the restoration of papal prerogatives.

The Romanian and Slavic Groups

In Eastern Europe there were several millions of Uniates, mostly belonging to the Austro-Hungarian Dual Monarchy, who even in the eyes of Rome were a natural bridge for the encounter with Slavic Orthodoxy.

Transylvania was the home of half a million Romanians, grouped in two dioceses of the Hungarian Church province of Gran; Blaj was their ecclesiastical and cultural center. Between 1782 and 1830 the position was held by John Bob, educated in the Josephine spirit, who put an end to Uniate Monachism which counted among its followers such eminent men as Peter Maior, one of the pillars of the Romanian cultural renaissance. He and his colleague Vulcan, bishop of Oradea Mare (Grosswardein) (1806–39), continued the reintegration into the Catholic Church of the schismatic parishes from the time of Maria Theresia and awakened in the secular clergy a new awareness of its pastoral obligations. In spite of receiving little help from Latin Catholics, they developed a network of educational institutions, which assured the flock of their Church an intellectual level far above that of the other Uniate Churches, as the synods of Blaj (1821 and 1833) attest. John Bob's successor, I. Lomeni (1833–50), continued his work by promoting the religious impact of his clergy and gathered able professors in Blaj to serve both religious and national aims.

Much more important was the group of the Ruthenians or Ukrainians who after the Union of Brest (1595) had fallen away from the Russian Church. After two centuries of uninterrupted Polish oppression, the Ruthenians had succumbed to the attraction of the powerful and rich Latin Church to a larger degree than the other Uniates and adopted a number of western customs in the area of devotional exercises and discipline. These were acknowledged and strengthened by the Council of Zamosc in 1720 and ultimately led to their clear differentiation from the Orthodox Church.

The Polish partitions at the end of the eighteenth century split the Ruthenians into Austrian and Russian groups. The Russian government understandably was hostile to the Latin and Polish strains of the Uniate Church of the Ukraine and immediately began efforts to lead them back to the fold of Orthodoxy through the use of force, attempts at conversion, and elimination of the clergy. Alexander I's (1801–25) desire to effect a union of the two Churches made possible a lessening of the tension, leading to a partial restoration of the hierarchy which had been suppressed almost totally under Catherine II. But the deterioration could no longer be stopped. The relation of the Holy See to the Uniate Church continued to be difficult, and the representative of the Catholic Church in Russia, Monsignor Siestrzencewicz, who viewed the end of the Uniates as inevitable, attempted to lead as many Uniates as possible to the Latin rite, mindless of the protests of the Ruthenian clergy and the prohibitions of Rome. At the time of the accession of Nicholas I in 1825, the Uniate Church in the Russian Empire was still represented by 1.5 million believers, two thousand priests, and six hundred monks, but it was in the process of decay. The deterioration was enhanced by the fighting between some secular clerical dignitaries, trained in the Josephine spirit at the general seminary of Vilna, with the pro-Roman Basilian monks, whose wealth was the envy of the others. Catherine II's plan of a radical Russification was disinterred. Under the pretext of strengthening the Uniate Church, its structure was refashioned in the likeness of the Orthodox Church by the ukase of 22 April 1828. The liturgy was adapted; the clergy systematically indoctrinated; and the episcopal sees were staffed, without paying any attention to Rome, with men who agreed with the government. After they had circulated among the clergy a petition with 1305 signatures in February 1829 at the Synod of Polozk a bill of union with the Orthodox Church was drafted. Opposition from the population was ignored, and a number of the opponents thereupon fled to Galicia, while others secretly maintained their loyalty to Rome. Only the diocese of Chelm escaped immediate integration, as it was located in the Kingdom of Poland and thus belonged to another governmental jurisdiction.

The fate of the Ruthenians of Galicia, subordinated to Austria, was a happier one. In order to make them immune to Russian influence, Pius VII in 1807 created a new Church province and revived the old title of the Metropolitan of Halicz which he awarded to the bishop of Lvov, with Przemysl and Chelm as auxiliary sees. Within this new framework, the Uniate Ruthenian Church of the Habsburg Empire, numbering 2 million believers in 1840, was able to reorganize itself. Pursuing the directives of the synod of Přemysl of 1818, they increased the number of parishes and schools and worked at a quantitative and qualitative improvement of the spirit of the Enlightenment. But the results of these efforts were limited, as the Ruthenians no longer had a leading class ever since the majority of the aristocracy had turned away from the Eastern rite in order to enjoy the privileges reserved to the Poles. People ultimately became accustomed to have the "peasant faith" of the Ruthenian serfs on one side and the "landlord faith" of the Latin rite on the other. The feeling of inferiority growing out of this situation was the reason for a greater inclination to adopt western rites. Yet the development did not prevent frequent tensions with the Latin clergy inasmuch as it favored the change of rite. The Latin clergy thus followed its own nationalistic Polish feelings and the conviction that in this fashion the Ruthenians could best be strengthened in their Catholic faith. The attitude of the Holy See, however, was more differentiated. It encouraged

Latinization, but did not wish to see the suppression of the Ruthenian rite. On the contrary, Gregory XVI in 1843 considered the appointment of a patriarch for the Uniates in the Habsburg Dual Monarchy, because he wanted to encourage the return to the Roman faith of many of the Orthodox still there (nearly 3 million, principally in Hungary) and to protect the Uniates better against the attraction of the Russian Church.

In the Habsburg Empire of the seventeenth century, there lived in Podcarpathia another group of several hundred thousand Uniate Ruthenians who had never belonged to Poland and whose customs therefore in some points deviated from those of the Galician Ruthenians. After 1781 they had their own diocese of Mukačevo. The growing number of converts moved Pius VII in 1818 to establish a second diocese in Prešov. Zealous and expert bishops, who towered above the intended mediocrity of the prelates of the Russian Ukraine, lent a new buoyancy to the religious life with the help of the Catholic revival of the Habsburg Empire. The rivalry between Austria, to which Galicia belonged, and Hungary, to which Podcarpathia was subordinated, prevented the connection of the two dioceses with the metropolitan see of Lvov. Thus, just as the Romanian Uniate dioceses of Transylvania, they remained part of the Latin province of Gran, with the result that regulations concerning the Hungarian clergy were also accepted by these Uniates.

The unsuccessful efforts of the Vienna government in Dalmatia, as well as the more effective support which it granted to the more or less Latinized reorganization of the Uniate dioceses in Transylvania, Galicia, and Podcarpathia, were part of a comprehensive larger plan aiming at the largest possible absorption of the remaining Orthodox groups in the Empire. It did not do so, as was the case with Rome, for confessional reasons, but rather for the political reason of preventing the formation of beachheads of Russian influence in the area of the Balkans and Danube. Such ulterior motives behind the Uniate policy of the Habsburg states for a long time to come poisoned the relationship between the Vatican and the Russian Orthodox Church.

CHAPTER 11

The Resumption of Missionary Work

The Beginnings of Restoration prior to Gregory XVI

The French Revolution had no direct catastrophic effect upon missionary work. Only a few French possessions in the Antilles and in India were affected by it. At home, however, the destructive consequences of the activity of the encyclopedists and the deists were more than evident.

At the turn of the century, the problems of the missions required particular attention because it was a time of growing turbulence. The uninterrupted wars following the French Revolution and especially those under Napoleon made normal communications between the central office of the missions and the non-European areas almost impossible, and even the work of the central office itself was seriously disrupted. This disruption occurred first in 1798, when General Berthier occupied Rome and the offices of the Congregation. Hardly reorganized after 1800, the Congregation was almost totally destroyed after 1808 when Pius VII was taken into French captivity. The estates of the Congregation became the property of the French state; the printing house was closed down and its valuable type was handed over to the French state printing house; and finally, the entire archives of the Congregation were transferred to Paris. Only after the fall of Napoleon and the return of Pius VII was the Congregation gradually able to resume its orderly function and, after 1817, to improve its financial situation slightly.

Although Napoleon's plans to transfer the Pope and the Congregation as well to Paris failed, they indicate that the Emperor appreciated the great importance of missionary work, at least as a political activity. In a letter to Pius VII of 28 August 1802, Napoleon offered the Pope the protection of France for all missions in the Near East and China. In a memorandum in the same year Minister Portalis spoke of the political value of French missionary work, citing concrete examples of English efforts to establish such a protectorate in China.

The leading circles in France soon added to this political interpretation by an understanding of the religious concern for the propagation of the faith. The savior of the mission seminary in Paris and future general of the Congregation, Denis Chaumont (1752–1819) was a quiet but successful spokesman for missionary work. From his exile in London he tried to revive the missionary spirit through strong exhortations and the publication of mission reports. In 1805, an imperial decree restored the Paris mission seminary together with the seminary of the Fathers of the Holy Spirit, who were chiefly active in the French Antilles.

This success was prepared by René de Chateaubriand's (1768–1848) *Le Genie du Christianisme* (1802). The work principally served to revive the Catholic religion in France and the missions, especially in America, with which Chateaubriand was personally acquainted.

The book by this romantic was proof of the intimate connection between a revived Catholicism and the activity of spreading the faith. This connection explains why the Church in France, although for a long time affected by rationalistic and anti-Christian forces, was gradually able to hold a position of supremacy in Catholic missions. The focus of spreading the faith increasingly shifted from the Iberian countries to France. Here new missionary orders and congregations sprang up. In 1805, the Congregation of the Sacred Hearts of Jesus and Mary (Picpus Fathers) was founded, a congregation which provided the first complete group of Catholic missionaries in Oceania, and in 1807 the Sisters of Joseph of Cluny began continuous work in Africa and Asia. In 1816, the Oblates of the Immaculate Virgin Mary became the modern apostles to Canada, and in 1836 the Marian Society (Marists) was given responsibility for a huge area in the South Seas.

While French orders and societies trained and sent out new missionaries, Marie-Pauline Jaricot (1799–1862) sought to help the missionaries by founding in

Lyon in 1822 the Association for the Spreading of the Faith. The Association offered its help through regular prayers by the members and through a collection of a weekly "penny for the missions." Although the initial efforts of Marie-Pauline Jaricot were made in close contact with the Paris mission seminary, as early as the founding meeting plans were made to encompass all Catholic missions, a plan heartily supported and inspired by the two French bishops in America, Flaget (1763–1850) and Dubourg (1766–1833). The fact of such "Catholicity" was probably the reason for the fast growth of the association beyond the French borders at first to the neighboring countries of Savoy and Piedmont, then to Switzerland (1827) and the Netherlands (1830), and ultimately to America, Portugal, and Spain. Due to the exclusively French direction and administration, independent associations sprang up in Austria and Germany, where several missionary circles had been formed. People in Vienna founded the Leopoldine Foundation in 1828; people in the Rhineland organized themselves as the Xaverius Society in 1834, and in Bavaria the Ludwig Society was founded in 1838. In 1824, the journal *Annales de la Propagation de la Foi* began to appear regularly, at first in French and then in translation throughout most of Europe. After the Congregation for the Propagation of the Faith had been looted twice, first by revolutionary troops and then by Napoleon, the Association for the Spreading of the Faith became the most important source of money for the missions in modern times.

The Bull *Solicitudo omnium,* published by Pius VII on 17 August 1814, restored the Society of Jesus. This was an act of the greatest consequence for the missions. Shortly after assuming office, the Pope had armed the existence of the order in Russia. The Society had continued to exist there under the protection of Catherine II, but only papal recognition brought about an increase in its membership in Russia. The restoration of the Society was intended to rejuvenate the old Jesuit mission to China as well. Together with that in Indochina, the China mission was the only one which, in spite of all obstacles, had maintained a vibrant religious life.

Of fundamental importance for all of China was the first synod in Szechuan conducted by the martyr Bishop Gabriel Taurin Dufresse (1750–1815) together with fourteen Chinese and three European priests. The minutes of the synod were approved and published by the Congregation for the Propagation of the Faith in 1822, and a decree of 1832 made the decisions of the synod applicable to all of China. Although this synod with its far-reaching decisions gave the impression of peaceful conditions in China, in fact, local chicaneries continued and in 1805 and 1811 grew into general persecutions. In addition to persecutions, the Franciscan missions in the north suffered also from internal difficulties.

However, despite persecutions, the external organization of the dioceses and vicariates apostolic in China not only remained intact, but the European and Chinese missionaries also managed to create new Christian centers. These centers were small and widely scattered, but, in the course of the nineteenth century, they expanded to regular communities. By 1815, eighty-nine Chinese and eighty European priests devoted themselves to missionary work and ministered to two hundred ten thousand Christians. The relatively high number of Chinese clergymen illustrates the active way in which the European missionaries had conducted their training and education.

Efforts by Pius VII to provide support for beleaguered Catholics elsewhere,

such as in South Africa, Australia, India and Oceania, had only short-lived results or were total failures. It was his missionary zeal, however, that reorganized
the Congregation for the Propagation of the Faith, restored the Society of Jesus,
confirmed new missionary societies, and aided the Association for the Spreading of the Faith. Pius VII prepared the way for the restoration period under the
pontificates of Leo XII (1823–29) and Pius VIII (1829–30).

The Restoration of Missionary Work under Gregory XVI (1831–46)

In 1831, the Camaldolensian Cardinal Mauro Cappellari was elected Pope. Since
1826 he had been prefect of the Congregation for the Propagation of the Faith, and
as such was well acquainted with the deficiencies, obstacles, needs, and tasks
of missionary work. As Pope, he was eager to promote and to instill new life into
the various missionary endeavors.

Gregory XVI saw as his first task the acquainting of the Church of the western
world with the duties and tasks of spreading the faith, a task which heretofore
had been conducted primarily by the use of patronage powers. To do this, the
Pope used his first papal mission Encyclical *Probe nostis* of 15 August 1840, extensive support of the Association for the Spreading of the Faith, and recognition
and support of the Holy Childhood Association, founded in 1843. The national
mission associations in Aachen, Vienna, and Munich also received support from
Gregory XVI, who attempted to subordinate them to the direction of Lyon.

One of the chief concerns of the Pope was to increase mission personnel.
Spain and Portugal, which in the past had provided most of them, in the course of
persecutions between 1834 and 1836 had dissolved almost all of the orders and
religious associations and expelled or imprisoned their members. These persecutions had detrimental consequences for the Spanish successor states in America
and for the Portuguese missions. Although the Jesuits were the most persecuted
group in the Iberian states, France and Switzerland, Gregory XVI sought help for
their beleaguered missions. The Pope's position was also adopted by the Jesuit
General Johann Philipp Roothaan (1785–1835), and found enthusiastic readiness
among the Jesuits just as in the sixteenth and seventeenth centuries. Ever since
the Dutch general had taken over direction of the order in 1829, it had become
internally and externally strengthened; and at his death it again numbered 5209
members. Even more important for the organic growth of the Church was the
fundamentally positive attitude of General Roothaan toward the central mission
office of the Congregation for the Propagation of the Faith. He engaged tirelessly in
completely adjusting the work of the Jesuit missions to this highest organ of missionary activity. His struggle for cooperation by both parties was to be of benefit not
only for all mission work, but also for the activity of other orders and congregation.
The end of this development saw a strategy in effect to this very day: the division
of missionary areas and their transfer to the various orders and congregations.

The Paris mission seminary also followed the new trend. Until the nineteenth
century it had provided the vicars apostolic for the Far Eastern mission areas,
but had sent missionaries only in isolated cases. Now the bishops were joined
by missionaries of specific societies, who took entire mission areas under their

care. In fact, the seminary became the principal mission society for the Far East in the nineteenth century.

The Society of the Holy Ghost operated entirely in the service of the blacks, who at his time were virtually without missionaries. In 1841, the association began its mission and pastoral work on the island of Mauritius and in 1842 on the island of Réunion. The first ten missionaries, seven priests and three friars, arrived in Senegal in West Africa in 1843, but within one year all but one of them had succumbed to the tropical climate. In spite of all losses the ranks were refilled again and again, and in West and East Africa one mission area after the other was entrusted to the Congregation of the Holy Ghost. The fruitful development of missionary work was due not only to the heroic efforts and the vision of the missionaries, but also to those who never lost sight of a native Church.

Anna Maria Javouhey (1779–1851) had begun the work of spreading the faith. In 1807, she founded the Congregation of the Sisters of Saint Joseph of Cluny with the purpose of reviving the languishing religious life in France. When she heard of the great misery in Africa, she sent her sisters to the island of Réunion in 1817 and to Senegal in 1819. Accompanied by six companions, she herself brought aid to the suffering in West Africa, organized mission work in Senegal and neighboring Sierra Leone and, after 1827, devoted herself principally to the blacks in America and Guyana. Mother Anna's enterprise laid the foundation for the work of the sisters in Africa. Moreover, not only did she act as the pathfinder for missions in Africa; the example of her sisters was also the signal for a general participation of women in the modern Catholic apostolate overseas.

Even before the dissolution of the orders in the Iberian countries, the shortage of missionaries had negative results in the vast reaches of Asia which were part of the Portuguese patronage. Gregory XVI, as former prefect of the Congregation for the Propagation of the Faith, was well acquainted with the local conditions and from the beginning of his pontificate sought to ameliorate the situation. When Portugal failed to respond to the papal request, the Pope himself undertook the reorganization of ecclesiastical affairs in Asia, beginning first in India.

After solving a number of problems which had originated in part from the participating orders and in part from the governments of Portugal and England, Gregory XVI in 1834 reestablished the vicariate apostolic of Bengal (Calcutta), where the British East India Company, which virtually ruled the area, had its headquarters ever since 1733. Here, in 1819, was created the first Anglo-Indian bishopric.

A similar situation existed in Madras, where the British had built a fort as early as 1641, and never had permitted admission to Portuguese missionaries. Pastoral care here was in the hands of French Capuchins. As in Calcutta, the establishment of the vicariate apostolic of Madras in 1832 did not fully untangle the jurisdictional problems. The same was true for the vicariates of Pondichéry, Ceylon, and Madura, all of which were established in 1836.

Rome's unusual and significant intervention in India's mission situation was not accepted well everywhere by the patronage clergy. Some priests and their communities refused to obey the new bishops, who in turn demanded from Rome an unequivocal decision which would put an end to the disastrous double jurisdiction. It was not until 28 April 1838 that Gregory XVI signed the Decree *Multa praeclare,* and he failed to inform Portugal and the corresponding administrative levels in India of his decree in the correct form. His brief dissolved the patronage bishoprics of Kotschin, Kranganore, and Meliapur in India and the bishopric of Malacca in Indochina. The effect was disastrous, and the sporadic opposition to the vicar apostolic now hardened to a united front and in the subsequent period resulted in increased confusion.

Multa praeclare shook Portugal out of its lethargy. The Portuguese government nominated the Benedictine José Maria da Silva Torres (1800–1854) for the archiepiscopal see of Goa, vacant since 1831, and in 1843 Gregory XVI accepted him. Unfortunately the Pope appointed Torres according to the example of earlier bulls and only a private letter *Nuntium ad te* obligated the new archbishop to acknowledge the Brief *Multa praeclare* and the subsequent reduction of the archbishop's jurisdiction. As a Portuguese national, the new archbishop was compelled to act in accordance with *Multa praeclare,* while the vicars apostolic acted according to *Nuntium ad te.* Thus from the beginning the two points of view clashed irreconcilably and poisoned India's religious-ecclesiastical climate.

Gregory XVI in 1834 established the vicariate apostolic of Sardhana and in 1845 the vicariate of Patna in the Capuchin mission of Hindustan. Less troublesome than the reorganization of the dissolved Portuguese dioceses of India was that of Malacca which, first joined with Burma (vicariate apostolic of Ava and Pegu) and then after 1840 combined with Siam, was divided into two vicariates in 1841.

The most vivid growth of Christianity in Indochina took place in the former empires of Tonking and Cochinchina. Under Emperor Gialong (died 1821), who had ascended the throne with the help of the French and notably that of the vicar apostolic Pierre Pigneau de Behaine (died 1799), the mission experienced a period of rest which enabled it to heal the damages of the persecutions of the eighteenth century. In 1830, under his successor, Ming Mang (died 1841), however, a bloody persecution began which claimed hundreds of Christians, twenty Vietnamese priests, nine European missionaries, and four bishops as its victims. Gregory XVI in 1839 directed a letter of consolation and encouragement to the persecuted Church and, in a public consistory of 27 April 1840, praised the Christian fortitude of the individual martyrs. The Church was able to continue its existence only under the protection of the forests and rivers.

In spite of persecutions and a shortage of missionaries, the China mission survived relatively intact during the first half of the nineteenth century. That this was so was owed principally to the uninterrupted maintenance of the office of the Congregation for the Propagation of the Faith in Macao. Another factor was that Gregory XVI dealt more circumspectly with the bishoprics there than in India.

It was also during Gregory XVI's pontificate that the first three missionaries of the recently reinstated Society of Jesus were sent out. In 1841 the missionaries arrived in Macao and soon became active in the diocese of Nanking. According to the plans of General Roothaan, the China mission was to be a bridge for the reopening of the mission in Japan. Korea, the nearest and most natural connection with Japan, was difficult to reach. Only in 1837 was a missionary priest able to step upon Korean soil, to be followed in 1838 by the first bishop. In 1836, the Ryukyu Islands were assigned to the Korea mission in the expectation that they would facilitate the entry into Japan. The Paris missionary Father Forcade was appointed in 1846 as vicar apostolic, but all attempts to establish a mission in Japan proper failed.

A new epoch in Chinese mission history was introduced with the Chinese-French treaty of Whampoa in 1844, which had arisen out of the unfortunate Opium War and the subsequent treaty of Nanking. At Whampoa, the French plenipotentiary De Lagrené succeeded in obtaining not only the freedom of action which France wanted, but also, albeit to a limited degree, freedom of religion as well. This treaty concluded the period of the old China mission. The new mission, especially in the second half of the nineteenth century and the twentieth century, stood in the shadow of the French protectorate.

In the Philippines, the spreading of the faith was continued during the nineteenth century within the framework of the established hierarchy, and in Indonesia, established in 1831 and designated as vicariate apostolic in 1842, was compelled to limit its activity to the European population. The missions in Oceania, however, found a vast new field. The first Catholic representatives, the Picpus Fathers, arrived in Honolulu in 1827; Protestant missionaries had been active there since 1797. In 1833, Polynesia became a vicariate apostolic, and in 1836 West Oceania was separated from Lyon for the benefit of the Marists, a portion of which was elevated to the vicariate of Central Oceania in 1842.

The contrast between denominations, so evident in Oceania from the very beginning, was accentuated by political differences as well, with the Protestants siding with England and the Catholics with France. Both denominations, following the example of the old Paraguay mission, had established autonomous theocracies in their areas, headed by native chieftains. But these social creations were not impervious to the increasing European penetration of the South Seas, and the missionaries were forced to look for new supports. They found these in their home states, with the Protestants looking toward England and the Catholics toward France, thus laying the base for the political attitudes of the future. On the other hand, it was often the Catholic missionaries who tried to protect their Christian flocks from French exploitation.

With colonial powers as well as missions expanding into the South Seas, the African continent, aside from a few areas on its rim, had not yet awakened any great colonial or missionary interest. In North Africa, after the French occupation, the diocese of Algiers was established in 1838 and the vicariate apostolic of Tunis in 1843. In Abyssinia, the Lazarist Giustino de Jacobis (1800–1860) resumed the long-interrupted missionary work, and the Capuchin Guglielmo Massaia (1809–89) was appointed by Gregory as vicar apostolic to the heathen Gallas. Missionary work in West Africa first began in Liberia, a new state formed with liberated slaves from America. Monsignor Edward Barron (1801–54) arrived in Liberia from the United States in 1841, as a result of the council of Baltimore in 1833, which had stipulated that Catholics in the United States should be involved in the establishment of black missions. In 1842, Barron also became vicar apostolic for Upper Guinea, but was unable to take care of this gigantic area. Almost all of the missionaries to Upper Guinea died within a short period of time. Senegambia and Gabun were ceded to the Holy Ghost Fathers in 1844, and Monsignor Barron returned to the United States a sick man. In South Africa, the vicariate of Cape Town was established in 1837, and the first missionaries ministered principally to the white Catholics. Although the Pope, who knew little about the still-unexplored continent, was able to take few positive actions on behalf of Africa, he nevertheless tried to help the blacks through his Apostolic Constitution of 3 December 1839, in which he condemned the slave trade.

The increased number of vicariates apostolic established during subsequent pontificates "renewed" all missions in the sense that they received a structure which they hitherto had not known. By assigning entire vicariates or mission areas to single orders or religious associations, a number of advantages ensued. Among these was that the earlier tensions between missionary orders and the hierarchy ended, because the new bishops were selected from the missionaries of the same order. Also, gradual separation of powers between superiors of Church and orders enabled the orders not merely to concern themselves with the religious-ethical life of their members but actually obligated them to do so. This practice involved the officials of the orders back home, to whom was left the task of appointing the superiors in the field, more closely than before in the missionary activity of their confreres. As a consequence, the home orders gave more material help to the missions and simultaneously enhanced their own spirituality. Finally, the logical consequence of this reorientation was that the entire academic and religious education of the missionaries was no longer a matter for the mission administration but instead for the individual orders themselves.

However, the new direction of missionary activity also harbored grave disadvantages. The missions now felt more acutely the effects of centralization and bureaucracy. Active missionary work became almost exclusively the concern of orders and congregations. The administration of the Congregation, however, with few exceptions, remained in the hands of secular priests who often lacked the most fundamental knowledge of missionary work. To this was added a new political direction. The Spanish-Portuguese influence had diminished, but its place was now occupied by the modern colonial powers, in particular England and France. Although connection with them was not sought by the missionaries, it was actively sought by the congregations and the vicars apostolic of the various countries. There can be no doubt that Gregory's close cooperation with the restoration and the conservative powers formed the basis for the political reorientation of the missions. The reason for any lack of missionary effort may be found in these political and spiritual ties.

The Awakening of Catholic Vitality

Roger Aubert
Chap. 13: Rudolf Lill

C H A P T E R   1 2

The Rebirth of the Old Orders and the Blossoming of New Congregations

Although by the end of the Napoleonic era all clerical institutions suffered from revolutionary unrest and its consequences, none of them was harder hit than the religious orders. Severely shaken in the second half of the eighteenth century by the spirit of the Enlightenment and Josephinism, the orders appeared to have received the coup de grace through the secularization measures in all of western Europe during the final quarter of the century. Although Bonaparte had dissolved only a portion of the monasteries, such was the case in France in 1790, in Belgium in 1796, in Germany between 1803 and 1807, in Italy between 1807 and 1811, and in Spain in 1809. A few countries escaped the storm, but the decadence of many monasteries in these areas had progressed so far that a resurgence was highly improbable. Within less than a generation, however, a restoration movement was initiated which "in breadth and complexity has no equal in history" (H. Marc-Bonnet) and which became one of the focal points of Church history in the nineteenth century. With the exception of the disappearance of some twenty houses, the old orders began to be restored, and particularly in France and in northern Italy numerous new congregations were formed. These congregations were better adapted to the needs of the time and provided an undeniable sign of a revitalized Catholicism.

A spectacular decision by Pius VII, himself a former member of an order, brought about a sudden change in events. The Society of Jesus, which since 1773 had been officially suppressed, was reestablished. In reality the Society had never

113

totally disappeared; with the tacit consent of Pius VI, it continued to exist in Russia and served as a haven for many former members. Pius VI had encouraged the diplomatic José Pignatelli to keep in contact with the Russian Jesuits, though without traveling to Russia.

Upon his return to Rome in 1814, Pius VII accepted a petition from the Jesuits asking for formal restoration. Encouraged by Cardinals Pacca and Consalvi, who had abandoned their old prejudices, the Pope immediately granted the petition. In doing so the Pope ignored all political caution, especially with respect to Spain and Austria, both of which could have been expected to advise postponement of the decision.

The Pope's action was greeted with strong reservations by such enlightened Catholics and romantics as Görres and his friends. Liberals also reacted with dismay to this act of "counterrevolution," and for several years the government in Vienna resisted the resumption of Jesuit activity in the Empire. Many bishops and the majority of militant Catholics, however, greeted the readmission of the Society of Jesus with acclaim. After 1805 the general of the order was Thaddeus Brzozowski. Brzozowski received many inquiries regarding the reopening of old colleges and residences of the order, and the now somewhat more heterogeneous membership increased. The general congregation, convened in Rome in September 1820, insisted on retaining the Society as an effective instrument for the Holy See, and Father Luigi Fortis was elected general (1820–29). The rules and constitutions of the old Society were adopted and an end was put to all attempts to refashion the Society. After Della Genga became Pope Leo XII, he returned the Collegium Romanum to the Jesuits and in 1826 confirmed their old privileges, including those in the area of exemptions.

Just as the material condition of the Society was restored, its activity in the areas of the colleges, preaching, and missions to the people were redeveloped. To be sure, growing opposition was encountered from the liberals in Spain, where the Society was once again banished during the three years of constitutional government from 1820 to 1823, and in France, where the "Black Men" were treated as scapegoats for all sins committed by the ultras; but the Society had the satisfaction of once again establishing itself in the Habsburg Empire.

While the Society of Jesus experienced a rebirth which was as rapid as it was brilliant, the reorganization of the old orders proceeded rather slowly. The problem was a dual one. It was necessary to reopen a number of houses for the surviving members and to provide them with the material conditions for the resumption of their communal life. In addition, in those provinces not affected by secularization a number of abuses which had spread for two hundred years and had become aggravated owing to the unusual circumstances of the past few years needed to be abolished. These were laxness of discipline and communal life; violations of the vow of poverty; neglect of choir prayer; and, in some convents, disregard of seclusion. The abolition of abuses was a rather difficult task, because of the obstacles posed by some of the more regalistic governments and by bishops who were anxious over their jurisdictions. These groups resented the interventions of the generals of orders established in Rome or the visitors sent by the Holy See. As a result of such problems, a genuine revival in Austria was possible only after the middle of the century.

In Spanish America as well, the monasteries, which had lost a good portion of their estates as a result of the wars of independence, were no longer able to maintain contact with their superiors in Europe. This had fateful consequences for their discipline and religious life and offered a further justification for systematic attempts at suppression by the diverse liberal governments during the course of the century. In Spain, the papal Bull *Inter graviores* of 15 May 1804 posed a special problem. Under the pretext that after the dissolution of a number of houses of the mendicant orders in western Europe the monasteries dependent on the Spanish crown (including the Philippines) were now in the majority, King Charles IV managed to obtain from Pius VII a separation of the Spanish provinces. It was agreed that the two groups were to be governed in turn by a general and a virtually independent vicar general.

After his return to Rome in 1814, Pius VII was eager to provide a model for restoring the orders. In the Papal States he created a special reform congregation and charged it with conducting disciplinary reforms as well as the regrouping of a number of houses in an effort to increase their vitality. For a brief time Pius even considered dividing all the monasteries of his state into two congregations, one for the black monks and another one for the white ones. The project was reconsidered by Leo XII and ultimately was not implemented. Pius VII also watched with great interest the revival of the large mendicant orders and more than once intervened personally, with differing results, in order to promote necessary reforms.

The mendicant orders emerged from the revolutionary age weakened from two causes. All monasteries in France, Belgium, and Germany, and some of those in Italy, had been dissolved; and the monasteries in Spain, the only other country beside the Russian part of Poland in which they had continued to exist in large numbers, were removed from the jurisdiction of the central administration and finally dissolved during the secularizations of 1834–36. The Dominicans, eager to save what they could attempted a regrouping of their Fathers in Italy. In this way, eighty of the five hundred monasteries in existence at the end of the eighteenth century were reestablished. For forty years these monasteries provided the order with new blood for its central administration and enabled it to safeguard its traditions, although in a somewhat attenuated form. At the same time a new beginning, was evident in England as well as in Holland where, in 1824, a school was opened. In the United States, Father E. A. Fenwick laid the foundation for the Province of Saint Joseph.

Unlike the Dominicans, the Franciscans managed to recover only with great difficulty. The Capuchins were able to revive themselves under the leadership of their energetic general, the future Cardinal Micara (1824–30), who pushed reform at the risk of his own life, and the order was able to regain a foothold in France in 1824. Only in 1844 was the Belgian province finally reconstituted, to be followed by France in 1850. The Clarissas, who except in Spain had almost totally disappeared, quickly rose again. Even before the fall of Napoleon the former sisters had begun to regroup, and the order quickly spread under the influx of new members. The same was true for the Carmelite Sisters, who reappeared in the first few years of the nineteenth century in France. The Carmelite Brothers, on the other hand, did not appear again until 1830, and were never able to regain the influence which they had exercised prior to the revolution.

The different branches of the Benedictine community as well as the monasteries of the regular canons were especially hard hit. The crisis of the resolution had come to them in an already attenuated condition. In most instances that vital force which the mendicant orders possessed in their tight organizations was also absent. Such organization among these orders either had never existed, as in the case of the Benedictines, or, as in the case of the Cistercians and the Premonstratensians, who had their seat in France, had been destroyed.

The Cistercians of the *observantia communis,* who had survived in part in Spain and Portugal, reorganized themselves in southern Germany. In 1821, Pius VII gathered the monasteries of Italy within one congregation. Inasmuch as Cîtaux had been dissolved, the Pope had appointed the abbot of one of the Roman monasteries as general superior in 1816. In 1816 also, the Grande Chartreuse was reopened. The Premonstratensians, who had regained their large abbeys in central Europe, revived slowly in Belgium and in France. It was not until 1869, however that they were able to convene their first general chapter.

The experience of the Benedictines was similar to that of the Premonstratensians, even though the Benedictines enjoyed the personal sympathy of the Pope. In the course of the revolutionary disturbances they had lost more than a thousand houses, and the remaining monasteries were beset by uncertainty in the face of the enmity of the regalistic governments in the Habsburg and Russian Empires and the temporary closing of numerous houses in Spain in 1809 and in 1820–23. It was possible to reopen twelve abbeys in Italy, and in 1821 the congregation of Monte Cassino was reorganized.

In contrast to the rapid revival of the Society of Jesus, therefore, the rebirth of the old orders of medieval origin proved to be much more difficult. Yet the foundations were laid at this time from which their renewal was to come during the two next generations. A few modern institutions, however, which were better adapted to the times, as early as the first decades of the nineteenth century profited from a development which would have been unthinkable during the Old Regime. This was particularly true for some charitable women's congregations such as in France the Sisters of Saint Joseph, inspired by Mother Saint Jean Fontbonne; the Daughters of Wisdom, led by Father Gabriel Deshayes (1820–41); and, especially, the Sisters of Saint Vincent de Paul. The last-named, after their official recognition by the government in 1809, spread outward from France and developed their specific religious character during the course of the nineteenth century.

Several male congregations also flourished at the beginning of the restoration. Among these were the Brothers of Christian Schools, who had retained only a few of their houses in the Papal States. In 1803, they were reintroduced by Brother Frumence, whom Pius VI had appointed in 1795 as vicar general. As early as 1810, the order held a general chapter and by 1814 already numbered fifty-five houses. Such a revival was experienced by the Redemptorists whom Klemens Maria Hofbauer (1751–1820) had introduced in central Europe, chiefly in Austria. Emperor Francis I, after his trip to Rome in 1819, guaranteed their safety, in spite of the Josephinist legislation inimical to the orders. From Austria, the order expanded to France (1820), Portugal (1826), Switzerland (1827), Belgium (1833), Bulgaria (1836), and the United States (1832).

The most noteworthy development during the period was the growth of new congregations. Frequently the influence of these congregations, especially in the case of women's congregations, did not extend beyond a diocese, and in many cases not even beyond a few parishes, but some of them developed both extensively and quickly and within a few decades assumed a place of prominence next to the great old orders. The male congregations were oriented chiefly toward two models: The school brothers followed the system introduced by Jean-Baptiste de la Salle during the preceding century. The priestly congregations followed French models of the seventeenth century, which allowed them a supple formula for many apostolic activities.

Among the women's congregations, it is noteworthy that there was an increase in a type of small congregation which devoted itself equally to charity and education. These congregations were in the immediate service of the parish clergy and generally were created by them for specific purposes such as the education of novices. Such small groups had the disadvantages of creating local splintering. The precise number of such communities has never been determined; nor would it be easy to discover it, because of the numerous fusions and splits and great similarity of names.

This phenomenon was particularly evident in France after the concordat, but could be seen everywhere in western Europe during the subsequent years. The surplus of women and the late date of marriage made possible a longer time for choosing a spiritual life; and the respect that women in orders enjoyed in the religious community, together with the expectation of upward social mobility provided especially in the teaching orders, made such a choice attractive. In contrast to the conditions under the Old Regime, most of the aspirants came from the lower economic strata and occasionally from the aristocracy. Rarely did the middle class choose the vocation.

Among the founders were many simple souls who passively had allowed themselves to be guided by a clerical adviser. But there were also among them some strong, complex personalities, who combined great spiritual abilities with a developed sense of action and organization.

The rapid development of numerous congregations, so different from the old orders and so often delayed in acquiring a definitive form, presented the Holy See with subtle problems of canon law. "The multiplicity of inquiries which frequently reach us from France," Leo XII explained to Mazenod in 1825, "persuaded the congregation to devise a special type of approval and to applaud and to encourage, without, however, granting formal approbation." The *decretum laudis,* the first step of a papal approbation, originated in this time in answer to problems of these congregations. The Holy See, long hesitant about women's congregations with simple vows and whose members were not secluded, changed its attitude when it was realized that this new type of order was especially well suited to many of the new conditions. The Sisters of Love of Ghent were the first to receive the special approbation from the Congregation of Bishops and Religious in 1816. Once again the circumstances of changing times provided the impulse to adapt canon law.

CHAPTER 13

The Beginnings of the Catholic Movement
in Germany and Switzerland

Historically speaking, the spiritual rebirth which the Catholic Church in Germany experienced during the first decades of the nineteenth century was more significant than the organizational reconstruction. This rebirth received its impulse from native forces, independent of the official Church. The common denominator was the determination to overcome the crisis caused by the radical Enlightenment. Redefinition of the essence and the tradition of the Church became a valid alternative to the rationalistic depletion of theology, tendencies toward secularization of society, and the far-reaching submission of the Church to the state. An important prerequisite was the existence of an unbroken tradition in all areas of the Church, especially outside of the courtly and urban elements of educated society. Some achievements of the moderate Enlightenment, such as the cultivation of positive theology, reforms of liturgy, preaching and pastoral care, as well as a basic ecumenical sentiment present in some localities also contributed their share. The experience of the French Revolution and its consequences shook the Church out of its lethargy and simultaneously heightened the defensive character of the incipient movement. Because of radical consequences of the Enlightenment and the modern theories of the state, both revolution and secularization made themselves suspect in the eyes of Catholics. From its beginnings, therefore, the Catholic defense had to aim at the two concrete goals of restoring ecclesiastical liberty and replacing destroyed centers of education.

Romanticism provided strongly differing impulses. In its universal aspects, romanticism reached back to early Christian ideas and values in the areas of the arts, science, and societal order. It emphasized the irrational, historic, and organic roots of the present. In contrast to the focus of the Enlightenment upon the individual, reason, and progress, romanticism often went to the opposite extreme of awarding primary value to community, feeling, mysticism, tradition, and continuity. The Church was again viewed as a living and historical organism, and romantic inclusiveness strove for a synthesis of religious and profane cultures. Among the Protestants, romanticism promoted the concepts of revival and nation, but many of its representatives were attracted by the Catholic Church, whose structure and forms of piety corresponded more closely to their ideals. Eminent converts had a decisive influence on the beginnings of the Catholic movement in Germany. The new appreciation of the Catholic Church was often a consequence of the rediscovery of the essentially Catholic Middle Ages and its artistic and spiritual creations. In addition, romanticism fostered the German patriotism of Catholics. Its emphasis on continuity and organic structures led to a concept of restoration which idealized Emperor and Empire and, following the wars of Liberation, the value placed upon people and nation allowed the growth among German Catholics of a feeling of affinity for religion and nationality.

Consonant with the customs of society at the time, the Catholic movement grew out of small circles, often in conjunction with attempts to revive religious studies. Roman influence was totally absent and French philosophy of restoration only began to play a role in the 1820s, primarily through the people involved with the Mainz seminary and associated circles in the Rhineland.

Even before the French Revolution, Princess Amalie Gallitzin (1748–1806), who had resided in Münster since 1779, gathered around her a number of people who were concerned with deepening their faith through imbuing it with emotion and who raised the reaction against the Enlightenment to the level of an antiintellectual belief. Among the advisers of the princess were the religious instructor and educator Bernard Overberg (1754–1826) and the canon Franz von Fürstenberg (1729–1810). Since 1762, Fürstenberg had administered the cathedral chapter of Münster in exemplary fashion, and, in contrast to his own bishop, who was also the Elector of Cologne and had freely opened his court at Bonn to modern ideas, had resolutely resisted the Enlightenment. After Fürstenberg in 1780 had been forced to give up his political offices, he concentrated on internal improvements and pedagogical reforms, aided by his close collaborator Overberg, whom he entrusted with the training of teachers. The Gallitzin circle, regarding itself as a *"familia sacra,"* also counted as members several professors of the academy founded by Fürstenberg. Among these were the Church historian Theodor Katerkamp and the exegete Bernard Georg Kellermann, as well as younger people who were deeply influenced by the circle, such as the brothers Droste-Vischering.

Close relations existed with the pietistic Lutherans, such as Matthias Claudius, Friedrich Perthes, Count Friedrich Leopold zu Stolberg, and Johann Georg Hamann. The Enlightenment had influenced the circle insofar as it had emphasized the common elements of the denominations, albeit the aims of the circle were of an anti-Enlightenment direction. The faithful were supposed to unite against rationalism as the common enemy. In 1800 Stolberg became a Catholic, and his conversion, the first of an impressive number, created a sensation. He settled in Münster and together with other members of the *"familia sacra"* wrote the *History of the Religion of Jesus Christ,* which interpreted Church history in a universal sense and as the passion and salvation of Christ. This interpretation reawakened in German Catholicism the historical consciousness buried by the Enlightenment. In spite of his apologetic approach, Stolberg also incorporated such Lutheran elements as the belief in salvation exclusively through God's mercy, and his concept of the Church was comprehensive and included episcopal elements.

The writings of Overberg, together with those of Sailer, founded a new Catholic pedagogy. Although Overberg favored educational discourse and growth of the students within the meaning of the Enlightenment, he saw the "higher assurance of the Christian faith" exclusively in revelation. For this reason he made revelation the focal point of religious instruction and acquainted a wide readership among teachers and families with this concept through his frequently reprinted *History of the Old and New Testaments.*

Under the impact of the rising against Napoleon (1809), Vienna developed into a radiating center of German romanticism. Through the circles around Clemens Maria Hofbauer (1751–1820) and Friedrich Schlegel (1772–1829) it also raised a new religious consciousness.

Schlegel, Müller, and their friends attempted to prove monarchical authority and hierarchical social order as natural and divinely inspired. For this reason they propagated a corporative state, based on religion and national characteristics and modeled on medieval concepts. State and Church were to be connected and equal partners. They saw the most legitimate guarantee of the preservation of continuity within the hierarchical order of the Catholic Church. They agreed with the objectives of de Maistre and tried to provide them with the deeper religious and philosophical support which they found missing in his writings. Schlegel, Müller, and Baader also derived the first postulates of social Catholicism from the corporative principle. Their demands for a just wage and the integration of the lower classes, for subordinating the economy to social policy, and for a just balance between agriculture and industry had no direct effect, but did have lasting influence upon the development of Catholic social theory.

While the Emperor, the government, and the majority of Austrian clergy, especially the prelates, still adhered to Josephinism, the Hofbauer circle initiated its spiritual conquest.

Hofbauer fought the Enlightenment with uncompromising and often abrasive vigor, and during the Congress of Vienna he was Wessenberg's most important spiritual opponent. The argumentative Redemptorist also favored the restoration of a church organization applicable to all of Germany. Moreover, his group was the first among the circles of Catholic revival to conduct this reconstruction in close collaboration with Rome. The circle was convinced that only the papacy, which was regaining its strength at that time, could provide the German dioceses with bishops who were free of the belief in an established Church and Febronianism. This position explains the group's strong defense of a centralistic and authoritarian church regulation. Secretly Hofbauer's circle informed on people who thought differently and thus started in Germany the denunciation of ecclesiastical opponents. It was an embarrassing accompaniment to ultramontanism.

Johann Michael Sailer (1751–1832), the leader of the Landshut circle, built upon the philosophical and literary heritage of the period and initiated the encounter of Catholicism with the modern intellectual culture of the nation. At the same time, his main concern was the intensification of traditional religion, and he early began to oppose deism. Sailer, an eclectic, adopted the moral philosophy of Kant, the religious philosophy of Jacobi, and the pedagogy of Pestalozzi.

Accused of illuminatism and being a proponent of the Enlightenment, Sailer was forced to leave the University of Dillingen in 1794. Five years later Montgelas, the defender of a bureaucratic established Church, appointed Sailer professor of moral and pastoral theology at the University of Ingolstadt, which, in 1800, was transferred as a Bavarian state university to Landshut. Sailer pleaded for a rejuvenation of the Church arising from its internal strengths, and it was his very acquaintance with the Enlightenment which qualified him as a credible opponent. He developed a theology of revelation and spirituality which was new for his time and which had a biblical and patristic basis. His concept of the Church attempted to mediate between Curialism and Febronianism. In his Bible-oriented pedagogy, Sailer, as had Overberg, transcended the Enlightenment.

Sailer was not only an effective teacher and publicist, but also a charismatic pastor and counselor. He gathered around him an unusually large circle of students and friends from all walks of life and faculties. Only after difficult negotiations between the government and the Holy See did he become auxiliary bishop and coadjutor of Regensburg in 1822 and bishop in 1829. Other clerics from Sailer's circle continued to promote his religious and ecclesiastical concerns.

Because Crown Prince Ludwig belonged to Sailer's admirers, the Landshut circle influenced Bavarian domestic policies. Crown Prince Ludwig ascended the throne in 1825 as Ludwig I. The King held fast to parity and established Church, but in all other respects he followed the path of romantic restoration. He also wanted to see Bavaria become the leading state of German Catholicism. Benedictines, Franciscans, and several women's congregations were permitted to return; teacher training was largely turned over to the Church; royal seminaries for priests were established; the missions received financial support; and numerous church buildings were restored.

Ringseis became the first president of the Bavarian State University, which was moved from Landshut to Munich in 1826, and his consistent policy of appointments made it into the most important Catholic center of the period. In addition to Ringseis, important leaders were found among the new professors, Josef von Görres, Franz von Baader, and Ignaz von Döllinger. These men prepared the ground for Catholic federations and fought rationalism and liberalism on the level of philosophy and history. To an increasing degree this group also fought an alliance between Protestantism, rationalism and liberalism. The anniversary of the Reformation in 1817 produced a first confrontation, and in general the revived Churches were developing a new denominational self-assurance.

The King's religious policy permitted the introduction of two Church newspapers, which also treated non-Bavarian matters and became very influential in Church policy. These periodicals, together with *Katholik,* founded a few years earlier in Mainz, constituted the first development of a German Catholic press.

With greater efficiency than Hofbauer's friends, a number of people in Mainz began to promote a centralistic-authoritarian rejuvenation of the Church. Its first leaders were Johann Ludwig Colmar (1760–1818), who had been appointed by Napoleon as bishop of Mainz, and Franz Leopold Liebermann (1759–1844). Both men had been part of Alsatian Catholicism, which had kept out of internal French developments but which finally was forced to undergo the most radical consequences of the Enlightenment during the revolutionary disturbances. In 1805, Colmar founded a Tridentine seminary headed by Liebermann in place of the theological faculty of the university, which had been destroyed by secularization. In 1816, another Alsatian and student of Liebermann, Andreas Räss (1794–1887), was appointed to teach there. In contrast to the other circles of revival, the leaders of the Mainz group were all clerics. Like all defenders of purely ecclesiastical concentration, they were opposed to theological departments at state universities. Because of this, they contributed greatly to the training of priests at seminaries in Germany, a method which was also desired by Rome. Their justification was that at many state universities theologians were teaching who were rationalistic and in favor of an established Church. Colmar and Liebermann based theological instruction upon a return to Scholasticism, while Räss and his friend Nikolaus Weis (1796–1869) also included French restoration philosophy. The Mainz circle was convinced that strict spiritual and organizational concentration of the Church was of the essence in the face of the Enlightenment and its consequent concept of an established Church. They pleaded for a retreat to the seemingly secure bastion of the old doctrine, coupled with an innovative activation of the faithful, while remaining unaffected by romanticism. Their program coincided with that of the "zealots" in the Roman Curia, who had gained the upper hand after the election of Leo XII in 1824. Since that time, the Mainz group had been even more in favor of close collaboration with Rome. Their simplistic belief was that episcopalism would lead to the established Church of the Enlightenment, while papalism would bring with it freedom of the Church.

In order to influence the clergy and laity toward the Mainz program, in 1821 Räss and Weis founded the monthly publication *Der Katholik*. Through *Der Katholik* and several popular pamphlets, the Mainz theologians fought against the Enlightenment, an established Church, and the forces of Protestantism. They also opposed Catholic lines of thought which were unacceptable to them, such as Hermesianism, which was spreading in the Prussian Rhineland. The authoritarian defense upon which they relied throughout this process was well suited to the exigencies of the period, but their generalizations contributed toward excluding the Catholic Church from intellectual developments and toward placing it within the very ghetto in which its enemies wished it to be.

The fighting spirit of the Mainz seminary also reached to Bavaria and influenced many another Catholic circle. At first such Catholic circles initiated internal revivals on the local level, but with increasing effectiveness they defended themselves against bureaucratic ecclesiastical regimens. The Rhenish circles maintained close contact with one another. Common to all of them was the hostility to the Hermes School which was pursued so markedly at Bonn. In Koblenz the first steps toward a modern Caritas were developed, while at Cologne attention was primarily directed to the maintenance of medieval-Catholic traditions and buildings.

Persons and forces contributing to the ecclesiastical renewal were later opposed or pushed aside by the strengthening Catholic movement. Wessenberg initiated a biblical-liturgical reform movement which was in force for a long period. Out of the Hermes School came a generation with an optimistic pastoral outlook; a generation which was convinced of the compatibility of the old faith with new ideas. Many outstanding bishops promoted internal reconstruction. By incorporating positive aspects of the Enlightenment and attempting to evade conflicts with the governments, they distinguished themselves from their pugnacious successors who stood under the influence of the revival movement.

The beginnings of the revival movement in Germany included the entire range of Catholic thought ranging from a universal interpretation resting on the spirit and the tradition of the Church to a defensive-hierarchical concentration. From this broad beginning, reaching into romanticism, it was possible for the last time in modern German history to have active cooperation in the shaping of the intellectual and artistic life of the nation. But for the inner development of the Church, the narrower and stricter direction was decisive. The circles around Hofbauer and the Mainz seminary understood how to provide a clear and easily acceptable program to the majority of Catholics, who were confused by the intellectual shifts and oppressed by the established Church. Recognizing the fundamentally conservative state, these circles demanded from it fulfillment of the promised parity. Within Catholicism they created the first modern mass consciousness in

Germany; a consciousness which achieved political relevance after the unrest at Cologne. The movement, initially varied, eventually joined the forces of the ultramontane restoration, which had come to the fore in Rome in the 1820s and were systematically supported by the papacy after the election of Gregory XVI.

The regrouping of the Swiss dioceses was only a prerequisite for the revival of Catholic life in Switzerland, a revival which was as urgent there as it had been in neighboring countries. However, the indifferentism of the Enlightenment and the anti-Roman stance of Wessenberg deeply influenced the minds of laity and clergy in many cantons. The reaction against philosophes and Jacobins and against the Febronian reformers was led in an especially active fashion by a group of professors of the Lucerne seminary. These professors, headed by J. Gügler, one of the first representatives of romantic theology, and by F. Geiger, the founder of the *Swiss Church Newspaper,* were students of Sailer. In addition, the Jesuits became active again in Brig in 1814 and in Fribourg in 1818 and, as the Capuchins had done, missionized the people and founded confraternities and congregations. Although the efforts of the governments to control the work of the seminaries did not simplify matters, pious and hard-working prelates effectively contributed to a revival.

Finally, the Catholic revival was accompanied, as in Germany, by a number of conversions. In spite of his voluntary exile in Paris from 1820 to 1830, a number of Catholic ultras gathered around K. L. von Haller, who, in violent opposition to Jean-Jacques Rousseau, the revolution, and liberalism, combined an irreconcilable ultramontanism with political concepts of a patriarchal and legitimistic inspiration. The majority of Haller's compatriots, however, turned toward a liberal progressivism.

CHAPTER 14

The Catholic Movement in France and Italy

The Catholic Action of the Laity in France

The French clergy counted on the strong support of the government, but saw no reason to remain inactive itself. Its efforts were effective especially within the framework of the parishes.

This priestly activity, however, could flourish only in the more backward rural areas; for the needs of urban populations it was inadequate. In order to appeal to them, a large number of organizations were created during the course of the restoration in which the laity assumed an eminent place. Of course, the clergy continued to hold a leading position in founding and direction of these works, but the laity played a great participatory role not only as executors but also as initiators and cofounders. This was a new phenomenon, and one must go back as far as the *Compagnie du Saint-Sacrament* in the seventeenth century in order to find an analogous event in France. The intrusion of the laity into a sphere long reserved to the clergy is in part explained by the lack of priests and orders, but it was also the result of an awareness of the new conditions of the apostolate. Here are the beginnings of the modern Catholic Action, an action directed toward a specific social environment.

At the beginning of many of these laymen's works stood the Congregation, whose description as the "Central Office of Catholic Action" may perhaps be overblown, but whose efforts on the national level resulted in a significant achievement. Founded in Paris in 1801 by an ex-Jesuit, it was banned by Napoleon in 1809 and ultimately reestablished in 1814. Approximately sixty similar bodies, often founded in provincial towns in connection with missions to the people, were associated with it. The Congregation charged its members with performing all kinds of charitable and apostolic works designed to influence the masses and represented by branches throughout the country.

The Congregation was attacked severely by opponents of what they called the "Party of Priests." It was accused of being a secret club, dominated by the Jesuits, for the purpose of controlling state and society. The Congregation as such always avoided any direct political activity and neither it nor its branches ever acted as lobby groups for the filling of influential positions. But there was also no doubt that the majority of the leaders of this organization were convinced that the religious future of France was closely tied to the Bourbon dynasty; this orientation gave Catholic Action an undeniable monarchical direction. A number of influential members of the Congregation were also, in conjunction with their official positions in the government or their prominent social standing, eager partisans of an ultramontane policy and active members of the secret monarchical Knights of the Faith. Thus the liberals were not wrong when they accused the people associated with the Congregation of being leaders of a secret club bent on acquiring control of the government.

Nonetheless, many of these lay works, even if they were not creations of the Paris Congregation, lived under its strong influence, at least until the death in 1826 of Mathieu de Montmorency, the leading personality of the first generation of the Congregation. After his death, which coincided with the great offensive of Montlosier and the liberals against the Congregation, a new generation took over its leadership, and introduced a new spirit. They exercised little influence on the government — which, incidentally, explains the quick decline of all those organizations which existed because of official support — and instead turned more directly to fashioning public opinion.

Catholic Publications in France

Several of the societies took it upon themselves to promote the distribution of good books, as the Catholics had clearly recognized the great importance of the press for winning public opinion on behalf of the Church. After being freed from Napoleonic censorship, Catholic publishing houses developed a remarkable activity. Reprints of apologetic works of the eighteenth century and publications of new apologies of the Catholic Church as well as of monarchical government became increasingly numerous, a process in which quality was often sacrificed to quantity. In addition to Lamennais, there were four figures who for a period of fifteen years radiated from Paris to the rest of Europe a political-religious ideology based on the combination of Catholicism and monarchical authority. It was an ideology which took the place of the earlier rationalistic and liberal ideology which likewise had emanated from France during the two preceding generations. It was characteristic for the intellectual condition of the Church in France toward the end of the revolutionary era that these four persons were laymen and that three of them were foreigners.

Count Louis de Bonald (1754–1840) throughout the restoration period continued his little-read but frequently quoted publications against the individualistic and critical philosophy of the eighteenth century. Tirelessly and with imperturbable logic he treated topics which for half a century became the focus and point of departure of political and social traditionalism on one hand and of philosophical and religious traditionalism on the other. The Savoyard Joseph de Maistre (1754–1821), a writer with a brilliant and sharp pen, who became for the Society of Jesus, under rather different conditions, what Pascal was for Port-Royal (Thibaudet); he paled much sooner, but was also much more appropriate for his time. From the excesses of the revolution he derived the necessity of monarchical absolutism and theocracy and became the defender of the infallibility of the Pope. The Swiss Karl Ludwig von Haller (1768–1854), opponent of Rousseau and defender of the principle of authority, arrived at a rejection of Protestantism through the extension of his ideas to the field of religion. Finally there was the Dane Nikolaus von Eckstein (1790–1861), who in 1809 converted to Catholicism and after 1816 resided in Paris. He was a prolific, often confused, but also occasionally original author, thanks to his German professors Schlegel and Görres, for the spread of whose thoughts in France he was largely responsible.

The Catholic champions intended to serve throne and altar not only through books and pamphlets. Lamennais as early as 1814 thought of founding a paper for the defense of Catholic interests, and on a regular basis he contributed articles to political newspapers which he regarded "not only as a tribune, but as a pulpit." Thus he contributed to Chateaubriand's *Conservateur,* to Genoude's and Bonald's *Défenseur,* and finally he published in *Drapeau blanc,* whose editor he was temporarily, eloquent indictments of the politics of concessions to the secular state as it had emerged from the revolution. Most of the Catholic papers founded during the period of the restoration were rather colorless.

In addition to the support provided by writers and a few journalists, Catholicism during the restoration could also count on poets who continued to travel the path first taken by Chateaubriand twenty years earlier. In his *Méditations,* which turned out to be the literary event of 1820, Lamartine demonstrated that and how religion illuminated the problems of human destiny. In the circle around Nodier, the leaders of the new romantic school, especially the young Victor Hugo, celebrated the beauty of the Bible, of Gothic cathedrals, and of Catholic liturgy.

The Appearance of Abbé de Lamennais

Several times the activity of Lamennais has been mentioned. In the course of the last years of the restoration he dominated to an increasing degree the Catholic movement in France and in other countries, chiefly in the Netherlands and Italy, and in some manner was connected with the beginning of the great intellectual development of Catholicism in the nineteenth century.

Félicité Robert de Lamennais (1782–1854) in 1804 found his way back to his faith and decided to work in the service of the Church in the future. He read extensively, especially the Bible, Bossuet, Malebranche, and Bonald. Interrupted by long periods of depression, together with his brother Jean-Marie he wrote a work against rationalism and another one against the religious policy of Napoleon. After long hesitation he finally allowed himself to be persuaded by his spiritual mentors to enter the priesthood in 1815. In addition to his collaboration with ultraroyalist newspapers he then turned to the writing of comprehensive apologetic works designed to establish an effective protection of religion and the freedom of the Catholic Church. In the *Essai sur l'indifférence en matière de religion* he attacked less the unwillingness of individuals to concern themselves with religious questions as the attitude of the government, which refused openly to defend the only true religion.

The first volume, published in December 1817, reveals an intimate knowledge of the mentality of his time. It was written in a style of concentrated emotion which to us may appear high-flown, but it met the taste of the readers of the *Génie du Christianisme* and in the following years became a gigantic success in spite of the reticence of the left as well as the right press. Overnight the young unknown priest had risen to the first rank of literary eminence. It was his pleasure to witness that under his influence several of the young romantic writers again came closer to the Church. The volumes subsequently published between 1820 and 1823 were written in a more sober style, confused the public, and displeased the critics. But they inspired a number of young priests, who in consequence of an inadequate philosophical training in the seminaries were without protection exposed to the thought processes of an apparently relentless logic. They believed themselves to have found in Lamennais the man of the future, able to breathe life into the religious restoration by adapting it to the spirit of the times.

To the same degree they applauded the passionate polemicist who in the press directed severe attacks against the weakness of a government whose policy, especially with respect to education, lacked sufficient Christian content. He also attacked the submissive spirit rooted in the Gallican influence with respect to the civil powers which prevented the bishops from taking effective action against this "treason." It earned Lamennais the first episcopal reprimand and he was excluded from the *Drapeau blanc.* But two of his initial admirers, the Abbés Gerbet and Salinis, pastors to the students, in January 1824 decided to take a page from models in Germany and Italy and founded an independent newspaper. With the cooperation of their master and with the intent to spread his ideas, it was designed to deal with religious, philosophical, and literary problems from a modern vantage point in place of political discussions. The resulting *Mémorial catholique* generated a vivid echo even in liberal minds, and was a surprise not only because of its "youthful verve and fervent proselytizing spirit" (Sainte-Beuve) but also because of the breadth and variety of the questions raised. It went considerably beyond what the remaining contemporary press had to offer, and strove to acquaint its readership with the most important foreign publications. But it had the disadvantage of introducing into ecclesiastical literature a belligerent, provocative, and frequently intolerant tone which characterized Lamennais and his adherents and a good deal of French publications in the nineteenth century.

It increasingly strengthened the opposition to Lamennais and the young reformers of the apostolate surrounding him. The bishops were enraged over the lack of constraint with which these "religious Jacobins" (Frayssinous) treated hierarchical authority in their attacks against Gallicanism. The Sulpicians were offended, and the Jesuits were not at all convinced; they feared that his intemperance could cause a reaction among the liberals, whose first victims they would be. Finally the clerics had to fear for the advantages which the Church derived from the protection of the civil power, and therefore they condemned the virulent attacks of the new school against the state. When Lamennais attacked Gallicanism more strongly than ever before and recommended that the Church separate itself openly from the government of the Bourbons, the overdrawn formulations especially attracted the young, who, as so often is the case, were exposed to great danger in an apparently favorable situation. With the electric effect of his writings, the prophetic character of his ingenious intuitions, and the magical charm of his personality, Lamennais succeeded in surrounding himself with an enthusiastic elite of young clerics and laymen. Among them were most of the leading minds of French Catholicism of the subsequent decades, even though more than one of them, as for example Guéranger, later preferred to treat these youthful associations with silence. Encouraged by the benevolent reception which Leo XII accorded the talented apologist and defender of ultramontane doctrine on the occasion of his journey to Italy in 1824, the sickly little priest became the leader of a new generation, and his influence ultimately was so great that Duine could speak of his spiritual dictatorship over the French Church.

One of the reasons for this extraordinarily great influence was that Lamennais, however much importance he attached to his intellectual work, in equal measure was concerned with the "Catholic Action" as the practical realization of his new Christian philosophy and the vital religious currents which inspired it. He wanted to encourage his followers in a complete reform of Catholic society and the work of the Church in the world by asking them to solve all problems of social life not with a respectful neutrality toward all opinions but from the vantage point of revealed divine doctrine. This former ultra eventually became the leader of Catholic liberalism, but still pursued the reconquest of society for Catholicism.

The Beginnings of Catholic Action in Italy

In Italy also the Catholic restoration, as in other countries of western Europe, was not only a political movement, but to an equal degree a manifestation of religious vitality in which laymen played a significant role. But there also, especially in the north, were a number of priests and laymen who placed all of their strength in the service of religious restoration. Some of them concentrated on preaching to the people according to the French example. Others devoted themselves to the apostolate among the young or tried to ameliorate the needs of the poor. Others attempted to influence the opinion of the educated and to make a front against the prevailing mentality at the end of the eighteenth century. They attacked philosophies which were hardly compatible with Christian spiritualism, turned against the *Illuminismo* which sailed in the wake of the encyclopedists and followed rigoristic tendencies in morality, and were opposed to regalism and to those who disapproved of papal prerogatives. Pio Brunone Lanteri (1759–1830), whom circumstances often forced to act secretly or anonymously, is least known. As a teacher he used a portion of his wealth to distribute small pamphlets, often written by him, in order to dispel the errors of his time.

It was primarily his efforts which brought back to life in completely new form in 1817 a society for the distribution of good books which had been founded forty years earlier by the ex-Jesuit Diesbach. This *Amicizia cattolica* was subsequently headed exclusively by laymen, without exception members of the nobility, and no longer placed the personal salvation of its members into the foreground but concentrated on mass action to be effected through publications. Several societies related to the *Amicizia* of Turin were created either under its direct influence (in Rome and Novara) or in imitation of its principles and methods. Among the latter a special place was occupied by the *Società degli amici* and its branches in Venice and Lombardy, founded in 1819 by Rosmini in Rovereto. Its attitude was neither fearful nor conservative, and it was oriented toward Italy. On the other hand, its aims were far-reaching; it wanted to devote itself both to charitable work and to an intensification of Catholic education.

After the unrest of 1820/21, Catholic publications received a new form through the founding of newspapers for the defense of Catholic and monarchical principles. But already by 1825, the mediocre results of these efforts brought about a weakening of the initial zeal; genuine journalistic talent was lacking and this also limited the power to influence. All of these papers, which unceasingly and in all areas countered social and intellectual anarchy with the principle of authority, were inspired, albeit with considerable variations, by the counterrevolutionary ideology developed at this time in Paris and Vienna. The editors of these Italian Catholic papers were more or less firmly convinced that the Church was the only and indispensable guarantee for social order. They also believed that the political revolution of 1789 was nothing more than the logical consequence of the religious revolution of the sixteenth century and that for this reason an integrated religious restoration was necessary. With the aid of this restoration they wanted to return, aside from all deviations of the Gallicanism of the Old Regime, to a medieval Christianity in which the Church, represented by the Pope, formulated the duties of the state.

Such ideas, which even some members of the Roman Curia considered excessive or at least inopportune under the prevailing circumstances, could hardly be to the liking of the regalistic governments of the time, and in fact the papers were suppressed one by one. The enthusiasm, however, with which these circles initially greeted the campaign of Lamennais in favor of theocracy and ultramontanism is easily understandable. Yet it was not Lamennais to whom they owed their convictions; they merely recognized in the French writer an excellent means to propagate their ideas.

The Italian, and above all the Piedmontese, Catholic movement of the restoration period lacked a certain cultural open-mindedness — the unequivocal opposition to romanticism is typical — and that sensitivity for new religious and political problems which lent the French movement of Lamennais its conquering dynamic. Their efforts were limited to a rather superficial concept of the activity of the Church in the world, assigning more significance to the Christianization of institutions than to the development of conscience. We see here — and this consideration justifies the importance assigned to this movement in spite of its lack of immediate success — the beginnings of the intransigent current whose strength in Italian Catholic life grew more important in the second half of the century.

Not all Catholic forces, however, oriented themselves in this conservative direction. On the other hand there were also convinced Catholics in the romantic movement which, in contrast to France and especially to Germany, in Italy had a much stronger continuity with the *Illuminismo* of the eighteenth century. The most striking figure in this context is Alessandro Manzoni (1785–1873). Manzoni moved from revolutionary encyclopedism to Catholicism by way of the moral endeavors of Jansenism and Calvinism. His frequently reprinted *Osservazioni sulla morale cattolica* (1819), in which he corrects the Protestant Sigismondi, who attributed the political decadence of the Italians to Catholicism, constituted the first remarkable manifesto of a cultural patriotism in Italy which openly was as one with the Catholic tradition. Even if Manzoni's thinking at this time cannot yet be called liberal, it implied liberal consequences which made Manzoni one of the most important originators of Catholic liberalism in Italy during the second third of the century. In an environment, then, which in essence remained reactionary, the seeds for a rejuvenation of Catholic mentality were planted which approached modern values with greater openness.

C H A P T E R   1 5

The Complex Revival of Religious Studies

The eighteenth century, although productive in the areas of exegesis, Church history, and pastoral care, was on the whole not a glorious time for theology. The following century began under even worse conditions. In spite of a rich apologetic literature, Catholic thought lacked force and determination. In Italy and Spain, theologians were absorbed by sterile polemics and religious thought languished in mediocrity. In France, the magical style of a Chateaubriand could not conceal the doctrinal poverty, and works which were tied to the classics were ill-suited to a modern mentality. In Germany, a majority of theologians, influenced by the rationalism of their environment, stood in danger of emptying Christianity of its supernatural content. In addition, the old centers of education were disorganized as a consequence of the French Revolution.

Between 1810 and 1820, the very depth of the crisis in Catholic thought, a crisis which could no longer be ignored, brought about a reaction. Within a few years, a number of initiatives were taken. Although inept, these actions were more impressive and positive than the Neo-Scholasticism at the turn of the century was willing to admit. They had as their aim the regaining for Catholicism of that esteem among the educated which it had lost almost completely. These attempts were strongly supported by the romantics, in spite of the inherent ambivalence of their philosophy. The literary and theological revival not only occurred simultaneously, but theology also received lasting influences from romantic thought and adopted such concepts as a sensibility to the coldness of reason, a mystical understanding of the universe, a reaction against individualism in favor of the values of the community, and a desire for the rehabilitation of tradition and history. This mentality was reflected in a somewhat exaggerated philosophy, which fostered a daring idealism in search of comprehensive harmonious syntheses and a history in which the organic development of the idea through the ages was accentuated. In theology, this attitude led to a revaluation of the confession of faith, occasionally even sliding into fideism; to a shift in emphasis in religion from the moralism of the eighteenth century to a mystical and supernatural position; to a view of the Church as a living organism which, although it had occasionally neglected the personality of the believer, was also the soil from which dogmas developed; to a rediscovery of the meaning of the past and especially of the Church Fathers; and even, in consequence of the admiration of the Middle Ages, to a renewed interest in Scholasticism. It was also recognized that there were internal connections and an organic unity between the various theological sciences, such as between dogmatism and morality, and exegesis and Church history. This new view led in similar fashion to a rapprochement between theology and profane culture. In spite of the profound differences which separated the two, in this area the strivings of the Hermes School and the Tübingen theologians coincided with those of a Lamennais in France or a Rosmini in Italy.

Germany: Between Rationalism and Romantic Idealism

In contrast to Austria, where the structure of the theological university departments had hardly been touched by the disruptions at the end of the eighteenth century, in Germany the secularization of the ecclesiastical principalities and abbeys in the wake of the suppression of the Jesuits had led to the dissolution of most of the ecclesiastical centers of education. Thanks to the firm organization of the Catholic theological departments at a number of universities the interruption was mercifully brief. The new arrangement whereby theology was studied at state universities, an arrangement which has lasted to this day, offered the Catholic scholars the opportunity of close contact with non-Catholic sciences; an exchange which turned out to be fruitful. However, the new order noticeably limited the degree of control over educational content exercised by the ecclesiastical authorities. This academic freedom occasionally promoted an exaggerated sense of independence and even actual deviations from correct doctrine. The danger was particularly great during the first years, when teaching appointments were made without adequate consideration of the orthodoxy of the candidates.

The Mainz seminary, which was reorganized by the French regime, under Liebermann became the center of the future Neo-Scholastic movement in Germany. Two strong and equally dangerous tendencies dominated theology and apologetics at the beginning of the nineteenth century. The rationalism of the preceding century, strengthened by the success of the great post-Kantian philosophical systems, still exerted a strong attraction. Many efforts to defend Christianity were characterized by an unjustified accommodation to the positions of the opponents and thus incurred the risk of unseemly concessions. In some cases the tendencies to make a compromise were very strong. The thinking of many pious theologians remained anchored in the Enlightenment or succumbed to Kantian criticism and idealistic pantheism. In contrast to these tendencies, however, there was a reaction against the dry moralism and the cold rationalism of natural religion. The concepts adopted by such philosophers as Jacobi and Schleiermacher, the Protestant "Court Philosopher of Romanticism," in spite of the superiority of their emphasis on the nonreducible originality of the Christian experience and religious dynamism, led frequently to an antiintellectualism which endangered the rational foundations of the confession of faith. In some cases, they encompassed a concordism which regarded Catholicism and Protestantism merely as two different aspects of the same mystical Church.

As always in turbulent times and intensive intellectual fermentation, a few probing attempts were made to combine the different movements of the period.

Johann Michael Sailer, professor of pastoral theology at Landshut from 1800 to 1821, is characteristic of the theologians of the transition from the Enlightenment to Catholic romanticism. Sailer was an eclectic, but possessed a certain creativity, and was one of the first to integrate theology with Christian spirituality again. Starting from a position still firmly imbedded in the views of the eighteenth century, he gradually moved from vivacious religiosity to the life of the Church by first discovering the patristic concept of tradition and then that of the Church as a spiritual organism whose supernatural life is shared by its members.

Between 1820 and 1830, Bonn, Tübingen, and Munich were the three centers of learning which most influenced religious thought in Germany. At Bonn, after 1819, the influence of a school founded by Georg Hermes (1775–1831) was to last for a generation. Hermes, who earlier had been a professor of dogma at Münster and a member of the circle of the Princess Gallitzin, was a priest with great apostolic zeal. He wished to contribute to the Catholic restoration by transcending the apparent antagonism between modern philosophy and the teachings of the Church. Although he recognized the great danger which Kant's criticism and Fichte's idealism posed for the Christian faith, he was too fascinated by these philosophical systems to discard them completely. Instead, he wanted to fight Kant with his own weapons. Hermes carried the criticism of human knowledge a step further than Kant by regarding agreement with the truths of faith as a neces-

sary conclusion of proof. He then proceeded to give an a priori description of all —
including supernatural — reality on a rational basis, consonant with the demands
of idealism. Because of his remarkable teaching ability and his priestly charisma,
Hermes was able to gain the enthusiasm of a portion of the young intellectuals.
Upon his death, he left convinced followers in more than thirty philosophical and
theological teaching posts and, in some cases, also in important positions in ecclesiastical life. But in reality, his work, which seemed so modern at the time, lacked
a sense of history. Hermes' limited interest in ecclesiastical tradition, coupled with
his concept of religion as a doctrine which could be understood rationally rather
than spiritually, caused him to regard the development of dogmas and the history of dogmas as genuine latecomers of the Enlightenment. Therefore, he had to
suffer not only the well-founded criticism of a few far-seeing minds who chided
him for his Pelagian and semirationalistic position, but also of those, particularly
those outside of the universities, who, influenced by romanticism, placed feeling
and heartfelt belief before cold reason or were under the influence of French
traditionalism.

While in the Rhineland Hermes was working on an apologia with which to
confront the problems caused by Kantianism and rationalism, a group of theologians at Tübingen, fascinated by the philosophy of idealism but determined not to
deviate from Catholic orthodoxy, sought a happy medium between the unhealthy
mysticism of many romantics and the narrow-minded rationalism of many late
students of the Enlightenment. They were courageous researchers, open to contemporary movements, who took advantage of the fact that certain terms of the
new philosophy were already theologically adapted by contemporary Protestant
thinkers. On this basis they presented a new theological synthesis which, although
critical of the basic positions of Protestantism, was both modern and traditional
and presented a bold program for the reform of liturgy and Church discipline.

In some areas the Tübingen theologians followed those precursors like Sailer,
whose profound influence on the theology of romanticism has become increasingly clear; Geiger and Gügler, Sailer's students at Lucerne, who may be regarded
as the link between the beginning of traditionalism and Hegel's philosophy;
and others. But only the Tübingen School managed to articulate the intellectual
currents and to combine the great topics of romanticism in a comprehensive
synthesis.

In reality, the Tübingen School stands out precisely because of its close blend
of positive and speculative methods. It attempted to understand dogmatism not in
the narrow sense of classical theology, for which it was merely a kind of catalogue
of orthodox doctrines, but speculatively as revealed realities which demonstrate
their inner harmony. The Tübingen theologians desired a more suitable instrument
for the expansion of Schelling's philosophy or Hegel's dialectic, then very much in
vogue, than was the case with regard to Scholastic philosophy. From Schelling's
philosophy, which closely related to the romantic movement, they took the idea
of life and the organism as well as the strong emphasis on mystical knowledge.
From Hegel they adopted, among others, the concept of a living spirit giving life to
the continuing unfolding of the "Christian idea." In fact, as a result of its encounter
with the writings of the Church Fathers, the history of dogma, together with the
concept of a living tradition, constituted a kind of collective conscience of the

Church acting under the effect of God's spirit. The development of a historical perspective became the characteristic method with which the nineteenth century approached all questions.

Three names dominated the Tübingen School. Its founder, Johann Sebastian Drey (1777–1851), was still tentative in his progress and tied to the ideas of Schelling and Schleiermacher. Yet his services were twofold; he incorporated the contributions of Protestant historians in his theology without falling victim to archeologism, and he developed a theology from the perspective of transcendental idealism in order to lead Catholicism back to a fundamental and comprehensive idea. He emphasized that this idea was not based a priori upon reason, but was grounded in revealed realities; and that it was not a pure idea, but God's eternal plan manifesting itself in time: a gift from supernatural life to man. These considerations led him to a treatment of the organic unity of the Church, its continuing development, and the life of the community inspired by the Holy Spirit.

Johann Baptist Hirscher (1788–1865) was a reformer of the pastoral and catechetical areas and developed daring and useful thoughts, some of which were rather far from reality. He was also a rejuvenator of moral theology and introduced, as Drey had, a social dimension into this discipline. Hirscher presented moral theology in a less abstract manner, which was reminiscent of Pauline kerygma, and strove for a close connection between dogma and spirituality in order to counteract the naturalistic moralism of the eighteenth century and the casuistry of the preceding centuries.

Johann Adam Möhler (1776–1838) towered above both Drey and Hirscher just as "genius surpasses talent" (de Grandmaison). In the course of his brief professorship he reformulated all topics which he treated: the basic dogmas of Christianity as much as the knowledge of faith, the supernatural, grace, and the Church. Not only did his thought grow in precision between his impressive early *The Unity of the Church* (1825) and his later *Symbolism* (1832), but also in the four later editions of this latter work, which came to be the most important treatment of controversial theology since the end of the sixteenth century. We see in him the unfolding of a theological renewal influenced in its beginnings by rich, deep, and tradition-molded insights but also including a nonreflective enthusiasm vulnerable in its philosophical assumptions. If Möhler was inferior to Drey in speculative thought, he was yet the greater of the two in that he succeeded in freeing his synthesis from the system-immanent pantheistic tendencies of idealistic philosophy. Thus his well-considered and balanced work, in a style which conveys an enthusiastic conviction, can be regarded as the most significant example of the intellectually awakened and fundamentally very Catholic theology of romanticism.

The University of Munich, transferred from Landshut in 1825, did not contribute to the theological rejuvenation of the first third of the century to the same degree as Tübingen. However, through the activity of King Ludwig I and his intimate friend Ringseis, the first president of the university, it grew within a few years into the most important intellectual center of Catholicism in central Europe in the areas of philosophy, history, literature, and the arts. Among its professors were Schelling, a Protestant who was very open-minded toward Catholicism and whose brilliant philosophical-religious synthesis of Christianity was universally acclaimed; the historian Döllinger; the able exegete Allioli; and the poet Brentano. In addition to these, two others, both laymen, drew attention. The philosopher Franz von Baader (1765–1841), enthusiastically acclaimed by some contemporaries as the rejuvenator of speculative theology, was closer in his work to theosophy than theology. Inspired by Thomas Aquinas and Meister Eckhart as well as by the Protestant mystic Jakob Böhme, his was a very religious, daring, and original mind. He was interested in bringing about a union of the Churches outside of the domination of the Pope.

The second influential layman was Johann Joseph Görres (1776–1848), a typical representative of the development which returned a number of young intellectuals to their faith. These young intellectuals, without losing the positive values of their intellectual positions, moved from a lack of faith, so popular in the eighteenth century, to a rediscovery of the spiritual demands within the atmosphere of romanticism, to the Christian faith, and finally to a vital and profound understanding of the Catholic Church. In 1826 Görres became a professor of history and literature at Munich and for about twenty years was the leader of an intellectually and artistically very active group. He also provided the stimulus for a German Catholic movement against an established Church. His lectures, conducted with a high degree of scholarship, were more concerned with the philosophy of history than with history as a science. He developed a universal view of history in the romantic style. These views became the foundation for Görres' work on *Christian Mysticism* (1836/42), a work which displayed very little critical spirit, but which for half a century was a point of departure for many scholarly works on speculative mysticism.

France: On the Way to a New Apologia

The revival of theological studies proceeded much slower in France than in Germany, as a result of the lack of an institutional framework. The suppression of the religious orders and the destruction of monastic libraries had occurred at roughly the same time as the disappearance of the theological schools of the Old Regime and most of the French centers of learning. For several generations, therefore, the entire intellectual training of the clergy was concentrated in the seminaries of the dioceses. There the curriculum left much to be desired for two reasons. Competent professors were not available, as a consequence of the interruption occasioned by the Revolution, and the shortage of priests compelled the bishops to be more concerned with rapid ordinations than with the quality of their education. Training of priests was of a purely practical nature. In seventy-five out of eighty seminaries, Church history was not taught at all, exegesis was generally limited to a devotional commentary without any critical content, moral theology was limited to the usual casuistry, and the study of dogma consisted of the memorization of simple and antiquated texts.

Louis Bautain (1796–1867) is generally regarded only as a champion of fideism. But in reality, his orientation toward Plato and Augustine made him much more differentiated. Bautain possessed a profound if somewhat fanatical mind, and his university education made him a rarity in those days. He was very much concerned with a unity of thought and life, and he attempted to solve the intellectual problems of his age with a truly Catholic spirit. Unfortunately, Bautain was not familiar with Scholastic tradition, a dangerous ignorance, but it allowed him a fresh and free approach to problems. Beyond a sharp criticism of rationalism, his work was designed to offer a genuinely theological synthesis from the perspective of German idealism. Reflecting upon the wealth of ideas contained in revelation, he attempted to describe the complete agreement of dogmas and to demonstrate how they explained the riddles of nature and human life. His theological wisdom, presented to the faithless as the only true philosophy, acquired an apologetic significance. Throughout this time, apologetic intentions dominated Catholic thought in France, where destruction as a consequence of unbelief had been greater than in other countries. In many instances, however, the need for a rejuvenation in the area of methodology was not recognized. The numerous editions of these works, many of which were merely mediocre efforts, point up how undemanding the ecclesiastical public was.

In a number of new books, two other laymen, Louis de Bonald and Joseph de Maistre, whose writings first appeared at the time of the Revolution, took up the topics raised since 1796. Their intention was not that of the classical apologists to prove the truth of religion, but rather its necessity. This they did by applying the pragmatic perspective of Chateaubriand to the area of politics. Not only does revelation satisfy to the highest degree the demands of the heart and man's noblest motives, but it also confirms through experience that it is the necessary foundation of the activities of spiritual and social life, just as the destructive nature of the revolution had proved the error of the philosophy of the Enlightenment. For Bonald, individual reason, incapable of arriving at the truth, must be replaced by external authority, divine in origin and social in its realization, a revelation transmitted with the aid of tradition. This concept became in France the impulse for the development of the study of the history of religion and of sociology and guided the attention of theologians to the social aspects of Christianity. De Maistre took an analogous but clearly differentiated direction. In a visionary fashion and without concern for early tradition, he examined the historical experience of the past few centuries in order to divine the laws of providence and the immutable principles of society. He also arrived at the conclusion that monarchy was the best form of government, but he insisted on the necessity of its association with Catholicism and warned that any attempt at independence with respect to the Holy See would necessarily lead to disruptions. In this way de Maistre became a champion of ultramontane revival as well as of that movement which favored the return of divided Christianity to Roman unity.

This counterrevolutionary apologetic, abandoning individualistic rationalism for social salvation based upon a return to a religion of authority, had much to offer a world which saw society shaken to its foundations. But in order to be truly acceptable, especially to the young, it had to be less dogmatic and had to be able to express itself in a language fitted to the romantic mentality. In addition, it had to be shown as less directly political and no longer primarily as justification for a monarchical social order. It must stand as a strongly intellectual system of Catholic philosophy. This task was left for Lamennais, whom we encounter once more in this connection in his *Essai sur l'indifférence en matière de religion* (4 volumes, 1817–23). Lamennais continued to be inspired by themes of the apologists of the seventeenth century: Pascal, Bossuet, de Maistre, and especially Bonald. These themes were newly expressed by Lamennais even if not newly thought through. In a remarkable way Lamennais understood the mentality and the difficulties of his contemporaries and for that reason allowed himself momentarily to be fascinated by the ideology of the eighteenth century. He returned to the Church, however, not out of a reactionary reflex as so many followers of de Maistre or Bonald had done, nor through a purely emotional attraction like Chateaubriand, but in the name of the demands of spiritual and intellectual freedom, which had been threatened by the despotism of the state and the domination of Napoleon.

This brilliant apologia of Lamennais, which articulated many commonly held ideas with prophetic force and enriched them with fruitful if immature insights, was paired with a philosophical traditionalism which in Lamennais' eyes constituted its irreducible rational foundation. Out of the genuine desire to provide the doctrine of the Church with a valid philosophical justification, he started with a theory of knowledge which, inspired by Bonald, placed the criterion of certainty in the *sensus communis* instead of with the insight of the individual and that of general reason. Lamennais saw his justification in a dimension of social reality which had been a constant part of the faith of humankind since its beginnings. For him, Catholic Christianity was its only valid form of expression. His system contained positive aspects which had been neglected in preceding centuries. These were the emphasis on the social character of religious man and on the historical perspective of the intellectual development of mankind; a demonstration of the thesis confirming the moral necessity of revelation; the thought, in contrast to the Protestant view, that tradition preceding the writing of Holy Scripture is the chief organ of revelation; and the working out of a non-a priori religious theory based on fact. But the passionate criticism of individual reason which is the basis for Lamennais' apologia contains dual dangers. One is fideism, which in the act of accepting religious faith suspends the autonomy of the individual conscience; the other is naturalism, which confuses the truths of general reason with supernaturally revealed truth and the authority of humankind with the authority of the Church.

The new system therefore not only earned the scorn of the rationalists but also the partially justified criticism of the theologians from Saint Sulpice who had remained true to the classical concepts. Lamennais, a self-taught man, who was "ignorant of the classics" (Lambruschini) and who stood chronologically and ideologically at the turn from the eighteenth to the nineteenth century, became the originator of a new Christian humanism. For a decade he was the leading spiritual power of the most dynamic wing of the young clergy. These young clergymen were equally interested in an unmerciful criticism of Gallicanism and in the new and more modern political theology which Lamennais presented in *De la religion considerée dans ses rapports avec l'ordre politique et civil* (1826). Lamennais' influence reached far beyond the borders of France.

The dynamic effect of Lamennais on the revival of speculative theology and philosophy in France resulted not only from his writings but also from his charisma. Convinced that one of the principal causes of the inferiority of Catholics in France for the past several centuries must be seen in the cultural and scientific backwardness of the clergy, together with his brother Jean-Marie he developed in 1828 the idea of a new congregation which was to take the place of the old orders which were no longer capable of meeting the needs of the time. Aware that the task surpassed the strength of any individual, he hoped to enlist the assistance of the young intellectuals who had gathered around him. Under a simple rule which would permit membership to priests as well as to laymen, the new congregation would train scholars according to the example of the Benedictines, college and seminary professors according to the model of the Jesuits and Sulpicians, and preachers according to the way of the Dominicans.

In order to solve the great problems of the nineteenth century through a reconciliation of science and faith, the new congregation was to intensify learning. The scope of study was to include philosophy, theology, exegesis, Church history, languages, and all of the profane sciences including mathematics and chemistry. Within this ambitious and rather unrealistic program, ideals frequently assumed the place of clear concepts and empty phrases replaced serious scientific work. A major cause was that Lamennais and his followers "like the whole clergy in France suffered from a lack of basic education in spite of their prophetic intuitions" (Leflon), and their activity proved it. Lamennais was a great initiator even though the concepts he presented did not have lasting value.

Among Lamennais' associates at La Chênaie, his closest confidant, Philippe Gerbet (1798–1864), was the outstanding theologian. His sharp intelligence impressed all who met him. As the most active promoter of the *Mémorial catholique* after 1826, Gerbet, employing Lamennais' theory of proof, developed an analysis of the act of faith which attracted the justified attention of theologians. More important was the publication of his *Considérations sur le dogme générateur de la piété catholique* (1829), a treatise of the Eucharist which was both a dogmatic and a devotional tract.

Italy: Renaissance of the Christian Philosophy

Despite the upheavals of the revolution, the ecclesiastical centers of education in Italy survived in greater numbers than in France. The scholarly tradition of the eighteenth century was continued laudably in the areas of patrology, epigraphics, and Near Eastern studies, but stagnated in that of theology. No rejuvenation could be expected from the northern university departments, which were strongly supervised by government. The Roman schools, reorganized by Leo XII, and especially the Gregorian University, which had been entrusted again to the Jesuits in 1824, together with the Spanish schools were almost the only ones preserving the Scholastic tradition in higher education. But it was an obdurate Scholasticism, corrupted by the doctrines of Locke and Condillac, whose views were very much in fashion among the Italian clergy at the beginning of the nineteenth century.

These conditions in Italy make understandable the enthusiastic attitude which the public held toward the work of Lamennais. The first volume of the *Essai sur l'indifférence* was received with great acclaim, and the sympathies for the author increased on the occasion of his journey to Italy in 1824. Yet the effect of Lamennais in Italy must not be overstated; it was less a case of influence than of a meeting of analogous thoughts. If Lamennais' views received acceptance it was because he expressed already existing ideas more fittingly and elegantly and because he was regarded as disseminating the ideas which le Maistre had already publicized for a number of years. Lamennais was admired as the defender of the Church against revolutionary rationalism, as the champion of theocracy, as the rejuvenator of the concept of authority, and as the apologist who voiced a general agreement with religious truth. The Italians evinced more reserve toward the philosophical system which he wanted to make the foundation of his intellectual revival. The doctrine of the *sensus communis* found a few adherents, but most were disturbed by the unclear relationship between the authorities of Church and humankind and by the consequences of a radical rejection of the possibilities of individual reason.

Thus at the very moment when the German Catholics were fascinated by post-Kantian systems and the French for a generation were involved with traditionalism, there grew in Italy, within a Scholasticism corrupted by Cartesianism and empiricism, tender shoots of a renascence of original Thomism. The center of this movement was Piacenza. After his "promotion" to provincial of Naples in 1831, Taparelli d'Azeglio entrusted Serafino Sordi with the teaching of philosophy at the school in Naples, which henceforth became a second center of this movement.

Other Catholic thinkers in Italy were convinced that traditional philosophy was in need of rejuvenation. This was the path taken by Pasquale Galuppi (1770–1846), who introduced Kant to Italy. His effort was continued in comprehensive fashion by Antonio Rosmini (1797–1855), one of the best Italian metaphysicians of the nineteenth century. Rosmini also began with the suggestion of a return to Thomism, but he gradually developed a more personal system in which Thomistic elements were combined with inspirations by Plato, Augustine, Anselm of Canterbury, Leibniz, and Hegel. He was a pious and ardent priest, a champion of the Catholic cause in the north of the Italian peninsula, a personal friend of Manzoni, and a skilled educator, whose *Dell'unità dell'educazione* (1826) is still regarded well today. Pius VIII encouraged Rosmini in his philosophical and theological work, and, in 1830, there appeared the first fruit of these labors, his *Nuovo saggio sull'origine delle idee,* which has become his fundamental work. The first reaction to his attacks upon contemporary idols was negative on the part of shocked laymen. Yet gradually Rosmini's philosophy, modern and religious in equal measure, was accepted. This acceptance was due in large part to the ease with which Rosmini's philosophy adapted itself to many characteristics of the national temperament. Between 1830 and 1850, large numbers of Rosminic groups of priests and laymen were formed. Their members admired in him the thinker as much as the priest. In the course of time, Rosmini's ideas were taught at the universities and in numerous seminaries of Northern Italy, where they remained strongly influential until the time of Leo XIII.

Part Three

Between the Revolutions
of 1830 and 1848

I N T R O D U C T I O N

Gregory XVI

Pius VIII died on 30 November 1830, at a critical point in European history. Even if the year 1830 was not as important a turning point as 1789, 1815, and 1848, it was nevertheless a significant caesura. The July revolution in France marked the victory of the middle class and of the parliamentary system over the vain attempts to restore the Old Regime, and caused a chain reaction in Europe: from Belgium, where the Vienna settlement was first breached, to Poland, Ireland, Piedmont, the Duchies of Parma and Modena, and the Papal States. This political fermentation, which soon involved the Iberian Peninsula with its dynastic and ideological conflicts, was only the symptom of a much deeper discontent. Intelligence and fantasy had advanced faster than the general development of a world whose economic and social structures were only just beginning to change and in which large landed estates continued to play a predominant role. New ideas of freedom and justice were born and raised expectations for the future. These new ideas were expressed in liberal newspapers and pamphlets, in the systems of utopian socialism, and in romanticism, which was, as Victor Hugo explained in his foreword to *Hernani* (March 1830), only "liberalism in literature." The desire for change was an overwhelming concern of the young intellectuals, whose dreams of transformations were impossible because they did not correspond to actual power realities. These suppressed desires came to the fore at the slightest opportunities and finally exploded in 1848.

The members of the Sacred College were as little able as any other statesmen of the period to analyze the situation in ways possible to the historian of a hundred years later. But all of them sensed that the Pope whom they had to choose would have to confront a particularly difficult situation. They sought a solution in traditional approaches, especially as the two parties opposing one another at the conclave of 1829 were present in virtually unchanged strength. There were the "politicals" who were still interested in a defense of the Papal States through close cooperation with Metternich's Austria, and the "zealots," who were more interested in the independence of the Church from governments than in diplomatic combinations. Of fifty-five cardinals, thirty-four were present at the opening of the conclave on 14 December 1830. Contrary to all expectations, the conclave lasted for fifty days. Pacca's candidacy was supported by the pro-Austrian party led by the old Cardinal Albani. Victory for Pacca seemed likely, especially as the hesitant reply given by the candidate of the "zealots," Cardinal de Gregorio, to the speech of the French ambassador, was received with disappointment and reduced his initially strong chances. On 28 December the "zealots" voted for Giustiniani, who received twenty-one votes. But on 9 January the Spanish ambassador rejected this candidate, because during his nunciature at Madrid he had defended the rights of the clergy so energetically as to arouse the hostility of the government. Now the "zealots" cast their votes for the Camaldolese Cardinal Cappellari, prefect of the Congregation for the Propagation of the Faith, who earlier had been considered one of the *papabili* but who so far had never received more than seven votes. Finally, the pro-Austrian party gave up the hope of winning a two-thirds majority for Pacca and presented Macchi as their new candidate. But his candidacy also lacked a good chance of success, as he was suspected by the French government because of his relationship with ex-King Charles X. The duel between Pacca and Cappellari continued for three weeks, in spite of the growing dissatisfaction of the Roman population and the worsening political situation in Italy. It required all of the skills of Cardinal Bernetti and the announcement of a rebellion in the Romagna to persuade Albani to give up. Thus Cappellari was elected Pope on 2 February 1831. He chose the name Gregory XVI.

Bartolomeo Alberto Cappellari, known in his order as Fra Mauro, was born on 18 September 1765 at Belluno in Venetia. In 1783 he had joined the Camaldolese, the strictest offshoot of the Benedictines, and for more than a quarter of a century devoted himself to theological studies. In 1799, at the nadir of the papacy, he published *Il trionfo della Santa Sede e della Chiesa contro gli assalti dei Novatori* (*The Triumph of the Holy See and the Church over the Attacks by the Innovators*). Directed against Febronians and Jansenists, it was to have great influence on the development of the ultramontane movement. Gradually this monk, theologian, and scholar became acquainted with the complexities of ecclesiastical affairs. After he had been sent to Rome in 1795, he became abbot of San Gregorio al Celio in 1805 and shortly afterwards procurator superior of his order. This position enabled him to show his administrative talents at a particularly difficult time. Shortly after his return to Rome in 1814, Pius VII followed the advice of Cardinal Fontana and appointed Cappellari as consultant to several congregations, including the Congregation for Extraordinary Ecclesiastical Affairs, and as examiner of candidates for the episcopate. After he had become vicar general of his order in 1823, Leo XII, who regarded his knowledge of doctrinal matters highly, made Cappellari a cardinal in 1826 and appointed him prefect of the Congregation for the Propagation of the Faith. As such he was concerned not only with missions in general, but also with the Churches in America, the Uniate Churches of the Near East and Russia, and Catholic affairs in England and the Netherlands. The secretary of state consulted Cappellari regularly, and frequently his opinion was decisive.

Although he had spent the greatest part of his life in a monk's cell, as Pope Cappellari was surprisingly well versed not only in the affairs of the Curia, but also with the concrete difficulties facing the Church almost everywhere. Cappellari was intelligent and quite capable of grasping the ramifications of problems, as long as their aspects were within the framework of his thinking, which was linked to the eighteenth century. He was also an educated man according to the standards of this century and encouraged scholarly work, especially archeological research. On the other hand, this monk had difficulties in his contacts with people and hardly any sensitivity for the interests of the laity of the Papal States. A further obstacle was that Cappellari knew no foreign languages, had never met any of the statesmen of his time, and did not know much about politics. This left him at the mercy of advisers who were not always either enlightened or nonpartisan. This strict theologian, who had gleaned all of his knowledge from books, was incapable of grasping the problems of the new currents swirling around him, harbored nothing but mistrust toward the liberal aspirations of the coming new society and resolutely took the part of the defenders of the established order.

One can better understand the general directions of Gregory XVI's pontificate if one keeps in mind his basic orientation. This obstinate and authoritarian doctri-narian, ascending the chair of Saint Peter in far better health than his predecessors, was determined to face the dangers against which the "zealots" had warned for half a century. Interested wholly in religious concerns, the Pope opposed vague romantic religiosity and, in particular, rationalistic naturalism. For the purpose of combatting them, he preferred to employ the religious orders, whose difficult re-birth he promoted with all of his strength. He saw the root of the evil from which the Church suffered in the secret societies. Tenaciously the Pope used his magis-terial office to remind people of the great traditional principles and to characterize as error whatever attempted to evade submission to the supernatural.

He also made himself the unbending defender of ecclesiastical principles and of the independence of the Church from all notions of an established Church. Energetically he opposed all governmental systems which asserted the right to subjugate the pastoral office to secular domination, especially in the area of nomination of bishops. Equally energetically the Pope rejected compromises in questions involving dogmatic principles, especially in the case of mixed marriages, which had been treated rather laxly by Rome for many years. With equal determi-nation he defended the supreme authority of the Pope within the Church. Without realizing the anachronism of such pretensions, he systematically employed the nunciatures to obtain the acknowledgment by the Catholic governments of papal monarchy, as whose savior he saw himself ever since the publication of his *Tri-onfo della Santa Sede.* Sharing the shortsightedness of the "zealots" concerning the changes modern society was undergoing; incapable of recognizing the weak-ness of the political and social system of the Old Regime, which he regarded as an expression of divine will; and haunted by the thought that the Papal States, in which he saw the guarantee for the spiritual independence of the Pope, could be destroyed by liberal aspirations, Gregory XVI was determined to mobilize all means at the disposal of the reviving papacy in order to stop all further advances of the "revolution." For the same reasons the Pope obstinately refused to cooperate with any "subversive forces," even in Poland and Ireland, where they seemed to work toward the liberation of Catholics.

The pontificate of Gregory XVI appears as a "pontificate of struggle" (Pouthas), in the service of a conservative, even a reactionary, ideal. Thus it is not astonishing that in contrast to the events half a century later under Leo XIII, laity and clergy engaged in initiatives aimed at a reconciliation of the Church with modern society without the participation of the papacy. They provided Catholicism with a face totally different from that of 1815. Among many people the impression grew that a new and more progressive attitude prevailed, and it is this impression which explains the many illusions during the first months of Pius IX's pontificate.

During the fifteen years in which Gregory XVI guided the fortunes of the Church, such a development was possible not only because the Holy See in contrast to the subsequent pontificate was not yet able effectively to restrain the tendencies of which it disapproved. It was also possible because the work of Gregory XVI had many positive aspects which were directed toward the future; so much so that in more than one case Pius IX only needed to pluck the fruits of the patient preparations undertaken by his predecessor. Gregory XVI's battle against the ex-cesses of rationalism, indifferentism, and Kantian subjectivism helped to achieve a balance between the sense of the supernatural and the value of human reason, and thus laid the firm foundations for the future development of the Catholic spirit and Catholic spirituality. By insisting inflexibly on the prerogatives of the Holy See and the independence of the Church, however, the Pope also prepared the way for those future successes of ultramontanism which ultimately stifled pluralism and endangered the collegial nature of ecclesiastical authority.

The immediate effect of Gregory's position, however, was the overcoming of that ecclesiastical nationalism in which the autonomy won by the regional Churches with respect to Rome had to be paid for with the submission of the Church to secular power. On the other hand, it must not be forgotten that in spite of the unyielding nature of the Camaldolese Pope, Gregory could be flexible in the practical applications of his principles. Gregory XVI demonstrated his suppleness in his Bull *Sollicitudo Ecclesiarum* of 7 August 1831. Although personally holding the legitimist view, he declared that in case of changes of political regimes the Holy See would negotiate with the governments in de facto possession of power. He employed this principle in the delicate case of the new South American republics, which had been a continuing problem for his three predecessors.

The Pope showed the same ambivalence with respect to past and future in the selection of his assistants and advisers. Cappellari, counted among the "zealots," chose as his first secretary of stare a former associate and friend of Consalvi. Cardinal Bernetti was a man of the world, little concerned with the religious aspect of problems, a pure technician of politics and diplomacy, who clearly recognized the deficiencies in the administration of the Papal States. Metternich valued his "knowledge of the needs of the time," while Lamennais accused him of giving in too much to the demands of governments. But, formed in the atmosphere of the first Roman restoration following the Jacobin interlude, Bernetti shared with the "zealots" the resolute hostility to liberal political regimes and the conviction that the only hope for a continuation of the Papal States rested in a conservative policy.

The growing opposition of the College of Cardinals, which accused Bernetti of attempting — like Consalvi — to centralize all power in his hands, caused Gregory XVI to dismiss him in 1836. His next choice, Cardinal Lambruschini, was a man of totally different character, a strictly pious son of the Church. Like the Pope himself, he sympathized with the pastoral aspect of problems and was closely allied with the Jesuits. But he belonged to those members of the Curia who most resolutely closed their minds to modern ideas. Yet if he was a reactionary as a result of his innate personality and his development, and very much intent on fighting unmercifully any legacies of the revolution, his diplomatic experience had taught him that in practice he must moderate the rigidity of his principles. This showed itself in the administration of the Papal States, as well as in his general ecclesiastical policy which, when necessary, he adapted to constitutional conditions.

One must also take into account that Gregory XVI, to a far higher degree than his predecessors, personally participated in the conduct of papal affairs. He worked hard and in addition to his secretaries also relied on other advisers. Lambruschini was chiefly responsible for the immobility characterizing the last years of the pontificate of Gregory XVI in many areas. It contrasted glaringly with the vitality which the Catholic Church outside of Rome displayed at this same time.

Section One

The First Phase of Catholic Liberalism

Roger Aubert

In the eyes of the Catholics of the restoration period, liberal concepts were identified with the revolution and needed to be rooted out. In France, the last remaining sympathies disappeared which a number of the Constituent clergy held for the liberal ideas of the eighteenth century. But around 1830, when in all of Europe the majority of the priests and of the faithful continued to see salvation for the Church exclusively in a restoration of the political conditions of the Old Regime and in the reconquest of the privileged position of the Church in society, a growing number of young clergymen and laymen began to question this course. Fascinated by the mysticism of freedom which jointly inspired the writers and artists of romanticism, liberal conspirators, and people opposed to the Holy Alliance, they began to wonder about the possibility of reconciling Catholicism with liberalism to a certain extent and, without betraying their own faith, of accepting a social order based on the principles of 1789. These principles were: personal freedom in place of despotism; political freedoms which were no longer conceded privileges but legally anchored; the right of peoples to self-determination; primacy of the principle of nationality over the principle of legitimacy; and, in the area directly concerning religious life, freedom of the press and freedom of religion together with a limitation of ecclesiastical privileges, possibly even separation of Church and state.

Some promoted the reconciliation of Church and liberalism for practical reasons. For them it was either a means of winning the young intellectuals back to the Church or an unavoidable necessity in light of irreversible developments which should be adapted in the best possible way to the interests of the Church. Some voiced the thought that in countries with a Protestant or Orthodox majority and in which Catholics were the victims of a system of established religions, the introduction of a more liberal government would result in noticeable advantages for the Catholics. Others pointed out that the same advantages would accrue in Catholic countries in which regalistic governments posed serious obstacles to the work of the Church. Thinking that from the apostolic point of view liberal institutions were to be preferred to the protectionism to which the union of throne and altar frequently degenerated, they believed it to be necessary not merely to tolerate the contemporary movement but to encourage it. In fact, where it had not yet started, they thought it ought to be provoked. Others favored closer relations between Church and liberalism for reasons of principle. They shared the optimistic confidence of the philosophes of the eighteenth century in man's potential and regarded the development of society in a liberal direction as progress. Put differently, they regarded the democratic ideal which inspired the liberals as a realization of the message of the Gospel which invites the replacement of the inequality of conditions with the equality of nature and the domination of a few with the freedom for all. Others would soon go even further and want to introduce liberal ideas in the Church itself: less authoritarian relations between bishops and flock; greater autonomy of Catholic thinkers with respect to the official theological systems; greater leeway for the clergy in relation to traditional pastoral methods. No matter of what type the concrete applications might be, they were fundamentally an outgrowth of the same freedom which inspired the reform efforts of Hirscher in Tübingen, of Raffaele Lambruschini and Rosmini in Italy, and of Lamennais in France.

This general movement, comprising some very different tendencies, was called "Catholic liberalism" or "liberal Catholicism." It was to develop into one of the main problems, especially in the Latin countries, which agitated Catholics throughout the nineteenth century. The solution was the more difficult as the liberals, when the ecclesiastical authorities refused to follow the path suggested by them, now became emphatic in their anticlericalism. In their eyes, the Church was the main obstacle to political freedom, intellectual liberation, and progress in general. This attitude in turn stiffened the backs of the leaders of the Church, who saw themselves confirmed in their view of the incompatibility of the Church with those forces which, in collaboration with Freemasons and the heirs of the philosophes of the eighteenth century, wished to overturn the established religious and political order.

The connection between Catholicism and modern liberties was systematically established in Belgium between 1825 and 1828. It did not receive its impulses from Lamennais' theories. On the contrary, the practical union between Belgian Catholics and liberals influenced the intellectual development of Lamennais. Yet Lamennais' ingenious intuition immediately grasped that the new procedure used by the Belgians to solve specific problems could be applied generally. He developed it into a theoretical system which included a new social philosophy, and he did not hesitate to urge the Church to follow the movement which was pushing nations toward democracy. By placing his considerable reputation in the service of this idea, he obtained for it the widespread attention which it had hitherto lacked and he continues to deserve to occupy a leading position in the beginnings of Catholic liberalism.

CHAPTER 16

From Belgian Unionism to the Campaign of *L'Avenir*

The Decision of Belgian Catholics in Favor of Liberty

Belgian Catholics in general and the clergy in particular had shown themselves very reactionary in 1815. The episcopate had gone so far as to forbid the oath of the constitution because it proclaimed freedom of the press and freedom of religion. This attitude had only served to increase the hostility of the liberals toward the clergy, which appeared to them as the defender of an anachronistic theocracy.

The remarkable aspect of the campaign ten years later against the seminary decrees of June 1825 was that, while it rested on an appeal to the right of the Church to train its priests, it soon took on broader outlines. At the end of 1825, Catholic parliamentarians and journalists liked to refer to constitutional freedoms. They demanded freedom of education as a natural extension of the freedom of conscience, and called for the independence of the Church from any governmental interference in the appointment of ecclesiastical dignitaries in the name of religious freedom. Publicists eventually discovered in freedom of the press the best protection against arbitrary governmental actions to which the Catholics were exposed. Even in entering this arena, though, the Catholics did not renounce their principles, which were very different from the ideals of the liberals who desired an increasing laicization of society. But in order to safeguard the permanent goal of instilling Christian values in public life, the Catholics considered it more realistic to resort to means other than those of the Old Regime. The Catholic view could be summarized as follows: In a parliamentary state, guaranteeing freedom of education and the press, Catholics would have the unrestricted right to influence consciences and to gain predominance legally. Laws passed by a majority would then enable them to construct a Christian society which heretofore had always depended exclusively on the good will of a Catholic sovereign.

In the course of 1826 the important Catholic newspapers began to emphasize the advantages of liberty. Adolphe Bartels used it to say that truth could prevail without official protection, and that the political desire of the liberals to have a government which expressed the will of the citizens and was no longer the governing instrument of a monarch was compatible with Catholic orthodoxy.

With the Catholics embarking on this course, some young liberals became convinced that the tactic of the old freethinkers of supporting the government in its chicanery of the Church was nothing more than a fool's paradise, as it enabled the government to pursue a policy of enlightened despotism. They considered it more important to oppose the absolutist tendencies of the monarchical government than to stifle the Church at any price. They thought of offering the Catholics a broad-based alliance on the following quid pro quo basis: We renounce any exclusion of the Church from education or any control over its activity aimed at limiting its influence on society; you, in turn, will no longer attempt to reach a privileged position in the state by way of a concordat or any other method, and will join us in demanding the exercise of modern freedoms.

When Devaux made this liberal appeal in the spring of 1827, many Catholics hesitated. At that very time they thought that they could reach a separate agreement with the King. But when it became clear four months later that the government was delaying an agreement, they began to have second thoughts. On 1 November the *Courrier de la Meuse* agreed to Devaux's offer and during 1828 the idea of a union of Catholics and liberals on the basis of the mutual demand for constitutional freedoms became widely accepted in the country, especially in Flanders. It did so without arousing the opposition of the clergy, which hated the government more than it disliked the liberals.

Hence by the end of 1828 Catholics had been won for "unionism," i.e., for the tactic of uniting with the liberals in order to demand the independence of the Church on the basis of modern liberty and its right to establish an educational system directed exclusively by itself. The unionists of 1828 regarded their alliance with the liberals and the acceptance of the liberal viewpoint only as a provisional arrangement and not as a system representing a permanent ideal. They had no intention of speaking of a "natural alliance between Catholicism and democracy," nor to raise their demands for freedom to the point of a complete separation of Church and state. Matters were very clear for the ecclesiastical authorities as well as for the young noblemen of the Robiana-Merode group, whose real intentions were revealed in their private papers. In no way did they favor the principles of 1789; on the contrary, they wished to have the Church once again assume the spiritual control of civil society. De Gerlache and Kersten also insisted on avoiding an overemphasis of human rights. They were unwilling to accept the principle of popular sovereignty, just as much as they viewed the union with the liberals merely as the smaller of two evils, dictated by the circumstances. To be sure, Bartels — with the approval of a number of Flemish clerics — continued to be progressive and in 1828 developed several theses which appeared in the writings of Lamennais in the following year. One of them was that the people had primacy over the King, but he qualified this by saying that he desired general liberty not as an inherent good but as the smaller evil. This was still quite different from the demand for liberty for its own sake, as *L'Avenir* was to champion it later. But the positions assumed by the Belgian Catholics in their opposition to William I were by themselves and in spite of their limited character a revelation for Lamennais.

Lamennais' Development as a Liberal

Lamennais, the reactionary editor of the *Conservateur* and the *Drapeau blanc*, appeared hardly destined to become the leader of Catholic liberalism. During the first decade of the restoration he was one of the most ardent advocates of a return to the Old Regime. His ideal of a protected Church in a divine-right monarchy was opposed to a free Church in a free state. When in 1826 in his book *De la Religion consideŕée dans ses rapports avec L'ordre politique* he advised the Church to cast itself free from the Bourbon regime, he did so because he thought that its compromises with liberalism would destroy it. His ideal was still a theocratic state.

Although in his articles Lamennais often wrote of freedom, and although his ultramontanism was based on the idea of freedom, he meant the freedom of the Christian against the powers of evil and the freedom of the Church with respect

to the government. It was not, a freedom for all, "but a freedom without toleration." In his writings before 1828 there is no sympathy for political liberalism or
democracy. But during this period Lamennais thought more theocratically than
monarchically. From this vantage point it becomes understandable that once he
grew disillusioned with monarchy — he found it easy to turn away from it. He associated the Church with the growing cause of the people and strove to achieve
what Verucci has called a "democratic theocracy." In this perspective, the Pope
appears as the protector of the weak and as the arbiter guaranteeing right over
might. This development must have come about the more easily as Lamennais
had already demonstrated in his apologetics the extent to which he understood
the mentality of his time and the necessity to adapt to it.

The struggles for the independence of the Church, especially in the field of
education, brought Lamennais to a tentative acceptance of the idea of separation
of Church and state. He openly defended it in his book *De la Religion* (1825/26),
at the same time as he began to develop the thesis that truth was more powerful
than institutions.

Under the impact of these diverse influences, Lamennais in February 1829
published his book *Des progrès de la Révolution et de la guerre contre l'Église.* He
still regarded an ultramontane Catholicism as the only solution for society, and
rejected liberalism, statism, and secularism. But he also touched upon a number
of new ideas. Liberalism, he wrote, could be different from the way it presented
itself in France at the time, and there was an essential inner connection between
Catholicism and a healthy liberalism which aimed at the liberation of people from
any suppression by other people. He stated that freedom of the press was a small
evil and could be advantageous for the Church, and that revolutions could be
instruments of providence for the purpose of discarding a number of antiquated
institutions under which the Church had suffered for a long time.

The book was a great success, and even if it encountered the violent opposition of royalists, jurists, and the episcopate, it confirmed his position in the eyes
of his young followers, who to an increasing degree were disgruntled with the
compromises the bishops made with the royal government. With rather romantic
optimism they concluded that only a few gestures by the Church were required
to give liberalism a different turn and to place this growing force in the service of
the Catholic apostolate. They expressed these sentiments with increasing vehemence in their journals *Mémorial catholique* and *Revue catholique.* The evolution
of the events in Belgium only confirmed them in these beliefs and soon they no
longer hesitated to go even further than the Belgians and to assert that the alliance
between Catholicism and liberalism was the only way of salvation for the Church.

These ideas fell on prepared soil. Baron Eckstein in his journal *Le Catholique*
emphasized the "admirable alliance" between Catholicism and a regime of political liberty. Historians have not properly gauged the influence which he thereby
exercised on a part of Parisian Catholic youth. Young noblemen, who had worked
with him and hardly ever had had contact with Lamennais, founded the *Cor-
respondent* in March 1829. In it they declared themselves in favor of religious
freedom for Protestants, which Lamennais had rejected, demanded the right for
members of orders to join together, emphasized freedom of education independent from a state monopoly, and pointed to the dangers of too close a relationship

between throne and altar. They did not go as far as Lamennais' followers later in demanding a complete separation of state and Church and a complete cessation of Church support in the state budget. It was these young people from the *Correspondant* who first received the appellation "liberal Catholics" from the editors of the *Globe* with whom they had opened a dialogue.

The July Revolution of 1830 and the outbreak of anticlericalism associated with it confirmed Lamennais and his followers in their conviction. The Church should welcome those political forms of government which replaced arbitrary action with control by the people, in order both to avoid accusations against it and to provide these new forms of government "with a soul." In the face of the hostile attitude of the government, separation of Church and state was more imperative than ever.

Harel de Tancrel, a young convert, suggested to Abbé Gerbet, Lamennais' most important assistant, the creation of a newspaper for the purpose of publicizing these views. Lamennais liked the idea greatly; even though he did not accept the position of editor, he settled near Paris at the College Juilly in order to be able to keep a close eye on it. On 20 August Gerbet announced the impending publication, an announcement which was received enthusiastically. The first issue of *L'Avenir* saw the light of day with a lead article from the pen of Lamennais.

The name of the paper said much, but even more its motto: "God and Liberty." The paper intended to fight a two-front war. On the one hand it gave the liberals the assurance to support impartially and enthusiastically the freedoms announced by the revolution of 1789. This was to be valid for all freedoms, however, including that of education, which many liberals were reluctant to concede for fear of aiding and abetting ultramontane propaganda. On the other hand, *L'Avenir* tried to make Catholics and clergy understand that it was time to dissociate themselves from the Old Regime and to turn to the future for the creation of a new humanism. A decided turn to modernity became indeed evident in all areas. *L'Avenir* proved itself open to the new romantic literature; it demanded general disarmament and the unification of Europe; and it supported the national revolts of the Belgians, the Irish, and the Poles in the name of the right of peoples to self-determination. Increasingly it accepted universal franchise and republican government, and emphasized the providential character of the revolutions then shaking Europe. It also displayed an open mind with respect to social democracy and underscored the connection between the independence of the Church and its voluntary poverty, as only through it could it feel solidarity with all of humankind and become meaningful to common and oppressed people.

On the political and religious level, *L'Avenir* at first limited itself to praising the regime of liberty and the separation — or better, the differentiation — of Church and state as the most suitable springboard for winning back the faithless. The paper presented this relationship between Church and state as a necessity, without, however, accepting it as the ideal. It demanded the renunciation of the concordat, because in a society "which God had forgotten" it actually hindered the freedom of the Pope and bishops. If the clergy were rid of this unholy tie, Catholicism would experience a new awakening, as Ireland had shown. By the spring and summer of 1831, the paper progressed to an acceptance of the liberal system as the ideal form of government for a mature society.

While the paper, whose circulation never exceeded three thousand, day by day spread its ideas with a zeal which cared little for concrete conditions, Lacordaire, Montalembert, and de Coux, not satisfied with a mere campaign of ideas, established a "general agency for the defense of religious freedom." It organized in the provinces a systematic campaign of influencing public opinion, attacking administrative chicanery about which Catholics had reason to complain, especially in the field of education. By doing so legally with small groups of people in the name of constitutional liberties, they succeeded in gaining the sympathies of the young clergy and in shaking a relatively large number of laity out of their lethargy.

Following a suggestion by the Dutch journalist Le Sage ten Broek, the campaign was quickly expanded to foreign countries, where it appealed for support of Catholics in Ireland, Poland, Germany, and the Netherlands. With the intention of creating genuine international solidarity in obtaining religious and political freedoms, and of opposing the Holy Alliance of Kings with a "Holy Alliance of Peoples," *L'Avenir* on 15 November 1831 published the draft of an "Act of Union, to be submitted to all who, despite the murder of Poland, still hope for freedom in the world and want to bring it about." It was a manifesto which governments interpreted as an instrument of international revolution.

To what extent were the religious-political ideas propagated by *L'Avenir* accepted in the neighboring countries? In Germany, Lamennais' philosophy was received with interest by the Munich group, but the leaders of the Catholic movement regarded the attempt to come to an accommodation with liberalism with suspicion. In Italy, the conservative Catholics who once had acclaimed the defender of throne and altar rejected his ideas. Liberal Catholics were disappointed by the ultramontane doctrines of *L'Avenir* and its defense of the secular power of the Pope; some members of orders, though, especially in Tuscany, greeted them with approval. In Holland, on the other hand, the campaign of *L'Avenir* was observed with wide acclaim. It was a justification for those who, in a country with a Catholic minority, had discovered the advantages of religious freedom while they lived under the French regime. But nowhere was the influence of *L'Avenir* greater and more effective than in Belgium.

The Belgian Constitution of 1831

Until the beginning of 1831, unionism was for Belgian Catholics nothing more than a tactic, a temporary coalition, from which they expected to derive the greatest possible advantages; it owed nothing to Lamennais. After the publication of *Progrès de la Révolution,* which in Belgium generated an unbelievable echo because a man as famous as Lamennais used Belgium as an example, a goodly number of Catholics began to hold a different view. Inspired by the recent publications by Lamennais and his associates, many people came to the conclusion that a regime of modern freedoms was inherently the best form of government. It corresponded to the wishes of the people in accordance with the principle of *vox populi vox Dei* and the views of philosophical traditionalism, and provided the essential connection between Christianity and freedom. Hence, on the eve of the September revolution of 1830, several currents of thought were in evidence among Belgian Catholics. There was the group around Lamennais, numerically clearly in the minority, which with its enthusiasm soon infected the majority of Catholics and was instrumental in renewing the somewhat loosened bonds between Catholicism and liberalism. In the group, were laymen as well as priests. Some of them openly acknowledged themselves as democrats or republicans. In opposition to episcopal directives they emphasized their personal freedom of interpretation in matters of theological tradition as long as defined dogmas were not involved.

There were also numerous conservatives who were unionists only from necessity. Unwilling to concede the natural character of an alliance between Catholicism and liberalism, they instead, as loyal monarchists, hoped for a quick return to the old unity of throne and altar.

Between these two extremes stood the Mechelen group. Numerically it was very small, but it became very influential through the support of the archbishop of the Belgian Church, the strong personality of his vicar general Sterckx, and the new bishop of Liège, Van Bommel. Their thought also spread to other dioceses. Although showing sympathies for Lamennais' theories, the adherents of this third group, relatively strongly represented in the clergy, were not persuaded by them. Quite realistically they concluded that a return to the Old Regime was no longer possible in view of the revolution which thinking had undergone. In fact, such a return was no longer even desirable. Mutual independence of the two forces seemed preferable, and all religious communities should be afforded religious freedom. The Mechelen group attempted to combine the advantages of the liberal system and the Old Regime in keeping with Van Bommel's view, who was thinking chiefly of financial subsidies, that "freedom should not exclude protection, and protection should not stifle freedom."

Now a constitution for the new state of Belgium had to be drafted. The bishops did everything in their power to assure that the constituent assembly had a Catholic majority. But many of the elected Catholics, open to the ideas of Lamennais, were more than ready to trust completely in liberty. The Mechelen group, however, which desired a certain protection of the Church within the framework of religious freedom, attempted to amend the first draft of the constitution with this objective.

But the atmosphere of the national congress, and the Catholics represented in it, was too strongly influenced by Lamennais as to be able to realize fully their program. But even if the Church was not successful in obtaining all desired concessions, especially with reference to religious congregations, the constitution adopted on 7 February 1831 granted it a rather advantageous position. Freedom of education was guaranteed (Art. 17), as well as the right to free association (Art. 20), i.e., freedom for orders. The state continued to be responsible for ecclesiastical salaries (Article 117). Article 16 guaranteed the Church a degree of independence unknown at this time in any other Catholic country. The state was permitted neither to impose any conditions for the appointment of bishops and the publication of papal announcements nor to attempt to achieve this control through a concordat.

The lifting of all ecclesiastical privileges, and especially the liberal atmosphere in which the constitution had been worked out, worried the Holy See. Warned by Capaccini, Sterckx, who meanwhile had become chapter vicar of Mechelen, wrote a skillful defense in which he pointed out that while the traditional union between the two powers no longer existed, the separation actually was only apparent and was not complete. He hoped that the Church in Belgium possessed enough respect to regain in practice what it had lost in theory. At least his intervention, supported by several Jesuits, succeeded in warding off a formal disapproval by the Holy See. Henceforth the Belgian constitution gained European significance for the future development of Catholic liberalism. For many years it was the ideal of many Catholics who likewise demanded freedom as it was practiced in Belgium.

Briefly summarized, the unionism of the Belgian Catholics in its beginnings intended to be only a temporary and tactical association with modern liberty. But a genuine Catholic liberalism developed in dual fashion in the years 1829–31. One resulted from the theoretical writings of Lamennais and his associates, especially in *L'Avenir*, and the other from the embodiment in the Belgian constitution of conditions which would prove the fruitfulness of these ideas.

CHAPTER 17

The Roman Reaction

The Appeal to Rome

Lamennais' polemics against Gallicanism and Scholastic philosophy earned him the animosity of bishops and theologians, especially the Sulpicians and the Jesuits. His liberalism and the campaign waged by *L'Avenir* for a reconciliation of Church and democracy increased the number of his opponents. They were additionally embittered by the provocative tone and the personal attacks of *L'Avenir*, which for longer than a generation were to be the hallmark of Lamennais' followers. The bishops were irritated because, being legitimists and Gallicans, they were unable to distinguish between what was false and exaggerated in this movement and what was reasonable. Most of them hesitated, however, to attack the well-known apologist and defender of the Roman cause with pastoral letters. But many of them purged their seminaries and pressured their priests to stop reading the paper. A number of older followers, actually in favor of a more open attitude toward liberal tendencies, were worried by the increasingly radical posture of *L'Avenir* in political matters.

The editors of *L'Avenir* attempted to clarify the situation with the aid of a declaration addressed to the new Pope, in which they extensively explained their philosophical, theological, religious, and political positions. But when Rome did not respond positively, cancellations of subscriptions increased and the financial condition of the paper became untenable. At the end of October it was decided to cease publication of *L'Avenir* and the activities of the agency.

An unexpected turn of events occurred when Lacordaire suggested that Lamennais present his case to the Pope personally. Then, equipped with a certification of his orthodoxy, he could return and begin anew with strengthened authority. On 15 November *L'Avenir* appeared for the last time, with the announcement that for the time being it would cease publication. One week later, Lamennais, Lacordaire, and Montalembert started on their journey to Rome.

Arriving in Rome on 30 December, the "Pilgrims of God and Freedom" visited a few well-disposed influential persons. They wanted to see Lamennais well received in spite of the "real errors" of his political writings, because they acknowledged his achievements as apologist, as champion of ultramontanism, and as defender of the freedom of the Church. They were also impressed by the evangelistic echo which *L'Avenir's* appeals to a poorer Church evoked. This view was shared by the Capuchin Cardinal Micara, a few other members of the Sacred College, a few theologians like Father Olivieri, *Magister Sacri Palatii,* and Father Ventura, who was once again totally reconciled with Lamennais and eager to help him.

The opponents were many and powerful. There were the secretary of state, whom the judgment of *L'Avenir* concerning his suppression of the revolts in the Papal States had offended, and Cardinal Lambruschini, who as former nuncio in Paris was regarded as the expert on matters affecting France. He was a decided reactionary, who found it easy to gather adherents for his indignation about this "arrogant spirit" who thought he could give lessons in diplomacy to experienced nuncios and lessons in religion to the Pope. There were several theologians and canonists, especially Jesuits were outraged by the condescension with which Lamennais treated respected theologians. Finally there were French legitimists — supported by the Austrian and Russian embassies — assembled around the auditor of the *Rota* and Cardinal de Rohan, who articulated the concerns of the bishops.

The role of the foreign diplomats was discussed heatedly, and Lamennais himself in his *Affaires de Rome* ascribed to them a predominant influence. Access to the archives has made possible a more balanced view. The French government did not intervene directly, but its hostility to *L'Avenir* was known, and Gregory XVI under no circumstances wanted to increase the tensions between the Church and the new government. It is true that Gregory XVI even before the complaints of Austria's ambassador in December 1831 was not kindly disposed toward Lamennais and regarded as unbecoming his presumption to demand from the Holy See a declaration concerning his case. But the intervention of the ambassador strengthened the unfavorable impression of the Pope. Metternich intervened several times during Lamennais' stay in Rome. Later, after the publication of *Mirari vos,* Metternich sent the Holy See numerous compromising letters which had been intercepted by his censor. Metternich had annotated them with comments and advice which corresponded to the personal opinion of the Pope and contributed to his hardening attitude. The vivid interest of the representatives of the Holy Alliance in Lamennais' case definitely convinced the Pope that he had to take a stand and publicly condemn the new school of thought.

Whatever the case may be, Lamennais and his associates met a wall of polite silence during their first weeks in Rome. The Holy See issued a polite plea to let the matter rest. Lacordaire understood immediately and decided to return to France without delay. But Lamennais, convinced that the opposition against him was exclusively of a political nature and that he was blameless with respect to doctrine, was determined to force Rome to reply. He extended his stay until July. When by that time he still had not heard anything, he decided, encouraged by some Roman friends, to resume publication of *L'Avenir.* He left Rome, bitter that he had been denied the opportunity to present his case personally. The fact that the authorities had systematically avoided any serious discussion convinced him that Rome, overly busy with problems of the day and purely secular problems, had no interest in the general welfare of the Church.

The Encyclical *Mirari vos*

Contrary to Lamennais' assumption, his case had been under serious investigation by the Congregation of Extraordinary Ecclesiastical Affairs since March. The report edited by Cardinal Lambruschini emphasized the international aftereffects of *L'Avenir's* campaign: discontent among the bishops of France and Belgium and concern in the cabinets of the Catholic powers. The advisers were unanimous in their view that the Pope could be silent no longer, as he otherwise might create the impression that he approved the subversive doctrine published by Lamennais during the past two years. Instead of compiling a list of the theses to be condemned, a process which would have taken too much time, the advisers suggested to the Pope that, without mentioning *L'Avenir* expressly, he condemn the theses about the legitimacy of revolution, the separation of Church and state, and freedom of religion and the press. The arguments set forth were primarily of a theological nature. The incriminated theories were accused of being derived from a "certain religious indifferentism, which faith must reject," and countered notions of popular sovereignty with texts like *"omnis potestas a Deo."* But it is likely that the cardinals and the Pope himself were also persuaded to intervene by extratheological factors, such as renewed remarks by the diplomats, renewed outbreaks of liberal agitation in the Papal States, and the Belgian problem.

The Encyclical *Mirari vos* of 15 August 1832 painted a pessimistic picture of the conditions which Gregory XVI encountered upon his accession to the throne. After a condemnation of rationalism and Gallicanism, which Lamennais also had opposed for fifteen years, the encyclical railed against liberalism in its various manifestations, "this false and absurd maxim, or better this madness, that everyone should have and practice freedom of conscience. It spoke against freedom of the press, "this loathsome freedom which one cannot despise too strongly" and from which to expect anything good would be an illusion, attacked the invitation to revolt against sovereigns (this point was developed with special pathos), and opposed the separation of Church and state. Yielding on any of these points was condemned. Neither Lamennais nor *L'Avenir* was mentioned directly, but all of their theses were rejected by connecting them erroneously with naturalistic indifferentism. The fact that Rome did not regard this encyclical as a condemnation of the Belgian constitution indicated a willingness to remain on the ground of principles and to accept a regime which tolerated modern freedoms, under the condition that the essential rights of the Church remained untouched. What was condemned was the assertion of the legal equality of all religions and that the freedom to dispense any doctrine was an ideal and progress. Equally, the doctrine of popular sovereignty was condemned, inspired more by the theoreticians of the divine right of Kings than by the Aristotelian positions of Thomas of Aquinas about the origin of power. It motivated a few Dominicans to react, even in Rome where they were not the only ones to question the opportunism of the encyclical or its authority.

Lamennais was sent a copy of the encyclical, accompanied by a letter from Cardinal Pacca, who explained that Lamennais was alluded to because of his tactics which he seemed to believe necessary for the defense of the Church, and because of his doctrines on religious policies. Lamennais received the message in Munich, where he wanted to make contact with some of his German followers. In agreement with his collaborators he published a declaration which recanted nothing but announced that, "devoted to the supreme authority of the Vicar of Christ, the battleground would be vacated on which for two years a loyal fight had taken place." The declaration satisfied Rome, which had feared a storm of indignation.

From *Mirari vos* to *Singulari nos*

The encyclical convinced a number of Lamennais' followers that they had been on the wrong path and they renounced the theories which heretofore they had defended. But Lamennais and many of his students believed that they were merely enjoined to silence and could continue to hold their earlier ideas without change.

The Belgian Catholics faced a special conflict of conscience, as for them Catholic liberalism was not only a theoretical system but was also embodied in a constitution whose concrete advantages were appreciated more every day. But the bishops were not worried at all. They rightly assumed that the declarations of principle concerning an ideal regime did not refer to the constitution, an agreement of civil and not theological nature. Soon the Catholic papers began to interpret the encyclical in the same sense, and some of them added that an encyclical was not binding for the faith. Some early unionists like Gerlache, out of loyalty to the Roman doctrine, felt obliged to give up their parliamentary activity; but most of them after a few weeks of contemplation decided that for them nothing had changed. Metternich was extremely incensed and did not hesitate to pass his alarm on to Rome, insisting that a new, clearer declaration was mandatory.

Numerous French voices also called for another papal intervention, one which would obligate the followers of Lamennais to a genuine recantation. They desired above all that the Pope condemn the list of fifty-six theses by Lamennais which Monsignor d'Astros had submitted to the Holy See in 1832 and which for this reason was known by the name of "Censure of Toulouse." But while some secretly hoped to compel Lamennais to throw off his mask and believed they could triumph over the rebellious apostle of ultramontanism, Gregory XVI preferred to wait. He agreed with the opinion of the Congregation of Extraordinary Ecclesiastical Affairs not to follow the "Censure of Toulouse"; instead, a brief was composed in which the

Pope confined himself to an expression of unmitigated joy over the way in which his encyclical had been received.

At the same time two other events occupied the center of attention. A Belgian paper published an excerpt from a letter by Lamennais in which he expressed his intention of resuming publication of *L'Avenir*. In spite of appearances, the letter actually was written prior to the encyclical, but in Rome the news was received as proof of his duplicity. The effect of this tragic misunderstanding was heightened by the shattering foreword of Mickiewicz's *Book of the Polish Pilgrims*. The papal brief to Monsignor d'Astros (8 May 1833) was immediately amended by the insertion of a statement directed at Lamennais. An exchange of letters between Lamennais and Rome followed. The Breton abbé, no longer concerned with religious freedom or the separation of Church and state, but now interested in the cause of exploited peoples and oppressed nations, was prepared to announce his submission to the Holy See in questions of faith, morals, and Church discipline. But he wanted to retain his full freedom of thought and action in the political sphere, even after the encyclical. Gregory XVI was unwilling to concede this, as he was of the opinion that the call to revolt against established authorities questioned moral and religious principles. Lamennais was therefore asked to agree expressly to the totality of the statements made in *Mirari vos,* including those concerned with political activity.

Physically exhausted by the weeks of tiring discussions, embittered by the intensified attacks of the Catholic press doubting his loyalty, and desirous of "peace at any price," Lamennais finally surrendered on 11 December. His private letters, though, reveal his true attitude: he was ready to sign everything, "even if it had been an acknowledgement that the Pope were God." It was the end of the process which had begun with his stay in Rome.

It is probable that the papal brief of June 1832 to the Polish bishops made a deeper impression on Lamennais than the condemnation of *L'Avenir*. The brief condemned the national insurgency and justified its brutal suppression by the Tsar in the name of the obedience owed to a legitimate rule. The Polish revolt was for Lamennais not only an attempt to liberate a people, but also a religious rising for the defense of the rights of Catholics violated by the Russian schismatics. He began to wonder to what extent a Pope could be believed who so clearly betrayed his spiritual mission for political reasons. Logically this led him to the question: "What is the Church?" Is it the hierarchy and the papacy, opposing the strivings of a people for its liberty, or is it all of humankind?" Henceforth the time had passed for him in which the papacy acted in the divinely sanctioned role of interpreter of the truth entrusted by God and humankind. Now it was necessary to await the coming of a new religious society, emerging from the Catholic Church like a butterfly from its chrysalis.

His outward submission gained him a few weeks of respite, but soon he began to accuse himself for his lukewarm attitude. From Ventura and other Roman friends he learned that even at the center of Catholicism the views of Gregory XVI were not accepted without reservations and that French and European policy was becoming increasingly reactionary. He decided to take an unequivocal stand. In April 1834, against the advice of his friends, he published a series of poems under the title *Paroles d'un croyant*. He had written them in order to proclaim in the style of the prophets of the Old Testament the arrival of a new age in which the renewed intervention of Christ would free the peoples from the tyranny of despots and rulers. This hymn to everything the Pope had condemned in *Mirari vos* made a great stir. Rome reacted without delay. Lambruschini was ordered to prepare a report, and although he came to the conclusion that a papal brief would suffice, and although the archbishop of Paris recommended total silence, the Pope on 21 June 1834 published the Encyclical *Singulari nos.* It recounted the events, extensively condemned the revolutionary doctrines of Lamennais' work, especially as these purported to be based on the doctrines of the Bible, and concluded with a short and rather generally worded condemnation of philosophical traditionalism.

Lamennais did not react immediately and his break with the Pope became evident only with the publication of *Affaires de Rome* in November 1836. Yet the influence of the movement started by Lamennais was a deep and lasting one in the Catholic Church. The impetus generated by the Breton prophet retained its influence on thought and action, notwithstanding the severe strain to which the impatience of its founder exposed it.

Section Two

Church and State in Europe
from 1830 to 1848

Chaps. 18, 19: Roger Aubert
Chap. 20: Rudolf Lill
Chap. 21: Patrick J. Corish

More than once it was assumed that the condemnation of *L'Avenir* in the Encyclical *Mirari vos* dealt a deathblow to Catholic liberalism. But this was not the case. Those followers of Lamennais who continued to be convinced of the viability of his ideas gave up developing theories about the ideal relationship between Church and state and ceased pursuing a systematic apologetics of the separation of the two powers. They turned to a translation of theory into practice by employing modern institutions in favor of religion and by demanding the application of common law instead of privileges wherever the freedom of Catholics was constrained as a consequence of governmental actions. At the same time, they tried to adapt Catholic culture to the movements and tendencies of modern society. The militant wing of Catholicism was resolutely engaged in this development, especially in France. It was also the policy of Belgian and Dutch Catholics, noticeably supported by their bishops. In Italy some attempted to take the same path. In the German states, only little influenced by Lamennais, there were parallel tendencies in the attempts of Görres and the Munich group to make Catholic thought palatable to Protestant intellectuals and to free the Church from the yoke of the regionalism of the Old Regime. It was not happenstance that the followers of Lamennais in France and Belgium observed the resistance of Prussian Catholics during the events at Cologne with enthusiasm. The second spring which English Catholicism experienced during these years was due above all to the Emancipation Act of 1829, a Catholic and liberal success. It had its origin in O'Connell's activity; his example convinced the followers of Lamennais, and Montalembert emphasized its significance. In spite of the prevailing reactionary atmosphere in Rome and Vienna the most important Catholic developments in western and central Europe during the fifteen years of Gregory's pontificate thus occurred under the banner of liberty.

CHAPTER 18

The Continuation of Catholic Liberalism in Western Europe

France

The July Revolution of 1830, replacing the alliance of throne and altar so beneficial for the French clergy with a regime in which the influence of the anticlerical and liberal middle class was predominant, caused great consternation among the clergy. Upon the advice of Austria and against the counsel of his Curia and the nuncio in Paris, Pius VIII quickly recognized the new regime, which promised to honor the concordat. But a few anticlerical institutional measures generated in the already suspicious clergy the fear that persecutions would begin anew. These measures were often of a local nature, but they were augmented by attacks of the Paris press and theaters on the clergy. Additionally, there was the tendency of some community councils, especially in the cities, to reduce clerical influence on public life. Actually, ecclesiastical reconstruction was consolidated during the eighteen years of the July Monarchy. In some areas — thanks to the sensible application of the tactic recommended by *L'Avenir* — there was even a continuation of the Catholic renewal which had begun during the restoration period.

Although they were indifferent in religious matters, neither the King nor his ministers were hostile to the Church. Not wanting anarchy to spread among the people, they made their peace with the clergy, whose influence in the countryside and the small towns remained considerable. In order to prevent the clergy from placing its influence at the disposal of the legitimist opposition it was necessary to prove that there was no intention of restricting its apostolic work. To be sure, at the beginning the government was not able to commit itself to a certain policy, as it had to be mindful of public opinion, but thanks to the skills of the internuncio Garibaldi it was possible to overcome the initial difficulties. To the degree that the government felt more secure, the authorities became more sympathetic.

This development was enhanced by the death in 1839 of the archbishop of Paris, who was one of the few bishops who resolutely refused to become reconciled to the "usurper." Increasingly the clergy was valued as the most important preserver of public order in the face of the threat of socialism. The ministries of religion also from the very beginning showed their good intentions.

The handling of episcopal appointments was characteristic of the improvement of relations. After the unfortunate selections of the first few months, the government agreed to make appointments with the advice of the bishops. The correspondence between Monsignor Garibaldi and Mathieu, archbishop of Besançon, reveals the important role played by the latter. He was effective in bringing about a genuine separation of the prerogatives of episcopal appointments between the secular and spiritual forces, a separation far exceeding the provisions of the concordat. Government and nunciature jointly tried to exclude the most intimate followers of the deposed King as well as those of Lamennais, the progressivists of the time. The majority of the seventy-seven bishops appointed by Louis-Philippe came from the middle class and were relatively young (between forty and fifty). The result was a solid and pious episcopate more concerned with administration than with problems of intellectual and pastoral accommodation caused by the new society. These bishops strove to keep the Church free from any political exposure and to maintain their independence from the government. Yet their conduct toward their clergy was often very authoritarian, as the concordat permitted them to act as they pleased. Their capriciousness was aggravated by a general ignorance of canon law. This led to a protest movement, meetings, and publications, started by the brothers Allignol from the diocese of Viviers. Their book *De l'état actuel du clergé de France* (1839) was moving proof of the precarious situation of the country clergy, the victims of dual dependence on lay notables and ecclesiastical superiors.

The numbers of active clergy changed dramatically. At first, the fear caused by the new government's hostility to the Church and the cancellation of stipends for the seminaries resulted in a clear reduction of ordinations, from 2357 in 1830 to 1095 in 1845. Unfortunately, the young clergy, were hardly better educated than the older clergy. Trained in seminaries whose standards continued to remain mediocre, the clergy did not adapt its pastoral efforts to new problems and its effectiveness remained limited.

The mediocrity of the diocesan clergy opened a wide field of activity for the orders which suffered from the July Revolution. But by 1835 tolerance gained ground. New male and female congregations devoted to elementary education and welfare were permitted, together with the old orders which had been absent since the great revolution. In 1833 Dom Guéranger again introduced the Benedictines in France, and when Lacordaire in 1841 did the same with the Dominicans, the government did not dare oppose the move, in spite of the warnings of anticlerical deputies and newspapers which pointed to the orders' illegality. The growing influence assumed by the orders in the French Church was not to the liking of all bishops. Some of them did not care at all for these "guerillas," who were not subject to episcopal jurisdiction and whose untimely initiatives could endanger the détente between Church and state. Moreover, the new congregations, frequently favored by the upper classes, siphoned off contributions by the faithful.

Even more than on the structural level, the vitality of the Church proved itself in the field of Catholic action. After the apostasy of Lamennais, the romanticists, representing the active wing of the literary movement, became alienated from the Church. Many people of the middle class respected the Church, but in their religious practices confined themselves to an uncommitted conformism and directed all of their attention to material pursuits. Protestantism competitively intensified its efforts and thanks to the dynamic of its revival movement was able to register some successes. On the other hand, the urban youth was frequently more open to religious impulses than it had been during the restoration period. In a few dioceses, able prelates contributed to the growth which had started even before 1830. But above all there was a growth of small but very dynamic elite groups led by noted personalities.

Additionally, there were the young student Frédéric Ozanam, who in 1833 together with E. Bailly organized the first Vincent Conference, L. Rendu, the creative force behind the *Cercle catholique scientifique et littéraire* (1840), and Abbé Ledreuille, the "workers' priest" and founder of the Society of Saint Francis Xavier

(1840), which comprised thousands of workers and even had branches across the country. The groups were numerous and their most active members were legitimists with ties to the notables. Their militant wing was formed by the disciples of Lamennais, who unmercifully made life difficult for a clergy trained in the old ways. Without having given up their old ideal of a reconciliation between the Church and the modern movements, they recognized that *L'Avenir's* mistake had been to propagate ideas for which the time was not yet ripe, and that it would be more productive to act in a practical way in order to prove the validity of the recommended methods. They advocated cooperation between laity and clergy in a joint struggle for the faith, realizing that effective work in the Church was possible only in agreement with the hierarchy and not in opposition to it. Between 1832 and 1848 their activity developed in two-fold fashion.

A number of young Catholics, inspired by the ambitious program of Lamennais at La Chênaie, continued to develop an academic basis for Catholicism to make it acceptable to future generations and to regain for the Church the respect of the intellectual world.

Montalembert, who had held back after *Mirari vos,* during the last ten years of the July Monarchy fought for freedom of education on the parliamentary level. He also was active on behalf of the right to existence for religious congregations, a right which was continually questioned by the authorities. In view of the lacking willingness of the authorities to make compromises, he sought the backing of the people instead of waiting for a solution through diplomatic negotiations between the Holy See and the King, a course of action favored by the Pope and most of the bishops.

The question of freedom of education, embodied in the constitution but in need of statutory regulation, had been discussed by *L'Avenir.* When at the beginning of 1831 the administration of Casimir Périer closed the music schools of Lyon, in which choirboys had been trained free of charge, the editors of *L'Avenir* decided to establish an elementary school without official permission in order to bring the question into the open. Two years later the Guizot Law of 28 June 1833 granted freedom of education for elementary schools and recognized members of orders as public teachers, thereby breaching the monopoly of the universities.

Montalembert's enthusiasm and oratorical gift succeeded in imbuing the French with a crusade mentality with respect to secondary schools, a mentality which was at work during the next several generations. For many years, Catholic newspapers and pamphlets accused the public high schools of being "breeding grounds of pestilence," offering "atheistic and materialistic" instruction, and changing children into "dirty and wild animals." In fact, the majority of the teachers were freethinkers, and in philosophy classes the eclecticism of Victor Cousin predominated.

At the same time, though, 5 percent of public teachers were priests, among them many principals, and more than 20 percent of the teachers were practicing Catholics. Montalembert, who in the Chamber of Peers had developed into a courageous representative of Catholic interests, decided to act on the basis of common law. He demanded for the Church neither the privilege nor the right — which many bishops still called for — to control public education, but only the constitutionally guaranteed freedom of education. Properly applied, it would permit the Church to organize its own school system, in addition to the public one, not only for future priests, but for all children. Many Catholics actually did not see the public schools in sinister colors, and public opinion initially was only hesitantly on Montalembert's side. A new attitude was also supported by the growing number of militant Catholics who demanded for Catholic education the same degree of unrestricted freedom which prevailed in Belgium after the adoption of the constitution of 1831. The struggle raged until 1847. Abbé Dupanloup also became reconciled with Montalembert. He was well known in Paris society and the clergy as the only one among the leaders of the Catholic movement in the July Monarchy who from the beginning had opposed Lamennais. He adopted Montalembert's tactic of regarding the question of education as part of the constitutionally guaranteed freedoms. Inasmuch as the new draft presented by Villemain conceded only limited freedom to Catholic education (it was denied to the religious congregations, specifically the Jesuits), Monsignor Parisis came out with further aggressive pamphlets and a petition campaign was organized in 1844 and 1845. Dupanloup issued a moderately worded brochure in June 1845, *De la pacification religieuse.* In it he developed in large outlines a kind of concordat for schools, resting on mutual concessions by Church and state.

But the lack of cooperation of chambers and government, which attempted to divert attention by a direct attack on the Jesuits, led Montalembert, in spite of his youth the leader of the Catholic movement of this time, to a change of tactics. Following the Belgian example, he tried to organize all Catholics in a large political party. He did so against the will of many bishops who, like the archbishop of Rouen, were of the opinion that laymen did not have any business in ecclesiastical matters, and the Holy See, which accused the leaders of the Catholic movement of jeopardizing with their loud methods Rome's attempts to reconstitute the former alliance between Church and state. Encouraged by his friend Lacordaire, Montalembert together with de Vatimesnil and de Riancey founded the Committee for the Defense of Religious Freedom. It became very active outside of Paris, in spite of the resistance of many clerics who were enraged by this direct intervention in parliamentary politics. With the support of the newspaper *L'Univers* Montalembert in 1846 achieved the election of 144 representatives who favored freedom of education. It also happened to be the time of the election of Pius IX, which dispelled the fears of Rome. But this success was not translated into victory; the fall of the July Monarchy took place before the question was settled. The long conflict, in many respects regrettable because it deepened the rift between clergy and public teachers, yet produced two tangible advantages. It reawakened the energies of laymen who became aware of their responsibility to defend Catholic interests in the parliament (although these interests were pursued in rather narrow clerical fashion), and it broke the ties of the French Church to a government which shortly was to be brought down by the revolution of 1848.

Belgium

With every reason, the leaders of the Catholic movement in France enviously looked to Belgium in 1840. There, in the years after achieving independence, a truly remarkable upswing took place. It was the result of a Catholic, even clerical offensive on the basis of the constitutionally guaranteed freedoms of religion and education. The systematic intervention of the clergy, especially in Flanders, gave the Catholics strong positions in parliament and government. Although a Protestant himself, Leopold I favored the Catholic Church, as he saw in it the best protection against the revolutionary spirit. His support assured the Church of an important position in the life of the nation, in spite of the constitutional regime which had an affinity for those who favored separation. Laws and agreements, concluded in a spirit of friendship between Church and state for the protection of morals among the people, Catholicized liberal institutions. The outstanding success of this policy was the law of 23 September 1842, concerning elementary schools. It established complete freedom of the Church in education and made religious instruction in public schools mandatory. The implementation of the law, thanks to the efforts of the Catholic minister de Theux, virtually gave the Catholic clergy control over education in elementary schools. In the area of secondary education, fifteen years after independence two-thirds of the seventy-four high schools of the country were directed by clerics or members of orders.

These results finally led to the recognition of the liberal constitution by all those who, through the Encyclicals *Mirari vos* and *Singulari nos,* had been strengthened in their opposition to everything which, rightly or wrongly, seemed to be inspired by Lamennais. The opposition was further strengthened by the unyielding attitude of large numbers of the Flanders clergy, which was very receptive to the democratic ideas of the lower middle class from which most of them came. By 1835, tension between the two camps was strong, but it soon was relieved. The majority of the former followers of Lamennais adopted a more conservative attitude as a consequence of the break between him and the Church. From a Catholic liberalism, retaining from the liberal ideal everything that appeared compatible with the Catholic faith, they changed to a liberal Catholicism which used liberty as a means for Christian activity. The useful system in place seemed a small evil in the opinion of the bishops, who clearly distanced themselves from the encyclicalists, to the great dismay of the nunciature, many Jesuits, and Metternich. But their supreme goal was pure: in spite of the mixture of politics and religion, characteristic of Belgian Catholicism for a century, they were above all pastors desirous of enabling the Church to perform its primary mission, the saving of souls. Nonetheless they were pastors who retained from the time of the Napoleonic regime and the enlightened despotism of William I the tendency to exercise their offices in strongly administrative and centralistic terms. They were also the heirs of a long tradition which knew how to combine an unconditional loyalty to the Pope with a remarkable independence from the Roman influence on the life of the local Churches. In this spirit they approached the planning of a reconstitution of diocesan administrations, taking account of the new situation but not always of canonical regulations.

The unity of action of the six bishops was guaranteed by an annual conference. It was the first of this type in Europe and in the eyes of the bishops replaced the provincial councils. But the unity of action of the bishops was guaranteed even more by the pressure exerted by the archbishop of Mechelen, Cardinal E. Sterckx (1831–67), on his auxiliaries. A pious and industrious prince of the Church without special theological training, he appeared with his prudent behavior as a "remarkable precursor of the bishops of our own time, the time of a free Church in a free state" (Simon). He respected the autonomy of the state and was conciliatory to the new currents of thought, but remained loyal to the Holy See.

The long vacancies in most of the episcopal sees during the era of the Dutch government retarded the Catholic restoration, which was so necessary in view of the indifference toward religion among the population. Immediately after the achievement of independence restoration was renewed with emphasis. The foundation for the effort was the parish missions. They had an undeniable success in the countryside, where the number of people participating in Easter Communion increased noticeably.

In their reconstruction efforts the bishops could count on a numerically adequate clergy, whose quality improved in the course of the years. After the turn of the century the Belgian priests accepted the increasing centralization of diocesan life with a greater degree of submission than their French brothers. Trained in seminaries whose programs were revised and unified in the years 1842–48, but taught by professors who were largely autodidacts and strongly under the influence of Lamennais, the Belgian clergy for a long time remained on a low qualitative level. But supported by annual exercises and monthly retreats which were reinstituted toward the end of the 1830s, the clergy was characterized by a strictness of morals, a simple and open attitude, the realism of its apostolic methods, and a piety which was regulated very methodically but contained few elements of mysticism. Even so, the main work of the parish clergy for a long time was confined to confessions, administration of the sacraments, and visits to the sick.

Owing to the constitutional freedom of association, religious congregations developed quickly. The bishops favored the small congregations, which were a valuable aid to them in education and welfare work, but they were much more reserved toward the older orders. The bishops wished to see their privileges restricted in order better to control their apostolic efforts. The Holy See proved very understanding in this respect and allowed the direction of the orders temporarily to be withdrawn from the superiors and entrusted to an apostolic visitor whom the archbishop wished to see selected from the Belgian clergy.

Orders and secular clergy could count on the cooperation of many influential laymen, serving the Catholic cause not only in parliament and communal councils, but also through their active participation in often subordinate positions and in those undertakings which were designed to keep the masses under the influence of the Church. In 1834 the bishops reopened the University of Louvain in order to assure themselves of a Catholic elite among the secular professions on which society rested in the nineteenth century. The reopening of the university was a consequence of freedom of education in Belgium, and quite consciously the bishops ignored the Roman desire to make it a papal institution.

But the successes which accrued to the Belgian Church from the skillful manipulation of constitutional freedoms could not conceal some weak points. One was the failure to understand the problem of the workers, especially regrettable in a country which was in the midst of industrialization. The few beginnings of a Christian socialism made by a few Flemish followers of Lamennais were quickly stifled by the conservative reaction introduced by Leopold I with the aid of the nunciature. Pastoral problems generated by the rapid development of workmen's districts in the industrial areas were ignored; the numerous new parishes in this period were generally created in the rural areas. It was not surprising, therefore, that the workers gradually lost touch with the official Church. In 1834 it was noted that a large proportion of the population in the Walloon area no longer bothered to receive the Sacraments. The liberal middle class, around 1830 still religious and practicing, also began to distance itself from the Church. The unfortunate circular of the bishops in 1837, which with the attitude of Catholic purism repeated the papal condemnation of the Freemasons, contributed a great deal to the rift between Catholics and liberals and strengthened the anti-Christian orientation of the Freemasons. But the reconciliation in 1840 of the ultramontanes with the constitutional freedoms was the primary impulse for a transformation of the liberal Catholic spirit. The goal of most clerics and militants was no longer freedom for all in everything in the sense of mutual toleration, but the greatest possible freedom for the Church so that it could exercise its influence on society under the best possible conditions. This attitude, appearing to many as a planned clerical offensive, unavoidably resulted in a reawakening of anti-clericalism, which after the middle of the century was ever more aggressive.

The Netherlands

After the end of the Dutch-Belgian union, the Dutch Catholics were again in a minority. While it took almost a quarter of a century to replace the mission administration with a diocesan organization, a continual development to a less anomalous situation occurred. In 1833, a former professor at the seminary of Warmond, Baron van Wijckerslooth, was ordained as bishop *in partibus;* his elevation made the Netherlands independent from foreign clerics with respect to confirmations and ordinations of priests. In 1840, a royal decree granted the Catholic Church certain subsidies, but under conditions regarded as controversial by the clergy. New vistas were opened by the accession of William II (1840–49). He was an intimate friend of the pastor of Tilburg, J. Zwijsen, and saw Catholicism as an antirevolutionary force; there was talk of a new concordat. Thereafter the influence of Lamennais and his followers, who had emphasized the great advantages of freedom, had strengthened the revulsion against a concordatic solution. But Rome was always in favor of such an approach, and in the fall of 1840 negotiations were begun by the internuncio Capaccini. After a few months the talks produced a partial success: the Dutch government accepted the principle of a concordat which was to bring about the establishment of a diocesan hierarchy in the southern provinces. But in view of the vehement opposition of the Protestants it was decided to postpone an agreement. In the meantime, the number of vicariates apostolic in these provinces was to be raised and their titulars were to receive episcopal rank, but without involving the King in their nomination in any way.

The good will of William II for the future development of Dutch Catholicism was significant. The lifting of the restrictions against the orders permitted their rapid recovery even to the north of Moerdijk, and especially the congregations of women active in education and charity flourished.

This blossoming was proof of the vitality of Dutch Catholicism and also became visible in the spiritual and intellectual growth of the clergy. It came about under the influence of the new director of the seminary at Warmond, F. J. Van Vree, and one of his professors, C. Broere. The latter was an able writer, deeply influenced by Lamennais, and placed his energies into the service of the Church.

In order to promote the growth of a necessary Catholic intellectual class, Van Vree and Broere in 1842 founded the newspaper *De Katholiek* which, while it did not succeed in breaking out of the isolation which characterized Dutch Catholicism for a long time to come, yet made a remarkable contribution to the Catholic revival for half a century. Three years later, Abbé J. Smits founded the daily *De Tijd* and gained the cooperation of two talented laymen: J. W. Cramer, and J. Alberdingk Thijm (an enthusiastic follower of the romantic movement, who contributed materially to supplying the paper with that cultural prestige and genuine national spirit which at the middle of the century was still very rare among the Catholics of the Netherlands).

The improvement of the condition of Catholicism in the Netherlands during the second third of the nineteenth century was without a doubt the fruit of the dynamic activity of such enterprising personalities as Le Sage and Broere, as well as of the zeal of numerous clerics like Zwijsen who were not particularly intelligent but conscientiously carried out their pastoral duties. Catholicism profited also from two broader currents which contributed to a change of minds in its favor, namely, romanticism and liberalism.

Under the influence of the novels of Walter Scott and studies by German philologists of Dutch literature during the Middle Ages, many Protestants became interested in their national traditions preceding the Reformation. Simultaneously, they gained an understanding of some Catholic values, as for example liturgy. Prejudices dissolved, the more easily as the romantic rediscovery of the Middle Ages was not the work of Catholics who actually for a long time were tied to a limited classicism, but of pastors and scholars without any connection to the Church. It freed them of any tinge of suspect apologetics.

Liberalism pilloried as anachronistic the Calvinistic attempts to preserve a privileged established religion, and at the same time actively supported the entrance of the Catholics into public life. With enthusiasm the writings of Lamennais had been greeted by some of the most important spiritual leaders of Dutch Catholicism. Especially Le Sage ten Broek was very liberal in his pronouncements before the publication of *Mirari vos*. Not satisfied with calling concordats useless and even dangerous, he did not hesitate to declare that "truth owed its victory to itself and therefore error must be permitted to be free." The condemnation by Gregory XVI effected a change. Le Sage conceded that "liberty has its dangers and excesses" and that wisdom must "set limits" for it. Ten years later he no longer even encouraged a détente between Catholics and liberals on the parliamentary level, although earlier he had seen Belgian unionism as a victory over prejudices.

If this reserved attitude predominated until 1848 in the traditionally more conservative southern provinces, such was not the case in the area north of Moerdijk, where many Catholics, without wishing to bring about a doctrinary reconciliation between Church and liberalism, felt that there were reasons to support the liberal opposition. The opposition's program corresponded to the interests of Catholics in trade and economics, strongly represented in the large cities and the religious indifference of many liberals fostered hopes for a more tolerant attitude toward the Church than that of the conservative Protestants in power. A significant role in this context was played by a man long overlooked: the intelligent F. J. Van Vree, the future bishop of Haarlem. Together with the journalist Smits he encouraged and carefully and tenaciously guided the development of the new Catholic populations of the northern provinces. They gathered in the movement "Young Holland" and contributed a great deal to the electoral victory of the liberals, which in turn produced the change in the laws in 1848. This change produced a double advantage for the Catholics. The introduction of ministerial responsibility provided protection from royal arbitrariness, and it gave the Church a hitherto unknown independence. Its first result was the restoration of the hierarchy in 1853, achieved independently from any concordat by the more or less conscious application of Lamennais' principle of a free Church in a free state.

CHAPTER 19

The Beginning of the Risorgimento in Italy

Ferment in the Papal States

The secretly growing discontent of the middle class and the young intellectuals after 1815 with the "priest government" continued to grow with Consalvi's resignation. The July Revolution in France and the revolution in Belgium brought it to a head. This double failure of the principle of legitimacy and the blow given to some important clauses of the Vienna Settlement encouraged renewed doubts about the maintenance of the traditional system of government in the Papal States as well as in the rest of Italy. On 4 February 1831, two days after the election of Gregory XVI, Bologna, following the example of Parma and Modena, rose in revolt and under pressure from the *Carbonari* proclaimed the end of the Pope's secular rule in the province. During the subsequent days the revolt extended to the entire Romagna, the Marches, and Umbria, i.e., to four-fifths of the Papal States. The revolution had been improvised by lawyers intoxicated by romantic notions, but it was not supported by the majority of the people. Thus it was quelled within a few weeks by an Austrian army for the intervention of which the papal government had asked after it had failed to put the revolution down with its own forces. The revolt had weighty consequences. It proved the uselessness of local plots prepared by secret societies, brought about the decline of the *Carbonari,* and led to the rise of a new national movement. This was Giuseppe Mazzini's "Young Italy," with the much further-reaching aim of establishing a united republic with Rome as its capital. The consequences on the international level were even more important, as public opinion saw the Roman question in a new light, which predominated until 1870. It was no longer as in the eighteenth century a matter of incompatibility of religious values with the problems of politics, but a concern for the interests of the subjects of the Papal States as part of the interplay of the two great Catholic powers of Austria and France, with the latter once again resuming a central role on the stage of European politics after a fifteen-year hiatus.

Occasioned by the Austrian intervention in the Romagna, the rivalry between the two states concerning supremacy in Italy surfaced again. An international conference was convened in Rome by the great powers of England, Russia, Prussia, Austria, and France, and in spite of differences of opinion, they drafted a memorandum and handed it to the secretary of state on 21 May. The document suggested a number of reforms regarded as absolutely necessary if the Roman government was to have the foundation required by the European interest. The Pope was irritated by the intervention of the European powers in the internal affairs of the Roman state and together with his advisers regarded the suggested program as too liberal. Consequently the edict of 5 July confined itself to a few unimportant changes in the administration of the municipalities and provinces and caused deep disappointment. Shortly after the Austrian troops left the Papal States on 15 July, fresh disturbances occurred in the Romagna. The brutal behavior of troops in Forli caused a general uprising. In order to quell it and without consulting with the Pope, the Austrians were asked for help, and once again they marched into the Romagna in January 1832. But this time France, interested in preventing the Papal States from becoming an Austrian satellite, reacted immediately and occupied Ancona. In spite of his indignation, shared by the other European governments, the Pope was forced to reconcile himself to the situation and agreed to the French occupation until the departure of Austria's army.

Propped up by foreign bayonets, the papal government ruthlessly punished the ringleaders, but afterwards was still confronted with the problem of reforms. These were demanded not only by the liberal governments of England and France, but from a different perspective also by Metternich, who was an enlightened and realistic conservative. In contrast to reactionary elements in Vienna and Rome he considered changes necessary if an end was to be put to the endemic discontent in central Italy. In his opinion, the discontent was largely caused by the incompetence of the Roman administration.

Gregory XVI and Bernetti were radical opponents of political reforms which would permit the population to share in the governing of the state and refused to entrust laymen with important positions, but they genuinely desired administrative and economic improvements. Thus they took some useful steps even though these were esteemed too highly by the defenders of the Holy See. In February 1833 the secretariat of state was reorganized by dividing it into two branches, one for internal and one for external affairs, each one headed by a cardinal. It was without a doubt the first step in the direction of significant reforms.

But even timid and long overdue reformism was too progressive for the majority of the "zealots." In 1836 they welcomed with satisfaction the replacement of Bernetti by Lambruschini. He was no blind reactionary and attempted to moderate police repression as well as to improve elementary education and the road system. Neither was he a total slave to the Austrians. But rot dominated the entire system. The policy of the secretary of state was limited to reserving the important positions and privileges for the followers of the government. This naturally embittered the liberals, who had no difficulty in presenting to the enlightened public opinion of Europe the backwardness of the government, in particular the refusal of Gregory XVI to permit railroads in his state. It was typical that most of the members of the committees of revolutionary Italian refugees came from the Papal States. There the situation grew worse in the course of the years. Special military courts were in session permanently, and thousands of people were persecuted, banished, and punished for their political opinions. But repression was not able to maintain internal peace. The suggested reforms were very moderate. But in his reply Lambruschini spoke of the "criminal declarations of a mad mob," revealing the depth of incomprehension which separated the papal government from the aspirations of a considerable portion of the people of the Papal States outside of the city of Rome.

The expressions of joy which greeted the news of the death of the Pope on 1 June 1846 provided a picture of the hatred of the Pope and the system of government embodied by him that had grown in the population. Discontent had been further fueled by the completely negative attitude of Gregory XVI and his secretary of state toward the attempts of Italian patriots to free the peninsula from Austrian intervention and toward the manifestations of national feeling which for a decade had grown mightily in the population, including the clergy.

The Catholics and the Problem of Italian Unity

A national consciousness, awake in Italy since the middle of the eighteenth century, gradually spread among a Jacobin minority when the French invasion toppled the dynasties. This national consciousness was fostered both by the revolutionary principle of the right of people to self-determination and the concrete experiences in the Kingdom of Italy. After 1815, the often rather vague concepts of unification of a peninsula liberated from the antiliberal Austrian yoke survived chiefly among the young from middle class backgrounds who longed for the Italy of Napoleon, but also among a part of the educated public living on the memories of the grandeur of Rome and the resistance of the Lombard cities to the German Emperors. The broad masses also were infected by the movement of the *Risorgimento,* fed by the atmosphere of romanticism which promoted historical awareness. The unrest of 1830/31 enlarged the number of Italian patriots; renewed Austrian intervention made it clear to all that constitutional and liberal aspirations could only be satisfied by a common front of all Italians. In subsequent years, the periodic congresses of scientists held in Italian capitals contributed to the breakdown of parochialism by pushing national questions into the foreground. The economic development, illustrated by the growth of railroads, tended in the same direction. Initially there were among the *Carbonari* convinced Catholics, even priests and members of orders. But between 1830 and 1840 the wish for the unification of all of Italy was represented chiefly by men who were hostile to the Church, either because they saw in the Pope the primary obstacle, or because under the influence of Freemasonry they regarded liberty incompatible with religion and viewed the priests as the main defenders of an authoritarian society opposed to their striving for popular sovereignty. There was also Mazzini, who in 1831 founded the organization "Young Italy." His program called for liberation from all dogmas and Churches, so that under the motto "God and People" a new religion of humanity could be created and with universal brotherhood a democracy of the future could be realized. The radical character of Mazzini's program, aimed at replacing the legitimate rulers with a democratic republic, tended to increase the distrust of many Catholics and explained the almost totally negative reaction of the hierarchy toward the national movement. Around 1840 a new development occurred under the influence of intellectuals who favored a somewhat vague but genuinely religious Christianity and realized that in Italy loyalty to Catholicism represented the foremost national tradition. Consequently they tried to bring about the unification of their country not against the will of the Church, but with its support. This movement of neo-Guelphism replaced with convergence, cooperation, and occasionally even uniformity the antithesis of the revolutionary left, which saw *Risorgimento* and Catholicism and Italy and Papacy as mutually exclusive hostile forces.

The starting point of neo-Guelphism was the conviction that the combination of religious and patriotic sentiments could form a powerful national lever, as had been shown by the examples of Spanish resistance to Napoleon, the liberation of Greece from the Ottoman yoke, and the emancipation of Belgium from Protestant Dutch domination. At the same time, historians were attempting to bring back into prominence the tradition of national Guelphism through dubious reconstructions of the resistance to the Hohenstaufen Emperors.

Only Tommaseo, banished to France since 1833, suggested in his work *Dell'Italia* (1835) that the Pope should take the lead in Italy's rebirth. He demanded the expulsion of the Austrians from the Italian peninsula, called for a united Italy, and proclaimed his belief in the unity of liberty and Christianity. The true initiator and spiritual leader of neo-Guelphism, however, was Vincenzo Gioberti, a Piedmontese priest who because of his publicly announced sympathies for Mazzini had been banished to Brussels. Later he had broken with Mazzini's followers. After praising in his book the genius of Italy and reminding the readers of its contributions to the cultural legacy of humanity, he announced that the rebirth of the country, which encompassed liberty, national unity, and independence, in cooperation with a moderate liberalism, should utilize the alliance between modern currents and existing institutions, i.e., between monarchy and Catholicism. From this vantage point he called for the unification of Italy in a federation of states, with the Pope as president. But never before had these thoughts been offered with such eloquence, and never before had the secular, political, and practical value of Catholicism and its main support, the papacy, been glorified as the spiritual source of national rebirth with such force. Of course, the book was not welcomed by anticlerical liberal circles; they had no difficulty in contrasting Gioberti's ideal Pope with the reality of Rome under Gregory XVI. Traditional Catholics also criticized the study because they were disturbed by its innovative views and its call for reform. For this reason Lambruschini quickly forbade the distribution of the book in the Papal States. But it was welcomed by very many Catholics and clergy, including some cardinals, and immediately after its publication it was said that the idea of Italian unification was no longer identified with Mazzini but with Gioberti. The book's surprising success was especially astonishing in view of its difficult style. It proved that its content corresponded to a widespread attitude. People longed to reconcile what previously appeared irreconcilable: attachment to the ancestral religion and the desire for political rejuvenation, national sentiment and the revulsion against revolutionary violence. In any case, for whatever reasons, neo-Guelphism for several years was considerably successful.

Gioberti's thoughts were seized upon by several Catholic writers. They regarded the continuation of the secular power of the Pope as the guarantee for the free exercise of his spiritual office, but they also thought that this principle could be reconciled with a federative Italy by a few changes in the statute of the Papal States.

It must be noted that in the case of all of these neo-Guelphs, national and unitary striving went hand in hand with the desire to create liberal institutions. These two aspects were intimately tied together since the beginnings of the *Risorgimento.* It explains to a large degree the mistrust and the often unconcealed hostility with which the movement was regarded by many members of orders, especially the Jesuits, and by the majority of the hierarchy. They could not permit this attempt, reminiscent of Lamennais, to "Catholicize the revolution." Yet the success achieved by the neo-Guelphs among a considerable portion of Italy's Catholic population on the eve of the pontificate of Pius IX proved that in Italy also, even though in forms substantially different from the various West European countries and in spite of the much less favorable political and social conditions, a liberal Catholic movement was in the making.

The Varieties of Catholic Liberalism in Italy

In spite of the agitation of a dynamic but numerically small portion of the middle class and intellectuals, liberal institutions were nowhere in Italy introduced before the big crisis of the middle of the century, and relations between Church and state continued to function within the framework of the Old Regime. There existed a privileged established Church, strictly supervised by the government, a situation confirmed by the various concordats and agreements from the time of the pontificate of Gregory XVI.

With exceptions, the majority of militant Catholics in France and Belgium went along with the liberal tendencies. The situation was fundamentally different in Italy, however. There, even in the northern provinces which were more receptive to modern currents of thought, militant Catholics joined the ranks of the counter-revolutionaries and traditionalists of the preceding period. It can be said that the failure of the revolutionary movements of 1831 actually strengthened the reactionary character of the "intransigents" and their alliance with legitimism. Weekly or monthly periodicals such as *La Voce della verità* in Modena (1831/41), *La Voce della ragione* in Pesaro (1832/35), and *La Pragmalogia* in Lucca (1828), were indicative of this attitude. These intransigent Catholics promoted a stiffer attitude toward the Protestants, especially in Tuscany and Piedmont, and were emphatically suspicious of all initiatives not hewing to the denominational line. They were opposed to the religious indifferentism of the Bible societies as well as to activities concerning education and charities, because they threatened the monopoly of the Church in these areas. They commended the essentially religious and essentially monarchial kind of education of the Jesuit colleges and attacked the custom of the schools to leave groups of students in charge of student monitors, as they did not keep the children under the "precious yoke" of authority.

Although these attitudes prevailed among the majority of people, there were also some Catholics in Italy during the two decades before 1848 who were seriously concerned with the problem of confronting religious beliefs with the liberal tendencies of the time. But they did not band together. On the contrary, they remained split in many small groups, with hardly any contact among them, attacked problems from totally different perspectives, and differed in many important respects.

There were indeed free spirits who raised the question of reform of Catholicism in its institutions and occasionally even in its dogmas, in order to adapt it to modern currents of thought. This was especially the case in Tuscany. They strove for tolerance, human progress, and a reduction of ecclesiastical power and its increasing spiritualization. But above all they desired a reform of Catholicism and papacy analogous to the principles of the Protestant revival movement. Plans developed for a reform of the Church which were as far-reaching as those of Ricci and Degola. Parishes were to be governed jointly by an elected parish priest and an elected lay consistory, both of them forming a counterweight to ecclesiastical power. Beyond such organizational reform plans, these men were opposed to a religion of authority and in favor of an intensification of Christianity, which they looked upon more as a force for individual ethical perfection than as a communal religion of salvation.

In addition to this liberal Catholicism, touching the limits of ecclesiastical doctrine and occasionally overstepping them and demonstrating certain similarities with contemporary liberal Protestantism, there were also reformers who not in the least wished to question Catholic dogma in its Tridentine formulation, but who were interested in a limited democratization of ecclesiastical institutions. They were primarily the spiritual heirs of the Jansenists of the preceding generation, whose aims in this respect coincided with certain liberal tendencies: priests or members of orders who demanded the election of bishops by the faithful and a greater degree of independence from their superiors. For this reason they demanded the separation of Church and state, not in the name of the laicism of the state, but in the name of the transcendentalism of religion.

Special mention must be made of the philosopher, theologian, and political theorist Antonio Rosmini. To be sure, there were also in Italy Catholics who were primarily interested in the question of bourgeois and liberal freedoms. But they approached them from a perspective quite different from that of their fellow believers north of the Alps. There it was chiefly a case of militant Catholics, for whom the reconciliation with the modern and liberal governmental systems come to power in the course of the revolutions of 1830 posed a problem of conscience, inasmuch as liberal thought since the end of the eighteenth century tended to be anticlerical and occasionally anti-Christian. Still, the Catholics north of the Alps were of the opinion that by making peace with the new regime the Church had more to gain than to lose. After all, reconciliation would allow it to defend its rights more effectively and provide it with the opportunity to perform its apostolic work in a sector of leading public opinion which was threatening to slip away.

In Italy, however, Catholics engaged in reform politics faced the task of replacing the still prevailing absolutist governments with liberal institutions. They were primarily concerned not with the defense and the rights of the Church, but with the victory of liberalism. Several historians have therefore suggested designating them as "liberals and Catholics" rather than "Catholic liberals," as they had no difficulty reconciling their liberal views with their religious convictions. After all, the Italian liberalism of 1825 was not Voltairean and certainly not atheistic. As for foreign influence, that of the Cortes of Cádiz was more a guiding factor than that of the revolutionary French assemblies. Besides, in Italy, where the demand for liberal institutions was concretely tied to the awakening of a national consciousness and a rejection of foreign influences, the support was appreciated which the clergy in Spain, in Tyrol, and even in Italy itself had provided for the resistance to the Napoleonic policy of conquest. Even the almost total counterrevolutionary attitude of the ecclesiastical hierarchy hardly posed a problem for these men. Many of them had learned from Jansenism how to separate their religious convictions from submission to the ecclesiastical authorities in nondogmatic areas.

The "liberals and Catholics" of this movement, standing between the followers of Mazzini who clearly had divorced themselves from Church and Christianity and the reactionary militant Catholics, had many followers among the intellectuals. Two persons among them stand out: Niccolo Tommaseo and Alessandro Manzoni. Tommaseo combined the influences of the Tuscan group, of Rosmini, and of Lamennais. His passionate work *Dell'Italia* (1835) was an echo to the motto of *L'Avenir:* "Christianity separated from liberty will always remain a slave; the combination of the two will be an indication of the nearness of world peace. Only the banner having both names on it will rise victoriously. . . . " It is difficult to define Manzoni's precise attitude toward Catholic liberalism. After his conversion under Jansenist auspices he discovered in religion the source of true spiritual liberty, the principle of autonomy of conscience with respect to those forces which exert pressure on it from the outside, and the leader of liberty who will keep it within reasonable boundaries and will prevent its descent into anarchy and tyranny as was the case during the French Revolution. This view is reminiscent of Lamennais' position in 1826–27. But Manzoni developed it completely independently from the French theoretician and fitted it into the framework of a national tradition reminiscent of Savonarola's aphorism: *"Unus ex potissimis vitae christianae effectibus est animi libertas."* There is also no trace in him and others of Lamennais' earlier theocratic tendencies. In the case of Manzoni it was not a matter of a renascence of society through a free Church, but of the development of the person owing to a free conscience.

Does this mean that there was in Italy no equivalent to the liberal Catholicism as it existed in France under the July Monarchy? That would go too far. The Lamennais of *L'Avenir* found no great response in Italy, and the liberals generally regarded with skepticism his hope to effect an agreement between liberalism and an excessive papal sovereignty.

Mirari vos put a quick end to the enthusiasm for Lamennais' doctrines among many clerics and laymen who were excited by the concept of a liberal ultramontanism. Possibly, though, the hopes awakened by Lamennais explain to a certain extent the success which the neo-Guelphs had ten years later among broad masses of the ecclesiastical world. Many people saw in neo-Guelphism an opportunity to reconcile their loyalty to Roman Catholicism with their patriotic and liberal tendencies, in spite of the skepticism of many liberals who immediately diagnosed the illusionary nature of the movement, which was a late product of romantic enthusiasm.

Finally, there were in Italy on the eve of 1848 also many Catholics whose principles were much like those of Montalembert. This was the case, for example, with the Jesuit Taparelli d'Azeglio. He not only unequivocally opposed despotism, thereby departing from the accepted political theology of the Society of Jesus and approaching that of Thomism, but also declared his confidence that a governmental system of constitutional liberties would bring advantages for the Church. He called upon Catholic laymen to organize themselves on the basis of common law for the defense of their religious interests. This proves that the ideas matured elsewhere slowly made their way and penetrated even to the Jesuits, of whom it was too quickly thought that in Italy they were always identified with the defense of reactionary absolutism.

Numerous Catholics were beginning to realize that in order to do justice to the new problems posed by modern society and modern civilization, it was no longer possible to be satisfied with a return to traditional solutions, but that a somewhat radical adaptation was unavoidably necessary. But while this conviction was widely accepted by many Catholics north of the Alps, it was present in Italy before the middle of the century only in a small circle of intellectuals, none of whom was able to find acceptance by the public. The only exception was neo-Guelphism at the end of this period, and even it was more concerned with national than with liberal considerations.

CHAPTER   20

The States of the German Confederation and Switzerland, 1830–1848

The July Revolution demonstrated to all who believed that revolutionary ideas had been overcome the continuing vitality of such ideas, put in question the political system of 1815, and raised fears of a new age of crisis. Its general impact was more significant than its concrete effects, which differed from country to country. Switzerland experienced profound changes, while the structure of the German Confederation and its member states generally survived the crisis. It had far-reaching consequences, however, which touched upon the ecclesiastical realm. Everywhere conservative forces found themselves on the defensive. More important, liberal movements, the efforts to acquire modern constitutions, and protests against the authoritarian use of power by the states were buoyed. Changed views also impinged upon the renewed Catholic movement. Resistance to the system of established Churches and demands for the realization at last of the religious parity promised in most constitutions were articulated more emphatically. Occasionally there was limited cooperation between liberals and Catholics against the common foe.

The Roman Curia held back until the 1840s, when it seized the leadership. Gregory XVI, in any case a full-blown reactionary, became Pope during the July Revolution which created the first crisis endangering the existence of the internally weak Papal States. For this reason the new Pope sought the backing of the authoritarian states even more than before. Gregory XVI shortly after his election influenced the development in Germany by the first German publication of his *Triumph of the Holy See.* It became one of the programmatic tracts of the movement of renewal and contributed substantially to its ultramontane orientation.

Clinging to the system of absolutist established Churches, most of the governments exacerbated the existing tensions. Denominational minorities resided mostly in areas acquired by the states between 1803 and 1815. Church policy, therefore, was part of the larger context of integrating these territories, and the opposition to the new authorities often combined ecclesiastical, regional, and historical desires for autonomy. This was most pronounced in the Rhineland, acquired by Prussia in 1815, where in the decade after 1830 the first great dispute between state and Church took place at Cologne. The occasion for it was the Roman condemnation of the Bonn philosopher Hermes and the problem of mixed marriages. For the population, the latter issue was a very weighty problem, as it affected ecclesiastical policy in no longer denominationally uniform states.

Count Ferdinand August von Spiegel, archbishop of Cologne, had invited Hermes to the University of Bonn and found in him as well as in many of his students suitable supporters for the spiritual and organizational reconstruction of ecclesiastical life. Strict opponents denounced Hermes' doctrine, Rome subjected it to lengthy examinations, and Gregory XVI condemned it in his summary Brief *Dum acerbissimas* of 26 September 1835. The Curia did not notify the state authorities of the brief, it was not published officially, and its implementation caused difficulties. For the Hermesians, the papal decision came as a great surprise. The nuncios at Munich and Brussels assigned the task of distributing the brief to the opponents of Hermes, who were most eager to do so and who used the brief as a weapon in their fight against an established Church. The Catholic press supported them, and the involvement of the nuncios was a clear indication of the expanding ultramontanism.

The strictly Tridentine law concerning mixed marriages proved impossible to maintain everywhere in the eighteenth century. Mitigation of the law was conceded to Prussia, whose government refused to apply the law in its original form; with respect to Silesia, Pius VI in 1777 had left the implementation to the bishop of Breslau. The clergy was generally content with the provisions of the Common Law Code of Prussia, according to which sons were brought up in the religion of the father, daughters in that of the mother. Even the declaration of 1803, according to which legitimate children were to be raised in the religion of the father, raised no objections. The government hesitated to take further steps before the ecclesiastical reorganization was finished; but in 1825 a cabinet order extended the declaration of 1803 to the western provinces where canon law applied and where an established Church of the Prussian type had no tradition. The order violated the guarantees which had been given to the Church when Prussia assumed possession of the Rhenish provinces and was a determined effort to Protestantize the western provinces, as almost only Protestant officials and officers were stationed there. Bishops and Curia did not dare resist, but many clerics, especially those close to the movement of revival, refused to carry out the order. Their appeal to freedom of conscience was also supported by many liberals. Because the government was unwilling to give up its claims and insisted on the clerical blessing of mixed marriages, it began new negotiations with the Curia, conducted by Christian Karl Josias von Bunsen (1791–1860), Niebuhr's active successor as envoy to Rome. With his *Brief Litteris altero abhinc* of 25 March 1830, Pius VIII tried to be conciliatory. He permitted priests to provide "passive help" in all cases in which a mixed marriage was not preventable in spite of attempts at dissuasion and in which agreement was not obtained to raise children as Roman Catholics. But the government refused the official acceptance of the papal brief, insisting on formal wedding ceremonies and renunciation of the priestly attempts at dissuasion.

Inasmuch as Rome now stuck to its position, the government attempted to persuade the Rhenish-Westphalian bishops to interpret the papal decision most liberally, using massive pressure in the process as well as promises which later were not kept. The bishops of Münster, Paderborn, and Trier gave in quickly; not so Archbishop Spiegel of Cologne, on whom everything depended and who was always interested in asserting the Church's independence. Eventually he also agreed, only because the Prussian emissaries were able to convince him that the Pope desired the most liberal interpretation of the brief possible. When the Prussian government then accepted the brief for transmission to the bishops, the Curia was convinced that it had won a victory. But on 19 June 1834 Spiegel and Bunsen signed a secret convention in Berlin which required for formal marriage vows no more than the "religious intention on the part of the Catholic partner to adhere to the faith and fulfill the duties involved in raising children" and limited passive assistance to cases of evident frivolity. Spiegel's auxiliary bishops concurred.

But the expected calming of the waters failed to occur. In fact, the protest against Prussia's religious policy, now combined with criticism of the archbishop's yielding and Rome's silence, only grew more vehement.

Clemens August Baron von Droste-Vischering (1773–1845) became Spiegel's successor in 1836. Because of his authoritarian regimen in Cologne he failed to win the sympathies of either subordinates or associates. The few advisers whom he trusted all came from the militant wing of the Catholic movement. Droste's first aim was the destruction of Hermesianism, which he had always distrusted; he also wanted to hurt the University of Bonn's department of theology. His distant goal was a type of Tridentine seminary for all theological instruction. To achieve his objectives, Droste used means which were illegal in the eyes of state and Church and maneuvered himself into a corner. In the spring of 1837 the archbishop seized upon the problem of mixed marriages, which appeared to him as a wonderful battle instrument to conduct his test of strength. He was determined to apply the Berlin convention, which by now as a result of better information was also contested by the Curia, only to the extent to which it corresponded to the brief of Pius VIII. He refused to be intimidated by the ultimatum of the Prussian government either to give in or to resign. Employing the means of an authoritarian police state, the government on 20 November 1837 had Droste arrested and incarcerated in the fortress of Minden.

Gregory XVI on 10 December 1837 protested against this act of violence in the solemn form of an allocution to the cardinals. At the same time he placed in question Prussia's entire conduct in the question of mixed marriages and rejected the convention of Berlin. But Görres with his polemic *Athanasius* (January 1838) was much more effective. The talented publicist succeeded in painting Droste as the great champion of freedom of the Church and to make his cause that of all German Catholics. Numerous brochures followed, and Church newsletters experienced a tremendous rise in circulation. In 1838 Görres and his friends founded the *Historisch-politische Blätter,* which under the leadership of Georg Phillips, Görres' son Guido, and Carl Ernst Jarcke laid the foundations for the Catholic-conservative doctrine of state and society. To an increasing degree the polemic was also directed to Protestants, the great majority of whom sided with the Prussian government; the events at Cologne contributed to a lasting hardening of the denominational fronts.

Out of the dispute over mixed marriages grew the first mass movement for freedom of the Church, finding support in the Pope, and forcing the Prussian state to the limits of its power in a way previously unknown. Within a few months after Droste's arrest the government had to endure "modest inquiries" about the Catholic education of children from mixed marriages. Immediately after the papal allocution, canon law with respect to mixed marriages was applied in the western provinces and soon it was also employed in the eastern provinces.

The ascension of the throne of Prussia by Frederick William IV in June 1840 brought about a fundamental turn of events. The new King was imbued with the thought of political romanticism and despised established Churches and bureaucracies. Believing in one Church with different denominations, he wanted to create a Christian state. He desired the independence of the Churches and their coordination with the state, and in Berlin he displayed an unusual degree of sympathy for specifically Catholic forms of worship and traditions. In negotiations with the Curia, in which Ludwig I of Bavaria and Metternich acted as mediators, the King quickly made far-reaching concessions. Gregory XVI's diplomacy thus succeeded in reaching the compromise in the summer of 1841 which granted the Catholic Church in Prussia a larger degree of freedom than it enjoyed in any other German state and which considerably enhanced the reputation of the Holy See in Germany. The Munich nuncio Viale-Prela acted as the prudent interpreter of Roman intentions and generally extended the influence of the nunciature to non-Bavarian dioceses. Prussia gave up the demand to approve and interfere in the practice of mixed marriages, the bishops were allowed to correspond freely with Rome, the freedom of episcopal elections was guaranteed according to the agreement of 1821, and a separate branch for Catholic affairs was created in the ministry of religion. Dunin was permitted to return to his office; Droste, whom the Curia was not loath to see pushed into the background because of his rudeness, had to be content with an apology.

The administration of the archbishopric of Cologne was assumed by the bishop of Speyer, Johannes von Geissel (1796–1864). Geissel energetically used the freedoms granted to the Church and integrated the impulses generated by the Catholic movement into his hierarchical concept. The unnecessarily harsh exclusion of the last remaining Hermesians was Geissel's first measure to achieve internal uniformity. Soon he began the creation of Catholic clubs which reached beyond the borders of his diocese; the founding of the Borromäus Association in 1844 was a promising beginning. Even before the revolution he achieved concerted action on the part of his bishops in a way which the government had not permitted before 1840. He was supported by Wilhelm Arnoldi (1798–1864), whose appointment as bishop of Trier in 1842. The sensible defense against German Catholic attacks was guided by Melchior von Diepenbrock (1789–1853), a student of Sailer, who became prince-bishop of Breslau in 1845 after having overcome strong reservations on the part of conservative clerics. In contrast to the belligerent and defensive activism of Geissel, Diepenbrock adhered to the conciliatory principles and broad ecclesiastical concept of his mentor and thereby gained the full confidence of Frederick William IV. In a period of ultramontane hardening, he preserved a decided awareness of episcopal autonomy.

The development in Bavaria at first proceeded totally within the course mapped out by Ludwig I. The revolution was followed by a more conservative policy. The King knew how to combine adherence to an established Church with strictly conservative ecclesiastical rejuvenation. As he strongly supported the Church, the Curia was willing to make concessions to his regalism, for example in the dispute over mixed marriages in which Gregory XVI initially attempted to have canon norms accepted. Pressured by the King and his government, the Holy See gave in with respect to this problem which was of such great importance to Catholic rejuvenation. An instruction to the Bavarian bishops of 12 September 1834 contained the same concessions which Pius VIII had granted the Prussians. Ludwig, in contrast to the government in Berlin familiar with the limits of Roman willingness to compromise, was satisfied.

The men led by Ringseis, Görres, and Döllinger reached their greatest effectiveness during the thirties; among the younger associates there were Georg Phillips, the lawyer Karl Ernst von Moy de Sons (1799–1867), and the theologian Friedrich Windischmann (1811–61). Phillips influenced Carl August von Abel (1788–1859), secretary of the interior after 1837. Abel continued the Catholic state traditions of Bavaria and followed an extremely conservative, and at the same time militantly Catholic policy; conversions were favored, and new creations of Protestant communities were hindered.

Abel's appointment was symptomatic for the reaction of Ludwig I to the religious events in Prussia. Especially during the Cologne disturbances, the King believed that he had to act as *defensor ecclesiae;* it was due to him and Abel that Bavaria presented the Catholic point of view. The Cologne events and Ludwig's partisanship had the effect in Bavaria of aiding the growth of the Catholic movement and especially of strengthening its intransigent wing. A short period of particularly close ties between Rome and Munich began; following the Prussian example Ludwig also in 1841 permitted the bishops of his state and the Curia to correspond freely.

In the appointment of bishops, Ludwig generally steered a middle course, but the nomination of the young Count of Reisach as bishop of Eichstätt in 1836 meant a strengthening of the militant forces. Reisach, personally close to Gregory XVI, was the first real curialist among the German bishops of the nineteenth century. While most of his fellow bishops wanted to retain a modest degree of autonomy even during the height of ultramontanism, Reisach was eager to adjust all ecclesiastical structures and forms to the Roman standards and examples.

While the King tried to follow a moderate course once the situation had become calm again, the Catholic leaders retained their militancy. Their intransigence, often protected by Abel, increased, they turned against Ludwig's established Church, endangered the internal peace of the state, and provided the strong liberal attacks on the ministry with nourishment. The consequence was a gradual alienation between the Catholic movement and the King, who remembered his earlier dislike of ecclesiastical excesses and once again exercised his prerogatives over the Church. A few months later the crisis erupted openly in conjunction with the Lola Montez scandal. When the attempt to give the King's lover citizenship became public, Abel and his colleagues were replaced by a liberal cabinet and leading Catholic civil servants and professors lost their positions.

In southwest Germany, the rigorously applied laws imposed on the Church in 1830 precluded any free development of ecclesiastical life. The bishops essentially were confined to the ordination of priests, diocesan coordination was impossible, and the bishop became alienated from his clergy because of his dependence on the state's authority. As in neighboring Switzerland, internal tensions complicated the situation. The rejuvenation of the Church gained ground only slowly; many clerics saw in Josephinist ties to the state a better guarantee for effective religious work than in closer ties to Rome; a considerable portion of the clergy derived radical consequences from Wessenberg's reforms and demanded far-reaching democratization; and frequently there was solidarity with parallel political movements.

The first two archbishops of Freiburg, Bernhard Boll (1756–1836) and Ignaz Anton Demeter (1773–1842), attempted to obtain concessions from the state through conciliation and continuation of Wessenberg's liturgical reforms. Demeter opposed the synodal movement; he obtained the establishment of a state school of theology and the appointment of two eminent theologians, the catechist Hirscher and the dogmatist Staudenmaier, at the University of Freiburg. Archbishop Hermann von Vicari, after the revolution an outspoken champion of freedom of the Church, during the first years of his long episcopate (1842–68) also had to make many concessions, but under the impact of the Cologne disturbances he was at least able to have the canon law on mixed marriages recognized.

The more important attempts to free the Church from supervision by the police state in southwest Germany were made by laymen. The process was accompanied by the first stirrings of a Catholic party. In Baden, Heinrich Bernhard von Andlaw-Birseck (1802–71) and Franz Josef Buss (1803–78, after 1836 professor of law in Freiburg) were active. And law was in favor of a strictly conservative course, Buss attempted a synthesis of conservative and liberal forces. Buss independently continued to develop the doctrine of a corporative state, and more strongly than the Viennese political romanticists he emphasized individual responsibility. He was the first to designate the solution of social problems, in addition to achieving freedom for the Church, as the chief task of German Catholics. In Württemberg, the Catholic nobility of Upper Swabia, with the hereditary Count Konstantin von Waldburg-Zeil and Baron von Hornstein in the forefront, led the mostly conservatively motivated opposition to the established Church.

After 1830, Metternich championed an alliance with the Church more strongly than before. He was doubtless motivated more by political sentiments than by religious conviction. He had become completely convinced that the universal authoritarian power of the Catholic Church and the supra-national monarchy of the Habsburgs had to take a common stand against revolutionary forces. He was also interested in a recovery of Austrian prestige in the Catholic world, obscured by Josephinism and its repercussions on Austria's international and German positions. It was easy for the chancellor to confirm Gregory XVI in his reactionary principles. The military aid given the Papal States in 1830–31 enhanced the solidarity. It was more difficult to make the concessions desired by the Pope and recognized as necessary by Metternich. The concessions were opposed by the liberal civil service, which continued to see in Josephinism the best guarantee for the monarchy. But the chancellor gained considerable ground domestically under the reign of the incompetent Emperor Ferdinand (1835–48). Besides, the ecclesiastical policy testament of Francis II, in whose formulation Metternich had had a hand, formally empowered him to revise Josephinist legislation. Metternich therefore strove for a cautious coordination of the two powers; the contradictions between the laws of the state and the Church were to be removed through joint agreement, and the demands of both sides were to be carefully separated. Carl Ernst Jarcke and the titular Abbot Joseph Otmar von Rauscher (1797–1875) aided him; Rauscher came from a family of civil servants with strong ties to the state and had received his intellectual impulses from Hofbauer. Viale-Prela, nuncio in Vienna after 1845, also was in close agreement with Metternich.

In Switzerland, the July Revolution put an end to the predominance of conservative principles of state, and in twelve cantons liberal democratic constitutions were introduced. In the process of change, many Catholics also expressed desires for reform along Josephinist-Wessenberg lines and found support among the liberals. The seven cantons which in 1832 had united for a liberal change of the federal constitution, in 1834 at the Baden conferences also formulated a joint program of religious policy. They demanded the sovereignty of the state over the Church to the same degree as achieved in southwest Germany. They also wanted a nationally influenced uniformity and autonomy of the Church, in particular the creation of a Swiss Church province with Basel as archbishopric, and the expansion of episcopal prerogatives vis-à-vis Pope and nunciature. Monasteries were to lose their exemption and were to pay taxes for social purposes.

The Articles of Baden lastingly aggravated the differences among Catholics as well as between Catholics and liberals They were condemned by Pope and episcopate alike, and a large majority of the Catholic population voted against them. In consequence, the radical-liberal forces grew more hostile to Catholicism, and the initially political opposition between liberal and conservative estates shifted to the religious area. The general anger of the Catholics, brought about the fall of the liberals in the canton of Lucerne. The new Catholic administration recalled the Jesuits, thereby arousing the ire not only of the radicals but of all Swiss Protestants. Both sides were increasingly dominated by militants. When in 1844 the radicals organized irregular troops for the purpose of toppling the Lucerne government and favored a far-reaching revision of the federal constitution in order to make it centralistic and liberal, the Catholic cantons formed a defensive alliance, seeing in the undiminished maintenance of their sovereignty the irreducible prerequisite for freedom of the Church. They refused the demand of the Diet to disband their league (1846/47). The Diet consequently resolved to use military force. In the short war of the Separatist League, the last religious war in central Europe the Catholics were defeated.

The liberal majority of the Diet was now in a position to pursue its program. The Protestant victory was cheered lustily by the liberals in all of Europe and stimulated the development of events in 1848. In several cantons monasteries were dissolved, several of the defeated cantons received liberal governments in favor of established Churches, and the federal constitution of 1848 contained the discriminating prohibition of the Jesuits. The Swiss Catholics were forced into a ghetto to which they adjusted spiritually and socially. The connection with Rome was intensified, the greatest possible internal cohesion was attempted, and all areas of life were dominated by the Church. Encounters with new ideas were avoided, and participation in public life was reduced to the absolutely essential. Catholic principles and interests were equated with those of the ultramontane and conservative movements.

CHAPTER 21

Great Britain and Ireland, 1830–1848

English Catholicism survived punitive legislation as a small community, dominated by a lay aristocracy. Even before the Emancipation Act of 1829, however, forces were at work which were to change its nature. Influenced by romanticism, there were a number of famous conversions, among them those of Kenelm Digby (1823), Ambrose Philips de Lisle (1825), George Spencer (1829), and Augustus Welby Pugin (1834), the neo-Gothic architect. Actually, these converts fit badly into traditional Catholicism, which continued to be suspicious of religious enthusiasm and only slowly emerged from its tradition of isolation from public life. The converts, finding their way to the Catholic Church via romanticism, raised hopes of mass conversions, but their influence was much smaller than that of the Oxford Movement. The Oxford Movement arose from a dissatisfaction within the Church of England, a dissatisfaction which turned more toward contemporary Rome than to the Church of the Middle Ages. There was general agreement on the need for reform of the Anglican Church, but it was not quite so clear from where the spiritual strength for reform was to come, considering that the Church in many of its aspects was controlled by Parliament. After 1829, Parliament was open to men of all Christian denominations. A crisis erupted in 1833, when Parliament dissolved a number of Protestant bishoprics in Ireland. The action of Parliament raised the general question of parliamentary control, and the possibility of disestablishmentarianism was discussed. A number of prominent people at Oxford concluded that the danger of submitting the Church to the state according to the theory of Erastus could be avoided effectively only if the Church reformed itself.

The leaders of this group were clerics belonging to the established Church. Some of them, like Keble and Pusey, remained loyal to it, but others, especially the representatives of the younger generation like Ward and Faber, converted to Catholicism. The most famous of these converts was John Henry Newman (1801–90). Although in no way an official leader of the movement, he became its spiritual and intellectual focus because of his character and his intellectual capacity.

Newman's all-encompassing sense of religion and responsibility for human beings, as well as his life-long concern with Scripture and Church Fathers, can be traced back to a spiritual crisis during his early years in 1826. In 1817 he entered Trinity College at Oxford and became a Fellow of Oriel in 1822, even though he did not achieve honors. He was ordained in 1825 and in 1828 was appointed vicar of the university church of Saint Mary's. It was during these years that he began to develop his ideas of the Church: the Church as connecting link between man and Christ, based on the teachings resting on its tradition, its sacraments, and the apostolic succession of its hierarchy. When the crisis came in 1833, he already had gained considerable influence in the religious circles of Oxford.

The protest began in July with Keble's sermon, "The National Apostasy." It was continued in the writings known as *Tracts for the Times,* as a result of which the Anglo-Catholics gained a powerful position within the established Church. The group met resistance, even though Newman in the tracts written by him interpreted the Anglican Church as the *via media* between the errors of Protestantism on the one hand and those of Rome on the other. The *via media* opposed both, and instead relied on antiquity, Scripture, and the Fathers. He opposed what constituted in his eyes a constant threat for Anglicanism, namely, the "liberalism" which wanted to submit revealed truth to human judgment.

Gradually he was forced to admit that age alone could not be regarded as a source of ecclesiastical authority in modern times. Catholicity, not age, was the sole measuring stick; but Catholicity, he asserted, was only incompletely realized in the Anglican, Roman, and Eastern branches of the Church, and Rome had deformed its Catholicity through accretions to the symbols of the early Church. Tract 90 appeared on 27 February 1841. It asserted that the Anglican 39 Articles were not incompatible with the nature of Catholicism. The tract created a storm of indignation and was condemned by the university and twenty-four bishops. In consequence, Newman retired to Littlemore near Oxford. Later he said that with respect to the Anglican Church he was at that time already on his death bed, even though he was becoming aware of this only gradually. Rome's accretions to the original symbols continued to be for him a real obstacle. There is only one faith, the Anglican in him argued, and Rome failed to preserve it; his reading of the Fathers always made him reject the Roman reply that "there is only one Church, and the Anglicans are not part of it. But by 1843 he was "very far more sure that England is in schism, than that the Roman additions to the Primitive Creed may not be developments, arising out of a keen and vivid realizing of the Divine Depositum of Faith." After his sermon in September on "The Parting of Friends," he quietly retired to the lay community in order to devote himself to what eventually emerged as his *Essay on the Development of Christian Doctrine.* Even before it was published, he was received into the Catholic Church on 9 October 1845, by the Italian Passionist Dominicus Barberi.

Influenced by Newman, a number of his friends took the same step; but hopes for a mass conversion, harbored by many, especially by Nicholas Wiseman, who in 1840 had become coadjutor to Bishop Walsh in the Midland District, were not realized. Wiseman, born in Spain as the son of an Irish father and a Spanish mother, received his education at Ushaw and the English College in Rome, whose dean he became in 1828. His London lectures, held on the occasion of a stay in England in 1835, received great attention not only because of their scholarship, but also because he presented in them something which went beyond the traditional and insular nature of Catholic England. In 1836, financially supported and encouraged by Daniel O'Connell, he founded the *Dublin Review* as the organ for Catholic scholarship. When he returned to England for good in 1840, it was only natural that he placed great hopes in the Oxford Movement. But at this time the most pressing problem for the bishops in England consisted of the growing number of Catholic immigrants from Ireland.

Irishmen had migrated to England in small numbers during the eighteenth century and had settled chiefly in London. The immigration quota rose with British industrialization, especially after the Act of Union in 1800. By 1840, there were four hundred fifty thousand Catholics in England and Wales. About half of them were native Irishmen, and about 80 percent were Irish by birth and extraction. In Scotland, there were about one hundred fifty thousand Catholics, 80 percent of them also of Irish extraction. Many Irish Catholics served in the army and the navy, but most of them worked in heavy industry, in railway construction, in ports and mines, and in steel and textile mills. Most of them were very poor and lived under confined and terrifying conditions in London and the industrial areas of the Midlands, Lancashire, South Wales, and Scotland. They were ill adjusted to English life, which began to develop into a democracy under the impact of the Reform Bill of 1832. The Irish proletariat was viewed with suspicion and fear as the germ cell of political and radical unrest. Catholic England was badly prepared for the spiritual care which they required, but it was precisely the needs of this Irish Catholic proletariat which broke the traditional mold far more than the conversions of Englishmen, no matter how important those might be. Although wealthy English Catholics proved themselves very generous, churches and schools in the industrial centers had to rely largely on the contributions of the poor. As long as England continued to regard education primarily as a task of the Churches, the schools could rely on a certain amount of state subsidies for whose optimal utilization organizations were founded. The rapid numerical increase of the Catholics and the pastoral problems connected with it led in 1840 to an increase in the number of vicars apostolic from four to eight. But the establishment of a diocesan hierarchy was only possible in 1850, given the suspicions by English Catholics of such an organization.

In Ireland, the emigration to England had contributed only little to the easing of the job situation. Ireland's population had grown from about 5 million people in 1780 to more than 8 million in 1840. But industry was present only in Protestant Ulster. In all other areas, cities and centers were in decay, as English manufactured goods drove out local industrial production. Two-thirds of the population were directly dependent on agriculture and, especially in the west, constituted a large rural proletariat subjected to very uncertain conditions of life.

The Catholic Emancipation Act of 1829 was of little significance for the poor. Political power was closely tied to property and that was largely in Protestant hands. The Protestant established Church continued tithing, even though its members everywhere constituted only a minority and in some areas only a very small minority. Daniel O'Connell decided to use his political organization, which he had built for obtaining Catholic emancipation, to achieve the repeal of the Act of Union. He argued convincingly that the clergy should support his new movement as it had supported the old one, because repeal was also a religious problem. His reason was that in return for supporting the union the Catholics had been promised full emancipation but had not been granted it.

Emancipation had been granted in 1829, because political opinion in the United Kingdom was generally convinced of its reasonableness and necessity. There was no such unity with respect to repealing the union, but O'Connell succeeded in building a mighty organization in Ireland. Although some bishops hesitated to support it, most clerics had no difficulty in doing so. It was most strongly supported by the influential bishop of Kildare and Leighlin, James Doyle. When he died in 1834 at the age of forty-eight, his place was taken by John MacHale, who in the same year had been appointed archbishop of Tuam despite the opposition of the government.

The government attempted to deal with the Irish discontent through such laws as the Tithe Composition Act and the new Poor Law, both passed in 1838. Neither of these laws was radical enough to be effective. The government also tried to keep the Irish clergy within bounds through pressure on Rome. But here it was in a difficult position; formal diplomatic relations were unacceptable, and the loyalty oath imposed on the Catholics in connection with the Emancipation Act forced them to swear that the Pope had no political authority in the United Kingdom. But the Curia of Gregory XVI feared the risks of revolution and in general was so badly informed about conditions in Ireland that it sharply remonstrated with MacHale.

When the Tories came to power in 1841 with Robert Peel as Prime Minister, they were determined to suppress the repeal movement. By this time, Archbishop Murray of Dublin (1768–1852) was almost the only bishop opposed to the movement. Additional laws were passed: the Charitable Bequests Act of 1844, the Queen's Colleges Act of 1845, and the Maynooth Act of 1845 for the increase of the state's subsidy to this college. Pressure on Rome continued and finally on 15 October 1844 led to a decree in which the priests were requested to keep away from politics. But the phrasing of the decree was cautious and vague and devoid of any judgment concerning the repeal movement and the right of Catholic laymen to support it.

Neither Rome's warnings nor the palliative laws were able to stop the support of the clergy for the repeal movement. In 1846 the organization Young Ireland was created as a challenge to O'Connell's unqualified rejection of physical force. By this time O'Connell's health was debilitated and his death in 1847, together with the great famine of that year, put an end to the problem of repeal.

Despite their poverty, the Irish Catholics built churches, hospitals, and schools. The modest repentance chapels were replaced. For the schools and hospitals, the new orders were of great help. In 1834 the Sisters of Charity opened Saint Vincent Hospital, the first Catholic hospital in Dublin.

Finances, especially in the field of education, were always inadequate. The first census in 1841 revealed an illiteracy rate of 53 percent, and whatever interpretation one wishes to give this figure, it can not have been far from the truth. The Stanley Act of 1831 created a governmental system of elementary schools by creating a national office for the administration of nondenominational schools and offering guarantees for the faith of the pupils. The Irish Catholics already had enough experience with state subsidies for education, designed to win the children for Protestantism, but the system of 1831 appeared to offer enough guarantees and was generally accepted. With its approval of state supervision it was far ahead of contemporary developments in England.

Book Eight

THE CHURCH IN
THE AGE OF LIBERALISM

Translated by Peter W. Becker

Part One

Between the Revolutions
of 1830 and 1848

Section One

The Continuation of
Catholic Renewal in Europe

Roger Aubert

C H A P T E R 2 2

The Progress of Ultramontanism and
the Growth of the International Orders

Progress of Ultramontanism

The fifteen years of the pontificate of Gregory XVI saw significant steps toward the victory of ultramontanism, and the weakening of ecclesiastical influence upon civil society turned the Church inward. During the Restoration period, the influence of these internal forces was already noticeable throughout Europe and in particular in France and Germany. From this time forward, the ultramontane movement enjoyed increasing encouragement even from Rome itself.

Resistance to the interference of the Roman Curia in the life of the national Churches continued far beyond the middle of the century, but increasingly it met with countervailing opinion. Many of the scholars and theologians in England clung fiercely to the concept of the national Church and rejected new customs coming from Italy and the doctrine of the personal infallibility of the Pope. Others supported by the first generation of liberal Catholics and Italian missionaries, developed contacts with Rome and favored the "new" continental exercises of piety. Thus the situation gradually changed. In Piedmont, where Josephinistic tendencies were still very much alive in the theological departments and seminaries, a number of young clergymen and militant Catholics began to charge that such tendencies constituted an expression of the despised Austrian influence and to represent an orientation toward Rome as an affirmation of membership in the Italian nation.

After 1830, true Gallicanism had few defenders in France. Relations between the bishops and the Holy See, however, remained at best tentative. That part of the clergy which had not been won by Lamennais continued to maintain the position of the bishop within the hierarchy as well as to adhere to special ecclesiastical customs, particularly in the liturgical and canonical areas. It was in this atmosphere, then, that during the July Monarchy the ultramontane campaign gained ground quickly and simultaneously at many different levels and in many different areas.

Abbé Combalot, a diocesan missionary, made himself the champion of Roman ideas among the lower clergy. On the other hand, the campaign for a Roman liturgy, led by Dom Guéranger with the support of some young priests, was directed chiefly against the Gallican sympathies still harbored by some members of the upper clergy. The fact that even before 1848 many dioceses rejected modern French liturgies seemed to be a victory for ultramontanism over ecclesiastical particularism. In the years between 1842 and 1849, Abbé Rohrbacher realized his intention to revise Fleury's *Histoire ecclésiastique* in an ultramontane direction for use by the young generation of clerics, but with more good intention than critical acumen. Rohrbacher's cell was the "Roman salon of Paris," and his library well represented that Gallican position. Two of the most zealous defenders of the ultramontane movement in the French episcopate, Monsignor Gousset and Monsignor Parisis, stayed with him on the occasion of their journey to Paris.

Many factors worked in support of the ultramontane campaign. Loyalty to the monarchy, that very foundation of Gallicanism, had lost much of its meaning with the fall of the Bourbons, and the anticlericalism of the July Monarchy was an added reason to look for support from Rome. In addition, the lethargy of certain bishops in the struggle for educational freedom also favored the Roman position. Montalembert and his friends won the Catholic masses to ultramontanism with the aid of the newspaper *L'Univers*. Another decisive factor was that the lower clergy disliked accepting the unlimited power of the bishops and desired nothing more than to have the Roman congregations provide protection against episcopal capriciousness. Even the bishops recognized the de facto privilege of the Holy See to intervene in doctrinal or disciplinary questions concerning the Church of France. The nunciature intervened ever more openly. Fornari, supported the militant ultramontanes fully even when their conduct was questionable. Not satisfied with opposing the demands of some bishops for independence in the liturgical and canonical areas, Fornari supported the vehement reactions which these demands evoked in many priests or monks.

The general approval which met the condemnation of the *Manuel de droit ecclésiastique* by Dupin in 1845 proved that political Gallicanism was completely discredited in France. The changes in the church treatise used at this time by Saint Sulpice, which was especially strongly tied to the traditions of the old France, as well as the revisions of the commonly used catechisms and handbooks were also symptomatic of the decline of theological Gallicanism. In practice, however, moderate Gallicanism continued to enjoy considerable sympathy. Prelates acting in this fashion were only a minority by the end of Gregory's pontificate and were regarded with mistrust by the younger clergy. The sympathies of a number of older priests, however, remained attached to the traditions of the old French clergy and its specific concepts of hierarchy, liturgy, and piety. These advocates became the most serious obstacle to the complete victory of Roman ideas in France, but the group lacked a cohesive core. In this respect the failure to reestablish the old theological departments destroyed by the Revolution was of great significance; had they succeeded, the encounter with the history of Christian antiquity could have resulted in a concept of the church according to the Gallican model.

In Germany, an analogous but much slower development took place. Here there was much more resistance than in France. Many theologians, however, continued to defend a moderate episcopalism, which in their eyes seemed to correspond better to the organization of the old Church as well as to the German concept of authority and society. They saw the relationship between the Pope and the bishops from the organic perspective of the Holy Roman Empire, where sovereign and feudal lords cooperated together in the Diet. Knowing from experience that the congregations generally failed to take into account the true situation in the Protestant areas, they tried to reserve decisions for themselves in cases which the Holy See regarded as its province. This was true the more so because the frequent appeals to Rome were often made by men notable for neither intelligence nor moderation.

Many of the opponents of the planned centralization of Catholic life in the Roman Curia resisted this development for various reasons both theoretical and practical. They were outmaneuvered, however, by those who believed that this resistance gave aid to a number of fearful and neglectful ecclesiastics and to governments that wanted to prevent the escape of the Church from their tutelage. Thus, as it had happened in France, albeit with a ten-year delay, a genuine ultramontane party was formed in Germany to which clerics as well as laymen could belong. The spiritual center of this party was at Mainz, where the influence of Maistre and Lamennais joined with a development arising from the Catholic Action. The leaders at Mainz, trailblazing in the area of the apostolate and clearly aware of the demands of the modern world, sensed that traditional ecclesiastical particularism was no longer tenable in a world which ignored national borders. They were convinced that the destructive power of the antireligious forces could be countered only through a mobilization of the masses, who were guided strictly and uniformly. Only the Holy See was capable of providing this guidance. Under the pressure of increasingly complex problems, Germany was developing from the collegiate and corporative system of the Old Regime toward modern centralization.

Strengthened by the so-called "Germanists," the former students of the German College in Rome which was reopened in 1824, this ultramontane party published its ideas in *Der Katholik* and experienced an increase of its reputation as a result of two circumstances. They gained the trust of the masses because the ultramontane bishops and priests successfully intervened with Protestant governments for greater religious freedom of the Catholics. The opponents of the ultramontanes, sympathizing with the doctrines of Hermes, lost their standing in the eyes of the faithful when these doctrines, after years of discussion, were finally condemned. Thus, the movement spread and new centers were formed.

In Austria ultramontanism developed even more slowly than in Germany. It is characteristic of the Austrian movement that as late as 1842, when four bishops were consulted whether to lift the ban of 1781 forbidding seminarists to study in Rome, two were opposed to a change and another had serious objections. But in Austria also the consciousness of the Church awakened, and the opposition of the militant Catholics, even though they were still in a minority, began to shake the foundations of the Josephinist system. A few years later the Austrian ambassador drew Metternich's attention to the growing threat to Austrian influence in Rome. He pointed out that the civil service in Vienna was determined to curtail the relations between the Holy See and the Church of Austria at a time when, as the Curia emphasized at every opportunity, France was in the process of relinquishing this antiquated system.

Rome, aware of its growing strength, no longer hesitated to influence and encourage firmly a movement which pointed both faithful and clergy toward the center of Catholicism. At times, as it did in Austria, Rome attempted to loosen the regalistic policies of governments; at other times, the nuncios supported the work of the ultramontane clerics and tried to increase the number of ultramontane seminarists at Roman colleges. In order to break down resistance, and to encourage the efforts of some and to hasten the development of others, a systematic policy was employed with great skill. This policy included direct and indirect pressure with a scale of finely differentiated expressions and briefs of approval and disapproval, tailored in each case to the special circumstances. It also included the awarding of benefices as well as the delay of honors and rewards. Rome's policy was developed by Pius IX, but it was inaugurated during the last years of Gregory XVI with increasing benefit.

The Large Orders

The Generals of the large international orders had since the Middle Ages had their seat in Rome and actively had assisted in the Roman centralization as well as provided able members for the congregations. Even if the mendicant orders recuperated only slowly and played only a secondary role in this connection, the pontificate of Gregory XVI was marked by a triple phenomenon whose consequences were of significance for the efficiency of the Holy See during subsequent pontificates. It consisted of the rapid growth of the Society of Jesus, the new impulse which the Dominicans received from Lacordaire, and the founding of the Benedictine congregation in France by Dom Guéranger.

Once the Society of Jesus had overcome its developmental crisis of the first decade, it experienced a remarkable growth under the generalate of the Dutchman Philipp Roothaan (1829–53). Roothaan was able skillfully to employ his great influence on Gregory XVI for the benefit of his order, while also fashioning it into a marvelously reliable instrument in the service of Roman unity and ultramontane ideals. In a very short time the Jesuits grew in numbers from 2,137 in 1830 to 4,757 in 1847. They reestablished their former provinces, and exerted growing influence upon the direction of ecclesiastical studies and piety in a post-Tridentine sense, that is, contrary to the spirit of the eighteenth century. Father Roothaan also urged the Jesuits in 1833 to devote themselves to missions among the heathens as they had done under the Old Regime.

Father Roothaan provided pious as well as skillful leadership for the society. He has been called its "second founder." He strove to reawaken in it the full spirit of its founder. He interpreted the spirit more narrowly, however, by placing emphasis more upon ascetic exercises than on mystical enthusiasm. Roothaan saw to it that the two years of the novitiate and the third year (terciate) were served under normal conditions. Beginning in 1832, he convened a meeting of all procurator generals regularly every three years in order to achieve a strict observance of the rules.

But the remarkable successes which the Society of Jesus experienced within only a few years were not without repercussions. Some bishops, especially in Belgium, regarded the society as too aggressive. The liberals in particular were uncomfortable with their rapid rise. What appeared to many as the Jesuits' tendency "to confuse revolutionary disorder with the inevitable tendency of the modern world to replace absolute monarchy with the principle and practice of national sovereignty" (Montalembert) provided their enemies with an easy pretext to incite the public against them. In 1834 the Jesuits again were expelled from Spain and Portugal. In 1845 the order experienced a general attack. But the storm was only of short duration; favored by the conservative reaction following the crisis of 1848, the progress of the Society of Jesus was even more rapid than before.

The mendicant orders, however, only slowly recovered from the crisis which had overcome them at the end of the eighteenth century. This was especially true because the Iberian peninsula, in which they had been able to retain their strong position, was now being shaken by the secularizations being conducted by Madrid and Lisbon between 1833 and 1837.

The Franciscans, counting about ten thousand members in Spain, were reduced to a few hundred; this enabled the Italians once again to regain their leading position in the order. The development of the order in the German-speaking and Anglo-Saxon countries became significant only in the second half of the century.

The Dominicans were reduced in numbers in Mexico, Russia, Portugal, Cuba, and especially Spain. A number of monks found refuge in the missions in the Far East, and the seminary of Ocana, their source of growth, remained open. Even the provinces of Italy, constituting 40 percent of the membership of the order, did not display great vitality. But under the pontificate of Gregory XVI a change of fortunes occurred. In 1838, Abbé Lacordaire, who had received great acclaim from the students of Paris as a result of his Lenten sermons at Notre-Dame, announced his intention to reestablish the order in France. His objective was a diverse intellectual apostolate in keeping with the movement of rejuvenation started by Lamennais and the Congregation of Saint Peter. Lacordaire envisioned sermons in town and country, the instruction of the young, and, in keeping with the temper of the time, the writing of religious and profane tracts from an apologetic perspective. After contacting Master General Ancaroni, Lacordaire published his *Mémoire pour le rétablissement en France des Frères Prêcheurs,* (7 March 1839), appealing to the country for freedom for the orders. He finished his novitiate in Italy and, armed with papal encouragement, returned to France, where the government, after some hesitation, treated him with benign neutrality. In 1850 he had a sufficient number of adherents to enable him to establish a French Dominican province. In the same year, one of Lacordaire's companions, Alexander Jandel, was appointed Vicar General by Pius IX (he became Master General in 1855), with the charge of reorganizing the order.

Another French initiative in the second half of the century led to an almost simultaneous rejuvenation of the Benedictine order, an event which met with a certain amount of resistance by the Curia, but eventually was supported by Gregory XVI. Moved by a romantic longing for the medieval past and the desire of Lamennais to reestablish the centers of cloistered scholarship so lacking in postrevolutionary France, Prosper Guéranger, together with three companions, ignored all legal hindrances and settled in the former priorate of Solesmes. In 1837 the Pope confirmed Solesmes as an abbey and recognized it as a focal point for a new Congregation of France. The constitutions approved by the Pope were essentially similar to those of the Maurists. Only on two points did Dom Guéranger go back to the old tradition which had been abandoned almost everywhere else: these were the autonomy of each house and the appointment of abbots for life, a request approved by Rome only after long hesitation. These positions, as paradoxical as they may seem, did not prevent him from becoming one of the strongest proponents of liturgical centralization and the most extreme ultramontane theses. Dom Guéranger had to overcome numerous difficulties: distrust because of his earlier connection with Lamennais and because of his vocal support of the ultramontane movement; the enmity of the bishop of Le Mans against the monastic exemption; repeated financial worries; and the internal disputes among his students, which were aggravated by his administrative mistakes. But Dom Guéranger's persistence succeeded in overcoming these obstacles. His abbey of Solesmes, in spite of its moderate size, became a beacon of influence toward a return to the traditions of the past, an influence which was felt during the subsequent decades throughout the various branches of the Benedictine family. Of course, such a tradition contained the danger of artificially reawakening a monastic life which had been created in a social and economic context totally different from a Europe in the process of developing an industrial society.

It was precisely this effort to meet the religious needs of a changing society which explains the success of the congregations devoted to education and the care of the sick. The educational congregations, in particular, experienced a marked revival during the course of the first decades of the century. Old congregations like the Daughters of Charity, experienced a new bloom. Many new congregations were founded also. The growth of these congregations contributed its part to the progress of Roman centralization. While under the Old Regime each convent and numerous smaller congregations founded during the first quarter of the century remained autonomous and subject only to the local bishop, Rome now encouraged the tendency to gather the novices and concentrate the members under the authority of a General Superior. It was an authority which, in spite of the protests of the diocesan bishops, frequently resulted in liberation from the supervision of the bishops and in direct submission to the authority of the Congregation of Bishops and Orders in Rome. This congregation, aware of the great dissimilarity of objectives and local conditions, very carefully refrained from forcing a uniform type of constitution upon the smaller congregations and convents, but left to each the formulation of its rules, as long as it could control them and suggest changes. Thus, there gradually came into being a new canon of members of orders, codified only much later, whose development after the second quarter of the nineteenth century occurred under the vigilant control of Rome. On the other hand, the increasingly important role assigned to the superiors of these new congregations in comparison to that of their ordinary members favored the development of a mentality which facilitated the progress of ultramontanism by placing emphasis more on authority and obedience than on collegial responsibility.

CHAPTER 23

Old and New in Pastoral Care and Moral Theology

The Modernization of Ecclesiastical Institutions

Historians have noted the lasting effect of Napoleonic institutions in a large part of Europe: wherever the French introduced them, they were generally retained, and occasionally they were imitated even in countries which did not experience any French occupation. This development was nothing more than the legal recognition of an irreversible economic and social evolution. The development in the ecclesiastical area was similar. Gradually the profound changes resulting from the nationalization of the estates of the Church and from the concordat of 1801 spread. The concordat turned the bishop into a "violet prefect." Geissel in the Rhineland, Sterckx in Belgium, and Mathieu and Bonald in France were characteristic of the new bishop's generation. These bishops had come to acknowledge that the restoration of disturbed Catholic life and the increasing complexity of problems needing solution demanded much more in the way of organization and administrative work than had been the case during the Old Regime. Clearly cognizant of their episcopal authority as it had been determined by Napoleon's Organic Articles, they were eager to guide systematically the pastoral activity of their priests.

In parallel fashion, the situation of the lower clergy also changed fundamentally. The priest without a precisely defined task became a rarity, in contrast to their high numbers under the Old Regime. The decline occurred less rapidly in the southern countries, where there were still too many clergy. Some of the priests continued to exercise their apostolate on the fringes of the diocesan clergy as preachers and private or public teachers. But most of them were now employed in the incumbency, where they began to constitute a parish clergy whose social status completely changed within a few years. Instead of receiving income from a benefice, the clergy in most countries were paid by the state. At the same time they were to a high degree exposed to the capriciousness of the bishops. Indeed, officialities and diocesan courts frequently played a much less distinctive role than at the time of the Old Regime, and in many countries most of the pastors had to endure being transferred against their will from one parish to another. In Austria, Bavaria, and southern Europe the obligation of advertising vacant positions continued and the canonical principle of being irremovable remained. Some bishops in Spain and Italy circumvented this rule, however, by declaring that they were the only irremovable pastors. This facilitated control of the administration of the parishes, but the system also gave rise to abuses which — especially in France — led to serious discontent.

The chapters also lost much of their independence and importance. Their members, personally selected by the bishop from the diocesan curia officials, were only subordinates and did not have the faintest intention of risking a conflict with their superiors. Besides, the tasks once carried out by the canons were more and more assumed by the secretaries, who, in conjunction with the vicars general, became the real assistants of the bishops.

Furthermore, the bishop, whose jurisdiction over his clergy was so strongly expanded, to an increasing degree was elected without any participation of the clergy. The concordats of the early nineteenth century generally granted the right of nomination to the governments, whose choice ordinarily was more influenced by administrative than by pastoral criteria. In countries like the United States or Belgium, where the governments were not interested in participating, the bishops selected the nominees without consulting the priests of the diocese in question. And even where, a chapter election, or a limited participation of the clergy was retained, the Holy See gradually took such suggestions less into account, a practice which was increasingly adopted after the middle of the century. It must be said, however, that Rome generally chose genuine pastors from all walks of life. Still, in fulfilling its pastoral obligations, the upper clergy remained interested in a limited independence from state officials. The bishops were also aware of the necessity to coordinate their actions with respect to the governments and their activity on the pastoral level. For this reason they attempted to revive the old practice of synods, which had fallen out of use because of the suspicion by the states and the Roman Curia.

The Methods of Catechetical Instruction

The transformations at the end of the eighteenth century occasioned profound and lasting changes not only in the area of institutions, but also in the various aspects of pastoral care. Added to them were the influences of the new currents of thought. This explains why the catechism, especially in the German states and in France, became the object of several revival efforts.

The introduction of compulsory education in Germany resulted in the transfer of catechetical instruction from the Church to the school. While this made it possible to devote more time to religious instruction, it changed this instruction to nothing more than another academic subject which was taught in a profane environment. Thus there was the danger of infection by the intellectualism and naturalism prevailing in the atmosphere of the Enlightenment. But it was the influence of the Enlightenment which caused educators to include biblical history in catechetical instruction and to adopt the Socratic method in order to accommodate themselves to the intellectual receptivity of the children. This method avoided the need to introduce concepts which had not been explained properly before, but it also held the danger of overlooking the transcendental character of God's word. The consequence was that at the beginning of the nineteenth century the dogmatic substance of ecclesiastical doctrine was almost eliminated from many catechisms, which were governed by moralism and more directed toward man than toward the gospels. During the first half of the century there was a reaction which attempted to deepen and to evolve the valuable impulses of the Enlightenment, but to exclude a too rationalistic way of thinking.

In Austria the legal situation of the state before the signing of the concordat in 1855 made it difficult to replace the official catechism of 1777. But efforts were made on the methodological level.

In Germany from 1817 to 1863 J. B. Hirscher was professor of pastoral and moral theology, first in Tübingen, then in Freiburg. He criticized as too abstract the catechisms inherited from the Counter-Reformation and demanded a greater consideration of the emotional side of the child. He emphasized as chief goal of catechesis the religious instruction and not the transmittal of an overly large body of knowledge. Throughout his entire life he urged that Christianity be presented as a message of salvation, as a doctrine of God's realm emerging from the biblical stories.

But Hirscher's promising beginning was negated within a few years by the new Scholasticism and the tendency once again to emphasize the doctrinal differences among the Christian denominations. In this kind of atmosphere the bishops, looking for uniformity in catechisms, accepted the catechism of the Jesuit Deharbe. It offered a short survey of Scholastic theology with clear and precise formulations, was concerned more with theological accuracy than with educational adaptation, was very strongly apologetic and anti-Protestant, and was free from all biblical and kerygmatic perspectives. After its appearance in 1847 and a revision in 1853, it was initially adopted by the Bavarian bishops, then adopted by most of the German dioceses, and used until 1924. During the second half of the century it was used also in several other countries: in England, the United States, Austria, and the missions in India and in China. After 1850, the practice of discussing the problems of the concepts and the content of the catechism was ended, and only purely didactic and educational questions were raised.

In France there were no chairs for pastoral theology and theoretical problems were much less debated there than in Germany. But on the practical level many interesting efforts were undertaken. The most interesting one started at the seminary of Saint Sulpice. J.-A. Émery, who had started Saint Sulpice again, returned to the tradition of J.-J. Olier and initially introduced young clerics to pastoral care by way of catechetical exercises in the parish. This method was adjusted to the new times by a few priests who understood the psychology of children. They knew how to make catechetical instruction come alive through the use of approving letters and other rewards and by interspersing it with songs and prayers. The direct heir of these innovators was Dupanloup, who was inspired by their example and their spirit and who added his own educational genius. Even if the old clergy accused the young vicar of adding too much drama and profane accents to his catechetical instruction at La Madeleine in Paris (1826–34), his method, aiming equally at the training of the religious sensibilities and the theoretical knowledge of the child, was gradually accepted.

On the whole, the French province lagged behind during the first decades of the new century. Only when the group of the Paris catechists was dispersed across the country as a consequence of successive bishops' promotions, did the catechetical movement spread there also. It was then anchored in the decrees of the provincial councils which met after 1848. But here and there interesting initiatives had been undertaken before. One needs to think only of the extraordinary success achieved before 1830 by the catechists of the Curé d'Ars, who stood out because of their continual attempt to speak a language which was understood by the common people.

Without a doubt, important catechetical work was being done in France during the time between the First and Second Empire. But it was hampered by a much too individualistic view of religion as the means to "achieve salvation" and the lack of a connection with liturgical life; its chief deficiency was that it was directed at the young communicants, in spite of the efforts at developing "catechismes de perseverance" for young men and women. During the July Monarchy first communion was dressed up as a spectacular celebration, which doubtless underscored its importance, but also produced the impression in children and parents alike that catechetical instruction was more a preparation for the rite of first communion than an introduction to the daily life of a Christian. The result was that after first communion many ceased practicing. Catechetical instruction, on which so much effort had been spent, was not adequately integrated into the totality of pastoral care.

Pastoral Theology and Pastoral Practice

In the theological departments of German universities emphasis was placed on theoretical considerations of how the Catholic Enlightenment could be overcome without doing away with its positive aspects. France was more concerned with practical initiatives, even if they were hesitant, unsure, and much more isolated. Their aim was accommodation to the new situation as it had resulted, on the one hand, from the transformations of the political revolution and the decisively changed position of the clergy in the nation, and, on the other hand, from the industrial revolution, gradually presenting astute Catholics with the completely new problem of pastoral care for the urban proletariat.

Moralism and the anthropocentric inclination of the Enlightenment left their mark on the first suggestions for pastoral theology in Germany. This was particularly true for the Church, which saw its mission from an almost exclusively sociological perspective. Sermons and catechesis were seen as nothing more than mere instruction according to the rules of the profane world, and liturgy was reduced to an exercise in the virtue of religion. From this perspective, the essentially Christian and supernatural aspect was lost sight of and pastoral theology was narrowed to a professional ethic for the use of the clergy, whose function seemed to be limited to the moral and cultural education of the parish members. A change came with Johann Michael Sailer at the turn of the century. As professor of pastoral theology at Dillingen from 1784 to 1794 and at Landshut from 1800 to 1822 he exerted great influence on the clergy of southern Germany. His teaching effected a break with the naturalistic pastoral of the Enlightenment, but he tried to retain the positive elements developed in reaction to the Jansenist mentality, the pietistic anthropology, and the excessive objectivism of the post-Tridentine pastoral. Although Sailer was also interested in an improvement of homiletics, he was primarily concerned with the content of the sermon. Instead of moralizing and dogmatically poor observations he demanded the preaching of the fundamentals of Christianity, free from Scholastic formulations which went beyond the understanding of the people and consisted of nothing more than scholarly commentaries on theological concepts. The best method to achieve the ideal consisted for him of direct and continual contact with Holy Scripture.

In spite of everything, Sailer was still strongly tied to the influence of the sentimental individualism of the "Sturm und Drang" period and the contemporary Protestant theology of "experience." The Tübingen School represented a step forward, as it emphasized the positive and historical character of Christianity as well as the ecclesiastical perspective from which the pastoral theology needed to be derived. Anton Graf added to the function of pastoral theology of sermon and catechesis the task of treating the entire range of activities by which the Church rejuvenates itself thanks to the work of the constantly present Holy Spirit, active among God's people. After 1850, the ecclesiological direction which Graf had wanted to impart to pastoral theology was neglected, and it became more and more a science of practical work in which psychological, ascetic, and canonical considerations won out over the theological aspects. Another indication of the development of this time, damaging the efforts at biblical and theological rejuvenation in Germany, was the success gained around the middle of the century by German versions of French works with characteristic titles. They were chiefly designed to supply the parish clergy with "recipes."

As long as it was not a matter of purely theological consideration of the pastoral, but one of practical realization, France was indeed the country which set the pace until, beginning with the middle of the century, the "movement of union" pushed Catholic Germany into the forefront. Increasingly, priests and laymen concerned with the rejuvenation of the forms and methods of the apostolate turned to the movement.

The pastoral, as it was understood by the French priest and his helpers during the first half of the nineteenth century, was filled with a longing for the past, governed by the desire to rejuvenate the Christian community and the express feeling of hostility toward the world. It was in fact a pastoral of preservation, which attempted not to lose all those who still clung to the Church, i.e., chiefly women and children. This emphasis was not without consequences. The center of gravity of pastoral care moved increasingly to the world of women and children, attested to during this time by many church songs, pictures of saints, statues, and religious paintings.

All too frequently priests were tempted to concentrate on the small loyal group of followers who were willing to bow to their authority without resistance. Yet they did not totally ignore the lost sheep. For this purpose they employed the missions to the people or parish missions from the preceding period. After an interruption of several years toward the end of the Empire, these popular missions were immediately resumed in France after the return of the Bourbons. The July revolution stopped this movement, which often had assumed a political character; gradually it was resumed with less fanfare but with greater emphasis on depth.

In Italy also the parish missions had developed into firm fixtures and were resumed almost everywhere after the end of the revolutionary upheavals. Italians introduced such missions to the people into England and Ireland after 1843. As a result of the limitations imposed by the governments, the missions in the German states were not very successful until the middle of the century. But after 1840 they were permitted to spread in Austria and after 1848 also in Germany. In the United States an Austrian Jesuit, F. X. Weninger (1805–88), conducted about eight hundred missions after 1848.

The organization of a mission was always an extraordinary event, and in between them the priests had to search for suitable means of drawing the people into the churches, where they could learn how to fulfill their obligations, to avoid sins, and to gain salvation. The parish priests of that time viewed their task in this formalistic fashion. A high point of the year was first communion, establishing a connection, strengthened by folklore, between parish, school, and family. An attempt was made to transform the ceremony into a kind of popular mission in order to induce indifferent families once again to partake of the sacraments.

But the popular missions were not the only institutions which the French priests of the nineteenth century, in admiration of the traditions of the old French clergy, wished to revive. They also tried to restore a number of former confraternities. It was above all the Marian congregations which experienced a lively revival in similar forms. They had been dissolved in France in 1760 under pressure from the Jansenists, but in the nineteenth century enjoyed the advantages of the veneration of Mary. The Association of Sons of Mary the Immaculate, which, between 1820 and 1830, was founded by the Daughters of Charity for the children of their boarding schools, but which after the appearances of Mary to Catherine Labouré and their official acknowledgment by Pius IX in 1847 became a worldwide phenomenon without regard to social class (six hundred thousand members by the end of the century).

In addition to these traditional forms, there were others which endeavored to take into account the new needs of an increasingly urban society. Of chief importance in this connection were the juvenile homes which attempted to compensate for the lack of moral and religious instruction among the common people.

In France and Belgium such protective pastoral organizations developed especially under the influence of the Society of Saint Vincent de Paul. The Vincentians, started by young French laymen, the best known among them being Frédéric Ozanam, had given themselves three goals: assistance for the poor, not only materially, but also psychologically through contacts between human beings; strengthening of the faith of the members through the common exercise of charity; and apologetic witness before the world by attesting to the viability of Catholicism through action.

The Vincentian Conferences were an enterprise in which laymen played the primary role. The increasingly large role played by laymen in the service of the Church was one of the most significant innovations in the pastoral of the nineteenth century, in the course of which this trend became more pronounced. They were the men and women, generally from the social elite, who placed their wealth or their active interest in the service of the parishes in order to preserve already existing institutions or to help with the creation of new ones. Year by year the number of journalists and parliamentarians increased who often quite selflessly defended the interests of the Church with word and pen. Laymen were necessary in order to regain contact with the world through the presentation and defense of the faith in a language understood by all. The use of laymen as mediators for the purpose of representing the Church in the nerve centers of the new society was imperative. These centers were located in parliamentary bodies, in the offices of the civil service, in communal administrations, and in the editorial offices of newspapers. In spite of complaints and lamentations based on old habits difficult to shed and on a too narrowly interpreted ecclesiology, the people who looked to the future with awareness hesitated less and less to identify themselves with Lacordaire when he wrote: "The layman has a mission; he must add whatever the secular clergy and the religious orders lack. The faithful must join in their efforts to defend truth against the continual influence of bad doctrines; their love must work together in order to repair the breaches in the Church and the social order."

The Reaction of Moral Theology
to the Rationalism of Enlightenment and Rigorism

As in so many other areas, moral theology and pastoral theology often have been characterized by the contrasting views of decadence on the one hand and restoration on the other in connection with the period of the Enlightenment and the first half of the nineteenth century. In reality, the reaction of numerous moralists of the eighteenth century against the reduction of moral theology to casuistry or against the discussions about probabilism also contained many positive values and justified objectives. But all too frequently there was the tendency to lose sight of the peculiar nature of Christian morality in comparison to a purely philosophical morality and to lend more weight to psychological considerations than to the biblical and ecclesiastical foundations of moral theology. This antidogmatic tendency was encountered in a number of German moralists of the first decades of the nineteenth century. There was also the parallel development both in moral theology and dogmatic theology of a growing reaction to rationalism. But even if the German moralists endeavored to seek their primary source of inspiration in Holy Scripture and increasingly to respect the entire range of doctrines of the Church, they were much more concerned with developing syntheses in close contact with the philosophy and the problems of their time than were their colleagues in the Latin countries.

In their argument with the naturalism of the preceding generation, they tried to restore biblical morality with its original force and to point out the intimate ties existing between it and the dogmas. But they also turned against the classical moral theology which seemed to limit itself to drawing the line between mortal and venial sins. As far as they were concerned, it was the function of moral theology to present the ideal of a Christian life in its totality. They did not consider the methods and the language of jurisprudence as suitable for a morality based on the gospel. Thus, Sailer's *Handbuch der christlichen Moral* (1817), written without much system and in an elevated style, yet filled with a host of original ideas, was a kind of introduction to a life of devotion. It was designed, as the subtitle explained, primarily for future Catholic pastors and secondarily for every educated Christian. In reaction against the casuistry of the Jesuits and also against the rationalism predominating in the universities toward the end of the eighteenth century, Sailer traced the essential nature of Christian law to the love of God without, however, adequately delineating the subjective conditions of this love. Hirscher surpassed his predecessor "in the acuteness of psychological observation, by the greater actuality and contemporaneity, and not least through the cohesiveness of the systematical presentation, even if he does not always reach Sailer's mystical drive" (B. Häring). It was his intention to reconstruct morality on the biblical concept of "God's realm" just as Drey had done with dogmatics. A critical examination reveals inadequacies without, however, detracting from his great achievement.

One finds traces of the influence of Hirscher, Sailer, and Möhler in the writings of several authors of the subsequent generation, who with their chief works appearing around 1850, partially returned to the classical tradition so strongly criticized by their predecessors, but they inherited from the Tübingen professors the concern of providing moral theology with its own organic unity in contrast to a merely external systematization. They also gained from them the conviction that the unique foundation of Christian morality must lie "in the nature of God's children, sanctified by the sacraments" (Jocham). Additionally, they emphasized the idea of development inasmuch as they show a moral life not based statically on fixed definitions and standards but rather dynamic, as a battle between grace, encouraging the perfect life, and the earthly forces pulling toward the darkness of sin.

Most of these moralists neither aimed at an approximation of morality with ascetic and mystical theology nor desired to have their books viewed narrowly as a guide for fathers confessor but wanted them to be regarded as useful scholarly works of edification for catechists, preachers, and educated believers.

The situation was totally different in the Latin countries. Here the classical form of the seminary textbook of a canonical-pastoral type was retained, designed to educate future fathers confessor and assembling a dry codification of obligations and sins on a casuistic basis. Here the innovation consisted of the replacement of the rigoristic or at least probabilistic principles by the moderate equiprobalistic doctrine of Saint Alphonsus Liguori in the French-speaking countries. This development, taking place in the second quarter of the century, was "one of the chief events of French Church history during the nineteenth century" (Guerber). It was in fact one of the primary factors for the victory of ultramontanism over the Gallican tradition. It also facilitated access to the sacraments for the faithful and revitalized Christian life.

The adherence by the moralists and the clergy to Liguori's system was promoted by the frequent favorable indications given it by the Roman authorities: the Congregation of Rites in 1803; Pius VII in 1816 on the occasion of the blessing of Alphonsus Liguori; Leo XII in 1825 in a letter to the publisher of his collected works; Pius VIII in 1829; the "Sacred Penitentiary" in 1831 in a reply confirmed by the Pope; and Gregory XVI in 1839 with the bull of canonization. Liguori's victory over the rigorism taught by the Sulpician seminaries was clue primarily to Abbé Gousset, a seminary professor at Besançon, as it was he who had occasioned the reply of the Penitentiary in 1831. But he was not the only one to spread Liguori's doctrines in France. Yet it touched only small groups and the clergy in the countryside were hardly influenced by the movement. But when Abbé Gousset in 1832 published his *Justification de la théologie morale du bienheureux Alphonse de Liguori,* he created a deep impression and during the following decade more than thirty thousand copies of Liguori's *Theologia moralis* were sold in France. After he became archbishop of Reims, Gousset added to this success by publishing a *Théologie morale à l'usage des curés et des confesseurs,* in which he presented Liguori's doctrines simply and impressively.

Probabilism was the prevailing doctrine in Belgium until the end of the eighteenth century. A few priests who had emigrated to Germany during the revolution there discovered Liguori's *Theologia moralis,* of which two editions were published in Mechelen and Antwerp in 1822. The settling of the Redemptorists in the country contributed to the success of Liguori's doctrine among the clergy in spite of persistent resistance in the seminaries and by the old clergy.

At the same time Liguori also was accepted in Germany, where he had always had a number of followers. A portion of the clergy became interested in good casuistic works.

C H A P T E R   2 4

Catholic Thought Searching for New Ways

As in the preceding fifteen years, attempts were continued under the pontificate of Gregory XVI to guide Catholic thought into channels more suitable to the modern way of thinking than Scholasticism. The result of such efforts was uneven in Germany, France, and Italy. The defenders of tradition resisted innovations passionately, and the Holy See, whose authority was growing firmer, after a long interval once again began to censor those Catholic theologians and philosophers whose writings it regarded as threatening the faith. Most of the theological discussions took place in Germany, such as the posthumous controversies over the theories of Hermes, the admiration for Günther and the attacks against him, and the influence of the schools of Tübingen and Munich. But the Catholic University of Louvain also rose as a new center of higher education in Belgium. The failure of Lamennais and Bautain in France must not let one forget that numerous, often hapless, often interesting initiatives were taken. They were a testament to the efforts of open-minded Catholic intellectuals to leave the old worn-out paths and to accommodate themselves to the thinking of their contemporaries. One of the most notable indications of such efforts is the growth of the Catholic press; not of dailies as yet, but of journals and periodicals. It is especially noteworthy that this phenomenon characterized all of western Europe.

The Hermesian Controversy

After the death of Georg Hermes on 26 May 1831, at the height of his fame, criticism immediately became stronger and more virulent. His opponents lacked the intellectual force for a precise limning of his errors, but they sensed that Hermes had assigned reason too high a place in the doctrine of faith. Anton Josef Binterim (after 1805 pastor in Bilk near Düsseldorf), one of the bitterest opponents of Hermes, succeeded in convincing the nuncio in Munich to warn the Roman authorities. Until then they had relied on the Cologne Archbishop Count Spiegel, who had defended the orthodoxy of the Bonn professor. But in consequence of the report by the nuncio, the *Philosophische Einleitung in die christ-katholische Theologie* was placed before the Index congregation. Toward the end of 1833 two German-speaking theologians, the Alsatian Kohlmann and the future Cardinal Reisach, were asked to translate the contested passages into Latin and to evaluate them. The nuncios in Munich and Vienna were requested to obtain the testimony of experts and to forward it to Rome. The Munich nuncio turned to two bitter enemies of Hermes, C. H. Windischmann and Binterim, the latter of whom was hardly competent to make a judgment. The Vienna nuncio consulted the Güntherian J. E. Veith, who was favorably inclined towards Hermes, but also the theologically untrained jurist K. E. Jarcke, who was very hostile to Hermes.

In Germany the controversy was renewed when J. A. Achterfeld in 1834 posthumously published the hitherto unpublished first volume of Hermes' *Dogmatik*. With public opinion being agitated, the examination of Hermes' doctrines continued. On 26 September 1835 a sharply worded papal brief globally condemned Hermes' writings as "absurda et a doctrina Catholicae Ecclesiae aliena." Branded were numerous errors concerning God, grace, original sin and ecclesiastical tradition, especially the method of using positive doubt as the foundation of all theological inquiry, and the rationalistic principle which sees reason as the only means of obtaining knowledge of supernatural truth. The papal document filled Hermes' opponents with joy and prompted them to demand the immediate dismissal of his students from all university teaching posts. But aside from the bishops of Osnabrück and Posen, the bishops took no action, as the brief had not been transmitted through governmental channels.

The Hermesians, totally unprepared for the condemnation and thunderstruck by the judgment as well as by the harsh language used in connection with their revered master, quickly went over to the counterattack. They declared that Hermes' doctrinal opinions had been badly interpreted and that the papal brief attacked only a heresy of the imagination. They asserted that the recent condemnation of Bautain's fideism by the bishop of Strasbourg justified Hermes and proved at the same time the weakness of the position of their opponents. The last was a point valid for many of the involved. For no matter how bitter their attacks, they still were not able to write a decisive refutation.

The controversy raged again after the appointment of Archbishop Droste zu

Vischering. In his youth he had belonged to the circle around the Princess Gallitzin with its mystic and Platonic tendencies. Now, quite unjustly, he suspected the Hermesians of making common cause with the Prussian government in order secretly to undermine Catholicism. The archbishop also intended to destroy the influence of the department of theology at the University of Bonn and to replace it with the diocesan seminary in Cologne. He demanded from the professors an express submission to the papal brief and from all ecclesiastical candidates a sworn agreement with the eighteen theses in which the errors condemned by the Pope were even more sharply formulated; they were in fact very tactlessly phrased. According to the anti-Hermesian Franz Werner, Droste also was guilty of a number of mistakes: he was incapable of recognizing what was correct in some of the scholarly demands of the Hermesians. But primarily he lacked the pastoral tact and the conciliatoriness which would have allowed the Hermesians a graceful retreat. He wanted to drive them to an unconditional surrender, but instead only succeeded in embittering them and confirming them in their excessive adherence to the doctrines of their teacher. They also were contemptuous of the archbishop's magisterial office, which desired to contradict with arguments of authority a philosophical system whose spirit it had evidently not grasped at all.

Toward the end of 1835 F. X. Biunde, professor at the seminary at Trier, established contact with Rome in order to enable the Hermesians to explain the meaning of the condemned writings, which, according to their opinion, had been misunderstood by the Roman censors. The result was that at the beginning of 1837 two delegates went to Rome. They were P. J. Elvenich, layman and philosopher, fully acquainted with the Hermesian system and also a capable Latinist, and J. W. Braun, a theologian of great erudition, "the best mind of the Bonn faculty" (Schrörs), with good connections in Rome. They were initially well received — much better than Lamennais — and asked to discuss their case with the Jesuit general Roothaan, who spoke German. But they quickly discovered that everything rested on a misunderstanding: The Roman authorities were solely interested in determining whether the Latin translation which the censors had used was correct, while Elvenich and Braun wished to explain the essential nature of the doctrines in order to justify them. The Index congregation refused to consider this approach and did not even wish to see the Latin summary, *Meletemata theologica,* which the two had prepared. Other misunderstandings and the intervention of Metternich, who saw in rationalism a danger to the principle of authority and feared that the religious ferment could degenerate into political disturbances, served to discredit them entirely. Their eleven-month stay ended in total defeat. Because they insisted that they agreed with the Pope in condemning all of the errors which he had cited, including the method of positive doubt, but denied that Hermes' writings contained such errors, Secretary of State Lambruschini in a letter of 6 April 1838 accused them of lacking obedience and of taking recourse to the Jansenist differentiation between *quaestio iuris* and *quaestio facti.* The letter, immediately published by their opponents, hastened the decline of Hermesianism which had begun two to three years earlier. Although the Hermesians active in pastoral care delivered excellent service, the majority of the clergy and the militant Catholics, who were increasingly ultramontane, distanced themselves completely from these "ivory tower theologians" who openly opposed the Holy

See. The intellectuals began to turn to Anton Günther, the new rising star, who also attracted some of the best speculative minds among the Hermesians. Nor were the rearguard actions by the uncompromising Hermesians to any avail. They believed that they had reasons for hope when Pius IX in his inaugural encyclical *Qui pluribus,* directed against the fideists, emphasized the importance of the rational basis of the act of faith. The Hermesians interpreted the passage as a revocation of the brief of 1835. But the Pope put a quick end to this tactical maneuver. The time of the Hermesians was gone irrevocably.

Rise and Fall of Güntherianism

Anton Günther (1783–1863), like Hermes a pious and concerned priest, attempted to reconcile faith and reason and to enable Catholic intellectuals to remain in the Church while they confronted the great philosophical currents of their time. Like Hermes he became the revered teacher of a whole generation of philosophers and theologians. And like Hermes he was accused — not without grounds — of semirationalism. But the differences between the two thinkers were considerable. Hermes endeavored to overcome Kantian criticism and to create a rational basis for the acceptance of revelation. Günther dealt with Hegel's pantheistic idealism and Feuerbach's materialistic monism in order to work out a philosophical justification of the great Christian dogmas. The differences between the two men were even greater when one considers their intellectual background. Hermes and his followers were late representatives of the dry rationalism of the Enlightenment of the eighteenth century, white Günther and most of his enthusiastic students were deeply influenced by the Catholic romanticism of the restoration period.

Günther was born in northern Bohemia and received his philosophical education in the rationalistic atmosphere of Prague. He developed an intense religiosity and began the study of theology with the help of the Redemptorist Clemens Maria Hofbauer. In 1821 he became a priest and settled in Vienna, where he lived as a private scholar until his death. He failed to obtain a teaching position in Vienna and rejected all offers coming from Germany. He lived surrounded by like-minded admirers, clerics, and laymen, who were equally attracted to his apostolic temperament, his metaphysical genius, and the charm of his discourse. Among them were the Cartesian naturalist J. H. Pabst, Günther's chief collaborator, and the famous preacher J. E. Veith, a former Jew.

With his numerous books, written in a very personal, sometimes very condensed, sometimes free and humorous style, Günther's influence reached far beyond this personal circle. Without much system they offered original and often far-seeing observations and astute criticisms of the most important philosophical systems, especially of Hegelianism. There is no doubt that Günther recognized the intellectual greatness of Hegelianism, but he also recognized the danger it presented much more clearly than most of the other theologians of his time. He was also convinced that Scholasticism was not only outdated but, like any philosophy of concepts, was connected to a kind of semipantheism, and therefore he devoted himself with unusual intellectual enthusiasm to a new scholarly proof of theology with an anthropological base. He presented Catholic dogma in the language of the "phenomenology of the mind" and tried to show how it is possible to understand creation through the Trinity and the Trinity through human self-consciousness. As in all of German idealism, the accent was placed on the concept of man as "nature and mind." During the 1840s Günther dominated the German Catholic intellectual world, the more so as the Prussian government appointed numerous Güntherians to philosophical and theological university teaching posts.

The chief centers of the movement were Vienna, Silesia, and the Rhineland. There were numerous sympathizers elsewhere. The Güntherians had an eager protector even in Rome in the person of Pappalettere, the abbot of Monte Cassino, who saw in them the agents for Germany's liberation from rationalism.

But soon there were also opposing voices. The philosophers, whom Günther had criticized mercilessly, were the first ones to counterattack. Then theologians became involved, accusing Günther of claiming to provide a rational proof of supernatural mysteries. The arrogance of Günther's students, many of whom did not share the deep religiosity and the apostolic dash of their teacher and who, as is often the case, emphasized the debatable aspects of many of his thoughts, only magnified the discontent. By 1845, the old front of the anti-Hermesians, who rigorously rejected any compromise with modern philosophy, deployed itself against Güntherianism. After the crisis of 1848, during which the Güntherians played a predominant role in the Catholic movement, they founded the new philosophical journal *Lydia* (1849–54) for the purpose of spreading their views. Attacks against them increased on the doctrinal level. When the controversy passionately agitated Germany's and Austria's theologians and philosophers, surpassing in acidity the dispute over Hermesianism fifteen years earlier, the archbishop of Cologne submitted the problem to the Holy See. Günther had powerful protectors, who were grateful to him for having freed Catholic intellectuals from their fascination with Hegel and who sensed the danger of offending the universities, which already viewed the official Church hierarchy with mistrust. Matters probably could have been settled satisfactorily had not Baltzer and Knoodt, authorized to defend their system in Rome directly, spoiled everything by their cool attitude toward the Jesuits and the contempt which they showed for the development of Roman philosophy. Still, Rome hesitated two years before it finally decided to act. The opponents of the Güntherians did not cease their attacks. Finally, in January 1857, Pius IX decided to place Günther's works on the Index, even though he paid strong compliments to the person and the intentions of the author. Günther submitted despite his deep disappointment.

Tübingen and Munich

Theological life in the German-speaking countries was not limited to the activity of the Hermesians and Güntherians and the controversies which they caused. Even in Bonn, one of their citadels, not all professors agreed with their teachings.

In southern Germany, theological life was concentrated chiefly in the theological departments of the universities of Tübingen and Munich. The generation of the founders gradually disappeared in Tübingen; their places were taken by younger men. J. E. Kuhn, professor of dogmatics after 1839, who for forty years remained the uncontested head of the school, impressing his students and the readers of his many books by the clarity and depth of his thoughts and the brilliance of his dialectic. In his evolutionary view, Scholasticism was a useful phase in the history of Christian thought, but now outdated. Inspired by Hegel's method, he tried to get to the bottom of the Christian mystery; but his faith-rooted speculation was based on the facts of revelation and took account of the history of dogma. Kuhn remained faithful to the principles of the Tübingen School and was also a talented metaphysician and thoroughly familiar with the Greek Church Fathers and Saint Augustine. He also was an able exegete and in 1832 published his *Leben Jesu wissenschaftlich bearbeitet* to counteract the book on the life of Jesus by David Friedrich Strauß. Kuhn was less tied to romantic idealism than his teachers and placed the concept of mind, spirit, intellect before that of life. In him and his younger colleagues of the Tübingen School "the movement gained speculative depth and systematizing power" (Scheffczyk).

The influence of the Tübingen School extended to other universities, especially to Gießen and Freiburg im Breisgau. The department of theology at Gießen was established in 1830 as a substitute for the Mainz seminary in spite of the protest of the chapter. From the beginning two Tübingen-educated professors left their imprint; Kuhn, holding the chair for New Testament studies from 1832 to 1837, and Franz Anton Staudenmaier, who taught dogmatics from 1830 until 1837, when he moved to Freiburg. In Freiburg he was joined by Hirscher, another respected Tübingen-educated professor. The influence of Staudenmaier, long neglected by historians of theology, was not any less than that of the Tübingen people. In his time his *Geist des Christentums* (1835), which saw eight editions within half a century and was a seminal work in liturgical theology, was even compared to Chateaubriand's *Génie de christianisme.* His *Christliche Dogmatik* (4 vol. [1844–52]) also was a very personal work, in which the central ecclesiological perspectives are grounded in a trinitarian theology and in a history of theology which replaces Hegel's dialectical philosophy of history with the living and free working of God among men as revealed by revelation.

In Munich it was the lay professors who initially played a role. Görres remained the center of the group until his death in 1848. Inspired by the native initiative of Sailer as well as the influence of Tübingen, especially Möhler's presence from 1835 to 1838, the department of theology also improved over time.

After 1826, Döllinger belonged to the faculty to which he had been appointed in consequence of Sailer's help. Connected in his youth with the Mainz group, he had become acquainted with Görres and for two decades stood in the forefront of the journalistic polemic for religious and academic freedom. He had a remarkable talent for dogmatic analysis, which he displayed in his doctoral thesis, *Die Lehre von der Eucharistie in den ersten drei Jahrhunderten.* Regarding university teaching as an apostolate, he turned to church history in the awareness that the Catholics were far inferior to the Protestants in this area. After initial work on Hartig's textbook he published his own *Lehrbuch der Kirchengeschichte* (2 vols. [1836–38]), which was acclaimed for the clarity of his presentation and the originality of his thought. Not merely chronicling events, it treated the development of ecclesiastical institutions in the areas of religion, discipline, and constitution. In 1837 Döllinger was elected as a member of the Bavarian Academy of Sciences. In

1842 he founded an Archive for Theological Literature as the organ of expression of the professors of the theology department.

In the course of the following years he was affected by the hardening of the denominational fronts which under the influence of the converts Jarcke and Phillips superseded the indifferentism of the Enlightenment as well as Sailer's irenicism and Möhler's dialogue. His first great work, *Die Reformation, ihre Entwicklung und ihre Wirkung* (3 vols. [1846–48]) was an anti-Protestant polemic. It was designed to refute the assertions made by Ranke in his *Deutsche Geschichte im Reformationszeitalter.* Based on a considerable number of primary sources drawn from the reformers, he attempted to show the destructive character of the Reformation and its unfortunate cultural consequences; yet he also tried to indicate the reasons for it. This portrait of Lutheranism was rejected by the Protestants because it only treated the dark side of the Reformation, but it caused Catholics to look upon the author as one of the outstanding champions of the Church and to regard Munich as the shining center of Catholic scholarship.

The Catholic University of Louvain

Soon after the creation of the Kingdom of Belgium, the episcopate, suspicious of the moral and religious atmosphere of the state universities, started an experiment which during the nineteenth century frequently attracted the attention of foreign Catholics. In October 1832 it decided to establish a Catholic university with academic freedom and two years later translated this decision into reality. In the attempt to avoid the impression among the liberals that profane education was subject to Rome, the episcopate refused to make it into a papal university. The decision was quite contrary to the usage under the Old Regime and worried the Holy See. Its fears that the new institution could grow into a citadel of Catholic liberalism were confirmed by the appointment of several of Lamennais' followers, among them the university president Xavier De Ram. Considering the lack of qualified personnel in the country, it was necessary to turn to foreign professors. They were won with salaries equivalent to those paid by the state universities. Although the faculty included several autodidacts, it became possible from the beginning to provide students with an education qualitatively comparable to that of the other universities of the country. Thanks to Xavier De Ram's intervention, the Belgian Jesuits were able in 1837 — after an interruption of half a century — to continue the work of the Bollandists. Twenty years later Renan assigned this enterprise first place among the products of the Catholic renaissance of the nineteenth century which he considered serious.

In the theology department, which quickly attracted students from the neighboring countries, the outstanding person was Jean-Baptiste Malou, professor of dogmatics from 1837 to 1849. He displayed his patristic scholarship in the book which he published a few years later on *L'Immaculée Conception de la bienheureuse Vierge Marie* (1857). Educated in Rome, he became at Louvain the defender of Scholasticism against his ontological and traditionalist colleagues.

Tentative Attempts by the Catholic Intellectuals in France

While Germany retained the considerable lead of the first decades of the century and even enlarged it, the Latin countries on the whole presented a sad picture.

In Spain, with the Church suffering the aftereffects of the chaotic political situation, theological studies stagnated. But the training of the clergy in the seminaries was clearly superior to that in France and Italy, even though it was limited to reading the great writers of the sixteenth and seventeenth centuries. Any openness to modern problems was lacking, with the result that Spanish theologians exerted no influence outside of Spain before the Thomist renaissance during the last third of the century.

Italy enjoyed three advantages: the scholarly tradition of the eighteenth century was not totally disrupted by the revolutionary events; it had in Rosmini a Christian philosopher of great stature; and the Roman College was for some of its theologians the means by which they attained international acclaim. But other scholars were not able to work within the framework of famous universities and this could not but have an impact on the quality of their work, no matter how meritorious it was.

Rosmini was admired by the educated public as well as in the Lombard seminaries, where he contributed to freeing instruction from Febronian tendencies. But after 1840 he saw his doctrines passionately attacked. In the area of philosophy he was accused by Gioberti and his students and the adherents of the Scholastic tradition of ontological inclinations; theologically he was attacked by the Jesuits, who, reacting sharply to the criticism to which Rosmini had subjected probabilism in his *Trattato della coscienza morale* (1840), polemicized against what they regarded as his erroneous concept of original sin, in which they saw the basis of his moral doctrines. Although Gregory XVI, asked by the Jesuits to intervene, in 1843 imposed silence on both parties, the spreading of Rosmini's thought in the Catholic circles under the influence of the Jesuits suffered in consequence of these polemics.

The Roman College, closed to innovation in methods and the perception of problems, offered a qualitatively disappointing education. The German professors complained about it and so did the general of the Jesuits. In philosophy the authors of the preceding century were studied without any originality, and the pioneers of the Thomist renaissance were ignored. In the field of theology, only two names stand out from the general mediocrity. They were F. X. Patrizi, professor of exegesis, a conscientious scholar whose *De interpretatione Scripturarum sacrarum* (1844) was the first Catholic monograph on the typological interpretation of the Bible, and Giovanni Perrone, from 1824 to 1848 professor of dogmatics. He was a vulgarizer without much originality who much preferred the dispute with the Protestants and the rationalists to genuine theological reflection. But it was to his credit that the relatively new treatment of the relationship between reason and faith was introduced into classical theology. He also sensed the importance of positive theology, which during the pontificate of Pius IX came to full bloom in the Roman College under his students Carlo Passaglia and Johannes Franzelin.

In France around 1830 there had been two hopes for renewal of Catholic thought: the School of La Chênaie and Malestroit under Lamennais and, on a much more modest level, the School of Molsheim near Strasbourg under Louis Bautain. Lamennais' condemnation was especially disastrous for his school because the Holy See had condemned both his church-political theories and his philosophical system, which constituted the basis for his program of renewal. In addition, of course, the vague and moderate condemnation was exploited extensively by his enemies. It did not immediately curtail the influence of philosophical traditionalism. But after 1835 most of Lamennais' students preferred practical work to now suspect speculations. Thus the changing of the guard which the school of La Chênaie had promised ultimately did not take place and instruction was mediocre, not least because Bautain's work, undertaken completely independently from Lamennais, gradually atrophied.

In 1832 Bautain published a pamphlet on *L'enseignement de la philosophie en France au XIXᵉ siècle* which became the manifesto of his school. He criticized in it both eclecticism and the Cartesian Scholasticism reigning in the seminaries. Bautain's numerous opponents asked the bishop of Strasbourg, Monsignor Le Pappe de Trévern, to intercede. His opponents consisted of Sulpicians offended by his attacks against their methods of instruction, Jesuits, followers of Lamennais who did not care for his criticism of the philosophy of common reason, a portion of the Strasbourg clergy, who regarded him as an interloper, and the seminary teachers of Besançon who were jealous of the competition by the Molsheim group. In the spring of 1834, Monsignor de Trévern, who for six years had had no complaints about Bautain, submitted to him six questions on the relationship between faith and reason. There is no doubt that Bautain, lacking adequate theological training, presented fairly correct views on religious knowledge in terms seemingly incompatible with traditional formulations, and that under the influence of Kantianism he was inclined to denigrate human reasoning. But the questions of the bishop were also unfortunately framed. The consequence was a dialogue among deaf people, carried on for years and worsened by personal dislikes. After the bishop had deemed Bautain's answers unsatisfactory, he published a notice on 15 September 1834 and sent it to the Holy See and to all bishops in France. But the exploitation of the notice by the Hermesians in favor of their semirationalistic views caused Rome to react circumspectly.

Bautain was convinced that the bishop was exceeding his jurisdiction, as in his opinion it was not a problem of dogmatic but only of philosophical questions. In addition he failed to comprehend how a philosophical doctrine based on faith could be accused of "destroying religion." He published a comprehensive work, *La philosophie du christianisme,* in which he presented the essence of his thought in the form of letters to his students. Except for some small exceptions, it was accepted by Möhler at Tübingen, which awarded him the title of doctor of theology. Toward the end of 1835 everything seemed to calm down when Bautain indicated his willingness to sign statements modified with the help of the auxiliary bishop of Nancy, Monsignor Donnet. But the Strasbourg bishop insisted that the new sentences were not really any different from his earlier formulations and sent Bautain's writings to Rome so that with the help of his friend Rozaven they would be placed on the Index. Following Lacordaire's advice, Bautain traveled to Rome in order to defend himself personally.

He was received politely, as Rome did not wish to give the Hermesians new food for thought. He also made an excellent impression during his three months in Rome with his declared willingness to submit himself to Rome's decision. The authorities limited themselves to requesting him to correct a few passages of his book and of a new one which he carried with him in manuscript form. Bautain was more than willing to do so, as the discussions with Roman theologians had revealed to him where he was exaggerating and as he had also discovered that condemnation of rationalism was a far cry from condemnation of reason. He acknowledged that it was possible to regard reason as a first step toward faith without denying the necessity of grace for the awakening of the soul.

From this perspective he published his *Psychologie expérimentale* (2 vols. [1839]), on which he had labored for longer than eighteen years and which he considered as the major achievement of his life. But the old bishop of Strasbourg refused to reinstate Bautain and his followers in their former positions in spite of a request from Rome. On 8 September 1840, Bautain signed a more refined version of his questionable propositions, drafted by Monsignor Räß, the new auxiliary bishop of Strasbourg, and retired to Paris. There, for a quarter of a century, he was active as a respected lecturer and preacher. But the long debate over a single point of his system diverted attention from the importance of his attempt to rejuvenate apologetics. Additionally, he failed to raise the standards of priestly education with respect to the problems caused by modern currents of thought.

Most of the seminaries clearly ignored these problems. Especially at Saint Sulpice "the cult of modesty and caution prevented any attempt at a spiritual rejuvenation" (X. de Montclos). The only notable exception was Charles Baudry, a great patristic scholar who liked to be innovative. In the episcopate as well there was only one man with any sensitivity for these questions: Monsignor Affre, who in 1840 became archbishop of Paris. Results, unfortunately, corresponded little to his intentions. He succeeded as little as his predecessor in breathing new life into the department of theology at the Sorbonne, and he was able only to plan a graduate school of ecclesiastical studies, subordinated to the archbishop. Newman detected in this plan the seed for a future Catholic university, but actually the plan found little echo in France.

Yet the overall balance of the July Monarchy was not only negative. Some — in view of the contemporary circumstances even much — of the vitality and originality of Lamennais' movement survived. It had the goal of reaching the intellectual standards of the Protestants and the faithless and to establish a new humanism in which Catholic dogma was to be the guide for all manifestations of intellectual life without putting the mind in a straitjacket. Even if the plan to send a number of young Catholic intellectuals to Munich (1833–34) was dropped again within a few months, it at least led to important translations. They enabled the French public to become acquainted with some characteristic writings from beyond the Rhine, among them Möhler's *Symbolik* (1836) and Döllinger's *Lehrbuch der Kirchengeschichte* (1841). It encouraged a few clerics — unfortunately many too few — to study at German universities. One who did so was Henri Maret, one of the few great French theologians of the next generation.

Gerbet founded in 1836 the periodical *L'Université Catholique,* with the intent of interesting a wide readership. Because a university independent from the state analogous to the Catholic University of Louvain could not be established in France, the founders of the journal wanted to offer the educated public the equivalent of lectures and presentations in the spirit of Lamennais: research capable of enriching the interpretation of dogma, and critical studies with the aim of refuting rationalistic propositions through extensive reliance on German research, especially that of the Munich School. One of the chief contributors of the new journal was Augustin Bonnetty, who also continued to publish his *Annales de philosophie chrétienne.* With prodigious amounts of labor he collected gigantic numbers of historical documents for the defense of Christianity. He became a precursor of comparative religious studies and his findings and documents were used by other authors for their successful books. Enthusiasm in the service of truth and the acknowledgement of the central importance of history in intellectual studies unfortunately did not provide for these self-taught writers the critical spirit and methodical discipline, the lack of which was one of the chief deficiencies of French Catholicism until the end of the century.

In the absence of genuinely scholarly works, it was nevertheless to the credit of French Catholics under the July Monarchy that they reissued the classical writers of ecclesiastical scholarship. Advised by clerics, a number of Catholic publishers issued collections of old texts, added fresh commentaries, and hoped to adapt traditional instruction to the progress of modern society. Among them was Jacques-Paul Migne. With the help of a number of excellent scholars and thanks to his own business acumen, Migne published three parallel series as tools for the clergy. These were: the most important Bible commentaries of the seventeenth and eighteenth centuries (25 vols. [1834–40]); a number of theological tracts of the sixteenth to nineteenth centuries (28 vols. [1839–45]); and the most important apologists from Tertullian to Wiseman (16 vols. [1842–43]). He also published a *Collection universelle et complète des orateurs sacrés* (99 vols. [1844–66]), an *Encyclopédie théologique* (52 vols. [1844–52], supplemented from 1851 to 1866 by another 119 volumes) which combined updated excerpts from old encyclopedias (like that by Bergier) with articles by contemporary authors, and finally the two famous Patrologia series (the *Series Latina,* 217 vols. [1844–55], and the *Series Graeca,* 161 vols. [1857–66]).

To a large degree Migne was able to publish the two Patrologia series owing to the assistance of a monk from Solesmes, Dom Jean-Baptiste Pitra, a scholar of high caliber. Unfortunately, Pitra remained an exception among the French Benedictines. Even Dom Pitra's work was handicapped by the financial difficulties of the monastery.

The French could be proud of a number of other original and contemporary achievements. Lamennais' former student Alexis-François Rio was concerned with the essence of Christian culture, for which he became what Winckelmann had been for the art of classical antiquity. His book *De la poésie chrétienne* (1836), in reality an introduction to early Italian art in which Schelling's aesthetics can be seen, had only limited success in France, but found great acclaim in Italy and Germany. With all of its preconceived apologetic opinions and methodological weaknesses, his book tried to demonstrate that the paintings of the Middle Ages were inseparably connected with a definite Christian view of man and life. Surpassing the *Génie du christianisme,* it wished "to cause a revolution in aesthetics equal to that which metaphysics based on original revelation had tried to cause in the area of philosophy" (Deré). Montalembert started a similar work in the field of Gothic architecture. He fought the demolition of monasteries and in his *Histoire de Sainte Élisabeth de Hongrie* (1836) he wrote a poetic hagiography in honor of the Christian Middle Ages. He intended to demonstrate the atmosphere of medieval piety through a representative which German romanticism had made accessible to him. At the same time he devoted pages of panegyrics to the Marburg Elizabeth Church, connecting the achievement of Gothic art with the religious sentiments of the contemporaries of Saint Francis of Assisi and Saint Louis. His book was similar to that which Ozanam, with greater scholarship, wrote on the literature of the Middle Ages. In his lectures at the Sorbonne on Saint Francis of Assisi, in his two books on Dante (1838 and 1839), and in his *Études germaniques* (1847–49) Ozanam, within the framework of comparative literature, always also taught religion and made "the long and arduous education which the Church imparted to modern peoples" the central topic.

It was another accomplishment of Ozanam that at the age of twenty he persuaded the archbishop of Paris to introduce at Notre-Dame on the occasion of Lent a style of preaching designed for the young intellectuals and radically different from usual sermons; additionally he convinced the archbishop to assign these Lent sermons to Abbé Henri Lacordaire. As a romanticist who completely grasped the attitude of the new generation, Lacordaire introduced a new style of preaching in 1835 and followed new avenues in apologetics. To a generation captured by the picturesque and by emotions, he offered the eloquence of paintings, colors, enthusiasm, and indignation. He knew how to speak of eternity in everyday language without fruitless bemoaning of the lost past and without condemning the values held by his audiences. He allowed himself to be guided by the experience of his own conversion. He accepted Christianity and the Church as givens by attempting to show how much they corresponded to the needs of the present as well as to the essential needs of human nature. His success indicated that he had found the right approach.

The Growth of the Catholic Press

The picture of Catholic achievements in the intellectual sphere is not complete without reference to newspapers and periodicals. It is useful to summarize the essence of these publications in order to show the universality of this phenomenon which started during the first quarter of the century and increasingly grew after 1830. In 1844, the *Revue des deux mondes* noted: "In order to preach more freely on topics other than morality and charity, the press was employed. Priests in large numbers entered the new arena; laymen became theologians and theologians turned into journalists. Today, journalism has become for some members of the clergy a branch of the pulpit in the recognition that the power of the press is mightier than sermons." This observation was true not only for France, but for all of western Europe.

In Germany some astute leaders of the Catholic movement like Lennig and Döllinger quickly grasped the importance of the press. Yet at first great obstacles had to be overcome. Quickly there appeared a number of journals which addressed themselves to clerics and educated laymen. Among them were *Der Katholik,* founded in Mainz in 1821 "for instruction. warning, and defense against attacks on the Church"; the journal *Eos,* edited by Görres in Munich and transformed by him into the organ of conservative Catholicism in southern Germany, treating both literary questions and church-political problems; the *Zeitschrift für Philosophie und katholische Theologie,* founded in 1832 in Bonn by Braun, a few other Hermesians, and a few bishops in order to provide Catholicism in Prussia with a respectable publication; the *Historisch-Politische Blätter* of Jarcke and Phillips in Munich, more accessible to the broad public but, in the view of Prussian Catholics, edited from a too strongly southern German perspective; and the *Rheinisches Kirchenblatt,* founded in 1844 in Düsseldorf as a monthly and converted into a weekly in 1848 in order better to spread Archbishop Geissel's views. The daily press, on the other hand, especially in the Rhineland, had a difficult beginning and for a long time was limited to papers with purely local circulation, edited in pronounced anti-Protestant, apologetic fashion. They only came into their own during the second half of the century.

In France there also appeared a few notable periodicals: the *Annales de philosophie chrétienne* (since 1830) and the *Université Catholique* (since 1836); also the *Revue européenne,* which between 1831 and 1834 took the place of the *Correspondant* and after the demise of *L'Avenir* — with the exception of political aims — served as forum for the followers of Lamennais; and *Le Correspondant* itself, reappearing in 1843 in order to support Montalembert in his struggle for freedom of education. There were also journals of more popular bent, such as the *Journal des personnes pieuses.* With the exception of *Le Correspondant,* the French periodicals were more concerned with the problems of ideas than with church-political questions. Such questions were treated in the daily press and especially in *L'Univers,* founded in 1833.

In Belgium also there were a number of Catholic newspapers in the provinces, but hardly in the capital. But in 1834 the layman Pierre Kersten founded in Liège a journal of general interest, the *Journal historique et littéraire.* This excellently edited monthly found readers even beyond the borders of the country. Shortly afterwards there appeared in the Netherlands the monthly *De Katholiek* (1842) and the daily *De Tijd* (1845), both of which were to have a long and productive lives.

In Great Britain, the first Catholic monthly appeared in 1831; but the regular Catholic press really began to appear only between 1835 and 1840. At first there was the *Dublin Review,* founded in 1836 by Wiseman with the support of two Irish laymen, as a counterweight to the strongly anti-Catholic *Edinburgh Review.* It was followed by the monthly *The Tablet,* founded in 1840. These were joined by a few less important publications.

Religious periodicals also appeared in the Mediterranean countries. In Italy this was due chiefly to the labors of the *Amicizia cattolica.* In Spain, thanks chiefly to Balmes, there appeared in 1830 in quick succession *La Civilización, La Sociedad,* and *El Pensamiento de la Nación.*

Even if the history of the Church in the nineteenth century in many areas was a series of missed opportunities, it must be noted that the Catholics in most countries quickly recognized that the press was destined to play a large role in modern society. But it must also be mentioned that owing to a lack of material and intellectual means, the journalistic achievements, especially with respect to the daily press, were only second-best compared to the freethinking press.

Section Two

The Ascension of Pius IX
and the Crisis of 1848

Chaps. 25, 26, 27/II: Roger Aubert
Chap. 27/I: Rudolf Lill

CHAPTER 25

The First Years of the Pontificate of Pius IX:
From the Neoguelf Mythos to the Roman Revolution

When Gregory XVI died on 1 June 1846, the religious situation of the Church posed no problems, but the political condition of the Papal State was tense. In view of the administrative and constitutional attempts at reform and the desire of patriots to free Italy from the tutelage of Austria, the regime represented by the late Pope and Secretary of State Lambruschini was at the nadir of its prestige. For this reason internal political considerations were of primary concern in the conclave, the more so as it was decided in view of the serious political situation to open the conclave immediately, without waiting for the arrival of the foreign cardinals. The intransigents favored the election of Lambruschini, as it would guarantee the continued support of Austria in the suppression of revolutionary elements. Others, led by Cardinal Bernetti, considered a few concessions to public opinion necessary and were in favor of a Pope from the Papal State in order to manifest their independence from foreign influences. The preferred candidate of this second group was Cardinal Mastai. On the first ballot, Mastai received fifteen votes, Lambruschini seventeen. Those who feared a victory of Lambruschini then rallied behind Mastai, who received a two-thirds majority on 16 June, the second day of the conclave.

   Giovanni Maria Mastai-Ferretti was relatively young; in memory of his benefactor Pius VII he chose the name Pius IX. He was born on 13 May 1792 in Senigallia in the Marches, and from the beginning of his clerical career demonstrated piety, pastoral concern, and administrative ability. A journey to South America (1823–25), undertaken as auditor of the apostolic delegate to Chile, provided him with insight into the new dimensions of missionary problems and into the difficulties which liberal, regalistically oriented governments could cause for the Church. But as archbishop of Spoleto (1827–32), and as bishop of Imola he succeeded in gaining the respect of the area's very active liberals. He was full of charity toward the members of his diocese, regardless of their views, he was open-minded, and he seriously tried to improve the antiquated nature and the police-state aspects of the government of the Papal State. Yet these administrative reforms were not designed to allow the public actively to participate in affairs of state, as this seemed to him incompatible with the religious character of the papal government. On the other hand, there is no doubt that he was open to the stirring of Italian patriotism. Contrary to the widely accepted view, he thought it impossible to implement the neoguelf program and thought that the Pope as the spiritual head of all Christians should not play the role of the president of an Italian federation. But he intensely felt the national enthusiasm which was being fed by the romantic movement, and the brutalities of which the Austrian troops were accused deeply hurt his generous soul. They brought him into agreement with the forces which desired Italy's liberation from the foreign yoke.

The first decision of the new Pope seemed to confirm the "liberal" attitude of which Rome's reactionaries accused this enlightened conservative: On 17 July he decreed a generous amnesty; he appointed Cardinal Gizzi, wrongly suspected of being a representative of Massimo d'Azeglio's ideas, as secretary of state; he selected Monsignor Corboli-Bussi, a young prelate with an open mind for new ideas, as his confidential adviser; he was generous to Father Ventura, the eloquent follower of Lamennais; he kindly received a number of persons known for their connection with the moderate liberals; and he fully agreed to some long-desired reforms, even though they were not part of a comprehensive concept.

In this heated atmosphere and at a time, just before 1848, when the romantic concepts of Catholicism joined with the goals of democracy, even these very limited gestures of the Pope received the acclaim of the masses. Ignoring the encyclical *Qui pluribus* of 8 November 1846, which again condemned the basic principles of liberalism, people preferred to see in Pius IX "a messenger of God sent to complete the great work of the nineteenth century, the alliance between religion and liberty" (Ozanam). Metternich, on the other hand, whose initial response to the attitude of the Pope had been favorable, was beginning to worry that the Church was headed by a man "with the fire of the heart, but weak in planning and without any real ability to lead." All of liberal Europe responded positively.

For several months the authority of the papacy was at a peak, the more so as at the same time a reconciliation between Rome and the Ottoman Empire seemed possible and the negotiations with Russia, begun in 1845 after a visit of Tsar Nicholas I to Gregory XVI, led to the signing of a relatively favorable treaty.

In Italy, where all demonstrations against the rule of the Austrians or against reactionary governments were accompanied by shouts of "Long live Pius IX," enthusiasm reached a high point. The myth of the "liberal Pope" acted like a catalyst for the disparate elements which before 1848 held progressive opinions; former opponents of the Church, Catholics won over to modern ideas, and the patriotic clergy, all were temporarily united in a common hope. Their disappointment was so much greater when facts began to speak and the actions of the Pope failed to fulfill the hopes which had been placed in him.

The disenchantment began in the area of internal reforms. Pius IX had to take account of the growing opposition on the part of most of the Curia prelates; although he was seriously concerned with an improvement of the situation of his subjects, he himself was not prepared to go beyond the limits of what can be called ecclesiastical paternalism. He was afraid that by relinquishing a part of his priestly kingdom to laymen he would limit the independence which the Holy See required for the fulfillment of its spiritual tasks. He remained far from a liberal attitude toward people and society and by no means wished to change the Papal State into a constitutional and modern state based on the precepts of 1789. A few activists, playing with great skill on his desire to be popular, succeeded in pushing him in this direction, without, however, changing his basic convictions. The results were freedom of the press, freedom of assembly, formation of a council of twenty-four notables in October 1847, and introduction of a lay element into the government in January 1848. Gradually he agreed to several concessions and also immediately attempted to circumscribe them as much as possible. But after the fall of Louis-Philippe in France he was forced to a hasty approval of the constitution which had been demanded for months. Even this decision appeared only as a half-measure and agitated more than it satisfied the increasingly impatient public opinion.

Such hesitation on the part of the Pope, who constantly wavered between advice from the right and the left and thought that he could avoid offending anyone with his decisions, was displayed also and with grave consequences in his attitude toward the Italian movement. Pius IX evidently could not accept Mazzini's idea of a unified Italian republic, as it would mean the suppression of papal sovereignty; equally unacceptable was the neoguelf program.

Still, after a period of tentative moves he agreed with some moderates who wanted to reduce Austrian influence in Italy and who wanted to establish the prerequisites for such a development through strengthening the bonds among the various Italian states. Therefore the Pope tried to give a political direction to the negotiations which began in August 1847 with the objective of establishing a customs union with Tuscany and Piedmont. The idea of a union of the Italian sovereigns in a defensive league, sponsored by Florence and supported by the Pope's chief adviser, Monsignor Corboli-Bussi, was also very agreeable to him. This solution automatically would have associated the Papal State with a national resistance in case of military intervention by Austria for the suppression of revolts which were threatening everywhere, without directly forcing the Pope into a declaration of war. But the ambitions of Piedmont, desirous of claiming for itself all of the advantages accruing from a war of liberation, prevented the formation of the league. Thereafter, events quickly overtook Pius IX.

What has been called the "miracle of 1848" rested in part on a misunderstanding; but for a few months it actually existed. A few remarks by Pius IX, contradicting the negative attitude of Gregory XVI, sufficed to awaken in many Italians the conviction that the new Pope was willing to implement the entire national program and was prepared, according to a promise by Gioberti, to place himself at the head of a crusade in order to drive the Austrians from the peninsula and to effect national unification. Such illusions were also nourished by the evident reserve which Pius IX since the beginning of his pontificate had exercised toward the Austrian ambassador; this reserve, however, stemmed not only from his sympathy for the Italian cause, but also from his dissatisfaction with the Josephinist religious policy of the Empire, especially in Lombardy. When on 10 November 1848 Pius IX in a public address attempted to lessen belligerency but at the same time implored God's blessing for Italy, public enthusiasm reached its zenith. Convinced that the Pope was on their side, the clergy as well as the faithful in all of Italy during the subsequent weeks of national agitation lent a large degree of support to the national uprisings. When the Piedmontese government went to war against Austria in support of the nationalists, it was expected that the papal troops would follow suit. A number of papal advisers in Rome encouraged such a step in order to avoid the displeasure of the people. But the majority of the Curia theologians and cardinals spoke out for neutrality, which seemed more fitting for the head of the Church. Pius IX himself, overcome by the events, was in conflict between his genuine Italian patriotism and the awareness of his religious responsibility, which went beyond national concerns. In order to clear the air, the Pope made his famous speech of 29 April, whose recently discovered draft allows us a direct glimpse at his contradictory feelings. In the first version of the speech the Pope said that while he could not intervene against Austria militarily because its subjects like his own were his spiritual sons, he had full sympathy for the Italian demands. The published text, however, probably corrected by Cardinal Antonelli, placed the chief emphasis on the first point and left the second one obscure. In his simplicity, Pius IX was unaware of the consequences of these changes, and when a few days later in response to the angry reaction of the Italian opposition he explained that his words had been designed to clarify the special position of the Pope and were in no way to be a disapproval of the national struggle, it was too late. The equivocal epithet of "liberal pope" was replaced by the equally erroneous designation of "antinational pope."

The situation was aggravated by the discontent caused by the economic crisis affecting the Papal State and all of Europe. It made the people an easy prey of agitators. Anarchy continued to spread. Political assassinations increased. To establish mastery over such a volatile situation would have required the abilities of an extraordinary statesman. Pius IX, however, very receptive to superficial suggestions, wavered between the reformatory advice tendered him by the likes of Rosmini and the fear of losing his religious independence. It was a fear fed by the reactionary party at the papal court and the result was a growing lack of morale. He finally consented to entrust the administration to the energetic Count Pellegrino Rossi, who wanted to form a constitutional government after the model of France. But he was unpopular with both the parties of the right and the left and was assassinated shortly after his appointment.

Now things happened quickly: The revolutionaries besieged the Pope in the Quirinal Palace and demanded the convocation of a constituent assembly and a declaration of war on Austria. In the city, cardinals and prelates were exposed to all kinds of threats. Under these circumstances the Pope decided on 24 November, primarily advised by Cardinal Antonelli, who feared that the Pope could be pressured into making ill-considered concessions, to leave Rome. Disguised, he went to the Neapolitan port of Gaeta in order to board ship for France. He was dissuaded, however, by those who feared that he would fall under the influence of a republican country, and instead accepted the invitation of the king of Naples to seek refuge in his kingdom, where he stayed for seventeen months. Two days after his flight Pius IX dissolved the government which he had left behind and placed Cardinal Antonelli at the helm of the papal administration with the title of prosecretary of state. For the next twenty-five years, Antonelli was in charge of the fate of the Holy See.

Antonelli was an easy-going prelate, ambitious and avaricious, and in spite of his genuine faith more a man of the world than a man of the cloth. He was industrious and energetic and possessed a limited intelligence, but without any perspicacity. He had those abilities peculiar to excellent civil servants. Sensitive and observant, cunning and winning in his ways, a diligent pupil of Bernetti, but without any convictions of his own, he now showed himself as a nimble diplomat. But his ability consisted primarily in finding excuses, in adjusting to the conditions of the moment, and in avoiding difficulties, rather than in attacking a problem at its roots and finding new solutions. He was by no means a reactionary and initially supported the reform movement introduced by Pius IX. But events convinced him that a partial laicization and liberalization of the government of the Papal State would not produce results and that the independence of the Pope as head of the Church could be guaranteed only by the return to a theocratic form of government. He thus decided to pursue a hard-line policy toward the politically active in Rome, and placed all of his hopes in a foreign intervention which would return the Pope to his throne. While Rosmini advised the Pope not to burn his bridges to the Roman parliament, Antonelli emphatically refused to receive a Roman delegation which wanted to ask the Pope to return to the capital. On 4 December he urged the European powers to use force in order to return the Pope to his temporal position. He then advised the Pope against a proclamation in the conciliatory form drafted by Rosmini and encouraged him to disavow the provisional government officially. Rosmini, who clearly recognized the disadvantages of a connection of the papal cause with Austria and the conservative powers, in vain advised the Pope to seek a solution with Piedmont as intermediary rather than through the aid of foreign troops. Antonelli, determined to achieve a solution through force, easily succeeded in exploiting the prejudices of Pius IX against the government of Turin and after a few weeks the rivalry between Rosmini and Antonelli ended with a complete victory of the latter. The Pope valued the devotion and skill which he displayed during the critical November days.

In Rome, where the flight of Pius IX made a very bad impression, Antonelli's inflexibility completely discredited the moderates and allowed the radicals to gain the upper hand. The constituent assembly, elected on 21 January 1849 with 134 against 123 votes, declared the Pope devoid of all claims to political power over the Roman state and proclaimed a republic. The government was entrusted to a triumvirate under the leadership of Guiseppe Mazzini. The people had been won over less because of the republican ideology than because of extreme irritation with the "government of priests" and the abuses associated with it. Mazzini's role had great significance, for it was he who, like a prophet, made Rome the focal point in the struggle for Italian rejuvenation, a role which it had not played during the time of Gregory XVI. It was now the ideological capital of the Risorgimento.

Joint military action by Austria, Spain, Naples, and France within a few months put an end to the republican government. The Catholics in France, encouraged by the events in Austria, were able to persuade Louis Napoleon to undertake the Roman campaign despite the opposition of the democratic elements. The conference of Gaeta (30 March to 22 September 1849) established the foundation for the restoration of papal power. The French government desired the restoration to take place in a liberal atmosphere. But while Antonelli considered a return to the form of government of 1848 impossible, he untiringly worked to prevent the implementation of the statute of March 1848 which the Pope had conceded. He was supported by the diplomats of the conservative powers; contrary to expectations, Austria's representative was not the most obstinate; in fact, he was very much aware of the dangers of an excessive reaction. The end result was the motu proprio of 12 September 1849, which promised great freedom on the communal level and reforms of the judiciary and the administration, but which brought no political freedom. The regulation, which in effect merely implemented the recommendations of the memorandum of 1831, was "about eighteen years behind the requirements of the present" (Ghisalberti). Even so, there was a large number of cardinals who considered even this regime as too progressive. They were supported by the Neapolitan court in their delay of the implementation of the recommendations of the motu proprio. They undertook repressive measures in an atmosphere of passionate prejudices, totally justifying the description of the papal restoration as reactionary and inept.

Even more remarkable than the obsolete character of the political restoration was the change in the attitude subsequently demonstrated by Pius IX. At Gaeta, in contrast to the people around him, his concern for a religious revival predominated and was the real cause for the ideas of political reaction. His advisers missed no opportunity to keep alive in his impressionable soul the memories of the bloody Roman revolution and especially the murder of Pellegrino Rossi, the defender of a far-reaching liberalization of institutions, by radical elements. Aside from the psychological level, the opinions of Pius IX also hardened, especially his distrust of principles whose dangerous consequences had become evident. More than ever before he was now convinced of the connection between the principles of 1789 and the destruction of traditional social, moral, and religious values. The new orientation began with the placing on the Index on 30 May 1849 of the works in which Gioberti, Rosmini, and Ventura had presented their reform program. The *Civiltà cattolica* became for the Pope, who very much encouraged its founding by a group of Jesuits, an instrument of doctrine and a carrier of propaganda effective far beyond the borders of Italy.

CHAPTER   26

The Consequences of the Events of 1848 in France

French Catholics initially were chagrined by the news of the abolition of the monarchy, evoking in them sad memories of the Terror. But then they noted with joy that the new government harbored no hostile sentiments and that the revolutionaries even displayed a respectful attitude toward the Church. It would be too simplistic, of course, to equate the insults hurled at priests in 1830 or the destruction of the residence of the archbishop in Paris with the appeal of 1848 which asked the clergy to bless the liberty trees, for the short period of friendship between Church and Republic was essentially limited to Paris. Yet there is no doubt that a change of mind had taken place since 1830 and that many people in 1848 as heirs of romanticism were motivated by a kind of Christian sentimentalism and were taken by the evangelical message of brotherly love and human equality. They were also impressed by the liberal stance taken by Pius IX at the beginning of his pontificate and by the fact that the clergy, less involved in politics than during the restoration period and even occasionally treated with coldness by the authorities, had come closer to the people. Thus, clergy and flocks, after a momentary disquiet, were calmed by the thought that religion flourished in the American republics and accepted the new government with sympathy. Numerous clerics, regarding themselves as successors to the priests of 1789, became candidates for the constituent assembly, which confirmed their initial hopes. Through the introduction of the universal franchise in a country in which many peasants were still under the influence of the clergy, the Church was assured of a larger political role than under the earlier class voting arrangement.

But the revolution of 1848 posed a much more difficult problem for the conscience of French Catholics than the simple acceptance of the Republic: it was its socialistic character which exercised a disturbing influence on the broad masses of the Catholics, especially in the rural areas, and among the petite bourgeoisie and the landowners. There were also a few groups who under the July Monarchy had become concerned with the problems of the workers. From the beginning these people favored the socialistic tendencies of the young republic. A few clerics and laymen, among them Ozanam and Lacordaire, were even willing to support them actively, and with the approval of the archbishop of Paris, Monsignor Afire, they founded the newspaper *L'Ère Nouvelle,* designed to defend not merely the principles of 1789 and the republican ideal, but also various social reforms, some of which were still rather daring at this time.

The program also found an echo in some Catholic newspapers in the provinces and initially was somewhat successful chiefly among the young clergy. But a large majority of Catholics were above all interested in the maintenance of order and the inviolability of property. Their worries, caused by financial impositions designed to pay for the initial social legislation, turned into panic after the June disturbances which were caused by the closing of the state-run workshops. They convinced the French Church for the next twenty years that religion, morality, and the traditional social order were threatened. Confirmed in its fears by the events in Rome, it essentially returned to a conservative position, and because of its fear of the

Socialists was prepared for all kinds of compromises. While the bishops painted democracy as the heresy of the nineteenth century and Louis Veuillot began to attack socialism, to which were attributed the areligious, antifamilial tendencies of some of its leaders, Montalembert became the leader of the countermovement against the radicals, in whose aims he saw a threat to the true concept of freedom.

This rapid development was favored by the Orleanist bourgeoisie, which now was perfectly willing to make common cause with the Church for the purpose of defending property. To be sure, Montalembert and Falloux, together with Thiers and Mole, the leaders of the large "party of order," were concerned about the preservation of the interests of religion and obtained significant advantages for the Church; but their clever calculation on the parliamentary level took insufficient account of the dangers inherent in this pact between religion and capitalist interests. On the other hand, French Catholics strongly supported the increasingly antidemocratic measures with which the National Assembly in 1849 and 1850 attempted to reduce the influence of the left. Thus they appeared not only as antisocialists but as antirepublicans as well and their attitude toward Louis Napoleon Bonaparte reinforced the impression. Without a doubt, they preferred him to Cavaignac as president because he promised them the freedom of secondary education and the support of France for the restoration of the secular power of the Pope. To the same degree that he revealed himself as dictator, clergymen flocked to him, as the traditionalist movement increased their sympathies for the authoritarian forms of power.

The attitude of the Catholics to the coup d'état of 2 December 1851 was therefore predictable. With a few exceptions — among them Lacordaire, Ozanam, Dupanloup, and the small group of Christian Democrats — they agreed after brief hesitation with Veuillot: "There is only a choice between Bonaparte as Emperor and the socialistic republic." Montalembert exhorted people to vote "yes" in the plebiscite "in order to defend our churches, houses, and women against those whose greed does not respect anything." But the praises to God which the clergy sang in public on the occasion of the coup d'état aroused the anger of the republican leaders. Unceasingly they denounced the "alliance between saber and aspergillum" and gradually imbued their followers with their violent anticlericalism.

For the moment, however, the four years of the Second Republic had clearly been positive for the French Church. The tactic employed by Montalembert during the July Monarchy had borne fruit. The Catholics, well represented in the parliament and needed against the left, succeeded in obtaining a number of institutionally and administratively favorable decisions. They were not able, as they had hoped initially, to do away with the so-called Organic Articles which limited the freedom of the Church, but the new constitution quite satisfactorily regulated some points important to the Catholic interests. Favored by generous legislation, orders expanded quickly. Relations with the authorities were easy and often even friendly. Advised by Dupanloup, Falloux appointed excellent bishops and they, strictly supervised by the nuncio, gradually grew accustomed to dealing directly with Rome without interference from the government, which in any case granted them more freedom than they had had under the monarchy. After brief hesitation, the government even gave in to the importunings of Monsignor Sibours and permitted the convocation of provincial synods, last held in 1727. These councils regulated a number of ecclesiastical administrative problems which had been left unattended for more than fifty years. They also provided proof for the clergy that large portions of the population had become estranged from the Church and that new methods of pastoral care needed to be employed.

The major advantage for the Church during the Second Republic was in the field of education. Fear of the "Socialist danger" and apprehension of the elementary school teachers, many of whom seemed to be enamored of socialism, drove the middle class to the Church which it had fought for so long. Thiers was willing to entrust the entire primary school education to the clergy, whose expectations had been far lower. In secondary education, however, designed for the children of the bourgeoisie, there were still numerous defenders of the monopoly of the state. At all costs they were determined to achieve a series of conditions which seriously would have restricted the freedom promised in Article 9 of the constitution. For four months the matter was discussed in a special committee created by Secretary of Education Falloux, but finally the skill of Abbé Dupanloup, Thiers, and Cousin succeeded in winning substantial concessions. The draft developed by the commission was adopted on 15 March 1850 in spite of the opposition of university professors and the left. The Falloux Law, for thirty years the basis of a dual school system, brought about a total reform of the state and private systems of education. It was based on two principles: freedom of private education, producing some very favorable conditions for schools run by the Church, and influence by the Church on the education system of the state.

The Falloux Law promoted an increase; in the number of Catholic schools and perforce gradually deepened the gap which ideologically separated the former pupils of the ecclesiastical colleges from the high schools of the state and the former pupils of the school brothers from the lay schools. By increasingly making the Church a rival of the state in the area of education, this law contributed to the formation of a broad anticlerical movement, which half a century later led to drastic measures against the orders, through which it was hoped to deliver a mortal blow to Catholic education. For the moment, however, the law was a great victory for the Church after forty years of a monopoly by the university.

But it was also a victory for Catholic liberalism. The tactic inspired by Montalembert had made success possible. On the other hand, the acceptance of this compromise law meant for the Church the official renunciation of its claims to the monopoly of education which it had had under the Old Regime and of which many still dreamed. A portion of the clergy, supported by intransigent journalists led by Louis Veuillot, regarded this "Edict of Nantes of the nineteenth century" (Lacordaire) as an unacceptable capitulation, signifying in an essential point the end of the system of an established religion. The discussions soon grew so heated that the Pope, warned by Montalembert and Dupanloup, had to force the episcopate to accept the law. It made the split in the Catholic bloc final and any small incident could not but deepen it.

CHAPTER 27

The Consequences of the 1848 Revolution in the States of the German Confederation and the Netherlands

The States of the German Confederation

Buoyed by the news from France of the revolution in February 1848, the liberal movement in Germany in March 1848 could have either taken over the government in various German federal states or gained a degree of participation. After general elections, the National Assembly met in Frankfurt in May, confronted with the double responsibility of creating a unified state and a liberal constitution. It wrote the constitution, but by the time it was passed in March 1849 the Assembly no longer had the strength to withstand the individual states, which had regained much of their power. In the larger states by this time the governments had managed to impose constitutions of their own — in Prussia in December 1848, in Austria in March 1849 — and while these realized many liberal demands, they actually started a counterrevolutionary phase.

Most of the German Catholics greeted the changes in March 1848 with approval. Brought up in the tradition of empire, they desired national unification and welcomed the fall of police state administrations which had oppressed the Church. The old ecclesiastical demands for freedom could be articulated effectively within the framework of the March movement and the leaders of the Catholics immediately took advantage of the recently decreed principles of freedom of the press, association, and assembly. From now on they pursued two large goals: The Church in Germany was to gain effective unity of action and lasting autonomy with respect to the governments; and in the desired national state the Catholics were to regain their proportional influence, lost after the secularization. Catholic activity was focused on the three new areas of associations, parliaments, and joint actions of the episcopate. Once again laymen and lower clergy were in the vanguard.

The first impulses which pointed the way were generated in Mainz. In March, the "Pius Association for Religious Freedom," was founded whose program was publicized by the *Katholik* and the *Mainzer Journal.* Several other associations followed, first in the Rhineland, in Westphalia, and in Baden, then also in Bavaria, Tyrol, and the east (Breslau and Danzig). By September there existed seven central associations and several hundred branches, many of them directed by laymen. In addition to religious freedom, the associations demanded social measures and some, especially in the Rhineland, also favored political liberalism. The most important daily papers founded in 1848 were the Greater-German federalist *Deutsches Volksblatt* (Stuttgart) and the *Rheinische Volkshalle* (Cologne).

During the elections for the National Assembly, the, associations, together with Catholic election committees and the active support of the clergy, worked for the election of Catholic candidates. When the role of religion was debated in Frankfurt in the summer of 1848, the associations generated a flood of petitions which made the public aware of the Catholic demands.

In Prussia, the movement was led by Archbishop Geissel. In consultation with his auxiliaries he adopted Lennig's suggestion of a synod of all German bishops and pursued it diligently. He drafted a religious policy program which attenuated the desire of liberal Catholics for a separation of church and state and held fast to a continued parallelism to the extent that it was useful for the Church. It demanded autonomy but simultaneously also the maintenance of protection by the state and of legal privileges for the Church. It had great significance for the future development of the Church in Germany.

The active Catholics among the Frankfurt delegates worked for the realization of this program. They belonged to different political factions and were therefore not yet a regular party but only a working group under the name of "Catholic Club."

Geissel, attempting skillfully to coordinate these forces, was a member of the Prussian Diet, where he led the Catholic representatives. At the same time the archbishop followed the path of direct negotiations with the government. As parliamentary work in Berlin made only slow progress and there were strongly anticlerical forces on the left, this way was realistic as well as programmatic. Most of the Church leaders wanted greater freedom, but they also wanted to maintain the alliance between throne and altar. Alternatives were not considered. Geissel was not in favor of cooperation between Rhenish Catholics and political liberalism, and he and Diepenbrock defended the threatened authority of the crown.

In Frankfurt the position of the Church also was debated vigorously, but in September a compromise was found which satisfied central demands of the churches. In the section on basic rights, all Germans were guaranteed freedom of religion and of conscience; all groups were permitted the public exercise of religion, and civil rights were neither a precondition of nor limited by religion. The greatest success of the churches consisted of being granted the right to regulate and administer themselves within the framework of general laws. Autonomy was achieved and separation from the state was avoided. Combined with the freedom for churches was their equality; the privileged existence of some denominations was abandoned. The liberal parliamentary majority also insisted on some core demands of its concepts of state and society, in the face of which the churches were pushed into a helpless defensive. Civil marriage was introduced, and all public education was placed under the authority of the state, with the exception of religious instruction. Private schools, however, were permitted.

In spite of the failure of the National Assembly, the religious policy compromise of the constitution was significant and even influenced the Weimar constitution. It also had direct results, thanks to Geissel's exertions. The Frankfurt concessions to the churches became part of the Prussian constitution imposed by the King. It renounced the right of approval, the right of the state to participate in the filling of clerical positions, and it facilitated the founding of orders. The revised constitution of January 1850 confirmed these rights. Under the influence of the conservative reaction it also accepted the Christian religion as the basis of all those state institutions which were connected with religion. It was generally assumed that this basis was provided by the two major denominations. The regulation of civil marriage was postponed until later (it was introduced only during the *Kulturkampf*), and for elementary schools consideration of denominational conditions was accepted. The relaxation of tension in the relationship between church and state thus reached its zenith.

During the celebration of the building of the Cologne Cathedral in August 1848, an affair equally ecclesiastical and national, Lennig's suggestion of a national meeting of the representatives of Catholic associations met with general approval. At the beginning of October the first German Catholic Conference took place in Mainz; it was characteristic for its structure that it was presided over by a layman, Buß, and that the bishop of Mainz did not take part in the proceedings. Twenty-three representatives came from Frankfurt, and Döllinger made a programmatic speech in which he demanded a greater degree of freedom for the Church than the National Assembly had granted. He pleaded for a uniform, nationally and historically based organization of the German Church; it would not limit papal primacy, but it would give the Church the weight it deserved. While the majority applauded the speech, the ultramontanes began to have their first doubts. They did not know how to reconcile such autonomy with their centralistic concept.

The Mainz Catholic Conference was the start of a lasting integration of German Catholicism. The most important concrete results were the creation of a central organization, the "German Catholic Association," and religious decisions which were directed not against the thrones but merely against the concept of established churches, demanding freedom of religion as well as guarantees under law. The Catholic Association was to be led by laymen and to pursue national goals. But the increasing anticlericalism of many liberals, the failure of the Frankfurt National Assembly, and the subsequent rise of a revolutionary radicalism allowed the growth of uncertainty with respect to political goals. The two Catholic conferences in Breslau and Regensburg in 1849 agreed on political neutrality and on concentration of energies on ecclesiastical concerns. The Regensburg conference declared religious freedom to be the prerequisite for national unity and accused the Frankfurt National Assembly of not having considered this historical truth adequately.

In 1848 Archbishop Geissel managed to convince most of his colleagues to convene a bishops' conference and to invite eminent theologians, among them Döllinger, and laymen as advisers. He designed a tentative program, calling for freedom of religion and reforms in ecclesiastical structure and preaching. Reiterating Döllinger, the archbishop came out in favor of a structural unity of the German Church, which measure was not to be understood as directed against Rome but only against tutelage by the state. He also favored greater rights for the lower clergy and laity and greater use of German in the liturgy.

The first German bishops' conference took place from 22 October to 16 November 1848 in Würzburg under Geissel's chairmanship and largely adopted his program. Of the Austrian bishops, only Cardinal Schwarzenberg (Salzburg) participated. In an extensive memorandum to all German governments the conference formulated its religious demands, thus placing the episcopate in the lead of the ecclesiastical movement for freedom. The memorandum contained a consistent maximal program for the emancipation of the Church from the state and thereby determined the direction for future disputes, especially in southern and southwestern Germany. After lively discussions the majority of the bishops voted in favor of a national organization under the leadership of a primate as well as for timely reforms of church regulations and liturgy. The Pope was asked for permission for a formal national council which was to implement the decisions.

The papal reply was half a year in coming and was negative. The novel initiative of the German bishops had caused suspicion and doubts in the Curia; in fact, Rome had tried to torpedo the conference. Pius IX was not prepared to grant the bishops supradiocesan responsibilities and in ignorance of the people active in Germany (including Döllinger!), shades of Febronius and of the Ems Congress were conjured. Suspicion was awakened and fed persistently by the intransigent Munich internuncio Sacconi and Archbishop Reisach, who closely cooperated with him. Their criticism was focused on the plans for a national church organization and the liturgical reforms and clearly presaged the internal divisions of the Church during the subsequent two decades.

The German bishops accepted the papal decision postponing a national council for an indefinite period of time. After all, they had not intended an action unacceptable to the Pope, and besides, national enthusiasm had considerably diminished in the meantime. Once again the Church had to deal with the individual states after the revolutions.

Thanks to the bold efforts of Anton Günther, Sebastian Brunner (1814–93), and Emanuel Veith (1787–1870), the association movement in 1848 spread to Austria. Cardinal Schwarzenberg, a disciple of Günther's, in August 1848 sent petitions to the Reichstag; after his return from Würzburg he intensified his efforts for the activation of the episcopate. Only when there was no longer any doubt about the victory of the counterrevolution did the Josephinist Viennese archbishop Vincenz Milde (1777–1853) ask the young Emperor Franz Joseph for the convocation of an all-Austrian bishops' conference. The Emperor, who in the Patent of 4 March appended to the Constitution had granted all Christian denominations the right to the autonomous regulation of their affairs, and the government led by Prince Felix Schwarzenberg, a brother of the Cardinal, agreed to the project. The conference took place in Vienna between 27 April and 17 June 1849; its chief participants were Schwarzenberg, Rauscher, and Diepenbrock, entitled to participate because of the Austrian part of Breslau. Basing itself on the Patent of 4 March, the conference appealed to Emperor and government for the dismantling of Josephinist legislation and for a concordat for the border areas. From now on, this was a persistent demand by the bishops. Franz Joseph, a pupil of Rauscher's, quite in keeping with the recommendations by Metternich, was desirous of assuring his restoration policy through an agreement with the Church. His decrees of 18 and 23 April 1850 satisfied the most important demands of the bishops (among others lifting of the *placet*, freedom of communication with Rome, free exercise of episcopal disciplinary powers), thus starting the Church policy which led to the concordat of 1855.

The Netherlands

The support given to Thorbecke's liberal party by the Catholic middle class in the northern provinces made a peaceful revolution possible, leading to the constitution of 1848. The Catholics, desirous of complete freedom in education, had to be satisfied with a compromise, but received full satisfaction in all other areas.

Owing to freedom of assembly, the last obstacles were removed for religious orders. In spite of the efforts of the conservatives among the Reformed to give the country the character of a "Protestant nation," the new constitution proclaimed the equality of all religious denominations before the law and the right of each denominational community to regulate its own affairs.

The restoration of a regular episcopal organization, on the agenda for longer than thirty years, had to appear as the crowning point of this complete and legal emancipation. But in reality it was not desired by many priests. In the rural south they were satisfied, ever since in 1842 the vicars apostolic had assumed the character of an *Ordinarius loci,* and in the cities of the north the archpriests and regular clergy feared the loss of their autonomy. The laymen of the north, supported by a few priests of the group clustered around Warmond and the bishop of Liège, Van Bommel, who was of Dutch descent, pleaded with Rome for real bishops. Their main reason was their wish to have a local authority capable of guiding them in all political questions touching the interests of the Church.

They all agreed in principle, but differed in the modalities. Those who were close to the office in The Hague responsible for the Catholic religion would have preferred a concordatory solution or at least an agreement with the state negotiated on the basis of the Mechelen School; the strongly liberal group of the young Papo-Thorbeckians of the *Tijd* chiefly desired the independence of the Church from the state, even at the cost of complete separation. The demands of the government, which had to take into account the rejection by the Protestants of the establishment of dioceses in the north, forced the Holy See to accept the second solution and to decide unilaterally how to restore the hierarchy. In order to offend the Protestants as little as possible, it was at first planned, in agreement with the suggestions of the internuncio and vicar apostolic of 's-Hertogenbosch, Monsignor Zwijsen, to establish only one diocese in the north and three in the south, including the see of the metropolitan. But the prefect of the Propaganda, on the occasion of a visit, convinced himself not only of the numerically growing importance of Catholicism in the north, but also of its dynamic nature, and it was finally decided in a kind of restoration of the pre-Reformation hierarchy to make Utrecht the archiepiscopal see and to add four auxiliary dioceses: Haarlem for the large coastal cities, Breda, 's-Hertogenbosch, and Roermond for Brabant and Limburg.

The establishment bull of 4 March 1853 caused a wave of protest on the part of the Protestants which became known as the "April Movement," but it had a more political than religious nature. The prejudices of many Calvinists against the Pope were exploited by the reactionaries opposed to the liberal cabinet which had made the Roman decision possible. These attempts to place in question the favorable articles of the constitution of 1848 nevertheless failed because of the hesitant attitude of King Willem II. The King held no sympathies for the Roman Church, but considered it dangerous for the unity of the country to drive the Catholics to the extreme.

Disregarding the Protestant agitation, the new bishops, under the directorship of Zwijsen, who was appointed archbishop of Utrecht, immediately began to rewrite Church regulations according to canon law. He was an industrious pastor, had no interest in intellectual pursuits, but possessed common sense and strength of character. During this difficult period these virtues were of use, but they also contributed their healthy share to the ultramontane, ghetto character of Dutch Catholicism for the next one hundred years.

Under the strict leadership of an episcopate whose authority was limited by neither government nor traditions, surrounded by a pious, active and steadily growing clergy, and ministered to by regular clergy of both sexes, whose growth was even greater, the faithful had hardly any opportunity to make efforts of their own. They accepted this clericalism, unthinkable in any other environment, without any hesitation and supported the clergy with remarkable generosity. For all areas of life the Catholics founded associations. Thus they guaranteed the maintenance of religious life, and non-practicing Catholics, aside from the workers, remained an exception. But at the same time these social organizations contributed to keeping the Catholics away from most expressions of national life.

The isolation was noticeable especially on the cultural level. While a small body of Catholic intellectuals came into being among the urban middle class, intellectual life on the whole stagnated. While Catholics were well represented in music and architecture — here as everywhere else the Neo-Gothic was in full flower — their contribution to literature was minimal. Much more serious was the fact that their shortsighted suspicions of educational literature mired them in an almost total ignorance of the great literary movements of the time. In philosophy and theology, Catholic Dutch publications hardly rose above the level of reference books for seminaries or popular apologetic writings. Only a few exceptions stood out from the prevailing mediocrity.

Part Two

The Catholic Reaction
to Liberalism

I N T R O D U C T I O N

Pius IX after 1848

Pius IX was still relatively young when at the age of fifty-four he was chosen Pope by cardinals chiefly concerned with a solution of the political problems of the Papal State. Yet in this very area he failed completely. On the other hand, his unusually long pontificate (1846–78) profoundly and lastingly affected the fate of the Catholic Church.

He was not at all a strong personality, such as his successor Leo XIII. But Pius IX managed rather effortlessly to win a large number of the clerics and of the faithful for his ecclesiastical, theological, and spiritual concepts.

His contemporaries were unanimous in agreeing on his fascinating charm. He loved being in contact with people and increased the number of audiences, during which with loving good nature he received not only a few notables, as his predecessors had done, but also numerous priests and laymen, who, owing to the improvement of transportation, flocked to Rome in ever greater numbers. The visitors, taken by their kind reception, after returning to their home countries broadcast their impressions, and consequently there developed a real papal adulation in the Catholic world. The adulation facilitated to a high degree the enthusiastic agreement of many to an increasingly centralized leadership of the Church and to a coordination of the regional Churches with a certain type of Catholicism preferred by Rome.

The Pope, because of his fervent piety, trust in providence, and strength of soul in adversity, praised by many as a saint during his lifetime, appeared to others, including many clerics and many a militant layman whose devotion to the Church was unquestioned, as no more than a vain autocrat or a puppet maneuvered by insensitive reactionaries. Both impressions are one-sided and simplistic.

Pius IX labored under three handicaps. In his youth he suffered from epileptic attacks which left him with an extreme excitability. It makes understandable many of his summary declarations and the fact that he frequently changed his mind according to the opinion last heard. Consequently, many observers regarded him as a hesitant and indecisive person. Only when he was convinced that it was a matter of consequence did he demonstrate unshakable resolution and boldly defend his position. The second handicap was that like most of the Italian clerics of his age, raised during the first two decades of the nineteenth century with the upheavals of the Napoleonic era, his education was rather inadequate. His superficial training often did not permit him to recognize the complexity of problems or the implications of many statements which he was expected to judge. This lack was partly compensated for by his Italian shrewdness, which allowed him to understand much without being very erudite. Thus Pius IX was able to apply common sense in assessing concrete situations, at least as long as they were reported to him accurately. Unfortunately, and that was his third handicap, his staff was not always able to inform him with the required care. His trusted advisers were generally conscientious and industrious, but also rather exalted and often viewed matters with the uncompromising attitude of theoreticians out of touch with contemporary views. Under these circumstances it is not surprising that Pius IX failed to adapt the Church to new conditions. These were on the one hand the profound evolution which was in the process of completely altering the structures of civil society, and on the other the totally changed perspectives by which certain theological positions needed to be viewed in light of the progress made in the natural sciences and historical research.

If the capabilities of Pius IX had undeniable limits, especially regrettable in a superior who increasingly was compelled to make solitary decisions in many areas, he must also be credited with qualities and achievements which cannot be regarded as small. This was first of all true on the personal level. Pius IX was a genuinely unpretentious and good person, equipped with a sensitivity which permitted him to make charming gestures and have happy ideas, without excluding, if he considered it advisable, a sometimes rude frankness. He was sufficiently supple to make occasional concessions which at first sight looked dangerous, because more than the tacticians in his environment, he relied on trust built on personal relations. He was not an intellectual, but was interested in all kinds of problems, and in his youth had read extensively. After he became Pope, he kept abreast of modern inventions. He knew how to pray, and the depth of his religious sentiments was undeniable, even if in this area, as in others, he combined weaknesses with virtues. He attached too much weight to prophecies and other manifestations of the miraculous, and tended to see in the political convulsions which involved the Church a new episode in the great battle between God and Satan instead of realistically subjecting the events to a technical analysis.

At the beginning of his priestly life, at a time when most young clerics are concerned with making a career, he completely renounced ecclesiastical honors and devoted himself to orphans and other poor. As bishop he impressed the people of his diocese by the apostolic strength with which he rose above party struggles in order to minister to everyone, including the enemies of the papal government. Even after he became Pope, his chief concern was to act as priest and pastor, responsible before God for the defense of Christian values, which were jeopardized by rationalism and the increasing ungodliness of laicism. He increasingly encouraged the ultramontane movement, but not for reasons of personal ambition or love of theocracy, which tempted him less than his successor Leo XIII. He was ultramontane only because this movement appeared to him as the prerequisite for a rejuvenation of Catholic life wherever the intervention of governments in the Church seemed to throttle it, and because he saw it as the best means to coordinate all vital forces of Catholicism for the struggle against the rising flood of anti-Christian liberalism. This attitude explains his resistance to liberalism and his ever more violent condemnation of it. The Pope was part of the political philosophy of the traditionalistic type prevalent among Catholics during the middle of the nineteenth century. As such he was incapable of differentiating among the confused strivings of his time between those of positive value, which actually prepare the ground for a stronger spiritualization of the Catholic understanding of faith, and senseless concessions to fleeting fashions or even unconscious compromises with ideologies which failed to correspond to the Christian spirit. Above all he lacked realism in his church-political ideal, which throughout his entire pontificate he chased with an uncontrollable energy better expended on a worthier cause.

In contrast to these doubtlessly grave defects and missed opportunities, which we can easily see from today's perspective, stands the fact that the long pontificate also had great positive effects. Many things changed in the world and in the Church after Pius IX became Pope. The strongest ecclesiastical change took place with respect to the quality of the average Catholic life, beginning with the spiritual and pastoral standards of the clergy, the chief instrument of preaching the faith in the view of that century. Pius IX also contributed a considerable share, primarily by providing his contemporaries with his personal example of piety and Christian rebirth, which characterized the second third of the nineteenth century. Even more important than his personal example was Pius' activity. Because a tough attitude in practical and doctrinal terms appeared to him as indispensable for complete success, he forced himself, in spite of a personal inclination to mediation and mitigation, to the reiteration of principles which constituted the basis of his doctrine. Occasionally he did so with a deplorable lack of subtlety.

No Pope, no matter how active and independent, can perform without advisers. Of those who for many years enjoyed the confidence of Pius IX there were chiefly Borromeo, Ricci, and Stella, devoted and scrupulous men, yet without great vision and guided by reactionary tendencies. Of greater weight were two foreigners, George Talbot, an Englishman related to Borghese, and Xavier de Merode, half Belgian, half French, who together with Prince Gustav von Hohenlohe were appointed in 1850 after the return of Pius IX to Rome for the purpose of underscoring the international role of the papacy. Talbot and Merode were intelligent men, holding less simplistic views with respect to modern society than was generally the case in Rome. But in their judgments both failed to consider the pros and cons and more than once encouraged the Pope, who placed great confidence in them, to assume an intransigent stance.

While Pius IX's immediate entourage thus played a larger, if unofficial, role than that of his predecessors and successors — "influence without responsibility" Dom C. Butler called it — a noticeable reduction in the importance of the College of Cardinals took place, both with respect to the secular administration of the Papal State and the religious direction of the Church. With respect to the Papal State, Antonelli conducted affairs; concerning the cardinals, their selection occurred under new criteria. When in 1850 Pius IX created ten foreign and only four Italian cardinals, he signalled clearly that the essential task of the Sacred College was no longer that of administering the Papal State. The internationalization of the College of Cardinals continued. At the time of the death of Gregory XVI there were eight foreign and fifty-four Italian cardinals; when Pius IX died, there were twenty-five foreign and thirty-nine Italian cardinals. The Italians by themselves were no longer able to produce the two-thirds majority required for the election of a Pope. The internationalization went hand in hand with another change. The representatives of the Roman aristocracy and the high functionaries in important administrative and political positions, who in the past had constituted the majority in the College of Cardinals, were gradually replaced by men of the Church of often modest background who excelled in pastoral work, theological knowledge, or ultramontane zeal. But in spite of this development the role of the College of Cardinals in the religious leadership of the Church grew smaller to such a degree that on the eve of the council the French ambassador wrote: "Never before was the role of the cardinals so modest and their influence so insignificant as today."

Pius IX liked to inform himself directly about matters and did not hesitate, in the process of reaching a decision, to ignore regular channels. Unfortunately, all too often he relied on informants who were partisan or who lacked a sense for the complexity of concrete situations daily facing the Church. While the meetings of the consistories and commissions of cardinals for the discussion of problems touching upon the Church became rarer, individual cardinals personally played a significant role. Some of them headed primary agencies — the most important of them were Giacomo Antonelli, secretary of state from 1848 until his death in 1876, and Alessandro Barnabo, the competent and energetic head of the Congregation for the Propagation of the Faith from 1856 until 1874 — others simply enjoyed the personal confidence of the Pope. Among the latter were Cardinals Gaude and Bilio, in charge of dogmatic questions, Mertel for legal affairs, Franchi for church-political problems, and Reisach for the concerns of German-speaking countries but especially there was Cardinal Patrizi, a friend of the Pope, who for thirty years had unhindered access to him. Patrizi was an example of virtue and piety, but with a rather narrow mind.

The continuing centralization of the Church naturally enlarged the importance of the nunciatures and of the Roman congregations. But most of the contemporary observers noted with regret the frequent mediocrity of the staff of both institutions. The men concerned were generally very respectable concerning their morals and piety and well versed in the subtleties of canon law and the theology of reference books, but overwhelmingly they lacked an understanding of the modern world and its developments. They "favored everything that was old, from dress to opinions, from labels to theology," Cochin wrote in 1862. They displayed a hostility toward critical methods which expressed not only their distrust of the new direction of philosophy, history, and natural sciences, but also the thoughtlessness with which they accepted and even encouraged denunciations of all who intellectually and religiously failed to share their conformist views. This well-meant but short-sighted attitude merely postponed the solution of problems, and the more open-minded approaches under Leo XIII often came too late. These could not completely make up for lost time, so that the actual roots of the crisis of modernism go back to the pontificate of Pius IX.

There were numerous positive sides. One of the most important was the intensification of Christian life, in which, in addition to local efforts, Pius IX and some of his collaborators had a large personal share. There now arose a large movement of popular piety and priestly spirituality. It has often been accused of too much superficiality, but this simplifying condemnation is contradicted by the flowering of church activities and the tremendous growth of orders. At the same time, during these three decades, the Church also became stronger externally. Promoted by the colonial expansion of Europe, there was on all five continents a missionary expansion under the centralizing impulse of the Vatican. The immigration of Catholics led to the creation of new Churches in Canada, Australia, the United States, and Latin America. The old Churches, existing under difficult conditions since the Reformation, were reorganized in England, the Netherlands, and above all in Germany. The resistance recorded during the *Kulturkampf* demonstrated the vitality which this Church was able to develop within a few years through its connection with the Holy See. For together with the quantitative expansion of the

Catholic Church went its closer ties with the Pope. The growth of Roman centralization, solemnly sanctioned by the Vatican Council, without a doubt represented
one of the most striking phenomena of this pontificate.

The triumph of ultramontanism caused the reaction of governments which
did not like the removal of the local clergy from their influence. Additionally, the
parties of the left mobilized against the Church in the wake of its compromises
with the antirevolutionary systems, underscored by sensational condemnations
of liberalism. Thus the last years of the pontificate were darkened by numerous
conflicts. At the moment of Pius IX's death (7 February 1878) it was easy to assume
at first sight that the Church was totally stranded in a sea of hostile public opinion.

But in reality it was not only consolidated internally, but had begun, precisely
at the moment when the disappearance of the Papal State eliminated the papacy from the traditional diplomatic chess board of Europe, "to become a world
power of which every policy must take account" (H. Marc-Bonnet). This was
demonstrated at the start of the pontificate of Leo XIII.

Section One

The Temporary Improvement
in the Situation of the Church

Chaps. 28, 30/II, 31, 32: Roger Aubert
Chap. 29: Rudolf Lill
Chap. 30/I: Patrick J. Corish

The Church appeared to have emerged with flying colors from the crisis of 1848, so worrisome to its officials, on two levels. In part it profited from a turn toward conservatism, which, concerned about the rise of democratic demands, expected from it assistance in stabilizing the bourgeois order. After all, Tocqueville's statement that "the fear of socialism has the same effect on the bourgeoisie as the Revolution had on the aristocracy," applied not only to France. At the same time the Church benefitted from the concessions to liberalism of which governments were compelled to take account through a moderation of their regalistic policies or even through the granting of complete independence to the Church. This stabilized condition enabled the Holy See to arrange a number of favorable concordats. The most spectacular one was that signed with Austria in 1855. Recognition of freedom of religion, already in effect for Belgium, Great Britain, and the United States, was also incorporated in the new constitutions of Prussia and the Netherlands and produced the same beneficial results for the growth of Catholicism in these states. Finally, systematically resumed missionary work, in conjunction with European colonial expansion, resulted in noticeable successes after the middle of the century. They permitted the impression that the Church had overcome the great crisis of the past one hundred years and could look optimistically to the future. But the euphoria was of short duration. The situation worsened again after the 1860s and again brought home the truth that it was always a mistake for the Church to rely too much on institutional advantages which it had obtained through nothing more than good fortune. Yet the favorable condition almost everywhere in evidence during the first years of the pontificate of Pius IX made possible the stabilization and spiritual intensification of the Catholic renaissance. In spite of the uncertainties in many countries this condition must therefore not be underestimated when one attempts to form an exact picture of the religious situation during the final quarter of the nineteenth century.

CHAPTER 28

The Seeming Success of the Church in France during the Second Empire and the "Moral Order"

The Privileged Status of the Church

The favoritisms extended to the Church under the Second Republic were increased at the beginning of the Second Empire. The Emperor and his advisers were not particularly interested in giving preference to the Church, but as conservative opportunists they were aware of the advantages of the moral and social force of religion in checking revolutionary propaganda. Moreover, association with the Church seemed to them a good way of binding legitimist circles to the Empire.

The government visibly enlarged the religious budget, made virtually no attempt to apply the Organic Articles, closed its eyes to the rapid growth of orders, suppressed antireligious tendencies in public education, and looked for opportunities to let the Church share in the prestige of the state. In response to the revolutionary excesses a good number of the middle class — and not only property owners — returned to the Church, seeing in it an effective guaranty for the maintenance of the social order. Having gradually regained its influence on the leading elements since the beginning of the century, the clergy now also obtained the assistance of many high officials. In an authoritarian regime their power was not to be underestimated and through them the benevolent attitude of the government toward the Church found strong expression. In addition, the universal right to vote, introduced in 1848, provided the lower clergy, which had maintained close contact with the people in the rural areas and small towns, a power which it had not yielded before.

But the clergy failed to exercise restraint, and to the extent that revolutionary threats diminished, the government began to be suspicious of the growing importance of clerics in public life. The tactless policy of Nuncio Sacconi (1853–61) and the systematic efforts of the ultramontane party to exclude completely any influence of the government in ecclesiastical matters led to a reawakening of the Gallican tradition of a Ministry of Religion. The crisis, present in embryo after 1856, erupted with the development of the Roman Question after the Italian War (1859). The leaders of the Catholic movement, having until now hailed Napoleon III as a latter-day Charlemagne, were very disappointed when the Emperor agreed to a division of the Papal State. They tried to raise a wave of protest in the country, but did not have much success. This convinced the government that the people no longer followed the lead of the clergy as much as before. It appointed bishops who refused to accept the increasing interference of the Roman Curia in France, stopped the further growth of orders and religious communities, and gave preference to the public schools. It increasingly resorted to chicanery in order to destroy the influence of the clergy, but ostensibly continued to promote religion in and outside of the country so as not to lose the confidence of the Catholic population.

The policy, moderated by the benevolent neutrality of many Catholic civil servants, created indignation among the clergy. It also succeeded in drawing a number of notables to the side of the opposition. The growth of the Republican

Party after 1863 therefore persuaded the government to return to a less hostile policy in order to regain the good will of the "Clerical Faction." While the cabinet continued to tolerate the attacks of the anticlerical press against the Church, it tried in other ways to regain the confidence of the clergy. It hoped that after the appointment of a number of Gallican-oriented bishops the clergy would less compliantly adhere to the increasingly intransigent positions of the Vatican with respect to problems of modern civilization.

Owing to the Roman Question and the convention of September 1864, this pacification policy did not have immediate results. But after the intervention of French troops in Mentana (1867) nothing stood any longer in the way of the reconciliation desired by both sides. The joint fear of the republican opposition led the two powers to cooperation. Once again it tied the declining Empire to the conservative force of the clergy, which, in turn, was apprehensive of the anticlericalism displayed by the republicans.

The reputable standing of religion and the improvement of the material and moral condition of the rural clergy, which until the middle of the century stood on the sidelines of Christian intellectual life, soon had its effects on the number of priests. This increase was also affected by the Falloux Law. The number of ordinations in France climbed by more than a third, and the total number of priests rose from 46,969 in 1853 to 56,295 in 1869. The increase enabled the bishops to fill numerous vicariates, to raise the number of clerics in public service.

The training of the clergy, however, remained deficient. In spite of the efforts of a few discerning bishops seminary instruction, imparted by insufficiently educated teachers, hardly rose above the level of a catechism taught in Latin. The priests trained in them were virtuous, but more inclined to minister to the "converted" than to make contact with the increasingly indifferent populace or to counter the prejudices of upwardly mobile people. It is not surprising, therefore, that the clergy — with the exception of a numerically limited elite — regarded Louis Veuillot as their model. With absolutely uncritical zeal they followed the directions of *L'Univers,* a paper which fed the clergy's ultramontane enthusiasm and its mistrust of the "modern world."

If the majority of the lower clergy after the 1850s became ultramontane, they did so primarily in the hope of gaining in the Roman Curia a counterweight to the authoritarian stance of the bishops. They strengthened controls, transferred personnel without consideration of their personal desires, put out detailed regulations on Church discipline and pastoral work, and left little initiative to their priests. This systematic and dutiful activity resulted from their wish to guide their dioceses in the best interest of religion, but in most cases their efforts regrettably were not matched by pastoral sensitivity. On the whole, the upper clergy was extremely colorless and — with a few exceptions, such as Dupanloup or Freppel — not at all the belligerent episcopate depicted by the anticlerical press. Instead of thoroughly rethinking the methods of the apostolate, the bishops were satisfied with the institutionalization of those methods which had proved effective during the first half of the century. Thus, disregarding the migration of people resulting from the industrialization, positions in the countryside were increased while there was a crying need for additional parishes in the burgeoning cities.

The work of the bishops and the clergy was much facilitated by the assistance of the orders. For them the Second Empire was a time of growth; this was especially true for the female congregations, which were favored by the law of 31 January 1852. Between 1851 and 1861 the number of nuns increased from 34,208 to 89,243; membership in the male orders rose from 3,000 to 17,656.

The rapid growth of orders and congregations provided the Church with the necessary manpower for reaching two goals. These were entry into public education and free education. The Church was not satisfied with the exercise of supervision of the teachers by the pastors; the practice was made possible by the Falloux Law, but gave rise to frequent friction. The Church wanted to obtain from communal councils, which were often kindly disposed toward the Church, permission to entrust public schools to the supervision by members of orders. Simultaneously, advantage was taken of a favorable tax law facilitating gifts of money and property to increase the number of Catholic schools and colleges. By preferentially admitting students from socially prominent families they attracted the attention of the middle class and contributed to a change in its attitude. Between 1850 and 1875 the number of children educated by teachers of orders rose from 953,000 to 2,168,000, while the number of students in the lay schools rose only from 2,309,000 to 2,649,000.

The dubious character of this achievement was clearly recognized by A. Latreille: "The kind disposition of the government of Napoleon III to congregations and their schools must be regarded as the most significant fact of the history of French Catholicism between 1830 and 1880. It provided the Church with a large degree of satisfaction and possibilities of influence which it had been denied ever since the Revolution. But more than anything else it contributed to the growing distrust of the Church." This distrust became militant especially after 1870, but even during the Second Empire the desire to stop the progress of the Church grew stronger among those who suspiciously watched the influence of the "clericals" (the expression was coined during this period). After a few years, during which public education in view of the republican sympathies of the public teachers consciously had been neglected, Rouland undertook his reorganization in order to fashion public schools into a viable competitor for the schools maintained by the congregations. In spite of repeated protests by the episcopate, Victor Duruy after 1863 with varying success obstructed the development of free Catholic education and freed public schools from the influence of the Church. His ministerial policy found a ready echo as the success of the *Ligue française pour l'enseignement public* attested.

Although the government was not willing to allow the Church to drive it out of charitable work, it nevertheless pointedly requested the Catholics to participate in this social work. Thus, in addition to poorhouses and hospitals, Catholic facilities of all kinds were established. There were welfare associations and works for poor sick people; mutual help associations, especially in southern France; youth homes and other organizations devoted to young laborers. The initiators of these enterprises generally were religious congregations (some of them founded expressly for this purpose), laymen from the rural nobility, and wealthy people from the middle class. Many of them were branches of the Society of Saint Vincent de Paul, whose legitimist orientation on the part of some of its leaders in 1861 occasioned sensational interference by the Ministry of the Interior, or of the *Société d'économie charitable.*

In addition to these charitable actions there were many others which, while very active, were too fragmented to achieve a national stature. There were apologetic works, directed against the "bad press"; missionary works which enjoyed particular popularity; and works of piety (eternal adoration, nocturnal adoration, priest associations, congregations of the Most Blessed Virgin, etc.), all of which showed that beyond the social utility of religion an elite of the French middle class rediscovered genuine Christian values. Finally, one event in the France of the Second Empire must not be forgotten: Lourdes in a very short time "became not only the most visited object of pilgrimage in a country already rich in historical holy places, but the world center of prayer and active charity" (Latreille).

This apparently magnificent condition was hardly affected by the fall of the Empire in 1870. The seizure of power by the republicans, almost without exception anticlerical and Freemasons, initially worried the Catholics, but the excesses of the Commune led, just as in 1848, to a shift to the right. The National Assembly, consisting largely of conservative rural nobility and upper bourgeoisie, was especially friendly to the Church. The government of the "Moral Order," whose leaders were friends of Monsignor Dupanloup, tried, much to the dismay of the paper *L'Univers,* to present Catholicism more as a useful social force than as the official state religion. But it did not at all object to the desire of the Church to infuse the state's institutions with a Christian spirit. Disregarding the republican concept of secularization, it strengthened the influence of the clergy in the army, public welfare, and education.

The Church was able to exploit its legal advantages because it could call on more personnel. There was also a dark cloud, however: except for a few secluded areas like the Jura or the southern part of the central region of the country, the number of seminarists was declining. Inasmuch as the mortality rate of the clergy was still low and the number of active priests increasing, the threat was not yet perceived. In 1870 the ratio of priests to flock was 1:730, by 1876 it was 1:654. Membership in the orders grew so much that M. Pouthas regarded the growth of the congregations as a characteristic of the Church during the beginning years of the republic. It enabled France to provide by far the strongest contingent of missionaries for the evangelization of the pagan peoples.

This large number of people alone, coming from all walks of life and signifying more than mere social climbing, together with the continued rise in piety and good works on the regional and national level, would be sufficient proof that the impression of a powerful Church was anything but a facade and that it still commanded large reserves of Christian strength. Actually, the religious awakening in 1870 extended far beyond this elite. Many people viewed the military defeats and the tragic convulsions of the Commune as divine punishment or at least as the logical consequence of the spread of "socialistic atheism" and the frivolity displayed by the Second Empire. The religious awakening found expression in more faithful attendance at Sunday services, greater morality, and in the growth of popular literature devoted to the adoration of the Sacred Heart of Jesus, Mary, and the saints. More spectacularly it was displayed in large pilgrimages of faith and repentance centered on the shrines of Lourdes, La Salette, and Paray-le-Monial.

It was through the efforts of the Assumptionists that Catholicism in these years again became popular and developed into the religion of the people. They took a long-range approach, addressed a broad public, moved the masses, and talked to them in plain language. After an interval of fifty years they resumed the work of the missions of the period of restoration. The visible crowning of their efforts was the construction of the cathedral of Sacré-Coeur on Montmartre.

The Ambivalence of the Actual Religious Situation

The favorable conditions just described should not obscure the truth, however. At the very moment when contemporaries were able to record these achievements, the signs of that religious crisis began to appear which was to emerge fully during the final quarter of the century. The seemingly brilliant condition of the institutions on one hand and the effects of a small spiritual elite on the other tended too often to conceal the actual condition of the great mass of the people, which, after all, was the important ingredient of the Church.

First of all, geographical differences must be considered. A large part of the west, the central region, the Alps, and the Jura, remained closely tied to their faith until the end of the century. Religion was practiced there by many men, the supply of recruits for the priesthood, missions, and orders was abundant, and the new types of piety were received well, especially in the rural areas. The populace, increasingly well integrated with a growing number of priests and a network of Catholic schools, resisted fairly well the blandishments of a society which tried to laicize it.

In other areas, even under the July Monarchy in the process of becoming alien-ated from Christianity, considerable efforts were undertaken to win them back. The efforts were guided by active bishops such as Dupanloup in Orléans, Dupont des Loges in Metz, and Parisis in Arras. These prelates were actively assisted by people specially trained for preaching in the parish missions. This intensive mis-sionary activity during the Second Empire, spurred on by the administration and high notables, in some cases resulted in a considerable revival of religious prac-tices, at least before 1870. But in essence it touched only the middle class of small towns and the stale parishes in devout areas. Elsewhere, the differences between the sexes became more pronounced. The women tended to take their religion seriously, while the men largely stayed away from Sunday and Easter services.

The situation was worse in the area of Paris, in the departments of the Charente, in the southeast, and in Provence, where religious practice, weak even before 1848, sank to a level below the present one, in spite of hundreds of missions which had been conducted there. In some parishes not a single soul attended Easter services; the religious practice of the men was close to zero; about half of all marriages took place in front of a civil registrar only; many boys no longer went to their first Communion; and processions were molested. As the years went by, such conditions became more widespread.

Seen as a whole, a considerable part of France fell prey to religious indiffer-ence, notwithstanding the efforts of the regular and secular clergy, an indifference generally accompanied by a relentless hostility to the Church. In the countryside the hostility was strengthened by the growth of the means of communication and the more intimate contacts with the new urban civilization which they facilitated. There was also the systematic drumfire of the anticlerical newspapers, only feebly countered by the Catholic press, which was not sufficiently popular. It was further encouraged by the frequent conflicts erupting in the villages over the establishment of Catholic schools and the expensive building of parsonages. Frequently a role was played by the clergy's lust for power and money, their identification with the legitimist landlords, and their rigoristic and negative habit of preaching morality.

The world of artisans and laborers, still a minority but visibly growing, adhered to a kind of Christian atavism; in most areas of the country their alienation from the Catholic Church grew more pronounced. Separated from their rural roots, the workers easily succumbed to the immorality and the anticlericalism of the burgeoning cities. Generally, the clergy neglected them. Scheduling of services and ecclesiastical customs were not fitted to the working conditions of the industrial proletariat. The proletariat was being pushed to the sidelines of the Church, and many priests of rural background were discouraged by the difficulties of the workers' environment. The active religious participation of these people, aside from a small female minority, was limited to the chief events in life. Doubtlessly, the workers were also repulsed by the paternalistic attitude of the middle class to social problems. While the mass of the workers had not yet articulated its discontent, the militants accused the Church of hindering the social rise of the working class. Priests and bishops, in their own view tied to a divinely inspired static and hierarchical concept of society, condemned the attempts to improve the lot of the working class as "antisocial" and only emphasized in their sermons that earthly miseries would be rewarded in the next world. The outbreaks of violence directed against the clergy after the fall of the Empire in Paris, Lyon, and along the Mediterranean coast, all in sharp contrast to their indulgent behavior in 1848, was an indication of the rapid change in the attitude of the workers. The proletariat increasingly developed its own class consciousness, felt alienated socially and psychologically from traditional Catholicism, and began to regard the priests as enemies in the battle against the conservative forces. Only a few areas were spared this development. In Lille and other municipalities in the east small but strong Christian workers' associations were formed, and around the turn of the century their membership constituted the first Christian labor unions.

While the Church lost ground among the mass of the people, especially in the cities, it could console itself with gains among the middle class. A large part of the middle class, especially in the provinces in which the population remained faithful to the Church, returned to a genuine Christianity, generously gave of its time and money for Catholic works, and provided young people for the orders. But many others returned to the Church only because romanticism had made cathedrals fashionable and because, after the great fear of 1848, they saw in the Church a guarantee for social stability. Their attitude was more clerical than believing and contributed to exposing the Church in the eyes of the people, the more so as its morality, left much to be desired.

On the other hand, religion, especially in the provinces, became an external sign of respectability, even though the professions largely continued to remain anticlerical. In fact, especially among the left, which was angered by the agreement between Church and the Bonapartist government, anticlericalism was on the rise. Among the important reasons for this attitude were the anachronistic character of the Papal State, stoutly defended by the clergy, and the publication of the *Syllabus,* which was seen as the manifesto of the unreasonable demands of traditionalistic Catholic circles on society. Even more serious was the fact that the intellectuals — writers, scientists, historians, and philosophers — influenced by rationalism and positivism, which had taken the place of romanticism, became alienated not only from the Church but from the Christian faith and religion itself. The success of the book *La vie de Jésus* by Renan (1863) was symptomatic.

At about the same time the spiritualistic Freemasons adopted that hostility to religion which was to become characteristic for them. The lodges became the active centers of the idea of laicization. Based on the progress of science, it was not only to free society from the clerical yoke but also to liberate the human spirit from the fetters of dogma and the false belief in supernaturalism.

The men responsible for the fate of the Church in France began to be concerned, but they failed to grasp the true situation and, especially after 1870, their views lagged far behind the developments in their country. Most of them believed that all difficulties would cease if only the government gave stronger support to the Church. Even the small group of liberal Catholics around the *Correspondant,* which was aware of the illusory character of state protection, was unable to go beyond considerations of principles. They did not initiate actions comparable to those started at the same time by German and Belgian Catholics.

The deficiencies of French Catholicism were. also evident in its intellectual life. Catholicism seemed to be incapable of countering lack of faith in its very own bailiwick of philosophy and the history of Christian origins. Apologetic literature as well as episcopal pastoral letters and sermons were characteristic of a vague and romantic phraseology, marked by the total absence of introducing the clergy to a critical spirit and the new methods of scholarship. The bishops refused to acknowledge the necessity of such acquaintance, and with few exceptions they feared that by attending universities no longer under the control of the Church the priests would absorb dangerous ideas. The negotiations for the reestablishment of theological departments at universities, on the other hand, were stalled because of the distrust by the Holy See of the continuation of Gallican tendencies in France. A. J. Alphonse Gratry wanted to select a few qualified priests for a kind of "apologetic workshop," but the Oratory of France, reestablished in 1852, was diverted from its original aim by the more practical enterprises of its superior. Only with the founding of Catholic universities, made possible by the law of 1875, was a serious attempt made fifty years later to remove the intellectual deficiencies of the Church.

A further weakness of the Church in France during the Second Empire was the increasingly bitter disagreements of Catholics in various areas. The opponents of an excessive Roman centralization, clinging to the traditional habits of the old French clergy, were worried about the aggressive stance of the defenders of neo-ultramontanism. Liberal Catholics, convinced that the Church could regain the respect of the new leading elements through being more open-minded, and intransigent Catholics, seeing in modern liberties the reason for the decline of religious practice, accused one another of being responsible for the worsening of the situation, but failed to seek concrete ways to alleviate it. Liberal Catholics condemned the ultramontane integralism, but could not agree among themselves. Consumed by internal disputes, the majority did not realize that not only the future of Catholicism but of religion itself was at stake and that it was most urgent to close ranks in intellectual and social areas, where delay had worsened the situation.

The convulsions of 1870–71, far from opening the eyes of the responsible people, contributed to a further intensification of opposing views. The most agitated element of French Catholicism, confirmed in its authority by the defeat of the minority at the Vatican Council, wanted to connect the movement of religious revival with a two-fold restoration from which it expected the secular and spiritual salvation of France. These were the elevation of the Count of Chambord to the throne of the Bourbons and the installation of Pius IX in his restored Papal State.

The tactless manner in which this restoration was promoted, less so by the bishops, who remained relatively reserved, than by the lower clergy and militant Catholics, quickly mobilized the moderates. They saw in the "most Christian King" a herald of theocracy and feared that France would be driven to "make war for the Pope." The friends of Dupanloup and Duke de Broglie recognized the danger and disavowed the anachronistic goals of the radicals. But their moderate approach, diametrically opposed to that of the ultras, angered many adherents of "political supernaturalism," who condemned such a policy as spinelessness. The dispute between liberal Catholics and intransigent Catholics grew even more bitter than it had been under the Empire.

While the clergy in this fashion involved itself in noisy and fruitless controversies over the ideal political form of government, it continued to ignore the real problems of the hour: the training of modern-minded laymen, capable of effectively serving the Church in a society undergoing rapid secularization; the definition of its position with respect to the material and intellectual progress which the Church, to the great dismay of the multiplying admirers of scientific discoveries, was disregarding; and finally, and possibly foremost, the problem of social development. Most Catholics were convinced that the anticlerical movement had not come about spontaneously. They believed that it had been thought up by a radical intelligentsia and was not a reflection of the actual feelings of the French people, whom they saw as still strongly tied to their religious customs. They concluded that the intellectual crisis could be ended through censorship of the press. They failed to see the close connection which after 1870 in a kind of "messianic hope for the egalitarian, fraternal, and laicistic republic" developed between the militant, radical, and anticlerical wing of the republican middle class and the progressive elements of the urban and agrarian working class. The workers actually remembered only with hate the brutal suppression of the Commune, for which they also held the clergy responsible, as it was sociologically related to the conservative classes. The peasants suspected the clergy of wishing to reintroduce the tithe of the Old Regime together with the restoration of the monarchy. The middle class, finally, was more than ever convinced of the incompatibility of modern society with a Church which looked upon the *Syllabus* as its ideal. The anticlerical offensive started in 1878 with the seizure of power by the radicals thus encountered a well-prepared soil.

CHAPTER 29

The States of the German Confederation and Switzerland, 1848–70

The years 1848–49 showed that the partial alliance between Catholics and liberals rested on a weak foundation. Political and philosophical liberalism were difficult to separate. The same liberals who were engaged in the struggle for greater freedom, which was also of benefit for the Church, in their majority also asked for separation of Church and state, civil marriage, and public schools. Thus, they fought against positions regarded by the Church as unalterable. Furthermore, economic liberalism hurt the lower middle class and the peasants who were still loosely tied to the Church. These opposing views and the reliance of Catholics on the Roman Curia with its reactionary concepts had grave consequences after 1848. While the leaders of German Catholicism were eager to preserve the freedoms obtained in 1848 and extend them to all German states, they also turned away from liberalism and democracy and toward patriarchal conservatism. The consequence of the failed German revolution for the Church was that once again it was compelled to negotiate with the restored states and to take account of their reactionary policies during the subsequent decades.

Following the Roman example, the German bishops and leaders of the lay movement became convinced that only a monolithic Church would be able to counteract the prevailing liberalism, rationalism, and atheism. They also therefore tried to erect barriers against the intrusion of new ideas; while these barriers succeeded in preserving much of ecclesiastical substance, they also promoted the very isolation desired by opponents. The Church could think of nothing better to counter the turn to political liberalism, experienced by most of the German states toward the end of the 1850s, than an authoritarian defense. Catholics no longer participated in Germany's intellectual development, which was increasingly influenced by the technical and historical sciences. Anyone who adopted the new historical view of the world came in conflict with the Scholastic-juridical concepts promoted by Rome.

The leadership of the Catholic movement more and more was taken over by the circles in Mainz and Munich which most thoroughly turned away from liberalism and most effectively propagated their departure in Heinrich's and Moufang's *Katholik* and Jörg's *Historisch-politische Blätter*. Only the Rhenish Catholics remained relatively close to political liberalism; they had ties with progressive western Europe and, as a minority in the Prussian state, could expect benefits from the application of liberal principles.

In the national question as well, of tremendous concern to a large number of people, an unbridgeable riff developed in the 1850s between liberals and Catholics. The majority of the liberals were predominantly in favor of a Little German-Prussian solution. The liberals hailed the Italian unification (1859–60), whose fundamental principles were their own, regardless of the fact that implicitly it was directed against Austria and the Papal State. It encouraged their own activity, and they denied the inherent validity of the Catholic protests against the

Pope's loss of territory. The majority of the Catholics continued to cling to the concept of a Greater Germany, even though hopes for unification under Austria's auspices were increasingly improbable.

In Prussia, thanks to the constitutions of 1848 and 1850, the Church gained a new stature and new life, which affected other German states. Geissel and Diepenbrock, the most important persons in the Prussian episcopate, were created cardinals in 1850, but Diepenbrock died in 1853. After that date, leadership was completely in the hands of Geissel, dynamic organizer and church politician. He tried to preserve and enlarge the legal position obtained in 1848, to intensify religious life with the aid of ultramontane forms of piety, and to coordinate pastoral care and fresh activities of laymen. He also promoted uniformity of action by the episcopate and was able to hold a provincial council in 1860 in which most of the bishops of northern and western Germany participated. Through the assistance of the bishops the association movement was able to spread, and religious orders and congregations returned, thus permitting the establishment of hospitals, orphan homes, and schools. Sacramental and rosary prayers, pilgrimages and processions were reintroduced, and the dogma of 1854 encouraged the veneration of Mary. The orders also enabled Geissel to revive the missions to the people, which had languished since the Enlightenment. After initial distrust, the missionaries were assisted by some state officials, as the preachers also defended conservative authority and spoke against revolution, socialism, and democracy.

The reactionary ministry of Manteuffel (1850–58) applied specifically Prussian and therefore often anti-Catholic traditions of state, and the largely Lutheran state bureaucracy continued to prevent the full implementation of constitutional parity. In 1852, Friedrich von Raumer, minister of religion, decreed a ban on studying at the Collegium Germanicum in Rome, established state supervision of foreign clerics and of parish missions, and confined the latter to purely Catholic areas. The decrees were primarily directed against the Jesuits, as a result of whose activities a reduction in the number of Lutherans was feared. Geissel and Bishop Müller of Münster protested immediately. In addition, a political opposition came into being, leading in 1852 to the formation of a "Catholic Faction" with sixty-two representatives in the Prussian Diet. Under this dual pressure the government moderated Raumer's decrees in a way acceptable to the Catholics. Subsequently the Catholic Section in the Ministry of Religion, successfully worked toward a better understanding between state and religious interests, but the increasing gravity of the differences between Catholicism and liberalism as well as between the two denominations began to hinder its work in the 1860s. The government tried to interfere in the election of the Cologne archbishop after Geissel's death (1864), when it was called upon for help by the liberal chapter minority against the ultramontane chapter majority, but ultimately it accepted Bishop Melchers of Osnabrück, who had the approbation of the Roman Curia. In Gnesen-Posen as well, Rome was able to place its candidate, Count Ledóchowski.

The leaders of the Catholic Faction (called "Faction of the Center" after the assignment of seats in the Diet), were interested in developing a general political party. The immediate goal of the faction was the defense of ecclesiastical freedom, and it was only sensible to argue for the observance of the constitution as a whole. This led to the splitting off of a number of noble representatives who began to support the Catholic-conservative movement propagated in Mainz and Munich. In its church policy and its Greater German attitude the Catholic Faction differed from the liberals, in its constitutionalism it differed from the conservatives. Its inability to formulate for all of its members a common position during the great Prussian constitutional conflict (1862–67), led to its demise.

In Austria, Emperor Franz Joseph, steadfastly converting his restoration policy after 1850 to a neo-absolutism, in religious questions also remained on the path taken in 1848–49. He started negotiations for a concordat, headed on the part of the state by Josef Otmar von Rauscher, who had become archbishop of Vienna; the negotiator for the Curia was Viale-Prela. Franz Joseph and his representative regarded the Catholic Church as the unifying factor in holding together the multinational state, and they also wished to make of Austria the preeminent political power of Catholicism; for this reason the Emperor strongly desired a concordat at any price. The Curia exploited this desire and successfully created a precedent for its negotiations with other states. The concordat was signed on 18 August 1855; it not only liquidated Josephinism and fulfilled justified ecclesiastical expectations, but it derived these from ultramontane principles. Throughout, it reflected the militantly defensive antiliberalism of both contracting partners. Literally duplicating the Bavarian concordat of 1817, the Catholic Church in the entire monarchy was guaranteed all rights to which it was entitled in keeping with "the divine order and canonical statutes" (ARTICLE 1), laws conflicting with the concordat were repealed (ART. 35), and all religious issues not specifically treated by the concordat were to be settled according to the doctrines of the Church and its regulations as authorized by the Holy See (ART. 34). The Emperor assured the Church and its institutions of his special protection (ART. 16), and he retained his right of nomination to episcopal sees (ART. 19) and most of the cathedral canonships (ART. 22). The appointment of bishops was clearly designated as a papal privilege; the permission to correspond freely with Rome was justified with the jurisdictional primacy of the Pope by divine right. The Catholic Church retained considerable influence on the education system: In General, instruction in the schools was to coincide with Catholic doctrine, and elementary schools were placed under the control of the Catholic Church (ARTS. 5, 7, 8,). The state agreed to the suppression of all books antagonistic to the Church (ART. 9), and marriages were subjected to canon law (ART. 10).

The legal monopoly of the Catholic Church engendered passionate opposition among liberals, Protestants, and Josephinist Catholics. Yet the Curia and the majority of the bishops believed that they had won a great victory. They failed to recognize that less would have been more and that this concordat could not but generate new and profound controversies.

Cardinal Rauscher, who in 1856 gathered the bishops of the monarchy in Vienna and subsequently guided the episcopate in authoritarian fashion, saw to it that the concordat was strictly implemented. Through it he wanted to preserve the Christian character of all public institutions. But the cardinal and the like-minded minister for religion and education, Count Thun, were faced with growing difficulties. The ratification of the concordat also saw the beginning of the struggle for its repeal or changes in it, a struggle which was to burden domestic Austrian politics for the next fifteen years.

The domestic and foreign policy defeats of the conservatives in 1866 intensified the controversies. Buest, the new chancellor, pointed to the concordat and its propagandistic exploitation by the liberals in Germany and Italy as one of the causes of Austrian defeat. As it was his intention to gain new respect and influence in German affairs through a liberal Austrian policy, he closely cooperated with the liberal parliamentary majority. In the spring of 1868 denominational laws were passed which once again subjected marriage and education to the state and guaranteed the free choice of religion. The most important clauses of the concordat were thus liberally modified.

While the revolution and its results in the two major states of the German Confederation produced liberalization of the legal position of the Church, the other German states continued to adhere to the practice of state regulation. Maximilian II, who became King of Bavaria in 1848, was a confirmed Catholic, but he also regarded himself as the guardian of parity and tolerance. He was determined to preserve the sovereign rights of the state, and disliked ultramontanism and its representative Reisach. He pursued moderate, liberal education and religious policies, but consulted advisers of different persuasions, among them C. A. von Abel, whose influence on the liberal-conservative ministry of von der Pfordten effected some concessions to the reactionaries. Only after Pfordten's resignation in 1859 was Bavaria's domestic policy guided by liberalism. King Ludwig II (after 1864) also was a liberal.

Archbishop Reisach attempted to satisfy the demands of the Würzburg bishops' conference in Bavaria. At a Bavarian bishops' conference in Freising (October 1850) a memorandum drafted by Reisach and Windischmann was passed, demanding the complete realization of the concordat and the repeal of the religious edict. Disregarding Döllinger's warnings — in spite of his differences with Reisach he still acted as adviser to the bishops — the conference also raised educational demands, such as participation in the filling of positions, which were unacceptable for a state pledged to parity.

The Freising demands caused a protracted debate. The government realized that the old system could not be maintained as it was and therefore looked for an acceptable compromise. The royal decisions of 8 April 1852 and 9 October 1854 met the bishops' demands with respect to priest seminaries and control of schools.

The Bavarian bishops met again in 1864 for the purpose of weighing defensive measures against the government's liberal religious and education policies; even in Catholic Bavaria, the Church had become rather isolated because of its undifferentiated resistance to the prevailing thought of the time.

Under the chairmanship of Freiburg Archbishop von Vicari, a conference of the Upper Rhenish bishops in March 1851 sent a memorandum to the government which was based on the Würzburg demands. It was published and seen as a fundamental attack against the concept of a state church. The government did not respond until two years later, when it offered a number of concessions, which, however, a further joint declaration of the bishops characterized as inadequate.

Inasmuch as the governments refused to give in or to accept the conference of bishops as a negotiating partner, the five bishops were compelled in the succeeding years to negotiate individually. In electoral Hesse, Bishop Kött of Fulda achieved a temporary agreement. In Hesse-Darmstadt, Ketteler, bishop of Mainz since 1850, had considerable success. He displayed an unusual degree of assurance, but also supported the government in its Greater German conservative policies and its battle against liberalism and democracy. Their mutual aversion to these movements produced an alliance, prudently employed by the bishop in the service of religious freedom. In 1851 Ketteler opened a theological studies institute at the Mainz seminary, thereby removing the reason for the existence of the state's institute at Gießen. The Dalwig government lodged only a verbal protest. In 1854 Ketteler and Dalwig signed an agreement which took account of the interests of both sides and kept religious peace for longer than a decade. The Curia in the meantime had begun to insist on the Pope's exclusive right to negotiate concordats and was irritated by the bishop's unauthorized action and his failure to make maximum demands; Ketteler succeeded in obtaining Rome's consent only after further concessions by the government.

In the negotiations with the governments of Württemberg, Baden, and Nassau, the Holy See, represented by Cardinal Reisach, was able to obtain some central objectives analogous to the concordat with Austria. This, however, went too far again: The concordats with Württemberg (1857) and Baden (1859) required parliamentary consent, which was obtained in neither state.

Subsequently, both states regulated the affairs between Church and state unilaterally in keeping with their prevailing liberal orientation. The legislation of 9 October 1860 in Baden for the first time reflected liberal goals in a German state; the compromise clauses of the National Constitution of Frankfurt, which served as a model, were interpreted to the disadvantage of the Church. The Churches were granted a position as public corporations and the autonomous regulation of their affairs (ARTICLES 1, 7), but otherwise they remained subject to the laws of the state; ecclesiastic regulations which affected "the rights of citizens" required the consent of the states (ARTS. 13, 15). Evidence of a "general academic education" became a prerequisite for the holding of a Church office; the government was entitled to reject applicants of whom it did not approve for "civic or political reasons" (ART. 9). Property of the Church was administered jointly by the Church and state agencies (ART. 10), the establishment of religious orders was subject to state approval (ART. 11). The entire system of public education was placed under the control of the state (ART. 6), even though the Church was empowered to establish parochial schools (ART. 12). Religious legislation in Württemberg, passed on 30 January 1862, rested on the same principles, but in a few points was more favorable to the Church.

Many of the new regulations were ambivalent; it all depended on how they were applied. In Baden, the administration of August Lamey (1860–66) was conciliatory, but the subsequent ministry of Julius Jolly (1866–76) used the legislation to start the first fundamental conflict between a liberal state and the Catholic Church in Germany.

Between 1850 and 1870, seventeen Catholic Conferences continued the work begun by the previous ones. They served to unite the Catholic forces, and enabled them to look at the associations, the press, and pastoral care; to an unprecedented degree, laymen became involved in ecclesiastical affairs.

Most of the associations were founded at the Conferences, such as in 1848 in Mainz the Vincent Association by August Reichensperger, and the Boniface

Association in 1849 at Regensburg upon the suggestion of Döllinger. The Vincent Association devoted itself to charity; the Boniface Association assisted the communities of the Diaspora. Active support was also given to the journeymen associations. Their founder, Adolf Kolping (1813–65), a practical-minded educator, after 1848 developed them into a network for young craftsmen, covering all of Germany and Switzerland. When they finished their training, the journeymen often joined these associations. Kolping's concern for craftsmen and skilled workers characterizes the middle class origin of the Catholic social movement, which one encounters also in the contemporary Catholic press and in Alban Stolz's apologetics. It was an attempt to preserve the old social order by improving it and by fighting against liberalism, capitalism, and socialism. Unfortunately, the movement had no solutions for the novel problems of an industrial society and its proletariat. Ketteler was the first one to address this problem and to say that traditional methods of charity were inadequate. He called for a state social program which would also engage the Church, and at the same time pointed to new areas of activity for it. He singled out such matters as pastoral care for the workers, diocesan workers' associations directed by the local bishop, and social-pastoral instruction for theology students. In 1869 Ketteler confronted the entire German episcopate with the problem of the workers, but failed to induce it to make a decision along the line of his suggestions. The bishops at the time were absorbed by the problems and controversies which had arisen after the announcement of the Vatican council; the plight of the workers took a second seat behind the struggle for papal infallibility.

The Catholic Conferences adhered to the decision made in 1849 not to become involved in everyday politics, but, interested in achieving the broadest possible effect by their attempt at rejuvenation, they voiced their opinions with respect to fundamental questions of public life. Defending the ecclesiastical status quo and opposing the spreading secularization, the Catholic Conferences and associations were increasingly pushed into the defensive by liberals and their Protestant comrades.

Controversies over the national question and the Papal State intensified the differences. The Conferences came out in favor of a Greater Germany. In a Germany which included Austria, the Catholics were in the majority and therefore in a better position to obtain the rights denied them by individual German state governments; contrary to liberal polemics, the Catholic Church was an intimate part of many national traditions and wished to participate actively in the nation's unification. But Döllinger's logical call for national ecclesiastical cooperation was met with reserve which grew to decided resistance with the gradual merger of German Catholicism and ultramontanism.

The combination of ultramontane religiosity and Greater German objectives was unable to make headway, because the non-Catholic majority in the non-Austrian German states favored a Little Germany and an alliance with liberalism. The German National Association (after 1859) organizationally and ideologically modeled itself on the Italian Risorgimento.

In this situation the defense of the Papal State, clearly enunciated for the first time by the Catholic Conference in 1861 at Munich, assumed an integrative character. Leaders and members of the movement were guided by their special feeling of solidarity with the Pope, a solidarity derived from the ultramontane concept of the Church. With dangerous oversimplification, only comprehensible against the background of the liberal attacks on papacy and Church, the liberty of the Church was seen as dependent on that of the Pope, and his, in turn, dependent on that of the Papal State. In the course of the actual injustices inflicted on the Pope it was overlooked that the Roman priest state went counter to the political and legal principles of the century. Modifying statements like those of Döllinger, who doubted the necessity of the Papal State, were rejected out of hand; they only fed the mistrust of the intellectual minority which objected to the growing Romanization of German Catholicism.

The reaction to the *Syllabus* (1864) was characteristic of the intellectual orientation of the Catholic movement. Without reserve the Catholics accepted the summary condemnation, in some points unjustified, in others inadequately reasoned, of ideological and political liberalism, even though a moderate interpretation, taking account of Germany's situation, was necessary. New disputes became unavoidable, for the papal document created tremendous excitement among liberals and Protestants, to be exceeded only by the dogma of infallibility. Although the *Syllabus* did not say anything new, it was seen as a declaration of war on the modern state and modern science, in view of its claim to authority and the sharpness of its formulations.

The political decisions of 1866 accentuated the contrasts further. Prussia's destruction of the German Confederation and exclusion of Austria from German affairs put an end to the political hopes of the Catholics. At first they looked upon the events more as a revolutionary break with legitimate tradition than as the beginning of a new form of national unity. The removal of Austria as a great power from the concerns of Germany and Italy was also a defeat of Catholicism. In the new North German Confederation the Catholics were only a minority; the Italian national state required only the remainders of the Papal State for its completion, whose disappearance was thus only a question of time. The change in Germany was heightened by the fact that liberal and Protestant publicists viewed the events as a victory of Protestantism; with dangerous simplification they viewed Prussia as the embodiment of progress and disposed of the Austrian Empire as a relic of the Middle Ages.

In 1867 the Catholic Conference took place at Innsbruck, and, employing the example of Tyrol to demonstrate the synthesis of Germandom and Catholicism, it once more came out in favor of a Greater Germany. But soon the realization gained ground that an effective representation of Catholic interests could only be made on the basis of the new realities and that national unification could be achieved under Prussia's auspices only. The first to plead impressively for the integration of Catholics with the North German Confederation was Ketteler; of the politicians only Peter Reichensperger seconded him. This integration during the subsequent years was much more of a fact than the polemics of the 1860s against what were called the "enemies of the nation" indicated. It was facilitated by Prussia's adherence to its friendly policy toward the denominations. Initially, Bismarck wooed the Catholics and for their sake denied Italy, Prussia's ally in the war against Austria, any assistance in Italy's hostile stance to the Papal State. But Bismarck's policies in 1866 also initiated his alliance with the National Liberals, which during the succeeding decade decisively influenced Prussian-German domestic politics and steered it into the *Kulturkampf.*

The political transformation and the announcement of the Vatican Council gave birth in the German episcopate to the desire for closer cooperation and to the plan of a joint conference like that of 1848. This realistic plan encountered objections only in Rome, but Cardinal Rauscher succeeded in removing them. The centralism of Pius IX refused to concede initiatives and jurisdictions to the bishops which transcended the borders of their German states. In September 1867 the bishops from the North German Confederation and the south German states met at Fulda; the most important outcome of their deliberations was the institutionalization of the bishops' conference, which was to be held every two years.

The gathering of Germany's Catholic scholars in 1863, suggested by Döllinger and observed with fearful mistrust by Rome, produced no understanding between the representatives of historical and Neo-Scholastic theology; the *Syllabus* and the announcement of the Vatican Council only served to intensify the contrasts. The monopolization of Neo-Scholasticism, eagerly promoted by Rome, was propounded by those who saw in Scholasticism the best ideological basis for their own antiliberal concentration. The Jesuit-directed theology department at the University of Innsbruck also established Roman Neo-Scholasticism.

But the larger majority of the German theology professors, including Döllinger, who had fought for religious freedom during the 1850s, resisted the Roman uniformity of thought with theological, historical, economic, and religious arguments. They feared that the extreme ultramontanism imposed on the Church by Pius IX's Curia would destroy legitimate religious structures and traditions and would produce an intensification of the conflict with the liberal forces which was as dangerous as it was unnecessary. In contrast to the Neo-Scholastics who were harking back to an idealized past, they sought a dialogue with other scholars and a reconciliation with modern thought in general. Next to Bishop Maret's French neo-Gallicans, the German theology professors were regarded as the most dangerous opponents of the Curial movement. Their enemies, with the Catholic masses behind them, fought, defamed, and largely isolated them. The Munich nuncio accused them frequently of rebellion against authority and of sympathies for Protestantism.

In Switzerland, the liberals consistently exploited to their advantage the victory of 1846–48 over the Catholics. Their policy, designed to narrow further the freedom of movement of the Catholic Church, was viewed as exemplary by the liberals of other countries and was imitated in the religious battles during the 1860s and 1870s; the first state to do so was neighboring Baden. After 1848 as well, a good number of monasteries and religious schools were closed, the curricula of the remaining schools and the administration of ecclesiastical property were placed under cantonal control, and the clerics were compelled to swear an oath promising to uphold the laws; some cantons suppressed religious instruction entirely. But the constitutional guarantee of freedom of religion made possible the establishment of religious communities in the Protestant cantons, aided by gifts from foreign Catholics.

The radical behavior of the governments met the approval of only a minority of the Catholics which had continued to develop Wessenberg's reforms in a democratic direction and which believed that it could do so in continued cooperation with the governments. Groups with such aims continued to exist in most of Switzerland's cantons and eventually joined the Old Catholic protest movement against the dogma of papal infallibility. Those antiultramontanes who remained in the Church were isolated. The liberals asserted to be fighting not against the Church as such, but only against hierarchism and ultramontanism, but actually their attitudes helped the growth of the movements to which they objected.

The closest possible cooperation with Rome seemed to be the best guarantee for development and continuation of religious life, and ultramontane activists dominated the situation.

The pressure exerted upon the Church strengthened the need for organization, which often was set up according to the German example. After the 1850s, Pius Associations and other charitable organizations sprang up.

The predominantly agrarian structure of the Catholic cantons, which burdened the struggle with the urban liberals with additional social tensions, did not permit much intellectual activity. Only Fribourg and the abbey of Einsiedeln under the leadership of Abbot Heinrich Schmid were productive.

CHAPTER 30

The Rise of Catholicism in the Anglo-Saxon World

England

In 1840 the number of vicars apostolic was raised from four to eight, but the solution of the problems of the Catholic Church in England, resulting from the growing number of Irish immigrants to the industrial cities, was possible only through the establishment of a diocesan episcopate. After the elevation of Pius IX, representatives of the vicars apostolic asked Rome in 1847 and in 1848 to give them immediate relief. But the Roman revolution and the exile of the Pope delayed a decision until 1850. In the meantime, the arrival of great numbers of destitute Irishmen following the great famine of 1847 burdened the ecclesiastical organization heavily.

The papal brief of 29 September 1850 established in England and Wales a Catholic hierarchy, with Westminster as the metropolitan see and twelve auxiliary bishops. Wiseman was named archbishop and cardinal. A few days before journeying from Rome to England, he addressed a pastoral letter to all English Catholics in which he expressed his tremendous joy "that Catholic England once again was placed in its orbit in the ecclesiastical heavens." He was by nature effusive and optimistic, but his letter merely confirmed many Catholics in their conviction that Wiseman basically did not understand the English situation and the English character. The news of the establishment of the hierarchy generally had been well received, but his letter caused irritation. The press reacted with an outburst of bigotry, and there were street demonstrations against what was called "papal aggression."

Wiseman poured oil on the waters, which he had roiled unwittingly, with his skillful and effective *Appeal to the Reason and Good Feeling of the English People,* published shortly after his return to England.

There were still conversions, but only in small numbers. The most notable one was that of Henry Edward Manning. But the primary concern of the hierarchy was not the proselytization of England, but the creation of a system of parishes and the construction of churches and schools for the impoverished Catholics in the industrial areas. More than half of all Catholics lived in Lancashire (dioceses of Liverpool and Salford), whose population had swelled as a result of the strong influx of Irishmen after the famine of 1847. The rest was concentrated in London (dioceses of Westminster and Southwark) and in the industrial area of the Midlands (chiefly the diocese of Birmingham). In the remaining part of England Catholics lived so dispersed and in such small numbers that it was almost impossible to establish a diocesan organization for them.

Much, however, was achieved at the three provincial synods of 1852, 1855, and 1859, convoked by Wiseman. The parish missions received their final status and the problem of obtaining priests for them was tackled. Some priests, of course, came from Ireland. In addition, Wiseman continued to employ regular clergy. This led to some difficulties, as the interests of the exempt regular clergy did not always coincide with those of the bishops. The cardinal himself founded a diocesan organization, the Oblates of Saint Charles, and appointed Manning as their superior. Additional problems resulted from the tendency of Wiseman and Manning to promote seminaries with strict Tridentine principles. Until then, it had been English practice to train candidates for the priesthood and candidates for lay occupations together. After an upsetting period of doubt and of changing methods, tradition finally won out.

When Wiseman died on 15 February 1865, it was the personal decision of Pope Pius IX to designate Manning as his successor, even though the chapter had chosen Errington for the post.

Manning, a man of iron will and firm determination, remained archbishop for twenty-seven years. Almost immediately after his conversion he had been ordained a priest and had then spent three years in Rome. There he developed extreme ultramontane views, but yet became a national figure in Victorian England. His social conscience and his concern for the poor were probably the outstanding features of his activity. This tendency had become clear even before his conversion and reached its zenith with his successful mediation during the great London dock strike in 1889. His life was also filled with the battle to obtain a fair proportion of public funds for Catholic elementary schools when, as a result of the Education Bill of 1870, public schools came into being. His genuine sympathy for Ireland also was of benefit for his pastoral care, as 80 percent of the English Catholics were of Irish descent.

Manning had a firm grasp of the intellectual problems of his age, but also a deep distrust of their effect on the Catholic faith. Although supported in the matter by almost all of the bishops, it was he who was responsible for the absolute ban on Catholics studying at Oxford or Cambridge. Three years after his death in 1885 the prohibition on Catholics attending state universities was lifted.

The problem of university attendance led to discord between Manning and Newman. Newman agreed with much of traditional English Catholicism; Newman and the Old Catholic group were brothers under the skin and viewed with distrust the enthusiastic ultramontanism of Manning and other converts.

After his conversion, Newman had studied theology in Rome. There he had become aware of his spiritual affinity to the oratory of Saint Philipp Neri, and after his return he founded the first English oratory in Birmingham. Its growth faced many obstacles. In view of the tensions between him and Frederick William Faber, the oratories in Birmingham and London developed independently from one another and even with a certain degree of hostility. In 1852, Newman accepted the invitation of Archbishop Cullen to go to Dublin as president of Dublin University. But his tenure was not very successful and in 1858 he resigned his position. But he left a lasting memorial to his presidency in the form of a series of lectures which he had given in May 1852 and which were published under the title *The Idea of a University.*

Returned to England, he founded the oratory school in 1859 and thus made a notable contribution to the tradition of Benedictine and Jesuit education. In the same year, his bishop, Ullathorne of Birmingham, asked him to take over the *Rambler,* a journal founded in 1848. The reason for Newman's appointment was ecclesiastical suspicion of the *Rambler,* but his own contribution to the July issue of 1858 was denounced by Rome, and George Talbot, the Pope's English informant, characterized Newman as the most dangerous man in England. During the next five years his attitudes were questioned, he was treated with disrespect, and became a man without influence. His earlier position was restored with the publication of his *Apologia pro vita sua.* It appeared in 1864 as a reply to accusations by the Rev. Charles Kingsley that Newman and the Catholic clergy did not regard "truth for its own sake" as a virtue.

The core of the reply bears the title: "A history of my religious opinions," and the honesty displayed by Newman was a very effective defense of his personal honor. He could hardly hope to have a similar success in 1864 when he attempted to refute the assertion that Catholic theologians were severely handicapped in their scholarly work. Two years later, Ullathorne offered him a church in Oxford, but the suggestion was blocked by Manning, Ward, and Talbot, who did not consider Newman sufficiently orthodox. In the following year, the Congregation for the Propagation of the Faith prohibited Catholics from attending public universities.

In 1870 Newman published *A Grammar of Assent.* He had spent twenty years on it, and it is perhaps his only work which was not written as an immediate response but was the fruit of long reflection. Its theme was the fundamentals of certainty and, more specifically, the reasons of faith: How can one believe something that is beyond comprehension or proof? His approach — the more interesting as it takes place independently from the Scholastic tradition — is essentially a psychological analysis of "moral proof, of a collection of probabilities," not a single one of which is proof in itself, but which as a whole can produce an act of faith based on what

Newman calls the "illative sense," the ability of reason to draw conclusions and arrive at judgments.

Also in 1870 there was a growth of tension between Newman and Manning with respect to the definition of papal infallibility. Newman had no difficulties with the dogma as such — in fact, in a very real sense it had been a motive for his conversion — but he feared that a formal definition would create hostility outside of the Church and discontent within it, especially if it were to be pronounced in the extreme form which he had reason to believe would be used. He had no difficulty with accepting the doctrine as defined by the council.

In 1877 he returned to Oxford after thirty years in order to accept the first honorary fellowship awarded by Trinity College. Two years later Leo XIII created him a cardinal with the unusual privilege of residing in Birmingham, even though he was only a priest. There he spent the last eleven years of his life in peace. His gravestone bore the inscription, which he had written himself "Ex umbris et imaginibus in veritatem."

Scotland

The number of Catholics in Scotland also grew noticeably as a result of Irish immigration to the industrial areas. In 1851, 18 percent of the population of Glasgow were Irish. Most of the immigrants came from the province of Ulster and brought with them the tension existing there between Catholics and Protestants. In addition, they encountered the hostility of the Scottish Presbyterians and were incapable of adjusting themselves to the native Catholics. Many of their priests came from Ireland and there was discord between Irish and Scottish priests. In 1851, the Irish in Glasgow started a newspaper, the *Free Press,* whose incessant polemics against Dr. Murdoch, the vicar apostolic, probably hastened his death. Murdoch's successor was John Gray, his former coadjutor. Rome suggested that Gray should choose his own coadjutor and hinted that an Irish priest would be suitable. But Gray was unwilling to do this and was supported by the other vicars apostolic, who, in the case of an Irish appointment, feared a general worsening of the situation of the Church in Scotland.

At the urging of Archbishop Cullen of Dublin the president of the Irish College in Paris, James Lynch, C.M., was finally appointed Gray's coadjutor. Regrettably, but unavoidably, the appointment increased tensions in Glasgow, where the Irish clergy followed Lynch and the Scottish clergy followed Gray. In 1867, Archbishop Manning suggested the transfer of both Gray and Lynch and thought that the Scottish problems could be solved only through the establishment of a diocesan hierarchy. But the government regarded such a step as premature and relayed its reservations to Manning and Rome.

Consequently, Rome hesitated to establish such a hierarchy in Scotland. The selection of the metropolitan see also proved difficult. Two-thirds of the three hundred fifty thousand Catholics lived in the metropolitan area of Glasgow. The next larger concentration was Edinburgh, Scotland's capital; Saint Andrews, the seat of the medieval archbishopric, was only a small town with very few Catholics. When the hierarchy was finally established in March 1878, an attempt was made to take all of these considerations into account. The metropolitan see was established in Saint Andrews and Edinburgh with four auxiliary bishoprics, and Glasgow as archbishopric without auxiliary sees was subordinated directly to the Holy See.

Ireland

It is generally taken for granted that the great famine of 1847 was a decisive turning point in the modern history of Ireland. It marked the beginning of a strong emigration which possibly raised the standard of living in Ireland slightly, but nevertheless still left behind a large agrarian proletariat, which had little hope of improvement as long as the laws concerning landownership remained unchanged.

Catholics constituted almost 80 percent of the population. The majority of the Protestants was concentrated in Ulster, while in most of the south and the west the population was almost totally Catholic. The predominant Protestants gave up their essential monopoly of wealth and political power only slowly. In 1873, a very important court judgment stated that papal jurisdiction in Ireland was still illegal, according to an unrepealed statute from the sixteenth century. In practice, however, civil courts respected the jurisdiction of the Church, as its decisions were easily accepted by the Catholics.

Under the force of the Penal Code and during the days of O'Connell, a feeling of closeness had developed between the Catholic clergy and the laity; it became stronger during the nineteenth century as a consequence of the fact that the large majority of the parish clergy was educated in Ireland, chiefly at Maynooth. Only a small minority attended the few seminaries on the continent which had been reopened after the French Revolution.

In 1849, Paul Cullen, head of the Irish College at Rome, was appointed archbishop of Armagh. In 1852 he was transferred to Dublin and in 1866 became the first Irish cardinal; he dominated the Irish hierarchy until his death in 1878. He was equipped with the authority of an apostolic delegate and thus empowered to convoke a national synod at Thurles in 1850. There, Church discipline and religious practices were adapted to common canon law and the prevailing ultramontane tendencies, the planned Queen's Colleges were condemned, and the political activity of the Irish clergy was restricted.

Attempts to define these restrictions were only partially successful and resulted in the complete alienation of Cullen and the influential Archbishop MacHale of Tuam. After 1860, there was the revolutionary movement of the Fenians, which, according to Cullen's conviction, posed the same threat to the Church in Ireland as the revolutionaries on the continent or in Italy. But even though the Fenians refused to continue to recognize the leadership of the clergy in Irish politics, they were not unbelievers.

In his opposition, Cullen was supported by the bishops, but the clerics in some instances hesitated to follow him, as they shared the anti-British sentiments of the people. But it was not easy for them to find a theological justification for the rebellion at the very time of the *Syllabus,* and therefore on the whole they refrained from openly supporting the revolutionary movement. After a failed uprising in 1867, many Fenians were imprisoned; now the clerics acted less restrained and participated in the public demonstrations of sympathy for the prisoners. In order to counter this threat, Cullen in 1870 managed to obtain a formal Roman condemnation of the Fenian movement.

Ultimately, Cullen was prepared to cooperate with the Liberal Party, then in the process of formation under the leadership of Gladstone, even though it was hostile to an ultramontane papacy.

English liberals and Irish Catholics were in agreement that the Protestant Church in Ireland should be disestablished. Both parties wanted to distribute its property to all Churches in Ireland. But Cullen insisted that no Church be subsidized by the state and that each should instead be a voluntary association before the law, just as the Catholic Church had been since the Reformation. This principle was embodied in the Irish Church Act of 1869.

Cullen's association with the English liberals remained more in the area of common interests than in common principles, and his support of a "free Church in a free state" was primarily based on his Irish thought and not on any principles of liberalism. This became clear in the question of education.

University education had long been a source of conflict. In 1850 the synod of Thurles had prohibited Catholics from attending interdenominational universities, known as Queen's Colleges. Cullen returned from Rome with the charge of establishing a university modeled on Louvain. Newman accepted the invitation to become its president, but the institution was always in trouble. There were many reasons. The government was unwilling to accredit the institution, and its degrees were therefore not recognized. The Irish Catholic middle class, which was ready to send its sons to this university, was numerically too small, and Newman's hope to erect in Dublin a Catholic university for all of Great Britain and Ireland was unrealistic. Some of the bishops denied the new university their active support, and MacHale was soon its bitter enemy. This aspect was particularly grave, as the finances of the university depended on church collections. With respect to practical matters, Newman could deal solely with Cullen, but the temperaments of the two men were too different. After Newman's departure in 1858 the Catholic University was constantly in difficulties. The government still refused to grant it a constitution, even though in 1879 it installed the Royal University of Ireland as a supervisory agency which examined the students of the Catholic University together with those of all other colleges for the granting of degrees.

The frailty of the Catholic University and the concentration of seminary training in Maynooth led to a strictly clerical orientation of the Catholic professors in Ireland.

Experience taught Cullen that it was impossible for a priest or bishop in the Ireland of the nineteenth century not to become involved in politics. But the involvement of the clergy in politics had a particularly sad consequence. The Protestants concluded that an independent Ireland would be ruled by the Catholic clergy and that "Home Rule" would in fact mean "Rome Rule." After 1860, the Orange Order, started in 1795 as an instrument of Protestant domination, was revitalized.

The break between the Irish Catholics and the Protestant Liberals over the question of university education in 1873 led to the fall of Gladstone's government. After six years of political instability, a number of bad harvests at the end of the decade once again raised the problem of the tenant farmers. Charles Stewart Parnell, a Protestant, acted as the leader of a strong parliamentary group which demanded agrarian reform and a limited degree of autonomy known as Home Rule. He gained the support of the revolutionary leaders and of the Catholic hierarchy, especially of Archbishop Walsh of Dublin and Archbishop Croke of Cashel. Gladstone, returned to office in 1880, was sympathetic, but the English conservatives, including some prominent Catholics, depicted the Irish movement in Rome as revolutionary. Papal intervention and condemnation made life more difficult, but the movement held together until 1889, when Parnell was named a corespondent in a divorce suit. The bishops declared that he could no longer act as spokesman, and the consequent split led to a further period of political instability. When it was overcome, it was recognized that the involvement of the clergy in politics, peculiar to the 19th century, had also passed.

The United States

During the second third of the nineteenth century, the Catholic Church in the United States was able to record some significant progress. After 1870 it was not only numerically the largest English-speaking Catholic group in the world, but it was also during this time that American Catholicism acquired its peculiar characteristics.

Originally consisting of former English and French settlers, and former Spanish ones in the southern states, the Catholic community of the United States gradually assumed different characteristics with the immigration of Irish Catholics. The great famine between 1845 and 1847 in Ireland speeded up this movement, and additional German immigrants journeyed to the United States in the wake of the 1848–49 revolutions. This dual movement, which coincided with the rapid economic development of the country, continued during the two subsequent decades. The majority of the Irish were Catholics, and so were many Germans. Although many of them, and especially their children, isolated in a Protestant environment, left the church of their fathers, the immigration, together with the natural increase, resulted in a growth of the Catholic population which exceeded all expectations. There were in the United States in 1840 approximately 663,000 Catholics, i.e., 4 percent of the total population; in 1870 there were 4,504,000 Catholics, corresponding to 11 percent of the total population.

But the distribution of the Catholics was quite different from region to region. While around 1870 one out of nine Americans was Catholic, the ratio in the southern states, which the immigrants avoided because of their black population, was only one in twenty-five or fewer. The immigration of Catholics benefited chiefly the states of the North, such as Pennsylvania, Ohio, Kentucky, Illinois, Wisconsin, Iowa, and Minnesota. The Germans, settling chiefly in the triangle between Cincinnati, Milwaukee, and Saint Louis, generally settled in rural areas, while the Irish, too poor for agrarian colonization, and dependent on immediate employment as workers or domestics, congregated mostly in the port and industrial cities of the North. Inasmuch as the Irish were by far the largest group, American Catholicism for a long time had an urban, even proletarian, character.

The steady stream of immigrants from Ireland led to a rekindling of the nativist campaign which had been declining in the 1840s, and under the new name of Know-Nothingism anticlerical violence started again. It reached its apogee between 1854 and 1855 and only came to an end with the Civil War.

The rapid increase of the Catholic population, together with the westward movement and the addition of Oregon, Idaho, Texas, New Mexico, and California, presented the ecclesiastical authorities with difficult problems of organization.

In the open areas of the Far West a new beginning had to be made, and in 1846 the Congregation for the Propagation of the Faith founded a new church province with Oregon City as its capital.

Even in the former Mexican provinces a new beginning needed to be made, for the Church had had to suffer grievously in these seemingly Catholic areas as a consequence of Freemason-inspired government action against the regular clergy and from a corrupt clergy. Through the establishment of the dioceses of Galveston for Texas (1847), Santa Fe (1850) for New Mexico, Monterey-Los Angeles (1850) and San Francisco (1853) for California, the situation was mastered. This was facilitated by the freedom of religion which prevailed in the United States and which permitted the Franciscans to resume their missions to the Indians.

In the largely rural areas of the Midwest and the South, in which the majority of the population lived dispersed in the country, the situation for a long time was similar to that of the missionary countries, as the few priests could travel through the vast areas only at long intervals. In spite of the sparse financial means and the lack of priests (at the beginning hardly more than ten), gradually there were established dioceses at Chicago, Milwaukee, and Little Rock in 1843; Cleveland in 1847; Saint Paul and Savannah in 1850; Springfield, Covington, and Alexandria in 1853; Marquette and Fort Wayne in 1857; and Green Bay, La Crosse, and Columbus in 1868.

In the states of the Northeast in which the majority of the immigrants was concentrated, the delicate question of trusteeism was only solved in the 1860s. His energy and his influence on the public enabled G. Hughes archbishop of New York, to obtain in 1860 a law for the state of New York which provided the Church with the desired degree of freedom and simultaneously maintained a sufficient degree of lay control over the property of the Church. Gradually the other states also adopted this law. But the main difficulty was posed for the Catholic authorities by the ever increasing stream of immigrants. The priests, although industrious and agile, could no longer do all of their work, and the great number of languages spoken by their flock confused matters totally. What is more, the poverty of the faithful, who earned their daily bread as workers or domestics, in spite of a high degree of altruism did not permit them to do more than supply a portion of the financial needs of the Church.

Fortunately, the American bishops, of whom two thirds came from Europe, excelled with their sense of the practical and their enterprising spirit, and Europe responded generously to their appeals. Irish priests arrived in great numbers and placed themselves in the service of their emigrated brethren. In 1857, at the request of Monsignor Spalding, a college was established at Louvain for the purpose of training European seminarians who volunteered for the apostolate in the United States. By way of these additions and the slowly growing number of native priests, the active number of clergy rose from about 700 at the time of the accession of Pius IX to 6,000 in 1875. A good number of new parishes were founded, but the Irish character of the Church in the United States, and especially the tendency of the Irish priests to treat their flocks as minors and to leave only little initiative to laymen in religious matters, was strengthened by this development.

At the same time that the clergy was growing, the continuous arrival of regular clergy (both men and women) from France, Belgium, and Austria, and the financial assistance of French, German, and Austrian missionary societies made possible the building of Catholic schools, the creation of charitable institutions for the reception of the immigrants in the ports, and the organization of parish missions according to the method which had proved itself in Europe.

The Civil War, in which the southern states rose against the Union between 1861 and 1865, tested the mettle of the young American Church. The Church had never taken an unequivocal stand in the controversy over slavery. In the South, the ecclesiastical authorities were not completely opposed to slavery as long as it was humane, and even in the North, where the attitude of the Catholic clergy was virtually the same as that of the Protestant ministers, many Catholics were irritated by the alliance between the abolitionists and the nativists. The official attitude of the hierarchy left the faithful with the complete freedom of decision, and itself was completely engrossed in maintaining the political neutrality of the Church in temporal affairs, a tradition reaching back to Carroll. The outbreak of the war, kindled less by slavery than by the concern to preserve national traditions, made the situation easier for the Catholics. Almost throughout, they followed the leaders of their respective states, and Catholics fought in both armies. The absence of a clear position among the Catholics, in a question whose moral relevance was evident, engendered fresh attacks by the Yankees against the Roman Church. Yet its standing was enhanced by the charitable activity in which priests and cloistered women engaged in the Confederate states as well as in the Union states. It was furthermore aided by the fact that the Catholic Church was one among the various religious communities which managed to maintain its unity, even though its faithful and occasionally its pastors — although on their own authority — declared themselves unequivocally for one camp or the other.

After the end of the war, the Catholics began immediately to heal the material and moral wounds.

One of the first actions of the Church after the end of the war was the convocation of a plenary council. It was held in October 1866 in Baltimore. Although it was able only partially to solve the difficulties confronting the Church in the United States during the last third of the nineteenth century, it at least strengthened the idea of a collegiate leadership of the Church. This was a concept rarely encountered in Europe at the time, but it became one of the characteristics of the American episcopate. In addition to many practical regulations, Spalding suggested the writing of a textbook-like explanation of the council, which amounted to a departure from earlier councils. The intention was to present the great topics raised in the encyclical *Quanta cura* and the *Syllabus* in a positive form and to adapt them to the American mentality, especially with respect to the demands which the apostolate was making on the Church in a pluralistic society.

Among the many council decrees, an entire chapter was devoted to the pastoral care of millions of blacks, whose sudden emancipation created great problems. The Protestant blacks suffered much less under the new situation, as their pastors belonged to their race. While in the South relations between black and white Catholics were cordial, the mutual embitterment carried separation of the races into the Church and resulted in a further decline of contacts. The blacks, constituting about 10 percent of the total population of the United States, were effectively lost to Catholicism in spite of the care which members of foreign orders lavished on them.

Another difficult problem with which the council of 1866 had to grapple was the membership of Catholics in secret societies. In addition to the Irish societies connected with the Fenian movement, other groups with philanthropic aims grew considerably. Although these groups, unlike Freemasons in Europe, did not have any revolutionary or anti-Christian objectives, their indifferentism posed a real threat. The bishops could not agree on a united stand and the decree of the council of Baltimore which attempted to formulate binding regulations was not very suitable in practice.

Most of the council's attention, however, was devoted to the problem of education. Since the constitution guaranteed religious freedom, the secretary of education, Horace Mann, at first attempted to include nondenominational religious instruction in the curriculum of the public schools. But in practice this plan encountered obstacles, and public instruction quickly developed in an almost exclusively laicistic direction. This convinced the Catholics that, following the Irish example, they had to organize their own schools, in spite of the heavy burden involved. The motto of Archbishop Hughes of "school before Church" was gradually accepted by most of the other bishops. Urgent appeals were directed to Catholic families to keep their children from attending public schools as much as possible. After 1870 some militant laymen, like the journalist J. McMaster and Miss Edes, who believed that some bishops were slack in implementing their demands, carried the matter to Rome. In November 1876 the American episcopate was informed by Rome that it must follow the same strict directives which then were valid in England and Ireland.

The emphasis with which the organization of Catholic schools was pursued was only one, albeit a fundamental, aspect of a more general policy, the objective of which was to keep the faithful in strictly closed communities, to avoid the use of Protestant institutions as much as possible, and to keep Catholics on the periphery of normal American society. Many priests and bishops, especially Monsignor Hughes, whose personal prestige among the Irish contributed to winning them to his side in opposition to the native American Catholics, thought that the faith of the immigrants, who in the majority were very simple people and in the past had been tied to the Church by environment and local traditions, was not capable of resisting the influence of a Protestant or indifferent environment. The inherited hostility of the Irish toward the Anglo-Saxons and the awareness of being a socially despised proletariat, an awareness that was constantly being nourished by the repeated attacks of the Nativist movement, as well as the mistrust of the traditionalist German farmers of the materialistic character of the new American civilization, finally drove the Catholics into denominational ghettos. The enterprising spirit of the Irish coupled with the organizational talent of the Germans resulted in the creation of a number of organizations: charitable organizations, hospitals, newspapers and journals, and societies of all kinds. Their growth received a further boost by the arrival after 1870 of numerous nuns whom the *Kulturkampf* had driven out of Germany.

Their encapsulation compelled the Catholics to develop a degree of activity that had no equal in the European Churches; an activity which simultaneously strengthened the vitality of their faith. Beneficial for the moment, this separation in the long run produced serious problems. For one thing, it held the vast majority of the Catholics at a very low cultural level, as at this time their lack of money and people did not yet permit them to establish a system of higher education. This low cultural and social level of the Catholic minority explained its relatively weak ability to influence the society around it.

As most of them came from countries in which for centuries they were looked upon as second-class citizens, the immigrants had a natural tendency not to proselytize. But the desire for a less passive attitude grew among the converts of American origin who also were influenced by the Oxford movement. One of the first to become engaged in this fashion was Orestes Brownson. He was a genuine American, upset by the Irish predominance in the Church, often eccentric and obstinate, yet one of the guiding spirits of American Catholicism in the nineteenth century. He was the founder and from 1844 until 1875 the editor of *Brownson's Quarterly,* a nonconformist and lively journal. In 1859, another enterprising convert, Isaac Hecker, together with some former Redemptorists who objected to the European mentality of their superiors, founded the congregation of the Paulists, whose chief objective was the proselytization of Protestants. But men like Brownson and Hecker were for a long time only exceptions.

It is part of the same development that the Catholics and above all the clergy in the United States did not participate in the solution of the great social problems. This was true for slavery and the movements directed against alcoholism and the attempts to gain greater social justice for the workers. At first sight this particular failure appears most astonishing in view of the connection of American Catholicism with the lower social classes.

The isolation of the Catholic minority in the United States on the periphery of American public life provided it with peculiar characteristics for a long time to come. Still, there was a gradual development after the Civil War; it began in the Midwest and spread to the East Coast. It was favored by the fact that in such places as New York and Baltimore the Irishmen Hughes and Kenrick were replaced in 1864 by the American-born McCloskey and Spalding. Simultaneously it became evident that the young American Church, which had so successfully applied the well-known formula of a free Church in a free state beyond all ideology, was beginning to assume a place of its own in the universal picture. The first time this happened was at the Vatican Council. When in 1875 McCloskey was elevated to cardinal, it was spectacular proof that the New World had at last outgrown the missionary phase.

Canada

The years after the Act of Union in 1840 were fruitful for Catholicism. The liberal inclinations of Governor Lord Elgin, embodied in the law of 1851, ended the official predominance of the Anglican Church, especially as the high birth rate of the French Canadians and the immigration of Irishmen into the Great Lakes area temporarily resulted in the numerical superiority of Catholics (650,000 vs. 550,000 in 1840). In the subsequent period, immigration favored the Catholics, but the absolute number of Catholics also continued to rise noticeably. The census of 1851 registered more than one million, and by 1881 there were 1,600,000, approximately 40 percent of the total population of 4,300,000. The numerical progression was reflected in the establishment of additional dioceses: four under Gregory XVI and five under Pius IX. The Church province of Quebec, founded in 1844 after lengthy negotiations, was gradually dismantled and three other dioceses took its place: in 1862 Halifax for the Maritime Provinces, in 1870 Toronto, and in 1871 Saint-Boniface in the West. Despite the premature attempt to establish a hierarchy on the Pacific Coast, which at the time of the death of Pius IX was inhabited by only a few thousand Catholics, the essential strength of Canadian Catholicism remained concentrated in the area of the Saint Lawrence. But even there they were unevenly distributed. At the time of the formation of the Canadian confederation in 1867, which on the whole was well received by the Catholics, they constituted 86 percent of the population in the province of Quebec, consisting of descendants of French settlers and fifty thousand Irish; they constituted 16 percent in Ontario, five-sixths of whom were English-speaking and economically weak; they were 24 percent of the population in Nova Scotia, chiefly of Scottish descent; and they constituted 33 percent of New Brunswick, largely as descendants of the French-speaking Acadians.

In the province of Quebec the development started at the end of the 1820s by Monsignor Lartigue, the first bishop of Montreal (1821–40), continued. The young clerics, influenced by the theocratic direction of the French ultramontane school of the restoration period and its subliminal social thought, turned the nationalistic reaction, which lost its initial liberal ties, to their advantage. They became the propelling force of a clerically oriented society with focus on the rural population. In the decade from 1840 to 1850, the Church slowly and gradually grew to be the strongest institution in French Canada, largely as a result of the numerical and qualitative growth of the clergy. In contrast to the United States, the native recruitment of clergy in Canada was high even before the middle of the century, and between 1840 and 1880 the ratio of 1700 Catholics per priest decreased to 520. Coupled with rising standards of training in the seminaries, priestly exercises were reintroduced in 1840, and a short time afterwards periodical meetings for the purpose of studying theological questions were begun. The Canadian clergy, which at one time had been extremely independent, during the second half of the century became highly disciplined.

This change in the attitude of the clergy, and especially its "Romanization," were hastened by the arrival of many French members of religious orders, both male and female, during the 1840s. They were invited by Monsignor Bourget, the enterprising, authoritarian bishop of Montreal (1840–76) and the outstanding ecclesiastical personality in Canada during the nineteenth century; for more than a generation he guided the religious fortunes of the province of Quebec in a strictly clerical sense. The enthusiastic ultramontanism and the reactionary political concepts of the regular clergy from France consolidated tendencies already present in Quebec. They fueled the embryonic religious-political struggles and led to difficulties with the native clergy. Their influence on the spiritual development was considerable; they were largely responsible for the acceptance of new forms of piety. They turned against the moralistic rigorism of the old priests; the establishment of new classical colleges contributed to the training of future clergy; and they promoted the founding and spreading of conventual orders like the Gray Sisters of Ottawa and the Daughters of Charity of Montreal, who later spread to all of North America and attested the vitality of the Canadian Church.

Within the entire Church, the province of Quebec constituted the unique case of a society which in the midst of the nineteenth century was formed by Catholic principles. In their desire to preserve their cultural heritage within an English-speaking and Protestant majority, the French-Canadians spontaneously accepted the influence of the Church in all areas of private, social, and political life. But this situation, in which the Church with a minimum of official privileges exercised an almost unlimited moral authority, also had its disadvantages. It very soon resulted in a clericalism which systematically prevented any efforts by laymen. Characteristic of this condition was the opposition of the hierarchy to the *Institut Canadien,* a series of public libraries organized by some young, liberal Catholics, and to the development of teacher associations. This attitude encouraged the development of a strictly conformist Catholic civilization, in spite of the founding by the first provincial council (1851) of a Catholic university in Quebec which became one of the few centers of a moderate Catholic liberalism.

In the province of Ontario, where the Catholics constituted a minority, the bishops were confronted with two problems at the middle of the century. One of them was the necessity to integrate the stream of immigrants, especially in the countryside, and the difficulty of priests and nuns, imported from France and Quebec for that purpose, in adapting themselves to an environment so totally different from their native soil. The other great problem was the question of Catholic schools. The Catholic campaign for the improvement of the status of the schools was intensified after the passing of legislation in 1850 under the leadership of the Toronto Catholic Institute, but the bishops themselves disagreed on how much to demand. The most active among them was the bishop of Toronto, Monsignor Charbonnel, who had recently arrived from France and whose sympathies in the discussions of the Falloux Law were more in keeping with the intransigence of Louis Veuillot than with the tempered realism of Dupanloup and Montalembert. Protracted negotiations with the government ultimately resulted in insufficient though noticeable improvements. In this instance as well as in the matter of Church property (clergy reserve) a solution was reached which combined the limited denominational protectionism desired by the Church with the American ideal of the complete neutrality of the state in religious affairs.

The appointment of an apostolic delegate in 1877 acknowledged the growing importance of Canadian Catholicism. Despite many problems which it had in common with the United States, such as immigration and borders, the mixing of races and languages, and secularization, Canadian Catholicism came to have its own peculiar characteristics. The factor chiefly responsible for this separate development was the French element, which was determined to survive in an Anglo-Saxon world.

Australia

Although more modest than in America, the progress of Catholicism in Australia within a single generation resulted in the growth of a new Church with half a million faithful (25 percent of the total population).

Initially a penal colony, Australia gradually also attracted free immigrants; the Irish were especially strongly represented in both groups. After the turn of the century the government permitted the dispatch of clerics, who naturally also were Irishmen. But after the Emancipation Act of 1829, the government insisted that the chief representatives of the new Church be Englishmen. Benedictines, in the majority from Downside Priory, assumed this function. John Bede Polding, the first vicar apostolic, appointed in 1834 and archbishop of Sydney after 1842, was an energetic man and full of missionary zeal. But the growth of the population made the realization of his dream impossible. At the time of his appointment in Sydney, 90 percent of the forty thousand Australian Catholics resided in New South Wales, but the increasing Irish immigration to other areas of Australia and the gold rush in 1851 in the area of Melbourne demanded an increase in the number of parishes and dioceses. These were by necessity primarily staffed with Irish priests and bishops of Irish descent. These, however, followed pastoral principles which were quite different from those of the Benedictines, inasmuch as they emphasized education and an increase in the number of elementary schools. Frequent tensions among the bishops; conflicts between the bishops and their active and independent-minded priests; misunderstandings between the English Benedictines and the Irish clergy, which often placed its patriotic feelings above obedience to superiors; and the opposition of some liberal laymen desirous of a more democratic organization of the Church; all of these resulted in frequent disturbances of the Australian Church during the second third of the century. But these troubles must not be permitted to overshadow the missionary efforts by all clergy, an effort which found a visible reward in the growth of religious activity. Nor should the devotion be forgotten of some lay people whose charitable work among the immigrants was admirable.

As in many other countries, the problem of education assumed a central role in Australia after 1865. The increased withholding of state subsidies for parochial schools, which led to the closing of many Protestant schools, hardly affected the growth of the Catholic elementary schools, which bishops and priests regarded as one of the most important foundations of pastoral care.

CHAPTER 31

The Easing of Tensions in the Iberian World

Spain

Spain lost much of its significance for the Holy See when its former American colonies declared their independence. Even so, it remained one of the three great Catholic powers of Europe. In fact, until the accession of Pius IX Spain was of greater concern to Rome than the France of Louis-Philippe or the Josephinist Austria of Metternich.

The crisis began in 1833 upon the death of King Ferdinand VII. He had annulled the Salic law and assured the throne for his daughter Isabella. But the "apostolic faction," afraid that the regency of María Cristina would return the liberals to power, supported the claims of Don Carlos, who was known for his reactionary political and religious views and also had the support of the regionalists of the northern provinces. The resulting dynastic war lasted until 1839, openly supported by most of the clergy of Navarre, León, and the Basque country. The war intensified the contrast between the liberals and the intransigent Catholics because Gregory refused to acknowledge Isabella. Partly out of a spontaneous sympathy for the traditionalist ideology represented by the Carlists, and partially under the pressure from Austria and Russia, Gregory openly took the side of Don Carlos.

Gregory was also motivated to do so by the anticlerical policy of the new government, even though during the first months of his regency the moderate Minister Martínez de la Rosa tried not to break with Rome and, without diverging from canonic forms, attempted to adjust the statute concerning the Spanish Church. This statute still conformed to the concordat of 1753 and corresponded neither to the ideas nor to the political realities of the present. But it was soon removed by the radicals. The change began with widespread outbreaks of violence, the burning of monasteries, the murder of regular clergy in Madrid, Saragossa, Murcia, and Barcelona, and violent acts aimed at the clergy in other cities. Beginning in 1835, the new minister, Mendizábal, proclaimed a number of anticlerical laws. The first, the confiscation of Church property, chiefly grew out of economic considerations and was an attempt to deal with the growing deficit in the state's budget. But all of the others had their origin in an ideology which combined the dreams of the Alumbrados of the eighteenth century and of the liberals of the nineteenth century. The laws effected the dissolution of all monasteries except those devoted to education and the care of the sick, the unconditional dissolution of the large orders, the confiscation of the property of the parishes and chapters, and the abolition of the tithe, which constituted the chief source of income for the clergy (approximately 400 million reales). The state, now expected to assume the tasks hitherto performed by the Church, failed to live up to its public welfare obligations. The government passed punitive legislation against the "abuse" of pulpit and confessional, and expelled with military force the prelates accused of opposition to the government. In no time at all the most important episcopal sees such as Toledo, Valencia, Burgos, and Granada were vacant. For the first time, the Protestants received permission to proselytize. Finally, a plan was conceived for a general reform of the Church according to the example of the French Civil Constitution of the Clergy of 1790.

The opposition of María Cristina resulted in three years of calm (1837–39) and an attempt to put the finances of the Church on a new footing. But eventually María Cristina was forced to flee the country, and under the regency of General Espartero (1840–43) anticlerical policy came to the fore again. Espartero not only refused to pay the clergy the salaries to which it had agreed in return for the confiscations, but also on his own authority established new parishes and without consulting the Holy See appointed administrators for forty-seven of the vacant sixty-two episcopal sees. His Catholic opponents, among them preeminently the Catalan canon Jaime Balmes, based their opposition to his policies on Espartero's own principles of liberalism. There was no doubt that the radicalism of this religious policy began to worry a good number of moderates in a country in which the Catholic faith was still deeply rooted even among the bourgeoisie.

After ten years of an uninterrupted degeneration of the old Spanish Church regimen, a relaxation of tensions set in with the return of the moderates. It lasted for a whole decade and began with the maturity of Queen Isabella, who had warm feelings for the Church. In 1844 the laws providing for the state's supervision of ecclesiastical activities were repealed. A short time later the expelled bishops returned and the court of the Rota was reinstated. The sale of Church property continued for a while, but was fully stopped during 1845. While the government was revising its policies, some sensible bishops like P. P. Romo, the new archbishop of Seville, began to recognize that a regime willing to allow constitutional freedoms would permit the Church to have a degree of independence which would more than compensate for the loss of certain privileges. They began to draft a pastoral program which better corresponded to the new mentality and whose objective was freedom of education. This attempt was facilitated by the open atmosphere prevailing in Rome during the first months of the pontificate of Pius IX. After it failed, the Spanish Church limited itself to regaining as fully as possible the restoration of the position earlier achieved in 1814 and 1825. But it was an erroneous expectation, as the change of thought among the middle class, especially among the university students, this time was much more profound.

In the meantime, negotiations with Rome had been started with a view toward restoring the relationship interrupted in 1835 and toward a new arrangement of ecclesiastical affairs. The most difficult point was the statute for the financing of the Spanish clergy, as it involved not only financial questions but fiscal ones as well. Additionally, the negotiations were handicapped by the mistrust of the Holy See toward a government which the papacy considered as too liberal and by some regalistic demands on the part of the Spanish government. A draft providing for some reforms was initialed in April 1845. Among them were the reopening of a few monasteries and the return to the secular clergy of unsold Church property. But the Holy See did not want to acknowledge the sale of Church property officially until the question of paying salaries to the clergy had been answered satisfactorily by the parliament. But, faced with the demand of the liberals to have the sales officially accepted immediately, the Spanish government refused to ratify the treaty. The government was also disappointed in not seeing included in the treaty several clauses, included in the concordat of 1753, which granted the state a number of concessions, particularly in the matter of the *placet.*

Yet both sides were interested in finding a solution, and the negotiations were resumed. After being interrupted by the death of Gregory XVI, they were continued in 1847 on a new basis and with a willingness on both sides to compromise. After extremely frank exchanges of views, the delicate question of salaries for the clergy was settled by the law of April 1849. Eventually the negotiations produced the concordat of 16 March 1851.

The agreement, in spite of some concessions to the spirit of the times, indeed confirmed Spain's Catholic nature. It also differed from the concordat of 1753 in removing the interference by the state in purely ecclesiastical matters and in granting the Church a large degree of autonomy. It thus was the "most liberal" of all Spanish concordats. It should also be noted that the loss of the majority of Church lands was a liberating experience for the Church and that after fifteen years of troubles the clergy felt closer to the Holy See than before. At the same time, the excesses of the liberals convinced the clergy that a guarantee of religion and social order could only be expected from the conservatives. This conviction moved the Church closer to the parties of the right, on whom the fate of the concordat seemed to depend. This was demonstrated clearly in 1854 when Espartero returned to power and immediately repealed the concordat with accompanying transgressions against Church property and religious orders. The debates of the new parliamentary assembly were the opportunity "for the first real discussion of the relationship of Church and state in the history of Spain" (Kiernan). But in the fall of 1856 the government returned to the hands of the moderates under the leadership of Narváez. Until the revolution of 1868, the Church was permitted to live in relative peace, sanctioned by an agreement with the Holy See.

The concordat granted the Church a decisive position in the state. It made possible a limited restoration of the Church, facilitated by the protection of Queen Isabella II. External reconstruction expressed itself in a high number of applicants for the seminaries, on whose reorganization the episcopate spent a large degree of effort. It was also shown by the founding of new active convents, especially in Catalonia, devoted to education and charity. But the underpinnings were provided by the genuine Christian sentiment among the masses. Unfortunately, the blossoming of the Church was only external. The clergy was still very numerous proportionally. Moreover, the clergy all too often was satisfied with a mere religion of rite and routine and frequently confused its apostolate with inflexibility. It maintained its claim to the moral leadership of the nation without justifying it with an adequate education, and by relying on an outdated Scholasticism which lacked any originality.

While during the preceding generation many anticlericals had remained believing Christians, after 1860 the number of intellectuals whose faith was shaken increased. Romanticism was introduced in Spain only belatedly after 1833 by the exiles who returned from France, at a time when its chief proponents were already alienated from the Church. It opened the way to free thought and under the influence of post-Hegelian philosophies found its Spanish expression in "Krausism." Many of the intellectuals were discouraged by a Catholicism which, under the leadership of the Neo-Catholics of Nocedal, the spiritual heirs of the Carlists, and their paper *Pensiamento español,* was fanatically antimodern. Their noisy conduct produced nothing but a stronger anti-clericalism among the educated middle class.

Portugal

The religious situation in Portugal during the pontificate of Gregory XVI developed parallel to that of Spain, just as had been the case during the restoration period. Portugal also had two pretenders: Don Miguel on one hand, and Don Pedro and his daughter Maria da Gloria on the other. The dynastic conflict was made graver by the ideological struggle between the absolutists, supported by clergy and Pope, and the constitutionalists, supported by the Freemasons. After the victory of Don Pedro in 1832, a number of anticlerical steps were taken: expulsion of the nuncio; establishment of a commission for the reform of the clergy, which in addition to sensible suggestions like a reduction of the overly large number of dioceses came up with projects of Gallican and Jansenist origin which were at direct variance with Roman ideas; suppression of the Jesuits, who had only just returned in 1829; and the closing of all monasteries, including those in the overseas possessions. Even graver was the fact that Don Pedro refused to acknowledge bishops who had been appointed by his rival Don Miguel, while on their part the majority of the bishops refused to cooperate with the liberal government. Many episcopal sees were soon declared vacant, and the government proceeded to noncanonical elections of chapter vicars. These came in conflict with the legitimate Church authorities, and priests and faithful who refused to recognize them were subject to persecution. A virtually schismatic condition existed for several years.

But, as in Spain, the political developments produced a relaxation of tension, starting in 1835. Even so, the negotiations with Rome, skillfully conducted by Monsignor Capaccini since 1842, made only slow progress. An agreement was reached only in October 1848 after the death of Gregory XVI; it dealt primarily with the question of the seminaries and the ecclesiastical jurisdiction in law. In 1857, the agreement was supplemented with a convention on the right of patronage by the Portuguese King with respect to the missions in India and China. Seminaries were reformed, a matter of dire necessity in light of the low standards of training of the clergy, whose conduct and pastoral negligence the nuncios had frequently criticized in their reports. In spite of the obstacles put up by the Freemasons, the orders, including the Jesuits, gradually regained a foothold in the country after 1858. Even more than in Spain, the common people remained faithful to the traditions of Catholicism. But the rationalistic orientation of the educated middle class became more prominent, and the indifference of the Portuguese Catholics to the attacks by the antireligious press stood in uncomfortable contrast to the Spanish endeavors to create a Catholic press during the second third of the nineteenth century.

The Spanish-American Republics

The dozen republics of former Spanish America were far from bringing much joy to the Holy See during the middle of the nineteenth century. While most of their constitutions continued to acknowledge Catholicism as the official state religion, the governments were unwilling to give up the tradition of a strict supervision of the Church and insisted that the Holy See recognize their right of patronage over the Church. At the same time they tried in the name of the new liberal ideology to reduce the influence of the clergy on the population, to do away with the clergy's legal privileges, and to incorporate the Church's considerable land holdings in the public economy. This attempt led to repeated conflicts and occasionally, as in Colombia and Mexico, to a rupture.

In some cases the conflicts were caused by the insistence of the Church on rejecting the state tutelage, which was incompatible with the new ultramontane ideas. But in most cases they resulted from a reactionary attitude of the clergy, which obstinately fought rearguard actions in defense of increasingly outmoded positions. Simultaneously, with the exception of Chile, the clergy, whose condition had changed radically, was no longer up to its tasks. There was a great lack of priests, especially in the rural areas. It grew worse with the break with Spain, especially as the immigrants were almost never accompanied by priests from their native homelands. In addition, there was a lowering of morality, a lack of discipline, and the total loss of a pastoral dynamic, leading to the total abandonment of the Indian missions within fifty years. The religious orders, which had remained after the secularization at the beginning of the century, were in full decline.

But after the deep crisis which had shaken these Christian communities during the wars of independence, a new beginning dawned by the middle of the century. It started with the pontificate of Gregory XVI. At first, the long-vacant episcopal sees were filled gradually. Apostolic visitors with extensive authorization were sent to restore discipline in the orders.

Restoration proceeded slowly but steadily. Pius IX, who had a vivid interest in these countries ever since his trip to Latin America, supported the initiatives. Additional dioceses made possible closer contact between priests and their flocks; Church provinces were reorganized in order to adjust them to the new political borders; attempts were made to regain control over the local clergy through the appointment of delegates who tried to ameliorate the crassest abuses, although only with limited success; regular clergy from Europe were encouraged to open schools, and in spite of obstacles put up by the governments their number increased gradually, even though their influence was limited to the propertied people. In Rome, the *Collegio Pio latino-americano* was established in 1858, with the aim of training an elite clergy obedient to the Holy See.

To be sure, almost the entire pontificate of Pius IX passed before official diplomatic relations between Rome and the most important South American republics could be established; prior to 1877, there were only a few delegates apostolic. But between 1852 and 1862 the Holy See succeeded in negotiating seven concordats or conventions. Some of them remained in effect only temporarily, but at least they brought about an improvement in the relations between the Church and the governments. This was usually the case both after the conservatives returned to power in the course of the second third of the century and after the subsequent triumph of the liberals during the final decades of the century.

This was especially true for Central America, where the dictator of Guatemala, General R. Carrera (1839–65), repealed the anticlerical laws introduced after 1829 by the liberal President Marazán. He restored the ecclesiastical privileges and the control of the clergy over the schools and the press, returned the land of the orders, and forced the smaller neighboring states to conclude concordats with the Holy See which were advantageous for the Church. This was also true, even though to a lesser degree, for Chile. There, Archbishop R. V. Valdivieso (1847–78), a diligent pastor, inflexible defender of the rights of the Church, and bitter antiliberal, complained unceasingly about the regalism of the government and the relief granted to the Protestants. But the Church received considerable compensation payments for the abolition of the tithe (1853), and during the twenty-five years that D. Portales was minister of education the influence of the Catholic Church in the schools was fostered, because Portales saw in it the best guarantee for public order. He also promoted the immigration of active orders from Europe.

In Venezuela the Church had to accept the loss of its own legal jurisdiction and of the tithe and the decision of the government to establish two new dioceses without consultation with Rome. But the conservative oligarchy which governed almost without interruption from 1830 to 1864 favored the clergy, culminating in the concordat of 1862. Bolivia almost concluded a concordat in 1851. In view of the small influence of the Church in public life, the government was friendlier than in many other countries, but refused to ratify the treaty when Rome insisted on "granting" the government the right of patronage over the Church, while the government demanded this recognition small influence of the Church in public life, the government was friendlier than in many other countries, but refused to ratify the treaty. Relations nevertheless remained cordial, because Rome tolerated the exercise of the national patronage de facto, without recognizing it officially.

In Peru the moderate liberal President R. Castilia was able to effect a compromise solution with the assistance of the conciliatory Archbishops F. X. de Luna Pizarro (1845–55) and J. S. Goyeneche (1859–72), in spite of the protests of a group of priests connected with the conservative party who tried to impose their reactionary views on the government. It was not possible to save the legal jurisdiction of the Church, the tithe, and the control of the Church over education, but the Church retained the majority of its property. Chiefly, however, the Church enjoyed an independence from the state which went far beyond that in any other South American state. Even in Argentina the end of the "golden age of the clergy" came with the departure of dictator Rosas in 1852. There, the clerics had adjusted to a pronounced regalism, but it was favorable to them. Still, the Church enjoyed another ten years of peace, because the constitution of 1853 contained several articles favoring the Church.

The Church registered a spectacular success in the years after 1860 in Ecuador. President García Moreno, a fiery but authoritarian Catholic, admired by the ultramontanes of the world, between 1861 and 1875 attempted to mold his country into a model Christian state. Legislation was fashioned along the lines of the encyclicals of Pius IX and especially of the *Syllabus*. For the implementation of his ideal the president to a large degree relied on European orders, in which he saw the guarantee for regeneration.

This policy clearly illuminates one of the principal weaknesses of Catholicism in Latin America throughout the nineteenth century. Social life, at least in those areas in which the Church had firm roots under the Old Regime, was inherently Christian. But these Christian traditions were not capable of making necessary internal changes. Local Catholicism, with few exceptions was passive and without vitality or originality culturally, socially, and apostolically. The reason was the absence of a middle class in these countries, the social structure of which was hardly changed by the political revolutions. It is chiefly to be found in the fact that the Church until the end of the Old Regime had retained a colonial structure too dependent on Spain and had become sterile and incapable of thought or action. Additionally, there was a very individualistic mentality, which under the influence of Freemasonry neglected organized ecclesiastical life in order to find salvation in a pietistic attitude toward faith.

Brazil

The Empire of Brazil was the largest and most populated state in South America, with a size of 3.3 million square miles and 5.5 million inhabitants in 1830, who grew to more than ten million by the end of Pius IX's pontificate. Under the regency and long reign of Pedro II (1831–88), the Church lived in relative peace, even though the government, which, following the example of Pombal, desired to govern the Church by protecting it, periodically created tensions. In 1844 the government appointed the archbishop of the capital contrary to canon usage. The measures against the old orders, "victims of internal abuses which without radical reforms inevitably would lead to their dissolution" (Y. de la Brière), were intensified in 1855. On the other hand, however, new active congregations were founded, and the European congregations which devoted themselves to education and charity were freely accepted. From the 1860s on, these congregations were able to conduct parish missions of several weeks duration, an undertaking very much needed, considering the profound religious ignorance of the people.

The regalistic mentality of the government was approved by the clergy until about 1860. But not everything was perfect. Freemasonry gained a considerable influence, even touching the religious confraternities. Another inheritance of the eighteenth century was the growth of rationalism and positivism among the educated and the deplorable situation of the clergy. The clergy was not only weak numerically; in 1872, there were fewer than one thousand priests. They were chiefly concentrated in the coastal cities, while in the interior of the country perhaps twenty parishes, covering thousands of square miles, were administered by a single priest and many faithful did not see a priest for ten years or longer. In addition, the morality of the clergy often left much to be desired. Until 1850, many priests were influenced by the ideas of Rousseau and the encyclopedists, and even if a portion of them turned away from Freemasonry on account of its hostility to the Holy See, by 1870 approximately more than half of the clergy still belonged to its adherents. Some of the bishops, of whom there were only eleven, tried to strengthen the seminaries, and gradually the Catholic lay leaders became better educated also. But on the whole the period of the Empire was a time of stagnation behind a facade of peace and quiet. In fact, more to the truth, it was a period of decay for Catholicism.

C H A P T E R   3 2

The Catholic Church in the Orthodox World

Unionist Prospects in the East

In the middle of the nineteenth century, two phenomena drew attention to the Eastern Churches. One was the development of the Eastern Question; the expected disintegration of the Ottoman Empire presaged profound political and religious changes. The other one was the clear recognition of the role which Russia's Pan-Slavic policy would play in connection with the budding nationalism of eastern Europe. Toward the end of the pontificate of Gregory XVI, a group led by Princess Volkonskaya, a wealthy convert residing in Rome since 1825, took up the question of the "return" of the separated Eastern Churches to Rome. Under the presidency of the prefect of the Propaganda, the group in 1847 suggested to Pius IX that he address a solemn appeal to the separated brethren in the East. The Pope combined this plan with his own intention to send an apostolic visitor who was to inform himself of the prevailing conditions in the East. In January 1848 he directed the encyclical *In suprema Petri sede* to the Eastern Christians. He informed the Uniates of the impending arrival of the apostolic visitor, who was well-known among the Catholic Armenians. He praised the customary advantages of the Catholic faith and invited the separated Uniates to join the Roman Church "as no conceivable reason could prevent their return to the true Church." The Uniates saw this document as a provocation. In May 1848 four partriarchs and twenty-nine archbishops wrote a negative reply in which they condemned Latin innovations, the pretensions of the Pope, and the proselytism of the Latin missionaries.

This failure did not discourage those, however, who regarded the upper clergy of the Orthodox Churches as no longer representing the true feelings of the people, who were in turmoil as a result of changes. At first they looked toward Russia, where they believed they saw a tentative opening for a rapprochement in the reforms of Alexander II and in the growing interest in Roman Catholicism among some noblemen who were searching for an effective antirevolutionary ideology. With the covert and overt assistance of this nobility, the writings of Joseph de Maistre enjoyed renewed popularity in Russia for a number of years and occasioned a series of foundations after the Crimean War (1854–56).

But it was especially in the Austrian Empire and France that a vivid interest was awakened in the "return" of the Eastern Christians to Rome (the problem of union was always approached in this way, going counter to any ideas of ecumenism). In Austria an attempt was made to draw the Orthodox believers in the border areas away from Russian influence and to orient them toward Rome; Franz Joseph and his advisers in this instance were motivated by both genuine religious concerns and reasons of state. Such attempts were also aided by some Slavic clerics in the Empire. Monsignor A. M. Slomšek, the bishop of Lavant, in 1851 in Slovenia founded the Brotherhood of Saints Cyril and Methodius, which quickly grew in Moravia also among the Ukrainians of Hungary and Galicia.

After 1860, the expectations with respect to Russia gradually disappeared. They were replaced by a new interest in the potential return to the Roman Church of the Christian communities of the Ottoman Empire. Such expectations were raised as a result of French intervention in Syria, and the model thought of were the Uniate communities. Public opinion was especially enthused by this question in France, where interest in the Christian East had grown for the past two decades. The issue had been kept alive by the speeches of men like Monsignor Dupanloup, by publications like the bimonthly journal *La Terre Sainte et les Églises orientales*, founded in 1864; and by the *Oeuvres des Écoles d'Orient*, founded in 1855 and given strong leadership by Lavigerie. Finally, in 1862, Father d'Alzon, at the request of the vicar apostolic at Constantinople and of Pius IX, engaged his Assumptionists in the unionist apostolate in the East. After a difficult beginning they played an important role for the next seventy-five years.

Rome could not remain indifferent to this interest in the East which agitated the Catholic world of the West, especially as the efforts of the Russians and chiefly the Protestant missions aided by the British were cause for concern. Much more serious were the efforts of Cardinal Reisach, who became interested in the Slavic problem by way of his contacts with Austria. He acquainted the Pope with the necessity of having available in Rome a number of specialists for the East. Following his suggestion, the Benedictine Pitra was ordered to undertake a study trip to Russia (1859–60), during which he was also to gather material for a broad documentation of the sources of Orthodox canon law. In 1862 Pius IX decided to divide the Congregation for the Propagation of the Faith into two sections, one of which was to concern itself with the affairs of the Churches of the Eastern Rite. Each cardinal belonging to the new section was assigned to a certain rite and asked to acquire competency in his area, and some of the best experts on the East were employed as consultants. There was no doubt that Pius IX and the leaders of the Propaganda genuinely desired to respect the different liturgical usages of the Eastern Churches in contrast to many Western missionaries who were bent on forcing the Eastern Catholics into loyalty Rome by making them replace their traditions with Latin customs, or in contrast to men like Father d'Alzon, who were convinced that the advance of European ideas necessarily would be followed by the disappearances of the Eastern rites.

Rome also tried to reestablish the influence of the Curia over the life of these Churches and gradually to gain entry for the principles of post-Tridentine Catholicism into the canon law of the Eastern Churches. But the optimistic expectations of a mass return of the separated Eastern Churches to the Church of Rome were not realized. In fact, the extreme centralization policy of Cardinal Barnabo by 1870 resulted in serious crises in the Uniate communities, crises which were intensified by the Vatican Council. Only in southeastern Europe and the Near East was Catholicism able to register some rather superficial progress, while its position in Russia once again deteriorated.

The Russian Empire

Contrary to the expectations which Gregory XVI at the beginning of his pontificate attached to the condemnation of the Polish rebellion, Tsar Nicholas I did not change his policy toward the Catholic Church; in fact, its condition behind "a curtain of silence" (de Bertier) grew worse. The Section for Religion at Saint Petersburg openly promoted the conversion of three Uniate dioceses of the Empire (1839) to the Russian Orthodox Church. Measures limiting the freedom of action of the Latin Church and its contacts with Rome in Poland and in the Russian Empire intensified from year to year. It is not to say too much that the Catholic Church legally was so integrated in the Russian state that it did not differ at all from any other state religion. While papal diplomacy in 1840 took up contacts with Polish conservatives in exile, through whom pressure was to be exerted on Russia, Gregory XVI's violent dislike of any revolutionary enterprise quickly regained the upper hand, and Rome returned to the usual method of secret negotiations through diplomatic channels.

In return for new concessions by Rome in 1841, Russia's envoy made some vague promises. In fact, however, nothing changed. The ukase of 25 December 1841, which secularized all property of the Churches in the western provinces and reduced still further the authorized number of regular clergy, only confirmed the failure of this method. Catholics in Russia, Austria, and western Europe could not understand the long silence of the Holy See. All questioned cardinals regarded a public protest as unavoidable. At this point, Gregory XVI again asked the Austrian Emperor and Metternich to mediate, only to learn that they were interested in a prolongation of the ecclesiastical abuses in the western provinces of neighboring and hostile Russia. This attempt having failed, the Pope in July 1842 published an address in which he complained to the world about the repressive measures applied to Polish and Russian Catholics and about the disloyal conduct of the Tsar.

Angry over the unexpected outburst, the Tsar, as many people had feared, began to intensify the measures against seminaries and orders. But upon the advice of Chancellor and Secretary of State Nesselrode, he started a policy of detente after a few months. He had two reasons. One was that at the very moment when Russia, in the eyes of a "revolutionary" Europe, tried to appear as a country in which, under the paternal authority of the Tsar, religion and order prevailed without compulsion, such an appeal to the world did not fit the Tsar's policy. He also feared that Austria would exploit the situation and would present itself to Rome as the only Christian great power. The recall of the Russian envoy from Rome (1843), his replacement by the moderate Butenev, and contacts made in 1844 through the mediation of the nuncios at Vienna and Munich paved the way for a personal encounter between Nicholas I and Gregory XVI. They met in December 1845, and Gregory XVI submitted to the Tsar an agenda which he had personally prepared.

Negotiations were started in November 1846 in Rome, after Nesselrode had made the necessary preparations first in Rome in talks with Monsignor Corboli-Bussi and Cardinal Lambruschini and then in Saint Petersburg with a special ministerial committee for Catholic affairs. Gregory XVI had died in the meantime, but Pius IX insisted that former Secretary of State Lambruschini, who was well versed in the problems, should continue to represent the Holy See. On the Russian side, negotiations were conducted by Bludov, former minister of the interior and justice, who was assisted by Butenev. The plenipotentiaries faced a difficult task; after all, they had to find solutions for the reconciliation of two powers with incompatible principles. Rome desired a total revision of Russian legislation, designed to return freedom to the Catholic Church. Saint Petersburg desired an improvement of its relations with Rome for the purpose of pacifying Polish agitation and winning the opinion of Europe for Russia. Russia was prepared to make some concessions, but was unyielding in the question of strict control over the Churches by the state. After twenty conferences (19 November 1846 to 1 March 1847), agreement was reached on some points, including the question of appointment of bishops. But the representatives of the Tsar again refused to discuss the suppression of the Uniate Church in the Ukraine. They insisted on demands unacceptable to Rome, among them those concerning mixed marriages and contacts of the bishops with Rome.

An impasse was reached, and both the Tsar and Lambruschini were willing to break off the negotiations. But the more conciliatory Nesselrode implored the delegates to resume their talks after a certain interval. At the same time the same opinion was voiced in Rome by a commission of cardinals headed by Pius IX. Considering that the Catholic Church in Russia was facing an extreme emergency situation, the opportunity for an ever so limited improvement should not be allowed to pass. Consequently, negotiations were resumed on 15 June and by 3 August 1847 led to a settlement. It listed all points on which the two parties had agreed, as well as those on which agreement had not been reached and which were reserved for future discussions. A completely satisfying concordat was still a long way off, but at least a clear break was made with the policy of unilateral decisions, followed by the Tsars since the beginning of the eighteenth century. The agreement, which Nicholas I in the absence of a better one ultimately signed, could be viewed as a success by the Holy See.

Yet the particular conditions made normalization difficult, the more so as after initial proofs of good will the administrative chicaneries increased as soon as the fears raised by the revolutions of 1848–49 dissipated. Even graver was the government's tactic of appointing to higher offices prelates who for reasons of cowardice or ambition were willing to do the government's bidding. Finally, in the 1860s, after the Crimean War, slavophile influences replaced the party friendly toward Rome, and a campaign for the conversion of Latin Catholics to the Orthodox Church was begun. There was no doubt that in the eyes of many Russians the western provinces of the Empire were seen as foreign bodies as long as Catholicism, which was called the "Polish faith," continued to exist. Even the insufficient attempts to adhere to the concordat were justification for the convinced Orthodox Russians to emphasize all those points which gave them reason for their opposition to "Romanism." This attitude produced a number of controversies among the intellectuals until the end of the century. They are reflected in Dostoevski's *Idiot* (1868), where Prince Myshkin evaluates Catholicism as worse than atheism.

As for Poland, the tsarist government understood that it could not eliminate Latin Catholicism, but was nevertheless determined to control all ecclesiastical life as much as possible. It kept episcopal sees vacant and tried to limit the contacts between bishops and Rome to a minimum. It forbade the bishops to convoke their priests in synods and to make public appeals in pastoral letters to the faithful. It intervened in the running of seminaries, which were badly off in any case owing to insufficient funds, and limited the number of postulants admitted to orders. At the beginning of 1862 the government created a committee for religion which strictly separated Catholics, Orthodox, Protestants, and Jews and, ignoring canon law and the Convention of 1847, deprived ordinaries of a majority of their jurisdiction.

It was not so much a matter of persecution of a denomination as one of regalistic practices. These had been a matter of course during the Old Regime in all of Europe, but in view of the developments in the Catholic world, for which the Austrian concordat of 1855 was a benchmark, appeared anachronistic and offensive. Thus, it was not surprising that priests and regular clergy, who had expected a democratic government to free the Church from its fetters, increasingly made common cause with the leftist opposition, which in addition to propagating social reforms knew how to exploit the Polish nationalism of the lower clergy. In spite of the reserved attitude of the Holy See and the episcopate, these patriotic priests with their revolutionary agitation discredited the Catholic Church and strengthened the distrust of the Russian officials and encouraged them to take stronger action against the Church. Yet, in spite of the growing discontent, the resistance of the Catholic people was not strong enough. Most important, however, was the absence of any foundation on which a movement could have developed. In this police state there were no political platforms, no newspapers, nor any other means by which information could have been disseminated. Additionally, many episcopal sees were either vacant or occupied by incompetent men who were willing to accept a mutilated canon law to the extent that their ecclesiastical training was determined by Josephinism and Febronianism. Finally, a number of the upper clergy, partially for reason of social conservatism, partially for reason of hostility to the Germans, regarded collaboration with Russia as the lesser evil.

The Holy See, very well informed of the difficulties of the Church in Poland by emigrants and its numerous contacts in the Hapsburg Empire, repeatedly protested to the Russian embassy at Rome against the violations of the 1847 agreement. At the same time, the Holy See tried to establish a nunciature at Saint Petersburg, in the expectation that it would facilitate the solution of many local problems and the supervision of the efforts of the Polish clergy, which the Holy See frequently regarded as unfortunate. The more liberal attitude of the new Tsar, Alexander II, seemed to justify such hopes during the initial period of his rule, and, in fact, negotiations had reached a promising state by 1862. But the Polish rebellion of 1863–64 once again put everything in question and thereafter relations between Rome and Saint Petersburg grew chillier.

The reaction by the Russian government to the assistance provided the rebels by the clergy was very strong. More than four hundred clerics, including several bishops, were deported to Siberia. Of 197 monasteries, 114 were closed; because the regular clergy was strongly allied with the rebels, bans of processions and pilgrimages multiplied, as did police surveillance of sermons and the confessional. Between 1866 and 1869, three dioceses were dissolved without the consent of Rome and were attached to neighboring dioceses.

Pius IX harbored as little sympathy for revolutionaries as Gregory XVI; but the brutality of the Russian reprisals against the Church angered him. On 24 April 1864 he lodged a strong protest. A complete rupture of diplomatic relations was delayed by Austrian mediation, but when the situation continued to deteriorate, the Pope again complained in a speech on 29 October 1866. It had been drafted by a commission of cardinals and was accompanied by rich documentation for the press. On 4 December the Russian government replied by revoking the concordat. In May 1867 it decreed that in the future all contacts of the bishops, including the Polish ones, with Rome were to be subject to official control by the Roman Catholic College at Saint Petersburg. The majority of the bishops was willing to comply with the new regulation, but the Pope described it as incompatible with the divine constitution of the Church. The Russian government in turn forbade the bishops of Russia and Poland to attend the Vatican Council. After the council, attempts were made by several factions to start a movement in favor of establishing a separate Slavic Catholic Church with a Latin rite, modeled after the Old Catholics. The project was utopian and the Russian government paid hardly any heed to it.

The Russian government, which since 1870 seemed to be interested in improving relations with Rome, from which it expected a pacifying influence on Poland, made a gesture of good will. It announced its willingness to reform the Roman Catholic College at Saint Petersburg in a way acceptable to the Holy See. But renewed attempts in 1877 to introduce the Russian language into the religion, as well as the discovery by the British during the Russo-Turkish war of police measures against the Uniates who refused to bend to the dictates of the "robber synod of Chelm," occasioned another Roman protest. It led to the final break between the two parties.

On balance, however, the situation was not as negative for Poland as it might seem. While the rationalistic influence of the Enlightenment was long in evidence among the educated people, the upper levels of society, who recognized the pacifying influence of the Church in relation to revolutionary social demands, experienced a development very similar to that which France had undergone a few decades earlier. This change of atmosphere, even though it was tied to certain interests, promoted a profound religious awakening. It was strengthened by the new wave of spirituality then coursing through all of Europe.

A more significant indication of the rejuvenation of the vitality of Catholicism was the development of the religious orders. Many among them bore unmistakable signs of decadence, which fully justified the measures taken by the Russian government. There were too many monasteries with too few people, and there was a lack of novicemasters. Violations of seclusion regulations and the vow of poverty and the admittance of candidates who had no real vocation and merely wished to escape military service were very frequent. On the other hand, the Capuchins, especially in Warsaw, performed extremely valuable work in the areas of piety — particularly as it concerned the Virgin Mary — charity, and social

work. After the middle of the century, there were also numerous new foundings of women's congregations, as for example those of the Felicians in 1856. The
movement continued even after the setbacks of 1864.

The Slavs in Austria-Hungary

As a country of nationalities on the borders of the Slavic world, the Hapsburg
Empire was a place of encounter and also conflict between Eastern and Western
Christendom. In 1870, the Empire comprised 24 million Latin Catholics, 3.5 million
Protestants, 4 million Catholics of the Eastern rite, and 3 million Orthodox. The last
two enjoyed freedom of religion and of organization, but both the government and
the Catholic hierarchy hoped that they would return to Rome.

In Croatia, where the Orthodox comprised 30 percent of the population and
were in close contact with their brethren still under Turkish domination, unionist
efforts were embodied by Monsignor J. G. Stroßmayer, Bishop of Diakovar from
1849 to 1905. A conscientious prelate and ardent patriot, he had gradually become
the moral leader of the Croatian opposition to the Magyar oligarchy. Instead of
becoming involved in fruitless political battles, he preferred to advance the Slavic
cause on the cultural level. He employed a majority of his high income to subsidize
journals and publications on Slavic literature, history, and folklore and to give his
country two important institutions, an academy (1867) and a university (1874).
His contributions earned him an incomparable popularity among all Slavs of the
south, Orthodox and Catholic alike. He intended to use his popularity to gain his
second objective, the unification of the Churches. As far as he was concerned,
this union was the prerequisite for the adoption of Western culture by the Slavs
without risk. In order to facilitate an approach, he favored the Roman liturgy in
Old Slavic and at the Vatican Council suggested a policy of decentralization of the
Church. But his irenic way of approaching the problem of unifying the divided
Christians met a favorable echo in Rome only during the pontificate of Leo XIII.

At the other end of the Empire, the growth of Pan-Slavism and the resultant
tension between Austria and Russia had repercussions on the Ruthenian Church
of Galicia. Its leader, Monsignor Lewicki, after 1813 archbishop of Lvov, was created cardinal in 1856; this dignity had not been awarded to a prelate of the Eastern
rite since the sixteenth century. The clergy, cognizant since 1848 of the humiliating condition which Poland had imposed on the Ruthenian people, increasingly
devoted itself to the political struggle in the name of Ukrainian nationalism. Some
saw in it a means to regroup all Uniates on both sides of the border for a more
effective resistance to the attractions of Russian Orthodoxy, but others, especially
among the young, began to view Orthodox Russia as the protector of the Slavs.
With the secret support of tsarist agents they viewed with sympathy the efforts
of Michael Popiel in the diocese of Chelm, because after the concordat of 1855,
which was binding for all Catholics of the Empire, the tendency to adjust Eastern
ecclesiastical regulations to Latin canon law was intensified under pressure from
the Vienna government.

In this atmosphere, the century-old controversies between the clerics of both
rites could not but become aggravated, but the resistance of the Ruthenian clergy

to the Latin pressures of Poland served to tighten the connection between Church and people. With the consent of the nuncio, the Galician bishops worked out a sensible plan for an agreement, which was presented to the Holy See in 1853. Regrettably, Rome did not make an immediate decision, and soon the situation worsened again when both sides accused one another of proselytism, especially in connection with mixed marriages. Only in 1863, under the impact of the Polish revolution, was an agreement finally reached.

The Ruthenian dioceses of Podcarpathia, living in complete peace until the middle of the century, now also began to feel the effects of nationalistic agitation. For it was at this time that an effort was started in liturgy to substitute Hungarian for those Magyars who no longer understood Old Slavic. The government in Budapest, interested in weakening the influence of Slavism in its territory, supported these efforts, while the Russophile propaganda was encouraging the awakening of Slavic consciousness and obtained a number of conversions to the Orthodox religion.

The Uniate Rumanians of Transylvania had to thank the hostility to the Orthodox Serbs for many conversions. Upon the suggestion of the bishop of Grosswardein, Monsignor Erdeli (1843–62), two new dioceses were established together with an autonomous province with its capital at Fogaras. The reorganization of this Church was undertaken in close cooperation between Rome and the Rumanian Uniate hierarchy. In 1858, the Congregation for the Propagation of the Faith directed three instructions concerning marriage law to the hierarchy, asking for urgent reforms. A Roman delegation headed by the Vienna nuncio went to Transylvania in order to examine the situation which had become doubtful in light of the right of the Emperor, acknowledged in the concordat of 1855, to intervene in various matters, including the election of bishops. After conferences between Monsignor De Luca and the Rumanian bishops it was decided to hold a provincial council. After some delay, but well prepared by the new Metropolitan Ioan Vancea (1868–92), an extremely active prelate with Roman training, and Monsignor J. Papp-Szilaggi, the author of one of the few handbooks on Eastern canon law of the sixteenth century the council met in Blaj in May of 1872. Its decrees were well considered and complete. In addition to this juridical rejuvenation, the clergy continued its efforts in the pastoral and cultural areas by becoming the ardent defender of the Rumanian language and national idea in the face of Magyar domination.

Progress of Catholicism in Southeastern Europe and the Levant

In 1860 it looked for a moment as though a new Uniate Church were to be established in Bulgaria. Faced with the consistent refusal of the Phanariot to allow the Bulgarians to have their own bishops as a first step to their cultural and political emancipation, the Polish Committee in Paris began to suggest that the Bulgarians could expect their religious emancipation only from the Pope; they propagated the union with Rome under the condition that Old Slavic be retained as the liturgical language. Pius IX was well disposed toward the suggestion; after he had personally consecrated the aged Hegumenos, J. Sokolski, as archbishop of the Uniate Bulgarians in April 1861, a conversion movement was started in which politics played as much of a role as did religion. But the intervention of Russia, which desired the emancipation of Bulgaria for Russia's benefit, and the tactlessness of the apostolic delegate, Monsignor Brunoni, soon nipped the movement in the bud. After the mysterious disappearance of Sokolski only a small flock was left, entrusted by Pius IX to the Assumptionists of Father d'Alzon and to the Polish Resurrectionists. When a new Bulgarian bishop was finally appointed four years later, the opportunity had passed.

In all areas which for centuries had been under Ottoman domination, Catholicism of the Latin rite made progress during the second third of the nineteenth century; in its own time it was very significant.

In Rumania, autonomy grew until the establishment of an independent monarchy in 1866. In the same way the activity of the regular clergy in Moldavia increased in spite of the occasionally justified criticism leveled against it, and within a period of fifty years increased the number of faithful from forty-eight thousand to seventy-five thousand. In the liberal atmosphere prevailing in 1859 during the reorganization of the Polish status of the principalities, the Catholics were granted civil and political equality. In 1864 the government, which wished to end the Austrian protectorate over the Catholics, even planned a concordat with the Holy See. But sensitivity on the part of the Orthodox did not permit the replacement of the apostolic visitor by the establishment of a diocese at Jassy before 1884. In the preceding year an archbishopric had been established in Bucharest, after the number of Catholics in Wallachia, insignificant until the middle of the century, had grown tenfold within a few decades.

But this progress on the level of institutions should not lead to false conclusions. The spiritual tension between the national Orthodox Church and the Catholic minority continued. The majority of the Latin clergy were foreigners and the mission of the Conventuals in Moldavia was accused of being a tool of Magyarization. In fact, there were people who, with reference to the Hungarian descent of a part of the Catholic population, for a long time tried to entrust the mission to Hungarian members of the order and to withdraw it from the authority of the Congregation for the Propagation of the Faith in order to place it directly under the ecclesiastical administration of Hungary. The government of the new kingdom in its striving for national independence insisted on the training of a native clergy, a demand which as early as 1842 had been acknowledged as justified by the Congregation for the Propagation of the Faith. For some time in this area, in which the priests because of their low numbers were not able to minister regularly to the faithful, who lived dispersed in many villages, a native organization had grown, the lay didascales. These were not only catechists and sacristans, but they also conducted Sunday prayer services, conducted funerals, and took the place of missionaries in civil matters. But as most of them were former seminarians from Transylvania and partisans of the Hungarian cause, the efforts to train the Rumanian didascales was persistently thwarted by the Hungarian Conventuals. It was accomplished only in the final years of the century.

In Bosnia, which until 1878 belonged to the Ottoman Empire, the long conflict between Vicar Apostolic Barišić and the Croatian Franciscans, who defended the South Slavic idea against Austria's influence, was solved in 1847 by dividing the country into the two vicariates of Bosnia (one hundred twenty-five thousand faithful) and Herzegovina (thirty-five thousand faithful.) However, the Catholics in these areas remained isolated and had only a small share in the improvement of the legal position of the Christians in the Ottoman Empire as a result of the decrees of 1839 and 1856.

At Constantinople and the ports of the Levant, the Catholic presence as well as the activity of Protestant missions was no longer concealed. In 1839, the new sultan, Abdul Mejid, following the advice of his liberal grand vizier, published the Hatti Sherif of Gulhané, which promised to all, regardless of religion or sect, complete safety of their lives, their honor, and their property. He wanted the Western powers to feel obligated and to assure himself of the loyalty of the Christians. The application of this regulation often was only theoretical, especially in the Balkan countries. But a first step toward emancipation had been taken, of particular benefit to the Uniate communities.

The Crimean War and the resultant Hatti-Humayun of 1856 produced another noticeable improvement in the legal position of the Christians, which improved even further after the Syria expedition of 1860. The holding of the regional Council of Smyrna in 1869, which brought together the Latin episcopate of Greece and the Greek islands, the vicar apostolic of Constantinople, and the archbishop, would have been unthinkable twenty years earlier. Nevertheless, the steady growth of the missions founded by religious congregations, most of which were of French origin, was surprising. In close contact with the French consuls, who under the Third Republic were even more concerned with limiting Italian influence in the Near East than under the Second Empire, the activity of the Lazarists, of the Christian Brothers, of the Sisters of Charity, and of the Sisters of Saint Joseph increased; and many other congregations joined them also. The Jesuits of Beirut were especially active. In an attempt to protect the educated classes from the Protestant influence, they founded a modern publishing company which published Arabic translations of Western religious tracts; they also established a large Catholic newspaper, the *Al-Bashir* (1871), and finally a modern college which in 1881 became the University of Saint Joseph.

It must be admitted that the Latin Catholics of the Near East, whose numbers increased very satisfactorily, were for the most part foreigners. They came primarily from Malta and Italy, and as they grew in numbers they were increasingly regarded as alien intruders. But at the time their progress was greeted in Rome with joy, and the Holy See tended to see in their growth the future of Catholicism in the East. In order to coordinate the multifaceted missionary work and to assure Rome of control over the organization of the various Catholic communities in the Ottoman Empire, the Congregation for the Propagation of the Faith put its hope in the work of the apostolic delegates. It also continued to send out visitors who supervised the implementation of reforms and reported back to Rome.

The Eastern Patriarchates

In the course of the third quarter of the nineteenth century two developments characterized the Uniate Churches. There was a quantitative growth and with it a continuation of institutional consolidation, but there was also the threat of new schisms as a result of Rome's intensified policy of centralization. This policy of the pontificate of Pius IX expressed itself in the interference of the Congregation for the Propagation of the Faith in the elections of patriarchs and bishops, in the alteration of decisions of the local synods, and in the introduction of reforms in traditional institutions. It also showed itself in the activity of the apostolic delegates in favor of an accommodation of Eastern ecclesiastical regulations to those of the Latin West.

This could be noted particularly in the Armenian Church. Numerous conversions, especially in Constantinople, raised the total number of the faithful in Turkey to about one hundred twenty thousand by 1870. Allowing for this progress, Pius IX in 1850 had created six new dioceses in northern Asia Minor and subordinated them to the primate archbishop of Constantinople. This archbishop, Monsignor Hassun, with enterprising energy and with the assistance of the Jesuits and other Western missionaries as well as the Armenian Congregation of Antonites, who were experiencing an incomparable growth, increased the number of churches and schools several times over. In order to crown this progress with a uniform canon discipline and a further improvement in the relations between Turkey and Rome, the Holy See after the death of the patriarch of Cilicia decided in 1866 to fuse the two supraepiscopal jurisdictions by the election of Monsignor Hassun as patriarch. But this very step, which seen from the Roman point of view would promote the cohesion of the Armenian Church, in fact caused a great crisis. The reason was that the document which reorganized the Armenian patriarchate, the famous bull *Reversurus,* also and fundamentally altered the Eastern laws with respect to the privileges of the patriarch and the method of election of the bishops. The upper crust of the laity after 1850 repeatedly had complained about the virtual abolition of its right of participation; now it protested again, supported by clergy and bishops who also accused the patriarch of despotism in the leading of his Church and too much subservience to the Congregation for the Propagation of the Faith. The opposition became stronger at the council which the patriarch convoked at Constantinople from July to November 1869. While Hassun was attending the Vatican Council, a dissident movement was formed under the leadership of the superior of the Antonites, Monsignor Kasandschan. After the opposition declared Hassun deposed, it obtained recognition by the Turkish government as the true Armenian Church, and took over a number of churches and schools. The schism lasted for ten years, until Leo XIII in 1880 replaced Hassun, who had been created a Curia cardinal, with the more flexible Monsignor Azarian.

The Chaldean Church was fortunate in being led between 1847 and 1878 by Joseph Audo, an energetic and dynamic person, even though he was an only moderately educated patriarch. At the Council of Rabban Hurmuz in 1853 the Church for the first time codified its canon discipline in a Latin form. Within a period of twenty-five years it grew from forty thousand members to sixty thousand, but was shaken after 1860 by the increasingly fierce conflict between Audo and the Congregation for the Propagation of the Faith. Rome objected to the patriarch's extending his jurisdiction to the Chaldeans of Malabar, who since the seventeenth century had been under Latin sovereignty. After a preliminary settlement of the question in 1863 and the recall of the apostolic delegate, who had exceeded his instructions, the struggle was renewed when the applicability of the bull *Reversurus* was extended to the Chaldeans by the constitution *Cum ecclesiastica disciplina* of 31 August 1869. Furthermore, the resentment caused by the Vatican Council was still smoldering. The Chaldean episcopate split into two groups, and in 1876 the aged and ill-advised Audo was about to break with Rome. But the loyalty of the old patriarch to Catholicism and a gesture of peace by Pius IX were able to prevent this catastrophe at the last moment.

The Syrian Church did not have to go through such a crisis, even though a tense atmosphere lasted throughout the pontificate of Pius IX. The founding of the patriarchate by Antonius Samhiri (1854–66), which was occasioned by the Council of Sarfeh in 1853, was accompanied by some disagreements and some new efforts. It laid the basis for the future of the Syrian Church, whose center was transferred from Aleppo to Mardin upon the request of Rome. But the succeeding patriarch, Philipp Arqus (1866–74), was hesitant and assumed a very vague and waiting stance in view of the uncertainties caused by the bull *Reversurus* and the Vatican Council.

The patriarch of the Melchites, Mazlum, heatedly opposed Roman interference with the rights of the patriarch. After the deaths of Gregory XVI and Cardinal Litta, who had personally known and trusted the patriarch, violent clashes took place, especially as the authoritarian and power-hungry Mazlum caused some of his opponents within his own Church to ally themselves with the Western partisans of a systematic Latinization. The Congregation for the Propagation of the Faith succeeded in having Clement Bahut (1856–64) chosen as Mazlum's successor. Bahut was very loyal to Rome, where he had studied, but he was more of an ascetic than a man of action. His ineptitude created a schism in his Church, but fortunately it was of short duration.

Fortunately, the massacres of 1860, in which the Druses were responsible for almost as many cruelties among the Melchites as among the Maronites, put an end to the squabbles. Everything was put right again by Bahut's conciliatory successor, the eminent Gregory Yussef (1864–97). One of his greatest concerns was the improvement in the education of the local clergy, which was still inadequate in spite of Mazlum's efforts. Through the establishment of native schools, designed as a counterweight to the education provided by the Protestants, he tried to counter the annoyance caused by the schools maintained by certain Latin missionaries for the Churches of the Eastern rite. But he did not convene a council, in spite of the advantages which would have accrued to his reorganization, because he would have required the help of Rome and did not wish to ask for it. There was no doubt that Yussef, although he was a former student of the college of the Congregation for the Propagation of the Faith at Rome, was convinced by the bull *Reversurus* and the undifferentiated program of the neo-ultramontanes at the Vatican Council that Rome desired the destruction of the traditional privileges of the patriarchs. The reorganization of the Melchite Church had been started by the Council of Jerusalem, but its decrees had not been ratified by the Holy See during the time of the sharp conflict with Mazlum.

The Maronite Church suffered heavily from the revolt of the Lebanese peasants against the feudal domination of the sheiks and the Druse massacres in 1845 and 1860. But the decline of the civilian leadership ultimately turned the patriarchate into the most important political power of the country. For half a century it was guided by Paul Masad (1854–1890), who combined great leadership qualities with considerable erudition. He opened his pontificate in 1856 with a national council at Bkerke under the chairmanship of the apostolic delegate; the council was attended by the superiors of the three Maronite orders, which at this time comprised about eighteen hundred members and eight hundred priests. The long-standing and close connection with France, the strong protector of Lebanon, prepared the ground for a good understanding with the Latin missionaries. The disagreements caused by the bull *Reversurus* and by the definitions of the Vatican Council only slightly disrupted the Maronite Church, whose connection with the Holy See went much further back in history than that of the other Uniates. Regrettably, little is known to this day about the inner life, the pastoral work of the clergy, the religious life of the faithful, and the development of the monastic customs of this vital Church, as well as of the other Uniate Churches.

Section Two

The Missions between 1840 and 1870

Johannes Beckmann

CHAPTER 33

The Strengthening of the Gregorian Restoration

The long pontificate of Pius IX, seen from the missionary point of view, was essentially a continuation of the reforms of Gregory XVI, but also an amplification. The actual work was done by Alessandro Barnabo (1801–74). Serving the Congregation for the Propagation of the Faith since 1831, Pius IX in 1847 made him its secretary and chose him as its cardinal prefect in 1856. He had a strong sense of duty and was a conscientious administrator, but not even his contemporaries, let alone posterity, knew much about his many accomplishments. Barnabo not only prepared all new foundings to the point of papal briefs and appointments, but also took care that missionary personnel were increased accordingly.

While during the first half of the nineteenth century new missionary institutes were established chiefly in France, it was Italy which became very much engaged in this area of activity during the second half of the nineteenth century. Until the twentieth century, all of the Italian foundations were rooted in the renewal and intensification of the religious life of the closing eighteenth and beginning nineteenth centuries, carefully nurtured through generations of outstanding priests and bishops. This explains the fact that all new religious foundations, created and carried by the secular clergy, had an apostolic-missionary character. Some of the institutions, owing to the Italian revolutions, could become active only after a long period of preparation.

The foundations by Giovanni Don Bosco (1815–88) of the Oratory and in 1859 of the Society of Saint Francis de Sales (Salesians) were primarily directed to local religious and social needs, but the apostolic spirit soon carried members beyond the borders of Italy to all continents, where they took over individual missions and also worked successfully as educators and journalists. Another institute, created solely for Africa, was that which Daniel Comboni founded in 1866 in northern Italy. It was the Mission Institute for Africa, which later was transferred to Verona and in 1885 renamed the Society of the Sons of the Sacred Heart. The impetus for it came from the Sudan mission established in 1846 in central Africa and maintained largely by Austrian secular priests. Monsignor Comboni's interest was to provide it with a stable foundation.

In France also new mission institutions came into being. Father Jules Chevalier in Issoudun established the Association of the Sacred Heart of Jesus, which devoted itself chiefly to the mission in the South Seas. In 1856 some clerics at Lyon joined the former Paris missionary and bishop in India, Melchior de Marion Brésillac (1813–59), to form the Society for the African Mission for the conversion of the blacks. Leadership at Lyon was assumed by the youthful Augustin Planque (1826–1907), who led the society through obstacles and sacrifices to a stable existence. The Holy Ghost Fathers and the Lyon missionaries were able to send missionaries only to the coastal areas of East and West Africa, as they lacked the personnel for missions in the interior. The farseeing and energetic Cardinal Lavigerie (1825–92) became their apostle. In 1868 he established the Society of the White Fathers, organized their first caravans to the interior of the continent, and fostered the work of the missionaries with his practical and prudent directives. In 1860 Pius IX confirmed the Society of Saint Francis de Sales (Salesians of Annecy), founded in 1833 at Annecy, which in 1845 had begun to send missions to Central Africa.

The founding of two other important missionary societies took place at about the same time: the Belgian missionaries of Scheut and the English missionaries of Mill Hill. In 1862, a number of Belgian secular priests offered themselves to the Congregation for the Propagation of the Faith for work in the missions. With them Theophile Verbist founded the Congregation of the Immaculate Heart of Mary (at Scheut/Brussels) and selected Mongolia for its work. The English Society of Saint Joseph (Missionaries of Mill Hill/London), founded in 1866 by the future Cardinal Herbert Vaughan, concentrated on the mission to the blacks in the United States. In 1892 it became an autonomous organization in America, but also extended its work to British colonies.

Beginning in the middle of the nineteenth century, after freedom of religion and proselytization were guaranteed in a large number of Asian states, the emphasis of the missions was placed on education and charity. For this reason it was natural to involve the Christian Brothers, especially the followers of Saint Jean-Baptiste de la Salle, in the Asian missions. In 1859 they began to work in India and gradually extended their activity to other countries as well.

The imposing number of new missionary institutions in this period could create the impression that the missions had enough personnel; comparisons with earlier periods show clearly, though, that these efforts were far from those of the Spanish and Portuguese during the sixteenth and seventeenth centuries. Other mission areas were worked only feebly or not at all. For this reason it was significant that earlier orders, whose apostolic impulses had gown feeble, renewed their missionary spirit. The activity of the Holy Ghost Fathers is a case in point. By opening apostolic schools, establishing a Portuguese province, and resuming missionary work in Angola, the Portuguese missions developed a fresh impetus.

The Weakening of the Portuguese Patronage
and the Reorganization of the Asian Missions

In the British Sphere of Influence

After the long period of struggle over the reorganization of ecclesiastical matters, especially in India, it could have been assumed that all seeds of discontent had been removed. Exactly the opposite occurred. The contrast between the patronage missionaries and the missionaries of the Congregation for the Propagation of the Faith grew increasingly intense. Even if the Goan unrest did not cause a schism in terms of canon law — obedience to the Pope was never in question — legal uncertainties constituted a heavy burden, especially in those areas where the interests of the two authorities clashed. A conciliatory step was taken by Portugal in 1849 when it recalled da Silva Torres, the archbishop of Goa. After arrival at Lisbon, he directed a letter of apology to Pius IX, who read it in open consistory and sent a friendly reply. During the vacancy of the see, the bishop of Macao, Jeronimo da Matta, exercised episcopal functions in the areas assigned to the vicars apostolic of Ceylon and Bombay, triggering a protest from them. The struggle between adherents of the patronage and adherents of the Congregation for the Propagation of the Faith reached its climax with the siege of the church of Upper Mahim, in which the vicar apostolic of Bombay, Anastasius Hartmann, remained confined for weeks. In a letter of 12 April 1853 he informed the vicars apostolic of India of the events, and after receipt of their replies he sent a letter of protest in all of their names to the Holy See.

During the conflict the British authorities observed strict neutrality in keeping with their principle of not becoming involved in religious matters in India. Finally, though, they gave in to the pressures of the Goanese and denied Bishop Hartmann the church of Upper Mahim. From Rome, the bishop had received only a temporizing reply which left him no option but to draw the consequences. In 1856 Bishop Hartmann returned to Europe. His willingness to turn over the vicariate of Bombay to the Jesuits and to devote himself to the organization of the Capuchin mission in the newly created position of a mission procurator allows the conclusion that this journey was the logical end result of the principles which he himself had enunciated in 1853.

The concordat of 21 February 1857 with Portugal settled the confusion in India, albeit in favor of Portugal's patronage. The Portuguese bishoprics of Cochin, Mylapur, and Malacca (in addition to the archbishopric of Goa) were restored, and the jurisdiction of the Congregation for the Propagation of the Faith was recognized only for China and individual parts of Malacca. In fact, Portugal obtained the concession of establishing additional patronage bishoprics in India.

In spite of the one-sided emphasis of the rights of patronage, the concordat of 1857 did not have any deleterious results for the Indian mission, in part because of the discretion exercised by the vicars apostolic, who tolerated the Goan communities in their dioceses and treated them generously according to their needs, in part because of the lack of Portuguese priests who might have ministered to the already established Christian communities and might also have won additional believers. Furthermore, with the experience of a century behind them, the British would not have liked to see an increased activity of the Portuguese; they placed no obstacles in the way of native Goan priests.

In close connection with the work of Bishop Hartmann and his secretary, future Bishop and Cardinal Ignatius Persico (1823–95), occurred an event which guided the Indian Church for many decades: a papal visitation. On 1 June 1858 the two Capuchin bishops directed a memorandum to the Congregation for the Propagation of the Faith concerning the deficiencies of the Indian mission and the means of removing them. In order to counter the lack of unity among the vicars apostolic and the missionaries of the Propaganda, they suggested a papal visitation. In August of the same year Pius IX appointed the vicar apostolic of Pondicherry from the Paris mission seminary, Clement Bonnand (1796–1861), as his visitor. He was charged with examining the deficiencies as well as determining the means of removing them in the areas subject to the Propaganda, all to be included in a detailed report of his own writing. He started upon his task with courage and optimism, but was not able to finish it because he died of cholera at Benares in March 1861. The vicar apostolic of Mysore, Monsignor Étienne Charbonneaux, carried the visit to its conclusion.

This visit of inspection was necessary not only in order to bring about greater harmony and cooperation among the visitors apostolic of various nationalities and orders, but also to instill renewed courage to persevere in the representatives of the Congregation for the Propagation of the Faith, who after the victory of the Portuguese in the concordat of 1857 felt deserted and betrayed. Within the Portuguese bishoprics there were at the time of the visitation the following dioceses under the direction of the Propaganda: in the west, Bombay and Poona under German Jesuits, whom Bishop Hartmann had invited in 1853, in the north the vast areas of the vicariates of Agra and Patna under Italian Capuchins, in the center Hyderabad and Visakhapatnam, the former under the new Milan mission seminary, the latter under the direction of the Oblates of Saint Francis de Sales of Annecy. In the south, the old Jesuit mission of Madura was revived; the Italian Jesuits worked in Mangalore. The Carmelites continued to minister to the two vicariates of Verapoly and Quilon, the Paris missionaries to Pondicherry, Mysore, and Coimbatore; there were also the earlier established vicariates of Madras, which later was taken over by Don Bosco's Salesians, and Calcutta under the Jesuits, who in 1856 were joined by the Holy Cross Fathers and in 1866 by the Milan missionaries in eastern Bengal. The suggestions of the visitors (establishment of a hierarchy and apostolic delegation) were implemented only after the pontificate of Pius IX.

Another point to which the visitors drew emphatic attention was the absence of a native clergy in the areas under the ministration of the Congregation for the Propagation of the Faith. Aside from Pondicherry, where since the synod of 1844 the training of a native clergy was being undertaken with vigor and which at the time of the visitation numbered fifty Indian priests, seven vicariates had no native clergy, and the others only a few, most of them in the ranks of their own orders. The Propaganda acknowledged the justification of the reproof. On 8 September 1869, in extensive instructions to the mission bishops, it reminded them not only of its own directives of 1845, but also demanded the formation of a capable native diocesan clergy.

The lack of an Indian clergy had to be the more detrimental as the numerically strong Goan clergy theologically and ascetically held views which closely corresponded to those of the European missionaries.

The external difficulties of the Indian mission included the relationship to the colonial power. The English East India Company had absolutely no interest whatever in missionary activity. It required a direct order from London before the work of Anglican missionaries in 1833 and of non-British Protestant mission societies in 1834 was permitted. The Catholic Church, which had been active in the country for centuries, did not seem to exist at all. The unceasing efforts of the Capuchin Bishop Hartmann showed how difficult it was to obtain limited just treatment of the Catholics in India — there never was any talk of equality. In 1857 Hartmann journeyed to London and with his brochure *Remarks on the Resolution of the Government of India upon the Catholic Affairs in India* commented on the government's declarations. Clearly and objectively he dealt with the question of the position of the Catholic bishops, the military chaplains and garrison priests, churches, schools, hospitals, and the unjust treatment of Catholic orphans. His efforts and those of other bishops were crowned with a minimum of success for the rest of the century.

When in the course of reorganization in 1834 the vicariate apostolic of Ceylon was set up, there were only sixteen priests, Goan Oratorians, for two hundred fifty thousand Catholics. The first bishops came from their ranks, but the initial fervor of the Goan priests declined. As a result of English pressure — Ceylon was English after 1796 — augmented by pressure from the Catholics of Colombo, Rome was compelled to appoint a European as auxiliary bishop. Considerately, an Oratorian, Orazio Bettachini (1810–56), was selected. Soon the Pope gave him jurisdiction over the northern part of Ceylon, the vicariate of Jaffna, established in 1847. In that same year he succeeded in gaining the cooperation of the Oblates of Mary Immaculate.

After Bettachini had finally been named vicar apostolic of Jaffna (1849), Rome appointed the Italian Silvestrin Giuseppe Bravi (1813–62) as auxiliary bishop of Colombo. The Oblates worked principally in Jaffna, the remaining Oratorians of Goa principally in Colombo. In spite of all machinations, the native vicars apostolic remained loyal to the Congregation for the Propagation of the Faith; but intrigues and messengers from Goa so poisoned the atmosphere that ultimately there was only one solution: the replacement of the decreasing number of Goan priests with European missionaries.

One reason for the decline of the once flourishing mission of the native priests was the inability of the Goans to adapt to new conditions. While the Catholics with increasing urgency asked for English schools and English education, their priests obstinately clung to the Portuguese language and culture. At the same time the Catholics faced the task of becoming better acquainted with the Sinhalese and Tamil cultures of the country. Credit is due principally to the Oblates that this education was provided and fostered.

In the Kingdom of Burma, which gradually fell to England in the course of the nineteenth century, Italian Barnabites were active from 1722 to 1832. Because of lack of personnel and means, they transferred the mission to the Oblates of Mary of Turin, who, for the same reasons, were forced to abandon the mission in 1856. The Congregation for the Propagation of the Faith immediately assigned the vast territory to the Paris mission seminary. The division of the area into three dioceses, earlier decided upon by the Propaganda in 1863, was implemented. The Paris missionaries in northern and southern Burma were joined by the Milan missionaries in eastern Burma, where they were active among the Karens.

After 1828, the Malay peninsula constituted a part of the British Empire. The bishopric of Malacca, established in 1558, did not have a bishop throughout the entire century. The activity of the patronage priests was limited to the Portuguese parishes in Malacca and Singapore. The missionaries of the Paris mission seminary devoted themselves chiefly to the Chinese and Indian immigrants. The focus of their work in the vicariate, which was established in 1841, was the expansion of the seminary at Pulo-Penang. The vicar apostolic generally resided in a neighboring parish. The unique arrangement of the parallelism of a patronage bishopric and a vicar apostolic in Malacca continued in existence.

The Kingdom of Siam (Thailand) owed its independence during the nineteenth century to the fact that the two colonial neighbors England and France were unwilling to either share domination over the Thais or to leave it to only one of them. Catholic missionaries had been active in the area since the sixteenth century. Although they were not able to register noticeable successes, the tolerance of ruler and people allowed them to develop the country into an important missionary base. This was true especially for Vicar Apostolic Jean Baptiste Pallegoix (1802–62), an expert on Siamese language and culture, who established close ties to the Siamese court. For fifteen years, Pallegoix maintained friendly relations with the abbot of a Buddhist monastery, who later ruled in Bangkok as King Mongkut (1851–68). His toleration and benevolence continued, with the result that the Catholic mission, almost at the point of extinction because of wars and lack of missionaries, revived again. Mongkut himself directed a friendly letter to Pius IX in March 1861; in October, Pius IX replied in the same vein, praising the tolerant attitude of the monarch toward Christianity. Yet with all of his gestures of goodwill to Christianity, Catholic and Protestant alike, the King remained a convinced Buddhist and used his newly won knowledge of Christianity for a thorough reform of Siamese and Hinayana Buddhism.

The strengthening of the Catholic Church in Siam, begun by Bishop Pallegoix, has lasted to the present.

In the French Sphere of Influence

After the death of Emperor Minh Mang in 1841, the Tonkin Church enjoyed peace under his successor Thieu-Tri (1841–47). The indefatigable vicar apostolic of West Tonkin, Monsignor Pierre Retord (1803–58), used this period to reassemble the dispersed and frightened Christians. But a new, even bloodier persecution afflicted the Church under Tu Duc (1847–82). Thousands of Christians had to pay for their faith with their lives, among them about fifty priests and five bishops. The first decree of persecution (1848) was directed against the European priests, the second decree (1851) against the Vietnamese priests, and the third one (1855) against all Christians. In order not to endanger their flocks directly, the missionaries had to live in the mountains and forests, where Bishop Retord, exhausted by flight and deprivation, died in 1858.

French intervention took place during this difficult period. After an initial failure, the French consul de Montigny asked Monsignor Pellerin, the vicar apostolic of North Cochin China (1813–62), who had fled to Hong Kong, to seek an audience with Napoleon III in order to obtain help for missionaries and Christians. Because in 1857 a Spanish Dominican bishop, Monsignor Diaz, was executed, the two powers intervened together. In 1858, the port of Da Nang in Tonkin was taken, and in 1859 Saigon was occupied by French troops. This action was the first step in the gradual occupation of all of Indochina by the French, culminating with the seizure of Hanoi in 1873. Although religious freedom was embodied in all treaties following each individual phase of the wars of conquest, the Church had to suffer its greatest loss of blood after the "pacification," especially in what is today Vietnam. It is not to be denied that missionaries caused the French intervention and that the suppressed and threatened Christians desired and expected it. But it is also clear that most of the missionaries and Christians did not die because of these political events and wars, but because of their faith.

In spite of the almost incessant persecution, Christianity made progress. The number of missionary dioceses was doubled during this period and so was the number of native clergymen. The clergy had been taught at Pulo-Penang, which was known by the name of *Seminarium martyrium.* As soon as the south of Indochina was calm, the Christian Brothers began their work in Saigon; in 1861, the first Carmelite house was established there.

The development of the Church in China took place on two levels: on the political/ecclesiastical, and the missionary/religious one. The concordat of 1857 with Portugal dissolved the hitherto Portuguese dioceses of Peking and Nanking, with only Macao remaining under Portuguese patronage. The replacement of the patronage missionaries by representatives of the Congregation for the Propagation of the Faith occurred without stir and without injury to the areas concerned. Nanking was replaced by the vicariate apostolic of Kiangnan and transferred to French Jesuits, Peking was given to French Lazarists. The Chinese provinces of Kwangtung and Kwangsi belonged to Macao. Only in 1858 was this area also split from the mother diocese. From then on, the entire China mission was directed by the Congregation for the Propagation of the Faith.

This development resulted in the virtual end of the Portuguese right of patronage in China. But the Treaty of Whampoa (1844) started a new political association, which, especially during the second half of the century, was to be unhappy: French patronage. The contractually agreed freedom of religion was at first valid only for the five so-called treaty ports. Other military action (especially in response to the rebellion of Taiping) led to the treaty of Tientsin (1858) and the peace treaty of Peking (1860). They extended religious freedom to the entire country and to all missionaries who carried a French document of protection. The Chinese were granted the freedom to accept and exercise the Christian faith. The weakness of these treaties and other agreements was, of course, that they were not concluded on the basis of equality but were imposed on the Chinese. All disagreements and persecutions in the course of the century were, in the final analysis, only expressions of hate directed at foreigners and not at Christianity, which was hardly known.

This fact becomes evident from a study of Chinese sources. The increasing number of "missionary incidents" after 1860 may occasionally have been caused by tactlessness, lack of comprehension, and pushy missionaries, but the real cause was the class of Confucian-trained gentry, mandarins, and large landowners. Ever since the seventeenth century they made common front against foreigners and Christianity and intensified their hostility' during the nineteenth century. By means of falsehoods and lies they tried to incite the ignorant masses against the strangers and the followers of foreign religions. Violent incidents led to negotiations with the foreign powers which lasted for years.

Such setbacks did not prevent the missions from expanding far into the interior of the country. Externally this was evident in the increase of the vicariates apostolic. Those orders already present in China strengthened their ranks.

In its instructions of 1845 concerning the education and training of native clergy, the Congregation for the Propagation of the Faith had emphasized the importance of regular meetings of the superiors of orders at local synods for the preservation of ecclesiastical unity and discipline. This general admonition was followed in June 1848 by an encyclical to the bishops of China and neighboring countries to gather for a synod at Hong Kong. In spite of additional reminders such a synod did not take place, primarily because to most of the bishops the conditions in the country for such a gathering were not favorable and the journeys too dangerous, but also because most of them did not see the need for such a meeting. Behind the scenes, the old protectionist power (Portugal) and the new one (France), insisted on their right to participate.

In the meantime, Rome tried to prepare for an eventual synod. Pius IX appointed Monsignor L. C. Spelta, O.F.M., the vicar apostolic of Hupei, as apostolic visitor. Unfortunately, he was forced to terminate his inspection and died in 1862 at Wuchang. A stronger impression than this visit was made in Europe by the journey of two Lazarists, E. Huc and Joseph Gabet, through Mongolia to Tibet (1844–46). After his return to Europe in 1848, Gabet directed a voluminous memorandum to Pius IX in which in plain language he told him the truth about China and the means whereby its conversion could be hastened. In essence, these consisted of drawing concrete consequences from the instructions of 1845 by the Congregation for the Propagation of the Faith. When Father Gabet submitted his report, he could look back upon ten years of missionary experience; as the founder of the Catholic mission to Mongolia he had worked in Mongolia since 1837.

In 1848 the first European sisters arrived in China. Their work in schools, hospitals, and orphan homes was the reflection of a profound change in missionary methods. Ever since persecutions had begun, especially during the past 150 years, the European missionaries had confined themselves to spreading the faith unobtrusively among moderate numbers of people. The pastoral care of families and women was left to Chinese girls. Beginning with the second half of the nineteenth century, the educational, social, and charitable institutions recruited members for the Christian faith indirectly. But it was precisely the (actually very beneficial) activity of European women which the Chinese regarded as alien and which they rejected. It is understandable, therefore, that the Chinese memorandum of 13 February 1871, which the government addressed to the foreign powers after the events of Tientsin, demanded more respect for Chinese sensibilities from the Europeans in general and the removal of the sisters in particular. The demand was decisively rejected by foreign powers and missionaries alike. The expansion of the missionary work was continued as before and characterized the Chinese mission until recently.

Korea was established as a vicariate apostolic separate from Peking in 1831. The remoteness of the country and the long access journey meant that it was not until 1836 that the first European missionary, Pierre Philibert Maubant (1803–39), arrived. The vicar apostolic of Korea, Bishop Barth. Bruguière, had died in Mongolia in 1835 on the way to Korea. In 1837, Father Jacques Honoré Chastan (1803–39) reached Korea, soon followed by the second vicar apostolic, Laurent Joseph Marius Imbert (1796–1839). All three died a martyr's death after the bishop had been arrested and the two missionaries voluntarily had turned themselves in to the authorities in order to protect their communities from harassment. During the next bloody persecution in 1846 the first Korean priest, Andreas Kim, became a victim. After finishing his theological studies at Macao, he had gone to Korea in 1845, accompanied by his bishop, J. Ferréol (1808–53), and a missionary. When new persecutions broke out in 1866, during which two bishops, seven missionaries, and about eight thousand Christians were slain, the young Korean Church numbered about twenty-five thousand members. It was to be ten years before the country would receive other missionaries and pastors.

Attempts to reestablish missions in Japan failed until the American admiral Matthew Perry opened the country in 1854. In 1858 France obtained the concession from Japan to allow freedom of religion for foreigners in port cities and in Tokyo. Father Girard (1821–1867) became the first priest and interpreter of the French Society of Paris Missionaries to settle in the capital. For foreign Catholics, small churches were established at other places as well, but attendance was forbidden to the Japanese.

Nagasaki allowed the presence of foreigners again in 1862, and the Paris missionaries built a small church. It was here that Father T. Petitjean in 1865 discovered surviving Christians, of whom about twenty-five thousand acknowledged themselves to the missionaries. Such an event could not be concealed from the Japanese authorities in spite of all precautions on the part of the missionaries. Anti-Christian legislation was still in force and was strengthened in 1869 by an imperial edict. Another wave of persecutions swept over the newly organized Christian communities, culminating in mass deportations and exile to distant parts of the country. Only pressure by the European powers effected a gradual diminution of the persecutions.

The discovery of the Old Christians produced internal difficulties, especially with respect to language. The faithful of Nagasaki still used prayers, hymns, catechisms, and religious literature in Spanish and Portuguese terminology. The muddled situation did not improve when Monsignor Petitjean, vicar apostolic of Japan after 1866, reissued old books from the Jesuit printing press. By about this time, Chinese terminology had become accepted in central and northern Japan, while the traditional Spanish-Portuguese terminology survived in southern Japan until the death of Bishop Petitjean. The problem was attenuated in 1876 by the division of Japan into two vicariates, North Japan and South Japan.

Philippines, Indonesia, Oceania, Africa

Although relatively autonomous and possessing their own religious administration, the Philippines until the nineteenth century were nothing more than an extension of Spanish-America to the Far East. Given this close association, the ideas of the French Revolution and of the American Independence movement could not but affect the islands. The first stirrings of political independence failed, in part because the dominant Spanish upper class was too weak to assume a leading role, in part because the Friars, especially the Augustinian Eremites, who since the end of the sixteenth century had carried the chief missionary and pastoral burden on the islands, maintained their strong position. Together with Franciscans and Dominicans they formed the most reliable pillar of Spanish rule. It was a paradox of history that Spain itself, especially after the revolution and the dissolution of all orders in 1835, began to weaken its own position in the country through the positive support of Freemasonry. The association of Philippinos with lodge brothers of the United States in the neighboring Asiatic countries, who were to serve only as allies in the struggle against the Church, produced in the islands new sources of unrest, fostered the movement for independence, and ultimately, much to the surprise and disappointment of all parties concerned, brought about the American occupation of the country.

Until the middle of the nineteenth century, the ranks of the Spanish missionaries could be filled with Spaniards, but after 1855 there were difficulties with recruitment. Queen Isabella II granted the reopening of the mission seminaries for the Philippines and the readmission of the Jesuits, whose first members arrived at Manila in 1859. They performed their work primarily on the islands of Yolo and Mindanao, where the majority of the population was Muslim. In addition to the already mentioned political paradox, there was also an ecclesiastical-religious paradox with ominous consequences. The orders had done good work in training a native clergy, whose numbers had grown to impressive proportions by the nineteenth century. Unfortunately, they left this native clergy in subordinate positions, without raising its social or economic standing. Thus they forced this educated class into the ranks of the malcontents and rebels.

A mission to Indonesia became possible only after 1807 when Louis Napoleon granted freedom of religion to Holland. But even after the establishment of the vicariate apostolic of Batavia in 1842, missionary work remained limited to the pastoral care of white Catholics. The colonial legislation of 1854 made any expansion of such work dependent on specific permission by the government. Only gradually, step by step, did Catholics achieve their missionary right to exist. In 1859 Portugal, in a peace treaty with Holland, ceded this island and others, but managed to insert a clause guaranteeing the care over native Christians. Further progress was made only during the subsequent mission period. The part of Timor remaining with Portugal and a few other small islands, raised to the bishopric of Dili in 1940, were administered by the diocese of Macao until recently.

The missions of Oceania continued to attract hosts of missionaries after the middle of the nineteenth century in spite of tremendous difficulties, such as immense distances, tropical diseases, and political and denominational contrasts. With most of them, genuine religious motives determined their preference for the Pacific islands, but some of them were no doubt also influenced by romantic adventurism and the image of paradisiac conditions. Polynesia remained the missionary field for the Picpus missionaries. Spreading out from Hawaii, they gained footholds on the Marquesas, Tahiti, and the Cook Islands, where independent vicariates were gradually erected. Subsequently, the missions gained world-wide attention through the heroic work of Father Damian de Veuster (1840–89), who, active in Hawaii since 1863, after 1873 worked among the lepers on Molokai. Easter Island, where missionary work began in 1864, was also part of Polynesia.

When in 1836 the vicariate of Central Oceania, comprising all of Melanesia and Micronesia, was established and handed to the care of the Marist Fathers, ignorance of geographical realities allowed people to believe that enough had been done. But missionaries on the spot quickly realized that by themselves they would never be able to take care of such an immense area. Operating from the Solomon Islands, the Marist Fathers tried to deny Protestant missionaries access to New Guinea; but the deadly climate put an end to their efforts. The mission was not resumed, and twenty-five years passed before fresh help arrived.

From their center in New Zealand, where they were trying to convert the Maoris, the Marist Fathers expanded their efforts to other, northern island complexes, especially to the Solomons, to Tonga, Samoa, Fiji, New Caledonia, and the New Hebrides. Gradually, independent dioceses were established in this area. The vast distances and new languages promoted local printeries, especially by the Marist Fathers.

The Marist Fathers never reached Micronesia, which had been assigned to them as a missionary area as part of the vicariate of Central Oceania. These islands, especially the Mariana Islands, where Christianity survived even after the expulsion of the Jesuits, ecclesiastically belonged to the diocese of Cebu in the Philippines (1814–98). Their Christian communities were tended by the Augustinian Recollects.

At this time, the Benedictines began their missionary work among the Australian aborigines. In 1859 the area became an apostolic prefecture, and later became an *Abbatia nullius.* The method employed by the Benedictines was the same as the one used by them in missionizing Germanic tribes during the Middle Ages.

Although Africa was geographically closer to the European mission centers and thus could be reached much more easily than the Pacific islands, missionary settlements in the dark continent were established only slowly, under great sacrifices, and with only moderate success. The vicariate of Central Africa, established in 1846, had a stirring and sorrowful history. Its establishment was suggested by A. Casolani, canon in Malta, who became its first vicar apostolic. He accepted the appointment on the condition that Jesuits accompany him as missionaries. By 1861, the new mission had cost the lives of forty missionaries. Only Daniel Comboni (1830–81), vicar apostolic of Central Africa after 1877, was able to create better conditions for his missionaries by moving his headquarters from Khartoum to Cairo. But the rising of the Mahdi in 1882 destroyed the entire mission.

Thanks to the loyalty of the missionaries of Verona, the flourishing Sudan mission emerged from the vicariate apostolic of Central Africa. In 1868 the new apostolic prefecture of Sahara and Sudan was created and subordinated to the archbishop of Algiers, Charles Lavigerie, as apostolic delegate. It can hardly be assumed that Rome, when making out the decree, which is not contained in any official collection of documents of the Congregation for the Propagation of the Faith, seriously thought of converting the Sudan. But the man to whom the seemingly impossible task was entrusted conceived of a daring plan to achieve this objective with the aid of the White Fathers, whom he had founded. First attempts to penetrate to Central Africa from the Kabylia mission in Algeria failed. Only after much more careful preparations did the White Fathers make their way from the East African coast to the area of the great lakes.

The areas which they had to cross in the east in order to reach their central African mission areas were under the jurisdiction of the Holy Ghost Fathers, who in 1863 worked in Zanzibar and after 1868 at Bagamoyo on the mainland. After the death of their founder, Father Ignaz Schwendimann filled the office of superior general from 1852 until 1881. Under his leadership the young society was strengthened and took a firm foothold on the African mainland. In addition to their initial areas in western Africa (Senegal, Senegambia, Gabon), they were given the vicariate apostolic of Sierra Leone in 1864. In 1849 the plan emerged to minister to the vacated Portuguese mission areas, but it was not until 1866 that the first Spiritans arrived in the Portuguese Congo and in Angola. In the Congo, they found traces of the Italian Capuchins who had worked there earlier. To the normal difficulties in tropical Africa was added the severe opposition of Portugal; only the tireless activity of Father Charles Duparquet (1830–88), residing after 1866 in Angola, effected the settlement of the Spiritans in Portugal and the establishment of a Portuguese province, thereby removing any obstacles.

With the arrival of the Oblates of Mary Immaculate in Natal in 1852, the areas of South Africa saw their first missionaries; until this time the area's secular priests had been able to minister to the white settlers only. In 1862 the Oblates made their way to Basutoland, which hitherto had been closed to Catholic missionaries, and eventually built up a flourishing mission. During subsequent decades they also became active in other areas of Africa.

With the Jesuits active on the island of Reunion and the islands around Madagascar, they sought ways and means to penetrate the interior of the large island itself. But the political and denominational contrast (England/France) as well as the difficulties posed by France and the long-established colonial seminary in Paris were so strong that initial attempts failed. Only in 1861 did the Jesuits settle firmly at Tananarive and begin the establishment of the Church in Madagascar.

It is perhaps astonishing that in a survey of missionary activity during the middle of the nineteenth century Africa occupies such a modest place. Of course, the difficulties to be overcome were great, but certainly not greater than in the Far East, the South Pacific islands, or in China and India. If the missions of the East were treated better, the reasons for this lie deeper. The optimistic missionary reports of the seventeenth and eighteenth centuries had surrounded the missions of the Far East with an attractive halo. The advanced cultures of these peoples, known particularly through the researches and reports of the missionaries, were valued as much as the tolerant character of the inhabitants. Unimaginable utopias exercised a great allure for the islands of the Pacific. Africa lacked such attractions. The great explorations of European investigators started only in the middle of the past century and were only cautiously exploited by Protestant and Catholic missionary circles. The languages and cultures of Africa, aside from the west coast and Portuguese colonies, were largely unknown. Finally, the burden of earlier times still rested on the shoulders of the black race. The African was largely regarded as a slave in Europe and the New World, and this was also the view of the Church. The descriptions of slave hunters and traders remained alive, at least subconsciously. To be sure, slavery was condemned and an attempt was made to lighten the lot of the blacks; but the continent exerted only minimal political and missionary appeal, a circumstance which explains the slow penetration of Africa.

C H A P T E R   3 4

The First Vatican Council and the Missions

The first Vatican Council from 1869 to 1870 was a mirrored reflection of the laborious missionary effort during the nineteenth century. In contrast to the Council of Trent, missionary countries were represented, even though the presence of missionary bishops was controversial. As it was, their principal concerns were not dealt with at all, in part because of the early termination of the council and in part because the council participants lacked preparation and knowledge.

Pius IX solemnly announced the impending council on 26 June 1867 in a public consistory, and a year later, on 29 June 1868, the bull *Aeterni Patris* invited the participants from throughout the world. Between these two events the decision was made to include the vicars apostolic, i.e., the missionary bishops. In its session of 17 May 1868 the preparatory central commission agreed that it would be proper to invite titular bishops to the council in keeping with the words "patriarchs, archbishops, and bishops" in the draft of the bull. But the commission did not address the legality of participation. This fact proved to be a hindrance for the position of the vicars apostolic at the council. Their position was inhibited by the polemics preceding and accompanying the council, denying the vicars apostolic the right to participate and mentioning their lack of education and manners. From the words of some missionary bishops we know that they became aware of their second-class standing only at the council itself. But the bad "missionary climate" at Rome was even more painful for the mission representatives than the journalistic sniping.

The idea of forming preparatory commissions had first been raised in 1865. Cardinal Bizzarri, the chairman of the central commission, primarily moved to engage members of the Roman Curia, as they were most conversant with the problems to be treated and with the traditions of the Apostolic See. Additional theologians and canonists could then be made members as necessary. As a result of the chaotic conditions in Italy, it was not until 1867 that five preparatory commissions were formed and approved by Pius IX.

In this context, the Commission for the Eastern Church and Missions is of primary interest. The chairman of the commission was the prefect of the Congregation for the Propagation of the Faith, Cardinal Barnabo (1801–74). It consisted of seventeen members: eleven Italians, three Germans, and one Englishman, Russian, and Oriental each. Upon the urging of the cardinal, the commission, which initially comprised only members of the Curia, specifically of the Propaganda, was expanded with three men who had practical experience. Both the men of the Curia and those with practical experience counted among them outstanding Eastern experts.

For the mission bishops arriving at Rome it was disappointing and paralyzing to learn that there was not a single expert or representative of the actual pagan missions on the commission. Moreover, in the very first session Cardinal Barnabo announced that the primary task of the commission was the application of the disciplinary rules of the Council of Trent to the conditions of the Eastern Churches. Aside from a few laudable exceptions, what was meant by this was a far-reaching Latinization of the Eastern Churches. "Mission" meant for most of the members of the commission, aside from a few laudable exceptions, nothing more than the Near Eastern mission. This narrow interpretation resulted from the fact that the older missionary nations like Spain and Portugal were not at all represented on the preparatory commission, while the bishops of the Portuguese and Spanish patronage, respectively their American successor states, regarded themselves as belonging to the European residential bishops, i.e., to the bishops first class, and not to the barely tolerated vicars apostolic. Only in January 1870 were two missionary bishops of the Paris mission seminary, Monsignor E .L. Charbonneaux, vicar apostolic of Mysore, and Father J. M. Laouënan, vicar apostolic of Pondicherry, appointed to membership on the commission. Both of them were renowned linguists and historians and had made names for themselves as associates of Visitor Monsignor Bonnand and continued his work.

The principal task of the commission was the drafting of a schema to be presented to the council fathers. Cardinal Barnabo had written to Near Eastern and Austrian bishops as early as February and March 1868 and asked them for ideas and suggestions. Of the replies, that of the Hungarian Bishop Roscovany demanded a thorough and effective promotion of the propagation of faith and a higher level of piety in the Christian countries. Other demands or suggestions reached the commission during the council. Among the home Churches, only France submitted a valuable postulate pointing to the future (signed by thirteen participants). On 23 January 1870, 110 members asked for a solemn recommendation by the council of the Association for the Propagation of the Faith. Thirty-five vicars apostolic voiced a similar concern for the Childhood of Jesus Association, and two postulates, one signed by thirteen, the other signed by sixty-one participants, were in favor of supporting the Association for the Support of Schools in the Near East.

By November 1869 a first draft of a mission schema was ready. Only the third draft of 26 June 1870 was accepted for distribution to those council fathers still at Rome. Following an introductory letter from Pius IX, there were three chapters: 1. On Bishops and Vicars Apostolic, 2. On Missionaries, 3. On the Means of Spreading the Faith. Appended to the text were the *Adnotationes ad Schema Decreti de Apostolicis Missionibus.*

The intervention of the representatives of missions to the pagans succeeded in changing many passages in such a way that they applied to all messengers of the faith. Yet other long passages, concerning only the Church and pastoral and missionary care among the peoples of the Near East, remained intact. The second chapter "On the Apostolic Missionaries" conformed precisely to the initial intention, i.e., the implementation of Tridentine rules.

This one-sided orientation toward the Near Eastern missions was further indicated by the writers listed in the *Adnotationes.* Writings concerning pagan missions were conspicuous by their absence.

Aside from the deficient treatment of the pagan missions and their problems, the centralistic orientation of the schema encountered opposition. It was less a question of papal infallibility, to which all representatives of the missions agreed, than of the concentration of jurisdiction and administration of the missions in the hands of the bishops and vicars apostolic, which implied the virtual exclusion of the orders. After the mission schema had been distributed toward the end of June 1870, twenty-seven council fathers submitted extensive observations. Almost all of them opposed the intended exclusion of the superiors of orders; this view was not only held by the generals such as the general of the Society of Jesus, Petrus Beckx, but also by representatives of the home episcopate of the secular clergy. Behind the tendency toward centralization, no matter how carefully and cautiously it was formulated, was concealed a noticeable rejection of the missionizing orders, especially of the Jesuits. After all, most of the members of the commission belonged to the Congregation for the Propagation of the Faith, and Monsignor Giuseppe Valerga, the Latin patriarch of Jerusalem, the most influential representative of the orders (O.F.M.), virtually spoke for the prefect of the Propaganda, Cardinal Barnabo. Additionally, a mission directory was to promote uniformity of missions in all mission areas; its precise constitution was left to the Congregation for the Propagation of the Faith. This suggestion also was made by Monsignor Valerga, who in his verdict acknowledged that while the *Monita ad Missionarios* contained valuable admonitions, it was incomplete and lacked the necessary authority.

Faced with this atmosphere, which was not exactly favorable to the pagan missions, the missionary bishops resorted to a kind of self-help in regional bishops' conferences. The Indian and Chinese bishops met separately. The eighteen vicars apostolic of India directed a petition to the Pope requesting him to do away with the Portuguese right of patronage, in which they saw the greatest obstacle to the conversion of India. But Pius IX did not think that he could accede to their request. The gathering of the Chinese bishops developed into a kind of synod. The soul of these meetings, which from 22 December 1869 onward took place once a week and then twice a week, was the vicar apostolic of Kweichow, Monsignor Louis Faurie, who also acted as the secretary of the gatherings. The basis of their discussions were seventy-two questions submitted to the bishops by the Congregation for the Propagation of the Faith. In addition, the participants were chiefly concerned with the relationship of the Chinese missions to the French government, respectively to the French protectorate. Some of the non-French bishops absented themselves from the sessions dealing with a letter of gratitude to Napoleon III.

The questions of the Congregation for the Propagation of the Faith dealt with by the bishops of China concerned the establishment of an apostolic delegation or nunciature, to which the bishops reacted skeptically and negatively, as they were jealous of their independence; the division of the Chinese mission into five regions, specifically with respect to the holding of regional synods; the appointment of a council for the vicars apostolic and of another council for mission estates and the regular clergy in missions; the Chinese clergy, its education and training, which should be of a kind allowing them to administer a mission or become bishops; liturgical questions; feast and fast days; the significance and spread of Christian literature and schools; and the administration of the sacraments.

On 14 July 1870 a final session of all Chinese bishops was called, the only one which was chaired by the cardinal prefect of the Congregation for the Propagation of the Faith. Thirteen problems were discussed; some of them had been discussed earlier, others were new, like the problem of opium and the use of Chinese hymns in liturgical and paraliturgical celebrations. All decisions of the Chinese bishops were to be submitted to the council fathers for final disposition. Considering the second-class standing of the missionary bishops, it is not astonishing that not one of them played an eminent role at the Vatican Council.

The weakness of the missionary climate of the council as a whole was shown by the single postulate on the African missions. It was short and impressive, carried a brief rationale, and demanded effective steps on the part of the council for the conversion of the blacks, especially in central Africa. The author was Daniel Comboni, the founder of the Missionaries of Verona, missionary, and future vicar apostolic of central Africa. It is dated 24 June 1870 and was signed by seventy council fathers. These signatures, especially in the context of what was said above, present a clear picture of the lack of interest in missions. Although Comboni rushed from man to man like a beggar, appealing for the conversion of Africa, he only met large-scale incomprehension. He was best received by the representatives of the Near Eastern Churches; together with the missionary bishops of the Near East, they provided thirty-one signatures. Of the residing bishops, twenty-five signed. Even of the actual mission bishops only fifteen signed their names: six from India and nine from Far Eastern countries.

Given the lack of interest in missions among the council fathers and the almost systematic displacement of the pagan missions to the margin of the council, no profound reflections on the missions were produced. Nevertheless, the Vatican Council acted as a stimulant and guide for mission theory during the subsequent period. Among the votes and postulates, especially of the French and Chinese bishops, there were programmatic suggestions, some of which were put into action under the more relaxed pontificate of Leo XIII, while others had to wait for the twentieth century and the Second Vatican Council. In their submission to the council, the French bishops considered deliberations on the dissemination of the faith as one of the primary, most significant and important matters with which the council ought to deal. At the same time, they anticipated their great responsibility for the missions. So that they could perform their tasks better, they asked for regular reports from the Congregation for the Propagation of the Faith concerning the status and problems of the pagan missions.

Section Three

Light and Shadows of Catholic Vitality

Roger Aubert

CHAPTER 35

Regular and Secular Clergy

Orders and Congregations

The pontificate of Pius IX saw a new and decisive phase in the internal reorganization of the old orders and an expansion of the new congregations. To be sure, the orders were hard hit by secularization measures in southeastern Europe, Poland, and Latin America, but in western Europe and in North America there was a continuing quantitative and qualitative growth. The orders constituted an essential factor in the flourishing of religious organizations and the intensification of spiritual life.

Pius IX himself was not a member of an order, but like his predecessors Pius VII and Gregory XVI, was concerned with the restoration of discipline. The consolidation during the first half of the century enabled him, with the assistance of Monsignor Bizzarri, the energetic and competent secretary of the *Congregatio Episcoporum et Regularium,* to raise his aspirations. Immediately after his election he established a commission of cardinals in September 1846 and charged it with restoring the life of the orders in those countries in which they had suffered as a consequence of disorder. In the next year he created the *Congregatio super statu regularium,* with the specific function of supervising the reforms. Two decrees of 25 January 1848 strengthened the precautionary measures taken to prevent the admission of unworthy candidates to the novitiate. An encyclical of 1851 tightened the requirements of communal life and of poverty (although prudently retaining the toleration of the *peculium*). The encyclical *Neminem latet* of 19 March 1857 extended a requirement to all monastic orders which heretofore was only applied to the Jesuits: the obligation to precede the solemn profession of vows with temporary vows. In order better to counter the loosening of morals and customs which had crept in during the preceding centuries, Pius IX did not limit himself to encouraging centralization within the orders and to emphasizing more strongly their dependence on the Roman congregations; in several cases he did not hesitate to appoint their superiors himself.

During his refuge at Gaeta Pius IX had noted the deplorable conditions prevailing among the Redemptorists in the Kingdom of Naples, where their generalate was located, in contrast to the progress of the congregation north of the Alps. For this reason he decided in 1853 to move their headquarters to Rome and to appoint their general, a function which normally would have been exercised by the chapter general of the order.

In order to remove the decadent features which had begun to characterize the Dominicans, he decided in 1850 to abolish the election of the master general. Much to the dismay of the Italian members, he named Father Jandel, one of Lacordaire's early associates, as head of the order. Jandel remained master general until 1872 and finished the movement of restoration. Characteristically, his efforts were guided by the initial concepts of the order, which the historical research of the eighteenth century had brought to light again. Thus, the closings to which the order had been subjected since the French Revolution and which in some countries continued beyond 1870 at least had the advantage of completely clearing the slate of the most recent past. The fact that the provinces of the order had to be restored from new houses facilitated the return to the original guidelines. This was not as simple as it sounds, as Jandel, who tended to cling to traditional forms, came in opposition to Lacordaire, who had a better feeling for the necessity of accommodation to the requirements of modern times.

Pius IX also repeatedly (1856, 1862, 1869) intervened in the designation of the general of the Franciscan order; in 1856 it resumed the long interrupted practice of chapters general and revised its statutes. Gradually the order reestablished itself in the various countries of western and central Europe. But the order also suffered new and serious losses in consequence of the secularization in the Latin countries. At the chapter of 1856, ninety provinces were represented, but in 1882 only thirty were still in existence, and the number of members during this quarter of a century decreased from twenty-five thousand to fifteen thousand.

Even though the reform attempts instigated or encouraged by Pius IX produced good results fairly rapidly in the centralized orders, the same efforts met resistance from the abbeys, especially in central Europe, which had remained largely independent. Yet the Premonstratensians gradually revived and former Cistercian abbeys were reopened and regrouped in new congregations. The young branch of the Benedictines, planted by Dom Guéranger at Solesmes, also began to bear fruit. While progress in France was slow and difficult and really came into its own only during the following pontificate, the brothers Wolter, who in 1863 founded the German abbey at Beuron, completed their training at Solesmes. As early as 1872, Beuron founded a branch monastery at Maredsous in Belgium, and additional foundings were made in Austria-Hungary during the *Kulturkampf.*

The example of Beuron demonstrates that it did not always require the initiative of the Holy See to revive old orders and congregations. Some of them, in fact, made remarkable progress on their own.

In particular, the Society of Jesus demonstrated its vitality. The first years of the pontificate of Pius IX were rather difficult for the order. On one hand the Jesuits had to meet general attacks on them in most of the European countries, and on the other they received only lukewarm support from the Pope. He was irritated by the covert resistance of many Jesuits to his concessions to the liberal cause. But the aftereffects of 1848 brought the Pope closer to the Jesuits again, especially after Father Roothaan, with whom the Pope did not get along too well, was replaced in 1853 by Father Beckx. For more than thirty years he led the society with prudence and intuition and saw to it that the Jesuits refrained from any polemics and avoided involvement in politics. The frequency with which his intervention was required indicated, however, that not all Jesuits agreed with him on this issue. Although the Jesuits suffered from fourteen cases of expulsions and confiscations during a thirty-year period in all Catholic countries of Europe, with the single exception of Belgium, and especially in Latin America, the society increased its membership from 4,540 in 1848 to 10,030 in 1878. The influence of the Jesuits steadily increased. On the level of the regional Churches they were effective in missions to the parishes and through other organizations; their colleges and sermons and their contacts with the upper classes were invaluable. On the level of the universal Church, the Gregorian University and the journal *La Civiltà cattolica* gave them an important voice. They also were involved in the Roman congregations, in which neither the secular nor the regular clergy had men as competent as the Jesuits. And finally there was the growing confidence of Pius IX, who after his earlier bias against them recognized the value of the discipline of their training and their devotion to the Holy See.

In comparison to the Jesuits, the new congregations and institutes attracted much less attention. Between 1862 and 1865, seventy-four new congregations and institutes received papal approbation, compared to forty-two such approvals between 1850 and 1860. Aside from the fact that many of them were destined to have a glorious future — the Salesians founded in Turin in 1857 by Don Bosco come to mind — the global significance of their capillary effectiveness in all areas of the apostolate must not be underrated. They were active in education, especially that of girls; the care of the sick; social work, which became increasingly specialized for orphans, old people, domestics, young working girls, prisoners, the blind, the deaf; catechetical instruction; publishing; and missions. The development, going hand in hand with the growth of the congregations founded during the first half of the century, was universal. There were the congregations of priests who followed the versatile guidelines of the sixteenth and seventeenth centuries in pursuing their many activities; the confraternity institutes, which were well attended at a time when admission to the high schools, which alone paved the way toward the priesthood, was still a privilege; and countless women's organizations, many of which placed themselves under the protection of the Virgin Mary.

Rome did its best to channel these forces and to limit the increase of tiny congregations, which occasionally created the impression of ecclesiastical anarchy. On the other hand, of course, they served the interests of many priests and of many women willing to place their energy in the service of charity, especially as they could do justice to the various needs on the local level. The *Congregatio Episcoporum et Regularium* continued to encourage especially those congregations which under a superior general could group together a number of communities whose activities were not confined to one diocese or even one country. But it also had to take account of the differences in languages and customs or of the objection that this necessitated excessively long journeys for the members of these congregations. Additionally, there was the fact that many countries objected to seeing their religious institutions under the control of foreigners. Monsignor Bizzarri knew how extraordinarily varied intentions and local customs were and was smart enough to avoid prescribing a uniform constitution. At least until 1860 he left it up to each congregation to draft its own statutes and limited himself to examining them and making occasional suggestions for change. Gradually and under the pressure of events a new rule for members of institutes emerged. It was codified only much later, as the Vatican Council, which was supposed to pass on it, did not have enough time to deal with the eighteen decrees prepared for the purpose.

The Diocesan Clergy and Pastoral Work

Without a doubt there were substantial differences between a French village priest, the vicar in an industrial area of the Rhineland or Belgium, the owner of a benefice in Austria-Hungary, a Spanish dean, a Sicilian priest, and an immigrant pastor in the United States. Somehow, from the various national traditions and the different life styles, there emerged over the years the classical type of Catholic pastor. The worldly priest playing the role of an intellectual in the salons of Paris, the scholar whose benefice afforded him enough leisure to pursue his studies, the rural parish priest with loose morals only distinguishable by his habit from the mass of his flock, all of them became, especially in western Europe, exceptional cases after 1850. The distinct rise in the spiritual standards of the clergy was one of the most characteristic aspects of Church history in the course of the pontificate of Pius IX. This development was dear to the heart of the Pontiff and he constantly returned to it in his encyclicals, speeches, and especially in his private correspondence.

This development of the clergy was the result of education received in the seminaries. Most candidates for the priesthood now had to undergo such an education and training, often starting in childhood. This was, of course, a hothouse atmosphere, rather deficient in intellectual content (only a part of the German and Austrian clergy still attended the regular universities), even though the clergy was imbued with high spiritual and pastoral ideals. The ideal had been formulated by Saint Sulpice, which directly or indirectly served as model for all of Europe and America. The clergy's development was also the product of the systematic efforts of many bishops with high standards of office. These episcopal objectives corresponded to the spontaneous efforts of a growing number of priests who gathered in associations, better to promote their aims. At the same time, the influence of the regular clergy over the secular priests grew. The two branches of the clergy cooperated better and the secular priests relied on the publications of the orders for their spiritual guidance. Thus the regular clergy tended to intensify the tendency among the diocesan priests to an otherworldliness inculcated in them by the seminaries, even at the risk of losing touch with the people among whom they exercised their apostolate.

Without a doubt, many priests in the villages and small towns everywhere confirmed the famous definition of Taine: "Loyal sentry duty in a guardhouse, obeying the watchword, and standing a lonely and monotonous guard." Their activity essentially consisted of celebrating the Mass-during the week only for a few women — of preaching the Sunday sermon, explaining the catechism to children, listening to confessions, and administering the last rites to the dying. But these conditions varied from country to country. A village priest in central or southern Italy was much more closely involved, occasionally much too much, in the daily lives of his flock than a French priest. In England and Ireland, the priests in the workers' quarters were not merely the spiritual fathers of their communities, but also acted as worldly advisers and occasionally were the leaders for their demands from the authorities. Even in those countries in which the restriction of the clergy to its purely ecclesiastical functions was most pronounced, there increasingly emerged, especially in the large city, an asceticism of action. It moved the clergy to engage in forms of the apostolate designed for conquest. Founders of religious congregations such as Father d'Alzon and Don Bosco clearly pushed their associates in this direction; but such thinking was not limited to the regular clergy. Dupanloup in his rural diocese encouraged his priests not to be content with waiting for the faithful in their churches, but to make home visits in order to arouse the indifferent; he tried to stimulate them to greater efforts through the introduction of social inquiries, of which he was a pioneer, even though not the only one. Although the focus of priestly work continued to be the parish, a new type of priest in addition to pastors and vicars came into being: the leader of socio-religious organizations. This was by no means the beginning of the specialized apostolate of the twentieth century, but many priests began to suit the method of the apostolate to the various groups to which they ministered, such as craftsmen, the sick, women, and children.

These efforts to reach the faithful more effectively unfortunately all too often suffered from a great deficiency. They were more oriented toward defense than to proselytization and urged the "good people" to withdraw unto themselves and to do nothing to shorten the gap between them and the bad Christians and the faithless. The latter were regarded as people without loyalty and faith, with whom any attempt at conversion would be fruitless. The same threat of confining Catholicism in a kind of intellectual ghetto, with its consequences for the apostolate, was also evident in the considerable efforts to develop a Catholic school system. The problem of education had already been raised during the pontificate of Gregory XVI, but the more education became common property, the more the clergy viewed education in a positively Catholic spirit as a necessity justifying any sacrifice. While in the German-speaking countries a solution acceptable to the Catholics was reached, the disappearance of Christian content in the public schools in many Latin countries, or their Protestant character in the Anglo-Saxon countries, caused the ecclesiastical authorities (at different rates in different countries) to establish a network of free Catholic schools. This was done parallel to the public school system and often in competition with it. In Great Britain, the system of parochial schools was generally confined to the elementary level of the parishes, but also comprised high schools, as in France, and even a Catholic university, as in Belgium. These efforts, repeatedly encouraged by the Holy See, had undeniably positive results, in spite of the dangers. C. Marcilhacy has pointed to the concordance between the establishment of parochial instruction and the growth of religious practice and noted that cause and effect became intertwined.

The conscientious zeal with which many priests devoted themselves to the three-fold tasks of parish, organization, and education was unfortunately devoid of the pastoral imagination necessary to rethink classical methods, allowing for the changes which civilization was undergoing. The lack of initiative was particularly worrisome in light of the problems posed by the growth of the large cities. While at the beginning of the nineteenth century there were only 20 cities with more than one hundred thousand inhabitants, they numbered 149 at the end of the century, among them 19 cities with more than half a million inhabitants each. Together they housed 47 million people in contrast to only 5 million in 1801. Although ever larger numbers of people moved from rural to urban areas and were cooped up in them, new parishes were established only slowly and belatedly.

Of course, the situation was not the same everywhere. In Great Britain and the United States, where Catholicism as a consequence of Irish immigration had an essentially urban character, serious work was accomplished. But in France, Italy, Belgium, and Catalonia the considerable increase in the number of only nominal Catholics was not seen as a sufficient reason for the division of a parish. During the final years of the century evidently only distances and transportation difficulties were considered, and rural areas were assigned a clear preference in pastoral organization. Inasmuch as the ecclesiastical authorities were chiefly concerned with what were regarded as the irreducible needs of the rural population, from which the seminaries obtained a large number of their students, they raised the number of pastors in the growing urban parishes only meagerly. Needless to say, this neglect made personal contact between the priest and his flock increasingly difficult. Finally, looking at the continuing urban de-Christianization, which eventually could no longer be ignored, only very few leaders of the Church recognized that an increase in the number of churches or in the personnel of the parishes was much less important than the discovery and application of new methods of the apostolate, which alone would make it possible to reestablish effective contact between the rootless masses of the proletariat and the Church.

Even though the clergy was very derelict in this respect, it at least quickly placed the periodical press in the service of the apostolate. During the second quarter of the century the clergy had encouraged the publication of periodicals for the educated class and had actively participated in such enterprises. Now a new, more popular type of publication was developed, the church newspaper, which indicated the hours of services in the various parishes of a district and listed the Catholic associations. This kind of publication had been in existence in Germany since the 1840s, including Catholic weeklies of general interest. These initiatives bore witness to a rather active clergy increasingly cognizant of its responsibility.

CHAPTER 36

The Growth of Piety

The second third of the nineteenth century was accompanied by a profound and lasting change in piety, especially north of the Alps. Turning away from the strict and rather cold piety preached in Germany by Sailer and his people, in England by the former students of the seminary of Ushaw, in France by the products of Saint Sulpice, and in Italy by the spiritual heirs of the Jansenists of the Synod of Pistoia, within a decade or two there emerged a religiosity which was more sentimental and less rigoristic. It emphasized a more frequent reception of the sacraments and a greater exercise of external forms of piety. From now on piety was increasingly directed to the compassionate Christ pointing to his heart "which loves man," to Jesus, "the prisoner of love in the tabernacle," to Mary, among the more intuitive aspects of Notre-Dame de Lourdes, and to a number of popular saints like Saint Anthony and Saint Joseph, whom Pius IX in 1870 proclaimed as the patron of the Church. Pilgrimages, which had lost much of their importance in the eighteenth century, gained appeal again.

Several factors contributed to the change, beginning with the romantic enthusiasm for everything that was reminiscent of the Middle Ages: veneration of Mary, adoration of saints, veneration of reliquaries, processions, pilgrimages, and other public displays of faith. But a large role was also played by considered actions, such as the influence of Pius IX, who strongly promoted the new love of indulgences and who multiplied the opportunities for jubilee indulgences; the influence of Roman-educated priests who in many popular publications told the world why they were so delighted with expressions of popular piety in Italy; the influence of those who disseminated the works of Saint Alphonsus Maria de Liguori, which were suffused with confidence in divine providence, love for the Virgin Mary and the Eucharist; but chiefly the influence of the Jesuits with their optimistic and anti-Jansenist theology, whose impact was multiplied by the fact that they had become the chief preachers at retreats for secular and regular clergy. It was partially owing to the Jesuits that piety became increasingly individualistic during the nineteenth century. But they also contributed much to the spread of the Sacred Heart of Jesus veneration, to the introduction of closed retreats, and to silent prayer according to the Ignatian method.

The new orientation of piety, branded by the adherents of the old customs as one of the main sins of ultramontanism, naturally also had its drawbacks: it was frequently insipid and infantile, as many simplistic church hymns and a whole range of devotional literature demonstrate; good intentions did not exclude mediocrity and bad taste. At the very time when German historians, with the tools of modern methodology, were in the process of rewriting Church history on the strict basis of authentic documents, devotional literature was written by authors who virtually had no such standards. According to the principle that any type of tradition must be accepted as long as it promotes piety, they became fervent defenders of the most improbable tales of saints, which the Bollandists and the Maurists had swept away a century earlier. On the other hand it must be acknowledged that this development, no matter how inept, was the healthy reaction of

Christian sentiment to an attenuated Christianity bordering on deism, which in the preceding century had gained many converts. Confessions on a regular basis and admonition to take Communion more frequently once again drew attention to the essentially sacramental character of Catholic life. The orientation of the new piety to the Christmas crib, to the cross, to the heart of Jesus, and to the Eucharist once again placed into the limelight the central reality of Christianity: Christ as the true God and true human being, the incarnation of divine love, who is asking each person to love him.

Eucharistic piety as yet had no feeling for liturgical life as a community-embracing aspect; instead, communion was seen as the wellspring of special grace and the real presence as the object of veneration. In France, Monsignor de Ségur became the fervent and tireless herald of frequent communion. His book *La très sainte communion* (1860), in which he advised the faithful to take communion at least once a week and, if possible, every day or every second day, created a storm of indignation among the old clergy. The encouragement for such dissemination came chiefly from Italy. In his *Il convito del divino amore* (1868), Frassinetti defended frequent communion in the name of Christian antiquity, and Don Bosco declared himself in favor of early communion, which had been fashionable in southern Italy for a long time.

Also from Italy came the various forms of venerating the sacrament of the altar. They became very popular during the second half of the nineteenth century and were adopted as their very own concern by a number of congregations founded during this period. The "Perpetual Adoration" officially recommended by Pius IX in 1851 was propagated in England, in Canada, and in the United States in the decade between 1850 and 1860. In France, it was already being employed at the time that Pius IX ascended the throne of Saint Peter. The Roman custom of nocturnal veneration was introduced in Germany.

In the case of the veneration of the Sacrament of the Altar, emphasis for a long time had been placed on the atonement for the humiliation inflicted on Jesus Christ. In France, this concept received a new interpretation: Atonement should be made no longer merely for the lapses of individual sinners, but for the attitude of the authorities, who were surrendering society to laicism. Engendered by this view, there emerged, also in France, toward the end of the pontificate of Pius IX, the idea of holding international Eucharistic Congresses. The reason behind the idea was two-fold. The apathetic masses were to be brought closer to the Eucharistic Presence by the drama of grandiose rallies, and make Catholics, intimidated by anticlerical policies, aware of their numbers and their strength. The original thought was to exploit the new interest in pilgrimages for the staging of special pilgrimages of atonement to the major sites which had been honored by a Eucharistic miracle. Various experiments were conducted on the local level between 1874 and 1877 and, publicized by sermons and pamphlets, gradually acquainted Catholics with this new type of mass demonstration. E. Tamisier then conceived the idea of combining the rallies with scholarly conferences in order to fashion them into genuine congresses with an international reputation. This idea was first put into practice at Avignon in 1876 and at Lille in 1881.

The devotion to the Sacrament of the Altar emphasized an especially important aspect of nineteenth century piety: It was more attracted to a union with the suffering Christ than to the glorious mysteries of the Easter message. In the spreading devotion to the Sacred Heart of Jesus several facets of this form of piety were addressed: deep sympathy with the pain of the pitiable victim of Golgotha, as the Middle Ages had felt it; compensation for the betrayal and the grave insults of sinners in the spirit of love and atonement; and, finally, the apostolic desire to complete what was missing in the suffering of Christ by assuming, as Christ's successors, the sins of humanity and their consequences. All in all a rather paradoxical aspect of this bourgeois, individualistic, and positivist century. This atoning and apostolic longing unfortunately had a weak theological foundation, which took too little account of the Corpus Christi mysticism and was too sentimental. The parish missions of the restoration period had spread the devotion to the Sacred Heart of Jesus, until then limited to a few elitist circles, to the parishes. But it was the pontificate of Pius IX which earned the nineteenth century the name of the "Century of the Sacred Heart," suggested by Monsignor d'Hulst. Actively promoted by the Jesuits, the Sacred Heart of Jesus devotion was eagerly taken up by the faithful. To them, the realistic mysticism of this veneration appeared as the best means to protest against the rationalistic and pleasure-seeking trends of their time. After 1870, a new element was added in France: the tendency to combine the atoning veneration of the Heart of Jesus with thinking of the "Prisoner in the Vatican" and with the recollection of national defeat. This dual aspect provided the grandiose demonstrations of Paray-le-Monial and, after 1876, of Montmartre, where the church of Sacré-Coeur in the first year of its existence witnessed the presence of three cardinals, twenty-six bishops, and 140,760 pilgrims, with a peculiar and frequently unpleasant coloration.

Even if the impulse driving the masses to a veneration of the Sacred Heart of Jesus was emotional, a few theologians, following the example of Perrone, began to find a place for the idea of the Sacred Heart of Jesus piety in the doctrine of the "Word which had become man" and tried rather ineptly to define the theological basis for the devotion to the Sacred Heart of Jesus. Pius IX encouraged the movement. In 1856 he agreed to the wish of many French bishops and expanded the Sacred Heart of Jesus feast to the entire Church.

The message of this mystic also contained a social element. Having long remained in the background, it was emphasized by ultramontane circles after the middle of the century. They tried to convince the entire world to acknowledge the absolute sovereignty of the Sacred Heart of Jesus and the obligation to strive for its social domination. In this context the musician Verboitte composed the famous motet: "Christus vincit, Christus regnat, Christus imperat." Two French Jesuits started the apostolate of prayer. They started an association whose members once a month prayed for a special and joint concern. The particular project was announced each month with the approval of the Pope and explained in the *Sacred Heart Messenger* (since 1861), a publication which twenty-five years later was issued in sixteen national editions and was duplicated in many other countries. The movement of the Consecration of the Sacred Heart was guided by the same considerations, although theocratic sympathies also played a role. After the consecration of individuals, families, and orders, states were also solemnly consecrated, and the consecration of the entire world to the Sacred Heart of Jesus was also demanded.

The rise in the devotion to Mary happened somewhat later than the Sacred Heart devotion. In Spain, the very strong current, sustained for two centuries, had grown feeble toward the end of the eighteenth century and was only revived in the twentieth century. In Italy, the few publications dealing with the matter were very weak from the theological point of view. In France, the Marian revival during the restoration period had remained superficial and without theological force, in spite of some pious initiatives. Then, within a quarter of a century, a complete turnabout occurred. It started with a number of appearances by the Virgin Mary. In 1830 she appeared to Catherine Labouré, signaling the beginning of the *Épopée de la medaille miraculeuse;* in 1836, also in Paris, she appeared to the pastor of Notre-Dame des Victoires, an appearance which resulted in the establishment of an archconfraternity which grew rapidly and within forty years numbered eight hundred thousand members; in 1846 she appeared to two children at La Salette in Savoy; and Bernadette Soubirous saw her at Lourdes in 1858. Marian congregations sprang up in all countries and May prayers became very popular after the 1830s. The discovery of Grignion de Montfort's manuscript on the *Traité de la vraie dévotion a la Sainte Vierge,* the first publication of which took place in 1843, provided the cult of Mary with another impulse. The final impetus was the solemn definition of the Immaculate Conception in 1854, the product of a number of petitions.

The intensity of the piety connected with Mary in the nineteenth century was also demonstrated by the names which religious congregations adopted when they were founded in this period. But there were dark sides to the cult of Mary as well. The forms assumed by the Marian rejuvenation were extremely uneven, sometimes infantile, and sometimes of such a nature that the Holy Office was compelled to take action. Mariological writings were of sad mediocrity. Only a few theologians came up with valuable contributions, among them Passaglia and Malou on the occasion of the definition of Immaculate Conception, and Newman and Scheeben somewhat later. But theirs were isolated accomplishments and received little attention at the time.

However, not only Mariological literature was generally mediocre. This was true as well for all of the spiritual literature of that time, especially in the Latin countries, where the tastelessness of the "art of Saint Sulpice" had its counterpart in the "ghastly pamphlets of piety," so aptly castigated by Ernest Hello. The best pieces that showed up in France prior to 1860 were the many reprints of works of the French school of the seventeenth century. The works of the Jesuit Jean Nicolas Grou fell into the same category. After 1860, the situation gradually improved.

The situation was somewhat better in England and Germany. England produced some original works, generally written by converts whose Anglican background had given them a much more pronounced knowledge of the Bible and patristics than was the case with most Catholics on the continent. Newman, Manning, Dalgairns, and Faber deserve mention. Faber's book especially, translated into various languages, spread in all of Europe and the Anglo-Saxon countries a spirituality which was inspired by the Italian school of Saint Liguori and the great Oratorians of the seventeenth century. In Germany, Görres' important book *Die Christliche Mystik* inspired a series of scholarly works on speculative mysticism. Scheeben's first books, were actuated by the Greek Fathers. But these were publications which were hardly accessible to the broad public. Yet, Germany could take the credit for introducing liturgical piety to the large mass of the faithful.

The liturgical renewal took its rise from the French Benedictine Dom Guéranger. The treasures which he collected in the volumes of his *Année liturgique* unfortunately remained restricted to a small elite in his country, probably because his perspective too strongly reflected the interests of an archeologist who was interested in the most complete restitution of the Middle Ages possible. In the German-speaking countries, the liturgical question had been raised in the 1830s and 1840s from the pastoral point of view. The return to liturgical piety occurred in Germany during the following generation in a form which closely corresponded to medieval tradition. In 1864, Maurus Wolter, one of the founders of Beuron Abbey, translated into German the famous *Exercitia spiritualia* by Saint Gertrude von Helfta, which were oriented toward annual and daily spiritual observations. In a long enthusiastic introduction, Wolter acquainted the German public with the movement started by Dom Guéranger in France and explained its principles. In the following year he published the small book *Choral und Liturgie,* quoting whole pages from the introduction to *L'année liturgique,* and devoting a large amount of space to a summary of Guéranger's principal thought concerning the incomparable wealth of the spiritual food involved in liturgy. His booklet had a great response among large segments of the population. Parallel to it, Wolter wrote a patristic commentary on the Psalms, *Psallite sapienter* (5 vols. [1871–90]), for monks in order to induce them to bring their spiritual life in step with liturgical life. What appears to us as a matter of course was very necessary at that time, for the influence of Ignatian methods had so profoundly affected the spiritual atmosphere of most of the Benedictine monasteries that worship often completely lacked the liturgical spirit.

CHAPTER 37

The Backwardness of Religious Studies and the Controversy about the "German Theologians"

In his famous lectures to a gathering of Catholic scholars at Munich in 1863, Döllinger stated that only Germany was "tending the two eyes of theology, history and philosophy, with conscientiousness and thoroughness." Comparing the two competing schools of thought, the "German" one and the "Roman" one, he asserted that the former was defending Catholicism with rifles, while the latter was still using bows and arrows. His allegation created consternation in many circles. Today, with the benefit of a century of perspective, it must be admitted that Döllinger was right. Even if the erudite historian exaggerated the theological decadence of the Latin countries slightly, it can not be denied that it was in a wretched condition. Although the efforts of the German scholars in teaching and research were not totally perfect, there is no doubt that the departments of religious studies in German universities were able to maintain and to enlarge the lead which they had gained during the first half of the century. Outside of Germany there were hardly any centers of Catholic scholarship which could measure up to the achievements of Protestants and rationalists.

Religious Studies outside of Germany

All observers, including those most devoted to the Holy See, were unanimous in deploring the extraordinary nadir of scholarship in Rome under Pius IX, the absence of organized libraries, and the lack of interest on the part of the papal leadership in teaching and research. Yet, as paradoxical as it may sound, it was in Rome that the most serious work outside of Germany was conducted. This was in part due to foreigners working in Rome. One of them was the French Benedictine Pitra, who published patristic editions (philologically not entirely free of errors), and numerous important works on Eastern canon law and Byzantine hymnology. Another was the German Oratorian Augustin Theiner, prefect of the Vatican Archives, a somewhat sloppy and restless spirit, who published several editions of sources which have been useful to this day. But there were not only foreigners. The Barnabite Vercellone (1814–69) published some valuable Biblical textual criticisms. Christian archeology was Rome's very own science. It had awakened to new life under the pontificate of Gregory XVI. After the reorganization of the Museum Kircherianum, Giuseppe Marchi somewhat clumsily had begun the scientific exploration of the catacombs, which had been totally neglected since the seventeenth century. Pius IX sanctioned the new beginning with the creation of the *Commissione de archeologia sacra* in 1852. Marchi's preferred student was Giovanni Battista de Rossi. Even though after Fausti's evaluation he can no longer be regarded as the originator of Christian archeology, De Rossi was responsible for its strict scientific methodology, and he defined the rules of Christian epigraphy to such an extent that he became its virtual originator. After he had published the *Inscriptiones christianae Urbis Romae* (1857) and founded the *Bollettino di archeologia cristiana* in 1863, De Rossi wrote the comprehensive *Roma Sotteranea cristiana.* It revived the whole history of the Roman Church from its beginnings, dealing with its doctrine, its hierarchy, its liturgy, and its art. According to Cardinal Pie it was a new *locus theologicus,* but with exemplary scholarly scrupulousness De Rossi refused to exaggerate the meaning of facts for apostolic purposes. His treatment was the best possible one at that time.

There was also the Roman College. If its teaching was more akin to that of high schools than that of German universities, and if the majority of the faculty was not known for its excellence, dogmatic theology at least was brilliantly represented. Passaglia, Perrone's best-known student and, according to W. Kasper, one of the most brilliant theologians of the nineteenth century, taught at the college from 1844 to 1858. His theology rested on an infinite knowledge of the Greek

Fathers. He made up for his unfamiliarity with German by having his young colleague Clemens Schrader keep him informed of the important studies appearing in German. Subsequently, Schrader largely followed the doctrines and methods of his older confraternity brother, albeit more Scholastically and rigorously. When Schrader was appointed professor at Vienna (1857) and Passaglia was forced to leave Rome because of his involvement in the Italian cause, their work at the Collegium Romanum was carried on by the Austrian Johannes Baptist Franzelin. He worked out a theology less striking than Passaglia's, but one that was more elegant and exact. It was based on criticism of the texts, monuments, and facts, utilizing the latest archeological discoveries, and employing his thorough knowledge of Eastern languages and the products of the German historical school. The solid and original works of these three teachers gave large room to positive theology and to speculation; their speculative theology was more concerned with an organic synthesis of the facts of faith based on the Bible than with a philosophical exploration of the truths of revelation.

Compared to their work, the *Instructions synodales sur les erreurs du temps présent* by Monsignor Pie, long regarded as one of the masterworks of French theology in the nineteenth century, made a pitiful impression. Fighting against the naturalism of the time by presenting the supernatural aspects of Christ's passion and salvation, Pie's instructions were long on beautiful rhetoric and short on scholarly spirit. Although imbued with great powers of persuasion, they are a testament to the tremendous weakness of Catholic thought in France under the Second Empire. The theologians were still using the oratorical methods of romanticism, while the thinkers of this period were increasingly influenced by the results of the positive sciences and the detailed analyses of historical criticism. Characteristic in this context is the weakness of the refutation of Ernest Renan's basically rather superficial *Vie de Jésus* (1863).

In the field of Church history, the inferiority of Catholics during the pontificate of Pius IX, with the exception of Germany, was most clearly visible. In Spain, the tradition of Flórez and Villanueva was interrupted for almost a hundred years. Italy also, aside from Christian archeology, lagged behind the eighteenth century. True, there were in France two or three good books on positive theology. This refers to the *Histoire du dogme catholique pendant les trois premiers siècles* (1852) by Ginoulhiac and the two volumes of Monsignor Maret's *Du concile général* (1869), which displayed a good knowledge of Christian antiquity and some critical faculties.

A good number of clerics used their free time for scholarly activity; most of them confined themselves to local researches and historiography, and as a consequence of their faulty training they rarely produced anything that exceeded the mediocre. More serious was the fact that the idea of apostolicity of the French Church, which had been discredited by the scholars of the seventeenth and eighteenth centuries, was taken up again in 1835 by the Sulpician Faillon, was again taught in the seminaries, found entrance in the history books, was supported by many bishops, and seemed to triumph with the appearance in 1877 of *Les Églises du monde romaine* by the Benedictine Chamard. At the same time, the lack of associates forced the monks of Solesroes to discontinue the publication of *Gallia christiana*. This backwardness in the scholarly field was not even balanced by acceptable works of synthesis.

The situation was somewhat better in Belgium. The university of Louvain continued to produce respectable studies in the areas of Eastern studies, patrology, and historical evaluations of canon law. The Bollandists, after having been restored in 1837, published six volumes of the *Acta sanctorum* between 1845 and 1867 and included Slavic sources and Celtic hagiography in their fields of endeavor. Their inspiration, however, the tireless V. de Buck, remained a gifted improvisor; only after his death in 1876 was the work of the group placed on a firm foundation by his successor, Charles de Smedt.

In philosophy, the "other eye" of theology, the situation was more complex. The systems which in their struggle against rationalism denigrated the powers of reasoning to an excessive degree lost a part of their prestige after the condemnation of Lamennais and the difficulties experienced by Bautain. But many Catholics saw the interventions of the Holy See merely as warnings against excesses, and traditionalism continued to exist in attenuated form until the Vatican Council. This was the case especially in Italy and France, where traditionalism was represented by A. Bonnetty and the brilliant Italian polemicist Ventura, whom the events of 1848 had forced to take refuge in France. In his *Annales de philosophie chrétienne*, Bonnetty continued to pursue his intention of proving the continued existence of original revelation. He sharply criticized the fateful influence of Aristotelian rationalism on the "hardly Christian" language of Scholastic theology. Ventura conceded that the existence of God, the immortality of the soul, and the foundations of morality, once they are established, can also be proved by reason, but in contrast to the "Semi-Pelagians of Philosophy" argued the necessity of revelation for their primary knowledge and the importance of God-given language for the thorough study of these concepts. Traditionalism continued to be successful in spite of the criticism advanced by the defenders of the rights of reason from among the Jesuits and the Sulpicians and in spite of a very hesitant renewed intervention of Rome. Its success stemmed not only from the continuing fascination exercised by Lamennais upon his followers, but also from the agreement of the traditionalist system with an ultramontane attitude and the authoritarian inclinations of many Catholics after 1848. It was from this perspective that the attempts of the French ontologists derived their meaning, even though in contrast to Rosmini's system theirs found only limited acceptance. It started with a group of intelligent priests, who recognized the danger posed by the growth of an authoritarian principle in philosophy for the future of Catholicism in a society determined to have intellectual autonomy. Dissatisfied with both the idealistic German systems and a positivism which closed its eyes to metaphysical problems, they attempted to restore intellectualism in a Platonic and Augustinian tradition. But the general of the Jesuits in 1850 put a quick end to the success of the ontological doctrines at the training center at Vals. While the attacks against Rosmini twice, in 1854 and 1876, ended with a preliminary acquittal, the Neo-Scholastic opposition in 1861 succeeded in obtaining from the Holy Office the condemnation of seven characteristic theses of French ontologism.

The reaction to traditionalism and ontologism was a result of the renascence of Scholasticism. It was promoted by the conservative wing of romanticism, which was captured by the ideas and institutions of the Middle Ages. Prior to 1870, many adherents of a return to Scholasticism were not yet genuine Neo-Thomists. Rather they were eclectics, desirous of a return to the philosophy of the Middle Ages, who wanted to rethink this philosophy, in the light of Suárez in Spain, and in the light of Cartesianism in France and Italy. Gradually the number of people desiring a return to a genuine Thomism increased. In Germany, this was the case from the 1850s onward; in Spain, there was the circle led by the Dominican Gonzalez, who founded the journal *La ciencia cristiana* in 1873; in France, there was Abbé Hulst's circle; in Belgium, there was the group led by the Dominican Lepidi, professor and regent of the research department at the training center at Louvain. The main impact occurred in Italy. While the Roman College remained a citadel of Suárezianism until the election of Leo XIII, the Jesuits of the *Civiltà cattolica* became fervent propagandists of Thomism. The two chief centers of Thomism were the Collegio Alberoni at Piacenza and the Jesuit Collegio Massimo and the Liceo arcivescovile at Naples. In 1846, G. Sanseverino established the Accademia tomista there and published the journal *Scienza e fede*. There were also other centers.

From the quantitative point of view, it must be noted that the Catholic authors of the third quarter of the nineteenth century devoted their best efforts to apologetics. For after the revival of religiosity and of sympathy for the medieval Church, characteristics of the generation of romantics, the intellectual world, beginning with the middle of the century, experienced a quick and different type of development. The historical claims of Christianity and the traditional authority of the Bible were questioned in the name of historical criticism and as a result of the discoveries of paleontology and Near Eastern archeology. The problem of the transcendence of Christianity was immediately raised by the comparative history of religions, and soon the foundations of theism and the idea of religion were attacked by Feuerbach and the liberal Hegelians. Materialistic explanations of the universe were widely disseminated in Germany by men like Ludwig Büchner, Karl Vogt, and Ernst Haeckel. Spencer continued the traditions of English empiricism and propagated the Darwinian evolutionary interpretation of the world, which theologians rejected categorically. In the France of the Second Empire, Auguste Comte's thoughts combined with English agnosticism and German materialism and were exported under the name of "positivism."

Under these circumstances it was not surprising that apologetics increased in significance in the course of the nineteenth century. The study of dogma, hitherto regarded as the essential task of theologians, began to appear to most Catholic thinkers as less urgent than the defense of religion and the foundations of Christianity. Even when they studied theology, they did so from an apologetic perspective. The speculations of Hermes and Günther, formally belonging to the field of dogmatics, were in reality guided by the aim of making dogma acceptable for people who had been won by modern philosophy. The scholarly studies at Tübingen and Munich as well were more directed toward a defense of the great Christian and Catholic theses against rationalistic and Protestant criticism than they were concerned with the origins of the Bible of the Fathers.

To be sure, apologetic works continued to be written and testified to the apostolic zeal of their authors; but most of them suffered from a total lack of adaptation. Elegantly in Germany, more superficially elsewhere, they incessantly repeated the same classical arguments. In view of the intellectual atmosphere of the time, they no longer had any impact; people were no longer receptive to them. It is sad to note the paucity of Catholic studies prior to the final twenty years of the century which competently treated the principal problem of adapting the Christian faith to the new science-based thinking. A first step was taken in 1875 by the Jesuit Carbonelle with the founding of the Scientific Society of Brussels, which drew together Catholic scientists from various countries.

Among the apologists who endeavored to understand the views of those whom they wished to convince were Father Félix and Alphonse Gratry. Between 1853 and 1869, the Jesuit Félix preached the conference sermons at Notre-Dame in Paris and in them developed an apologetics which took account of contemporary realities. He analyzed the trends of the time with astuteness, especially the enthusiasm with which progress was regarded. He tried to show that Christianity, far from hindering any legitimate striving of humankind, was actually the only way for it to achieve what it was blindly seeking. Gratry tried in vain to realize an idea by Lamennais to gather a number of priests in a kind of *atelier apologétique* by reestablishing the *Oratoire de France* in 1852. In many of his publications he anticipated the path taken during the next generation by Ollé-Laprune and Blondel.

One man surpassed all others by the power and force of his genius and his ability to look into the future: John Henry Newman. He paved the way for the acceptance of new demands and fresh values of human reason in the service of faith. In his *Essay on the Development of Christian Doctrine* (1845) he emphasized the value of and the need for historical thought; in his *Grammar of Assent* (1870) he wrote of the value of the spontaneous power of reason, based on a convergence of judgments and practical life experience; he demanded a "Dialectic of Conscience" and the psychological preparation of people for the acceptance of faith justified by reason. In his essay *On Consulting the Faithful in Matters of Doctrine* (1859), the *Letter to the Duke of Norfolk* (1875), and two volumes of the *Via Media* (1877) he brought out the importance of the meaning of Holy Scripture and the Christian Fathers for the Christian mystery as the basis of all religious knowledge. Unfortunately, there was no one at the time to follow him on the paths whose importance for the future Newman anticipated. Moreover, his employment of the essay made his studies less accessible to professional theologians. Lastly, there were the suspicions which were cast on his orthodoxy. They were one of the most unpleasant aspects of the intellectual policy of the Roman Curia under Pius IX and persisted until the elevation of Leo XIII.

Scholastics and Germanics vs. the "German Theologians"

One of the major achievements of the Tübingen School was that Catholic dogma was rethought with pronounced attention given to the historical dimension, the discovery of which was a main characteristic of the intellectual life of the nineteenth century. What counted from now on was not merely critical scholarship or chronology, but a sense of becoming and the awareness that events, institutions, and doctrines are what they really are only when they are placed in the context of time and when their historical development is taken into consideration. Following the example of Drey and Möhler, theologians increasingly discussed the consequences of seeing Christian events and Christian revelation in the context of history. This did not mean that speculative considerations disappeared, not even among those who remained tied to Scholastic tradition. Still, as the century advanced, theological sciences became more concerned with historical theology and became more interested in the vitality of dogma than its metaphysics. The redirection to a less speculative theology than had been pursued during the first half of the nineteenth century was hastened by apologetic interests. While Protestant historians developed a critical method which enabled them to question many traditional attitudes toward the origins of Christianity and the Middle Ages, some university departments, especially at Tübingen, developed a radical exegesis and a Hegelian interpretation of the history of dogma, originated by Ferdinand Christian Baur. In close contact with their opponents at the universities, Catholic theologians grasped quickly that it was essential to enter the arena on which the battle was fought, to fight them with the same weapons employed by them, i.e., with facts, texts, and documents, and to revise positions incompatible with the facts.

In the field of exegesis, seen as a whole, the achievements of Catholics, even though not insignificant, remained far behind those of the Protestants.

In the area of the history of dogma and Church history, on the other hand, good work was done. This was the case at Tübingen, where Karl Joseph Hefele worked on studies ranging from the apostolic Fathers to Cardinal Ximenes and wrote his monumental *Conciliengeschichte* (7 vols. [1855–74]). Also at Tübingen there was a group of young scholars who wrote for the *Theologisches Quartalschrift* and employed the new critical methods in order to delineate the stages of progress in Christian thought. Another center of activity was Munich, thanks to the great influence of Ignaz Döllinger, the uncontested leader of the German Catholic historical school.

In the course of the events of 1848, Döllinger emerged as one of the most important Catholic leaders both with respect to politics and religion. But he was disappointed by the trends of the Catholic movement under the leadership of the men from Mainz and the growing influence of the Jesuits in the Church. He withdrew from public life and devoted himself to scholarly work, always from an apologetic point of view. *Hippolytus und Callistus* (1853), a masterful example of historical criticism receiving the acclaim of all German scholars, was designed to shore up the Catholic conscience in the face of objections to the papacy which Protestants like Christian Karl von Bunsen believed to have found in the recently discovered *Philosophoumena*. Similarly, *Heidentum und Judentum. Vorhalle zur Geschichte des Christentums* (1857), the first scholarly Catholic attempt to present the origins of Christianity within their historical context. He wanted to demonstrate that, historically speaking, no development of Greek or Jewish origin could explain the rise of Christianity. His *Christentum und Kirche in der Zeit der Grundlegung* (1860), a book with a genuine religious flair, contained a number of passages concerning the papacy which were clearly directed against Protestants. Even more than through his publications, Döllinger's influence, whose tremendous extent it is difficult to understand today, was spread by his lectures and was carried by his students to many professorships at universities in Germany, Austria, and Switzerland. In his personal contacts, the richness of his thought, the clarity of his views, and the simple demeanor of the man captured his discussion partners, and his correspondence touched upon the scholarly works written in German, English, and French.

Döllinger, Hefele, Kuhn, Günther, and most of their colleagues and students who were in close contact with the academic world were primarily animated by the desire to liberate Catholic intellectuals from the inferiority complex which the flowering of Protestant and rationalistic scholarship had given them. They expected to accomplish their aim by suggesting to them to compete with the same weapons and to give them the feeling of complete intellectual freedom, aside from the relatively few questions of dogma. They hoped to win a degree of influence for the Church in the world of the mind which corresponded to the influence which the Church was in the process of gaining through public political action.

But a part of the German clergy, among them Bishop Ketteler of Mainz and his advisers Lenning, Heinrich, and Moufang, saw matters differently. They had in mind the mass of the Catholics, the peasants, the craftsmen, and tradesmen, whose Christian beliefs, consolidated by a pious and active clergy, was to find expression in a mighty movement of well-disciplined associations. These were to subordinate themselves to the Holy See, able to carry out the decisions of the hierarchy down to the lowest levels of society. The supporters of this movement were more interested in having good priests than educated ones, and therefore were very much opposed to the German system, which forced young clerics to study in the departments of theology attached to public universities. They wanted to replace this system with the system of diocesan seminaries used in France and Italy, the same system which Ketteler had reintroduced in his diocese. Beyond this, many of them wished to withdraw young laymen from the atmosphere of public universities, where the vast majority of the faculty was Protestant. They called for the creation of a Catholic university which for the German Catholics was to play the same role as the University of Louvain in Belgium. These plans were supported by all people and publications associated with Bishop Ketteler. Headed by Döllinger, Ketteler and his supporters were opposed by all other German Catholics who realized that the faith needed clergy completely conversant with the latest knowledge. They also recognized the danger of educating young Catholics in complete isolation, as it would deny them access to all of the scholarly tools which only the universities could provide. They feared the cutoff of Catholics from the intellectual life of their time, if the point of view of Ketteler should prevail. Döllinger's fear was the greater as his opponents openly demanded a return to Scholasticism, failed to comprehend the urgency of the problems raised by historical criticism, and believed that speculative thought in Germany had reached a dead-end street with Kant's philosophy.

A return to Scholasticism was the major concern of the Mainz journal *Der Katholik,* which was edited by professors appointed by Ketteler in 1849 when he reopened the Mainz seminary. The pioneers of German Neo-Scholasticism were the dogmatist Johann Baptist Heinrich and the philosopher Paul Leopold Haffner. At Bonn, the movement was supported by the young belligerent layman Franz Jakob Clemens. At Munich, the *Historisch-politische Blätter,* Archbishop Reisach, a former student at the German College in Rome, and Vicar General Windischmann were behind the movement. Windischmann had long pointed to the dangers of Güntherianism. In Austria Neo-Scholasticism was encouraged by Cardinal Rauscher, who in 1857 appointed the Jesuit Schrader and the Dominican Guidi to positions at the University of Vienna. After 1857 Neo-Scholasticism had an active center in the department of theology at the University of Innsbruck, which was directed by the Jesuits. It was in fact the Jesuits who everywhere became the most ardent supporters of the Neo-Scholastic restoration, assisted by the success of Kleutgen's books *Die Theologie der Vorzeit vertheidigt* (5 vols. [1853–70]) and *Die Philosophie der Vorzeit vertheidigt* (2 vols. [1860–63]). In an original and thorough fashion, Kleutgen rethought the doctrines of Saint Thomas, but he also tackled problems which Thomas had not foreseen, and occasionally was guided by Suárez as well. He demonstrated that Thomas' traditional doctrines could be applied to new problems and how they fit into other great philosophical systems. It was his great achievement that he cleared away antiquated methods which made them unacceptable to modern minds.

The fact that many people favored this Scholastic orientation is in part explained by the real weaknesses of theological instruction at the universities, as for example in the rationalistic and historicistic approach of some professors, but especially in the neglect of the leadership role, which in theology must be assigned to the magisterial office of the Church guided by the Holy Spirit. In the subsequent generation, Matthias Joseph Scheeben showed that Neo-Scholasticism was not only of defensive utility in the fight against the excesses of the "German theologians," but also produced works of real spiritual and religious value. Karl Werner's books proved that adherence to Scholasticism did not have to exclude solid historical scholarship. Yet it must be conceded that most of the products of Neo-Scholasticism remained on a rather low level. Even when they attempted to integrate historical knowledge — which almost always was only secondhand — with the speculative treatises of classical authors, they failed to integrate them truly and to evaluate them historically and theologically. The retreat to the bastion of a timeless valid system cost theology its actuality and representation in the modern world.

This last aspect was particularly regrettable, as the opposition to university theology came in part from men who were not merely worried by the occasional excesses of "German scholarship," but were indifferent or hostile to scholarship in general. This was, of course, not true of all of them. Some harbored genuine admiration for scholarship, as long as it was orthodox; but many former students of the Collegium Romanum, called "Germanics" because they had resided in the Collegium Germanicum when they were in Rome, failed to make use of the perspectives which the teaching of Passaglia and Franzelin had made available to them. They refused to acknowledge that the advances of historical methods required new attitudes in many different areas. Even less did the survivors of the fideistic and traditionalist currents, influential in Archbishop Geissel's circle, favor the aim of the "German theologians" of confronting Christian thought with the great Neo-Kantian philosophical systems. They refused to undertake a serious review of the texts which modern historical criticism required. These texts were usually adduced by the Catholics for the defense of their traditionalist positions, but were too often confused by them with ecclesiastical tradition itself.

More serious was the fact that many defenders of Neo-Scholasticism, irritated by the contempt in which the academic world held them, tried to strengthen their arguments and objections by an appeal to the supreme foreign ecclesiastical authority. The notes which they increasingly sent to Rome were not always generated by the desire for truth but stemmed from personal intrigues and rivalries. The first great success of the Scholastic reactionaries was the condemnation of Güntherianism in 1857. The Neo-Scholastics were supported by the nuncio at Munich in their increasingly bitter attacks, and in the Roman Curia they found allies in Cardinal Reisach and Kleutgen. As consultant to the Congregation of the Index, Kleutgen was particularly influential.

Günther's condemnation encouraged the ultramontanes to attack those theologians and philosophers who insisted on continuing their studies without taking account of ecclesiastical directives. When Kuhn asserted the right of philosophy to be independent, Clemens was assisted by *Der Katholik,* which kept a close eye on doctrinaire currents. The front of the universities was breached in 1854 with the appointment of Heinrich Denzinger, a former student at the Gregoriana, to the chair of dogmatics at Würzburg. He was soon joined by two other "Romans": by the Church historian Joseph Hergenröther and the apologist Franz Hettinger. All three of them worked in the spirit of total subjection to ecclesiastical authority. Denzinger's collection of ecclesiastical decisions, *Enchiridion Symbolorum et Definitionum* (1854), reminded the German theologians of the importance of the decisions of the magisterial office, including those which were not infallible.

Numerous German professors in the name of academic freedom refused to bow to the authority of the Church, unless it was a question of defined dogma. Their attitude created consternation in Rome, where academic concerns were of little interest and the struggle against liberalism was in full swing. In this connection, many works were placed on the Index after 1857. In 1862, Pius IX directed a letter to the archbishop of Munich in which he discussed the errors of the Munich professor Jakob Frohschammer and lamented that Frohschammer was not the only one who demanded "a freedom to write and to teach with which the Church hitherto had been unacquainted." Separated by the geographical distance, Rome's distrust of German academics increased and eventually encompassed even Germany's leading professors, including Döllinger.

For several years, the eminent historian had been the subject of accusations. He, in turn, was offended by Rome's centralizing tendencies, which coincided with the aggressive behavior of the Neo-Scholastics. The most zealous among the ultramontanes suspiciously watched this theologian, who used such un-Roman methods, tended to think that serious ecclesiastical studies were only conducted at the German universities, and considered the growing influence of the former students of the Collegium Romanum in Germany's ecclesiastical life as a victory of obscurantism. For the time being, however, at least until his two lectures which he gave in 1861 at Munich, the ecclesiastical authorities respected his stance. The two lectures had essentially a pastoral goal. Convinced of the impending decline of the Papal State, he wanted to calm the Catholics with the assertion that by no means would such a decline constitute a decline of the papacy as such, no matter what the Protestants were saying. But he did not confine himself to the presentation of positive views concerning the importance of papal primacy and the recognition of the attempts by Pius IX to bring about improvements in the Papal State. He explained the hostility toward the secular power of the papacy with the obvious deficiencies of the archaic and clerical papal government. Many observers interpreted Döllinger's remarks as open support for Cavour and some seized this opportunity to take action against him. They organized a protest campaign and tried to discredit the scholar in the eyes of the Catholic people, who were still devoted to the Pope in spite of his shortcomings. Dismayed, Döllinger tried to correct the situation, but was not successful in eradicating the initial negative impression. Subsequently, criticism of his theological positions became more overt, the critics being secure in the knowledge of having the ear of all those who placed the defense of the privileges of the papacy at the top of their objectives.

It annoyed Döllinger that his prestige among Catholics had been hurt and it displeased him that his academic work was questioned by absolutely incompetent people. Yet in spite of his growing hostility to the policies of the Curia, he remained a devoted son of the Church. But it bothered him that the German Catholic intellectuals were fighting one another instead of making common front against the increasingly radical attacks by secular academics. Thus, a reconciliation of the two Catholic groups was urgently necessary. For years the idea of a congress of German Catholic scholars had been in the air. Therefore Döllinger, Alzog, and Haneberg, ignoring the skepticism of the Tübingen group, the reserve of the Mainz circle, and the open hostility of the Jesuits, invited the Catholic scholars of Germany, Austria, and Switzerland to gather in Munich in September 1863. In the meantime, unfortunately, the distrust of Döllinger had grown, primarily because of his book *Die Papstfabeln des Mittelalters* (1863). In it he revealed the legendary character of some of the traditions of the medieval papacy and used the weaknesses of Pope Liberius and Pope Honorius as arguments against the thesis of papal infallibility.

In his remarkable opening address on "The Past and Present of Theology," justifiably described by Goyau as a "Declaration of Rights" of theology, Döllinger described various methods of theology and demanded complete freedom of movement whenever faith was not directly affected. "For scholarship, such freedom is as essential as air is for the body," he said, and called for purely scholarly weapons in the struggle against theological error, instead of ecclesiastical censures. Just as among the Hebrews prophets and priestly hierarchy had existed side by side, there should be in the Catholic Church as well an extraordinary power in addition to regular authority. This, he asserted, is public opinion, the molding of which was a matter for theologians. Inasmuch as at the same time he spoke of the complete decline of theology in the Latin countries, he created the impression that he was demanding the actual intellectual leadership of the Church by the German theologians. The theologians from Mainz and Würzburg did not allow such assertions to pass without protest, but finally a vague compromise concerning the rights of authority and of liberty was formulated.

Many participants returned home convinced that the chief objective of the congress of scholars, namely, an understanding with the "Romans," had been effected. The first reaction of Pius IX, who had feared that the congress might degenerate into a declaration of war against the Roman congregations, also was rather favorable. But the reports of the nuncio and other opponents of Döllinger about the atmosphere at the congress, at which the students of Döllinger constituted a majority, and the text of Döllinger's addresses produced an immediate change in the attitude of the Pope. For a time, placing the proceedings of the congress on the Index was even considered. Ultimately, however, Pius IX only sent a brief to the archbishop of Munich in which he denounced the attacks on Scholasticism and deplored that a gathering of theologians had taken place without explicit request from the hierarchy, "whose task it is to guide and supervise theology." He stated further that Catholic scholars were not only bound by solemn definitions, but actually were obligated to take into consideration the magisterial office, the decisions of the Roman congregations, and the common doctrines of theologians.

Döllinger's attempt at conciliation had failed, and the tone of the polemics of the two camps immediately doubled in stridency. On one side were the men who were convinced that the chief task was to regain the respect of the educated Catholics for the Church by painstaking applications of the historical method and by a presentation of Catholic dogma convincing for modern philosophical attitudes. The Tübingen group also shared this dual ideal, but disapproved of the radicalism of the Munich group and assumed a more passive stance. The aggressive vanguard of the Munich group consisted of Döllinger's friends. Soon they had their own journal, the *Theologisches Literaturblatt,* founded in 1865. On the other side was the "Roman" party, which thought that the chief task was to provide Catholics with a complete doctrinary system of unquestionable orthodoxy. Their main centers were the seminary at Mainz, the seminary at Cologne, the seminary at Eichstätt, and the training center of the Jesuits, where Joseph Florian Riess in 1864 founded the *Stimmen aus Maria Laach* for the purpose of commenting on the *Syllabus.*

Only a few people succeeded in maintaining good relations with both sides. Tension increased from year to year and the smallest incident gave rise to sharp polemics which held no trace of disinterested scholarship or of the milk of human kindness.

Döllinger, constantly worried about the serious threat to the freedom of Catholic scholars, grew bitter when he noticed that his popularity was disappearing. It looked as though he himself were trying to justify the attacks of his opponents by announcing loudly his compromises with Protestant scholars and anticlerical administrators and by his malicious comments on everything that emanated from Rome. Some of his disciples, the "young Munich School," as it was called, created consternation through their arrogance and their lack of Catholic sympathies.

The responsibility for these conditions was to be found on both sides. The intransigence and narrow-mindedness of many defenders of the Roman position contributed a great deal to worsening an already delicate situation. There were indeed moderate men among them, but there were also men whose fanaticism had deplorable consequences. They included Kuhn in their attacks and thus carried suspicion to the Tübingen school. They prevented the Tübingen group from exercising the moderating influence of which it would have been capable. It did not suffer from the historicism and the rationalism of the Munich school and could have supplied what the Neo-Scholastics lacked in the way of Biblical and historical thought and a sense of mystery.

Section Four

The Altercation between Catholicism and Liberalism

Chaps. 38, 39, 41: Roger Aubert
Chap. 40: Rudolf Lill

The confrontation of liberal ideas with the traditional positions of the Church, which had started in the 18th century and continued to grow with the Declaration of the Rights of Man and the Citizen in 1789, reached its peak under the pontificate of Pius IX. Shortly after the end of the idyll of 1848, the antagonism on both sides increased on the ideological and practical levels. The revival of the Roman Question could not but inflame the hostility further. Even though its true roots were found in the national enthusiasm of the Italians and partially also in the political ambitions of Piedmont, the sovereignty of the Pope was officially questioned in the name of the new freedoms — the right of peoples to self-determination and the liberal concept of the state. The two problems could very well have been kept separate, as proved by the attitude of the people led by Montalembert and Dupanloup; but in fact they were looked upon as intertwined.

CHAPTER 38

The Roman Question

From the Papal Restoration to the Italian War

The restoration of the authority of the Pope in the Papal State after the brief interlude of the Roman Republic had taken place in a clearly reactionary atmosphere. The new form of government, worked out by Cardinal Antonelli in a number of laws passed between 10 September and 24 November 1850 followed the principles of Cardinal Bernetti. The secretary of state subsequently regarded him as his mentor in political matters. He envisioned a number of reforms, but they consisted exclusively of improvements of existing institutions and produced no genuine changes in structure. In the failure of 1848 Antonelli saw final proof of the incompatibility of the maintenance of the temporal power of the Pope with even only a partial liberalization of the governmental system. For this reason he rejected all entreaties by the Paris and the Vienna governments at least to take the path of a moderate constitutional reform. Yet it must be acknowledged that Antonelli's government had its merits on the level of administrative accomplishments. De Rayneval, French ambassador to Rome, mentioned that Antonelli started or inspired a number of steps which demonstrated great vitality and good will. This view was confirmed by the investigation of Dalla Torre, even if he is too apologetic. Other foreign observers also noted with satisfaction that some of Antonelli's measures were far-sighted. But many of these endeavors were only partially realized and remained on the level of the enlightened despotism of the eighteenth century and were not able to prevent people's minds from being dominated by the two thoughts of a liberal growth of political institutions and the realization of Italian unity.

The first years were relatively calm. But after the Congress of Paris (1856) the problem of necessary reforms in the Papal State was pushed into the foreground of the concerns of the Italian public by the skillful propaganda organized by Cavour and supported by England. In spite of the misbehavior of the Austrian troops charged with maintaining order in the northern provinces, the common people, who could note a slight increase in their standard of living and appreciated the popular modesty of the Pope, actually were not terribly dissatisfied. The middle class, on the other hand, found it increasingly more difficult to endure a government which not only denied it any political responsibility but also filled all important positions with clerics, and whose legislation was still oriented to medieval canon law.

That was the situation in the summer of 1859 when the Italian war broke out. Several provinces revolted, encouraged by the Austrian defeat, and demanded to be annexed to the Kingdom of Piedmont, in which throughout the entire country all those people had placed their hopes who wished to see a unified Italy governed according to modern constitutional requirements. Assured of the support of Napoleon III, who for several reasons wanted to see the temporal power of the Pope maintained, albeit in a smaller, essentially only symbolic state, the Piedmontese government tried to exploit the situation to the utmost. Victor Emmanuel demanded from Pius IX not only that he accept the situation in the Romagna, which spontaneously had placed itself under Piedmontese sovereignty, but he also asked him to turn over effective governmental powers in Umbria and the Marches, which were to remain under the nominal sovereignty of the Pope. But the Vatican refused any accommodation. On 19 January 1860 Pius IX in his encyclical *Nullis certi verbis* exposed to the eyes of the Catholic world "the sacrilegious attack on the sovereignty of the Roman Church" and demanded the "unlimited restitution" of the Romagna. After the Pope had been assured once more by Cardinal Antonelli that there was only one solution, i.e., "to restore what had been taken," he on 26 March placed under the ban the usurpers who had violated the laws of the Holy See.

The Roman Question had now become acute. Even though it was more a problem for diplomacy than for the Church, it was nevertheless a heavy psychological burden for the remaining eighteen years of the pontificate of Pius IX. The opposition of the Vatican, which was more one by Antonelli than by Pius IX, to any compromise could do nothing but confirm the attitude of those who suspected the Church of being fundamentally opposed to the ideas of the modern world. It contributed its considerable share to the further reduction of papal prestige in non-Catholic and indifferent circles. Additionally, the Roman Question preoccupied the energies of the most dynamic Catholics in France and Italy with a political problem and for a whole generation distracted them from religious concerns. To be sure, the Roman Question contributed to tying all engaged Catholics even more closely to the Pope, and in this way it played an important role in the ultimate defeat of Gallican and Josephinist tendencies; but it did so in an atmosphere of passionate involvement, which on its part contributed to giving the ultramontanism of the time an emotional coloration which was rather objectionable from the doctrinal point of view.

From the Establishment of the Kingdom of Italy to the Occupation of Rome

While Antonelli, in the hope of saving what could be saved, cautiously engaged in diplomatic negotiations with the French government, his attempts were compromised by the Pope himself. The plan was hatched by Monsignor de Merode, a decided opponent of Napoleon who was destined to raise the ante in the ambiguous game which Napoleon III during the past months had played with the Holy See. For several months de Merode had tried to convince the Pope to give up the protection of the French troops and to raise his own army by recruiting volunteers from the entire Catholic world. Antonelli was too much the realist to approve of this plan. But Pius IX, deeply disappointed by Napoleon's unreliable policy, was not prepared in this time of crisis to heed the cautious secretary of state. He did not remove him, as was expected by many, from the general direction of affairs, but ordered his opponent Merode, together with the legitimist French general Lamoricière, to organize the new army. But within a few months the campaign of Garibaldi and the fall of the Kingdom of Naples hastened events. Italian troops quickly occupied Umbria and the Marches after they had defeated the small army of Lamoricière at Castelfidardo. A short time later a national parliament proclaimed Victor Emmanuel King of Italy.

The Papal State was now reduced to Rome and its environs (about seven hundred thousand inhabitants contrasted to the earlier 3 million), and there was little hope of ever regaining the lost provinces. The moment seemed to have come to bow before the inevitable and to seek a reasonable compromise. This was the opinion of the French government, but also of many Italian Catholics and even clerics. Cavour, who could count on active sympathy in the Curia, was eager to complete his work by offering Rome an agreement on the following basis: the Pope was to renounce voluntarily any temporal power, which in any case would soon be a matter of the past; Italy in turn would renounce the last remaining traces of regalistic influence on ecclesiastical life and replace earlier legislation by the concept of a free Church in a free state. But from the beginning the negotiations suffered from a lack of willingness on the part of Antonelli and in March 1861 ended in total failure.

The position of the Holy See was now determined for a long time to come: it consisted of total rejection. Antonelli, failing to recognize the degree to which political conditions and ideas had changed during the preceding ten years, was still hopeful of saving the Pope's temporal power. He expected to be able to do so through a repetition of the policy which had been successful at Gaeta, namely, an appeal to the Catholic powers on the basis of legitimacy and the immutable right of the Pope to his state. But for this policy to be effective it was necessary to remain on the foundations of international law without causing the impression that the possibility of a compromise would be considered. By assuming this strictly legalistic position one could gain time by placing the European governments in a difficult position. The secretary of state, secretly encouraging Neapolitan resistance, probably hoped, as did so many others at the time, that the young Italian state would quickly break apart again and present new possibilities.

For Pius IX the problem was of a totally different nature. In contrast to his secretary of state, he had preserved deep sympathies for the national aspirations of Italy. But for him the question was not one of the independence of Italy from Austria, but the enforced centralistic unification under the leadership of anticlerical Piedmont which led to the dissolution of the Papal State. Pius IX was not so much concerned with temporal power for its own sake as that he saw in it the indispensable guarantee of his spiritual independence, and the outraged reaction of Europe's ultramontane press confirmed him in the belief that this power was something for which he had to answer to the Catholics of the whole world and of which he could not dispose according to his private wishes. He was fed by the conviction that the political upheavals, which included him, were merely another episode in the great struggle between God and Satan, which, of course, could only end with the victory of the former.

The conflict between a liberal Italy and the Pope's temporal power was transformed in his eyes into a religious war in which resistance to what increasingly he liked to call "the revolution" was no longer a question of the balance of diplomatic, military, and political forces, but a question of prayer and trust in God. The almost mystical fervor with which some of the leaders of the *Risorgimento* conducted the struggle against the demands of the Church confirmed him in the conviction that all of this was preeminently a religious problem. In order to emphasize in solemn fashion the religious character of the Roman Question, he in May 1862 convoked a gathering of more than three hundred bishops. In response to a papal allocution, in which Pius IX attacked the rationalism and materialism of the period and sharply criticized the Italian government, they agreed to an address which, while it did not condemn liberalism as unequivocally as the Pope had desired, described papal temporal power as an indispensable institution of providence for the well-being of the Church. It refrained, however, from raising temporal power to a dogma of faith.

But neither the protests of the bishops nor the on the whole rather sparse recruitments of papal mercenaries could stop the unavoidable course of events. Nor could this be done by the protestations of the Catholic press, which only with difficulty could conceal the indifference of the Catholic masses or the more or less open sympathies of a number of Italian faithful or even priests who were forced into a painful conflict of conscience between their patriotic strivings and the directives of the Church. The unexpected death of Cavour on 6 June 1861 and the fact that his successors lacked diplomatic skill, together with the hesitant policy of France, effected a brief delay of the decision. Napoleon III, forced to take account of Catholic agitation and hoping for the election of a Pope more willing to make concessions than the ailing Pius IX, did not wish to offend anyone. But finally, on 15 September 1864, he signed a convention with the government at Turin in which it obligated itself to respect the remnants of the Papal State; the agreement included the possibility of the recall of the French garrison from Rome. The agreement, concluded without knowledge of the Pope, appeared as a hardly concealed disavowal, and the defeat of Austria at Königgrätz in 1866, which destroyed any remaining expectations from this side, caused ultimate despair for the defenders of temporal power. The French intervention at Mentana, 3–4 November 1867, which blocked an attempt by Garibaldi to seize Rome, and the categorical declaration of Minister Romher were a pleasant surprise, but the extremely reserved attitude of most of the European powers, including Austria, confirmed that the days of temporal power were numbered. Less than three years later the collapse of the French Empire at Sedan opened the way for the Italians to Rome; on 20 September 1870 they entered the city, and a few days later they annexed it.

In spite of the advice of some hotheads, Pius IX obediently followed Antonelli's advice not to leave Rome. But his reactions to the new accomplished fact produced, as could have been predicted, fresh excommunications, diplomatic protests, an appeal to the Catholic and conservative powers, and a repeated invocation of the immutable rights of the Holy See. Similarly, he refused to accept in the following year the law of 13 May 1871 "for the guarantee of the independence of the Pope and the free exercise of the spiritual authority of the Holy See," because the guarantee appeared to him as absolutely inadequate. In fact it must be noted that to contemporary liberals, even the moderate ones, the necessity of an unconditional renunciation of temporal power, no matter in what form, appeared as an absolutely untouchable "dogma," and a solution of the type of the Lateran treaties of 1929 would not have been acceptable to them. In order to do justice to the intransigence with which Pius IX repeatedly presented demands to the world which today seem immoderate to us, one must be aware of this lack of understanding on the part of official Italy for the concerns of the Holy See for independence in the exercise of its spiritual mission. But the senescent Pope was again and again buoyed in his hopes for a "miracle" by the illusionary thoughts of his entourage and the enthusiastic demonstrations of the growing numbers of pilgrims who cheered "the Prisoner of the Vatican." He was equally angered by the narrow-minded fanaticism of Italian religious policy. Increasingly he connected his demands for the spiritual freedom of the Holy See with growing radical criticism of liberal assumptions, which he untiringly castigated as the source of the misfortunes of the Church. Such an attitude could not but strengthen the belief of those who held that in its innermost core the Church was in solidarity with the governments which had been swept away by the progress of the centuries and that it was still striving for the general restoration of a theocratic regime.

CHAPTER 39

The Offensive of the Liberal Governments in the Non-German-Speaking Countries

The Secularization Policy in Italy

Until 1860 Italy was nothing more than a geographical expression; its religious-political condition as well as the religious life and the mentality of the clergy varied greatly among the different states.

In the Kingdom of the Two Sicilies the Church maintained its privileged position, and the reaction after 1848 only served to strengthen the tutelage of education by the Church. Yet, in spite of the cordial relations between the court at Naples and the Holy See, the regalistic attitude of the civil servants diminished only very gradually, especially as the local episcopate, in contrast to the bishops of the north, was quite content with this situation. Moreover, the anti-Roman traditions of the eighteenth century were still quite alive in many seminaries, and the very specific conditions under which priests were recruited in the south exemplified the lack of discipline and the lax morals of a still numerically strong clergy. Side by side with wealthy, almost empty monasteries there existed a clerical proletariat, consisting of parsons in small villages, priests without a clearly defined function, Capuchins and others. Many of these deserted their spiritual calling after the arrival of Garibaldi.

In Tuscany, on the other hand, the standards of the also numerically very strong clergy were clearly above the average; but its frequent attempts at reform often disregarded the boundaries of orthodoxy. Under pressure from the Grand Duke, who had shared exile with Pius IX in Naples and revered him, the government in 1851 reluctantly signed a concordat; it put an end to the regalistic legislation which had come down from Pietro Leopoldo. But Rome's success was more theoretical than practical, for while the Tuscan bureaucracy had made concessions in principle, it regained a great portion of its earlier control over religious matters. For eight years both sides conducted an unreal and fruitless dialogue: Florence continued to deliberate from the perspective of the eighteenth century and Rome did so from the standpoint of the medieval Church. Characteristic in this connection were the attempts by the Vatican to prevent the emancipation plans of the Jews. Symptomatic of the progress of ultramontanism was the fact that a few bishops, especially Cardinal Corsi, gradually began to resist the government.

In 1857 an agreement was reached with the Duke of Modena which effected a limitation of the right of asylum by the Church and in return made concessions on mortmain, a problem which had become acute on account of the many monasteries on the peninsula.

In the Lombard-Venetian kingdom the dislike by many clerics of the Austrian government sprang from Italian national feelings and the hostility toward the Josephinist system. Subsequent to the concordat of 1855, the Church regained some of its freedom of movement. This development was noticeable especially in Venetia, where the clergy had little contact with the lay world. In Lombardy, where the priests were better educated and less open to authoritarian arguments, many of them continued to sympathize even after 1848 with the national and liberal aspirations of the middle class, and after annexation to Italy they constituted a strong bloc of resistance to Roman directives.

In Piedmont — according to Doubet "the people which in Italy took Catholicism most seriously" — apostles like Don Bosco, Cafasso, and Murialdo were only the most outstanding examples of a great number of pious and diligent priests who, thanks to their education in the Ecclesiastical Convent of Turin, clearly surpassed all of the Italian clergy, including the Papal State. Charitable and apostolic works continued to flourish and often imitated French examples; the brilliant figure of Rosmini was surrounded by a veritable elite of intellectuals drawn from the laity and the clergy. But under pressure from a middle class increasingly hostile to ecclesiastical privileges, even though it was a more devout middle class than in France, the state was subjected to a policy of secularization against which the clergy, especially in Savoy, fought in vain. The initial steps taken by the moderate government of Massimo d'Azeglio, were in no way extreme. Despite Rome's opposition in principle, which was based on the clauses of the concordat, a majority of the Catholic public approved of the legislation. The people were irritated by the clumsy obstinacy of the archbishop of Turin, Fransoni, and in any case were used to accepting papal directives with simultaneous emphasis of their own independence. But the atmosphere was poisoned by the inept conduct of the Turin government, the inflexibility of the Roman canonists, who had no feeling for the spiritual situation, and the Machiavellianism of Cardinal Antonelli, who thought it fitting to exploit the case of Fransoni (at first imprisoned and then expelled) for the benefit of his political design, but in the process neglected to take account of long-range religious concerns. The situation worsened when Cavour allied himself with the anticlerical left. The latter demanded civil marriage, began the secularization of education, and forced, over the hesitation of the King, the passage of the law of 22 May 1855, which dissolved a number of monasteries. While the Vatican broke off diplomatic relations and excommunicated the authors of the law, there also grew a Catholic opposition. Following the example of Montalembert in France, it attempted in part to gain strength on the parliamentary level, but principally was concerned with stirring up public opinion with the aid of newspapers organized along the lines of Louis Veuillot's *L'Univers*.

Cavour was reluctant to enlarge the struggle. He had supported the more regalistically than liberally inspired policies of the anticlerical left only in order to gain its parliamentary support for his Italian policy. He had no intention of limiting the activity of the clergy, provided that they confined themselves to purely religious work. His goal was a mutually agreed-upon separation of Church and state, with the Church having the freedom to regulate itself autonomously. In Rome, where Pius IX had resumed the concordat policy of Pius VII and Consalvi, minds were not yet open to a solution of this nature. Without a doubt, however, a modus vivendi would eventually have emerged if the development of the Roman Question after 1859 had not irrevocably disposed the government of Turin against the Holy See.

In fact, from now on Piedmontese religious legislation was applied in all of Italy, and its quick application in the former papal provinces was the more painful to Rome as the reformist tendencies of Cavour's successor, Ricasoli, who belonged to the Tuscan group of Raffaele Lambruschini, produced the unfounded suspicion that he intended to Protestantize the country. But there still existed possibilities for a rapprochement. On the Italian side many moderates, although forced to make concessions to the radicals, in all seriousness wished to find a basis for agreement with Rome. They desired it in part because of their religious convictions and emotional traditions, in part because they regarded the activity of the Church as a guarantee of social stability. On his part, Pius IX was of the opinion that a satisfactory regulation of Italy's ecclesiastical affairs was more important for the Church than the restitution of the provinces annexed in 1860. He was sensitive to the dangers which would accompany a permanent break: denial of approval of new bishops by the government and thus an annual increase in the number of vacant episcopal sees (in 1864 this was true for 108 out of 225); disturbance of seminaries and diocesan life in consequence of arrests of refractory priests; flooding of secondary and high schools with infidels and apostate priests; and other actions. The mutual hostility of the anticlerical left in Florence, which had become the capital of the Kingdom, and of the bitter opponents of the new Italy in Rome, in the spring of 1865 brought about the failure of Vegezzi's mission. But the protracted hesitation of the government to apply the law of 7 July 1866, which dissolved religious corporations and confiscated ecclesiastical property, demonstrated clearly that the bridges had not yet been burned. After Tonello's mission at the beginning of 1867 Rome harbored the justified expectation of a mutually acceptable agreement, especially as there grew in some Roman circles the willingness to reconcile. But the opposition of the radicals, who desired no separation on a friendly basis, but rather a throttling of the Church, made a failure also of this renewed attempt. The second Ratazzi cabinet initiated a new period of a bitter anticlericalism. It produced the law of 15 August 1867, which was clearly Jacobin-oriented and whose consequences were to be a heavy burden on religious policy for years. This was especially the case after 1870 when sectarian elements forced the King and the government, in spite of their desire for a pacific development, to enforce this law with increased harshness, and thereby hurled fresh insults at Pope and clergy.

It was in this tense atmosphere, in which liberalism appeared as the oppressor of Church and even of Christian values, that the Catholic press developed and the Italian Catholic Action had its beginning. Ever since the restoration there had existed a number of Catholic periodicals, but daily newspapers were published hardly at all. But while in other countries Catholic newspapers were generally under the guidance of laymen, in Italy the founders were almost invariably priests. In fact, frequently they were directly dependent on a bishopric, a characteristic which tended to strengthen their clerical orientation. This remained a peculiarity of the Italian press far into the twentieth century. The vast majority of those who shared the opinion of the Holy See about the new government withdrew resentfully and passively awaited the impending collapse of the Kingdom, which daily was prophesied by an increasingly aggressive press. A few irreconcilable laymen from Bologna, led by the lawyer Casoni, wanted to take action. Dusting off the slogan "neither cast a ballot nor allow yourself to be elected," which a few years earlier had been used in Piedmont to keep people from voting, they wanted to organize in all of Italy an extraconstitutional movement with the aim of first re-Catholicizing society and then of seizing political power. The idea gained ground only slowly. It was supported by the founders of the Society of Italian Catholic

Youth. It was to lead in 1874 to the convening of the first Italian Catholic Congress, modeled after the German Catholic Conferences and the congresses of Mechelen. Confronted with a middle class which increasingly turned away from a Church which seemed to disapprove of modern trends, the militant wing of Italian Catholicism decided against compromises along the line of Catholic liberalism and in favor of a militant movement on the basis of the principles of the *Syllabus,* whose anathema against liberal society had reawakened the energies of the intransigents. They could count on the strong support of a new generation of clerics, faithful to Rome, which had taken the place of the numerous conciliatory priests who were the heirs of the neoguelf illusions of 1848.

This change of mind in the clergy in the 1860s was the result of systematic action on the part of the episcopate. With the support of the Holy See it throttled in sometimes despotic fashion the liberal tendencies and the strivings for a democratic reform of the Church which could frequently be observed among the priests of the 1848 generation. Much absorbed by these attempts and numerous administrative difficulties which governmental policy imposed upon them and even though there often were agreements on the local level, the bishops were unable to deal with other tasks which by themselves would have been enough to absorb their energies. To be sure, the question of de-Christianization was not yet as acute as in France, but there were other problems: the disappointing condition of the old religious orders, which at least in the north was partially compensated for by the founding of some very dynamic new congregations such as the Salesians of Don Bosco and the African missionaries of Comboni; the backwardness of Italy in the number of female religious; the unpleasant behavior of many priests, particularly noticed by foreigners, and the high number of apostates; the extremely inadequate education of the clergy (worse in the south), which to a large degree had not attended any seminaries at all; and the low standards of these seminaries. This was in part caused by the small size of some dioceses; the frequently still very archaic forms of pastoral methods, which rested on an external control of religious practices and which left the Christian masses to their own devices when they were confronted with the secularization of public life and especially of schools, although there were a number of significant private initiatives; and finally, with the exception of a few centers which actually had been more active in the 1850s than they were in 1870, the recognizable lack of a Catholic culture of a genuine Italian and simultaneously truly Christian character. In this connection, the reaction of the Jesuits to the adherents of Rosmini, who were suspected of liberal sympathies, passed up an opportunity which would not soon present itself again. The delay of the solution of these urgent problems in part doubtlessly resulted from the inadequate structure of the Italian Church, which, like many European countries at this time, had too few centers of pastoral reflection and remained split into too many small dioceses. But to a substantial degree it was also the indirect consequence of the long political-religious conflict which agitated Italy during the entire pontificate of Pius IX, a consequence which was much graver than the loss of obsolete privileges, on whose defense the ecclesiastical authorities vainly concentrated their best energies.

Anticlericalism in Belgium and in the Netherlands

The Church of Belgium in the middle of the nineteenth century "through its strength and independence had become a model, a kind of ideal for the other European Churches" (Pouthas). The continuing growth of the secular and regular clergy throughout the pontificate of Pius IX made possible the encouragement and development of all kinds of activities in addition to the ordinary and regular growth in the number of parishes and in Catholic education. Despite some differences between several bishops and the Jesuits, who in the view of some people had gained much too much influence, their cooperation was generally excellent. Charitable efforts, in continuation of the Vincent conferences, were made to ameliorate the suffering of the industrial workers and to influence the youth of the lower classes in the cities. Publishing companies and newspapers tried to make up for bad literature. After 1850 there were also an increasing number of works of an edifying nature, thanks to the initiative of young ultramontane laymen who through the deepening of their own religious life and through publicly witnessing their faith intended to re-Christianize all social and cultural life.

But while the Catholics thought it the most natural thing in the world that under the protection of freedom the Church de facto, if not de jure, was able to exercise a growing influence in the country, the liberals soon became convinced that matters could not be allowed to proceed in this fashion. In order to return to what they justifiably considered the letter of the constitution, they held a congress in June 1846 at which they unequivocally presented their program: "actual independence" of the civil power from the Church and especially "the establishment of a comprehensive system of public education under the exclusive authority of the civil power . . . and rejection of the interference of priests on the basis of their jurisdiction in a school system organized by the civil power (Le congrès libéral de Belgique [1846]).

The first indication of this new secularization policy was the law of 1 June 1850 dealing with secondary schools. It was far less favorable for the Church than the law of 1842 dealing with elementary education. Without intending to exclude religion from education, the new law provided for public education totally independent from any ecclesiastical control. Many liberals, who in the future wanted to pay their respects to religion, had hoped to effect their policy of secularizing institutions through a friendly agreement with the Church. But the implacable attitude of most of the bishops, in spite of the willingness to compromise on the part of Cardinal Sterckx, to the new education legislation destroyed such illusions, and the attitude of Rome deepened the disappointment. The government of Rogier-Frère Orban, in office from 1857 to 1870, passed a number of laws which, supplemented by administrative decisions, dealt in secular fashion with the problems of charitable foundations, cemeteries, and church boards. In the eyes of the bishops these were nothing but falsifications of constitutional freedoms. Simultaneously the liberals, encouraged by such radical groups as the Education League, which was founded in 1864 in advance of a similar organization in France, intensified their efforts in the communities with a liberal majority for a "correction" of the law of 1842 through administrative decisions. Their purpose was to limit the rights which had been conceded to the clergy in the area of elementary education.

While liberalism thus was increasingly more determined and militant, the Catholics defended every foot of the religious bastions which they had succeeded in restoring or maintaining within the civil institutions. Their resistance was weakened, however, by lack of unity in their ranks and the diffusion of their efforts. Disregarding the exhortations of his colleagues, at first by Van Bommel and then also by the young militant bishops who had been appointed after 1850 and received their directives from Rome, Cardinal Sterckx refused to unify Catholics in a denominational political party, for fear of strengthening liberal suspicions even further. He preferred the individual activity of laymen on the parliamentary level and within the framework of ecclesiastical works. On the other hand, the sympathies of a part of the Catholic population for the intransigent attitude of Louis Veuillot, which admittedly was largely identical with that of the Pope, after twenty years of quiet had once again fanned the discussions between ultramontanes and Catholics loyal to the constitution. The debates grew more bitter by the year.

In the expectation of being able to unify all Catholic forces in practical matters, some laymen, in the years 1863, 1864, and 1867 organized large Catholic congresses, designed to coordinate the activity of ecclesiastical works which had grown without guidance, and to inspire a powerful movement of public opinion for the support of Catholic resistance on the parliamentary level. Encouraged by the aged cardinal and, in spite of the caution of the ultramontanes, effected through the spectacular intervention in 1863 of Montalembert, these congresses undeniably contributed to awakening Catholic energies. An attempt was made to make up for omissions in the area of the press and to establish immediately — at least in the dioceses of Bruges, Ghent, and Tournai — a network of free schools directly under the authority of the clergy. They were intended to counter public instruction, whose ideological tendencies were, with a good deal of exaggeration, regarded as fundamentally incompatible with the Catholic faith. They also changed the status of the "Catholic Circles," chartered by the state, into political organizations and united them in a national federation. It produced the electoral victory of the Catholics in 1870 which kept them in power until 1878.

This amounted only to a delay on the parliamentary and legislative levels, however, for the situation in the country had become increasingly worse since the beginning of the 1860s. As in all of western Europe, the gap between the masses of the workers and the Church had widened, indifferentism made progress in the rural settlements, which were strongly affected by Freemasonry, and religious practice was retrogressive in the large population centers. Much graver, however, was the fact that while a portion of the Catholic middle class was much more willing to testify to its faith, the new liberal generation after 1860 increasingly tended toward a militant anticlericalism. The reason for this was the conviction that there was an incompatibility not only between the Church and modern freedoms (this was underscored in 1864 by the *Syllabus*), but also between science and faith. The young generation instead turned in part to a demythologized Protestantism, but more frequently to a scientific and a religious humanism — the first society of this kind, Free Thought, was founded in 1863 — and also to a socialistic atheism. For these young liberal intellectuals it was no longer simply a matter of liberating the civil power from the grasp of the Church, but of "rescuing intelligence from the darkness of obscurantism." In order to achieve this goal, they called for public control of all Catholic activities.

In view of the development of liberalism in the direction of intolerance, the Catholics once more were split in two camps. While one group, as before, saw the only effective protection against the aims of the radicals in the constitutional freedoms, the others responded that this was nothing more than a fool's paradise in that the state was actually under the control of the enemies of the Church. This second group, led by Professor Perin (Louvain), who was being encouraged by Pius IX, started a campaign against the constitution and its "freedom to be destroyed." It was only a minority, but a very vocal minority, which around 1875 made many people believe that at the moment that liberalism under the influence of the radicals would turn away from the compromise solution which was hailed in 1830, the Church also would turn away from it, but in the opposite direction, in order to regain at least partially the standing which it had enjoyed under the Old Regime. Thus, the situation was extremely tense and the entire relationship between Church and state once again seemed to be in question.

In the Netherlands, the situation developed quite similarly, even though somewhat more slowly and although the position of the Catholics in the state was rather different. The parliamentary alliance between Catholics and liberals lasted until 1866; but more so than in Belgium the rapprochement was determined by tactical considerations rather than by a change of conscience. Soon wide differences of opinion surfaced. On one side stood the intolerant behavior which a liberal anticlericalism adopted in all European countries and which in the Netherlands was enhanced by the continuation of an abiding hostility to the Pope. On the other side stood the increasingly reactionary orientation of the pontificate of Pius IX and the influence of the antiliberal polemics of Veuillot, which Cramer echoed in the *Tijd* by making it virtually obligatory for Catholics to divorce themselves from modern civilization. While a generation earlier Broere and Van Bommel had been responsible for some efforts at rethinking Catholicism with a view toward new ideas, the condemnation of Lamennais had interrupted this first attempt at intellectual modernity, and the excesses of the anticlerical polemics on the occasion of the publication of the *Syllabus* confirmed those in their views who insisted on the incompatibility of Catholic philosophy and the principles of 1789. It was the problem of education over which the final break occurred.

The Catholics did not have enough money to establish their own school system and therefore had to choose between those who wanted to preserve the Calvinist character of the public schools and the liberals who demanded the neutrality of public instruction. Preferring the latter to a Protestant parochial school and hoping that in the end it would be characterized by the Christian spirit, many Catholics, not without criticism by other members of their faith, supported the liberals. Together they passed the law of 13 August 1857, which for the first time in Europe introduced absolute neutrality in education. But after a few years hard facts could not be denied: neutral education in reality had turned largely into a completely secular, even a religious type of instruction. Now the bishops, encouraged by the encyclical *Quanta cura,* at first at the Provincial Council in 1865 and then in a joint pastoral letter in July 1868, proclaimed the right of a Catholic child to be raised in a Catholic school. The right of the child had its complement in a corresponding obligation of the parents, and the bishops legally began to increase the number of free schools. In order to meet the tremendous expenditures which this policy necessitated, the parishes organized active school boards; the joint demand for public money for the free denominational schools brought Catholics and Protestants closer to one another. Now that the liberals had replaced the religious outlook of 1850 with a rationalistic and positivist attitude, the "common foundation" (A. Kuyper) of Calvinists and Roman Catholics was suddenly discovered; while it was not yet strong enough to form the basis of an ecumenical dialogue, it was sufficient for a "Christian coalition" to gain religious objectives. However, the goals were not achieved immediately. To the contrary: inasmuch as the elections of 1877 gave the liberals a strong majority, the radicals became eager to translate their ideas into reality and managed to pass a law which jeopardized free education.

It was a severe defeat for the defenders of Christian schools and impressed upon the Catholics the necessity of having an organization of their own and of closing ranks in a political party.

The Confused Situation in the Iberian Peninsula

In Spain as well as in Portugal the situation of the Church had improved since the unrest which it had experienced under the pontificate of Gregory XVI, but peace was only temporary and was constantly endangered. In Portugal there were repeated scandalous interferences by the government in ecclesiastical affairs. After 1865 the Freemasons under the leadership of Count Paraty started a campaign in favor of civil marriage.

In Spain serious disturbances took place. The liberals refused to accept the predominance of the Church, which it had regained with the concordat, and their hostility was heightened when the clergy attempted to arrange itself with the increasingly reactionary Narváez government. Between 1854 and 1856, when Espartero was in power, this hostility had known no bounds; but it was even worse after the revolution of 1868, when the Provisional Government quickly fell under the influence of the radicals; it meant the end of intellectual and political moderation. There was not only the immediate repeal of the concordat; much more serious was that as a result of acts of violence by the people against priests and regular clergy the growing gap between the proletariat of the large cities and the Church became visible. The Church was subjected to a number of legal restrictions, introduced civil marriage and a relative freedom of religion, and contained measures directed against the orders, especially the Jesuits, and the Vincentian Conferences. Much more significant than these obstacles, however, was the spirit in which they were rooted. It was actually strengthened by the obstinate reaction of the hierarchy to the anticlerical steps which followed one another after October 1868, as well as by the declaration of the infallibility of the Pope in 1870.

After the fall of the republic in 1874 Canovas del Castillo was interested in reinstituting the concordat, but considering the confusion it seemed impossible to him to return without adjustments to the conditions which had existed before 1868. Consequently, the constitution of 1876 included the principle of freedom of religion, despite the vehement protests of the clergy and of Pius IX. If one takes into consideration that the constitution, among other things, left the Church in control of education, even at the universities, religious freedom was only a minor concession to the liberals. Still, it was one more defeat for those who saw in the *Syllabus* the ideal of a Christian society, a defeat for which to a large degree the antiliberal Catholics were responsible.

Regalistic Liberals and Freemasons in Latin America

The relative easing of tension, noticeable in many Latin American states by the middle of the nineteenth century, was not universal. Especially in two countries, Mexico and Colombia, in which the Church ever since colonial times held a particularly strong position, the liberals incessantly and successfully tried to break its power, a power which benefited the large landowners, who in turn relied on the army.

In Mexico, the most densely settled republic in Spanish America, where the conflict was aggravated by the racial hatred harbored by the Indians against the Spanish, V. Gómez Farias as early as the 1830s had attacked the orders and the privileges of the clergy and had secularized a part of its great wealth. The principal consequence was that the flourishing missions of the Franciscans in California were almost totally destroyed, but the economic and political power of the Church was hardly affected. After a conservative interlude, the success of the reform movement, which had grown since 1845 under the leadership of the Indian Benito Juárez, a convinced Freemason and anticlericalist, led to the resumption of an earlier policy. Its aim was to replace the corporate society, in which denominational groups and especially the orders occupied a privileged position, with a regime of individual rights. Its ultimate aim was to laicize the state, which in spite of earlier disputes was still subject to the Church. The recalcitrance of the clergy, which on its own had been incapable of introducing unavoidable reforms and correcting the most flagrant abuses, could not have been more pronounced. Utilizing the tenuous pretext of the utopian character of the democratic program and its evident social failure in a preindustrial society, the clergy continued to place all of its hopes in the vain attempts by the conservative reaction. In its intransigence, encouraged by Nuncio Meglia and the new archbishop, P. A. Labastida (1863–91), it refused to support Emperor Maximilian (1864–67) when he wanted to maintain freedom of religion and the press and to ratify the nationalization of Church estates in the hope of winning the moderate liberals to his side. After his return to power, Juárez, aware of the slumbering strength of Catholic traditions in the common people, was sensible enough to enforce anticlerical legislation with moderation. But after his death in 1872, his successor wanted to strengthen them through incorporation in the constitution. Subsequently, civil marriage, laicized education on all levels, separation of Church and state, and the nationalization of Church lands, having been embodied in articles of the Mexican constitution, became sacrosanct. But considering the close ties which a majority of the population still had with Catholicism — provided that its demands were not excessive — and considering the generosity of the faithful, the reality was much less tragic than it appeared according to the law; but there was no question that the secular power of the Church finally had been broken.

In Colombia also the situation, which had not been good under Gregory XVI, became increasingly worse during the pontificate of Pius IX. After 1845 anticlerical steps followed in quick succession: abolition of the tithe and of canonical jurisdiction; expulsion of priests and bishops if they attempted to resist this legislation; separation of Church and state in 1843, the first decision of this kind in Latin America; nationalization of Church property; and the dissolution of all monasteries in 1861. These measures were accompanied by extensive restrictions on the activity of the clergy, in spite of the contradiction that was involved with respect to the official separation of Church and state. This genuine *Kulturkampf* lasted until 1880.

The other South American republics, with the exception of Bolivia and Peru, after 1870 also experienced a revival of militant anticlericalism and secularization policies. It was now no longer merely a matter of the nationalization of Church property, the abolition of canonical jurisdiction, or the control over the appointment of bishops and parish priests, but of the introduction of civil marriage, freedom of religion for the Protestants (whose numbers in some countries increased because of immigration), reduction of the influence of the Church on education, and total separation of Church and state. Just as in the preceding generation, the rationale of these policies was the attempt of the liberals, who almost everywhere had regained power, to reduce the political and social influence of the clergy. This was the result, in part, of the clergy's support of the conservative parties in the interest of defending the "established order" and its hierarchical and paternalistic concept of society. It was in part also caused by the introduction of two new elements which created hostility to the Church: the influence of the members of orders who had come from Europe and who advocated ultramontane ideas which conflicted with an increasingly sensitive nationalism, and the unmitigated claim by the Church to regulate the life of civil society as recently laid down by the *Syllabus;* also there was the progress of Comte's positivism, which in some instances changed the church-political conflict into a regular battle against the Christian faith, which a part of the educated middle class was beginning to reject. In Venezuela President Guzmán Blanco, a fanatic sectarian, in 1870 began the fight for laicized schools and attempted to create a national Church totally dependent on the state, in which the archbishop would be elected by the parliament and the parish priests by their parishes. In Guatemala the sentiment was not quite so radical, but here also there began after the fall of President Cerna (1871), the great protector of the Jesuits, a policy of laicization which reached its apogee in the constitution of 1879 and soon was imitated by the other republics of Central America (except for Costa Rica). Chile followed the same path under the presidency of Errazuriz (1871–76), as did Argentina after the success of the National Autonomist Party in 1874. It was centered on the landed gentry, which makes evident that the roots of South American anticlericalism were not only of a social nature; Ecuador after the assassination of García Moreno in 1875 also took this direction.

C H A P T E R   4 0

Preliminary Phases of the *Kulturkampf* in Austria, Bavaria, Baden, and Switzerland

During the 1860s the conflict between liberalism and the Catholic Church in several German-speaking countries reached that ideological confrontation which Rudolf Virchow characterized as *"Kulturkampf."* Consequently, liberalism, which had grown to be the predominant political power, began to implement one of its central concerns: the liberation of state and society from ecclesiastical tutelage. The chief opponent seemed to be Catholicism with its ultramontane coloration, highlighted by the dogma of the Immaculate Conception and the *Syllabus,* which had been augmented by the dogma of papal infallibility. The contrast emerged particularly sharply in countries with mixed denominations. German and Swiss liberalism, having grown out of Protestantism and being especially doctrinal, considered a frontal attack necessary. In the process, the power of the state was often ruthlessly applied, in violation of liberal principles. To the ideological contrast there was frequently added an economical-social one: the liberal urban middle class confronted the lower middle class and rural populations, who had close ties to the Church and felt disadvantaged by the beginning industrialization.

Both sides were responsible for aggravating the situation. Neither was prepared to recognize the autonomy of the other in its own area; liberal politicians and Church leaders attempted to define "the borderline between state and Church" in such a way as to be most beneficial to each group.

Catholic states on the whole were content to acquire sovereignty over the borderline areas claimed by the Church, such as education and civil registries, and to retain the surviving parts of the system of state Churches. Non-Catholic politicians went much further; they wanted to replace the cooperation for which the Church had fought with a complete return to the earlier state Church, a move which they justified with the claim to the absolute legal authority of the modern state. Frequently these liberals, imbued by national ideologies, tried to substitute such national Church organizations for the supranational principle of Catholicism.

In Austria, the denominational laws of the year 1868 continued to undermine the concordat but did not affect the inner sphere of the Church. Emperor Franz Joseph endeavored to avoid a break with Rome, yet could not prevent the extremely sharp condemnation of the laws by the Pope. In Austria itself voices were raised in objection and not only by conservatives. The belligerent Bishop Franz Joseph Rudigier of Linz (1811–84) became the focal point of a popular opposition movement. Such a development was new for Austria, but it found imitation in other states where the struggle against the liberals was being waged; the Catholic faction in the parliament at Vienna also grew stronger. Because he exhorted people to disregard the law, Rudigier was found guilty by a court in 1869, but was immediately pardoned by the Emperor; nevertheless, the brief imprisonment of the bishop had a jolting effect on the Catholic masses.

The Emperor continued to effect a moderate application of the laws, and his constant communication with Cardinal Rauscher also had a calming effect. Although polemics from both sides continued with unabated stridency and the liberals in 1869 succeeded in passing a national elementary school act which reduced the number of denominational schools, Emperor and cardinal working together prevented the outbreak of a real *Kulturkampf.* Rauscher's auxiliary Johann Rudolf Kutschker contributed greatly to his cardinal's policy of understanding. He was also in charge of Catholic ecclesiastical matters in the Ministry of Education, a dual position which can only be comprehended by looking at Josephinist traditions.

The constant objective of Chancellor Friedrich Ferdinand von Beust was revenge for Prussia's victory in 1866. For this purpose he needed both the support of the liberals and an alliance with antipapal Italy. Among other matters, the concordat was an obstacle to such goals, but all attempts to move the Curia to a voluntary renunciation of the treaty were in vain. In the summer of 1870 Beust finally used the dogma of papal infallibility as a pretext for disavowing the concordat and was supported in this move by the liberal minister of religion, Stremayr. After some hesitation, Emperor Franz Joseph on 30 July 1870 declared the concordat as no longer valid. He argued that as a consequence of the dogma the Roman partner had changed his character, that a contractual relationship was impossible with a partner who claimed to be infallible, and that it was the state's responsibility to counteract the dangerous consequences of the new dogma. This legally untenable step rested on a much too broad interpretation of the dogma, although it was plausible as a result of ultramontane declarations. It can be assumed that the Emperor resorted to it only because he was deeply disappointed by the results of the Vatican Council and the Curia's hardening attitude, both of which harmed ecclesiastical peace. His disappointment was deepened by the resigned attitude of the Austrian bishops when they returned from Rome.

The attempts of the liberals to intensify the struggle after Beust's resignation were only partially successful. They reached their legislative peak with the religious laws which were introduced in 1874 by the liberal ministry of Auersperg and accepted by the Emperor. The passage of the laws was preceded by intense arguments in which the Pope intervened in the form of an encyclical to the Austrian bishops and a letter to the Emperor. While Cardinal Schwarzenberg favored vocal protests, Rauscher and Kutschker negotiated quietly and succeeded in the striking of several unpalatable clauses.

The laws strengthened the state's supervision of the Churches and effected the equality of denominations, without, however, crossing the line established by the legislation of 1868. They left to the Catholic Church the position of a privileged public corporation and assured it of freedom of education and worship, the free exercise of its jurisdiction in the ecclesiastical sphere, and the free development of the orders and parochial school systems. The ecclesiastical part of the public schools was merely placed under state supervision. Thus, the Austrian laws were considerably milder than the *Kulturkampf* legislation in Baden and Prussia. Additionally, transgressions required neither prosecution by the state nor a "dismissal" of the offending cleric; at most, the offices of such clerics had to cease public activity.

Emperor Franz Joseph was convinced that these laws adequately protected the rights of the state and resisted all additional anticlerical legislation. A law in the spring of 1874 which established the state's right to dissolve monasteries was not sanctioned by him. The Curia also was willing to be flexible, not least thanks to the judicious reports of Nuncio Jacobini, who had been sent to Vienna in 1874. It was recognized that the Austrian laws struck a balance between state and Church and that despite a premature papal complaint conditions in Austria were not the same as in Germany. This did not mean that the ideological struggle between liberals and Catholics ceased; it continued and damaged not only the Church. The Catholic ability to resist, exemplified especially in the Christian-Socialist Party, founded in 1880, proved to be far stronger than opponents had assumed.

Prince Chlodwig von Hohenlohe-Schillingsfürst (1819–1901), after 1866 Bavarian minister president, was a Catholic, but just as antiultramontane as his brother, who resided in Rome as a Curia cardinal. He clung tenaciously to the remainders of a state Church. It was his intention to transform Bavaria with the aid of an emphatic liberal domestic policy and to strengthen South German autonomy. Only when this proved to be unattainable was he willing to enter into a closer relationship with the North German Confederation. In 1868 the right of the Church to supervise schools, which had been conceded in 1852, was repealed and the entire elementary school system was taken over by the state; Jesuit missions were banned. 1869 also saw theological and political resistance to the dogma of infallibility emanating from Munich. Hohenlohe, extensively but one-sidedly informed of the Roman happenings by his brother and Döllinger, tried to persuade the other powers to take a collective stand against the planned definition. As was the case with other liberals, Hohenlohe feared that the dogma would not be confined to the theological sphere but would claim papal jurisdiction over princes and states in nonreligious questions as well. But because of the disinterest of most of the governments, Hohenlohe's initiative failed; Beust as well as Bismarck replied evasively.

Opposition to Hohenlohe's Little German and anticlerical policy in 1869 led to the founding of the Patriotic People's Party under the leadership of Joseph Edmund Jörg. Its membership was almost exclusively Catholic, and on the first try it won the majority of the seats in Bavaria's parliament. Its rapid successes rested on the support given to it by the Catholic associations, a lesson which was applied shortly afterwards in the foundings of Catholic parties in Baden and Prussia. The Patriots, whose agitation very much contributed to making the liberal press equate Catholic with particularistic, in January 1870 achieved the fall of Hohenlohe. The government's course did not change, however, as the new administration, backed by King Ludwig II, was under the influence of the National Liberal minister of religion Baron Johann von Lutz (1826–90). He resolutely continued Hohenlohe's religious policy and even intensified it after the publication of the dogma of papal infallibility. He protected the incipient movement of the Old Catholics, and on 9 August 1870 he decreed that the new dogma could not be announced from the pulpits; owing to the objections of the bishops, the decree could not be implemented. However, in 1871 Lutz introduced a bill in the Federal Council of the new German Empire which outlawed the misuse of the pulpit for political purposes; it became law on 10 December 1871. The Bavarian government also played a leading role in the passing of the second imperial law of the *Kulturkampf* which allowed the dissolution of the Jesuit organization and the expulsion of Jesuits from

Germany. Yet Lutz did not openly endorse the conflict in Prussia; he was satisfied with conducting a kind of creeping *Kulturkampf*. Its apogee was a royal edict of 20 November 1873 which restored the previous supervision of the state over the Churches. Considerable tension, especially in connection with the appointment of bishops, continued for a long period of time. But an open break was avoided, as both King and government honored the concordat. The government tolerated that Bavaria's bishops temporarily gave refuge to Prussian priests and students of theology to whom the May Laws had denied the exercise of office and the opportunity to study.

The majority of the bishops appointed by the King, under the leadership of Archbishop Gregor von Scherr of Munich-Freising, assumed a conciliatory stance. Only Archbishop Michael Deinlein of Bamberg (1800–1875) agreed to the veto right of the government. Bishop Ignatius von Senestréy of Regensburg (1818–1906), whose strictly ultramontane attitude was shared by Bishop Baron Franz von Leonrod of Eichstätt (1827–1905), remained an intransigent fighter against liberalism and the state Church.

Earlier and more completely than in any other German state, middle-class and Little German liberalism had assumed a dominant role in Baden. After 1860, the administrations of Lamey and Jolly, in cooperation with the liberal parliamentary majority, determined domestic policy and fashioned the relationship to the Churches. The law of 9 October 1860, which took the place of the concordat rejected by the Chamber, formed the foundation; still, the majority of the liberals was not satisfied with it and neither were many Catholics. In 1864 a struggle over education erupted. Especially among the active liberals in Baden there were eminent proponents of the principle of the absolute legal authority of the state; inasmuch as Jolly headed the government after 1866, they were able to implement their program. The religious legislation of Baden in the years 1868–76 transferred to the state many duties hitherto exercised by the Churches and subjected the Churches to a far-reaching system of state supervision. The laws of Baden influenced the *Kulturkampf* legislation of Prussia and other German states; conversely, the laws passed in Baden after 1871 followed the example of the legislation of Prussia and the German Empire.

From beginning to end, religious legislation in Baden was characterized by the claim of the liberals to jurisdiction over education. The elementary school law of 8 March 1868 changed parochial schools into nondenominational schools and made the establishment of parochial schools dependent on a special law; eight years later, the education law of 16 September 1876 made nondenominational schools mandatory. On 21 December 1869 a civil marriage law was passed which, like the first of the two education laws, was more a legal consequence of the secularization of society than a belligerent measure. The same could not be said of the foundation law of 5 May 1870. It arbitrarily differentiated between secular Catholic foundation property (school and charitable foundations), which was transferred to the administration of the municipalities, and actual church property, the administration of which was merely placed under supervision by the state.

The most trenchant incursions in ecclesiastical life took place in 1872 and 1874. Regulations concerning the religious orders of 2 April 1872 forbade members of orders to teach school, and forbade any pastoral activity to members of orders which were not legally registered in Baden. The law of 15 June 1874 concerning Old Catholics was based on the fact that the anti-Roman traditions of a minority of Baden Catholics had led a number of clerics and laymen to join the protest movement. The members of the new community were assured of all rights which they had held as Catholics. Clerics turned Old Catholic were allowed to retain their benefices and income; Old Catholic communities were permitted to use Catholic churches and were granted a share of the community property, the extent of which was determined rather arbitrarily by the state authorities. The high point of *Kulturkampf* legislation occurred with the law of 19 February 1874 on the legal position of the Churches in the state. After an academic examination according to the law of 1860 had been ordered in 1867, admission to a clerical office was now made dependent on graduation from a secondary school and a three-year course of study at a German university, as well as on a discriminating public examination in the fields of philosophy, history, and German and classical literature (ARTICLE 1). The Churches were permitted to retain only institutions for the theological-practical preparation of prospective clerics; hostels for theology and secondary school students, which the liberals accused of isolating the students from the national education of the German youth, were closed (ART. 2). For transgressions, ART. 3 decreed fines and imprisonment, in severe cases also withholding of salaries and removal from office; in addition, the attempt to influence elections by clerics was also made subject to fines.

Ecclesiastical opposition to this law was led by the aged Archbishop von Vicari, whose last years were also filled with a battle over the appointment of his cathedral dean, whom he also wanted to act as his auxiliary bishop. In 1867 Lothar von Kübel (1823–81) was named director of the hostel, and after Vicari's death in 1868 headed the archdiocese as chapter vicar for thirteen years. The election of the archbishop foundered on the rejection by the government of all but one of eight candidates nominated by the cathedral chapter. Kübel filed legal objections to all of the laws. Together with a large majority of the clergy he also passively resisted them, a resistance which was not even broken by the law of 25 August 1876 which suspended all financial subventions by the state. Chapter vicar and clergy refused any cooperation in implementing the religious law of 1874; jailing of clerics, numerous vacancies, and growing pastoral emergency conditions were the result.

Liberal anticlericalism in Baden also affected the political activation of Catholics. The Catholic People's Party, founded in 1869 by Jakob Lindau, sent five delegates to the Chamber and two years later raised this number to nine; its chief publication was the *Badischer Beobachter,* founded in 1863. In opposition to the oligarchical structure of the liberal system and in accordance with the democratic traditions of Baden, the party demanded not only religious freedom but also liberal and democratic basic rights which the liberal government had delayed, such as the universal, equal, right to a secret vote.

Jolly's first religious law found a positive echo among the liberals outside of Baden. There was no change in the official religious policy of Prussia before 1871–72, but to the degree that Bismarck's alliance of 1866 with the liberals became firmer their anticlericalism also spread. When in the spring of 1869 Rome's intention to seek definition of papal infallibility at the impending council was made public, liberal declarations became angry and Protestant-conservative warnings added to the furor. As for the German Catholics themselves, the passionately discussed issue of infallibility divided them into two camps.

It was in this tense atmosphere that the German bishops gathered at Fulda in September 1869. Other urgent items on the agenda, such as Ketteler's social solutions, receded into the background behind the question of infallibility; the latter forced the episcopate into a one-sided and unnecessary fighting posture. But the conference at least discussed the events in Baden and declared its solidarity with Kübel.

As for the definition urged by Rome, the majority were disinclined to agree with it; of twenty bishops present or represented at Fulda, fourteen presented their views to Pius IX in vain. Their joint letter to the Pope was drafted by the recently appointed bishop of Rottenburg, Hefele, who together with Ketteler lectured on the issue of infallibility. Ketteler actually anticipated some postulates of the minority at the Vatican Council by demanding that the evidence of tradition in the definition meet scientific criteria and that the infallibility of the Pope be proved in connection with that of the Church. Hefele used historical arguments, denying a positive cause for the definition as well as its timeliness. If the dogma of infallibility were accepted, he said, it would make a reunification of the divided denominations much more difficult, would weaken the unity of German Catholicism, and would intensify the religious struggle in the political arena. The waves of controversy which after the summer of 1870 broke over German Catholicism justified his views.

In Switzerland, the battle between liberalism and strict Church adherents and between the liberal minority and the ultramontane majority of the Catholics ever since the 1840s was marked by a *Kulturkampf* intensity which grew even more bitter in the decade before the Vatican Council. The basic disagreement there also was the council itself and the issue of papal infallibility. The official announcement of the dogma was made more difficult in some cantons, in others it was forbidden altogether. On the other hand, the agitation against the council, which prepared the ground for the Old Catholics, was allowed to unfold unhindered, initially in the "Freethinking Catholic Associations" in which political motives often outweighed religious ones. The reason for this was that many Catholics, whom the *Syllabus* offended in the core of their thought and action and whom it completely alienated from an authoritarian Church, saw in the opposition to the dogma a welcome opportunity to move the Church in the direction of a democratic and national Church. Only in 1873 was a theologian, the former Lucerne professor of theology Edward Herzog (1841–1924, after 1875 bishop of the Christian Catholic Church of Switzerland), enabled to assume the leadership of the protest movement. It was largely due to him that the movement excluded the radical elements and as the Christian Catholic Church followed the tradition of Wessenberg's reform program.

Bishop Eugène Lachat of Basel (1819–86), whose seminary was closed in the spring of 1870, in 1873 was "dismissed" and expelled from five of the seven cantons which comprised his bishopric because of his advocacy of the new dogma and the excommunication of Christian Catholic opponents; he withdrew to Lucerne. In the overwhelmingly Catholic Jura the Berne government expelled all pastors when they sided with Lachat. They were replaced with clerics loyal to the state, among them several foreigners, but were rejected by the parishes so that a schism was avoided. Pius IX acted very unwisely in 1873 when he appointed the auxiliary Gaspard Mermillod as vicar apostolic of Geneva. He liked Mermillod because of his unquestioned ultramontanism, but his appointment partially anticipated the establishment of a bishopric, an action illegal under the constitution. Mermillod was immediately expelled by the Federal Council. To the papal condemnation of the injustices inflicted on the Church in the encyclical *Etsi multa luctuosa* (21 November 1873), the Federal Council replied by completely severing diplomatic relations with the Vatican.

The *Kulturkampf* was carried over into the new federal constitution of 29 May 1874. The establishment of new dioceses was made dependent on permission by the Confederation. Confederation and cantons received summary authorization to preserve peace among the denominations and to take the requisite steps to prevent violations of the rights of citizens and state by ecclesiastical authorities (ART. 50). The events of 1870 had shown that even the publication of principles of faith and the excommunication of opponents were viewed as such violations. The Society of Jesus and all organizations "affiliated" with it were excluded from the entire territory of Switzerland and its members were forbidden to be active in church and school (ART. 51). The establishment of new monasteries and the restoration of closed ones was also declared impermissible (ART. 52). The maintenance of civil registries was turned over to the exclusive care of the government (ART. 53), canonical jurisdiction was declared abolished (ART. 58), and elementary education was placed exclusively in the hands of the state (ART. 27).

Although the *Kulturkampf* politicians quickly had to acknowledge that the National Church-Old Catholic movement constituted no more than a minority, anti-Catholic legislation was dismantled only slowly; fundamental moves for a relaxation of tension in Switzerland were made only under the pontificate of Leo XIII.

CHAPTER 41

Internal Catholic Controversies in Connection with Liberalism

Catholicism and Liberalism after 1848

The crisis of 1848, which pointed out the degree to which the traditional order of society had been shaken, and the subsequent wave of reaction only intensified the great problem which had confronted Catholic thought for half a century. What was to be the attitude to the world which had emerged from the revolution and its advertised governmental form of freedom? Could one reconcile with it or did its nature require that it be rejected? Many Catholics were fascinated by the memory of the Christian Middle Ages, which a Catholic Romanticism had impressively displayed before their eyes in idealized fashion, were haunted by the thought of a recurrence of the unrest which once again had troubled Europe, and were profoundly disappointed by the failure of the attempts by Pius IX to guide liberal demands into acceptable channels through concessions. They were also troubled by the almost universal decline of religious practice, in which — as moralists and not as sociologists — they saw a consequence of the errors spread by an "evil press." Thus, they gradually became more and more convinced that the restoration started at the beginning of the century could only be successful if one resolutely forgot about the social philosophy of the eighteenth century and returned to those concepts on which the strength and greatness of the "century of faith" rested. Justification and confirmation for this mistrust of liberal principles existed in the continuance of the political philosophy which the Scholastics of the Spanish Counter-Reformation had developed. It was also found in the still strong influence of Maistre and Bonald, which was used to counter the seditious character of the rationalistic Cartesian-inspired systems, and in the aversion of many clerics to the new civil society, which was identified with excessive stock market speculations and the search for material pleasures. In short, political and social notions, pastoral prejudices and traditional thought combined in varying proportions to lead a considerable number of the clergy and a few militant laymen to an authoritarian Catholicism. Its aim was to preserve and to regain privileges and external prestige for the Church within Catholic states freed from the pressure of anti-Christian currents, such as in the Spain of Isabella II, in the Empire of the Habsburgs, and until 1859 in several Italian states. The official publication of this intransigent Catholicism was the *Civiltà cattolica,* published by the Roman Jesuits. Its guiding principles were those outlined in the essay "Ensayo sobre el catolicismo, el liberalismo y el socialismo" (1851) by the Spaniard Donoso Cortés, which also became available soon thereafter in French and German. *Civiltà cattolica,* founded in 1849, had as its principal goal the complete restoration of Christian principles in the life of the individual, of the family, and of society.

In contrast to 1815, the monarchical and reactionary governments which were totally devoted to the Church by the middle of the century had lost the support of the young. Thus, there were many Catholics who, deeply sympathetic with the currents of their century, attacked the intransigent group by arguing that the attempt to return to the concepts of the restoration period was not only dangerous but also futile. Most of them pointed out that a significant number of the leaders in the state no longer practiced their religion and that for this reason it was utopian to expect disinterested aid and protection from the state; at best the Church could hope for a benevolent neutrality. Some of them went further. In light of the genuine values and of the real humanitarian progress which liberalism in spite of some excesses had produced, they were prepared to accept the modern concept of greater rights for the individual. It hardly needs mentioning that they were not always aware of the danger that the excessive autonomy of the individual could result in the claim of man's total independence from God.

Gradually there arose two opposing Catholic groups which, while both were intent on serving the Church, completely differed in how best this could be accomplished. One group saw the modern world of its century as an historical epoch with its own peculiar organizational form and thought it necessary to be its advance guard. Tactfully the members of this group threw a veil over the condemnations in the encyclical *Mirari vos,* the memory of which was beginning to pale, and demanded that the Church embrace liberalism just as in earlier times it had done with Greco-Roman civilization, the reaction of the parishes to the feudalism of the Middle Ages, and the humanistic endeavors of the Renaissance. The others, regarding the modern world as the anti-Christian legacy of the revolution, preferred to avoid error by breaking off all contacts and desired a tightening of prohibitions in order to avoid infection. They insisted on the solemn repetition of the earlier condemnation of liberalism and other modern errors by the magisterial office. They were oblivious of the dangers of such a course of action, which could only intensify the ambiguities as a result of which many liberals had come to the firm conviction that a society in keeping with the demands of the time could only be built if the Catholic Church was deprived of all influence.

Conflicts between the two groups were unavoidable. They were aggravated at the same time by the intrusion of additional debates which split the Catholic elite in many countries. In France, where political problems easily assumed an ideological and religious character, it was the question of reconciliation with the Empire after the coup d'état; in Italy it was the Roman Question; in Germany it was the growing contrast between university theologians and defenders of Scholasticism, in which could be seen the same spiritual opposition which separated the believers in progress with their sense of history from those who preferred to trust the methods which previously had been approved by a hierarchical authority.

The Division of the Catholics in France

Internal Catholic controversies over modern liberties reached their high point in France. Elsewhere the problem was dealt with as a practical one. Rome conceded under Pius IX as well as under Gregory XVI that on this level attitudes could be different, depending on each case. While liberal legislation in Piedmont was formally condemned, it was tolerated in Belgium and even appreciated in countries with a Catholic minority, such as the United States, England, and the Netherlands. But such practices confused the French, who with their logical bent desired coherent theories which could be raised to the level of universal validity. Revived by the differences of opinion swirling around the Falloux Law, whose proponents and opponents indulged themselves in treating the matter on the level of fundamentals, the old debates over the ideal Christian society, which ever since the condemnation of Lamennais had receded into the background, once again began to agitate some people. Numerically weak, their influence nevertheless stretched far beyond the borders of France.

The Catholics who believed in freedom in turn were divided over several important issues. There was the group which in 1855 had reorganized the newspaper *Le Correspondant.* It was headed by a few anti-Bonaparte laymen who were closely allied with Orléanist circles: Falloux, and primarily Montalembert, who thanks to their personal qualities, their social position, their influence in political life, and their great services in the cause of Catholicism also influenced people who did not sympathize with all of their ideas. This group, "academic and in vogue" (Planque), which in some respects approached the ideal of "devout humanism," was also represented in the provinces and in the great orders. Among the Dominicans its views were championed by Lacordaire, among the Oratorians by Gratry, and even among the Jesuits by P. de Ravignan and the first editors of *Études.* But above all it profited from the support and the growing prestige of Monsignor Dupanloup, the eloquent and active bishop of Orléans, whom his defense of the temporal position of the Pope after the Italian War placed in the forefront of Europe's religious politics. Dupanloup's liberalism was highly relative. Basically his aim, as that of the Belgian bishops and of Ketteler, was to employ new methods and institutions which corresponded to liberal aspirations and under the circumstances were the only possible ones, in order to create a modernized Christian society in which liberty "was regarded as the guarantee for the activity of the Church" (Gadille). Yet he was viewed by the ultramontane press as the religious leader of the "liberal Catholic faction," while conversely many moderate Catholics, convinced that they were in agreement with the spirit of the century, accused him of a lack of logic precisely because he refused to apply liberal principles to the solution of the Roman Question.

A much more consistent liberalism was represented by the clerics led by Monsignor Maret, the dean of the theological faculty at the Sorbonne. On the one hand, they did not hesitate to proclaim a "Catholic and liberal reform" within the Church, which was to rejuvenate the old institutions like synods and councils which limited authority and to free Catholic research from the stranglehold of the Index. They made no secret of their sympathies for the constitutional efforts of the Romans or of their conviction that the temporal power of the Pope was more damaging than useful for the exercise of his spiritual mission. On the other hand, in the question of the relation between the two powers, they openly adhered to the concept of the modern state, which was allied with the principles of 1789, which, "correctly understood, were rooted in Christianity just as much as in philosophical reason" (Maret). These neo-Gallicans saw in the concordat an instrument of cooperation in freedom between the Church and a secula:ized society. But such also were the ideas of a majority of the Catholic middle class which was frequently willing either to exclude or to ignore of the official doctrines of the Church whatever happened to be too much of a burden for its intellectual and political concepts.

These groups were opposed by those who in contrast to the liberal Catholics proudly designated themselves as "nothing but Catholics" and thereby emphasized their loyalty to the Roman standpoint, whose hard line they wanted to strengthen. They remained faithful to the counterrevolutionary traditionalism of the first third of the century and lacked the power of discrimination to detect the kernel of truth inherent in liberalism. They tended to judge political decisions according to absolute principles, from which they deduced their logical consequences, instead of searching for compromises adapted to concrete situations varying according to time and place. The leader of this group was Monsignor Pie, who in his *Instructions synodales sur les erreurs du temps présent* (1855–71) ceaselessly pilloried naturalism, which wanted to alienate God and the Church from the concerns of the world. Inspired especially by Dom Guéranger, he developed a political supernaturalism which was based on the Kingdom of Jesus Christ in this world and the glorification of the Pope-King. He did not advocate theocracy as such, i.e., the exercise of direct political power by the Church, but while admitting that the complete attainment of a Christian society would not come before the end of time, he nevertheless demanded the renewal of faith in the individual and the family as well as the Christianization of the state and the state's agencies. They did not hesitate to proclaim the direct sovereignty of Church and Pope over all of civil society. They expected that with the aid of Bourbon President Chambord a Christian state, as the Middle Ages had seen it, would soon be established.

These extreme ideas were spread with an absolute lack of differentiation and were often accompanied by unjust condemnations of Catholics who thought differently. The leading journalist who acted in this fashion and intensified the polarization was Louis Veuillot. Veuillot's achievements are undeniable: his devotion to the Pope, his personal altruism, and the great accomplishment when through his sarcastic contempt of anticlericals he helped to free the average Catholic from the inferiority complex which had burdened him for so long. But he also did more than anyone else to poison the atmosphere. The intransigence of his Catholicism — that of a convert — all too often made him forget the requirements of Christian charity and led him to a wholesale condemnation of modern civilization, for which he held the foolishness of the freethinkers of his time responsible. While the bishops were reluctant to admonish this journalist who often criticized them for what he regarded as their lack of orthodoxy, he quickly became an oracle for the provincial clergy, which valued his popular language and his massive criticisms. With this clergy acting as an intermediary, Veuillot's influence was effective with a limited, but not to be underestimated, number of the faithful. For a long time they maintained a stance of clerical intolerance and systematic defamation of civil authority.

Catholic Liberalism outside France around 1860

The debates in Belgium proved most similar to those in France. There also around 1860, under the influence of the bitter press polemics which agitated French Catholicism and of the domestic political situation, the question about the bearable extent of Catholic accommodation to the system of modern freedoms was translated from the level of tactics to the level of ideas. While those with personal contacts to Montalembert and his friends continued to praise the extremely liberal constitution as the ideal, others began to worry over the change of Belgian liberalism to an anticlerical radicalism which no longer had anything in common with the unionism of 1830. They raised the point that the traditional privileges of the Church had been surrendered and that the opponents had gained freedom for the unlimited propagation of their ideas, but that they, after having achieved the legal majority, now systematically prevented the Church from taking advantage of the concessions which it had been promised in return. Even if the Catholics should regain the majority in the parliament, they argued, it would be impossible for them to conduct an unequivocally Catholic policy as long as they were obligated to respect the freedom of evil. Without agreeing in all points with the extreme positions of Veuillot — a comparison between the newspapers *L'Univers* and *Le Bien Public,* the chief paper of the Belgian ultramontanes founded in 1853, is very revealing — and clearly distancing themselves from the antiparliamentarism of the French polemicist, they began to talk of the necessity of amending the constitution as soon as circumstances permitted it. Between these two extremes stood Cardinal Sterckx and the canonists of Louvain, who drew attention to the practical advantages of the constitution, which guaranteed the Church a unique independence from the civil authority. They had to overcome the growing resistance of many younger bishops, trained in Rome, who regarded the Catholicization of some aspects of liberalism as impossible.

In Italy the problem was quite different. After the collapse of the neoguelf movement, which by many had been seen as the meeting point of the Catholic sentiment and the liberal sentiment, the development of the Roman Question made a reconciliation between liberal endeavors and Catholic loyalty to the faith much more difficult. The idea, propagated by Montalembert and the Belgian Catholics, of a Christian reconquest of society with the help of political freedoms found only few adherents in Italy. On the one hand, many patriotic and constitutional Catholics, disappointed by the "betrayal" of Pius IX, without reservation joined the liberal camp, i.e., the moderates, and for the achievement of their political ideals allied themselves with the anticlerical left "by leaving everything religious behind them and being concerned with it only in the last hour when the priest is called" (Curci). On the other hand, the indignation of many over the more statist than truly liberal policy of the Turin government, which de facto constituted a serious infringement of the rights of the Church and a limitation of its freedom even in the spiritual sphere, led to a reaction of embitterment and an indiscriminate condemnation of liberalism, no matter how moderate it might be. This intransigent direction enjoyed the complete approval of Rome and was spread throughout the country by such belligerent newspapers as Don Margotti's *Unità cattolica* and Don Albertario's *Osservatore cattolica.* Under the pontificate of Pius IX, after the passing enthusiasm of the "mediating" priests immediately after 1860, it won most of Italy's clerics and militant Catholics.

But even if the circumstances in Italy prevented the formation of a liberal Catholic party which, like those in France and Belgium, could have been politically influential, a Catholic liberal spirit, which believed in the possibility of a reconciliation of the Catholic faith with constitutional institutions and modern civilization, had not quite disappeared. This liberal Catholic spirit, strongly determined by the differences of cultural traditions in the various parts of Italy and the preferences of individuals, could be found in many groups. Behind these leading figures was ranged the great number of those who continued to receive the sacraments, but who on the religious level combined the principle of authority with freedom of conscience and wanted to assure the independence of civil society within its own sphere. They were also the ones who, openly acknowledging the historical benefits which the Church had bestowed on Italy, were yet of the opinion that the status under which the Church had existed since the Middle Ages was not sacrosanct and that it was perfectly legitimate to adjust it to the requirements of the nineteenth century. This adjustment meant for some a clearer demarcation between the realms of religion and politics and, despite the protests of the Holy See, the cancellation of archaic ecclesiastical privileges, and for others the introduction of separation of Church and state and the renunciation of the exercise of the temporal power of the Pope.

In Germany the reconciliation between Church and state within a liberal framework occasioned fewer dramas of conscience than in the Latin countries. The reason for this was in part the fact that the German Catholics as a minority demanding religious freedom, unlike France or Belgium, did not seem to favor error but to the contrary seemed to support Catholicism. Furthermore, the German Catholics, influenced by Catholic Romanticism, in their praise of freedom harked back less to the principles of 1789 than to corporative freedom as it had existed prior to the absolute monarchy. Finally, unlike the Latin countries, religious freedom for them did not include the freedom of unbelief, but simply implied a nondenominational state with a Christian way of life. Despite a certain worry in conservative circles and some reservations in Austria and Bavaria, the disagreeableness of the petty bureaucratic interferences in the life of the Church was considered fairly balanced by the official recognition which the support of the state lent to the Church. Thus, the militant Catholics and the defenders of the principles, strengthened by the experience of Prussia after 1848, agreed to acknowledge the religious advantages of constitutional freedom, which they were careful not to label "freedom to lose," even though this did not keep them from directing fierce attacks on the anti-Christian character of ideological liberalism. This moderate position, represented by Ketteler in his work *Freiheit, Autorität und Kirche* (1862), for a long time was accepted by the large majority of German Catholics and even at the time of the *Syllabus,* when only a few extreme voices on the right (Austrian Jesuits, among others) and on the Left (Döllinger's group) muddied the waters of unity.

But violent controversies took place in the German-speaking countries over the question of academic freedom and ecclesiastical authority. Some representatives of the Catholic renascence, led by Döllinger, wanted to free Catholic intellectuals from the inferiority complex which a flourishing Protestant and rationalistic scholarship had given them. They thought it absolutely necessary to provide them with complete freedom of research, aside from the few questions which touched upon defined dogma and which they tried to avoid as much as possible.

Their intentions were genuine and their attempt to withdraw scholarly work from the control of the Inquisition was justified. But they insisted on seeing only one aspect of a complex situation. A reaction was therefore unavoidable; unfortunately it originated with men who often were ignorant of the new methods of scholarship and in some instances were actually hostile to them. Some people now opposed any intervention by the ecclesiastical magisterial office on principle and wanted to escape from all control by the ecclesiastical authorities. In this way there developed on the soil of classical liberal Protestantism a tendency among Catholic intellectuals which had its equal only in the small English group of *The Rambler.*

The journal *The Rambler* was founded in England in 1848 by the convert Richard Simpson with the objective of countering the intellectual inferiority of English Catholicism. Repeatedly the journal was the outspoken advocate for a limited autonomy of laymen in the Church. Its iconoclastic tendencies were reinforced in 1859 when the young John Acton assumed the directorship. He was a student of Döllinger's and for a period of fifteen years embodied English Catholic liberalism. He characterized himself as "a man who has renounced everything that is incompatible with freedom in Catholicism and with the Catholic faith in politics." The independent position of the journal (and also that of *Home and Foreign Review,* which followed it in 1862) with respect to academic freedom, the Roman Question, and numerous other burning religious issues provoked the reaction of Wiseman and Manning, both of whom were avidly supported by W. G. Ward, the English emulator of Veuillot, and his *Dublin Review.* One of the saddest consequences of this controversy was the fact that it compromised Newman, who could not be further away from religious and political liberalism and who had attempted the role of mediator in vain.

The *Syllabus* and Its Consequences

The different manifestations of liberalism in Catholic life, often incautiously expressed and occasionally accompanied by openly equivocal conduct, were an irritant for the men of faith. Confronted with this "religion of freedom" and a "religion of learning," they endeavored once again to confirm the "rights of God over minds and society." They were deeply worried because, as conservatives almost instinctively tied to the past, they had great difficulty distinguishing between eternal verities which must be preserved at all cost and contingent structures of the ecclesiastical and civil order. Many others were additionally shaken by the fact, no longer to be glossed over by 1860, that whenever liberals came to power, anticlerical legislation soon followed. This aspect worried the Romans especially, whom the events after 1848 in Italy confirmed in the belief of a close connection between the principles of 1789 and the destruction of traditional values in the social, moral, and religious order. Pius X came to believe that he had to take action so that his silence would not discourage the few Catholic nations which to some degree had remained faithful to the — in his eyes best — system of a privileged Church protected by the state. Inasmuch as circumstances had forced him to make practical concessions in several countries, he now considered it so much more urgent unmistakably to draw attention to principles. Additionally, however, the idea of a comprehensive condemnation of all ideas of modern society regarded as erroneous gained ground gradually. It was started in 1849 by Cardinal Pecci and

later taken up by the *Civiltà cattolica.* After the revival of the Roman Question in
1859 it was promoted again, and in the fall of that year the Vatican asked some
trusted churchmen like Monsignor Pie, Dom Guéranger, and the president of the
University of Louvain, Xavier de Ram, for suggestions as to which errors ought to
be condemned and which points of doctrine ought to be emphasized.

On the basis of the replies, a first draft of the *Syllabus errorum in Europa vi-
gentium* with seventy-nine propositions was prepared by the spring of 1860. But
in the fall Rome received a long pastoral letter from Bishop Gerbet of Perpignan.
The document under the title of "Instruction sur les erreurs du temps présent,"
contained a list of eighty-five erroneous statements and appeared to the Pope as
an even better basis for his own solemn project. According to P. Martina, he did
so wrongly, as the first draft dealt more with principles and had a more comprehensive character. Several successive commissions of theologians and cardinals,
whose work was closely observed by the Pope, for more than a year worked on
the theological justification of Gerbet's propositions. Disregarding the pronounced
reserve of many Curia cardinals, who would have preferred a return to the first
draft, Pius IX decided to present the new list of sixty-one propositions to the bishops who visited Rome in the summer for the purpose of lending support for the
Pope's temporal power. The list was based on Gerbet's pastoral letter and summarized the most important modern efforts to liberate philosophy, morals, and
politics from the control of religion. Although the information was provided on a
confidential basis, some of it was leaked. The premature disclosure of the document occasioned a storm of indignation in the anticlerical press against Rome's
obscurantism. Episcopal reactions, few in number, were rather reserved. Nonetheless, the Pope insisted on his original idea and the commission continued work
on Monsignor Gerbet's propositions. Still, it proceeded so slowly that it seemed
that the great condemnation of modern errors was being postponed to a later
day; some hoped it was sine die.

But in the summer of 1863 two unfortunate speeches once more brought the
problem to the fore. One was the apology which Montalembert, impatient with
the "timidity" of his friends, made at the international congress of Belgian Catholics in Mechelen in defense of a "free Church in a free state." The other one
was Döllinger's bold demand for the independence of Catholic scholars from the
ecclesiastical magisterial office, which he presented in Munich. The first speech
received a strong echo and was a challenge to all those who saw the chief danger
of their time in liberal Catholicism. They now insisted that Rome react clearly and
unequivocally. Several interventions spared Montalembert a public censure, but
Pius IX more and more became convinced that he needed to take a solemn step in
order to calm the excited spirits. Several factors then delayed his pronouncement
by a full year. The French intervened diplomatically, fearing that public opinion
would be offended; the Belgians were worried that it might look as though Rome
condemned the constitution, and just before elections this would only play into
the hands of the liberals; and finally there were the apprehensions of Cardinal
Antonelli that some non-Catholic defenders of the temporal power of the Pope,
like Adolphe Thiers, might become discouraged. Pius IX was not deaf to these
considerations, but this so very impressionable man was also subject to other
influences. There was the increasing tendency of many Italian Catholics to take

a neutral position; there was the success of Renan's book *Vie de Jésus,* which graphically made evident the dangers of freedom of the press; there were the recent violations of the rights of the Church in Poland and Mexico; there were Ketteler's warnings of the spiritual independence of the German theologians; and, more generally, there was the threat of promoting radicalism through passivity on the part of the Catholics. The convention of September 1864 was then the final straw which decided Pius IX to hesitate no longer.

Consulted again in August 1864, the cardinals of the Inquisition had renewed their objections to the list of Gerbet's propositions and had suggested a different approach. They thought the Pope should repeat his earlier condemnations in summary form. The Pope decided to follow the new suggestion and within a few weeks there was drafted, with the special assistance of the young Barnabite L. Bilio, an encyclical and a list of excerpts from addresses and writings of the Pope which he had made since the beginning of his pontificate and in which he had a|ready condemned the various "modern errors." At the end of December the encyclical *Quanta cura* was published; appended to it was a catalog of eighty unacceptable propositions under the title *of Syllabus errorum.* In it the Pope condemned pantheism and rationalism; indifferentism, which regards all religions as equal in value; socialism, which denies the right to private property and subordinates the family to the state; the erroneous concept regarding Christian marriage; Freemasonry; the rejection of the temporal power of the Pope; Gallicanism, which wanted to make the exercise of ecclesiastical authority dependent on the authorization by the civil power; statism, which insists on the monopoly of education and dissolves religious orders; and naturalism, which regards the fact that human societies no longer have respect for religion as progress and which demands laicization of institutions, separation of Church and state, and absolute freedom of religion and the press. The last aspect in particular impressed the public, as the propositions of the *Syllabus,* taken out of context, often were bewildering: and justified the evaluation of Dom Butler that "it was a most inopportune" document.

The majority of non-Catholics at first were confirmed in their belief in the incompatibility of an ultramontane Church with the ways of life and habits of thought of the nineteenth century. The ultramontane press, jubilant over the *Syllabus,* heightened the impression to the point that many Catholics began to ask themselves whether conditions were really as they were depicted.

Actually, though, excitement was not very strong everywhere. In Italy, the press engaged in verbal skirmishes but the public remained calm, some because long ago they had stopped paying attention to the strictures of the Vatican in political questions, and others because they realized that an exact interpretation of the Roman document required careful exegesis. Generally the document was debated in connection with the Roman Question, and was seen less as a stand against modern society than against the convention of September. In Great Britain the non-Catholic public was virtually unanimous in finding the Pope's campaign against modern society totally ridiculous, primarily because he had condemned virtually everything. English Catholics, on the other hand, attempted, not very successfully, to argue that Pius IX had condemned the doctrinal errors and excesses of liberalism, and not the liberal institutions as England knew them. A similar situation prevailed in the Netherlands. Although there the Catholic newspapers also adopted this interpretation, the papal document contributed to increasing Protestant hostility to the papacy and to the hastening of the break between Catholics and liberals in parliament.

The situation was different in the German-speaking countries. The Austrian government initially feared that, emboldened by the encyclical, the clergy would demand an even more favorable application of the concordat. Döllinger and friends deplored the *Syllabus;* but the Mainz faction, whose influence reached the broad mass of the Catholics beyond the range of the intellectuals, noted the condemnation of atheistic philosophers and of bold theologians with satisfaction. With few exceptions, however, they took the justified position that the rejection of anti-Christian liberalism was no obstacle to continued exploitation of constitutional liberties. This interpretation also quickly gained ground in Belgium, even among the ultramontanes, but in the initial period the despondency of the constitutionally inclined Catholics was very great. In France agitation lasted for several weeks. Many moderate liberal Catholics were severely shaken in their convictions. Others were aware that the reminder of the principles on the whole did not really change the situation, but they also were despondent as the exaggerated comments of Veuillot's press forced them to observe the widening gap which separated the skeptics from the Church. Many bishops immediately wrote to Rome, pointing to the dangers of ambiguity, and demanded a clarification. Some of the others, among them Darboy and Maret, in the interest of preventing extreme interpretations on the part of their colleagues, persuaded the government to forbid the official publication of the encyclical under the pretext that its condemnations were directed against the constitution of the Empire. With the genius of the born polemicist, Dupanloup, assisted by Cochin, used this anti-liberal measure to write a mitigating commentary on encyclical and *Syllabus* in the form of a defense of the Pope, who was being unjustly attacked by a hostile press and equally hostile cabinet ministers. Beyond this he was sufficiently skillful to woo the Romans by adding to his commentary an eloquent indictment of the recent convention in which the French imperial government had promised the Italian government to evacuate Rome. This "translation of the encyclical into contemporary language" (A. Dechamps), in which the severity of the original was attenuated somewhat, was highly successful in Europe and even in America and within a few days persuaded public opinion to reject anticlerical criticisms. Pius IX, grateful to Dupanloup for his sharp attack on the imperial government, sent him a brief of commendation. The brief was very carefully formulated, but in conjunction with the praises of numerous bishops it gave Dupanloup's pamphlet the veneer of a more or less official interpretation of the *Syllabus,* even though many who disagreed with it attempted to belittle its significance. This fact has a certain importance for the later history of Catholic liberalism, and for this reason Dupanloup's brochure deserves more than a merely anecdotal interest.

For the moment the storm subsided and theoretically both factions were back where they had started, inasmuch as Dupanloup's action had saved the liberal Catholics from seemingly inevitable retreat. For this reason they were able to maintain their position until the accession of Leo XIII, even if in the meantime they were forced to strike their sails. Many also acknowledged, in con-

Internal Catholic Controversies in Connection with Liberalism361

sequence of the papal condemnation, that in their utterances they occasionally had been too radical or imprecise. Above all they recognized the necessity of discretion in order not to anger the aging Pope, who was increasingly irritated by the growing sectarianism of those who called themselves liberals. Toward the end, Pius IX, who almost daily condemned liberalism as the "error of the century," was no longer able to see the radical difference between Catholic liberalism and liberalism as such. While regular liberalism, even if its adherents practiced their religion, was naturalistic and wanted to separate man as much as possible from his religious ties, liberal Catholics both intellectually and practically were guided by the demands of their faith and accepted, sometimes somewhat unwillingly, their subjection to the decisions of the Church. Pius IX admitted the difference, but only unwillingly. "Catholic liberalism," he declared in 1874, "has one foot in the truth and one foot in error, one foot in the Church and one foot in the spirit of the century, one foot on my side and one foot on the side of my enemies." He was willing in many cases to tolerate the "hypothesis," but could not refrain from showing his dislike of those who in his eyes too easily decided for this option and now could proceed from practically admissible concessions to a surrender of principles. The full favor of the Pope was reserved for the "Knights of the Absolute," who, without consideration of intellectual developments or of local requirements, maintained what was supposed to be the "right of a Christian society." The frequent encouragements which Rome sent to their leaders finally convinced them that the Pope had entrusted them with a genuine mission. Liberal Catholics had escaped condemnation, but they were clearly aware that they were in disfavor. For the next fifteen years the scene was dominated by extremists — liberal radicals and intransigent ultramontanes — who were equally intolerant and wanted to force their thinking upon everyone else.

Antiliberalism and Social Catholicism

Recent investigations have revealed that the Catholic opposition to liberalism was not always only confined to negative criticism. To be sure, there were among the opponents of the liberal Catholics many closed minds without any understanding of the times; but the more flexible among them, who succeeded in gaining the attention of a considerable segment of the Catholic public, were imbued with a two-fold positive ideal. For one, they wanted to react to the timidity of many of their brethren who seemed to be reconciled with the liberal view that religion was a private matter without any impact on social life. For another, they demanded the right to the "actual state," compared to the "legal state," which was dominated by a numerically small oligarchy. This makes understandable why from the second third of the nineteenth century onward these "reactionaries" in particular undertook more social initiatives than the liberal Catholics, of whom it might have been thought that they had more in common with democratic ideals. It also explains why these efforts were primarily directed toward the immediate amelioration of the poverty of the working class rather than to a solution of its real problems through structural reforms. The intention was to obtain the sympathy of the workers and their support in the battle against the anticlerical bourgeois state. It finally also makes clear why these efforts were more often inspired by the nostalgic ideal of a return to an idealized, patriarchal, and corporative past than by a realistic accommodation to the new situations created by the Industrial Revolution.

The connection between antiliberalism and social efforts was shown early in the *Civiltà cattolica,* in which, for example, Father Taparelli in 1852 held the view that the corporations dissolved by the French Revolution were rooted in natural law. Pius IX devoted one paragraph of the encyclical *Quanta cura* to the unmasking not only of the illusions of socialism, which wants to put the state in the place of providence, but also of the pagan character of economic liberalism, which in the relationship between capital and labor eliminates the moral factor.

Such ideas inspired several of the first initiators of the Catholic movement in Italy, who in this as yet hardly industrialized state were concerned chiefly with the pitiful situation of the rural masses, and whose initiatives actually reached their full effectiveness only under the subsequent pontificate.

In France during the July Monarchy there had existed an early form of Christian socialism in addition to the *Société d'économie charitable,* in which Viscount Armand de Melun had gathered legitimate representatives of social work who, while genuinely touched by the misery of the proletariat, were also rather reticent to call for an intervention by the state in economic life. But the movement received a mortal blow by the general reaction to everything which resembled the kind of socialism which developed after the crisis of 1848. Thus, for a period of twenty years social Catholicism was represented almost exclusively by conservatives who were decided followers of the paternalistic approach. They tried less to change the condition of the workers for reasons of justice than to lead the workers back to the Church and to maintain the established order at the price of a few improvements in their material situation. The majority of the engaged men of the Second Empire, who were often met with the indifference and even the mistrust of the broad masses of the faithful and of the clergy, were inspired by the theories of Le Play, whose scholarship left much to be desired and which, in conjunction with a narrow interpretation of the *Syllabus,* served to lead these social Catholics to a "counterrevolution" opposed to the doctrine of human rights and democratic egalitarianism. In this fashion much personal generosity was wasted without actually reaching the working class. On the contrary, the working class now strove to take its fate and the battle for its liberation into its own hands.

In Belgium the situation was hardly any different. The few progressive Catholics who suggested a few hesitant legal measures in favor of the workers met general rejection at the congress of Mechelen.

It is paradoxical that the origin of a more realistic Catholic social movement lay in Germany, although its industrial development started only later. The German social movement had an open mind toward labor unions and approved of a restriction of economic liberalism through social legislation, the first steps toward which were outlined in the encyclical *Rerum novarum* of Leo XIII. There was no denying that the German Catholics, like the others, were at first primarily interested in maintaining order, but what they desired — in contrast to France, where all too many Catholics only wanted to preserve external order and to subjugate the workers to the current situation — was a traditional order, the organized society of the "good old days," which no doubt was not at all democratic but which at least had the advantage that it protected the little people against an unlimited exploitation by the rich. At first, until about 1870, most German Catholics in their attempt to bring the Church to the people and the people to the Church were mostly concerned with the defense of the independent artisans and the organization of the farmers. But gradually attention was paid to the problem of the workers. In 1837, the militant Catholic Franz Josef von Buß of Baden pointed to the dangers of uncontrolled industrialization and demanded action by the state in order to improve the situation of the workers. In his opinion it was up to the Church to assume the defense of the workers, who had no official representation.

In 1846 Adolf Kolping, a former shoemaker's apprentice turned priest, founded the first journeymen's association. Thanks to outstanding collaborators and the active participation of the journeymen themselves, whom Kolping allowed broad participation, the organization grew rapidly with the support of Cardinal Geissel of Cologne. From the Rhineland it spread throughout Germany and to Austria and Switzerland. Gradually other social institutions were founded in the industrial areas of the Rhineland, culminating in the founding of the People's Association of Mönchen-Gladbach. To the care and saving of souls and amelioration of need there was now slowly added the effort to establish a professional organization and a solid action foundation for the activity of the workers. These, it was hoped, would lead to a change of working conditions.

In this development, which presented the problem of the workers to the German Catholics more as a question of institutional reform and less as a matter of mere charitable help, the dynamic Bishop Ketteler of Mainz played a significant role. He was frequently misunderstood and the prelate was often depicted as a pioneer of Christian democracy and as initiator of the booming social works in Germany during his life. Actually, many of these activities, started in the Cologne area, were begun without him. Even if Ketteler in his practical work was occasionally inspired by Socialist doctrines, especially by the form which Lassalle had given them, and even if he adopted some of Lassalle's arguments and indictments of capitalism, he harbored no sympathies for modern democracy. Speaking out against the oppression of the economically weak, which society permitted, this Westphalian aristocrat had in mind a return to the corporative society as it had existed in the Holy Roman Empire of the Middle Ages. Yet Ketteler's influence on the social Catholicism of his time was tremendous. In his book *Die Arbeiterfrage und das Christentum* (1864), the fruit of fifteen years of reflection, he did not limit himself to proposing a few concrete reforms, but attempted to demonstrate that the solution of the workers' problems was only possible by a cooperation of state and society, acting in direct opposition to liberal individualism and to the totalitarianism of the modern centralized state. Energetically he attacked the solutions suggested by middle-class capitalism and statist socialism. Instead, under the influence of Catholic Romanticism, which had marked him deeply in his youth, he glorified society as a living hierarchical organism, strongly molded by the unity of faith, in which the artisans were organized with a view toward the general welfare and economic life was freed from the iron law of greed and profits. Thus Ketteler was the first theoretician of a social order based on corporatism, which for more than half a century formed the basis of Catholic social doctrine. Its opposition to the individualistic ideal of economic liberalism after 1870 in more than one case — especially in the social wing of the Center Party, in the Austrian School, and with La Tour du Pin — was more unequivocal than the practical mistrust of and the theoretical objections to socialism.

The Victory of Ultramontanism

Chaps. 42, 43: Roger Aubert
Chap. 44: Rudolf Lill

CHAPTER 42

Ultramontane Progress and Final Gallican Resistance

The Ultramontane Movement around 1850

The fifteen years of Gregory XVI's pontificate were a decisive phase in the progress of ultramontanism. Yet not all resistance had been removed. The great mass of the clergy and of the faithful were convinced of the advantages which accrued to the Church as a result of its liberation from the tutelage of the governments and of closing Catholic ranks around the Pope. Still, the question was occasionally asked whether it was at all advisable to have such a concentration of power in consequence of this rather extreme centralization. Such a centralization inevitably had to result in a reduction of the authority of the bishops, in uniformity of Church discipline and liturgy, even piety, all of which would mean the complete renunciation of revered local customs and the adoption of a "religious way of life" for the entire Church, analogous to Italy's.

It is of great importance not to lose sight of the complex character of the ultramontane movement and its concrete reality. Its adherents propounded theological and canonical doctrines concerning the special privileges of the Pope and the prerogatives of the Church over the civil power, developed a program for turning the ecclesiastical organization into a more authoritarian and centralistic one, favored restriction of the freedom of scholarship in philosophy and theology, and demanded a new outlook on piety which consisted less in an inner attitude than in frequent receipt of the sacraments and an increase in external devotions. While the ultramontane movement and its opposition to the heritage of the regalism of the Old Regime met with general acclaim, it encountered various forms of resistance because of the ecclesiastical problems posed by it. The resistance originated with the theologians whose minds were closed to dogmatic progress and who refused to see why the Pope now should occupy a more important place in the Church than during the first centuries. But there was also resistance by people who, tied to old religious customs, preferred the particularism of the past to a future with a predominantly supranational character. And finally there was also the opposition of upper clergymen who feared the loss of their historical rights and occasionally wondered whether the traditional character of an episcopate based on divine right was still safe.

Such pockets of resistance could be seen almost everywhere. They could be found in England, where among some Old Catholics the insular thinking of the eighteenth century lived on, and in Lombardy and in Poland, where Josephinist thought continued to be propounded in the seminaries and universities. They held on especially strongly in France and the German-speaking countries, where latent opposition was incited by the very excesses of the ultramontane faction. In essence, though, these were no more than rearguard skirmishes, incapable of stopping the victory of the ultramontane movement.

In France during the Second Republic, the ultramontanes became stronger, ably assisted by Nuncio Fornari. The bishops appointed by Falloux largely thought "Roman" thoughts and helped them to victory at the various provincial councils. At these councils the Holy See succeeded in having some decrees changed and thereby implicitly achieved recognition of its claim to such control. The newspaper *L'Univers,* edited by Parisis and Gousset, eagerly supported every move made by the Holy See in this connection, and thereby strengthened the impulse with which Catholics had looked toward Rome for years.

The defenders of ultramontanism found considerable support among the lower clergy, which was dissatisfied with the arbitrariness of many bishops. In order to protect themselves, the priests were demanding the restoration of church tribunals, which had been abolished after the French Revolution; the provincial councils of the middle of the century met some of their demands through the reinstitution of officialates. Dissatisfied with the way and methods of episcopal jurisdiction, the parish priests began to turn to the Roman tribunals even in the smallest of episcopal decisions whenever they did not meet the approval of the pastors. The tribunals in turn were only too happy to oblige and to interfere in the internal affairs of French dioceses, going over the heads of the bishops. The tendency to resort to Rome was promoted by some canonists and publications like *Le Rappel* and *La Correspondance de Rome,* which in France publicized the decisions favorable to the lower clergy which the Roman congregations had made in the name of universally valid canon law.

Returned to Rome at the beginning of 1851, Cardinal Fornari emphatically continued to support the attempts of the ultramontanes by defending the papers *L'Univers* and *La Correspondance de Rome* against the attacks of some bishops, and by promoting the inclusion of Gallican-oriented works in the Index.

The vociferous enthusiasm with which the ultramontane press greeted these steps, and the application of often rather insensitive methods led to a counter-reaction. In 1852, a Paris theologian wrote *Mémoire sur la situation présente de l'Église gallicaine relativement au droit coutumier,* which concerned itself with the most important questions discussed at the time, such as the problem of particular rights as against the universal right of the Church, the reform of liturgy, and the interference by Roman congregations. At the same time, steps were taken to silence those journalists who expressed themselves too loudly in favor of the ultramontane cause. The time was well chosen, inasmuch as many, even non-Gallican, bishops were becoming concerned about priestly agitation; they detected in it the spirit of rebellion which, by appealing to Roman authority, was trying to escape from the supervision of the bishops at home. Additionally, they were shocked by the action of Catholic laymen who presumed to substitute a learning Church for the teaching Church, and became angry over the arrogance with which some journalists assumed they could dictate how the bishops should carry out their duties. Pius IX himself was required to counsel Veuillot to moderation. Errors in leadership by Dupanloup and Sibour, the archbishop of Paris, necessitated the Pope's intervention. In April 1853 he published the encyclical *Inter multiples,* concerning the problems raised in France. It was a clear disapproval of Gallicanism, even in its moderate form, and of all those who, for whatever reasons, were resisting the ultramontane current.

Rome's Systematic Activity

The publication of the encyclical *Inter multiples* signified a change in the attitude of Rome. Like most of the great movements in Church history, the ultramontane movement had started from below. Initially the Holy See had confined itself to noting its progress without active interference on its part. But during the final years of Gregory XVI a development was initiated which became notably intensified under the pontificate of Pius IX.

The personality of the Pope alone contributed to it. His charm and open nature, so different from the reserved behavior of his predecessor, together with the aura of a "martyr," which the problems arising from the Roman Question lent him, gradually gave him among the Catholic peoples of the world a popularity such as no Pope had known before him. This singular phenomenon in Church history explains in part the enthusiasm with which all of the clergy and of the faithful accepted the doctrine of papal infallibility after it had been unclear for centuries. It also explains the favorable reception of ecclesiastical centralization, which, as everyone knew, also was desired by the Pope.

But Rome was not satisfied with allowing favorable circumstances alone to do the work. The course of the 1848 revolution inevitably meant that at the close of the crisis a systematic plan would be developed to prevent future revolutionary attempts. In its implementation the Jesuits, who had become very influential in the Curia, played a great role. The professors at the Gregoriana in their works emphasized the classical theses of the primacy and infallibility of the Pope. Like Passaglia in his *Commentarius de prerogative B. Petri* (1856), which served as the model for analogous publications, they strove for a more scholarly foundation by returning to the Scripture and the Fathers. Or, like Schrader, they developed the ultramontane positions to an extreme, giving them a clearly theocratic perspective. The number of their students continually grew, thanks to the increase

in the national seminaries at Rome, and they in turn spread these ideas throughout the world. *Civiltà cattolica* effectively popularized them. The proclamation of
the Immaculate Conception (1854) can also be seen from the perspective of the
increasingly emphasized infallibility of the Pope. This event, which strongly influenced the Catholic world, in singular fashion affirmed the prerogatives of the Pope
and his growing importance in the life of the Church.

Even more than on the doctrinal level, Roman activity proceeded systematically in the practical area of discipline. Rome seized every opportunity to support
and strengthen the efforts that were being made by ultramontanes in the various
countries to effect closer ties to the center of Christianity and a strengthening of
papal power. While nuncios in earlier times had acted as diplomatic liaisons to
governments, they now also took a hand in the internal affairs of the Churches in
the countries to which they had been assigned. Pro-Roman priests were supported
and, if necessary, protected against the accusations of their bishops; frequently
they were appointed as prelates in order to raise their standing. The obligation
for periodic visits, which had fallen into disuse, was revived, and the increasing
contacts with the bishops were augmented by the large assemblies of 1854, 1862,
and 1867. Hundreds of bishops gathered in Rome and each time the assemblies
appeared as the apotheosis of papal power and Catholic unity. Everything possible was done to stifle regional differences in ecclesiastical life by discouraging all
calls for the convocation of national councils, by favoring a return to the integral
observation of universal canon law, and by recommending appeals to the Curia,
even in unimportant matters. The Pope increasingly appointed bishops without
considering the opinions of the local higher clergy, and more than once gave preference to mediocre men of whom he could be sure, rather than appoint able men
with an independent view; what made the difference was the Roman education
and pliability of the candidates.

It was even attempted to increase Roman influence in the election of Eastern
bishops. The opportunity for this move was provided by the Ottoman government
when it withdrew Catholics of the Eastern Rite from the civil jurisdiction of schismatic patriarchs and thus made sure that the election of bishops and patriarchs
had secular significance. It was necessary to take steps to prevent the elections
from taking place under the pressure of influential laymen who conceivably had
their material interests more in mind than the spiritual welfare of the Church.
The Armenian patriarch Hassun suggested to Rome a transitional solution which
would simultaneously enhance the role of the apostolic delegate and preserve
the essentials of the traditional system. The majority of the consulted cardinals in
Rome agreed with this approach, but Cardinal Barnabo, the prefect of the Congregation for the Propagation of the Faith, and some of his supporters tended to
see a schismatic factor in the slightest autonomy in ecclesiastical discipline and
were unwilling to grant the Uniates more than their liturgical peculiarities. Pius IX,
personally agreeing with Barnabo, consulted Valerga, the Latin patriarch of Jerusalem, on the matter; Valerga came out in favor of a radical reform of the Eastern
patriarch statute in order to give it a centralistic tone. The Pope used the presence of all patriarchs during the festivities of 1867 in Rome to inform them of his
intentions. From now on, the lower clergy and laymen would no longer participate in elections, the patriarch elected by the bishops alone would assume his

position only after being confirmed by the Pope, and the appointment of bishops would be in the hands of the Holy See. It would select one candidate from a list of three names submitted by the patriarch, the bishops, and the Congregation for the Propagation of the Faith. The immediately following protest by the Maronite and Melchite patriarchs resulted in a postponement of the application of the measure in the jurisdictional area of the two patriarchates; but for the Armenian Church it went into effect immediately with the papal bull *Reversurus* of 12 July 1867. The announcement that these steps, amounting to a reversal of the status expressly granted by Benedict XIV, would soon also be extended to other patriarchates created profound consternation in all Uniate Churches. This worry was added to the displeasure with the pressure which increasingly was applied in favor of an adaptation of Eastern Church discipline to the canon law of the Latin Church. It became evident in the commission which was charged with preparing the decrees of the Vatican Council for the Uniate Churches. The attempts violated the venerable traditions of the East too much not to cause considerable resistance, but in Europe they could easily be enforced through the joint actions of the nuncios, bishops, Catholic movements, and ecclesiastical press.

In Austria, the concordat of 1855 had liquidated Josephinist laws and had made possible the reorganization of the educational system in keeping with the wishes of the Holy See. Consequently, Cardinal Rauscher, the archbishop of Vienna, together with the support of his colleagues Rudigier, Gasser, and Fessler, was able to influence the numerous Catholic associations in an ultramontane direction and to promote the activity of the Jesuits and Redemptorists. In Innsbruck, whose department of theology was entrusted to the Jesuits in 1857, Moy and Vering established the Archives for Catholic Canon Law as a strong outpost of Roman ideas, in Budapest F. Hovanyi made the theology department into a center for the reaction to the Josephinist tentacles in Hungary, and in Vienna the most radical ultramontane theses were defended at the University of Vienna by the Jesuit theologian Clemens Schrader and the canonist Georg Phillips. In his *Kirchenrecht* (7 vols. [1845–72]), Phillips, like Schrader, betrayed an unabashed romantic enthusiasm for medieval theocracy, identified the Pope with the Church, and expressed a rather legalistic and superficial view of the Church and its unity. The work was only second-rate from an academic point of view, but is proof of an educated mind; it was largely responsible in the German-speaking countries for widely popularizing the doctrine of the infallibility of the Pope and of his universal episcopal office and the doctrine of the indirect sovereignty of the Church over the state.

In Germany, Ketteler assumed the leading position, which Geissel held until his death in 1864. Mainz was still the vanguard of the movement, but Moufang and Heinrich, assisted by the nuncio in Munich and Reisach, who in 1854 had become a Curia cardinal, elsewhere also had supporters who worked toward the same goal: the Jesuits with their increasing numbers and influence, the Germanists, and the priests trained in Innsbruck under the guidance of the Jesuits. All of them, who liked to think of themselves as the sole possessors of the Catholic spirit, gradually impressed their views on the Catholic masses. They imparted to them their ideas about the prerogatives of the Pope and the authority of the Roman congregations in the life of the national Churches, as well as about the ideal image of a good Catholic. Within the span of a few decades they produced a profound change in German Catholicism. The place of the old view of piety, centered around inner spirituality and the exercise of virtue, was taken by a new way of religious life which emphasized superficial exercises, membership in confraternities, and the strict observation of church regulations. Sailer's irenics yielded to an attitude which emphasized the gap between Catholics and non-Catholics by once again applying the old maxim of "Extra Ecclesiam nulla salus."

In England, the persistent Manning, assisted by the *Dublin Review,* succeeded within a few years in winning the majority of the Catholic faithful to a very unpretentious and radical ultramontanism, in spite of the opposition of the liberals at the *Rambler* and the hesitant stance of Newman and other traditionalist bishops. In Ireland, Cardinal Cullen, who was a total adherent of the centralistic plans of the Holy See, carried the day for the Roman concepts.

In France the encyclical *Inter multiples* played a decisive part in the victory of ultramontanism. It became possible because of the benevolent neutrality of the government at the beginning of the Second Empire, the extension of Dom Guéranger's campaign in favor of the Roman liturgy, the Rome-oriented development of Saint Sulpice, which trained a majority of the young clergy, and the establishment of the French Seminary at Rome. The last was accomplished in 1853 with the support of Monsignor de Ségur, whose writings greatly helped in spreading the "Roman spirit" in France. Louis Veuillot's newspaper *L'Univers* grew into a battle instrument of the movement. It started a campaign to win the lower clergy for a theocratic concept of society in which politics would be in the service of religion, and for a Church in closer contact with the papacy; in this way it would be better prepared to withstand the dangers of "revolution." Ultimately Veuillot succeeded in creating among French Catholics a "cult of the papacy" as could be found in no other country. At the same time the works of Bossuet, of the Maurists and their students, and of the Jansenists, which in earlier generations had formed the foundation for the training of the clergy, were replaced by an ecclesiastical literature whose academic content was virtually nonexistent, but whose orientation was clearly ultramontane.

The Excesses of Neo-Ultramontanism
and the Reaction in Germany and France

As all other movements, ultramontanism also was not able to avoid excesses. Thoughtful ultramontanes clearly recognized the weaknesses of Gallicanism. More clearly than their opponents they realized that the development of ecclesiastical institutions had not come to an end with the conclusion of the patristic period. They were of the opinion that Rome's intervention in the affairs of the national Churches, which would be able to resist the encroachments of the governments only with difficulty, was justified. They desired a clear centralization, convinced that it was indispensable for the solution of religious problems on the only level where this was possible, namely, on the supranational one. But they also often lacked moderation and occasionally a sense of the fitting in their methods and ideas. After 1860 certain tendencies became clear which Wilfrid Ward and Dom Butler suggested be termed "neo-ultramontanism." Some people wanted to see the role of the bishops reduced to an intolerable point; some portrayed the most extreme theses of medieval theocracy as divine law; others wished to extend the infallibility of the Pope to all of his pronouncements, even those which concerned religious policy, or they developed forms of papal veneration which amounted to "idolatry of the papacy." The Pope was referred to as the "Vice-God of Mankind" and as the "Permanent Word Incarnate." Monsignor Mermillod preached on the "three incarnations of the Son of God" in the womb of the Virgin Mary, in the Eucharist, and in "the old man in the Vatican." The *Civiltà cattolica* went so far as to write that "when the Pope meditates, it is God who is thinking through him." All of these exaggerations and flatteries, to which Pius IX did not object, were splashed throughout the Catholic press, to the great disgust of those who were incapable of realizing that these unfortunate formulations were not merely thoughtless expressions emerging from the simple soul of the masses. They certainly did their part in fortifying the last remaining centers of resistance.

The stupidities of neo-ultramontanism angered the German professors the more as they already had great difficulty in swallowing the more moderate views of Bellarmine's followers. As they tended to see ecclesiastical reality only in historical terms, their view in general was too retrospective. They ignored that, considering its involvement with history, the Church perforce had to adapt its institutions to contemporary times. As experts on Christian antiquity, they refused to recognize as legitimate the development of papal prerogatives in the course of the centuries. Their view was supported by the questionable nature of many of the arguments advanced by the representatives of ultramontanism, whose scholarly pronouncements often were not able to keep pace with Catholic thought. They were accused of being a group of fanatics who, while they had a certain power as a result of the support of a considerable number of pious laymen, nevertheless were discrediting the standing of the Church in the eyes of society's leaders. Additionally, there was the hostility between the "German theologians" and the representatives of Scholasticism, which had assumed the form of conflict between Rome and Germany.

The opposition of the Catholic scholars to the growth of ultramontanism could have confined itself to the type of passive resistance which the professors at Tübingen exercised. But under the influence of Döllinger, the intellectual leader of the movement of reaction to the incursion of the "Romans" into Catholic scholarship and the administration of the Church in Germany, it assumed the character of an open battle. The last word on Döllinger's development during these years, which step by step led him from a theological to a dogmatic opposition, has not yet been spoken; there can be no doubt, however, that on the Catholic side there was too much of a tendency to simplify matters. Once Döllinger had become suspicious of the centralizing tendencies of the Romans, which were in line with the aggressive orientation of the Neo-Scholastics, his apprehension of papal absolutism made him increasingly fearful. The *Syllabus* confirmed his fears of the dangers to academic freedom and of the introduction of a medieval theocratic system as an article of faith. He was convinced that the future of Catholicism itself was in danger if there were no change in the behavior of the Church. At the convention of Catholic scholars in 1863 in Munich he collided with the Neo-Scholastics. Now there arose the question of whether the ultramontane faction, disregarding ecclesiastical institutions, was not in fact falsifying the religious ideal of Christianity. But the very virulence of his polemics against the "papal system," which he portrayed as a creation of the Middle Ages, incited the bishops against him, including those who, like Rauscher and Ketteler, also regarded certain forms of Roman centralization as excessive. Thus, open resistance to ultramontanism in Germany remained essentially restricted to the universities.

In France, on the other hand, a group of decided opponents of ultramontanism within the episcopate once again came to the fore during the final years of the Second Empire. It had two different roots. The dean of the theological faculty at the Sorbonne, Monsignor Maret, who identified with the ecclesiological views of Bossuet, was deeply concerned about the absolutist and theocratic manipulations of the neo-ultramontanes. He surrounded himself with a small group of intelligent priests with liberal and moderately Gallican views, and through his close relationship with Napoleon III succeeded in having several of them appointed as bishops. Although the effectiveness of these bishops was limited by the Roman enthusiasm of their clergy and a majority of their flocks, they nonetheless constituted a very intimate association of opponents of Roman policies. They were led by Monsignor Darboy, archbishop of Paris after 1863. Indignant about the behavior "of these strange Catholics whose piety consisted mainly of greeting the Pope from afar in order to insult the bishops near by," Darboy several times, and with a frankness to which Rome was no longer accustomed, informed the Pope of his profound consternation with regard to the interference of the Roman congregations in episcopal administrations. He condemned this as an attempt to introduce in France "the regimen of mission countries."

Raised in a totally different theological climate and having long been cool toward the Bonapartist bishops, the liberal Catholics of the *Correspondant,* who once had seen in ultramontanism the guarantee for the freedom of the Church, now began to move closer to the group around Maret and Darboy. They saw ultramontanism represented and personified in *L'Univers* and the *Civiltà cattolica,* in men, that is, who had not the slightest inkling of the true requirements of modern society and who favored absolutism in Church and society. Even men as devoted to the Holy See as Dupanloup, who more than once had stated his belief in the infallibility of the Pope, now began to fear its final formulation. They feared that it would lead to a consolidation of the positions of the *Syllabus* and other documents which assumed religious-political views incompatible with the modern mind. Thus, the extent of the ultramontane victory in France led to the formation of a new Gallican front, whose most active members were precisely those men who twenty years earlier had been the champions of this victory.

CHAPTER 43

The Vatican Council

Preparation

The decision of Pius IX to convoke a council must be seen from the pastoral perspective of the reaction to naturalism and rationalism which he had pursued since the beginning of his pontificate. As painful and retrogressive the modalities occasionally might be, essentially it was his intention once again to provide Catholic life with a focus on the fundamental events of revelation. Additionally, he intended to undertake the highly necessary adaptation of canon law to the profound changes which had taken place during the past three centuries since the last ecumenical council.

The idea of a council as a cure for the crisis from which the Church was suffering had been suggested to Pius IX as early as 1849, and slowly matured. At the end of 1864 he consulted a number of cardinals, who happened to be in Rome, about the advisability of the matter. In spite of some qualifications, their opinion on the whole was rather positive, and the Pope decided to pursue the issue carefully. He asked about forty bishops, selected from the most important Catholic countries, and a few bishops who held offices in Churches of the Eastern Rite to submit suggestions for an agenda. Gradually he then formed four commissions, which he charged with working out the details of the program. A majority of the Curia, however, was not very enthusiastic about the papal plan, and their reticence caused the Pope to hesitate for more than two years. He was also moved by the not totally unjustified fear that the contrasting tendencies evident in the Church in many areas, such as the question of modern freedoms and the growing Roman centralization, might come to a head at the council. But finally, encouraged by a number of respected bishops, the Pope on 26 June 1867 publicly made known his intention, and one year later he invited to Rome for 8 December 1869 all Catholic bishops and those people who had the right to participate in a council.

During the consultative deliberations, more than one bishop suggested that the council be used to attempt contacts with the separated Christians. This was in part based on the hopes of a return of the Orthodox, which grew out of the changes in the Slavic world and the Near East. Similarly, with respect to the Reformed Churches, the continuation of the Oxford Movement in the Anglo-Saxon countries and the crisis which the progress of liberal Protestants had caused in the German Lutheran Church had occasioned unionist thoughts on all sides. It is true that the Holy See reacted rather reservedly and during the 1860s, especially under the influence of Manning, several times stiffened its attitude. Nevertheless, Pius IX and several of his advisers continued to hope for a return of the separated Christians and they believed that at least in the Near East there were some opportunities which should not be allowed to pass. With this possibility in mind, a letter was directed to all Orthodox bishops in September 1868, in which they were asked to return to Catholic unity in order to be able to participate in the council; a few days later a global letter was sent to Protestants and Anglicans. But this clumsy and double procedure was generally badly received and to us, today, from an ecumenical point of view appears as one of the saddest cases of missed opportunities.

In the Catholic world the announcement of the council quickly intensified the opposition between the currents which for a number of years had been facing one another: Gallicans and liberal Catholics on one side, ultramontanes and opponents of the modern freedom on the other. The selection of the consultants who were supposed to prepare the conciliar decrees — sixty Romans and thirty-six foreigners, almost all of them known for their unequivocally ultramontane and antiliberal views — worried those who had hoped that the council would give the bishops who stood on the periphery the long-awaited opportunity to achieve a limited opening of the Church to modern ideas. Instead they believed that they saw a certain tactic at work: a secret preparation of the council beyond all conflicting debates and only with exclusive consideration of the point of view of the Curia, and then discussionless acceptance by the council fathers of all proposals, worked out beforehand down to the smallest detail. A misunderstood piece of news the "Correspondance de France," which on 6 February 1869 was published in the newspaper of the Jesuits, the *Civiltà cattolica,* seemed to confirm this prognosis by announcing the definition of papal infallibility by acclamation and therefore without any possibility of clarifying the matter through discussion. Reactions were violent, especially in the German-speaking countries and even in the circles which normally could not be accused of harboring any systematic hostility toward Rome. Döllinger, whose hostility to the Curia had grown noticeably during the last several years, under the pseudonym of Janus published a critical and partisan book attacking the primacy of the Pope and the Roman centralization. In France also press polemics appeared, somewhat milder in tone, because the liberal Catholics considered a definition of papal infallibility as inopportune and the ultramontanes viewed it as desirable. In this fashion the problem, initially virtually not intended to be on the program, during the months preceding the council moved into the foreground of activity. Several respected bishops like Monsignor Dechamps, archbishop of Mechelen, and Monsignor Manning, archbishop of Westminster, demanded immediately that the council be utilized solemnly to define the truth of this publicly contested point. Monsignor Dupanloup, on the other hand, after a long silence came out against the definition because he deemed it inopportune. The majority of the German bishops at their annual conference at Fulda in September 1869 also expressed reservations about the future definition of the personal infallibility of the Pope.

Several governments on their part feared decisions of the council concerning civil marriage, secular education, and constitutional freedoms, and were apprehensive over a possible reconfirmation of certain medieval prerogatives of the Church over the civil authority. The request by some bishops, which was received positively by Rome, to make the *Syllabus* of 1864 the basis for council deliberations, could not but intensify such fears. All those in the Church who were afraid of the triumph of the ultramontanes at the council tried to reinforce the suspicions of the governments, hoping thereby to cause diplomatic admonitions and warnings. For a while France considered appointing an ambassador extraordinary for the council as it had done for the Council of Trent, and in April the minister president of Bavaria, Prince Chlodwig zu Hohenlohe-Schillingsfürst, tried to bring about a joint intervention of the European governments; they, however, preferred to barricade themselves behind an attitude of watchful waiting.

Infallibilists and Anti-Infallibilists

The council opened on 8 December 1869 in the presence of about seven hundred bishops, i.e., of more than two-thirds of those entitled to participate. Among them were 60 prelates of Eastern Rites, for the most part from the Near East, and almost 200 fathers from outside of Europe: 121 from America, 49 of these from the United States, 41 from India and the Far East, 18 from Oceania, and 9 from the missions in Africa. It should be noted, however, that while the prelates from the other parts of the world amounted to about one-third of the council, many of them, especially the missionaries, in reality were European, and that with the exception of the bishops of the Eastern Rites there were no native bishops from Asia and Africa. Within this European predominance there was a Latin predominance. There were some significant English-speaking groups (among them the Irish element predominated) and about seventy-five Germans and Austrians, but disregarding the Spaniards and Latin Americans, who comprised about one hundred members, the French constituted about 17 percent of the assembly (for many missionaries hailed from France) and the Italians constituted a whopping 35 percent, so that the French and Italians together amounted to more than half of the council fathers. The overwhelming Italian predominance, which was strongly criticized, interestingly enough had no tactical rationale; it was merely the result of historical circumstances. In antiquity the number of dioceses established in southern and central Italy was high, in more recent times a large part of the Catholic apostolate in the Greek and Turkish islands was entrusted to Italian missionaries, and Italians occupied a large number of the positions in the Curia. The Italian prelates by themselves constituted not only one-third of the assembly, they also provided two-thirds of the consultants and experts, all of the secretaries, and all five presidents; only one important position that of secretary general, was entrusted to a foreigner, to the Austrian Fessler.

The controversies which in the course of 1869 swirled around papal infallibility and especially the clumsy interference of Monsignor Dupanloup in the middle of November soon after the opening of the council resulted in the replacement of national groupings, which had begun in the first few days, with an ideological grouping. On one side stood the fathers who did not doubt, who in fact expected, that the council would again emphasize those principles which in their view in an ideal Christian society had to form the foundation for the relationship between Church and state and who desired a solemn definition of the infallibility of the Pope. Even if they were not in agreement with all of the centralizing steps of the Roman Curia and thought of some manifestations of papal veneration as ludicrous, many father were convinced that the Gallican and Febronian theses which called for a limitation of the papal primacy in favor of the episcopate would be a regression. It would go counter to the old traditions favored by a number of unequivocal statements in Scripture (for example: "Tu es Petrus"), by some formulations stemming from the time of the church Fathers (for example: "Roma locuta est, causa finita est"), and by all of the great Scholastic teachers, from Thomas Aquinas to Bellarmine and Alphonsus Liguori. Confronting some of the difficulties of a historical nature with the living faith of the Church, they were especially impressed by the almost universal agreement of the Church of their time with the thesis of the personal infallibility of the Pope, a concept which in the preceding twenty years had been affirmed by provincial councils several times. Under such circumstances it appeared quite normal to them that controversies which they considered fruitless should be nipped in the bud. Extratheological reasons lent additional weight to the conviction of many prelates. In addition to their veneration of Pius IX, they were convinced that emphasis on the monolithic character of the Roman unity would send non-Catholics to the Church, because they were confused by the hesitation of the Churches separated from Rome or by the contradictions in modern philosophical systems (this aspect was emphasized particularly by the convert Manning). Noticeable also was their endeavor to emphasize the principle of authority as strongly as possible in a world undermined by democratic efforts, which in their eyes were nothing more than a milder form of anarchy, inspired in the main by Protestantism. Finally, given the developing crisis before their eyes, they desired to see an increasingly centralized organization for the offensive and defensive strategy of the Church.

Precisely the same mixture of considerations of a theoretical-doctrinal kind and extratheological factors brought other bishops to the conviction that such plans would be a shock for the traditional constitution of the Church and threaten civil society in its most legitimate aspects. The number of these bishops was relatively small and for this reason they were known as the "minority," but they enjoyed a high prestige because of the sees which they occupied and because of their theological scholarship. Some continued to adhere to the semi-Gallican concept of the ecclesiastical magisterial orifice, the starting point of which was that the Pope could never treat a question of doctrine independently from ratification by the episcopate. The influence of the tradition of Bossuet, the episcopal mentality passed down from the Febronian theologians and the canonists of the preceding century, historical difficulties such as the condemnation of Pope Honorius, an archaic theological attitude which clung too much to the sources and had little understanding for dogmatic developments, led them to the conclusion that either the Pope did not possess the privilege of personal infallibility or that the problem at best was still obscure and its treatment therefore premature.

More widespread seemed to be the legitimate, albeit occasionally exaggerated worry about the second element in the divine structure of the ecclesiastical hierarchy. The proposed definition of the infallibility of the Pope appeared to many fathers as the separation of a partial aspect from an indivisible whole, the effect of which would result in the virtual abolition of the episcopate. The way in which the council had been prepared seemed to justify their apprehensions. Did the agenda, determined by the Pope and, in contrast to the Council of Trent, not by the fathers, sufficiently respect their freedom of action? And could the bishops expect to play more than the role of extras in a scene staged in advance by the Curia?

There was additional concern about the fact that several of the best known supporters of the definition wanted to include in the subject area of the infallibility of the Church, i.e., of the Pope, a number of "Catholic truths" which did not belong to the *depositum fidei* and had only indirect connection with it. This was particularly the case in the religious-political area. Many people indeed noted that the definition of papal infallibility in the extensive form suggested by its proponents would strengthen the authority of such documents as the bull *Unam sanctam,* the declaration of Sixtus V concerning the right to depose sovereigns, and especially the *Syllabus,* whose judgments were a special burden for the council. Both European and American newspapers were extensive witnesses to this concern. Besides, the way in which the question of infallibility was being dealt with by the ultramontane papers was enough to justify the belief of those who were convinced "that it was the intention to declare the Pope infallible in matters of faith in order to give him the appearance of infallibility in other matters as well" (Leroy-Beaulieu). It was expected that the governments would not tolerate such a course of events without voicing their opposition, but of course this would be to the disadvantage of the local Churches. Beyond the question of immediate tactics there was also a question of principle. It was raised by those who believed that the political future belonged to the liberal institutions, and that the Church, as long as it showed itself as a defender of an autocratic authoritarianism, stood to lose everything. Finally, there were the ecumenical aspects: the proposed definition would add to the difficulties of establishing closer relations with the separated brethren, especially of the Christians in the East; it would promote the aggressiveness of certain Protestants; and could even provide a new schism in the intellectual circles of Germany which were strongly impressed by Döllinger's arguments.

If the feeling of discontent which showed itself at the beginning of the council rapidly resulted in an organized opposition, this was in part the result of some misunderstandings, but to an overwhelming degree it was the result of a regrettable maneuver of the infallibilists. For the purpose of preparing the election of the dogmatic commission, the so-called *deputatio de fide,* which was to deal with the question of papal infallibility, two different election committees had been formed: one by Dupanloup, the other one by Manning. The latter insisted on the exclusion from the deputation of all fathers who were suspected of opposing the definition. A list compiled under his supervision and approved by one of the council presidents was distributed to the fathers. For the most part they had no personal knowledge of the other members of the council and on 14 December elected the proposed members in good faith. This procedure, which excluded from the deputation such competent men as Cardinal Rauscher and Monsignor Hefele, the learned author of the *Conciliengeschichte,* was a gross mistake. It put an end to the possibility of a dialogue between the two opposing positions and by its partisanship angered the members of the minority who, erroneously, believed that this maneuver by Manning's group had been engineered by the Curia. Even more, it created the impression outside of the assembly that the elections had only been a guise. From this moment on there were many who began to doubt the freedom of the council.

First Council Debates

After three weeks of exhausting formalities, the discussion concerning the first constitutional draft "against the many errors stemming from modern rationalism" was begun on 28 December. It immediately became the object of strong criticism. To many fathers it was obscure, insufficiently pastoral and too aggressive, and went far beyond the points that had been discussed freely by the theologians. Criticism originated both from the infallibilists and the minority, an advantageous fact in that it gave hope that the council would proceed less inhibitedly than had been feared. After six sessions of debate, the presidents announced on 10 January that the schema was being returned to the deputies for revision. Some men were astonished that the decision was made without prior advice from the assembly, which in its majority probably would have adopted the draft with only minor changes. That this was not done shows clearly that the Roman leaders — contrary to the intention of which they were accused even before the opening of the council were far from exploiting the obedient majority and that they tried to achieve the best possible result even at the cost of some humiliations.

In order to occupy the fathers during the time which the revision of the first doctrinal schema required, discussions were begun on the schemata concerning church discipline and the adaptation of canon law. Many of the fathers believed that this adaptation to the new circumstances of the nineteenth century was the principal task of the council. For this purpose, twenty-eight schemata or draft proposals had come from the disciplinary commission, even though most of them were of a picayune nature and failed to display any openness to the future or any pastoral imagination in the search for truly new formulations; eighteen additional ones had been worked out by the commission dealing with the religious orders, which thanks to the leadership of its authoritarian and effective president, Cardinal Bizzarri, had done fruitful work. Furthermore, the preparatory commission for the missions and the Churches of the Eastern Rite had prepared three schemata and the commission for political-ecclesiastical problems had worked out eighteen schemata which concerned topics of genuine interest and often were more timely than the ones which had been prepared by the commission for church discipline. Only a few of the eighty-seven schemata were distributed to the fathers during the council and ultimately there was not enough time to pass even one of them.

For an entire month, beginning on 14 January, the first four schemata were debated. Because no time limit existed, many fathers were tempted to lose themselves in details and to discuss purely local problems. A number of interjections were of interest, however. Some of the Eastern bishops, for example, raised the question, one which did not seem to have occurred to anyone, as to what extent the disciplinary schemata were relevant to the Eastern Churches. Once again it was realized that seemingly quite neutral questions could involve ecclesiology. This became even more evident in the course of the discussions of the fourth project, dealing with the expediency of the drawing up of a universal catechism which was to take the place of the numerous diocesan catechisms: the proposal, which had not originated with the Roman Curia, was viewed as a sign of mistrust of the bishops.

The dissatisfaction of many fathers with this proposal was aggravated by the distribution on 21 January of the constitutional draft *"De Ecclesia Christi."* The draft had its good qualities — the patristic sources of its chief author, Clemens Schrader, were clearly discernible — but it also had regrettable weaknesses, especially in the disproportional number of passages devoted to the episcopate and to the papacy, a deficiency which was noted with regret even by some members of the majority. The final chapters as well, concerning the relationship between Church and state, were rejected by many because of strongly theocratic views offensive to the modern mind.

Work on the schema on rationalism, which had been revised by Kleutgen, was resumed on March 18, after the sessions had been interrupted for three weeks to make needed improvements in the acoustics. The new version was favorably received by the fathers, and only small details needed to be ironed out. Aside from a violent incident, caused by the passionate remarks of Monsignor Stroßmayer, and some complaints about the unseemly hurry with which ballots were taken on requests for amendments, the discussions took place in an atmosphere of equanimity. On 24 April the council, despite the last-minute hesitation of the most mistrustful of the minority, solemnly and unanimously approved the first dogmatic document, the constitution *Dei Filius*. It opposed pantheism, materialism, and modern rationalism with a compact and enlightened presentation of the Catholic doctrine concerning God, revelation, and the faith. For almost a century it was to be the basis of standard theological textbooks.

Agitation concerning Papal Infallibility

While inside the council auditorium texts were prudently debated which caused little excitement, outside of it the discussions concerning infallibility, which soon became the center of attention, were in full sway. During the last days of December, Manning, Dechamps, and some German-speaking bishops began to circulate a petition which asked the Pope to put the item on the council agenda. The preparatory commission, however, was not disposed to placing the issue on the agenda itself. During January the petition was signed by more than four-hundred and fifty people.

This maneuver, organized by a group acting independently from the Curia, was the occasion for the opponents of the definition to organize resistance from among splinter groups which had not yet clearly articulated their views. Monsignor Dupanloup labored under the illusion that his appearance alone would suffice to make him the center of the various discontented groups, but even the feverish activity in which he plunged himself after his arrival in Rome had only very limited success. The actual leader of the minority was a layman, John Acton. As a historian he shared with his teacher Döllinger the objections to the new proposed dogma, but even more than Döllinger he feared the potential indirect consequences on the future development of Catholicism in a society whose preoccupation with the idea of freedom was growing. The recent publication of Acton's correspondence with Döllinger has confirmed the assertions of the English diplomat Odo Russell concerning the preeminent role played by the young English lord in the organization of the council minority. Thanks to his numerous international connections and his linguistic abilities he was largely responsible for the fact that at the very beginning of the council the most important leaders of the opposition, many of whom hardly knew one another, were brought together. His acquaintance with parliamentary procedure allowed him to point out to them the possibility of joint action, suggest several operations to them, draw their attention to several intrigues which were being hatched in the opposing camp, supply them with historical documents for the buttressing of their position, and play the role of mediator between the leaders of the minority and several foreign governments. It was due to his initiative that together with Archbishop Haynald — a member of the Hungarian House of Lords and therefore also familiar with parliamentary practices — an international committee was formed which was to guarantee the collaboration of the various opposition groups. Several times a week it served as a meeting place for about ten Austrian, German, French, British, Italian, and American bishops. The committee circulated a counterpetition which demanded from the Pope that he forego the definition of his infallibility. The counterproposal garnered 136 signatures, i.e., one-fifth of the assembled fathers. It did not, however, prevent Pius IX from deciding on 1 March to include a formal definition of the infallibility of the Pope in the draft of the "Dogmatic Constitution of the Church."

The leaders of the minority did not confine themselves to increased personal contacts with those fathers whom they hoped to win for their cause. Convinced of the disastrous consequences for the Church of the proposed definition, and believing that they were justified in using all possible means of preventing it, some of them thought it advisable to mobilize public opinion in the hope that it would exert the necessary pressure on the council leaders from the outside. Several Roman salons turned into veritable snake pits of intrigue in the service of this or that view, for the proponents of the definition quickly, with the agreement of the Vatican, imitated the tactics of their opponents. But if in this still very aristocratic society the salons occupied a very important place, the newspapers constituted an even more potent instrument. Both camps tried to enlist the press, especially as the interest of the public in the affairs of the council had become evident.

Among the journalist polemics, particularly those of Louis Veuillot in favor of the definition and those of Monsignor Dupanloup in opposition to it, the "Roman Letters" assumed a special place. Döllinger published them in the *Allgemeine Zeitung* of Augsburg under the pseudonym of Quirinus. As a kind of council chronicle they were designed, by way of a tendentious depiction of participants and events, to discredit from the beginning all the decisions at which the assembly might arrive. Acton supplied Döllinger with the necessary information, which he received from some bishops who did not consider the obligation of secrecy, which the Pope had unilaterally decreed, as binding.

The feuds of the press were augmented on both sides by continuing publications of brochures which, like those of Dechamps or Gratry, were identified by name, but which more often remained anonymous. There were also attempts by some members of the minority to enlist the support of the governments in Vienna, Munich, London, and especially Paris. Everyone was aware of the tremendous weight of Napoleon III, whose military and diplomatic support was absolutely essential for the survival of the remnants of the Pope's temporal power. The various attempts by some bishops to cause their governments to intervene were a failure with respect to placing the item of papal infallibility on the agenda, but it can justifiably be assumed that they were not quite without influence. Cardinal Antonelli was in any case concerned with the matter, but now the attention of several members of the Curia and a number of the majority moderates was drawn to the influence which the agitation occasioned by the proposed definition had in the secular world on the discussions concerning the legitimacy of modern freedoms and the right of the Church to intervene in civil affairs. An effort was made to restrict the question of infallibility to the strictly doctrinal area in order to dispel the worries of any who were afraid that, once the Pope was acknowledged as infallible, he would be in the position, as one of them said, "in the future to decree [as infallible] any syllabus, even the most controvertible one."

With public and governmental concern growing on the fringe of the council, the assembly continued its work; but it soon became clear that, considering the speed with which progress was made, the chapter dealing with the primacy and the infallibility of the Pope would reach the discussion stage in the following spring at the earliest. Therefore, new petitions in March demanded that this chapter, which greatly disturbed the council, be dealt with immediately after the conclusion of the discussion on the constitution concerning rationalism. Although three out of the five council presidents were reluctant to do so because they did not wish to anger the minority, Pius IX, whose irritation with the opposition was growing, decided in favor of the petition.

The Constitution *Pastor Aeternus*

In order to gloss over the extraordinary procedure involved in giving chapter 11 priority, it was decided to reformulate it in such a way that it became a small constitution, especially devoted to the Pope. The discussion was opened on 13 May by the moderate expert opinion of Monsignor Pie. The general discussion, even at this early stage, essentially reduced itself to a debate of the expediency of the definition and in places was conducted with great passion. After about fifteen sessions, in which the presentations of Manning and Dechamps and the criticisms of Hefele, Stroßmayer, Maret, and Darboy stood out, the assembly proceeded to a discussion of the details of the text. It was especially concerned with the fourth chapter, which contained a definition of papal infallibility which the commission had already improved, but which failed to take sufficient account of the legitimate role of the episcopate, in addition to the Pope and in conjunction with him, as part of the supreme magisterial office of the Church. Fifty-seven members addressed the measure, presenting theological arguments and historical difficulties, and pointing up the practical advantages and disadvantages of a definition under the prevailing conditions. These often tiring debates, which took place in increasingly unbearably hot weather, at least permitted more precise formulations and removed some obstacles.

In the meantime the negotiations in the hallways outside of the auditorium had grown in intensity, and it was hoped that a compromise formula could be found which would prevent the divisions within the assembly from becoming known to the public. Indeed, many defenders of infallibility in the meantime had acquired a better grasp of the complexity of the problem and the necessity of greater differentiation, while the opponents learned that the faith of the Church in this matter was broader and firmer than many of them had thought at the beginning. But primarily the greatest part of the fathers basically consisted of moderates for whom all of the agitation was painful and deeply worrisome. Far from being intent on the destruction of the opponents, they desired only to find a middle ground on which a compromise was possible. This was especially true for the majority of the Italians, who constituted one-third of the council participants and who had not taken a definite position in the initial maneuvering to include the infallibility issue on the agenda. By dint of their numbers they lent decisive support to the informal compromise faction. This group, conciliatory from the outset, finally succeeded in having a more flexible formula accepted, which occupied a middle ground between the neo-ultramontane and the anti-Curial extremists, and which allowed for adjustments in the future. It is quite likely that an even greater portion of the minority would have voted for the ultimately adopted solution if Pius IX, who in the course of the last months had intervened increasingly openly in favor of the definition, had not been so intransigent.

Whatever the extent of his personal responsibility, it is a fact that the attempts at achieving a reconciliation with the opponents failed, in spite of the good impression made by the summary which Monsignor Gasser had prepared in the name of the theological commission. It was an authorized commentary which even today is of essential importance in grasping the nuances of the council text. In the preliminary balloting, 451 *placet* votes were cast, together with 88 *non placet* and 62 *placet juxta modum* votes. Hoping that the size of the opposition would provide a reconsideration, the minority made a final appeal to Pius IX in order to obtain the elimination of a controverted expression in the canon concerning papal primacy and the addition of a few words in the definition of the infallibility of the Pope which would imply the close cooperation of the Pope with the Church as a whole. But Pius IX, who was pressured in the opposite direction by the extremists of the majority, proved unyielding and inflexible. For this reason about sixty bishops decided to leave Rome before the final vote in order to avoid having to cast their *non placet* in front of a Pope who was personally affected by the issue. The other members of the minority believed that, despite the inclusion of an unfortunate phrase which designated the Pope infallible "ex sese, non autem ex consensu Ecclesiae" — designed to dispel the slightest suspicion of Gallicanism — the most serious objections had been removed as a result of the various textual improvements and Monsignor Gasser's commentary. They decided to approve the final version, which on 18 July was solemnly and almost unanimously passed by the members present.

During the subsequent weeks the council continued its work at a slower pace; because of the heat and of the Franco-Prussian War, most of the fathers left Rome during the summer. The occupation of Rome by Italian troops on 20 September terminated the council, and on 20 October the Pope announced its adjournment sine die.

The end of the debates, however, did not produce an immediate acquiescence. Agitation continued for some time and there occurred some regrettable apostasies, especially in the German-speaking countries. Led by university professors who took their cue from Döllinger, the so-called Old Catholic schism came into existence. Among the bishops of the minority some, like Hefele and Stroßmayer, hesitated for a while, but ultimately none of them denied his approval of the new dogma.

CHAPTER 44

The Rise of the Old Catholic Community

The internal Catholic protest movement against the dogma of the universal episcopate and the infallibility of the Pope spread after the summer of 1870, especially
in Germany and Switzerland. It experienced several stages, and contrary to the
initial intentions of its leaders culminated in the establishment of its own Church.
The nucleus was formed by the university theology professors Döllinger, Johannes
Friedrich, and J. A. Messmer of Munich, G. J. Hilgers, F. P. Knoodt, J. Langen, and
Franz Heinrich Reusch of Bonn, Johann Baptist Baltzer, Joseph Hubert Reinkens,
and T. Weber of Breslau, A. Menzel and Friedrich Michelis of Braunsberg, Eduard
Herzog of Lucerne, and a layman, the Prague canonist and legal historian J. F.
von Schulte. Sectarian radicalism, which had characterized German Catholicism,
was at first alien to the professors. They regarded themselves as conservatives
adhering to the old Catholic faith in the face of erroneous innovations; some of
them had been close to Günther's theology.

At the council, primarily historical objections had been raised against the doctrine of infallibility and the way it was dealt with. The protesting theologians were
now joined by some noted historians who as Catholics in a liberal age had earned
their right to academic equality. Among them were F. W. Kampschulte and C. A.
von Cornelius with his students A. von Druffel, M. Ritter, and F. Stieve.

The professors were joined virtually only by academicians and middle-class citizens. Some of them were guided by the same religious and scholarly impulses,
others more by a religious liberalism which had begun to split away from the
Church even before 1870. This burdened the movement as much as the nationalism of many of its members which reflected the climate of the founding of the
German Empire. Old Catholicism was and remained an elitist movement; in the
1870s it reached its peak in Germany with about sixty thousand members. After
all, the Catholic masses and their organizations had contributed to the development which culminated in the Vatican Council; after the annexation of the Papal
State they felt even more impelled to stand by the imperiled Pope. The political
leaders, who prior to 1869 had warned against the dogma, also made their peace
with the decrees of the council.

In August 1870 more than one thousand three hundred Rhenish Catholics
protested against the council; in Nuremberg thirty-two professors appealed to
an "ecumenical council, true and free, and therefore to be held not in Italy but on
this side of the Alps." Expectations of support by the episcopate diminished when
at the end of August the majority in Fulda agreed on a pastoral letter, temperately
defending council and dogma; they disappeared totally only in April 1871, when
Hefele as the last German bishop published the council decrees.

The agitation over council and dogma, in which the entire liberal press took the
side of the opponents, experienced a renewed intensification after the temporary
diversion of the Franco-German War. The reason was that several bishops after the
fall of 1870 proceeded against the opponents of the council by withholding the
missio canonica, suspension, excommunication, and denial of the sacraments.
The victims appealed to the state for assistance. The governments granted them

protection and guaranteed them the continuation of temporal and ecclesiastical offices; the ensuing feud with the bishops led to the *Kulturkampf*.

In September 1870 the first congress of Old Catholics was held in Munich with three hundred delegates from Germany, Switzerland, and Austria. The participation of guests from the Orthodox and Anglican Churches and the small Utrecht Church signified not only the joint opposition to Rome which the Vatican Council had intensified, but also a novel ecumenical content which Döllinger and his friends consciously promoted by appealing to the common Christian tradition of old. Döllinger's program underscored the conservative nature of the protest movement and claimed for it the right to continued equal membership in the Catholic Church. Döllinger passionately advised against division, and he himself never formally joined the Old Catholic Church. Schulte, Friedrich, Michelis, and Reinkens, on the other hand, called for the establishment of an emergency community, and the majority of the congress participants agreed with them.

In Rome, the momentous decision, which, like the whole movement, confirmed old prejudices against the German professors, determined future development. At first local Catholic Associations were formed. The Second Congress in 1872 in Cologne, which officially adopted the name "Old Catholic," decided to establish regular pastoral care and appointed a commission for the preparation of the election of a bishop. On 14 June 1871 the Breslau professor Joseph Hubert Reinkens was chosen. He was consecrated by a bishop of the Utrecht Church and thus entered into the apostolic succession.

Reinkens, placed under interdict by Pius IX, established an episcopal administration in Bonn, assisted by Reusch as vicar general. He was acknowledged as a Catholic bishop by Prussia, Baden, and Hessen-Darmstadt; legislation passed in these states during the *Kulturkampf* assured the Old Catholics of their share of Catholic Church property and use of Catholic churches. Only to the extent that the *Kulturkampf* was acknowledged as a mistake and was dismantled after 1878 did the support of the states flag; earlier than other proponents of the *Kulturkampf*, Bismarck recognized that as an ally against Rome Old Catholicism was too weak.

The constitution drafted by Schulte according to old Christian models granted legislative powers and the right to elect bishops to the synods, formed of representatives of the clergy and laymen. After approval by the Third Congress in 1873 in Constance, it was ratified by the first synod in 1874 in Bonn. The synods of the subsequent years with respect to doctrine remained based on the undivided Church of the first millennium; tempered and timely reforms were introduced into worship and after 1880 German was employed in the liturgy of the Mass. Against the will of Reinkens, Reusch and other fellow champions, liberal forces in 1879 succeeded in abolishing celibacy.

In Switzerland, where the conditions were particularly favorable, Reinkens and Michelis actively participated in the establishment of a Church. In 1875 the first synod gathered in Olten and established the "Christ Catholic Church of Switzerland." In doctrine it followed the German model, in its constitution it was more democratic. In 1876 Eduard Herzog was elected bishop and during almost fifty years of work established a Church oriented to Bible and Eucharist. The theological university established in 1874 in Berne by the government as an instrument in the *Kulturkampf*, with Herzog's authoritative assistance grew into a considerable theological center which after the turn of the century was influential far beyond the borders of Switzerland. The reason for this was that the German leadership came to an end with the expiration of the outstanding scholarship of that generation. All attempts to maintain the theological faculty at Bonn, which, except for one member, was totally Old Catholic, failed; after the death of Reusch (1900) and Langen (1901) the remaining chairs were filled again with Catholics.

In Austria, where the government remained passive and where the bishops, especially Rauscher, avoided a confrontation by extremely lenient treatment, the protest movement developed very slowly. After 1872 there existed four Old Catholic communities, to be officially recognized by the state in 1877. An increase occurred during the 1890s in consequence of the more nationally than religiously inspired Away-from-Rome Movement. In 1879 its first synod took place and it adopted the German patterns. After 1881 the small Church, whose constitution was also drafted by Schulte, was guided by an episcopal administrator.

The Old Catholic bishoprics and the Utrecht Church, which prior to 1870 had been totally isolated, in 1889 formed the Union of Utrecht. It is an autonomous union of national Churches free from Rome, whose honorary primate is the archbishop of Utrecht. A joint declaration again accepted the faith of the first millennium and the kind of Roman primacy which then prevailed. It repeated the protest against the dogmas of 1854 and 1870, as well as its readiness for the "removal of the differences existing since the schism." Döllinger's internationally recognized scholarship and his ecumenical efforts in 1874–75 resulted in the Bonn conferences of union consisting of Old Catholic, Russian Orthodox, and Anglican theologians. In the nineteenth century they were a bold attempt at interdenominational theological discussions and thus a precursor to ecumenism, in the service of which the future international congresses of Old Catholics placed themselves. But the practical result of the conferences was small; they suffered from their small basis and from the resentful and antiecumenical polemics against Rome, which for a long time characterized Old Catholicism.

Book Nine

THE CHURCH IN
THE INDUSTRIAL AGE

Translated by Margit Resch

Part One

The Problem of Adapting
to the Modern World

I N T R O D U C T I O N

The World Plan of Leo XIII:
Goals and Methods

Oskar Köhler

The Conclave

The conclave after the death of Pius IX meant a turning point in the history of papal elections because, for the first time, the head of the Catholic Church was to be elected after the factual loss of the *Patrimonium Petri.* The late Pope had explicitly indicated his choice as to the election site. The alternative was to meet in Rome or in a foreign country. During the first congregation (8 February 1878), a minority of only eight cardinals voted for Rome as the election site. The following day, Cardinal di Pietro indicated in a speech that, even though no foreign power had issued an invitation, Italy had been given a guarantee of nonintervention. The cardinal had been nuncio in Lisbon and belonged to the politically "liberal" group of the College of Cardinals. When the matter was put to the vote, five cardinals voted for Spain and thirty-two for Rome.

Italy was not interested in it, despite radical efforts to expel the Pope from Rome. The guarantee was, therefore, trustworthy. The foreign powers had, for different reasons, an interest in a smooth transition and a politically obliging successor to the Holy See. Therefore, the new situation of the Catholic Church was distinctive in world history because the conclave played a minor role this time in diplomatic correspondence. A conciliatory Pope was wanted. Even the "Catholic powers," who stood in the background, would consider the idea of exercising the right of exclusion only if a disciple of Pius IX's politics were to be elected.

Did the Curia assess the situation correctly when discussing whether the election should take place outside of Italy? Four years after his election and after the riots which occurred one night in 1881 during the transferal of Pius IX's body from Saint Peter's to S. Lorenzo fuori le Mura, the new Pope would discuss with a delegate from the court in Vienna whether Trent or Salzburg could offer him asylum. He received an invitation which implied, however, that he should not accept it (1882). The alternative of having the papal elections in Rome or in a foreign country, which was apparently deemed serious on 8 February 1878, turned out to be no alternative. One could continue to reject the Italian guarantee law of 13 May 1871, but one had to live with it and worry that it was here to stay.

On 18 February sixty of the sixty-four cardinals moved into the Vatican for the conclave. Twenty-five of them were non-Italians, in accord with the ecclesiastical world plan of Pius IX. The preparatory congregation had decided on 10 February to elect an Italian; probably the only possible solution in this situation. The insinuation in Paris that a non-Italian, but certainly not a German, could be elected met with no support in Vienna. Pius IX had chosen the cardinals for the thirty-five positions created since 1868 mainly from the zealots. But even they tended to lean toward a man who would be capable of easing the political and theological tensions which had increased during the previous pontificate. Due to the efforts of Cardinal Bartolini, the conclave's leading member, the conclave was able to focus quickly on one candidate. Gioacchino Vincenzo Pecci had been bishop in Perugia since 1846 (cardinal since 1853). During the lifetime of Pius IX, Pecci had moved up to a promising position within the papacy because he was regarded as the representative of the moderate line. However, he was not allowed to enter Rome until Antonelli died. Pecci's competitor, Cardinal Bilio, had been close to Pius IX and had participated in drafting the *Syllabus.* He had, apparently, been chosen by Pius to be his successor. But because of Bartolini's attitude, the intransigents were unable to agree upon a candidate from their midst, and Bilio was threatened with a French and Spanish veto. The candidate of the "liberal faction" was Cardinal Franchi. He had become a legate to Spain in 1850, nuncio in 1871, and was respected in matters related to Church policies. His side was taken by the Spanish cardinals, in accordance with their government. Bartolini was able to win their votes for Pecci (Franchi was appointed secretary of state on 5 March 1878, but he died that August).

On the morning of 20 February, Pecci was elected Pope with 44 votes, a two-thirds majority. So far, this was the shortest papal election, a few hours shorter than that of Pius IX.

The new Pope chose his name after Leo XII (1823–29), to whom he was grateful for furthering his studies at the Roman seminary. Observers felt he indicated his program in the fact that he did not call himself Gregory or Pius.

Leo XIII did not deliver the benediction *urbi et orbi* from the outer loggia toward the Saint Peter's Square but toward the Basilica. There were indications that the problem of relations between the Church and the postrevolutionary world articulated itself most strongly in the Holy City: festive illuminations stood in contrast to protest demonstrations. This was true also during the coronation (3 March), held in the Sistine Chapel and not in St. Peter's because the Italian authorities could not or would not guarantee security. The Pope's choice of a name inspired the mockery, "Non è Pio, non è Clemente, Leone senza dente." Leo sent individual inaugural letters to Catholic as well as non-Catholic heads of state in which he indicated his desire to settle disputes. The Italian government was ignored and in turn did not recognize the new Pope officially.

Despite the strong positive response of the world to Leo XIII's election, it is questionable whether the Catholic Church really began "to develop into a great world power which politics had to take into account." Above all, Catholicism certainly had to incorporate domestic politics, especially as long as it was capable of establishing itself as a social group. But it was the goal of the Pope, sixty-eight years old at his coronation, to present the Catholic Church and the papacy to all of mankind as *the* "great world power" with an intellectual and spiritual mission.

The Career of Gioacchino Pecci

Gioacchino was born on 2 March 1810, the son of Colonel Lodovico Pecci. The bishop of Anagni was his godfather. Together with his older brother Giuseppe, he attended the Jesuit school in Viterbo from 1818 on. After his graduation with honors in 1824, he studied rhetoric, philosophy, and theology at the Roman seminary which Leo XII had just returned to the Jesuits (among his teachers were Perrone and Patrizi). His brother entered the *Society of Jesus* the same year. It was in accord with his talents that Gioacchino Pecci, during the jubilee in 1825, was allowed to head a delegation to the protector Leo XII and deliver a Latin address of gratitude. As was in keeping with someone who had a church career in mind, Gioacchino Pecci studied law at the *Accademia dei nobili.* He concluded his doctoral studies in 1837 with the remarkable topic of appeals to the Pope. The same year, Cardinal Odescalchi ordained the promising young man to the priesthood. Pecci had found influential patrons in Cardinal J. A. Sala, in Cardinal Bartolomeo Pacca, and in Secretary of State Lambruschini.

The year of his ordination, the twenty-seven-year-old Pecci was appointed domestic prelate by Gregory XVI and given three offices, one of which was consultant at the Congregation of the Council.

The nunciature in Belgium was Gioacchino Pecci's first failure (1843–46). The task demanded too much from the scarcely thirty-three-year-old man, despite his efforts to adjust to the situation he faced. After all, he had acquired his experience under totally different circumstances. In Belgium, the understanding, developed since the nation's founding between so-called Liberals, the liberal Catholics, and the moderate ultramontanes, began to crumble. Pecci's predecessor, who had been transferred to Paris, knew very well how to maneuver in this terrain and had been on good terms with Prime Minister Nothomb. When Nothomb was overthrown by the Conservatives in 1845, he blamed the new nuncio. Pecci's generally fine relationship with Leopold I and the royal family had its drawbacks because the conservative attitude of the monarch was not the only one in the web of political forces. This prompted the ultramontane clergy to accuse the nuncio of opportunism. The fact that Pecci did not avoid Vincenzo Gioberti, who was living in Brussels at the time, pleased neither the liberals nor the clergy. It was even more difficult for the nuncio to get along with the University of Louvain, which was Catholic but not papal. During this time, the confrontation of the ontologists and the representatives of philosophical traditionalism with the Scholastic renaissance began to develop at the university, and its leading publication was opposed by the Jesuits. By demand of the royal court, Archbishop Pecci was recalled in 1846 because he had supported the episcopate against the King in the question of the university's examination commission.

One had to have a great deal of imagination to predict the tiara for the failing nuncio. In January 1846 he was given the bishopric of Perugia, located "in remote tranquility" (Schmidlin). He was honored with the cardinalate *in petto* in 1853. It is not without reason that we call Gioacchino Pecci an outstanding bishop who was especially concerned with the education of his clergy (which includes the founding of the Academy of Saint Thomas). He intensified pastoral work through the establishment of missions and he furthered charitable institutions through his strong administrative talents. As a result of such activities, he would hardly have received emphasis in Italian Church history. His decisive opposition to the revolutionary movement (1848, destruction of the papal castle) and to the Piedmontese regime (established 1860 in Perugia) shows a dedicated bishop, who had the same experiences as his fellow bishops. Pecci simply expressed the general ecclesiastical conviction in his pastoral letter of 12 February 1860, when he wrote that the time before Constantine the Great was a legitimate epoch, "because the highest spiritual power of the papacy carried the seed of secular power from its inception." Though he did not even enjoy the favor of Pius IX, Bishop Pecci was also instrumental in the efforts which brought about the *Syllabus*. A characteristic new tone, however, was sounded in the pastoral letters of 1874–77, which maintain that a reconciliation between the Church and modern culture, provided modern culture is understood correctly, is possible and desirable. The letters spoke of human progress, e.g., relaxation of the penal code, and they praised technological accomplishments.

Long before such demonstration of insight, however, Cardinal Giacomo Antonelli, secretary of state since 1850, had put the bishop of Perugia on the list of men within the hierarchy who seemed suspect to him. Antonelli did not even allow Pecci to venture to suburbanized Albano. His attempt to do so indicated that he did not possess the kind of nature which would be satisfied with the ecclesiastical duties facing him in Perugia. On the other hand, one can conclude from Antonelli's opposition that he sensed in Pecci an important personality and opponent of his politics. After Antonelli's death, Pius IX, who had to reckon with his own death, appointed Cardinal Pecci camerlengo on 21 September 1877. Through this gesture, the Pope documented his evaluation of the man from Perugia and his confidence that Pecci possessed the skills necessary to meet the danger of the interregnum. The appointment somewhat diminished the feasibility of Pecci's becoming Pope because, traditionally, the camerlengo has virtually no chance in the conclave. Gioacchino Pecci lived in Umbria more than thirty-one years.

The Pontificate

Pope Leo XIII led the Catholic Church into a world which had risen from revolution. With an attitude which can only adequately be termed "optimistic," he attempted to reconcile an uncompromised tradition with the modern spirit. One may say that he opened up a new epoch in the history of the Catholic Church and set a precedent with courage deeply rooted in faith, without which his successors to the see of Saint Peter would not have been conceivable.

On the other hand, it should be noted that the image of Leo XIII in Catholicism, as it was passed on in popular and in scholarly history, was instilled with success by some sort of pressure, which may be informative about the situation and historical self-awareness of Catholics after this pontificate. "Peace Pope" and "Pope of the Workers" are the two most significant appositions crystallizing the tradition of his image. Placed between Pius IX, Pope of the *Syllabus,* and Pius X, Pope of the Borromeo encyclical, Leo XIII is historically illuminated in a fashion which does not correspond to the reality of the concluding *Kulturkampf.* Josef Schmidlin characterized this pontificate more comprehensively: After "the harmony between the two spheres [Church and culture] dissipated, and after both were alienated from each other because of the polemical attitude toward modern philosophical accomplishments under the papacy of Pius and Gregory, the progressive peace Pope considered it his foremost task to restore a close union and understanding to the realm of ideas" and to re-build a "Christian *Weltanschauung"* based on speculative reason and positive history. In his scholarly writings, he was supposed to have developed in a unique way "the governmental program of gain and conciliation, which means Christianization of modern life and modernization of Christian life," a program which he outlined in his inaugural encyclical. "With inner ties he chained the modern world again to the tiara" and strengthened the moral greatness and authority of the papacy even more "than the medieval *dominium temporale* had been able to do" and more than the "anti-revolutionary reactive faction" was intending to do. J. Schmidlin speaks about the "indestructible accomplishment of Leo's pontificate," which "was to imprint upon the twentieth century his domination of modern man and mankind's reconciliation with the Church." Fernand Hayward, considered the reconciliation of Catholicism with the age, without the abandonment of Catholic teachings, to be the hallmark of this pontificate. Such evaluations, like most others from the first half of the twentieth century, have their roots in the obvious need of a group to escape isolation while remaining true to itself and while having to live within the confines of a society to which it belongs but to which, in the final analysis, it cannot belong. Leo XIII appeared to be the Pope who had created this possibility which seemed so vital that, to a large extent, its realization had to be historically verified. There are also considerations, however, usually presented as qualifications, which delve deeply into the problems of this pontificate. Wilhelm Schwer, who dealt with the social teachings of Leo XIII, noted that the Pope, for quite some time, tended "to attribute all material progress to Christian and ecclesiastical influences, more than a precise analysis of the participating forces will permit." This insinuates more than an incidental error in historical interpretation.

Leo XIII was a political Pope and it is, therefore, correct to say that he enjoys a position among the "masters of politics." To be sure, he was fortunate that Bismarck himself had an interest in terminating the *Kulturkampf* in Germany. The political chance had to be taken advantage of and had to be pursued to its very end with determination and skill. In so doing, papal politics could not deal exclusively with Bismarck but also had to take into account the ideas of the German episcopate and those of the Center Party, the latter not seeing itself as an extension of the Curia. There is no question about the personal credit due to Leo XIII for the termination of the *Kulturkampf.* In Switzerland, the relatively limited *Kulturkampf* was essentially ended at the onset of the pontificate, thanks to the election victories of the Conservatives and the cooperation of moderate Liberals. After 1883, only the Geneva question and the nomination to the bishopric of Basel-Solothurn had to be settled; but even that was not possible without compromise. In Belgium, however, at the beginning of his administration, Leo XIII had to face the severe school conflict, and as a result of his intention to avoid intensification, differences with the Belgian episcopate emerged. In this case, success was due, first of all, to the Belgian Catholics, who, strengthened by their devotion to the Pope, brought about a devastating defeat for the Liberals in the elections of 1884. But the style in which diplomatic relations were resumed in 1885, after they had been discontinued in 1880, was typical for the polite ways of Leo XIII. Much more difficult was the task facing the Pope in Spain. The problem was not so much the various governments during the era of the Spanish "restoration," which vacillated between liberal-conservative and moderate left; nor the tensions which resulted from the censorship of text books, and the admission of religious who had been expelled from France. The problem was rather a group who believed themselves to be more papal than the Pope and who fought their political enemies as if they were traitors. With political perspicacity, the Pope recognized that the constitution of 1876 provided the Church with relatively optimal operating possibilities. Papal politics also avoided unnecessary aggravation in Portugal, the land of Pombal, while negotiating the new circumscription of the dioceses (1881) and the rights of patronage in the Indian mission (1886). From the central-European perspective, Leo XIII's success with his stance toward the changing conditions in the Latin American republics was generally underestimated. It was the prerequisite for the possible success of the pastoral plans of the plenary council of 1899.

It was in keeping with the confessional, ethnic, and political situation in the Slavic world that the politics of Leo XIII could only obtain slight relief for the Catholic population there. But it is probable that the arrangement with Russia, which the Austro-Hungarian ambassador to the Vatican, Revertera, called a "Midsummer Night's Dream," was all that could be achieved. In this matter Leo XIII also had to deal with the concerns in Vienna, where the strengthening of Pan-Slavism and additional tensions were feared. The situation was most delicate in areas where the Pope collided with the union of national and Catholic consciousness, especially in the Russian and Prussian parts of Poland. The clergy and the population believed themselves betrayed by the Pope to Russification, particularly because Leo XIII encountered very little understanding for his cooperation in Petersburg. In view of the serious differences between Czechs and Germans in Bohemia and Moravia, the Pope had hardly a choice but to admonish the episcopate, in 1901, to keep the Catholic faith out of those differences. Like the Poles, the Slovenes and the Croatians had found their historical identity within the Slavic world in a union of confessionality and nationality. The idea of a Catholic Greater Croatia was completely contradictory to the Pope's intentions. He wanted the Croatian College in Rome, which was just being changed and renamed, to be a center for the movement to unify the Church. Aside from the confessional questions in Hungary, which had been increasing since 1886, the policy of Magyarization was a difficult component of Leo XIII's religious policy in Eastern Europe.

One can compare the attitude of Leo XIII toward Polish Catholicism under Russian influence with his attitude toward the Irish, who were suppressed by Great Britain. In both instances, there was a revolutionary situation. The difference was that Britain had Gladstone, which gave the Pope a chance to pursue an effective pro-Irish policy. Thus the question should be asked as to which the Pope better understood: the principles according to which every revolution needs to be rejected or the terribly violent resistance of the Irish toward the injustices inflicted upon them. The relations of Leo XIII with Great Britain were even better when the liberal de-anglicanization of public life provided greater freedom for Catholics. The reputation of the papacy in the Anglo-Saxon world grew remarkably during this pontificate; and it was more than just an act of courtesy when Cleveland, then president of the United States of America, sent a copy of the Constitution to Leo XIII for the anniversary of his ordination in 1887. The Know-Nothing Party and the Ku Klux Klan were to fight Catholicism publicly and secretly for a long time to come, but their influence on public opinion was counterbalanced by the prestige of Leo XIII.

At the jubilees in 1883, 1887, 1893, and 1903, the Pope could enjoy the Catholics' demonstrations of loyalty and the good wishes of almost all other nations. However, it characterizes the historical situation that the original countries of the Christian West, France and Italy, could not be listed in the index of success, even though Leo XIII considered these countries especially important in the perspective of his world design.

Perhaps the central question in the historical evaluation of this pontificate deals with the opportunism which even benevolent historians denote as a characteristic of Leo XIII. This question can only be answered in the context of Leo XIII's total concept. Is it correct to say that his policies and his ecclesiastical leadership were solely determined by the desire to restore the Papal State? No doubt this was a legitimate goal, but if this had been the ultimate goal of Leo XIII, according to which his devotion to modern society is to be judged, then he would have been neither a "master of politics" nor an important Pope.

It is obvious that the Italian question is a primary motif which, with extreme fluctuations from cautious hope to inscrutable resignation, ran through the life of Gioacchino Pecci after he was enthroned on the chair of Saint Peter. It would be misleading to see his advances toward Bismarck from this perspective only. From an agreement with the "great conservative statesman," this "ingenious, courageous, strong-willed man, who knows how to procure obedience," Leo XIII expected the establishment of a bastion against the revolutionary tendencies in Europe. But the papal words *finis impositus,* from his address on the termination of the German question (23 May 1887), were spoken in the fatal year when, after many disappointments for the Pope, the end of a greater alliance had come. After the shameful events of 13 July 1881, Austria as well as other powers refused the expected help against Italy; and in October King Umberto was a celebrated guest in Vienna. What other hope had he placed on Bismarck, a Protestant, yet an admired politician? At first, the Pope was not alone in his opinion of the weakness of the House of Savoy. But just when the Pope spoke of an asylum in the Habsburg Monarchy with the Austrian special emissary (1882), the Triple Alliance between Germany, Austria, and Italy was about to be ratified. The support of the House of Savoy — a child of the revolution to Leo XIII — was presented to the Pope as an act of conservative politics, and Austria pressured the Vatican to settle the German question. The Pope's reliance on Bismarck grew considerably when the latter asked him to mediate the negotiations with Spain concerning the Caroline Islands, one of Leo XIII's most important functions in the last phase of the *Kulturkampf*. Its conclusion was announced in a papal address of 23 May 1887, ending with the expression of hope that "harmony" could now also be restored to Italy stressing the condition that the Pope's authority should be subject to no one else's. Obviously, the Pope felt, at that moment, that the time for such a solution to the "Roman question" had come: crowning the peace with Germany. However, Crispi refused immediately. In October the Italian prime minister was Bismarck's welcome guest, and the Triple Alliance was renewed. The Pope, though "abandoned by the powers," returned to his old demands. But with what political power could they be realized? On 2 June 1887 Mariano Rampolla was appointed secretary of state. On 4 October 1887 the French ambassador reported to the Vatican that the Cardinal had spoken with France *d'une entente cordiale*. At the end of the year Pope Leo XIII himself called France *sa fille privilegiée* in the presence of the ambassador. As early as 1884, the letter *Nobilissima Gallorum gens* had intoned such language. In the year 1888, when Wilhelm II visited the Pope, the Pope called Bismarck a great revolutionary during an audience with the French ambassador. After the report of the Austrian special emissary (6 August 1888), Leo XIII told him, "If the government cannot dispatch any troops for my protection, they should at least hoist their flags on the walls of the Vatican when danger is imminent." In connection with a war feared at that time, the Pope advised Vienna and Paris that an alliance with the Vatican would be to their advantage. In 1890 the policy of *ralliement* began: reconciliation with the French Republic. Rampolla explained to the French delegate that the establishment of an Italian republic might clear the situation for the Vatican because the Pope would not have to reckon with a monarch next to him in Rome. The second political alliance failed with the *ralliement*. That it had little to do with a trend toward democracy as such can be deduced from the report by Revertera, the Austrian ambassador to the Vatican, according to which the Pope, two weeks after the encyclical *Au milieu des sollicitudes* (1892), declared his principal support for a "monarchical restoration in France," were it at all possible.

During the New Year's reception in 1897 at Count Revertera's, Leo XIII expressed two hopes: before the end of his days, he wanted to see the dawn, at least, of a unification with the Christian peoples outside of the Church and the beginning of a solution to the Roman question. So as not to diminish the political problems of the Papal State or to cloud one's view of the greatness of the Pope by isolating the problem from his total portfolio, it is necessary to see both hopes as one. Naturally, one must understand the Pope's hope for unification from the perspective of what was then historically feasible. The Pope did not expect mutual sympathy from the separated Christians, but rather a mass movement toward conversion. The movement was the horizon on which the validity of the Anglican ordinations was discussed. After he received reports from the Balkans in 1887, Leo XIII believed he could count on the movement. He had oriented his policies toward Russia according to his expectations. Even without calling Leo XIII a "mortal enemy of Protestants" (R. Seeberg), one could reject such a perception of Christian ecumenism. But given the Catholic self-concept, the city of Saint Peter was the essential component of a Christian unification. However Leo XIII may have envisioned the solution to the Roman question at different times, in detailed or in general terms, it was not only a matter of a "small principality," but of the Holy City as the center of the world Church and the episcopal see of its sovereign, subject to no other power. Rome of Saint Peter's successor and Christ's deputy — or Rome of the Freemason "plague"; that was the question. "La Roma nostra," Leo XIII used to say. And when the Pope spoke about finding asylum in Austria or Spain, he repeatedly used Ambrose's words "Ubi Papa, ibi ecclesia"; however, he thought primarily of a future triumphant return to Rome.

If one wants to understand all aspects of this pontificate, it seems necessary to start with Leo XIII's very pronounced awareness of the history of the papacy. He repeated, again and again, in his encyclicals that the papacy formed the Christian West, and what the nations, especially Italy, owed to the papacy. It is self-evident that the Popes Leo the Great and Gregory the Great were especially mentioned, and, likewise, that Leo's predecessors since the French Revolution occupy the most space in the list. Upon examination of the actual content of the frequent traditional mentioning of predecessors, one might find it worthy of note that quotes by Innocent III abound, almost all of which show the personal handwriting of Leo XIII. In the encyclical *Inscrutabili Dei* (28 May 1878), Innocent III appears together with Leo the Great, Alexander III, and Pius V as models for the new pontificate. Leo XIII, referring to Innocent III and other popes in connection with his unification plans for Eastern Churches, provokes historical comparisons which were, of course, not intended. *Nobilissima Gallorum gens* (1884), written after the conclusion of the Triple Alliance, anticipates subsequent French policy (in the introduction, the *Gesta Dei per Francos* is mentioned). Interestingly, Innocent (together with Gregory IX) is cited in a quotation from the letter to the archbishop of Rheims. In it he speaks of the preferential love of France and her obedience to the Apostolic See, which outdoes all other empires. In 1892 Leo XIII had the remains of Innocent III transferred from Perugia to the oldest and most sacred church in Rome, the Lateran Basilica, which he had been restoring and expanding in grand style since 1881. In the same year, the *ralliement*, the second big attempt to solve the Roman question, was in progress, as well as the creation of a papacy which would, in this revolution-ridden world, resume the universal historic task from which it had profited during the Middle Ages. With the appropriate adjustments, the papacy could win back "moral-religious hegemony in a new Christian world empire" (G. Schmidlin). In 1892, on the anniversary of his coronation (3 March 1878), Leo XIII justified the transfer of the remains of his great predecessor, Innocent III, in a speech to the cardinals. During his episcopate in Perugia, his favorite idea had been to honor the memory of this man, and he realized the idea that year, so that his voice might be heard from the Lateran Basilica, the "symbol of Christian unity." Immediately afterwards, he mentioned the great goals of Innocent's pontificate: the "conquest of the Holy Land and the independence of the Church." Under the "freedom of the papacy," he said, the Christian faith, "like our blood, revitalized the social and political organism" and tied the "peoples" to the authority of the Church, the "moral center of the world." Is not "a strong faith, verified in the conscience of the peoples, rather than the restoration of medieval institutions," the way to achieve final victory? The differentiation of medieval and contemporary conditions reflects the discussions about the guilds which were conducted in Socialist circles and paid attention to in *Rerum novarum* (1891).

It seems especially important that, in these instances, peoples rather than nation states were referred to. This was in line with hopes placed on the "Catholic
masses" since 1887 and with a remark by Rampolla on the "clearly democratic
trend of an era, which the Church should not face with animosity." Rampolla's
opinion was supported by the worker pilgrimages. We do not know, specifically,
what Leo XIII knew about the pontificate of Innocent III, whose great universal
goal it had been to lift the papacy "in the realm of *christianitas* to a sacerdotal-royal
position," with himself "as head of the super-national *populus christianus,* which
would be his direct responsibility." It would be misleading to single out Innocent III
merely on the basis of the quotations from Leo's predecessors. But Innocent III's
memory accompanied Leo XIII from his birth (Anagni was the native bishopric
of Gioacchino Pecci) to Perugia, to a dramatic turning point, the transfer of Innocent III's body to the Lateran Basilica (1892), to Leo's own burial (on the right
side of the Basilica opposite the tomb of Innocent III). Thus, Innocent III offers
access to the universal conception of Leo XIII, who felt that another personality
from the Middle Ages, Thomas Aquinas, had completed "Christian philosophy,"a
return to which would be the way to cure modern society. Perhaps this explains
Leo XIII's "temptation to theocracy."

From this background it is understandable that, in an age of imperialism,
against all political reality, Leo XIII highly valued the prospects of an international
office for arbitration. Such an office he claimed principally for the papacy. Already,
in *Diuturnum illud* (1881), one is reminded that, at the time of the Holy Roman Empire, the Church as *conciliatrix* had tamed the political passions of peoples partly
through clemency, partly by exerting authority. Bismarck's offer of papal mediation (1885) in the dispute between Germany and Spain over the Caroline Islands
was, naturally, significant for Leo XIII, mostly because he interpreted the gesture of
the Chancellor as recognition of his temporal sovereignty. The Pope, who tended
to attach high hopes to the offer, underwent the experience of Spain's refusing
his arbitration under international law and conceding merely to mediation. In his
letter of 29 May 1899, Leo XIII referred specifically to this diplomatic action. He
was answering a letter from the Dutch Queen Wilhelmina, who, at the initiative of
the Tsar, had wanted to include the Pope in the peace negotiations in the Hague,
and had asked him for "moral support." Leo XIII explained in his letter that it was
the duty of the papal office not only to provide the conference with moral support,
but also to "play an effective and active part in it." This, he wrote, was in keeping
with the tradition of the papacy, whose authority transcended all national borders.
Despite opposition, he was going to pursue this duty and not seek any fame other
than "de servir la cause sacrée de la civilisation chrétienne." The invitation failed
because of Italy. Other countries were also perplexed over this view of papal duties. They believed it to be limited to arbitration. Confirmation of the papal mission
had been drawn into demonstrations of loyalty by Catholic congregations, yet it
would lead to complications if it was to be applied to a concrete situation. It was
a delusion to project this political world onto a "Christian civilization" and to want
to redesign it as a union of nations unified in the Christian faith.

The significance of the encyclical *Rerum novarum* (1891) is correctly evaluated
and not in the least diminished if placed in the context of Leo XIII's great world
design. Certainly the experiences the Pope had with the conservative monarchies,

specifically in the years 1887/88, play a role. The monarchies did not want to assist him against the Italian upstart. And Leo XIII, despite his general utterances in reference to political philosophy, was adverse to democracy. Likewise, the change in tone after 1901 toward *Graves de communi* is evident. The negative turn of events exposes the overall goal: a cure for the social and political disruptions in the modern world, which was plunging into a state of deep resignation around the end of the nineteenth century. The cure was hoped to be the recognition of the moral authority of the *vicarius Christi*. It involved the inevitable liberation of the *proletarii* from oppression by *classes dirigeantes* as well as their right to unionize. The "question of the workers" is only one part of the general renovation of society based on Neo-Scholastic social philosophy. For Leo, renovation was feasible only if the authority of the Church would be respected again by everyone. As much as the workers' pilgrimages to Rome meant to the Pope in view of the Piedmontese sovereignty, it is absurd to interpret the patriarchal papal involvement in the workers' question as a mere means of pragmatic politics in the "Roman question."

Leo XIII was not only a political but also a seigneurial Pope. His first secretary of state, Alexander Franchi, whose appointment may have had something to do with the papal elections, was the most distinguished secretary of state before Rampolla. In 1880, two years after Franchi's death, Lorenzo Nina, who also belonged to the intransigents, incurred displeasure and was in office only a short time. Secretary of State Ludovico Jacobini (1880–87), formerly nuncio to Vienna, had a cautious nature and "his personality could neither succeed in the Vatican nor with the Pope himself" (Engel-Janosi). He had to follow the changing initiatives of the Pope in his policy toward Bismarck. Leo XIII also expected that his nuncios would be recognized as executive representatives of his authority, through which he ruled the world Church in a centralized manner. To strengthen his position toward the ecclesiastical opponents of the Spanish constitution, the Pope stated the point clearly in a letter on 15 April 1885, delivered by Secretary of State Jacobini to Rampolla, nuncio to Madrid since 1882. "In respect to the faithful in the country and their ecclesiastical affairs," the nuncios have an "authoritative mission," whose extent is determined by the Pope — the constitution *Pastor aeternus* is referred to. Domenico Ferrata, one of Leo XIII's outstanding diplomats, became nuncio to Paris after his duties in Switzerland and Belgium (1891–96). In 1894 he declared to French President Périer that the nuncio represents the Pope as the "true spiritual sovereign of the Catholics in the respective country," and that he, the nuncio, differed fundamentally from other ambassadors. Another man especially favored by the Pope was the diplomat Luigi Galimberti. As special emissary of the Pope, he played a major role in the conclusion of the *Kulturkampf,* and his behavior toward Windthorst, which he could not have afforded at his own expense, documented the individual style of government of this pontificate. That his rival Rampolla became secretary of state in 1887 and that he himself had to go to Vienna as nuncio (until 1893) were the result of the major policy changes in papal politics. As long as the Vatican archives until 1903 are not generally accessible, it cannot be determined accurately, among other matters, which position Secretary of State Rampolla took toward Leo XIII. It is possible that he had great influence on Leo XIII's activities during the final years.

With this diplomatic apparatus, Leo XIII sought to assert the power of his moral authority. In the beginning of the 1880s, he had to realize that the conditions for such assertion were not present because the conservative forces did not consider this authority indispensable to their survival in the face of revolutionary tendencies. After the nineties Leo XIII noticed that turning directly to the people could strengthen his authority over Catholicism. But his hopes for the expansion to turn into conversion movements were not fulfilled, much less his expectation that he would be respected as the moral authority by all men. It was one of his favorite plans to establish diplomatic relations with China. He had already designated Antonio Agliardi, later nuncio to Vienna, as the apostolic delegate when his letter to the Emperor of China (1 February 1885) received a positive response. His immediate motive had been the protection of the Catholic missionaries. But the ultimate goal was the inclusion of this world culture into his universal concept. The plan failed because France, the only power generally recognized to protect the Christians in the Orient, saw her interests endangered and threatened the Vatican with a break in diplomatic relations.

One must see the consecration of the entire human race to the Sacred Heart, on the occasion of the jubilee in 1900, in the perspective of Leo's world plan. Even though Leo XIII was a "political Pope" and as such subjugated to the conditions of politics, this pontiff cannot be understood if his goal is defined as "the domination of all of mankind by the Catholic Church," unless one understands "domination" as the kind of mutual permeation of religious and political concepts which characterized the political theory of the West before it dissolved in the later medieval period. One cannot say that his pontificate distinguished itself through the creative forces of spirituality, even though Leo XIII's deep religious piety is proven beyond doubt. Traditional forms, which Marie-Thérèse of Lisieux picked up and internalized during her life of suffering, were developed further and incorporated in the service of public worship. But the character of this pontificate is distorted if one misunderstands the "politicization" as an ideological manipulation of religiosity. This is contradicted by the astonishing attraction which most religious orders and congregations exerted, so that they were able to keep winning many young people for extensive social work with religious motivation.

The world design of Leo XIII found its most magnificent expression, revealing its innermost moments, in the apostolic letter *Praeclara gratulationis* of June 1894. It is one of those utopias without which historical greatness is not possible. The end is marked by the bitter letter *Annum ingressi sumus* of 19 March 1902," in which Leo XIII bemoans the insults inflicted upon the Church. But it was not just the fanatic hatred of individual Freemasons and the animosity of the whole organization toward the Catholic Church. Reconciliation of the modern world with tradition was no longer in anyone's power. The so-called "tragic failure" of Leo stood under a world signature. His successes were fewer than he had hoped. But that he had hoped for much was the basis for his achievements. To the faithful "he gave a new feeling of inner security toward the world" (Fülop-Miller). This constitutes his historical significance. "Though his reign, in retrospect, may not appear to be as unique as it was presented elsewhere, Leo XIII is unquestionably the most important Pope of his century and the most important Pope between Benedict XIV and Pius XI" (G. Schwaiger). His policies and the changes in his policies, his political and social encyclicals, his reclaiming the great philosophy of

Thomas Aquinas, his centralized orientation of Catholicism and the Church toward Rome, his involvement in the world mission, his hopes for a great conversion movement: all these were testimony to his grandiose desire for *restauratio;* no longer by way of political restoration as at the beginning of the century, but by turning to the modern world because of his basic concern for the salvation of mankind. The fact that the election of the new Pope after Leo's death on 20 July 1903 stirred the political powers much more than those in the year 1878 was a result of the respect which Leo XIII had gained in the world for the papacy.

The Situation in the Various Countries until 1914

Chaps. 45, 47: Rudolf Lill
Chap. 46: Erika Weinzierl
Chaps. 48, 51–54: Oskar Köhler
Chap. 49: Mario Bendiscioli
Chap. 50: Jacques Gadille
Chap. 55: Bernard Stasiewski

CHAPTER 45

The *Kulturkampf* in Prussia and in the German Empire until 1878

Nowhere in Europe was the struggle between Church and state fought as vigorously as in the German Empire of 1871. This battle considerably impeded inner consolidation for the next two decades. Since most of the controversial issues continued to be subject to the legislation of the individual states, the struggle took place on their terrain, and most vigorously in Prussia, the dominating power in the new Empire. There were two momentous determining factors: ideological contrast between the ultramontane Catholic Church and liberalism, which was controlling spiritual and political life, peaking in the years of the *Syllabus;* and the continued disparity within the Prussian state. The confessional disputes had further increased; the Prussian bureaucracy, partly Protestant, partly liberal, had only reluctantly executed an ecclesiastical policy of parity, as defined by the constitutions of 1848 and 1850. The strengthening of Catholicism as a social force awakened old and new adversaries. In the late sixties, attacks against confessional schools, cloisters, and other Church institutions occurred more and more often. Mutual misunderstandings due to insufficient knowledge of the opponent and lack of flexibility and moderation were contributing factors.

One direct cause of the conflict was the creation of the Center Party, which Bismarck falsely regarded as a conglomerate of the Empire's adversaries. Other causes were the dispute over the dogma of infallibility, the alliance with the National Liberals, designed by the chancellor to consolidate the Empire, and his fear of an anti-German coalition of Catholic states.

The political tensions within the Church increased and were nurtured continuously since the end of 1869 by news from the Council in Rome. These tensions and the fear of more severe anti-Catholic measures, as demanded by the Liberals, seemed to necessitate the political consolidation of Catholics in Prussia as well. The movement seeking to found a party since the summer of 1870 was headed by Hermann von Mallinckrodt and Peter Reichensperger. Against the opposition of integralistic circles, they insisted on a political, not primarily a Catholic, party: a principle they had already defended in the fifties. Nevertheless, in response to the particular initial situation, Church affairs took precedence in the first program of the Center Party: the immunity of the Church as defined in the Prussian constitution, the guarantee of confessional schools and freedom of instruction. Other, more important resolutions demanded the preservation of the federal constitution of the German Empire, governmental decentralization, protection of workers, and social welfare. On the basis of this program, fifty-eight deputies were elected to the Prussian Diet in November 1870.

The founding of the Center Party coincided with the Franco-Prussian War. Even the majority of the German Catholics and their leaders regarded this war as a legitimate opportunity to ward off ever increasing threatening pressures. In a similar vein was the pastoral letter of the episcopal conference in Fulda in the summer of 1870, which was addressed particularly to the opponents of the dogma of infallibility. In contrast to the fraternal strife of 1866, the war against the "arch-enemy" was quite popular, especially in the Catholic west and southwest of Germany.

Those who had approved the war could not reject its predictable consequence, the founding of the Empire. Indeed, in 1871 the sentiments of most Catholics differed from those of most other Germans only by reason of an increasing fear of Church conflicts. They also wanted close contact between the Empire and Austria. At the Catholic Convention in Mainz (September 1871) its President Friedrich Baudri and Bishop Ketteler gave recognition to the Emperor and the Empire. Urgently responding to the actual increase of controversies caused by the dogma of infallibility, which had already invaded imperial legal territory, they demanded from the state justice for the Church and protection from assaults by the Liberals. Similarly, Ketteler expressed himself in a political program written in 1871, but not published until 1873. He welcomed the "partial unity of the German people," created by the founding of the Empire, "because it satisfied, partially, a right of the German people and it made amends for the injustice inflicted upon them."

At the first session of the *Reichstag* (March 1871), the Center Party already represented the second strongest faction (with fifty-eight deputies). The program, which had not been substantially modified since the previous year, and Ketteler's words (in 1871/72 he was a member of the *Reichstag*) showed the reservations of the Center Party as it proceeded with its work. They were sufficient to create an almost irreconcilable opposition to the dominant National Liberals. This was clearly proven by the exclusion of the Center Party from the Presidium. The situation was intensified when the Center immediately accepted some Guelph guest listeners and, soon afterwards, supported other minorities as well (Poles, Alsatians). Continual controversies about the new dogma, about the ecclesiastical censure of orthodox adversaries, and about the growing Old Catholic Church were part of the efforts of the new Empire to gain a historical self-understanding. After 1866 National-Liberal, National-Protestant, and also Protestant-Conservative writers presented the results of 1870/71 as a victory for the social principles essential to Protestantism and a consequence of Protestant Prussian history. The Habsburg dynasty, the papacy, the Jesuits, and the Counter Reformation were held responsible for actually or allegedly leading German history astray.

The Center Party itself had introduced these disputes over principles into the first session of the *Reichstag.* This was instigated by the problems of the Papal State, which stirred everyone's emotions, especially after the annexation of Rome (September 1870). The numerous demonstrations and pilgrimages of the Catholics were meant to assure the Pope of their solidarity and to ask their governments for support. The Liberals took this as a challenge, since they considered the completion of unity in Germany and Italy as a victory of the modern concept of the state.

Since help could neither be expected from Austria, which tried to come to terms with Italy, nor from now Republican France, Pius IX had asked the King of Prussia for assistance in the fall of 1870. Archbishops Melchers and Ledóchowski had turned to Wilhelm I and Bismarck with the same request. In Berlin Queen Augusta (Empress since 1871) expressly supported the papal desires. She was guided by a conservative awareness of the law as well as the wish to integrate Catholics into the Prussian-German state. The conservative Minister of Religious Affairs Heinrich Mühler (1813–74) agreed with her, but intended to intervene only together with other political powers. King Wilhelm I (Emperor since January 1871) was not disinclined toward the considerations of his spouse, but had to agree with Bismarck's arguments, who, during the persisting war with France, strictly refused any anti-Italian intervention. However, he was willing, if necessary, to grant asylum to the Pope.

In the Emperor's speech before the first *Reichstag,* Wilhelm disavowed any kind of intervention into the domestic affairs of other peoples. In the draft of a reply addressed to the Monarch, the National-Liberal majority formulated the principle of non-intervention, which was in accord with the national self-understanding and the needs of the Empire in regard to her foreign policies, but clearly oriented against the Pope and the Papal State. The Center Party attempted a modification which would not fundamentally exclude intervention in favor of the Pope. Constitution-minded Ludwig Windthorst (1812–91), former cabinet minister of Hannover, stood out in this debate. In the following years, especially after Mallinckrodt's death in 1874, Windthorst became the great leader of the Center Party and Bismarck's most important parliamentary adversary in the *Kulturkampf* Windthorst declared papal independence, as guaranteed by the Papal State which was created under Charlemagne, founder of the First German Empire, to be of vital interest to German Catholics. The majority's address to the Monarch was approved with 243 to 63 votes. Although the failure of the Center Party's motion was predictable, the fact that it was pursued anyway was not only due to the antipapal tone of the majority draft. The deputies of the then strongest Catholic party seemed to believe that they could draw inopportune conclusions from the commitment of solidarity with the Pope, which had always been part of an ultramontane Church concept. Once again, more trenchantly than in 1866, did the Roman-Italian aspect of the decision of 1870 affect and burden German Catholics and their relations to the nation-state.

The debate on the address resulted in the isolation of the Center Party, which was immediately intensified during the deliberation about the constitution. The faction reiterated demands for the inclusion of certain fundamental rights in the federal constitution, among them articles 15 and 18 of the Prussian constitution, guaranteeing immunity for the Church. As early as 1867, after the creation of the North German Confederation, several Catholic deputies had voiced these demands.

The debates on the address and the constitution anticipated the parliamentary fronts of the *Kulturkampf.* Bismarck found his suspicions concerning the Catholic party verified. It seemed to him that the party's alleged "international" character and its first initiatives endangered the consolidation of national unity. He hated the "Guelph" Windthorst. He was particularly suspicious of the protection which the party provided the Poles who had been forced into total opposition since the founding of the Empire. Attempts to denounce the Center Party in Rome as conspirators of revolution and compel the Pope to chastise the party were only partially successful. After some ambiguous remarks, Cardinal Antonelli expressed his appreciation for the party in a letter which Ketteler had effected. Bismarck thereupon fought an open battle, which was primarily motivated by political, not by religious reasons. The Center Party did not suit Bismarck's plans; confessionally based on the masses, it was socially heterogeneous. It had also legitimized itself as a democratic body and was therefore intent on parliamentary rule, which Bismarck despised. The "ultramontane" party was the first which the Chancellor embellished with the term "foes of the Empire," fighting them with unreasonable vehemence. Bismarck's opposition to these groups was responsible for the integration of the other parties in accordance with his governmental policies.

The Prussian government, especially Bismarck and the conservative Minister of Religious Affairs Heinrich Mühler, regarded the Vatican Council and its resolutions as domestic affairs of the Catholic Church. A position was not taken until the bishops began inflicting penalties upon opponents to the impairment of their civil or social status. Mühler completely avoided conflict, regretted the recent internal developments within Catholicism and sided with the reprimanded professors in Bonn and Breslau and the other clerical teachers. Prince-Bishop Forster of Breslau had acted especially harshly, though he had been a vehement opponent of the dogma of infallibility himself. He had submitted, finally, and expected the same from his clergy.

Bishop Krementz of Ermland took steps not only against Professor Michelis of Braunsberg, but also against all the teachers of the local Catholic high school. The principal and the religion teacher, were excommunicated. Students subsequently boycotted religious instruction and were forced by the government to leave the school.

The government used the controversy for its first administrative maneuver of far-reaching consequences. On 8 July 1871 the Catholic department of the Ministry of Religious Affairs was dissolved and combined with the Protestant department to form a department for ecclesiastical affairs. Bismarck and the liberal press accused the functionaries of the Catholic department, vainly defended by Mühler, of two offenses: in the latest controversy they did not adequately represent the position of the state and they did not energetically combat the expansion of the Polish clerical influence in the schools of the eastern provinces.

In the meantime, Bismarck's alliance with the National Liberals had solidified because the Conservatives had taken a reserved stand toward his domestic policies, fearing a diminution of Prussian autonomy. The radical political program directed against the Church, which the Chancellor explained to Mühler in August 1871, a few weeks after his official "declaration of war," was completely in accord with the new constellations. The program combined Bismarck's typical desire to restore the old Prussian sovereignty over the Church with the extensive adoption of the ecclesiastical maxims of liberalism. Bismarck wanted to combat the ultramontane party, especially in the eastern provinces. He was aiming at separation of church and state and of church and school. He wanted to transfer school inspections to nonclerical supervisors and abolish religious instruction in the schools. Henceforth, ecclesiastical affairs were to be administered by the Ministry of Justice.

The Prussian bishops in a direct petition tried to prove the legitimacy of their measures against the Old Catholics and to clarify the misunderstandings caused by dogma. But they were unable to accomplish anything against Bismarck's intentions. Ketteler, after a conversation with Bismarck in November 1871, had to recognize that the conflict had become irreconcilable. The Chancellor seemed to be convinced that the Curia and the Center Party were conspiring against the Empire.

A legal strategical initiative had meanwhile emanated from Bavaria. In October 1871 the *Reichstag* opened its second session. Minister Johann Lutz presented a bill introducing a pulpit paragraph which was ratified 10 December 1871 (ARTICLE 130a of the penal code). The clergy was forbidden, when in office, to deal with public affairs "in a way which would endanger the peace of public life." In previous passionate debates, Windthorst, Peter Reichensperger, and Ketteler had justified the opposition of the Center Party. Lutz had explained that it was a question of who was in command: the state or the Roman Church. Almost all National Liberals agreed. Their chairman admitted in confidential consultation that he wanted to provoke the clerical faction to act with more rigor.

Meanwhile, Bismarck and his colleagues had proceeded to realize their program in Prussia. Only with reservations did the Emperor join in. But Bismarck was able to convince him that the interests of the state left no choice. Augusta's numerous and well-founded warnings of the conflict accomplished nothing. Mühler resisted Bismarck consistently. He wanted to introduce the law on school supervision by the state, which Bismarck desired so urgently, only under the provision that a general school law be passed which would preserve the Christian character of the school system. Mühler had to resign in January 1872. He was succeeded by Adalbert Falk (1827–1900), a disciple of the liberal political concept. He had strong support from the National Liberal Party and was the driving force next to Bismarck in the *Kulturkampf.* On 11 March 1872, the school supervision law was passed. Now, the state had the right to supervise all public and private schools and to appoint school inspectors (ART. 2), who had earlier been employed by the Church. This law, like the Baden school law of 1868, was not so much a result of the *Kulturkampf* as of the liberal desire to remove all ecclesiastical influence from public affairs. It was discriminatory because of the circumstances under which it was passed. Bismarck, Falk, and the liberal press left no doubt that they wanted to strike out against the Catholic Church and the Polish population of Prussia. Nevertheless, this law caused the break with the Conservatives which embittered the Chancellor. The Conservative majority rejected the new dogmatic developments within Catholicism. But they also rejected a conflict knowing that it would turn against the Protestant Church and, generally, against the alliance of throne and altar.

In the following months, the government increased antiecclesiastical administrative measures introduced under Mühler. Prominent victims were Bishop Krementz, whose salary was withheld in spite of the Emperor's reluctance, and Bishop Namszanowski, military ordinary to the armed forces. Namszanowski had discontinued services in the garrison's church, St. Pantaleon in Cologne, which the state had allowed to the Old Catholics. He had also forbidden a curate, who opposed the dogma, to perform the duties of his office. The Defense Department did not understand the clerical responsibilities of the military ordinary and considered his actions illegal transgressions from his area of competence. When Namszanowski participated in the episcopal conference in Fulda (April 1872), the Department charged him with leaving Berlin without permission "on unofficial business." The government suspended the bishop, but the disciplinary court did not confirm it. The appeal was decided by the Ministry of State itself. On 26 June 1873, the Bishop was placed under suspension, after the cabinet decree of 15 March 1873 had already dissolved the military ordinariate. A diplomatic protest by the Vatican (Antonelli's letter of 28 August 1872), with whom the establishment of the ordinariate to the armed forces had been arranged, received no answer. This diplomatic insult of the Vatican had been preceded by a worse one in the spring of 1872. Bismarck had tried to force Cardinal Hohenlohe as ambassador upon the Pope, though in 1870 he had fallen out of favor with Rome. After papal rejection of the cardinal, only a chargé d'affaires remained in the Vatican. By the end of 1872, he was also recalled because of Pius IX's vehement protests against the unrelenting execution of the Jesuit laws. In 1875, at the peak of the *Kulturkampf,* funds for the embassy to the Vatican were stricken from the state budget.

Intensification of the already tense situation in 1872, painfully felt by the Vatican and the majority of the German Catholics, brought about the Jesuit law, the second federal law of the *Kulturkampf* (4 July 1872). The Society of Jesus and related orders (Redemptorists, Lazarists) were forbidden in the Empire and existing foundations were dissolved (ART. 1). The members were subjected to residence restrictions, and the foreigners among them faced expulsion from the country. This was precipitated by a storm of petitions by Old Catholics, the Association of Protestants, and many National Liberal groups. The Jesuits were charged with responsibility for the *Syllabus* and for the dogma of infallibility, and they were exposed as opponents of the modern state and civil liberties. The leaders of south German liberalism, Lutz and his predecessor Hohenlohe, launched concrete initiatives in opposition to the law, but confined them to the residence restrictions for the Jesuits. In spite of the strong resistance by the Center and some Conservatives, the National Liberal majority of the *Reichstag* pushed through a law of prohibition without any time limitations. Like the Socialist law, passed in 1878, the Jesuit law was an exceptive law which violated the constitutional principles of liberalism. Nevertheless, only a few National Liberals advised against it, and the majority of the leftist-liberal Progressive Party. The fact that the majority of the National Liberals voted for the exceptive laws damaged their credibility and prepared the party's crisis, facilitating the conclusion of the *Kulturkampf.*

The Catholic reactions to the Jesuit law were sharp. Shortly before its passage, Pius IX, in a address to the German Catholics, urged resistance to the "persecution of the Church." The most important protest was contained in a memorandum drafted by Ketteler and accepted by the entire German episcopate in Fulda in September. The memorandum called the recent measures of Prussia and the Empire violations of Church immunity, as defined by the constitution and international law, and highly detrimental to the current judicial system. In no uncertain terms the bishops brought to mind ARTS. 15–18 of the Prussian constitution, which guaranteed ecclesiastical autonomy. From the divine endowment of the Church the bishops derived the claim that the Church "existed within the integrity of its constitution and its very essence." The charge that the Church, Jesuits, and Center Party were enemies of the Empire, and therefore dangerous to the state, was rejected once and for all.

The Prussian government had to concede that its religious policies, practised since 1871, were in violation of the constitution. But since the government intended to adhere to its program, it answered the Fulda memorandum with the law which limited the guarantees of ARTS. 15–18 (5 April 1873). ARTICLE 15 was amended to the effect that the autonomy of the churches recognized therein would remain "subject to the laws of the state and to its jurisdiction." The state's prerogative to regulate by law the rights of the Church regarding the training and employment of the clergy and its disciplinary authority restricted the Church's freedom to staff ecclesiastical offices (ART. 18).

Thereby the conditions for the actual laws of the struggle were set. They were passed in May 1873 after stormy debates in the Prussian Provincial Diet and in the House of Lords, imposing upon the Church a closed system of governmental supervision. Since taking office, Falk had been preparing these laws.

The law regarding training and appointment of the clergy (11 May 1873) made the appointment to a clerical office dependent on German citizenship, on education at a German university, and on approval by the state (ARTS. 1–3). All clerical educational institutions were placed under the control of the state (ARTS. 6, 7, 9–14). Theology students had to pass an additional state examination in philosophy, history, and German literature (culture examination ART. 8). The bishops had to report each candidate for clerical office to the appropriate functionary (Notification Law). In case of objections, the appointment could not take place. Objections could be made on the basis of facts justifying the assumption that the candidate might violate the law or disturb the peace (ARTS. 15–17). Each vacant incumbency was to be filled within a year (ART. 18). Violations were punished with stiff fines (ARTS. 22–24).

The law regarding both ecclesiastical disciplinary power and the establishment of a Royal Tribunal of Ecclesiastical Affairs (12 May 1873) excluded all non-German Church institutions, primarily the Pope and the Curia, from disciplinary power over the German clergy (ART. 1). Consequently, all ecclesiastical disciplinary measures could be made subject to the control of the state (ARTS. 5–9). Those affected by such measures had the right to appeal to the newly created Tribunal of Ecclesiastical Affairs, which could declare the appealed decisions void (ART. 10–23). The Tribunal could also dismiss clergymen who had violated the law or a civil regulation to such a degree that their activity appeared incompatible with law and order (ARTS. 24–31).

Above all, the state veto of clerical appointments and the right to remove clergy from office were severe attacks on the constitution of the Church as well as freedom of belief and conscience. Both the National Liberals, whose animosity toward the Church had been strengthened by the dogma of infallibility, and the bureaucracy, which was still adhering to the common provincial law, cooperated in reimposing a historically obsolete state church in an expanded fashion, enabled to do so by the political power of the modern state. The Church was of course compelled to oppose these measures, and thus these first two May laws kindled a long and passionate fight.

The Prussian bishops decided quickly, justified by the memorandum of Fulda in 1872, to practice passive resistance to the May laws. They rejected and forbade any kind of cooperation in their enforcement. With the exception of a small minority (so-called state priests, state Catholics), the clergy and the laity followed these directives. Directors of seminaries refused state supervision, theology students rejected the culture examination. The bishops themselves appointed priests, ignoring the provisions of the May laws. The state reacted by closing most clerical seminaries. In December 1873 a new oath was ordered for bishops and episcopal functionaries, which required absolute submission to all laws. Soon indictments began against bishops and clergymen who had been appointed illegally. Prohibition of appointments turned into termination of office. Falk, the liberal lawyers supporting him, and the Prussian bureaucracy enforced these laws relentlessly and without constraint. The Chancellor also appreciated the useful aid of many journalists who, contrary to Bismarck's political goals, brought the ideological struggle into the limelight, and who advocated the supremacy of the national state and the superiority of the "German mentality" against the "Rome-serving" Catholics.

Bismarck, Falk, and their aides completely misjudged the Church's will and strength to resist. Under the concentric pressure by the state, Catholics from all walks of life flocked around their bishops and the Center Party, which was able to increase its mandate considerably *(Reichstag* 1871: 58; 1874:91 deputies; Prussian Diet 1870: 58; 1873: 90 deputies). Under Windthorst's leadership, the Center became the primary opponent to the Chancellor, fighting him uncompromisingly on constitutional grounds. The Vatican persistently supported the Prussian Catholics. Pius IX and Antonelli, finally forced into the defensive by 1870, confined themselves to fruitless protests, hardly adequate in view of their opponents' arguments. They refused to recognize that their intransigence had contributed to the intensification of the differences. The Pope acted very unwisely, when, in a letter to Wilhelm I, he justified his right to criticize the May laws with the questionable identification of Papal Church and Christianity: "Everyone who has been baptized belongs in some way to the Pope." This hurt the Emperor, who personally did not exactly favor the *Kulturkampf,* and the conservative Protestants, who felt likewise but remained silent because of their deeply rooted loyalty to the Prussian state. They were forced into the camp that was fighting the *Kulturkampf* and trying everything to exploit the confessional differences.

In order to break the Catholic resistance, the May laws were intensified in 1874. However, this step was unsuccessful. Since the penal sanctions of the law of 11 May 1873 had proven insufficient, the Prussian government passed an expatriation law for the whole Empire (4 May 1874), which violated the bill of rights severely. Clergymen who continued practicing in office after their dismissal by the state were threatened with expulsion from certain places or areas. In case of extreme insolence or contravention, they would be threatened with exile or loss of citizenship. On 20 May 1874, the Prussian Diet passed a law concerning the administration of suspended bishoprics. According to this law, an episcopal administrator (capitulary vicar) could only operate until the state-approved appointment of a bishop, provided he could document his qualifications according to the law of 11 May 1873, and provided he swore an oath of obedience to all laws. If no capitulary vicar were elected by the chapter, a state commissioner had to administer the bishopric. Since no chapter was willing to execute the law, such commissioners had to be appointed for all vacant dioceses. Immediately, the law concerning the declaration of the law of 11 May 1873 (21 May 1874) followed. It placed the burden of proof on the clergymen who had been charged with illegally taking office, and threatened to confiscate all property if an office were filled against the provisions of the May laws. The judicial and administrative struggle against the Church seemed complete.

The National Liberals used the intensification of the conflict to realize an old postulate of their social doctrine. By law (9 March 1874), civil marriage became obligatory in Prussia. Wilhelm I approved, with serious reservations. A year later, civil marriage became an imperial law — the culmination of the *Kulturkampf* (6 February 1875).

In the meantime, prosecution of the bishops and priests in violation of the laws was continued. Since bishops were fined whether they did or did not fill an office illegally, the sum of fines reached proportions which could neither be paid through compulsory auctions nor with voluntary contributions from the faithful. In this situation, the Prussian bureaucracy did not refrain from employing imprisonment. In 1874/75, five out of eleven Prussian bishops spent several months in prison. The imprisoned bishops were worshipped as martyrs.

The Catholics' political convictions suffered disillusionment, and they grew increasingly bitter when the government decided to apply even the most extreme May laws, forcing the royal tribunal, created in 1873, to dismiss the bishops who were still practising resistance. Dismissals began with Ledóchowski in 1874. In 1878, only Bishops Krementz (Ermland), von der Marwitz (Kulm), and Sommerwerck (Hildesheim) were still in office. The episcopates of Fulda, Osnabrück, and Trier had been vacant since the death of their incumbents. According to Church law, the six dismissed bishops remained in office, but they could not administer officially and, thus, went into exile, where they tried to rule over their dioceses with the help of secret delegates.

The final phase of the *Kulturkampf* was ushered in, at the end of 1874, during the trial of former ambassador and Bismarck opponent Count Arnim, when the text of a "papal election telegram" became known. It was sent by the Chancellor in May 1872. Bismarck therein suggested to the European governments an agreement regarding conditions for the recognition of a new Pope. He justified his initiative by stating that, since the Vatican Council, the bishops of all countries were merely functionaries of the Pope. In February 1875, the German episcopate responded with a declaration based on a thorough analysis of the Vatican decrees. It stressed the direct authority of each bishop within his diocese, justified by apostolic succession, and was, soon thereafter, approved by Pius IX. Shortly before, the Pope had used the sharpest means at his disposal against the Prussian religious policies. The encyclical *Quod numquam* (5 February 1875) declared the May laws invalid, insofar as they contradicted the divine constitution of the Church, and decreed excommunication of everyone who participated in their creation and execution. At the same time, Pius rejected any kind of dissent against the authorities in secular matters.

Prussia answered with a new series of penal laws. The so-called breadbasket law (22 April 1875) decreed discontinuation of all state funds to the Catholic Church (ART. 1). It provided the possibility of resumption in individual dioceses only in the case of a written assurance by the responsible bishop or episcopal administrator that the laws would be obeyed (ART. 2). Individual clergymen also could only receive the state funds due to them if they provided such declarations (ART. 6). Few state priests were willing to make such promises, and, therefore, an almost total cessation in state payments occurred, welcomed by the Liberals as an important step in the separation of church and state.

The law concerning religious orders of 31 May 1875 hurt the Catholics most. It excluded orders and congregations from Prussian state territory. Existing settlements were not allowed to accept new members and were to be dissolved within six months. In case of orders whose members were teaching, the deadline could be extended up to four years (ART. 1). Exempted from the decree were hospital orders, whose place of residence, however, could be seized at any time and placed under state control (ART. 3).

On 18 June 1875, ARTS. 15 and 18 of the Prussian constitution were abolished. On 20 June, a comprehensive law regarding the administration of the estate of Catholic parishes was passed. Its aim was to debilitate the hierarchic system of the Church and extensively adopt evangelical parish principles. The administration of Church estates was democratized (ART. 1) and turned over to a vestry board consisting of the pastor and elected members (ARTS. 5–8). Important decisions were dependent on the approval of a board of local representatives (ART. 21). The Church could tolerate this law, since most elected mayors tried to cooperate with the ecclesiastical authorities.

The final law dealt with the ecclesiastical property of the Old Catholic parishes (4 July 1875). It assured the Old Catholics the use of property and churches belonging to the Catholic parishes wherever they had gained a "considerable number" of new members (ARTS. 1, 2). Priests who had become Old Catholic could keep their benefices (ART. 3). Since the Catholics continued to reject the use of their churches by the seceded minority, and since the bureaucracy usually interpreted the law in favor of the Old Catholics, serious controversies occurred. Catholic services were discontinued in churches given to the Old Catholics.

The year 1876 brought only amendments to the pulpit paragraph and to the law regarding the administration of diocesan property. Also, a ministerial order was issued by Falk, subjecting religious instruction in elementary schools to state supervision (18 February 1876).

Otherwise, the struggle began to stagnate. The Catholic Church organization in Prussia was demolished, more than one thousand parishes were without pastors. But the passive resistance of the Catholic population, their cooperation with the clergy and the hierarchy, and the active resistance of the Center Party remained unbroken. These were not the only reasons why, in the middle of the 1870s, the *Kulturkampf* turned out to be a failure. Liberal ideology and bureaucratic perfection had given the *Kulturkampf* an edge, originally not intended by Bismarck, which deeply affected internal peace and forced Catholics and other minorities into a ghetto, to the disadvantage of the Empire. The struggle against the Catholic Church furthered de-Christianization of society, which did not suit Bismarck's authoritarian concept. Favored by the *Kulturkampf,* a new and dangerous adversary appeared — social democracy. In addition, Prussia had lost its reputation as a tolerant state, a reputation twice as valuable in the impending age of public opinion. The arrests and expulsions of bishops, clergymen, and members of orders deepened the mistrust toward Bismarck outside of Germany, even in anticlerical circles. The Napoleonic methods of his "founding the Empire from above" had had the same effect.

Slowly and strategically motivated, the Chancellor, therefore, turned away from the *Kulturkampf.* If the Center Party could not be conquered in open battle, then he had to try to integrate it into government politics or separate it from its roots among the masses either via political concessions or agreements with the Vatican.

Bismarck's experiences, resulting from the *Kulturkampf* contributed greatly to his estrangement from the National Liberals, which was further determined by the renewed disagreements over parliament, constitutionalism, and economic policies. Another contributing factor was the crisis of the liberal system, beginning in the middle of the seventies. At any rate, the Chancellor was preparing a conservative turn of events which would determine his domestic policies from 1878/79 on. He did not take an initiative for a compromise in religious policies because he wanted to avoid, at any cost, the impression of a pilgrimage to Canossa, and because a settlement under Pius IX seemed impossible to him (and to other politicians). Both sides strengthened their positions.

The political failure was completed by the fact that Bismarck had not succeeded in involving foreign countries in the *Kulturkampf.* Bismarck had placed high hopes on the leading statesmen of Austria and Italy because of local disputes involving religious policies. But they were too realistic and too familiar with the nature and the strength of the Catholic Church to agree to a bureaucratic persecution in the Prussian fashion.

During the liberal five years after the founding of the Empire, the *Kulturkampf* was able to spread to other federal states, however with characteristic differences. Most similar to the Prussian development, though less consequential, was the one in Baden. Its school, marriage, and Church laws of 1868–74 were fashioned after the Prussian laws or followed them verbatim. — In Bavaria, "a covert *Kulturkampf*" had begun already before 1870, rooted in the tradition of a liberal-Catholic regalism. It was led by Lutz's ministry (1870–90) with consistency and the intent to avoid open conflict. He did not go beyond restoration of previous state supervision (1873). Bavarian parishes and seminaries accepted clergymen and theology students who had to leave Prussia. Only because they were vacant for several years did the bishoprics of Speyer and Würzburg attract some attention. Pius IX had rejected the appointment of candidates for these sees who were nominated by the King and who leaned toward the state-church concept. Following Prussia's example, Hesse-Darmstadt and Saxony passed liberal religious laws in the years 1874–76.

The two other German states with a large Catholic population, Württemberg and Oldenburg, refused to become involved in the *Kulturkampf.* In Württemberg, within the boundaries set by the Church law of 1862, there existed an exceedingly good relationship between Church and state, cultivated carefully by King Karl I (1864–91) and Bishop Hefele. In Alsace-Lorraine, whose very difficult integration into the Empire would have been complicated even more by the *Kulturkampf,* the administration, dependent on Berlin, backed away from sharp measures.

CHAPTER 46

Tensions in the Austro-Hungarian Monarchy (1878–1914)

After the denominational laws of May 1874 came into force, all further attempts by the Liberals to design the Cisleithan legislation concerning religious policies according to their concepts failed. The bill to regulate the exterior judicial system of the monastic societies miscarried. The marriage clause, also miscarried. Such projects were tabled in favor of other legislative tasks and the occupation of Bosnia and Herzegovina. All other attempts by the Liberals to achieve a change in legislation regarding religious policy came to nothing.

The Catholics, on the contrary, had considerable success concerning the school question. On 5 February 1880, Prince Aloys Liechtenstein, deputy of the Conservatives introduced a school resolution requesting the government to revise the elementary school taw. The goals of Liechtenstein's reform plan were: decrease of expenditures, increase of the individual states' influence on the school system, and consideration of the population's religious, moral, and national needs.

The government bill was finally passed by Parliament in April 1883 and ratified by the Emperor in the following month. The amendment was significant for the organization of the school system and gave particular consideration to the religious denomination of the students. The government's attitude was emphatically reinforced by the Austrian Social Democrats, who were then on their way to unification. However, the Christian Socialists, heeding their voters from the German-speaking parts of Czechoslovakia, denied Badeni their support for his attempt to oblige the Czechs with his language ordinances. Thus, the Christian Socialists contributed to Badeni's overthrow. Their leader, Dr. Karl Lueger (1844–1910), had meanwhile become mayor of Vienna despite the resistance of the upper clergy and the royal court. This did not prevent the radical German Nationalists under the leadership of Georg Ritter von Schönerer from exploiting the sympathies of the Alpine Catholic People's Party for the Slavs' desire to propagate the Away-from-Rome movement. Thus, for the Liberals, the desired elaboration of the denominational legislation became unattainable. There is no doubt that the Emperor and, finally, both the government and the bureaucracy respected the feelings of the enraged Catholics who had decided seriously to resist the state. The denominational appeasement is partially due to the understanding which Cardinal Rauscher and his successors, the Viennese Archbishops Kutschker, Ganglbauer, and Gruscha, had offered to the state even after the repeal of the concordat of 1870. In addition, the Liberals suffered an almost total loss of their nearly omnipotent position after Auersperg's ministry was overthrown in 1879.

The neutral conservative cabinet of Eduard Taaffe maintained good relations with the conservative Right in the Parliament and had mostly Christian social reformers such as Count Egbert Belcredi and Aloys Liechtenstein work out the social legislation set in motion by Taaffe. This legislation was compatible both with the clause regarding the elementary school law of 1883 and the Catholics' school demands. During Taaffe's era (1885) there followed provisionary legislation by the Congruists to improve the poor material condition of the clergy.

This spirit of conciliation marks the ecclesiastical legislation of all Cisleithan governments after Taaffe. In this area, laws were only enacted when it was absolutely necessary for practical reasons or to avoid hardships, and as such included the amendment to the law regarding religion teachers (1888), the so-called Forensen law (1894), and the Congruist law (1898), which still did not quite fulfill the wishes of the lower clergy and was therefore improved in 1902 and 1907 through amendments. Until the collapse of the Monarchy, the Austrian religious legislation was essentially based on the denominational laws of 1868 and 1874, whose moderation and generally benevolent execution by the government finally compelled the Catholics to be more or less content with them.

In the ensuing open controversy between the Conservatives and the Christian Socialist Party, as it was called since 1889, almost all of the bishops — as well as the Emperor — faced the new Catholic party with utter mistrust, if not animosity. Since the beginning of the 1890s, the upper clergy, represented by Cardinal Schönborn of Prague, together with the Emperor's diplomats, continually brought charges against the Christian Socialists in Rome. However, thanks to the mediation of the Viennese Nuncio Agliardi and the good will of Secretary of State Cardinal Rampolla, these accusations had no disadvantageous consequences, but resulted in Rampolla's explicit approval of the Christian Socialist program, provided, to be sure, that the radical anti-Semitism propagated by the party during its rise and endorsed by many priests be alleviated. Nevertheless, Cardinal Gruscha probably gave moral support to Franz Joseph, with whom he got along splendidly, when the Emperor tenaciously refused to confirm Lueger's election as mayor of Vienna. Gruscha bitterly opposed the Christian Socialists. Lueger, in turn, at a campaign meeting in 1901, did not refrain from severely criticizing the "obedient" attitude of the Austrian episcopate regarding religious policies. Only under Archbishops Nagl and, above all, Piffl, did the relations of the episcopate to the party substantially improve. After all, the party had started out representing the middle classes; then it won over the farmers, united with the Conservatives in 1907 and was finally the only representative of Church interests in the Republic. Of course, these were also advocated by the Catholic organizations springing up in the last two decades of the nineteenth century (Catholic University Society 1884, Catholic School Society 1886, Christian Workers Movement 1892). In 1905, through the initiative of Viktor Kolb, S.J., the Pius Society was founded to protect the Catholic press, which, after the First World War, joined the Catholic People's Union (founded in 1909). Around the turn of the century, Catholic farmers' unions were organized. In 1917, several Catholic youth groups from the prewar years were combined in the Imperial Union of Catholic German Youth of Austria. Also the Austrian Catholic conventions, taking place at irregular intervals after 1877, served from the beginning as a platform to declare ecclesiastical (specifically Catholic) demands, even though they might not coincide with the government's policy, for reasons relating to foreign politics. This was the case in 1889, when the second Catholic convention made the need of freedom for the Holy See the subject of a memorandum directed against Italy, a member of the Triple Alliance.

The Habsburg Monarchy's position regarding Italy and its problem of nationalities was the dominant question arising in the discussions between Austria-Hungary and the Vatican during the pontificate of Leo XIII. According to information from the Austrian Legate Johannes von Montel (1831–1910), Cardinal Manning and Cardinal Simor, primate of Hungary, were instrumental in the election of Leo XIII. The newly elected Pope soon complained in his first political letter to Franz Joseph about "the constantly increasing hostility" of Italy against the Holy See; he asked the Emperor to intervene on behalf of the threatened papacy. The Emperor responded favorably but without committing himself. Since it was decided in Vienna to include Italy — arisen from revolution — in the circle of conservative powers, Austria, among others, refrained from condemning the scandal occasioned by the transport of Pius IX's body in July 1882. In the spring of 1882, through his special legate, Baron Hübner, the Emperor offered the deeply disappointed Pope the Monarchy's hospitality in case of need. However, Hübner was also to prevent the Pope from making use of the offer for asylum. This difficult assignment was successful enough for Leo XIII to say to Hübner: "My hopes, my love, and my trust I place, next to God, in his Majesty, the Emperor of Austria."

As a matter of fact, within the Triple Alliance Austria refused to guarantee Italy the possession of Rome. In 1888, the Emperor, through Hübner, again offered the Pope, who was being pressured by the Crispi government, asylum in Austria. Once again, quite in line with Austria's expectations, Leo XIII did not accept, but he gave serious thought to Salzburg in 1882 while still considering Trent as his place of asylum.

Under Secretary of State Rampolla, however, relations between the Monarchy and the Vatican cooled down considerably. The Vatican's pro-French and pro-Slavic politics had been noted with dismay in Vienna. Aside from that, there were continuous frictions with the Curia over a series of questions regarding the Monarchy's ecclesiastical policies, as, for instance, in the case of appointments of bishops. The Emperor's right to nominate was largely claimed by the royal and imperial bureaucracy. The Emperor nearly always agreed with its political leanings and, after 1880, was more and more oriented toward the problem of nationalities. Therefore, Italians and Slavs from the coastal areas and Dalmatia, unpopular Ruthenians in Galicia, but mainly men whose loyalty to the government was believed to be absolute were nominated bishops. Above all, the Curia created difficulties when bishoprics in Hungary and in the coastal areas were to be filled. Compromises were often reached only after exhaustive negotiations and mutual rejection of the candidates, as in the case of Hungarian Primate Simor's succession in 1891 and the occupation of Zagreb (1894) or Zadar (1902). In Zadar, there was a question of the imperial right of transfer of bishops, a matter which was energetically defended by Catholics as ardent as Max von Hussarek, who functioned as adviser to the Division of Religious Affairs in the Department of Education. Occasionally, there were also tough battles about the appointment of cardinals, as in the case of Archbishop Dr. Josef Samassa of Erlau, who had been nominated by the government. Samassa, in the opinion of the Vatican, had not appropriately opposed the Hungarian bill about civil marriage. He had also come out in favor of the imperial veto regarding the papal election to the Hungarian delegation in 1894. Therefore, Samassa was not granted the honor of cardinal until Pius X's pontificate. The efforts of Foreign Secretaries Aehrenthal and Berchtold to raise the number of cardinals in the Monarchy from six (four in the Austrian and two in the Hungarian part of the Empire) to seven were not successful.

On the other hand, those bishops of the Monarchy, "whose voices were gladly heard in the Vatican," did not enjoy the sympathies of the Austrian government. Among them were Bishop Stadler of Sarajevo and Bishop Stroßmayer of Djakovo, both spokesmen and protectors of the Croatians. Important was the question of the national liturgical languages, especially of the Slavic language in the Croatian-Dalmatian dioceses with Latin rites. The government considered it a means, intentionally employed by many bishops (e.g., Stroßmayer), to unite the Slavs or at least the southern Slavs on a national level "through the bond of the Catholic Church."

Another source of political and scholarly controversies between the Vatican and Vienna was the use of Hungarian as the liturgical language in the Greek dioceses of Munkács and Epirus by Magyarized Ruthenians. The Vatican finally forbade the use of the Hungarian liturgy. This did not prevent Rome from quietly tolerating its usage in the bishopric which was established in 1912 for the Greek-Catholic Hungarians in Hajdudorog, although the successor to the throne, Franz Ferdinand, had explicitly disapproved of it.

The Austrians also reacted sensitively to the Monarchy's right to protect the Christians of the Balkans and the Middle East. The Vatican's negotiations with

Turkey about the conclusion of a concordat for Albania failed because of Austro-Hungarian opposition. Austria-Hungary saw a violation of its protectoral rights in such an agreement.

All these differences lose their importance when compared with the most consequential controversy the Monarchy had with the Holy See during the pontificates of Leo XIII and Pius X: the fight over Hungary's legislation regarding religious policy. It goes back to 1890, to the so-called decree of abatement of former religion through baptism. Its goal was to obtain obedience to the law of 1868 pertaining to the religious denomination of children from denominationally mixed marriages. According to this law, children were to follow by sex their father's or mother's denomination; but it became common practice for the Catholic priest to "abate" the denomination through baptism. Already at that time, Rome had refused the transfer of baptismal records to the appropriate clergymen as was required by the state. This stand was evident in 1891, when the demands for civil marriage, civil matriculation, and general religious freedom were recapitulated in the Hungarian Parliament. The government succeeded at the end of 1894 in pushing through both houses of Parliament civil marriage, civil matriculation, and an amendment to the law of 1868. The Emperor ratified the new laws. In contrast to the radical-conservative Hungarian People's Party (founded in November 1894) and to many tendencies of the liberal Bánfly government, both Secretary of Foreign Affairs Count Kálnoky and the Austrian Ambassador to Rome Count Revertera tried to prevent an open quarrel with the Holy See. When Nuncio Agliardi of Vienna came to Hungary in April 1895 for an official visit, he pleaded with the Catholic leaders of Hungary in several speeches to side with the clergy in the ensuing fight with the government. This was followed by an interpellation in the Hungarian House of Representatives. In his answer, President Bánfly declared that the nuncio had overstepped his authority. The nuncio's behavior was seen as "tactless." Rome, on the other hand, refused to recall Agliardi, "provided that the insult inflicted upon the Holy Father in the person of His deputy be compensated," as Secretary of State Cardinal Rampolla explained to Revertera. Even though Rome disregarded an expressed apology by Vienna, it was not until 1896 that Agliardi was appointed cardinal and thus recalled from Vienna. Meanwhile in Hungary, the laws concerning the acceptance of Judaism and general freedom of religion had been enacted and, at the end of 1896, ratified by the Emperor. One could argue whether the changes in the Hungarian legislation regarding religious policy from 1894 to 1895 should be assessed as a *Kulturkampf* or a reform. Without a doubt, however, the long and at times dramatic controversy between Church and state could have been at least alleviated. Its acuteness was probably rooted in the fact that the Church was not only interested in defending the sacrament of matrimony and Catholic education, but also its dominant position in the Empire of Saint Stephen, which, according to Rampolla, "was never to be relinquished to the Calvinists and Jews."

The longer Leo XIII's pontificate lasted, the more powerful the secretary of state became. In Vienna, he grew more and more unpopular, not to say hated. Even the Imperial Ambassador Revertera, extremely loyal to church and Vatican, differed from him again and again. It was certainly not easy to get along with the proud and sensitive Sicilian. The animosities of the Austrian diplomatic corps seem to have originated in the burden imposed upon the Monarchy's domestic policy by the problem of nationalities, which was constantly increasing, especially during Leo XIII's pontificate, and reached a climax during the Badeni crisis of 1897. Rampolla sympathized with the Slavs, the Italians, the Christian-Socialists, and the respective Catholic democratic parties within Austria and Hungary. He granted France and Russia an important role in the foreign policies of the Vatican. Therefore, he had to be *persona ingrata* not only with the conservative and liberal politicians and with several Austrian bishops, but also with the Emperor himself. It remains to be decided whether, through the years, the Emperor remembered the cardinal's initial refusal to give his son Rudolf a church funeral. One thing is certain: never before had there been such accord on the use of the imperial veto as during the papal elections of 1903. As of the evening of 1 August, Rampolla was ahead with twenty-nine out of sixty-two votes, and was already greeted as the new Pope. One has to assume, then, that the Austrian veto announced by Cardinal Puzyna of Cracow on 2 August deprived him of the tiara. Giuseppe Sarto, patriarch of Venice, was finally elected Pope on 4 August 1903. He quickly fulfilled several of Austria's long-standing wishes; for instance, the promotion of Archbishop Samassa to cardinal. Yet more quickly (in January 1904, through the constitution *Commissum Nobis*), Pius X declared invalid the right of veto which France, Spain, and Austria had traditionally claimed, and imposed extremely harsh penalties upon participation in such an act.

The battle against "modernism," which Pius X fought so passionately within the Church, "was of no great consequence for the relations of this pontificate to the Habsburg Monarchy" (Engel-Janosi). Indeed, there was a "literary battle" in Austria; there were people who were accused of "modernism" and suffered harm because of it. Even the Viennese Archbishop Gustav Piffl was denounced in Rome as a modernist by integralists from the Viennese Commer-Kralik group. He had opposed the establishment of a Viennese subsidiary of Benigni's infamous organization *Correspondance de Rome,* whose purpose was denunciation. The tempest over modernism never reached the dimensions it did in France, Germany, or Italy. However, the Austrian public took an enormous interest in a case which was supposedly dramatized by the unauthorized and certainly undiplomatic action of Granito Pignatelli di Belmonte, nuncio to Vienna. Professor Ludwig Wahrmund, specialist in canon law from Innsbruck, who had published a study about the veto right of the Catholic powers in 1888, interceded in favor of reform Catholics Ehrhard and Schell in his lectures of 1902. On 18 January 1908, he gave a "scientific" speech for the general public in Innsbruck about the "Catholic world view and free scholarship," which was directed against the *Syllabus* and Pius X's encyclical *Pascendi* and was a masterpiece of massive anticlericalism. Moreover, Wahrmund published this speech in Munich after it was confiscated in Austria. Consequently, Nuncio Belmonte did not just call on Foreign Secretary Aehrenthal, but also announced to several newspapers that he had asked Aehrenthal to remove Wahrmund from his teaching position. He insisted on the truth of this statement even after Aehrenthal's official denial. As a result, Wahrmund became the hero of an enraged liberal public, and the Department of Education could not afford to dismiss Wahrmund had it wished to do so. Aehrenthal, in turn, demanded that Belmonte be recalled. Pius X, apparently feeling offended himself, pounded the table and declared: "I am not a diplomat, but I am immovable. I cannot allow Monsignor Belmonte to leave Vienna now. If his mother were on her deathbed, I would not give him leave at this time." Then he deplored the Josephinism which continued to exist in the Habsburg Monarchy. In 1911, when it was his turn, Belmonte became cardinal and was thus officially recalled from Vienna, though he was not received any longer by the Austrian foreign secretary. Nevertheless, Pius X generally expressed himself with benevolence towards the monarchy, giving it his unequivocal sympathy at the outbreak of the world war he had feared for many years.

On the Austrian side, in those "last years of a great power," when the bishops of the Monarchy paid homage to Franz Joseph on the occasion of his sixtieth anniversary of government in 1908, the Emperor once more emphatically acknowledged the alliance of throne and altar for which he had strived since the beginning of his reign.

C H A P T E R   4 7

The Conclusion of the *Kulturkampf* in Prussia and in the German Empire

Leo XIII considered himself to be a political Pope and wanted to break the isolation of his predecessor as quickly as possible. Considering his foremost task to be the conclusion of the German *Kulturkampf,* then the most pressing political burden of the Church, he initiated immediate action. On the day of his election (20 February 1878), he wrote a letter to Emperor Wilhelm I and other princes of states struggling with tensions concerning religious policy in which he suggested mutual attempts to restore the previously good relations. Berlin's unwillingness to compromise did not deter him. Supported by a few trusted men, such as Secretary of State Cardinal Franchi and Monsignor Czacki, he hurriedly drafted his program. The Pope and his advisers appreciated Bismarck's anti-revolutionary policies and were convinced that only a statesman of his caliber was capable of ending the *Kulturkampf,* which he himself had started.

The Pope's immediate and constant goal was to restore his freedom of movement, which the Church needed for its spiritual mission. If necessary, he was willing to grant the state concessions consistent with the Church constitution. An equally legitimate task, in his opinion, was the preservation and strengthening of the conservative social order. In an alliance between the papacy and a monarchal power such as Prussia and the Empire, Leo saw the most effective defense against socialism and revolution. He hoped for a comprehensive contractual agreement.

Convinced of the state's need for peace, he prematurely expected that Bismarck would more or less share his views and meet a conciliatory Pope halfway in these urgent controversies. The self-conception of the modern state, the complex political structure of Prussia and Germany, and the numerous psychological obstacles in the way of appeasement found little consideration in the Vatican. Neither the nuncios in Vienna and Munich who were fairly informed about the situation in Germany, nor the Prussian bishops were consulted. The politicians of the Center Party who were carrying the main burden of the struggle were not consulted either. The Pope considered himself, and only himself, the appointed guardian of ecclesiastical rights, believing that he alone was competent to conduct negotiations and make decisions in a struggle of such fundamental significance as the *Kulturkampf.* From a treaty between papacy and Empire, Leo also expected a strengthening of his claim to sovereignty, which he decided to cultivate more rigorously than his predecessor, who tended to give way to resignation. In addition, an agreement with the strongest European powers could facilitate the conclusion of the conflicts with other states.

The strength of Leo XIII's program lay in his insight that the Church should not be permitted to be content with the belligerent situation which it had inherited from Pius IX. Its weaknesses were the exaggerated assessment of his own possibilities and his insufficient knowledge of the situation in the various states, such as Germany. Only after setbacks which could have been avoided had the situation been analyzed in time and with realism did the Vatican come to the understanding that political reverses had to be accepted. The Pope, attributing greatest significance to appeasement, was more willing in a tight situation to compromise than his collaborators.

Of the reasons which compelled Bismarck not to reject Rome's peace attempts, only one partially agreed with the Pope's motives: the weakening of the monarchical state system through the *Kulturkampf* was increasing and filled the imperial court and many conservative circles with concern. More important for the Chancellor were the failure of the *Kulturkampf,* the changed situation as a whole, and his new domestic plans. The change of course from free trade to protective tariffs, which he initially thought necessary, could only be enforced against the will of the liberal allies in the *Kulturkampf* and required new alliances. Bismarck was used to discarding partners who had done their duties. He was already reapproaching the Conservatives. Now he planned to either attract the Center Party or to pass them over through negotiations with the Pope and to separate them from their ecclesiastically motivated mass base. Since the change of pontificate, the conditions for this move seemed more favorable than previously. His speculations on the Center Party and his consideration of the Conservatives indicate the larger framework of domestic politics primarily determined by the growth of social democracy. The change of economic policy was only part of the conservative turn and consolidation of the Empire's structures which were introduced by the Chancellor in the spring of 1878. Included are the Socialist law and the repression of all efforts to parliamentarize the Empire. A modus vivendi with the papacy and the Catholic Church suited this new domestic turn, as did the simultaneous new direction in foreign policy taken through the Dual Alliance with Austria-Hungary. The open struggle was to be ended, but the state's supervision over the Church was to remain. The harshest features of the May laws were to be eliminated; this was to be done, however, through unilateral laws. Bismarck never contemplated the treaty which the Pope envisioned.

The problem-ridden conclusion of the *Kulturkampf* took place in three stages: in the first, through negotiations between the Holy See and Prussia (1878–80); in the second, through discretionary mitigation laws (1881, 1882, 1883); in the third through the two Peace Laws (1886, 1887).

1. Bismarck reacted to the signals from the Vatican with utmost dispatch. He knew how to keep the Pope in the dark about his true intentions for a long time and entice him down the path of concessions through harmless advances, as for example the Roman question. Leo's obvious desire for peace put the trumps in the hands of the adversary.

Nuncio Aloisi Masella of Munich, the Prussian delegate Count Werthern, and Bismarck's Bavarian adviser Count Holnstein established the first contacts, expressing the Chancellor's wish for an honorable peace. Crown Prince Friedrich Wilhelm, representing his father, who had been hurt in an assassination attempt, wrote a letter which led to the main negotiations. It also contained Bismarck's program in its entirety, the implications of which were at first not understood in the Vatican. The Crown Prince explained that the laws of the state could not be adjusted to the Catholic dogmas and that a fight over principles was out of the question. He suggested, however, solving practical controversies together. In the summer of 1878, a meeting between Bismarck and Aloisi Masella was arranged in Kissingen, where the incompatibility of the two viewpoints became clear for the first time. The nuncio asked for the return to the status quo of 1871, which was characterized by the legal rule of the state Church. The Chancellor demanded papal recognition of the May laws regarding the duty to announce to the state candidates for clerical office and, in turn, offered restoration of diplomatic representation to the Holy See in order to conduct further negotiations about practical solutions. The prospect of a nunciature in Berlin was also held out. Though Leo XIII was very interested in diplomatic relations with Berlin, he could not agree to this offer because it preserved the entire legislation of the *Kulturkampf.* In addition, his peace policy had at that moment, lost its strongest supporter when Franchi suddenly died. Therefore, Aloisi's talks led to an atmospheric improvement. In place of negotiations, intentionally dilatory letters by Bismarck were exchanged between the new Secretary of State Cardinal Nina and the Chancellor until the summer of 1879. By order of the Pope, Nina demanded contractual guarantees for the autonomy of the Church, especially a free exercise of their ministry for bishops and clergy and the return of those who were expelled including religious as well as clergy. He also asked the state to waive its claim to interfere in the education of the clergy and religious instruction in schools.

Bismarck's anti-Polish attacks were skillfully handled by the Vatican, the Chancellor's hopes for papal influence on the Center Party seemed to have a chance of being fulfilled. Leo XIII's program left no room for independent action by the party. Above all, so the Vatican soon indicated, the party was to oblige Bismarck politically in order to facilitate the negotiations between Rome and Berlin. Only if these negotiations should stagnate was the party to exert pressure on the Chancellor. The first differences between the Curia and the Center Party occurred in the summer of 1878, when the party, against Rome's wish, refused to approve the Socialist law. Matters did not improve when the Cathedral Canon Moufang of Mainz, a respected man in Rome, explained the motives of the Center to the Curia. He said that the party wanted to keep political and ecclesiastical questions separate, that it was willing appropriately to fend off the socialistic danger, but that it did not want to approve Bismarck's exception laws because of its constitutional principles. At the end of 1878, Windthorst himself approached the Curia several times through the Viennese Nuncio Jacobini, who was rather open-minded toward the party, and suggested parliamentary procedures to revise the May laws. He believed that the cooperation between Center Party and the Conservatives favoring Bismarck's new economic policies had created propitious conditions. He concluded that, in a constitutional state, a party, with its influence on the parliament and the public, was able to offer better guarantees for the Catholic minority than treaties between the Vatican and the government could. To Windthorst, the time for a separation of Church and state seemed to be right. Such proposals were not in keeping with Leo's wish to come to terms about the question of sovereignty. From the improved parliamentary constellations, the Vatican drew the opposite conclusion. The Center was urged to form a close coalition with the Chancellor. This was the first climax in the attempts to influence the party, but they were unsuccessful. The leadership of the party, supported by the episcopate, insisted on its political independence.

As a result, Leo XIII agreed to negotiate details as Bismarck had demanded since Kissingen. New hopes were raised when Falk, Minister of Religious Affairs and the embodiment of the *Kulturkampf,* resigned and was replaced by highly conservative Robert von Puttkamer (1828–1900), who disliked the *Kulturkampf.* Falk's resignation was primarily caused by his differences from the orthodox faction of the Protestant Church, which was influential at the imperial court. In the negotiations conducted since the summer of 1879 in Vienna by Jacobini, the German Ambassador Prince Reuß, and canonical experts, both positions regarding the resolutions of the May laws were formulated. Both standpoints continued to be essentially irreconcilable. The Chancellor, however, did openly declare his sympathy for the papal claim of sovereignty. Henceforth, several concessions were announced during the talks in the following months. The ecclesiastical tribunal was to be abolished, the state was to resume payments, the extradition law was not to be enforced any longer, the oath for administrators of bishoprics was to be eliminated. Under state supervision, convents and seminaries were to be reopened. Denominational organization of elementary schools and teacher training were allowed, the prospect of assigning local school inspection to the pastors was held out.

Before the Pope was able to make his objections, Bismarck broke off negotiations. Apparently, he had just wanted to ascertain the positions of his opponent. His pretext was the opposition of the Center to several bills proposed by the government. In order to save some portions of his concept, Leo XIII went so far as to concede his duty to announce clerical appointments in advance and thus to make the very concession which both the Prussian bishops and the Center feared would result in the subjugation of the entire ecclesiastical life to the state bureaucracy.

2. Meanwhile, the Chancellor decided surprisingly to move ahead unilaterally.

In March 1880, discretionary legislation was announced, which was to empower the government to apply several resolutions of the May laws with moderation. To the Curia and the Center, the discretionary powers of authority seemed unacceptable because they aimed at regulating pending controversies without cooperation from the Church and substituted the arbitrary decisions of the bureaucracy for the severity of the current laws. Over the joint reactions to Bismarck's new plan there arose a relatively good collaboration between the Vatican and the party.

The bill, introduced in May 1880, was to make possible the state-controlled organizational reconstruction of the Catholic Church. The most important enabling acts proposed by Bismarck and Puttkamer pertaining to new regulations of the culture examinations and the readmission of dismissed bishops had to be stricken because the National Liberals believed that they went too far, and the Center, upon instructions from Rome, continued to reject them. The first moderation law, passed on 19 June 1880 by a four-vote majority, authorized the government (until the end of 1881) to employ episcopal administrators and bishops without an oath of obedience, to terminate the state's administration of the property belonging to newly filled dioceses, and to resume financial support by the state. The time limitation was proposed by the Conservatives, who wanted to characterize the discretionary legislation as a temporary arrangement. The law enabled state-approved clergymen to perform office as substitutes in vacant parishes and reinstated nursing orders without a time limit.

After his transfer to the Department of the Interior (1881), the new Minister of Religious Affairs, conservative Gustav Goßler (1838–1902), continued the strategy of gradual concessions. However, against the Center's wishes, he insisted on the state's authority in all matters concerning schools. In 1891, Goßler became the highest civil official of West Prussia. But only in the eastern provinces did Goßler proceed with his usual harshness. The second moderation law (31 May 1882) extended the enabling acts of the summer of 1880 to 1 April 1884 and contained the concessions which had earlier failed because of Liberal opposition.

The definite revision of the *Kulturkampf* laws demanded by Rome and the Prussian Catholics was postponed again. The government required complete realization of the May laws appertaining to the announcement of clerical candidates before it would consider revisions. Several initiatives by the Center were unsuccessful. In April 1883 Windthorst received the majority in the Provincial Diet for a resolution which demanded the "organic revision of the May laws." Bismarck and Goßler, however, succeeded in parrying the effects of the resolution by quickly enacting the third moderation law (11 July 1883). According to this law, conferring of clerical offices whose incumbents could be recalled and the arrangements for a substitution were no longer subject to report to the bureaucracy, and the state's right to veto the nomination was abolished. This was a rather remarkable accomplishment toward progress. The temporary filling of vacant parishes was now possible without time limitations. The Church had to be content with having to apply for the candidate's dispensation from the culture examination demanded by the May laws.

The first moderation law rendered possible the filling of the bishoprics of Fulda, Osnabrück, Paderborn, Trier, and Breslau, which, through the death of their incumbents, were canonically vacant. This required new negotiations between Berlin and the Vatican. Leo XIII was still disappointed about Bismarck's change of course. He agreed to negotiate only after some hesitation and upon the advice of the Center's leadership. The party pleaded for constructive use of the present accomplishments while reiterating further demands from the state. In the summer of 1881, Kurd von Schlözer (1822–94), then the Empire's envoy in Washington, negotiated with Cardinal Jacobini, who had meanwhile become Leo XIII's secretary of state. Schlözer knew how to deal with the prelates, and therefore Bismarck wanted him in Rome at all times. As the first head of the Prussian Legation to the Holy See, reopened in February 1882. he energetically participated in negotiations for the following five years. The restoration of diplomatic relations was a clear step toward normalization, though Leo XIII had hoped for more in this important area: he had hoped that the Empire would establish an embassy. The Chancellor tried to appease the Liberal opposition in the Provincial Diet by stressing that the function of the legation to the Vatican was simply one of concern with Church matters and, thus, with domestic affairs. At the same time, he had to convince the Vatican that the legation did indeed mean recognition of papal sovereignty. To stress this point, Bismarck avoided, as did Austria, giving Italy a formal guarantee of her territorial claims, which had been requested during the negotiations for the Triple Alliance in the spring of 1882. This would have meant a direct recognition of the annexation of the Papal State. Nevertheless, the treaty of the two imperial powers with Italy deeply disappointed the Pope, because it consolidated Italy and raised her political value. Now the Pope could not expect from Bismarck effective help on the question of the Papal State.

The concrete goal of Schlözer's mission was only reached gradually and with new difficulties. At first, the Holy See enabled only the cathedral chapters in Osnabrück and Paderborn to elect capitular vicars, who were able to assume office in February 1881 without state interference. In Trier, where an election was subsequently ordered, Philipp de Lorenzi, who had been chosen by that chapter, was rejected by the government. The negotiations were difficult and complicated by the differences between the liberal, pro-government minority and the ultramontane-intransigent majority. But the government and the Curia agreed to appoint bishops in Trier and Fulda who were nominated by the Pope directly, circumventing the chapter's right of elections. In choosing the candidate, a momentous compromise was arrived at: in Trier the Curia insisted on the staunchly ultramontane Alsatian Michael Felix Korum; in Fulda, the government insisted on compliant Georg Kopp. Korum established close contacts with exiled Archbishop Melchers, with Bishop Krementz from Ermland, and with the Center Party. He also led the opposition of the episcopate's majority to Berlin's religious policy. Kopp, ready to make concessions, represented the other side of papal policy. He felt just as responsible to the state as he did to the Church. Reconciliation of state and Church was of great concern to him. But since he felt that considerable concessions were necessary to realize this goal, he soon found himself in opposition to his colleagues and to the Center, which he accused of sterile opposition.

When these bishops were appointed, when Bishops Blum (Limburg) and Brinkmann (Münster) were pardoned and returned (in 1883–84), when government payments to the dioceses with state-approved bishops were resumed, and when vacant parishes were filled temporarily, the restoration of the Catholic

Church organization as desired by the government had indeed begun. After 1883 the shortage of priests was rapidly relieved. Many important questions, however, were still unresolved. The *Kulturkampf* continued to smolder, while the involvement of the faithful due to granted relief threatened to decrease in time. The gravest difficulties were caused by the state's continuous claim to the right of veto regarding the filling of offices, the training of the clergy, the question of religious orders, and the new appointments for the bishoprics of Cologne and Gnesen-Posen. According to the government, seminarians were to study only in the theology faculties of the state universities, a choice also preferred by liberal Catholics, while the Curia and the majority of the bishops insisted on seminaries controlled by them. The state bureaucracy and the National Liberals resisted the return of the religious orders. In Berlin reinstatement of Archbishops Melchers and Ledóchowski was felt to be a question of the state's prestige and was categorically refused, even though neither archbishop reacted any differently to the *Kulturkampf* laws and Leo XIII's concessions from the majority of his colleagues. In Gnesen the government wanted to name a German archbishop.

For the time being, neither side was willing to give in. In 1883 and 1884, the Pope and Secretary of State Jacobini declared several times that freedom in the matter of ecclesiastical jurisdiction and the training of priests was essential. Essentially, Leo XIII took the same position in this matter that the majority of the episcopate, led by Melchers and Korum, and the Center faction under Windthorst maintained.

3. In 1885 Leo XIII changed his mind, which led to the last phase of the conclusion of the *Kulturkampf*. Bishop Kopp had prepared the Pope diplomatically, corroborating his old notion that the *Kulturkampf* should be terminated as soon as possible in cooperation with rather than in opposition to Bismarck. He also declared the resignation of the archbishops a prerequisite for salvaging a situation that had run aground. He regarded preliminary concessions as inevitable, even as justifiable, since he trusted Bismarck. Just as important were the power shifts within the Vatican. As a result of his illness, Secretary of State Cardinal Jacobini, who tended toward the Center, had lost some of his influence. In 1885 the Pope was busy defending himself against severe criticism from intransigent Catholics, and therefore decided to continue his strategy of negotiations with even more persistence. Last but not least, because of the intensification of Italy's anticlerical politics, the Pope desired more and more urgently immediate and evident successes. Monsignor Galimberti, of Cardinal Franchi's school, had taken over the factual direction of the Congregation for Extraordinary Affairs in the summer of 1885. The Pope found in Galimberti an adviser who was as devoted as he was able. Monsignor Boccali, head of the papal secret cabinet, eagerly supported him. Both monsignors entertained close relations with the Prussian delegate, with Montel, Austrian Auditor of the Rota, who was also a friend of Schlözer's, frequently mediating.

Strengthened by his advisers, the Pope made his old program more concrete. Like the leaders of the Center and the majority of the Prussian bishops, he feared only the continuation of the *Kulturkampf*. While the former deduced from this that one should continue to demand the *status quo ante* and that compromises would eventually end in the Church's submission to the state, the Pope drew the opposite conclusion. He did not believe, as Windthorst did, that time would work in favor of the Church. He decided to make concessions in several areas. As soon as possible, he wanted to achieve a solution which would guarantee at least the more important ecclesiastical demands. On this level he met Bismarck, who was also interested in a speedy appeasement, considering the consolidated alliance with Austria and the impending international crisis in 1885. Both the Pope and Bismarck had to overcome the resistance of the intransigents within their respective camps and, therefore, used only the reliable aides. Kopp especially, who was trusted by both sides and who in 1887 had been appointed to the Prussian House of Lords with the Pope's approval, henceforth mediated between Rome and Berlin, bypassing his colleagues and the Center.

The deadlock was overcome in the summer of 1885, when Leo called Melchers to Rome as a cardinal of the Curia and appointed Bishop Krementz his successor in Cologne, even though no satisfactory solution was in sight for Gnesen. Krementz followed the principles of his predecessor, but that was not as relevant as the prestige the government had gained by removing the speaker of the episcopate in the years of struggle. Nevertheless, the decisive impetus came from Bismarck a few months later, when he offered the Pope to mediate between Germany and Spain in the controversy over the Caroline Islands, an offer he accepted with alacrity. The "prisoner of the Vatican" was officially recognized thereby as sovereign, and, for the first time, Leo could perform the international office of arbitration in the service of peace, a function which he hoped to secure for the papacy for good by way of returning to politics. The Pope thanked Bismarck for his help by awarding him the Order of Christ, an act that was interpreted, not only in governmental publications, as a demonstration of reconciliation.

During the following months, the foundations for the two decisive peace laws were laid in secret meetings, from which were excluded the Center Party, the majority of the Prussian bishops, Cardinal Jacobini, and the members of most of the duly qualified authorities of the Vatican. The original alternative of appeasement by treaty or law was replaced by a combination of both, as Bismarck had wanted. After consultation with the Vatican about what could be demanded from either side, the state enacted laws which legally validated the content of those consultations.

The draft of the first of these two laws was debated from February until March 1886 and encountered reservations similar to the first moderation law six years earlier. But now the changed constellation had its effect in the localities where the decisions had to be made. Contrary to parliamentary procedure the draft was initially not debated in the Provincial Diet, but in the House of Lords, where Kopp and some aristocratic "state Catholics" could appear and conservative governmental forces were in charge. Windthorst, Korum, and Krementz were ignored, even though they continued to be backed by the great majority of the Prussian Catholics. In previous years, visits and letters from Trier to the Curia had been welcomed, but now the attempt to send one of the bishops to the Vatican and convince the Pope to take a stricter stance failed. Bismarck and Leo XIII, Galimberti and Kopp succeeded and achieved a great deal: the law (21 May 1886) disposed of the ecclesiastical tribunal and the culture examination for theology students. In most dioceses, seminaries and convents were allowed to reopen without the state supervision required by May law, thus widening the restricted work of the religious orders. Even before the law was published, Leo XIII assented to Bismarck's renewed request appertaining to the duty to report candidates for permanent positions in pastorates.

The fierce discussion over the second law was also encumbered by the septennate controversy. Bismarck maneuvered the Center Party into this struggle, assisted by Leo XIII and his advisers. The Chancellor used the crisis in foreign policy to further enlarge the armed forces and, above all, to effect another septennate, i.e., the commitment of the military budget for seven years. As on similar former occasions, Bismarck wanted to limit the *Reichstag's* right to appropriate funds. The antiparliamentary course of 1878 was consistently pursued. Under the pretext that a Franco-German war was on the way, Bismarck persuaded the Pope to exert massive influence on the Center in favor of the septennate. In this matter, as in the question of the Caroline Islands, Leo was guided by his exaggerated concept of the papal mission of order and peace. The Center, however, insisted upon its political independence. According to its constitutional fundamental concept, the party, along with the Freethinkers, did not want to sanction more than a three-year military budget. Such a compromise did not satisfy Bismarck. The *Reichstag* was dissolved; the government presented the new elections (21 February 1887) as being a decision for or against Germany's defense preparedness. Through this demagogical tactic, the Chancellor accomplished the alliance of the National Liberals and the Conservatives, the so-called cartel. It was not difficult to accuse the two opposing parties of animosity toward the Empire. The Pope did not wish a catastrophe for the party and was alarmed by the startling criticism on the part of Korum and Bishop Senestréy of Regensburg. Therefore the Center endured but an insignificant defection, mostly noble Catholics from the right, who sympathized with Kopp's course in any case. Thanks to his solid voting block, he could return to the *Reichstag* with ninety-eight deputies (previously ninety-nine), while the Freethinkers, under pressure by governmental propaganda, lost half their mandate. In March 1887, the cartel parties, who had emerged from the election campaign with new strength, helped the septennate to victory.

The Pope directly intervened in the final preparations for the second law by sending Galimberti to Berlin, where he also expressed the Pope's wider political desires. They ranged from the restoration of the Papal State to papal arbitration for the purpose of avoiding war. As had happened on former occasions, Bismarck's simple and polite approval awakened exaggerated hopes and further willingness to compromise in as yet unresolved controversies. Again, there were serious disputes over the next moves between Galimberti and Kopp, who were essentially satisfied with Bismarck's offers, and Windthorst and his faction, who wanted to continue fighting in order to gain more. By order of the Pope the Center finally supported the bill of the Chancellor, who took great efforts to overcome the resistance of the liberal advocates of the *Kulturkampf.* The law, enacted on 29 April 1887, limited, as far as the state was concerned, the duty to report candidates and the government's right to veto the permanent filling of pastorates. At the same time, it waived the obligation to fill them permanently. Seminaries and convents were allowed again in all German-speaking dioceses; most religious orders could return and were given back their property, which had been taken into custody by the state.

The state had thus abandoned most of the discriminatory measures of the

Kulturkampf. Remaining from the *Kulturkampf* legislation, but in moderated form, were the state supervision of schools, civil marriage, the pulpit paragraph, the Jesuit law (until 1917), and the duty to announce candidates, but in moderated form; the Church paragraphs of the constitution were not reinstated. The state's control over the Church was consequently preserved to a degree which went far beyond the situation of 1871, but Bismarck was not able to reinforce this control. The Church, relieved of the shackles of the *Kulturkampf,* could no longer be kept dependent through the remaining restrictions. In the following years, a status quo of balance between Church and state, acceptable to both sides, was reached. In that respect, Windthorst, Korum, and their disciples had been too pessimistic. Leo XIII handled the concrete controversies quite realistically. The relatively favorable conclusion of the *Kulturkampf* did indeed increase the Vatican's diplomatic prestige, which Leo was particularly interested in, since, in 1887, Francesco Crispi became the head of the Italian government. He was strongly anticlerical and desirous of further isolating the Vatican. The Pope rightfully called the second peace law an *aditus ad pacem,* expressing in this manner his hopes for further moves by the state. His hopes for such moves were fueled by the enforcement of his pro-Prussian politics of 1886–87 through important decisions pertaining to personnel. Circumventing the suffrage of the cathedral chapters, which primarily tended toward the Center's course, he appointed progovernment bishops in Limburg and Kulm. In Gnesen-Posen, for the first time, he appointed a German archbishop in the person of Julius Dinder from Königsberg, Kopp, so bitterly opposed by the Center, was promoted to Prince-Bishop of Breslau a few months after the achievement of the compromised peace which he had supported so diligently. Following Cologne, Breslau was Prussia's most prestigious episcopal see. But Leo XIII's other wishes and far-reaching political expectations remained unfulfilled. The Chancellor had reached his goal and, therefore, did not think of further concessions. The Pope made it easy for the Chancellor to deceive him. Nevertheless, Bismarck, in complete command of the current situation, did not sufficiently contemplate the long term effects of his actions. The Pope's final disappointment in Bismarck and German politics form the background for the pro-French reorientation, which Leo XIII and Jacobini's successor Rampolla launched soon after.

Bismarck also did not succeed when he attempted for the last time, on the occasion of the septennate, to force the Center Party into submission and thus force a strong opponent out of the front which was pressing for parliamentarism. The party of the Catholics had supported the Chancellor on many issues, such as his fledgling policies of worker protection. In the eighties the party had already become an important and stable factor in German politics, which could only be hampered for a few years by the cartel of 1887.

Therefore, the *Kulturkampf* was one of Bismarck's worst mistakes in regard to domestic politics, aside from the persecutions of the Socialists. However, he was able partially to compensate for it through a skillful termination of the conflict. The *Kulturkampf* laws and the exceptive laws diminished the trustworthiness of the state and the ideas concerning law of the Germans. The timely evolution of state structures as well as the integration of the Catholics into the nation-state was delayed unnecessarily. The relations between the denominations as well as between the Germans and Poles were lastingly affected, especially as the fight in the eastern provinces was continued as a struggle between nationalities. Thanks to the mobilization of new political forces and Leo XIII's diplomacy, which was dependent on these forces, German Catholicism survived this test of strength. Nevertheless, militant liberalism reached a goal which it had pursued since the sixties: the Catholics had been completely isolated spiritually and socially in those years of struggle.

As groups tend to do when pushed into a ghetto, they reacted by relying on their own strength and by refusing to recognize that some of the liberal initiatives merely corresponded to increasing secularization, which negation could not forestall in the long run. The most important new creations of the *Kulturkampf* period were the *Görres-Gesellschaft* and the *Volksverein.* That the defensive attitude of most Catholics was not unjustified was proven, last but not least, by the founding (1886) and activities of the *Evangelischer Bund.* It embraced those Protestants who felt the termination of the *Kulturkampf* to be a capitulation to the Catholic Church, and initially enkindled extreme denominational polemics.

C H A P T E R   4 8

The Development of Catholicism in Switzerland

The defeat of the Catholic cantons in the War of 1847 significantly determined for generations to come not only the external but also the internal situation of Swiss Catholicism. The federal constitution of 1848 assigned the regulation of Church relations to the cantons on a federalistic basis, in spite of increased centralism. But in the elections, majority suffrage (election by proportional representation first in 1918), deliberate division of constituencies, and, last but not least, domestic differences among Catholics rather favored the Liberal candidates. The occurrences after 1848 were especially radical in the canton of Fribourg. But the reaction of Catholics was just as resolute: in the parliamentary elections of 1856, the Conservatives were overwhelmingly victorious (sixty-four versus three radical representatives). Bishop Marilley of Lausanne-Geneva, expelled in 1848, was able to return. The development in the canton of Lucerne was similar. There, the teaching sisters of Baldegg had to be readmitted, and the Conservatives were successful in May 1871 despite the First Vatican Council. Special problems existed in Ticino because it belonged to the dioceses of Como and Milan. In 1861 a law regarding schools could be enacted which was favorable to the Catholics. In the 1859 elections in Unterwallis, the Conservatives were successful. It should be noted, however, that liberal cantons with Catholic minorities (e.g., Basel, Zurich, Winterthur, Berne, Lausanne, Geneva) practiced toleration (moderated, to be sure, by the ecclesiastical law of the state) even though the denominations were frequently financed through secularizations. These were the external conditions for intensive pastoral work in respect to the diaspora.

To find the pragmatic middle of the road between centralism and political federalism, essential to the Catholic cantons, was a difficult task for Swiss Catholicism in view of this cantonal situation. The Catholic *Schweizerischer Studentenverein* (Swiss Student Association), founded in 1841 in Schwyz, was the first organization to expand throughout all the cantons. Patrician Theodor Scherer-Boccard (1816–85) of Solothurn directed the editor's office of the *Schweizerische Kirchenzeitung* and became chairman of the *Schweizerischer Pius-Verein* (Swiss Pius Society), founded in 1857 in Beckenried. The Benedictine monks transformed the cantonal school in Sarnen (Obwalden) into a reputable secondary school, and the monasteries at Einsiedeln and Engelberg enlarged their curriculums.

The *Kulturkampf,* occurring at the same time as the First Vatican Council, is closely related to the occurrences in Germany. Before it ended, *Die katholische Stimme aus den Waldstätten* (The Catholic Voice of Waldstätten) appeared in Lucerne, following Döllinger's argumentation. After 1873, professor J. H. Reinkens of Breslau, since 1873 bishop of the Old Catholics in Germany, founded in many cities in Switzerland "societies of free-thinking Catholics," from which sprang the Christian Catholic Church of Switzerland, founded in 1875–76 in Olten. But one should consider the specific social differences within Swiss Catholicism itself, the resistance of Catholic patrician families to the constitution of 1848, and the differences between agrarian Catholic cantons and the predominantly liberal urban bourgeoisie, whose Catholics, to a large extent, had rejected Pius IX's *Syllabus.* Eduard Herzog, professor of theology in Lucerne, born in Schongau, was a very devout representative of the Christian Catholics, but had hesitated to accept his election as bishop in Often. Local conflicts usually broke out because the Christian Catholics demanded the right to use the Catholic churches.

While the cantonal governments in Zurich, Lucerne, and Saint Gall exercised restraint, severe conflicts flared up in Berne and in cantons belonging to the diocese of Basel-Solothurn, especially at the bishop's see of Solothurn, where, in 1870, Eugen Lachat was forced to accept the closing of the seminary (which had just been opened in 1858) by the "Diocesan Body" (representatives of the canton governments). On 29 January 1873 the "Body" dismissed Lachat because he refused to keep in office the clergy who opposed the dogma of infallibility. The cantons of Lucerne and Zug did not support his dismissal. In Aargau and Solothurn convents and monasteries were closed and the many developing Christian Catholic congregations were favored (especially in the canton of Aargau, where whole congregations often followed their priests on the path away from the Roman Catholic Church). The Benedictine monks from Maria-Stein who emigrated across the French border were able to continue to administer their parishes in the cannon of Solothurn. The canton of Berne proceeded with severity against the priests in the Jura who were loyal to deposed Bishop Lachat (living in Lucerne), eighty-four of whom were expelled from Switzerland; others had to conduct services in secret hiding places.

Aside from Bishop Lachat of Basel-Solothurn, Gaspard Mermillod (1842–92) was also the object of harsh struggles regarding ecclesiastical policies. In Geneva, the overthrow of the patrician government by the Liberals turned out to be advantageous for the Catholics. Subsequently, the congregations, strengthened by immigrants, expanded quickly in the fifties. In Notre Dame, a church dedicated in 1859, Mermillod delivered moving sermons, and in 1864 Pius IX appointed him titular bishop of Hebron, auxiliary bishop of the diocese of Lausanne, and vicar general of Geneva, replacing Bishop Marilley of Lucerne, who resigned in 1879. The cantonal government regarded this as a circumvention of the constitutional decree forbidding the establishment of new bishoprics. Oriented toward the leftist Liberals since 1870, the government dismissed Mermillod in September of 1872 as priest of Geneva's Notre Dame. In January 1873 the Pope responded to this move by appointing Mermillod apostolic vicar in Geneva. In February 1873, the government, having already enacted a radical state-church law in 1872, expelled Mermillod from the country. He continued his activities, however, from Ferney, on the other side of the French border. The Federal Council immediately answered a papal letter to the Swiss Catholics of 21 November 1873 by severing diplomatic relations. A centralistic revision of the constitution in 1874 intensified the state's Church law.

The *Kulturkampf* in Switzerland did not last as long as in Germany. At the end of 1875, the Federal Council gave permission to the clergymen who had been expelled from the Berne Jura to return, and after 1878 they were allowed to perform their office without disturbance. The leftist liberal canton government in Geneva suffered several defeats in 1878. In Bellinzona (Ticino) a conservative government was formed in 1875. Thus Leo XIII's diplomat Domenico Ferrata found a favorable situation when he came to Switzerland as a result of the Federal Council's appeal to the Vatican. The Geneva question had already been solved in 1883: when the successor of Bishop Mermillod (who had resigned) passed away, Leo XIII was able to appoint Mermillod bishop of Lausanne-Geneva, gaining approval of the Federal Council, but sacrificing Pius X's Geneva plans (the apostolic vicariate was abolished). That Ferrata had difficulties later on adjusting to the local situation was due to internal affairs within the Catholic Church. The Basel and Ticino questions were resolved through pragmatic unification. At first, the person of Bishop Eugen Lachat presented a problem: the non-Catholic cantons of the diocese of Basel-Solothurn wanted peace, but rejected Lachat's return from exile in Lucerne. Gioacchino Pecci, as bishop of Perugia, had demonstrated his sympathy for papally loyal Lachat, and now, as Pope, he had to sacrifice Lachat for the sake of a political arrangement. Ferrata's investigative mission resulted in Lachat's being persuaded to resign. Ferrata's visit permitted the bishop to save face before the outraged members of the diocese. In Ticino, separated by the Provincial Diet from the dioceses of Como and Milan (in 1859, Austria had lost Ticino to Piedmont), the problem was that the Catholic conservatives of Bellinzona wanted their own bishopric, while the Federal Council insisted on annexation to the German-Swiss diocese of Basel-Solothurn. Ferrata and Swiss politicians, led by the Protestant Conservative deputy Emil Welti (of Aargau), agreed at a conference (1884) that the Pope should appoint a persona grata (F. Fiala) to the bishopric of Basel-Solothurn, at least for the time being, and that Lachat should become apostolic administrator in Ticino with a temporary office in Balerna. The Ambrosian liturgy was to be preserved together with the Roman liturgy. After Bishop Lachat's death (1886) the Ticino question had to be renegotiated. In 1887 Ferrata (meanwhile named nuncio to Belgium) had to deal with two Freethinkers in Berne, discretely indicating to them that the administrator from Ticino could be expelled and possibly govern from Italy. It was agreed that the parish church of Saint Laurenz in Lugano be elevated to the Cathedral of Ticino, and that an apostolic administrator be appointed who had to be from Ticino (triple nomination) and required the approval of the bishop of Basel.

In the eighties, a new generation of Swiss Catholics came to the forefront. In 1888 three fellow students, Kaspar Decurtins from the Grisons (1855–1916), twenty-six years old and the youngest senator, Ernst Feigenwinter, a lawyer from Basel (1853–1919), and theologian Josef Beck (after 1891 professor in Fribourg) founded the *Verband katbolischer Männer und Arbeitervereine der Schweiz* (Catholic Federation of Men's and Worker's Unions of Switzerland). This group intentionally addressed itself to Swiss Catholicism as a whole, turning away from the Pius societies of the Catholic cantons with their traditional leadership. The first plenary meeting in 1889 — held in Zurich — behaved as if it were a Catholic convention with an address by the Pope, so that the president of the Pius societies, A. Wirz, had occasion to complain. In the course of the growing conflict, Wirz pleaded for "the kind of prudent policy following conservative Catholic principles we inherited from our forefathers." This was an allusion to the fact that Decurtins and his friends had been founding members of the *Schweizerischer Arbeiterbund* in Aargau, which had a large membership of Social Democrats. For Decurtins, Catholicism was a house with many mansions, and he lived in the "left" wing.

In the nineties, the competition between the Pius society, now calling itself *Schweizerischer Katholikenverein,* and *Männer- und Arbeiterverband* increased rapidly. A union of both organizations was rejected. The idea to direct the rural and the conservative urban population toward the *Katholikenverein* and the industrial areas toward the *Männer- und Arbeiterverband* was utopian as well as characteristic. A new initiative emanated from Saint Gall, where, in 1899, Prebendary Johann B. Jung (1861–1922) founded the first *Christlich-soziale Arbeiterverein* and where the first *Christliche Gewerkschaft* was formed. Both organizations were combined in 1903 in the *Zentralverband christlich-sozialer Organisationen,* whose president was Dr. Alois Scheiwiler (1930 bishop of Saint Gall). The *Christliche Gewerkschaften* were interdenominational, though the Protestants were rather in low profile. Starting in 1903, the Christian-social *Zentralverband* spread from east Switzerland throughout the entire Swiss confederation. In 1904 the *Katholikenverein* and the *Männer- und Arbeiterverband* were combined. This move was introduced in September 1903 at the first "general" Catholic Convention in Lucerne. In 1905, the *Katholikenverein* counted 40,983 members. Kaspar Decurtins remained stubborn. Decurtins had gained a reputation in Rome for his involvement in the social-political Catholic *Union de Fribourg.* After 1906, the Christian social groups in various cantons began to form a political party which cooperated, in spite of differences, with the Conservative People's Party established throughout the cantons in 1912. The separation of church and state proceeded essentially without problems. Catholics received the status of an association under civil law; the Protestants and Old Catholics fell under the law applying to public bodies — a distinction that was generally made according to the individual cantonal situation. Bishops' conferences took place annually.

The Swiss Catholics accomplished a goal to which the Germans had aspired in vain: they created a Catholic university. Leo XIII hesitated to support the idea as can be seen by his "cold and short" treatment of the intermediary on 6 June 1889. His behavior was not based upon monetary demands. On 4 November 1889 statesman Georges Python succeeded in prevailing upon the cantonal government in Fribourg to found and finance a department of law and philosophy. Mermillod was absent during its creation. Behind his back, Decurtins traveled to Rome in December 1889 to solve the delicate matter of the theological faculty which Mermillod wanted to have established by the bishops. Python and Decurtins miraculously persuaded President Ruchonnet to have the Pope appoint the professors of the theological faculty from members of the Dominican Order (he was interested in preventing students from studying theology in foreign countries). On 21 January 1890 the Pope gave his approval and donated 100,000 francs and a golden chain for the president. It had not been easy to recruit professors for this university. After a fruitless attempt in Louvain, Decurtins concentrated his efforts especially in Germany, where Gustav Schnürer accepted a position in history. This resulted in 1898 in the "German crisis" at the university: eight professors submitted a collective resignation because they felt encroached upon by Dominican censorship. Decurtins acted rather pompously in this matter and spoke about the German "royal gibberish." The Dominicans' lust for power was proven by the fact that they demanded from the Swiss theology professor J. Beck that he propagate the order's mission. It was necessary to find a replacement in Austria. In 1906 Pius X had occasion to praise the university and the Dominican order for their theological position.

In the *Neue Züricher Nachrichten,* the talented writer Heinrich Federer, under the pseudonym "Senex," sharply condemned the extremely conservative contemporary Catholic literature. He made common cause with Bishop Schmid von Grüneck of Chur, who called Carl Muth a "modernist" when he visited the bishop on the advice of the prior of Einsiedeln.

C H A P T E R   4 9

Italian Catholics between the Vatican and the Quirinal

The *Non expedit* at the Time of Leo XIII

The political and sociological situation in unified Italy did not show any fundamental changes. Attempts were made to adjust to the new institutions, which were very liberal and lay oriented. Suffrage was rather limited: in 1871, of a total population of 25 million, only 600,000 were listed on the register of voters. The parliamentary deputies came from well-to-do social classes, where the different interests of the industrialized North and the rural South clashed. They also did not stand up, to the same extent, for the lay orientation as represented by the state. The Catholics, obedient to the hierarchy, maintained a critical distance from the unified state because it had annexed the Papal State and enacted anti-clerical laws (church marriage was not recognized by civil law; the orders were suppressed and their properties confiscated; ecclesiastical welfare organizations were secularized; religious instruction in schools eliminated). In this manner, Catholics declared their solidarity with the protests of the Holy Father and the excommunications imposed by him on the "usurpers." These intransigent Catholics developed their ecclesiastical societies according to the uniform directives formulated by the *Opera dei Congressi e dei Comitati Cattolici;* but, obeying the *Non expedit* of the Vatican, they refrained from political life and election campaigns. With their newspapers, they wanted to be the spokesmen of the "real country," demanding, above all, freedom from want. This was quite in contrast to the "legal country" of the parliament, the government, and government-dependent authorities, which represented only 2 percent of the population due to the electoral system and which were under the influence of Masonic anti-clericalism. Therefore, the "obedient" Catholics were happy with the symptoms of weakness which the new state demonstrated, because they felt it was indicative of its decline. The political development of Italian society and the state, proceeding hand in hand with the economic development, brought about changes precipitated in the Catholic movement through new directives and several new structures.

But there were also the "liberal," "disobedient" Catholics, who disapproved of the lay principles of the state derived from the *Risorgimento.* However, they were of the opinion that this state represented the historical reality to which one needed to adjust. They therefore founded a conservative party in order to support the principles and institutions of the national Catholic traditions in the spirit of loyal cooperation with the official authorities.

Some of the ways in which the open attitude of Pius IX's successor expressed itself were: the fact that he resumed and strengthened diplomatic relations with the states, that he approved and furthered Catholic initiatives in social and political areas, and that he used gestures and words to address the Italian people and their statesmen which were conciliatory or, at least, efforts toward easing the tensions. The *Non expedit,* strongly adhered to in 1886 (participation in political elections was not allowed), was gradually regarded as a tactic in the relations between conscientious Catholics and the national unified state. In 1880 the official *Osservatore Romano* (11 June) was already interpreting the *Non expedit* as an active element, as "preparazione nell'astensione" ("preparation with temperance"). Expanding voting rights to new segments of the population (1882) worried several bishops, who feared that the leftists, under the influence of the Freemasons, could be strengthened and that anticlerical politics could be radicalized, unless the voices of the Catholics, excluded through the *Non expedit,* were able to create a countermeasure for the purpose of defending the religious and social order. Pope Leo returned to his rigid position and demanded the restoration of the temporal power of the Pope and, especially, the return of Rome (15 June 1887).

The directive "preparation with temperance," which exceeded the rather passive and polemical motto "nè eletti nè elettori" ("neither the elected nor the voters"), expressed by the *Osservatore cattolico* of Milan, entertained the idea of prospects for political activities, however remote they might be, and created the division of militant Catholics into three groups: some concentrated on purely religious activities; others waited for an occasion to expand these activities to the political sector; while others turned to social areas. But the Holy See immediately expressed its preference, requesting action in the service of the defense and preservation of the faith, love for one's fellow man, and traditional Christian morality. The arbitration proposals, intended at least partially to restore the Papal State and grant to the Kingdom of Italy the remaining territory, were rejected, even by less sectarian politicians, who, affirmed Italy's claim to all of Rome. The anti-ecclesiastical lay legislation also hurt the works of charity, emanating from faith and animated by it. It forced them to be absorbed in congregations of charity, which excluded the pastor and were administered by the community (1890). This happened at a time when Catholics increasingly concentrated their efforts on the administration of congregations for which the *Non expedit* was invalid.

Thus the Italian Catholics were called upon to apply their strength and abilities to religious social activities. For this purpose, the existing organizations were further developed, especially the Catholic youth society, certified in 1886, the *Società della Gioventù cattolica italiana,* which had been joined by the more polemically oriented *Associazione Cattolica per la libertà della Chiesa* of 1866. According to its motto "prayer, action, sacrifice," the association was especially active in the area of piety and edification. Aside from this, Catholic parish committees (*Comitati cattolici parrocchiali)* sprang up, which were religiously active and often joined the traditional confraternities which were not affected by the suspension laws. They referred their members to new areas of activity and bound them more strictly to obedience toward the Pope and the bishops and to solidarity with the protests of the "prisoner of the Vatican." Soon, in Rome, Pavia, Genoa, Milan, and Pisa, Catholic university groups were formed (*Circoli universitari cattolici*). In all these associations, a stronger social sensitivity — the new sign of loyalty to the Catholic faith — was combined with religious activities and strict adherence to ecclesiastical regulations regarding the observance of holidays and fast days. This expressed itself primarily in new institutions, like the "Vincent Conferences" which Ozanam also organized in Italy. A certain militant spirit was included.

For the purpose of coordinating these parish and diocesan committees, the *Opera dei Congressi e dei comitati cattolici* was added in 1874. Soon this league became the driving and constructive force of the Catholic movement in Italy. In 1884 Leo XIII gave this organization, established under the pontificate of Pius IX, a new structure, which reflected its progress. It was divided into five sections: Organization and Catholic Action, Christian Social Economy, Instruction and Education, Press, Christian Art. Because of the industrial development, which caused the workers to demand social legislation, the second section (*Dell'economia sociale cristiana*) was of special importance. In dealing with liberal and Socialist economic theories, Giuseppe Toniolo designed a Christian social program in which he presented the medieval guilds of the Christian past as models of socio-economic institutions.

The *Opera dei congressi* — the name implied the annual meetings of the diocesan and regional committees — was supported by the more active parish clergy of northern and central Italy. It was further aided by the "notables" who followed, according to family traditions and by conviction, the directives of the hierarchy and did not relate to the new political leadership class (landed proprietors, noblemen, independent professionals). The *Opera dei congressi* was also endorsed by the people, especially the rural population, who identified with the Church institutions which were affected by the suspension laws, because they did not see their standard of living improved by the new laws, particularly by the tax laws and the military draft. Therefore, they were willing to lend an open ear to the Pope's protests against the secular state and to agree with them. Thus the *Opera dei congressi* was able to pursue detailed action for the purpose of deepening the consciousness of faith and to inspire the activities of Catholic societies by enforcing and coordinating local diocesan and regional initiatives.

The Catholic movement, stimulated in this fashion, not only made use of the hostile press in the large metropolitan centers of Turin, Milan, Florence, Naples, and Venice, but also in provincial cities like Brescia and Bergamo. The polemics and ridicule of scandals, which resulted in confiscations and law suits, were followed by discussions of the actual problems and the possible solutions according to the principles of the Christian conscience and the institutions inspired by it.

The leaders were all strong personalities, firmly rooted in their convictions. Therefore they often had differences of opinion regarding organizational questions, the interpretations of papal decrees, or the selection of the cadre. Most of all, they fought over merging the Catholic movement into the socio-political reality of the Italian state under the regime of the *Non expedit.* The new orientation took the socio-political efforts of the Catholics north of the Alps as a model and tried resolutely to promote Catholic action in the social and economic area (banks, companies, publishing houses, trade schools, etc.). The encyclical *Rerum novarum* of Leo XIII was cited. This group, however, encountered the opposition of the intransigent wing, which feared infection by the liberal spirit and compromises with the institutions of the secular state. The area most likely to cause controversies between the two positions was the administration of communities and provinces which were open to Catholics. It was the task of the Catholics, voted into these administrations, to protect the primary schools, which were subject to the community, from sectarian and laic influences, to appoint as administrators of charitable institutions men who would respect their religious goals and arrangements regarding church services, and to make sure that the hospitals, especially psychiatric clinics were staffed with members of religious orders. The need of gaining control in the communities and provinces by appropriate election preparations played an increasingly important role for the Catholic movement in Italy and created emotional tensions.

Along with the intransigents, who strictly adhered to the papal decree forbidding cooperation with the secular state, there were the transigents, who, like the intransigents, relied upon their own religious conscience. They were, however, of the opinion that the interest and the duty of the Church demanded that they not seek refuge in the ghetto and flee the world and its progress in the socio-economic and political institutions. Instead, they were to delve into the new realities and work from the inside out, in order to bring to bear the motives and forces of the Christian tradition and thus to shape these realities in the Christian spirit. These transigents were partly spiritual heirs of the "New Guelphs," of the first Gioberti, like Cantú and Tosti, and partly confirmed supporters of the liberal Catholicism in accord with the ideas of Montalembert, Lacordaire, Görres, Newman, and Lord Acton. Many of them had shared the patriotic enthusiasm of 1848. They had held political offices in the decade of 1848–59 and in the first years of the Italian kingdom and had thus participated in the *Risorgimento* movement. Some of them, e.g., Lambruschini and Capponi, identified spiritually with Jansenist circles of the early nineteenth century or they advocated the reform programs of A. Rosmini (which were both religious and socio-political). They were members of the educated clergy, personalities who had a reputation because of their education, their profession, or their wealth; reputable members of one of the two chambers; mostly Liberal Conservatives who had many supporters, particularly among the middle class. There were also personalities of the hierarchy among the transigents. The transigents had certain elements of the press at their disposal, among them respected daily papers, such as the Milanese *La lega Lombarda.* They were also heard by papers of the conservative right, like the *Perseveranza,* appearing also in Milan, where they could present the intentions and motives of their "moderate" position compared to the anticlerical radicalism of many proposed laws and several divisions of the state bureaucracy. The numerous faithful Catholics who held offices in the administration, in the military, and in the different branches of government were able to effect a moderate interpretation of the anticlerical laws and apply them appropriately. Moreover, these transigents were in the position of offering their services as arbitrators to the state authorities, to the politicians, and to the public administration. They were also able to negotiate formulas and procedures which made it possible for Vatican-appointed bishops, for instance, to maintain their sees and to receive the appropriate revenue without having expressly to submit to the statute of the guarantee law requiring the *Exequatur* by the government.

There were also issues on which the transigents (liberal, middle-of-the-road Catholics) and the intransigents agreed: they both pointed to the necessity of public order; both fought socialism as a socio-political doctrine and as an organization devoted to class struggle. The majority of their "notables" came from the same circles, primarily in Piedmont and in certain areas in southern Italy. Both sides respected the monarchy and relations with the personalities of the House of Savoy. Beyond the polemics of the Roman question and the legal regulations, which were to be valid for the ecclesiastical institutions, these common features found expression in the election alliances between clerical and moderate groups. In the administrative elections, they seriously defeated the coalitions of radicals and Socialists and their lay program.

During the last two decades of the nineteenth century, in a unified Italy, further crass economic and socio-political disparities appeared, not only between the north and the south, but also between the different social classes. The transition from an artisan to an industrial economy, which had to compete with the more productive branches of industry north of the Alps and was largely dependent on their finances, their machines, and their technicians, occasioned constant disquiet and anxiety. The organization of the working class under both the flag of Marxist socialism and the banner of the most radical revolutionary syndicalism, took place even in the rural areas. Strikes, civil unrest, and suppressive measures followed one after another in all parts of the country and found a strong echo in the press. The expansion of suffrage, which in 1882 increased the number of eligible voters from 2 to 10 percent of the population, provided the Socialists, in coalition with the Radicals, representation in parliament. In 1891, the official founding of the Italian Socialist Party took place. Its program represented the demands of the workers, but also contained a lay anticlerical policy. All this favored the draft of a social legislation which was in line with the encyclical *Rerum novarum* and was therefore energetically promoted by the Catholic movement, especially by the Christian Social Economy section of the *Opera dei congressi* and by the *Unione cattolica di Studi sociali,* founded by Tonioli. With this kind of sponsorship, the Catholic societies, in accordance with the demands of the social-political situation, produced new institutions: workers' cafeterias, parish houses, employment agencies, trade schools, societies for mutual assistance, production, credit, and consumer agencies, banks for the support of various professions and institutions, and workers' associations with a union character, which competed with their efforts toward socialistic associations. On the theoretical level, the *Unione cattolica di Studi sociali* formulated in 1894 a "program of Catholics in regard to socialism" which mirrored the demands and the experiences of the agricultural and industrial world of Lombardy, Emilia, and Tuscany.

All this had an effect on the *Opera dei congressi,* whose organization and program was severely criticized by the young. They insisted that the defensive attitude, the predominantly religious and devotional orientation, the nagging paternalism, and the gap between the secular state and the democratic organizational forms should be abandoned in favor of greater latitude regarding decisions and freedom of movement. Even the *Non expedit* was now open to various interpretations: distance from the secular state meant obligation to an autonomous social and political organization, which obviously had to agree completely with the principles of Christian morality. On the basis of the formula "preparation with temperance," this line was already being presented by the three most active centers of the Catholic movement: in Bergamo with Medolago Albani and the newspaper *L'Eco di Bergamo,* in Milan with Filippo Meda and the *Osservatore cattolico,* in Brescia with G. Tovini, G. Montini and the *Cittadino di Brescia.* This increased the demand for more extensive efforts in the political field. The motives were provided, on the one hand, by the need to insure the socio-economic principles of the movement in legislation and to enforce social laws which would agree with the Christian maxims of cooperation between the various social classes. The other motive was the need to fight socialism and its associations on their own ground. The contentions between the young and the old increasingly vitalized the Catholic congresses, with the result that the Vatican more and more emphatically demanded harmony and unity.

In 1898 (the year of war between Spain and the United States) disturbances flared up here and there in Italy because of an increase in bread prices. In Milan, they were violently suppressed with the help of military forces dispatched solely for that purpose. Among other measures, the radical Socialist and Catholic opposition newspapers were suppressed and their editors imprisoned. Thus the year 1898 put the Catholic movement to the test: personalities of the intransigent wing tried to keep their distance from the mass disturbances and their spokesmen and made efforts to restore the Church and Catholicism as guarantors of the existing social order. Therefore, the government in Rome took measures only against some Catholic organizations in the north, not, however, against the presidency of the *Opera dei congressi,* which was still dominated by such socially backward intransigents as Count Paganuzzi. This resulted in rapprochement between the conservative intransigents and the conservative governmental authorities. The young, however, saw in the need of the people an opportunity to attack the "secular hunger state" even more vehemently and were preoccupied with the idea that social action could serve as a springboard for seizing power for the benefit of the masses.

The Holy See took careful note of everything that was going on in the Catholic movement. It was obvious that the Curia harbored differing opinions. Some supported a trend which tolerated or even favored the expansion of Catholic action in the social field and, though with more constraint, even in the political arena. Among them were cardinals, who pointed to the model and the accomplishments of the Catholic movement in Belgium, Germany, Austria, and the United States, and to whom Leo XIII gave ear. But there was also an opposition group which still regarded every political and social action employed to overcome the tensions present in Italy, every instance of cooperation with the existing authorities, and every exploitation of state laws as support of the "Italian revolution," a minimization of the problem of the Roman question, and an undermining of the *Non expedit.* According to their opinion, the *Non expedit* was to be strictly adhered to, so that the Vatican could exert pressure on the Quirinal. Particularly in view of the energetic demands from outside their ranks (meaning the laity), these opponents of the movement liked to point to the fact that quite a few bishops rejected it also. The men in the Vatican preferred to confine themselves to the confirmation of general directives and to the admonition to activity in the spirit of harmony.

That very year, 1898, a new leader of the Catholic movement appeared with the publication *Cultura sociale,* which was intended to be for the Italian Catholics what the *Neue Zeit* represented for the German Socialists. This leader was Don Romolo Murri. Born in August 1870, he received his doctorate in theology from the Università Gregoriana in Rome and founded the Catholic university circle there in 1894. But soon he extended his activities to the social field. He remained intransigent in regard to the Roman question, considering it a symptom of the deep schism between the Christian and the modern "heathen and materialistic" concept of life and culture. The contrast between the dome of Saint Peter's Basilica and the tricolors upon the Quirinal were for him the "sign of conflict between two different and mutually antagonistic cultures, "the secret of the inner history and the future of the Church." With this statement he recommended fighting the liberal, secular state to the bitter end. The boycott of the ballot boxes was, therefore, not just an act of obedience toward the Pope, but also the conscious rejection of the freedom-persecuting state.

Murri's general promotion of social action was close to Toniolo's heart. Yet Murri's call for autonomy was more urgent and he demanded the expansion of social programs in the area of politics, suffrage, and legislation. Thus, the demands for autonomous action in the spirit of a "Christian democracy" were voiced more and more at the congresses of the *Opera dei congressi* in Milan (1897), Ferrara (1899), and Taranto (1901). It encountered vehement reactions by the individuals and currents which, in this ferment, were forced to reformulate their motives and forge new alliances, not only in the central, but also in the regional diocesan and local committees and related organizations.

At stake was the traditional domination of Paganuzzi, Medolago Albani, and both Scottons from Venetia, who were all in contact with militant groups in Venetia, Lombardy, Piedmont, Tuscany, and Rome. In 1899, a Christian democratic union (*Fascio democratico cristiano*) was formed in Milan, and in Turin an "action program" containing twelve points was formulated outside of the *Opera dei congressi.* They all referred to the papal decrees, the *Rerum novarum* and the subsequent "instructions." They interpreted them as they saw fit and mobilized their friends in high Vatican circles to have their program confirmed.

From within the Congregation for Special Church Affairs, Leo XIII appointed a "permanent commission to regulate the Catholic movement in Italy" and entrusted it with the task of examining the many documents pertaining to the presidency of the *Opera dei congressi,* to its various sections, the subgroups, and the numerous bishops who had expressed their need for help and had asked for directives. The main point of controversy was "Christian democracy" as a name and a program. It was typical for the methods of Leo XIII that he was able to assert his already clearly defined decision. Basically, he was siding with the young, in whom he saw vital energies of the Church. But even though he approved and recommended the social action arising from below, "he was intent on having the inspiration and coordination filter down from above, from his will" (D. Secco Suardo).

In this manner, Leo XIII prepared his intervention, followed by the encyclical *Graves de communi* (18 January 1901). With reference to *Rerum novarum,* his circular letter insisted that the action of the Catholics proceed in unity, to the exclusion of all politics, in conjunction with a central organization, and in submission to the Pope and the bishops, who had the right to take practical measures "according to the local and personal situations." In the "fundamental theoretical and practical points," which were to be publicized among the people, the following was declared: "Christian democracy shall not have any political significance; it advocates the welfare of the lower classes, but also pays attention to the upper classes; it does not support plans for insubordination and opposition to public authority; rather, it proposes to put all its energies into easing the hard lot of the manual laborers, gradually enabling them to provide their own livelihood" (D. Secco Suardo).

The success of the movement's social and religious action, which enforced the people's loyalty to the Pope, affected the people's conscience and procured more political impact for the movement. This provided the Vatican with greater influence on the Italian government. In December 1901, as a result of its concern for public order, the government proceeded toward a policy of exceptive laws, which both the Socialist radicals and the younger members of the Catholic movement rejected with determination.

Leo XIII's attempts to mediate between the various factions of the Catholic movement in order to preserve unity and identity encountered difficulties. The customary compliancy toward the Pope was not able to break the opposition of the conservatively inclined older generation, who tried to justify the existing economic and social order by referring to the events of 1898. They alluded essentially to paternalistic motivations, since they were only concerned with love and charity. The boisterous younger generation, on the other hand, was reluctant to adhere to the institutions organized and ruled from above. Inspired by Murri, they undermined the homogeneous structure of the *Opera dei congressi* which was less and less representative of the Catholic movement in Italy.

CHAPTER 5 0

The Failure to Reconcile Catholics and the Republic in France

The Ecclesiastical Policy of the Republicans

During the enthronement of Leo XIII, everything indicated that the existence of the Republic in France, formed in 1875 under such tremendous difficulties, was secure. The elections of 1875 brought a Republican majority into parliament which held 64 percent of the seats in the Chamber of Deputies. Moreover, the failure of the *coup de main* of 16 May 1877, shortly before the papal elections, was a successful prologue to the take-over of the provincial diets and the offices of the mayors. These victories of Gambetta's friends were bound to be followed by the overthrow of the senate majority in January 1879 and by the massive invasion of a group of deputies who held, after the elections in the summer of 1881, 83.6 percent of the seats. In the following years, the government successfully survived an economic crisis and an attack by the Boulangists. But now, the Church leaders had to recognize that it would be prudent to come to an understanding with a Republic on whose demise they could not count.

The Republicans, in turn, were eager to secure their election victory through a "republicanization" of the upper administration (e.g., the State Council and the large institutions, the army and the judiciary). The Catholic Church was especially affected by this policy of the "Republican defensive" in view of the farspread social influence which it had gained through preaching and charity, through its schools and, most of all, through the religious orders. This impact was feared by the leaders of the Republican majority, and therefore they placed systematic secularization of public life at the top of their ideological and political program. During the budget debate of 1877, a plan was presented, and consequently a fund was provided to finance an investigation into the significance of the orders. This investigation, carried out in 1878. It showed that the total number of order members amounted to at least 30,000, among them 3,350 Jesuits. The congregations of women included about 128,000 persons who cared for approximately 16,500 girls schools. There were three times as many religious priests as secular ones, and it was discovered that this number approximated that of 1765, when the number of religious priests had peaked in the eighteenth century. Most of the congregations were not legally authorized. This explains why, on 15 May 1879, the Minister of Education Jules Ferry supplemented his bill regarding the introduction of a generally obligatory, secular primary education with ARTICLE 7, which prohibited the nonauthorized congregations from any kind of instruction. It also explains why he enforced this prohibition through appropriate decrees, at first directed against the Jesuits, who were expelled in 1880, and then, in the following November, also directed against the other nonauthorized male congregations.

The struggle between the Republic and the Church erupted most vehemently over the issues of religious orders and schools. The bishops, in turn, waged a campaign against the laicization of elementary education, which was resolved on 28 March 1882, and against the cancellation of payment in connection with the abolition of official manuals for public instruction. But in many other areas, religious demonstrations in public were forbidden or strictly regulated. Processions, preaching, lay societies, courts, hospitals, and cemeteries were supervised, and the Magnet Law regarding divorce was finally passed after intensive debates (19 July 1884). The cardinals of Rouen and Paris declared in festive *Observations* (1 June 1882) "that more than twenty bills regarding the regulation of religion had been proposed."

The aim of such a policy was, in fact, the suspension of the concordat. Separation had already been the main theme of the election campaign in the summer of 1881, and, when the two chambers were combined, a bill was introduced, reiterating the proposals of four deputies who had also demanded the dissolution of the concordat. Those responsible for Republican policies, however, hesitated to make this extreme move. Ferry especially adhered to a concordat policy which, in June 1879, he had called "a strict application of the treaty of 1801 and which was to satisfy everything and to secure a rigorous defense of the rights of the state."

This caution resulted from an analysis of the country's religious and political situation deduced from the three important series of reports. They clarified the very obvious regional differences in the religious practices in urban areas, which, from the vicinity of Paris, extended toward the north up to Normandy and to the northern and northeastern region bordering the Central Mountains and which were characterized by increasing separation from the Church; as well as in the wooded and mountainous rural areas (Lyon and the eastern border of the Central Mountains, the Savoy Alps, etc.), where a general religious practice continued to dominate. In addition, the reports listed a stronger tendency for separation in the areas bordering the *departements* Yonne, Sâone-et-Loire, and, above all, in the Mediterranean region from Narbonne to Nice. This separation rarely affected the religious situation directly, and even in the most de-Christianized areas, as in Haute-Vienne, religious practices continued. Among the peasants, there was a general and widespread mistrust of the priests' meddling in the political and social arena, and of everything conventionally called the "government of priests." This mistrust existed even in the most devout areas. It increased according to the extent to which the clergy itself demonstrated through remarks and behavior that it was intransigent, generally in southern areas. In the vicinity of the bishops' sees, the reports often detected a social class with such intransigent and vehemently anti-Republican sentiments, where the lay dignitaries and society ladies were competing with each other. These groups were often under the leadership of the respective vicar general, who, simply on the basis of his age, often controlled large elements of the clergy. They were also able to make themselves heard in the *Semaines religieuses,* and were intent on exerting direct influence on the leadership of the dioceses. The only authority which these circles obeyed and which was able to suppress the opposition of the clergy was the bishop, mainly through the full powers of authority which the concordat had bestowed upon him. This was the reason why the government had conceded special importance to the figure of the bishop and the role he could play as a mediating factor. The prefect emphatically pointed out the advantages of a direct agreement with the bishop in order to avoid unpleasant incidents. For dioceses where the clerical opposition could possibly increase, the responsible agencies of the Republic systematically appointed bishops who were interested in a settlement. The reports finally showed that alongside the priests in Mayenne who were strongly influenced by the nobility, a new generation of priests was growing from among the lower clergy, mainly in the western parts of the country, who were conciliatory and Republican. In the poorest areas, the intransigence of the clergy was moderated by the traditional high esteem for the ruling authority, which in the eyes of the people, was the guarantor of an ordered life and of respect for the individual.

Thus the concordat treaty continued to be firmly rooted in the political reality of the country, in the almost universal loyalty of the peasantry toward their religion, and in the desire of a certain segment of the upper and the lower clergy to be cooperative. The government wanted to preserve the concordat in letter and in spirit.

Thus the French found themselves in the paradoxical situation of having to deal with two powers which, in theory, had opposing political and philosophical principles, but, in practice, made efforts to bring about a reconciliation. In spite of those representatives of the Republican state and the Church who regarded the separation as inevitable, both parties had one interest in common: preventing the break as long as possible. Thus this alliance was only a temporary endeavor based upon expediency and de facto situation, a weak base, which was threatened as soon as the conflicts were stronger than the desire to agree.

The Politics of Reconciliation (1878–92)

The further development in the relations between the two powers was also subject to fluctuations which were based upon both French domestic politics and the opposing influences within the Curia which affected Leo XIII. In the first period, embracing the years 1878–90, politics was marked by mutual efforts to avoid alienation. The French government and especially the Foreign Office made attempts at the Vatican to diminish the significance of anticlerical pronouncements and the majority's legislation. The kind of politics which part of the Concordat Commission expressed in their definite rejection of the desire for separation asserted itself on every occasion. In the spring and summer of 1880, attempts were made to incite the congregations' political declaration of loyalty, which would have limited the application of ARTICLE 7 and thus allowed a reduction of expatriations. After the enactment of the law of March 1882, pertaining to obligatory and laicized elementary instruction, Jules Ferry's pronouncements defined the neutrality of schools in a way which paid respect to the freedom of conscience. The government tried to negotiate the cancellations of salaries which it had ratified after the incidents regarding the manuals for state instruction. Finally, the government seized every opportunity to emphasize that it was willing to pay a certain price to prove that its foreign policy served the defense of the Catholic interests.

The Holy See and the ecclesiastical hierarchy were intent on preventing the defense of the Church's rights against the anticlerical laws from developing into an open opposition to overall policies. In this respect, Leo XIII's efforts to keep the ultramontane press in check and to counterbalance it with the "liberal" press were of great importance. So was his attempt to tie the leadership of the Church once again closer to a responsible hierarchy. On every occasion, the Pope protected the Nuncios Czacki and di Rende against the attacks of the intransigent Catholics. He did the same for those bishops who championed the policy of reconciliation.

When the elections of October 1885 seemed to offer a favorable chance for the formation of a Catholic party, Leo XIII expressed himself negatively, because the well-known statements of its main advocate, Albert de Mun, would have, without doubt, stamped the party with an anti-Republican imprint. In 1889, the Pope, encouraged by French domestic politics and the international situation, believed that the time had come amicably to conclude his policy of reconciliation with France. The philosophy of Henri Bergson, *"Les données immédiates de la conscience,"* and the literary prose by E. M. de Vogüé and Paul Bourget had undergone a spiritual renaissance. Finally, the Holy See felt that the policy of coalition within the Triple Alliance made the need for close cooperation even more urgent. Leo XIII requested Monsignor Domenico Ferrata, whom he appointed nuncio to Paris in June 1891, to report to him personally about the state of these efforts. Called upon for comment, the cardinals of Paris, Lyon, and Rennes declared that they were not competent. It took no less than five appeals until Cardinal Charles de Lavigerie, in October 1890, was willing to deliver a declaration, ignoring the dangers which such an involvement entailed for his missionary work. When, on 12 November 1890, he received the officers of the Mediterranean fleet in Algeria, he proposed a toast to the French navy, suggesting to the French Catholics the "unconditional acceptance of the Republic," and added that "they would surely not have to experience the disapproval of any authority as a consequence." Rome endorsed this viewpoint only semiofficially, and Leo XIII let fifteen months pass before he expressed himself similarly in his encyclical *Au milieu des sollicitudes* of 17 February 1892, following a brief to the French cardinals on 3 May 1891. This hesitation can certainly be explained by the cool reception with which the leaders of French Catholicism responded to the papal attitude.

The term *Ralliement* had a different significance in the deliberations for Leo XIII and for the French Catholics. For the Pope, in line with his "political" encyclicals of 1881, 1885, and 1888, it was not at all a question of "baptizing" the Republic, but rather of accepting this government as a tool to re-Christianize legislation and the social institutions. For him, it was also not a question of founding a Catholic party, but rather of combining the Catholics of all persuasions and the Republicans in one comprehensive conservative union. This union, with the parliamentary power it represented, was to contribute to re-Christianization within its constituency. Such a concept, however, was difficult to accept for the majority of the bishops and the leading lay representatives of the Catholic public. The tradition of the "religious defensive," which they embraced, compelled them rather to form a Catholic party. From this arose the *Union de la France chrétienne,* which was founded in April 1891 and which refused the succession to Charles de Lavigerie, archbishop of Algeria.

In the Catholic public, however, the pressure in favor of the policy of the "toast" became more and more noticeable. Several bishops had already taken such a position; and some newspapers and individual groups from Paris and Bordeaux were working toward a reconciliation. The appearance of *Rerum novarum,* primarily, introduced a change in the political attitude of the Catholics. The existence of groups which had formed years ago and wanted to take the same path of social action accounts for the response which this encyclical encountered. Among them was the *Association Catholique de la jeunesse française* (ACJF), which, under the leadership of Albert de Mun, was able to fill even part of the aristocracy with enthusiasm and, above all, the committees which had been established by the newspaper *La Croix* since 1887. With the help of these committees, Abbé Théodore Granier awakened the interest of the Catholic public to the fate of the workers and farmers, which created the foundation for a union which was constituted in 1892 as the *Union Nationale.*

The Pursuit and the Failure of Reconciliation (1892–99)

At the time when Leo XIII commented on the occurrences in France, the voices within the Catholic public had become more conciliatory. The intransigent wing of the newspaper *L'Univers* defected and founded the paper *La Vérité.* On 12 May 1892 the *Assemblée des Catholiques* dissolved the *Union de la France chrétienne.* Two of their most important leaders, Albert de Mun and Armand Mackau, joined the *Ralliement,* ignoring the criticism of their friends from the monarchic right. The moderation of these men during the Panama crisis and during the anarchist crisis was received by the Republicans with satisfaction, and they gave their official approval to this policy. Everything seemed to indicate that the reconciliation would be confirmed by the people's vote at the elections in August 1893.

These elections, however, turned out to be a disappointment. Only about thirty advocates *of Ralliement* were elected, and not one of the Catholic leaders who had so courageously expressed his opinion was among them. The reason for this may lie in the fact that they had not succeeded in agreeing on a parliamentary level, which would have enabled them to form a "unified front" in the election campaign. But Albert de Mun, leader of the *Association Catholique de la jeunesse Française* wanted primarily to stress the common denominator of Catholicism in regard to the constitutional engagement of the *Ralliement,* and he opposed the ACJF to the Catholic League. Another deputy supported by several liberal Catholics mainly from the southwest of the country, finally began paving the way to the moderate Republicans through the Catholic League. There was no election coalition between the two groups, and even after the election, no link could guarantee the cohesion between the various groups of the *Ralliement.* They divided and dispersed, joining the various factions of the Chamber, and (since their leader did not belong to the Chamber and they were without help) were finally absorbed by the moderate majority which enjoyed relative stability.

After the failure of the attempt of 1893, there was no more hope for the success of a policy which aimed at a parliamentary coalition. Thus a second phase began, during which, in view of the impending elections of 1898, the reconciliation was to take place on the stage of public opinion. This phase was, indeed, the great time of the "second Christian democracy." Representative of this trend was a group of young clergymen who tried to create new possibilities for pastoral work. They recognized the political power of their apostolic involvement. Fruits of their work were the organization of congresses for the Christian Democrats, the first of which took place in May 1903 in Rheims, and the founding of newspapers like *La Justice sociale, Le Peuple française,* and *La Démocratie chrétienne,* which appeared until 1908. In September 1893, in the northern area of Hazebrouck, one of these democratic clergymen, was elected in place of a respected Catholic. This election was an example of the awakening of the Republican consciousness of a large part of the clergy and the farmers of this area marked by Christian faith. The Christian Democrats' centers were in the north, where there was a connection to the Belgian Catholic social movement, and in the area of Lyon close to the *Chronique du Sud-Est.* The impact of this newspaper extended over the *departements* of Ain, Loire, and Ardèche and into the Mediterranean area, where a paper was founded in Montpellier with the significant title La *sociologie catholique.* Another active center existed in the area around Bordeaux. Simultaneously, and often in connection with the Christian Democrats, the local boards of the newspaper *La Croix,* whose owners were Assumptionists, reached the peak of their development in the year 1895 with 3,000 local subsidiaries. The great number of local editions of *La Croix* (approximately 100 in 1897) and its wide circulation, which secured a total of almost 700,000 per issue, made this press organ an important support of these committees. *La Croix* did also reach the middle classes, but mainly the lower middle class, the workers, and the rural population. Having the same basis as the Christian Democrats and the ACJF, the members of these committees insisted on a definite political engagement. At a congress held in 1895 an election committee of *La Croix* was formed under the name Comité Justice-Égalité.

Now the congresses of the Christian Democrats, in turn, founded an election federation in Rheims (1896) and Lyon (1897). It was actually a question of organizing all those groups, which had grown rapidly since 1890, and of placing them under a common leadership while preserving a certain autonomy. However, the elections of May 1898 resulted in the same failure of the *Ralliement* as the elections of 1893. The following months brought the end for the federation and the decline of "Christian democracy" in France.

Very much to the disadvantage of the "new spirit," there continued to be considerable sources of tension between the Catholics and the Republicans. They were passionately nurtured by the readers of *La Croix.* Two points were of importance: the government of Alexandre Ribot had imposed additional taxes on the religious congregations, the so-called *Abonnement,* which had incited a wave of protest. Primarily, it was anti-Semitism which provoked the Catholic masses against the Republic. Édouard Drumont charged the Republic with being in the grip of a "Jewish-Masonic" conspiracy, which was sneaking into the higher ranks of the military, thus threatening religious values and national integrity. This partly explains why the revision of the sentence for the Jewish Captain Dreyfus, attaché in the War Ministry, had drawn such attention from the public. Dreyfus had been falsely accused of delivering military secrets to Germany and, in 1894, had been sentenced to deportation for life. The episcopate did practice noteworthy constraint in this affair; but this cannot be said about the lower clergy and the masses of Catholics, among whom only a small minority courageously confessed to be *"dreyfusards."* Recent research has shown that Édouard Drumont's articles in the newspaper *Libre Parole* had found an undeniable echo in Catholic circles, and that the anti-Semitism of *La Croix* was indeed of a different nature, but nonetheless very real. The newspaper unconditionally took the side of the army when, in 1899, heated debate flared up about the trial of the Court of Justice of Rennes. Even among the Christian Democrats anti-Semitism was strongly represented.

The nationalistic excesses in the spring of 1899 turned against the person of President Émile Loubet. That was not unexpected, since a coalition had been formed in Parliament whose anti-clerical program was directed against the religious congregations. It was the motto of the "Republican concentration" which achieved a majority for Pierre Waldeck-Rousseau on 26 June. Their Republican leaders did not hesitate to blame the Catholics' intrigues for the sentence which prevented Dreyfus' acquittal in August and resulted merely in a reduction of his punishment. In November, the houses of the Assumptionists in Paris and the offices of *La Croix* were subject to a police search. The suppression of the Assumptionists, following a trial in the District Court, and Leo XIII's decision to deprive them of the direction of the *Bonne Presse* have to be seen in the context of the influence they had had in the previous ten years. The Assumptionists were the first religious congregation to be affected by the measures which finally led to the separation of Church and state.

Now the Republic returned to its policy of persecution, which, in the eyes of the general Catholic public, it had never completely given up. This poses the question of whether French Catholicism in its majority was ever really ready for reconciliation. The anti-Semitic wave and the corresponding press propaganda allow the conclusion that the Catholic population itself was, to a large extent, responsible for the failure of the reconciliatory efforts by causing an anticlerical feeling within the committees and the administration of the Republicans.

CHAPTER 51

On the Road to Conservatism:
Belgium, the Netherlands, and Luxemburg

Belgium

Around the turn of the century, thanks to the constitution of 1831, Belgian Catholicism had been able to flourish so intensely that Belgium was practically a Catholic country, at least in regard to the classical arena of struggle against liberalism: the school system. This constitutional reality, however, deviating from the liberal statutes, was endangered. The ecclesiastical circles, on the one hand, regarded the political status quo merely as an opportunity; and the Liberals, on the other hand, forgot the time of common resistance to the Dutch Monarchy and reacted with increasing anticlericalism. There were also indications of considerable differences between the agrarian and the early industrial areas, between the Flemish and the Walloon areas regarding religious practices. The radical-liberal government of Rogier and Frère-Orban (1857–70) was overthrown because the powerful Catholic congressional movement, organized by the laity, was also politically transformed, and the domestic differences within Catholicism pertaining to the question of the constitution could temporarily be settled.

But the conflict continued to intensify. Pope Leo XIII, who was familiar with the Belgian circumstances through his nunciature (1843–46), believed, when taking office, that peace could be preserved in Belgium. After the June 1878 election victory of the Liberals, he still tried to prevent an intensification of the situation, while requesting respect for the constitution. A pastoral letter by the Belgian episcopate in December, quite contrary to the intentions of Leo XIII, was composed in a sharp tone, which coincided with the belligerent attitude of Archbishop Victor-Auguste Dechamps of Mechelen, who had also intervened in the German *Kulturkampf.* On 10 July 1879 the law regarding nondenominational elementary schools was enacted, followed by a law pertaining to public secondary and high schools. The Belgian bishops excommunicated those parents who sent their children to public elementary schools and did the same to teachers who taught there. In vain the Pope attempted moderation. A papal letter to Dechamps of 2 April 1880 finally recognized the attitude of the episcopate, which Leo could not disavow. But since he had promised the Belgian ambassador to the Vatican a compromise, the government felt deceived and broke off diplomatic relations in June 1880.

The school laws were simply a failure, especially in Flanders. By the end of 1880, 580,680 children went to free Catholic schools and only 333,401 to public schools, which were being increased to no purpose. The ecclesiastical sanctions against the communal school system could usually anticipate religious obedience and willingness to make sacrifices (e.g., dismissal of civil servants). The people also complained about the financial burdens which were the consequence of the state's rather irrational school policies. In the elections of 10 June 1884 the Liberals suffered a devastating defeat, which was to be a determining factor for a long time to come.

In February 1885 the Belgian government sent a special delegate to the Vatican, and in May, Domenico Ferrata, who had earned diplomatic credits in Switzerland, came discretely to Brussels as nuncio. On 21 June, during the Te Deum on occasion of the jubilee of the Belgian kingdom, he was already able to function as the doyen of the diplomatic corps. He preluded Lavigerie's famous toast by a toast to the royal couple during the anniversary of the railroad, receiving the applause of the Liberals who had approved the budget for the Vatican Embassy in 1886. The discussion of two questions pertaining to canon law during the nunciature of Ferrata (until 1889) is indicative of the Leonic pragmatism. The liberal government of Frère-Orban had suspended denominational cemeteries in 1879. Since Beernaert hesitated to change this, the Pope recommended to his nuncio to wait and see. More crucial was the fact that in 1876 the Holy Office, via the French episcopate, had prohibited the Catholic judges in France from cooperating in divorces (legalized again in 1884) even if it required their resignation. Neighboring Belgium, where divorce had been legalized in 1809, was worried about this, and therefore Ferrata informed them that the decree was only binding for the French bishops, not for Belgium.

In reference to Belgium it was noted that the difference between liberal and social Catholicism was not as general as it seemed. The delay in social activity was said to have to do with the Lamennais crisis of Catholic Liberalism in Belgium. The Catholic bourgeoisie was energetically involved in the enormous industrial growth going on since the sixties, which after 1880 could continue only with strict economic concentration because of the European protective tariff policies. Therefore King Leopold II, who had done much for the country, encountered strong resistance when he wanted to introduce compulsory military service within the framework of his military policy, because he did not anticipate again having the good fortune which had guided him in the war of 1870. The socio-political aspect amounted to the fact that everybody could free himself from military duty by financing a substitute, which was naturally not possible for a worker or a small craftsman.

Moreover, the gradual removal of the property qualification had to be accomplished in spite of the opposition of the Catholic Conservatives and their allies, the Liberals of Frère-Orban's persuasion. The pioneers in this struggle were the younger Liberals, but it was primarily the Socialists whose demonstrations forced the government, dominated by the Catholic party, to introduce general though still limited suffrage in 1893. The Conservatives did not expect that the Catholics, rather than the Socialists, would profit from this law, especially in the Flemish-speaking areas.

The signal for a social reform which could no longer be ignored (unusually low wages, long working hours) was the general strike, starting in Liège on 18 March 1886 and commemorating the Parisian uprising of the commune in 1871. There was violence, and military forces were dispatched. The Beernaert government was now forced to design reform laws against the opposition of the extreme right, led by Charles Woeste, an intransigent convert. Liège became the center of the Catholic social movement which recognized that traditional paternalism, often enough just a phrase, was no longer adequate for the growing industrial society. In East Flemish Ghent in 1875 a group of young workers came together, from which the Anti-Socialist League emerged. By 1911 the organization had one hundred thirty-five staff members, its own daily paper, and productive social institutions.

The Socialists felt that this organization was breaking class solidarity and consequently collisions occurred. Among the first of the Catholic labor leaders who belonged to the working classes themselves was the weaver Léon Bruggeman from Ghent, who, together with printers, founded a Christian-oriented union in 1882. In 1886 and 1887, the first two socio-political congresses took place in Liège, endorsed by Bishop Doutreloux, who was a good-natured priest but not a fighter. Charles Woeste called these events "exaggerations," but he assessed them correctly as an opposition, since people were a great deal more realistic in Liège than in France. The Liège Congress (1890) enjoyed sizable international participation and was quite lively. The discussions concentrated around the generally controversial state intervention, which Woeste exposed as *"Césarisme,"* and the equally delicate question of whether employers and employees should form joint or separate organizations. It was this question which again divided Belgium's Catholics into two vehemently opposed groups. Without meaning to establish their own party, the approximately one hundred Catholic workers' societies combined to form the *Ligue Démocratique Belge.* Charging Woeste with being interested only in an increase of the state budget for the Church's sake and the public support of the Catholic schools is probably a polemical exaggeration. But there is no doubt that the power of the *Parti Catholique* was determined until World War I by the strong interests of the middle-class Catholics, against whom the Christian social forces had difficulties bringing their interests to bear, especially since they were often enough in disagreement and looked for a coalition with either the Conservatives or the Christian social movement on the left. It was also due to the abstract style of the encyclical *Rerum novarum* (1891) that it could become the object of particularly serious controversies in respect to its interpretation. Bishop Doutreloux had defined papal principles in a pastoral letter in the beginning of 1894. Leo XIII, in a letter to the Belgian episcopate of 10 July 1895 suggested a conference which took place in March 1896 in Mechelen and decided on a rather inappropriate compromise. Meanwhile a group of young Catholic deputies had formed to the left of the Democratic League, indebted with respect to its definite social demands to the Dominican Rutten, one of the "social chaplains" of that era, later the first secretary general of the *Confédération des Syndicats chrétiens,* which had gown out of local groups between 1904 and 1912. Significant for the existing insecurity was Cardinal Goossens' inquiry in Rome in connection with the Congress of Mechelen in 1896: did the employer commit a sin, and to what extent, if he preferred cheaper labor and did not pay family-adequate wages in the fight to compete on the market? It was the Belgian primate's inquiry, rather than this particular problem (widely discussed among western European Catholics), which was remarkable, as well as Cardinal Zigliara's answer that a "fair wage" was to be paid according to equity.

Leo XIII in 1895 refused to receive Abbé Daens. But the ultraconservative Charles Woeste also was by no means persona grata. However, the Pope's chances of alleviating the extremes within Catholicism were even more limited in France than in Belgium. The Conservatives were in power and had the financial means, which the bishops used for ecclesiastical projects and did not intend to relinquish. This situation intensified critically in 1898 when A. Verhaegen implored the Church in Rome to authorize a political oath. There he encountered the opposition of Woeste, but also the benevolence of Rampolla, who mediated his audience with the Pope. Leo XIII promised to send a letter on behalf of Verhaegen to the Belgian episcopate. But while Cardinal Goossens and the bishops again assured the *Ligue Démocratique* of their friendly disposition, they did not want to risk a public congress for the purpose of unification. As in the case of Abbé Daens, the Belgian episcopate in view of these tensions was chiefly interested in preserving the unity of the *Parti Catholique* and its majority in Parliament.

The social differences within Belgian Catholicism were difficult to overcome because, in contrast to comparable parties in other countries, the Catholic party had the clear majority and external forces of integration were lacking. In 1905 a majority of Christian-Social and Socialist deputies carried through the Sunday-rest law in spite of the opposition by the Catholic chief of the cabinet, and in 1907 the government was defeated in the question of the eight-hour day for miners, which enraged the middle-class Catholic press.

The Catholic societies developed slowly under the dominance of the *Parti Catholique,* which seemed to offer security for the Church. In 1903 the *Association de la Jeunesse belge* was founded in Louvain. At first it was a loose group, whose goals were not particularly directed toward the youth. A change was effected by young Abbé A. Brohée. He sharply separated religious from political action, and at the congresses of 1911 and 1913 almost no one but young people gathered. The first beginnings of the *Jeunesse ouvrière chrétienne,* developed in the vicinity of Brussels and itself an appeal to the youth, was interrupted by World War I. In contrast to the societies, religious orders and congregations flourished, especially when the Belgian Congo offered them new tasks. In 1829, 4,791 religious were counted, as compared to 38,140 in 1910. The Jesuits could do their work here undisturbed. The society of the Salvatorians, founded in 1881 by the Alemannian Johann Baptist Jordan and expanding rapidly, also took root in Belgium. A flourishing center of monastic life was the Benedictine priory in Maredsous (abbey since 1878), which Maurus Wolter had founded in 1872 with the help of the Desclée family (entrepreneurs from Tournai). The priory was closely associated with the abbey at Beuron, whose hindrance by the German *Kulturkampf* forced attention to foreign affairs. Abbot Maurus Wolter of Beuron (since 1875) appointed his brother Placidus abbot of Maredsous and became the instrument of the liturgical inspiration which he had during a sojourn in Solesmes (1862). In 1878 Gérard van Caloen published the first lay missal in Maredsous (*Missel des fidèles*). In 1888 the abbey's church was consecrated by a cardinal legate in the presence of Nuncio Ferrata and the entire Belgian episcopate. When Maurus Wolter died (1890) and his brother Placidus succeeded him as archabbot of Beuron, Hildebrand de Hemptinne took over the direction of Maredsous. When he was consecrated abbot by Cardinal San Felice in Montecassino, he was also given a comprehensive papal commission. In the same year, a priory was founded in Steenbrugge (1896, abbey). The priory of Mont-César in Louvain (1890) would later become, next to Maredsous, an important abbey in the Belgian congregation. From here emanated, in 1909, the liturgical movement inspired by Lambert Beauduin.

That the first eucharistic congress did not take place in Belgium was due to reservations Cardinal Dechamps had during the Frère-Orban government. But after the third congress, which took place in Liège in 1883, where E. Marie Tamisier had a protector in Bishop Doutreloux, Belgium and France became the main areas of this movement.

The Catholic University of Louvain enjoyed the special benevolence of Leo XIII and had a financial patron in Cardinal Goossens. In 1882, Désiré Mercier, who had studied theology there, became the first professor to hold the chair for Thomistic philosophy which had been established upon the Pope's request, and after the ontological crisis he inaugurated a new phase in the history of the institution, which gained great significance in historical and biological studies as well. Between 1890 and 1905, the theological faculty received acclaim especially in the fields of biblical research and patristics. As archbishop of Mechelen (cardinal, 1907), Mercier determined the ecclesiastical situation in Belgium on the basis of a Neo-Scholastic interpretation of society.

In spite of all this, an increasing de-Christianization of life in Belgium cannot be overlooked, even in rural areas, but mainly in the industrial regions, where only a few churches were built in the workers' quarters. Not only did the attendance of Sunday services decrease, but even birth, marriage, and death were often no longer included in ecclesiastical life.

Amidst the mostly decadent spiritual literature of these decades, the poetry of the Flemish priest and poet Guido Gezelle (1830–90) shone like a star. Filled with the intimate experience of nature and an original religiosity, Gezelle broke with all conventions and kept aloof from all fashionable styles.

The Netherlands

Catholicism in the Netherlands, after the area's separation from Belgium, constituted a sizable minority of nearly 40 percent. The liberal circumstances permitted the development of religious orders and schools, and in the forties the establishment of a press. Next to these ecclesiastical issues, economic considerations were decisive for the coalition with the Liberals. The leading ranks of Dutch Catholicism were comprised of men from business and trade. Thus the Catholics had a remarkable share in the success of the Liberals under the leadership of Thorbecke and in the state's basic law of 18 September 1848, which fundamentally strengthened the power of Parliament and ended the Calvinistic character of the Netherlands. The Catholics profited from the freedom of association in all areas of life. In the Netherlands, as elsewhere, the question of schools was the key issue in the relationship of Catholics to modern society. As an alternative to the Calvinistic parochial school, a group of Catholic politicians endorsed the school law of 1857, which indicated a radical ideological neutralization. However, this resulted in the *verzuiling,* which characterized Dutch society, because of a-Christian, even atheistic beliefs developing within liberalism, and because of the Calvinistic and Catholic orthodoxy's joint opposition. A letter drafted by both in 1868 requested the increase of free Catholic schools.

Shortly before the school conflict in Belgium, the left-liberal Kappeyne government enacted a law which was emphatically and successfully opposed by the Reformed clergyman Abraham Kuyper (he gathered 470,000 signatures). In 1888, as leader of the Anti-Revolutionary Party, he established connections with the Catholic priest H. J. M. Schaepman (1844–1903), who had been voted into Parliament in 1880. The Kappeyne government was overthrown. This conservative coalition, rather than Leo XIII's admonition directed toward the Dutch Catholics in April 1888, effected the school law of 1889, which placed the principle of free schools on a realistic foundation: free schools would receive state support and, after 1920, unconditional equality. The church-minded Protestants and Catholics, who were in agreement over the necessity of parochial schools, constituted a political cooperation which repeatedly resulted in formations of government. In 1896, Monsignor Schaepman founded the *Katholieke Staatspartij,* which developed into an exceedingly powerful factor in Dutch politics. Leo XIII made use of the now strong and pro-Rome Catholicism of the Netherlands for his fight in Italy. His relations with the royal court were friendly, and neither the widowed Queen nor Leo is to blame for the failure to invite the Pope to the first general peace conference, which took place in The Hague in 1899 and was opposed by Italy.

Since industrialization, at that time, was much slower than in Belgium and socialism did not play as important a role there, social Catholicism lagged behind for a long time. This was not Monsignor Schaepman's fault, who had indeed recognized this growing problem, but the fault of the lobby within his party. The occasion which led to the founding of the Catholic People's Union by W. J. Pastoors, later deputy to the Parliament, was trivial: the Catholic workers and the lower middle class were angered by the high price of tickets which the wealthy prominent Catholics had charged in 1888 for the celebrations in Amsterdam of the tenth anniversary of Leo's pontificate. That same year the Catholic social priest A. Ariens organized a workers' league in the textile city of Enschede, whose goals were religious education, social gatherings, and financial assistance through a relief fund. The Socialist propaganda prompted him by means of a strike (1890) to transform the league into a denominational union. His alliance with the Protestant group of 1895 seemed to be the beginning of an interdenominational Christian union in the Netherlands, and for several years the union, with its joint executive board and treasury, had considerable success. But the denominational party structure as well as the ecclesiastical opposition, especially of the Catholic episcopate, gave this attempt no chance. In 1895, a congress of the Catholic workers' movement combined forty-nine Catholic unions which had emerged locally since 1891. In 1910 Monsignor H. Poels, founded a Catholic workers' union in Limburg, a city which had recently been discovered by industry. Thanks to Poels, de-Christianization of the workers did not proceed as quickly in the Netherlands as in other countries.

Compulsory elementary education was not enacted until 1900, which was partly due to the opposition of the conservative parties and their press, from which Monsignor Schaepman was completely isolated. In 1905, parochial high schools also received state subsidies.

Dutch Catholicism retained its conservative hallmark (developed since the middle of the nineteenth century) far beyond World War I. The Catholic Convention in Utrecht in 1889, strengthened the religious self-identity in connection with the political victory, which was little touched by the problems of the era. The awareness of unconditional dependence on the papacy increased during the pontificate of Pius X, who established a regular hierarchy in the Netherlands in 1908. The *Maasbode* represented an extreme integralism, and Pius X found himself able to praise the Dutch episcopate when, thanks to its alertness, the "modernistic plague" did not find a stronghold there. The Catholic University of Nijmegen, founded in 1923, is historically rooted in the educational system which was created by H. Moller at the beginning of the century. Its spiritual open-mindedness was along the lines of the publication *Van onzen tijd,* which had been founded by laymen, especially by the Klarenbeekse Club.

In the history of the Catholic Church, the Netherlands enjoyed the reputation of being, at that time, a haven for the persecuted, who were of a different persuasion from those during the time of the Enlightenment. Arnold Janssen, born in the Lower Rhine area, founded the *Societas Verbi Divini* (Society of the Divine Word), which was to grow into the most important missionary institute. With the approval of Bishop J. A. Paredis of Roermond and Archbishop A. J. Schaepman of Utrecht, he transferred the institute across the Dutch-German border to Steijl (1874). The Jesuits, who were absolutely forbidden in Germany from the conclusion of the *Kulturkampf* until 1904 and officially forbidden in Switzerland until just recently, could work in the Netherlands and Belgium without interference, and therefore they transferred their exile college in Ditton Hall, England, to Valkenswaard in 1894.

Luxemburg

The Concordat of 1801 made Luxemburg part of the bishopric of Metz; but after its promotion to grand-duchy in union with the Netherlands in 1815, it was assigned to the bishopric of Namur (1823). Following the Belgian revolution, it lost its position as a diocese because King Willem I of the Netherlands did not want to divide Namur. Following a provisionary arrangement for the city of Luxemburg and after the surrender of the Walloon area to Belgium (1839), the rest of the country became an independent apostolic vicariate (1840). The appropriate desire to promote Luxemburg to a bishopric, which Willem II favored on account of the concession for free papal appointments, failed because the proposals of the concordat were not sanctioned by Rome. Pius IX's unilateral move of 27 September 1870 encountered the opposition of the Luxemburg State Council. Not until 23 June 1873 was the establishment of a bishopric ratified through a royal grand-ducal resolution by Willem III. The school law of 1881 suspended the inspection in which the clergy participated, as well as the right of the local priest to supervise the teacher, and it authorized community commissions, including a priest, to supervise the schools. This law, which was revised in 1898 in favor of the Church, demonstrated the delayed development in Luxemburg. But the law of 1912, which Bishop J. J. Koppes (1883–1918) opposed, though it did respect the Christian faith, caused the separation of school and Church. Consequently, religious instruction was administered outside of the school. According to the example of the neighboring countries, Catholic organizations now developed.

The desired course of the interdenominational Christian union in Luxemburg did not succeed. During World War I, however, the workers left the weak specialized sections of the workers' societies and joined neutral associations, which is why in 1920 independent but denominational Christian unions were founded. The development of the iron industry in the region of Esch caused an increase in the membership of the Social Democratic Party, founded in 1900. The ecclesiastical alienation of large segments of the population was due less to the relatively moderate Luxemburg Liberals of the eighties than to the Socialists. But Luxemburg did not lose its Catholic character.

ARTICLE 26 of the Constitution of 1848 resolved that the religious societies needed a legal license. But the regulation was usually interpreted amicably, so that, during the *Kulturkampf* in Germany and in the wake of the laws of 1901 and 1904 in France, the faithful could find refuge in Luxemburg.

CHAPTER 52

The Church of the Iberian World between Revolution and Reaction

Spain

The leading ranks of Catholicism in Spain were preoccupied with waging war against each other, in spite of Leo XIII's constant admonitions. The descendents of the "Apostolic Party" and the Carlists, such as the journalist Nocedal in his *Siglo futuro* or the publication *Ciencia Cristiana,* charged the liberal conservative Catholics with betrayal of the faith. In 1881, under the aegis of Cardinal Moreno of Toledo, a national pilgrimage to Rome with many committees was organized. It was to serve as a demonstration of their own power rather than of their loyalty to the successor of Saint Peter. This caused Secretary of State Jacobini, on 13 February 1878, to request purely diocesan groups of pilgrims. The rather reform-oriented *Partido Socialista Obrero Español,* founded in 1878 under the leadership of Pablo Iglesias, was not adequately assessed by the belligerents, at least not at first; but it flourished. So did the violent anarchism which had sympathizers and disciples especially among the totally impoverished farm hands on the large latifundia in Andalusia and in Catalonia. There were numerous assassinations and terrorism. The activities reached a climax on 7 June 1896 in Barcelona when, during a Corpus Christi procession, a bomb killed six people and seriously wounded forty-two.

In reference to religion, the constitution contained a compromise between the Catholic state religion and the freedom of religion, but in spite of this and despite the significant ecclesiastical rights regarding education, Pius IX and the Spanish clergy rejected it. The governments between 1875 and 1902 were alternately formed by Cánovas' liberal-conservative party and by the monarchical Liberals under the leadership of Sagasta. The censorship of books was either introduced or abolished, depending on the government. But both parties had their political base in the Bourbon monarchy and in the representative constitution.

A serious conflict between Church and state arose in 1899 when, in violation of the law of 1880, numerous members of the orders and congregations from France had immigrated to Spain because of persecution. The question of civil inscription of orders, which were not licensed as was required by the laws of 1867, was solved in 1901 through the conciliatory stance of Secretary of State Rampolla and the Spanish nuncio. The vitality of the Church in Spain during Leo XIII's pontificate was demonstrated by the exceedingly strong development of the female congregations.

The chief theme of Church history during this period in Spain involved the political differences within Catholicism itself. In January 1882, Rampolla occupied the nunciature in Spain, and on 8 December, Leo XIII, in an encyclical, implored the politically divided Spanish Catholics to make religious peace, and requested that they develop Catholic organizations under the direction of the bishops, as was done in other countries. But in 1884 and 1885, Rampolla was exposed to vicious attacks in the press by Nocedal. A minister of the Cánovas government had given a speech in Parliament about the temporal sovereignty of the Pope, which complicated relations with the Italian government and upset the Vatican. In this context Nocedal wrote that the nuncio evaluated the circumstances in Spain regarding ecclesiastical conditions much too optimistically instead of fighting the entire system of Cánovas, including the constitution of 1876. The controversy became a matter of principle when Nocedal characterized the function of the nuncio as a purely diplomatic one, which required his subordination to the episcopate in questions pertaining to the domestic affairs of the Spanish Church. Bishop Casas of Plasencia had written a strongly worded pastoral letter. In a note of April 1885 to Nuncio Rampolla, Secretary of State Jacobini termed Nocedal's ideas Febronianism and declared, in reference to the constitution *Pastor aeternus,* that the Pope had the right to interfere at any time in the affairs of the bishoprics, even through the nuncios whose competence he alone determined. In the case of Bishop Casas, Rampolla also received the desired letter from Jacobini, in which the bishop was reprimanded for disturbing the internal peace of the Church.

Around this time, it was Leo XIII's general intent to prevent the formation of exclusively Catholic parties. He became increasingly reserved toward the *Union Católica,* led by Alejandro Pidal, which he had still recommended in 1881, because he wanted to be considerate of the Carlists whom Pidal had failed to win for his union. In their press, the Carlists waged a venomous war against the *Union Católica* because they did not regard it as sufficiently Catholic, since it recognized the Bourbon Kingdom. The Pope's support of the *Union Católica* could have only increased the tensions in Spanish Catholicism. Leo XIII brought his authority with the Spanish episcopate to bear in order to prevent the Carlists from acting up after the death of Alphonso XII (26 November 1885) and to assure the reign of the widowed Queen María Cristina.

The Pope concentrated his special attention on the internal renovation of the Church, especially on the improvement of clerical education, which was to be handled by the following metropolitan seminaries: Toledo, Tarragona, Seville, Valencia, Granada, Burgos, Valladolid, Santiago de Compostela, Saragossa. The Jesuit seminary in Salamanca was authorized to award doctorates. The University of

Comillas (near Santander) was established in 1890 as a papal institute and gained influence in Latin America. In 1892, the "Spanish College" was opened in Rome.

After Rampolla's appointment as secretary of state (1887), the conflicts within Spanish Catholicism increased considerably. In 1889, the Pope had reason to write to the bishop of Madrid, the cardinal of Saragossa, and the bishop of Urgel; and he urged the *Revista popular* to end its polemics. The great pilgrimage to Rome in 1894 was tarnished by the previous Carlist disturbances in Seville, which caused vehement discussions in the press and in Parliament. In spite of the intransigent ecclesiastical attitude of the Carlists, the Pope refrained from taking sides and asked the Spanish pilgrims to accept the constitution of 1876 and to devote themselves to religious and cultural tasks.

There was no lack of the kind of tasks the Pope had spoken of. In 1887, 81.16 percent of the Spanish population was illiterate (1900: 71.43 percent). The negligence of the state and the communities was not compensated for by the efforts of the Church. The initiative emanated from the liberal philosopher of law Francisco Giner de los Ríos of Madrid (1839–1915), who rejected any kind of political agitation. But his *Institucíon Libre de Enseñanza* (since 1876) had developed a small but tremendously effective school complex, in which the liberal intelligentsia was nurtured. The outstanding representative of ecclesiastical Catholicism at that time was a professor of literary history in Madrid, Marcelino Menéndez y Pelayo (1856–1912). In rediscovering the *Siglo de Oro,* he wanted to overcome the contemporary controversies within Catholicism, which were paralyzed with clichés, and he intended to resurrect the great traditions of Spain. In his speech commemorating Calderón, he recalled the great ideals of Spanish history: the Catholic faith, the Spanish monarchy, the Latin race, and Iberian liberty. In his *Historia de los heterodoxos españoles (1881),* he wanted to present a sharp critique of all the spiritual phenomena which endangered Spain's tradition. He refrained from actual disputations because he relied on a creative restoration which would speak for itself. In his later work, *Historia de las ideas estéticas,* he attempted a Christian interpretation of Hegel.

The defeat of Spain in the war with the United States in 1898 meant the political and intellectual end of the restoration period which was passionately criticized by the "generation of 98." But a figure like Miguel de Unamuno (1864–1936) makes clear the complexity of the new spiritual development then breaking through which cannot be imagined without Spanish Catholicism. However, the fanatical integralism of the *Siglo futuro* continued to live, and Cardinal Sancha y Hervas of Toledo was accused of liberalism because of his counsel urging internal peace. Consequently, he had to ask for the Pope's protection, who, on 22 August, clearly reprimanded those people who wanted to determine autocratically who was Catholic and who was not. Leo XIII witnessed the enthronement of sixteen-year-old King Alphonso XIII on 17 May 1902 and he had reasons to worry about Spain's future. During Pius X's pontificate, the internal controversies within Catholicism continued. The Jesuits had supported the integralistic line of Nocedal until Leo XIII intervened through the general of the order. But when the Jesuits, in their publication *Razón y Fé* (since 1901), endorsed some sort of probabilism in the election of the deputies, they were defended by the Pope against the intransigent Conservatives.

It was not surprising that the encyclical *Rerum novarum* (1891) encountered little interest in Spain. The *Círculos Católicos Obreros,* which copied the institutions founded by Albert de Mun in France and were promoted after 1876 by Bishop Ceferino Gonzáles of Córdoba, developed very slowly. At the Church Congress of Tarragona in 1894, the encyclical was on the agenda, among other things; and in 1895, the *Consejo Nacional de las Corporaciones Obrero-Católicas,* the central organization of the worker societies was formed. Its lack of efficiency has to be judged in view of the fact that the interest for social problems was rather slim in all parties down to the leftist Liberals; the strongest interest existed in Cánovas' party. Around 1900, only about 30 percent of the population belonged to the industrial complex of the Spanish economy. But it was especially devastating that the agrarian production did not correspond to the increase of the population, which was negligible compared to other countries. The ruling class knew, without admitting it, that the anarchistic assassinations were by no means singular incidents. This is proven by the fact that there was hesitation in publishing the result of an investigation by the workers in 1884. This made it even more necessary for the Church to get involved. But, to Leo XIII's sorrow the interests of the Church were almost completely absorbed by the differences within the ruling ranks. The de-Christianization in the middle class, increasing since the sixties, began to extend into the industrial world. The bombing attack during the Corpus Christi procession in Barcelona in 1896 had only been a prologue. The great crises of the twentieth century drew closer. In the left wing of the dividing parties appeared the group of Alejandro Levroux, who, in the name of the Republic, proclaimed the now fashionable version of *"Écrasez l'infâme!"* and incited his *jóvenes bárbaros* to act. Thirteen years after the strike against the Corpus Christi procession, the masses of workers of Barcelona burnt seventeen churches, twenty-three monasteries, sixteen parochial schools, and four asylums. They brutally shot monks and nuns who tried to flee through a city blocked with street barricades and desecrated their bodies. The uprising of July 1909, following a general strike, was suppressed by the military forces dispatched from Valencia and Madrid. The repeated call for a dictatorship became louder and louder.

In the years following 1902, ecclesiastical policies of the alternately conservative or left-liberal governments were concerned with the question of admitting or limiting the religious communities, a question which was intensified by the return of Spanish missionaries from Cuba and the Philippines. The overthrow of the liberal government made possible the Convention of 1908, which was followed by the creation of a Vatican-Spanish commission, under the chairmanship of the archbishop of Toledo, empowered to investigate the monastery and school question. The conflict came to a head again when J. Canalejas (murdered in 1912) prohibited the founding of religious orders for the next two years, abolished the religious vow in December 1910, limited religious instruction in public schools, and recalled the ambassador to the Vatican. During the Eucharistic Congress in Madrid in 1911, King Alphonso XIII consecrated the Spanish people to the Sacred Heart. By this act and by its festive repetition in 1919, he won the Carlists for the Bourbon monarchy.

Portugal

The parallel between Spain's and Portugal's development continued into the last third of the nineteenth century, but in the beginning of the twentieth century remarkable differences developed. The agreement of 1848 between state and Church could essentially be preserved and was hardly impaired by the alternation of the two monarchal parties heading the government of the apolitical King Luis I (1861–89); the conservative *Regeneradores* and the *Progresistas*. The economic difficulties of the sixties under the conservative ministry of Antonio María de Fontes (1871–77) were turned into a brilliant recovery. The exhaustive negotiations between the Vatican and Lisbon under the liberal government of Braacamp (1879–81) resulted in a new circumscription of the dioceses through the papal constitution of 30 September 1881: the seventeen dioceses were reduced to three archbishoprics (Lisbon, Evora, and Braga) with nine auxiliaries. At the end of another conservative government came the new convention of 7 August 1886 regarding the rights of royal patronage in the Indian missions. At the University of Coimbra, having been anticlerical since Pombal, the theology faculty renounced Church supervision in 1885, solidly supported by the other faculties.

In the last decade of the century, Portugal's crisis began in spite of the political wisdom of King Carlos I, who refrained from visiting King Umberto I in 1895 because, as Rampolla had indicated, it would be against the Pope's wishes. The crisis was partly due to public debts (bank crisis) and partly to the erosion of the two-party system and the resulting power of the radical forces. The liberal-conservative ministry decreed in 1901 that the clerical societies be limited to those which were devoted to teaching, charity, and mission in the colonies. Leo XIII had opened a Portuguese College in Rome in 1900. In a brief of Easter 1902 addressed to Cardinal Neto of Lisbon, he praised the episcopate for having sent an address to the King concerning the religious orders' legislation. Carlos I and the Crown Prince fell victim to an assassination on 1 February 1908. This was the actual end of the Portuguese representative system. In the land of Marquis de Pombal, all radical forces had gathered around the Republican party, founded in 1876. Its partners were the Freemason lodge *Gran Oriente Lusitano Unido* (formed from scattered groups in 1869) and the violent *Carboneria.* While revolutionary groups were organizing in the underground, willing to lay their lives on the line, Portuguese Catholicism had spiritually collapsed despite its membership in the rural areas.

The Republic, proclaimed on 5 October 1910, experienced terrorist acts against the churches and monasteries, robberies, arson, and murder (as it had during the Spanish uprising in 1909).

The minister of justice declared: "Within two generations, Portugal will have eliminated Catholicism totally." The law of 20 April 1911, following the French model, carried out the separation of Church and state. The bishop of Oporto, Antonio Barroso, was arrested because of a pastoral letter; the archbishops of Lisbon and Braga, the bishops of Portalegre and Lamego were expelled. the constitution of 21 August 1911 limited the freedom of religion and suspended religious instruction. On 24 May 1911 Pius X sharply condemned the separation law in an encyclical to the Portuguese episcopate. After the tensions in the Sidonio Paes government had eased somewhat, Pius X recommended to the Catholics the recognition of the Republic. In 1913, the papal nuncio was expelled. Portugal's long internal turbulence ended with the Conservatives' coup d'état in 1918, resulting in the dictatorship of General Carmona (resumption of diplomatic relations to the Vatican).

Latin America

The *Collegio Pio latino-americano,* founded in 1858 in Rome, was not very successful in changing the religious situation in Latin America. To be sure, the orders and congregations tried to strengthen their establishments with immigrants from Europe or with new foundations. They wanted to ease the chronic and extreme lack of priests, which was a result of earlier negligence in training the native clergy and had been intensified drastically by the expulsion of the Jesuits and subsequent revolutionary occurrences, especially since the clergy were concentrated in the cities. The population of the South American continent increased from 20 million in 1825 to 65.7 million in 1900. But a religious revitalization could only be expected if the ecclesiastical forces within the Latin American countries themselves were activated. With this insight and after amazingly thorough preparations, Leo XIII convened the Latin American Plenary Council, which met from 28 May until 9 July 1899 in Rome and organized twenty-nine general congregations and nine solemn sessions. Within several years, a comprehensive report of more than one thousand articles had been worked out. It was sent to the Latin American episcopate for comments, which, in turn, were examined by the consultants in Rome. The strongest influence came from the Catalan Capuchin Vives y Tutó (1854–1913), who had endorsed a staunch antiliberalist line in the Curia (since 1884) and was promoted cardinal in 1899. Twelve archbishops and forty-one bishops of the one hundred four Latin American hierarchies came to Rome, which seemed to be the only feasible place for a meeting in view of the political situation. The constitutions of the Council, which included sixteen titles with 998 decrees, were sanctioned by Leo XIII on 1 January 1900. The Council's resolutions dealt with: bishops' conferences and provincial as well as diocesan synods, the canonical conduct of the often undisciplined clergy, the regionally varied pastoral work (especially in reference to the young), the charitable institutions, the dangers to the faith which secular books and newspapers, neutral schools, and the Freemasons represented, and with positivism (which had gained significance in Latin America). The Council also ruled on the principles of relations between Church and state, whereby the full authority of the nuncios in reference to the country's episcopate was emphasized, on the temporal rights of the Church regarding property, and on the claim for ecclesiastical jurisdiction. All these issues had long been the object of public debate in the Latin American states. The decrees were preceded by the consecration to the Sacred Heart and to the Immaculate Conception.

Toward the end of Leo XIII's pontificate, the Plenary Council had without doubt touched upon the main ecclesiastical problems in the Latin American countries. But the structures of society were and continued to be so rigid that the social prerequisites for a fundamental religious renovation were absent, especially since the Christianization of the people had stagnated and the European enlightenment had seduced the intelligentsia. As history proves, it was only natural in such a situation that as a rule the Church had its alliance with the great landholders in the provinces representing the Federalists in contrast to the liberal Centralists in the urban centers. The masses, even the poor white population, remained passive until the end of the nineteenth century, and the Church was unable to activate them because they were either not willing or too weak. For a long time, there was no middle class. Until World War I, there was little social welfare. Even if the Church had acted with less conformism after the secularizations, it would hardly have been in the position to effect a change of circumstances beyond its conventional Christian work of charity.

By 1880, Argentina, Chile, and Brazil were the leading Latin American countries, chiefly because of their economic growth, but also thanks to a relationship between Church and state which was essentially peaceful, in spite of repeated tensions. The Argentinian constitution of 1853 remained in force until 1920. It declared the Catholic Church to be the state religion and provided financial compensations for secularizations. It did, however, tolerate other denominations. President Domingo Sarmiento (1868–74), who was greatly interested in improving the backward educational system, opened the country to European influences. After his overthrow and emigration to Chile, the political anticlericalism of the Liberals was strengthened by a minor, but intellectual group. Nevertheless, Leo XIII was able to establish, with the approval of the government, the bishoprics in La Plata, Santa Fé, and Tucumán. Argentina's situation was strongly determined by immigrants: in 1869, 1.8 million inhabitants were counted; from 1874 to 1880, approximately 45,000 people, from 1880 to 1881 approximately 70,000 people came into the country annually, mostly Italians and Spaniards. At times, in the following period of speculation, 300,000 people immigrated per year. It was difficult to organize proper pastoral work, and the increase of bishoprics (under Pius X three additional ones) was actually a facade. In 1910, a Catholic University was established in Buenos Aires. In the same year, the liberal lawyer and politician Joaquín V. González, founder of the University of La Plata, wrote his book *El Juicio del Siglo,* in which he analyzed the path the country took from the culture of the Spanish aristocracy via barbarism down to the "return": it emphasized the continuity of *hispanidad,* transcending anticlericalism.

The ecclesiastical situation in Chile resembled the one in Argentina because it had a similar constitution (1865). Basically tolerant of other religions, Catholicism was still the official religion, even for the regalists, whose belief in regard to the state church law was rooted in the tradition of the patronate's law. During the pontificates of Leo XIII and Pius X, the Chilean ecclesiastical situation was characterized by the fact that the masonic anticlericalism of the Radical-Liberals eased up considerably. An example of such curious alliances is the purely political one of 1890 between the strictly Church-oriented Conservatives and the Radicals.

The establishment of the Republic in Brazil by the Radical-Liberals came about peacefully. This can be partly credited to the Pope's diplomacy; he was, however, totally ill-disposed toward Emperor Pedro II (1831–88) and his tolerance of non-Catholic sects. The Pope recognized the Republic and diplomatic relations were resumed. The constitution of 1891 guaranteed the Church freedom and property, but, following the separation law, all financial aid was disallowed. The Brazilian

Church now had to rely on its own resources (like the Church in the United States), and it had to centralize the revenues and donations of its diocesan treasuries. Of greatest concern, however, was the augmentation of the clergy, whose number (in 1872 not quite one thousand priests) was especially depressing compared to the rapid growth of the population under Pedro II because of heavy immigration (from approximately 6 to 14 million). The Church was also interested in raising the standards of religious education, which had suffered greatly in the era of rationalism. The Pope favored the settlements of European orders in Brazil, such as those of the Premonstratensians of Averbode in São Paulo and the Benedictines of Maredsous, who strove to renovate the Brazilian congregation of Olinda. In 1894 and 1895, G. van Caloen made visitations, the results of which were discussed in Beuron's mother house in Maredsous. Leo XIII employed his authority to this end (*est mea voluntas*). In 1899, the Pope appointed van Caloen vicar general to the Brazilian Archabbot Machado with the right of succession for life. From 1892 until 1902, Leo XIII established eight new bishoprics in Brazil. In 1905, Pius X appointed the archbishop of Rio de Janeiro, Arcoverda Cavalcanti, cardinal, the first one in Latin America.

Bolivia was weakened by frequent military revolts and the loss of its coastal province of Atacama to Chile. Only after World War I did it recoup on account of its tin production. Even in the last third of the nineteenth century, the ecclesiastical situation remained unchanged and the Franciscans continued their missionary work among a population which consisted mainly of Indians and half-castes. Though freedom of religion existed in principle, the Catholic Church was the only one supported by the state. Coupled with this support, however, was a large amount of interference, against which the Pope protested in 1906. In Peru, where a papal delegate was allowed to reside in Lima (also responsible for Bolivia and Ecuador), conditions similar to Bolivia prevailed until the turn of the century, when the situation was clouded by the introduction of civil marriage (1898).

It is interesting to compare ecclesiastical development in Colombia and Venezuela with that in Ecuador and Guatemala. Colombia was the first Latin American country which instituted a radical separation of Church and state (1853). Since the presidency of R. Núñez (1880), relations with the Church were exceedingly friendly, and, in 1885, diplomatic relations with the Vatican were resumed. After the constitution of 1887/88, amended in 1892, the Catholic Church became the official religion and enjoyed independence. Compromises were agreed upon in controversial questions, such as the clergy's civil jurisdiction and the Church's competence in regard to cemeteries. The separation law of 1853, however, was not suspended. In the years from 1880 until 1900, Leo XIII established six new dioceses. Between 1899 and 1902, the country was once again shaken by a violent civil war, resulting in the secession of Panama, supported by the United States, from Colombia. After 1904, General Rafael Reyes ruled rather dictatorially. But he is fondly remembered because he removed the consequences of civil war. He demonstrated his good relations to the Catholic Church by constructing a building for the nunciature in Bogotá (1908), where a Eucharistic Congress took place in 1913.

Venezuela also experienced the evolution of religious toleration after the regime of Guzmán, who was hostile toward the Church and had expelled Archbishop Guevara from the country in 1870. The activities of the religious orders flourished under his reign; not, however, under the dictatorship of Cipriano (1899–1908), at least not in respect to foreign relations. The seminary which was planned at a bishops' conference in Caracas (1904), was opened in 1913.

The relationship between Church and state fluctuated in Ecuador and Guatemala. Even after the murder of Ecuador's President García Moreno (1875), whose work created what was called a "model Christian state," the Church continued to be favored under the more or less conservative governments. In 1881, the Concordat of 1862 was revised and Roman Catholicism in its capacity as the state religion was given extraordinary rights, as in regard to the supervision of schools. An additional agreement in 1890 allotted 3 percent of the state's property to the episcopate. In return, Leo XIII promised to use his influence on the bishops during the elections; this was generally the quid pro quo in Latin America, and it was particularly difficult because the appointment of priests was often under the direction of the ruling classes. However, the radical-liberal revolution of 1895, under the government of the otherwise moderate General Eloy Alfaro, produced severe measures against the previously favored Church, confiscating properties and expelling religious orders. After the enactment of civil marriage in 1902, the separation of Church and state was declared official (1904).

The development in the Central American republic of Guatemala proceeded more quickly. Following the presidencies of Carrera and Cerna, who were amicable toward the Church and dominated by the Conservatives of the white minority, the Liberals introduced a lay regime with the new constitution of 1879. With prophetic pathos, Archbishop Casanova y Estrada excommunicated President Justo Rufino Barrios, who had confiscated ecclesiastical estates, expelled the Jesuits, forbidden clerical dress in public, and mobilized the Indians and half-castes constituting the great majority of the population. He was exiled in 1887. The subsequent presidents essentially followed the same line. Dictator Estrada Cabrera (1899–1919) built a "Minerva Temple" for state celebrations.

Probably the most extreme changes in the relations between Church and state took place in Mexico. After the failure of the politically respectable program of pure-blooded Indian Benito Juárez the lay laws regarding the separation of Church and state, constitutionally validated by his successor, remained in force. But this separation had rather advantageous effects during the economically successful dictatorship of Porfirio Díaz (1877–81, 1884–1911). The wife of Díaz, Carmelita, who was friendly toward the Church, played an important role. The members of the orders and congregations were allowed to return more or less legally, and in the period between 1880 and 1902 Leo XIII established the bishoprics of Oaxaca, Monterey, and Durango, as well as eleven other bishoprics. It was in accord with the Indian tradition that Leo XIII decreed the consecration of the shrine of Nuestra Señora de Guadalupe in 1886, whose veneration (the name was taken after a Spanish shrine) was never disturbed by political disorders after 1531. In 1896, a provincial council took place. According to the European model, Catholic Congresses were organized in Puebla (1903), Mérida (1904), Guadalajara (1906), and Oaxaca (1909). At the Congress of Zamora (Mexico) of 1913, the program of the *Confederación Nacional de los Círculos Católicos Obreros* was developed. Some of the social principles may have had an influence on the constitution of 1917 which arose from revolutionary chaos. However, ARTICLE 3 contained resolutions regarding the radical laicization of education and Art. 27 the nationalization of Church property.

There are many reasons for the failure of the religious regeneration of Latin America during this period. Without a doubt, the ecclesiastical forces concentrated too much on the relations between Church and state and on the hope of finding protection from the conservative governments, which, when given, was often rather questionable. Unfortunately, it is just as certain that the native clergy was qualitatively and quantitatively too weak, and that help from Europe not only came too late but brought ideas which did not match the Latin American circumstances. It was said that the wives of the politicians of all colors did go to church and that an open belligerence toward religion did not exist until the twentieth century. One may add that Latin American Catholicism is so basic a phenomenon that it is evident even in the non-Christian literature, not to mention the Chilean poet Gabriela Mistral (Lucila Godoy Alcayaga). But this traditional Catholicism was exposed to consistent erosion after the middle of the nineteenth century due to the philosophy of Auguste Comte. Around 1880, positivism was the acknowledged faith of nearly the entire intellectual elite and of a large part of the liberal politicians (though with a different interpretation); it prevailed far beyond the turn of the century. Whoever lifted himself into the educated classes, which expanded considerably in the decades after 1880, would generally go the same route. The revolutions at the beginning of the nineteenth century had been a great disappointment, especially to Simón Bolívar. Now, it was hoped, the breakthrough would proceed past traditional Catholicism and succeed with the help of education.

C H A P T E R   5 3

Catholic Self-Awareness in the British Empire

England and Scotland

In 1912 England had 1.79 million Catholics and Scotland 0.54 million, totalling 2.33 million within a population of 40.8 million (not counting Ireland). Around 1878, approximately 0.35 million Catholics lived in Scotland. Ireland aside (80 percent Catholic including Ulster), the Catholics were a small minority, which was concentrated for a long time in certain areas: in England, in Lancashire, London, and the Midlands; in Scotland, mainly in the vicinity of Glasgow and Edinburgh. After England had been granted an official hierarchy in 1850, Leo XIII, as one of the first acts of his pontificate (4 March 1878), established in Saint Andrews-Edinburgh the Scottish metropolitan see with four auxiliaries and in Glasgow an archbishopric which was directly responsible to Rome. This division was implemented with consideration for the significance of Irish immigration relative to the English Catholics, who were frequently of Irish descent. This explains why most Catholics were poor. To be sure, there were a large number of wealthy Catholics in England, which increased as a result of the conversion movement, but there was only a small representation in the middle class.

It is due in part to these sociological conditions that growing Catholicism was imprinted with the political genius of Henry Edward Manning rather than with the spirit of John Henry Newman. Manning (born in 1808), was the son of an entrepreneur, an English patriot who was shocked by Newman's conversion in 1845, and a friend of Gladstone, who also could not understand Manning's conversion. The archbishop of Westminster (1865) was elevated to cardinal in 1875. That Manning was able smoothly to combine his English patriotism with his activism on behalf of Pius IX is, on the one hand, based on the religious tolerance of the Victorian period; on the other hand, it rested on Manning's social involvement which he considered a Christian as well as a national matter. This was facilitated by the fact that in Great Britain only a fool could have conceived of the idea of instituting a Catholic social movement. It was quite natural that Manning appeared as the speaker at the anniversary celebration of the British and Foreign Anti-Slavery Association in 1884 and that he was a member of the "royal commission for securing better housing for the poor." His main concern was not Catholicism as such, but social problems which were becoming increasingly urgent and had major political relevance in view of the election reforms. Manning, not withstanding his religious motivation, was interested in the matter itself, which can be said of only relatively few Catholics. By no means did he prefer political action to social action; in fact, he refused to combine secular politics with ecclesiastical politics. For Manning, as for his friend William E. Gladstone (1809–98), the great leader of the Liberals, Irish home rule was a matter of both fairness and political prudence. To sacrifice it for the sake of the papal diplomacy of the eighties was just as unthinkable to Manning as the idea of developing the overtures, exchanged during the fiftieth jubilee of Queen Victoria (1887), into diplomatic relations as envisioned by the conservative English Catholics. He had no confidence in missionary work conducted from above. "So far, the world has been ruled by the dynasties. Now it is time for the Holy See to negotiate with the peoples" (Quoted in K. Buchheim).

In close cooperation with Leo XIII, Cardinal Manning resolved the difficulties which regularly occurred in the process of transition from the ecclesiastical structure under the Propaganda Fide to that of an official hierarchy. There were tensions especially between the episcopate and the Benedictine monks as well as the Jesuits, whom Manning disliked. In the constitution of 8 May 1881, pastoral work and the administration of Church property were reserved exclusively to the episcopate. Manning's concept of the spirituality of the secular priesthood, whose activities he protected against the criticism of the religious orders, must be seen in this. Neither theological speculation, one of the elements of tension between him and Newman, nor the isolated priesthood was of interest to Manning. "The clergy are in danger of becoming mere Mass priests and hucksters of sacraments." What he wanted was a simple profile of Catholic basic principles, which were not to be concealed by secondary issues; no useless disputations, but expansive directives for action.

As everywhere else, the educational system was an important issue. The liberal religious policies of Gladstone, who even in his later years adhered to his Christian persuasion, contained an ambivalent aspect for Catholicism in Great Britain. On the one hand, it was to its advantage that the Anglican Church, which dominated the school system and received public funds for it, began to lose its preeminence. On the other hand, the education law of 1870, which required that public nondenominational schools were to be financed by the state, resulted in the "provided schools" of the state dominating the field (general compulsory education was not introduced until 1880). The parochial private schools decreased, except for the Catholic ones, which dominated in Saint Leonard's on the Sea (Sussex), among other places. There, they were cared for by the Sisters of the Child Jesus. But it was not until 1902 that the Catholic schools received state funds (if they followed the general school curriculum).

In Great Britain, there were at least two different ways of dealing with the status of a minority; in fact, there were two sociologically different philosophies of Catholicism facing each other in the ecclesiastical world as it developed in the eighties and in the mentality of those who favored the attempts of an alliance with the Anglican Church (1895).

There was the kind of Catholicism in Great Britain which, with great sacrifice, supported the clergy and its schools. It was the Catholicism of the lower classes, much more so than in the United States. This social climate was a determining factor in Cardinal Manning's activities. "The coming age will belong neither to the capitalists nor to the commercial classes, but to the people. The people are yielding to the guidance of reason, even to the guidance of religion. If we can gain their confidence, we can counsel them, if we show them a blind opposition, they will have power to destroy all that is good." What is characteristic in this statement is that Manning was able to see the social problems of the industrial revolution as a universal problem. In 1880 he had already formed a theoretical foundation in *The Catholic Church and Modern Society*. In this sober analysis, the son of an entrepreneur identified himself with the cause of the industrial worker. This, not esteem for the high priest of the papal Church, is the background for the popular story dealing with the arbitration of the dockworkers' strike which broke out in London on 13 August 1889. In this instance, Manning fulfilled the "duties of citizens and patriots," whose rejection by the Catholics even after 1828 he called "a dereliction of duties in and of itself illegal." The question of denominational or Christian unions was of little importance in Britain, since the trade unions were not oriented toward Marxism. The membership of Catholic workers was taken for granted. The Catholic Social Guild, founded in 1909 by H. Parkinson, president of Oskott College, and by the Jesuit C. Plater, was devoted to the religious training of workers for the purpose of halting the spreading de-Christianization. Following the model of the *Katholischer Volksverein* in Germany, "penny-pamphlets" were to be distributed. The beginnings of the Catholic Social Guild were difficult. Five thousand members had been expected, but by 1912 there were only a thousand, though some were group memberships.

The rest of organizational activity in Great Britain was rather limited, even though it extended over a multiplicity of social groups: 1910, The Catholic Medical Guild, with 200 members; 1911, The Catholic Stage Guild. The Catholic Young

Men's Society of Great Britain had 22,000 members in 1912, including the Catholic Boy Scouts. The Catholic Women's League reached a membership of 8,000 in 1912. A very bourgeois-conservative affair was The Catholic Association, founded in 1891 under the presidency of the Earl of Denbigh. It was related to the Catholic Confederation, which appeared in 1910 and was socially more embracing and above partisanship.

It was said that Manning's social activity stands isolated, and that is true to a certain extent, because Catholicism's scholarly exchanges in the social question in Britain were not intensified until after 1900, in conjunction with the political growth of the Socialists. But this has to be placed in the context of general history. Gladstone, who was consumed by the Irish question and in a legal sense favored the development of the trade unions, "was not a social reformer in the strict sense of the word, and the needs of the working class hardly concerned him" (P. Kluke). Benjamin Disraeli, who is said to have had sympathies for Manning, was a rather unique figure among the Tories for his social sensibilities (the Labour Party was founded in 1900). There was only a small number of Catholics to be found in the upper reaches of society.

The Catholicism of the upper classes was somewhat sympathetic toward the English Church Union, an organization founded in 1844 by the Anglo-Catholics within the Anglican Church. Its president (after 1868), Lord Halifax, personally inclined toward the Roman Catholic Church, had met the French Lazarist Fernand Portal, a student of Dupanloup, in 1890 on Madeira. In their correspondence during 1892, they searched for a way to unify the Roman Catholic and the Anglican Church in the near future. A discussion about the validity of Anglican orders was to serve as "a means toward that goal." In July 1892, Halifax paid the archbishop of Westminster a visit in order to present his plan. Herbert Alfred Vaughan (in 1872 bishop of Salford, after March 1892 archbishop of Westminster, after 1893 cardinal) came from an old Catholic aristocratic family. In 1857 he had joined the Ambrosians, a society of the secular clergy, founded under Charles Borromeo, which Manning had introduced in Bayswater the same year. Vaughan differed from Manning and had lifted the prohibition for Catholic students to study in Cambridge and Oxford, which Manning had effected in Rome in 1895. Nevertheless, he was in agreement with his predecessor in terms of ecclesiastical policy and definitely endorsed the doctrine of infallibility in the *Tablet,* which he purchased in 1866. Compared to Manning, he was less interested in social questions. From the beginning Vaughan made it clear that, in contrast to the Anglicans, the recognition of papal primacy was the decisive element. Portal published *Les ordinations anglicanes* under a pseudonym in 1893 in Paris, in which he termed the consecration of Matthew Parker (appointed archbishop of Canterbury in 1559 by Elizabeth I) valid in terms of the "historical facts," but expressed doubt concerning the "intentions" of the consecrator. Church historian L. Duchesne used Catholic teaching on the sacraments to argue against this treatment of the question of intention and declared that one could consider the ordination as valid. Since Portal was able to anticipate the Catholics' objections to his arguments concerning the intention, as one would expect from an educated theologian, his essay was termed "a tactical move" (J. J. Hughes) to get the discussion going. In 1894, Portal visited Halifax, who introduced him to the Anglican bishops. The archbishop of Canterbury, E. W. Benson, was very cool and just as aware of his convictions as Cardinal Vaughan, who was also annoyed because Portal did not follow up his invitation to visit him. In September 1894, Portal was asked by Cardinal Secretary of State Rampolla to come to Rome and be introduced to the Pope. Portal's suggestion that Leo XIII should propose a conference to the Anglican episcopate was discarded. Instead, Rampolla wrote a letter to Portal, praising his desire for ecclesiastical unity and expressing hopes for "England's return to the only center of unity." Portal's second visit with the archbishop of Canterbury was even cooler than the first one. On 21 March 1895, Lord Halifax had an audience with the Pope, in which he proposed a direct offer (not through Cardinal Vaughan) to the Anglican episcopate, which was graciously noted. But in February, F. A. Gasquet, O.S.B., a Vaughan aide, was given the task of composing a papal letter which was not to be addressed to the Anglican episcopate. Vaughan, who had arrived in Rome in 1895, used all means at his disposal to exert pressure against Portal's intentions. Basically his and Lord Halifax's plan had already failed in view of the apostolic letter *Amantissimae voluntatis* of 14 April 1895, which was addressed *Ad Anglos* and urged using the "means" of discussing the ordinations in order to achieve a conference which could initiate the reunification. The letter, recalling Pope Gregory the Great, spoke with restraint about the Reformation ("Anglia . . . gravissimum vulnus accepit . . . , divulsa a communione Apostolicae Sedis, dein ab ea fide sanctissima abducta est"), praised the efforts toward unity of all Christians, and finally granted indulgence in a prayer to the Virgin Mary which was intended for the *Fratres dissidentes* and asked that they unite *summo Pastori, Vicario in Terris Filii tui.* The conclusion of the letter was composed by Merry del Val, who, as a young man, had been much favored by Leo XIII. In spite of this conclusion, the letter was generally well received in England; even Benson spoke of an "honest appeal," but noted the important fact that it did not mention the Anglican Church. In the papal commission, appointed in 1896 for the purpose of investigating the question of Anglican orders, Merry del Val played a significant role as secretary to the president, Cardinal Mazzella, and as middleman to Vaughan. The six (later eight) members were selected equally from both parties; the one side was led by Gasquet, the other by Duchesne. However, Cardinal Mazzella, who rejected an application for admission of the Anglicans then present in Rome, and his secretary were definite opponents of the recognition of Anglican orders. The vote took place on 7 May. Voting for recognition were Duchesne and the Jesuit A. M. de Augustinis (professor of dogmatics at the Roman College); Pietro Gasparri (in 1880 professor of canon law at the *Institut Catholique* in Paris, later cardinal secretary of state) and another member expressed through their vote that the validity of the ordinations was "doubtful." The Vaughan group voted against it. The validity of Anglican orders was rejected in the papal bull *Apostolicae curae* of 13 September 1896, which was composed by Merry del Val. The expectations of some that the conversions would increase if submission to the authority of the Pope was clearly demanded were not fulfilled. The hopes of others for an impending reunification of the Churches as such was an illusion in view of the contemporary historic situation. Except for the situation of the Anglican Church, oscillating between conservative and liberal tendencies, Wilfrid Ward, a moderate disciple of Vaughan and mediator to Halifax, analyzed the situation in England and Ireland clearly: "Should we be surprised that the descendants of those whose lives were ruined . . . or who died the death of a martyr . . . could muster only little under-standing for the argument that their persecutors and judges belonged to a Church which, all in all, was possibly in agreement with them?" (Cited by J. J. Hughes).

Leo XIII's conciliatory pragmatism was also responsible for the existing illu-sions, which include the Pope's own on unification. It is interesting that nearly one month before the papal bull, on 23 August 1896, Leo XIII sent a letter to Car-dinal Vaughan dealing with the problem of the economic situation of converted Anglican clergymen. Here, his intentions were clearly expressed. He speaks about the "heroism" of those clergymen who converted without any consideration of the economic consequences. But there were also others who did "not possess as much courage," but yet were close to taking this step. Therefore he suggested establishing a relief fund. The Converts Aid Society, however, was not very suc-cessful because of the extraordinary financial burden placed upon the Catholics and because its purpose was misunderstood. Cardinal Francis Bourne (1903–35) organized this action after World War I with great interest. In 1898, analogous to other national institutions, Leo XIII founded the Beda College in Rome, and on 13 November he elevated the Venerable Bede to the rank of Father of the Church.

In 1905, following the victory of the Liberal Party, which had been rejuvenated by youthful forces, the question of schools came up again. The objective of the education law of 1870 was reiterated insofar as the Rosebery cabinet wanted further to repress the traditional Anglican predominance in education. But now Cardinal Bourne aligned with the Anglicans and the conservative opposition in the fight against the deconfessionalization of schools (religious instruction was to be given in the classroom, but not to belong to the general curriculum) and, consequently, the bill miscarried in the House of Lords. But these were tactical alliances. The Eucharistic World Congress of 1908 in London, which was attended by Cardinal Legate Vannutelli, was correctly analyzed as a "brilliant expression of the unified power" of the island's Catholics (K. Waninger). But this was also the way a large part of the London public understood it, and thus protests occurred, and Lord Herbert Asquith, promoted from chancellor of the treasury to prime minister (1908), warned against carrying the monstrance in the procession. It was clear to the seasoned episcopate in Great Britain, which also held back in the dispute over modernism, that the founding of a Catholic party, as Leo XIII desired, would only harm ecclesiastical life.

Ireland

During the first year of Leo XIII's pontificate, Cardinal Paul Cullen, the head of the episcopate in Ireland, died. In 1880 Gladstone took over the government after the victory of the Liberals in the elections, in which the Irish National Party was able to increase its seats from fifty-nine to sixty-five. In spite of Gladstone's conflicts with the Irish episcopate over the question of the universities in 1873 and his reaction to it (published in a flyer which became known all over Europe), his personal involvement and current events entangled him once again in the Irish question. Bad harvests and the intensification of the political battle resulted in 1882 in nearly one hundred attempted assassinations and twenty-six murders.

The terrorism in the battle for justice was also directed against those Irish who did not obey the directives of the organization. This has to be taken into consideration as well as the impoverishment of the Irish tenant farmers, whose lot could only gradually be improved by a land act which Gladstone enacted in spite of the terrorism. Otherwise, the solidarity of a large part of the episcopate and Leo XIII's interventions cannot be adequately assessed.

On 3 January 1881 the Pope sent a letter to Archbishop MacCabe of Dublin, no doubt repeating, in reference to Gregory XVI, more of the *debita obedientia* and the *Cupiditates in seditiones flammam,* than was prudent in view of the situation created by the recently enacted land act. The letter of 1 August 1882, addressed to the entire Irish episcopate, endorsed the condemnation of the terrorist acts; however, in blaming them on the "secret societies," he showed little understanding of the necessity for organized resistance in such a situation, even though the Pope generally approved of the desire for justice. Incidentally, the Irish episcopate had good reason to suggest that Rome should not altogether trust the information from London. After MacCabe had been elevated to cardinal on 27 March 1882, the Pope, in a letter of 1 January 1883, admonished the episcopate to act in concord and the clergy to obey the bishops. The intrigues of the conservative Catholic deputy from Ireland, Errington, at the Vatican showed what kind of impact the massive interests of the landlords had, even on the Church's treatment of the Irish question. How venomous the atmosphere was in the Church itself is documented by the case of Archbishop Walsh of Dublin, who had to undergo an interrogation in 1885 in Rome before he was confirmed. The Vatican critic Gladstone was able to foresee for the next decades that the Irish question could not be solved merely by improved reform laws, but that the request for home rule had to be granted. In the beginning of 1886, he failed to win support for his bill providing for the suspension of the union of 1801 and for Ireland's own Parliament (with the exclusion of trade, foreign affairs, and the military). The bill miscarried because of imperialistic resistance, even within his own ranks. The Home Rule law of 1912/14 came too late because of the war. It brought revolution. Leo XIII carried part of the responsibility for this. The old grievances did not return after Gladstone's defeat, but Ireland's being chained to Great Britain and the interests of the Unionists persisted, so that the unrest was aggravated, a consequence from which the episcopate could not escape. Nevertheless, the Pope, counseled by the Prefect for Propaganda Simeoni and the Irish College, showed little understanding for Ireland's increasing national, rather than economical demands. On 20 April 1888, the Congregation on the Inquisition answered negatively an inquiry about whether a boycott by the tenant farmers was permissible, and requested an attitude of charity and fairness. However, in a letter of 24 June 1888, addressed to the entire episcopate, Leo XIII emphasized that the matter was not only subject to the authority of the bishops but also to his own authority, and he resented being insufficiently informed. The Irish question had critically entangled political issues, characterized by a mixture of right and wrong, with ecclesiastical aspects on all sides. At the same time, it was an example of the dilemma of Leo's direct policies, and thus it continued to smolder.

The liberal Asquith was able to achieve in 1909 what the liberal Gladstone had failed to accomplish in 1873. In addition to the Queen's University of Belfast, he established the National University of Ireland, with its three colleges in Dublin, Cork, and Galway, which were both fundamentally supra-denominational, but the school in Dublin was, for all practical purposes, Catholic.

At that time, Catholicism in the United Kingdom of Great Britain and Ireland was sociologically hardly homogeneous. This is evidenced by the biographies of a line of significant writers who knew they belonged to Catholicism, but cannot be regarded as its exponents without serious reservations: C. K. Patmore, G. M. Hopkins, Francis Thompson, G. K. Chesterton, and Hilaire Belloc.

Canada

In Canada, the Catholic part of the total population decreased slightly from 42.9 percent in 1871 to 39.4 percent in 1911. The Franco-Canadian Catholicism in the province of Quebec, which had developed a pronounced conservative stance during Pius IX's pontificate and actually dominated public life with its strong ecclesiastical authority, was suffering from serious tensions in the last quarter of the century, which were at least partly ignited by its relations with France. The French-Canadian economic relations were increased after 1890, and at that time, Franco-Canadian society was more and more influenced by an image of France based on the Restoration rather than the Revolution. It was the spirit of Victor Hugo. As a result, the controversies within French Catholicism, the pro and con in reference to Leo XIII's *Ralliement* politics, and the ecclesiastical policy of the Third Republic were considered by the Canadian Catholics to be much their own affair. These backlashes combined with inner Canadian differences in the episcopate. E.-A. Taschereau, from 1871 until 1898 archbishop of Quebec, held from the beginning of his episcopate a more differentiated opinion of the relationship between the civil society and the Church than Bishop J. Bourget of Montreal, who had died in 1876. The Conservatives, therefore, suspected him of liberalism, and he had to defend himself against immigrant extremists by demanding their return to France. The owner and editor of *La Vérité*, J.-P. Tardivel (1851–1905), had chosen Louis Veuillot as his model. After 1881 he fought, together with his friend Fr. J. Grenier, S.J., anyone who, in his opinion, was not exclusively oriented toward Rome. Both Veuillot and Tardivel inspired a comparison with Taschereau and Dupanloup. The basic attitude of Archbishop Taschereau was more in line with Leo XIII's intentions than those of his opponents, and thus Leo appointed him cardinal in 1887.

In the nineties French Canada also experienced a school struggle. But it differed from similar conflicts because of the conditions there: the dominant position of the Church in education. In 1886 the Sulpicians had been accused of undermining the congregations of teaching brothers by supporting a stronger participation of laymen in education. In 1893 it was demanded that the clergy pass the same examination as the laymen, from which they had been exempted in 1846. Moreover, the traditional humanistic curriculum became more and more the object of controversy. The Prime Minister of the Dominion of Canada, John A. Macdonald, who had been in office since the British North America Act (1867), was replaced in 1891 by the liberal Wilfrid Laurier. When the liberal president of Quebec, F.-G. Marchand wanted to establish a department for education in 1889, a furious public reaction occurred and the project was unable to secure a majority in Parliament. In 1889 Leo XIII seized the initiative and elevated the ecclesiastical University of Ottawa (founded in 1849), where Archbishop J.-T. Duhamel taught (1874–1909), to a papal institution. The University, recognized by the state in 1866, was the first in Canada to teach in English and French. On the other hand, an increase in animosity toward the Church is evident, which came partly from Ontario, whence anti-Jesuitism spread to Quebec, and partly from France. The anti-Catholic Equal Rights Association founded a group in Montreal and the radical Grand Orient lodge founded a branch in French Canada. The conflicts survived the death of Cardinal Taschereau (his successor in Quebec was L.-N. Bégin, 1898–1925), corresponding to the political development in France. In 1911 the first plenary synod was aimed at demonstrating the inner cohesiveness of French and English Catholicism in Canada. The opening address of the premier of Quebec, L. Gonin, at the Eucharistic Congress of 1910 showed what kind of authority the Church still possessed in spite of a certain intensification of liberalism: "The Canadian State does not consider the Church an enemy to be fought as a rival; it considers the Church an ally and its best support."

Australia

Catholicism in Australia entered a new period of growth, when P. F. Moran was appointed archbishop of Sydney (in 1885 he became Australia's first cardinal). In spite of a decrease in Irish immigration, the portion of the Catholics in the growing white population remained fairly constant. It was of great significance in 1888 that Cardinal Moran could found and open Saint Patrick's Ecclesiastical College in Manly (north of Sydney), thus providing for the training of the native clergy. This contributed to easing the tensions which the religious orders and secular clergy from Europe had brought into the country. It also diminished the Australian Englishmen's fear of French settlements. But the process of deconfessionalizing education had more negative consequences for the Catholic schools in Australia than it did in Britain. The cancellation of state subsidies could not easily be compensated for by individual efforts, and the Australian bishops had to solicit the assistance of European teaching orders. Until the middle of the twentieth century, the congregations were usually represented in branch foundations.

Among the original Australian foundations are the Sisters of Saint Joseph (in 1882 in Goulburn and in 1883 in Lochinvar) and Our Lady's Nurses of the Poor (1913). Cardinal Moran followed the example of Leo XIII's pontificate and organized regular plenary synods in Sydney (1885, 1895, 1905). The growing social awareness of Australian Catholicism expressed itself in the congresses taking place after 1900, having an active leader in their cardinal, who was a supporter of the constitution of the Commonwealth of Australia. It was in accord with the social status of most Catholics in Australia that Moran favored the Australian Labor Party and showed sympathy for the strikes of the nineties, even though that gained him the reputation among the Conservatives of being a Socialist.

Like the rest of the population, the Catholics concentrated in New South Wales and in Victoria. There were difficulties in establishing an ecclesiastical organization in West Australia, where natural conditions in the southwestern part favored a stronger density of population. There, the Irishman M. Gibney, who had been a priest in West Australia since 1863, was appointed Bishop of Perth in 1887 (a bishopric since 1845). The use of Trappists from the abbey of Sept-Fons in the Beagle Bay Mission proved to be impractical. In 1901 they were replaced by the Pallottines. Lacking crucial internal or external tensions, Catholicism was able to develop favorably, and Cardinal Cerretti, during his visits in 1915/17, found a flourishing Church.

CHAPTER 54

The American Way

In 1820 there were one hundred ninety thousand Catholics among the total white population of 7.8 million. In 1900, there were about 12 million Catholics in the total population of 78 million; they had tripled since 1870. For the year 1957, there was an estimate of 25.7 percent Catholics.

In view of the growing mobility of the industrial age, pastoral work in regard to immigrants, especially in the United States, had been recognized as an important task. At the Catholic Convention in Mainz 1871, the Saint Raphael Society for the Protection of German Emigrants was founded, mainly upon suggestion of the businessman Peter Paul Cahensly (1838–1923; 1885 deputy of the Center Party). Journeying to the United States in 1874, he occupied steerage in order to investigate the situation of the emigrants. Encouraged by Leo XIII, he repeated this trip in 1883. In Italy, which was harder hit than Germany, G. B. Scalabrini, bishop of Piacenza after 1876, took the initiative and founded the *Pia Società dei Missionari di S. Carlo per gli Italiani emigranti* (1887). Cahensly, who had presented his case to the Congress of Liège in 1887, made contact with Scalabrini, who founded the *Società S. Raffaele* in 1890. It is the name of the rather active German Cahensly that comes to mind in connection with the controversy about "Cahenslyism" (which was unreasonable, but its proponents had good intentions), rather than the name of the diligent Scalabrini, in whose spirit Francesa Saveria Cabrini (1850–1917) worked. During the Saint Raphael's Convention in Lucerne in 1890, the international character of which was somewhat diminished by the absence of the Americans, a memorandum was composed which stated that, as a result of the pastoral situation in the United States, 10 million Catholic immigrants had been deprived of the practice of their faith. Cahensly sent the memorandum to the Pope and increased the number of victims in a letter to Rampolla to 16 million. As a remedy he suggested placing the national parishes under the authority of a bishop of their respective countries.

The reaction of the episcopate as well as the general public in the United States was vehement. As for an objective diagnosis, Archbishop Ireland, who was probably more aware because of his pride in America, came closest to the truth in his estimation that 1 to 1.5 million immigrants had lost the practice of their Catholic faith, and this figure should be considered accurate.

The controversy concerning the immigrants' pastoral care was already on the horizon of the great conflict of the nineties, and it illuminates the central problem of Catholicism in the United States at that time. The difficulties of a minority in an often aggressively hostile society were intensified by its national heterogeneity. On the other hand, the groups of the various immigrants found a certain security in their national parishes, so that the development of a total Catholic consciousness as well as its acculturation to American society was problematic. But these tendencies, fostered by the European mother countries, stood in contrast to existing social conditions, especially for the second generation of immigrants. The result was the emergence of problems related to parochial jurisdiction whenever there was the desire to change the parish and thus the *rector ecclesiae.* The language problem seems to have played a relatively minor role. The Irish spoke English, and the Germans, next to the Irish the most important group up to the eighties, quickly learned the language of the country, at least in the second generation.

The situation was more difficult for the Italians and the Eastern Europeans. But the command of the English language did not erase the differences which were, last but not least, a matter of clerical estate. The German Roman Catholic Central Society (founded in 1857), for a long time the only Catholic umbrella organization in the United States, played an important role in American Catholicism. This caused understandable resentment among the Catholics of Irish descent, who were highly influential in the hierarchy, constituted the great majority, and refused to tolerate special groups. The question of parish membership was delayed by the Propaganda Fide in 1887 and finally resolved in 1897, with the understanding that children of non-English-speaking immigrants born in America could, upon reaching maturity, leave the parish of their parents and join an English-speaking parish; and that English-speaking immigrants could become members of an English-speaking parish and were not subject to the pastor of their national congregation. The increasing social mobility gradually drew the Catholics into the American melting pot. An unreliable census in 1916 counted 5,660 Catholic national parishes. English sermons were delivered in 3,502 of them, and sermons in one additional language were even delivered in some. The Irish episcopate aimed at the sensible goal of totally Anglicizing Catholicism in the United States, but this achievement was hampered by national emotions.

The leaders of the Church in the United States during Leo XIII's pontificate were born in the thirties and were mostly of Irish descent. James Gibbons (1834–1921) was the son of an Irish immigrant in Baltimore, though he grew up in Ireland between 1837 and 1853, because his parents had returned there. A priest since 1861, he was consecrated bishop in 1868 and participated as the youngest council father in the first Vatican Council. In 1872, he was appointed bishop of Richmond. His book, *The Faith of Our Fathers,* appeared in 1876 and was a great success among American Catholics, even though, theologically, it was insignificant. Gibbons was a master of well adjusted apologetics. As coadjutor of J. R. Bayley, an Anglican clergyman who converted in Rome in 1842, Gibbons succeeded him in 1877 as archbishop of Baltimore. Cardinal (since 1886) Gibbons was in many respects Manning's American counterpart, and was repeatedly helped by him in his ecclesiastical endeavors. He was convinced of the papacy's mission and entertained no doubts concerning his episcopal responsibility, as he saw it, in the framework of the specific situation of Catholicism in the United States. The constitution of the United States was for him a sort of secular Bible: "I would not expunge or alter a single paragraph, a single line, or a single word" (1897). His reserve toward some German-speaking Catholics was not unfounded. He contributed considerably to the development of American Catholicism and to its esteem in the total society.

It is much more difficult to assess John Ireland (1838–1918). Born in Ireland (Burnchurch), he came to the United States with his parents in 1848. The French bishop of St. Paul sent him to study at the preparatory seminary of Meximieux in France, which gave him an education in the spirit of Dupanloup. Upon his return to St. Paul, he was ordained a priest in 1861; in 1875 he was named auxiliary coadjutor and in 1884 bishop. In 1888 he persuaded other bishops to sign a petition to elevate St. Paul to an archbishopric. His patriotism was not as natural as that of Cardinal Gibbons and often approached exaltation. In spite of their different opinions and temperaments, Gibbons and Ireland were united in their efforts toward an indigenous American Catholicism. Ireland's address to the Council of Baltimore (1884), "The Catholic Church and Civil Society," became famous. His love for writing was documented by the collection of essays *The Church and Modern Society.* Ireland's endorsement of the missionary concept of I. T. Hecker was probably less controversial in respect to the dispute over "Americanism" than was his behavior after Leo XIII's letter of condemnation to Gibbons, *Testem benevolentiae,* of 22 January 1899. The Irishman John Keane (1839–1918) also belonged to this influential group of the American episcopate. It was thanks to his initiative, supported chiefly by Ireland, that the Catholic University of America was founded in Washington in 1889. He was its first president, but also one of the first victims of the "Americanism" disturbances, and was relieved of office in September 1896. From 1900 to 1911 he was archbishop of Dubuque. An important role in the controversies, intensifying in the nineties, was played by the president of the American College in Rome, Denis Joseph O'Connell (1849–1927). He was born in Ireland and was a close friend of Gibbons and his liaison man at the Vatican, where he was considered a "Liberal." Gibbons had to agree to O'Connell's dismissal from the College in 1895, and he could only save his friend's and his own reputation by appointing him rector of his titular church in Trastevere. In 1903, he made him president of Catholic University and continued to maintain the friendship. The limitations of the cardinal became obvious when, in 1890, he wanted to promote John Lancaster Spalding, bishop of Peoria and cofounder of Catholic University, to archbishop of Milwaukee, but failed because of the Curia's opposition. The leader of the opposition in the American episcopate was Michael A. Corrigan (1839–1902), whose Irish father had immigrated in 1828. Between 1859 and 1863, he studied at the North American College in Rome (founded by Pius IX) and was ordained a priest in the Lateran by Cardinal Patrizi. Under the patronage of Vicar-General McQuaid (later the bishop of Rochester), he was consecrated bishop (at age thirty-four) in Newark, where he had taught dogmatics since 1864.

He promoted the Jesuit College in New Jersey and organized the first American pilgrimage to Rome (1874). After the Council of Baltimore (1884), he published the pastoral letter on "true freedom." Coadjutor, by 1880, Corrigan was appointed archbishop of New York in 1885. In various controversial questions he held a very intransigent view. While Gibbons, Ireland, and Keane were upset about the approbation of Charles Maignen's devastating book, which increased the American tensions coupled with the French ones, it was welcomed by Corrigan.

In this milieu of people and movements, Catholicism in the United States matured. The issues of the first Plenary Council of Baltimore in 1866 were, to a large extent, still discussed at the third Council in 1884. In the previous year, Leo XIII had invited part of the episcopate to Rome in order to give the archbishops directives through the Propaganda Fide, and he planned to have the council chaired by a cardinal of the Curia. The Americans were able to realize their desire to entrust the chairmanship to James Gibbons, who occupied the see of Baltimore, the most prestigious archbishopric, but was rather indifferent toward the project (J. T. Ellis). Symptomatic of the change in the structure of American Catholicism is the portion of American-born bishops at the Council: in 1852, there were 9 out of 32; 1866, 14 out of 45; 1884, 25 out of 72, 15 of them of Irish descent. Aside from these 15 prelates, there were 20 who were born in Ireland, so that the Irish almost had the majority (8 Germans, 6 Frenchmen, 4 Belgians).

A specifically American question concerned the procedure for the appointment of bishops. While the Curia wanted to transfer the European model of the cathedral chapters to America, there were also strong efforts to introduce an election system by the clergy. The council decided that the "diocesan consultors" (half appointed by the bishop and the other half elected by the clergy) together with irremovable pastors were to make a list, to which, however, the bishops of the ecclesiastical province were not obligated when making a proposal to the Pope. This remarkable procedure was in effect until 1918 (new codex). In the years between 1880 and 1903, Leo XIII intensified the ecclesiastical organizations by establishing 23 dioceses and 3 prefectures. After Pius X's establishments, there were now 82 bishoprics in 14 ecclesiastical provinces. While the Plenary Council of 1884 took place without a papal legate, Leo XIII used the occasion of the centennial of the American Catholics in 1889 to send Francesco Satolli (1839–1910), an adviser from Perugia and a strict Neo-Scholastic, as his representative to Baltimore. On the occasion of the World's Columbian Exposition in Chicago in 1893 (a celebration of the four-hundredth anniversary of the discovery of America), organized by the United States, Satolli, now titular archbishop, came a second time in order to deliver Vatican documents. Satolli, who returned to Rome in October 1896 and was replaced by Archbishop Sebastiano Martinelli (1889 Prior-General of the Augustinian Hermits, 1901 cardinal).

More crucially than in Catholicism elsewhere, the school question stood in the foreground of American interests. The constitutional right to found private schools, its necessity for the Catholic minority's development of self-awareness, the financial difficulties in this extensive country form the background for the history of the school system. At the Plenary Council of 1884, the responsibility of the parents was emphatically defined as an episcopal decree, and the tendency to excommunicate offenders was repressed. Episcopal dispensation had to be mentioned because there were not nearly enough Catholic schools. By 1900, the two hundred primary schools of 1840 had increased to 3812; yet, more than half the children went, more or less by necessity, to other schools. Moreover, the standards of public schools improved considerably. The Jesuits were particularly concerned with higher education. Around 1880, they had four thousand students altogether, and in 1890, five thousand five hundred. The small increase was caused by the fact that the Jesuits had not adjusted their organization and curriculum to the public schools, which was partly corrected by the initiative of the second president of Catholic University, Thomas Conaty. An increase of scientific subjects failed in spite of the efforts by Notre Dame University, founded in 1842 under the direction of the Congregation of the Holy Cross. The Sisters of the Sacred Heart, who from the middle of the century until 1890 had founded ten girls' high schools, tried to adjust within limits. It is natural that education became one of the areas of conflict in American Catholicism's attempt to gain identity. During the congress of the National Education Association in 1890, John Ireland surprised the public and his friends-in-faith with the suggestion to integrate the Catholic parochial schools with the system of the public schools, whereby religious instruction was to be given outside of the general lessons. To some, this seemed like a betrayal, to others a malicious Roman attack on the free republic. Patriotism and the worry of increasing the Catholic schools' incompatibility had joined hands in Ireland. The idea was realized in the parochial schools of Faribault and Stillwater in the Archdiocese of St. Paul, which were leased on notice to the local school board for one dollar a year as part of the public school system. The school board was also responsible for the salary of the Catholic teaching sisters (except for the religious instruction to be given in the schools). The professor of ethics at the Catholic University of America, Thomas Bouquillon, and the group of the episcopate around Gibbons supported the "Faribault plan," but Bouquillon's colleague, the German professor of dogmatics J. Schroeder, and the Jesuits opposed it vehemently. The majority of the German Catholics' resentment was based upon the *Kulturkampf*, rather than concern about the preservation of the German language. Rome, to which the controversy had been transferred, decided (in April 1892) in favor of a *tolerari posse*, referring at the same time to the resolution of the Council of Baltimore. But Ireland's idea had failed.

In Baltimore, in 1884, the founding of a Catholic national university was planned, an idea which Gibbons viewed with reservations (J. T. Ellis). At first Bishop John Lancaster Spalding and Bishop John Keane supported the idea. Opposed to the plan were Archbishop Conigan and the bishop of Rochester, Bernard J. McQuaid, as well as a good part of the Jesuits, because they feared a liberal spirit. The donation of a young female convert amounting to three hundred thousand dollars facilitated the efforts to gain the Vatican's approval. On 13 November 1889, the Catholic University of America in Washington (the founders had wanted this location, while Gibbons had favored Philadelphia — outside of his dioceses) was inaugurated in the presence of President Harrison. Keane relinquished his bishopric in favor of the presidency. But internal Catholic animosities within the institute continued. Within the faculty, the German Joseph Schroeder, who taught dogmatics, was the head of the opposition against Keane and his friends in the episcopate. He had emphatically supported Cahensly's criticism of America and created the teaching chair for German literary studies, which was to be filled in accord with his ideas defined in the essay "Liberalism in Theology and History" (1881). Ireland succeeded through the Apostolic Delegate S. Martinelli in having Schroeder, who was supported by Corrigan, recalled. The German dogmatist Josef Pohle had already returned to Europe in 1894. Leo XIII's recall of Keane from the presidency on 15 September 1896 is part of the crisis of American Catholicism. In 1904, after the presidency of T. Conaty, the university, in spite of the efforts by Denis O'Connell, was driven into a catastrophic situation due to the mismanagement of its treasurer, a situation which it could not overcome until ten years later. The comparatively older universities in Georgetown (since 1805) and St. Louis had trouble adjusting to the general development. Most successful was the University of Notre Dame.

Another complex problem discussed at the Plenary Council of 1884 was the question of which societies with Freemason-like rituals Catholics would be allowed to join. This was an old problem, with which the Provincial Council of 1875 in San Francisco had dealt. They suggested that the father confessors permit membership in a society in doubtful cases, but demand withdrawal as soon as the respective "secret" society was forbidden by the Church. The discussion was bound to get more serious after the encyclical *Humanum genus* (1884), which contained an especially sharp condemnation of the Freemasons. But since their rituals were customary in many American societies, there was only the alternative of leaving the decision to the conscience of the faithful or to proclaim a list of forbidden societies, which was exceedingly difficult. An archiepiscopal conference in 1886 approved the Grand Army of the Republic (a society of Civil War veterans whose president was a Catholic and the brother of a bishop) and the Ancient Order of Hibernia. The explicit prohibition of other societies was debated at the conferences, but no agreement was reached. In Boston, in 1890, the majority around Gibbons decided to forbid only Freemasons, a rule that was protested by other episcopal parties (Corrigan, McQuaid, and others). Archbishop Katzer of Milwaukee complained in Rome. After the Church provinces of New York and Philadelphia had autocratically forbidden, respectively, three and four societies, the question was turned over to the Curia in November 1892 (meanwhile Satolli had arrived as papal delegate), since no agreement had been reached. After some time, on 20 August 1894, the Holy Office proscribed three societies. Rampolla's simultaneous letter to Satolli, stating that the execution of this decree was left to the judgment of the metropolitans, only caused confusion. In December 1894, Leo XIII, through Satolli, ordered the promulgation of the decree. Gibbons traveled to Rome in vain (1895) — the crisis was on the way. Now, societies like The Knights of Saint John or the more important Knights of Columbus were promoted — a separation which was against the principle of accommodation. The fact that individual bishops were suspicious of such organizations, and that the entire episcopate did not support a federation of the individual Catholic societies until 1905, is indicative of the social attitude of American Catholicism before World War I.

The struggle over a closer definition of the "secret societies" was also one of the elements in the controversy about the association of the Noble and Most Holy Order of the Knights of Labor, which was founded in Philadelphia in 1869 and spread quickly under the leadership of the Catholic Irishman Terence Powderly (since 1879). Two thirds of its members were Catholics. When Gibbons was able to prevent Rome's condemnation of this society in February 1887, it was already (for several reasons) on the decline. Therefore, the historical significance of these events was not embedded in the history of this association as much as in the relation of American Catholicism to the socio-political question of which association was representative.

It was said that the "ever-present and recurring earning potential" of the United States had prevented the social embitterment that had occurred in Europe. Although the question of salaries and working conditions was pertinent, the main long-term problem was the accumulation of capital in the hands of the lower classes and the way in which this wealth was accumulated. Concentration in the agrarian sector produced a growing rural proletariat, which was welcomed by industry. There, however, the workers were victims of a ruthless labor market and had to pay the price in times of crisis as a result of legislation, jurisdiction, and an administration which exclusively served the interests of the entrepreneurs. Cheap labor was plentiful among immigrants, "freed" black slaves, and children. The formation of unions was hampered by legislation and the lack of solidarity among the heterogeneous labor force. The Knights of Labor was the first significant worker movement, though vehemently attacked by American society as a whole, in spite of its sensible demands (equal wages for women and blacks, an eight-hour day, a labor arbitration court) and its reserved attitude in regard to strikes. The same sentiments were shown by the conservative segment of the clergy, who, moreover, associated the Knights of Labor with the "secret societies" which were forbidden by the Church because they copied the secular "mores" of the Freemasons. Because the Catholic workers were urged, on the occasion of parish missions, to leave the associations, T. Powderly (son of an Irish worker with twelve children) changed the title of his association. In 1884, upon his inquiry in Rome, Taschereau (archbishop of Quebec, after 1887 cardinal) received the reply that membership in the Knights of Labor was forbidden by the Church. The American episcopate discussed whether this prohibition applied to Canada only and decided to present the question again to the prefect of the Propaganda Fide, Cardinal Giovanni Simeoni. In Canada, where Archbishop Lynch of Toronto favored the organization, it was discussed whether the reply referred to Quebec only. The answer from Rome in 1886 was "general prohibition." Gibbons' letter of 20 February 1887, which he signed himself, but had composed in collaboration with Ireland, Keane, and Denis O'Connell, effected in Rome a toleration of the Knights of Labor. Gibbons' recollections thirty years later showed which internal and public problems in regard to Church affairs he had had to face. But soon more radical organizations successfully competed with the Knights of Labor. The radicalization of the social differences was one of the causes for increasing de-Christianization slightly veiled with Christian slogans. The encyclical *Rerum novarum* (1891) found little attention among the American Catholics. But there were a few clergymen who called the social problems by their names, in the first place John Ryan (1869–1945), son of an Irish immigrant, who had already attracted attention at the Catholic University of America in 1906 with his dissertation "A Living Wage: Its Ethical and Economic Aspects." In 1916, his main work, *Distributive Justice,* was published. During the twenties he reached the peak of his public career. One of his allies was

Peter E. Dietz (1878–1947), son of a German immigrant, who cooperated success-fully with some of the union leaders and founded a social section in the *Deutscher Katholischer Centralverein.* The fact that he founded a Catholic union (Militia of Christ for Social Service), in accord with the encyclical *Singulari quadam* of 1912, should be viewed in this context. In 1923, the Catholic members of the Chamber of Commerce persuaded Archbishop J. T. McNicholas of Cincinnati to force Dietz to close his Social Academy.

The case of the New York priest Edward McGlynn (1839–1900) turned into a the-oretical social conflict with strong ecclesiastical and political overtones. McGlynn had lobbied for the land reform theory of Henry George and for his candidacy (1886) as mayor of New York. The fact that Archbishop Corrigan had forbidden it only promoted fanaticism. After two citations ordering him to come to Rome, which he did not obey, McGlynn was suspended (1887). But in 1892, as a result of Gibbons' approval (mediated by Delegate Satolli), he was reinstated. Since Cor-rigan had failed to secure approval for his proposal to place the writings of Henry George on the Index because Gibbons' group opposed it, this act was a serious disavowal of the archbishop.

The concept which Gibbons and his friends held of the relationship between the Church and society as a whole finds its most definite expression in their active participation in the Religion Congress of 1893 in Chicago, which was organized in the context of the World's Columbian Exposition. Jews, Moslems, Hindus, and followers of other religions had been invited. Its president was the Presbyterian J. H. Barrows, who declared that no one was expected to sacrifice even the most insignificant part of his faith. Gibbons' position in the public of the United States of America is illuminated by the fact that he recited the Lord's Prayer after his welcoming speech. John Keane, one of the twenty speakers (among them Ireland and Hecker's biographer, Elliot), gave the concluding speech, which he repeated in 1894 at the Catholic Congress of Scholars in Brussels. None of the participating Catholics was religiously indifferent, but they were all of the conviction that the Roman Catholic faith could not be absent from the register of world religions in the United States of America. Writing to Satolli in September 1895, Leo XIII stated that so far he had tolerated interdenominational conventions quietly; he preferred, however, Catholic events to which non-Catholics were invited.

It was the first year of the crisis. The long brief *Longinqua Oceani* of 6 January 1895 was full of praise for the United States and the religious zeal of the Catho-lics. However, it contained a paragraph which was understandable in view of the Pope's opinion of the relation between Church and state in "Catholic" countries and especially in view of his expectations in regard to France. At the same time, it questioned the sociological foundations of American Catholicism. It may be ac-ceptable to say that the separation of Church and state as practiced in America was not the best of all possibilities under any circumstances. But the Pope's re-mark that the fruits of the development of ecclesiastical life would be a lot more plentiful if the Church would enjoy, aside from freedom, the favor of the law and the patronage of the public authorities, offended the secular creed of every citizen in the United States. Even Corrigan wrote to Gibbons that it was fortunate that the non-Catholics had not taken offense. But this was not only a matter of concern for the non-Catholics. One cannot assume that the paragraph in the Pope's letter was incidental. That same year, Denis O'Connell was recalled from Rome; in November the same happened to Satolli, and in September 1896, Keane was dismissed as president of the university. In connection with the conditions in France and the situation in general, the "American way" turned into the ecclesiastical problem of "Americanism."

Gibbons' concept had failed. On 6 June 1911, the fiftieth anniversary of his ordination, thousands of visitors assembled, among them President W. H. Taft and former president T. Roosevelt, whose visit in Rome the previous year had resulted in complications with the Vatican. But Gibbons no longer held center stage. In 1911, William H. O'Connell (1859–1944), whom Gibbons had made the successor of Denis J. O'Connell at the American College (1895), was elevated to cardinal of Boston, after an official hierarchy had been established in the United States in 1908 through the apostolic constitution *Sapienti consilio.* In 1905, following the Russo-Japanese War, William H. O'Connell visited the Emperor of Japan on a special mission for Pope Pius X. He diligently supported the organization and funding of missions at the congress of 1908 in Chicago and of 1913 in Boston. He was a man of the new era.

CHAPTER 5 5

Catholicism in the Slavic World until 1914

Russia, as one of the great powers, lost its supremacy in Europe after its defeat in the Crimean War, but it preserved its leadership over all Slavs and propagandized for the liberation of all Slavic peoples in the Austro-Hungarian Empire and Turkey by employing, aside from foreign politics, pan-slavic idealism. The Orthodox Russian State Church, with its representation at the Holy Synod, left little chance for development to the Catholics within the Russian area of influence; the Poles especially were oppressed. Because of the impact of liberalism and nationalistic tensions, Catholic Slavs found themselves in a difficult position in the Austro-Hungarian Dual Monarchy, in the small countries in southern Europe, and in the areas of Turkey remaining after the Balkan Wars. Their efforts to preserve the mother tongue in education and preaching, which they had a right to according to Church laws and decrees, created widespread conflicts, which had been caused by state orders and which could only partially be resolved.

The Russian Empire

Following the Polish uprising in 1863/64, the introduction of the Russian language into schools and church services in 1869–77, and the close collaboration of some Polish prelates and the Russian government, a break between the Holy See and Russia occurred.

By announcing to the "Highest Emperor and King" Alexander II (1855–81) his coronation on 20 December 1878, Pope Leo XIII tried to loosen the rigid political fronts and establish diplomatic relations with Russia. He gave his Nuncio Ludovico Jacobini full authority to conduct preliminary talks in Vienna. These resulted in a settlement reached on 24 December 1882. The partners agreed on the administration of the bishoprics of Minsk, Podlachia, and Kamieniec under the jurisdiction of the archbishop of Mogilev and bishop of Luck-Zytomierz, on the subordination of seminaries and the Clerical Academy of Saint Petersburg to ecclesiastical direction and state supervision, and on lifting the government strictures against the clergy decreed in 1865–66. The regulation requiring that studies in Russian language, history, and literature should be increased in ecclesiastical academic institutions and indifference to the controversial problems of the oppressed Uniates foreshadowed future conflicts in spite of the agreements achieved. Moreover, the Chief Procurator made no secret of his dislike of the agreement and deplored the concession to the Catholic Church, which he presented as a danger to the existence of the Russian state. As the tutor of Alexander III (1881–94), who came to power after the assassination of Alexander II, he exerted great influence on the young Tsar. He was filled with the ideals of the "Holy Russia" of the old Moscow, and wanted to overcome the internal strife within Russia by reenforcing the Orthodox State Church and by fighting against the liberal reforms and revolutionary elements. Since he rejected Catholicism, which had, traditionally, deep roots in many areas in the country, he regarded the agreement with the Vatican as pandering to revolutionary elements. He considered disastrous an alliance between the Pope and the Orthodox State Church, which, in his opinion, offered the only defense against the autocracy of the Tsar, even though others recognized the restoration forces of the papacy. Anxious to offer moral support against revolutionary currents and to conclude the *Kulturkampf* in Germany and Russia, Leo XIII endeavored to come to an understanding with Alexander III. His first success was the reorganization of the Church hierarchy by preconization of twelve prelates with whom he filled the vacancies in the archbishopric of Mogilev, in the auxiliary bishoprics of Kovno, Luck-Zytomierz, Tiraspol, and Vilnius, as well as in the archbishopric of Warsaw, in the auxiliary bishoprics of Kalisz, Kielce, Lublin, Plock, Sandomierz, and Seyny. The new pastors tried to eliminate the obstacles to ecclesiastical life posed by the Russian State Church.

The measures of the state against the Uniates and the pressures to employ the Russian language in preaching and instructions as well as the regulations of 16 January 1885 regarding the appointment of clergy (who could function only after the respective governors or governors-general in the Vistula regions had given their approval), effected another break in diplomatic relations between Russia and the Vatican. They were not resumed until after 1887/88. In 1890, Leo XIII appointed a number of new bishops for Russia. On 18 June 1894, Alexander Izvolsky, Imperial Russian diplomatic agent in the Vatican since 1888, became resident minister to the Holy See. Count Frederick Revertera, the Austro-Hungarian ambassador to the Vatican, called the papal efforts in regard to an understanding with Russia a "midsummer night's dream," but Leo XIII was able to ordain seven more bishops for Russia in 1896. The accession of Nicholas II (1894–1917) seemed to warrant new hopes. In 1899 the Tsar gave his permission for the construction of a new church in Saint Petersburg. But the erection of a nunciature, which the Pope desired, did not follow.

By 1900, 70 percent of the Russian population were members of the Orthodox Church. After them, the Moslems and the Roman Catholics formed the strongest religious groups. Of the approximately 10 million Catholics, two-thirds were Poles; the rest were Lithuanians, White Russians, Ukranians, Latvians, and Germans. At the beginning of the twentieth century, state funds for the Orthodox Church amounted to about 30 million rubles, while the Catholics received only about 1.5 million rubles. Payment of state salaries to the Catholic clergy through the Roman Catholic Clerical College in Saint Petersburg considerably limited their independence. The entire correspondence between the Church administration and the Curia was conducted through the Ministry of the Interior. The preconized bishops (in each case it took exhaustive negotiations in order to find a candidate who was acceptable to both the tsarist government and the Vatican) were appointed by the Tsar. He also had to confirm in office all canons and other dignitaries. An instruction from the minister of education of 1900 demanded that the topics for final examinations in seminaries be in the Russian language and include history. Since this regulation was not followed by the Polish bishops, numerous clergymen could not be employed.

A manifesto, issued on 22 February 1903 by Nicholas II, expressed religious toleration and acknowledged the freedom of the Catholic Church to act, but it did not alleviate the distress of the Catholics in any way. Only after defeat in the Russo-Japanese War of 1904/05 and the proclamation of a constitutional system of government at the end of 1904 did the Tsar decide to issue a statement in which reforms were promised (e.g., freedom of belief and conscience). On 30 April 1905, he published a belief and toleration edict, which was followed by amnesties for religious offenders; this filled the Catholics with confidence. The Orthodox Church was termed the prevailing Church; it was allowed to maintain the right of propaganda; the penalties against those who left the Church and converted to another religious congregation were abolished. The Russian Old Believers, who had been cruelly persecuted since their separation from the Orthodox Church in the second half of the seventeenth century, could relax. The situation of the Catholics seemed particularly to improve, since the Tsar, in a manifesto of 30 October 1905, ordered the government "to give the population immovable foundations of civil freedom according to the principles of absolute inalienable personal rights, freedom of conscience and speech, and the right of assembly."

The optimism of the Catholics was soon shaken. At first, some relief was given them, for instance in the controversial language question. In 1906, the Curia yielded to the pressures to use the Russian language in preaching, and on 22 July 1907 it came to an agreement with Russia concerning Russian language, history, and literature in the Catholic seminaries in Poland.

The regime survived the year of crisis (1905/06). But after its stabilization, it stunted the growth of parliamentary life by suspending the First and Second Duma (1906/07), and through certain regulations and administrative measures it turned the relief granted to the non-Orthodox churches into an illusion. At the fourth Missions Congress in Odessa in 1908, Orthodox bishops demanded that the bishops be reprimanded and that the toleration edict be voided. In 1907, Eduard Baron von Ropp, since 1904 bishop of Vilna and a member of the First Duma and of the Catholic Conservative party, which he had founded, was recalled by Nicholas II because he had resisted the introduction of the Russian language into Catholic church services. He was replaced by an administrator sent by the Curia. In 1909, Bishop Cyrtovt of Kovno, together with three hundred clergymen, was accused of having failed to comply with the required formalities when converting from the Orthodox to the Roman Catholic Church. In 1910 the Catholic bishops were forbidden to deal directly with the Curia and to publish papal decrees without the permission of the government.

On the eve of World War I, the Catholics were being suppressed in Russia just as they had been in the nineteenth century. The Roman Catholic Clerical College in Saint Petersburg, which was responsible for the joint affairs of the dioceses, consisted of the archbishop of Mogilev and two members appointed by the Tsar from among the higher clergy and from assistants elected in the various dioceses. The government maintained a controlling influence, especially the Department of Foreign Cults in the Ministry of the Interior, in spite of the papal protests that the jurisdiction of the College be limited to merely material affairs. The hierarchy consisted of 15 bishoprics, including the archbishopric of Mogilev with 7 and the archbishopric of Warsaw with 6 auxiliary bishoprics. Each bishop took care of a seminary. After the suspension of the Warsaw Academy (1867) there was only one academic institution of university rank, the Roman Catholic Clerical Academy in Saint Petersburg, which earned a reputation through its scholarly and ascetic training of qualified clergymen (53 bishops came from this restitution).

The effectiveness of the bishops and the secular and regular clergy in dealing with the faithful entrusted to them and in securing their loyal observance of Catholic traditions was wasted by their defensive stand against state pressures. The Russification measures, which were mostly aimed at the Catholics of Latin and Uniate rites, showed that Catholicism was merely tolerated. Catholicism was exposed to new burdens by the war, the consequences of the October Revolution of 1917 relative to ecclesiastical policies, and the growing independence of Poland and the surrounding Baltic areas after World War I.

The Three Polish Territories

After the fourth division of Poland at the Congress of Vienna, Russia possessed 82 percent, Austria 10 percent, and Prussia 8 percent of the Polish-Lithuanian Empire, which had been dissolved through its partitioning at the end of the eighteenth century. The Polish question kept the European cabinets busy until the Republic of Poland was founded in 1918. The passionate determination of the Poles to retain their language and their heritage, the activities of the emigrants, the hope of recovering freedom and unity by being doubly loyal toward the three dividing powers (after the failure of the uprisings in 1831, 1846, 1848, and 1863/64), the dissolution of the Russian Empire, and the defeat of the Central Powers were essential prerequisites for the restoration of the national independence of Poland. During these efforts, the Catholic Church formed a unifying link, transcending political boundaries.

In Russian territory, after the failure of the uprising of 1863/64 in which several Catholic clergymen had participated, the governor general of the western provinces enforced a rigorous regime, with reprisals against the bishops and priests continuing throughout the next decades: the closing of monasteries, the dissolution of the Uniate bishopric of Chelm (1875), the supervision of pastoral work, and measures aimed at the introduction of the Russian language into the Church. Leo XIII tried to relieve the predicament of the Polish Catholics by direct negotiations with the Tsars Alexander II and III and Nicholas II. The Poles were afraid that their national interests were being threatened by the Pope's agreement with the Russian government. In a public consistory on 19 February 1889, Leo XIII tried to defend himself against these charges. At the same time, through one of his directives, he impressed upon the newly appointed Polish bishops that their mission was to serve the mutual accord and friendly harmony between spiritual and secular powers. In spite of agreement concerning the appointment of bishops and official willingness to comply with the wishes of the Curia, nothing changed in regard to the curtailment of freedom for Polish Catholics.

In 1886 the regulation requiring that the construction of a church could be allowed only by the minister of the interior, after consultation with the responsible governor and Orthodox bishop, was extended to Polish territory. The regulation was also valid for other non-Orthodox religious congregations. The government placed special emphasis on religious instruction conducted in the Russian language. The law of 4 March 1885 regarding the Polish elementary schools left the decision to the curator of the Warsaw school district. He was to share the decision with the governor general whether Catholic religious instruction was to be given in Polish or Russian. In higher schools, the Orthodox teachers taught in Russian, since the Catholic priests refused to abandon their native language. In 1892, all Catholic parochial schools were placed under the supervision of the minister of national education. The result was the founding of secret Catholic parochial schools. To prevent the construction and maintenance of these illegal schools, penal regulations were enacted and again enforced in 1900. The instructions of the minister of national education regarding examinations in seminaries were disobeyed, with the result that the governor general in Warsaw did not recognize the examinations and the appointment of newly ordained priests. When Tsar Nicholas II allowed them to reapply for the examination, there was no response. By 1905 the number of unemployed priests had risen to 156, the number of vacant parishes to 263. When, in the same year, the instruction was cancelled, the authorities declared their willingness to confirm even those candidates who had not taken an examination in the Russian language.

Nicholas II's edicts of toleration of April and October 1905 were enthusiastically welcomed by the Poles, since it seemed that the free development of their ecclesiastical life was now guaranteed. On 3 December 1905, the Pope addressed the Polish bishops of the Russian Empire, praising them for their loyalty to the Apostolic See and demanding that they stand up for the preservation of peace, justice, and Christian education. The tensions regarding the language questions were eliminated, as can be deduced from the convention signed in Rome on 22 July 1907. The number of houses of religious, which had rapidly decreased in the first decades and had only slowly risen at the end of the nineteenth century, increased again. Charity centers and social activities commenced.

The majority of the Catholics forced into Orthodoxy and belonging to the dissolved (1875) Uniate bishopric of Chelm had to suffer from the Russification measures and wanted to call upon the toleration edict of 1905. Since they were forbidden to return to their faith, about two hundred and thirty thousand converted from the Orthodox Church to Roman Catholicism between 1905 and 1910. In other parts of northwestern and southwestern Russia, people who earlier had been forcefully converted to Orthodoxy now rejoined the Catholic Church. The Orthodox bishops, supported by the Holy Synod, organized counter-propaganda. The Orthodox Bishop of the recently created eparchy of Chelm, a diligent representative of the Russification policy, convinced the Third Duma to create the province of Chelm, a new ecclesiastical entity comprised of parts of the provinces of Lublin and Kielce (1912). The purpose was to halt the expansion of Catholicism. As early as 1908, an Orthodox mission congress in Kiev had demanded the revocation of the toleration edict. The Association of the Russian People of 1906 requested in 1909 that the false interpretation of the Easter manifesto come to an end and that freedom to proselytize be granted only to the Russian State Church. In 1912, the Orthodox Bishop of Warsaw declared in the State Council that the historic task of the Russian state used to be and still was the Russification of everything non-Russian and the conversion to Orthodoxy of everyone who was not a member.

The growing pressure against Polish Catholicism was evidenced by the fact, among other things, that foreigners who had established religious orders after 1905 were expelled in 1910. When, on 21 January 1911, the priests came to Lublin to take the antimodernist oath, they were forced by police upon their arrival to depart immediately. They were informed that the papal directives were not valid in Russia, since they had not been announced via the proper channels of the state authorities.

In order to weaken Catholicism, the government and the Orthodox Church patronized the Mariavites, who had developed from a society of nuns founded by Felicja Kozlowska (1862–1921) and an association of secular priests founded by Jan Maria Kowalski (1893), which strove for religious renewal among the clergy and people. The Mariavites' Eucharistic and Marian devotion tended toward mysticism and therefore the organization was not approved by Rome. The association of priests was proscribed by the Holy Office in 1904; on 5 December 1906, Jan Kowalski, Felicja Kozlowska, and forty priests were excommunicated. As minister general, Kowalski organized a Marian Union, which on 28 November 1906 was recognized by the Russian cabinet council as a special Catholic religious community. In spite of repeated condemnation by the Roman authorities, the Mariavites spread quickly because of their support by the state; in 1909 a law regarding Mariavite parishes secured their position. Negotiations between Kowalski and the Utrecht Union resulted in the acceptance of the union by the Old Catholic churches. Kowalski had the bishop of Utrecht, Gerhard Gul, consecrate him as bishop and he established a new hierarchy with four bishoprics. The number of Mariavites may have reached a maximum of three to four hundred thousand when the Russian government and Orthodox dignitaries were supporting them in any way possible in order to halt the influence of the Roman Catholic Church. Even before World War I, many had left the new church. In spite of decline due to internal and external problems it is still in existence.

In Galicia, one of the Cisleithan crownlands of the Habsburgs, the Catholics were not as defensive as in Russia. In the first half of the nineteenth century, they were exposed to the effects of the state church, Viennese centralism and Germanization. However, they were aided by the self-government which the cities and rural communities had been granted in 1849, by the concordat between Pius IX and Emperor Franz I, concluded in 1855, but annulled in 1870 by Emperor Franz Joseph, and by the constitution of 1867, which favored Polish aspirations toward autonomy. Count Agenor Goluchowski, governor of Galicia, decreed the introduction of the Polish language in the schools, the courts, and civil offices. Numerous Poles were promoted by the Austrian government to the ministerial ranks and two of them to minister president. The Polonization of the two national universities in Crakow and Lemberg (which had Catholic theological faculties), the founding of the Crakow Academy for the Sciences (1872), and the collaboration of the conservative Galician aristocracy with the imperial court secured the political superiority of the Poles (about 45 percent of the total population of over 43 percent Ukrainians, 11 percent Jews, and 1 percent Germans).

Polish Catholicism of the Latin rite, which consisted of about 3.5 million faithful in 1910, had a somewhat tense relationship with the approximately 3 million Uniate Ukrainians because of national differences. Even though the solution presented by the Concordat of 1870 resulted in several difficulties within the Catholic educational system and in other areas of the Church's public activity, the ecclesiastical organization of the archbishopric of Lemberg with the auxiliary bishoprics of Przemysl and Tarnow and the prince bishopric of Crakow, which was placed under the jurisdiction of the Holy See in 1880 and expanded in 1886 through several deaneries of the diocese of Tarnow, could be enlarged.

The Polish educational system made possible the development of an academic staff in science, art, and journalism. Aside from theological, mostly pastoral publications, the monthly *Przeglqd Powszechny* (General Review) appeared in 1883 under the direction of the Jesuits, in which prominent Catholics wrote leading commentaries on fundamental questions of current interest. It became the main publication of Polish Catholicism known beyond the borders of Galicia.

Since Galicia's economic development did not keep pace with its intellectual and spiritual life, and the large increase in population could not be absorbed by industrialization, the peasantry was in danger of progressive deterioration. The Church was aware of its duties in dealing with social problems. The social encyclical *Rerum novarum* of 15 May 1891 received attention here as well.

Religious life was influenced by representatives of the older orders and younger religious communities. Jesuits who had been expelled from Prussia during the *Kulturkampf* found a new sphere of activity in Galicia. The Pallottines tried to establish a press apostolate in Lemberg in 1908. The Redemptorists formed an independent Polish province in the same year. Several new communities appeared: the male and female Albertines; the Sisters of Archangel Michael (*Michaelitki*), and the Fraternity of the Blessed Virgin Mary, the Queen of the Crown of Poland.

In the Prussian territory, the differences between the Protestant government and the Catholics, particularly the Polish-speaking population, had increased through the decades. After settlement of the conflict with Archbishop Martin Dunin of Gnesen-Posen (1831–42), his successor, Archbishop Leo von Przyluski (1845–65) persistently stood up for the restoration of Polish rights. The colonizing and Germanization tendencies of the Prussian state contributed to the growth of the Polish national consciousness. After 1870, the Polish policy of the German Empire created a struggle of nationalities in the eastern German regions, which continued (with few interruptions) until 1918. The school supervision law of 1871 and the decree requiring the use of German in the Polish schools of Silesia (1872), Posen, and West Prussia (1873), the systematic abolition of the Polish language in higher schools (1872–90), the introduction of German as the only official language; in all public offices and businesses (1876), the anti-Polish measure during the *Kulturkampf* burdened the situation in regard to Church policy.

Archbishop Miecislaus Ledóchowski of Gnesen-Posen (1865–86), who endorsed Polish religious instruction in high school classes and paid no attention to the so-called May laws, was the first bishop to be arrested (on 2 February 1874) and to be dismissed by the State Court of Justice in Berlin. In 1875, the time of his imprisonment in Ostrowo, Pius IX created him a cardinal for his courageous defense of the faith. After his expulsion he proceeded to send directives from Rome to his areas of jurisdiction and was subsequently penalized with fines for having usurped episcopal rights. During the negotiations to end the *Kulturkampf,* he was willing to resign. Aside from Ledóchowski, both his auxiliary bishops, Janiszewski of Posen and Cybichowski of Gnesen, together with nearly 100 clergymen were arrested during the *Kulturkampf,* so that 97 parishes were vacant and 200,000 Catholics were deprived of proper pastoral care. The diocesan administrative offices were maintained by secret delegates empowered with special plenipotentiary authority. In spite of state pressures, the Polish Catholics were not discouraged by the *Kulturkampf.* They accepted the challenge and intensified their efforts to expand their social, cultural, and ecclesiastical independence.

After Ledóchowski's resignation, Pope Leo XIII made an attempt to eliminate the *Kulturkampf* laws by appointing Pastor Julius Dinder of Königsberg (originally from Ermland), archbishop of Gnesen-Posen (1886–90), and the only German in a long series of bishops who wanted to alleviate nationalism in the controversies regarding ecclesiastical policy. The Pope's attempt failed.

The expulsion of twenty-six thousand foreigners (1885–86) from the eastern provinces, the settlement law of 1886, the East Marches Society of 1894, the fireplace law of 1904 (which was to limit new Polish settlements), the law regarding societies of 1908 (which required that even Polish societies use the German language in their statutes and meetings), and the expropriation law of 1908 intensified the national struggle. During this time, the Poles were able to preserve and strengthen their national characteristics with determined efforts, through parliamentary activities of their factions in the Prussian Provincial Diet and the German *Reichstag,* and through cooperative societies and business organizations. Prelate

Piotr Wawrzyniak (from 1892 until his death in 1910 president of the Polish savings bank cooperatives) and other clergymen tried to prevent the purchase of real estate from Polish hands and pursued a successful Polish settlement policy on parcelled latifundias.

Above all, the Poles demanded the reinstatement of Polish as the language of instruction in elementary schools, especially in religious instruction. Their demands for the use of their own language were supported by the Center Party and the German Catholic conventions. Archbishop Florian Oksza-Stablewski of Gnesen-Posen (1891–1906) advocated the preservation of Polish as the language of religious instruction. He also objected to government measures requiring that the twelve- to fourteen-year-old pupils of elementary schools in Wrzesnia speak German during religion classes, which had resulted in the Wrzesnia school strike (1901). He also protested the decree demanding that 20 schools in the administrative district of Posen and 183 schools in the area of Bromberg use German during religious instruction, which had resulted in an extensive school strike in 1906. In a pastoral letter of 8 October 1906, Oksza-Stablewski gave a summary of his efforts toward the protection of Polish religious instruction. He asked parents and clergy to devote more energy to the catechization of the young. He did not witness the end of the school strike, which lasted into 1907. At the beginning of the strike, 90,000 of the 241,000 children received religious instruction in Polish. In 1906, nearly 47,000 Polish children refused to attend 750 schools in the province of Posen. Since the government took rigorous steps against the parents and clergy, the tensions remained.

From 1906 until 1914 the archiepiscopal see of Gnesen-Posen remained vacant. At the outbreak of World War I the government approved the nomination of Auxiliary Bishop Edward Likowski as archbishop (1914/15) in order to appease the Polish population.

In the struggle between German and Polish nationalities, the Polish population succeeded in improving its position. The portion of Germans receded from 41 to 38.4 percent between 1871 and 1905. The Polish Catholics directed their energies toward the preservation of their national identity under the leadership of their archbishops of Gnesen-Posen and prominent prelates within and without ecclesiastical life. In addition to their insistence on the use of the Polish language in schools, they expanded their press. After 1879, they published the *Ecclesiastical Review* (*Przegląd Kościelny*). In 1895, Archbishop Stablewski provided the initiative for the publication of a weekly paper, the *Catholic Guide* (*Przewodnik Katoliki*). In 1906, at his suggestion, the new *Preacher Library* (*Biblioteka Kaznodziejska*), published between 1872 and 1894, was continued with the publication of the *New Preacher Library* (*Nowa Biblioteka Kaznodziejska*). He placed great emphasis on the training and continuing education of the clergy. The old Lubrańsk Academy in Posen had served as a seminary from 1780 to 1896. During the *Kulturkampf* it was forced to close its doors and it was not allowed to open them again until 1889. In 1896, the theology students were provided with a new building, where they attended theological and pastoral lectures after receiving basic philosophical training in Gnesen. In this context it is worth mentioning Polish scholarly societies and their publications, in which clergymen decisively participated. By means of lending libraries and book clubs, the clergy managed the distribution of religious writings.

The monasteries were centers that radiated Polish religiosity. The Community of Servants of the Blessed Virgin Mary, which was founded by Edward Bojanowski (1814–71), a Polish nobleman, and devoted to the care of the sick and the orphans, expanded. After the conclusion of the *Kulturkampf*, the orders and religious communities resumed their drastically confined activities.

The Poles of the German eastern provinces were a source of inspiration for the other Polish territories. Their tightly organized and concentric efforts towards national identity were highly esteemed by the Poles in Russia and Galicia. In view of the different political developments in the three territories, ecclesiastical life contributed to the internal consolidation of Polish Catholicism. Polish self-confidence was strengthened by reports of the activities of the chief pastors and the clergy in numerous parishes, as achievements of the orders and other religious communities, and the successes of associations on various levels. Adherence to the Catholic faith and to Polish nationalism merged into one inseparable entity, in spite of all social differences and parties. The Polish Catholics looked toward the popes as advocates of their national interests, even though the popes practised caution in their addresses and letters in order to avoid conflicts with the governments. Cardinal Miecislaus Ledóchowski, who, after 1883, worked in the papal Secreteriat of State, was their influential spokesman at the Curia.

Austria-Hungary

The dual Habsburg Monarchy of Austria-Hungary, with its many nationalities, harbored numerous internal and external political problems in the decades preceding its decline at the end of World War I. These problems greatly affected the Slavic population in regard to the development of its ecclesiastical history. In 1900 Austria was estimated to have 23 million Roman Catholics, 3 million Uniates, and 600,000 Orthodox. At the same time Hungary was estimated to have 9 million Roman Catholics, 2 million Uniates, and 3 million Orthodox. In addition there were 700,000 Orthodox and 350,000 Catholics in the Turkish provinces of Bosnia and Herzegovina, which had been occupied in 1878 and annexed in 1912. The Orthodox and Uniate Christians belonged to Slavic nationalities. Slavs of the Roman Catholic creed were mainly the Poles in Galicia, the Czechs and Slovaks in Bohemia, and the Croatians, Slovenes and some of the Serbs in the south of Austria-Hungary.

The Austro-Hungarian *Ausgleich*, adopted due to pressure by Hungary in 1867, was criticized by Slavic politicians who endeavored to change the Monarchy into a federation of free and equal nations as giving unjustified preference to the Magyars. By 1871 the Czechs voiced their claims against the centralistic German guardianship. In 1880 they effected a language ordinance for Bohemia which required that even in purely German areas each application had to be filled out in the language of the applicant and trials had to be conducted in the language of the accused. In 1882/83, they succeeded in having the University of Prague divided, and after 1891 there existed a German and a Czech Catholic theological faculty with eight professors and one lecturer each. In April 1897 language ordinances for Bohemia and

Moravia followed. Not until 1913, under the impact of the impending World War, was the way paved for successful German-Czech negotiations for a compromise in the language question.

In the course of these efforts, the Catholics worked for an expansion of their rights in the following areas: in the archdiocese of Prague, which in 1886 established a Czech seminary for boys in Pribam, in the diocese of Leitmeritz (with 75 percent Germans and 25 percent Czechs), and in the archdiocese of Olmütz, where Czech was spoken exclusively in the east and south. Since the election reform of 1907, Christian forces emerged as rivals of the old national parties (Old and Young Czechs), which formerly claimed exclusive representation, especially among the rural population. From the beginnings of the Czech Christian Socialist party formations at the end of the nineteenth century, which took shape in 1904, arose the conservative wing, the People's Party (*Lidová strana*) in Bohemia (1911) and the Catholic National Party (*Katolicko-národní strana*) in Moravia. In order to alleviate the tensions between the German- and Slavic-speaking clergy, Leo XIII turned to the bishops of Bohemia and Moravia with his letter of 20 August 1901, asking them to nurture their inherited language, to care for all of the faithful with equal love, to avoid the language controversies, to prevent disagreements in seminaries, and to seek harmony in their dioceses.

Toward the Slovaks, who gradually voiced their claims for autonomy, the government of the Kingdom of Hungary showed no kindness. It oppressed all non-Magyar nationalities and conducted a strict policy of Magyarization, which extended into the ecclesiastical realm.

Like the Slovaks, the Carpathian Ukrainians, Rumanians, and Serbs suffered under the Magyarization process, which also included the educational system which made no exception for religious instruction. Not until 1914 did the Hungarian government give in to the pressures of the disadvantaged nationalities. It permitted religious instruction in the respective mother tongues in all elementary and civil schools as well as in teacher seminaries.

In the south of the Dual Monarchy, life for the Slavs was extremely tense. The majority of the Croatians belonged to the Kingdom of Croatia and Slavonia, bound to the Austrian crown; one part belonged to the Cisleithian-Austrian half of the Empire in Istria and Dalmatia, the other to Bosnia-Herzegovina, while the Slovenes belonged to the western part of the Empire in Carniola, in the south of Styrh, and in Carinthia. The Serbs, who had achieved absolute independence at the Congress of Berlin in 1878 and had formed their own kingdom in 1878, tried to attract the minority in the south of the two Austro-Hungarian portions, mainly from Bosnia and Herzegovina, and they propagandized a Great Serbian South Slavic Empire, which was to include Serbs, Croatians, and Slovenes.

While the Slovenes and Croatians had their roots in Western culture and Roman Catholicism, the Serbs were rooted in the East and in Orthodoxy. After centuries of oppression by the Turks, all three nationalities were filled with a tremendous desire for freedom and left no stone unturned to achieve their political, cultural, and religious independence. Attempts failed to buffer the alternating pressures of the South Slavic question by reorganizing Austria-Hungary along federalistic lines or according to a triadic empire concept in place of the current dualism (Austria-Hungary).

By the beginning of the nineteenth century the Slovenes had created a uniform written language. Their awakening national consciousness is reflected in their societies, cooperatives, and in the Sokol movement. Together with the Croatians, they attempted a solution within the framework of the Habsburg Empire. Dr. Anton Korošec (1872–1940) founded the Slovenian Farmers' Party (1907), approved a southern Slavic agreement, and accepted in 1918 the chairmanship of the Slovenian-Croatian National Council.

The Croatians were much more active. They were not satisfied with autonomy in regard to administration, education, and the judiciary, which they had been granted through the Hungarian-Croatian Agreement of 1868. Franjo Rački (1828–94), who was the first president of the Croatian Academy of Sciences in Zagreb (1866–86) and leader of the Croatian People's Party since 1880, and Bishop Josip Jurij Strossmayer (1815–1905) were the spokesmen of their national interests for decades.

The bishopric of Djakovo was headed by Bishop Strossmayer, from 1849/50 until his death, according to his motto "all for faith and country." In 1900, 253,770 Catholics of the Roman rite, 29,000 Uniates, and 169,000 Orthodox lived there. Of ninety parishes, fifty-five were Croatian-speaking and three German; thirty parishes had a mixed Croatian-German population and two a mixed Croatian-Hungarian population. In spite of his political and cultural dedication to his people, Bishop Strossmayer tried to bridge differences for the sake of a union with Rome by demonstrating his loyalty to the Habsburg Monarchy, furthering the Uniates and pursuing the idea of uniting all southern Slavs, even the Orthodox Serbs. In 1872, he retired from active politics. He opposed the Hungarian claims and the hegemony of either Croatians or Serbs, and furthered with his patronage the development of Croatian culture. This can be demonstrated by his donations to the University of Zagreb (1866), the Croatian Academy of Sciences (1867, opened in 1874), and the art gallery in Zagreb. Furthermore, his support was valuable to scholarly publications and instrumental in the construction of a representative cathedral in Djakovo, which was inaugurated in 1882. In view of the concepts of the governments in Vienna and Budapest, his Catholic pan-Slavism brought about conflicts with the national Croatian politician Dr. Ante Starčević (1823–96), who ruthlessly fought the Serbs and demanded a Greater Croatia, which, in addition to its native land, was to include Bosnia, Herzegovina, and Dalmatia. It was to be on an equal footing with Hungary. Strossmayer reestablished the Croatian Institute *S. Girolama dei Schiavoni* in Rome, which Leo XIII, upon a motion by the Croatian episcopate, renamed *Collegium pro gente croatica,* hoping, as did his secretary of state, Rampolla, that it might become a stepping stone for the ecclesiastical unification movement among the Balkan Slavs.

In contrast, Joseph Stadler (1843–1918), after 1881 archbishop of Sarajevo, expected the college to be a nursery for a Catholic Greater Croatia. He carefully pursued the development of the ecclesiastical organization aided by Jesuits, Franciscans, and several religious orders of women. In 1904–11 he wrote a textbook on Scholastic philosophy in the Croatian language. During the reorganization of the ecclesiastical arrangement after the occupation of Bosnia and Herzegovina (in 1895 a census counted 675,000 Orthodox, 55,000 Moslems, and 350,000 Catholics), Leo XIII established the archdiocese of Sarajevo with the auxiliary bishoprics of Banja Luka and Mostar. During the decades before World War I, the number of Catholics increased to almost 400,000 because of the influx of Catholic civil servants, soldiers, and businessmen. They were cared for by the archbishops of Sarajevo and the bishops of Banja Luka in Bosnia. The bishops of Mostar were the chief pastors in Herzegovina.

The constitutional annexation of Bosnia and Herzegovina in 1908 did not change the ecclesiastical situation, but the resulting international tensions led to World War I, in spite of the agreement between Austria and Turkey concerning the Serbian "Great Power" aspirations and because the European powers were ready for action. During this war, Catholic Slavs fought on both sides. The majority of the Slavic Catholics was supported by Austria-Hungary, while the Orthodox Slavs were protected by Russia.

Section Two

The Development of Catholicism in Modern Society

Oskar Köhler

C H A P T E R   5 6

Catholicism in Society as a Whole

During the pontificate of Leo XIII the Catholic movements, arisen from the confrontation with modern society as it evolved from revolution, formed themselves into social groups in various countries within society as a whole and thus gave rise to what today is called Catholicism. The idea of restoration had failed; the revolution of the bourgeoisie could not be revoked, having achieved its last victory with the occupation of Rome, which, in conjunction with the commune uprising in Paris, marked the beginning of the revolution against the bourgeoisie. It was an epoch-making turning point in the history of the Catholic Church, representing, at first, a fundamental change in its relation to the "world," touching its very essence and self-awareness. From the time of Constantine the Great until the French Revolution, the Church was able to absorb all political figures into its own organism, assimilating them. Indeed, in the early stages of the West, it was even capable of portraying the *imago imperii*. This is no longer true in the age of the liberal and democratic constitutional state and the "growing industrial society with its continuous changes in its stratification" (C. Bauer).

The cultural forms of Catholicism of the various countries took their classical shape during the pontificate of Leo XIII and were typical until the first third of the twentieth century. The multiplicity of denominational associations, especially in Germany, proved statistically to be rather successful. So was the press, ranging from daily papers to intellectual periodicals, whose circulation, with the exception of religious mass literature, was not competitive but did have dedicated readers supporting it. All this was an expression of a strong self-awareness, which, in turn, could affect daily life through solidarity. G. Goyau glorified the *Catholicisme social,* to be understood in a general sense, as a "society of saints" in the midst of the modern world, turning away from the individualism of Chateaubriand toward a *fraternité,* which he said was a definite reaction to the concept of a lay society, and he related his vision of the human society to the *société surnaturelle:* the dream of the old relationship between reality and its image. But he was compelled to bewail the misfortune of the Catholics in his country, who appeared to be the rearguard of society, but were in reality the vanguard. But it is exactly this assessment, be it from the point of view of the liberal bourgeoisie or the Socialists, which defines a deficient relationship to society as a whole. Even though Catholicism took initiatives, particularly in reference to the social question, it simply used the sociological and political configurations of the post-revolutionary world rather than accepting them from within, at least initially. This is also valid for the popular movements, for the workers' pilgrimages to Rome, for the nonecclesiastical lay societies and their activities, which are, after all, phenomena of an increasingly democratic society. Their tendency toward independence boded conflict with the clerical claim for leadership. The terms in which Catholicism expressed itself were borrowed, and its self-righteous expectations of asserting itself within the total society by means of its re-Christianization were illusory.

In this context belongs Catholicism's realization of its internationality, which was demonstrated at congresses when foreign guests of the same religion were welcomed. In reality, the national differences were quite substantial, even if one ignores the effects of international political factors. Of course, the concept of internationality was realized in the sovereign common to all Catholics and, no matter how controversies about certain issues regarding ecclesiastical policies arose, the authority of the Pope within Catholicism was not questioned during Leo XIII's pontificate. It was intentionally nurtured by observing certain anniversaries and was extensively interpreted by the Pope when he defined the competence of the nuncios, as well as by lay representatives. At major public events such as the Catholic conventions and Eucharistic world congresses (as soon as they were fully developed), the idea of the *Ecclesia militans* as the Church of the martyrs took an outspoken militant turn.

The forms of Catholicism, to be sure, were not merely at odds with the principles of the liberal bourgeoisie but were also struggling with more or less fierce internal conflicts. These differed according to the specific historic situation and obstructed an international consensus. Attempts were made to divide the Catholicism of the various countries where the pre-revolutionary Church had been the "established Church" (like Spain, Portugal, Latin America, France, Italy, and Austria-Hungary), and the countries whose recent history did not accord the Catholic Church this kind of status and therefore "had fewer difficulties in adjusting to the new political conditions of the nineteenth century"(J. N. Moody). This general typology certainly provides some useful insights, but distinctions must be made. Catholicism in Bismarck's Germany, for instance, where the Church was never "established," significantly differed from Catholicism in the United States. What the different forms of Catholicism had in common in all countries — varied according to their respective social structures — was that they were composed of the same social strata, although less so among the upper classes, as society in general. This posed the problem to what degree Catholicism could act as an integrating force on the conflicting interests of society's subdivisions. The strength of identity of each group depended on the extent to which, in addition to the issue of Church and state, social contrasts could be bridged. A strong, distressed minority could exploit this circumstance.

Between Total Revision and Reform

It is a characteristic mark of Catholicism that it always saw the "social question," in a narrow sense in the "perspective of the total society" and the labor question as part of the "integral social reform question." This view was only held by some theoreticians in areas where Catholics were in the extreme minority, as in Great Britain and in the United States. Therefore, it is necessary to integrate the Catholic social movements into the concept of the total society. Only then does the dilemma which Catholicism faced wherever it had to strive for more than the civil equality of a small minority become visible. Either it had to inculcate fundamental changes within the total society in which it was embedded (since it was clearly not of the same spiritual descent), or it had to content itself with realizing its principles by way of reforms within the plurality of the total society, foregoing its own concepts and making compromises along the way. This dilemma survived the turn of the century and was resolved, depending on the situation of the individual countries. Even though the differences between the countries have to be considered, the "changes in the socio-political realm of ideas relative to German Catholicism in the nineteenth century," as Clemens Bauer described them, can be regarded as a model case. Change meant primarily Christianization and re-Christianization, which was difficult to equate with charitable activities as proletarization grew in a capitalist society and was increasingly recognized as a general condition that was not absorbed by the "labor problem." When Edmund Jörg termed liberalism the "ruling spirit of our time," and the "natural son of the new national economy," thus closely connecting political and ideological liberalism with the capitalist economy, a "total social reform" could indeed be regarded as the main task of Catholicism, whether "class inspired" in a sentimental social sense or impregnated with socialistic features, whether it was called Christian or not. However one chooses to assess the "newly created socio-economic reality," the desire for fundamental structural alterations of society had to either vanish in utopia or, without admitting it, take on a revolutionary character. How deeply Catholicism was affected by the idea of developing a concept that would embrace all of society and putting it in competition with a liberal bourgeois ideology is documented by the encyclical *Rerum novarum*. It was penetrated by only a few ideas about a "total social reform," but was able to revitalize the principal disputes within Catholicism, which had acquiesced to the facts of capitalism under the leadership of the Center Party and followed the path of social reform.

The Problem of Toleration

The "broken relationship" of the Church to the liberal civil society is a phenomenon which is characteristic of all forms of Catholicism, though not so much in the United States during the Gibbons era where the leading segments of the episcopate, although opposed by the Corrigan group, were firmly anchored in the Constitution, i.e., in the principles of human rights. The reasons for this attitude were not merely based on ecclesiastical policy and tactics. In reference to modern society, this is one of the Church's basic dilemmas which the teaching authority had to face in view of internal Catholic tensions as well as the position of the Church in the secular world. Since the opposition put forward by the *Syllabus* was clear, only requiring refined interpretation, was there an alternative? *Tolerantia,* in accordance with the *Syllabus,* was a negative term for Leo XIII and the majority of Catholics (wherever they were not an extreme minority) because it was equated with a concept wherein truth and untruth, morality and amorality are equally valid. The positive term, being alien to the *Syllabus,* is the *patientia* with which the Church is in waiting until mankind discovers the one and only truth, Catholic truth. This principle is applied to religious freedom, which, when indiscriminately granted (*promiscue*), will result in atheism. It applies to the freedom of speech, the press, and education, upon which the state is obligated to place limits, not withstanding the Church's inalienable freedom to teach. All principles of liberalism, which were fundamentally condemned, were banned in the *Syllabus* in the same manner as in the encyclical *Libertas* (1888). However, and this is the only difference, the latter speaks of the consideration of "human weaknesses" by the "maternal judgement of the Church," which does not ignore the course of events and therefore does not condemn the state's occasional indifference toward certain events which do not comply with truth and justice in the interest of eventual good and prevention of evil. It is clear that even a liberal who was willing to practice his principles in the face of the Catholic Church was misunderstood as long as his idea of truth was identified with a radical indifferentism and his world view was tolerated by the Catholic Church as the lesser evil. He had to fear that "patience" would only last until an opportunity for the dogmatization of public life arose again. But Leo XIII created a modus vivendi with respect to society's pluralism, and more could not be expected in this particular historical situation. At the same time, he offered a formula for resolving internal Catholic controversies. The test case was Catholicism in the United States. It is indeed understandable that the notion that the American conditions should be considered a model for the Church was discarded as an error. But the limits of an essentially unrealized adjustment were evident in the remark that the Church could reap a rich harvest if it were granted, "aside from freedom," also "the favor of the law" and the "protection (*patrocinium*) of the state." This required the Catholic who adhered to the constitution of the United States to reconcile the irreconcilable. In the papal proclamations on the problem of the relation between truth and freedom there were certain shifts in emphasis, but there was no essential progress.

The Doctrine of Property

The doctrine of property is of as much importance to liberal civil society as is the principle of toleration. In this respect, however, recent research in Neo-Scholastic social philosophy has affirmed that the teaching of Thomas Aquinas regarding personal property was transmitted in a truncated form and eventually fell under the rather strong influence of a liberal economic theory. This is the area where the real theoretical decisions have to be made regarding the question of whether Catholicism should follow its own total conception of social order or whether it should comply and pursue a social reform policy (though, to be sure, in different versions, reflective of its relationship to a capitalist industrial society). It was noted that the individualistic idea of property had its predecessors. Luigi Taparelli (died in 1862) had already presented it in his exemplary work on the Natural Law. He was the teacher of Gioacchino Pecci, who even as Pope remained loyal to his basic concepts, although he did not agree with the reference to the instinct with which the dog will defend its food. "The exaggerated emphasis of the individual side of the concept of property, which neglected the social side ..., did indeed have an impact on papal documents like *Rerum novarum*" (O. v. Nell-Breuning). Nevertheless, in Leo XIII's theoretical writings after 1878, a considerable shift in emphasis can be noted. In the beginning, he discusses the lower classes' wanting to occupy the palaces of the rich without thinking about eternal life. The tone of the social encyclical is essentially different, even though Matteo Liberatore (1810–92), the master of Roman Neo-Scholasticism, who placed the natural right to personal property at the center of his social philosophy had a considerable influence on the history of its creation. Two factors especially seem to have determined the Neo-Scholastic theory of property. Like Leo XIII's encyclical, it basically proceeds from agrarian property: "it is not an exaggeration to maintain that the concept of possession, property as we understand it today, basically was the result of the French Revolution" (idem.). Perhaps this is why the essentially academic question (in which the Pope remained neutral) of whether personal property, as Suárez claimed, was to be attributed to *ius gentium* is of concrete importance insofar as the historical background of the respective specific property law is concerned. If only the "ability to possess property," thus the fundamental right to have personal property, is determined by Natural Law, then there exists a great deal of leeway in which to regulate property and the proper proportions of personal and community property. In addition, Leo's social encyclical places definite value on the property of the "have-nots." That was "surprising for all those who wanted to secure their monetary interests under the patronage of *Rerum novarum.*" Yet Leo XIII "did not distinctly see the two groups of capital and labor as two social classes in the technical sense of the word" (idem.), though these groups were of fundamental significance in the formulation of this modern question. Moreover, in spite of the Pope's efforts in terms of social criticism, he did "speak in the tone of a grand seigneur and a patriarch, almost with a voice descending from the realm of eternity, full of fatherly mercy and kindness when addressing his dear children, especially the workers"; (Idem.) and, without a doubt, his voice grew more "fatherly" after 1878. It was often noted that Leo XIII did not intend to develop a social theory in his encyclical, but the unquestionably strong systematic elements stem to a great extent from the Neo-Scholastic social philosophy of Liberatores, and this is the point of contact for Catholic moral theology as far as the doctrine of property is concerned.

The other factor which needs to be considered when assessing the Catholic doctrine of property in those decades is the polemical dispute over socialism, that is, socialism as a complex phenomenon with all of its ideological components. Unquestionably the logic in Catholic social theory was to a large degree determined by this confrontation. Nevertheless, when attempting a historically adequate evaluation of the total situation, one cannot say that the rejection of socialism "from the perspective of the civil society" should be "called a vital error of the theology of the nineteenth century" (F. Beutter). That, indeed, was precisely the question: Would Catholicism under the given historical conditions of the nineteenth century be able to arrive at a comprehensive concept of society or would it have to assert itself defensively against the mutually contradictory currents of the time, against liberalism as well as socialism, in order possibly to influence reform efforts? Nonetheless, the definite rejection of ideological liberalism did not preclude a more or less strong coloration of the doctrine of property through liberal individualism.

Social Theories

The social theoretical works of the moral theologians often went through numerous editions. But few gained as much international significance for Catholicism as Charles Périn's (1815–1905) *De la richesse dans les sociétés chrétiennes* (first edition 1861). This Catholic economist from Belgium, who also strongly influenced the social activists in France and western Germany, was ideologically and politically a confirmed antiliberalist. But in his principal rejection of state intervention, which was augmented by his opposition to the liberal constitutional state, he acted as representative of economic liberalism. However, he did want this liberalism amended by his concept of "Christian property," meaning the social ties of charity. He accepted the concentration of property in one individual as a result of the progress of civil freedom but he saw the possibility of achieving congruity in respect to self-interests in the sense of sacrifice natural to Christian asceticism. Of course, he deemed the ideal to be moderate wealth, which was most likely to be found among the middle class, and that shows clearly how he underestimated the process of industrialization. The French social scientist Frédéric Le Play (1802–82) had an effect reaching far into the last third of the nineteenth century. Through his sociographical investigations of the family life of workers and craftsmen in France, England, Germany, and Russia, he dealt with an issue that was the central point of Catholic social doctrine. The family is intact when the patriarchal authority of the father is unimpeded. The family is also the model for society as a whole with its "social authorities," including the entrepreneurs. The rejection of liberal human rights and the constitutional state could consistently merge with economic liberalism of a distinctly paternal character, while still implying a serious aspiration toward social justice. The ideas of Le Play were predominant in the *Association des Patrons du Nord.* The antiliberalism of the philosopher and economist Giuseppe Toniolo (1845–1918) had an entirely different background. Professor in Pisa in 1889, Toniolo founded the *Unione cattolica per gli studi sociali in Italia,* which prepared the Catholic social congresses in Italy. In 1891 the *Società operaie cattoliche* included 284 local chapters and was especially popular in northern Italy. The Christian social program, designed under the guidance of Franz Schindler (1847–1922), who was a professor of moral theology in Vienna in 1887, was sent not only to Rampolla, but also to Toniolo. In contrast to Rampolla's sober and pragmatic reaction, Toniolo approved, regarding as essential the program of profit-sharing among the workers. He also gave his basic consent to an "organization of society according to occupations," but took exception to the idea of having infinite competition controlled through corporations by arguing that occupational egotism could ruin the consumer. Being strongly influenced by the historical school of German economics, Toniolo is not so much important for the originality of his doctrine as for his influence in Italian Catholicism and with Leo XIII.

Just as Charles Périn's social theory radiated toward the West, so did the influence of the early Viennese school under Vogelsang toward France. Catholics in countries like France, Belgium, and Austria who tried once more to create a universal order of society in the Christian image of man had something in common: they categorically rejected the liberal civil society. This "reactionary" attitude was affected by various political configurations and thus presented one facet during the Third Republic of France, where such social criticism amalgamated more or less by necessity with antirepublicanism. It had a different appearance in the Habsburg Monarchy, where such criticism was suspect with the liberals as well as the conservatives, so that it came to be associated with revolutionary tendencies. This, as well as the East-West gradient in the process of de-Christianization, has to do with the fact that the Christian impetus was more direct, as it were, in France than in Austria, where socio-political objectives were approached in a more direct manner. In Germany, the defense against the *Kulturkampf* absorbed most theoretical and practical interests and the conclusion of the dispute later coincided with the turn toward a social reform concept. However, even here existed an incipient individual program relative to society as a whole. Most of the leading activists and theoreticians belonged to the aristocracy: in France mainly Albert de Mun, and Latour du Pin, in Germany Prince Karl zu Löwenstein, in Austria Count Franz Kuefstein and Counts Revertera and Belcredi, who were mainly interested in politics, and the North German converts Count Blome and Carl von Vogelsang, who during his odyssey had found a protector in Alois zu Liechtenstein, also called the "Red Prince." The background of these men can easily prompt the sweeping conclusion that an attempt was being made to turn back the wheel of history.

In the social theory of Carl von Vogelsang there are elements from the social doctrine of the Romanticists (especially Adam Müller); and his hypothesis of a "social kingdom" as an alternative to "state socialism" was possible only in the central European regions. However, Gustav Gundlach was justified in observing that the first representatives of a system which later was called "order by occupations" cannot be understood merely on the basis of such deductions. Catholicism produced only one original concept of a constitution embracing all of society. This was intended to be a creative draft of a defense against liberalism as well as socialism. It should be noted that only traces of this concept entered into the encyclical *Rerum novarum.* The practical decision to take the path of Catholic cooperation in the social reform of the capitalist society had already been made. Though the successes accomplished were impressive and cannot be disputed, an assessment of this concept regarding society as a whole cannot be reached on this ground alone. In order to confront the real dilemma of Catholicism, one has to consider that the realization of this concept would entail the abolition of the capitalist society and would therefore not have been accomplished without revolutionizing society. Moreover, these strictly antiliberal and thus anticapitalist theoreticians, mainly located in Vienna, knew rather little about economic realities.

What Vogelsang and his friends wanted to achieve (not through upheaval but "through a gradual transformation from within") was the following: the elimination of "exploitation" through capitalism "whose only purpose of economic activity is net profit"; the formation of occupational "corporations" in which capital and labor, employer and employee are united, forming a "social institution of society and state"; the replacement of the "horizontal stratification according to class by a vertical one according to occupations, which would be characterized by a "republican cooperative relationship"; elimination of "purely private, absolute, capricious property which is robbing God, society and the state." At the top of such economic and political social order was to reside the "social kingdom" as an integrating element. Vogelsang rejected suffrage by census as asocial and general suffrage as dispersing the "historical and political" individualities into "random sections divided according to external geographical criteria," and he also assigned propaganda to the "corporations." Their structure was certainly conceived from the perspective of the trade guilds, which Vogelsang wanted to modernize and organize into reliable production and sales cooperatives so that they could compete with industry. He believed that it was possible to transfer this modernized model to industrial enterprises. Austrian anti-Semitism, too, had one of its roots in the Christian social movement because Vogelsang and others saw the Jews as the main perpetrators of the "exploitation of the workers." Vogelsang's social concept solicited a limited amount of attention in other social study groups of Catholicism, particularly through Blome and Kuefstein. Considerable differences existed not only within these circles but also in the individual groups.

During a social study course of the *Volksverein* in Barnberg in 1893, Franz Hitze called Carl von Vogelsang the kind of "teacher" Germany lacked. The same year, Hitze became professor of Christian sociology in Münster and thus inaugurated the tradition of a new teaching chair in the theology faculty. Next to Wilhelm Hohoff, he was "the first Catholic sociologist who thoroughly studied Marx and recognized his significance" (J. Höffner). To him it was inevitable that "socialism would come, either the absolute, social-democratic version of the state or the relative, conservative, healthy version of the social classes" (Idem.). Hitze rejected the theory of surplus value, but the criticism of capitalism found in his early writings follows the very phraseology of Karl Marx. Like Vogelsang, he bases his theory on the model of the medieval guilds. But he believes they have to be placed on an "expanded economic and democratic foundation," which meant the evolution of industrial enterprises into productive associations autonomously controlled by all participants. Only in this manner could a situation in which the entrepreneur has the advantage and the employee the disadvantage be changed. Hitze opposed Charles Périn's theory with determination. He also saw danger in the idea of the "company as a family," which, through its social provisions, could adversely tie the worker to his place of work. The fact that during the trade union controversy at the turn of the century some representatives of the Catholic workers' societies criticized his idea of an "organization of society on a Christian basis by occupations" was a bitter pill for Hitze to swallow. For, after divorcing himself from the idea of a reunification of capital and labor and embracing the concept of social reform within a capitalist economy, he advocated the functioning of trade unions as "sales cooperatives" (of labor) and justified striking as a withholding of the commodity of labor. The controversy between young Franz Hitze and Georg von Hertling foreshadowed the victory of reform politics with the existing economy over a fundamental rejection of liberal bourgeois capitalism. Abandoned was the "corporative" idea, according to which the relation between capital and labor was not to be determined by the market conditions but by a social contract in the spirit of natural law, because labor was not to be degraded to a form of merchandise. Abandoned also was the conception of the mixed trade unions of "employers" and "employees" as presented mainly by Albert de Mun. The question yet to be answered was how the then clearly weaker partner, labor, could be protected. The following controversy over the state's intervention was dominated by paternalistic ideas (which were particularly persistent in western European Catholicism), but primarily by the relationship to the respective states. In this situation, the Pope, in the encyclical *Rerum novarum,* had to find a moderate position from which to mediate. Now the comprehensive "social question" of Catholicism turned into the more specific question of the workers.

Catholicism had finally evolved into a group within the total liberal civil society and it was responsible for resolving its internal differences over economic interests (the problem of its political parties). The representatives of "Christian socialism" existed in the background; but the idea of an "order according to occupations," along with its "revitalization" (Gundlach) in the magnificent encyclical *Quadragesimo anno* (1931), became essentially a theoretical affair.

Catholicism's multiple efforts in the seventies and eighties toward the design of a comprehensive social system were often mutually exclusive, but their fundamental significance could not be erased by mere pragmatism. They were the work of various study circles, whose ideas merged in the *Union catholique* of Fribourg (founded in 1884 by Mermillod). The image of unity which Catholicism presented in its defense toward the "modern world" needs to be modified considerably if one is adequately to appreciate the difficulties which had to be overcome in formulating *Rerum novarum.* The Neo-Scholastic abstract character of many parties has its explanation in the need to cover the rather contradictory concepts within Catholicism itself as they came to light, for example, at the international congresses in Liège, particularly in 1890. Only by placing it in the total historical context of these decades can we comprehend the significance and the limits of this encyclical in historical terms. Perhaps its greatest significance lies in the recognition of the workers' right to organize, along with its cautious affirmation of the state's right and duty of intervention.

Marriage and Family

Although tensions between Catholicism and liberal individualism on the one hand and collective socialism in the economic realm on the other hand were deep, doctrinal authority was united regarding the sovereign origin of the family. In the dispute with socialism, theories which aimed at revolutionizing the traditional concept of the institution of marriage were occasionally offered by bourgeois Catholics and had to be fended off. There was concern that the parents' rights and obligations regarding the care of their children could be diminished or suspended by state measures. The struggle against liberalism in this respect referred to the legalization of divorce, a prerequisite for which was the introduction of civil marriage. Leo XIII pointed out that marriage, insofar as it served the maintenance of human society, created civil correlationships which the state had a right to regulate. But matrimony is primarily a sacrament and as such subject only to ecclesiastical authority. This poses a problem in view of the de-Christianization and the pluralization of society at large. A solution aiming at differentiating the civil contract from the sacrament, which was respected as such, was rejected by the Pope. In respect to the extrasacramental "relation" (*coniunctio*), he said that in this manner a "rightful marriage" (*iustum matrimonium*) could not be constituted. No less important for the family than the dwindling attitude of society regarding the institutional character of marriage were the changes of the economic conditions resulting from growing industrialization as they affected the family. Leo XIII in *Rerum novarum* spoke only in general terms about a fair wage. He also said that the *paterfamilias* had to be able to support his family but aside from the economic problems it was probably the patriarchal concept of the family which prevented the amount of wages from being determined as a "family wage" according to natural law. To be sure, industrial female labor from the perspective of the worker's protection is an important aspect discussed among groups studying the social problem in Catholicism. But this kind of work was basically considered an evil which had to be alleviated. For a long time, the changes in the family structure of the industrial society were ignored and the family of the agrarian society continued to serve as a model. In this context belong representations of the image of the "Holy Family" in Nazareth. Women's emancipation was diagnosed by Christian social doctrine as a symptom of decline.

The School Question

The classical battlefield of the Catholic Church, society, and the modern state is the school and especially the elementary school. This fight is a defense against the state's claim, having come to full force through the French Revolution, to educate its adolescent citizens in accord with its needs and concepts. In the eighteenth century the predominant part of education had still been, at least indirectly, a Church matter. But the purely defensive character of the ecclesiastical school struggle was demonstrated by the fact that it focused principally and, above all, factually on the religious element of instruction. The parents' right and duty to

raise their children authoritatively was not defined in general terms but according to Christian mores. The ecclesiastical ideal was a Catholic school financed
by the state, which the state had the right to exert influence upon, but only as
far as it was congruent with its innate authority. In the sense of choosing the
lesser evil, these ideals were infringed upon when non-Catholic schools were
also admitted. Bordering the tolerable was the system wherein only Catholic private schools were allowed, even if, as was the case in the United States, they had
the same constitutional status as other schools. The "neutral schools," which,
as a rule, were antiecclesiastical, continued to be principally condemned, even
if it was permissible to administer religious instruction within or outside of the
school building during the time off. The achievements in the individual countries
differed according to the respective political situation: In France, education was
largely secularized by the turn of the century after initial favorable interpretation
of the law of 1882 by J. Ferry, because Catholic private schools were, in spite
of quantitative increases, considerably limited by the laws enacted against the
religious orders and congregations. In Italy, the Catholic victories in the local elections slowly counteracted the prohibition of religious instruction in elementary
schools. In Belgium, the Liberals were defeated in the school question with their
very own political principles. In the Netherlands, the political coalition of Catholics and Protestants prevented a de-Christianization of the schools. In Bismarck's
Germany, the school was the responsibility of the *Länder,* and either in practice or
through legislation the predominant problem of denominational diversity could
be solved while preserving the Christian character of the school, even though
the school laws were still vehemently debated after the *Kulturkampf.* In Great
Britain, the liberal de-Anglicanization of schools gave the Catholics some leeway
(which they took advantage of), assisted by state subsidy of private schools. But
the rising standards in education here as well as in the United States made it
more difficult for the Catholics to remain competitive. This was not only a question of financial means. At the Catholic Convention in Aachen in 1879, Prince
Karl Löwenstein presented the motion to form a commission which was to develop learning goals and corresponding teaching plans for universities and all
the way down to elementary schools. Though it was modeled after the school
of the Middle Ages, it was an outstanding motion, but it faded out after being
handed over to the *Görres-Gesellschaft.* The Jesuits, who were especially active in higher education wherever they were admitted, finally adopted *nolens
volens* the existing school plans, but they were, except where absolutely necessary, not able to develop their own modern concept. With good reason, the
shortcomings of teachers' training were pointed out. Without a doubt, education in all its stages was one of the most important areas in which to halt the
rapid or slow process of de-Christianization. This is why the tensions between
Catholicism and society as a whole became most vigorous in this sphere. The
dilemma which Catholicism had to face relative to its various relations to the total society became especially apparent: the dilemma of the desire to adapt until
a special society could be developed, a desire which arose from the hope for
re-Christianization.

Catholic Associations

The history of the Catholic Church since the middle of the nineteenth century is partially, at least in Europe, a history of Catholic associations. Even here national differences are considerable, depending on the political situation. In France, which was not particularly friendly toward associations, the internal political tensions within Catholicism, among other things, impeded a strong development. Aside from the social associations, the *Association catholique de la Jeunesse française* was probably the most important. It was founded in 1886 and grew considerably after 1899 because the organization reached out toward the social classes as well as to all age groups. The impact of the political problem shows most clearly in the two major movements emerging around the turn of the century: the religiously inspired *Sillon* of Marc Sagnier and the *Action Française,* in which monarchal Catholics and representatives of classical culture in the sense of Maurras joined hands. Whichever concept they followed, the French Catholics were always interested in the whole of France. Germany became primarily the classical land of the Catholic association movement because Catholicism there, in contrast to Anglo-Saxon countries, was such a strong minority that it could organize itself successfully within the general society, especially since it maintained certain regional strongholds in spite of the confessional mixture, and because it could not ignore the historical decisions of 1806, 1866, and 1870, and had to come to grips with the Protestant Hohenzollern Empire. The most famous organization was the *Volksverein für das Catholische Deutschland* [People's Society for Catholic Germany] of 1890, which also impressed many Catholic leaders in France and Italy. It also encountered criticism, but was regarded by many important forces in Switzerland and Austria as a model worth emulating. The founding process involved considerable internal struggles because the conservative agrarian politician Felix von Löe and Bishop Korum of Trier were striving for a society to "teach the German people about the religious and social errors of the present" according to the apologetic of Tilmann Pesch, S.J., who opposed the strongly anti-Catholic *Evangelischer Bund* (Evangelical Union) of 1887. Windthorst saw in it a danger to the Center Party, striving, together with others, for an extensive association for the masses which was to be separate from the Center Party (no election funds, no participation in the election campaign), but was to follow the same goals. This organization succeeded. The association became intensely active with publications, training institutions (for which lecture material was provided), and its "people's offices" (counseling places; after 1900). These activities with their emphasis on reform and decidedly social accent were instrumental in fending off the impact of social democracy on the Catholic workers. Most Catholic employers took a distant or negative stand toward the association, similar to the segment of the episcopate which was suspicious of an association not officially established by the Church, and especially of its democratic concepts. The *Volksverein* had, in 1891, nearly 109,000 members, and in 1914: 805,000. One should consider that the demands on the members of a mass association are necessarily minor. The association's stronghold was in the Rhineland, while Bavaria kept aloof. There were several conflicts with the many other associations of German Catholicism. The *Volksverein* continued to have one handicap: it was not altogether successful in mobilizing the laymen in the organization itself. The official ecclesiastical suspicion of lay participation should not mislead one to imagine that the activities of the laymen were too intensive. A good part of pastoral work was consumed by care for the associations. But the fact that the associations established without Church direction were a product of the postrevolutionary era, in spite of their significance for the Church in modern society, was not overlooked. Leo XIII emphasized the *summa potestas* of the Pope in his magisterial role even though the laity (*privati*) were allowed *industria nonnulla.* He underscored the fact that they could assume only a "resonance" of the teaching authority. The real reason for this statement was certain tendencies of the *Opera dei congressi,* which was divided after 1884 according to function and placed under strictly hierarchical command despite the lay presidency.

The Catholic Press

The daily press was also a child of the Enlightenment and the Revolution. When one pastor spoke of the "authority of the masses" which "threatens to silence the preacher," he was passing the same judgment that the *Historisch-politischen Blätter* expressed on an elevated level: a "specifically Catholic press" was a "necessary evil," having emerged because Christian society was not "in its normal condition." The remark that Catholics had neither "the writers nor the readers" was valid for some time and with respect to subscribers generally continued to be a problem, especially since this reflected on the revenue from advertisements. But the "evil" increased in terms of necessity. It had another aspect: Catholic journalism reflected and compounded internal strife within the various forms of Catholicism. In this respect, the *Kölnische Volkszeitung* and the Berlin *Germania* in Germany were competitors. The *Kölner Richtung,* joined the dispute that had broken out in 1906, endorsing the principally supradenominational character of the Center Party and its political freedom in the face of direct ecclesiastical instructions. The paper took an analogous position in the controversy over the "Christian trade unions." In Austria, the conservative *Vaterland* (founded in 1860) and the Christian-social *Reichspost* (founded in 1893) opposed each other (the papers united in 1911). A false image of journalism in German Catholicism is created when only the leading organs are considered and not the weeklies and the many small local papers. In 1865, the total number of subscribers was estimated to be about 60,000; in 1890, about one million were reported. Nevertheless, these numbers were relatively low: the *Berliner Tageblatt* alone had 250,000 subscribers. The *Kulturkampf* had effected a significant breakthrough. Of course this was related to the fact that the Catholic daily newspapers after 1870 were practically the mouthpieces of the Center Party. This and the bishops' desire to have a direct impact on the editorial staff resulted in an emphatic recommendation of the Church papers at the Catholic Convention in Metz in 1913. These were a medium of the Church authority itself, but they had to try to address Catholics of all political persuasions and therefore generally refrained from sharp polemics in areas outside of the religious and moral spheres. In the Catholic press which represented intransigent conservative viewpoints — in Belgium *Le Bien Public,* in the Netherlands the *Maasbode,* in Spain the *Siglo futuro,* in Canada the *Vérité* of Tardivel — the French newspaper *La Croix* stands out, not just because of its circulation (in 1897: seven hundred thousand, including the nearly one hundred local editions), but also because of its sometimes almost fanatical attitude. In the realm of journalism, the dilemma between Catholicism as a socially, politically, and philosophically coherent group and the essentially universal orientation of the Catholic Church is also evident.

The Enemy

Even if one were critical of a "world conspiracy," refrained from regarding the Grand Master of the Italian Freemasons, Andriano Lemmi, with his pathological hatred of the Church, as representative of all lodges, and made a distinction between the Roman and all the other organizations, it must be stated that we are dealing here with the intellectual leaders of the time who waged a ruthless war against the Catholic Church, no matter how the humanitarian ideals of that movement are evaluated. This and the successes of the Freemasons within Catholicism itself, especially in Latin America, cannot keep us from considering what impact the intensity of the Catholic struggle against the Freemasons had for the consolidation of group-consciousness in the face of the enemy. Even Leo XIII differentiated in his encyclical *Humanum genus* (20 April 1884) between individual *Sectatores,* who, he said, are not without blame, but do not participate in the malicious actions and do not have a clear picture of the ultimate goals of Freemasonry. But the encyclical begins with a reference to the *Invidia Diaboli,* and it ends with the request to the world episcopate to uproot this "wicked pestilence" (*impuram luem*) because an attack as vicious as theirs requires an equally vicious defense. In the first paragraph, the Pope places God's realm in opposition to that of Satan. The accusations against the "naturalists" are basically the same as those which the Pope had earlier brought against the "Socialists and Communists" and which he would bring against liberalism a year later, only that he describes it as work in solitary darkness comparable to that of the Manichaeans. Leo XIII reiterates the prohibition of membership under penalty of excommunication which his predecessors had proclaimed.

The positive definition of a Freemasonic lodge led to complications in Canada and the United States. For the Catholic Convention in Amberg in 1885, Prince Löwenstein, according to the account of his biographer, could not find a bishop who was willing to give a speech appropriately warding off the Freemasons. After the papal letter *Praeclara* of 20 June 1894 which repeatedly condemned the Freemasons (who had now emerged from the dark into the light), Bishop Korum himself was of the opinion that the leadership of the planned Anti-Freemason Congress in Trent had to be the responsibility of the laity. Gabriel Jogand-Pagés, an ex-Freemason who, with reference to the papal encyclical *Humanum genus,* had been opposing the lodges since 1885, was to appear there. As "Leo Taxil," Jogand-Pagés invented a Miss Diana Vaughan, who had supposedly penetrated the secrets of the Satan cult and since her conversion was forced to live in hiding in order to escape death at the hands of the Freemasons. Jogand-Pagés' accomplice was the physician Charles Hacks who, as Dr. Bataille, published the essay "Le Diable au XIXme siècle." The revelations of one Domenico Margiotta about the Italian Grand Master Andriano Lemmi drew the attention of some French bishops. An excerpt appeared in German translation, as well as the sermons of the Dominican Monsabré who demanded a crusade against the lodges. As president of the "Committee for Roman Affairs," Prince Löwenstein tried at the Catholic Convention to circulate such publications in Germany. But Bishop Korum and others expressed reservations toward such "disclosures" about the Satan cult. Italy initiated the international congress, which took place from 20 September to 30 September 1896 in Trent under the patronage of Cardinal Parocchi. Löwenstein was convinced that in the fight for the Church it was his obligation to take over the chairmanship. Yet some scepticism toward "Leo Taxil" was still brought forward as the result of information which arrived just in time. A Roman investigative committee established in Trent pronounced judgment on 22 January 1897: the existence of Miss Vaughan could neither be proven nor disproven. On 17 April "Taxil" revealed his hoax. It was the general problem which came to light through this affair, rather than the psychology of this man, which is important: large parts of Catholicism found themselves facing a basically anti-Christian and antiecclesiastical world. A difficult path had to be followed between adaptation and absolute resistance.

On another yet not completely separate plane are the anti-Semitic tendencies which permeated various parts of Catholicism, especially in Austria and France. The reasons are complex: a subcutaneous anti-Semitism in the history of Christianity surfaced due to the animosity of liberal, Jewish writers toward the Church, and this anti-Semitism joined with a general social resentment toward the Jewish world of finance and business. In France, both the right and the left wing of Catholicism were affected. In Austria, a middle-class mentality and Christian social reform ideas joined together. In France, in 1899, Abbé Gayraud called the Jews "la nation malfaisante et parasitaire."

CHAPTER 57

The Social Movements

In the second half of the nineteenth century, social organizations emerged from the forms of Catholicism which dealt with the needs and interests of the farmers, the middle-class, and the industrial workers. The attempts to meet these needs were primarily inspired by religious motives. The activities were actually initiated by the clergy and individual laymen, less so by the workers and farmers concerned. The fact that after the first third of the twentieth century the religious aspects became more or less insignificant in comparison to the economic ones does not allow the original combination to be considered ideologically suspect. Instead, it refers to the problem of the relationship between Church and state in the sense of the image and the model. In this context, it is important that the leadership of the organizations was more and more transferred from the clergy to the laity. This process, viewed objectively, was appropriate, but it resulted in the predominance of the representation of economic interests over the initial religious motivations.

Farmers

In Germany, beginning in the sixties, Wilhelm Raiffeisen (1818–88) devoted himself to the development of a rural cooperative system. Raiffeisen was a church-minded Protestant. In 1862 the Catholic aristocrat Burghard von Schorlemer-Alst (1825–95) founded an interdenominational (according to its statutes) Farmers' Association in Westphalia. It spread so rapidly in the areas with a Catholic population because of its limitation by the *Kulturkampf,* since the social union was impeded by the state, the Catholic farmers became even more active in their local societies.

In Italy the movement began in Venetia, where Cerutti founded a cooperative credit bank in 1880. This institution, (1904: 855 credit institutions) together with the already existing supporting funds of the *Opera dei congressi,* became the foundation for the development of the farmers' associations. In accord with the agrarian condition in Italy, there were societies for farm laborers and for farmers (in 1904:33 and 43 respectively). In Belgium, the *Boerenbond,* founded in 1889 by G. Helleputte and the priest Mellaerts, achieved considerable significance (1902: 359 local "guilds"). In 1896, a Catholic farmers' union was founded in the Netherlands. In France, in 1892, E. Duport and L. Durand created a rural system of cooperatives in the vicinity of Lyon, and rural youth groups were active. From these activities emerged the *Ligue agricole chrétienne.* Its goal, formulated in the statutes of the Farmers' Society of Schorlemer-Alst, was "to further the members in religious, moral, intellectual, social and material respects." It was applied in all rural organizations and, in its universal formulation, was especially pertinent in areas where de-Christianization had already early affected large parts of the rural population, mostly in western Europe. The organization of the credit system, buying, and selling played a special role in the Christian farmers' movement. This was a result of modern economic exigencies which also affected the agrarian sector. However, after World War I, the religious character of the farmers' societies survived only in Belgium and in the Netherlands. Consequently, economic interests were intensified.

The "Middle Class"

The term "middle class" needs to be defined in generous terms, because the ecclesiastically active industrial entrepreneurs and businessmen (the denominational statistics themselves mean little) were running only medium or small businesses, and with regard to their social policies they stood isolated from their colleagues especially from the those in higher ranks. This explains aside from socio-theoretical questions, why the idea of the mixed trade unions and paternalistic ideas dominated Catholicism for a long time. The entrepreneur regarded his small business (in which he knew everyone) as an sort of extended family. Since there were only minor economic differences, it was possible for employers and employees alike to belong to the Catholic organizations of this social stratum. (While farmers were among the self-employed, they constituted a separate category.) The journeymen's union of Adolf Kolping followed the tradition of the class of craftsmen, and the journeymen who were promoted to masters continued to be special members of the union. A similar situation existed in the mercantile associations within Catholicism. In 1884, an association of Catholic entrepreneurs emerged in the north of France, and in 1889, Léon Harmel and the priest Alet founded the *Union fraternelle du Commerce et de l'Industrie,* which consisted mainly of shopkeepers and small manufacturers who, because of their religious affiliation, also wanted to help each other economically. The members of such associations were largely paternalistic, and entrepreneurs who liked to experiment incurred displeasure.

Since the interests were different in the various economic sectors, a central federation with various special sections was founded in 1901. Abbé Puppey-Girard had suggested this federation, and in 1892 he also initiated the union of young engineers, the *Union sociale des ingénieurs catholiques,* which became a trade union in 1902. In the Netherlands, at the beginning of the twentieth century, Catholic employers' combines emerged in the tobacco and mechanical engineering industries. In Belgium and Germany, given the political partisanship, there was no need for such organizations. In Austria, in the nineties, the Christian Socialists emerged in opposition to the Conservatives. They were interested in the labor question, but they themselves were a decidedly middle-class movement, in which many employed and independent people of the petite bourgeoisie gathered.

At the beginning of World War I, the two Catholic industrialists Léon Harmel (1829–1915) and Franz Brandts (1834–1914) died. As heads of their own companies and in their capacity as organizers they had tried to find a solution to the labor question. They both used a patriarchal style, though it was different in each case because of the situation in their respective countries and their personal ways of thinking; and they were both from the textile industry. These men are not at all representative of their colleagues of the same denomination, but they document what was a serious paternalistic reform. Harmel, *le bon père,* was theoretically indoctrinated by Le Play, and he endorsed and practiced himself a certain form of workers' participation in company policies (the *Conseil professionel* of 1888 changed to the more precise term *Conseil d'usine* in 1891). Harmel also tended to induce the workers to execute their own initiatives. His distant goal was a corporation of employers and employees, but, in contrast to Albert de Mun, he believed that it could only be accomplished if the idea of trade unions was accepted. He was critical of state intervention, but also of his colleagues, whom he charged with being idle in terms of the workers' question, except for their customary charitable activities. He formulated his principles in the *Catéchisme au patron* (Paris 1889). Harmel was one of the main organizers of the French workers' pilgrimages to Rome, and after 1895 he was the president of the *Oeuvres des cercles catholiques d'ouvriers,* which he wanted to lead out of the conservative conception of de Mun in order to win the workers themselves. Through F. Brandts' recommendation he served as consultant during the founding of the *Arbeiterwohl* in Mönchen-Gladbach, an association of "Catholic industrialists and friends of the workers" (1879). Through this association and its publication, the German textile entrepreneurs wanted to propagate their socio-political ideas. Members of the executive board were Georg von Hertling and Prelate F. C. Moufang of Mainz, who brought with him the traditions of Ketteler. In 1880 Hitze, who had just returned from Campo Santo, joined the group as its secretary. Hitze had great impact on the social policies of the Center Party and was able to carry through the "Mönchen-Gladbach concept" over the Viennese Vogelsang school and the clerical "Berlin concept" (in 1890, Brandts became the chairman of the *Volksverein*). Brandts was also a patriarch, and as such, in 1886, he moved with his family to the Saint Joseph's House. in whose original structure he had accommodated the welfare institutions of his company in 1878. He was well aware that all the social works of the company would not suffice. He was a decisive representative of the state's right and duty to intervene, and, after initial reservation toward his resistant colleagues, he finally pulled his weight to grant the workers the same right to form coalitions in the trade unions that the employers enjoyed. However, the legal reform was needed to assure that "the activities of the trade unions would be restricted once the fight was launched."

The Socio-ethical Justification of the Workers' Movement

In regard to this topic, concepts were being formulated which emerged from the socio-theoretical debates within Catholicism, and, in spite of continued differences, found a magisterial basis in the encyclical *Rerum novarum* (1891). The endorsement of state intervention in this document represented a fundamental decision toward the liberal capitalist society and now left it up to the Catholics to act within the political parties of the constitutional state according to the principles of ecclesiastical sociology. How this was reflected in specific individual decisions (for instance, when designing a social insurance plan, or in parliamentary coalitions) is a matter of general history and belongs to Church history only insofar as it resulted in conflicts with the hierarchical claim to a magisterial role. The other, equally important directive of this encyclical, the recognition of the workers' right to form coalitions, had a direct effect on the social structure of Catholicism and had to go through a process of critical assessment. In this respect, the Pope elaborated on the title of the encyclical (*De conditione opificum*) by turning to the workers themselves. In the paragraph on the "workers' associations" (*sodalitia artificum*), Leo XIII dealt with the discussions of the medieval guilds, but he also stressed the necessity of adapting to modern conditions. This was of pressing importance at the time and had practical implications because it expressly left unsaid whether the societies were to be exclusively composed of workers or were to be mixed organizations. Since the formation of such associations is justified on the basis of the natural law, the state has no right to forbid them, and the state is warned not to misuse its right to justified intervention under the mere pretext of public interest.

Leo XIII considered a strike categorically evil because it harms the employer and the employee as well as the public welfare (*mercaturae, rei publicae utilitates*), especially since strikes usually entail violence. It is the duty of legislation to eliminate the causes of such conflicts. The subsequent discussion of Catholic social theoreticians proceeded from the paragraph on employees, who are to fulfill absolutely the work contract which they signed voluntarily and under the conditions of equity (*libere et cum aequitate*). At this point, the encyclical clearly expressed that the wealthy do not require the protection of the state to the extent that the *miserum vulgus* does, and there was no doubt that work contracts had to be consented to which were anything but voluntary and fair. Moreover, the encyclical could and did deal with the question of fair wages only in very general terms. The problem of strikes, to be sure, touched on a fundamental aspect of a stratified society. With which *ordo* could this phenomenon of antagonism be met?

Leo XIII strongly emphasized that the fostering of piety was to be the priority of the workers' associations and that, in the name of episcopal authority, the clergymen, in regard to the associations, were responsible for everything that had to do with pastoral work. For the early Catholic workers' movement, this was hardly a problem, since many socially concerned clergymen devoted their energy to the workers' questions in a comprehensive sense, even though they did not always meet with the approval of their superiors. However, the rural and middle-class organizations of Catholicism practiced religious solidarity primarily in regard to economic questions. Their mutual assistance in economic distress strengthened the religious solidarity of the Catholic special groups within the de-Christianization of the society at large. Therefore, the workers' movement, whether it was Marxist or not, was on the whole an anti-middle-class bellicose movement. Is it true that the more the Catholic workers' movement was religiously determined, the less it was a workers' movement according to the above definition? On the other hand, was its religious character as a *Catholic* workers' movement less pertinent when it was more belligerent, as in the "Christian trade unions"? This touches on the key question of the Catholic workers' movement, the only one, incidentally, Leo XIII spoke about. Were its religious character and the character of a necessarily belligerent movement compatible? In case of a possible conflict, was it not necessary to separate the representation of interests from the Catholic workers' societies and transfer it to the trade unions? What reason was there for representing economic interests in religious form? The "Christian trade unions" wanted to distinguish themselves through this particular name from then mostly atheistic socialism without giving expression to a strongly religious motivation in regard to their concrete goals. The subsequent controversy about the "Christian trade unions," above and beyond the denominational issue, had its basis in the lack of such differentiation and also partially in the rejection of the idea of trade unions per se.

Industrial Workers

If one were to superimpose the European map which delineates the industrial centers developed after the second half of the century onto the map of the Catholic denomination, one would find that the following areas coincide: Upper Silesia, the plains of the Po river around Milan and Turin, the areas around Barcelona, Bilbao, and Oviedo as well as the southern regions from Hamm to Dunkirk. In Upper Silesia, associations emerged in whose publication *Robotnik* purely pastoral goals were pursued; and in Spain, there were no or only very insignificant Catholic workers' organizations (Barcelona became a showplace of horror). In Italy, the institutions of the *Opera dei congress* concentrated in Venetia and Lombardy and, around this time, 170 workers' associations were counted. The ecclesiastical conflicts were kindled by the question of leadership and the character of the organizations. The stage of the Catholic workers' movement during Leo XIII's pontificate was essentially the Rhenish-Westphalian, the Belgian, and the northern French industrial areas.

Around 1880, the *Cercles catholiques d'ouvriers,* founded in 1871 by de Mun, had about 40,000 members. They declined as a result of the political differences within Catholicism in France and revived slightly in 1892 through the *Ralliement.* In 1906, there were about 60,000 members in 418 workers' societies. The relatively small numbers are not as decisive as the social status of the members. In a speech before the then entirely bourgeois Catholic youth association, de Mun said: "The simple folk, gentlemen, the workers in the cities, the factories, and the fields — this is the great problem which you should keep in mind!" But this appeal found little response except with the interested Catholics of the landed gentry and the upper middle class. Moreover, it did not succeed in "taking root in the world of the workers"; it continued to be "agir de l'extérieur." The reasons were partly of a political and partly of a specifically French nature. Even when de Mun, in 1885, in response to the Pope's wish relinquished the idea of founding a Catholic party, and even though he had sacrificed his political convictions during the *Ralliement,* the following goal remained decisive: to unite the Catholics in the "defense religieuse" and the "action sociale." Indeed, it was a question of a "religious, social, and political counterrevolution" which could not, however, break the economic liberalism predominant in the upper ranks and was therefore not approved by the antibourgeois working class. But the incorrect assessment of working class political psychology was compounded by the problematic question of which way the bourgeois spirituality (aside from its political implications) could match the mentality of the working class. The symbol of the *cercles* was a combination of the cross and the Sacred Heart. It had been almost impossible to touch the workers, let alone impress them. This was the candid word of a candid man, and he should not be blamed for the fact that for many of the northern-French patrons this religious activity was only an escape from the social question. The first beginning of a Christian trade-union movement was the *Syndicat des Employés du Commerce et de l'Industrie* of 1887, whose executive board, in 1891, rejected a protective committee of Catholic employers, as well as a clerical advisory body. From this and similar organizations emerged the *Confédération Française des Travailleurs Chrétiens* (CFTC).

In Belgium, the meeting place of the international Catholic social conferences, Bishop Doutreloux of Liège with his charitable activities and the establishment of the *Aumôniers du travail* (1895), the political Professor G. Helleputte with his workers' guilds, the social priest Pottier in Liège, and Fr. Rutten initiated a Catholic workers' movement which was not concerned with the political problems of the

French and was much more pragmatic, but which could only assert itself against the supremacy of the conservatives through the increasing influence of the *Ligue démocratique belge* (since 1891). But here as well, the de-Christianization of the working class spread more and more. In the Netherlands, two movements developed: the one of Leiden, which was oriented toward trade unions, and the one of Liraburg, which pursued a religious-social program.

"During this trip through Belgium, my sojourn in Aachen and the tour up the Rhine river I have come to the conviction that we have to combat the clerics vigorously, especially in the Catholic areas.... The scoundrels are flirting with the workers' question whenever it seems appropriate (e.g., Bishop Ketteler in Mainz, the priests at the Congress of Düsseldorf, etc.)." Karl Marx wrote this to Friedrich Engels on 25 September 1869. This observation about the enemy is also a warning against underestimating the efficiency of the Catholic workers' movement in the northwestern corner of the European continent. So was Bismarck's remark condemning the numerous "so-called Catholic local newspapers," which were often edited by chaplains and mocked the state measures against the "workers' intrigues" even though the uprising of the Commune in Paris should have opened their eyes. In 1869, Chaplain E. Cronenberg of Aachen working together with Chaplain Dr. Litzinger, who had been transferred from Essen (Chaplain Laaf had been called from Aachen to Essen), founded the *Arbeiterverein vom heiligen Paulus* [Workers' Society of Saint Paul]. Cronenberg carried on a controversy in his *Christian Social Voices* against the *Christian Social Newspaper* in Aachen, edited since 1869 by Chaplain Joseph Schings. Cronenberg was of the opinion that "the Christian workers should take the workers' question into their own hands" and that, in spite of their Christian affiliation, the social problems should be considered relatively independently. Around 1875, the *Paulusverein* in Aachen had a considerable reputation with its approximately five thousand members. That is when the battle began over the nomination of a Center Party candidate, which, at first, was won by the middle class; in 1877, in Essen, the worker J. Stötzel won and was elected to Parliament by a great majority. The final breakthrough of an independent Catholic workers' movement did not occur until 1884, at the Catholic Convention of Amberg (thanks to Hitze's efforts). The unification into regional associations was accomplished between 1892 and 1910 (at the Catholic Convention in Mainz, a cartel association was formed in 1911). This development already stood under the sign of the struggle over the "Christian trade unions."

The trade unions were the problem of the religious workers' associations and these, in turn, were the problem of the trade unions;. This was not primarily a question of belief, which was only pertinent in Germany. It was also not just a question of the direct ecclesiastical leadership which was claimed by the integralistic concept during Pius X's pontificate in Germany as well as in other countries. The key issue becomes clear when considering the disputes which were carried on during the organizational period of the "Christian trade unions" and when assessing the situation after the first third of the twentieth century. During the general meeting of the leaders of the German workers' associations in 1892 in Mainz (Hitze's participation had considerable impact), it became obvious that religious education was to remain a priority, that occupational questions were to be dealt with separately, and finally that the struggle was part of the essence of a true workers' organization. The "individual trade sections" within the Catholic workers' associations differed from the "individual trade sections" in Berlin during the subsequent trade union controversy. This is substantiated by the fact that the participants in Mainz accepted a strike as the inevitable "last resort," but they believed strikes not to be feasible under "local and denominational limitations" (of the workers' associations). At the Catholic Convention in Cologne in 1895 they spoke about the "individual trade sections" as being the first step toward the "professional organization of the industrial worker on a Christian foundation" (H. Brauns). But this was the opinion of a minority. At the Catholic Convention in Bonn in 1900 it was difficult to arrive at a compromise: "Catholic workers' associations and Christian occupational organizations," avoiding the term "trade union," intended to include "the entire economic life." Yet, in 1899 the first congress of the *Christliche Gewerkvereine Deutschlands* [Christian Trade Unions of Germany] had taken place in Mainz, which later caused the reaction in Berlin. The men initially involved in the Christian trade union movement showed "true denominational courage" in the struggle with atheistic socialism on the one hand and the (mostly Catholic) employers on the other hand — not to mention the opposition of bishops Korum and Kopp. But did Brauns not imply more than just the German denominational problems when he differentiated between the "spiritual attitude" in the "Christian trade union" and the "moral-religious attitude" in the workers' association? In other countries such as in Belgium and Holland, one followed the path discussed in Mainz in 1892, differentiating between "league" and trade union within one and the same Catholic workers' organization (in the trade union, the clerical leader was merely a "councilor"). In 1921, Cardinal Gasparri remarked that the Catholic workers' movement in Holland, Belgium, and Switzerland had sensed more acutely than elsewhere "that the personal development (the foundation of a Christian class movement) would be subjugated more and more to the predominant economic activities if there were no common authority to keep the balance." But whichever path was taken, the Belgian, the German, the French (which only led to a Christian trade union in the broadest sense) or the Italian (where the *Associazioni Cristiane Lavoratori Italiani* remained a purely educational movement) the historical result was basically the same everywhere. The Christian trade unions remained in the minority as compared to the others, and on the battlefield of labor they were in competition with them, which made it more difficult to assert their own principles. Within Catholicism itself, the Christianity of the trade unions only rarely permitted the antagonism of the class society to take on a different appearance; the religious "personal development" became insignificant in comparison to the fight for labor, or it was limited to a small circle, and this happened even more where the general development of trade unions took its own course.

The fact was often discussed that industrial workers especially were becoming alienated from the Church, and with good reason. The apathy of bourgeois Catholicism was deplored, clearly recognizable in the opposition which the Catholic workers' movement had to overcome within the ranks of its own fellow believers. But two points have to be made: The process of de-Christianization extended over all of society, but appeared more pronounced among the industrial workers because here, instead of a "fourth class," a new class, which essentially differed from the agrarian civil society, was emerging. Therefore, it was unable to relate to the Church traditions through which a conventional form of Christianity could yet survive for decades. Above all, the industrial workers were earlier and more directly than any other class affected by technology and thus by the epoch-making break with tradition which affected all of society.

This explains why the general problems entailed in the relationship of Catholicism to modern society as a whole so oddly climaxed in the Catholic workers' movement. Its religious urge to exceed the goals of the trade unions caused it to be felt as a foreign body within the general workers' movement, even in the non-Marxist movement. Its efficiency, to be sure, was not the showpiece of Catholicism. But it represented Catholicism's utmost effort to reconcile tradition with a radically secularized world, or at least to demonstrate the feasibility of such reconciliation. The question remains whether an independent Catholic workers' movement that was able to combine religious education and the inevitable belligerent goals regarding labor was indeed possible. In a similar situation, the Socialist movement was able to combine the party and its trade union. However, it also remains to be noted that, varying from country to country, Catholic workers' movements significantly contributed to counteracting the de-Christianization and social radicalization within society at large.

CHAPTER 58

The Relationship to the State and the Parties

The encyclical *Graves de communi* of 18 January 1901, which does not contain a trace of the political meaning implicit in the term "Christian democracy," is often assessed as a document of the later period of Leo XIII's pontificate demonstrating a departure from the initial program. Indeed, in those years the style, the climate, and the emphasis changed in nearly all aspects of ecclesiastical leadership. But when the pragmatic democracy," is often assessed as a document of the later period of Leo XIII's pontificate demonstrating a departure from the initial program. Indeed, in those years the style, the climate, and the emphasis changed in nearly all aspects of ecclesiastical leadership. But when the pragmatic conciliatory attitude in the Pope's earlier statements regarding the democratic form of government is carefully interpreted, a change of course in the true sense can hardly be found. Yet it is misleading to systematize the didactic statements which Leo XIII made throughout his pontificate in regard to the various questions of politics and social life, especially if one consequently neglects to differentiate between principles and the respective pragmatic adaptations to situations in individual countries. Above all, however, the exceedingly vague term *Démocratie chrétienne* could simultaneously have different, even contradictory implications at different times and in different countries. It could be taken religiously, in the sense of social reform, or even from the perspective of constitutional politics (from the constitutional and parliamentary monarchy to the republic); in short, it covered a highly diffused area of meanings. Subsequent to the encyclical *Rerum novarum,* the usage of the term (it had been used in connection with the revolutionary events of 1830 and 1848) considerably expanded, because it had become a verbal signal in the Catholic social movements of the various countries, often interchangeable with *Catholicisme social* or "Christian social." It was also significant that this development coincide, with the Pope's *Ralliement* policy regarding the French Republic. A fundamental interpretation of this policy was able to raise the value of the political content of the term "Christian democracy" to the point that it caused considerable complications. The Pope himself never made official use of the term (after its circumscriptive usage in the address of 1898) except in *Graves de communi,* and Rampolla's instruction *De Actione populari christiana seu democratico-christiana* of 27 January 1902 not only underlines the papal confinement of "Christian democracy" to Christian charity, but also emphasizes that this was not at all a *cosa nuova.* What had started out as an attempt to interpret the democratic ideals of equality and freedom (in accord with political theology) as the realization of the gospel ended here with the observation (which was meant to define the conflicts within the *Opera dei congressi* in Italy but was more encompassing), that a relationship between Church and democracy is not possible in the same manner as it had existed between the Church and the sacred monarchy.

Nonetheless, there existed in Leo XIII's pontificate a certain *cosa nuova,* but it had already taken place twenty years earlier and was anything but a way toward "Christian democracy." The encyclical *Diuturnum illud* of 29 June 1881 mentions the *cupiditates populares* which had emerged from the unfortunate doctrine of the people's sovereignty; and according to this encyclical, the patriarchal monarchy is unquestionably the ideal form of government, perfected at the time of the *imperium sacrum,* when the popes consecrated political power in a unique way. But it does not contradict the Catholic doctrine stating that in certain cases the principal representative of civil authority can be elected "according to the desire and the judgment of the masses," whereby power is not transferred, but rather it is determined who will execute it. With this contrivance, democracy is introduced as an ecclesiastically tolerable form of government. But at the same time it is deprived of its historical essence; that is, its revolutionary character is eliminated. It should be noted (and this is true for all encyclicals which attempt an accommodation with the modern era) that this piece of text is short and enclosed in a voluminous traditional text. The polemics against the social contract and the people's sovereignty clearly have priority.

More so than the encyclical of 1881, the encyclical *Immortale Dei* of 1 November 1885 is composed, with respect to France, in order to avoid at least an intensification of the situation regarding Church policies and to prevent the separation of Church and state. In fact, its aim is to find a way of reaching an agreement which would lead toward Leo XIII's ultimate goal: re-Christianization of the modern, democratic world. Also in this encyclical, the paragraphs in which the democratic form of government is recognized as equal to the other systems stand isolated within the main theme "Church and State" (*utraque* [*potestas*] *est*

in suo genere maxima), and the doctrine that the elected official need only execute the will of the people is rejected. But these paragraphs are rather positively
flavored, for instance when the Pope says that it is not worth a reprimand per se if
the people (*populos,* not *multitudo*) more or less take part in the government. In
fact, "at certain times" and "under certain laws" it may not only be useful but also
the duty of the citizen to do so. This argument was used to justify the opposition
toward the founding of an antirepublican party. This attitude is called an expression of ecclesiastical *lenitas* and *facilitas.* Also the encyclical *Libertas* of 20 June
1888, in which liberal human rights are condemned, concedes at the end that is
not per se a violation of one's duty to prefer a democratic system of state.

The contemporary disciples of a politically understood "Christian democracy"
did not sufficiently consider in their interpretations (or perhaps they wanted to
overlook it) that the Pope indeed accepted the democratic form of government
(among others), but in spite of differentiations, he recognized it merely as a fait
accompli. Leo XIII had always imagined that democracy was the result of revolution. In the encyclical *Quod Apostolici muneris* of 28 December 1878, which
primarily turned against socialism and preached obedience toward the state's
authority, the Pope brought to mind that the Church, even if the princes did not
execute their authority *ultra modum,* refused to tolerate an autonomous rebellion
against them (*proprio marte*). Even if the situation were hopeless, there is only
Christian patience and prayer available to expedite rescue. Obedience can only
be refused if the demand contradicts the law of God and nature. The encyclical *Libertas* (1888) exceeds the admonition for patience. It speaks of the "unfair
power" which oppresses the citizens or denies freedom to the Church, and it
calls lawful (*fas*) the request (*quaerere*) for "another constitution" which would
permit action "in freedom." It is not said in this context how this *quaerere* is to
occur, since unfair regimes are not in the, habit of resigning voluntarily. At the
same time, the violent resistance of the oppressed Irish is condemned. But the
encyclical letter to the French episcopate, the clergy, and all French Catholics, *Au
milieu des sollicitudes* of 16 February 1892 and the letter to the French cardinals
Notre consolation of 3 May 1892, which inaugurated the *Ralliement,* cannot speak
in such general terms to the land of obviously irreversible revolution, especially
since it requests loyalty to the French Republic "comme representant le pouvoir
venu de Dieu." Of what was called "venu de Dieu," the sons and grandsons of
the age of the "great Revolution" — however they felt about it — had very precise
memories. The questions in regard to the *Diuturnum illud* (1881) whether the
rejection of the people's sovereignty only meant to condemn Rousseau or also
the theory of Suárez, was answered rather cautiously by Rome. However, now
it was stated that all authority emanated from God, though this was not to be
taken to mean that the divine designation defines "always and directly the way
power is transferred, nor the contingent forms and personalities." The *modes de
transmission* were naturally the decisive element. Who affects them? "Time, this
great transformer of everything which exists here below." This is probably the
only place in the encyclicals of Leo XIII where he does not refer exclusively to
history, be it to bring to mind the achievements of the papacy for the benefit of the
West and specifically for Italy, or to characterize the devastating consequences
of the Reformation. He also invokes history to facilitate an understanding of his

request to accept this Republic "comme venu de Dieu." Compared to this, the Neo-Scholastic remark about the "pouvoir considéré en lui même," not touched by the "innovation," appears weak and abstract. The most remarkable statement by the Pope with respect to the Revolution as such is the one maintaining that the *changements* of the era — Leo XIII refers to the Eastern Empire of antiquity — are far from ever having been legitimate. Indeed, it is difficult to say that they are legitimate ("il est même difficile qu'ils le soient"). Not one word is said to restrict the doctrine of the Church which states that the Church does not permit rebellion against the authority in power; instead, the actual power having emerged from the Revolution is to be accepted for the sake of the general welfare ("le pouvoir civil dans la forme où, de fait, il existe").

Leo XIII noted that internal pacification in France was not only in the interest of the Catholics but in the interest of the entire country, even though the religious goal was not only the ultimate but also the only sufficient motive. Of course, this raised the question of whether the acceptance of the Republic as a mere fact still allowed the traditional conception of the relations between Church and state. In his political encyclicals, the Pope repeatedly evoked the medieval image of the relationship of body and soul, though he did refrain from mentioning the papal theories of the late Middle Ages. In *Au milieu des sollicitudes* he happens to mention that form of separation of Church and state in which the Church is reduced "to the freedom to live according to the common law of all citizens." What was apparently practiced in "some countries" — he obviously meant the United States — implied great "inconveniences," but it also offered some advantages, especially if the legislation allowed itself to be inspired by Christian principles due to a "fortunate inconsistency." The principle of separation continued to be false even though the aforementioned situation "was not the worst of all." But France, a "nation catholique par ses traditions et par la foi présente de la grande majorité de ses fils," was not to be brought into this "precarious situation." In spite of the somewhat relatively favorable results recorded by an investigation of the ecclesiastical and religious attitudes conducted by the state in the years between 1879 and 1888 in France, the question needs to be asked whether a country which, at the end of the nineteenth century, according to denominational statistics, was nearly homogeneous can really be called a "Catholic nation." The term *grande majorité* stems from the preamble of the Concordat of 1801, while the term *nation catholique* ignores the fact that almost one hundred years earlier other sects had been provided with equality before the law. Meanwhile, the process of de-Christianization continued. This did not necessarily result in the separation of Church and state, and certainly not in hostility. But the old image of the correlation between body and soul — no matter how much Leo XIII stressed that each power was the highest in its area of competence — was a contrivance which clouded an essential condition of the constitutional state, namely, that the position of the Church had become dependent on the majority standing of the political parties in a pluralistic society and was not dependent on the degree to which the constitution pronounced the Catholic faith to be the state religion or not. This is closely related to the complex problem of the Catholic parties in a democracy which is partly determined by the alternation of position and opposition and by the relations of the substantially differently structured Catholic Church to such political entities.

In 1885, Leo XIII inhibited the founding of a Catholic Party in France through Albert de Mun, and on 12 May 1892 a few days after the papal letter *Notre consolation,* the anti-republican *Union de la France Chrétienne* was dissolved. Both incidents should initially be seen from the perspective of the papal *Ralliement* policy and the attempt to close the cleft in French Catholicism between republicans and monarchists. But it contradicted Leo XIII's principles to involve the Church in the battles of the political parties (*Ecclesiam trabere in partes*) because he presumed that religion (i.e., the Catholic faith) had to be sacred and inviolable to everyone. There is no doubt that on purely political grounds (*in genere politico),* the Christians can fight for the success of their respective opinions (*opiniones*), "given the observation of truth and justice." But the Church cannot become a party because it is common to every one. This is applicable to the differences within Catholicism in France, Spain, and Italy, where each group operated under the assumption that it alone represented the rights of the Church; and to the papal admonition aimed at furthering the unity of the Catholics so that they could form a phalanx against the enemies of the Church. But his goal was the universal re-Christianization of state and society, where religion will be sacred to every one and the Church does not have to be represented by a party. There is a close connection between the tactical viewpoint that political party formations entangle Catholicism in internal strife and the principle that religion is not a matter of parties at all, because it has priority for all citizens.

An equally important problem in the relationship between the Church and the Christian parties was the concept of the hierarchical authority of giving directives. The Vatican's attempt to comply with Bismarck's wish and exert influence on the Center Party relative to the antisocialist law and the question of the septennate failed because of the political self-awareness of this party, which surpassed all other political entities of Catholicism in its cohesiveness. But this attempt was characteristic of Leo XIII's idea about the universal responsibility of the papacy. Ferrata's ecclesiastical internal policies exceeded such intervention. He was not content with prohibiting the French monarchists from a religious and ecclesiastical argumentation; rather he demanded the sacrifice of a fundamental political conviction. It was in accord with the character and range of this problem that the Pope in Italy reserved the right to make the decision in the question of the *Non expedit* and its exegesis to himself and to censor all special actions. But it was also in keeping with this policy that the movement of the *Opera dei congressi,* which was strictly organized in 1884, became the battlefield for all political questions whose resolution was therefore subject to, hierarchical directives. In comparison to other countries, the interpretation of the competence of the nunciatures practically resulted in a *potestas directa* over political matters which had been rejected in Leo XIII's theory concerning the relationship between Church and state.

Since the Church had to deal with very different political constitutions, only the recognition of all forms of government could be decreed didactically, given the known conditions. On the other hand, if, on the basis of the historical situation, Christian motives regarding the transformation of social conditions should coincide with political convictions, then both the French and Italian "Christian democrats" and — though in a different manner — that part of the episcopate which did not merely respect the constitution of the United States but also on principle accepted it, faced a dilemma between the necessarily abstract ecclesiastical political doctrine and their concrete political conviction. The term "Christian democracy" grew enriched in content when the paternalistic social practice flowing from top to bottom was replaced or at least supplemented by a social reform movement from below, conducted by the disadvantaged themselves. This enrichment essentially meant that the term also gained a political profile. This did not necessarily affect the form of government as such. But the state itself changed when the "self-liberation of the classes" began. The Christian republican, in turn, derived a good deal of his political convictions from the view that the paternalistically oriented social activities of the monarchists missed their target, and a real social reform was only possible in a democracy. A de-politicization of the term "Christian democracy" did not merely affect the form of government, but also the concept of politics in general.

However, wherever Catholics gathered in parties, as in Belgium, the Netherlands, Germany, Switzerland, and Austria, they were confronted with the task of balancing the various social interests if they wanted to gain political weight as a "people's party." This difficult process was only successful when the common Christian belief became the catalyst of the development of a political will. One can certainly say that. in France "the *Démocratie chrétienne,* in turn, repeated the mistake of the monarchists when it entered the political arena and turned the problem of the form of government into a question of religious principle."

The first time Leo XIII discussed the problem of "Christian democracy" was in his address on the occasion of a French workers' pilgrimage on 8 October 1898, wherein he was apparently responding to an "allusion a la démocratie." If democracy would be inspired by a belief in enlightened reason, if it accepted in "religious humility" and as a necessary fact ("comme un fait nécessaire") the difference between classes and living conditions, if when seeking a solution for the social problems, it would never lose sight of the superhuman love ("charité surhumaine") that Christ held to be a sign of his followers, then if democracy wanted to be a Christian democracy ("si la démocratie veut être chrétienne"), it would bring France peace, well-being, and fortune. The dangerous evil, from which this "democracy" is distinct, is socialism. In March 1896 Rampolla had still supported the abbés and laymen in France who were political believers in democracy. But since they failed to make Catholic voters agree upon promising candidates, the election of May 1898 was not successful. The *Ralliement* policy had failed and, in the address of 8 October 1898, no longer played a role. The tone in the socio-political questions also was quite different from that in *Rerum novarum.* The de-politicization in the sense of *religieuse resignation* was extensive. The speech reminds one of the encyclical *Quod Apostolici muneris* of 1878, which was subsequently quoted (before *Rerum novarum*) in the introduction to the *Graves de communi* of 18 January 1901. This letter was actually occasioned by the tensions in the *Opera dei congressi,* but the key sentences have a general character. The differentiation of the terminology is interesting: the Pope states that the term "Christian socialism" was rightfully abandoned; *Actio christiana popularis* is evaluated positively; it is used in the Italian "Congressi" organizations for which episcopal leadership authority is emphasized. Of the two terms "Christian socialism" and "Christian Democracy," the second one, "not so much" the first one, is said to have caused displeasure *apud bonos plures* because of its "ambiguity" and its "danger." One fears that it could "favor the people's state" (*popularis civitas foveatur*) and that it could be preferred to other forms of government. After the encyclical had emphatically differentiated between the *democratia socialis* ("social democracy") and the *democratia christiana,* it clearly rejects "the distortion" of the latter "into a political term" (*ad politica detorqueri*). "Democracy," in contrast to the general usage, could in connection with "Christian" only mean "beneficial Christian action for the people" (*beneficam in populum actionem christianam).* The earlier statements that democratic constitutions are just as feasible as any others are amended with the negative statement that the Natural Law and the Gospel are not dependent on any constitution. In this respect, none of the basic teachings of the Church is changed. But it is added that the Catholics would neither theoretically nor practically want to prefer one form of government to another or introduce a new one (*catholicorum mens atque actio*). With respect to social politics, the climate had changed even more compared to the address to the French pilgrimage of 1898. The Pope not only emphasized that the Church has to be available to all classes and may not prefer the lower, but also stated that in spite of shorter working hours and higher wages the workers' life is "crowded and miserable" (*anguste et misere*), which does not indicate an intensification of social reform but means that the workers still live with "rotten morals" and without religion. The fight against socialism dominated the intention of the encyclical.

If the principal statements in all of Leo XIII's magisterial writings are distinguished from the modifications incited by the given situations, the following transpires: democracy is a result of the "transformer time" with which one can and has to come to grips for the sake of ecclesiastical goals if the hierarchical leaders deem it opportune. Also the Christian social reform policies are less interested in the economic conditions of the working class than in a defense against atheistic socialism, which includes the elimination of social misery. These, in fact, are also the essential goals to be pursued by the official teaching of the Church. In the framework of his splendid universal program, aimed at presenting the papacy to the world as a moral, spiritual, and clerical authority and freeing this institution from the negative aspects of the *Syllabus,* Leo XIII had to confront the actual problems of his time, and he had to do so in the face of a society which was involved in a continuous dialectical process, oscillating between political parties and economic classes, and in the face of a Catholicism struggling with its own internal differences. The French monarchists were reported to be closer to his own political-clerical persuasion than the Catholic supporters of the Republic. But Leo XIII expected that they, as he had done, would sacrifice their conviction for the sake of a higher goal and that they would accept the democratic constitution, which he had officially only tolerated (along with others), restricting it by adding "per se."

In Neo-Scholastic social philosophy the Pope believed to have found a generally binding synthesis based on Natural Law which could confront the antagonisms of the time. In reality, however, Catholicism represented special groups within the general, increasingly secularized society, and it had its own problems of integration, with or without identifying with a political party. Since the religious aspects were decisive in this respect, a dilemma regarding the universality of the Church

could possibly emerge if the religious motives were combined with certain social and political goals whose actuality could only coincide very generally with
the Neo-Scholastic social philosophy. The dilemma increased the more Christian
faith and social political convictions were tied together and the more they were
simultaneously intent on changing inherited conditions. Each in his own way,
Leo XIII and the political "Christian democrats," were unable to see that the old
relationship between Church and world, that is, the world as a duplicate of the
Church, was not real any longer. This is the ultimate reason for the conflict which
resulted from the subsequent pontificate's interpretation of hierarchical magisterial directives in political questions. This conflict was already on the horizon in
Leo XIII's pontificate.

CHAPTER 59

The Position of Catholicism in the Culture
at the Turn of the Century

The relationship of Catholicism to its various national cultures in the last third of the
nineteenth century and at the beginning of the twentieth century varies greatly.
What was classified as cultural "ghetto-Catholicism" existed only in Germany,
because there the confessional minority was strong enough to develop a sound
self-consciousness, and its social structure was considerably different from that of
the society at large. For Irish Catholicism in England the Anglo-Saxon culture was
foreign for religious reasons; moreover, in its social isolation it did not even have
a chance to deal with this culture. In Ireland itself, the "revival" around the turn of
the century clearly documents that the affiliated writers were born Catholics, but
the movement, spiritually indebted to France, divorced itself from Irish traditionalism by emancipating itself from the Church. The two smaller Catholic groups in
England, the Old-English Catholics and the converts, belonged to the Anglo-Saxon
culture, conducted their intellectual disputes in the English language, and the significant poets were immersed in the tradition of English poetry. Catholicism in the
United States, itself culturally scarcely creative, tried to adapt to society as a whole.

In the Catholic countries of France, Spain, Italy, Austria, and Poland it is difficult (regardless of the intensive national Christian traditions) to determine which
phenomena should be viewed as Catholic in an ecclesiastical sense and what
distinguishes those who cannot be understood outside general Catholicity from
those who are almost or completely alienated from the Christian tradition.

This is especially true of France. The poet Charles Baudelaire (1821–67) with
whom modern French poetry begins stands at the beginning of the epoch treated

here. This man whose career ended so early dominated the field for generations to come. He is certainly not to be reckoned in the same category as Chateaubriand as representative of the Christianity of the restoration. Yet it cannot be denied that the author of the *Fleurs du Mal* which he originally called *Limbes* and who saw abandonment of the idea of original sin as the basic evil of the age was at heart a Catholic, yet no one would ascribe *catholicisme* to him. At the end of our era stands Charles Maurras (1868–1952), who was entirely different from Baudelaire. But he is an example of how wide the borders of French Catholicism range. Working for conservative newspapers in his early years, he lost his faith in Catholicism, but not in the monarchy or classical literature. He was an opponent of Romanticism and democracy and, in 1899, founded the *Action française,* which raised the hopes of many conservative Catholics in France and not just *their* hopes. He confessed to having lost the Christian faith, but he belonged to a *catholicisme,* which (he said) had saved mankind. But even if one proceeds from such marginal personalities into the middle of the cultural life of French Catholics at that time, one does not find an extraneous group, but members of the *Littérature française:* converts, not in the usual sense of the word, but men who had experienced their *conversio,* and this in the middle of their engagement in one of the literary trends which they shared with other Frenchmen. In this respect, the *Renouveau catholique* differs essentially from the literary movement in German Catholicism. But an apologist writer such as Paul Bourget (1852–1935), who from the start wanted to describe the demoralization of the middle class of the French Republic, the adultery, the hypocrisy of the anticlerics, and the asocial individualism of the liberal bourgeoisie; even he was considered "for thirty years an original representative, as it were, of the French novel as created by Balzac and George Sand. G.-P. Fonsegrive-Lespinasse (1852–1917) (philosopher and writer, editor of the publication *Quinzaine* [1896–1907]), who had to be protected by Leo XIII against his conservative critics, said toward the end of his life that "thirty years ago one could barely detect in the French public the kind of interest in spiritual questions that has surfaced now" (in the *Renouveau catholique*). The Jesuits also saw in the *Études* of French cultural Catholicism a form of new ecclesiasticality, though L. Laberthonnière, a strict disciple of Blondel, appeared very sceptical. As in the case of all cultural forms of Catholicism, one would have to distinguish between the profit gained from making Catholic existence possible in the modern world and the effect it would have on general society, which had abandoned its aggressive anticlericalism only because its apathy had become too great.

M. de Vogüé, in the *Revue des Deux Mondes* (1901), described the "two contradictory concepts of national history" in France. This does not apply to Spain of that same time period. Even the famous "Generation of 98" does not permit overt discussion of "two Spains." Therefore, the appeal of the politician Joaquín Costa (died in 1911) "Lock the grave of El Cid with three keys!" was immediately opposed by the true representatives of this generation, even though they were open to modern currents. Above all, it was rejected by Miguel de Unamuno, a Spanish Catholic who did not agree with Church dogma but had nothing in common with the Catholicism of Charles Maurras ("El Cristo de Velázquez," 1920). The Civil War of the twentieth century destroyed the unity of the spirit of the *Hispanidad.* In comparison, Italy was split so deeply because of the Roman question that even Dante's greatness as reflected in the various interpretations by national writers was no longer a unifying element. The intransigent Pope-supporting Catholics had become homeless in their national culture because they had nothing to counteract the positivism invading Italy from France as well as Hegelianism, and they had to stand by and watch while the Tuscan Giosuè Carducci, a fanatical anticleric, was celebrated as the poet of the new Italy. Alessandro Manzoni (died in 1873) had overcome the Enlightenment, had confessed his Catholic belief in fiery language in the *Inni sacri* (1812–22), and had written the Italian national novel, *I Promessi Sposi* (1827). His heirs could not understand the *Non expedit* for the same reasons which compelled Manzoni, the great pioneer of the religious-national unification of Italy, to become silent. Antonio Fogazzaro (1842–1911), the most outstanding of them all, in his main work *Piccolo mondo antico* (1895) described the Italian fight for freedom against Austria with as much national as religious enthusiasm. His novel *Il Santo* (1905), equally filled with deep religious sentiment, was condemned because of the four evils of the Church described therein. In 1887, during the critical year of Leo XIII's pontificate, forty sentences from the work of the famous theologian and philosopher A. Rosmini-Serbati, to whom Fogazzaro was very much indebted, were extracted and censored. Thus, cultural life in Italy was dominated by verism, G. d'Annunzio (the successor of G. Carducci), and the neo-Hegelians.

In Poland, after the failure of the uprising of 1863, the identity of creed and nation had become stronger, but the disappointment created a mood which was a fertile ground for western European positivism (Comte, Taine, Darwin), which seized "Young Poland." Thus emerged a fierce opposition between the leftist liberals and the conservatives. Their most eminent representative was H. Sienkiewicz (1846–1916), the author of historical novels about the era of Polish wars in the seventeenth century and of the internationally famous novel on the early Christian period, *Quo Vadis* (1896).

In Austria, the names Grillparzer and Stifter characterize the tradition of the kind of Catholicity which, in spite of its liberal and at times even anticlerical features, derives from a Catholic spirit. Catholicity is most strongly represented in the writings of Hugo von Hofmannsthal (1874–1929), who, in the spirit of Grillparzer and Calderón renounced the "magical power over the word" in symbolization and returned from his areligiosity to the great tradition of the West, whose historic tragedy he witnessed in the decline of the Habsburg Empire. This can be compared to the unfortunate poet Georg Trakl of Salzburg (1887–1914), who wanted to find the world's secret harmony in the language of the symbolists. A contemporary of these nonecclesiastical poets was the convent-bred Enrica von Handel-Mazzetti (1871–1955). Her novel *Jesse und Maria* (1906), dealing with the era of the Counter-Reformation, incited after its serial publication in the *Hochland* (1904) of Carl Muth a "literary controversy" because in this novel the Catholics as well as the Protestants are guilty. The novel was written with deep Catholic conviction, but it broke with the tendentious literature which had become popular in German Catholicism after the Romantic period.

At the general meeting of the *Görres Gesellschaft* in Constance in 1896, its president, G. v. Hertling, said: "But what we need now are not so much apologists but rather real scholars." Until Carl Muth, this was true not just for scholarship but for literature in general. When Hermann von Grauert, at the Catholic Convention in Munich in 1895, expressed his envy of French Catholicism of Brunetière (while Germany was dominated by Nietzsche), he referred to the wide public reputation which the French literary critic had acquired. What was later called the "educational deficit" in German Catholicism of that time had several causes. Lessing, Schiller, Goethe, Kant and the philosophy of idealism, J. G. Herder and Humboldt, the representatives of the German spirit, were Protestant. The significance of Catholic features in Romanticism is not easily assessed. Its Catholic spokesman, the convert Friedrich Schlegel was a protean figure, who turned to gnosticism in the last phase of his life in Dresden and died in 1829. In this movement, the Catholics had been as much a part of German literature as the ecclesiastical Catholics had been of French literature. Not just converts, but also born Catholics such as Clemens Brentano and Eichendorff participated. In his later years, the Silesian poet wrote about the "event in Cologne" (1837): here emerged what "the Romanticists had dreamt of and did not possess themselves: a Catholic spirit." But prophetically he had also warned of the "rigors of ecclesiastical restrictiveness," which, of course, was to some extent unavoidable in the belligerent position which German Catholicism as a minority group was forced into by a largely Protestant society, and which it brought upon itself by its awareness of being a strong minority. This is another point which explains the isolation of German Catholicism after the second third of the nineteenth century. This was the price that Catholicism paid for being able, unlike other sects, to structure itself within society. The German Catholics were underrepresented in higher education and especially at the universities (particularly if one ignores theology). This was the result of cultural and historical development and at the same time the cause of its intensification, especially if the socio-cultural and the socio-economic facts are combined. It was correctly pointed out then (1803) that secularization was a catastrophe for Catholic education; the academic career of Catholics at universities was, even after the *Kulturkampf,* greatly impaired by the intolerance of the Liberals. But one has to see the whole complex situation at once if one is to understand the reaction of Catholics in the overall cultural world during these decades. One has to isolate the key issue from the polemical global reproach of "inferiority." German Catholicism had at its disposal pertinent means of communication, and it was an internal matter when the "calendar for time and eternity," published by the Alemannian priest Alban Stolz (1808–83), and his own strongly autobiographical essays, which contain more than the usual polemics against liberalism, were pushed aside by a sort of literature of which *Das Opfer eines Beichtgeheimnisses (The Sacrifice of a Confession)* by J. Spillmann is an example (Spillmann's novels appeared between 1882 and 1903 and were a great success). It is Friedrich Wilhelm Weber's (died in 1894) *Dreizehnlinden* (1878), rather than Heinrich Hansjakob's true-to-life folk story *Der Vogt auf Mühlstein* (1895), which is representative. This work, written in concise language that was meant to satisfy sophisticated demands, could be found into the twentieth century in the bookcases of Catholics who had to live in the limited circumstances for which history had destined them. Yet the situation is not so much characterized by clumsy attempts such as that of Weber, but rather by the respectable effort, as it were, to offer a decent selection in the "library of German classical writers for school and home," for which the inclusion of

Lessing's *Nathan* must have been a difficult decision. The breakthrough brought about by Muth in *Hochland* resulted in conditions much like those in France: the works of these writers ceased to appear in Catholic publishing houses because the authors — once again to a large extent converts — wanted to be part of the general German literature.

The scholarly works in Catholicism gravitated naturally toward theology, philosophy, and (Church) history. Here, tradition provided a starting point and Neo-Scholasticism, which had become official through Leo XIII's Thomas encyclical, offered not only an international basis but also the possibility of developing, beyond the disputations and apologetics over the *zeitgeist,* an independent and even partially creative system and of giving the retarding forces a positive orientation. Also, the old and the new universities, founded during Leo XIII's pontificate, made attempts toward a comprehensive modern curriculum. Louvain distinguished itself in Near Eastern studies as well as in biology; Fribourg (1889) had started a philosophy and a law faculty and, in 1896, established a mathematics and natural science faculty; Washington (1889) developed its sociological emphasis, which was also pursued in Louvain. In France, the Catholic universities in Paris, Angers, Lille, Lyon, and Toulouse, founded around 1875, had to change their name to *Institut catholique* following the law of 1880, according to which the title *université* was reserved for state institutions. But with imperturbable enthusiasm they held on to their academic programs; and the plan also to establish schools of medicine was not a symptom of ambition but of the realization that intellectual decisions were particularly at stake in this field. Of course, grave technical difficulties stood in the way. That the establishment of theological faculties occurred subsequently is primarily a result of their problematic relationship to the diocesan seminaries. The names of the scholars affiliated with the individual institutions represented the rather different spirit of each institution.

In 1810, the University of Salzburg was closed, and attempts to expand the theology department, installed in 1851, into a full university were not successful, in spite of Leo XIII's encouragement through briefs in 1890, 1900, and 1902. However, the *Görres-Gesellschaft,* founded in 1876, the year of Joseph Görres' one hundredth birthday, may be called one of the most significant societies of Catholic scholars. The initiative had come from Georg v. Hertling (1843–1919), in 1867 lecturer of philosophy in Bonn, in 1882 professor at the University of Munich. With his Neo-Scholastic philosophy of law, politics, and society and as a Center Party politician (in 1875–90 and 1896–1912 member of the *Reichstag),* he was one of the most intelligent leaders of German Catholicism, a man who knew how to combine determination and restraint. The *Görres-Gesellschaft* enjoyed the ecclesiastical patronage of the incumbent of the diocese of Cologne, but it was founded as a private society. It renounced a theological section, although theologians formed a great part of its membership. The original four sections were devoted to philosophy, history, law, sociology, and natural science. The Austrian *Leo Gesellschaft,* founded in 1891 by J. A. Helfert and named after the ruling Pope, published mainly studies of the general and ecclesiastical history of Austria. In Germany and Austria it was of special significance that the theology faculties had remained in the academic structure of the universities. Thus, they were in a better position than the diocesan seminaries to preserve for Catholic theology a place in the general scholarly and scientific public. In spite of the conflicts within "reform Catholicism" and "modernism," into which theologians were drawn, there was rarely a real schism (contrary to the time of Döllinger).

The numerous scholarly publications in all forms of Catholicism, which received fresh impulses and were newly founded, document that Catholicism had defined its self-concept more in the realm of scholarship than anywhere else, even though the natural sciences came up for discussion more indirectly in the apologetic literature. There were a few exceptions, such as at the University of Louvain (the only Catholic institution which was a full university), the research on ants by the Jesuit E. Wasmann (published in the nineties), and the astronomical works of the Jesuits Hagen, Kugler, and others. Wasmann's studies of Haeckel's monism was based on his own scientific research. Tilmann Pesch approached the same problem on the basis of his natural philosophy (*Die großen Welträtsel,* 1883–84). Although the questions posed by the natural sciences were taken quite seriously, the many French Catholic scientists were more directly affected by the discussion taking place in Bible exegesis, which, since the nineteenth century, had resulted in more and more radical interpretations within liberal Protestant theology. It is understandable that they did not succeed in carrying out their intention to exclude this complex of questions at the international congresses of Catholic scholars and scientists in the last decade of the nineteenth century. This failure, in conjunction with the crisis of modernism and integralism, ended an attempt which could have become quite significant for the development of a common Catholic intellectuality able to confront modern problems decisively. The idea had emanated from Duilhé de Saint-Projet (1822–97), who in 1875 had been one of the men instrumental in the founding of the Catholic universities in France. In his *Apologie scientifique du christianisme* (Toulouse 1885) he developed a program for international congresses, which was worked out in detail in conversations with the first president of the *Institut catholique* in Paris, Maurice d'Hulst. Of course, he encountered strong reservations, because there was fear that at such congresses nontheologian participants would ask questions about dogma and exegesis and thus create great confusion. As always in such cases, Leo XIII was optimistic and asked Maurice d'Hulst for his expert opinion. D'Hulst suggested excluding the treatment of all questions concerning ecclesiastical teachings, but he emphasized the necessity of discussing the contemporary status quo of the sciences, and in 1887, the Pope approved the plan.

The first congress in Paris in 1888 proceeded to everyone's satisfaction, even though its international makeup was limited, as was the second one, which took place in 1894 (also in Paris) under the presidency of Bishop Freppel. During the third congress in Brussels in 1894, a paper by M. d'Hulst attacked the theologically controversial material which had accumulated. He warned against minimizing dogmatic statements of the Church. He strenuously advised against exaggerating them and suspecting everyone of rationalism who did not share one's own opinions. During the fourth congress in 1897 (in Fribourg), which was able to attract three thousand participants under the presidency of G. v. Hertling, the participants had the courage to form, aside from newly founded sections, a special group in which "exegesis and related disciplines" were to be discussed. What the *Görres-Gesellschaft* had avoided when it renounced the creation of a theological section happened here. The convention in Munich in 1900, which attracted even more participants, parted with the expectation of convening again in Rome in 1903. This was an illusion. The *Istituto cattolico internazionale per il progresso delle scienze,* which had been announced in the encyclical *Pascendi* for 1907 and for which Pius X had appointed Ludwig Pastor secretary general, failed to survive the initial stages.

Forms of Piety

Chaps. 60–62: Oskar Köhler
Chap. 63: Günter Bandmann

CHAPTER 60

Externalization and Internalization of Nineteenth-Century Spirituality— Beginnings of the Eucharistic Congress Movement— Veneration of Saint Thérèse of Lisieux

The forms of piety which had developed in the second third of the nineteenth century grew in scope during Leo XIII's pontificate. They were invigorated through demonstrative gestures in ceremonies of consecration, through liturgical festivities, and through the confirmation of congregations and fraternities. They were valued as socially integrating factors in the forms of Catholicism taking shape within the various countries. And yet their significance cannot be recognized unless they are valued as the daily religious nourishment of the faithful who were living in a strange or hostile environment and who, in those pious exercises, found the strength to remain loyal to a faith which was finding less and less support in the secular world. Depending on the country, the situation was quite different, of course, and cannot generally be differentiated according to urban and rural areas. There were rural areas in France where de-Christianization had progressed far, and the development during the course of the Third Republic was characterized by juxtaposing the "déchristianisation du peuple" and the "rechristianisation de la bourgeoisie." Agrarian concentrations in southern Spain resulted in the rural proletariat's alienation from the faith. In the German-speaking area, the Catholic rural population remained untouched by the modern spirit. The political development in France toward the end of the nineteenth century contributed to the revitalization of the consciousness of faith. However, during the same period in Germany, a partial paralysis could be detected, because the stimuli of the *Kulturkampf* were missing.

Contemporary observations regarding the significance of the political battle (including its national variations) are applicable to the style of religiosity in all forms of Catholicism, whereby we have to consider that the conservative group consciousness in religious life was accompanied by a subjectivism which, on the one hand, was generally embedded in the spiritual trend of the outgoing nineteenth century after the disappointments of the bourgeois revolutions, and which, on the other hand, was consciously nurtured by the pastors as a defense against the materialistic-collectivistic spirit of the time. This juxtaposition of sociality and subjectivity is one of the reasons for the late emergence of the liturgical restoration. Also significant is the positivistic concept of the "sanctity of the Church," which was believed verified through reference to the catalog of beatification and canonization examinations conducted by the Congregation of Rites of 1901. Moreover, since for the most part religious orders and congregations promoted the canonization of members and since they predominated among the Latin peoples, the picture was distorted. Reflected in this naive quantitative interpretation is the idea of the Catholic "membership" movement, which was necessary for the development of Catholicism and represented the result of often tremendous efforts as well as a mere reaction to processes in the secular society. That the organizational element remained "fashionable" to the extent "that the inner life, the grace, the mystery were frightened away" (Mayer-Pfannholz) also had an effect on the organization of devotional practices. Religious devotional art was quite popular at that time and is a difficult phenomenon to assess. In its precise meaning, this kind of popular devotional art appears for the first time in the late nineteenth century as the result of certain cultural and historical conditions. Favored by the possibility of reproduction, popular devotional art demanded and furthered participation in conventional art which was simultaneously isolating itself from society. These demands could not be satisfied. Therefore, they were appeased by elevating popular devotional art one step above banality — a phenomenon which cannot be compared to the disintegration of high art, sustained by an elite, into handicraft. Upon investigation of the mystical essence underlying Eucharistic piety and the Sacred Heart devotion of that time, it becomes clear that the faithful were overtaxed by this bid for sophistication. It is also evident that they were given an acceptable version with the best of intentions and thereby possessed an adequate means of expression in the art forms of the Nazarenes, who had fallen below their original level of quality. These conclusions are comparable to the analysis of secular popular art. Notwithstanding the nationalistic aversion to "the French," the fact remains that these expressions of piety, stemming from the Latin mentality, could only be transferred with difficulty to Germanic countries. The close relationship between art and religion is unquestionable; yet drawing conclusions from this assumption alone would result in a simplified judgment about the religiosity of that period: the faithful of the middle and lower classes were pious in regard to traditional forms of expression. An assessment of the religious quality itself escapes historic evaluation.

The considerable increase of charitable activities in all countries, flourishing in individual parishes, in diocesan societies and (especially in France, Italy, and Germany) in national organizations, can be measured by the number of institutions and participants. Lorenz Werthmann (1858–1921) received encouragement from France and the organizational forms of the Protestant "Home Mission" when, in 1897, he founded the *Deutscher Caritas-Verband* and propagated its goals in the publication *Caritas* (since 1896). He had to defend himself against the often-heard reproach that Christian charity had to take place without fanfare, and he had to fend off the envy of the episcopate, which did not recognize the organization until the conference of Fulda (1915) and Freising (1916). This placed it under episcopal supervision and suggested the formation of diocesan branch organizations. The organizational amalgamation of the many charitable institutions did not only aim at the concentration of the various enterprises, but proceeded from the assumption that in the age of industrialism the initiative to help your fellow men was by no means dispensable. However, in the interests of maximal effectiveness, a theoretical investigation of the economic conditions was unavoidable. The *Dictionnaire d'économie* was a model for Werthmann, the first president of the association, whose headquarters he moved to Freiburg in Breisgau.

How vital it is not to interpret the organizational features of piety as mere externalizations is documented by the emergence of the Eucharistic congress movement. E. Marie Tamisier (born in 1834 in Tours) was one of those restless religious personalities who could not easily be pressed into institutional molds. After having had first a gentle and then a rather rigorous pastor, she was finally fortunate to meet Gaston de Ségur, who assigned to her Eucharistic youthful piety the proper area of activity. Ségur designed a plan of operations entitled "France at the feet of the Most Holy Sacrament," in which he listed the locations of Eucharistic miracles. Upon the industrialist Philibert Vrau's suggestion, a central pilgrimage to Douai was decided on at Lille in 1874. The site of miracles, Avignon became in 1876 the stage for the first Eucharistic mass demonstration. During an event in Favernay, Besançon in 1878, the first beginnings of the movement's internationalization emerged. Finally, on 17 January 1881 in Paris, at the deathbed of Ségur (the Jesuit Verbeker, a Belgian enthusiast for the cause, had come for the occasion), it was decided to organize the congress in France after all, that is in Lille. On several occasions, Leo XIII had given his blessing, but not until 16 May 1881, scarcely one month after the date was announced internationally, did he give his approval. Three hundred sixty-three clergy and representatives of the laity came, yet the French were in the great majority, in spite of participants from Belgium, Holland, Austria, Switzerland, and Italy. The opening address was entitled "The Social Kingdom of Jesus Christ." The concluding procession was accompanied by about four thousand of the faithful from Lille. Upon Cardinal Dechamps' invitation, Avignon was followed by Liège in 1883. The congress in Fribourg in 1885 was presided over by Mermillod, who had meanwhile become president of the congress movement. This event for the first time included the entire public. The movement's center of gravity remained for the time being in France (in 1888 in Paris) and in Belgium (in 1898 in Brussels with Cardinal Goossens). National congresses took place in Italy (1891: Naples, 1896: Orvieto, under Cardinal Parocchi, 1897: Venice, under the chairmanship of Patriarch Sarto). The first event to be attended by a papal legate was the congress of Jerusalem in May 1893 under the leadership of Cardinal Langénieux. This congress was characterized by the efforts of the Pope regarding the Near Eastern Churches (fifty Latin bishops in contrast to eighteen Uniate Eastern bishops). At the regional Congress of Washington, Protestants were admitted for the first time. The international congresses in London (1908) and in Amsterdam (1924) resulted in vehement anti-Catholic reactions.

These boisterous events were in curious contrast to the old and now rejuvenated idea of Perpetual Adoration. But in this form of piety, which happens in complete quietude, the idea of religious reparation was coupled with something like a silent protest. In Rome, in 1883, the "Society of Reparation of the Catholic Nations" was founded, which allotted to individual countries certain weekdays for worship in order to unite the whole world in support of the "imprisoned" Pope. The principal fraternity of daily "Perpetual Adoration," founded in 1890 in the Franciscan church of Turin, was extended in 1893 to all of Italy and in 1909 to include the Catholic world. More congregations and fraternities in the same vein emerged. The Eucharistic encyclical of 28 May 1902, *Mirae caritatis* places the institution of the Last Supper at the end of Christ's life in curious analogy to the impending end of the author's life. The encyclical points to the papal approval in regard to Eucharistic institutions and confines itself in other respects essentially to general practices. A few paragraphs, however, point into the future: Mass, though somewhat set off, is placed in line with the other traditional forms of Eucharistic worship, but it is also indicated that it had been the Church's wish all along "that at every Mass the attending faithful should go to the table of the Lord." Three years earlier, in his encyclical *Annum Sacrum* of 25 May 1899, Leo XIII had ordered the consecration of all mankind to the Sacred Heart (after elevating it in 1889 to the liturgical rank of a feast day). This encyclical hardly suggests the mystical love between the Lord and his own because the nonbaptized are "still sitting as the unfortunate ones in the shadow of death," so that only the power of the sovereign and the law can be applied to them. In this respect, the Pope adhered, with Thomas Aquinas, to the medieval conception of the pagan world. Also characteristic is his mention of the cross as the Constantinian sign of victory, replacing it with the "Most Sacred Heart, transcended by the cross surrounded by the splendid halo of a fiery wreath." In 1891 the church of Sacré Coeur on Montmartre in Paris was completed. The restraint with which Pius IX had reacted to the desire for a worldly dedication had been abandoned, and Leo XII, in the conclusion of his letter, supplemented the new motives with a "purely personal, yet noteworthy and valid reason," namely, that God had just recently delivered him from a serious illness. Societies that had an impact on both Americas were favored. The Jesuits were especially involved in the propagation of this form of piety. In 1872, they had consecrated all provinces of their society to the Sacred Heart. Unquestionably, the demonstrative and seigneurial character of this worship under Leo XIII's pontificate intensified; but no one can determine in which way it was the source of true piety for each individual.

Leo XIII had devoted nine encyclicals and seven apostolic letters to the rosary. Their individual tones were rather different. A great portion of the letters deals with the spiritual guidelines for this prayer and only occasionally contains polemic passages. The encyclical *Octobri mense* of 22 September 1891, introducing the daily rosary for the month of October, recalls the "murders and outbursts of hatred" of the Albigensians, who could only be conquered through the power of the rosary; similar incidents are called to mind as well (such as the victory of Lepanto). The Albigensian *impii* were none other than the Freemasons. An interesting token of social criticism is contained in the *Laetitiae sanctae* of 8 September 1893: previously, "the undisturbed security of life was considered the reward for one's toils; today, the masses are only interested in filling this life with a maximum of pleasures, laboring under the illusion that the government system could be perfected to the extent that everything unpleasant would be eliminated." While the October encyclical limited an extreme Mariology through a *fere,* this period, as did others before and after, witnessed extremes regarding Marian worship (e.g., when the rosary became an independent cult). The entreaty *Regina sacratissimi Rosarii,* introduced in 1883 to the Litany of the Blessed Virgin, referred directly to Mary herself. In addition to the Eucharistic congresses, there were now also Marian congresses with international attendance. At the same time, along with the consecration to the Virgin of individual nations, the movement beginning with Pius IX to dedicate the whole world to the Heart of the Virgin grew stronger, intensifying at the congresses between 1908 and 1914. Throughout the nineteenth century, many ecclesiastical societies were founded and dedicated to the Virgin. There is no question that the increasing Marian devotion entailed abuses far into the twentieth century, particularly sentimentalizing prayers and hymns; but even though the longing for motherly warmth expressed therein could tempt one to withdraw into insular illusion, this form of piety has to be understood in its historical context.

The fact that the figure of Saint Joseph played a role in the education of workers, especially in France, was the reason for French postulates under Leo XIII to enter his name in the *Confiteor, Suscipe,* etc. This circumstance was also mentioned in the encyclical *Quamquam plures* of 15 August 1889, where Saint Joseph, after 1870 the patron of the whole Church, was labeled the model of a good husband and father and a consolation to "the proletariat, the workers, and all people in modest circumstances." The Pope emphasized that they had the right "to strive for an improvement of their situation with all legitimate means," but they had no right "to overturn the order ordained by divine providence." As popular as the devotion to Saint Joseph was in all levels of society, this manual laborer of a patriarchal period of history could not be made a model to be realized in an industrial society; neither could the image of the "Holy Family," as numerous as the foundings of religious societies named "Holy Family" may have been at that time.

The Catholic enlightenment did not just reduce the multiplicity of forms of piety, it often eliminated them entirely. The reaction to this in the Catholic restoration created even more institutions to practice the numerous new forms of worship whose style was often an expression of the contemporary popular taste, but which differed markedly from the Baroque because they were isolated from the culture as a whole. It is equally significant that while in the wake of the French Revolution class differences between the hierarchy and the people had been eliminated, the clericalism of the nineteenth century established new barriers. This is demonstrated clearly in the focal point of Catholic piety, the Mass. The political implications were expressed by the fact that the liturgical indications of enlightenment are called "communion of the divine service" and furthermore by the statement that the "Catholic temple" would maintain its eminence even if the congregation would never gather there, "because it is not the congregation that is the inspirational principle of the Catholic temple, but rather the indwelling of the All Holy and the sacrifice of the priest" (Jungmann). The polemical mentality, which was implicit in the expiatory sacrifice, is documented by the fact that Leo XIII added the prayer of St. Michael to the Marian prayer, which Pius IX had introduced as the conclusion of the Mass. Part of the Catholic restoration were Prosper Guéranger's efforts in Solesmes to restore the liturgical text, to eliminate Gallicisms and to return to the Roman liturgy — efforts which had very fertile effects in later years. They aimed primarily toward a renovation of monastic life, similar to the efforts of the Benedictines, inspired by Solesmes, in their new monastery at Beuron. The distance between the officiating priest and the people, which had a history of a thousand years, was confirmed by the prohibition against translating the text of the Mass, but violations were not seriously prosecuted any longer. The prohibition was quietly dropped when Leo XIII did not mention it again in the revision of the Index of Forbidden Books in 1897. But the translation of the canon of Holy Scriptures and even more so that of the consecration text was postponed until the twentieth century. By then, however, translations appeared whose subsequent significance could hardly be anticipated at that time. In 1878, the *missel des fidèles* by Gérard van Caloen was published in Maredsous, where, among others, the Beuron monk Anselm Schott resided during the time of the *Kulturkampf.* His *Meßbuch der heiligen Kirche,* published in 1884, had already sold one hundred thousand copies by 1906. It took a long time, however, until the "Mass devotions" in the prayer books were supplemented by liturgical texts. Diocesan prayer books multiplied in Germany during the nineteenth century, but they were only very slowly introduced to the public because of the Holy See's regulations. They contained a wide variety of Mass devotions for special occasions, which were often far removed from the liturgical process itself, even in regard to their psychological interpretation. A German specialty was the "sung Mass," which had been compiled during the period of Enlightenment and now had a very subjective flavor, especially the songs for Communion. Even though Leo XIII pointed out that Communion was a part of the sacrifice of the Mass, "spiritual communion" continued to be recommended. The separation of special prayers of preparation and thanksgiving at the Communion remained the custom until far into the twentieth century. In view of the hectic economic, social, and spiritual developments, one was, as in all areas of ecclesiastical life, intent on devotional writings, which were often carried so far that a differentiation between essential and incidental issues was said to be a "deeply devastating illusion." But in retrospect, even progressive ideas can be discovered. Rare pastoral thought remained, for the time being, the privilege of the theologians who were in fact the real pioneers, especially in regard to the significant scholarship in liturgical history.

Even though the statistics of canonizations do not constitute a "century of saints" like the seventeenth century, the very few outstanding spiritual personalities constituted, together with the great number of anonymous devotees, a historical "balance," without which a period cannot be understood. Charles de Foucauld (1858–1916) was one of them, no matter whether the impending beatification process will be finalized or not. After his conversion in 1886, the officer lived at first as a Trappist in France and Syria (1890–96), then, until 1900, as a hermit in Nazareth. In 1901, he was ordained priest. His idea of realizing Jesus' message entirely through the example of his own life without any physical protection in the midst of a Moslem world (which remained closed to all missions from the beginning to the present day) can be seen as a prophecy of the conditions of Christian life in the future, despite — or because of — the fact that Foucauld died in absolute solitude (he was shot by Tuaregs).

In contrast, Thérèse Martin, the saint of Lisieux (1873–97), was completely a witness of her own time, in spite of her effect on the twentieth century. It is probably no exaggeration to say that Thérèse of Lisieux embodied the entire structure of piety as it had developed since the second third of the nineteenth century. This piety was propagated by the *milieu* Catholicism which was to be ridiculed later, at a time devoid of understanding. It was expressed in the tasteless pictures of her time, embedded in the clan spirit and subsequent exuberant sentimentality of a devout French family. The extraordinary feature of this saint was her conventionality, which caused her to take the "narrow path" of mystical love for God, like Teresa of Avila, who remained a stranger to Thérèse and her friends. Though remaining in the Carmelite tradition, Thérèse activated it, however, when she recognized that the clergy, revered "like gods," required intercession. But in spite of her submersion in the New Testament, she did not depart from the contemporary image of Jesus. However, and this is crucial, there is no difference between Thérèse Martin's influence, which was quickly felt all over the Catholic world, and her own religious existence.

C H A P T E R   6 1

The Organization in the Old and New Orders — Inner Reform and the Power of Attraction

Even though Pius IX had repeatedly interfered in the reorganization of the Franciscan order (O.F.M.), it was not possible to bring about the necessary revision of the statutes in view of the more or less anachronistic discussions within the order. At the general chapter of 1862, one proposal received a great majority, but appeared in 1882 only as a draft. A memorandum presented at this chapter, according to which the Observants, Reformed, Discalced, and Recollects were to unite under the name "Franciscans," was rejected as inopportune. Only at the general chapter in 1889, which took place in the new Collegium S. Antonii in Rome, were uniform constitutions passed. After the interpretation of the order's poverty was accepted by the Recollects, a general secret vote turned out in favor of the union by 77 to 31 votes, a result which changed considerably after subsequent "yes" votes (8 no,

100 yes). Leo XIII ratified the resolutions on 15 May 1897, and he issued the constitution *Felicitate quadam*. In the eighties, the order counted only 14,000 friars; by 1907 there were 17,092 (8,152 were priests) in 1,460 houses. Pius IX's plan to unite the Conventuals and the Capuchins failed. The Conventuals still had 1,481 members in 1893 (in 1884, they succeeded in uniting with the Spaniards). In 1907 the nuns of the Order of Saint Clare (Poor Clares), which was mostly destroyed after the French Revolution, numbered 10,204 sisters in 518 cloisters. The Third Order developed remarkably after 1883, when Leo XIII had modernized the rules, reducing, on the one hand, the regulations for prayer exercises and fasting, on the other hand, requiring monthly confessions (previously only three per year). It is estimated that around the turn of the century 2.5 million belonged to the order, which tried to differ from the activities of other orders primarily by intensifying religious life.

"The day we become centralized will be the day when a reform will be impossible. The lively spontaneity will be eliminated and replaced by bureaucracy, which may be very well, but it imitates life and is not life itself"; this idea, attributed to Prosper Guéranger, the founder of the Abbey of Solesmes (1837), is more than a social theory of the constitution of the Benedictine order. It is the expression of a spirituality of contemplation, which is impossible without spontaneity. Conversely, the spirituality of activism requires organizational concentration. Significantly, the following sentence belongs in the context of this statement: "What is strength for the Jesuits, is a danger for us." In 1862, Prior Maurus (Rudolf) Wolter was in Solesmes for three months, where he was deeply moved by the spirit of Guéranger. Wolter had just negotiated with the royal court of the Prince von Hohenzollern-Sigmaringen to transfer the secularized Augustinian Beuron monastery to his as yet very small community of monks. After the catastrophes of the Revolution and the secularizations, and for internal reasons also, the Benedictine order had difficulties recovering. This is evidenced by the efforts both in France, where Solesmes certainly inspired new foundations, and especially in Bavaria, where Ludwig I encountered little response to his desire to revive the Benedictine order (1830: reopening of Metten Abbey, beginning of the Bavarian congregation, which flourished in the course of the nineteenth century). Here, it was a question of revitalizing old monasteries; Solesmes and Beuron in form and concept were new foundations. The theoretical and practical inclination to the liturgy as the focal point of spirituality was at first an internal monastic affair; but finally, this renascence was to penetrate the public life of the Church. In view of the small number of order members, the tendency to found more and more filial monasteries and to achieve the status of a congregation is striking. The Swiss monks from Einsiedeln were welcomed in Indiana, where, from the Abbey of Saint Meinrad (1871), they devoted themselves to the mission of the Sioux Indians. In 1884, this abbey joined, within the Swiss-American Congregation, the Swiss branch of the Engelberg monastery in Missouri, which had likewise been elevated to an abbey. The eagerness of the young Beuron Abbey to found more branches was given ample opportunity in Maredsous in 1878, where (in the same year) Placidus Wolter became the first abbot. The mission monastery of Reichenbach (Upper Palatinate), under episcopal jurisdiction, was transferred in 1887 to Saint Ottilien (near the Ammersee) and elevated to independent priory (1902 abbey) by the Propaganda Fide after some controversy (1897). Thanks to the transferral of the apostolic prefecture, which, upon Bismarck's suggestion, was established in Zanzibar (German East Africa), it became the starting point of the *Kongregation von Sankt Ottilien,* which developed world-wide missionary activities. The first archabbot of Saint Ottilien, which became the largest abbey of the order, was Norbert Weber (1902–1930).

The historian of the Dominican order rightly remarked that Leo XIII involved himself in the affairs of the Franciscans (1892) and the Benedictines (1893) much "deeper" than in those of his own order. The papal plan in regard to the Benedictines had been prepared for some time after the congregations had negotiated in vain. In 1886, a congress of the abbots of the Monte Cassino congregation took place in Rome. After separating from the congregation of Subiaco (1871) in order to realize a stricter observance under Abbott Casaretto, this congregation had gone through a process of rejuvenation. The main issue was the renewal of the College of Saint Anselmo as a Benedictine world center. It opened in 1888 temporarily in the *Palazzo dei Convertendi* under the leadership of Archbishop J. Dusmet, O.S.B. (born in Palermo), to whom Leo XIII had explained his ideas of a totally Benedictine college in 1887 (Dusmet was elevated to cardinal in 1889). The next step was the ordination of Hildebrand de Hemptinne in Monte Cassino as abbot of Maredsous, after Placidus Wolter had become archabbot of Beuron and thus successor to his brother, who had died in 1890. A brief of 9 December 1892 called all Benedictine abbots of the world to convene for the occasion of laying the foundation stone of Saint Anselmo on the Aventine in Rome in April of the following year. During a trip in 1887 by order of the Pope for the purpose of preparing the congress, O'Gorman, prefect of the English Benedictine congregation, encountered considerable resistance from the Benedictine abbots. In spite of that, Leo XIII decided to act. In a speech on 20 April 1893, Cardinal Dusmet interpreted the intentions of the Pope, stating that the *Societas quaedam* should not abolish the individual characteristics of the congregations. The abbots were to make a decision on the following points: the election of an abbot primate to represent the entire order in Rome (after consultation with the abbots; election of a *repraesentans* [rather than a primate] with a two-thirds majority [however, in accordance with Leo XIII's wish the first primate was appointed by the Pope]); the abbot primate to reside in the College of Saint Anselmo, which does not belong to any congregation and represents its own community, composed of various congregations (consultation with the abbots: the confederation should not imply dependence on a certain congregation); the primate's term of office to be twelve years (the term of the abbot prefect heading a congregation: six years). On 12 July, the "confederation" was confirmed. by the papal brief *Summum semper.* The confederation meant a deep invasion of the old structure of the Benedictine monastic life and certainly did not correspond to Prosper Guéranger's ideal. Even Pius XII had to deal with the constitution of the confederation.

After the Beuron congregation had sent at first only a few monks to the desolate Brazilian abbeys, van Caloen made two inspection tours in 1894/95, reporting about them to the Beuron general convention in Maredsous. Olinda, where van Caloen became abbot, was the point of departure for the rejuvenation of the Brazilian congregation, whose headquarters was the abbey of Saint Benedict in Rio de Janeiro. The archabbey of Beuron, which was chosen by the abbot primate in 1896 as the place for a convention of the abbots, initiated the establishment of Maria Laach, whose church Emperor Wilhelm II gave to the Beuron monks in 1892 after an audience with Placidus Wolter.

The membership of the Dominican order had diminished; even by 1910 it had barely reached the status of 1844. The general chapter of 1885 in Louvain decided to purchase a new residence for the general in Rome in the Via San Sebastiano. Shortly before his death, Larroca became "somehow" entangled in the controversy regarding papal politics toward the Italian state, having made some positive statements about Bonomelli's (bishop of Cremona) translation of the *Homiliae* by Monsabré, who had been the preacher of Notre Dame until 1890. As with the Franciscans and Benedictines, Leo XIII had also directed his attention to the rearrangement of the Dominicans, and in a letter of 31 May 1889 he impressed upon them the observance of the *vita communis*. The general chapter, whose residence determines the office of the vicariate general, was convening in Lyon. At the general chapter, the greatest majority of votes went to Andreas Frühwirth, who had just been made provincial of the Austrian imperial province for the second time. The Styrian Andreas Frühwirth (1845–1933) had joined the order in 1863, had studied in Graz and Rome, and became provincial of the imperial province for the first time in 1880–84. Until 1904 he was to the Dominicans an equally energetic and diplomatically adroit general, who prevented the order from showing any signs of weakness, and who was eager, primarily, to make himself indispensable for Neo-Thomism. Frühwirth devoted himself with special passion to the establishment of colleges. In a letter of 4 October 1893, Leo XIII made the Dominican order solely responsible for the edition of Thomas Aquinas. After three years, in 1882, the commission of cardinals appointed for this edition had published the first volume, and, in April 1903 the Pope received volume XI from the Dominicans.

During the generalship of Frühwirth there occurred the initial controversies regarding the Dominican M.-J. Lagrange. His first attempts to develop a "critical method" for interpreting the Pentateuch produced often crude suspicions after the Congress of Fribourg in 1897. Frühwirth, who had given Lagrange the title of "Master of Theology" in 1901, provided his research with some protection in his capacity as general of the order (until 1903). However, Pius X assigned the leadership of the new Biblical Institute not to the Dominicans, but to the Jesuits. In terms of spirituality, the order went along with the consecration to the Sacred Heart and the pledge to recite the rosary as was the general trend of the time.

After the death of the general of the Jesuits, P.-J. Beckx (1795–1887), during whose long term in office (since 1853) the number of members had increased remarkably (in spite of the prohibitions), the Swiss A. M. Anderledy, assistant for German-speaking provinces, took office. His successor, the Spaniard Luis Martín (general 1892–1906), deserves credit for the history of the order, and he assigned the edition of the *Monumenta Historica Societatis Jesu* to the Spanish provinces. The Society of Jesus still preferred to think of philosophy as *ancilla theologiae* rather than theology itself, which theme the Jesuits concentrated on in terms of the question of grace and an ecclesiology oriented toward the papacy. During Leo XIII's pontificate, however, the tendency of the Gregoriana toward positive theology, and against speculative theology, was corrected, and as a result the Pope's brother, Giuseppe Pecci, left the Jesuits (he was reinstated shortly before his death). The general congregation of 1883 decided to choose the encyclical on Aquinas, *Aeterni Patris,* as its guideline, and in 1886 Leo XIII confirmed the privileges of the society. The traditional emphasis on moral theology proved fruitful in dealing with the problems of modern society, with Jesuit authors providing important contributions. Wherever Jesuits were allowed to be active in schools, especially in the United States, lively discussions were held about curricula, primarily the relationship of humanism to the exact sciences. These debates essentially ended in 1906 with an adaptation to the secular schools.

It is a remarkable phenomenon that the Jesuits continued to have relatively large numbers of new recruits in spite of the prohibitions. In Portugal the Jesuits had only a short period of activity from 1880 until 1908. In France, schools had to be closed in 1880, because the order could not accept the school laws. In Italy, where the general of the order had been expelled from the professed house al Gesù, and had to settle in Fiesole, the Jesuits were prohibited or at least inhibited from living together. New members were scarce, in contrast to Austria, Germany, and Switzerland, where the order obtained many new members for its activities in foreign countries, particularly in the United States. A majority resolution of the German *Reichstag* (168 to 145) for reinstatement was voted down in the *Bundesrat.* However, the Redemptorists, who had turned to Latin America after their suppression in Europe, were not considered an illegal organization any longer. Rather unencumbered, the Jesuits were able to develop in Austria-Hungary after 1820. There they had high schools, and also the college *Stella matutina* (since 1856) in Feldkirch and the theological faculty of the University of Innsbruck, centers of learning that influenced Germany also. In the province of England, which was combined with Ireland, Maryland, New York, and Missouri through a vice-province, conflicts arose concerning pastoral work, which were intensified when the College of Chelsea was established through direct papal authority over the heads of the episcopate; consequently the Jesuits did not have Cardinal Manning as a friend.

Since the Cistercians of the Strict Observance and the Reform congregations could not come to an agreement, the Reformed Cistercians (Trappists) separated in 1892, a separation which Leo XIII confirmed in his brief of 17 March 1893 and the decree of 1902, including the privileges of the old order. In 1898 they were able to obtain the original monastery of Cîteaux. The Cistercians of the old observance still possessed at the end of the nineteenth century thirty-two monasteries, most of them in Austria-Hungary. Papal unification tactics, successful with the Franciscans, would have been out of the question in this case.

The extraordinary activity regarding the new establishment of congregations had peaked by the middle of the century. Most congregations were unable to extend their local impact. The Christian Brothers, one of the older congregations, achieved significant success and could be found all over the world toward the end of the century. The Redemptorists experienced a similar upswing. By 1900 they had 132 foundations, 30 of them in Italy, and after 1894 they were also admitted in Germany. The Salesians of Don Bosco, who counted 774 members in 57 foundations in 1888 at the death of their founder, expanded also outside of Italy, and by 1900 they had gained about 2,000 members in 300 houses (since 1903 also in Austria). They intensified their activities, begun in 1875, in the foreign mission.

The Pallottines (finally confirmed in 1904) experienced a more rapid development only after World War I. In terms of members, the Sisters of Charity (Vincentians) were leading all female congregations. They suffered civil restrictions relatively rarely and in general only for short periods of time, because everyone was dependent on their hospital care. At the end of the century, they counted approximately thirty thousand sisters in 2,500 houses. The Sisters of the Sacred Heart, founded in Paris, began in 1879 the beatification process of their founder Sophie Barat.

It was a character trait of the activities of the Dominican general Andreas Frühwirth that he paid special attention to the financial situation of the provinces of his order and the office of the general. Economic foundations had always played a significant role in the history of the orders and the congregations, but it was only natural that the conditions of the industrial age had an impact in this area as well. However, two other enterprises were able to develop unencumbered by political factors, even though they were not confirmed by the Church until the beginning of the twentieth century: the *Societas Divini Salvatoris* (S.D.S., Salvatorians) and the *Societas Verbi Divini* (S.V.D., Society of the Divine Word). Even through the hagiographical style of the biographies of the societies' founders one can sense that genuine religious engagement was combined with the virtues of an industrial manager.

The founder of the Salvatorians, Johann Baptist Jordan, was an ornamental painter, who had privately obtained a high school education and in 1878, as a priest, received through his pastor a stipend in Rome. The Alemannian, born on the Rhine River near Baden (1848–1918), got an audience with Leo XIII in 1880 (arranged by Cardinal Bilio). He extensively expounded the papal blessing of the founding of his *Apostolische Lehrgesellschaft* in Rome. He secured his position through recommendations by Cardinals Hergenröther and Parocchi. With the help of his publication *Der Missionär,* which he managed and which was approved by the bishop of Linz but directed from Rome, he wanted to establish an "association" whose program was to show no clear contours, but which was to have a diverse membership. His main problem was to find trained priests, and he therefore wanted to educate young people speedily, using his own career as an example. In spite of considerable difficulties, including financial ones, he was able to establish one foundation after another after obtaining a mission in Assam.

Arnold Janssen (1837–1909), founder of the Society of the Divine Word, was the son of a transport business owner on the Lower Rhine River. In 1861 he became a priest and a high school teacher and began his activity by also founding a publication called *Kleiner Herz-Jesu-Bote* (1874). After a fund-raising trip through Germany and Austria in 1875, Janssen purchased a piece of property with an old inn in Steyl, a town in the Netherlands near the border. Together with a carpentry apprentice, a Franciscan brother, and his real brother (a Capuchin from Münster), he founded a society here. His plan encountered great scepticism among the clergy and bishops, and with his autocratic style he caused most of his fellow members to leave in 1876. The same year, Janssen found a capable economist, the future superior general Nikolaus Blum, and so he began the construction of Steyl, even though he had only one tenth of the construction funds at his disposal. Within a few years he had accumulated three hundred thousand marks worth of debts. When the construction of Saint Michael's with its double church was completed in 1886, his debts were repaid. To the publication of the *Herz-Jesu-Bote* he added the magazine *Die heilige Stadt Gottes* and a calendar, printed in his own press, for which the lay brothers provided cheap labor. In 1888, he founded Saint Raphael's in Rome, 1889 Saint Gabriel's in Vienna, 1892 Heiligkreuz near Neisse, 1898 Saint Wendel's in the Rhineland, 1904 Saint Rupert's near Bischofshofen. Janssen acted according to the principle that it is not a question of the availability of funds, but of the necessity of the building.

Because the congregations for women were, aside from education, primarily active in charity and hospital care, they were, as a rule, less touched by state laws. Because of that, and thanks to their active religious willingness to make sacrifices, they were able to develop under the pontificate of Leo XIII. The Sisters of Mercy of Saint Charles Borromeo had founded, via their original congregation in Nancy, new congregations in Germany, Austria, and the Netherlands, which developed considerable activities (the Saint Hedwig hospital, founded in 1846 in Berlin, took care of 5,500 patients in 1895). Aside from the largest female society, the Sisters of Charity (Vincentians), smaller societies like the Niederbronn Sisters (1880 the general mother house in Oberbronn/Alsace) and the Ingenbohl Sisters (1894 confirmed by the Pope) also had an excellent reputation across religious borders.

Looking at the history of the older religious societies and the new foundations during the pontificate of Leo XIII as a whole, one cannot ignore the desire for an internal rejuvenation of the Church (not least in the foreign mission) and for a social impact upon education, hospital care, and social action. There was also the amazing attraction of the religious life for a considerable part of the youth in the Catholic Church in spite of the political tactics of suppression, the general attitude of the time, the continuously increasing resignation and scepticism, and the way of thinking which resulted from the growing role of technology in life. But the religious societies found in Catholicism, which had meanwhile reached self-awareness, a resonance of resistance to the secularization of life and a religiously motivated willingness to devotion which bore witness to the vitality of the Catholic Church. This vitality is particularly obvious in the societies with "simple vows," which by now found full recognition. To gather these impulses, to eliminate or prevent sterile divisions, and to make use of these societies for the ideals of his pontificate were the goals of Leo XIII's ecclesiastical legislation, whose most significant feature was the concentration of orders and congregations in Rome. It is historically understandable that such efforts were most difficult in regard to the oldest order of the West, the Benedictines. Its decentralized structure had corresponded to the specific liberties of a feudal society. The principle of centralization was the principle of a growing highly industrial society — and it was also the principle of Leo XIII and his successors in the sense of an economy of spiritual powers. Most religious societies were induced to transfer their headquarters to Rome. In 1908 Pius X established the *Sacra congregatio negotiis religiosorum sodalium praeposita* as the highest authority for orders of the Latin Church, to whom the religious of both sexes were subordinated.

CHAPTER 62

The Dispute over Church Music

Since church music is directly connected with the liturgical action, the question of how musical forms of expression of the *zeitgeist* can be incorporated in the Church service is much more crucial than in regard to the fine arts. Indeed, the religious subjectivity of the sacred music of a Franz Schubert does correspond to the subjectivity of general piety; however, it is certain that as the representative musical creations of Classicism and Romanticism emerged from the modern spirit born in the Revolution, frequently Christianity was simply the occasion for their creation. In France, the interest in the Gregorian chant of the Benedictines at Solesmes was primarily an esoteric and historical matter, and the *Schola cantorum,* which had just been introduced in all Romance countries according to the model of the Lateran Church (1868), lived in harmony with the well-known plain-chant, a popularization of the chorale. Even Charles Gounod's *Cecilia Mass* (1882) or the romantic harmony of César Franck, (died in 1890) did not give offense. However, in German Catholicism, a movement developed which wanted to restore the "pure" sacred music, believing that a musical reform, which was unquestionably necessary, could only be achieved by turning away from modern developments. The German example found an echo in many other forms of Catholicism (the Netherlands, Belgium, Ireland, North America), but not in Austria, where attempts were made to apply contemporary forms to the ecclesiastical spirit. Pierluigi da Palestrina (died 1594 in Rome) was for the revival of church music in the nineteenth century what Thomas Aquinas had been for philosophy and theology. Composition and declamation of the "Palestrina style" were renewed in the first half of the nineteenth century. Regensburg, the episcopal see of Michael Sailer, was the leading center, a city from which spread the tradition which Karl Proske (died 1861) started with his editions from the sixteenth and seventeenth centuries. That musicians who composed in the "Palestrina style" (such as M. Hailer [died 1915 in Regensburg], who was called the Palestrina of the twentieth century) were unable to produce important works is due to the process of superficial imitation. It is more important that, through the efforts of the highest church authorities, the *a capella* music of vocal polyphony was canonized, which was equally a historic misunderstanding of the great master Palestrina and a disregarding of artistic originality.

At first, there was criticism of the church music which was composed of elements of the symphony and the opera. Now, by separating the *musica sacra* from the *musica profana,* the church was separated from the world. In regard to instrumental music, as it was then composed by the church music directors, and which continued to be played, though not as often, the Belgian Edgar Tinel (died 1912) stands out, because he refused to follow this separation. During the Catholic Convention in Bamberg in 1868, the priest F. X. Witt (1834–88) founded the *Allgemeinen Cäcilienverband für die Länder der deutschen Sprache,* which Pius IX confirmed in 1870 as an organization under papal law with a cardinal protector. The brief contains the society's statutes as presented. Its first and foremost obligation is: "Gregorian chant (*cantus planus*) is to be cultivated intensively everywhere. Polyphonic arrangements for several voices (*cantus figuralis*) of older or newer compositions are to be furthered, as long as they comply with church regulations." Palestrina was not mentioned in this document, but he was the idol of the Cecilian movement. The society was thus authorized to determine in its catalog what sacred music was. The struggle over true Catholic church music was considered one of the most important ones in the battle with the *zeitgeist.* Deviations were condemned with extreme intolerance and with reference to the Church. Even the German Catholic church hymn, which treasure had been rediscovered by the Romanticists, partly fell under the influence of Cecilianism, and especially the convents of women added popular, sentimental songs. F. X. Witt, who, in spite of his aggressiveness, was one of the more forward-looking minds in the movement, did not want to see instrumental music excluded and hoped for "a Palestrina of modern orchestral music." He probably had Franz Liszt in mind, who respected him. The great value and impact of Cecilianism consists of the fact that it recognized the problematic relation of Classical and Romantic music to the liturgical ceremony. Its attempts to solve the problem, which should be seen in the historical and ecclesiastical perspective of that time, were inadequate. This is nowhere more obvious than in the fact that Anton Bruckner (1824–96), who as a Romanticist created his sacred music with liturgical objectivity, was not accepted by the movement.

Supported by papal authority, Cecilianism spread in the last third of the nineteenth century through most countries, after the Gregorian Society had been founded in the Netherlands in 1868. Its impact was particularly strong in Ireland. In the country of Giuseppe Verdi (1813–1901), where the influence of the national opera was especially problematic, the *Regolamento per la Musica sacra in Italia* of 1884 ruled: Except for the organ, only trombones, flutes, and drums and "similar instruments popular with the Israelite people" were permitted. They concentrated on cultivating the chorale, which was supported by ecclesiastical decrees. Cecilianism also exerted a certain influence.

Almost two decades after Palestrina's death, the Stamperia Medicaea in Rome, a printing office founded by Cardinal Fernando Medici and G. B. Raimundi, published an edition of the Roman gradual in which Gregorian melodies had been adapted to contemporary principles. This little-known publication was adopted in Mechelen in 1848, but it did not have any historical significance for the Church until after 1871, when the publishing house of Pustet in Regensburg prepared reprints. The inspiring and driving force was the priest F. X. Haberl (1840–1910) who, after sojourns in Rome, became cathedral conductor in Regensburg, where he founded a church music school in 1874. The Congregation of Rites offered Pustet a thirty-year imprimatur, even though the historical validity of the *Medicaea* was already being questioned at that time. A decree of the Congregation of Rites of 14 April 1877 bestowed upon the edition a somewhat official character.

In the meantime, the Benedictine J. Pothier (1835–1923) had conducted his research on chorales in Solesmes by order of his abbot, Prosper Guéranger, intending to do away with Gallicism and to restore tradition. After the publication of the principles of Solesmes, a congress was organized in Arezzo in 1882, to which the Congregation of Rites reacted on 10 April 1883 with a reiteration of the legitimization of the Regensburg edition. This was expressly confirmed by Leo XIII with the statement that papal directives be taken as mandates. In Regensburg, Witt and particularly Haberl fought passionately for their concept, and they did not fail to refer to the Roman authority. But after the termination of the imprimatur, Leo XIII seized the opportunity and found a way out of the dilemma with his brief *Nos quidem* of 17 May 1901, addressed to the abbot of Solesmes. The motu proprio *Inter pastoralis officii* (1903) of Pius X introduced a new phase in the understanding of the Gregorian chorale.

CHAPTER 63

Church Art
in the Nineteenth and Twentieth Centuries

Since the beginning of Church history, ecclesiastical art has carried the hallmark of the contemporary relation between the Church and the world and of the different forms of the notion of salvation, according to their epochal and ethnic background. In that respect, a work of art preserves in visualized form something from a past situation and can therefore serve, provided it is interpreted correctly, as a source for Church history. Art is particularly informative when it reports incidents that were not considered worthy of literary treatment or remained in the subconscious.

There is good reason that Church art should be chosen as a topic of investigation in the nineteenth and twentieth centuries. The previous, almost naive function of Christian art has become more and more the object of serious study and decrees and is thus a special section of Church history.

Architecture

After the Council of Trent, the Church developed an awareness of the specific character of its artistic activities, especially in the countries north of the Alps, which, having been affected by the Reformation, externalized its forms of expression. Stained glass and ribbed vaults continued to be considered "ecclesiastical," even though they were not customary any longer in secular architecture. In those areas in which the Reformation had left its mark, but which had been recovered by the Catholic Church, clear relapses into medieval architecture can be observed. The result is a "sacral style" with historical dimensions. However, Church art in consistently Catholic countries generally runs parallel to the contemporary development of style. It also does not lose touch with aesthetics, which grows more and more independent, even though the concept of beauty is no longer a theological one as in the Middle Ages. But since 1588, beginning with the activities of the Congregation of Rites, the Church in these countries felt compelled to publish papal and episcopal decrees, edicts, and recommendations on artistic activities in order to draw the line against Protestantism and the secular areas which were in the process of emancipation. The demands relate essentially to preservation of or connection to the Christian tradition, to avoidance of offensive presentations or recommendation of instructive ones, and to the observance of ethnographic customs (*usus*), provided they do not contradict liturgical regulations. The interpretation of these regulations and recommendations leaves a great deal of latitude and allows strict traditionalism as well as the recently increasing influence of the individual artist. The artistic context in general was thus able to be preserved by the Church throughout the Baroque and Roccoco eras, and during the secular Classicism of the end of the eighteenth century, in which the Enlightenment erected or at least designed its own edifices of art for the "Supreme Being" or the gods of "nature" and "reason."

Corresponding to the turn toward Greek art within the context of Classicism, churches, like palaces, theaters, and museums, decorated their entrances with a Greek temple facade in the form of a portal of columns with a pediment. In Classicism this mixture threatened to obscure the borders of profane architecture and to cloud the sacred purpose. But it also offers the opportunity to find from this vantage point the transition to early Christian architecture.

While the Classicism of the Enlightenment was understandably unable to influence Church art deeply, the sympathy for the Middle Ages emerging from the Romantic countermovement succeeded in defining the sacred art of the entire nineteenth century. This enthusiasm for the Middle Ages, furthered by the corresponding belles lettres, was almost from the start determined by Christianity. But the first beginnings of art are rooted in the secular realm, in the Gothic ruins of the eighteenth century erected in English gardens as symbols of *vanitas* to inspire meditation, or in the Gothicized garden houses which served as temporary shelter for Romantic poets. Wherever enthusiasm for Gothic elements in church buildings was aroused, it was devoid of insight into the sacred character of this architecture. Goethe discovered in 1772 in the facade of the Strasbourg Cathedral a "Babel-thought" of the Promethean architect Erwin von Steinbach, with which the human genius may win his freedom "on the confined and dismal clerics' stage of the *medii aevi.*" The Gothic architecture, once mocked by Vasari as *maniera tedesca,* is now in a positive sense celebrated as German or Germanic architecture, determined by the forces of natural growth and striving to illustrate the majestic and infinite. At first, interpretations of the Gothic church in a historically adequate and theologically symbolic sense are the exception.

An exemplar of the diverging motives in evaluating Gothic architecture is the story of the restoration of the Cologne Cathedral, which had been in a state of incompletion since the beginning of the sixteenth century. The motives for its completion were very different. The choir, completed in 1322, is seen as an intense image of the forest, which as an element of nature bears witness to the direct manifestation of God, but at the same time is also a reminder of the prehistory of man, who built himself his first hut out of branches and tree trunks, thus creating the Gothic style. Moreover, the cathedral is the "most elevating symbol of eternity," whereby the term eternity is to be understood in a general philosophical, not in a specific Christian sense. Primarily, however, the cathedral is a document of German history, striving again for national unity after its decline at the end of the Middle Ages and after its wars of independence. In the proclamation inspired by Sulpiz Boisserée and written by Joseph Görres, which appeared on 26 November 1814 in the *Rheinische Merkur,* the Cathedral is seen as "a symbol of the new Empire that we want to build." When the foundation stone was laid in 1842, Friedrich Wilhelm IV celebrated the planned completion as the "work of brotherhood among all Germans and all creeds," and the art historian Franz Kugler saw in it "a unifying sign for all people of the German tongue to gather around." In resuming medieval architecture and in view of Classicism, there is a feeling of progress from heathenism to Christianity, from things Hellenic to things German. Occasionally, the national impulse dominated the Christian medieval spirit to such a degree that there was talk about the victory of the Reformation, especially in view of the active participation of the Protestant Prussian government. One also bewailed as a contradiction the fact that the "slaves of Rome" were permitted to turn the edifice into a "place of Jesuit stupefaction and mendacity." Because of these and similar opinions, the Catholic population of Cologne remained demonstratively absent from the final celebration on 15 August 1880, at the time of the *Kulturkampf.* The first railroad bridge across the Rhine River, built between 1855 and 1859 at the King's wish as a continuation of the cathedral's axis and as a symbol of the new time connecting medieval history and technological progress, was inaugurated by the equestrian statues of Friedrich Wilhelm IV (1861–1862) and Wilhelm I (1867). Through the demolition of two churches and sixty-nine houses, free space was created around the cathedral.

Even though it had been shown in 1830 that Gothic architecture did not originate in Germany but in France and though it was recognized shortly after that the Cologne Cathedral had been constructed according to the Cathedral of Amiens, Gothic architecture continued to be considered German for some time.

More enduring than the national motive proved to be the perception of the Gothic as a specifically Christian sacral style suited for the construction of churches. The Cologne Cathedral construction office, managed after 1833 by Ernst Friedrich Zwirner (1802–1861), sent out numerous architects now familiar with Gothic construction principles, who renovated old churches and erected new ones in the Rhineland and elsewhere, and who went to revive construction offices in Strasbourg, Vienna, and elsewhere, or who were appointed to teaching chairs at technical colleges.

In Italy, the revival of the Gothic was sporadic.

For a very long time, the Gothic style was *en vogue* in America. Actually, it was not used until around 1900, and only receded in church construction in the fourth decade of our century. There, as in Germany and England during the Romantic period, many Protestant artists converted for aesthetic reasons.

In view of the freedom that church regulations offered by recommending that only the form handed down by Christian tradition be followed, an extensive, partly polemical dispute about the choice of proper style evolved. Reichensperger and many others advocated Gothic because they considered it progressive in contrast to the old Christian and Roman architecture, and they rejected the Renaissance because it was based on heathenism. Others recommended the architecture of the Italian Renaissance, since this era was not a Protestant one and had produced, moreover, outstanding saints. The popular handbook of liturgy by Franz Xaver Thalhofer preferred the Gothic because the German Renaissance was not of sufficient quality. This demonstrates once again how independent of each other art and worship had grown, and how the blending of the two had moved into the realm of the aesthetic and the arbitrary.

In Protestantism, the connection to Gothic style was even more definite, having nothing but Gothic examples in mind since the Eisenach Regulations of 1856 had recommended the model of a "historically evolved Christian architecture." But in the first half of the century, the Protestants also used Classical elements and toward the end of the century they built structures copying the Baroque. The Eisenach Regulations of 1908 finally did away with recommendations of a certain style and simply suggested "sincere and noble simplicity in form and color."

In spite of this change around the turn of the century, there is no doubt that, even after a definite rejection of historicism, the Gothic and its elements remained effective in the construction of churches in the twentieth century, not only during the time of Expressionism in Germany, as in the case of Dominikus Böhm, but also in the numerous Gothic structures after 1950 which incorporated versions of ribbed vaults, rose windows with tracery, and, above all, extensive stained glass.

The definitions of the Christian sacral style of the nineteenth century included, aside from the Gothic and old Christian, Romanesque and, last but not least, Byzantine architecture. Classicism provided a natural transition from old Christian to modern architecture; Romanesque architecture was given attention predominantly in the Rhineland with its many structures from the Hohenstaufen period; Byzantine elements are occasionally found in France. Since historicism was a frequent topic of contemplation in the nineteenth century and since antiquity and medieval Christianity were not always considered opposites, it occasionally happened that one artist would make proposals using both styles for one and the same church (e.g., Sacré Coeur, Paris). There were also attempts to harmonize the principles of several styles.

This eclectic principle had a unique kind of ethos, which became especially effective in the second half of the century. The blending of several styles in ecclesiastical architecture was seen as a simile for Christianity, embracing time and space. In secular architecture, it was considered an expression of the cosmopolitan tendency of the nineteenth century with its tremendous progress in the area of technology and with its radiant expansion in all scientific and humanistic disciplines, especially history.

Church Interiors

Similar tendencies can be observed in regard to church interiors of the nineteenth century which conformed to the liberal ecclesiastical regulations. An attempt was made to match the furnishings of the church with the historical style of the architecture. But in the first half of the century, contemporary art concepts were applied, for instance in the use of large frescoes that did not exist in the Nordic medieval Gothic. In this case, the insufficient archeological knowledge of the immobile and mobile furnishings of medieval churches as well as the intention to combine elements of the north and south may have played a role.

In the second half of the century, when architecture also began to copy old plans, the interior design appeared more and more orthodox, thanks to the old book collections and drawings published in the meantime. Numerous collections of medieval ecclesiastical treasures, obtained since the secularization, were created with the express goal of offering adequate models to the artisans. This was the foundation for many of our craft museums. One even began to follow the instructions of medieval treatises in order to make utensils and tools in the proper style.

In architecture, Romantic enthusiasm for the Middle Ages responded to secular and rational Classicism with a revival of the Gothic. Likewise, young painters from various countries reacted with new concepts to the aesthetic dogmas originating in antiquity which they had learned at the academies. They turned to the "divine" Raphael and the older Italian paintings of the quattrocento and trecento, to the Germans Dürer and Holbein, and to old German paintings. Subsequently, Johann Friedrich Overbeck (1789–1869) and similarly minded people founded a Saint Luke Fraternity (1809) in Vienna in opposition to the local academy. The society soon moved to Rome and settled in the isolated monastery Sant'Isidoro in voluntary monastic communion. They wanted to rejuvenate painting on the basis of religion. Because of their beards and long hair they were known in Rome as "Nazarenes." Like the poets and architects, many of them converted. Especially popular were motives in which medieval piety and the new concept of nature as a divine manifestation could be combined. The popular hermit theme of Caspar David Friedrich's gloomy pictures with monks and ruins, down to the last pictures at the end of the century combined nature and religion, historical contemplation and private worship. It should not be ignored that the general trend toward genre in the art of the nineteenth century included religious art. In spite of its sentimental or even trivial effect, it created a type of picture which, according to its function, can indeed be compared with the devotional paintings of the fourteenth century. Theological didacticism in church art was less prominent than sensitive private piety. The Nazarenes placed figurative Christian stories in the foreground, while in the Protestant north nature inspired religious devotion.

Not only thematic-iconographic preferences, but also those for a particular genre became recognizable. The monumental art of mural painting, which had disappeared from the churches during the period of Classicism, was revived again. They wanted to "fill the lonely chapels and high cathedrals with life" and so designed large sequences of frescoes with pictures of biblical stories.

The paintings of the Nazarenes soon fell below their original level of quality due to their increasing popularity. The impersonal schematicism of their composition and the flat brush technique conquered some of the art academies in Germany, but in view of the new movement of Realism around the middle of the century and later Impressionism, the Nazarenes found their art more and more limited to the often trivial problems of Christian utilitarian art. Likewise, in Italy, the *puristi,* comparable to the Nazarenes, had become academic and could not endure the new trends.

To be mentioned in France are Puvis de Chavannes (1824–1889), who painted

the great Genevieve series in the Pantheon in Paris (1874–1878). Puvis de Chavannes started a new style, which had an effect on the church art of the twentieth
century via French Post-Impressionism and Symbolism, represented primarily by
Maurice Denis (1870–1943). There are connections between Maurice Denis and
Father Desiderius Lenz (1832–1928), the founder of the art school in Beuron, and
the two symbolists Jan Toorop (1858–1928) and Jan Thorn-Prikker (1868–1932),
whose frescoes, mosaics, and glass paintings laid an important foundation, in
connection with a new church architecture, for the religious art of Expressionism.

The relationship between nineteenth century art and the new styles after 1900
in France can also be found in England, where Edward Burnes-Jones (1833–1898)
founded the Society of the Pre-Raphaelites, following the model of the Saint Luke
Fraternity of the Nazarenes and adopting many of their religious and moral principles as well. But in contrast to the Nazarenes, this community of artists, including
Millais, Hunt, Rossetti, and others, kept in touch with the progressive forces of its
time. They also adhered to the Nazarenes' ideals of national and religious restoration and often made use of sentimental and symbolic genre painting, but at the
same time they demanded "truth to nature" and were thus able to keep contact
with the basically secular Realism of the middle of the century. It became customary to paint outdoors and even in religious paintings precision of archeological
detail was demanded. William Holman Hunt (1827–1910), the most important
among the artists, went to Palestine for several years in order to familiarize himself with the location for his biblical pictures. The century of the exact sciences,
photography, and historical "truth" also challenged religious historical painting to
provide reliable information. "Not Christ, the supreme judge, but Jesus, the son
of the Jewess Maria" was to be represented. Even in the progressive nineteenth
century, the traces of the Pre-Raphaelites did not fade, in spite of the early dissolution of the Society, because at the same time their patrons John Ruskin and
William Morris pioneered the great art revolution of 1900 and ushered some of
the principles of the Pre-Raphaelite artists, such as craftsmanship and teamwork,
into the new era.

In Germany in the second half of the century, an area of church art arose that
was to have an effect in the future. Not unimpressed by the art of the Nazarenes,
but keeping an apparent distance, Desiderius Lenz had founded an art school in
the Benedictine monastery of Beuron. This school was intent on creating in the
monastic realm the liturgical unity of an artistically designed space, of music regen-
erated through the study of Gregorian sources, and of the devotional ceremony.
They wanted to replace the contemporary principle of *l'art pour l'art* with the
humble *l'art pour Dieux*. They were convinced that the stylization of artwork (primarily in abstract art, using "universal shapes" like the equilateral triangle) gave
the composition an air of sacred solemnity and quiet by suppressing the individual and allowing man to submerge himself in God. Intending to create "timeless"
art, they used elements from Byzantine art, from the mosaics of Ravenna, and
from Egyptian murals to produce the Maurus Chapel near Beuron (1868–1870),
the furnishings of the Emmaus monastery in Prague (since 1880), the furnishings
of the abbey of Maria Laach, populated again by Beuron in 1892, and the grave of
Saint Benedict and Saint Scholastica in the vault of Monte Cassino (1899–1913).
The contemporary interest in Art Nouveau, and also in the beginnings of the litur-

gical movement, the intense encounter of Maurice Denis and Desiderius Lenz, and their collaboration with Paul Verkade (1868–1946), as well as the last vestiges of the Pre-Raphaelites and the Dutch and Belgian symbolists created an art circle between 1880 and 1910 that was to become the basis for an artistic renewal in the twentieth century. The significance of the art school in Beuron lies, last but not least, in the fact that the church interior was not exclusively determined any longer by murals and glass paintings, as was the case in the previous century, where any other kind of design was considered a "craft" and entrusted to craftsmen's skills. This school subjected everything, even textiles, paraments, liturgical utensils, and furniture to one unifying design concept. This was a direction which the church art of the twentieth century carried on, paying particular attention to the vessel, which is so important for the liturgy.

With his strict rejection of all art in the style of Giotto, his rejection of all expressive phenomena of the past (El Greco), and of the present, Desiderius Lenz overextended himself, causing his former disciples in the twenties to disperse. Subsequently, polemical treatises appeared (as in the nineteenth century) which, in view of the broad framework of ecclesiastical regulations, turned against Expressionism in general and demanded a harmonic Naturalism, or accepted certain elements of the art form called "expressive," but which would not permit anything unusual or shocking. Finally, there were several advocates of absolute Expressionism who originated, in connection with the simultaneous renovation of church architecture, the truly modern features of church art. The appreciation of individual creative achievements provided the chance to entrust even non-Catholic artists with tasks related to church art.

In regard to sculpture and plastic art of the time in question, we have to say that it was bound to play a more important role than painting and that the creations of Thorwaldsen (1786–1844) and Dannecker (1758–1841) largely determined the conceptions of Christ. Through Neo-Gothic, the cathedral construction offices inspired a more thorough study of medieval sculpture of the thirteenth and fourteenth centuries, since the Cologne Cathedral, for example, required a number of new figures for its completion. The historical assessment of these masters, who also created tomb art, has not progressed very far due to the fact that they had to subject their work to the unity of the entire structure. Iconographically significant for furnishing Neo-Gothic churches in the nineteenth century with sculptures is the solution offered in the typological programs of the Middle Ages. Aside from characters of the Old Testament, those figures of the Passion and Salvation of Christ are preferred who impress in a special way through their human fate. Remarkable in regard to church sculpture is a certain phenomenon that occurs rarely in older art after the sixteenth century: large groups of several figures on an altar without any retable or frame, giving expression to the idea of the memorial, which was preferred by and characteristic of the nineteenth century.

New Art Forms

Around the turn of the century, an art revolution caused the rejection of historicism because not the traditional, but the "living" form was deemed more effective. This change occurred in church construction later than in secular architecture, because ecclesiastical resolutions and recommendations were continuing obstacles. Moreover, many worthy forms of past church architecture — like the semicircular apse, the basilican succession of steps, and extensive glass paintings — retained their fascination and continued to be frequent design elements.

A first indication of the change in attitude is the fact that the utility of the space used for the purposes of liturgy — for the celebration of the Eucharist for administering the sacraments and for preaching — always having been required by ecclesiastical decrees, was put more and more into the foreground after 1900. The statement, made frequently after 1896 by Cornelius Gurlitt, that the liturgy is the architect of the church, was taken up by the Protestants at the Second Church Architecture Convention (1906) in Dresden, which was connected with an exhibition of appropriate liturgical utensils. Gurlitt's idea also became the main motto of the simultaneous liturgical movement, which intended to increase the congregation's active participation in the liturgy. The consequences for church construction, especially for the spatial arrangement, were impressive, particularly since the new structures were usually community churches, while medieval church construction (a model for historicism) was essentially determined by monastic churches, in which the needs of the choir service prevailed and the question of the congregation's ability to see the ceremony (around the altar) and hear the oral part of the service, was never taken into consideration.

In accord with these tendencies of the liturgical movement was the simultaneous general architectural theory whose highest maxim required that justice be done to function, material, and construction. The same perspective of religious and artistic reform around the turn of the century evolved from the ability to understand and appreciate any kind of form, including the liturgy, as an organic entity; an ability that was furthered by the development of sensitivity and perceptual psychology in the second half of the nineteenth century. In regard to church architecture, the new maxims meant that quality and effectiveness of the final creation were no longer considered dependent on their approval by history. At first, the fixation on the Gothic style was criticized; later on, the slightest historical reminiscence fell victim to objection. The goal and the basis for evaluation are not the precise correspondence with the architectural model but, on the contrary, the impact of the new building materials of the advancing technological age on form and construction. Thus, the use of iron for support beams and ribbed vaults in the Church of Saint Eugene in Paris (1854–1855) or the use of a reinforced concrete framework in the Church of Saint Jean de Montmartre (begun 1894) were praised as progressive. accomplishments, even though the innovations in these basically Neo-Gothic churches came about principally for practical and financial reasons. Nevertheless, the abandonment of the exclusive use of raw stones was regretted.

This process of emancipation of formerly profane materials and related construction principles, which may no longer be obscured by traditional decorations, has not ceased yet, even though, as mentioned, the aftereffects of individual historical forms and formulae can still be observed. These allusions and reminders, however, turn into pliable elements in the hands of the individual architect who does not feel obligated any longer to the theological symbolism of the structure and its parts, but tries to transcend the material composition of the church by means of the individually designed form and to instill it with "sacred poetry" (R. Schwarz). The sacred character of the edifice is, therefore, created by the individual's sensitive interpretation of form. The natural conflict between ecclesiastical traditionalism, which does not allow, for example, "unusual" pictures and demands consideration of the *formae a traditione christiana receptae et artis sacrae leges,* and the individuality of the artist are thus resolved in favor of the artist, at least as long as his creation complies with the demands of the liturgy. Naturally, the new demands of the liturgy (in regard to church architecture: abolition of the choir rails and altar pieces, new seating arrangements for the congregation and relatively free ground plans, abolition of the multiplicity of altars and much more) was subject to the changes in theological concepts, which, in turn, are not independent of the general tendencies of the time. This opened up welcome opportunities for change to contemporary church architecture. However, this change, no longer encumbered by traditionalism, according to which the church structure belonged to the "external aspects of the liturgy," entailed threatening consequences for churches of the past which are still in use today and stand in high esteem as art works.

In church architecture, the new principles of architectural theory, as aforementioned, succeeded less swiftly than in secular architecture. An early example of the attempt to bring form "to life" is the continuing construction of a church in Barcelona which was begun in 1867 and was dedicated to the Holy Family, carried out by Antonio Gaudí (1852–1926).

Only after 1920 did Germany and France build churches that corresponded to the altered demands.

Since about 1960, new architects took their place who were likewise disciples of the aesthetic maxims of modern times, but who were not compelled by the same need for expression as were their predecessors, who had been imprinted with the spirit of the youth movement of 1919–1933. Moreover, the need and the capability for worship seem to have diminished as well.

The resolutions of the Second Vatican Council regarding Chapter VII of the liturgical constitution of 4 December 1963, which refrained from dependence on a certain historical sacred style (Article 123) and desired the structure to be an "external aspect of the liturgy," "dignified and functional" (Art. 128), confirm what has been in existence for a long time and is possibly facing another change even now.

Teaching and Theology

Chaps. 64–68: Oskar Köhler
Chap. 69: Bernard Stasiewski

CHAPTER 64

The Encyclical *Aeterni Patris*

The encyclical *Aeterni Patris* of 4 August 1879 was not just a specific doctrine about the philosophical and theological orientation of Catholic schools, but also the foundation of the entire program that Leo XII wanted to pursue in his pontificate. One can easily refer all subsequent doctrines and activities to this document. Otto Willmann called this encyclical the "ripe fruit of spontaneous regeneration attempts"; it reiterated earlier efforts to continue not just any form of medieval Scholasticism, but specifically to revive the philosophy of Thomas Aquinas. However, the encyclical did, indeed, initiate a philosophical movement whose most important representatives were able to revive Aquinas as one of the greatest thinkers of Hellenic-Occidental philosophy. To follow the encyclical and refer to Thomas Aquinas himself required tedious historical research. But philosophical thought itself also had to internalize the true work of Aquinas, that is, to include it in the philosophical process. Thus, the encyclical *Aeterni Patris* contains two aspects: It speaks from tradition, but this tradition must be revived in order to be able to do justice to the problems of the modern world.

The heading of the encyclical reads: *De philosophia christiana ad mentem sancti Thomae Aquinatis Doctoris angelici in scholis catholicis instauranda.* Of this "Christian philosophy" and its creator, Thomas Aquinas (died 1274), Pope Innocent VI, six hundred years later, is quoted as having said: Aside from its "canonical doctrine," this philosophy distinguished itself from all others by its peculiar vocabulary, its *modus docendi,* and its truthfulness, so that those who followed it never left the path of truth, and those who rejected it became suspect (*de veritate suspectus*). Thomas alone (*unus*) succeeded in overcoming all errors of previous times and in providing "invincible weapons" to combat future ones. This school was replaced by the method of a "a certain new way of philosophy" (*nova quaedam philosophiae ratio),* which, however, did not have the desired effect. Instead, philosophical directions have increased to a large extent, causing doubt and finally errors. Even Catholic philosophers, eager to imitate, have fallen victim to this revival mania, instead of replenishing the "inheritance of ancient wisdoms." This does not exclude making use of the treasure of new thoughts in order to perfect this philosophy (*novorum inventorum opes ad excolendam philosophiam).* Later, in regard to natural sciences, Innocent VI said that the Scholastics had learned that human intelligence could only be elevated to the capacity of knowing spiritual beings by way of the sensible world; they had also studied nature with great interest, as Albertus Magnus proved. This and statements by natural scientists themselves allow the conclusion that Scholastic philosophy has nothing to counter it. The *artes belles* and the *artes liberales* also are at home in this philosophy.

By reviving the philosophy of Thomas Aquinas, the encyclical claims to offer a universal solution to all problems of the modern world, last but not least for social problems: Whatever Thomas Aquinas taught concerning the true nature of freedom and the divine origin of authority possessed an "invincible power" to overcome those principles of the "new law" (i.e., revolution) which harm order and public welfare. Scholastic philosophy could be the remedy because Thomas Aquinas differentiated properly between reason and faith and at the same time, combined the two in "friendship" and because he perfected reason to the utmost degree, so that it could not easily be improved. From this, the encyclical concludes, the rationalists could be led to faith against their resistance, provided they were taught the highest rationality of Thomistic philosophy. "Aside from the supernatural assistance of God," nothing is as effective against error as this philosophy.

The encyclical clearly differentiates between the philosophy of Thomas Aquinas and that phase of Scholasticism in which the philosophers proceeded *nimia subtilitate,* referring to the period of decline of the *disputatio.* The encyclical suggests that the wisdom of Thomas Aquinas be drawn from other sources. But the development of Thomistic philosophy is described as a totally continuous process, leading smoothly from the old Christian apologists via Augustine to culmination in Aquinas, to whom we must return. Modern questions should be incorporated and the doctrine should be refined, but the intellectual world was perfected in the thirteenth century (in a classical sense). *Aeterni Patris* refers to everything, to society and politics, to the natural sciences and aesthetics; however, it leaves out the problem of history, as contemporary Neo-Scholasticism generally continued to do. It is remarkable that the famous historian of Scholasticism, Franz Ehrle, in his commentary on *Aeterni Patris* (his first great work), should present the historical development toward Thomas Aquinas as uninterrupted progress (in accord with the encyclical); later, however, when dealing with the subsequent fate of Thomas' work and the history of Scholasticism, he expressed his historical appreciation for the pro and con of the struggle, no matter how Thomas, as the *princeps,* is evaluated. Ehrle emphasized most of all that the older Spanish Scholastics of the sixteenth century were "for the most part intelligent, independent scholars, not inclined for reasons of mere piety to close themselves to the challenges of good arguments, and far removed from the kind of devotion which was to become characteristic of the newer Dominican school after Báñez." It should be noted that the interests of the order were involved in this matter; yet this commentary from 1880 shows that the Thomistic renascence was interpreted as a historical, creative process, not as a classical copy. By commissioning the edition of St. Thomas (*Editio Leonina*), appearing since 1882, Leo XIII earned significant and everlasting credit in the field of historical Thomas scholarship. Unfortunately, understanding Thomas as an entity removed from his historical context (which later led to canonical regulation regarding the instruction in Catholic schools) partly prohibited a philosophical and thus a real acquisition of Aquinas.

Following the *Constitutio de fide catholica* of the First Vatican Council, the significance of true philosophy for theology was strongly emphasized. This is evident in the title of the encyclical *De philosophia christiana*. Quoting Clement of Alexandria, the encyclical states that the doctrine of the Savior, being God's wisdom and in and of itself perfect, can not acquire more force through Greek philosophy, but by means of the proper philosophy the truth of the revelation could be defended. Moreover, it maintains that the use of philosophy compelled theology to attain the character, the appearance, and the spirit of a true science (*requiritur philosophiae usus, ut sacra Theologia naturam, habitum, ingeniumque verae scientiae suscipiat atque induat*). This feature of theology is based mainly on the fact that the Neo-Scholasticism of the period when the encyclical was written arrived at theology via philosophy, causing Neo-Scholastic theology to be largely characterized by the application of the terminological tools of the Neo-Scholastic philosophy, at least until Biblical theology forced its way in the course of the twentieth century.

Stubbornly and energetically, Leo XIII implemented his encyclical. On 18 January 1880, he ordered Cardinals A. de Luca, Simeoni, and Zigliara, O.P., to undertake the editing of the works of Aquinas, as well as the commentaries by Cajetan (1507–22), who was (even by Neo-Scholastics) considered the definite expositor of Thomas, thus making it difficult to dispute his authority by using Thomas himself. In May of the same year, under the presidency of Giuseppe Pecci, the Pope's brother, the Accademia Romana di San Tommaso was opened and well funded in order to enable it to educate the next generation. The foundation became the model for the Catholic world. Leo XIII emphatically supported the theologians of his program. In 1884, at papal request, the University of Louvain established a teaching chair for Thomistic philosophy, which was first occupied by D. Mercier, and developed one of the most important centers of creative Neo-Scholasticism. In Piacenza in 1880, the periodical *Divus Thomas* began a series of new Thomistic publications: the *Philosophisches Jahrbuch der Görres-Gesellschaft* (1888), *Pastor Bonus* (Trier 1888), *Revue Thomiste* (Paris 1893), *Revue néo-scolastique de philosophie* (Louvain 1894), *Rivista di filosofia neo-scolastica* (Milan 1909). There were plenty of channels for a Thomas renascence.

CHAPTER 65

Neo-Thomism, Neo-Scholasticism, and the "New Philosophers"

The necessary conceptual differentiation between "Neo-Scholasticism" and "Neo-Thomism" indicates that Scholastic-systematic philosophy and theology in the Catholic Church of the nineteenth century and also during Leo XIII's pontificate do not represent a monolith, as most of the publications seem to suggest. However, they often simply claim to be written *ad mentem S. Thomae Aquinatis.* But the traditions of Duns Scotus (especially with the Franciscans) and of Suárez (especially with the Jesuits) continue to thrive. There is also a difference between the often sterile letter-bound Neo-Thomism ("Paleothomism" [Steenbergen]) and the attempts of those, in the minority though they were, to proceed not formally from Thomas and thereby deduce the actualizing conclusions but rather to reverse the process and return to the great tradition of a real live questioning of contemporary problems. The picture becomes much more variegated if one considers that the other great (and older) tradition of Catholic thought, leading from Augustine via Bonaventura to Pascal, had not died out, even though those men who lived in it, as for example Maurice Blondel, could cause conflicts if they were not willing to subordinate the great father of the Church Augustine to the now dominant doctrine by quoting him occasionally. However, it took time to recover the entire wealth of tradition and thus the freedom to philosophize in the Catholic Church.

In Rome itself, the encyclical was unable to give rise to a Neo-Thomism which could be compared to the significance of Matteo Liberatore. This is partially due to the difficulties of changing the current school traditions, partially to the tendency of formally arguing with Aquinas' authority, and to not taking modern philosophy and science seriously. The influential Jesuit Camillo Mazzella advocated in his extensive treatise a Suárezian Scholasticism (Grabmann). G. Cornoldi, who participated in the founding of the Accademia Romana di San Tommaso, fought against the disciples of Rosmini, charging them with a "synthesis of ontologism and pantheism," a dispute which, in 1887, in conjunction with the political problem of the "Roman question," brought about the ecclesiastical censure of forty of Rosmini's propositions. Two years before the encyclical on Thomas, the Collegio di S. Bonaventura was established in Quaracchi (Florence). There, the works of the Franciscan Doctor of the Church (since 1588) were published and an international research center was developed. This did more to overcome a stagnation of philosophical-theological tradition than narrow-minded anti-Thomist polemics.

In Germany and Austria, Neo-Thomism also had numerous, often rather belligerent representatives who contributed a great deal to the failure of the intention underlying Leo XIII's encyclical. Matthias Joseph Scheeben (1835–88), by far superior to the theologians of his generation, was an unusually open-minded spirit and a deeply devout dogmatist from the Rhineland. He left a gap in this period in Germany which will never be closed. It is questionable whether Scheeben, who incorporated post-Tridentine theology and the Tübingen school as well as Neo-Thomism into his creative, original, and modern work, should be included in

"Neo-Scholasticism." But excluding him from this category would mean isolating him in a manner which is not in accord with the movement as a whole. It would mean presenting "the theology of the past as a multiplicity of efforts exerted by devout thinkers" (J. Höfer). Many of Scheeben's main works had already been published long before *Aeterni Patris,* penetrating an area of action that had been inspired by the encyclical among groups who did not interpret the letter as a request for "repristination." When Scheeben was completely himself, "he thought, like no other Neo-Scholastic, purely from faith and 'unapologetically,'" (K. Eschweiler) from the "childlike faith" (Scheeben) which was to him the perfection of religious belief. This, of course, did not comply with the kind of conclusion theology which dominated Neo-Scholasticism. The "double form" of theology — devotion and intellectual agreement — remained a problem for Scheeben, which he faced through the influence of Kleutgen and Schäzler.

With the exception of Scheeben, all German Neo-Scholastics of that period are outranked in significance by the scholars of medieval Scholasticism (Franz Ehrle, Heinrich Denifle, Clemens Baeumker, and Martin Grabmann), whose early activities still belong in this period. The Dominican Denifle from Tyrol (1844–1905) and the Jesuit Ehrle from the Allgänu (1845–1934) collaborated (after 1880 in Rome) in the publication of the *Archiv für Literatur und Kirchengeschichte des Mittelalters:* from 1885 until 1900 seven volumes of "eternal value" (Grabmann). Denifle deserves special credit regarding mysticism (Eckhart, Tauler, Suso), and Ehrle demonstrated with his scholarship and editions the variety of Scholastic thought. The historian of philosophy Baeumker showed the connection between Scholasticism and Moslem philosophy and called attention to the continued existence of Platonism, which he demonstrated in his main work on Witelo (1908) and his metaphysics of light in the thirteenth century. Now the stage was set for an extensive study of the Scholastic method, which was presented by Grabmann (1875–1945). Included in this group of scholars is the Belgian Maurice De Wulf (1867–1947), a pupil of Désiré Mercier, who founded the collection *Les Philosophes belges* (Louvain 1901ff). Even though the Neo-Scholastic systematists initially ignored these efforts, they kept the Thomistic renascence from stagnating into a classicism.

In France, most of the Neo-Thomists, strictly following the Gregoriana, did not go beyond their sterile disputations. An exception was the *Institut catholique* in Paris where Maurice d'Hulst seized upon Duilhé's idea of trying to avoid spiritual provincialism and to prove the productiveness of the Neo-Thomist method by holding international congresses for Catholic scholars. In this respect, the spirit of the center took effect where this particular period succeeded in an actual encounter with Thomas Aquinas: the spirit of the University of Louvain and Mercier (1851–1926). This scholar from Brabant, after studying philosophy and theology, became interested in psychiatry, which had an impact on the curriculum which Mercier taught after 1882 in his position as professor or Thomist philosophy, which had been created by the Belgian episcopate at Leo XIII's request. The thirty-one-year-old professor fascinated his students, including nontheologians, with the decisiveness with which he responded to the ultimate questions posed by the natural sciences, and with his efforts to "philosophize for one's contemporaries." Of course, his extensive use of psychology raises the question whether this approach is appropriate for Thomist ontology. However, Mercier tried most of all to come to terms with Positivism, so popular those days, and he was just as interested in it as he was in Kant's philosophy. He was intent, however, on preserving theology's independence relative to philosophy. The *Institut supérieur de philosophie,* established in 1889, was the result of a proposal by Mercier to Leo XIII in 1887. Mercier was also its first president. The *Revue néo-scolastique,* founded in 1894, achieved international repute.

The picture of a united front does not entirely match the reality of Neo-Scholasticism. This is evidenced by the effort in regard to Bonaventure, the rather aggressively defended positions of Suárezianism which the Jesuits (often somewhat artificially) tried to coordinate with Thomism, and Scotism to which the Franciscans were devoted. Such differences were still confined to Neo-Scholasticism. However, within the tradition of occidental thinking, attempts were made by individuals (consequently isolated people) to break, so to speak, the anthropocentric concept of the world from the inside and to prove the terminologically absolute opposite of immanence and transcendence to be an apparent opposite by using the argument of concrete existence. This resulted in a dispute with strangely inverted fronts: These philosophical theorems are based on the Christian mystery of Incarnation and on the belief in the support of the Holy Spirit, even though they were clearly philosophical or, at least, intended to be. They were rejected by the Neo-Scholastics as "modernistic" and categorized under different, hostile "isms." Neo-Scholastic philosophy and theology, on the other hand, often contained a goodly measure of rationalism, which could only seemingly be brought in tune with the Christian belief in revealed religion. These disputations often entailed quite subjective assessments of Neo-Scholastic efforts. The German theologian and religious philosopher Herman Schell taught that "in the acknowledgement of the Holy Spirit as the essential manifestation of Deity the principle of immanence and the idea of transcendence are intimately linked and the intrinsic worldliness of action is combined in superior harmony with the nontemporal power of creation." Rejecting any form of pantheism, Schell developed an image of God as "being completely in Himself and of Himself." He did not believe that the dynamics of this image could be grasped by the terminology of academic tradition. Thus he conceived the term God as *causa sui,* which he later (after being put on the Index) replaced with "self-reality," without terminologically relinquishing the actuality of God and His being active-in Himself. This concept of God was the foundation of Schell's personalism: In God's living personality rests all human personality. This Augustinian tradition was transmitted by German Idealism, while the philosophy of Maurice Blondel (1861–1949) was supported by Blaise Pascal, who survived in the background of French philosophical life, and by Nicolas de Malebranche, who influenced Leibniz. One of Leibniz's key problems was the topic of Blondel's first and fundamental work: the *Vinculum substantiale.* Blondel's basic philosophical theme dealt with the attempt "to overcome the static and concrete concept of substance and to define substance both as a unifying force and as a metaphysical entity," thus evading Idealism as well as the all too material Realism. Blondel's philosophy tried to solve the problem of transcendence by integrating the triple reality of life, of thought, and of being in existence. In contrast to objectivism, Blondel believes knowledge and existential revelation to be tied to subjectivity. He does not accept the opposition of immanence and transcendence, but rather finds them unified in "action" (existential realization), from which immanence automatically reaches out toward transcendence. The "supernatural" in the Christian message is not an *extrinsécism,* something which approaches human reality like a stranger from the outside, rather it corresponds to reality, and is thus logically necessary, even if this logic does not say anything about the freedom of divine revelation and the freedom of human acceptance of it.

Blondel's teacher was L. Ollé-Laprune (1839–1898), professor in Aix-en-Provence from 1896 to his death, who from 1875 on had taught philosophy at the École normale supérieure in Paris as a disciple of Malebranche: The conflict between faith and knowledge can only be overcome in personal experience, which is inaccessible to dialectic analysis.

Both the initiative to revive the Thomism that was inspired by Leo XIII and that was productive in significant ways, as well as the efforts of these "new philosophers" have to be seen in context, in spite of their opposition to Neo-Scholasticism, if one intends to obtain a historically adequate picture of the sincerity of the philosophers and theologians of those decades and of their efforts regarding the intellectual conditions under which the Christian faith can be experienced and justified in the modern world.

C H A P T E R   6 6

The Theory of Church History

The "almost turbulent expansion and specialization of Church history" (H. Jedin) corresponds to the general interest in history, developing in the last third of the nineteenth century and continuing into, the twentieth. Prerequisite for research was the publication of new sources of Church history in which secular institutes participated. Following the extensive editions of A. Theiner of Silesia (1855 — 70 prefect of the Vatican Archives), and after Leo XIII opened the Archives to scholars in general in 1881, a new era began. The prefect at the time, Cardinal (after 1879) J. Hergenröther, had considerable difficulties solving the technical problems of using the Archives. The rules of 1878 and 1888 regarding the use of the Vatican Library were helpful, as was its significant expansion after 1890 through the Borghese and the Barberini Libraries. In 1895 the medievalist Franz Ehrle (1922 cardinal) was appointed prefect. The opening of the Vatican Archives, which was followed by the founding of a series of national historical institutes in Rome was one of the most important moments for the rich deployment of editions and books on Church history.

As is the case in all aspects of life, history has to inquire about the relationship which Catholicism had established in regard to this academic discipline since its introduction to the modern world during Leo XIII's pontificate. The superficial debate concerning historical "objectivity," which many Catholic authors at that time felt compelled to discuss in their forewords, had no theoretical basis after G. Droysen's *Historik,* which in the meantime was rendered obsolete especially since its advocates from the nineteenth century could be proven guilty of a natural subjectivity of their own. But just how problematic the Catholic study of history could be is shown by a remark made in 1889 by the influential apologist A. M. Weiß, O.P. He justified the fact that the textbooks of Church history still consti-tuted an extreme minority compared to the systematic theological textbooks by asserting that "this fact is in accord with the nature of this matter. For us, exe-gesis and the description of the traditional doctrines of faith and morals are the essential elements in theology. History can only be granted the rank of an ancillary science." The historical-theological thought of the Tübingen school was replaced by the essentially ahistorical Neo-Scholasticism. The question remains whether and in what respect "the world" could be conceived "as history." It was not a question of selecting the documents, but rather of the futility of letting the sources themselves speak. "Historical understanding" was the new hallmark of histori-cal studies. Janssen had a better comprehension of this understanding than the otherwise much more important papal historian Ludwig Pastor (1854–1928), who was "seized by the material aspect to such an extent that he continued to work" on his sixteen-volume *Geschichte der Päpste seit dem Ausgang des Mittelalters* (first volume 1886) "undisturbed by all intellectual developments around him, and unconcerned about the changes in historical theories." "Negating the historical development, he unfolded a detailed concept of the centralistic Church and pa-pacy and projected it on the past" (C. Bauer). This endeavor separated him later in Innsbruck from the general development of German Catholicism, but it endeared. him to the Rome of Pius X (less that of Leo XIII), where he exerted considerable influence on the ecclesiastical personnel policy in Germany and Austria.

Leo XIII did not grow tired of including in his letters and encyclicals rather lengthy passages about Church history and especially the history of his predeces-sors and their service to the Western World. In the brief *Saepenumero* of 18 August 1883, he explained what he expected from the historians: a defense against ac-counts of the papacy written in *mendaci colon.* He trusted that the *incorrupta rerum gestarum monumenta,* if studied without prejudice, would successfully defend the Church and the papacy *per se ipsa.* With special regard to Italy, he called to mind the papacy's achievements during the time of the barbarian mi-grations, in the struggle against the medieval Emperors, and in the Turkish Wars. He also mentioned the preservation of Roman and Greek literature by the popes and the clergy. The Pope spoke with conviction when he said in 1884 "Non abbi-amo paura della pubblicità dei documenti," scornfully calling the sceptics around him "small minds." But, as a sharp observer noticed, Leo XIII could only say this because he did not understand the "historical method" (P. M. Baumgarten). It is completely erroneous to judge this as a "gap" in Leo XIII's education. In spite of the complex quality of his personality, there was no room for historical thinking. In Leo XIII's opinion, the first law for writing history demands that nothing false be said, furthermore, that the truth not be hidden, and, lastly, that any suspicion of either favoritism or hostility be avoided. But in view of indeed widespread hostility toward the Church and particularly the papacy, he presented these principles an apologetic context which permeated all of *Saepenumero.*

German Catholicism lost its edge in the area of critical historical method after the conflict with Ignaz von Döllinger, even though certain scholars tried to continue the historical method. The fundamental deliberation of these issues took place in France, because there the problem of the relation between revelation and history was debated by including the "Biblical question" and the history of dogma.

Charles de Smedt, S.J. (1864–76 professor of Church history at the Jesuit College in Louvain, 1882–1911 president of the Bollandists), developed certain principles of philological criticism which were used by his tremendously successful collaborator (after 1891) H. Delehaye, S.J. Per se, these principles were not problematic, even though de Smedt had to defend them, presenting them in his work *Principes de la critique historique* (Liège 1883) in the perspective of the total problem. However, Louis Duchesne (1843–1922), the famous Church historian and professor at the Institut Catholique in Paris from 1877 to 1885, got into a critical situation with his lectures on the history of dogma, creating debate and painful consequences. In 1895, he became the director of the École française de Rome. In 1882, Abbé Rambouillet attacked Duchesne for his theory of the development of the dogma. Duchesne's response was supported by Maurice d'Hulst. While universal inerrancy was the issue of the "biblical question," historical change was the problem in regard to the history of dogma. Billot rejected even the term itself. The debate, which continued into the crisis of modernism, included in its arguments the famous essay by John Henry Newman dealing with the personal tradition of faith in history, in contrast to the unfortunate concept of Vincent of Lérins, which is purely biological and develops an "unhistorical theory of tradition" (J. Ratzinger). Joseph Tixeront, after 1881 professor of the seminary of Lyon, carefully furthered the method of his teacher Duchesne. Pierre Batiffol (1861–1929), a friend of Albert Lagrange and patronized by Duchesne, studied early Christian history in Rome and became rector of the Institut Catholique in Toulouse in 1898, a position which he had to relinquish in 1907 after his book about the Eucharist (1905) was put on the Index. In his *Études d'histoire et de théologie positive* (1902), he had attempted a theoretical solution to the problem. In Germany, the problem was ignored.

Because of the methodological specialization, several disciplines were singled out from general Church history, such as patrology, a large area which, after the Vatican Council, was put aside for the time being along with the history of councils. However, with few exceptions, the history of dogma within Catholic theology was unable to divorce itself from dogmatics. This circumstance is significant for the condition of Church history as a whole. The fundamental problem was, on the one hand, to overcome an ahistorical concept of tradition implying Church historiographical positivism, and on the other hand, to avoid falling victim to relativistic historicism. The largely methodical critical work of Church historians regarding editions and research during Leo XIII's pontificate set the scene for a theoretical solution of the problem of Church history.

CHAPTER 6 7

The Question of the Bible

While the Protestant Bible societies in Germany, England, and the United States developed with increased activity at the beginning of the nineteenth century, the efforts toward a Catholic biblical movement were suppressed and pastoral use of Holy Scripture fell behind the Scholastic question-and-answer catechism. Readings of the Epistle and Gospel during Sunday Mass were generally bilingual, which was of less significance if they were considered part of the "pre-Mass" and had no relation to the sermon. "Biblical history," which was introduced to religious instruction in Germany and generated a great deal of familiarity with the Holy Scriptures, had a continuing impact in that country.

Both the position of Holy Scripture in everyday religious and pastoral life and the position of biblical studies in Catholic theology have the same origin: "Since the Reformation, Catholic theology in general and biblical studies in particular considered their foremost task to be confrontation with Protestant theology" (A. Wikenhauser) This resulted in the dilemma of whether biblical studies, in accord with the Catholic idea of the Church, were "to play a role inferior to" that of theology. It is part of the Catholic self-awareness that the First Vatican Council reiterated the Tridentine decree regarding the use of the Holy Scripture, requiring that the ecclesiastical teaching authority had the exclusive right to decide on the "true meaning" and interpretation. However, this purely negative definition did not exactly encourage the desire for biblical research, regardless of conflicts. This is demonstrated by a glance at the bibliographies relating to biblical studies at that time, when Catholic works represented a clear minority, not to mention their quality. This situation intensified in proportion to the phase difference between the defensive attitude of the teaching authority (which was understandable in view of the radical biblical criticism of David Friedrich Strauß[died 1874], Bruno Bauer [died 1882], Ernest Renan [died 1892], and others) as contrasted to the development of biblical studies according to principles about which everyone is in agreement nowadays.

Among the Bible translations in German-speaking countries, Joseph Franz von Allioli's, published between 1830 and 1832, was able to maintain its leading position throughout the nineteenth century and beyond. It follows the Vulgate "with reference to the basic text." The French translation by Jean-Baptiste Glaire was also based on the Vulgate. It was later incorporated by Fulcrain Vigouroux (1837–1915) into his *Bible polyglotte* (Paris 1897–1909). The translation of the original texts by C. Crampon gained in significance (NT 1885, OT 1894–1904). The efforts to approach the original texts by using handwritten manuscripts, i.e., philological-critical Bible editions, causing research to progress swiftly in the last third of the nineteenth century, were made almost exclusively by Protestant scholars. A "decisive impact" on the stimulation of biblical studies in France was accredited to the Sulpician Vigouroux, whose *Manuel Biblique* appeared between 1879 and 1890. His *Bible polyglotte* (8 volumes, in Hebrew, Greek, Latin Vulgate, and French) is derived from the Protestant *Bielefelder Polyglotte*. Vigouroux was totally occupied with the battle against biblical criticism and he fought it in every way possible.

Of prominent influence in German-speaking areas was the exegete F. P. Kaulen from Bonn (1827–1907). He was especially interested in the history of the Vulgate (1868), emphasizing this text as the "valid expression of biblical revelation" and describing the edition of the Benedictines of Tournai (1885) as "almost without errors." Like Kaulen, almost all exegetical collaborators of the Church lexicon took an extremely conservative viewpoint.

The participation of Catholic exegetes in historical-literary biblical criticism was closely related to the concept of inspiration. Lenormant's attempt to limit the correctness of the Bible to dogmatic and moral statements failed, as did the complex undertaking of Salvatore di Bartolo to differentiate between facts, which are an integral part of dogma and ethics, and incidental, possibly erroneous data. Statements of "profane truth" in the Bible were usually considered nonerroneous, even though, in regard to the six-day creation, it was conceded that there was "no need for clinging anxiously to the letter of the text." However, in cases where an undeniable error could be noted in regard to "perfectly certain facts of natural history, geology, and chronology," the explanation had to suffice that the inspired original text had been perverted in the course of tradition. A fundamental problem existed in the Holy Scriptures regarding the relationship between God, the inspiring "author," and the human author. The Neo-Scholastic theologian Johann Baptist Franzelin, S.J., in his *De divina traditione et scriptura* (1870) defined the term "inspiration" so broadly that in fact, in accord with tradition, only the verbal inspiration was excluded. This theory dominated the textbooks to the end of the nineteenth century. In the middle of the nineties began the kind of criticism that was especially advocated by the Dominicans with reference to Thomas Aquinas. To avoid mixing revelation itself with the process of inspiration, there were attempts to define the latter as a *motion inspiratrice,* thus expanding the freedom of the writer. But the Jesuit theologians continued to adhere to their theory of inspiration. The work *De inspiratione* (Rome 1903) by Louis Billot, S.J., one of the most influential theologians (from 1885 to 1911 professor at the Gregoriana), opposed the modernistic exegesis, but also the efforts of scholarly biblical studies by authors who stayed within the ecclesiastical tradition. However, it was precisely the inspiration of the Bible on the whole that motivated critical Catholic exegetes to discover the "true 'literal meaning' " of the Bible. This, however, put them for a long time in the extremely difficult position of vacillating between liberal biblical criticism and general ecclesiastical traditionalism.

The defense of Alfred Loisy's first writings by Maurice d'Hulst (1841–96), rector of the Institut catholique in Paris, where Loisy was a member of the faculty, in his article "La question biblique," which appeared in 1893 in *Correspondant,* caused a severe controversy, which was also carried on by the daily press. D'Hulst tried, according to his character — he was a monarchist, opponent of the *Ralliement* and in terms of church policy a liberal — to bridge the differences and to define in regard to the Bible question a "middle-of-the-road school," from where he was trying to mediate between the *école étroite* (the thesis of the equal inspiration of the Bible) and the *école large,* which he defined similarly to the attempts by Salvatore di Bartolo. Opposition came from all sides.

In November of the same year, the encyclical *Providentissimus Deus* appeared, stating that the defense against the rationalistic enemies of Holy Scripture, the "sons and heirs" of the Reformation, was especially urgent, since there are some men among them who want to be known as Christian theologians. It is an unreliable approach to overcome "difficulties" by admitting that the inspiration only referred to questions of faith and morals; such interpretations originate from the erroneous opinion that the primary goal is the discovery of why God said a certain thing. Referring to the Council of Trent and the Vatican Council the encyclical states that the "authentic parts" of the Bible do not contain any errors. Positively, the letter demands that biblical studies, *ad temporum necessitates congruentius,* be furthered carefully but decisively. The improvement of the Vulgate is encouraged by a quotation from Augustine. To determine the meaning, the encyclical suggests consulting, aside from parallel passages, the findings of related sciences; Eastern studies are to be strengthened. The exegeses of the Church Fathers, including the allegorical ones, are to be respected, which does not exclude *ultra procedere.* It is wrong to prefer the studies of "heterodox scholars," even though they may be useful at times; however, the untainted meaning cannot be found outside of the Church. The *Critica sublimior,* which judges parts of the Scriptures according to "internal motives" is rejected; only the *historiae testimonia* is important. One passage of the encyclical was particularly interesting to those who interpreted it for the purpose of finding assistance. Here, a quotation of Thomas' regarding questions of natural science serves to express the idea that the sacred author followed physical phenomena, similar to popular speech. In regard to historical problems, the encyclical reiterates the thesis that errors are the fault of the copyists; moreover, the original meaning of a passage could remain ambiguous. Also, the phrase stating that the Holy Spirit inspired and motivated (*excitavit et movit*) the biblical writer was interpreted to indicate a theory of inspiration which favors the human collaborator.

The encyclical found practically no opposition among Catholic theologians, but it was still short of solving the problems. The necessary effort made to agree with the encyclical resulted in artistic interpretations. But this raised the decisive question: What was the historical place and time when inspiration struck the biblical authors? This was the point of departure from which the historical positivism in the arguments of the "error debate" had to be overcome. It was unfortunate that the term *vérité relative,* which can be correctly understood and was used to replace the term historical or scientific "error," met with the twilight of modern relativism. In this regard, the "quotation theory," according to which a biblical author sums up other texts, was an expedient in view of the unsolved question of inspiration. This and other theories, also used by Lagrange and Hummelauer, were solidified into a system by the French Jesuit Ferdinand Prat (1857–1938). The Jesuits Delattre and Fonck, who rejected this theory, pursued with particular vehemence the Dominican Lagrange, who had studied Eastern cultures in Vienna from 1888 until 1890 and had founded the *École Biblique* in Jerusalem by request of his order. Lagrange planned to make his series of monographs, the *Revue Biblique* (1892) and the *Études Bibliques* (1903), to be scholarly-critical as well as Church-minded. A fateful trial for Lagrange was his occupation with chapters 1–6 of Genesis (published in manuscript form, Paris 1906) and especially the Pentateuch. He followed his principles of the "historical method" and was convinced that it was no longer possible to hold the opinion that Moses had composed the

whole Pentateuch, as we know it; that while the antiquity of the Ten Commandments in their substance and their proclamation by Moses be adhered to, the
Pentateuch be differentiated according to various editorial levels, of which a large
part is younger than Moses. Lagrange's importance is substantiated by the fact that
he is one of the few older exegetes who is still quoted in basic scholarship. However, at that time he encountered the bitter animosities of the Jesuits, and even the
Dominican order no longer authorized his refutation, written in defense against
the attacks by A. Delattre, S.J., *Éclaircissement sur la Méthode historique* (1905,
only published in manuscript form). He suffered the most painful blow when his
order requested his withdrawal from the exegesis of the Old Testament. Another
important center for similar efforts was the University of Louvain, where the Old
Testament scholar A. van Hoonacker had started a course in 1889 called "Histoire
critique l'Ancien Testament." His significant book *Le sacerdoce lévitique dans la
Loi et dans l'histoire* (1899) won him European recognition. His work about the
Hexateuch, written in Latin, was not published (Bruges 1949) until after the encyclical *Divino afflante Spiritu* (1943). Among the founders of the *Cursus scripturae
sanctae*, a collection of commentaries published after 1888 and not finished; the
most outstanding of them was the Jesuit Franz von Hummelauer (1842–1914),
who deserves special recognition for his serious definition of literary genres and
who proceeded from the conviction that "every (literary) genre possesses its very
own unique truth, which is the only thing we are justified in demanding from it."

When revising the regulations of the Index, the apostolic constitution *Officiorum ac munerum* of 25 January 1897 declared that, according to experience,
translations of Holy Scripture edited by Catholics in the language of the people
usually do more damage than good, as long as distinctions were not made (*sine
discrimine*). Therefore it was decreed that these Bibles contain *adnotationes* from
the Fathers or Catholic scholars. In 1902, the Society of Saint Jerome for the Propagation of the Holy Gospel was founded. Its chairman, Giacomo della Chiesa, was
a member of the Curia from 1887 to 1907 and later became Pope Benedict XV. In
the first year, one hundred eighty thousand copies of the New Testament were
sold in Italy. On 30 October 1902, the apostolic letter *Vigilantiae* was issued, on
the basis of which the Pontifical Biblical Commission was established, so that
the studies might be conducted *auspicio ductuque Sedis Apostolicae* and new
problems, not covered by doctrine, be solved according to ecclesiastical norms.
The intention to safeguard during disputes the "limits of mutual love" could be
sufficiently realized. Members of the Commission were the Cardinals Rampolla,
Parocchi, Satolli, Segna, and Vives y Tutó. Two of the secretaries were the very
conservative Vigouroux and the Franciscan Fleming, who had an open mind for
exegetical problems. Leo's plan was oriented toward mediation, which is shown
by the fact that the *Revue biblique* was originally intended to be the organ of
the Commission. The forty consultants comprised an international committee, to
which men like Lagrange, Prat, and Hummelauer were appointed. The intention
of the founders was supervision (to preserve the faith) but also the support of
truly scholarly studies. However, the question was whether the optimistic words
which the Pope addressed to d'Hulst and which were recorded by Baudrillart
would have an impact.

CHAPTER 68

The Condemnation of "Americanism"

The term and theory of "Americanism" originated in French academic circles. This is the reason for the content of the papal letter *Testem benevolentiae* of 22 January 1899, addressed to Cardinal Gibbons, which condemned "opinions, the sum of which some call 'Americanism.' " In 1897, Walter Elliot's biography of the founder of the Paulists, Isaac Hecker (1819–88), which appeared in 1891, was published in France in a shortened version prepared by the author himself from the French text. It was made "more attractive" by Abbé Félix Klein (1862–1953), who was professor at the Institut catholique in Paris from 1893 to 1907. The original edition had been given a special importance because the introduction was written by Archbishop Ireland, but it had not received particular attention. However, by calling Hecker the "priest of the future" and thus presenting the "American Way" of Catholicism as a model for the French traditionalists, Abbé Klein, in his foreword, gave a signal which aroused the indignation of the conservatives, who were already deeply wounded by the papal *Ralliement* policy. The book soon went through six editions. In the spring of 1892, Ireland, who spoke fluent French since his youth, was invited by the advocates of the current *Ralliement* policy in France to speak. He impressed Abbé Klein, who, in 1894, published a selection of his lectures under the title *L'Église et le Siècle.* Finally, he was contacted by those forces in French and American Catholicism which hoped to find the remedy for Church life by opening up toward the modern spirit that had arisen from the Revolution. This contact was expedient, if only because the Gibbons-Ireland group had been in trouble since 1895. In 1897, Ireland tried in his speeches to fend off the "retractors," charging them with rebelling against the Pope in conservative disguise.

The term "Americanism" was not defined by those who tried to follow the "American Way" in practice more than in theory, but rather by the French ultraconservatives. It began with a series of articles on *Américanisme mystique* by Charles Maignen, an opponent of the *Ralliement,* published under the pseudonym "Martel" in the conservative Paris paper *Vérité Française.* In a course of sermons, the Jesuits of Paris warned of the danger of "Hecker's Americanism" threatening the Church. In 1898, Maignen published his newspaper articles and other essays under the title *Études sur l'américanisme. Le Père Hecker, est-il un Saint?* Since Cardinal Richard refused the imprimatur, Maignen obtained approval from the *Magister Palatii,* the Dominican A. Lepidi in Rome, which was interpreted as papal sanction. Gibbons, Ireland, and Keane protested to Rome against the book, considering it a defamation of the American Catholicism they represented, while Archbishop Corrigan welcomed it. The controversies reached Belgium, Germany, and Italy and compounded the respective territorial tensions. The most vehement opponents of Hecker's friends were, among others, the Jesuit A. Delattre, who also sharply condemned the moderate biblical criticism of Lagrange; the Belgian Benedictine L. Jannsens at the Anselmianum in Rome; Merry del Val, who was promoted by Leo XIII and had been consulted in the battle against the validity of the Anglican ordinations; and especially Cardinals F. Satolli and Camillo

Mazzella, S.J. (1833–1900), who taught dogmatics in Georgetown and Woodstock (after 1868) and at the Gregoriana (after 1878).

The Pope rejected the request to put the Hecker biography on the Index and he appointed a Commission of Cardinals; representatives of the American episcopate were not included. The text of *Testem benevolentiae* was mainly written by Mazzela. The Pope changed the beginning and the end of the letter in order to avoid the impression of condemning the Gibbons group and the American situation. Whether Gibbons' telegram and Ireland's trip to Rome came "too late" (T. T. McAvoy, C.S.C.) or whether the letter could not be retracted by any means cannot be determined.

Leo XIII's letter to Gibbons began with a few words about the Hecker biography, especially its translation, noting that it had caused innumerable controversies because of certain opinions about the Christian way of life; these problems the Pope would treat extensively later. He condemned the following views: dogmas that are incomprehensible to contemporaries should not be denied, but rather be emphasized less or ignored; the ecclesiastical office is to refrain from authoritative statements to ensure the freedom of the individual through whom the Holy Spirit speaks more distinctly today than ever; natural virtues which promote activity are more important than supernatural ones; contemplative orders used to be justified, however, today, active virtues are needed; vows in the older religious orders kill the freedom to make decisions, which are so necessary today; the apostolate has to relinquish the old methods if operating among non-Catholics.

None of the suspects identified with these condemned opinions. But it wounded them deeply that the *cavenda et corrigenda,* though in a quotation, was cited *Americanismi nomine.* On 27 February the tactful Ireland wrote to the Pope that all "misunderstandings" had been cleared away and "true Americanism" was only "what was so called by the Americans." The letter by Cardinal Gibbons to the Pope was published *post festum:* "I do not believe that there is a bishop, a priest, or even a layman in this country who knows his religion and utters such enormities. No, this is not, has never been, and will never be our Americanism." The opponents of the Gibbons group, however, among them the German Archbishop Katzer of Milwaukee, who compared the "Americanists" with the Jansenists, thanked the Pope for having saved the Church in America from a great danger. Even though it was not put on the Index, the Paulists took the Hecker biography off the book market.

A distinction was drawn between "dogmatic" and "historical" Americanism, the latter being defined in Abbé Klein's words as *une hérésie fantôme.* However, one may question whether it was proper to extract papal doctrinal authority in this manner from its exceedingly complicated context; after all, the letter was addressed to Cardinal Gibbons. It is also questionable whether one could speak of a connection with modernism; this depends entirely on the definition of "modernism" and the customary terminological distinctions. In the perspective of the Roman procedure, it was noted that the "basic tendency and method of defense against modernism had largely been anticipated."

C H A P T E R   6 9

Papal Hopes for Unification —
The Independent Eastern Churches and the Uniates

Papal Hopes for Unification

The unions formed with Eastern Churches by the Popes of modern times were felt by most Eastern Christians to be violations of their traditions, which go back to the first centuries. The Holy See recognized the dignity of the old liturgies, but its efforts toward unification were based too strictly on the Tridentine concept of the unified Church and did not consider sufficiently the evolutionary character of the national churches of the East, thus creating a "Uniatism" which was an obstacle to the organic unification of the independent Eastern Churches separated from the Roman Church. The unionist initiatives which had arisen in the middle of the nineteenth century and had been partially adopted by the Propaganda Fide failed to develop.

Pius IX's proclamation of unification of 6 January 1848 in his encyclical *In suprema Petri Apostoli Sede* was harshly rejected by the four Orthodox patriarchs for its authoritarian tone. His brief *Arcano Divinae Providentiae consilio* of 8 September 1868, addressed to all Orthodox bishops, suggesting a return to Catholic unity and participation in the council, also failed; the Patriarch of Constantinople Gregorios (1867–71) bemoaned, for instance, the lack of respect for apostolic equality and brotherhood. Cardinal Alessandro Barnabo, prefect of the Congregation for the Propagation of the Faith, presided over the Commission for Missions and Churches of the Eastern Rites, one of the five subcommissions for the preparation of the First Vatican Council. This commission convened thirty-seven plenary sessions between 29 September 1867 and 9 May 1870. At the first working session, Barnabo declared that the negotiations were to avoid everything that could possibly injure the feelings of the Orthodox. However, the topic, debated by the seventeen consultors for months concerned the possibility of applying the disciplinary canons of the Council of Trent to the Uniate Church and was therefore little suited to pay tribute to the spiritual heritage of the Christian Middle East. The commission's task, to deal simultaneously with problems of missions and the Uniate Churches, must have been shocking to the Eastern Churches. The Latin patriarch of Jerusalem, Archbishop Giuseppe Valerga (1813–72), participated energetically in the formulation of the mission plan, which had been prepared by the commission and, after several revisions, on 26 June 1870, was extensively debated by the Council's fathers. More than half of the text (forty-four folio-size pages) dealt with the Uniate Churches, the rest (thirty-five pages) with the Latin mission in the Middle East. Valerga was intent on equating the Uniates with the Latin Church as far as canon law is concerned, but he wanted to let them retain their liturgical customs. At the request of the cardinals' commission, Valerga wrote a report on the manner in which the upcoming council was to handle questions regarding the Eastern Churches. At the council itself, the Uniate hierarchs were not united. The Melchite patriarch, Gregory II Jussef Sayyur (1864–97), the Chaldean patriarch, Joseph II Audo (1848–78), and the Syrian patriarch, Philip Argus (1866–74), left Rome before the final voting on the dogmatic constitution *Pastor aeternus* of 18 July 1870. Later, they agreed to it, but they remained indignant because of insufficient consideration of the patriarchs' traditional rights and privileges.

The pontificate of Leo XIII, who pursued liberal conciliatory policies in the political and social arena and hoped for reconciliation with the Anglicans and independent Eastern Churches, began a new phase in the relations between Rome and the Eastern Christians, reflecting the results of scholarly research and productive dialogues between open-minded experts. The reunification of those separated from the Church by belief and obedience was one of the Pope's main objectives, which he advocated in 6 encyclicals, 7 apostolic briefs, 14 pronouncements, and 5 addresses. Reunification was an integral part of his mission as peacemaker. In his encyclical *Grande munus christiani nominis propagandi* of 30 September 1880, on the Apostles of the Slavs, Cyril and Methodius, the Pope drew attention to the close relationship between those two men and the Holy See and to the Pope's interest in the Slavic peoples. He had special concern for the Eastern Churches and his most ardent wish was for them to unite with us and be committed to the eternal bond of unity (*concordia*)." The Uniates welcomed the encyclical with enthusiasm, for instance at the pilgrimage of fourteen Slavs on 5 July 1881 in Rome. It was led by Bishop Josip Jurij Stroßmayer of Djakovo, who had impressed the Pope with his ideas on ways of uniting with Russia and the Slavic faithful. Catholic Panslavism, which Stroßmayer supported and which originated in the Brotherhood of Saints Cyril and Methodius (in existence since the middle of the nineteenth century), encountered resistance in Russia, where it was feared its influence on the Slavs in the Habsburg Monarchy and on the Balkans would suffer a setback.

England's occupation of Egypt in 1882 and the Russian Orthodox Imperial Society of Palestine, founded the same year, turned Leo XIII's attention to the Near East. The Greek government asked that the Pope no longer appoint bishops *in partibus infidelium* for vacant episcopal sees in the Greek territories. The Pope granted the wish on 10 June 1882, using the term *episcopus titularis* in his apostolic letter *In suprema*.

In 1883, he received two extensive reports concerning the resumption of contacts with the Orthodox Churches. One was written by the apostolic delegate of Constantinople, Serafino Vannutelli. His motion regarding "the best available means to lead the dissidents back to the Catholic Church" demonstrated the failure of the Latin missionaries in the Near East and criticized their Latinization measures. The other report was written by Carlo Gallien, the Turkish consul general in Rome. He suggested sending new missionary societies into the respective areas, once their members had been made aware of the basic problems. The papal brief *Abbiamo appreso* of 4 January 1887, addressed to Giuseppe Benedetto Cardinal Dusmet, O.S.B., archbishop of Catania, seemed to be the first to be inspired by this proposal. In this brief, the Pope congratulated Dusmet, praising him for reopening the College of Saint Anselmo and including it in plans for the Christian Near East.

New ideas came from the Eucharistic Congress in Jerusalem of 14 to 21 May 1893. Bishop Victor Doutreloux of Liège (president of the Permanent Committee for Eucharistic Congresses, which prepared the Jerusalem Congress together with the Superior General of the Assumptionists, François Picard), expected the participation of representatives of the Eastern Churches paying homage to the Eucharist, and hoped for the return of the separated brethren to the great Catholic family. Leo XIII avoided expected diplomatic complications by informing Sultan Abdul Hamid (1876–1909) and Emperor Alexander III of Russia (1881–94) (via a French mediator) about the planned congress and by assuring the governments in Berlin, Vienna, and London that the meeting had a strictly religious purpose. He appointed Cardinal Benedict Maria Langénieux, archbishop of Rheims, his legate and president of the congress, which was attended by thousands of Catholic pilgrims, several cardinals, fifteen dignitaries of the Roman Catholic Church, eighteen representatives of the Uniate Churches, and twenty priests of the independent Eastern Churches. In his opening address, the cardinal legate emphasized the fact that his mission was marked by the sign of love and piety, implying an invitation to unite in faith. The congress submitted to the Pope eight desiderata, including Eucharistic prayers of Eastern liturgies in manuals of Roman Catholics, the encouragement of studies on the religious problems of the Eastern Churches with a view to church union; and the strengthening of relations between the faithful of the East and West and their clergy.

The Pope had ordered Cardinal Langénieux to inquire into the situation of the Uniates, the impact of the Latinization measures, and ways and means of overcoming the separation of the Eastern Churches from Rome. On 23 May, the Melchite Patriarch Gregory II Jussef Sayyur delivered a complaint concerning the Latinization measures, claiming they hindered the task and mission of the Uniate Churches. On 2 July, the cardinal of Lourdes sent a secret report to Rome on his investigations. Remembering the consequences of the Crusades, which are still felt today, he mentioned the Eastern Christians' mistrust of private interests and political goals. He also reprimanded Latin missionaries, whose behavior often contradicted apostolic directives, and expressed regret over the predominance of the Latin rites over the Uniate rites. He described the lack of authority and power of the Uniate Churches, which suffered from a lack of support and whose clergy was insufficiently trained. He reiterated the objections and opinions voiced by Latin missionaries, claiming that the theory of the apostolate of Uniate Christians in the Eastern Churches was a utopia. He was convinced of the future of the Uniate Churches, hoping that their revival could overcome their inferiority and link the Roman Catholics with the Eastern Orthodox. To disperse the prejudice of the schismatics and to strengthen the Uniates, he stressed the publication of an encyclical that would clarify papal principles regarding Eastern Christianity.

The apostolic brief *Praeclara gratulationis* of 20 June 1894, which Leo XIII addressed to all sovereigns and peoples on occasion of the 50th anniversary of his consecration as bishop, clearly reflects the ideas that were inspired by the Jerusalem Congress. He recalled the original unity of the Church, challenging the Eastern Christians to restore it. All Christians in the East and West, he said, recognized the Roman bishop, the successor to Saint Peter, before their separation. He promised that he and his successors would not touch their rights, the privileges of the patriarchs, their rites and customs. The Pope devoted one paragraph to the Slavic peoples, pointing out that the papacy had supported them since the time of Cyril and Methodius, but that a great segment had been alienated from the Roman belief; he therefore challenged them to unite. As far as the Eastern Churches were concerned, this programmatic letter contained the "first appeal for ecclesiastical unity with acceptable arguments" (J. Hajjar).

To use the results of the Congress in Jerusalem to strengthen further the Uniate Churches and reunite with the Eastern Churches, Leo XIII organized and chaired several conferences with Uniate patriarchs (24–28 November). In attendance were the Melchite Patriarch, Gregory II Jussef Sayyur, the Syrian Patriarch, Cyril Behnam Benni (1893–97), the patriarchal vicar, Archbishop Elias Huayek (replacing the aging Maronite Patriarch, John Hagg [1890–98, born 1817]), Cardinal Secretary of State Rampolla, the Cardinals Galimberti, Langénieux, Ledóchowski, and Vincenzo Vannutelli, who had been sent as papal legate to Saint Petersburg in 1882 on the occasion of Tsar Alexander III's coronation. These patriarchal conferences clearly defined the competencies of Latin missionaries and the rights of Uniate dignitaries. They also prepared the papal brief *Orientalium dignitas* of 30 November 1894, which relinquished the adaptation of rites and disciplines to Latin. "The preservation of the Eastern rites is more important than one is led to believe. The honorable age which distinguishes the various rites dignifies the entire Church and confirms the divine unity of Catholic belief." In thirteen theses, the Pope gave guidelines for the preservation of the old liturgies. He strengthened his intention to expand the Uniate seminaries and colleges for the native clergy.

In his letter *Christi nomen* of 24 December 1894, Leo XIII referred to his expositions in the apostolic brief *Praeclara gratulationis* of 20 June, stressing his efforts toward unity with the Eastern Churches and asking for support and training of a qualified Uniate clergy. In the motu proprio *Optatissimae* of 19 March 1895, he decreed that a permanent cardinals' commission for Uniate rites and reunification, chaired by Cardinal Ledóchowski, continue the deliberations of the patriarchal conferences of the fall of 1894. The brief *Provida matris* of 5 May 1895, on preparation for Pentecost, the extensive encyclicals *Satis cognitum* of 29 June 1896, dealing with the unity of the Church, and *Divinum illud munus* of 9 May 1897, concerning the Holy Spirit, elaborated his theological thoughts and practical suggestions pertaining to the union. On the occasion of the publication of the encyclical of 29 June 1896, Leo XIII had a medal struck, the front of which displayed his image with the inscription *Pontifex maximus* and the year of his pontificate (*anno XIX*) while the reverse side showed an allegory of Church unity with the words: "May there be one fold and one shepherd."

All these pronouncements differed from earlier papal utterances in their tone and their expression of sympathy for the Eastern Christians. They avoided terms like "schismatics" and "heretics," instead using words like *fratelli separati* or *dissidenti;* they distinguished themselves by respect for the rites and ecclesiastical laws of the East and prepared the climate for reconciliation. These papal efforts of appeasement were supported by Catholic diplomats (the Belgian Baron d'Erp), princes of the Church (Cardinals Langénieux and Vincenzo Vannutelli), bishops (Doutreloux of Liège and Stroßmayer of Djakovo) and theologians (Abbé Fernand Portal), who passionately pleaded for closer relations between the Catholic Church and the Anglicans as well as the Eastern Christians. Portal was a friend of Lord Halifax's and was inspired by the ideas of Russian religious philosophers, especially those of Vladimir Soloviev (1853–1900), who, as an Orthodox Christian, recognized the Pope and supported unification with Rome, the traditional center of the Christian world. For Soloviev, the papacy was a *mysterium unitatis,* the center of apostolicity, universality, and ecumenicity, the temporal manifestation and metaphor of the great secret of *Sophia.* In his philosophical works he strove to make his doctrine of the sophic world-soul agree with Christian theology. His convictions regarding the Russian Church's mission to unify all the churches evoked no response in the Eastern Churches during his lifetime, but his writings have had an ecumenical impact to the present day.

Leo XIII's intentions were published in numerous theological periodicals which provided a wealth of information, documentation, historical and theological research. By virtue of their scholarly integrity and theological sensitivity they rendered a clear picture of the history and the current situation of Eastern Christianity.

Generously, Leo XIII supported the Assumptionists, Benedictines, Dominicans, Jesuits, Capuchins, Carmelites, Lazarists, Lyon Missionaries, Redemptorists, Salesians, Christian Brothers, and White Fathers, who actively advocated the union in their pastoral work. The Pope also founded or restored colleges in Rome to train the Uniate clergy, such as the Armenian College (1883) and the Maronite College (1891). He carefully placed suitable candidates in the Propaganda College and in the international academies of orders, such as the pontifical Benedictine academy, the Anselmianum. He established Uniate seminaries and schools for the Copts in Cairo, for the Melchites in Jerusalem, for the Bulgarians in Plovdiv and Adrianople, for the Syrians and Chaldeans in Mosul, for the Greeks in Constantinople, Kadikoy (formerly Chalcedon), and in Athens. He willingly donated considerable funds for the development of these educational institutions.

Even though the Uniate Churches did not increase in their membership to any considerable extent in the last decades of the nineteenth century, the Pope emphasized their unique value within Catholicism as a whole. In his encyclicals and many other writings, Leo XIII traced their historical descent from early Christianity and the first Christian centuries to the missionary popes of the early Middle Ages who assured the Slavs their own ecclesiastical language, to the re-union councils of the early and high Middle Ages, the Second Council of Lyon in 1274 and the Council of Basel-Ferrara-Florence-Rome in 1431–45, and to the popes of modern times who struggled for union, especially Benedict XIV. These references alleviated the Uniates' inferiority complex; they no longer felt isolated, but were confirmed in their conviction of being recognized members of the universal Catholic Church, and entrusted with the task of building a bridge to the separated Eastern Christians. Their patriarchs, who had suffered under the Latinization measures instituted by Rome and under disciplinary regulations, were relieved and, because of the papal kindness and its accompanying proclamations, they felt themselves to be on equal footing with the Roman Catholic episcopate.

The Pope expected his unification program, his personal involvement on behalf of reunification with the separated Eastern Churches, and the expansion of the Uniate Churches to be successful. But many external and internal difficulties obstructed the realization of his ambitions. Turkish, French, Austro-Hungarian, and Russian interests clashed in the Balkans and in the Middle East. The cultural protectorate, which had developed from an institution of international law into a protectorate of foreign countries over Christians living in Turkey, enabled

France (since the sixteenth century) and Austria (since the end of the eighteenth century) to obtain certain privileges, particularly since numerous churches were under their protection and financed by them. The attempt to win over the Orthodox Slavs had to take Russia into consideration. When favoring the Uniate Slavs in Austria-Hungary, the delicate situation in this multi-national state could not be ignored. By order of their governments, diplomats intervened and expressed their anxieties over possible conflicts, as did, for instance, the Russian representative at the Vatican, Alexander Izvolsky (1888–96), and the Austro-Hungarian ambassador to the Vatican, Duke Friedrich Revertera-Salandra (1888–1901).

At the Curia, Leo XIII encountered resistance to his unification efforts and rejection of his personally benevolent attitude toward the Eastern Churches. He was unable to transfer his hopes to his immediate environment and the lower levels of his administration. Also, the penal regulations regarding Latinizing missionaries contained in his encyclical *Orientalium dignitas* were not very successful because they were not obeyed by the order members who devoted their efforts to traditional Latinization. Yet the Pope adhered to his ideas. According to Revertera's notes of New Year's Day 1897, Leo XIII desired to attempt the ecclesiastical unification with the Christian nations outside of the Church. This, Revertera said, would be very difficult in Russia: "He could not hope to witness more than the first dawn of a future which he so ardently desired" (F. Engel-Janosi).

Leo XIII had no illusions about the impending reunification with the Eastern Churches. Yet he strove for the unity of all Christians in the one and only Church, a characteristic of all his ecclesiological thoughts, which were the focal point of his theological concepts. When he died in 1903, the Uniates lost in him a pioneer and protector. His initiative prepared an ecumenical foundation which led to detente between Rome and the separated Eastern Churches, was continued by his successors, was reinforced by Pope John XXIII, and is still in effect.

His successor, Pius X (1903–14) proved to be primarily a pragmatic spiritual adviser. As Pope, he renewed the unification efforts of Leo XIII. He put the Roman churches San Lorenzo ai Monti and San Salvatore alle Capelle at the disposal of the Uniate Russians and Rumanians. He personally took charge of the protectorate over the Greek abbey of Grottaferrata near Rome, for which his predecessor, in 1881 had decreed the use of the original Greek-Byzantine rite. In 1904 he attended the celebration of the nine hundredth anniversary of the abbey, and he supported it throughout his pontificate. He anxiously observed the situation of the Uniates in Galicia and the propaganda of Russian missionaries in favor of unification with the Orthodox Church. For the Uniate Ruthenians, who had emigrated to the United States of America from Galicia and Hungary, he issued the bull *Ea semper* of 14 June 1907; that year, he appointed Vicar Apostolic Stephan Soter Ortynski and (in 1912) he sent, on behalf of the Ruthenians in Canada, Niceta Budka to be the bishop of Winnipeg.

By order of the Pope, Cardinal Vannutelli prepared festivities in Rome to honor the fifteen hundredth anniversary of the death of the patriarch of Constantinople, John Chrysostom, who was venerated by Christians in both the East and West. On 12 February 1908, in Saint Peter's Cathedral, Melchite Patriarch Cyril VIII Geha (1903–16) and his bishops and archimandrites celebrated the liturgy in the presence of the Pope, who sang the benediction, which according to their rite was to be delivered in the Greek language by the highest dignitary present. The next day he spoke to the numerous Uniates who had come to Rome of the Holy See's respect for the dignity and glory of the Eastern rites; he assured them that the Pope would guard the preservation of their national customs, that the congregation for the Propagation of the Faith would annually send a number of native priests to the East with the message to remain loyal to national rites and to avoid conversion to the Latin rite, and that he admired the accomplishments of great Eastern men and intended to make efforts to revive their heritage.

In his apostolic letter *Ex quo* of 26 December 1910, the Pope declared that the interest of the Holy See in the problems of the Eastern Churches had not ceased, that his predecessors had passionately desired the end of the separation, and that all Catholics were obligated to support the reunification. In 1910 he approved the world prayer octave for the unification of the separated Christians, which was to last from 18 to 25 January and had been initiated by the Anglican clergyman Paul J. Francis Wattson (1863–1940), who had converted in 1909 to the Roman Catholic Church together with the Brother- and Sisterhood of the Reconciliation, which he had founded. The octave was observed after 1908 by the Anglican and Catholic congregations in the United States and spread in the next decades to most of the Christian Churches.

After 1910 the monks of Grottaferrata published the periodical *Roma e l'Oriente,* which proselytized for the union of the Eastern Churches with Rome and was subsidized actively by the Pope. He was not always in agreement with all its articles. Yet in 1914 the Pope wrote to the editor: "Continue with your work on behalf of a difficult and frustrating cause and always apply the necessary wisdom."

In 1912 he established for the Hungarian Uniates the diocese of Hajdudorog. On 14 September of the same year, in connection with his liturgical reforms which earned him the sobriquet "Pope of the Liturgy," Pius X published the apostolic constitution *Tradita ab antiquis,* dealing with the receiver and administrator of Holy Communion. He gave the faithful the choice whether they wanted to receive the Eucharist in the form of leavened or unleavened bread, and, if possible, they were to receive Communion according to their own rites during Easter and the last viaticum.

Under Pius X's pontificate, the interest in the independent churches and those united with Rome was not as pronounced as under the pontificate of his predecessor; yet the papal hopes for reunification did not cease. The Pope assessed the possibilities of realizing his ambitions more sceptically and more realistically than Leo XIII. He did not share the optimism which had permeated Leo's proclamations. He was worried about the division of the Uniates into smaller churches where the lay element exerted great influence. He carefully observed the political development in Galicia and Southeastern Europe, and the attempts of the Orthodox Church to convert the Slavs of Dalmatia. He doubted whether Austria-Hungary would be able to preserve its cultural protectorate in the Balkans and feared the annexation of the Slavs to Russia, which he considered the greatest enemy of the Church. Therefore, he urged that the Uniates be bound closer to the Holy See and that they strengthen their religious life.

It was Benedict XV who finally created institutions which, taking Leo XIII's appeals seriously, could reliably carry out papal unification policies in the twentieth century. These institutions were the *Sacra Congregatio pro Ecclesia Orientali* (the result of the motu proprio *Dei providentis* of 1 May 1917) in which the Uniate Churches were freed from the union with other Roman congregations and placed under their own cardinals' congregation; and the Pontifical Institute of Oriental Studies (the result of the motu proprio *Orientis Catholici* of 15 October 1917), which was devoted to the study and teaching of all Eastern Churches and trained men to serve the reconciliation of the churches.

The Uniate Eastern Churches

In spite of all the schisms between the Eastern and Western hemispheres of Christianity, the Popes tried to restore unity. When they finally succeeded in concluding union treaties with the Orthodox Churches in Eastern Europe at the end of the sixteenth and in the seventeenth century, they expected to reduce the hardened barriers between the papacy and the Christian East, and unions with the Near East, Ethiopia, and India were established. But in spite of some success they had to endure backlashes. The pontificate of Leo XIII, oriented toward the future, opened new perspectives toward unification. Around 1900, approximately 8 million believers were jurisdictionally assigned to the Armenian patriarchate of Cilicia, the Maronite, Melchite, and Syrian patriarchates of Antioch, the Chaldean patriarchate of Babylon, the Uniate Coptic patriarchate of Alexandria, and to several archbishoprics and bishoprics in eastern and southern Europe, in Lower Italy and in southern India. On the basis of their liturgical languages they were divided into five groups: the Byzantine, Alexandrian, Antiochic (West Syrian), Chaldean (East Syrian), and Armenian rite. They were defined by the liturgies within and without the Byzantine Imperial Church in Christian antiquity.

The Byzantine Rite

The different versions of the Byzantine rite, also called Greek rite, were most popular among the Ruthenians, Russians, Rumanians, Hungarians, Serbs, Bulgarians, Greeks, Melchites, and Georgians.

The inclusion of the Orthodox metropolis of Kiev and all of Ruthenia into the Catholic Church through the Union of Brest in 1595/96 was the foundation for the reunification of the Ruthenians (Ukrainians) with the Roman center. The efforts in this respect were continued in Uzhgorod (1646), including the Carpatho-Ruthenians, Slovaks, Hungarians, and Rumanians.

Russia, penetrating into eastern central Europe in the eighteenth and nineteenth century, forced the Ruthenians living under its rule to convert to the Orthodox Church. In 1875 the only remaining diocese, Chelm, was dissolved. In spite of ruthless persecutions, 50,000 believers remained loyal to the union and in 1904 sent a delegation to Pius X. Their expectation that Nicholas II's edict of toleration would be applied to them was not fulfilled. They were only allowed to convert to Roman Catholicism.

In the Habsburg Monarchy, in Galicia, in Hungary, and in Transylvania, the

Ruthenians were able to develop their Church organization. In the archbishopric of Lemberg (Lvov), a second bishopric (Stanislav) was formed within the auxiliary bishopric of Przemysl. The reform of the Basilian order, the Provincial Synod of Lemberg of 1891, the founding of the Ruthenian College in Rome in 1897, the two archbishops Sylvester Cardinal Sembratovitch (1882–98) and Duke Andreas Szepticki (1900–44) led to the golden age of their Church (counting over 3 million believers within its three dioceses). The golden age was documented by the establishment of new orders (the Studites, an eastern branch of the Redemptorists, the female Basilians, the female Studites, the congregation of the Servants of the Immaculate Virgin Mary), new theological institutions, periodicals, schools, and charity centers. Basilian Archbishop Szepticki was known beyond Galicia's borders for his pastoral and missionary ambitions, his patronage, and primarily for his efforts regarding unification. His pastoral letters of 1907 and 1908 dealt with the theme of unity, which he tried to realize in the spirit of tolerance and love. After 1910 he was president of the Welehrade Union Congress. He became one of the outstanding figures of the union movement and was admired as the patriarch of the Ruthenians.

Szepticki supported White Russian students in order to restore the torn ties between the Ukrainian and White Russian people. In 1907 he traveled incognito to White Ruthenia, to the Russian Ukraine, and to Moscow. Through talks and negotiations, he initiated a new union movement of the Byzantine Slavic rite, which was expressly approved by Pius X the next year. Centers for the Russian Uniates were Saint Petersburg and Moscow.

As in Galicia, the Uniate Ruthenians in Hungary's bishoprics of Munkács (Slovak: Mukachëvo) and Eperjes (Slovak: Prešov) enjoyed an upswing through their own initiative and state aid. In the small bishopric of Kreutz (Croatian: Krizevci), established in 1777 for the Uniates of Croatia, Slavonia, and Batschka, almost half of the faithful were Ruthenians who had emigrated from Galicia and Carpatho-Russia to the south of Hungary.

In Transylvania, in the church province of Alba Julia-Făgăras, with its auxiliary bishoprics of Oradea Mare, Lugoj and Szamos Ujvár, the Rumanian Byzantine rite was used. Like the Uniate Ruthenians, the Rumanians expanded their educational system, their press, and their charity. But while trying to preserve their national identity, they had to struggle with the Magyarization measures of the administration.

The Uniate Hungarians, belonging partly to the Ruthenian dioceses, partly to the Rumanian dioceses, after 1868 demanded their own ecclesiastical jurisdiction and introduction of Hungarian as the liturgical language. In 1873 the vicariate of Hadjudorog, composed of thirty-three congregations, was established for the Hungarian Uniates. Pressured by the Hungarian faithful and the government, Pius X through the bull *Christi fideles Graeci ritus* (1912) created the diocese of the same name and demanded that it use Old Greek as the liturgical language. He approved Hungarian only for extraliturgical functions. Nevertheless, the liturgy was celebrated in the people's language. After World War I, the diocese was reduced by turning seventy-seven parishes over to the Uniate Church in Rumania, which also incorporated the archbishopric of Fogarasch and parts of the Slovak bishopric of Mukachëvo. The rest of this diocese and the bishopric of Prešov were given to Czechoslovakia. After the end of the nineteenth century, many Uniate Ruthenians and Rumanians emigrated to South and North America, where they created their own hierarchy.

Bishop Josip Jurij Stroßmayer of Djakovo helped the Uniate Serbs and stood up for them even outside of his bishopric.

According to the census of 1910, the number of Uniates in Austria was 3.5 million, in Hungary 1.9 million, and in Bosnia-Herzegovina 8,000.

In Bulgaria the union movement, initiated by Titular Archbishop Joseph Sokolski (1860–61), could not develop because of Russian intervention. Under Raphael Popoff (1865–76), the movement took hold in Macedonia and Thrace, assisted by the Assumptionists, Lazarists and Resurrectionists. In 1883 Leo XIII established an Apostolic Administration in Constantinople, which was responsible for two vicariates apostolic in Macedonia and Thrace. The approximately 15,000 faithful suffered from the pressures of the Bulgarian exarch, the Orthodox bishops, and the Turkish government.

The Uniate Greeks had even less of a chance to expand. They owed their internal organization to Hyacinth Marango's efforts, who founded a periodical in Constantinople in 1865 and established two congregations. The Assumptionists continued his work in the seminary of Kadikoy and through the periodical *Échos d'Orient*. In 1909 John Papadopulos was appointed vicar general of the Apostolic Delegates of Constantinople for the Uniate Greeks. In 1911 he was ordained bishop and entrusted with the independent administration of the small congregations. Hyacinth Marango also made propaganda for the Uniates in the Kingdom of Greece, but because of the anti-Catholic animosities of the Orthodox population he was only moderately successful. Leo XIII's efforts regarding the educational institute in Athens patronized by him and the work of several orders essentially failed. The Catholic archbishop of Athens was responsible for 2,000 Uniate Greeks in his capacity as apostolic delegate.

The Italo-Greeks and the Italo-Albanians, centered in the Basilian abbey of Grottaferrata near Rome, in Calabria, and Sicily, were threatened by Latinization measures or mixtures of Latin and Byzantine liturgies, but their independence was supported by Leo XIII. He decreed the elimination of any liturgical additions which did not agree with the Byzantine rite.

The Melchites were headed by the patriarch of Antioch. Maximos III Mazlum (1833–55) after 1838 also was the incumbent of the two Uniate patriarchal sees of Alexandria and Antioch. Gregory I Jussef Sayyur, whose jurisdiction over all Melchites was expressly recognized by Leo XIII in 1894, Peter IV Geraigiry (1898–1903), and Cyril VIII Geha (1903–16) improved the organization of the four archbishoprics and eight bishoprics with the help of the patriarchal vicars of Alexandria and Jerusalem. They provided a good education for the secular clergy in the Seminary of Saint Anna in Jerusalem and made sure that the orders could expand. Among others, the three Basilian congregations and the congregation of the Paulinists, founded by Archbishop Germanos Moakkad of Baalbek (died in 1912), excelled in their educational, charitable, and missionary activities. They succeeded in bringing together all the faithful scattered throughout the Near East and Egypt (1907: 140,000) and to affirm their loyalty to the Apostolic See, in spite of the social differences among the believers and demands from the laity for more participation, according to the Orthodox model. The Synod of Ain-Traz in Lebanon (4 April to 8 July 1909) dealt with dogmatic and pastoral questions in order to improve religious life. The results of the thorough deliberations were defined in 1,017 articles, which were sent to Rome in a Latin translation, but failed to be approved because of some questionable points. The Synod favored the further development of the Melchites in organizational and spiritual respects. The Arab paper *The Good Will,* whose publication was decided at the Synod, carried the basic concepts to the public.

In Georgia, Theatines (after 1629) and Capuchins (after 1662) had solicited support for the union. In 1848, the 50,000 Georgian Catholics were subordinated to the bishop of Tiraspol. Ten thousand of them were Uniates, mostly Armenians, and only a small portion adhered to the Byzantine liturgy. In 1886 the Russian government forbade this liturgy as well as the use of the Georgian language in sermons and public church service. After World War I, some priests took care of these faithful, who subsequently suffered the reprisals of the Soviet government.

The Alexandrian Rite

This group of liturgies includes the Uniate Copts and the Egyptians. The union of the Copts, initiated in the eighteenth century by the Franciscan Friars, progressed when Leo XIII supported the union in his apostolic letter of 11 July 1895, and when he responded to the request of a delegation under the leadership of Cyril Makarios of 26 November by restoring the Alexandrian patriarchate. Aside from the patriarchal bishopric, he established the dioceses of Hermopolis and Thebes. In 1899 he made Cyril Makarios patriarch. With resolutions regarding the faith, liturgy, and hierarchy, the Synod of Cairo of 1898 laid the foundation for the organization of the Church. Its reconstruction was interrupted when the ambitious patriarch resigned in 1908 and converted to Orthodoxy. He was replaced by an apostolic administrator. The number of Uniate Copts increased from 4,630 (1897) to 14,576 (1907).

For the Uniate Ethiopians, who were cared for since the middle of the nineteenth century by French Lazarists and Italian Capuchins, Leo XIII, in addition to the two existing vicariates apostolic, created an apostolic prefecture for the area of Eritrea (1894), which had become an Italian colony in 1890. In 1896 he sent Cyril Makarios to Addis Ababa, who asked in his behalf for the release of Italian prisoners. In his correspondence with Emperor Menelik II (1889–1909) he tried to improve the situation of the Uniates which, for political reasons, was difficult. Pius X also appealed to him in 1906. In 1910, by order of the Pope, the first native Ethiopian, Abuna Kidana Maryam Kassa, was ordained as bishop of Asmara. After 1911 he headed the vicariate apostolic of Asmara for the 4,000 Uniate Ethiopians.

The Antioch Rite

This group of rites included the Uniate Jacobites and Maronites. After 1783 these Syrians (West Syrians) from Syria, Mesopotamia, and Egypt had been subject to the patriarch of Antioch, who resided in Mardin after 1854. After the settlement of internal disputes at the Synod of Scharfa, where the ecclesiastical situation was newly regulated, the patriarchs gave their Church a clearer profile. With the help of four metropolitans, six bishops, and foreign and native orders, they improved the training and material security of the clergy and expanded the educational system. Aside from Patriarch Cyril Behnam Benni (1893–97), Ignatius Ephraim II Rachmani (1898–1929) also contributed to the stabilization of the union through his historical and liturgical studies as well as the addition of a Syrian ritual. When the faithful in Turkey (80,000) were threatened by persecutions during World War I, their number decreased, and dwindled further through emigrations. The patriarchal see was moved from Mardin in Turkey to Beirut.

The Maronites, in the only patriarchal Uniate Church without a parallel separated Eastern Church, had strongly increased in the eighteenth century. In 1885 there were 1,050 secular clergymen, 800 monks in 45 monasteries, and 8 convents. Around 1900 there existed 9 dioceses, 3 patriarchal seminaries, 6 diocesan seminaries, and a flourishing native order system, following the rules of Saint Anthony. Under Patriarch Paul Masad (1854–90) and Patriarch Elias Peter Huayek (1899–1931) the religious life of the Maronites improved, and was further strengthened by the Maronite College in Rome, which had been founded in 1584 and renewed by Leo XIII in 1891.

The Chaldean Rite

The Chaldean and Maronite rites belong to the East Syrian group of liturgies. The center of the Chaldeans (Uniate Nestorians) was located in Mesopotamia. Under their Patriarch Joseph II Audo (1848–78), residing in Mosul, an internal crisis broke out. It began with the patriarch's attempt to extend his jurisdiction over the Uniate Malabars, and the crisis was intensified through the Holy See's interventions in the administration of the Chaldean Church, reaching its climax in 1869 when Joseph II Audo refused to ordain two bishops appointed in Rome. In 1870 Pius X offered him the alternatives of either consecrating the bishops or resigning. Even though he yielded in this matter and in regard to controversies about the wisdom of the definition of infallibility, new tensions developed pertaining to the Uniate Malabars. These tensions first decreased under Elias XII Abolionan (1879–94) and Joseph Emanuel II Thomas (1900–47), when Leo XIII assured them of his benevolence. Under those two patriarchs, many Nestorians found their way to the union, so that in 1914, 100,000 believers belonged to the Chaldean Church in four archbishoprics and eight bishoprics. Aside from Dominicans, Capuchins, Lazarists, Carmelites, and Pallottines, two native congregations intensified the internal life of the Church.

The Malabars had difficulty disassociating themselves from their dependence on the Latin hierarchy. Patriarch Joseph II Audo's efforts to replace the Latin Carmelite missionaries with Bishop Mar Rocco as head of the Malabar Church failed. In 1874–76 about 24,000 believers assembled around Chaldean Bishop Elias Mellus of Accra, whom his patriarch had sent to Southern India. They separated from the union and joined the Nestorian Catholicate in 1907 (neo-Nestorian Church; 1914: 14,000 members). In 1887 Leo XIII withdrew the Uniates from the supervision of the Latin bishops and created for them the two vicariates apostolic of Trichur and Kottayam, which were at first entrusted to Latin prelates until, in 1897, the Pope filled three independent vicariates apostolic with native bishops. Their rites were cleansed from Latin additions. In the following years, their numbers rose from 200,000 (around 1900) to 300,000 (1914).

The Armenian Rite

In 1867, when Pius IX combined the two Uniate Churches of Constantinople and Cilicia, a crisis broke out among the Uniate Armenians, causing the nomination of a competing patriarchal candidate after the First Vatican Council and the conversion of numerous Uniates to Monophysitism. The crisis was finally settled when Leo XIII appointed Patriarch Anthony Peter IX Hassan (1867–80) cardinal of the Curia and Stephen Peter X Azarian (1881–99) his successor. At a synod in 1890 dogmatic, ritual, and organizational matters were discussed. The Pope supported the reconstruction of the patriarchate (2 archbishoprics, 13 bishoprics) by erecting the Armenian College in Rome (1883), which had already been planned in 1584 by Gregory XIII, and by approving the constitutions of the Viennese Mechitarists (1885). He also helped those Armenians who were threatened by the Turks (1894–96). In 1911 new controversies erupted, ignited by the differences between Patriarch Paul V Peter XIII (1910–31) and the laity in the Church administration who demanded more participatory rights. The patriarch was expelled by the Turkish authorities. In 1911 he held a synod in Rome, which was unable, however, to settle the internal difficulties. The atrocities inflicted upon the Armenians during World War I, killing about 50 percent of their clergy, paralyzed the further development of the 100,000 believers in the Armenian patriarchal Church. More favorable was their situation in the Armenian archbishopric of Lemberg (2,500), in Rumania (30,000), and in Russia (40,000). After World War II, however, they succumbed to Soviet ecclesiastical policies.

The spiritual Latinization of the Eastern Churches was finally stopped by Leo XIII after the First Vatican Council. He had recognized the unique qualities of the Uniates beyond their liturgical customs. The strengthening expected by the Pope, however, was hampered by internal and external difficulties. The superimposition of the Latin liturgy on the Syrians, Malabars, and Maronites continued to exist. The lay portion of the Church administration, customary in the independent Eastern Churches, caused tensions. The possibilities of growth were curtailed by continuous state pressures, especially in Russia and Turkey, and by the persecutions of the Armenians, Chaldeans, Georgians, Maronites, and Syrians. Only the Ruthenians and Rumanians in Austria-Hungary, as well as the Malabars in Southern India improved their Church organization. All Uniate dignitaries tried to elevate the educational level of their clergy, to return to the original liturgy of their Churches and to devise contemporary spiritual care. The help they received from Leo XIII and Pius X had positive effect on their initiatives and defined the position of the patriarchs, bishops, and secular and regular clergy.

Part Two

Defensive Concentration of Forces

Pius X, a Conservative Reform Pope

Roger Aubert

When the conclave which was to elect Leo XIII's successor opened, the Sacred College faced a situation much more complex than in 1878. A significant group of cardinals was convinced that the *Pontilex Maximus,* who had improved the reputation of the papacy to a great extent, was best replaced by electing his secretary of state, Cardinal Rampolla. They considered him to be intimately familiar with his thoughts; also he had collaborated in all prominent plans and activities of the last fifteen years. This was the opinion of those Church dignitaries who desired a continuation of the conciliatory policies which the deceased Pope had exercised toward contemporary philosophy and modern institutions; this was also the conviction of one segment of the intransigents who held Rampolla in esteem for being a relentless opponent of the Italian government. But the failure of Rampolla's French policy was not in his favor. Many cardinals thought it necessary to take an entirely different path, though they were not always in agreement as to the direction. Some, likewise contemplating political expedience, wished the Holy See to take a less rigid stance toward Italy because they considered it idle to speculate on its impending collapse. They also preferred the Church to rely on the assistance of Catholic Austria and the German Center Party rather than on Orthodox Russia, whose increasing influence in the Near East they feared; instead, they suggested taking a chance on anticlerical France. Others, who were more concerned with the principle at stake, worried about the liberal trends in exegesis and theology, about the danger of democratic ideas as propagated by the secretary of state threatening the principle of authority, and about the extent of the concessions he was ready to make to governmental authority in order to solicit its support or at least its neutrality. Therefore, they demanded a return to intransigence, the hallmark of Pius IX's pontificate. Still others, conservatives as well as reformists, believed that after so many years of giving preference to the "Ministry of Foreign Affairs" it was high time to think of the "Ministry of the Interior." Therefore they desired a pope who had matured in the office of bishop and would be most interested in pastoral questions, in a better administration of the dioceses, and in the improvement of ecclesiastical works.

Of the candidates nominated by Rampolla's opponents, Cardinal Serafino

Vannutelli was mentioned frequently. For years, Austria's friends had assembled around him, and he was, as everyone knew, well disposed to the Quirinal. Named most often was Cardinal Gotti, prefect of the Propaganda, a Carmelite who was conservative in regard to doctrine, yet liberal in respect to Church policy and a very able administrator. Some, however, spoke of the saintly patriarch of Venice, Cardinal Sarto, who was not well known to the public and the foreign cardinals, but had been discreetly and repeatedly named by Leo XIII as his successor. He was also supported by those Italian cardinals who did not belong to the Curia, especially since they knew that the government approved his candidacy and considered him "the more pliable of the inflexible candidates."

The problem was further complicated by the significant role which the diplomatic factor played. In 1878 the great powers arrived at the conviction that the Pope's function in the European political configuration had ceased to be significant since the Papal State had been dissolved. Therefore, they limited themselves to the request that a man be chosen who was moderate and committed to conciliatory settlements of the conflicts between Church and state. However, due to Leo XIII's intelligent policies, the great powers had to admit once again that the moral support of the Pope, meaning the Vatican, was still potentially of great value. Consequently they were not as indifferent toward the election of the new Pope as they had been twenty-five years ago.

The votes cast for Sarto rose from 21 to 24, and on the morning of 3 August increased to 27, surpassing Rampolla and practically eliminating Gotti. For a while, the cardinals feared Sarto would refuse to accept the responsibility which he himself felt exceeded his strength, but he could, in the end, be persuaded, and, on the morning of 4 August, he was elected, receiving 50 votes to the 10 cast by those who had remained loyal to Rampolla. Sarto declared that he would choose the name Pius X in memory of the Popes of the same name "who, in past centuries, had courageously fought against sects and rampant errors." This indicated the direction he intended to take in his pontificate.

The new Pope was born in 1835; he rapidly climbed the ladder of a pastoral career. Finally, in 1893, he became patriarch of Venice and cardinal. Wherever he was active, he left the impression of a virtuous and diligent spiritual adviser, indeed, almost of a holy man of great benevolence; yet at the same time he was energetic, moved by a strong sense of duty, and highly intelligent. He did not think much of innovations, such as the new trends in the area of exegesis and apologetics originating in France, as well as the program of the young Italian Christian Democrats who had assembled around Murri. As bishop he tried to inspire his priests, especially in regard to instruction in the catechism, preaching, and frequent Communion, and he encouraged the laity to get involved as much as possible in ecclesiastical activities, insisting, however, that this collaboration was subject to the strict control of the clergy. From the clergy, in turn, he demanded absolute obedience, even toward the minor directives of their bishops. Sarto was intensely interested in Socialist charges against the traditional religious foundations of society and did not hesitate to descend to the level of city politics and demand an alliance between the Catholics and the moderate liberals in Venice in order to erect a dam against the rising flood of radicals.

This course of action gave rise to the expectation that the new Pope would take a more conciliatory stance toward the new Italy than his predecessor. And indeed, his pontificate inaugurated a slow but gradual improvement of the relations between the Vatican and the Quirinal. The question which attitude the Pope would adopt in regard to the Roman question was only secondary in the spiritual orientation of the Pope because the concepts which guided his pontificate differed drastically from those of this predecessor. While Leo XIII derived pleasure from the delicate games of diplomacy and politics, Pius X did not enjoy them at all and was not willing to succumb to the compromises which are part of the game. In his estimation, Leo XIII's policy of reconciliation with the governments and royal courts had generally failed, and he was determined to concentrate on the problems of the Christian apostolate and religious life. Moreover, there was a glaring difference between the new Pope and his predecessor in all other respects, even physically, but particularly in essential matters. Leo XIII was known as the "Pope of the royal courts, the chancellories, the bishops"; his successor, in contrast, would prove to be the "Pope of theology and canon law, of the simple folk and the pastors" (J. Fèvre). Pius X liked to portray himself as the "good rural pastor" and his opponents were quick to take him at his word. Unquestionably, he lacked a university education, which would have allowed him to be more receptive to the critical method in the crisis of modernism and to be more independent of the narrow-minded opinions of his informants. But everyone who had contact with him was astonished at his intelligence, certainly a "rather more robust than subtle intelligence" (Baudrillart), but one which functioned clearly and precisely, grasping the essential point of a problem and supported by "a healthy common sense, almost a man of genius" (Briand). Prince Bernhard von Bülow declared that he rarely encountered such penetrating insight into human nature and into those forces which dominate the world and modern society.

No less remarkable were his moral qualifications. Many of the characteristics reported by eyewitnesses leave the compelling impression that this man possessed a wealth of virtues ranging all the way to heroism. Thus, the ceremony of his canonization in 1954 merely officially confirmed what many of his contemporaries had felt spontaneously. One point above all must be emphasized: the deep commitment he felt toward his responsibility as spiritual director enabled him to become a man of prayer as well as of action, a man of relentless will, ready to bear the criticism of the public if he felt the interests of the Church to be at stake. Often his energy could have been enhanced by a good measure of flexibility. The often rather pressing awareness of his responsibility may explain the rather authoritarian government of this otherwise friendly and social man, who "prepared the dictatorship that would save the Church," as one adviser of Cardinal Mathieu said. Indeed, Pius X was firmly convinced that the service of God and the salvation of the faithful required a serious change in many areas.

Pius X instinctively mistrusted progressive endeavors. It was clear to him that the liberal policies of his predecessor regarding the modern world should not be condemned in principle, but these seemed to him to have been conducted with insufficient precautions and to have run risks which would shortly incur regrettable consequences. Thus he considered a certain reactionary policy absolutely necessary, giving his pontificate from the start the hallmark of retreat into "wholesome isolation" and a "Catholic defensive," which was reflected mainly in relations with various governments, in the attitude toward the Christian Democrats, and in the suppression of modernism.

Regarding the governments, with the exception of Italy Pius X returned to a rigid and inflexible stance. Relentlessly and without consideration of political expedience or eventual, direct, and harmful consequences, he insisted on the rights of the Church. This was most apparent in the case of France: with regard to the separation of Church and state, he prohibited any settlement via negotiations or arbitration, in spite of the opposing views of a considerable segment of the episcopate and the public. Also in Spain and Portugal, his policies of decisiveness and inflexibility prevailed. In both countries, he risked an actual break in relations. In spite of his sympathy for the old Emperor Franz Joseph, Pius X was at one time on the verge of breaking off diplomatic relations with Austria because the government in Vienna hesitated to suspend from office a professor of canon law in Innsbruck who openly sympathized with modernistic trends. This again confirms how far the Pope was willing to remain inflexible if matters of religion seemed to be at stake.

At first glance, the Pope's reaction to the Christian Democrats was even more puzzling. After all, he had sprung from the common people and had always been a friend to the poor. He found it simply impossible to accept the fact that there were Catholics who wanted their social action to be more independent of the hierarchy and more self-reliant, or that some priests tried to orient social action more and more toward the political arena. However, various papal acts unquestionably demonstrate the Vatican's temporary devaluation of democratic ideas in favor of a paternalistic solution to social problems. The Pope also expressed preference for a hierarchical conception of society and at the same time demanded intensified attempts to keep the professional organizations of workers under the strict control of the clergy. All these aspects are rather characteristic of the ecclesiastical climate in Venetia, which Pius had never left before his election.

In regard to the suppression of modernism, it is unquestionable that there are troublesome aspects to the various reform movements at the beginning of the twentieth century and that the dishonest action of many a pioneer of these movements forced the Pope to call to mind certain principles and warn of blunders. However, one has to admit that the various measures employed to hold back the tide of modernism must be assessed negatively. Many men loyal to the Church were mercilessly banned and only few were relatively quickly rehabilitated, such as Father Lagrange. But more serious than these personal fates were other facts: for a long time the undifferentiated suppression of modernism kept the majority of the clergy from pursuing intellectual investigations. This prevented a gradual clarification of the intellectual processes taking place in the Catholic intelligentsia until around 1900 and kept them from learning to differentiate the constructive from exaggerations or even errors. The gap between Church and modern culture widened. The solution of fundamental problems was postponed, and by simply ignoring them nothing was won, but, on the contrary, harm was done.

The way in which Pius X pursued his main interest, that is, concentrating on the internal affairs of the Church, and the way in which he insisted under any circumstance on "demanding for God's sake omnipotent power over man and beast" (inaugural encyclical), disregarding political or diplomatic contexts, and primarily the spirit of the methods with which he pursued this program, especially in the last years of his pontificate, caused and are still causing rather different assessments. Some critics praise the saintly Pope as the fearless defender of orthodoxy and of ecclesiastical rights. Others, in contrast, sharply criticize the stubborn intransigence and narrow-mindedness of the Pope, claiming that he did not know how to treat the grave problems confronting the Church from a new perspective; instead he tried, using more and more authoritarian methods, to preserve the Church's reactionary and clerical concepts, which were in flagrant contrast to the historical development. Whatever the future judgment of Pius X's defensive actions may be, it would be historically incorrect if the meaning of this pontificate were limited to this hotly disputed aspect.

No matter how often the fact is emphasized that Pius X did not think much of the rules of politics and diplomacy so dear to his predecessor, one must not forget that he was by no means disinterested in the political dimension of these problems and that he even presented certain ideas in this regard which make him appear to be a forerunner. For Pius X, spirituality determined policies, and they had to be Christian policies. With this decisive resolution toward a political theology, he rejected, on the one hand, the pretenses of the lay liberalism of the nineteenth century; on the other hand, because of his extraordinary restraint toward the tendencies of "political Catholicism," he was in agreement with many justified trends of that same liberalism. Not only did he have grave reservations toward the politically engaged priests, but he believed even less than Leo XIII in the usefulness of denominational parties. Thus, it is typical that a sharp critic such as Falconi should praise him, claiming "he was the first in history to practice an *idealismo antitemporalistico,* even after the memory of such idealism had gotten lost in the first centuries of the Church."

However, more significant and of fundamental importance is the fact that Pius X appeared to his contemporaries as not very modern and rather conservative, which indeed he was in many respects; yet in reality he was one of the great reform Popes of history. This explains, by the way, why he was enthusiastically welcomed by a great number of people who strove for religious renewal, at least during the first months of his pontificate. Their first impression was one of religious resurrection rather than return to obscurantism. The motto of this Pope was *instaurare omnia in Christo;* and the restoration of the Christian community — this was the point in question — included, in his opinion, a rigorous defense of the rights of Christ and the Church as well as positive reform activity and initiatives with essentially pastoral goals, intensifying the communities' internal life and ensuring a more effective utilization of its potential. To this end, he issued the decrees regarding frequent Communion and the Communion of children, measures to improve the instruction of the catechism and the sermon, reform of Church music and revision of the missal and the breviary, and reorganization of seminaries to improve the training of the clergy. Though inspired by an obsolete conception of the lay world, many guidelines and directives made Pius X a pioneer of Catholic Action in the modern sense of the word. In this context belong the adaptation and codification of canon law and the reorganization of the Roman Curia, intended to enable the central administration of the Church better to fulfill the more and more difficult tasks imposed on it by the development of ecclesiastical centralization. Pius X dealt with all these different problems utilizing forty years of practical experience in multiple areas of pastoral work far away from the Curia, a background that is rare for a Pope. Thus he was able to apply to his new office the experience and energy which he had already displayed as head of the dioceses of Mantua and Venice. He could not be held back by bureaucratic routine; rather, with authority he enacted reforms within a few years which had been requested for centuries or were considered almost revolutionary in his time.

According to the unanimous testimony of all his advisers, Pius X played an important role in the design of such plans and in their rapid execution. Naturally, like every Pope, he had to rely on assistants. He made sure that they shared his ideal of religious renewal and therefore recruited them preferably from among the orders (but not only from the ranks of the Jesuits, as his opponents like to maintain). Consequently, the portion of religious priests increased in the Roman congregations. From among the bishops he chose co-workers whom he had known for a long time to be opponents of liberalism of whatever version. They were virtuous and diligent men, but often narrow-minded. They were completely devoted to the Holy See, but their ambitions sometimes lacked the proper insight, and their understanding of the real situation of the Church and the intellectual processes beyond the horizon of the small Italian ecclesiastical world was small.

Among the Pope's men, the four personal secretaries deserve special credit. They enjoyed his full trust and, driven by "somewhat exaggerated ambitions" (Della Torre), they reinforced more than once the intransigent orientation of the papal decisions. In addition, several particularly influential cardinals played a great role.

Of greatest influence, however, was the severely criticized triad of Vives y Tutó, Gaetano De Lai, and Merry del Val. First place must go to the Capuchin Vives y Tutó, of the group of Spanish integralism which produced the book *El liberalismo es pecado.* In 1884 he was assigned to the Roman Curia and, during the crisis of the Italian Catholic Action, he supported the campaign of Paganuzzi. He was a hard-working man of outstanding knowledge, a favorite adviser of the Holy Office, and prefect of the Congregation of Orders from 1908 until 1912. One of his followers was the feared creator of the reform of the Curia, Cardinal De Lai, an energetic and tireless organizer, who succeeded in concentrating in his hands a power unequalled in the history of the Curia. Since the time the Pope had been bishop of Mantua, De Lai had been his friend and he used this friendship to extend his already considerable power as prefect of the Consistorial Congregation by invading the authority of the Congregation of the Council. He dictatorially controlled the appointments of bishops and supervised the dioceses and seminaries. His principle was to proceed rigorously rather than softly when evil was to be eliminated. The third man in the triad was Cardinal Merry del Val, secretary of state at thirty-seven years of age. He occupied this office throughout the pontificate and was envied by the Holy Office for having been assigned to this office at such a young age, particularly as a foreigner, which was something unheard of. In contrast to the secretaries of state of the last two centuries, he was much more involved in the religious policies of the pontificate. Merry del Val was a devout and moralistic priest, a distinguished and polite aristocrat, and totally devoted to the Holy See. He faced the modernistic tendencies with an untroubled but rigid intransigence. He was more familiar with abstract principles than with the complex conditions of reality and, moreover, fairly isolated within the boundaries of the Curia. Thus he often gave the impression that he was unable to keep up with the times. However, Pius X respected this diligent, unconditionally loyal co-worker, who was from the start receptive to his own ideal of Catholic renewal and shared his conception of an authoritarian Church government. Thanks to his intimate relationship with the Pope, Merry del Val possessed immense power, which assisted him in extending the Secretariat of State's rights of intervention, which in turn resulted in more incisive reforms of the Curia. This created many enemies for him, even in Rome.

The texts and various documents collected during the process of beatification contradict the "legend of the secretary of state who brainwashed a benevolent and pious Pope with intransigence, the same Pope who had entrusted him with the reins of government." Yet this does not mean that Pius X was not at all directed by his environment or that he was solely responsible for all measures taken, even the most draconic ones which accompanied the antiliberal reaction so characteristic of his pontificate. He was justified when he turned indignantly against everyone who quietly maintained that the Church was led by "three cardinals," and he repeatedly asserted his complete independence. However, these protestations only prove his good faith, as G. Martina observed; they leave the problem of the real responsibility completely open. Today it cannot be disputed that many of his assistants were carried away by misguided ambitions, exceeding the Pope's intentions when applying certain decisions and using certain methods. On the other hand, it should be clear that the Pope based his decisions in more than one case on biased and tendentious information given to him by men in his trust. Holiness is no guarantee of the best ecclesiastical policies, and a Pope who thinks he has to make decisions for the Church single-handedly is unfortunately the prisoner of his informants and the executive body, loyal and devoted as they may be. An additional observation should be made: Many an assistant of Pius X may have exceeded his intentions; yet there were others who often countered his impulses with passive resistance or at least somewhat softened his intolerant directives. In the last months of his life, Pius X complained about this, especially when the antiintegralistic reaction became apparent even in Vatican circles. But at the beginning of his pontificate, several of his reform measures had encountered the passive resistance of the conservatives, who were just as opposed to the changes demanded by the highest authority as they were to the reformism of the progressives. In view of such cases, impressively illuminating Pius X's occasional difficulties in moving even those men toward obedience who considered themselves the pioneers of the defense against democratic anarchy, É. Poulat spoke of this Pope as having a "strong will and weak authority." Even though this may be exaggerated, the wording shows that the problem of relations between the Pope and his assistants is much more complex than most of his admirers and his slanderers — each in the opposite sense — would care to admit.

The Reform Work of Pius X

Roger Aubert

Immediately following the death of Pius X, the London *Times* wrote: "It is not an exaggeration to say that G. Sarto instituted more changes in the administration of the Catholic Church than any of his predecessors since the Council of Trent." Even if one must note that most of the significant decisions of this Pope date from the first five years of his pontificate and that his reform program was slowed down by his excruciating efforts effectively to fend off the threat of modernism, it is nevertheless clear that he took numerous and versatile initiatives and even realized many of the relevant goals. Immediately after his election, he had taken several steps to attain the reorganization of the diocese of Rome and to eliminate the many abuses committed by the clergy of Rome. However, this is merely an indication of the more general and urgent matters which he openly professed and which caused, initially, a great wave of hope among those who, after Leo XIII's "political" pontificate, expected a renovation of the Church in a more religious direction. In the course of 1905, however, in this optimistic atmosphere, an entire series of pro-reform pamphlets appeared in close succession. The exaggerated expectations of pro-reform groups, however, were disillusioned to such an extent that they often completely lost sight of the positive impact, by no means insignificant in spite of limitations, especially at the pastoral and institutional level.

CHAPTER 70

Reorganization of the Roman Curia and Codification of Canon Law

As pastor and bishop, Pius X often had occasion to discover that a reorganization of ecclesiastical institutions was urgently needed in order better to enable the clergy at all levels, from the top to the bottom, to fulfill their tasks. Thus, without much ado, he proceeded with this task, making good use of his organizational talent and the administrative experiences he had acquired in eighteen years as chancellor of the diocese of Treviso.

There is no need to list all the individual measures Pius X took in the course of his pontificate, even though they often had significant consequences. Only two undertakings of great impact shall be treated in depth: the reform of the papal administration and the reform of canon law.

The organization of the Roman Curia, essentially instituted by Sixtus V, was in dire need of change. In the course of three hundred years, it had turned into a heterogeneous assemblage of thirty-seven agencies whose rights and responsibilities were often totally undefined and who were constantly in conflict with each other, because each one dealt individually with administrative and judicial problems and controversies of the administration, and their areas of jurisdiction were often incompatible. Moreover, the elimination of temporal authority rendered some of these agencies totally superfluous. Pius IX and his successor had limited themselves simply to isolated reforms. On the other hand, however, the progressing Roman centralization in the course of the nineteenth century and the expansion and improvement of the possibilities of communication had essentially strengthened the contacts between the center and the periphery, making the development of certain offices desirable. Furthermore, the administrative methods were completely obsolete, inflexible, out-of-date, and quite costly, in spite of Leo XIII's modest attempts to lower the expenses of the Holy See. Moreover, many did not consider work within the Curia a challenging and demanding ecclesiastical pastorate conducted in the service of God's people, but rather a career promising the cardinal's hat, provided everything went well.

The idea of reform was in the air and not only in progressive circles, as was recently proven by a newly discovered plan which had been devised in the Vatican a year before Leo XIII died. However, this reform idea offended the principle *Quieta non movere,* honored by all administrations of the world, and it was rejected by all who saw their interests threatened. Facing a difficult financial situation, Pius X hurried to remedy the most glaring abuses, but that was not all. He began with several partial reforms which seemed especially urgent. On 17 September 1903 he suspended the obsolete special congregation *De eligendis episcopis,* founded by Benedict XIV and renewed in 1878 by Leo XIII. The Holy Office became responsible for the appointment of bishops in those countries which were not dependent on the Congregation for the Propagation of the Faith (the Propaganda) or subject to the regulations of a concordat. On 26 May 1906 he also suspended the two relatively new congregations *Super disciplina regulari* and *De statu regularium,* with the result that everything concerning the members of religious orders was concentrated in the Congregation of Bishops and Regulars. But he had already planned a much more extensive reform, as was requested by several prelates who had assembled around Cardinal Agliardi. His intentions were probably impelled by the idea of stopping the criticism of the radical front by taking the wind out of its sails. The radicals had begun to question the insufficient functioning of the Curia as well as its fundamental right of existence because they saw it as an obstacle between the Pope and the bishops. In the early summer of 1907 he decided to take steps which introduced a rapid development of the matters at hand.

A commission of cardinals was to be created to which Gaetano De Lai, secretary of the Congregation of the Council was assigned; De Lai was the chief supporter of this reform from the beginning to the end. According to the directives personally drafted by the Pope, the commission pursued the following goals: the abolition of superfluous offices and agencies and the creation of appropriate new ones as necessitated by the development of the situation; the separation of administrative and judicial responsibilities; the absolutely clear and rational definition of the responsibilities of each dicastery, assigning to one single organ all affairs pertaining, among others, to the bishops, the clergy, the orders, the sacraments, the missions, the simplification and thus the efficiency of the activities of individual offices; the assignment of a certain number of consultants to prepare resolutions; the coordination of criteria needed to come to a unanimous conclusion, and, finally, the standardization of fees and salaries of officials, which had been different depending on the individual functionary. The first plan drawn up by the Pope himself was presented to the commission in November. Concerning the Roman congregations, he relied extensively on a draft by Monsignor De Lai. In regard to the Secretariat of State, he followed Cardinal Merry del Val's standpoint: On the one hand, several countries were incorporated into the area of responsibility which had been subject to the Propaganda, even though they were no longer mission countries (Great Britain, the Netherlands, the United States, Canada); on the other hand, the Secretariat of State was assigned two previously independent agencies: the Congregation for Extraordinary Ecclesiastical Affairs and the Secretariat of Briefs. These expansions increased the significance of the Secretariat of State considerably. Finally, in order to separate the administration and the judiciary, the Pope revived the old medieval jurisdiction of the *Rota Romana,* which had been hobbled through the proliferation of the congregations equipped with judicial power to such an extent that its responsibility had been confined to liturgical questions (since 1870). In the course of the next months, the basic draft was repeatedly revised, but the changes did not impair the economy of the original plan: The Congregation of Matrimony became the Congregation of the Sacraments; the section of the former Congregation of Bishops and Regulars which had charge of the bishops was incorporated into the Congregation of the Consistory, so that all questions pertaining to the members of religious orders were now handled by a special congregation (the case of the Congregation of the Missions caused debates); the Congregation of the Index, at Pius X's request, was separated from the Holy Office "in view of the great number of books to be examined"; the Congregation of Rites and the Congregation of the Canonization of Saints were combined in one congregation.

On 29 June 1906 the constitution *Sapiento consilio* was published. The experts admired the "constructive and simplifying genius of Pius X" reflected in it (Torquebiau). From now on, the Curia was to include a triad of agencies: eleven congregations, three tribunals, and five offices. Within the area of congregations, the Congregation of the Sacraments was completely new. The former Congregation of the Council had been remodeled so drastically that it was also practically new; at the time of its establishment, it was to supervise the execution and interpretation of the decrees of the Council of Trent; but in the future it was to be in charge of the general discipline of the clergy and the faithful. The consistorial congregation's functions were considerably extended; it was even assigned the supervision of seminaries (in 1915, Benedict XV entrusted this function to the Congregation of Studies, whose only responsibility had been universities). The competence of the Propaganda was now limited to the mission countries in the true sense of the word; moreover, it had to relinquish all matters regarding marriage to the Rota and problems pertaining to sacraments to the Congregation of the Sacraments. For jurisdiction there were to be three responsible agencies: the Rota and the Apostolic Signature (as court of appeal) were to deal with the external forum, which had gradually been taken on by the Sacred Penitentiary; the internal forum was to be the responsibility of the Penitentiary. The five offices included the Apostolic Chancery, the Apostolic Datary, the Apostolic Camera (with very limited responsibilities), the Secretariat of Briefs, and the Secretariat of State as the most important. The constitution, which was amended by a detailed *Ordo servandus* (all together about eighty pages of small print), outlined precisely the functions of the new organs: appointments to the respective offices, schedules and statutes, the specific dispositions of the many subdivisions, and frequent reports, which often had to be presented to the Pope himself before a decision would be made. In order to facilitate the speedy preparation and execution of matters it was required that only the most important problems were to be submitted to the plenary session of the respective congregation. Other affairs were to be handled by the *Congresso,* a committee limited in number and consisting of high officials and the cardinal prefect of the congregation.

The practical application of the new regulations began immediately and was closely observed by the Pope himself. The fact that De Lai, who was created cardinal in December 1907, was given responsibility for the reorganization in a special commission was received with some amazement. Though many believed that the conservative Pius X proved to be rather revolutionary, the reform was generally received with satisfaction. Of course, the desire for a clear separation of administrative responsibilities and judicial functions was only partially fulfilled. The court of the Rota, indeed, confined itself to matters of matrimony; however, the congregations continued to handle controversies in other areas and issue penalties via administrative channels. Unquestionably, the basic structure of Sixtus V's organization was not as decisively changed as would be the case half a century later under Paul VI on the occasion of the reform of the Curia. Among other things, there was no mention of giving bishops who actually responsibly managed a diocese a position in the sections of the congregations dealing with practical matters. But even considering these obvious limits and shortcomings of Pius X's reform, the point must be clearly made that for the first time since the sixteenth century the entire Curia was reorganized according to, all in all, truly rational criteria.

These measures did not only possess a unique character, they were also of symbolic significance. They appeared to anticipate another highly crucial undertaking, the general reorganization of ecclesiastical law, in preparation since the beginning of Pius X's pontificate.

For several centuries, the idea prevailed of revising canon law and formulating a code that would systematically compile the entire body of law adapted to the contemporary situation. This code was to replace the immense, often inaccessible and obsolete collections of papal decrees. At the Vatican Council, a number of bishops had made certain requests in this respect; and shortly before this council convened, Pope Pius IX had issued the constitution *Apostolicae Sedis* (12 October 1869), thoroughly revising the legislation regarding ecclesiastical censures. Leo XIII had annulled or amended numerous obsolete regulations and even undertaken some partial codifications, using certain schemes prepared in view of the upcoming Vatican Council. His changes primarily affected the constitution *Officiorum ac munerum* (25 January 1897), codified and moderated in the legislation regarding censorship of books, and the constitution *Conditae a Christo* (8 October 1900), which finally afforded the religious congregations with simple vows a precise legal statute. Private canonists made several attempts.

"Two or three days after his election" (Merry del Val), Pius X was already expressing a desire to follow this path of reform.

He was strongly encouraged by Monsignor Gasparri, one of the best canonists of his time, and by Cardinal Gennari. On 19 March 1904 the Pope announced through his motu proprio *Arduum sane munus* the formation of a commission of cardinals, to be aided by a certain number of consultors, which was to adjust ecclesiastical legislation to the present circumstances and to codify it. In the following week, a letter was sent to all archbishops asking them to consult with their auxiliary bishops regarding the main changes which were to amend the present law and to send their recommendations to Rome, including additional nominations for consultors. A few days later, he also solicited the cooperation of Catholic universities throughout the world.

The announcement of this plan caused totally different reactions: satisfaction from those who witnessed in daily life the many-sided disadvantages of the present system; scepticism from the many scholars, mainly in Rome and Germany, who had better insight into the difficulties and thus predicted failure. The latter were supported by the famous editor of the *Corpus Iuris Canonici*, the Protestant Emil Friedberg, who charged the Pope with (among other things) attempting to extend in this way his power even further. Others feared that the sections dealing with ecclesiastical civil law and with the relations between Church and state could appear in a new edition of the *Syllabus* and lead to new confrontations with governments. Other Catholic groups, e.g., in Spain, criticized the project for attempting to copy the Napoleonic codes of law, which were considered an expression of liberal individualism. But Pius X remained unperturbed and made sure that everyone set to work at once.

From the very start, the chief promoter of this undertaking was Monsignor Gasparri, secretary of the Congregation for Extraordinary Affairs. The Pope appointed him secretary of the papal commission and president of the College of Consultors, and he was the heart and soul of the project until its conclusion.

To speed up the work, the consultors were divided into two commissions working next to each other. One was led by Gasparri with Eugenio Pacelli as secretary; the other one was headed by Cardinal De Lai with F. A. Sapieha as secretary. As of 13 November these commissions met weekly, comparing and discussing the editorial drafts for each chapter, which were presented by two, sometimes even three or four consultors working completely independently of each other. Proceeding from the different texts and opinions voiced, the president wrote a new draft, which was again discussed and reworked. Usually, this procedure was repeated at least three or four times, occasionally even ten or twelve times. To save time, the texts were first sent to the consultors for their critical examination and written comments. When they finally agreed on one version, Gasparri presented it to the commission of cardinals, which did not reveal its comment until after it had studied the text twice. The entire process took place in strict secrecy. One or two chapters or paragraphs, however, were published in the form of a papal constitution or a decree of a congregation either because the Pope considered the matter urgent or because he wanted to test the effectiveness in real life, trying to find out how the texts were received.

By 1912 many parts had been amended to the point that Gasparri was able to propose sending them to the bishops and heads of the orders asking them for their comments. In spite of the resistance of several cardinals fearing new delays, the Pope agreed. This consultation, where the bishops, in turn, could confidentially consult with two or three men in their trust, proved to be very useful. On 20 March 1912 Books I and II were delivered; on 1 April 1913 Book III; on 1 July Book V; and finally on 15 November 1914 Book IV. At that time Pius X had already been dead for three months. The final, conclusive version would take two more years.

Doubtless this project had its limits. Today, we see it as a new step in the direction of centralization and extreme uniformity of the Latin Church. Some, however, regret that it fails to make reference to the Holy Scriptures or the Church Fathers, in contrast to the ancient canonical collections. Even from a strictly juridical standpoint, a threatening insecurity in the terminology itself can be found, "even regarding concepts which are expressly defined" (G. Schwaiger), in spite of abundant discussions and subsequent revisions. Concerning the main content, a more radical further questioning of certain positions inherited from medieval law or from modern absolutism would have been desirable. However, one must admire the extent of a task executed in record time. After all, this work represents a well-structured summa, including the entire legislation of the Latin Church, excepting a portion of the liturgical material and excluding the particularly delicate problem of the relations between the Church and the respective state. It distinguishes itself through clarity and precision of style and seems to be inspired by civil codes of law. It reveals the attempt to synchronize the various segments of canon law with the demands of modern times and to give it the benefit of achievements in the field of learning and of the accomplishments of contemporary juridical practice. One must also praise Pius's interest in cooperating, from the beginning to the end, with the episcopate throughout the world and with the non-Roman canonists. Proof of his realism and moderation are the decisions made between the overly specialized position of the theoreticians and the extreme pragmatism of many a practitioner.

CHAPTER 71

Eucharistic Decrees and Liturgical Renewal

At the beginning of the twentieth century, a clearer perspective in favor of frequent Communion had been conceived. Yet the disputes between its advocates and opponents continued. Even Leo XIII's encyclical *Mirae caritatis* (1902), encouraging the "frequent use of the Eucharist" and protesting against the "contrived reasons for relinquishing Communion," did not succeed in settling the controversy, which was especially intense in France and Belgium. Some stressed the absolute necessity of doing away with premeditated venial sin before one could expect to be admitted to frequent Communion. Others advocated the concept, according to which the Eucharist is not "a reward for achieved virtue, but on the contrary, the means of achieving virtue." From this perspective, they strictly distinguished between the absolutely necessary and the desirable spiritual disposition.

As an admirer of Don Bosco, who had been an enthusiastic defender of the frequent and early Communion of children, Giuseppe Sarto had made the development of the celebration of the Eucharist the key issue of his program as bishop. Thus it was not surprising that as Pope he tried to realize this program for the Church at large. On the occasion of the international Eucharistic Congress, convened in Rome in June 1905, he approved a prayer "for the propagation of the pious custom of daily Communion," bringing to mind that "Jesus meant to be the daily remedy and the daily food for our daily shortcomings." The most decisive act, however, was the decree of the Congregation of the Council of 20 December 1905, *De quotidiana SS. Eucharistiae sumptione,* which provided the appropriate settlement of the impending controversy, specifying that two conditions for receiving Holy Communion be sufficient: the state of grace and the proper intention. At the same time, the faithful were asked to communicate "frequently and even daily." By order of the Pope, this decree was sent to all bishops and heads of orders, instructing them to "send it to their seminaries, parishes, religious institutions, and priests and to let the Holy See know what they had done to assure its execution." In the course of the next few months, other decrees encouraged the communicants by granting absolution (14 February 1906), by dispensing the sick confined to bed for more than one month from the Eucharistic rule of fast (7 December 1906 and 6 March 1907), and by defining the term "all faithful" used in the decree to include the children who had attended First Communion (13 September 1906).

The "age of reason" required for First Communion continued to be controversial. Frequently consulted about this disputed question, the Congregation of the Sacrament prepared a decree for which the Pope showed great interest, even though he anticipated strong resistance. After discussing the problem from a historical, dogmatic, and practical point of view, the decree *Quam singulari* (8 October 1910) declared that it is sufficient for children to be able "to recognize the difference between the Eucharistic Bread and common bread, and that it is unnecessary to postpone First Communion until the age of ten or twelve or even fourteen, as was done frequently at that time. This meant the new application of a principle on which all Eucharistic reforms of Pius X were based: Communion is not the reward for virtuous living, but the food to effect virtuous living according to the theological maxim *ex opere operato.*

Issuing appropriate decrees was not enough. It was necessary to apply this legislation to practical life. The new regulations were not at all as revolutionary as they seemed to be at first glance. Nevertheless, they turned many old customs upside down and encountered definite resistance in many countries.

Instigated by the Fathers of the Blessed Sacrament, a league of priests was founded in April 1905 for the purpose of enforcing the application of the decree about frequent Communion. Six years later, more than 50,000 priests had joined this league. Furthermore, immediately after the issuance of the decree *Quam singulari,* a Pious Union for the Communion of Children was founded in Rome, soon joined by many other national organizations (Italy, Spain, Belgium, South America, the United States, Canada). As of 1907 the Pope demanded the annual convention of a Eucharistic triduum in each diocese and if possible even in every parish. This was to draw the attention of the clergy and the faithful to the significance of the decree of 1905.

Pius X also used the international Eucharistic congresses to promote the acceptance and propagation of the Roman decrees. Originally these congresses were meant to be public manifestations to inspire the enthusiasm of the Catholics for all versions of the veneration of the Most Holy Sacrament and to liberate them from their fear of public judgment through clear and official testimony of Christ's Kingdom embracing all mankind (which was rejected by the followers of laicism). Since the beginning of Pius X's pontificate, however, another aspect came to the foreground, which had been only faintly present under Leo XIII: the desire to encourage the faithful to receive Communion frequently, even daily.

The utilization of the Eucharistic congresses bore increasingly rich fruit because their effect on the public grew considerably during the pontificate; the number of participants, their reputation and influence rose tremendously: in 1914, no fewer than six cardinals and two hundred bishops came to Lourdes, which approached the total number of participants of the first congress in 1881. Above all, the congresses became more and more international in character; of the first fifteen congresses, nine had taken place in France, four in Belgium, and one in Switzerland, areas which were generally considered an extension of France. To be sure, the Congress of Jerusalem in 1893 had been an exception, but one must not forget to what degree France had felt at home in the Levant. Nevertheless, Pius X, always very interested in the program of the congress, decided to hold it in 1905, the year of its twenty-fifth anniversary, in Rome. The next meeting places of the congress were determined: Metz (1907, German at that time), London (1908), Cologne (1909), Montreal (1910), Madrid (1911), Vienna (1912), and Malta (1913). Not until 1914 did the congress return to France, to Lourdes. Similarly, the significance of the foreign delegations attending the respective congresses increased. This expansion was needed in view of the fact that efforts had been made for several years also to organize national Eucharistic congresses almost everywhere. Therefore the international congresses were forced to emphasize their difference from the national congresses more clearly and to obtain a higher degree of internationality.

The Eucharistic decrees of Pius X, independent of their liturgical context, interpret Communion mainly as food for the individual Christian. On the other hand, Pius X played an important role in the rediscovery of the real position that the liturgy should take in Catholic life. The first significant reforms in the area of liturgy since the Council of Trent were owed to Pius X. Under his pontificate and partially under his influence, the so-called "liturgical movement," so far limited to a small elite and developing in the confinements of Benedictine abbeys, began to invade parishes.

One of the first acts of the pontificate of Pius X was the motu proprio *Tra le sollecitudini* of 22 November 1903, on the subject of Church music. However, its significance by far extended this area so that it is justified to speak of it as being the "charter of the liturgical movement." As bishop, the future Pope Pius X tried to combat "orchestral opera music," which had infiltrated Church music (more so in Italy than elsewhere), replacing it with classical polyphony and mainly with Gregorian chants, that is, the traditional chorale of the Church, whose true character the monks of Solesmes had gradually retrieved from the numerous changes they underwent in the course of the centuries. But he was not satisfied with such reforms instituted in his dioceses of Mantua and Venice. Thus in 1893 he proposed to the Congregation of Rites a motion about the reform of Church music, which text had been prepared (with the help of some monks from Solesmes) by Father A. De Santi, a Jesuit with connections with the *Civiltà Cattolica;* De Santi became more and more the "mover of the Gregorian reform" under Leo XIII's and Pius X's pontificates. Following the advice of Santi and with his assistance, a motu proprio was drafted in November 1903 which reiterated the text of the motion. It defined the true essence of Church music, its sources of inspiration, its exterior form, and its execution, and it banned from the ceremonies of worship everything that did not conform to these principles. Gregorian chant in "its original and pure form, to which it has been appropriately restored by recent efforts" was presented as the "perfect model of Church music": A church composition is more ecclesiastical and liturgical when it approaches Gregorian chant in its composition, its spirit, and its inner attitude; on the other hand, the more it deviates from this model," the less it is worthy of the house of God." However, even though Gregorian chant was propagated as the norm, Pius X inhibited its exclusive use, in contrast to many of the executors of his will who kindled illusions about the possibility of turning the monodic church chant into song truly accessible to the people, as subsequent experience was to show.

Through a second motu proprio of 25 April 1904, likewise inspired by Father De Santi, Pius X entrusted the Benedictines of Solesmes with the preparation of an authentic Vatican edition of the Gregorian melodies, under the control of a special Roman commission led by Dom J. Pothier, who had become abbot of Saint Wandrille in 1898. He requested that the melodies "be restored in their integrity and purity according to the oldest manuscripts, but also with special consideration of the legitimate tradition which had permeated the manuscripts in the course of time and of the practical use in present liturgies." This statement, inspired by Dom Pothier, caused endless debates in the commission. As a matter of fact, there were two camps, and not only within the ranks of the theoreticians, but mainly on the practical and pastoral level: Should one demand, as Dom Mocquereau and most of his fellow brothers of Solesmes did, literal adoption of the oldest manuscripts for an edition to be used in liturgy, even if these manuscripts did not agree with modern sensitivities, or should one request, as did Dom Pothier and the Germans (mostly Father Wagner), acceptance of the modifications and moderations later introduced by "living traditions"? The disagreements between the members of the commission were intensified by personal conflicts. Moreover, the question of whether the systematic study of the old manuscripts would not necessitate many years of scholarly research, thus postponing the publication of the official edition, which, according to the Pope's intentions, was to standardize the practice of Church music in the entire Catholic Church, was legitimate. In order to solve this problem, the Pope, actually favoring the second solution, decided to proceed from the edition published in 1895 by Dom Pothier. In 1905 Pothier was asked to take charge of the final preparation and completion of the new edition. The Vatican commission ceased its work. In October 1905, the *Kyriale* was published, followed in 1908 by the *Graduale* and in 1912 by the *Antiphonarium*. Several decrees of the Congregation of Rites reinforced the order to observe the regulations carefully, and the bishops were forbidden to allow future editions whose melodies did not conform with the Vatican edition.

The significance that the Pope attributed to the restoration of Church music does not only have aesthetic reasons — "provide a prayer with a beautiful background," he said — but rests mainly in the desire to awake in the faithful love for the liturgy and for solemn Church prayer, which the Pope considered "the first and irreplaceable source of Christian strength," according to the wording of the motu proprio of 1903. This intention compelled Pius X, who had been a man of the Church all his life, to institute several liturgical reforms. From the perspective of the second Vatican Council, they may seem rather modest, but they required a certain measure of courage and, in any case, provided the first, not insignificant guideline for the great liturgical awakening of the twentieth century.

The expedience of certain liturgical reforms or at least their revision had been in the air since the Vatican Council, which had offered the opportunity of a series of *vota* regarding the reform of the breviary. The progress of historical studies in Catholic circles during the last decades suggested a revision of the martyrology and certain readings of Matins. For this purpose, Leo XIII had founded a Historical-Liturgical Commission (1902). Pius X was not indifferent to this problem, and the benevolence with which he treated the school of Solesmes was partly due to the fact that this school endeavored to restore the purity of the old Roman music on the basis of thorough studies of the manuscripts. His interest in the liturgical discipline, however, was primarily of a pastoral nature. Moreover, the reform, which he began after successfully concluding the restoration of Church music, was not primarily designed to eliminate the historical errors contained in the breviary, but rather to upgrade the prayer of the weekly psalter and to restore Sunday to its rightful place in the liturgical cycle.

The festivals of saints or other more recent feasts with their own unique attributes had increased to such an extent that the Sunday or ferial office was rarely celebrated; consequently, numerous psalms were not recited any longer. Recently, Leo XIII had made the situation worse by conceding the votive office *ad libitum,* practically destroying the liturgical yearly cycle. Various undertakings led to the establishment of a papal commission to reform the psalter (July 1911).

This commission was ordered to work independently of the Congregation of Rites, whose tendency to cling to tradition would have made any serious reform impossible. The commission was also to work independently of the historical-liturgical commission which Leo XII had established. This documented the wish not to let objections by the historians get in the way. The commission was chaired by the new secretary of the Congregation of Rites, C. La Fontaine, a pastor who was intimately familiar with the liturgy but not with its history. The commission went to work at once. Working according to his own unique method, only assisted by a few advisers, Pius X was able after several months to publish the bull *Divino afflatu* (1 November 1911). It not only undertook the restructuring of the Divine Office in the spirit of tradition, but it also paid attention to the reasonable request to ease the burden of the breviary for the priest serving a parish. Matins was shortened from eighteen psalms on Sunday and twelve on weekdays to nine psalms or pieces of psalms. No holy days were suspended, but Sundays took a special place from now on; on most holy days, the ferial office was to be used along with the hymn of Matins, the lessons, and the concluding prayers. The *Proprium de Tempore* was restored to significance, readings of the Holy Scriptures were allotted more time, and the entire Office became more varied, even though it was considerably shortened and simplified, unfortunately sacrificing many traditional elements.

However, this was only the beginning. Despite the opposition of Monsignor La Fontaine, who claimed that an incisive reform required the consultation of the episcopate, Pius X adopted the more far-reaching concept of Piacenza and extended the duties of the commission to include a complete reform of the breviary and the missal. The execution of such an extensive program required thorough studies. The pressures by the publishers anxious to publish the new model edition of the breviary as soon as possible finally forced the Pope to find a temporary solution which emphasized the Sunday and ferial office, especially during Lent (motu proprio *Abhinc duos annos* of 23 October 1913). In the beginning of 1914, the reform of the missal was begun; however, the death of the Pope brought everything to a standstill, especially after the commission was strongly criticized for its working habits. The liturgical historians charged that it had sacrificed many time-honored values, for example, the prayer of Psalms 148–150, recited every morning at dawn. The pragmatists thought that the revisions, forced upon the concerned groups without consulting them, had been made "hastily" (Della Chiesa), without paying sufficient attention to the difficulties of application.

The role Pius X played in the restoration of the liturgy is not confined to his legislative work, as significant as this may have been for the reevaluation of the celebration of the Christian mysteries in the context of the annual cycle. In his motu proprio of 1903, regarding Church music, the Pope said that the first source to feed the Christian life of the faithful was to be found in "active participation in the mystery of worship and in the common and solemn prayers of the Church." From this statement the Belgian Benedictine Lambert Beauduin derived the inspiration and the foundation for founding the liturgical movement of Mont-César (Louvain) on the occasion of the Congress of Mechelen around 1909. He was supported by Cardinal Mercier. Since Beauduin possessed remarkable organizational talents and a contagious optimism, he succeeded (in his own special way) in interesting the parishes in the liturgical life. He distributed among the masses tens of thousands of pamphlets containing the translation of all Sunday Masses and their annotations. At the same time, he trained the pastors with both a journal, doctrinal in character, and the *Questions liturgiques.* He also organized yearly liturgical conventions, which grew more and more successful until the outbreak of the war. These meetings contributed a great deal to the spread of the movement for the liturgical pastoral outside of Belgium. It was to reach its peak in the course of the next quarter of the century.

CHAPTER 72

Concern for Pastoral Improvements:
Seminaries, Catechetical Instruction, Catholic Action

All popes of the nineteenth and twentieth centuries were intensely interested in improving the spiritual and moral level of the clergy and inspiring their pastoral enthusiasm. No pope was more systematically devoted to this task than Pius X. He continuously issued new memorandums and offered advice in this matter and again and again took new practical measures.

In March 1904, on the occasion of the thirteen hundredth anniversary of the death of Gregory the Great, he defined in an encyclical "the ideal of the true priest," as Gregory had described it in his *Regula pastoralis;* and he ordered for all of Italy apostolic visitations which were to bring to light the shortcomings of the clergy in order to eliminate them. A few months earlier, he had recommended to the priests joining the *Unio apostolica,* a fraternity of priests "whose usefulness and excellence he had tested himself." The questionnaire, prepared in 1909 by the consistorial congregation under his direction, focused on the clergy's observance of their duties and the situation in the seminaries. The bishops were to answer this questionnaire during their *visitatio liminum.* In view of the reaction of the national episcopate, Pius X did not make the wearing of the cassock mandatory all over the world, and he did not introduce everywhere the Italian custom of prohibiting the seminarians from returning to their families during vacation (in order to better protect them from worldly indoctrination). But he constantly reminded the bishops to use stricter standards when recruiting priests and to expel those young seminary candidates whose spirit of obedience gave cause for serious doubts.He urgently wanted the priests to concentrate on their ultimate religious task, and he took several measures for the purpose of releasing them and preventing them from participating in all activities of an economic or political nature. In order to improve the spiritual guidance of the clergy, he did not hesitate to ease the traditional rules regarding the tenure of the pastors.

Several of these measures may give the impression of a sort of police system of surveillance and espionage, and of an overestimation of obedience at the cost of a free exchange of opinions. However, we must not forget that Pius X was always guided by a very high, positive ideal. This ideal found an especially remarkable and eloquent expression in *Haerent animo* (4 August 1908), an urgent reminder to the clergy, representing the true spiritual charter of the priesthood and remaining authoritative for a long time to come. It was written entirely by the Pope himself on the occasion of the fiftieth anniversary of his ordination as priest, and it took only "about fourteen days of the few moments of free time at his disposal" (Merry del Val). He drew a truly traditional picture of the priesthood; but he incorporated the rules of the priest's office which evolved in the course of the nineteenth century, challenging the clergy to follow them zealously. This does not change the fact that this saintly Pope, with his totally unique flair for challenges, instilled in the pastoral ministry a new spirit, the effects of which could be felt long after his death.

Impelled by the desire to improve the quality of the clergy, Pius X dealt particularly with the question of the seminaries, including the preparatory seminaries; except in German-speaking countries and in Belgium, they trained most candidates for the priesthood from ages twelve to thirteen. The instruction offered in these seminaries was completely antiquated. The situation was worsened by the fact that most teachers were autodidacts. They were in no position to prepare future priests for coping with the problems of the modern world. These grievances had been pointed out for several years by various people. Especially in Italy reforms were urgently needed, because the great number of small dioceses made the situation worse. Many bishops of this country faced the dilemmas of financing and recruiting the faculty. Shortly before his death, Leo XIII discussed this problem before the episcopate in a motu proprio of 8 December 1902; Pius X was completely open-minded toward these problems; after all, in Treviso and as bishop of Mantua he had tried hard to improve the diocesan seminaries. In January of 1905 the bishops were asked to think about the interdiocesan reorganization of the seminaries, and a papal commission was ordered to prepare reform plans analyzing and utilizing the reports of the inspectors.

Eventually some improvements were made. Among them were: the consolidation of smaller institutions, adaptation of the high school curriculum to that of state institutions, introduction of a preparatory year at the beginning of theological studies, emphasis on the significance of a spiritual adviser and on the genuineness of vocations (especially urgent in countries where the clerical profession often meant social advancement). A new group of apostolic visitors was ordered to supervise the consequent execution of the Roman regulations. Unfortunately, the reform did not produce the results expected, especially in southern Italy. Qualified staffs were lacking, and the radical purge in reaction to modernism reduced the number of suitable men. The establishment of regional seminaries proved to be more difficult than had been expected, even though the Holy See financially assisted many bishops who did not have the necessary means at their disposal.

All these measures pertained only to Italy, but in the opinion of the Pope they could be taken as models elsewhere. All instructions received by the congregation entrusted with the control of the seminaries required that the regulations initially issued for Italy also be applied worldwide. Certain explanations in this regard specified the Pope's intentions.

Pius X's restoration efforts regarding a more effective pastoral extended over other areas as well. Holding the conviction that good bishops are a must if one wants good priests, he did not confine himself to pious reprimands, as contained in the encyclical *Communium rerum* (21 April 1909), in which he represents Saint Anselm of Canterbury as a model pastor, fervently drawing the picture of the ideal bishop. He also tried to improve the recruitment of the episcopate by revising the methods of appointments. He issued precise directives for the maintenance of the candidates' personal file, studying each one personally before making a decision. On the other hand in order to increase his control over the activities of his bishops he tightened not only the rule on the periodical *visitatio liminum* whereby every bishop was obliged, according to a strictly determined alternating schedule, to appear at the Vatican every five years. The bishop was now obliged to present a detailed report on the conditions in his diocese based upon a minutely detailed questionnaire.

Instruction in the catechism was also one of Pius X's concerns. Clearly recognizing the situation, the Pope drew attention to the fact "that it is much easier to find a brilliant speaker than a catechist who is an excellent teacher." He did not grow tired of reminding the priests to present Christian doctrine clearly and simply, and to deal thoroughly with the catechesis for adults, which had been greatly neglected in the nineteenth century because the instruction of children took precedence. As always, he did not confine himself to issuing a solemn encyclical regarding this problem; rather, he devised a series of measures, demanding, among other things, the more frequent employment of lay catechists, a novelty at this time. His words were followed by his example and, as he used to do, he personally explained the catechism every Sunday. Listeners came by the thousands wanting to hear the Pope who had not forgotten that he was also the bishop of the diocese of Rome.

Pius X also instigated the preparation of a new catechism, pointing out the elements which were to be considered. After examining the draft personally and correcting it with care, he introduced this catechism as the required text in the ecclesiastical province of Rome. At the same time, he expressed a wish to adopt it in all dioceses, because he was interested in fulfilling the desire for a universal standardized catechism which had been repeatedly voiced after the First Vatican Council.

The interest in catechismal instruction, which Pius X had displayed continuously as a young priest and in later life, was in line with contemporary concerns. In 1889 the first Italian catechetical congress had taken place in Piacenza. But it was primarily in German-speaking countries that an active movement in search of new directions emerged. Journals found good response even in non-German-speaking countries, and the catechetical societies, whose mouthpiece they were, organized important congresses in Munich (1906) and in Vienna (1912). Gradually, under the influence of H. Stieglitz, a new method was developed which had been inspired by the Protestant pedagogue Johann Friedrich Herbart and was known as the Munich catechetical method: an inductive method no longer proceeding from the text, which is explained, but from what the child knows already or perhaps (but at that time rarely) from a story in the Bible that was to be added to the text of the catechism. However, some time passed before the majority of catechists adopted the new ideas, and it took even more time before interest in the pedagogical problems related to the method were replaced by the more fundamental question of the content to be taught: What should really be taught, a religious knowledge verbalized in Scholastic terms or a message of salvation in Christ as presented in the Holy Scriptures?

It has already been pointed out that Pius X requested the frequent employment of lay catechists. But instruction in the catechism was not the only area in which he appealed to the laity. "Today, it is most important that every parish have at its disposal a group of enlightened, virtuous, decisive, and truly apostolic laymen." As a priest and bishop, Pius X knew from experience what effective help laymen, aware of their Christian responsibility, could provide the clergy regarding the vitalization of a parish and the modification of society.

Emphasizing the importance of the organized lay apostolate, Pius X may indeed appear to be a forerunner. Yet he proved to be conservative in the way he tried to implement this idea. "The activities assisting the spiritual and pastoral office of the Church...must be subject to Church authority in every detail....But even the other works undertaken to restore the true Christian civilization in Christ and forming Catholic Action in its aforementioned significance cannot be understood without the counsel and the high leadership of the ecclesiastical authority." This passage from the encyclical *Il fermo proposito* is characteristic of Pius X's viewpoint: he was aware of the indispensable effort of the laity to instill Christian principles into secular life; but he did not yet realize the specific character of the action of the Catholics within society, seeing it almost exclusively as an expansion and extension of the action of the clergy. He was inspired by certain formulas which had been successful during his time in Venetia, and he propagated an organization of Catholic Action according to a more or less uniform model which did not grant the laymen more than the role of an executor under the very strict control of the bishops. The Catholics were to join in certain groups in order to begin their various activities not only in the area of the religious apostolate, but also in the area of the social organizations, the press, or even political elections. But those were always strictly denominational organizations, incorporated into the framework of the parishes and the dioceses and dependent on the episcopate, which, in turn, was subject to the directives from Rome. By necessity, such a clerical conception of Catholic Action was bound to encounter clandestine or open resistance almost everywhere, depending on the situation. The most sensational oppositions of this kind were the crisis of the *Opera dei congressi* in Italy, breaking out in the first months of his pontificate, the affair concerning *Le Sillon* in France a few years later, and finally the conflict pertaining to the Christian trade unions in Germany.

Section Two

The Modernist Crisis

Roger Aubert

It is increasingly clear that the definition of modernism in the encyclical *Pascendi* offers in abstract terms a uniform system which is rightfully declared to be in conflict with the Catholic faith, offering the historian nothing but a somewhat inadequate framework, because, while the theologian assesses documents and formulas from an absolute perspective, the historian has to make an attempt to understand mankind in its actual multifariousness, its deeper aspirations, and its spiritual concerns. However, there is another reason: The Jansenism of the seventeenth century was nothing more than the marginal phenomenon of an often absolutely orthodox, but sometimes simply anachronistic Augustinian movement. Likewise, the restoration movement, developing within the Church at the turn of the nineteenth century, showed rather different kinds of tendencies: Some of them were certainly legitimate, even though they may have confused people moving along in traditional ways; but other tendencies were dangerous because of their lack of proper distinctions, even though they may have had sound principles. Others were extremely heretical and in some cases completely lacking in Christian content.

The term "New Catholicism" (later "modernism") embraced a series of concepts reflecting, in the opinion of contemporaries, the liberalism of the nineteenth century: renewed questioning of the traditional conception the Church had of the political and social order; the *aggiornamento* of the ecclesiastical institutions, the forms of the pastoral and the life style of the Christians living in and committed to this modern world; and the restoration of exegesis, theology, and religious philosophy. In this very general sense, modernism could be defined as "the meeting and confrontation of a long religious past with a present which found the vital sources of its inspiration in anything but this past" (É. Poulat). In this respect, the effects of modernism could be seen in Christian socialism and even in Christian democracy, in Sillonism, in Americanism (at least in the French version), and in the many different, often independent currents of an ecclesiastical reform movement as it appeared around 1900 in Germany, Italy, and France. One chapter in this section is entirely devoted to German Reform Catholicism, because in this area, especially at the beginning of the twentieth century, tendencies came to light originating in the confrontation of Catholicism with the currents of a changing society. Most of all we must investigate the religious and cultural crises transpiring primarily in France, occasionally in Italy, and in some Catholic groups in England, caused by the unexpected collision of traditional Church doctrine with modern religious studies that had developed independently of and often even in opposition to the control of the churches.

The crisis with which we must deal at this point is comparable to the one that broke out half a century earlier in the churches of the Reformation under the name of "liberal Protestantism." However, this crisis was on a much larger scale. While certain groups, often called "Progressives," confined themselves to placing the newest discoveries of religious studies into the service of the traditional faith, other, more radical groups (the modernists in the true sense of the word) considered it necessary to give this faith a new form of expression, which was to do justice to the changes of the human mind, whose symptom and driving force were precisely the very development of these new studies. Such attempts were considered by certain adventurous minds as the dawn of a new era. To others, especially to most of the ecclesiastical authorities, they appeared to be the beginning of an impending catastrophe.

Here are the roots of the bitter antimodernistic reaction. This bitterness cannot be solely explained by the methods of Church leadership and the delight of the contemporary press in sharp polemics. It was also caused by the realization that the Church felt deeply shaken and that, aside from some particularly acute men, no one could anticipate, sixty years before the Second Vatican Council, that the outcome of this renewed questioning, induced by a collective change of mind, would not necessarily lead to a total elimination of the essence of the Christian faith.

C H A P T E R   7 3

Reform Catholicism in Germany

Since the German clergy received a much more thorough training than the clergy in Latin or Anglo-Saxon countries, Germany was practically untouched by the phenomenon of modernism in the true sense of the word. However, in the two decades preceding the outbreak of World War I, the Catholic intellectuals were seized by a liberal current and a reform movement which wanted to reverse German Catholicism's trend of retreating within its own confines. This isolationism, the consequence of resistance to the *Kulturkampf,* had resulted in a kind of reaction that was inimical to the modern spirit and especially to its manifestation in German national liberalism. But these movements also wanted to combat clerical and authoritarian tendencies which had permeated the Church since the victory of ultramontanism under Pius IX's pontificate, and they planned to be more open-minded toward the modern world and its aspirations. Also called "present-day Catholicism" or "critical Catholicism" (in contrast to a blind submission to Church authorities), these reform efforts in the German Catholic Church toward the end of the nineteenth century and throughout the first half of the twentieth century were usually described by the term "Reform Catholicism." It was precisely this term, by the way, which contributed to its ill repute among those who were intent on emphasizing the differences between the Catholic Church and the Evangelical Reformation.

It is true that the term "Reform Catholicism" is a "collective name for many diverse, mostly unrelated tendencies" (Hagen), including: liberal elements who wanted to instill Christianity with the rationale of the natural sciences or strove for a diminution of authoritative dependence in theological research; theologians and philosophers who were interested in an exchange with modern thought and therefore disapproved of the pressure Rome exercised in favor of Neo-Scholasticism; historians who were sensitive to the evolutionary aspect of things, thus provoking the majority of the ultramontanes, who wanted to keep the thought and life of the Church prisoner of the norms which had been determined in the Middle Ages or at the time of the Counter Reformation; opponents of the centralistic Church regime who had not followed the Old Catholics in their schism with Rome but agreed with many of their demands; heirs of the reform movements in the area of the liturgy (use of the German language), of Church discipline (among other things, the question of clerical celibacy), of the training of future priests, heirs, therefore, of ideas which had been posed and supported by followers of the earlier ecclesiastical enlightenment and, in the course of the first half of the century, by men like Hirscher; laymen who had involved themselves in the life of the Church and wished for more independence, especially in regard to social and cultural affairs and decisions, often also in regard to the organization of life in the parish or in the selection of pastors; patriots who were proud of the growing power of the new German Empire and wanted to reintroduce to the Church the rich heritage of German cultural and intellectual life, seemingly alienated from German Catholicism since the middle of the nineteenth century; religious men, partially rooted in the tradition of German Romanticism, who wanted to replace the legalistic Church, mired in organizational matters and Church politics, with the apostolic Church of love or the Church of the spirit, as they called it. All of them shared a certain anti-Roman, especially anti-Jesuit attitude, often even an animosity to the "political Catholicism" organized in the Center Party, and furthermore a "naive overestimation of the scholarly characteristics of the nineteenth century" (G. Schwaiger). They also shared their loyalty to the Catholic Church and, in contrast to the modernists in the true sense of the word, the intent to respect unconditionally the basic structures of the faith and the Church. Some aspects of their demands and efforts were unquestionably narrow-minded and dictated by the circumstances of the time, but they "were loyal to the revelation and the Church, even though they dealt with the problems of the time more decisively and sometimes more obstreperously than their contemporaries."

In all these efforts, certain parallels can be detected to the demands voiced by men such as Monsignor Ireland or Father Hecker in the United States, the disciples of Americanism, some Sillonists in France, F. von Hügel in England, Monsignor Bonomelli, the followers of Rosmini or the Milan group of the *Rinnovamento* in Italy whose work had some response in Germany. All in all, German Reform Catholicism developed rather independently of the foreign reform movements of that time. It was oriented toward the tradition of German Catholicism, its own situation after the *Kulturkampf,* and its subsequent problems.

In view of the multiplicity of phenomena, the polemical terminology was especially disastrous. In the course of the following years these undefined efforts gained ground, but they were confined to certain academic circles, mainly in southern Germany, and they were usually unrelated. They were represented by three outstanding personalities: F. X. Kraus, H. Schell (above all) and later A. Ehrhard.

Franz Xaver Kraus, a brilliant professor of Church history and essayist, was at that time "the head and soul of the theology faculty in Freiburg" (H. Schiel) and one of the respected informants of the government in Berlin as far as Church policy was concerned. With unending loyalty he stood by the Church, no matter what his opponents maintained; but he was unable to understand the viewpoints of those who did not adhere to his ideas. He judged the general policies of the Church on the basis of his personally inimical sentiments. He was convinced that the future of the Church was threatened by the narrow-minded attitude and the fanaticism of the ultramontanes, and he branded them the Pharisees of our time, who "placed the Church before religion and were willing to sacrifice a clear decision of their conscience in favor of the decisions of an external authority." As a "liberal" in the sense that the word had in the nineteenth century (C. Bauer) and with the Dantean distinction between "religious" and "political" Catholicism, he sharply opposed the policies of the Roman Curia and the Center Party, not only in numerous anonymous articles, but also in his ecclesiastical-political "Spectator Letters," which appeared from 1896 until 1900 in the *Allgemeine Zeitung.*

Even though Kraus moved away from the Reform Catholicism J. Müller had praised as the "religion of the future," and even though "his own ecclesiastical-political principles and concerns dealt principally with questions other than the struggle of the antimodernists," (H. Schiel) his dissatisfaction with the existing situation and his sharp criticism of ultramontanism earned him the honor of carrying the banner for those liberal Bavarian Catholics who had founded, in 1904, under the name *Krausgesellschaft,* a "society for the advancement of religion and culture," which combined a naive admiration of "independent scholarship" with strong anti-Roman accusations and prejudices.

Herman Schell, after 1884 professor of apologetics, Christian art history, and comparative religious studies in Würzburg, attracted many enthusiastic admirers. He was an outstanding intellectual of tireless energy, anything but a polemicist, but a sincere and original philosopher and theologian, who has been discovered today as a forerunner of Christian existentialism because he emphasized the personal and vital aspect and the inwardness of Catholicism without in the least denying the visible and hierarchical aspects of the Church. He developed theories which were somewhat unfamiliar to the theology of his time, for example, about religious freedom, the apologetics of immanence, the role of the Holy Spirit, and the position of the laity in the Church; and he introduced religious studies to the ecclesiastical disciplines. Within a few years, he published amazingly varied and voluminous works, whose audacious constructs were often subject to justified criticism, but it was to his credit that he presented the traditional doctrine in personalistic categories, and that he was inspired by the continuous desire to "baptize" modern philosophy and science and to prove that they were by no means incompatible with Catholic belief. These declarations were made in the name of an "ideal Catholicism" and supplemented by a program for applying his theses to the areas of religious, intellectual, and political activities. He criticized the methods of the Church government more directly, and he expressed his conviction that the Church, provided its core was unchangeable, must rejuvenate itself continuously through dialogue with the world. On 15 December 1898 his most important works were put on the Index. Schell submitted, and he was allowed to continue teaching. His prestige grew. However, the bitter polemics against him continued in an "unworthy manner" (Schwaiger), his loyalty and his faith were doubted, and as a matter of fact, he was charged with planning "to revolutionize the clergy." According to his doctor, all these intrigues impaired his health, and he died in 1906, only fifty-six years old.

In the meantime, other progressive voices were making themselves heard. There were even attempts made to organize the liberal forces. In 1901 a former colleague of Schell's, patrologist Albert Ehrhard, published not just a pamphlet, but a larger, scholarly work with the significant title *Der Katholizismus und das 20. Jahrhundert im Licht der kirchlichen Entwicklung der Neuzeit* (Catholicism and the 20th Century in Light of Ecclesiastical Development in Modern Times). Based on his solid knowledge of the past, this work attempted to prove the thesis that it is possible to overcome the conflict unquestionably present between Catholicism and the modern world of thought, provided that, on the one hand, modern thought relinquish its anti-Christian prejudices, and that, on the other hand, the Church cease to conceptualize the Middle Ages in absolute terms. In Ehrhard's opinion, the Middle Ages do not represent the climax of Christianity's development. Its religious institutions had only relative value, and Neo-Scholasticism would have to fail if it was conceived merely as an unqualified restoration of the past. He also had reservations about the Society of Jesus. His work was very successful (twelve editions in one year), but almost the entire Catholic press in Germany and Austria criticized Ehrhard. Albert Ehrhard, not faced with any critics of his caliber, responded harshly with his new ingenious work: *Liberaler Katholizismus? Ein Wort an meine Kritiker* (1902).

Several other less prominent professors joined in the controversy in the following years, taking Ehrhard's side.

After 1901 the avant-garde gathered around several journals: *Renaissance* (1901-7); *Zwanzigstes Jahrhundert* (1902-9), whose motto was: "religion, Germanity, culture," perpetuated by an active minority of young Bavarians. *Hochland* had an entirely different format (1903-71; forbidden in 1941, continued in 1946). This journal opposed the criticism which, thanks to the powerful organization of the Borromeo Society, dominated most of the Catholic literary productions and was perpetuated by the clergy. Instead, *Hochland* advocated a literary evaluation, which emphasized aesthetic aspects over moralizing concerns. This journal greatly benefitted the alleviation of the ghetto literature mentality of German Catholicism, aside from its contributions to good literature.

The reactions of the hierarchy toward reforms were mostly of a negative nature. The hierarchy, interested in preserving its structures and strict orthodoxy and fearing the religious confusion of the masses, resisted change as such. This was also true in view of Reform Catholicism at the beginning of the twentieth century. The problem was aggravated by the fact that the latter, aside from justified demands and healthy efforts, succumbed to ill-advised or vague proposals and exaggerated criticism. This gave rise to the occasional, but usually completely unjustified question of whether these men, if only de facto, worked hand in glove with the Away-from-Rome movement raging through Austria at that time, and whether they were not striving for a Christianity practically independent of Rome. Even Bishop P. W. Keppler of Rottenburg, a prelate who was certainly not considered a reactionary (formerly professor in Freiburg) and who had approved, though with reservation, the publication of Ehrhard's disputed work, thought it necessary to intervene in the controversies with a public lecture "About the True and False Reform" (1 December 1902). He conceded that certain things in the Church needed improvement. However, his sharp, barely disguised criticism of men such as Kraus, Schell, and Ehrhard was astonishing. This lecture was fatefully influenced by the very successful writer Julius Langbehn (the "Rembrandt German"), an anti-Semitic forerunner of the "conservative revolution." To the dismay of the ultramontanes, Rome kept quiet for a long period of time. However, Pius X was more and more disturbed by the developments in Germany, especially by indications that the reform efforts were gaining ground. One such symptom was the founding of a society in Münster in the spring of 1906 which was joined by an elite of Catholic laymen (such as several leaders of the Center Party) and pursued the goal of prompting the Holy See to change the Index procedures. Another symptom was the support given to two bishops, about thirty seminary professors, and prominent laymen by a committee established for the purpose of erecting a memorial for Schell. After the Austrian theologian E. Commer had published an extremely aggressive book against Schell following his death, the Pope sent him a brief on 14 June 1907, praising him for the great service he had done for the Church. In this same brief, he charged the advocates of this memorial with "laboring under a misapprehension of the Catholic truth" and "resisting the authority of the Holy See." The appointment of the former Dominican General Frühwirth as nuncio in Munich at the end of 1907 was to serve both as a bulwark against the feared progressing decline of Catholic Germany toward liberalism and as an introduction to a reevaluation of the situation.

However, the turbulence and polemical controversies did not cease. They were even reignited through the disputes over the encyclical *Pascendi* and later over the antimodernist oath. In 1909 the *Zwanzigstes Jahrhundert* was renamed *Das neue Jahrhundert* with the significant subtitle: *Organ der deutschen Modernisten*. After a few months, however, a change occurred under the leadership of Philipp Funk, an idealistic young layman from the Catholic youth movement who was characterized by "a mixture of belligerence and religious inwardness" (Spörl). He turned away from the purely negative and polemical tendency of the journal, differentiating it sharply from French modernism and the Austrian Away-from-Rome movement and declaring that Reform Catholicism had to remain "a matter disputed *within the confines* of the Church."

Of all the personalities involved in Reform Catholicism around 1910, one man stands out for his energetic, unique character and his fearless and unconditional advocacy of the truth: S. Merkle, professor of Church history in Würzburg, whose lectures had incited conflicts between the boards of seminaries and the episcopal administration. In 1902 Cardinal Steinhuber had complained that most of the Munich "reformists" came from the ranks of Merkle's students. Merkle was the pioneer of a new, more positive Catholic evaluation of Luther and the ecclesiastical enlightenment. His viewpoints had not been accepted amicably in ultramontane circles whose dismay climaxed in 1912 when he opposed their plans for an exclusively Catholic university, instead defending theological faculties incorporated into the state universities. One of his chief arguments for maintaining the faculties was that they contributed greatly to the preservation of religious peace in Germany, but the effect of the indignation stored up during the *Kulturkampf* intensified the denominational differences among the heirs of the Mainz faction. They felt strengthened in their convictions by the support Pius X had given the opponents of the interdenominational trade unions during the trade union controversy. Thus the political and social conflicts in Germany on the eve of World War I intersected with the controversies over Reform Catholicism, as had been the case several years before in France in the course of the modernist controversy.

C H A P T E R   7 4

The Beginning of the Crisis in France

With justification Loisy wrote: "The *Histoire du modernisme* by Houtin rests on fiction: on the agreement of Duchesne's ideas about the early history of the Church conceived between 1881 and 1889 with my thoughts on the history of the Bible and Hébert's concepts of philosophy." It is a matter of fact that there was initially no concentrated action, even on a purely national level. Rather, there existed various concepts that had spontaneously developed during the last years of Leo XIII's pontificate and were favored by the general atmosphere of reconciliation between the Church and modern society, a climate seemingly confirmed by several papal initiatives. The controversy over Americanism had been in this respect symptomatic.

Influenced by Neo-Kantianism and believing to have found their ultimate master in Maurice Blondel, whose ideas were often falsified, philosophers strove to replace Scholastic intellectualism with a doctrine that would include the forces of the heart and the actual processes of life. Some of them remained under the vague influence of a religious symbolism based on Schleiermacher, combined with the evolutionism of Hegelian or Spencerian inspiration. They declared that theology has to relinquish unalterable concepts and devise new interpretations in order to preserve contact with steadily progressing life. Philosopher Marcel Hébert, priest and director of a large Paris college, joined this movement, which was strongly affected by A. Sabatier's work *Esquisse d'une philosophie de la religion d'ápres la psychologie et l'histoire* (Outline of a Philosophy of Religion according to Psychology and History, 1897), a book disseminating the concepts of German liberal Protestantism even in France.

Parallel to this philosophical movement, publicized through the *Annales de philosophie chrétienne,* young theologians, familiarized by Duchesne with historical criticism, discovered that German non-Catholic scholars, applying the principles of historical criticism to the documents and history of the beginnings of Christianity, had called in question certain traditional interpretations, such as those pertaining to Moses' work, to the history of Israel's religion, to the teachings of Christ, and to life among the first Christian generations. From this arose the problem of the compatibility of Catholic belief with the results of modern exegetic scholarship. The encyclical *Providentissimus,* issued by Leo XIII in 1893, had provided several principles for solving these problems, but certainly not all of them. The Pope's warnings against exaggerated criticism encouraged even the conservative forces to brand all attempts to apply the critical methods to inspired texts as thoroughly infested with rationalistic prejudices. Yet more and more exegetes upheld the conviction that the application of the critical method to this field was not sacrilege. On the contrary, intellectual righteousness and honesty demanded the application of the tested principles of historical method to studies of the Holy Scriptures, even at the risk of consequently having to change traditional postures in the controversies between believers and rationalists by making new fundamental distinctions between the (sometimes acceptable) literary and historical results of critical investigations and a conception of Israel's history and the origins of Christianity that would systematically erase the supernatural aspect.

From this perspective, Duchesne's student Alfred Loisy (1857–1940) devoted himself after 1883 to the study of the Old Testament and then the gospels, and M.-J. Lagrange founded in 1890 the École Biblique in Jerusalem, publishing two years later the *Revue biblique.* Lagrange confined himself to the world of experts and was intent on demonstrating the identity of his research results with the official doctrine of the Church (which did not prevent his critical appraisal by the conservatives and denunciation in Rome). Loisy and several of his collaborators, on the other hand, were less cautious. Convinced that Catholic apologetics, in view of the progress made by so-called "independent" criticism, had to completely revise its concepts, they did not hesitate to abrogate, even in popular journals, a great number of traditional doctrines. In spite of his efforts not to impede the progress of the investigations, Leo XIII deemed it necessary to send a letter to the bishops of France warning them, among other things, of "the alarming tendencies attempting to invade the exegesis of the Bible." This document incited the French Jesuit J. Fontaine to rebuke the "Protestant infiltrations" of the French clergy in a series of articles. He turned mainly against the *Revue d'histoire et de littérature religieuse,* founded in 1896 by Loisy, and against Loisy's articles concerning original revelation, the development of Israel's religion, or the development of dogma, published for the general public in the *Revue du clergé français.* Several interventions by the Pope caused a certain détente. This was shown through the creation of the Pontifical Biblical Commission at the end of the summer of 1901 (officially constituted in October 1902). The appointment of the Franciscan Fr. Fleming as secretary of the commission, the first consultants, largely chosen from the ranks of the progressive exegetes, and the original plan to make the *Revue biblique* the public relations channel of the commission illustrate the constructive rather than repressive character of this initiative. However, this was merely the calm before the storm. Several weeks later a new intervention by Loisy rekindled the controversy even more violently.

Loisy was a scholar of extraordinary intellectual prominence. Thoroughly informed and endowed with a penetrating critical mind, he was also a talented writer, possessing a very unique gift for words. Because of the encyclical *Providentissimus* he was forced to relinquish his chair at the Institut Catholique in Paris. He utilized the time afforded him through this suspension from office in transferring his research from technical exegesis to the more general problems posed by Holy Scriptures, investigating the divine truth and the value of the Church expressed and preserved therein. The French translation of Adolf Harnack's lectures on "The Essence of Christianity," published in 1902, gave him the opportunity to present a synthesis of the systems of Catholic apologetics that he had prepared shortly before. He promulgated this in a small book entitled *L'Évangile et l'Église* in November 1902; it caused more sensation and excitement in the world of religion than all but a few other books (F. Klein).

Like the famous Protestant historian Harnack, Loisy was convinced that the content of a critically interpreted Gospel and the various forms of historical Christianity were not necessarily identical. However, he wanted to prove that this disagreement was not a distortion, as claimed by the Protestants. Quite the contrary, the evolution of Catholicism, showed in three respects (institution, dogma, and cult), based inextricably in the authentic message of Jesus Christ, how this identity could be restored through history. However, this continuity differed fundamentally from that upheld by traditional apologetics.

Loisy was inspired by the thinking of the German eschatological school, revising their arguments in a novel way and declaring at length that it was not Jesus' intent to organize a new religious community to continue his work on this earth; rather, he endeavored to proclaim the impending establishment of the kingdom of heaven. However, things turned out differently from what he planned: "Jesus announced the coming of the kingdom and what transpired was the Church." Yet the Church sustained messianic hope, assuming the responsibility of nurturing and organizing this expectation, since the hour of salvation was a long time coming. From this adaptation of the term "kingdom" to the variable conditions of time and place, Loisy said, arose the successive formulations of Church dogmas, the development of its hierarchical institutions and the deployment of its sacramental rites. These experiences of the past show, Loisy added, that the essence of Christianity had to be seen in its evolution, not in a rigid core, as Harnack proposed. Consequently the future harbored the possibility, even the likelihood of new discoveries. Since the dogmas of the Church reflected "the general state of the knowledge of the times and the people who devised them," the conclusion was justified that a profound change in the state of scholarship could necessitate "a new interpretation of old rules," especially since it was obvious that "dogmas are not truths descending from heaven" but merely symbols of the eternal truth.

Those who were familiar with the difficulties which Loisy wanted to solve generally reacted positively to his theses: finally, here was someone to prove, on the basis of a strictly scientific method and in the face of the arrogant appraisals of liberal Protestants, that the Catholic Church was indeed the only legitimate fruit of the Gospel. Other readers objected primarily to the nonconformism of this new branch of apologetics, raising the question to what extent it was compatible with Catholic orthodoxy. They objected to many of his constructs, in spite of the various precautions which the author took to indicate rather than clearly to define them. Thus praise was quickly infused with criticism and rejection, voiced not only by the conservatives, whose "strong language often concealed complete *ignoratio elenchi,*" but also by open-minded experts such as Lagrange and especially Batiffol, who turned his Institut Catholique of Toulouse into a "stronghold of the struggle against modernism," contributing to the embitterment of this struggle for reasons as yet indiscernible.

On 17 January 1903, Cardinal Richard, archbishop of Paris, condemned Loisy's work, claiming that it threatened "to confuse seriously the faithful's belief in the fundamental dogmas of the Catholic Church." However, the episcopate at large preferred, with four or five exceptions, not to take issue; so did Leo XIII. The atmosphere in Rome changed during the summer after the election of Pius X, who had anxiously observed the theological and exegetical dissent in France for a long time.

The controversy flared up again even more seriously in the fall, when Loisy published a new volume justifying the first book: *Autour d'un petit livre.* Loisy's main concern in this book was the liberation of Catholic historians from a tutelage that he called anachronistic, expressly confirming the autonomy of biblical criticism of theological doctrine. But this was not all. He stated with even more precision, contradicting the pretensions of classical apologetics, that Christ's divinity evades history; so does his resurrection, his conception by the Virgin, or any other personal intervention of God in the course of human affairs. According to Loisy, the subject of history is not the existence of the resurrected Christ, but solely the disciples' belief therein, a belief undergoing progressively precise definition. While suggesting differentiation between the Christ of history and the Christ of faith, he did not declare, in contrast to the assertions of his Catholic opponents, that faith deemed true what seemed to be false to the historian. Though he believed, on the one hand, that the impact of faith acting in Christian consciousness did not just mean a development of ecclesiastical institutions, but also an idealization of the person of Jesus Christ, he also held the notion, on the other hand, that this phenomenon of a collective consciousness and its objective basis are commensurable.

However, these declarations did not alleviate the anxieties; on the contrary, they intensified them; and this time, the little book encountered the almost unanimous opposition of the theologians and the episcopate. On the other hand, interventions in favor of Loisy were offered in Rome by Baron von Hügel, a longtime admirer, and by Monsignor Mignot, one of the few French prelates who conceded that it was absolutely essential to make room for these new critical methods in the framework of ecclesiastical studies. Nevertheless, on 16 December 1903, the Holy Office condemned Loisy's works, but used rather ambivalent terms apparently indicating that the Vatican still hesitated to get seriously involved. Shortly afterward, Loisy made known that he would submit. For three years, he held aloof from the controversies he had incited, but, in seclusion, he devoted himself to the preparation of his great commentary on the Synoptic Gospels (1907–8).

Later he declared repeatedly that he had lost faith in the divinity of Christ and even in the existence of a personal God long before the publication of *L'Évangile et L'Église,* but he had preferred to conceal his true opinions, hoping to initiate more successfully a reform of the Church from within, deeming it useful for humanity. His biography by Houtin, who knew him well, seems to confirm his declaration at first glance. Houtin's text, unpublished for a long time, was edited by É. Poulat, some of whose discerning statements suggest that it was precisely the existence of this manuscript (of which Loisy knew more or less without ever having seen it) that partially explains the reconstruction of his religious development, which he wanted to promulgate a posteriori, after having abdicated all positive faith. This impairs the trustworthiness of the exegete's statements about the exact date when he ceased to believe, and it proves that many people were only too eager to believe his own explanations. In any case, the fragments of letters and his memoirs, published by R. de Boyer de Sainte-Suzanne under the title *Loisy entre la foi et l'incroyance,* confirm his distance from Renan, whose scientistic rationalism he despised, or from Houtin, who was an evil spirit in many respects. In 1900 Loisy already differentiated clearly between *foi* and *croyance,* between faith and belief.

Whatever Loisy's personal opinions may have entailed, it is a matter of fact that he became the catalyst of the anxiety spreading among the Catholic intelligentsia and that his two "little books" and their condemnation incited a dispute which rippled outward after 1908 and extended far beyond France's borders.

These revolutionary ideas found a resounding echo in certain intellectual groups, especially among the young clergy. They were fascinated by these suggestive concepts, fundamentally differing through their sensitivity toward the diversity of historical truths from the superficial character and the naivete of the "Lives of Jesus" and the stories about early Christianity available to the Catholic public. The (often misunderstood) thoughts of Newman concerning the development of the Christian doctrine and on the relationship between faith and reason, propagated at that time by Bremond in France, seemed to them a guarantee — the guarantee of a cardinal — for the new apologetic path Loisy had described and for his less abstract conception of revelation. In addition, they had a presentiment of the entire terrifying implication of the assurance that the Gospel was no historical scripture in the true sense, but a document of a catechetic nature expressing the belief of the first Christian generations as it was trying to formulate itself. Their misgivings were compounded by the realization of some Christian democrats that, on the one hand, their efforts to integrate the Church into modern society were comparable to Loisy's work of restoration on the theological level, and that, on the other hand, his demands for the autonomy of the exegete or the historian of dogma from the ecclesiastical teachings paralleled their own demands for the autonomy of the laity and civil society from the clerical autocracy.

Many of Loisy's enthusiastic admirers thought like Bremond, who responded to the deluge of rationalistic criticism with the following words: "He is a true Noah, and the Church should be happy to possess his ark." However, many were worried, and not only in the conservative camp. Many a progressive agreed with

Loisy as to the need for an incisive revision of traditional Catholic apologetics and to a series of his critical conclusions. Yet they refused to agree to his radical idea of the total autonomy of criticism from ecclesiastical teachings and to question, as he did, the basic concept of orthodoxy. This was the case with Batiffol, for instance, who apparently just wanted to restore his reputation in Rome, and with Blondel, whose articles entitled *Histoire et dogme* emphasized the true concept of tradition in the Catholic system and still appear to be especially acute.

Even though Loisy was the focal point of the controversy animating the world of Catholic intellectuals in the first decades of the twentieth century, and even though it may be justified to call him "the father of modernism" (Heiler), the question of the Bible and dogmatic history were not the only areas at that time to incite fundamental controversies, which some considered indispensable to rescue what could be rescued of Christianity, while others believed that they would destroy the essence of the Christian faith as they understood it.

The controversies over Blondel's proposals at the end of the nineties regarding a renovation of apologetics by using the philosophical method of immanence (immanence apologetics) gradually subsided. One of his students, Lucien Laberthonnière, revived these disputes and extended them to include the entire complex of the problem of religious cognition. In two collections of articles entitled *Essais de philosophie religieuse* (1903) and *Le réalisme chrétien et l'idéalisme grec* (1904), Laberthonnière criticized the philosophy of "essences," intending to replace them in the name of a moral dogmatism with a philosophy of action and personal inspiration. At this point, he also discussed one of the fundamental questions raised by the modernists: the question regarding the originality and character of Christianity as a revealed historical religion. However, his conception of philosophy compelled him to subject Thomism, which he hardly knew, to a radical appraisal and to correlate the natural order and the supernatural so closely that it appeared as if he wanted to fuse them. He was also inspired by Blondel's critique of "extrinsicism," charging the Church with proceeding in too authoritarian a manner. He gave theologians adhering to tradition good reason to oppose him, especially when his influence began to grow (around 1905) after he had accepted the management (together with Blondel) of the *Annales de philosophie chrétienne* and founded the *Association d'études religieuses,* an association which regularly brought together Christian philosophers and scholars open toward modern thought.

A member of this very group, Édouard Le Roy, a mathematician, philosopher, and a student of Bergson, preoccupied with religious problems, incited one of the most passionate disputes of these troubled years between Catholic theologians and philosophers. At the beginning of 1905, he published an article entitled "Qu'est-ce qu'un dogme?" challenging philosophers and theologians to think about the impact that the dogmatic rules offered to the faithful by the Church may have on a modern scholarly mind. Once again he questioned the classical conception of the dogma, which he felt was related to the Scholastic philosophy inherited from the Middle Ages and to its static concept of an eternal truth. He stressed the radical incommensurability of the mysteries and the human spirit and suggested assigning to dogmas an essentially pragmatic significance. Consequently it would no longer be a matter of speculative conceptions to be forced upon us, but one of rules pertaining to ethical and religious actions. Presenting us with such dogmas, the Church would merely ask us to believe that the religious reality indeed contained the arguments for justifying the obligatory mental attitude. Outstanding thinkers such as the Jesuit de Grandmaison or the Dominicans Sertillanges and Allo showed understanding; but most theologians reacted adversely to this "pragmatism," taking it, in ignorance of Le Roy's constructs, merely as profound agnosticism. Therefore they vehemently opposed this trend, particularly since Le Roy did not conceal the fact that he considered a series of Loisy's conclusions to be certain, and moreover, since he did not hesitate, once again in the name of the demands posed by a modern attitude, to bring the traditional concept of the miracle and its apologetic significance up for debate.

Thus within a few years, "the Tridentine peace of an entire Church world" (A. Dupront) was suddenly and almost simultaneously shaken in regard to a whole series of essential issues: the nature of revelation, the inspiration of the Holy Scriptures and religious cognition, the person of Christ and his true role in the birth of the Church and its sacraments, the nature and role of oral tradition within the Catholic system, the limits of dogmatic development, the authority of ecclesiastical teachings and the true meaning of the term "orthodoxy," and the value of classical apologetics. Those were indeed serious questions calling for an answer. The answers provided by Loisy, Laberthonnière, and Le Roy contained acceptable and often leading elements, as was proven through the subsequent development of theology and certain initiatives taken by the Second Vatican Council. But these positive elements were not sufficiently thought through and often presented without the imperative detailed differentiations or with inappropriate vocabulary, causing the nonconformists to be confused and bewildered. Moreover (especially in Loisy's case), sometimes truly ambiguous affirmations had to be dealt with, which could either be interpreted as erroneous and, in the final analysis, destructive to any Christian belief, or as being concerned with innovations, yet basically orthodox and really liberating in view of rather pertinent difficulties caused by the progress of religious studies. Those men defending the innovators believed that the latter had paved a promising path through obscurity, notwithstanding their rashness and their insufficient clarifications. Their opponents saw only the first possibility of interpretation and presumed that the ambiguous wording corresponded to the true thoughts of the authors. Their battle against these tendencies became increasingly fierce because the initial confusion turned more and more into blind panic. This panic had its origin in the ambiguous literature which was carrying the existing controversies (without clearly defined positions) into wider and wider circles. The consequences were devastating, especially among the clergy, who, because of very superficial training in the seminaries, were ill prepared to remain cool and whose increasing "outbursts" pleased the observers. Considering that Church authorities at that time had to fend off particularly vehement anticlerical offensives and that the emergence of socialism gave impetus to the right wing to resist any kind of innovation, the almost all-embracing confusion of responsible Catholics can be better understood, especially since the opposition took on progressively international dimensions.

C H A P T E R   7 5

The Crisis in England

In contrast to its manifestations in France and Italy, modernism in England displayed some unique characteristics. Even when the movement had reached its peak, the modernists there comprised a modest group; this is also true if the term "modernism" is defined in the sense of abstract immanentist heresy used in the encyclical *Pascendi.* Such a condition was to be anticipated in a country where Catholics were in the minority, including, in turn, a small minority of intellectuals. Yet on the continent and particularly in Italy, British modernism, by virtue of its quality, exerted an influence disproportionate to its numerical strength. If Loisy, on the one hand, deserves to be called the "father of Catholic modernism" due to his accomplishments in the area of exegesis and dogmatic history, the question arises whether Tyrrell does not deserve this title for his achievements in the area of fundamental theology and religious philosophy. On the other hand, all historians agree that von Hügel is the most prominent link between the modernists and the progressives of various countries and, at least at the beginning of the crisis, between the progressives and the ecclesiastical authorities. After all, no respected British modernist leaned toward an agnostic rationalism. The British modernists affirmed to the very end the definition Tyrrell, who has been more accurately appraised by recent scholars than by those of previous generations, had espoused in *Christianity at the Cross-Road.* "I understand a modernist to be a Christian of any denomination who is convinced that the essential truths of his religion and the essential truths of modern society can enter into a synthesis." At this point, the definition formulated by Maud Petre may be added: "Modernism is not only searching for a synthesis of modernity and religion, but also of modern religion and the Church."

The struggle for a synthesis between loyalty to the Catholic Church on the one hand, and the affirmation of modern culture and academic freedom on the other hand, had already in the sixties of the past century caused tensions within the core of British Catholicism, the so-called *Rambler* group; tensions that relaxed rather quickly, however. After a recess of about two decades, religious liberalism awakened again to new life under the pontificate of Leo XIII. In 1892 the Catholic journalist E. J. Dillon had begun to criticize the policies of the Roman Curia in the *Contemporary Review.* In 1896 Wilfrid Ward, son of the pioneer of the strictest ultramontane movement, had founded the Synthetic Society in reaction to the ghetto mentality of his religious brothers, a society in which Catholics joined with Anglicans and Protestants. In 1897 F. von Hügel, highly respected in the British Catholic world, had presented to the international congress of scholars in Fribourg a report concerning the sources of the Hexateuch, essentially following Wellhausen's viewpoints. In the course of the next years, he succeeded in soliciting within his circle more and more disciples of Loisy, with whom he communicated regularly by mail. Hoping to seize control again, the bishops issued a joint pastoral letter dealing with "The Church and Catholic liberalism," proclaiming the defense of the Roman congregations and emphasizing the difference between the "teaching

Church" and the "learning Church." The predominantly negative character of this document only increased anxieties, in spite of an affirmative brief by the Pope.

A prominent figure among the progressive Catholics in England at the beginning of the twentieth century was Friedrich Baron von Hügel (1852–1925). For a long time, Baron von Hügel was quite critically appraised by the Catholic historians for his unquestionable sympathy toward the fundamental tendencies of the emerging modernism and for the devoted support he gave for many years to its most prominent leaders, even the most compromised ones. In the meantime, his well-deserved rehabilitation was in progress, and more and more he appeared to be one of the most illustrious religious personalities of his time. He always stood apart from the religious subjectivism of several of his friends and from their efforts to reduce religion to the human problem of the inner self. He described his own ideal in a letter of May 1903: "Not only as simple a thing as honest scholarship, but also as complex, costly, and consoling a thing as honest scholarship must be lived and created in and with a sincere religion deeply anchored in history, and in and with a living Catholicism." More understanding than original, he felt better than most how important it is to remain equally loyal to the demands of a tradition embodied in an ecclesiastical community and to the demands of a thoroughly honest rational criticism, knowing at the same time how necessary it is to witness in the depths of one's personality as a human being and as a devout Christian the tension between those two aspects, instead of striving for a close balance of the two. This openness toward all true values may have been the most characteristic feature of Baron von Hügel's rich personality. His concern not to lose any of these values explains his will never to destroy the bridges to and to preserve the bonds with even those who were in error, in his opinion, for their exclusive claims, but who deserved credit for having drawn attention to an aspect of reality or a real problem that should not be ignored.

Friedrich von Hügel was the son of an Austrian diplomat and a Scottish mother who lived in London after 1871. In his youth he overcame a severe spiritual crisis thanks to the aid of Abbé Huvelin, who gave him the guideline: "For you, nothing but the truth, never orthodoxy." Therefore, he was deeply concerned throughout his life with preserving the independence of scholarly research within the Church. This rationality did not prevent him from being deeply pious and invincibly loyal to the Church, because he believed life in the Church, administering the sacraments, to be an indispensable source of any truly religious life. He was an autodidact, like many aristocrats of his generation. His religious education exceeded that of many clergymen. He combined German thoroughness with the English empirical method, thus becoming a forerunner of the "existentialist" thinkers of the following generation. He was no expert in any special field, but, rare at that time, he was equally competent in the area of biblical criticism, religious philosophy, and the history of spirituality. He also possessed the very special talent of shaking up spirits and souls, stimulating people, through restraining criticism as well as inspiring exhortation, to search sincerely for the truth. It is even more remarkable that he was able to utilize his complete fluency in the major international languages in the service of establishing constructive relations between exegetes, theologians, and philosophers searching for such truth in France, England, Germany, and Italy. For this purpose, he carried on an extensive correspondence and made frequent journeys to foreign countries. Many of these men stimulated von Hügel's thinking and became his best friends, while he, in turn, tried to help them with unequalled understanding, perspicacity, and sensitivity. He was not as erratic as many of them, looking for balance and rejecting radical concepts on principle. Thus he succeeded in evading condemnation, probably assisted by his social rank. He did his best to defend his friends to the bitter end; he rejected the improper and often superficial criticism that some of his friends were exposed to by the conservative wing, and he felt the Vatican's authoritarian methods to be shocking to a religious person of the twentieth century.

George Tyrrell (1861–1909) was a respected preacher and spiritual leader, author of devotional books of rare sensitivity and writer of apologetic essays reflecting in a remarkable way the attitude of his contemporaries. Mainly through von Hügel's influence he became familiar with biblical criticism and Neo-Kantian philosophy. Having turned to these pursuits, he began questioning a series of essential theses of fundamental theology. Tyrrell was of Irish descent. To his Celtic temperament he owed the critical spirit that occasionally played tricks on him, but also endowed him with the astonishing capability of investigating the secret depths of the supra-rational forces nurturing religious experience. At the age of eighteen he converted from the Anglican to the Catholic Church and joined the Society of Jesus. Two prayer books, *Nova et Vetera* (1897) and *Hard Sayings* (1898), establishing his friendship with Baron von Hügel, and a collection of spiritual lectures given to the students of Oxford, "External Religion, its Use and Abuse" (1899), established him as a writer. But precisely at that time he encountered difficulties with ecclesiastical censorship. Tyrrell, overly sensitive and irritable by nature, even more irritable because of the first symptoms of Bright's disease, of which he eventually died, was highly incensed by the narrow-minded limitations imposed upon his intellectual pursuits. Consequently, he began to doubt the authority of the ecclesiastical hierarchy. The extensive reform movement developing on the continent inspired him in his questioning. At the same time, other matters entered into his awareness: the all-too-frequent identification of the Catholic faith with its medieval forms of expression, the unique character of the individual's approach to truth, including religious truth, and, finally, the contrast between the static conception of dogma espoused by the Scholastics and the significance of the development of Christian doctrine in the context of history, all of which he had been exposed to through new books. From then on he was of the opinion that the classical concepts of the *depositum fidei,* the inspiration of the Bible, and revelation had to be analyzed from an entirely new perspective, placing emphasis on the mystical element of religion. With moderate restraint, he tried to prove that Christ did not appear as a teacher of orthodoxy and that Catholic theologians were mistaken when they considered faith to be a spiritual affirmation of the historical and metaphysical assurances given by a theology that was apparently revealed and miraculously saved from error; dogma was merely a human attempt to express the divine force within man in intellectual formulations. Under the pseudonym E. Engel, he promulgated these ideas in a brochure entitled *Religion as a Factor of Life* (1902), dedicating it to a friend with the words: "Something that preserves the strength of my faith under the rubble of my orthodoxy." A year later, under another pseudonym (Hilaire Bourdon), he published a more extensive book, the most radical of all his works, *The Church and the Future.* In it he opposed the system of despotic authority concentrated in the Roman Curia and the conception of the Church as an official institute of truth; according to him, the Church must be seen as nothing more than a "school of divine love on this earth" and its only task is continually to translate the inspirations, which the divine life effects in the hearts of its members, into new temporary rules. These publications found wide response in the modernist circles of France and Italy. At first, Tyrrell was left alone. However, in 1906, he was expelled from the Jesuits. *Lex credendi* (1906) and *Through Scylla and Charybdis* (1907), two works which he published in the following months in an effort to find a middle way between the extreme dogmaticism of the theologians and the all-too-human pragmatism of certain philosophers, did not contain anything particularly subversive; in fact, the former was praised in a review in the *Month.* His vehement protests against the encyclical *Pascendi,* published in the national press, and his opposition to the inquisitorial attitude expressed therein resulted directly in his excommunication. He intensified his communication with the modernists of the continent, above all in Italy, where he had numerous admirers, trying to organize a "strong force of excommunicants who were to form a living protest against the papacy." But the submission of the majority and the inclination of most others toward a Socialist humanitarianism or toward an immanentist rationalism were bitter disappointments to him. Moreover, his progressing disease deprived him of the ability to continue to play an active role. On 15 July 1909, death prematurely concluded the tragic career of a man who was for many years one of the most promising figures of British Catholicism.

Modernism in England involved but a small segment of the Catholic public. This is proven, for instance, by the lack of journals modernistic in nature or at least somewhat open to modernist interests. There is no reason to believe that modernism in Britain died with Tyrrell. Maud Petre, devotedly caring for Tyrrell in the last years of his life, was not the only one to refuse to take the antimodernist oath demanded by the bishop and continued her opposition, even though she was denied the sacraments in her diocese.

C H A P T E R   7 6

The Crisis in Italy

The restoration of the world of Catholic intellectuals in Italy around the beginning of the twentieth century proved to be more urgent than the one in France. Caused by the timid, negative attitude of the intransigents toward the liberal revolution, the cultural stagnation had left a void; on the other hand, a longing for greater intellectual freedom that gradually developed in the course of two generations could be felt among those persuaded to defend the new cause. The first indications of such awakening became visible during the last few years of Leo XIII's pontificate. This awakening was accelerated by various foreign influences: by exegetical publications in France and through Tyrrell's works, whose impact in Italy was much stronger than that of Loisy; by the personal impact of Monsignor Duchesne, who had settled in Rome in 1895; and above all by Baron von Hügel, who often sojourned in Italy. For too long the originality of this restoration movement, contemptuously called a "by-product" by Rivière, was belittled. The conclusions of recent research and the publication of documents, both of which greatly increased in the last decade, have illuminated the unique characteristics of Italian modernism. Firstly: this modernism rested in a long tradition which followed the *risorgimento* and stood for political liberation and religious reform. Two aspects of this tradition have particular significance: the desire for liberation from ecclesiastical tutelage, felt to be more oppressive in Italy than elsewhere, and an effort to present the Church as a community of the faithful, replacing the traditional concept that was oriented toward the hierarchy. Secondly: the French modernists were mainly interested in bringing ecclesiastical studies up to par by attempting to find solutions to the new problems that had emerged from the development of religious studies. Italian modernism, however, was characterized by extensive efforts to propagate the new discoveries among the masses, which partially explains why the contacts between the modernists and the Christian Democrats were closer there than in France. There is another difference: while the French modernists put the emphasis on reason, serving as a guideline for the modern academic culture, many Italian modernists were rather fascinated by the mystery of the charismatic Church and inspired by the ardent desire to return to original Christianity.

Within the Italian reform movement, developing in the first years of the twentieth century, roughly three tendencies can be distinguished: (1) young priests and friars, especially numerous in central Italy, tried to bring ecclesiastical studies up to date; (2) fanatics trained in the ranks of the intransigent *Opera dei congressi* realized the practical shortcomings of this movement and its ideological limits and tried to overcome them by developing the cultural foundations of a true Christian democracy; (3) against this movement, several young laymen, mainly from Lombardy, joined the liberal and national trends, trying to forge a link between Catholicism and the tendencies of the modern world.

Within the first group, scriptural studies were (for the most part) represented by three individuals: Giovanni Genocchi and Umberto Fracassini, two brilliant Catholic scholars, whose great intellectual open-mindedness was coupled with strict loyalty to the Church, and Salvatore Minocchi, a young, courageous priest, who did not intend, however, a reform to exceed the framework of the Catholic system. In 1901, in Florence, Minocchi had founded a journal entitled *Studi religiosi,* whose subtitle precisely defined the program: *Rivista critica e storica promotrice della cultura religiosa.* This journal offered space to all ecclesiastical studies, including religious philosophy, but the main portion was reserved for scriptural studies. Without question, the journal often merely translated eloquently the thoughts of Loisy, Lagrange, von Harnack, Houtin, Tyrrell, Blondel, Laberthonnière, and Le Roy, sometimes elaborating upon them. However, Minocchi possessed the art

of indulgently making allowances for the sensitivities of the guardians of orthodoxy, while also stressing that readers of his reviews of new books contemplate
the insufficient solidity of numerous traditional positions. In spite of the criticism
voiced by the *Civiltà cattolica,* Minocchi's journal soon became the center of the
enlightened and progressive young priests.

One of them was Ernesto Buonaiuti, a brilliant mind, endowed with extensive knowledge and possessing an extraordinary gift for assimilation besides. He
was to become the most outstanding figure of Italian modernism. In 1905, Buonaiuti published, directly in Rome, a similar journal, the *Rivista storico-critica delle
scienze teologiche.* Apparently, its purpose was to take a *via media,* a middle-of-
the-road between the progressivism of the *Studi religiosi* and the conservatism
of the *Civiltà cattolica,* providing more room for scholarly erudition. However, in
reality, the young, eminently dynamic editor strove for leadership of the entire Italian reform movement. Emphasis was primarily placed on the history of dogma
and of the Church, rather than the question of Scripture.

One of the leading collaborators of Minocchi and Buonaiuti deserves mention:
Giovanni Semeria, was an extraordinarily gifted friar. Close to Baron von Hügel
and several personalities of the academic world in foreign countries, he played
an important mediating role in the field of the early history of Christianity as well
as in religious philosophy, since he was more successful than most in assimilating
the results of contemporary research and in presenting them in a series of brilliant
lectures, immediately published in book form, to the general public.

Disregarding the different viewpoints and levels of education, we surprisingly
find in all these agents of the intellectual renewal of Italian Catholicism one common and apostolic concern, which distinguished them from similarly inclined
Frenchmen, who appeared rather to be bookworms. The Italian modernists were
less interested in competing with Protestant or rationalistic scholarship, but rather
in improving the religious education of the average Catholic, knowing full well
that the lack of religious education was the cause of the superficiality of Italian
religiosity.

Similar concerns of a cultural nature are visible in one of the most prominent
figures of Italian modernism, in the young democratic priest Romolo Murri. He
joined the modernist movement rather late, and his membership was simply a
transitional episode in his stormy career. He started in the *Opera dei congressi,*
where those antiliberal Catholics assembled who longed for a society of theocratic
character. Murri was not very interested in the tendencies that inspired Minocchi,
Buonaiuti, and their friends; however, he was convinced that the lack of intellectual maturity disabled the Italian Catholics and, above all, the members of the
clergy in dealing effectively with the problems confronting the Christian in regard
to the activities of his public life. He adopted the premature conclusions of religious criticism in order to be able to preach, surrounded by the halo of a prophetic
message, the spiritual and religious renovation of a Catholicism reconciled with
the modern world in the worship of freedom. By "returning to the Gospel," Catholicism was to be liberated from all its obsolete elements. Thus, his orientation
intensified in proportion to the development of his social and political activities
and gradually merged with an atmosphere of total intellectual and disciplinary
freedom outside of the control of the hierarchical authority. His ideas attracted

a number of priests who demanded more or less radical reforms in the Church, e.g., reduction of the number of dioceses, modification of the Index procedures, reform of the seminaries and traditional apostolate methods, suspension of sacerdotal celibacy, etc. The progressing development of a simple reform movement in the direction of a so-called "social modernism" finally compelled many to proclaim, at first rather awkwardly, the "autonomy of the temporal realm," as it is called today. Yet they later considered religion a problem of the inner self, so to speak, and the Church a civilizing and morally progressive factor rather than an institution of supranatural salvation. These ideas were also espoused by the group of the *Socialismo cattolico,* to whom Buonaiuti lent his support after the promulgation of the encyclical *Pascendi.*

Fundamentally different in origin was the group of reformists from Lombardy, the heirs of liberal Catholicism from the period of the *risorgimento.* Among them were men of action, such as the promoters of the *Opera Bonomelli,* a charitable institution for Italian emigrant workers. These men did not exercise as much restraint as the old bishop whose patronage they enjoyed. But most of the disciples of this group were intellectual laymen, passionately interested in religious problems, rare in Italy at that time. Most attractive to the general public was Antonio Fogazzaro, a brilliant writer full of mystical idealism, who stood in close contact with Semeria, Genocchi, and von Hügel, and was a great admirer of Loisy, Blondel, and Tyrrell, but also strongly influenced by Rosmini and his ideals of a religious reform movement as described in his book *Cinque piaghe della Chiesa.* Fogazzaro was also interested in coordinating Darwin's theory of evolution with Catholic dogma. In 1905 he published the novel *Il Santo,* whose hero appointed himself the apostle of a reform based on the spirit of love, love that was to permeate all areas of religious and social life. This novel contains numerous remarks about the nature of religious feeling, about the role of the priest, about the true Christian spirit, and the formalism of Catholic worship. However, the climax of this work is a long discourse on reform, addressed to the Pope, in which the four evil spirits, having invaded the Church, were branded: the spirit of dishonesty, closing his eyes to the light of modern scholarship and indicting the best defenders of the truth; the spirit of omnipotent power, changing paternal authority into a terrible dictatorship; the spirit of avarice, a mockery of evangelical poverty; and, finally, the spirit of rigid adherence to tradition, fearing any kind of progress and driving the Jewish rabbis to reject and condemn Jesus. The novel became a great success and was translated into several languages. However, it also led to violent controversies.

Less spectacular, but more profound, was the effect of the journal *Il Rinnovamento.* It was founded at the beginning of 1907 by a few young Milanese encouraged by Fogazzaro and Semeria. The journal emphasized the primacy of conscience over external authority, without negating the rights of the latter. In addition, it promoted freedom of scholarly research and the position of the laity in the life of the Church. Following post-Kantian philosophy, it stressed the significance of subjectivity, which was badly neglected by Scholastic thinking. True to liberal traditions, it espoused a new conception of the relations between Church and state in reaction to the "confusionism" of the previous centuries. The staff of the journal tried to extricate the values of secular education from all areas and to give them practical applications in the fields of philosophy, history, research methods, and law. At the same time, its publishers attempted to awaken interest in religious problems, since most intellectuals of that time found religious indifferentism to be a matter of course. Though being as open-minded as possible toward the contemporary trends and the solid accomplishments of religious studies, these intellectuals were nonetheless to remain loyal sons of the Roman Catholic Church, forming, so to speak, a "third" party, that felt its way around between the incomprehension of the integralists and the exaggerations of the radicals.

As in France, the ideas proclaimed by the leaders of the movement to renovate ecclesiastical studies found a positive response among the young clergy in Italy. Around 1906 it often happened in central Italian seminaries that when a priest was ordained, not only were works by Semeria and Lagrange chosen as gifts, but also those of Loisy and Tyrrell. Since the hierarchy in Italy was even less equipped than that in France to effectively deal with contemporary problems, their confusion was even greater. And as always in such cases, reaction raged against everything that deviated in the slightest from the traditional paths, that is, against the moderates as well as against the radicals. Even a man so above suspicion as Francesco Lanzoni became the target of allegations and denunciations simply because he wanted to apply the principles of historical criticism to the study of hagiography. The moderates, mostly loyal followers of the Church, submitted quietly; the more progressive, however, tried to organize resistance. To that end, they attempted to unify, both outwardly and inwardly, the movement that aimed at cultural and religious renovation, to give it a unity it was largely lacking. For the purpose of such unification, Murri, Buonaiuti, and Fracassini called a meeting in the summer of 1907 in Molveno that was also attended by Baron von Hügel. A week later, the encyclical *Pascendi* was issued; it forced the group to attempt to coalesce its divergent opinions and concepts, resulting in its dispersal.

CHAPTER 77

Intervention of Ecclesiastical Authority and the Integralist Reaction

Roman Intervention

The solemn condemnation of modernism did not take place until 1907. However, there were plenty of indications of the impending papal ban. During the first months of the pontificate, on 13 December 1903, Loisy's main works were put on the Index. Some months later, the encyclicals *Ad diem ilium* (2 February 1904) and *Iucunda sane accidit* (12 March 1904) urgently warned against the *novarum rerum molitores,* who, with great scholarly efforts, questioned the history of early Christianity. In December of the same year, the Pope admonished the bishops to practice uncompromising severity toward seminarians with overly liberal attitudes who lacked the proper respect for the scholarly efforts made "by our great teachers, Church Fathers, and interpreters of revealed doctrine." Similar warnings were contained in a letter, addressed to the rector of the Institut Catholique in Paris at the beginning of the following year, and in a lecture to the students of the French Seminary in Rome containing a rather overt reference to Loisy. In the fall of 1904 two excellent exegetes, Father Genocchi of the Roman Seminary and Father Gismondi of the Gregoriana, were replaced by two professors who fundamentally rejected the application of critical methods to the text of the Holy Scriptures. One of them, Father A. Delattre, had just sharply criticized Father Lagrange and the "new exegetical school." In August 1905 Father Fleming was replaced as secretary of the Biblical Commission by Dom L. Jannsen, a Scholastic theologian who did not possess specific competency in the field of exegesis, and overtly conservative consultants were appointed, eliminating the original balance between the various factions. The consequences of these changes were soon noticeable. While the first two reports of the commission regarding actual sayings in the Bible (13 February 1905) and biblical stories that only seemed to be historical (23 June 1905) handled the problem with moderation, the subsequent conclusions regarding the Mosaic authenticity of the Pentateuch (27 June 1906) and the Johannine authenticity of the fourth Gospel were much more reactionary in nature. Both schools, even in Rome, negated each other, because one recommended tolerance and patience in order not to discard the wheat with the chaff, while the other was uncompromising, focusing on the most radical viewpoints. This school more or less enjoyed the trust of the Pope, especially since the imprudence of many of the Italians who disseminated the new ideas had led him to believe that orthodoxy, for which he carried the responsibility, was seriously threatened, even though he had to admit that, in the field of exegesis, circumspective open-mindedness was prudent.

After 1904, in Rome, the Swiss K. Decurtins launched a vehement struggle against Blondel, Laberthonnière, and others. By the end of 1905 Loisy and the progressive exegetes had particularly attracted the curiosity of the Holy See. But the wave of the reform movement in Italy vacillated, enlarging the list of urgent concerns and drawing attention to other problems that were discussed more and more frankly. In December 1905 the bishops of the provinces of Turin and Vercelli issued a joint pastoral letter, which, for the first time in an ecclesiastical document, used the word "modernism." The following year brought additional measures: While the Congregation of the Index, on 14 April, condemned the novel *Il Santo* by Fogazzaro and Laberthonnière's books, by now several years old, Monsignor De Lai and Cardinal Gennari instigated systematic control of the Italian seminaries. Several professors were recalled from their teaching chairs without being granted an opportunity to defend themselves. Thus a gloomy atmosphere of suspicion developed in Rome. Everywhere, the approaching storm was felt.

This storm finally broke in the course of 1907. Within a few months more and more solemn *acta* were issued. On 17 April, in the context of a consistorial address, Pius X turned rigorously against the *neo-reformismum religiosum,* which was spreading with increasing audacity. At the end of the same month, the prefect of the Index Commission issued a warning to the Milan group of the *rinnovamento.* On 14 June Pius X sent a brief to the Viennese Professor Commer, congratulating him for having hacked to pieces the errors of the main representative of Reform Catholicism, Herman Schell. On 17 July the decree *Lamentabili sane exitu* was published by the Holy Office, over which it had been brooding for several years, containing a revealing list of statements which two Parisian theologians had extracted from Loisy's "little books." The decree condemned sixty-five theses concerning the authority of the ecclesiastical teaching office, the inspiration and historical value of the books of the Holy Scriptures, the terms revelation, dogma, and faith, certain aspects of Christological dogma, which had been questioned in recent disputes, the origin of the sacraments, the constitution of the Church and the nature of Christian truth in general. And finally, on 8 September, the encyclical *Pascendi* was issued. Since its intent was not to describe exactly the thoughts of the individual instigators of modernism, but rather to present the reflection of their ideas in the consciousness of the community, it started out with a somewhat contrived synthesis of modernism, blaming the various errors on agnosticism, which disputes the value of the rational argumentation in the religious realm, and on the philosophy of immanence, which ignores that the origin of religious truth rests in the needs of life. This philosophy created the dogma unfolding in the course of life on the basis of reason and experience. Likewise, the need "to give religion a *corpus* perceivable through the senses" created the sacraments; the books of the Holy Scriptures contain the experiences collected by the faithful of Israel and by the first disciples of Christ; the Church is a fruit of the collective consciousness, and the only task of authority is to give expression to the emotions of the individual. The encyclical stigmatized the modernistic conception of biblical criticism and the purely subjective methods of apologetics, as well as the demands of reform modernism. It concluded its third, disciplinary part by enumerating a series of practical measures ("remedies") to halt the further spread of evil, above all in the seminaries (renewed obligation to study Scholastic philosophy and theology, supervision of reading material, *consilia vigilantiae* in every bishopric).

The encyclical was immediately greeted with exuberant expressions of joy by the conservatives, who had desired it for a long time. Many moderates deplored the purely negative tone of the encyclical, yet they were glad that ambiguities, which gradually threatened to become dangerous, had been eliminated. Those who were attracted by the exponents of modernism reacted much less vehemently than had been expected, even though they almost unanimously considered the encyclical "a caricature rather than a picture of modernism" (Sabatier). Tyrrell believed himself able to predict that the encyclical would compel the "right wing of modernism to align itself more closely with the left wing," since the encyclical did not differentiate between reasonable progressivism and the "rendezvous of all heresies" based on agnosticism and immanentism, simply schematically reconstructing both. In reality, the opposite happened: For some, this painful condemnation by the Pope was the criterion revealing to them the fact that they implicitly stood outside of the Church. Consequently, they openly broke with the Church, depending on the individual case, with more or less restraint; and since they had to abandon hope of being able to reform the Church from within, some carried the radicalism of their viewpoints even further, quickly ending up in pure rationalism.

In most of them, however, loyalty to the Church was victorious. Thus most everyone submitted, creating the impression later on that the modernist crisis had simply been a matter of individual, rather isolated personalities. Unquestionably, the masses of believers had not been seized by the wave of modernism. But at least in France and, to a lesser extent, in Italy, the clergy who were informed about the development of scriptural studies, and a number of young Catholic intellectuals had felt strongly attracted to the new movement. These people were dissatisfied with the theological training at that time and conscious of the need for adjusting to the circumstances. Therefore they were enthusiastic over the pioneers who had paved the way. In contrast to some of these very pioneers, they would never have thought of continuing their research outside of the Church.

The agnostic and immanentist system, superficially reconstructed by the encyclical, was so obviously in contradiction to traditional Christian belief that it was fully normal for many true progressives to depart openly from it and renounce it. Even though submission to the anathema of the encyclical took place within a large framework, it was nevertheless extremely painful for many who observed an increase of hope for an impending adjustment of Catholicism to the changing attitudes, and therefore felt the danger of a more profound schism between the Church and the intellectual world of the West. Many shared the opinion of the "Erasmus of modernism" (J.-M. Mayeur), Monsignor Mignot, who had declared: "There is no Christian conscience that does not reject with the whole force of its faith all errors condemned by the encyclical." However, he also wrote that this encyclical erred in "limiting itself to condemnation without defining what one can say without being a modernist." Or they thought like the philosopher V. Delbos, a marvelous Catholic layman: "The encyclical has one all-too-visible *lacuna:* it consists of the negligence toward or the ignorance of the deeper causes which incited the so-called modernist movement."

Even though almost everyone submitted to the ecclesiastical authority, there were a few residual pockets of resistance. Loisy published a new little book, *Simples refléxions sur le décret Lamentabili et l'encycle Pascendi,* the tone of which was as ironical as it was aggressive. In order to stress the significance of the booklet, he published simultaneously two thick volumes on *The Synoptic Gospels,* which were far more radical than his previous studies. But it was precisely this development which caused many of his former admirers to fail away; and his excommunication on 7 March 1908 made him a loner. Tyrrell suffered the same fate, after having already been denied the sacraments by his bishop at the end of October 1907, following the publication of several articles in opposition to the encyclical in the *Times* and in the Italian press. At first Minocchi submitted, announcing he would discontinue the publication of his *Studi religiosi.* But after having been charged by his friends with servility, he soon held a public lecture on the earthly paradise and the dogma of original sin. He achieved a great deal of attention because he negated the historical character of the first chapter of Genesis. After the *suspensio a divinis,* Tyrrell rejected submission, and in October 1908 he took off his clerical garb. From then he strove for a more socialistic humanitarianism, seeing in Christianity nothing more than a contingent form of the religion of the absolute.

In Germany and Austria, a number of leading personalities of Reform Catholicism also protested against the encyclical: Monsignor Ehrhard, professor at the theological faculty of Strasbourg, turned against the practical measures forming the last part of the encyclical, since they prohibited, in his opinion, any kind of scholarly work; Professors Schnitzer of Munich and Wahrmund of Innsbruck opposed in harsher terms the misdeeds of ultramontanism and Roman absolutism, but these were overt manifestations of academic liberalism and not doctrinary modernism.

Aside from these open protests, there was a series of anonymous criticisms. The most remarkable, though rather superficial throughout, were, in France, the brochure *Lendemains d'encyclique,* in which Monsignor Lacroix, the very liberal bishop of Tarentaise, had collaborated, and particularly, in Italy, *Il Programma dei modernisti — Riposta all'enciclica di Pio X,* a document published on 28 October 1907 and quickly translated into French, German, and English. Monsignor Fracassini collaborated on the scriptural section, but the author was Buonaiuti, who, in contrast to other leading modernists, preferred to stay in the Church in order to continue from within the reform work that he had started. It is uncertain where the true Buonaiuti really revealed himself, in the *Programma,* the tone of which was rather moderate, or in the much more radical *Lettere di un prete modernista,* published several months later, likewise behind the veil of anonymity.

These pockets of resistance, which were rather insignificant, inspired the antimodernist reaction that had long remained sporadic and isolated. But since the modernist movement was confined to the circles of intellectuals, only a very few bishops deemed useful the effort of devoting a pastoral letter to it. Nevertheless, with the exception of Germany, they organized the *consilia vigilantiae* required by the encyclical in order to prevent suspect publications by the clergy. There were also isolated attempts to expose the modernist authors hiding behind a pseudonym. On the other hand, numerous theologians dealt with commentaries on the papal documents, but their refutations usually referred to abstract modernism as presented in the encyclical. Only a few seemed to have recognized the real problems that were maladroitly posed by the modernists; and even if their studies intended to exceed the level of mere general comprehension, their arguments frequently appeared to be rather simplistic. Among the laudable exceptions in France were the articles of the Jesuits Lebreton and de Grandmaison, as well as the *Lettres sur les études ecclésiastiques* by Mignot, in which he tried to prove to what extent the condemnation of modernism justified new scholarly studies; in Germany, the exceptions were an article by F. X. Kiefl published in *Hochland* and a collection of lectures held some time later at the University of Freiburg and published under the title *Jesus Christus.*

The systematic suppression of the modernist movement's last vestiges after the issuance *of Pascendi* was mainly the work of the Holy See itself, living for several years in an atmosphere of panic. With more and more reactionary leanings, the Index Commission as well as the Biblical Commission intensified their activities. Furthermore, new apostolic visitations in the Italian seminaries directly responsible to the Curia were decreed and suspect teachers were recalled, often merely on the basis of unfounded denunciations. Even though, according to Loisy's own words, modernism was in a state of "complete dissolution," two years after its condemnation in 1907, Pius X was still greatly worried about the continued existence of certain clandestine operations, which were extremely exaggerated. Thus he believed the Church was still "in a state of siege" and he deemed it necessary to take further measures. On 1 September 1910, in his motu proprio *Sacrorum antistitum,* the Pope demanded from all the clergy a special oath, the so-called antimodernist oath. This involved a statement of faith that had been adjusted to the already condemned versions of modernism, including the statement formulated by Pius IV. The first section formulated in five points the proof for the existence of God, the value of the basis for faith, the founding of the Church through Christ, the immutability of dogma, and the intellectual character of the act of faith. A second part demanded submission to the decree *Lamentabili* and the encyclical *Pascendi* and called for their affirmation. This text did not add anything essential to the *acta* of Pius X; however it was an official summary, the goal and purpose being to request from every priest his expressed solemn affirmation, in order to expose the crypto-modernists. The clergy submitted without much open resistance. In the Church at large, there were not more than approximately forty exceptions. In Germany, however, this measure caused considerable unrest in the name of scholarly freedom; and finally, upon the request of the episcopate, the German theological universities were relieved of the oath.

The results on the whole were not as negative as is sometimes maintained. Even in the field of exegesis, where serious studies were largely condemned to sterility in spite of the founding of the Pontifical Biblical Institute in 1909, some remarkable achievements were made: In 1908, *Biblische Zeitfragen* was founded, a popular collection; in 1912 there followed the founding of the *Alttestamentlichen und Neutestamentlichen Abhandlungen;* the publication of *La théologie de S. Paul* by F. Prat, S.J., (1908–12); and the commentary of Father Lagrange regarding the Gospel of Saint Mark (1911). In the area of patrology and dogmatic history, French authors were gradually able to compete with names like Ehrhard, Bardenhewer, and Rauschen: J. Tixeront, a student of Duchesne, published, between 1905 and 1912, a *Histoire des dogmes,* which, for its time, was not without merit. Father J. Lebreton did pioneering work with his *Origines du dogme de la Trinité* (1910). The same applies to J. Lebon in Louvain and his *Monophysisme sévérien* (1909). The growing interest in Near Eastern Christian literature was reflected in the *Corpus scriptorum christianorum orientalium,* continued by the Catholic universities of Louvain and of America after its establishment by J.-B. Chabot in 1902. In 1907 the *Görres-Gesellschaft* under the leadership of Monsignor Kirsch opened a Section for Archaeology, aimed at furthering Christian, classical, and Near Eastern archeological studies and the research of problems posed by religious history. In 1912 F. J. Dolger at the University of Münster established a new teaching chair for General Religious History and Comparative Religious Studies, and he investigated in his lectures the extent to which Christian thought and the original Christian rites felt the influence of the paganism surrounding them. A year earlier, while in France the first Catholic textbook on the history of religions, *Christus,* was published under the direction of P. Huby, P. W. Schmidt, S.V.D., founder of the journal *Anthropos* (1906), had collaborated in Louvain with Father Bouvier, S.J., in the organization of the first Catholic Week for Religious Ethnology; and another German, J. Schmidlin, had founded the *Zeitschrift für Missionswesen* and the first Catholic *Institut für Missionswissenschaft.* Literary history was brilliantly represented by the

German Baumstark, the Englishmen Bishop and Fortescue, and the French Benedictines Cabrol, Férotin, and Leclercq. The last mentioned published, in 1907, the
Dictionnaire d'archéologie chrétienne et de liturgie, followed by the *Dictionnaire
d'histoire et de géographie ecclésiastiques* 1912. The appearance of new journals
was another sign of the scholarly activities in these difficult years.

The modernists had posed real problems for discussion, problems that could
not be solved by merely condemning modernism. After all, they questioned the
relationship between theology and its sources (the Bible, documents of the old
tradition, decisions of the ecclesiastical teaching office) and the nature of their
homogeneity with divine revelation, down to its technically most sophisticated
form.

Of the few theologians trying to find a positive answer to the questions raised
by Loisy, Tyrrell, and Le Roy, two merit special mention: Father Léonce de Grandmaison, S.J., who, in this difficult time, helped with his moderate and reasonable
(in the opinion of Blondel and Loisy) articles to lead the confused public through
the treacherous cliffs of modernism and integralism, however without totally penetrating the problems; and primarily Professor Father Ambroise Gardeil, O.P., who,
despite his limitations, appears more and more as the forerunner. His influence
was initially confined to France, but later, thanks to his students, radiated far beyond French borders. His work reached a peak in the two studies of apologetic and
theological methodology long to remain classics: *La crédibilité et l'apologétique*
(Paris 1908, second completely revised edition: 1910), which became the object
of vehement controversies, above all on the part of Blondel; and *Le donné révelé
et la théologie* (Paris 1910), a study intended to resume the work done by Cano
regarding the problems of the beginning of the twentieth century. Germany and
Austria, the first to deal with historical theology, did not contribute a lot to these
methodological discussions.

Integralism

Hand in hand with the suppression of modernism by Church authorities went
a campaign of denunciations that increased throughout the pontificate and poisoned the atmosphere of its last years. It may seem peculiar that this campaign
unfolded from the very moment when modernism, after the condemnations of
1907, seemed to be in the process of decline.

Where did "semimodernism" begin? And where, moreover, did the "modernistic tendencies" and the "modernistic mental constitution," as the *Corrispon-
denza romana* called it, begin? The danger of abuse was particularly great because
most of these irresponsible censors were not very competent in the area of theology and especially in the field of exegesis. Furthermore, they belonged to those
minds who are completely indifferent to foreign ideas. Several months after the
publication of *Pascendi,* Cardinal Ferrari already had to take a strong stance against
the excesses, writing in his pastoral letter of Lent: "It is sad that some are obliged,
even publicly, to act excessively, detecting modernism almost everywhere and
denouncing it, and that they even want to suspect men of modernism who are
far from it." There was hardly a single Catholic scholar who was not exposed to

their attacks in the course of these years, to accusations that violated, in many instances, justice as well as love of one's fellow man. Even many deserving institutes were victims of such regrettable polemics, such as the École Biblique of Jerusalem, the theology faculty of Fribourg (almost suspended by Pius X), the Institut Catholique of Paris, numerous seminaries that had made efforts to improve the quality of studies, and many others.

These zealots have entered history under the nickname of "integralists." They called themselves "integral Catholics": in contrast to the efforts of liberal Catholics and modernists (whom they often threw in one and the same pot) wanting to water Catholicism down, they intended to confirm "the integrity of their Romanism: the entire Roman Catholicism (doctrine and praxis) and nothing but." Whatever their debatable methods may have been, many of them were more than just theologians envious of competitors who might want to deprive them of the favor of the younger generation. In view of the dangers threatening their faith, they simply considered their crusade a sacred duty, and the repeated encouragements they received from the Pope were bound to strengthen their convictions.

On the one hand, the integralists had no scruples over denunciations, clandestine methods, and even espionage; on the other hand, they fought with their visors open: with books and brochures, like those of the Jesuit J. Fontaine, whom É. Poulat considered "a remarkably well-preserved witness of an intellectual species, whose role is supposed to have been important," and with a series of journals (with rather limited circulations) controlled more or less by the integralists. In Italy, there was the *Unità cattolica,* financially supported by Pius X, *Verona fedele* and the *Riscossa* of the Scotton brothers; in France, *La foi catholique* by B. Gaudeau and *La critique du libéralisme* by É. Barbier, both appearing in 1908, *L'Univers,* looking for revival in integralism, and, after 1912, *La Vigie,* both journals dependent on the Assumptionists, thanks to Father Salvien; in Belgium, the *Correspondance catholique* of the lawyer Jonckx; in the Netherlands, *De Maasbode,* whose chief editor M. A. Thomson was the soul of Dutch integralism; and in Poland the *Mysl Katolicka.*

To what extent were all these activities coordinated and directed by one center and what role did the Holy See really play? In view of the fact that the integralists worked partly in the dark, the answer has remained unclear for a long time, especially since the Roman archives were made accessible to the general public with considerable delay. New information was provided in 1950 on the occasion of the beatification of Pius X. A tremendous step toward the illumination of the situation was recently made by É. Poulat with exemplary professional conscientiousness. He succeed in analyzing the workings of the "international antimodernist secret operations" that had been organized by Monsignor Benigni, a prelate of the Secretariat of State: the *Sodalitium Pianum,* often simply referred to by its initials S.P., or by the camouflaging name *La Sapinière.* After the discovery of 1921 there was a tendency to consider Benigni as the soul of the entire integralist movement; he was supposed to have acted without the knowledge of Pius X, who is said to have known nothing of his often disputable methods. Today the reality appears much more modest and at the same time more official than had been presumed. Except for the *Correspondance de Rome,* which was to provide the world press with religious news written in "the right spirit," the confidential bulletins promulgated by Benigni were but a "cascade of unfortunate attempts," and the S.P. had never more than about fifty members in all of Europe. However, the group was in contact with a number of individuals who formally did not belong to it, but shared its convictions. With other opponents of modernism, however, the relations of this group were a lot more reserved. The documents published in the meantime have thrown a completely new light on the often rather fundamental differences separating the minds summarily labeled with the collective term "integralists."

In his investigations, É. Poulat succeeded in dispelling the myth about the infamous integralist conspiracy. He discovered that the situation was much more complicated than had been presumed for a long time; mainly, he was able to "reduce the S.P. to its real dimensions" and to prove that the ideological world of integralism went far beyond the circle of the *Sodalitium Pianum* and its sympathizers. It was also proven that there was no longer a reason to maintain that Pius X had no knowledge of Benigni's activities. It is certain that the Pope supported *La Sapinière* and that he not only knew of the activities of its founders, but also approved and encouraged them. Benigni informed him daily through Monsignor Bressan and was regularly ordered to make delicate inquiries. It also seems to be obvious that the Pope never reprimanded Benigni seriously for the manner in which he conducted the tasks entrusted to him, as he had often done with other militant integralists; and that he personally covered up a sort of ecclesiastical secret police, one which does not seem permissible to us today, but which he appears to have deemed justified in view of the dramatic situation that he felt the Church was entangled in.

The integralistic reaction reached its climax during 1912 and 1913. In 1912, Father Lagrange, among others, was forced to leave Jerusalem, and the *Revue biblique* almost had to cease its publication. At the beginning of 1913, the entire fifth series (1905–13) of the *Annales de philosophie chrétienne* was put on the Index, a measure that was intensified a few weeks later when its director, Father Laberthonnière, was prohibited from publishing anything whatsoever, without being given the opportunity to defend himself. The same decree of 5 March 1913 had also put the *Sainte Chantal* of Abbé H. Bremond on the Index, a condemnation which was less serious, but nonetheless significant. Bremond also attempted a renewal in the field of hagiography, that is, he wanted to replace the traditional picture of a saint with a human face, but now, every attempt at renovation was suspect; this attitude applied not only to areas directly involving the faith but also to the manner of representing Church history or the life of the saints, if these manners were inspired by "secular methods." The Bollandists narrowly avoided condemnation only because of the powerful protection of Cardinal Mercier.

For the integralists, the danger of innovation and secularization did not exist only in the fields of exegesis, theology, philosophy, or Church history, but also in the area of relations between the Church and society, at that time called "sociology." In the efforts of the Christian Democrats, no matter of what persuasion, they saw the spirit of liberal Catholicism, stigmatized by Pius IX in the *Syllabus*, revived in a new version. Unfortunately, they made no distinctions between men like Murri, the French *Abbés démocrates,* the *Sillon* group or the trade-union headquarters in Mönchen-Gladbach. The program, presented to the collaborators of the *Sodalitium Pianum,* climaxed in the following declaration: "We are opposed to the exploitation of the clergy and the Catholic Action with the intention of luring them from the sacristy and rarely allowing them to return." At first glance, one may be surprised at such a viewpoint when observing that several integralistic leaders, such as Benigni in Italy, Maignen in France, Decurtins in Switzerland, and many others had been ardent admirers of *Rerum novarum.* But it is precisely Leo XIII's first program of social Catholicism to which they remained loyal. In this program, the Pope expressly contrasted, for the benefit of the bourgeois world which had emerged from the revolution of 1789, the Christian social order resting on Christ's Kingdom over human society to "social atheism." These men charged the Christian Democrats of the new generation with increasingly using their social concerns and their conviction of the independence of secular life as a pretense to liberate themselves from ecclesiastical tutelage.

These facts, in the context of which the term "pragmatic modernism" was sometimes used, increasingly engrossed the integralists, and even the Holy See, especially after the condemnations of 1907 had diminished the threat of doctrinaire modernism. It is interesting to find that problems of such a nature were the almost exclusive subject of Benigni's international correspondence, which has recently become available.

Naturally, in the various countries these incidents, labeled "blunders," were more varied than had been the case in regard to the problems of dogma. In Italy, attention was first directed toward the action that Murri and his disciples intended to carry on in the political arena. After they had failed and the ecclesiastical authorities had regained control of the Catholic movement, the Catholic press became their main concern. There were two opposing opinions regarding the press: According to one opinion, the Catholic newspapers, under direct control of the clergy, were to be official interpreters of the Holy See's thoughts and to preach to "a peaceful audience of devout citizens" (M. Vaussard) a strict policy of "religious defense," in agreement with the Catholic "thesis" regarding the rights of the Church within society; according to the other opinion, the Catholic press was to try to reach the ear of the upper class, which had largely adopted the liberal concept of society in order to make it familiar with the Catholic viewpoint concerning problems at hand. The controversy was: *stampa di concentrazione* or *stampa di penetrazione.* The Pope preferred the first solution, as represented by newspapers such as *Osservatore Romano* and the *Voce della verità* in Rome, the *Unità cattolica* in central Italy, and the *Difesa* in Venetia.

In France, numerous attacks were launched against "social modernism," supported by the *Action française* and others. Through the assistance they received from Rome, many victims finally succeeded in evading a condemnation.

In view of the international interest that the case of *Le Sillon* aroused then and continues to arouse today, *Le Sillon* is still worth a closer look. This movement owes its founding to a few young people who, like many other students, strove for reconciliation between Catholicism and a society indoctrinated by the ideas of 1789. One of these young men was Marc Sangnier, who, having a profound influence on his comrades, turned the original study group into an active movement (1899). He took various initiatives which, due to his extraordinary energy and his noble eloquence, were immediately very successful. He founded circles for social studies, in which young intellectuals and young workers got together on a basis of equality. He established institutes which entered into competition with the Socialist peoples' universities, and he organized public debates about problems and questions of the day. The movement, thanks to some strong local personalities also invading the provinces, quickly took on the form of a crusade aiming at the re-Christianization of Democracy by winning the masses back for the Church and by reconciling the Church with the Republic. At first, the movement kept its distance from the liberal Catholics, being too far removed from the world of the workers, and from the Christian democrats, whom it charged with doing little more than preferring reforms of the institutional order to the more urgent task of morally educating the individual, in whom, assisted by the indispensable intellectual forces, the true spirit of democracy should be developed, without which democratic institutions would be delivered to a disastrous fate. Internal disputes did not impair the impact *of Le Sillon.* A serious crisis appeared on the horizon after 1906, when the movement began to be active in politics, propagating a program according to which Christians in a pluralistic democratic society were to strive for a particularly strong influence, of course with mutual respect for different opinions. This new orientation changed the denominational group, essentially based on the apostolate, into a movement that invited, often in a rather provocative manner, non-Catholics, Protestants, even freethinkers to participate (Sangnier called this new institution *le plus grand Sillon).* By necessity, this development had an unsettling effect on the ecclesiastical authorities who tried to keep the Catholic youth under their exclusive control. Young priests and seminarians joining a movement that wanted to constitute itself without any official sanction by the hierarchy posed new problems, especially since many of them utilized Sangnier's declarations about the citizen's freedom of conscience in order to justify their independence from their superiors in other areas as well. Several bishops had already reacted to the new situation in 1907, and from this moment on the Vatican also acted. At first, Pius X had expressed his sympathy for these young Catholics' idealism, oriented toward religious activities; but he grew increasingly uncertain, especially since he was informed rather tendentiously. To be sure, there were incidents that justified concrete charges, such as the relentless criticism with which *Le Sillon* attacked those Catholics who did not share in its enthusiasm for republican democracy, or the intention to declare this democracy an obligation derived from Christian morality rather than the subject of free elections. Carelessness in terminology and Sangnier's increasingly harsh procedures completely compromised the movement. In February of 1909, Cardinal Luçon, the archbishop of Rheims, sent a serious reprimand to Sangnier, which resulted in the intensification of the campaign launched for months against him by the conservative press headed by the integralists. Encouraged by Benigni, Abbé Barbier took great pains to create the suspicion that *Le Sillon* smacked of modernism, since it paid homage to the concept of democratic authority condemned in the encyclical *Pascendi.* On the other hand, Pius X considered the new orientation of *Le Sillon,* with which it wanted to evade the ecclesiastical authority, unacceptable. For the Pope, any plan aiming at a modification of society was a matter of the moral order for which the Church alone was responsible. On 25 August 1910 he sent a letter to the French episcopate, in which he defined three kinds of errors on the basis of authentic Sillonist texts, which had been frequently "distorted or simplified"

(J. Caron) because they were taken out of their objective or historical context: (1) statements that are not in agreement with the traditional Catholic doctrine of society, since they are reminiscent of the "theories of the so-called philosophers of the eighteenth century, of the Revolution, and of liberalism, which had been often condemned"; (2) an illegitimate demand for autonomy from the ecclesiastical hierarchy in regard to areas belonging to the realm of morals, a demand worsened by the eclecticism of the alliance with non-Catholics; (3) finally, as a consequence of this work, "promiscuity": modernist infiltrations which would compel the Sillonists to forget Christ's divinity and to "speak only of His sympathy for all human suffering and His urgent appeals to love thy neighbor and to practice brotherhood," and which would result in the Sillonists forming only "a scarce tributary to the great flow of apostasy which had been organized in all countries for the purpose of establishing a world Church that would have no dogma, no hierarchy, and no rules governing the spirit."

Received with enthusiasm by the entire rightist press, this condemnation was taken by the leftists as a confirmation of the incompatibility of the Church and the modern tendencies within society. This impression was fortified by the fact that numerous influential circles in Rome and Pius X himself were benevolent toward the *Action française,* a royalist group of the extreme right that was led by Charles Maurras and usually supported the integralist opponents of Christian democracy. "It advocates the principle of authority, it defends the order," the Pope told the Catholics of the left who saw the *Action française* as an un-Christian conception of the state, aimed at elevating the reason of the state to the ultimate value. The Pope was grateful to Maurras for his sarcastic assaults on the kind of democracy perpetuated by the anticlerical parliaments of France and Italy and he was grateful that he had created a "teaching chair for the *Syllabus*" in order to preach a counterrevolutionary concept of society based on tradition and the hierarchy. He even went so far as to call this agnostic "a good defender of the Holy See and the Church," without taking into consideration the fact that Maurras had praised the Catholic Church for having succeeded in moderating the destructive content of the message of the "Hebrew Christ" through wisdom derived from ancient Rome. In 1913, after another offensive against Maurras that was supported by several bishops, "leading personalities" interceded with the Pope, presenting the denunciations as "a trap set by the demo-liberals." Nevertheless, after initial hesitation, the Pope sent Maurras's works to the Congregation of the Index; yet, though the congregation unanimously agreed on a condemnation (26 January 1914), he did not issue it, because he was afraid that a condemnation of the journalist who, in his opinion, was one of the strongest opponents of the modernists and the anticlerical groups, would only serve their cause.

Germany, scarcely affected by the modernist crisis in the true sense of the word, did not have to suffer too much from the antimodernist reaction on a doctrinal level, even though some Catholic scholars were subject to measures which hardly seem justified today. In the last years of Pius X's pontificate, Germany was violently shaken by integralist assaults of a political and social nature. This opposition was dealing with tensions between the Berlin group that had remained loyal to the old formula of the Catholic worker association and the much stronger Cologne group demanding interdenominational trade unions that would be willing to cooperate with the Socialists to defend professional interests. This double conflict required a fundamental decision as to what extent the laity was able to take on responsibility for its activities in the secular realm without the hierarchy's intervention. The integralists were convinced (and Pius X agreed) that religion was indeed the foundation of social order. Therefore, if one were to solve the political and social problems outside of the control of the ecclesiastical authorities, one would question the traditional concept of the "Christian civilization" and thus run the risk of committing an error in the area of doctrine. Consequently, the Christian trade unions, organized as they were everywhere in western Europe around the turn of the century, were charged with emphasizing their economic and social tasks instead of their ultimate moral and religious purpose. They were especially indignant about the Cologne group's going so far as to organize the defense of the workers on a neutral professional basis, enabling cooperation with non-Catholics and even with Socialists.

On the one hand, Pius X wanted to uphold the principles that, in his opinion, should guide every Christian society, and therefore he assailed the efforts to declericalize secular life. On the other hand, he had to take into account the strength of the Cologne group, which was backed by the majority of the German episcopate and enjoyed the clandestine support of the nuncio in Munich. For those reasons, the entire situation was fundamentally different from that of *Le Sillon.* Therefore, the Pope looked for a compromise and, in September 1912, issued the encyclical *Singulari quadam,* unconditionally sanctioning the Berlin proposal, but conceding that the other plan could also be "tolerated" to prevent a more serious malady, that is, thesis and hypothesis. However, this papal intervention did not succeed in easing the controversies raging over several years; on the contrary, it agitated the situation even more, since both parties had reason now to cheer. The conflicts also flared up again in France. There, the integralists took advantage of the encyclical, using it to revive their assaults against Christian democracy. Then the *Civiltà cattolica* published two articles by P. G. Monetti, a theologian to whom the Pope liked to listen. These articles were directed against the principle of the trade-union system and culminated in the statement: "It includes many things absolutely opposed to the true spirit of the Gospel, and there is no use in baptizing it Christian; when two terms are so ill-matched, one should not try to combine them." This article was obviously inspired. It was a test, a prologue for a new, much more pointed papal document. This document was intended to warn the Christian trade unions of a development that would drive them gradually away from the social ideology which Pius X considered the only legitimate one, since it agreed with the Catholic concept. However, this was denied by several apologetic historians. Those people, who were convinced that the Pope had been victimized by an obsolete "model" in the sociological sense of the word and was intent on proceeding with the adjustment of the Church to the development of modern society, tried to forestall this new threat. Cardinals Maffi and Mercier, the general of the Jesuits, Fathers Wernz, Toniolo, Harmel, and others discreetly interceded, and Pius X himself finally preferred to postpone the scheduled measures. Thus, the Christian democrats had finally been victorious over their integralist opponents in this "last great battle of the pontificate" (É. Poulat).

At that time, the excesses of the "witch hunt" had gradually caused a resistance that, in contrast to frequent appraisals, did not wait for the pontificate of Benedict XV in order to manifest itself more or less openly. This resistance progressively focused on a few prelates who had been concerned for years over the development of the situation and the direction it had taken, and around a number of Jesuits who had anticipated that Pius X's successor was bound to continue this development and that this turn of events also had to be anticipated. Several respected journals of the Society of Jesus such as the *Stimmen der Zeit*, publicly risked protests after 1913, in which Father Lippert brandished the "hunt for heresies" as one of the most regrettable phenomena of the antimodernist reaction. Likewise, the *Civiltà cattolica* published the complaints, issued by Prince zu Löwenstein on the occasion of the Congress of Metz, regarding the assaults of "certain" integralists against the social Catholics. A little later, the French Jesuit journal severely criticized "denunciations without any kind of discernment." For those who were informed, it was no secret that the Jesuits, reacting in this manner to the excesses of the integralists, were backed by the general of the society and two of his main assistants, Fathers Ledóchowski and Fine.

Pius X, whose bitter complaints about his "isolation" in the struggle on behalf of the integralist orthodoxy can be better understood in this context, did not conceal his dissatisfaction. In October 1913 he had assigned the management of the *Civiltà cattolica* to Father Chiaudano, who wholeheartedly shared his opinion, and of whom the integralist paper *La Vigie* wrote that he would lead the Roman journal back to the "relentless determination" from which it wanted to depart and that he would "revive the beautiful days of Pius IX." The brief addressed to the Society of Jesus on the occasion of the centennial celebration of its restoration did not leave any doubt, by virtue of the indifference with which it was composed, about the Pope's disappointment about the "blunders" with which he felt compelled to charge the Society. It appeared as if he even contemplated relieving Father Wernz of the direction of the Society and replacing him with Father Matiussi, who had close contacts with the integralists. But at this very moment, the almost simultaneous death of the "white Pope" and the "black Pope" brought an end to this particularly painful aspect of the suppression of modernism by the antimodernists.

The Holy See and
the European Governments

Chap. 78: Mario Bendiscioli
Chap. 79: Rudolf Lill
Chap. 80: Jacques Gadille
Chap. 81: Roger Aubert

CHAPTER 78

The Roman Question and Italian Catholicism—
The *Non expedit* in the Pontificates of Pius X,
Benedict XV, and Pius XI (until 1925)

Giuseppe Sarto, later Pope Pius X, participated as bishop of Mantua and subsequently as patriarch of Venice in the struggle of active integralism regarding the Roman question and the critical, aloof attitude toward the unified Italian state. However, he was quite sensitive toward the basic problems of the political society of Italy's being dominated, after the bloody incidents of May 1898 and the King's assassination in 1900, by anxieties, antagonism, and accusations. The Pope was worried that during the elections the Socialists would support the radicals who stubbornly continued their anticlerical campaign, inspired by the Freemasons, and refused to allow the Church to influence social life (education, schools, social welfare, charity) with respect to the essential internal national aspect of the "Roman question." In order to create a counterweight against such alliances between the radicals and the new social forces in the spirit of more open-mindedness for the democratic authorities, but also of a more aggressive laicism, Cardinal Sarto approved agreements for the purpose of defending religious values and institutions, to be concluded with the liberals on the occasion of the administrative elections. Moreover, in Mantua and Venice, Sarto had an opportunity to observe and appraise personalities, situations, and programs of the militant Catholics, and he did not entirely reject contacts with "transigent" and arbitrating groups.

Also as Pope, Sarto adhered to his guidelines of "conservative reformism" in the face of Catholic activism (Aubert); he was amicable toward the demands of the most ardent activists, but only within clearly defined limits and in a certain framework, thus keeping in check the initiatives and the men who perpetrated them and put them in action. As far as the Catholic movement in Italy is concerned, Pius X forced those men who had supported the policies of Leo XIII to step into the background, and he introduced new methods of government that were oriented toward direct, unbureaucratic relations with the leading figures of the movement and the spokesmen of various factions. These contacts were made via the Secretariat of State. Officially, however, the secretariat of state continued to be responsible, even though Pius X knew that its new leader, Cardinal Merry de Val, was not familiar with Italian Catholicism and was primarily anxious to preserve its authority, the discipline, and the direction from above.

In this manner, Pius X mainly preferred the personal leadership of men of his special trust who stood outside of the Secretariat of State and its offices. Among these advisers, some Fathers of the Society of Jesus were given particular responsibility. Moreover, as editors of the *Civiltà cattolica,* they obtained increased influence for this journal by making it the voice of the papacy. These men were Fathers Santi, Passavich, and Brandi. They had direct access to the organization and the successes of the organized Catholics, one of them in regard to Germany, the second one in regard to Belgium and France, and the third in regard to the United States. They were ordered to prepare drafts of papal documents and served as intermediaries between the papacy and the leaders of the Catholic movement, obtaining reports and declarations and passing on suggestions and reprimands.

It was the wish of Pius X as well as his predecessor that the decisions made at the top, according to his concept of papal authority, should emanate from the people; however, the laity and the active circles of the clergy were in disagreement and tried to drive a wedge between the members of the Curia and the Pope himself, causing the official directives to be somewhat contradictory and ambiguous. In 1904 it was decided that the *Opera dei congressi,* celebrating its thirtieth anniversary, be suspended. At the same time, the dependence of the Catholic movement and its organizations on the ecclesiastical authority was increased through instructions for the reorganization of the centralized cadres, based on the encyclical *Il fermo proposito* (11 June 1905). The Pope found himself bitterly disappointed as far as the people and institutions acquiescing in his intentions were concerned.

Also in regard to the formally approved *Non expedit,* Sarto began to introduce innovations; case by case, mitigations and exceptions were permitted aiming at the elimination of radical and Socialist candidates. At the general elections, the liberal candidates were supported, provided they had agreed to assent to the demands of the Catholics regarding schools, family (rejection of divorce), and the religious institutions. By backing the liberal deputies constituting the parliamentary majority of Prime Minister Giolitti, Pius X wanted to make a gesture of détente toward the Italian state. In return, he expected some kind of willingness to oblige in the Roman question, if only in two respects: in regard to the bilateral regulation of the position of the Holy See in Rome and in regard to a mutual agreement about the definition of the legal status of ecclesiastical institutions in Italy.

However, the expectations were not fulfilled. The prime minister from Piedmont indeed pursued a policy of cooperation, assisted by an obliging parliamentary majority despite opposition throughout the country and in the Chamber of Deputies. He listened to the demands and employed ecclesiastical spokesmen in his service. Yet in regard to relations between Church and state, and consequently the relations to the Holy See, he adhered to the customary attitude. He upheld the theory that state and Church could be compared to parallels determined to run abreast of each other without ever meeting. Therefore, the Vatican also returned to its formal and rigid stance. Concerning the Catholic movement, this resulted in a stronger emphasis of its dependence on the Holy See, but also in an intensification of the public activities of Catholics in the communal administrations and in economic and social organizations (savings and loan banks in the country, worker auxiliaries, emigrant welfare, community halls, the political-religious and popular polemical press, professional organizations, e.g., of elementary school teachers). All these activities resulted in more and more frequent contacts with the world of politics; in public opinion and in peoples' representations, the programs were synchronized and there were meetings pursuing the goal of exerting pressures on the official authorities in favor of the groups that were represented.

Thus, on the level of administrative elections (which had been strongly supported all along) as well as in the area of "political" elections (handled more indirectly), the problem of elections became the priority of the movement, whereby, aside from the "economic-social union," an "election union" was particularly significant during the preparations for the elections.

One of the last decisions made by Leo XIII was the appointment of a new president of the *Opera dei congressi,* Count Grosoli of Ferrara, a man who was sympathetic toward the ideas of Toniolo and to the demands of youth. As the editor of Catholic daily papers, he was bound to occupy an outstanding position. This meant that Leo XIII had begun to employ more venturesome principles of social democracy, and that he finally regarded as a social movement what had seemed to him to be a religious-clerical movement. At the Catholic Congress of Bologna (November 1903), the new democratic spirit had had an opportunity to assert itself through motions and democratic ballot procedures, persuading everyone that the groups had moved closer and that the progressive ideas and their authors had found followers. This was not the case within the traditional five actions. On the contrary, following Paganuzzi, who had been replaced by Grosoli, the "old ones" had incited an alarmist campaign against the new leadership, and in the following year they succeeded in taking the majority of the central committee of the *Opera dei congressi* away from Grosoli. Nevertheless, the Pope confirmed him; but shortly afterward (19 July 1904), the *Osservatore Romano* disapproved of a letter which Grosoli had sent to the Catholic Committees on 15 July 1904. Referring to the statement that "the matter of absolute, effective freedom and independence from the Holy See was the main goal of Catholic Action," Grosoli had insisted in this letter that the Catholics were subject to the authority of the bishop not only in regard to their religious, but also their economic and social initiatives, and that they were to abstain from political elections. However, significantly evoking their national consciousness and referring to demands regarding changing realities, he said: "Within the inalienable rights of the Holy See, Catholics consider historical epochs and events milestones on a path leading into the future and they are intent to assure that their work, carried on in this life, not be hindered by matters that are dead in the national consciousness."

Grosoli again handed in his resignation, and this time it was accepted. Subsequently, in a letter by Cardinal Secretary of State Merry del Val to the Italian bishops, the *Opera dei congressi* was declared suspended, with the exception of its second section, which was still chaired by Medolago Albani. The Catholic Action was to be dependent on the hierarchy of the Church. It had to relinquish the principle of determining the leadership through elections and to forego regional autonomy, thus returning to rigid Roman centralism and an organization of dioceses. "At general congresses and at smaller meetings, parliamentary procedures had to be abandoned and decisions could no longer be made through plebiscite" (A. Gambasia).

Grosoli did not succeed in persuading Murri to return to the organization and to adopt the guidelines of the *Opera dei congressi.* Through the problems he had raised, he had caused a crisis of conscience among the militant Catholics. This was not only of concern to the organization, its goals and methods, and forced it to decide whether Catholics were to follow the directives of the *Opera dei congressi* or Christian democracy; but it also called into question the validity of the *Non expedit* and the restrictive measures of the Vatican regarding the democratic activity of the Catholics.

At this point in time, in July 1904, the social movement showed a balance that was impressive even after being divided regionally: a total of 2,432 organizations, 642 of them in Venetia, 677 in Lombardy, 106 in Tuscany, 27 in Umbria, 99 in the Marches, 37 in Latium, 17 in the Abruzzi mountains, 37 in Campania, 17 in Apulia, 5 in the Basilicata, 8 in Calabria, 3 in Sardinia, and 125 in Sicily. These 2,432 organizations consisted of 774 associations established for the purpose of mutual assistance, 21 people's secretariats, 107 productive and consumer-oriented associations, 170 professional unions or workers' associations, 33 farm labor societies, 43 farmers' associations, 29 associations for collective tenants, 69 banks, 855 rural loan associations, 40 workers' banks, 154 cattle insurance federations, and 187 democratic propaganda societies.

The Catholic movement was now facing a dilemma: on the one hand, it had to continue to intensify the multiplicity of social work, and the organizations and their organizers had to take into account the demands raised by the world of workers and farmers. These groups were primarily affected by industrialization, subjected to new living conditions, and repeatedly overrun by crises emanating from the existing worldwide crises. Moreover, the Catholics wanted to establish themselves according to the model of the Socialist organizations, trying to show them that Christianity possessed the social strength to liberate the masses from their misery and utilizing all means at their disposal. On the other hand, Catholic activism, by virtue of its loyalty to the Pope, had to follow the papal directives that were spelled out in *Il fermo proposito* of 1905 and in the new "statutes" that had been painstakingly prepared by laymen in 1906. These statutes were the result of intensive consultations with Pius X's advisers and obviously tried to copy many aspects of the Catholic organizations with experience in foreign countries.

The overall structure had been simplified; in place of the five sections of the *Opera dei congressi,* three great national unions were formed. The biggest and most extensive union was the People's Union, comparable to the *Volksverein* of the German Catholics. It consisted of individual members and intended to train them socially and religiously through the traditional values of piety and love. It replaced the first section of the *Opera dei congressi,* unfolding its activities during the Social Weeks, according to the French model. The second section of the *Opera dei congressi* had been essentially retained under the new name Economic Social Union and had the task of educating people as to the principles of an economic order (based on Christian ethics rather than liberalism and socialism) and of creating the appropriate organizations. The activities of the Catholics in the administrative field, gaining more and more significance, were to be furthered and directed by a third organ that was significantly called the Election Union of the Italian Catholics. In regard to practical procedures, the main emphasis was placed on the disciplinary element, which was to curb the drive toward extensive social action and toward political involvements.

The task of adjusting the movement to these structures and the duty to obey the directives of the hierarchy, without sacrificing its vitality and impetus, were challenges to leaders and groups alike. In the spirit of Murri, the more active and impatient ones among them subsequently broke away from the movement and divorced themselves from the Catholic Action, ultimately joining forces with the radicals and Socialists. This precipitated the loss of many members. The most crucial point troubling them was the matter of autonomy. It caused the most tensions, if only because the demand for autonomy included the limitations imposed by the encyclical *Non expedit,* with all its principle and tactical requirements. In 1905, autonomous groups of "Christian democracy" were formed.

In view of the election of deputies in 1904, some people who, like Bishop Bonomelli under Pope Leo XIII, had pleaded for reconciliation with the government, asked the new Pope to cancel the *Non expedit.* They were joined by laymen who were more successful as spokesmen of the well-meaning, yet impatient activists from the provinces. One of them, Bonomi, the future deputy of Bergamo, was also asked to mediate the issue by advisers of Minister President Giolitti and Minister Tittoni, who compared the degree of Catholic voting in the administrative elections to the degree of abstention in political elections and took account of the political strength of the Catholics. In a conference dealing with the *Non expedit,* Bonomi was told by Pope Pius X: "Follow your conscience, the Pope will be silent." Subsequently, the Catholics participated in the parliamentary elections in Bergamo, Cremona, and Milan, gaining several chamber seats for Catholic deputies, thanks to agreements with the liberals.

On the part of the Holy See, this was a small concession, eventually resulting in the suspension of the *Non expedit.* The Vatican reserved the right to grant dispensations whenever the bishops deemed them necessary and demanded them. This was a consequence not so much of sympathy with the liberals as of fear of the advancement of socialism, which was considered a threat to the religiosity of the people and to the stability of the foundations of the Italian state, a state that was now felt to be stable and in need of protection from the turmoils of revolution.

The Catholic movement continued to take a defensive stance. It protested against any kind of assault on the authority and reputation of the Church, as well as on the religious convictions and customs of the common people. It charged liberal principles with such assaults and showed its strength in unanimous co-operation with the Pope. Not without tensions, this strength consisted of several factors, such as class identity, the progressive ascent of the lower classes, religious devotional enthusiasm, and the pastoral policy of the hierarchy. The leadership was dominated by those who loyally upheld the faith and wanted to lead it to victory. These factors also affected the political action in regard to its spiritual as well as its practical application.

This line was particularly extolled by the moderate clerical group that was part of the Catholic movement and of the Italian politics dominated by Giolitti and his governmental methods. It had a parallel in the so-called "reformist" tendency of socialism, provided that this kind of socialism wanted to take the democratic route toward the realization of its economic and social goals and distanced itself from revolutionary syndicalism and anarchism. The moderate clerical group was a re-sult of the meetings of Catholics and liberals that took place under the auspices of the journal *La rassegna nazionale* (founded in 1879), an official mouthpiece of the Catholics favoring reconciliation. Under Pius X this journal was brought into ill repute for its sympathies toward Reform Catholicism. Advocates of an election alliance with the liberals were conservative "intransigents" who were concerned with the economic and social order threatened by the collectivist program and the syndicalist agitation of the Socialists, as well as with the so-called "progressive intransigents," who felt driven to political action in order to be able to influence the official institutions in the spirit of Christian social ethics. The alliance's criteria per-taining to the characteristics expected of the candidates were defined by the Pope himself in 1908 when he said to the future bishop of Bergamo, Radini Tedeschi: "If they are neither sectarian nor Socialist candidates, if they offer sufficient prospects for being elected and pledge to uphold the principles of order and public welfare, they should be supported; if Freemasons, anticlerical, Socialist, or even worse candidates run for election, Catholic candidates agreeable to amicable factions should be nominated." These directives can be found in the so-called *Patto Gen-tiloni,* which was signed prior to the elections of 1913 (the first elections in which all men, i.e., 24 percent of a population that had increased to 36 million, had the right to vote). The *Patto* was given the name of Gentiloni, the current president of the Catholic Election Union. It demanded of the liberal candidates the following: the private educational system is not to be burdened with difficulties; the introduc-tion of religious instruction in community schools is to be favored; the institution of divorce is to be rejected; social legislation is to be furthered; and the candidate should be concerned with representing the Catholic professional associations in governmental employment bureaus. Customary defensive concerns took prece-dence over the social program. This reflected consideration for the liberal allies, as was demanded by the conservative wing, but not condoned by the Catholics, who had a socially more progressive attitude. Gradually the Christian trade-union system, supported by laymen and young priests, made itself felt through unions of farm laborers and of male and female workers, especially in the textile factories of northern Italy, who were accustomed to agitations for wage demands and knew how to use strikes as a weapon. Thanks to the Gentiloni pact, thirty-three Catholic representatives moved into Parliament and, no less significant, about two hundred deputies of the government party were elected due to the votes of Catholics.

Several Catholic groups in the southern part of Italy leaned toward political action as a natural consequence of the social movement, yet were predisposed against an alliance with the Liberals. Their spokesman was a Sicilian priest, Don Luigi Sturzo (born in 1871 in Caltagirone), who justified the opposition of the Catholics against the lay state based on dissatisfaction with the economically disadvantaged south, which was dominated by shrewd businessmen. Sturzo's restraint toward the liberal state rested on the fact that this state was engaged by Giolitti for the purpose of power in a system of business interests and such corruption that the prime minister from Piedmont was named "minister of corruption" by Socialists who also came from the south. Out of opposition against this centralistic, bureaucratic state, Don Sturzo recommended furthering the local autonomy of the communities and counties under the regime of the *Non expedit.* According to his intentions, the incorporation of Catholics into political life was to proceed in an autonomous manner, and one was to work toward the goal of "preparing with restraint." This goal was reached in 1919 with the founding of a nondenominational (formally not subject to the hierarchy) Italian People's Party (*Partito Popolare Italiano*).

Murri proceeded from a different position, totally rejecting the liberal, lay state and sharing in this regard the ideas of the intransigent circles. However, he soon planned to create, in opposition to the *Risorgimento* government, a political organization within the Catholic movement that was to put into action the Catholic social program by seizing power through elections. In a sensational campaign, Murri, the priest from the Marches, rejected the structural, hierarchical rigidity of the Catholic Action precipitated by the "instructions" of Pius X. Murri founded a denominational Catholic party, the *Lega democratica nazionale,* giving it a program that was aimed not only at a reform of the state but also of the Church. Through this, he risked two condemnations: a religious-political condemnation, following the collapse of Catholic unity, and the dogmatic condemnation threatening him as a disciple of modernism. With the support of the radicals, Murri was nominated as a parliamentary candidate. But in 1907 he was suspended *a divinis* and in 1909 excommunicated, even though personalities of the Curia continued to give him respect and understanding.

This National Democratic League was soon abandoned by intellectuals, trade-union leaders, and members of community and provincial administrations who could not accept Murri's "political modernism." In 1911, supported by Don Sturzo, they founded the Christian Democratic League; it was one of the elements from which the Italian People's Party subsequently emerged.

There was another significant meeting between the Catholic movement and political organizations: Catholic personalities and representatives of institutions patronizing the missions and the care of Italians in foreign countries met with the proponents of the new nationalist tendencies who considered such institutions instruments of national significance to be utilized in the age of colonialism for purposes of foreign politics. This resulted in the furthering of several Catholic works that were concerned with religion and culture in foreign countries and especially with the care of Italians who had emigrated to North and South America (in 1911 alone, the number of emigrants amounted to over half a million). The consequences of this were closer relations between Catholic leaders and the *Risorgimento* state.

Nevertheless, the active Catholics were still distrustful of and disappointed with the Italian state. The religious-social efforts of the Catholics encountered resistance and the Giolitti government was determined to keep the Catholics, in contrast to the Socialists, from advancing in politics. Therefore, it avoided making concessions to the Vatican that could have compelled Pius X to give the activity of the organized Catholics more leeway. The conciliatory gestures of the bishops and Catholic organizations on the occasion of the fiftieth anniversary of the unified state in 1911 entailed reprimands of the Vatican that sounded almost intransigent.

The Catholic movement had in the meantime invaded the cultural realm. In academia, it was represented by Toniolo and Contardo Ferrini, professor of Roman law, who was sympathetic to the Milan circles, as well as by the philosophers Petrone in Naples, Acri in Florence, and Bonatelli in Padua. Highly respected even in university circles were the conciliatory Cardinal Capecelatro, the astronomer Cardinal Maffi of Pisa, and Monsignor Talamo who was trying to establish contact between the Neo-Thomist renaissance and social studies in the *Rivista internazionale di scienze sociali.* Finally there was the young biologist Agostino Gemelli, who had converted from militant atheism to become a Franciscan friar. After 1909, he emphasized that the Catholic movement must also permeate the universities, thinking of his own plan of a Catholic university which he indeed founded in 1921. The problems of religious consciousness appeared also in literature committed to the cause. The plea for a merging of modern culture and Christianity in the area of historical studies and scriptural exegesis grew increasingly more intense within the circles of the movement. The most representative groups were those of Buonaiuti, Genocchi, and Fracassini in Rome and the Milan group gathered around the journal *Il rinnovamento* and including T. Gallarati Scotti, A. Casati, and A. Alfieri, who were in contact with the Barnabite Father Semeria and Bishop Bonomelli. However, this cultural orientation of the Catholic movement fell victim to the suppressive measures against antimodernism because it was reminiscent of concepts that were condemned by the encyclical *Pascendi.* The Catholic movement for decades to come was affected by these steps.

As the Catholic movement knew how to interpret the currents in the educated classes as well as in the masses, it succeeded in assuming leadership in the social and political upswing. From then on, its own development coincided more and more with the history of Italy as it emerged from the *Risorgimento.* Its exponents in both chambers, in the administrative bodies, in the press, in the pastoral management of dioceses and parishes soon faced the world conflict that confronted Italy with a choice between war and peace. At first, the Catholics were inclined toward neutrality, in part because of solidarity with the new Pope, Benedict XV (Della Chiesa), who decisively announced his neutrality. People who played an outstanding role and circles that were politically most committed, especially those who were close to the nationalists, were carried away by the appeals to intervene in the war and to fight on the side of the Allies against the Central Powers, on the grounds that this would bring about the completion of national unification. Remembering the spirit of the *Risorgimento,* the Catholics found intervention in the war to be an opportunity to prove their loyalty to the state. The government soon realized the political weight of the practicing Catholics and took their representative Filippo Meda into the Boselli Cabinet (1916).

In August 1917 the Pope called for a peace that would know neither victors nor vanquished, terming war "a senseless slaughter." This reflected negatively on the Catholics and raised doubts about their loyalty, even though, in agreement with the attitude of the Holy See (declarations of Cardinal Secretary of State Gasparri in 1915), they had rejected attempts of foreign powers to raise the Roman question to an international level.

Willing to deal with the problems of the postwar years pertaining to religious, moral, and socio-political issues, the exponents of the Catholic movement in 1919 founded the Italian People's Party (*Partito popolare italiano*). They approached the problems at hand with a concept of state and society that had matured in the course of their study of the struggles and experiences of the previous four decades. With the approval of the Holy See, the party declared itself "nondenominational," thus removing the last obstacle set up by the *Non expedit.* As a result of Catholic Action under the direction of the bishops, the various Catholic organizations were able to pursue their responsibilities to the different sectors of religious education and culture. Members of the People's Party were all Catholic representatives, the leaders and active members of Catholic societies and "white" trade unions. From this time on, their influence was obvious. It was not coincidental that this very same year, at the Peace Conference of Paris, the first deliberations over negotiations regarding the Roman question took place between Prime Minister Orlando and Monsignor Cerretti. These talks were interrupted by the government crisis and the stubborn resistance of certain anticlerical elements.

The success of the Catholics, due to the proportional representation of 1919 in the elections (the People's Party furnished over one hundred deputies), gave the Catholics a very strong position and the equally responsible task of aligning the parliamentary majority behind the government in the event of a major economic and political crisis. At the same time, in complete independence, the "white" trade-union organization unfolded, but not without slogans of class struggles and a radicalism that negatively affected the People's Party and relations to the hierarchy. The Catholics had to accept sharing the responsibility for the government in an atmosphere that was tense because of the emergence of new political forces and factionalism, which prevented the emergence of any dominant majority. In the elections of 1921, under Prime Minister Giolitti, the People's Party refused to enter into agreements with the liberal government party. Strengthened (with 107 deputies), it returned to the chamber and forced a compromise regarding a temporary government that was rejected by Giolitti. Pressured, on the one hand, by Socialists who had in mind the model of the Russian proletarian dictatorship and, on the other hand, by Fascist combat veterans who were soon assisted by the economic and political right wing, a government crisis emerged in which Catholic solidarity broke down. The conservative faction that had allies in the hierarchy and even in the Vatican, refused to align itself with the Socialists in Parliament, instead pressing for the acceptance of the alliance offered by the Fascists and their supporters. The Fascist program had, on the one hand, antidemocratic and nationalistic features, but was, on the other hand, ill disposed toward the Freemasons and benevolent toward the institutions and personalities of the Church.

Under the new Pope, Pius XI (Ratti), who was raised in a middle class and tolerant environment, the Vatican lessened the impact of the coup d'état of October 1922, legalized by King Emmanuel III, and allowed the formation of a wing of "national" Catholics in the People's Party that favored the new political course. Leaders of this wing joined Mussolini's "national" government in 1922.

The revision of the anticlerical traditions of the *Risorgimento* state had been initiated by the Catholics; the Italian People's Party had continued it systematically through legislation and administrative measures. However, now it seemed as if the renovation in important areas was conducted by forces that were unrelated to the Catholic movement or actually stood in opposition to it. Thus it was Mussolini's government that had the Cross installed in schools and courtrooms, reintroduced religious instruction in elementary schools, made denominational schools equal to public schools, officially recognized the Catholic University of Sacro Cuore in Milan, increased the state subsidies for the salaries of the clergy, exempted the higher clergy from military service, increased state subsidies for ecclesiastical buildings, paid greater respect to Church dignitaries, and participated in the great religious celebrations. The new government was also willing to revise the legislation regarding the Church system according to the wishes expressed by the clergy. In view of these concessions offered to Church life in Italy, the Holy See simply consigned the People's Party to the fate of an opposition party, its purpose, in the eyes of the Vatican, having been the political defense of religious ecclesiastical interests. Its leader, Don Sturzo, was asked to resign. In his capacity as priest, he was not to give rise to misunderstandings but clearly demonstrate that the Vatican, despite the opposition of the People's Party, took a benevolent and reserved stance toward Mussolini's government.

The maintenance of religious ecclesiastical interests toward the state was assumed by the hierarchy, and the new government indicated that it preferred to deal with ecclesiastical authorities rather than the representatives of an opposition party. But the attitude of the Holy See was not without reserve. In 1924, for the benefit of Mussolini's government, the Pope reprimanded the anti-Fascist collaboration between the *popolari* and the Socialists that resembled the collaboration between the Center Party and the Social Democrats in the German Empire and specifically in Prussia, but distanced himself from the government by condemning the Fascist violence that was perpetrated on individuals and institutions of the Catholic Action and by voicing his objections to the new totalitarian trade-union legislation, which resulted not only in the termination of the People's Party but also in the end of the Catholic workers' movement. When Minister A. Rocco set up a commission for the reform of the law on ecclesiastical matters, to which, with the tacit agreement of the Holy See, three clergymen were to belong, the Pope personally emphasized (in an address on 18 February 1925) that no decision by this commission could be accepted as long as the Roman question was not solved, whereupon the Minister announced (May 1925) that the problem would be taken up again on "a broader basis."

This implied a confirmation of the *Non expedit,* i.e., of papal control over Italian politics. This resulted in a new climate for a bilateral examination of the Roman question, which was regularized eventually in the Lateran treaties of 1929. In the meantime, directly through the bishops, the Holy See intensified its influence on Catholic attitudes and institutions. Even the structure of the Catholic Action underwent a reform that on the basis of a *Non expedit* emanating from the other side limited the Catholic movement. But the Catholic movement continued to exist, though with somewhat abated energy, especially among the youth and the student associations which were willing to offer resistance to the harassments of the government and Fascist violence. Dissatisfaction with and accusations against the hierarchy even reached the Lateran treaties, which introduced (in a certain sense) yet another phase in the Catholic movement of Italy, the phase of reconciliation (*Conciliazione*), which was interpreted and experienced in different ways.

C H A P T E R   7 9

German Catholicism between *Kulturkampf* and World War I

In 1886/87, peace in the matter of Church policies was restored, and until the end of the Empire it would not be seriously questioned. Bismarck's successors Caprivi (chancellor of the Reich from 1890 until 1894), Hohenlohe (1894–1900) and Bülow (1900–09) successfully wooed the Center Party; Caprivi, who tried to alleviate the internal tensions that had built up under Bismarck, made concessions to Poland. In 1891, a Polish prelate was assigned the episcopal see of Gnesen. Some of the severities of the retained sections of the *Kulturkampf* legislation were moderated. In 1890 the Expulsion Law was repealed and the exemption of theologians from active military duty was granted. In 1891 the Prussian dioceses were repaid the funds that had been suspended during the *Kulturkampf.* In 1894 the Redemptorists and the Holy Ghost Fathers, who had also been included in the Jesuit Law, were allowed to return; however, the efforts of the Center Party regarding the suspension of this exception law were only partially successful: In 1904 at least ARTICLE 2, which had permitted the internment and expulsion of individual Jesuits, was stricken. In 1902 a Catholic theological faculty was established at the Imperial University of Strasbourg. It soon received papal approval. However, the resistance of the Liberals to the Elementary School Bill drafted by Minister of Cultural Affairs von Zedlitz-Trützschler (1892) in agreement with the Center and the Conservatives showed all too clearly the limits of the compromise; reverting to the most ardent *Kulturkampf* polemics, this opposition involved the struggle "against the obscurantist spirit" and was finally successful.

In spite of this, the process of normalization was probably furthered by Wilhelm II and Pius X alike. During his thirty years in office, the Emperor stressed in his many often ill-conceived statements the Protestant character of his House and the Empire; but he also found understanding words for the Catholics and for Catholic institutions. He sincerely wished the mitigation of the denominational differences. He was particularly interested in the Benedictine order and the Catholic missions, since they were also useful in terms of colonial policy.

The state's right to participate in the appointment of high Church officials, as well as the election of bishops and the nomination of voting cathedral canons during the "royal" months was still exercised, but the bishops' elections that had burdened the relationship between Church and state until the *Kulturkampf* were not interfered with any longer. The government of Wilhelm II successfully effected the elevation of Prussian bishops to cardinals, and the Emperor himself had a vital interest in the improvement of the German influence in Rome, which had always been minor. His wish to have a German cardinal appointed to the Curia was not fulfilled, because the Emperor's own adviser on Church policy, Cardinal Kopp, skillfully opposed this plan. Kopp had refused since the conclusion of the *Kulturkampf* to share his role of mediator between Rome and Berlin with anyone.

In spite of concentrating on internal Church reforms, Pius X never neglected diplomacy, and thus he endeavored to establish good relations with the antirevolutionary Empires of Austria and Germany. On several occasions he demonstratively assured Wilhelm II and Bülow, the guarantors of the existing order, of his sympathy, which survived the break of the Center Party with the Chancellor (1906). The Vatican repeatedly confused the political with the ecclesiastical sphere. This was the case when Erzberger and other Center Party deputies criticized the imperial colonial administration, causing a break (that was also provoked by Kopp), and when the Vatican reprimanded them for ingratitude toward the Chancellor, who was friendly toward the Church. Supported by Kopp, Bülow entertained good relations with Rome. All in all, the example set by Bismarck in the septennate controversy continued to have an effect in Berlin: The Reich's government often tried to solicit internal political assistance from the Vatican and to preserve or increase the distance between the Curia and the growing democratic tendencies. Bülow's successor Bethmann Hollweg (after 1909) adhered to the ecclesiastical political balance. A temporary cooling off between Rome and Berlin only occurred because of the backlash that was caused in Germany by the struggle of the Curia against modernism. The efforts of Pius X (less intense than those of his predecessor) regarding the establishment of a nunciature in Berlin were not successful. They failed because of the opposition of the Berlin imperial court and many influential Protestant circles; but Cardinal Kopp and the Center Party, still fearing for their independence, did not want a nuncio in Berlin either.

After the nineties, the German Catholics and their political representatives began to integrate the Church into the national state. In spite of earlier scepticism, Windthorst had made the first steps in this direction. His successor Ernst Lieber

(1838–1902) led the party completely out of the opposition into which it had been forced during the *Kulturkampf,* making it an indispensable support for the policies of Caprivi, Hohenlohe, and Bülow. In pursuit of this aim Lieber disengaged himself from the governmental minority, consisting predominantly of noblemen from Silesia and supported by Cardinal Kopp, and introduced more national, but at the same time more democratic policies. In the spirit of Windthorst, Lieber's course aimed at strengthening the *Reichstag* and at the complete parliamentarization of the Empire, from which his party could expect the most effective increase of its influence. Moreover, there were tensions among the right wing that had already come to the fore in the trade-union controversy and resulted (after 1918, when the majority of the party had begun to favor the republic) in the migration of the Catholics of the right toward the German Nationals. Following the end of the *Kulturkampf,* the number of Catholics voting for the Center Party slowly and steadily decreased. The essential motives for the existence of the party were no longer valid.

The Center Party did not only support the social policies of Wilhelm II because they were compatible with its old objectives. Only the Center's approval enabled the enactment of all the great "national" legislative bills, ranging from Caprivi's trade treaties, the Civil Code, and the improvement of the navy, to the imperial budget reforms under Bülow. The sanctioning of Wilhelm II's navy policy was an expression of the unconditional will to fulfill a national duty. This was an understandable reaction to the earlier charges of "hostility toward the Empire,"a reaction that reflected the mood of the citizens at that time, yet was doubtful in terms of its impact. Nonetheless, the Center Party on the basis of its experiences collected during the *Kulturkampf* continued to promote civil rights, a significant contribution to the constitutional development of Germany. The Catholic association system, especially the *Volksverein,* also supported the democratization of society.

The Center Party managed to enter "the antechamber of power" by way of its national policy, but it did not proceed further. The leadership positions in the Empire and Prussia remained inaccessible to the Catholics; and also in the other areas of state administration, they were unable to achieve participation on an equal footing. Even in Bavaria it was not until 1912, after forty years of liberal regimes, that Hertling, an exponent of political Catholicism, occupied the highest position of government. Weighty remnants of *Kulturkampf* legislation continued to exist. It was not until 1917 that the Jesuit Law was completely suspended. The Center Party's so-called toleration proposal failed to introduce to the imperial code of law the guarantees for ecclesiastical liberty provided by the Prussian constitution that had been suspended during the *Kulturkampf.* Consequently it also failed in suspending the restrictions to which the Catholic Church in some predominantly Protestant federal states (e.g., Saxony, Mecklenburg, Brunswick) was still subject.

The most prominent figure in the Prussian episcopate until World War I was Cardinal Kopp. It was only in the last years of his life that he was increasingly isolated, mainly because of his inflexibility in the trade-union controversy. The differences between him and the bishops of the Rhineland, a remnant of the last phase of the *Kulturkampf,* had been moderated. After all, the bishops had to concede that the mediation of Kopp, criticized by them, was totally compatible with Leo XIII's intentions. Korum, Kopp's opponent in the game of Church policies at that time, was later to become Kopp's frequent ally. The integralism they had in common brought them together. Kopp's relations with Cardinals Krementz and Antonius Fischer of Cologne (1840–1912, in 1902 archbishop, 1903 cardinal) remained cool, even though both sides were in agreement about most ecclesiastical matters. The archbishops of Cologne and the majority of their auxiliaries were largely influenced by the Center Party of the Rhineland and the *Volksverein* with its democratic tendencies, as far as their political and socio-political stance was concerned. They also supported the Christian trade unions that had emerged in the nineties from the Catholic workers' associations in western Germany and continued to be backed predominantly by Catholics, though they were interdenominational. The militant atheism of the free (social-democratic) trade unions had caused the formation of the new organization. They enabled the Catholic and Protestant workers efficiently to represent their professional interests while respecting their religious convictions. The workers' associations led by priests now dealt only with the spiritual care of their members. The Christian trade unions employed all means necessary for the workers' struggle, even the strike. But since they only strove for evolutionary improvements rather than revolutionary change of the existing system, they were supported by the Prussian government in many instances. Their public relations were handled by the *Volksverein*. This reformism of the West, often merging with the remnants of critical distance toward the Prussian state, went too far according to Kopp's opinion. He insisted on patriarchal authoritarian concepts and wanted to integrate Catholicism unconditionally into the state of Wilhelm II and its rigid backward social structure. He was assisted by those magnates whose influence on the Center Party's politics was fading. Kopp knew how to deal with the power of the Center. However, his relationship to the party leadership, from which he frequently tried to extricate the representation of ecclesiastical interests in the political arena, was always tense and grew increasingly worse after Erzberger's rise.

In Bavaria, Archbishop Franz von Bettinger of Munich (1850–1917, archbishop after 1909) supported the *Volksverein* and the Christian trade unions. That he did not become cardinal until 1914 was due to governmental doubts about his leanings. The government would have preferred the elevation of the younger, more intelligent and at the same time more conservative Bishop Michael von Faulhaber (1869–1952) of Speyer, who owed his office to royal nomination. Among the bishops of southwest Germany, Paul Wilhelm Keppler (1852–1926, since 1898 bishop of Rottenburg), respected by his contemporaries as a religious writer, must be mentioned. He had inaugurated a constructive biblical and homiletical renewal, but occupied a very conservative position in the controversy over Reform Catholicism. Cultural inferiority, the most crucial inheritance of the *Kulturkampf,* was a heavy burden for the Catholics. That it grew worse for a while had two causes: The perpetuators of the predominantly Protestant or liberal national culture denied the Catholics full participation. Moreover, most Catholics remained, often preferred to remain, in the self-sufficient isolation that they had escaped to from the onslaught of the liberal offensive. The authoritative defensive of papal doctrine that had climaxed in Pius X's struggle against modernism aggravated or hindered the new ideas of the modern world. Thus the German Catholics were initially unable to provide adequate answers to the growing self-criticism of liberalism. Instead, they retreated into a superficial adaptation of the sham culture of the Wilhelmian era. The criticism of capitalism voiced by apologists and social reformers remained defensive and espoused obsolete concepts of society. The antiliberalism of the convert Julius Langbehn, temporarily supported by Bishop Keppler, contained, aside from the irrationalism and voluntarism which initially affected the developing youth movement, ambivalent elements that appeared in different places around the turn of the century and eventually paved the road for totalitarian ideologies.

Likewise, around the turn of the century, an active minority took up a more ad-equate rational confrontation with the intellectual forces of the time. The initiatives were provided by the representatives of Reform Catholicism, some of whom, out of opposition to papal centralism as well as to political Catholicism, had ventured too far into nationalism. The most significant contributions were provided by Carl Muth and his friends, who initiated in *Hochland,* founded in 1903, the liberation of Catholic belles lettres from an apologetical and backward-looking parochial-ism. Their opponent in the ensuing literary controversy was Richard von Kralik, representing the traditional concepts in *Gral.*

The controversy over Reform Catholicism and *Hochland* carried on through-out the last decade led to vehement disputes over the political or denominational character of the Center Party and over the permissibility of interdenominational Christian trade unions. These had partially grown out of older differences, but were also caused by the integralism of Pius X and his disciples. The liberal-democratic "Cologne Faction" and the patriarchal-integralistic "Berlin-Breslau Faction" con-fronted each other in the "Center Party controversy" as well as in the "trade-union controversy." Members of the first group were the West German Center Party with its paper *Kölnische Volkszeitung,* the *Volksverein,* the Christian trade unions, and the West German Catholic workers' associations. A minority was integralist, chiefly the association of Catholic workers' societies, located in Berlin, that claimed to represent their members socio-politically, but actually served the interest of the employers through its patriarchalism and by neglecting to utilize the weapons of the trade unions. The integralists were supported by Cardinal Kopp and Bishop Korum. Through Kopp, as well as through the international organization of Prelate Benigni, they had contact with the Vatican, whose full approval they enjoyed.

It was typical of the integralists thoughtlessly to doubt the loyalty to the Church of people who disagreed with them. The leaders of the integralists, especially Be-nigni and his assistants, were known to have spied on their internal ecclesiastical opponents and to have accused them of heresy. Theological modernism, which developed primarily in France, Italy and England, was condemned in 1907. After this date, they turned their full attention to German developments. The procedures of the Cologne faction were considered just as dangerous as the theological in-novations that had not gone quite as far. As a matter of fact, the Center majority pursued the declericalization of public life feared by the integralists, and the objec-tive separation of the spiritual and the temporal. Pius X considered this a serious danger. He insisted that all organizations sustained by Catholics should remain in direct dependence on the hierarchy.

When the Center Party was founded, the leadership and the majority insisted that it be a political party, claiming and obtaining independence from the ecclesiastical authority in political matters. But after Lieber's death, an integralist minority again voiced the demand, favored by the new course Pius X had taken, for more consideration of Catholicism in regard to party policy. In order to counteract this, Julius Bachem (1845–1918), after 1869 editor-in-chief of the *Kölnische Volkszeitung,* in 1906 wrote the famous essay "Wir müssen aus dem Turm heraus" ("We have to get out of the tower") published in the *Historisch-Politische Blätter.* This caused a dispute. Bachem warned against unrealistic conceptions of the Christian state and against abuse of the denominational principle. He demanded political and socio-political cooperation between Catholics and Protestants and the expansion of the party toward an interdenominational Christian people's party. His proposal, based on Windthorst and the tradition of the Center Party, became the program of the Cologne Faction. Its forerunners, among them many clergymen, were of the opinion that the Church was to interpret the general norms of morality, but that their actual application to politics and socio-politics was a matter to be dealt with by Catholics versed in these areas. The main paper of the "Cologne Faction," the *Kölnische Volkszeitung,* was supported by most publications of the Center Party, by the *Historisch-Politische Blätter* and *Hochland.*

The integralists accused the Cologne Faction of curbing papal authority, of wanting to deprive public life of ecclesiastical influence, and of threatening the integrity of Catholic Germany. Some, especially in the Benigni circle, went further. They took up Counter-Reformation slogans, maintaining that the Cologne group was propagating a national Catholicism that would lead to Protestantism. Cardinal Kopp, encouraging and supporting the integralist offensive with the increasing stubbornness of old age, spoke of the "infestation of the West," claiming "that *Hochland* was de-Catholicizing the educated classes, while the *Volksverein* was accomplishing the same within the lower classes through its support of the trade unions." All in all, the *Volksverein* and the Christian trade unions were rejected most vehemently because they dealt with tasks the Church was claiming without, however, paying attention to the hierarchy. The trade unions were repudiated because they were interdenominational and used strikes, a weapon that was revolutionary in conservative eyes. The outcome of the dispute would have been clear had it been carried on in Germany only. The great majority of the politically active Catholics, especially in the west and south of Germany, rejected integralism. Bishops Kopp and Korum were unable to persuade their colleagues. Cardinal Fischer protected the *Volksverein.* Furthermore, in 1910, he effected the resolution of the Bishops' Conference in Fulda, permitting membership in trade unions, provided they did not violate Christian morality and would not meddle with religious matters.

But the integralists refused to recognize these limitations. It was to the advantage of the Church's opponents, who profited from the controversy. The integralists clung to the dispute and carried it to the Curia, involving it for the last time in an internal German ideological struggle. In Rome, the mood was different from Fulda. Pius X and Merry del Val disapproved of the Cologne Faction. They disapproved of the *Kölnische Volkszeitung* because it had contradicted the Curia in the controversy involving Ehrhard and Schell. A papal brief addressed to Cardinal Fischer confirmed the freedom of the German Catholics in nonreligious matters. However, Pastor, following a papal audience in 1907, remarked: "I noticed clearly that the Pope did not approve of the German Center Party's request for absolute independence from any kind of ecclesiastical authority. Indeed, such political independence is too easily transferred to the ecclesiastical realm." Five years later, at the peak of the trade-union controversy, Pius X, in a conversation with Pastor, reiterated "that he absolutely refused the efforts of Julius Bachem and his disciples. He said openly that his reprimand was not directed against the many loyal Catholics of Germany but only against those who followed the *Kölnische Volkszeitung.* It was not their opponents who were disturbing the unity of the Catholics, but rather this very paper." Merry del Val went even further, including in his criticism Cardinal Fischer and the majority of the German bishops, as well as Nuncio Frühwirth of Munich, who was said to lean too far toward the Cologne Faction. Frühwirth, the general of the Dominican Order until 1904, was quite antimodernistic. However, in Munich after 1907, he had become convinced that the belligerent manner in which the integralists conducted themselves in the controversies concerning literature, the Center Party, and the trade unions was not justified. The Pope and his chief political adviser were not willing or able to examine critically the great amount of information that was forwarded. They believed only what they wanted to believe. Nonetheless, the Pope directly intervened in the Center controversy only once, in 1914, when the Cologne faction had essentially established itself. Derived from a lecture, the essay by the leader of the Center in Baden, Pastor Theodor Wacker (1845–1921), and entitled "Zentrum und kirchliche Autorität" ("Center party and ecclesiastical authority") was put on the Index because its emphasis on the independence of the party could be misunderstood. The disproportional severity of this measure suggests that the men around the Pope had indeed waited for an excuse to act. In other respects, the Pope had to exercise restraint; on the one hand, because the political independence of the Center Party had been recognized by his predecessor and confirmed, after all, by himself after Vannutelli's speech; on the other hand, because the party acted with caution in regard to Rome, taking the initiative in ecclesiastical matters only after consulting with the bishops.

Nonetheless, Pius X's course severely burdened the Church policies of the Center Party. In particular, the party had to cushion the various vehement parliamentary debates that had been caused by the Borromeo encyclical and the antimodernist oath. The encyclical *Editae saepe* (29 May 1910) issued on the occasion of the three hundredth anniversary of Borromeo's canonization, honored Saint Charles Borromeo as a model of a true reformer, as opposed to the false reformers such as the modernists and the men of the Reformation of the sixteenth century, against whom Borromeo had fought. The latter were charged in the encyclical with revolt against ecclesiastical authority and blind obedience to the sovereign. This metaphor, taken from the vocabulary of the religious struggles of the sixteenth century and congealed into a cliché in the Curia, incurred the outrage not only of the German Protestants. The efforts toward interdenominational cooperation suffered a severe setback. Following protests of the governments the Curia finally did not insist on the official publication of the encyclical in Germany. The Pope himself felt obliged to appease Germany. Through his secretary of state he explained that the Curia had not intended to insult the German nation. With respect to the antimodernist oath, a compromise was necessary also. Following similarly vehement discussions, the theological faculties of the state universities were exempt from the oath. Even Kopp had supported this compromise, because otherwise the continuation of the faculties would have been seriously threatened.

For the integralist efforts toward Roman intervention, the trade-union controversy, with its moral-theological implications, was more appropriate than the essentially political Center Party controversy. At that time, the Vatican was not sufficiently familiar with the problems of a modern economy. Following a trip to Rome, Cardinal Fischer believed it possible to announce in a pastoral letter the Vatican's neutrality in the controversy of the two German factions, but a papal pronouncement of May 1912 clearly sided with the Berlin group rather than the Cologne one. With insufficiently deliberated arguments the Pope reasoned that religion must penetrate the whole individual and therefore his economic enterprises as well. Cardinal Kopp and his allies almost obtained a formal papal condemnation of the Christian trade unions then struggling for a Christian as well as a democratic solution to the labor problem, offering at that time the only effective alternative to the antiecclesiastical workers' associations. At the last minute, Cardinal Fischer and his close ally, the Franciscan Bishop Bernard Döbbing, an adviser to the Pope, were able to reach a limited compromise.

The encyclical *Singulari quadam* (24 September 1912), concluding the controversy, began with a warning against the "undefined interdenominationalism" and continued with the reiteration of the reminder of the principle that the social problems could not be solved without recourse to religion and moral law. The Pope unconditionally praised the ecclesiastical workers' associations, supporting their monopoly in Catholic countries. However, subsequently he conceded that in other countries Catholics were allowed to cooperate with non-Catholics in order carefully to elevate the working class (*cautione adhibita*) and that, in the exceptional case of Germany, interdenominational trade unions could be tolerated. He made the membership of Catholic workers dependent on their simultaneous membership in the Catholic workers' associations and on the proviso that trade unions would not interfere with the doctrine of the Church. The first of these conditions unnecessarily burdened the workers, the second one ignored the goals of the trade unions. At least they were now able to continue with their activities. They had no difficulties adhering to the conditions of the *Singulari quadam* and preventing further conflicts with Rome. In spite of the Vatican's sympathies for the integralists, the trade-union controversy helped the progressive faction in German Catholicism achieve partial success. But the distrustful *tolerari potest* of the Pope encouraged the integralists to continue to discredit the trade unions, thus causing more unrest. Shortly before his death (4 March 1914), Cardinal Kopp himself rejected a conciliatory interpretation of the encyclical. In 1913, the trade unions already had to defend themselves against assaults by the opposition in a sensational trial that was played up by the antiecclesiastical press.

Cardinal Fischer died on 30 July 1912. Thus he was unable to witness the results of the action initiated by him. Due to the Curia's drastic interference with the suffrage rights of the cathedral chapter of Cologne, he was succeeded by Bishop Felix von Hartmann (1851–1919, after 1911 Bishop of Münster), who was close to the integralist, as well as to the national-conservative course of Cardinal Kopp, but who did not possess his leadership qualities. But even in this manner, full success could not be achieved: Hartmann tried hard to contribute to the preservation of the existing political and social structure, thus apparently establishing a good relationship with Wilhelm II. However, he had to pay attention to the realities of his new diocese and to be content with the activity of the Christian trade unions and the *Volksverein.*

C H A P T E R   8 0

Separation of Church and State in France

Voting on the Separation Law (1899–1905)

The emotions aroused by the Dreyfus affair had played a significant role in the failure of reconciliation. Likewise, the separation of Church and state in France was the result of a series of circumstances that gradually deteriorated the relations between the two powers. Basically, neither Pierre Waldeck-Rousseau nor Émile Combes, his successor to the ministerial office in 1902, intended a separation. However, they were led on this path by their personal decisions as well as by political measures demanded by the majority and the compelling force of circumstances. Certainly, many had long regarded the annulment of the concordat a natural consequence of the development, especially after the fateful outcome of the *Ralliement.* However, the internal and external reasons for avoiding the schism were just as strong during the time of the Republic as they had been twenty years before, even though the regime had meanwhile found stronger support among the Catholic voters. When Pius X categorically refused to recognize the law of 2 December 1905, a law introducing into France the "most radical separation system imaginable," the republican government was willing to make a few concessions in order to limit the effects of the law and to avoid at any cost the danger of a religious conflict.

An investigation must first deal with a series of legislative measures whose severe amendments resulted in the separation laws. The "logic of the laws" must not conceal the deep emotions with which these measures were enacted and applied. The ministries stood under the supervision of the majority in the parliament that was ready to strike as soon as the question of congregation and Church was raised. The elections of April 1902, which concerned this topic, resulted in a majority of 339 deputies who belonged to the "bloc" (composed of the Democratic Union, Socialists, Radicals, and Radical Socialists). The strong core of this "bloc" (200 deputies) was comprised of the representatives of the bourgeoisie of those medium-sized and small cities that were radically anticlerical. One of their loyal representatives was Émile Combes. Formerly a seminarian, he had left Catholicism and turned to medicine and propaganda for the Radicals. This brought him a senatorial seat in his department of Charente-Inférieure. The usual fanaticism of both parties, raked by the press with relentless personal assaults and caricatures, was not without influence on the attitude of the politicians. Preceding the separation, the expulsion of about twenty thousand members of religious orders between 1903 and 1904 nourished radicalism on both sides. The population frequently supported the resistance of the order members. The demonstrations often ended in bloodshed.

In November 1899 Waldeck-Rousseau proposed his bill on the religious congregations. He did not intend it as an aggressive interpretation of the policy of the *défense républicaine.* He had long desired to remedy the lack of any kind of regulation regarding the freedom of association in French law. His aim was to eliminate a new coalition, favored by legal uncertainty, between the nonauthorized congregations and an antirepublican social elite. He was intent on precluding the kind of threat to which the republicans had been exposed on 16 May 1877 and during the appeal of the Dreyfus trial. Moreover, as a statist jurist, he wanted to bring the various forms of ecclesiastical life under the control of the state. This was the background for the measures against the Assumptionists, the prohibition of bishops appointing members of orders to teaching posts and seminaries, and, finally, for the investigation of the property of congregations which he had ordered to be registered in the fall of 1900. In Toulouse, on 20 October, he reiterated the statement on the clandestine social influence of the congregations on education and the upper echelons of government.

The bill proposed by Waldeck-Rousseau on associations required religious congregations to obtain a license from the government, but at the same time it opened up possibilities for numerous agreements. However, supported by a delegation of groups from the left, the commissions of both chambers gave the bill an expressly anticlerical character. From then on, the admission of congregations which, according to ARTICLE 14, were prohibited from playing an educational role required legal authorization. The law of 1 July 1901 was, in terms of its spirit, far different from the draft of Waldeck-Rousseau. The religious associations were excluded from the freedom generously granted to others. After the autumn, several congregations had dissolved themselves voluntarily, but 700 foundations of female congregations and about 150 male congregations had applied for their authorization. After the enactment of the law, the minister proved to be indulgent and obliging, after Théophile Delcassé had left him in no doubt that for reasons of foreign policy the French did not want a break with the Holy See.

The situation was different in the case of Delcassé's successor, Émile Combes (after 1902). Waldeck-Rousseau was quick to make clear that he did not want the religious struggle launched by Combes. On 27 June 1903, before the Senate, he declared his opposition to Combes's absolutely rigid and uncompromising policy of execution. From all officials Combes demanded, in his words, "strict republican discipline." Contrary to the promises of his predecessor, he declared in June/July 1902 that all schools opened within the period of one year by congregations, even though licensed, were in violation of the law. In the following months almost 12,000 schools were closed, resulting in spontaneous protests especially in Brittany. This total laicization was crowned by the law of 7 July 1904, which denied all members of orders the freedom to teach. Again, 2,500 schools, among them the popular ones of the *Frères des Écoles chrétiennes,* had to be closed. In regard to the congregations, the Chamber approved a government proposal which provided for the denial of all licenses, with the exception of five missionary congregations. The dissolution of congregations was planned for Easter 1903. Some congregations preferred voluntarily to dissolve themselves. However, many others exercised passive resistance in order to draw attention to the coercion concealed behind these measures. Often, the religious who decided to emigrate were cheered by demonstrations of sympathy by the local inhabitants.

The vehement protests of the episcopate against all these measures compelled the government to attack the hierarchy. In the summer of 1902, after almost all seventy-four bishops had signed a petition for the purpose of defending the congregations and protesting the interpretation of the law regarding cooperatives, the officials resorted to the regulation that prohibited the bishops from joining together and presenting requests as a legal body. They turned all signatures en bloc over to the council of state which was applying the old and senseless procedure of the *appel comme d'abus* against the bishops. The income of the three initiators of the petition was canceled. During the last months of Leo XIII's pontificate, the standing conflict over the government's right to nominate bishops for elections also flared up again.The rigid attitude of the aging Pope in this matter was symptomatic of his situation. Pius X, on the other hand, clearly meant to prove his desire for peace when he accepted the rule that officially sanctioned the nomination by the government. Nonetheless, in June 1904 Rome did not hesitate to summon the two bishops of Dijon and Laval who were charged by their subjects with excessive indulgence toward the state authorities and experienced difficulties in their relations with the clergy and the administration of their diocese. The government forbade the two prelates to travel to Rome. These "summons" were issued a few weeks after a serious diplomatic incident had occurred on the occasion of Émile Loubet's (president of the Republic) visit to Rome. For the first time in the course of improving relations with Italy, the government had agreed to this official visit to the Quirinal, disregarding the advice Cardinal Rampolla had offered in the last months of the previous pontificate and giving no consideration to the Vatican. The fact that this questioned the presence of the nuncio in Paris was considered a challenging threat by the left. With a majority of 427 votes, the Chamber resolved to recall the French ambassador to the Holy See. This was the prologue to the break in diplomatic relations following the citation of the two bishops of Dijon and Laval to Rome on 30 July.

Combes's ministry came to an end on 14 January 1905 when the Socialists refused to endorse the anticlericalism of the Radicals. Combes' bill of 10 November to separate Church and state was replaced by a new, more liberal one under his successor J.-B. Bienvenu-Martin. During the debate extending from March into the summer, Aristide Briand, reporting for the commission, pleaded for the absolute neutrality of the state in religious matters in order that the Church "be completely at liberty to organize itself, live, and develop in accordance with its rules." Things changed at the end of April when a large majority voted in favor of ARTICLE 4. According to the article, religious communities were to follow the general organizational structure of their religion after they had announced their intention to adhere to its rules. This article precluded any attempt to form a state church that would have challenged the established churches. Instead, it amounted to a spiritualistic interpretation of the revolutionary tradition.

The entire legislative package, approved by the Chamber on 3 July and by the Senate on 6 December, was not applied until a year later. The law perpetuated the spirit of the legislation of the Revolution: neutrality and complete continence on the side of the state in religious matters, including salaries and subsidies. The buildings were declared property of the state or the community. Partially, they were given to the communities to practice their religion, but in the case of conflict, the council of the state, whose hostile attitude was well known, had the right to make a decision.

Execution of the Separation Law (1906–24)

The majority of Catholics considered this law a predatory incursion devised by the state. They had reason to assume that this law created the basis for the destruction of religion and its social impact. Nonetheless, at the end of the nineteenth century, certain groups within Catholicism were still willing to establish contact with the democratic society. They were agreeable to cooperation with the liberal efforts of certain advocates of the law, hoping to achieve with their help a tolerant execution of the law.

Jaurès himself relied on the support of certain groups of the clergy, " . . . without having to go as far as Loisy . . . with François Lenormant, the great Christian and scholar, or with Monsignor d'Hulst, or even with Abbé Duchesne, or with the Institutes of Toulouse and Paris, which tried, not without risks, to utilize some of the results of modern criticism for the benefit of traditional exegesis. If only some priests, enthusiastic democrats with liberal spirits, were to stand up and be supported by their religious communities. . . . "

Around 1900, Marc Sangnier, a young engineer from the Parisian middle class, founded a study group that courageously appeared in public with discussion groups, congresses, as well as a project designed to educate the people. The group intended through spiritual indoctrination to prepare the faithful to practice personal responsibility in a democracy. In 1905, the *Sillon* movement had five strong regional groups outside of Paris: in the north, the east, in Limousin, Aquitaine, and Brittany. This movement, whose efforts included sound spiritual and intellectual education as well as social activities, gained some support among the lower and middle classes of the cities and in the rural areas of the east and Brittany. Since 1904, in the region of Lyon, the *Chronique du Sud-Est* had supplied the staff of the *Semaine sociale,* a sort of traveling university which conducted annual seminars on topical or fundamental issues. At that time, the *Chronique* included two hundred groups scattered throughout the Rhone Valley. In 1904, the Jesuit Fr. Leroy founded another movement in Rheims, whose purpose was to disseminate information and be active among the workers. Its *Action populaire* as well as the *Semaines sociales* exist to this day. The Catholic Action of the French youth also undertook a program of social and trade-union related activities. This social involvement was enhanced by lively intellectual activities. When preparing the law, Jaurès had especially the centers of Paris and Toulouse in mind; but the *École de Lyon* that evolved around the new journal *Demain* (1905/07) should be included. The vitality of this group turned again to biblical (Lagrange), historical (Duchesne), and philosophical (Blondel and Laberthonnière) studies. After the elections of 1902, the *Action libérale,* founded in 1901 by Albert de Mun and Jacques Piou, held its ground in the field of politics. The *Action libérale populaire* gained many supporters in the north and in Isère.

These movements were forced to take a somewhat reserved stance toward the separation law. The Catholic press intensified its aggressiveness and, within the right wing, the *Action français* separated from *Sillon* at that time. The leading ranks had no difficulties convincing the rural population that the Republic was persecuting religion itself. This idea was also propagated by the majority of the clergy. Among the bishops, however, many shied away from a situation which entailed a complete break with the official authorities and, after the elections of 1906, many of them searched for a modus vivendi. The opposite opinion, rejecting any kind of concession to the political situation at hand and having come to terms with the predicted separation, was extolled by those prelates who referred to "liberal" traditions as well as those who had taken an intransigent attitude. Their number increased by the new bishops who were exclusively appointed and installed by the Pope, especially those seventeen bishops whom Pius X had appointed at the same time in 1906. In 1906 the antimodernist condemnations increased in Rome. They foreshadowed the encyclical *Pascendi* and the letter of 25 August 1910 in which the Pope asked M. Sangnier to dissolve the *Sillon* movement. The bishops lobbied for this intransigence because they were alarmed by the infiltration of modernist tendencies, which found disciples among the seminarians and the younger clergy. In view of these conditions, the forces of resistance from the leading ranks of the French Catholics down to the common people had a great deal of significance. However, restraint had to be practiced in this regard, because the elections of May 1906 assured the return and even an increase of the majority of the "bloc." These elections focused not on the religious question but rather on the social problem which remained in the forefront until 1914.

The execution of the separation law was dependent on the Roman directives. Its enactment was almost immediately followed by its condemnation through the encyclical *Vehementer nos* of 2 February 1906, but this did not preclude the possibility of searching for a solution which would insure the religious life of the Church. Such attempts, however, could not imply the recognition of a law prepared without the Holy See. Rome was suspicious of everything that could be taken as acceptance of a precedent and thus influence the concordat situation of the Church in other countries. On the other hand, the government, when preparing the execution of the law, had taken a rather inept and insulting measure. It ordered the churches to take an inventory of all their properties, which were to become that of the state. In March 1906, after a smooth start, these inventory practices caused grave incidents in Paris, Marseille, and especially in the rural areas. They took place, above all, in areas with strong religious practices (in the lowlands of the west and in the south of the Massif Central, in the Jura, and in French Flanders). This incipient revolt in the Christian rural areas compelled the government to back down and the inventory activities were discontinued. These incidents were related to the second condemnation of the law through the encyclical *Gravissimo officio* of 10 August 1906. Under these conditions, the negotiations over the wording of a law that was impossible from a legal point of view were extremely difficult. This was the reason for convening three consecutive episcopal conferences in May and September 1906 and in February 1907. None of the conferences could come to an agreement about the kind of diocesan associations that had been attempted in some dioceses. After the law had been enacted, both parties rejected the alternative of "usufruct," which considered the Catholics in their churches users without legal title. When they refused to obtain the official permission required for public gatherings, this offense was ridiculed as a "Mass delict."

The total refusal to cooperate forced the legislators to interpret the law moderately, unless they desired to worsen their already questionable position. The communities were required to let the faithful use the cult buildings free of charge. State council and courts referred to ARTICLE 4, assuring the right of the bishops to stop encroachments of schismatic religious communities that had formed in Toulouse, Lyon, and in the west around some pastors who were rebelling against the diocesan authorities. Thus, when executing the law, the administration even functioned as an "executive organ of the episcopal jurisdiction" (Axel von Campenhausen). The Roman intransigence not only forced it to practice a liberal course, but caused a strengthening of the authority of the hierarchy over the lower clergy, of the clergy over the faithful, and, one could add, of Roman authority over the Church of France.

Nonetheless, the overall balance of the first years was very disquieting to the Church. The confiscation of buildings and the lodgement of bishops and parish priests at their own expense in other buildings entailed material losses and great administrative disorder. The cancellation of stipends and salaries especially caused a rapid decrease of clerical appointments, because the seminarians, mostly of humble background, were unable to cover the cost of their education. The seminaries' student body was reduced by half, and even in areas with traditionally numerous clerical candidates a decline was felt. The spontaneously developing organizations for clerical appointments, seminary associations and associations of priests were indications of the seriousness of a situation that could not really be improved through such measures. Before the outbreak of World War I, the school conflict flared up again and was intensified by the attitude of the nationalists, who were willing to make the interests of the Church their own business.

In spite of this difficult situation, which was intensified until 1914 by the antimodernist criticism of the renewal efforts, the French Catholics found ways and means to respond to the severe challenges they were facing. The statement that the disestablishment of the Church of the concord, radically changed the Church's behavior within French society is justified. In this respect, it is significant that the initiatives in the nineties to strengthen the social impact of Christianity increased. They were supported by prelates. The societies that considered it their duty to waken the Catholics' interests in social affairs and to educate them accordingly, increased their activities. Especially prominent were the *Action populaire,* headed by P. Desbuquois, the *Semaines sociales,* whose activities attracted a large audience, and the social secretariats existing in Paris and the provinces after 1908. The *Action Catholique de la Jeunesse française* was asked to delegate apostolic responsibility to its lay members (Pius X's letter to J. Lerolle of 22 February 1907). Finally, most scholars, unperturbed by the ecclesiastical censures during the modernist crisis, insisted on bearing witness to the truth of the Catholic Church. This is documented by the *Annales de philosophie chrétienne* (until 1913) and the *Bulletin de la semaine.* Characteristic for these prewar years is the revival of religious interest within the intellectual circles, mainly among the youth and even at the universities, as was documented by Joseph Lotte, a friend of Péguy. Finally, the war slowly brought the various social groups closer together again. Comradeship in the trenches, where believers and nonbelievers, priests and laymen fought side by side, contributed substantially to the alleviation of anticlerical prejudices. In 1919, the population of Alsace-Lorraine was not forced to accept the separation law, in order to spare religious feelings. There, priests and pastors continued to receive their salaries from the state, and religious instruction was offered in public schools. This exception, motivated by political expediency, contributed to normalizing the relations between Church and state. It was also significant that during the enforcement of the separation law French schools in foreign countries, especially in the Near East, continued to enjoy the support of the French state.

The contacts between Paris and the Vatican were officially resumed in 1915, especially after the mediation of the superior of Saint Louis des Français. After Clemenceau had resigned from the political scene, Briand restored diplomatic relations. The new nuncio, B. Cerretti, was solemnly received in Paris in May 1912. At the same time, a deputy of the leftist Center, Célestin Jonnart, was appointed ambassador to the Vatican. Jonnart declared that the government intended "to let the moral forces dominating the world compete to restore peace," without infringing upon the republican laws *(Le Radical* of 29 May 1921). The Holy See granted the French government the right to examine the credentials of episcopal nominees. Finally, in November 1922, exhaustive negotiations began, dealing with the plan to replace the religious associations of parishes that had fallen under the influence of laymen with diocesan associations that were to be subject to episcopal jurisdiction. Thanks to the very active preparations of the texts by Louis Canet, adviser for religious affairs at the Quai d'Orsay, and to the subsequent memoranda of the bishops of Nice and Arras, the resistance of the majority of the French episcopate and the restraint of the Holy See could be overcome. At the beginning of his pontificate, Pius XI was persuaded to relinquish guarantees in the form of legislation so that the plan would not fail in the wake of reviving anticlericalism. The diocesan associations were finally constituted through administrative channels. They were headed by the bishop and entitled to administer Church property as well as to accept donations and bequests. On 18 January 1924 the Pope gave his approval by issuing the encyclical *Maximam gravissimamque,* which was endorsed through a letter of 6 February 1924 by the French bishops.

This resumption of relations and this modus vivendi did not mean that anticlerical tendencies had died down. But this was to be the "last crisis of the Third Republic that was receptive to the revival of the spirit of 1904" (André Latreille). The agreement reached during the postwar era reflected the spiritual development within the Church, which concerned itself with social activities that were more and more divorced from political goals, as well as among the Republicans, who subscribed more and more to a laicism of action rather than belligerent anticlericalism. This marked the establishment of a regime which was entrusted with the relations between the two powers in France in the course of the twentieth century.

C H A P T E R   8 1

The Outbreak of World War I

At the level of international relations, Pius X's pontificate coincided with the "time of crisis" (Duroselle). In 1903, King Alexander of Serbia was assassinated by a group of anti-Austrian officers who tried to make their country the center of Yugoslavian nationalism. From 1905 until 1914 there were five increasingly severe crises: the Franco-German crisis following the Tangier demonstrations of Wilhelm II in 1905, the Austro-Russian crisis following the annexation of Bosnia and Herzegovina in 1908, the Agadir crisis in 1911, the Balkan Wars of 1912–1913, which increased Serbia's prestige, and finally the crisis of July 1914 that caused World War I. Even though there was new hope every time that war was successfully circumvented, the approach of a catastrophe could be felt, the approach of a war that would be much more devastating than earlier ones, due to progress in armament and the general introduction of conscription. In the last years of his life, Pius X spoke more and more about the imminent catastrophe.

In view of the increase in nationalism and imperialism and the increasing threat of an expanding conflict, the reaction of Catholic groups appears disappointing in retrospect. In the course of the two years before the war of 1914–1918, ecclesiastical groups as well as the faithful themselves joined more and more openly in the glorification of national feeling. This chauvinism and the general resignation explain the enthusiasm with which the Catholics from both camps (with few exceptions) unanimously supported the fighting, rejecting, all in all, Benedict XV's repeated attempts to end this "useless slaughter."

In Germany, many Catholics followed the leaning of Protestants and became more and more receptive to everything relating to "national greatness." To be sure, the Catholic associations stayed away from Pan-Germanism and occasionally even condemned its excesses, but the Center Party had relinquished its opposition to armament policies after 1897, and, in 1904, Chancellor von Bülow praised the party for its "German national policies." The development of the international situation in the following ten years, coinciding with the incorporation of the Catholics into the bourgeois national state, encouraged this development, and Erzberger was one of its representatives.

In Austria, the Catholic intellectuals shied away from such chauvinism. However, nationalism was very active among the members of the Christian Socialist

Party between 1909 and 1914. The leading ecclesiastical circles showed no evidence of pacifist tendencies; rather they placed their moral influence with few exceptions in the service of the dynasty and the preservation of the old Empire, which was being undermined by the demands of the various Slav minorities.

In Italy, the weight of the Roman question often kept the Catholics from manifestations of patriotism. But by the turn of the century, a patriotic development had commenced. It intensified in view of the colonization efforts in Libya, which even the *Civiltà cattolica* presented as a crusade against Islam, though the Holy See had tried to compel the Catholic press to practice restraint. But from then on, the Catholics wanted to prove almost everywhere that no one could compete with them in terms of patriotism. Moreover, the incidents of conflicts between the organized Catholic movements and the extreme nationalists of Corradini increased. In 1910, when trying to solicit the support of the Catholics, Corradini had only found response among the disciples of Murri. In the elections of 1914, he campaigned as a candidate in the region of Vicenza, supported by the episcopate and Catholic Action.

In France, the majority of the clergy and the large Catholic journals emphasized the supposedly close relation between religious experience and patriotic enthusiasm. Following the Dreyfus affair, it was commonplace to consider "the enemies of the army," "the friends of Germany," and "the destroyers of Catholicism" to be one and the same. Demonstrations of this kind multiplied on the occasion of the beatification of Joan of Arc in 1909. In 1911, Secretary Caillaux suggested a policy of détente toward Germany and giving it a small part of the French colonial Empire. But he found that almost all French Catholics and a great number of Christian democrats and Sillonists turned against him. The *Société Gratry pour le maintien de la paix entre les nations,* when founded in 1907 by Vanderpol, an engineer from Lyon, could only solicit seven hundred members. Two years later, it changed into the *Ligue des catholiques français pour la paix.* When Vanderpol, supported by the bishop of Liège, tried to organize an international Church congress in order to pave the way for better Franco-German relations, only four French bishops were willing to send a representative. This was the reason why Vanderpol decided in 1911 to expand his plan and establish a *Ligue internationale des pacifistes catholiques,* which was to work on public opinion to try to prevent a forced solution of the problem and to insist on the use of international arbitration. In view of the situation, the league was located in Brussels and the positions of president and secretary general were entrusted to Belgians.

The aloofness of many Catholics toward pacifist movements cannot merely be justified with the old medieval tradition according to which military bravery is closely related to Christian virtues. It also rests in the fact that the instigators of antimilitary demonstrations around 1900 were almost always Socialists, anarchists, or Freemasons. At that particular time this meant: enemies of the Church. It is characteristic that Pius X principally granted approval to the Carnegie Endowment for International Peace, an American foundation of Protestant origin (letter of 11 June 1911), while rejecting a similar request by Vanderpol's *Ligue Internationale.* To be sure, the Pope had repeatedly condemned the use of weapons as a means to settle conflicts between nations and had demanded arbitration. When Cardinal Vannutelli praised the conquest of Libya by the Italians as a crusade, the

Pope called him to order. However, one cannot but concede that the Holy See did not try seriously enough until 1914 to curb the general tendency of the European Catholics to be enthralled by the nationalistic movement. The Holy See's benevolent attitude toward the *Action française* of Maurras and Daudet, pioneers of the *nationalisme intégral,* supports this impression.

The attitude of the Holy See at the moment of the outbreak of World War I is still a topic of discussion. When the Austrian ambassador informed Pius X about the ultimatum that was issued by Vienna and sent to Sarajevo on 23 July, the Pope declared his willingness to arbitrate between the two countries and he emphasized his intention to exercise a moderating influence on both governments. But what did really happen in the course of the following days?

Aside from rumors, for which "reliable documents are missing that could prove their authenticity" (Hudal), there are two documents at our disposal which are more reliable, but pose problems of interpretation. On the one hand, we have the letter of the Bavarian legate Baron Ritter, who wrote on 26 July: "The Pope approves the decisive steps Austria took toward Serbia." On the other hand, there is the detailed report of the Austrian legate Count Pállfy (of 29 July) regarding a conversation he had had two days earlier with Cardinal Merry del Val: "The memorandum addressed to Serbia was considered extremely harsh by the cardinal, but he approved of it nevertheless, at the same time indirectly expressing hope that the Monarchy would be able to endure the conflict. The Cardinal thought that it was a shame that Serbia had not been 'crushed' earlier because at that time it might have been accomplished without taking unforeseeable risks." The diplomat added: "This statement coincides with the Pope's ideas, because in the last few years His Holiness frequently expressed regret about Austria-Hungary's failure to put her dangerous neighbor in its place." When these texts were published, the Cardinal countered with a summary of the conversation: "It is true that I said to Count Pállfy after the terrible crime of Sarajevo that Austria had to remain firm and that it had a right to authentic reparations and the protection of its existence, but I never expressed the hope or the opinion that Austria would not take up arms."

What can we conclude from these texts? Unquestionably, we have to consider that a diplomat tends to declare a carefully phrased or simply implied opinion to be an official statement in order to prove that he has succeeded in persuading his opponent that his country was perfectly justified. One should also take into account that some people might have been of the opinion that the Holy See's restraint would finally remove the old Emperor's last inhibitions. On the other hand, it is clear that the slogan "Austria has to remain firm," which Merry del Val admitted to have used, was conducive to encouraging Vienna to impose its reign on Belgrade, even though Serbia had already responded to the Austrian ultimatum in conciliatory terms (25 July). Even on 27 July, the secretary of state and other diplomats were justified in assuming that a confinement of the conflict would be possible, at least as long as Russia had not taken a clear stand. When she finally did, she caused a chain reaction of hostilities all over Europe.

In any case, one fact can not be disputed: "A number of documents prove that in the decisive months of the summer of 1914 the Vatican was rather favorably inclined toward Austria-Hungary, in fact, one is tempted to say: surprisingly favorably" (Engel-Janosi). It would be exaggerated to speak about the Vatican's dependence on Austria. This can be documented by the fact that, on 24 June 1914, a concordat with Serbia was signed, even though the Austrian diplomats had tried persistently to prevent this because they considered it to be an encouragement for Yugoslavianism. Pius X, however, had great respect for the old Emperor Franz Joseph. After all, just a few years ago, he had appeared as the model of a Catholic sovereign when he walked in the procession of the Most Blessed Sacrament of the Altar on the occasion of the Eucharistic Congress in Vienna wearing his full-dress uniform. The Pope had placed even more hope on the Austrian successor to the throne, Archduke Franz Ferdinand. His assassination deeply disappointed him. Above all, since France's break with Rome, Austria was the only large Catholic state in Europe. Moreover, Austria provided protection against German Protestantism as well as against Orthodox Slavism. There are indications that Pius X and Merry del Val considered Serbia the malignant cell that would eventually infect even the existence of the Habsburg Monarchy. They believed that a weakening of the Austrian influence in the Balkans and on the Danubian plains would favor Russia, the main enemy of Catholicism in the Near East.

Is it possible that the sympathies the Pope and his secretary of state expressed for Austria (which does not necessarily mean that they intended war) also included Germany? In certain French circles, Pius X was charged with having been "the Pope of the Triple Alliance." It is true that the Pope, as a result of his more conciliatory stance toward Italy, did not have the same reasons to bear a grudge against the allies that Leo XIII had. It is also true that the German influence in the Vatican increased during his pontificate. On the one hand, this development was the normal consequence of the break of diplomatic relations by France and of the discontent of the leadership of the religious orders in this country with the measures taken against the congregations. On the other hand, this development resulted from the fact that Rome tended to favor the "safe" principles and dogmas of German Catholicism as opposed to the dangerous French progressivism in the matter of exegesis and philosophy. It is quite possible that the Vatican found satisfaction in the idea that the godless and immoral French would learn a lesson. In view of imminent war, the Pope did not raise the voice of a prophet condemning war, but rather confined himself to a somewhat meek appeal to all peoples to pray. He certainly did not restrain himself because he watched the approach of a catastrophe with pleasure, but rather because he reasoned that the Holy See's position was diplomatically weak and did not permit initiatives such as Pius XII would attempt twenty-five years later at the dawn of World War II. He may also simply have been too tired and old, lacking the energy necessary to act in a hopeless situation.

In fact, a month earlier, Pius X had celebrated his eightieth birthday, and for the last year his health had been a cause of concern. He died almost unexpectedly on the night of 19 August and left his successor with the new and difficult problems that the commencing war posed for the Church.

Part Three

The Expansion of Catholic Missions from the Time of Leo XIII until World War II

Jakob Baumgartner

The striking lack of representation of missionary interests at the First Vatican Council reflected the fact that ecclesiastical circles were caught up in European interests. As we demonstrated earlier, the participating missionary bishops were active, but in terms of numbers and influence they were a small group. The fact that the Council adjourned abruptly and the missionary proposals were never presented is not the reason for the fact that no effective initiatives for the propagation of the faith emanated from it. The real impulse came from outside, especially from the growing and prevailing imperialism or colonialism, in whose wake the missions had recently assumed truly worldwide scope. The earlier colonial powers, England and France, were joined by a united Germany. Russia expanded its empire in the east and south and thus exercised an antimissionary influence because, in agreement with Western powers, especially England, it impeded the preaching of the Gospel in such countries as Tibet and Afghanistan. In Africa, the Islamic faith, a political force in the Ottoman Empire, penetrated even the black population.

CHAPTER 82

Missions in the Shadow of Colonialism

Initially, a false understanding of the missionary concept impaired worldwide and open-minded missionary activities. This concept originated during the First Vatican Council among the authorities of the Congregation for the Propagation of the Faith. Missionary work was primarily understood to mean activities among the Christians of the Eastern churches and the Catholic immigrants in North America. In the context of the last few years of Pius IX's pontificate, this attitude is understandable; but it can still be found in the first years of Leo XIII's reign. While the Near Eastern Churches enjoyed papal attention (the Pope sent several proclamations and directives), the pagan missions, according to Roman archives, were neglected. On 3 December 1880 the Pope issued the encyclical *Sancta Dei Civitas,* but it is incorrect to call it a missionary encyclical. In 1884, he praised the activities of the missionaries and called them *Evangelii praecones.*

This view of the pagan mission changed after the reform of the Curia by Pius X on 29 June 1908; as a result of it, the activities of the Congregation for the Propagation of the Faith were principally limited to non-Christian areas. The reform deprived the Congregation of its authority over seven archbishoprics and forty-seven bishoprics in Europe (England, Scotland, Ireland, Holland, and Luxemburg) and thirty archdioceses with 147 auxiliary bishoprics in Canada and the United States. As far as the Near Eastern Churches were concerned, the system of 1862 remained in force. They continued to be subject to the prefect of the Congregation for the Propagation of the Faith, with its own special secretary. Finally, in 1917, a Congregation for the Eastern Churches was established, thus relieving the Congregation for the Propagation of the Faith of its last responsibility. On the basis of the reform of 1908, missionaries as missionaries were subject to the Congregation for the Propagation of the Faith. However, as members of religious orders they were responsible to the Congregation for Religious. Moreover, a number of areas for which the Congregation for the Propagation of the Faith had been responsible (e.g., matters of faith, of marriage, of rites and liturgy) were now transferred to other administrative branches.

During the pontificates of Leo XIII and Pius X, home missionary activities were increased and strengthened. This was necessary for two reasons: because of the expansion of missionary tasks (especially after the colonization of Africa) and because of the new Italy depriving the Congregation for the Propagation of the Faith of some of its responsibilities. Therefore, the existing missionary societies were strongly recommended and supported by popes and bishops alike. However, since several of these organizations (e.g., the *Leopoldinen-Stiftung* in Vienna and the *Ludwigs-Missionsverein* in Munich, etc.) served almost exclusively the American and Near Eastern missions, new societies arose.

In conjunction with the increase of material support, the number of missionary personnel increased. The first third of the nineteenth century was marked by the founding of French missionary societies, while the second third was marked by the establishment of new Italian associations, which were later joined by the missionaries of Parma (Saveriani, 1895) and the *Consolata* missionaries of Turin (1901). The German missionary groups were (for the most part) formed in the last third of the century. Because of the *Kulturkampf,* the first group settled in nearby Holland, where Arnold Janssen founded the Society of the Divine Word (Steyl, 1875). From here, he tried to move into Germany. In 1889, he began work, with permission of the government, in Mödling near Vienna and in 1892 in Neisse (Silesia). The actions of the missionaries in Steyl signaled the creation of German provinces by French and Italian societies.

Conceived differently was the missionary work started in 1882 by the Austrian Trappist Franz Planner and his disciples in Mariannhill (South Africa). From this community of Trappists, elevated to abbey in 1885, there grew over the years the nonmonastic missionary society of Mariannhill. In 1883/84, the Swiss Benedictine monk from Beuron, Andreas Amrhein, laid the cornerstone for similar monastic missionary communities, first in Reichenbach and later in Saint Ottilien. His intention was to develop the missionary component prior to the monastic.

Home missionary activities were also closely involved with the ecclesiastical efforts to improve the relations between Church and state that were disrupted after 1870, especially in Germany during the *Kulturkampf* and in France during the Republic. The establishment and development of German missionary societies or religious provinces was related to this problem. They owed their establishment to the legislation terminating the *Kulturkampf* and the improved relations between Bismarck and Leo XIII. Two outstanding diplomatic accomplishments of Leo XIII deserve mentioning: his role as arbitrator in the controversy between Spain and Germany over the ownership of the Caroline Islands, a role which he had been offered by Bismarck and in which he decided in favor of Germany; and his open and courageous support of Lavigerie in his campaign against slavery. The diplomatic successes and the receptive personality of Leo XIII permitted him to turn to such non-Christian sovereigns as the Emperor of Japan and Dowager Empress Tz'u-hsi of China and thank them, in writing, for their goodwill toward the foreign missions. While Leo XIII put his diplomatic skills into the service of propagating the faith, Pius X's chief concern in regard to the missions was of a pastoral nature. He recognized the potential of crossfertilization between home country and missions.

The propagation of the faith abroad was totally dependent on the colonial power which directly or indirectly dominated the country or the area. All colonies conquered by Russia, even those solely populated by non-Christians, were off-limits to Catholic missions, as were the countries of the Ottoman Empire and its successor states. These countries, especially England and France, pursued a rather ambiguous missionary policy. Among the non-Islamic populations they tolerated missionary activities, after the turn of the century openly supporting and furthering them. However, among the Islamic populations they forbade and hindered any kind of missionary work.

Everywhere, the missionaries were incorporated into or subjugated to the imperialist system. Real freedom of propagation of the faith barely existed in any of these countries. These facts, which had not been discovered until recently, do not mean that the missionaries voluntarily supported the political and economic systems. According to contemporary reports, most missionaries were scarcely aware of the political impact of their work. And even those who seemed to later generations to have been particularly active in the political arena simply wanted to demonstrate their patriotism, which was constantly questioned by the colonial administration.

Asia

The amalgamation of political power and apostolic activities produced numerous difficulties. The patronate in Asia offers ample evidence for this. After the unpleasant circumstances around the middle of the century and the controversies of the Congregation for the Propagation of the Faith with Portugal, Leo XIII finally succeeded in 1886 in settling the unfortunate conflict through a new concordat, at least in principle. Of course, this was a compromise, because the King managed to obtain the confirmation of the patronate through the archdiocese of Goa, which had been elevated to patriarchate, and through its auxiliary bishoprics (Damao, Cochin, Meliapur). Consequently, the double jurisdiction continued, and Lisbon succeeded in assuring its right to nominate candidates for certain episcopal sees. On the other hand, the government relinquished its right to claim the non-Portuguese areas in India and it recognized the authority of the Apostolic See. Taking advantage of this freedom, the Pope immediately established a proper hierarchy with seven church provinces (Goa, Agra, Bombay, Verapoly, Calcutta, Madras, Pondicherry), and in Ceylon he set up the archbishopric of Colombo. This marked the beginning of visible growth, solidification and strengthening of the Indian Church, which was furthered by the founding of the Papal Seminary of Kandy (Sri Lanka) by the Belgian Jesuits and the instructions of the Congregation for the Propagation of the Faith to the episcopate regarding methods of proselytizing. The Uniate Mar-Thomas Church also grew, obtaining its own apostolic vicariates (Trichur and Kottayam) in 1887. Extraordinarily successful was the mission of Chota Nagpur in the north, especially among the natives, the Kols. The conversion movement, accelerating after 1880, was consolidated by the Flemish Jesuit K. Lievens through a multiplicity of activities (training of catechists, writings in the language of the area, and social work). In the seventies, the Jesuits reported a considerable increase of members in the diocese of Madura, where they maintained the most important school in all of southern India: Saint Joseph College, located since 1881 in Trichinopoly. They succeeded in converting many Brahmans, thus penetrating for the first time the world of Hinduism. The Mill Hill Missionaries, the missionaries of Milan, in India since 1863, started a sizable conversion movement at the end of the century among the Telugus in the vicariate of Hyderabad. After Leo XIII's reorganization of the Indian mission, the development progressed rather slowly under the following pontificate.

Indochina, under British dominion, included Burma, with three vicariates established between 1866 and 1870 by missionaries from Paris and Milan. Here, the Karens were converted, while the true Burmese, mainly Buddhists, were less susceptible to Christianity. Moreover, the Malay peninsula fell under the control of the British. It was restored to bishopric in 1888. As in Burma, Christians were not recruited from the ranks of the indigenous population, but from among the Indian and Chinese immigrants, who joined in considerable numbers. This is also true for Siam, which, after a trade agreement with France in 1867, experienced a period of benevolent acceptance of the missions, especially under the long government of King Chulalongkorn, who visited the Pope in 1897 and, upon his return, recommended that the Christian messengers be welcomed as friends. Yet even here conversions took place mainly among the Chinese, while the Thais could not be converted. Even though the French colonial administration frequently put obstacles in the way of the missions, the Church of Laos, after 1899 apostolic vicariate, was able to grow. The Christians of Annam particularly suffered from the consequences of colonial politics. Following the peace treaty between King Tu-Duc and France (1862), there was a decade of relative peace, followed by renewed acts of bloody suppression (which can partly be blamed on some missionaries), one in 1872 and another one in 1886, when the final occupation of the country took place. In the course of these persecutions, 20 missionaries, 30 native priests, and 50,000 Christians lost their lives. In spite of this tragic history in the nineteenth century and the many intrigues by the colonial governments, the number of baptized Christians grew after World War I to about one million and the ecclesiastical hierarchy increased to twelve apostolic vicariates headed by the Parisian Dominicans and to two vicariates headed by the Spanish Dominicans.

Similarly fatal events and, for the future of Christianity, even tragic consequences resulted from the Christianization that followed the colonization of China.

The treaties imposed upon the Far East by the Western powers marked the beginning of a new era in missionary history. The various agreements paved the way for the missions throughout the entire country and, aside from acceptance and protection, it provided the Church with financial and social advantages. Yet such missionary policies proved to be harmful as well. The missionaries made insufficient efforts to fashion the communities with the Chinese spirit and sensitivities in mind, and many a conversion was inspired by material motives (the so-called rice Christians). In addition, the disciples of a white religion were suspect to the population (e.g., in regard to orphanages) and deeply hated by certain segments, especially the Mandarins and scholars, whose national pride was hurt. The resentments exploded during the Boxer uprising in 1900, an incident which cost the lives of thousands of Catholics and numerous priests. In spite of these setbacks and the revolution of 1911, which put an end to the Manchu dynasty but hardly affected the religious communities, the Catholic Church had 1.4 million members around 1912 (the number had doubled since the turn of the century), and the native clergy included 724 clergymen.

Almost twice as many foreign (especially French, Italian, and German) missionaries devoted themselves at the same time to missionary work all over China.

In order to further the expansion of the Chinese mission, which claimed Leo XIII's particular attention and love, the Pope divided it into five regions (1879), keeping in mind the future local synods that had been negotiated at the First Vatican Council. He also increased the dioceses by fifteen and, in 1883, issued more detailed instructions to the missionaries in China. It was indeed necessary to awaken the missionary spirit because in many cases the interest was not in gaining new territory, but consolidation within the established area. Therefore, the regional synods, appointed after the eighties, strongly emphasized the conversion of the pagans. The meetings were also important for the closer collaboration of the often colorful missionary personnel and for a more uniform organization of missionary procedures. The synods all attempted to eliminate other shortcomings, such as the missionaries' insufficient training and acclimatization to the land and its people, the neglect of the upper classes and intelligentsia in the press and the schools, and the rather arbitrary and not sufficiently planned way in which the Chinese Church was provided with a clergy and episcopate. The elimination of these inadequacies was demanded by a group of missionaries who were attracted by the positive characteristics of the Chinese and, supporting the so-called Tientsin method, advocated turning away from Europeanism. The establishment of a nunciature was to serve the same purpose, but the plan proposed by the Chinese failed because France opposed it. The often abused protectorate was opposed by Vincent Lebbe (1877–1940), who was extremely active, but also assailed by many. He was a disciple of the spirit of the Gentry group and can be considered the pioneer of a new direction of missionary work in China: thorough indigenization.

At the end of the century, the Western powers and Japan concluded treaties with Korea as well; they proved to be beneficial to the Church. Following the persecutions (1803–13, 1827, 1838–46, 1866–69) and the last edict (1881), Christianity was able to gain ground on the basis of the agreements of the eighties, in spite of some reverses in Taikyu in 1887. Religious freedom was not impeded after 1895 by the establishment of the Japanese protectorate, although the authorities attempted to propagate the official Shinto cult. Monsignor Félix-Clair Ridel, after 1869 vicar apostolic of Korea, was arrested and deported to China. Like his successors Blanc and Mutel, he was a member of the Missionaries of Paris who, disregarding the hostile atmosphere on the peninsula, had sent more and more personnel there. Mutel held the office of vicar apostolic of Korea from 1890 until 1911. After the division into two dioceses, Seoul and Taikyu (1911), he administered the former. The growth of the new Church was furthered by the founding of vocational and trade schools by the Benedictines of Saint Ottilien, located in Seoul after they established their monastery there in 1909.

Due to the influence and pressures from outside (treaties with the Européan powers) and the ensuing accessibility of the country to modern Western civilization, the Church in Japan seemed to face a promising future. By 1889 it enjoyed full religious freedom. The persecution decrees had been abolished in 1872/73. The improvement of the situation was aided by the friendly relations between both Leo XIII and Pius X and the royal court. Slowly conversions increased: in 1882, there were 28,000 Catholics, by 1890 the number had grown to 54,000. The Japanese bishops met that same year for their first synod in Nagasaki and, in 1891, Rome proceeded with the establishment of a hierarchy, with Tokyo becoming an archbishopric and Nagasaki, Osaka, and Hakodate auxiliary bishoprics. In 1896 the Trappists, the male as well as the female branch, began their prolific activities in Tobetsu near Hakodate. However, most of the work still rested on the shoulders of the Paris Missionaries. They were soon joined by other missionary societies: the (German) Jesuits founded the Sophia University in the capital (1913).

These groups all devoted themselves to the care of the Christians, the training of the Japanese clergy and the catechists, the education of the converts, the press, and social work. Around the turn of the century, however, the disillusioned and disappointed missionaries had to admit that their high hopes could not be fulfilled because the number of baptized had decreased and the number of converts were very few. The reasons for this are numerous. Money and personnel were lacking. However, the underlying causes are more complex. Among them were the religious scepticism of the Japanese, their passionate desire for purely material, economic progress, their resentment of European teachers, and the fact that they considered Christianity an intrusion. Moreover, there was the identification of the Japanese national character with Shintoism. After the decline of Buddhism, Shintoism became the state religion, the embodiment of the national ideal and the supporting pillar of the new empire. It was an obstacle to the development of the Church, especially since it was extensively propagated throughout the educational system, the military, and all schools. Finally, the missionary process itself had its flaws, which were recognized by a few of the missionaries: The Japanese world had not been penetrated sufficiently, the religions of the country had not been studied, and indirect work, such as literary endeavors, had been neglected. A more thorough study of language and culture, especially of the religious concepts of the Japanese, was needed.

The only Asian country with a Catholic majority, the Philippines, went through the most critical phase of its ecclesiastical history around the turn of the century. If one is interested in the cause of the events which almost brought the Church to the brink of its existence there, one will have to investigate, on the one hand, the characteristics of the political-ecclesiastical constellation within the Spanish colonial empire and, on the other hand, the American intervention, with its many detrimental consequences. Without diminishing the astonishing accomplishments of the Iberian mother country and especially the missionaries, one is compelled to notice that the system, especially on the ecclesiastical level, had considerable shortcomings: it did not aim at independence, but rather tried to preserve dependence on Spain by employing paternalistic methods. Supported by the Freemasons, nationalistic tendencies opposing the foreign dominion grew stronger in the course of the nineteenth century. The native clergy took the same direction because, having been confined to inferior positions, it felt disadvantaged. This placed the clergy into growing opposition to the Spanish religious orders whose members clung to their old (economically lucrative) positions and who seemed to guarantee loyalty toward the political power. What was originally devised as a colonial reform, slowly took a course toward separation and, in the struggle with the religious, developed even anticlerical features. Pressured by the rebels, Spain deported the monks and expropriated their estates (1897). However, it was too late. Asked for help by the nationalists, America declared war in 1897. But instead of being given into the hands of the patriots, the country became the property of the United States.

The presence of the new power produced drastic changes for the Church: the separation of Church and state (for which the faithful were not prepared), lay legislation which prohibited religious instruction in schools and thus caused religious deprivation, stress on ideological neutrality of the state university (founded in 1911), which alienated the educated from the Church, the infiltration of Protestantism and numerous sects, and, last but not least, the antagonistic attitude of groups indoctrinated by America who considered Christianity a thorn in their side. Finally, in 1912, in the course of the nationalistic turmoils and under the leadership of Gregorio Aglipay, a secular priest from the Philippines (1860–1940), some of the Catholics separated from Rome and formed the *Iglesia Católica Filipina Independiente.* After initial spectacular successes (50 of the 825 Philippine priests and about 1 million of the 8 million Catholics converted to Aglipayism), the membership slowly declined, especially after 1907 when the Church began to recover from the setback. Aware of the critical situation, Leo XIII had begun in 1902 to reorganize Church life, establishing an apostolic delegature and four new dioceses. On the basis of a treaty with Rome, the missionaries, even the Spanish ones, could return. The old orders, continuing their activities, were aided by more recent missionary societies, following the urgent appeal of the Pope to alleviate the dire need for priests. At the Thomas University in Manila (licensed in 1916), the Dominicans resumed their work. Pius X himself made efforts to convene a plenary council, which met in 1907 in the capital, headed by the delegate Ambros Agius. The real missionary work was done by the Jesuits (on Mindanao), the Scheut Fathers among the Igorots (northern Luzon), the Negritos, and the immigrant Chinese, while the Divine Word Missionaries, with equal success, took care of the Abras.

Under the rather intolerant colonial power of the Dutch, the Catholic Church was able to develop in Dutch East India after it resettled there in the first half of the century. In the twentieth century, the Jesuits were the only ones, supported by a few secular priests (after 1859), to work in the apostolic vicariate of Batavia, which included the entire huge area of the archipelago. After the formation of the first ecclesiastical districts and the arrival of new societies, the Catholics were able to compete with the Protestants, especially on the Lesser Sunda Islands, where exceedingly active communities developed. Progress was also due to the work of the various female congregations. Planting the seeds for the later growth of the Indonesian Church, these pioneers included a respectable number of missionaries who excelled in the area of language.

The missions in the Pacific also had to cope with the explosive atmosphere of colonial expansion. The fact that all islands in the Pacific were divided among the Western powers had its impact on the course of Christianization. Due to the presence of the greatest colonial power, Great Britain, Protestantism had a considerable head start, which motivated the Catholics, particularly the French, under the pontificates of Leo XIII and Pius X, to increase their activities. Continuing into most recent times, the denominational competition was occasionally intensified by national rivalries, the Protestant missionaries relying on England and the Catholic ones on France. Because of this, they were accused of political activities, but today scholars assess the situation with more restraint. Though taking advantage of the assistance of the protective and colonial powers, the missionaries were mainly interested in assuring the success of their work: the Christianization of the people in question.

All in all, we can say that each one of the three societies primarily involved in missionary work settled in a different geographic area. The Picpus Fathers settled in the eastern Pacific. Even though their vicariates on the Hawaiian Islands (where Damian Deveuster died in 1889 in the service of the lepers on Molokai) and on the Gambier, Society, Marquesas, Paumotu, and Tubuaï Islands were all stagnating, they reached out toward the Windward Islands (1888) and later the Cook Islands (1894). In the central Pacific, the Marists (1887) expanded their area of work to the New Hebrides. When establishing the vicariate apostolic (New Hebrides, 1904), they had only twelve hundred faithful. However, at their headquarters on the Wallis and Futuna Islands, the life of the Church flourished. It also developed satisfactorily on the Fiji Islands under Julien Vital (after 1887 vicar apostolic) and on the Tonga Islands. They did not return to the Solomon Islands, which they had to abandon after forty years of difficult trials, until 1897 when the apostolic prefecture of the Southern Solomon Islands was established (in 1912 a vicariate apostolic). During the revolt of 1878 on New Caledonia, they shared the fate of the colonial power and, fleeing under the protection of the French, paid their share with a number of lives. Pierre-Marie Bataillon (1810–77), bishop of the Marists, deserves credit for having dared to improve the education of the native clergy. Failures and setbacks did not discourage him. He made his last and most decisive move when founding the seminary in Lane (Wallis Islands), where his successor was privileged to ordain the first four Polynesian priests in 1886. In the western Pacific, we find mostly the Sacred Heart Missionaries. From 1881 on, they took care of the huge Melanesian Micronesian dual vicariate. On the Bismarck Archipelago, New Britain, New Ireland and the Admiralty Islands, they witnessed a remarkable increase in their communities around the turn of the century, and they were also successful on the Gilbert Islands under Monsignor Joseph Leray (after 1882 vicar apostolic of those islands). However, the apostolate on the Marshall Islands did not prosper.

On Guam (Mariana Islands), German Capuchin friars replaced the Augustinian Recollects who had been driven out by the Americans in 1898. From Australia, the Sacred Heart Missionaries traveled to New Guinea, settling first on Thursday Island (1884) and later on Christmas Island (1885). From here, Fr. L.-A. Navarre, later vicar apostolic, and Fr. St. E. Verjus (1860–90), who was well known and later elected chief, Christianized the British area. In the Dutch section, we find the Sacred Heart Missionaries after 1903. In German New Guinea, the Society of the Divine Word laid a solid foundation for Catholic Christianity at the end of the last century. The Marists continued their work among the Maoris in the south of New Zealand (Wellington), the Mill Hill Missionaries in the north (Auckland). There were only three somewhat significant missionary attempts among the aborigines of Australia: the efforts of the Jesuits after the eighties in the north, of the Benedictines of New Norcia, who received the new vicariate of Kimberley in 1887 and founded the daughter mission of Drysdale River, in 1910 and, finally, the attempts of the Trappists in Broome, which was given to the German Pallottines in 1900.

An important first step in all these missionary enterprises was the establishment of the apostolic delegature for Australia, New Zealand, and Oceania. At the outbreak of World War I, the number of Catholics in the nineteen mission districts of the South Seas was one hundred ninety thousand, a truly unique accomplishment in the history of missions, demonstrating the endless optimism of the pioneers of the faith in an area that presented more difficulties than anyone could imagine.

Africa

During the same period, the African mission experienced a similarly stormy development. Although it had been in the background in the middle of the nineteenth century, it now became a focal point of interest. On the one hand, it profited from Europe's growing interest in the dark continent. On the other hand, it took advantage of the possibilities which opened up when the colonial powers occupied large areas of land. Not infrequently, conflicts arose with the administration because the missionaries felt obliged to represent the side of the Africans. The Gospel was not always preached with the same enthusiasm and success. In White Africa (north of the Sahara) it gained hardly any ground, but, along the equator, Catholicism encountered the strongest response. Toward the south, the response gradually decreased.

In North Africa Christianity encountered the strongest resistance. From here the Islamic faith was to start its victorious course into the center of the continent. It was an element which the Christian churches had to face in many areas. Out of concern for the Muslim population, the authorities did not permit missionary activities in many areas or they imposed restrictions (e.g., in British Sudan, today's Ghana, and in Cameroon). For a long time, there was no real Islamic mission, until Cardinal Lavigerie became archbishop of Algeria in 1867 and introduced drastic reforms. In his first pastoral letter, he demanded the right to deal with the Arabs and he was, indeed, given greater freedom. In 1800, he was allowed to educate and baptize orphans whom he had collected in villages (Saint Cyprian,

1873, and Saint Monica, 1875). He also founded the first missions among the purely Muslim Berbers. His disciples, the White Fathers, were supported by the Jesuits, for whom their general, Fr. Roothaan, a genius with vision, had devised a bold program. Subsequently, the White Fathers moved toward the southeast, toward Shanija (three stations). The White Sisters opened a hospital in Biskra. By 1906, the number of Muslim converts had increased to eight hundred and the catechumens to two hundred within thirteen missions. This seems to be a small number, but in view of its principal significance, it represents an important achievement.

Lavigerie formulated his methodical principles regarding missions in his instructions to the missionaries (1878–79). Essentially, they are still valid, and they also inspired other societies in their behavior toward the Muslims. He initially forbade preaching a specifically Christian message, as well as the baptism of individual candidates. He recommended instead the indirect apostolate (charity, schools, orphanages, visits with the natives), hoping to prepare the ground gradually. The same course was taken by the "Apostle of the Sahara," Charles de Foucauld (1858–1916). The primate of Africa demanded of his sons that they know the language, adapt to the life-style of the people who were to be converted, and practice friendship and active charity. Foucauld tried to put these principles into practice in Beni-Abbés and later in Tamanrasset. The White Fathers moved their post into the Sahara desert, where they settled in Gardaia, El Goléa, and Uargla, thus adding to the vicariate of Sahara (1891) the prefecture of Gardaia (1901), which was served by the hermit Foucauld.

In West Africa, the activities of Catholic missionaries began in the black independent state of Liberia. The efforts made on behalf of this country show what kind of obstacles were in the way of missionary work: unhealthy conditions, the Islamic faith penetrating from the north, the strong presence of Protestantism. In many places, the colonial administration added to the difficulties. After their missionary attempts in the first half of the century failed, American secular priests and the Holy Ghost Fathers returned in 1884. But the tropical climate decimated their numbers and they were replaced in 1903 by the Montfort Fathers. When they gave up, the prefecture was given to the Society of African Missions, headed by the courageous Étienne Kyne. The two societies, the Spiritans and the Lyon group, took care of a number of areas in West Africa around the turn of the century. Some of them seemed promising (southern Nigeria, the Ivory and the Gold Coast, Lower Volta, Dahomey, the Bight of Benin). More missionaries arrived, such as the Pallottines in Cameroon in 1890. It was important for them that they began in 1901 to take care of the Yaundes. They contributed a great deal to the acquisition of large communities through farming and the development of small businesses, as well as an extensive school system where German was spoken almost exclusively. The female Pallottines took care of the women. In the north, in Adamaua, the priests of the Sacred Heart from Sittard took on responsibility, while the Divine Word Missionaries, mostly of German descent, moved into Togo in 1892, where they taught, developed agriculture, trained craftsmen, and worked a printing press (in Lomé).

After 1839, when France began to sign treaties with kings and chiefs in the territory around the equator, gradually expanding the French Congo, the first missionaries started to arrive. The Spiritans took care of the vicariate of Loango on the coast and the vicariate of Ubangi, which was responsible for the northeastern, the largest part of the colony (1890). This district was first headed energetically by Bishop P.-P. Augouard (1852–1921). In spite of the lowliness of the population, he never doubted their Christianization. Suffering great privation, he took daring trips throughout the huge territory, founding missions in strategic places. Though he was always concerned with the well-being of the missions, he also rendered outstanding political service to his country, but France did not reward him.

The area around the equator and central Africa belonged to those regions of black Africa that had been a focal point for preaching the Gospel since the fifteenth century. Libermann, Monsignor Bessieux, Mère Javouhey, and Monsignor de Marion-Brésillac planned to explore the Sudan, the enormous territory between the Atlantic ocean, the Sahara, Abyssinia, and the Congo. Even though they were unable to penetrate the interior of the continent, their attempts resulted in solid foundations on the coasts of Guinea and Senegal. Others planned to approach the center of Africa from the north along the Nile River, instead of from the west. In 1847, a year after the vicariate apostolic of Central Africa was established, the Congregation for the Propagation of the Faith itself sent out pioneers: Monsignor Annetto Casolani, Maximilian Ryllo, S.J., Emmanuele Pedemonte, S.J., and two trainees of the Congregation, Ignaz Knoblecher and Angelo Vinco. They made it all the way to Khartoum, where they failed in the attempt to found a mission. There was another point from which some attempted to reach the desired goal. After a 999–day trip, Stanley had explored the course of the Congo River and discovered its mouth near Boma (1877). Africa's secret was found. Now, the missionaries were able to penetrate the Congo area from the west.

In this enterprise King Leopold II (1865–1909) played a unique role. In 1876 he invited the Geographic Conference to Brussels. He was primarily interested in maintaining control of the initiative to explore the interior of Africa, pursuing the idea of Belgium's colonial expansion. During the debates about the establishment of international strongholds, most participants held the opinion that missionaries should help the explorers and traders to civilize the country. Leopold made sure that the final decisions were not in the hands of the missions because he had his own plans in this regard. Since the Belgian Catholics were sceptical, he informed the Holy See. Pius IX and his successor welcomed the royal plan. Trying to pursue his policy, the monarch established the *Association Internationale Africaine.* In 1885, on the basis of the Berlin Conference, the independent state of the Congo was created. At first it was the private property of Leopold; after 1908 it became part of the Belgian kingdom. Aside from abolishing the slave trade and elevating the morals of the natives, the King was clearly interested in their Christianization. For that purpose, he pursued the establishment of the vicariate apostolic of the Belgian Congo (1888), which was assigned to the Scheut Fathers because the King gave preference to his countrymen.

The Congregation of the Immaculate Heart of Mary began its work and, subsidized by the government, gathered primarily slaves and children in closed settlements. This system was used in the Kasaï mission (1904, apostolic prefecture), one of the most beautiful settlements of the Scheut Fathers. A similar method (the so-called *Fermes-chapelles,* including economic and cultural institutions) was employed by the Jesuits, settled in Kwango after 1893. Thanks to the efforts of the Scheut Missionaries and the King it was possible to attract new missionary personnel. Here they were joined by many missionaries from other orders and societies than anywhere else in Africa in the twentieth century. In spite of the enormous difficulties (slave trade, "Congo tortures," the population's stubborn belief in paganism, tropical diseases), the number of Christians increased (1910: fifty thousand; 1921: three hundred seventy-six thousand). In several areas, missionary activities began rather late, for instance in Ruanda-Urundi (around 1900), but after the twenties they were marvelously successful. These results give an impression of the efforts made by Catholic Belgium on behalf of its colony.

Another advance into the interior of Africa was made from the east, after Livingstone had explored new possibilities and Leopold II's initiatives had aroused the interest of missionary circles. Three societies offered their services to the Congregation for the Propagation of the Faith, proposing to Christianize these promising regions. In 1877, Fr. Augustin Planque (1826–1907), the first general of the Lyon Missionaries, offered to pursue this task. A year earlier, his priests had settled around the mouth of the Nile with the special assignment of reporting the results of the explorations, which were immediately known in Egypt, to the Roman authorities. In 1878 Lavigerie wrote his extensive *Mémoire secret* for the Congregation for the Propagation of the Faith. In it he suggested ways and means for swift Christianization and the elimination of slavery. The (tendentious) article resulted in the assignment of the missions in central Africa to the White Fathers on 24 February 1878, four days after the election of Leo XIII. The third person to promise establishing missions in the area of the great lakes was the vicar apostolic of central Africa in Khartoum, Monsignor Daniel Comboni, who, in contrast to Lavigerie, was in favor of the efforts made in Brussels. These areas belonged to his district.

In 1878, starting from Zanzibar, the first caravan of White Fathers headed toward the interior of Africa. In Tabora, they separated into two groups. One traveled toward Lake Tanganyika. The other group turned toward Lake Victoria. Fr. Simeon Lourdel (1853–90) succeeded in negotiating with King Mtesa of Uganda. After a fine beginning, the mission got caught in the net of politics. Upon pressure by the Muslims (around the middle of the nineteenth century, the Arabs had entered the area via Zanzibar) and because of Mtesa's fear of British aggression, the missionaries had to leave the country in 1882, at least until after Mtesa's death (1884). His son, suspicious that the European missionaries were pioneers of the colonial powers, agreed. In October 1885, the Anglican Bishop Hannington was murdered, and in May of the following year, a large number of Christians became victims of the persecutions, among them even servants at the court of Charles Lwanga. In 1894, when Britain took charge of the protectorate, a period of peace returned. However, particularly during the time of turbulence, the number of baptisms increased, in spite of the strict requirements by the White Fathers. Thus the threat of the Muslims in the period before World War I was eliminated and Christianity was on the way to becoming a Church of the people.

The Congregation for the Propagation of the Faith responded to this upswing by dividing the old district Nyanza into three vicariates, North Nyanza (Uganda), South Nyanza, assigned to the disciples of Lavigerie, and the Upper Nile, which was given to the Mill Hill Missionaries who used similar methods successfully. The Consolata Missionaries in near-by Kenya (since 1902) were hampered by the fact that the coast was totally Muslim. Toward the south, in East Africa (today Tanzania), Germany had colonial interests. Its protectorate received its final borders in 1890 through the Helgoland Treaty. In spite of bad setbacks (during the uprisings of 1889 and 1905), the German Benedictines of Saint Ottilien (after 1888) developed a new mission in Dar es Salaam (1902: vicariate apostolic), which pursued pastoral, educational, and agricultural activities. During the first East African Episcopal Conference in Dar es Salaam, in July 1912, it became clear that the area, with its seven flourishing vicariates, was outgrowing its status as a mission and that seeds of a native Church had sprung up, for which a well-structured catechumenate and the diligent cultivation of religious and liturgical life were characteristic.

In the middle of the nineteenth century, a simply catastrophic situation had resulted from the practice of the patronate in the territories of Portugal in West and East Africa. As good and as necessary as it may have been at one point, this institution was largely to blame for the decline of the missions, running parallel with the collapse in the motherland. The efforts of the Spiritans to take over the abandoned areas found little response until, in 1865, they received permission to work there. One year later they were able to begin. There were five priests in all of Angola. The leadership of the order gradually arrived at the conviction that only missionaries under Portuguese leadership were able to produce fruitful results. Therefore, the Swiss Father J. G. Eigenmann set out to found a settlement or a school of his order in Portugal. In 1869 he was appointed head of the Congo seminary in Santarem, the birthplace of the Portuguese province of the Holy Ghost Fathers. The first priest from the school of Eigenmann, Father José Maria Antunes, went to the mission in Huila (south of Angola) in 1882 to reorganize it. The revolution in the homeland (1910), followed by the separation of Church and state, destroyed a large part of the work abroad. The situation was even worse in the Portuguese part of East Africa, where, after the expulsion of the Jesuits, only a few secular priests were left, mainly Goans, to assure the religious care of the Christians. The Jesuits turned to the heathen missions again in 1881 in the lower portion of the Zambezi River. Due to the relentless climate, they lost thirty-seven members in twenty years. Nevertheless, they managed the founding of several new centers and smaller communities, until they had to leave in 1911. It is not surprising that there were only about five thousand Catholic Africans in this vast country at the beginning of World War I.

Eight of the Jesuits who had been driven out of Mozambique, mostly Austrians and Poles, settled in 1910 in neighboring northern Rhodesia. The Society of Jesus had long endeavored to found a permanent settlement there. Fathers Joseph Moreau and Jules Torrend from the Zambesi mission (in southern Rhodesia) were permitted to settle in Tongaland. Pioneers of the agricultural development of northern Rhodesia, they taught the population modern methods of agriculture and cattle breeding. They were also accomplished in the areas of linguistics and ethnology, especially Torrend, who gained a reputation with his research of the Bantu languages.

In 1879, the Zambezi expedition set out from Cape Town. Headed by the Belgian Jesuit Father Henri Depelchin (1822–1900), an experienced Indian missionary, the group of six priests (among them the German Fathers Anton Terörde [died in 1880] and Karl Fuchs) and five laymen arrived at Victoria Falls in 1880. They established the first station in the land of the Tongas. In spite of the massive reinforcement of fifty-one members which the Society received the following year, they were unable to hold their ground in the northern part of the Zambesi until the beginning of the twentieth century. In the northern region of today's Zambia, the area between Lake Bangwenlu and Lake Nyasa, the White Fathers laid the foundation for their mission among the Bembas (1895). Even though the "wild" tribe of the Bembas had to be trained to settle down, the mission, mainly by way of education and new agricultural methods, reached a remarkable level (1911: six thousand Catholics, fifty-seven catechumens, eighteen thousand pupils). From the beginning, a number of White Fathers qualified as linguists and their studies rendered invaluable services to their successors.

Aside from the Muslim north, the Catholic missionaries did not encounter anywhere the kind of difficulties they had to cope with in the south of the dark continent. Since they appeared rather late (middle of the nineteenth century), the Roman Church had trouble catching up with the headstart of the Protestants who had worked in these areas intensively. This situation was aggravated by the customary intolerance of the Boers, partly by the British residing in the country since 1806, by the racial differences, and by the numerous sects and African splinter groups which had begun before the turn of the century. In the northern part of German South West Africa, the Oblates of Mary Immaculate arrived and began work in 1896 (at the end of the seventies, the Spiritans had failed) in the prefecture of Lower Zimbabwe, founded in 1892. They also succeeded the missionaries of Lyon north of the Orange Free State (1882) and worked in Transvaal. But progress was slow, even though the Jesuits and Dominicans sisters who had been called from Augsburg to Grahamstown to organize a college could report modest success around 1876 among the Xhosas (east of the Cape of Good Hope area). Statistics may illuminate the situation: in 1911, the number of Catholics in the South African Union (with 4.7 million non-Europeans) was thirty-seven thousand; the Protestants had 1.4 million faithful.

The work was difficult, yet there were two areas in which the Catholics excelled: Basutoland deserves first mention (Lesotho). The Oblates, active in this mountainous and remote region since 1862, managed to establish an influential position, partly owing to their friendly relations with the chiefs. The Sisters of the Holy Family, who arrived in 1865, trained a dozen native sisters by 1912. After 1908, the Menzingen Sisters assisted with social work. The other flourishing mission was located in Natal, which had been assigned to the Oblates in 1850 as a vicariate. This was the center of Mariannhill founded in 1882 by German Trappists. Their life-style, based on Benedictine rules, facilitated social and economic activities which were mandatory in view of the local circumstances. They acquired a large complex of land, settled Bantus, and organized an impressive educational system (with a school, seminary, small businesses, printing press, and hospital).

Finally, the island of Madagascar should be mentioned (elevated to vicariate apostolic in 1885). Experiencing difficulties due to pressures from the pro-Protestant governments of the sixties and seventies, the Jesuits were nevertheless able to expand their activities. After they were temporarily deported during the occupation of the country by France and during the turmoils at the end of the century, they received assistance in 1896 from the ranks of the Lazarists, two years later from the Spiritans, and in 1899 from the missionaries of La Salette.

In 1906, the French *Kulturkampf* affected the East African islands and dealt the Church a severe blow. This did not stop its growth, however, but rather caused a constructive process of internal cleansing.

Reviewing the missionary activities under the pontificates of Leo XIII and Pius X, one must describe this period as epoch-making and highly important for Africa as well as the Pacific. Almost everywhere, new communities were established. Quantitatively as well as qualitatively remarkable feats were accomplished in such a short time span. But the missions were now outgrowing the first phase and trying to achieve independence and a character of their own. Even though the missionaries were indebted to the spirit of their time, they remained loyal to their true mission, the preaching of the Gospel.

CHAPTER 83

The Development of New Churches

World War I clearly interrupted the missionary activities. The missionary work that had seemed so very promising before the outbreak suffered severe reverses during the upheaval. After the peace was signed, missionary work experienced a decisive new orientation. Well aware of the multiplicity of relationships and tensions between colonialism and missions, the chief authorities of the Church were intent on de-politicizing missionary work. On the other hand, they focused more and more on the independence of the established communities. The period of the pontificates of Benedict XV and Pius XI entailed a basic rejection of Europeanism and can be called an era of increased adjustment to the peoples who were to be converted. Even though the past still had its effect here and there, the model of the native church was clearly in everyone's mind.

The consequences of the war were first felt in the economic sector and in personal life. The subsidies from the home countries decreased considerably or dried up completely. The countries directly involved in the war were affected, while the neutral countries, at least partially, filled the gaps. In spite of an early hope that the colonies might be spared the devastations of the war, hostilities also broke out in the German protectorates. In those areas where no actual fighting took place, the missionary activities suffered noticeably from the recall of numerous missionary personnel. This was particularly true in the case of French citizens, whose departure left many a region abandoned, and in the case of the Italian missions, though to a less devastating degree. The missions of the Germans were particularly burdened by the events of the war. In many places, the missionaries were expelled, imprisoned, or deported, which affected the settlements badly. The

German missionaries in British India suffered a similar fate. However, they were able to stay in German South West Africa and, to some extent, in the Far East. The spiritual damages of the war had more impact than the material and personnel losses. The belligerent Western nations, representing Christianity, also infected the missions with the idea of nationalism. In their disunion, they presented an annoying picture to the non-Europeans, causing the halo that had surrounded the white races to fade.

In order to heal the wounds inflicted by the war, many missionaries returned to their communities after the peace treaty, particularly from the victorious countries, such as the French. The Catholic Church found it easier to recruit replacements for those areas that the missionaries had been forced to leave. This allowed the Church (in some areas) to catch up more rapidly than the Protestants. On the basis of ARTICLES 438 and 122 of the Versailles Treaty, the German missionaries found their missionary freedom limited. However, in retrospect the destruction of the unity of mission and colonial power was a salutary move, even though it was one-sided. At least this was the beginning of the dissolution of the close ties between national and missionary interests, of the liberation of the missions from the burden of colonialism, and of once again focusing on the supranationality of the Church and its mission.

It is to Benedict XV's credit that he dealt with this question courageously. In a situation of extreme national pathos, he offered clarification, rigorously uncovering the weakness of the missionary activity of the Church (the nationalistic attitude of individual representatives and the colonialist missionary methods). Since he partially overcame Europeanism, also introducing a change in missionary theology, he deserves the name "Missionary Pope" as much as his successor, who, following Benedict's ideas, set out to realize the program outlined in *Maximum illud*. There is no doubt that the apostolic letter of 30 November 1919 was the Magna Carta of the modern missions.

During the time of Leo XIII, who loved openness and space, the universal responsibility of the Church was already clearly visible. Through his concern for the salvation of all mankind, he brought the missions back into the fold of the Church, integrating the doctrine of the mission into that of the Church. At the same time, in contrast to his predecessors, he assessed the situation of the non-Christians more positively. Pius X, on the other hand, almost completely neglected the "others," therefore hardly perceiving their true nature. He seemed to turn exclusively inward and did not include the missions in his reform plan — a fatal limitation of the idea of restoration, which caused Church and mission to be separated again and appear to be divided and unrelated entities. This was changed by Benedict XV, who resolutely opened the Church to the missions and restored them as a basic function of the Church itself. His reintroduction of the plural *ecclesiae* into the ecclesiastical perception of the Popes (the expression had previously been used in an abstract sense) had far-reaching consequences for his concept of the missions. The recognition that the entire Church is composed of individual churches suggests that one not speak of the propagation of the faith in merely general terms but that one plan in concrete terms the formation of new individual Churches. In the final analysis, this view emanated from the fact that the Church was taking its catholicity seriously.

With his new ecclesiological, missiological concept, Benedict offered a basic answer to the postwar conditions. In *Maximum illud* he focused on a series of urgent individual problems. First, he clearly rejected the nationalistic attitude of certain missionaries, emphasizing the ecclesiastical nature of the missions. Those, he said, who "think more of the worldly than of the heavenly fatherland" and confuse the interests of the nation with those of the Gospel bring Christianity under suspicion of being the concern of the foreign state under whose mandate and as whose agents the missionaries act. He did not hesitate to stigmatize such an attitude as *pestis teterrima.* The truly "Catholic" missionary is intent only on representing Christ, not his own nation. The Pope developed a missionary strategy that was rooted in mercy: The missionary will never meet anyone with disrespect, no matter how lowly he may be. Rather, "through all the kindness of Christian mercy" he will try to win him to the Gospel. When he defined missionary activity, Benedict also emphasized its ecclesiastical character. It is not exclusively the Pope (as was the case with his predecessors) who stands in the place of Christ and obeys his missionary order, but the Church as a whole. He therefore impressed on the missionaries (mainly their leaders) not to be satisfied with their achievements, but "to strive for the salvation of all people without exception." In order to accomplish this, the leader will, in the true "Catholic" spirit, involve other missionary institutions, if necessary, regardless of whether they are a member of a foreign order or nation. This was clearly aimed at the narrow-minded esprit de corps of the missionary societies. With his recommendation to discuss and resolve common problems with the neighboring areas, the Pope tried to combat any kind of particularism, replacing it with the spirit of cooperation.

The goal of missionary work, as the Pope envisioned it, is, in addition to the conversion of individuals, the founding of churches. This requires a native clergy that could "one day take charge of its people." Because the future of new churches is dependent upon the existence of thoroughly trained priests, this task, resting on the universality of the Church, demands the special attention of the responsible missionary staff. Benedict considered this the only way to acclimate the Church and the only possibility to do justice to the characteristics of the people or to harvest its treasures for the benefit of the Church. Unfortunately, the life of the Christian communities is neglected by the papal considerations — they are merely the *terminus ad quem* of the missionary efforts and their own significance does not come to the fore. Nevertheless, the Pope attempted not only to turn to the Church at home, but contemplated the problems from the perspective of the missions themselves.

The principles outlined in *Maximum illud* were completed in the instructions to the Congregation for the Propagation of the Faith, entitled *Quo efficacius* (6 January 1920). Referring to the classic passage according to which Christianity should not be alien to any nation, these instructions remind the missionaries to understand their task as a spiritual and religious one. They are asked to practice strict neutrality in political matters and forbidden to propagate their own laws and customs in the foreign country. Benedict tried to instill new energy into apostolic activities. This is demonstrated, on the one hand, by his measures to increase the missionary hierarchy (he established twenty-eight apostolic vicariates and eight prefectures as well as a delegation for Japan, Korea, and Formosa [1919]) and his order to conduct apostolic inspections (e.g., in China and South Africa); and, on the other hand, by his initiatives regarding the missionary relief system at home. In order to make the papal project more effective for the native clergy, he assigned its supervision to the Congregation for the Propagation of the Faith, thus locating it in Rome. The *Unio Cleri pro Missionibus,* founded in 1915 and approved in 1916, was incorporated in 1916 in the Roman headquarters. The Union of Priests and Missionaries quickly expanded into Canada, Germany, and Switzerland. Finally, during this pontificate, several missionary seminaries were established (for the purpose of founding missions manned by secular priests), such as the seminary of Maynooth-Galway (Ireland, 1917), of Almonte (Canada, 1919), of Burgos (Spain, 1919), of Montreal (Canada, 1921), and of Bethlehem Immensee (Switzerland, 1921). Many of these progressive activities under Benedict XV and later under Pius XI came about thanks to the open-mindedness of Cardinal Willem van Rossum, who is rightfully considered the pioneer of the Catholic "world mission." After all, he did away with Europeanism, pushed for adaptation, and worked toward the training and development of the native clergy under the supervision of native bishops.

The missionary programs that Benedict XV initiated during his relatively brief pontificate were continued by Pius XI and put into action. The prefect of the Congregation for the Propagation of the Faith of both papal administrations made sure that a continuity was preserved. By emphasizing certain aspects initiated by his predecessor, Pius XI shifted the focal point to the theme of universality, to the independence of the new churches and to their growing roots in the native soil, thus to indigenization. The preaching of the Gospel all over the world is the most essential task of the papal office, Pius XI declared at the beginning of his pontificate. In cooperation with the Pope, the entire episcopate has an obligation toward the task of mission because it represents the universal Church. The Pope required the same efforts from the priests, telling them at the first international congress of the *Unio Cleri* in Rome (3 June 1922) that the missionary apostolate is not just to be pursued by a special task force but by the entire Church, so that every church would gradually develop into a cell active in missionary work. According to the Pope, the secret of the universality of the Church rests in charity. Love of God and one's fellow man extends it and allows it to grow roots in areas where the population does not yet know Christ. The Church is not primarily self-serving, but exists to serve all. According to his maxim that missions should have priority among Catholic works, he opened during the Sacred Year the mission exhibition of the Vatican, which lived on in the founding of a missionary ethnological museum in the Lateran (1926). Furthermore, in order to awaken the missionary spirit in the entire Christian community, he declared in 1927 the second to the last Sunday in October to be observed as Mission Sunday. In 1922 he moved the Society for the Propagation of the Faith to Rome, incorporated it into the Congregation for the Propagation of the Faith and elevated it to a papal work (with new statutes). In 1929, he also initiated the coordination of the three most important organs (Childhood of Jesus, Propagation of the Faith, and Work of Saint Peter). He probably did this hoping to solicit more funds and to distribute them more fairly, but also in order to dissolve the regional national ties of the large missionary societies.

Another matter to which the Pope devoted his attention was outlined in detail in Pius XI's encyclical *Rerum Ecclesiae* (1926). Its main passages deal with the founding, solidification, and independence of the new churches. Three years earlier, the Congregation for the Propagation of the Faith sent directives to the missionary societies that clearly aimed at the assimilation of the church into the missionary district. The work of the foreigners could be considered concluded as soon as the new foundation had established its own leadership, churches, native clergy, and funds, in short, as soon as it no longer needed the help of others. At that stage its existence would no longer be threatened if the missionaries should be deported or fresh recruits from Europe should be reduced. For the creation of a church, *Rerum Ecclesiae* demanded: an autochthonous clergy that would be compatible with the European clergy; autochthonous orders that would correspond to the expectations and interests of the natives as well as to the regional conditions and circumstances; an autochthonous monastic system because the contemplative monasteries offer irreplaceable contributions to the development of an individual church; autochthonous catechists, and an elite of laymen whose careful training could be of invaluable importance for the future of Church and country. The words of Pius XI's encyclical were carried out in practice. In 1926, at the celebration of the Feast of Christ the King, he himself ordained six Chinese bishops, one year later a Japanese, and in 1933 three more Chinese, a Vietnamese, and an Indian. In spite of all obstacles, this was a decisive breakthrough toward independence. This tendency was also noticeable in the intensive development of the missionary territories: by the end of his pontificate, there were 116 new vicariates and 157 prefectures. The Pope pursued the goal of stabilizing the growing churches by sending out apostolic delegates and by convening local synods which tried to apply the directives from Rome to the respective situation.

In a letter to the ecclesiastical leaders in China (16 June 1926) Pius XI expressed another first principle: the idea of accommodation. In order to fend off the persistent charges that missionaries were pursuing political interests, the Pope once more emphasized in this letter the purely religious character of ecclesiastical activities. He continued stressing that no one could dispute the fact that the Church demonstrated the desire to adapt to the character of a people. The justified aspirations of a nation with a rich culture and tradition, he declared two years later in a message to the same country, should not be ignored. Two other initiatives by Rome point in the direction of indigenization. The "exceedingly Catholic initiative" requesting that the religious activities be adapted to Japanese characteristics and tradition is praised because the risky enterprise of a Christian Japanese art was somewhat crucial for the Church on these islands. On the other hand, the missionary leaders encouraged the artistic creativity of the natives on the occasion of the first exhibition of religious art in the Congo, justifying it as an expression of the catholicity of the Church, which was willing to absorb the spiritual values of a nation into its tradition. This document demonstrates the spirit of accommodation of the Roman headquarters. Finally, in view of the missions in Africa, a letter of 1938 should be mentioned, because it favors the adoption of burial ceremonies (Matanga) in the Belgian Congo and thus advocates the liturgical adaptation which was finally turned into a program by the Second Vatican Council.

To what extent were the ideas propagated by the two Popes and espoused in numerous proclamations applied to everyday missionary life? The ecclesiastical documents show a certain discrepancy between theory and practice. But if we want to be fair, we have to admit that, particularly between the two world wars, the Roman declarations had an effect on history, though maybe to a different degree, depending on the case. First of all, they succeeded in interesting Christians in the world apostolate, for instance the Dutch, who were exceedingly active, and the Catholics in the United States, who developed more and more missionary responsibility, or Spain, which sent many friars to South America. If the Church as a whole had not become more missionary in nature, we would not be able to understand the expansion of the missionary work during this period in which catholicity was realized to a unique extent.

However, in another area the positive influence of the two Popes was more visible: in the energetically pursued education of a native clergy and the assignment of the Church leadership to local bishops. This breakthrough at that time can be considered an epoch-making event in the recent history of the missions, even though a lot may have been lacking in regard to the independence of the new Churches. The principles extolled by Benedict XV and Pius XI (regarding the need, possibility, and usefulness of a native clergy and episcopate) were not new, they were embedded in a three-hundred-year-old Roman tradition. However, particularly regarding the demands pertaining to the office of bishop, these principles seemed shocking to many, sometimes even revolutionary. Opposition did not fail to appear: some used the tactic of procrastination, others, for reasons of racial prejudice, warned of hastiness. Disregarding the opposition, Rome helped the cause to succeed. The statistics are striking proof of this. Two examples may serve the point. First: China, which proceeded quickly after 1920. By 1939 it had more than two thousand autochthonous priests, and in approximately twenty districts natives were responsible for the fate of the Church. A historic milestone was the establishment of the hierarchy (1946): twenty-one Chinese were appointed bishop and seven apostolic prefects. Second: After many disappointments and unsuccessful attempts, Africa had, after World War I, 148 native clergymen. By 1939, their number had grown to 358. The first two black bishops (Madagascar and Uganda) were consecrated in 1939 under Pius XII. While the natives were entering the ranks of the clergy and the episcopate, the large orders, such as the Franciscans, Dominicans, and Jesuits opened their doors to the communities in the Far East. Furthermore, the natives were granted independence through the constitution of provinces and monasteries, or they were allowed to develop their own branches within the monastic system. At any rate, there the Church demonstrated that it was overcoming racial prejudice, which certainly did not free it from the responsibility to develop individual ways of training the clergy, depending on the various peoples, in order to break away from an all too Western education.

Finally, if we consider the efforts made toward a qualitative catholicity, which means the Church's willingness to get involved in the cultural, social, and religious traditions of the mission countries, we have to admit that between 1914 and 1939 this was not the dominant concern. Certainly, a native clergy and episcopate were created with indigenization in mind. But precisely this step had to be made first. Foreigners cannot completely adapt the Church to the characteristics, customs, and traditions of a people. This is essentially the task and the obligation of a matured native elite. The urgent need for acclimatization and decolonization in terms of spirit and religion did not surface to the level of awareness until the era of political colonialism approached its end. Nonetheless, the missionaries laid the foundation for such a change, and in that regard they followed the directives of the Pope, though perhaps not always with the (in retrospect) desirable energy. To vindicate them one could say that the will to adapt to the mentality of the land and the people was in many respects a lot stronger than we can imagine. This is proven by the efforts regarding the languages and the native literature (which cannot be praised enough), the creation of a Christian terminology, the indigenization of the Bible, and research in the area of ethnology and religious studies.

The new theological discipline called missiology participated energetically in the efforts toward the formation of new churches in the period between the wars, primarily through an eloquent defense of the native clergy and episcopate. The creation of missiology was, on the one hand, an expression of the strengthened desire of the Catholics for missions; on the other hand, it had a stimulating and cleansing effect on missionary activities. The Protestants conducted mission studies much earlier. In 1867 Alexander Duff (1806–78), a Scottish missionary who used to work in India, succeeded in establishing a missiological teaching chair in Edinburgh, which only lasted until 1905. The international mission conference in Edinburgh in 1910 made a new start by stressing the importance of this discipline for activating the home base. Above all, the Protestants of the United States followed the appeal and, by 1930, sixty out of sixty-eight schools taught missiology in one form or another. Gustav Warneck (1834–1910) is considered the true founder of the discipline on the Protestant side. He introduced it to its rightful place in theological teaching.

Under Warneck's influence, Joseph Schmidlin, an energetic man from Alsace (1876–1944), seized the Catholic initiative in Münster. After 1910 Schmidlin was lecturer for mission studies and, after 1914, the first Catholic full professor. He attended in a critical and systematic manner to the entire discipline with its various branches (theory of mission, missiology, missionary history, law, etc.). After some resistance, he took charge of the editorial office of the first Catholic missiological periodical, the *Zeitschrift für Missionswissenschaft,* which he published (with the exception of one short period) without interruption until 1937, making it the voice of many a thorough study. The basic works of the new discipline gradually emanated from his work for the journal: *Einführung in die Missionswissenschaft* (1917, 1925), *Katholische Missionslehre im Grundriß* (1919, 1923) — called "an event" in the Catholic world — *Katholische Missionsgeschichte* (1925), and the two-volume *Das gegenwärtige Heidenapostolat im Fernen Osten (1928).* Assisted by the *Internationales Institut für missionswissenschaftliche Forschungen,* founded by Schmidlin in 1911, the *Bibliotheca Missionum* was published. It is an exemplary tool, which now includes about thirty impressive volumes. In regard to recent literature, it should be supplemented by the *Bibliografia Missionaria* (Rome 1935ff.). Because of his opposition to National Socialism, Schmidlin was forced to retire in 1934 and to resign from the *Zeitschrift für Missionswissenschaft* in 1937. He died in 1944 in the Struthof concentration camp near Schirmeck.

The tireless efforts of this innovator bore fruit. His students especially carried missiology across the German borders. Their success was probably aided by recommendations from Rome. Indeed, after Münster, missiological teaching chairs were established in Munich (1919), in Rome (1919 at the Congregation for the

Propagation of the Faith), Nijmegen (1930), Ottawa (1932), Vienna (1933), Comillas (Spain), and Fribourg (1940). At other universities, lectures were given, as at the Institut Catholique of Paris after 1923, in Louvain after 1927, and in Lyon. Real missiological departments were established in 1932 at the Gregoriana and the Propaganda College in Rome. Elsewhere, but not until after 1939, academic institutes were added (Fribourg, Nijmegen, Ottawa). By the outbreak of World War II, thanks to these institutions and the efforts of individual scholars, this new academic discipline already had a sizeable number of missiological journals, series, and compilations, especially regarding sources. In the meantime, practitioners and experts debated acute problems at conventions such as the *Semaines de Missiologie* (Louvain, since 1922).

During the first phase of the development of Catholic mission studies, Germany produced men who made the young discipline respectable. Among others, Anton Freitag, S.V.D. (1882–1968), the first one to get his Ph.D. under Schmidlin, devoted his energy thenceforth to missiology. Johannes Peter Steffes (1883–1955) enriched the discipline by incorporating religious studies. Subsequently, Schmidlin expanded his journal after 1928 to a *Zeitschrift für Missionsund Religionswissenschaft.* Wilhelm Schmidt, S.V.D. (1868–1954) offered new ideas through ethnology and philology when founding *Anthropos.* Through Thomas Ohm, O.S.B. (1892–1962), at first professor of missiology in Salzburg, later in Münster, the scholarly investigation of foreign religions became the focal point. Missiology was relatively weak in France. In Italy, a student of Schmidlin, Giovanni Battista Tragella (1885–1968), mediated German missiology by translating several books and thus instilling new impulses into the missionary system at home. Pioneering studies in the area of Sinology and Chinese missionary history (especially about Matteo Ricci) were made by the Jesuit Pasquale d'Elia (1890–1963), professor at the Aurora University of Shanghai and subsequently at the missiological department of the Gregoriana. Essays valuable in regard to missiology and ethnology are contained in the *Annali Lateranensi* (after 1937), which was edited by Michael Schulien, S.V.D. (1888–1968) for three decades. In Louvain, missiology could only settle on the fringes of academia. Beckmann's interests included all aspects of his discipline, but his exceedingly rich work is also dominated by history. In Spain, missiology flourished unexpectedly after the Civil War, especially missionary history, so that the *Archivo Ibero-Americano* (1914–1936, 22 vols.), which was important for the missionary history of the Franciscans, could be continued after 1941. Aside from the Franciscans, the Catholics in the United States paid little attention to this discipline, in spite of the general upswing of missions in this country. It was regrettable that this branch of theology was also lacking in the mission churches themselves. But this is understandable in the case of a discipline that is still struggling for recognition, even though the missions needed it most.

It is obvious from the names mentioned that the strength of missiology during the period of its consolidation lay in the area of mission history, even though it accomplished a great deal in other areas as well, e.g., in mission studies. By investigating the past as objectively as possible and thus creating a benevolent understanding for the missionary efforts within the other camp, the intensive historical research in regard to missions resulted in a relaxation of the often tense relationship between Catholics and Protestants. This was quite an accomplishment. Aside from theoretical debates which are still carried on today, two problems played an important role. The first was the question of the missionary goal. Against the background of complicated interrelations, the discussion is dominated by two major trends: the theory of the *Plantatio Ecclesiae* and the salvation of the non-Christians. However, the viewpoints gradually merged and one could say that the missionary goal is the implantation of the Church with the conversion of the people in mind. The other frequently discussed problem deals with accommodation. The urgency of this matter resulted from the changes within the missionary field, the rejection of Europeanism. Several things were realized: adaptation is the requirement for the implantation of Christianity into the people. Adaptation emanates by necessity from the essence of the Church itself. It is the realization of its catholicity and occurs when cultures meet. This complex of problems became more complicated after World War II, when the exceedingly difficult situation of the countries in the Third World began challenging the new discipline to provide new answers.

Book Ten

THE CHURCH
IN THE MODERN AGE

Edited by Hubert Jedin and Konrad Repgen
Translated by Anslem Biggs

Section One

The Institutional Unity
of the Universal Church

Chaps. 84, 86: Hubert Jedin; Chap. 85: Konrad Repgen
Chaps. 87–88: Georg May

CHAPTER 84

Popes Benedict XV, Pius XI, and Pius XII—
Biography and Activity within the Church

Benedict XV

Giacomo Paolo Battista Della Chiesa was born at Genoa on 21 November 1854, the son of the Marchese Giuseppe. From 1869 as an extern he studied philosophy in the archiepiscopal seminary and then, at the University of Genoa, the laws, in which he took his doctorate in 1875. On 21 December 1878 he was ordained a priest and until 1882 continued his studies in the Accademia dei Nobili. After he had finished them, he was accepted, on Rampolla's recommendation, into the Congregation for Extraordinary Ecclesiastical Affairs. In 1882 Rampolla took him along as secretary to the Spanish nunciature. In Madrid he was known to the poor as "Curate of the Two Pesetas" because of his generous alms.

When in 1887 Rampolla was appointed cardinal secretary of state, Della Chiesa became his close collaborator, first as *minutante* and from 1901 as *Sostituto* (undersecretary of state). The undersecretary of state survived Rampolla's fall, because the latter's successor, Merry del Val, could not do without the experienced *Sostituto.* Only in 1907 was he named, not nuncio in Madrid, as he had wanted, but archbishop of Bologna. His episcopal ordination by Pius X in the Sistine Chapel on 21 December 1907 called forth the expression that, while he had to yield to the new course in the Secretariat of State, he still possessed the personal good will of the Pope.

Giacomo Della Chiesa was small of stature, slight, and somewhat misshapen, but of an active mind, clear thinking and clever, a finished diplomat, filled with zeal for souls. He took his removal from the Vatican well, visited the 390 parishes of his diocese, held conferences of deans, and twice, in 1910 and 1913, convoked his auxiliary bishops in council. Not until seven years after his appointment as archbishop of Bologna did he receive the red hat, on 25 May 1914.

In the conclave (31 August to 3 September 1914) the norms decreed by Pius X were strictly observed. The tenth ballot brought the decision: thirty-eight votes out of fifty-seven for Della Chiesa. The adherents of Rampolla had carried the day.

None of the papal garments on hand was small enough for the newly elected Pope. In memory of his great predecessor Lambertini, who had likewise come from Bologna, he called himself Benedict XV. Familiar with persons and the spirit of the Vatican because of his long activity in the Secretariat of State, from the first moment he moved with assurance and awareness of his goal. He transferred his coronation on 6 September to the Sistine Chapel, named as his secretary of state the former nuncio at Paris, Ferrata, and, after the latter's death on 10 October, Gasparri. The Pope's first pastoral word on 8 September and his first encyclical on 1 November were calls for peace.

In the next four years the world war put narrow limits on the Pope's activity within the Church. Not until after the armistice did there come the doctrinal letter on Saint Jerome (15 September 1920) and the naming of Saint Ephrem the Syrian as a Doctor of the Church (5 October 1920); he honored Dante on the six-hundredth anniversary of his death and the founder of the Order of Preachers, Dominic, who is buried at Bologna, on his seven-hundredth. The canonizations of Margaret Mary Alacoque and Joan of Arc were regarded by the French as a triumph of victorious Catholic France.

In accord with the program of Leo XIII, he founded Catholic universities at Lublin and Milan. The ecclesiastical event of the pontificate that had the widest influence was the new codification of the canon law, planned since the close of the sixteenth century but again and again postponed. The Uniate Eastern Churches were removed from the competence of the Congregation for the Propagation of the Faith in 1917 and a special Congregation for Seminaries was founded in 1915. The greatest merit of the skillful, diplomatically experienced Pope was that he had piloted the ship of the Church through the reefs of the First World War and was able to maintain the neutrality of the Holy See. He died on 22 January 1922.

Pius XI

Achille Ratti came from the industrial middle class of Lombardy. His father was employed as a factory manager in the silk industry. Born on 31 May 1857, he was his parents' fifth child. He was ordained a priest in the Lateran on 20 December 1879.

Having returned to Milan in 1882, he worked for five years as professor of homiletics and of dogma at the seminary until in 1888 he was admitted to the College of Doctors of the Ambrosian Library. In 1907 he succeeded Ceriani as prefect. The fruit of his scholarly works was the *Acta ecclesiae Mediolanensis,* with Charles Borromeo as the center, and the *Missale Ambrosianum.* As an Oblate of San Sepolcro he was active in the care of souls, and he was on friendly terms with Catholic intellectuals, such as Contardo Ferrini.

He became vice-prefect, then in 1914 prefect of the Vatican Library. But as early as the beginning of 1918 he was removed from this activity and named apostolic visitor in Poland, which was at that time still occupied by German and Austrian troops. By way of Munich, Vienna, and Berlin, where he called on Imperial Chancellor Hertling, he reached Warsaw on 30 May 1918. Politically much was in a state of flux: the visitor assured the bishops whom he called on and the Polish people of the Pope's good will. After the Republic of Poland had been established, he became nuncio and titular archbishop of Lepanto; on 19 July 1919 he presented his credentials to President Pilsudski.

Nuncio Ratti succeeded in restoring five bishoprics that had been suppressed under Russian rule, in seeing to the appointment of new bishops, and in bringing about the first episcopal conferences. When in August 1919 the Bolshevik armies stood before Warsaw, the nuncio remained at his post. He was able at least to mitigate the oppression of the Ukrainian Uniates but not, however, to go into the Soviet Union and Finland. Appointed apostolic visitor of the area of Upper Silesia that was subject to a plebiscite, he went to Oppeln in April 1920 and in July also into the part of East Prussia that was subject to a plebiscite. His conduct in the struggle over the plebiscite satisfied neither side. When on 29 November 1920 Prince-Bishop Bertram of Breslau (Wroclaw), with the Pope's consent, forbade political propaganda to the Upper Silesian clergy of both nations, under threat of suspension, the Poles obtained the recall of the nuncio.

There followed a sudden rise. Appointed archbishop of Milan and cardinal on 13 June 1921, he entered his diocese on 5 September 1921 after a month of quiet recollection at Monte Cassino and immediately displayed an almost feverish-seeming activity: when visiting the monasteries and ecclesiastical institutes he sometimes preached from five to ten times a day. On 8 December he opened the Catholic University of the Sacred Heart. He held up as models of his episcopal work the two great bishops of Milan, Ambrose and Charles Borromeo, with whom he had occupied himself as a scholar. But only five months of episcopal activity were granted to Ratti in his home diocese. The death of Benedict XV called him to Rome for the conclave of 2 to 6 February 1922. Fifty-three cardinals took part in it, including thirty-one Italians. Neither of the parties could achieve the two-thirds majority. This reason procured for the compromise candidate, Ratti, an increasing number of votes from the eleventh ballot. He was elected on the fourteenth ballot, 6 February 1922, with forty-two out of fifty-three votes. He chose as his motto *Pax Christi in Regno Christi,* which was explained in his first encyclical, *Ubi arcano,* and was later enlarged on in the encyclical on the Kingship of Christ in 1925: Christianity and Church must not, as liberal laicism wished, be excluded from the life of society but must be active in it.

He was the first scholarly Pope since Benedict XIV. He was recommended by his broad knowledge, his considerable knowledge of languages and international relations, and not least his acquaintance with modern scientific investigation. But not only by these gifts. As a pious priest, he had constantly been active in pastoral care, and as nuncio he acquired experience of ecclesiastical politics. His special energy gave promise of initiatives in many areas of ecclesiastical life. His health was excellent, his springy gait, even when he was in his seventies, made clear that he had succeeded in maintaining it by regular walks in the Vatican gardens.

"Life is action" was one of his maxims; another was "Don't put off until tomorrow what you can do today." Of a character like granite, "born to command," the formerly reserved Pope radiated inner assurance and a strong consciousness of authority. With strict objectivity and painstaking order he carried through in deliberate calmness his program of work, in which the several hours of constant reception of pilgrimages, which he addressed if at all possible in their native languages, occupied a broad, perhaps too broad, part. He did not think much of delegating the preparation of papal decisions to commissions: not entirely without reason was he reproached for an authoritarian, even autocratic, conduct of his office. The College of Cardinals was strongly deemphasized. Still another maxim: "Laws are to be observed, not to be dispensed with" (Confalonieri). Was he a fighter? It is certain that, where Christian principles and the Church's basic rights were at stake, he was as unflinching as his model, Ambrose. His devotion was "una pietà all'antica"; even at the age of eighty he held fast to the exercises of piety with which he was familiar from his seminary days: the breviary, the rosary, visit to the Blessed Sacrament, retreats. Lest even the suspicion of nepotism should appear, he received his relatives, not in his private apartments, but in the official reception halls.

The pontificate began with a surprise. Pius XI, as he called himself, because he was born under one Pope Pius and had come to Rome under another Pope Pius, imparted the blessing "Urbi et Orbi," customary at the proclaiming of the election, from the external loggia of Saint Peter's Basilica, thereby indicating that he intended to move toward a solution of the Roman Question. Even before his coronation on 12 February, he confirmed the previous secretary of state, Gasparri, in his office and thus made known that he planned to maintain the previous direction of Church government; when he sent him to Loreto as papal legate, he called him "the most loyal interpreter and implementer of his will." Even more decisively than Benedict XV, he held himself aloof from certain measures during the strife over modernism, in which he rehabilitated Francesco Lanzoni and without advance concessions restored to Albert Ehrhard the prelatial dignity he had been deprived of. The scholarly Pope regarded the promotion of science and of serious scholarship as his peculiar duty. He had the reading rooms of the Vatican Library modernized and enlarged; he gave the purple to his predecessor in the position of prefect of the library, Franz Ehrle, and to his successors, Giovanni Mercati and Eugène Tisserant. The Oriental Institute founded by Benedict XV and the Papal Archaeological Institute established by himself obtained sumptuous sites near Santa Maria Maggiore. For the Vatican collection of paintings he erected the new Pinacoteca. The means for all this were provided by the indemnity payments agreed to by the Italian government in the Lateran Treaties.

The Italian bishops were instructed to take care of a better preservation and organization of existing archives. In order to complete the collection of papal documents to 1198, begun by Paul Kehr, he established the *Piusstiftung* in Switzerland. Of great importance was the reform of priestly formation, into which modern scientific methods, for example, the employment of seminars and the production of scholarly dissertations, were incorporated. A historical section for the completing of the processes of beatification and canonization was added to the Congregation of Rites. The Pope took into account the significance of the natural sciences, with the results of which he was completely fascinated, by founding in 1936 an Accademia delle Scienze, into which were admitted important students of science from the entire world.

The Pope exercised the apostolic teaching authority in numerous encyclicals, which in part were related to historical anniversaries. In his first encyclical of 23 December 1922 he admonished the victors of the world war to reconciliation of peoples. On the occasion of the ecumenical conferences of Stockholm and Lausanne he warned against vague formulas of union and urged unity in faith.

Other encyclicals recommended participation in retreats, devotion to the Sacred Heart of Jesus and the rosary, or inculcated the bases of Christian education and Christian married life. The encyclicals on Catholic Action and against atheistic communism advanced still farther into the social field. Out of the conviction that in Fascist Italy no political but only a religious association of Catholics was possible, he sought to realize this insight in the whole Catholic world. For Italy a Central Council of Catholic Action had been appointed as early as November 1922: it supervised the activity of the organizations, of the diocesan commissions, of the youth organizations, and of the university federations. During the succeeding years Catholic Action was introduced in many countries — Spain, Portugal, Poland, Yugoslavia, Austria. In Switzerland and the Anglo-Saxon countries there were hesitations, because its basic aim had already been realized. For the same reason there existed doubts in already overorganized Germany; nevertheless, the Pope pressed for the introduction in his letter to Cardinal Bertram of 13 November 1928. That it was not to be understood as a withdrawal of the Church to a ghetto was made clear by the encyclical *Quadragesimo anno,* which attached itself directly to the social program of Leo XIII.

The "Pope of Jubilees" celebrated three Jubilee Years: the Jubilee falling according to the cycle in 1925, for which more than a half million pilgrims came to Rome; the missionary exposition organized at the same time attracted seven hundred fifty thousand visitors; the Holy Year closed with the instituting of the solemnity of Christ the King. Extraordinary jubilees were celebrated on the occasion of the Pope's golden jubilee of his priesthood in 1929 and in memory of the Incarnation and Redemption by Jesus Christ from Easter 1933 to Easter 1934; in the following year it was extended to the whole world. The world Eucharistic Congresses at Rome in 1922, Amsterdam in 1924, Chicago in 1926, Sydney in 1928, Carthage in 1930, Dublin in 1932, Buenos Aires in 1934, Rio de Janeiro in 1936, Manila in 1937, and Budapest in 1938 made people aware of the universality of the Church.

In the allocutions customary before Christmas the Pope took care to give to the College of Cardinals summaries of the most important ecclesiastical events of the year. Thus in 1923 he spoke of the aid to the populations of the Central Powers and of Russia, in 1926 and at other times of the persecution of the Church in Mexico, the menacing development in China, but also of the important happenings in Europe. He strengthened the College of Cardinals by eight members in his first creation; in the next years he filled up only with difficulty the vacancies caused by death and extended, though again only slowly, the representation of other continents in the college: in 1924 through the elevation of the archbishops of New York and Chicago, in 1930 of the archbishop of Rio de Janeiro. Not until 1935 did there follow a great promotion of twenty cardinals, but there were only two non-Europeans among them — Buenos Aires and the Syrian patriarch of Antioch. He left to his successors the step discussed by him toward a numerical internationalization of the College of Cardinals.

Noteworthy among the numerous beatifications and canonizations are those of Robert Bellarmine, beatified in 1923 and canonized and declared a Doctor of the Church in 1930; Peter Canisius in 1925, when he was also declared a Doctor of the Church; Albertus Magnus in 1931, also a Doctor of the Church; the curé of Ars in 1925; Don Bosco, beatified in 1929 and canonized in 1935; Conrad of Parzham in 1934; Bernadette Soubirous, beatified in 1925 and canonized in 1933. In addition to many founders of religious institutes, martyrs in the missions were preferred. The most imposing canonization of this sort was that of the English witnesses to the faith, John Fisher and Thomas More, in 1935.

Through all the internal ecclesiastical activity of Pius XI there runs like a red thread the awareness that the Church, to a degree never achieved before in its history, had become a World Church. This fact found expression in the extension of the international relations of the Holy See.

Already marked by a mortal illness, the Pope planned an address that was to be delivered on the anniversary of the "reconciliation" with a fierce protest against the ecclesiastical policy of Fascist Italy, but he died on the previous evening, 10 February 1939. His successor was his secretary of state, Pacelli.

Pius XII

Pius XII came from a family of Roman jurists closely connected with the papacy.

Eugenio, born on 2 March 1876, was ordained to the priesthood on 2 April 1899 by the cardinal vicar of Rome in the latter's private chapel. He celebrated his first Mass in the Borghese Chapel of Santa Maria Maggiore, and on the next day a Mass at the tomb of Saint Philip Neri in the Chiesa Nuova. This procedure is informative for his later career.

Favored by Cardinal Vannutelli, a friend of his father's, after the completion of his legal studies at Sant'Apollinare (1899–1902), he entered the Congregation for Extraordinary Ecclesiastical Affairs as a *minutante* in 1904; its secretary, Pietro Gasparri, requisitioned him for cooperation in the codification of canon law. Pacelli became undersecretary in 1911 and secretary of the congregation in 1914. Parallel to this, from 1909 to 1914, he was teaching at the Accademia dei Nobili and performing pastoral work as confessor, preacher, and lecturer.

The career of the young Pacelli was exclusively carried out in the area of Rome and the Vatican until on 20 April 1917 he was appointed nuncio in Munich. Benedict XV himself ordained him as archbishop of Sardes on 13 May 1917 in the Sistine Chapel and thereby made clear that he enjoyed the full confidence of the Pope in the discussion to be undertaken by him of the aims of the war with the German government. On 26 June the nuncio conferred with Imperial Chancellor Count von Hertling and on 29 June he was received in the imperial headquarters.

After the overthrow of the monarchy, Pacelli was on 22 June 1920 made the first nuncio to the German Republic, while retaining temporarily the Munich nunciature, and, as its occupant, on 29 March 1924 he signed the Bavarian concordat.

Not until 1925 did he move definitively to Berlin. The reputation and influence of the "perhaps most skillful diplomat of the Curia," as the German evangelical *Korrespondenz* put it, grew from year to year.

Recalled at the end of 1929 and created a cardinal on 16 December, on 7 February 1930 he became Gasparri's successor as secretary of state, and as such he signed concordats with Baden and Austria as well as the concordat with Germany. On 25 March 1930 he was named archpriest of Saint Peter's as successor of Merry del Val. He became known to the Universal Church through legations to Buenos Aires in 1934, Lourdes and Lisieux in 1935 and 1937 respectively, and Budapest in 1938. In 1936 he visited the United States in a private capacity. And so, at the end of Pius XI's reign he was the best known cardinal, and in the College of Cardinals there was a consensus that he was preeminently qualified to guide the Universal Church through the storm of the threatening war, as had Benedict XV, who had had a similar career, during the First World War. The conclave lasted only one day, 2 March 1939: Pacelli was elected as early as the third ballot, with forty-eight out of sixty-three votes, and assumed the name Pius XII. No secretary of state had obtained the tiara since 1667. His coronation on 12 March took place, out of regard for the masses of people whom Saint Peter's could not hold, on the loggia over the principal portal. It was the first to be carried on radio. As his secretary of state the new Pope named the Neapolitan Luigi Maglione, who had been nuncio at Paris until 1935.

When in the summer of 1939 the danger of war grew more real, the Pope in a radio broadcast to the world on 24 August urged peace: "Nothing is lost through peace; all can be lost through war." The appeal was made in vain. When the new Pope's first encyclical appeared on 20 October, the Second World War had begun. While it raged, the Pope, relying on his moral authority, could only urge peace again and again and demand a just and humane treatment of the civil population in the militarily occupied areas. The information bureau set up in the Vatican collected the names of prisoners of war and the missing and supplied information on them to their families — from July 1941 to December 1946, 1,162,627 particulars were furnished. After the bombing of 19 July 1943 the Pope personally visited the severely hit city quarter of San Lorenzo and succeeded in getting the Italian government to declare Rome an "open city." In order to improve the providing of foodstuffs to the city crowded with refugees, provisions were brought from central and upper Italy in Vatican truck convoys.

Like Benedict XV after the First World War, so also Pius XII did not regard the time as suitable for filling the vacancies in the College of Cardinals until after the concluding of the armistice. In order to make of this a "living image of the universality of the Church," on 18 February 1946 he named thirty-two cardinals from all parts of the world, among them Armenian Patriarch Agagianian and the archbishops of New York, Saint Louis, Toronto, São Paulo, Rio de Janeiro, Santiago de Chile, Lima, Havana, Sydney, Lourenço Marques, and the Chinese Tien; the Pope displayed courage by giving the purple also to three Germans: to Archbishop Frings of Cologne and Bishops Count Galen of Münster and Count Preysing of Berlin. A further step toward internationalizing the College was the promotion of twenty-four cardinals on 19 January 1953. Among them were the archbishops of Los Angeles, Montreal, Quito, Bahia, and Bombay. The proportion of Italians dropped to one-third.

In the thirty-three canonizations which Pius XII performed, French and Italians predominated, among the latter being Pius X in 1954.

Unaffected by the war was the exercise of the papal teaching office, which in several respects prepared the ground for the Second Vatican Council: the encyclical *Mystici Corporis* of 29 June 1943 on the Church, followed on 30 September of the same year by the encyclical *Divino afflante Spiritu* on Holy Scripture, which encouraged the investigation of the literal sense and regard for literary forms and allowed biblical scholarship more freedom than had been permitted it during the defense against modernism. The constitution *Sacramentum ordinis* of 30 November 1947 defined as the essence of the Sacrament of Orders the invocation of the Holy Spirit through the imposition of hands; the symbolic presentation of chalice and paten do not pertain to it. The bull *Munificentissimus Deus* of 1 November 1950 defined, without eliminating all the scientific difficulties, the dogma of the bodily Assumption of the Mother of God into heaven. The constitution *Sempiternus Rex* of September 1951 laid the foundation for the encyclical *Haurietis aquas* of 15 May 1956 on devotion to the Sacred Heart. The encyclical *Humani generis* of 12 August 1950 basically accepted theological progress but warned against the relativization of dogmas and the all too close accommodation to the trends of the day. The constitution *Sedes sapientiae* of 31 May 1956 extended the circle of theological departments of study in accord with the demands of modern pastoral work.

No Pope before Pius XII treated as often and as forcibly as he in his numerous and always carefully prepared addresses to pilgrims, participants in congresses, and members of the most varied professions the general themes of Christian life — human dignity, formation of conscience, marriage and the family — and questions of professional ethics — jurists, physicians, natural scientists, and others — and referred to the importance of the mass media — press, film, radio, and television. To the Lenten preachers of Rome he took care to speak on the sacraments as sources of sanctification. He remained rather reserved in regard to the ecumenical movement that grew so powerfully after the war.

But his liturgical reforms were epoch-making. Accepting the basic idea of the liturgical movement, the encyclical *Mediator Dei* of 20 November 1947 demanded the active participation of the faithful in the Sacrifice of the Mass, declared the reception of Communion to be desirable, though not necessary, and rejected the move to do away with cult forms that were unknown in antiquity. The Evening Mass, granted during the war out of regard for nocturnal bombardments, was definitively allowed by the constitution *Christus Dominus* of 6 January 1953, and at the same time the Eucharistic fast was modified. But perhaps the Pope's greatest deed in this field was the decree of the Congregation of Rites of 1 February 1951, which restored the Easter Vigil Liturgy. The new translation of the psalms, introduced in 1945, eliminated the translation mistakes in the Vulgate, but in the next years had to be again assimilated to the text made sacred by tradition. In September 1956 the First Liturgical World Congress met at Assisi.

Of the exhaustive legislative activity of the jurist Pope, to be singled out because of their general importance are the new decrees on the conclave and the papal election: photographic and radio apparatus could not be brought in, and television speakers and writers could not be employed; one vote over the two-thirds majority was needed to elect the Pope. A step on to new ground was the constitution *Provida Mater Ecclesia* of 2 February 1947: it laid down rules for secular institutes, whose members bound themselves to the observance of the evangelical counsels without living in community.

The slender, ascetically active Pope with the Roman head, who always took great care of his external appearance, was without doubt in the succession of Popes of the twentieth century the most brilliant phenomenon, admired by non-Catholics even more than by Catholics. The Romans never forgot that in the most difficult days of the war he had stayed with them and had been their single protector. Although he had three Germans in his immediate entourage — the Jesuits Robert Leiber and Augustine Bea and the former leader of the Center Party, Ludwig Kaas — and as his housekeeper Sister Pasqualina of the Congregation of the Swiss Sisters of the Cross, and although he employed the German Jesuits Gundlach and Hürth as advisers, he was far from favoring Germany or even of pursuing a pro-German policy. Earlier than many Germans, he had recognized the threat to Christianity from National Socialism, although the threat from Bolshevism seemed to him still greater. He, and only he, piloted the Universal Church; in his hand all the strings of the Church's direction ran together. As time passed, the College of Cardinals was more and more removed from transactions. In his relations with people he astounded them by his unerring remembrance of persons and charmed them by his amiability. His undoubted deep personal piety was strongly Marian under the influence of the apparitions at Fátima and misled opportunistic theologians to an excessive Mariology. Painful indiscretions of the physician overshadowed his last days and his death on 9 October 1958 at Castel Gandolfo.

C H A P T E R   8 5

Foreign Policy of the Popes in the Epoch of the World Wars

The First World War and the Postwar Years: Benedict XV

Benedict XV has frequently been called a "political" Pope in contrast to his predecessor, who was a "religious" Pope. This is correct to the extent that Benedict XV, who was likewise a "religious" Pope, was confronted in foreign policy by problems of greater impact than was any of his predecessors since 1815. As early as the beginning of September 1914 the war had expanded beyond the boundaries of Europe and become a "world war." It soon took on proportions for which historical memory could find no comparable examples. Two-thirds of the Catholics of the time were directly involved in this war, 124 million on the side of the Entente, 64 million on the side of the Central Powers. The third of the Catholics living in countries not engaged in the war were, except for German-speaking Switzerland and Spain, under the overwhelming propaganda influence of the Entente Powers.

It goes without saying that the war, with its presumed consequences, constituted a powerful criterion for the voting of the cardinals in the conclave of 1914, which was able to take place without hindrances, but it was hardly the decisive factor. Thus, the papal electors from the Central Powers were from the start for Della Chiesa, but the ecclesiastical questions — integralism and its problems — were more important to them than political considerations.

For the new Pope the question of the correct foreign policy course never became publicly a problem for the solution of which there would basically have been alternatives. From the first hour three points of orientation determined his answer to the challenge of the war: strict neutrality, charitable measures of assistance, and the call for peace and reconciliation.

Neutrality

The basis of political neutrality can be precisely grasped in the papal allocution of 22 January 1915. In it the Pope claimed for himself without restriction the right to be "summus interpres et vindex legis aeternae." He also declared in the abstract that he in no way sanctioned violations of rights but condemned them. He avoided with difficulty a concretizing and actualizing in regard to the problems which the war had raised. Hence he did not take a stand on the question of war guilt and of the infringements by German troops in Belgium or of the Russian occupation in Galicia. The war was by no means made less demanding: it was rather a "butchery" than a fight. To intervene with papal authority into the confrontations of the warring parties was, however, neither significant nor useful; on the contrary, the Holy See must remain neutral, however difficult this might be. Christ died for all men; the Pope is the Vicar of Christ for all men and on all sides of the war has children for whom he bears responsibility. And so he must not look at the *rationes proprias* separating them, but he must pay attention to the common bond of faith which unites them. Should the Pope act otherwise, he would not be promoting the cause of peace but further jeopardizing the interior unity of the Church. To be sure, he called emphatically and urgently for peace and reconciliation. Earlier the first encyclical (1 November 1914) had invited rulers and governments to peace negotiations: There are better means and ways to restore violated rights than war.

This program, to which the Pope held firm during the succeeding years without essentially new arguments and ideas, was the opposite of a preaching crusade: incomparably moderate and temperate in goals and hence without any emotional force of enthusiasm. The war was still young, and the propaganda organs were running at full speed. At this moment few were ready to listen to the Pope; in fact, he was reproached with the charge that his peace-preaching crippled the moral power of resistance against the (unjustified) attack of the enemy among his (own) Catholics. The Pope presumably was under no illusions as to the direct effects of his appeal. But the essentially pastoral outlook enabled him to look beyond the clamor of the day.

Pius XII followed this fundamental orientation in the Second World War. It may seem today in retrospect as a sheer foregone conclusion, but it was at first nothing of the sort. To establish and stick to such a tradition required considerable and continuous efforts. Of course, in regard to ecclesiastical interests and understanding, there were no acceptable alternatives.

A withdrawing from the principle of neutrality would necessarily have meant taking one side or the other. Just as the Pope would have had to establish this morally, legally, and politically, so right and wrong, guilt and innocence were by no means one-sided, clear, and undoubted in this or that warring coalition of powers. The Pope could identify himself with none of them. But even if this should have been possible, the Vatican, in the translating of such a concept into practical political activity, would soon have run up against scarcely surmountable barriers. The papacy of the High Middle Ages had not been able to realize *in praxi* the theoretical claim to be judge of the world. Between 1914 and 1918 the word of the Bishop of Rome meant incomparably much less. Among non-Catholics the political authority of the Holy See had dropped to its nadir under Pius X. Then people listened all the less to the Pope when even Catholics loyal to the Church did not collectively turn to Rome politically either predominantly or exclusively. This was especially true of the levels and groups that were then in any way "modern." Because a nationalism extending even to chauvinism was the prevailing tendency of the age, whoever wanted to obtain "contact" with his "contemporary age" could let himself be swept along easily and far by the nationalist movements. To accuse the Holy See that before 1914 it did not proceed energetically enough against this probably overestimates the possible influence of the ecclesiastical leadership and the political conduct of the faithful in purely political matters and leads ultimately to the posing of the question to which history from Gregory VII to Boniface VIII had already given a clearly negative answer. Hence, even with regard to the real ability to implement, neutrality was the only Vatican foreign policy that was available. A prudent judgment of the moral-legal situation of the military leadership and a skeptical evaluation of the readiness of the Catholics to echo the concrete political postulates of the Pope corresponded with Benedict XV's understanding of his office. This successor of Peter could and would "act [only] as the merciful Samaritan, not as judge of the world."

As a consequence of the Vatican's neutrality and the Pope's reserve with statements containing concrete proposals, much political latitude was possible for the Catholics and their organizations in the different countries. For most of them identification with the cause of their own state, regarded as good and just, was important. Hence the Pope hardly determined the political attitude of the Catholicism of the countries and nationalities affected by or participating in the war in the specific problems which the war raised. Whether this may be regarded as a failure of papal policy is questionable, for in this regard Benedict XV probably had no wish to lead. Conversely, his neutrality was the indispensable presupposition for extensive humanitarian measures of assistance and for diplomatic activities to prevent the spread of the war and for the restoration of peace.

Papal Measures of Assistance

Humanitarian measures of assistance fade easily and fast in historical memory. But, especially in war time, they require much patience, time, energy, and flexibility. The papal measures of help were supplied without regard to the religious, national, or ethnic membership of those affected, as the cardinal secretary of state had expressly prescribed on 22 December 1914.

In the First World War cruelties occurred in the Mideast which recall the Second World War, but were and are only lightly regarded by the historical memory of the Western world. For example, after the retreat of the Russians from eastern Anatolia one hundred twenty-five thousand Assyro-Chaldeans were first driven into western Azerbaijan and from there back into the area of Mosul, modern Iraq, where most of them starved. Deportations and massacres among the Armenians cost about 1 million human lives. A like fate was spared the Christians of Lebanon, but they too were decimated by hunger. The Pope could not prevent these happenings. But by avoiding branding them publicly, he continued in his neutral position and for this reason and by means of personal letters to Sultan Mehmed V he was able to bring about the partial halting of the massacres, to save from execution those condemned to death, and to insure that surviving children of the victims were cared for. An orphanage set up for this purpose in Constantinople received the name of Benedict XV.

On the other hand, the war in Europe was on the whole oriented in some degree to the contemporary norms of international law. Accordingly, the Vatican's measures of assistance in this sphere bore the charitable character of "normal" war care. First, from the spring of 1915, an exchange of prisoners unfit for military service succeeded by means of Switzerland, then the liberation and exchange of interned civilians, then the lodging of sick and wounded prisoners of war in neutral countries, to a total of over one hundred thousand, and finally the exchange of prisoners of war who were fathers of families of many children and the permitting of consumptive Italians to return from Austro-Hungarian prisons. In addition, collections of money prepared the way for these measures, and the Vatican's own resources were given to a total amount of approximately 82 million gold lire. Furthermore, efforts were undertaken or supported to put into motion again the postal exchange between the occupied and the unoccupied areas of a state, and, above all, corresponding institutions were established for the pastoral and charitable care of prisoners of war. Not least of all, with the help of these institutions the Vatican took part in the search for the missing. Measured by the misery of the years-long war of attrition for soldiers and the civilian population, such measures of assistance were, to be sure, only a palliative. But in the framework of what was possible much was attempted and far more was accomplished than in the field of "pure" foreign policy.

Efforts for Peace

The Holy See's strivings for peace were first concentrated on Italy, the history of which in the period from September 1914 to the declaration of war on Austria-Hungary on 23 May 1915 is nothing other "than the history of the overwhelming of a reasonable but impassive majority by an enthusiastic or unscrupulous, but in any case tirelessly active minority," in which it was not clear "who had used or compelled whom: the active minority the government, or conversely" (E. Nolte). Benedict XV was fundamentally interested in the outcome of these internal Italian struggles. It was of course unclear whether and how the Prisoner in the Vatican could at all continue the central government of the Universal Church if a state of war occurred in Italy. Besides, for the Italian Catholics loyal to the Church the Bishop of Rome had a special moral and political leadership responsibility. Finally, in the event of an Italian defeat in the Appenine peninsula there loomed the threat of a revolution from the left; in the event of an Austro-Hungarian defeat the collapse of the Hapsburg Empire and hence the end of the last great Catholic monarchy. Hence the Pope's aim was that Italy should stay neutral.

The conservative intransigents loyal to the Pope within Italian political Catholicism consistently upheld this goal. The other large groups, the moderate so-called *Clerico-Moderati,* who sought a compromise with and an integration into the liberal state, conformed to all the changes of the government; they began with neutrality and ended with interventionism. The other, smaller groupings were partly for and partly against entry into the war. This variety and these oppositions were apparently accepted by the Pope without his pressing for a uniform formation of purpose in the sense of the Vatican program and carrying this through. He did not prevent substantial portions of Italian Catholicism from coming out for intervention from March 1915.

On the other hand, Benedict XV made intensive use of the traditional means of diplomacy to move the Dual Monarchy to timely and adequate concessions to Italian nationalism and to keep the Italian government from joining the Triple Entente. He was unable to put across these aims, either at Vienna or in Rome. Austria-Hungary only proposed negotiable offers for Italy when the Kingdom had long before committed itself to the Entente in the London Treaty of 26 April 1915. ARTICLE 15 of the treaty, of which the Vatican learned as early as the end of 1915 and which the Bolsheviks published in *Izvestia* on 28 November 1917, was at first secret. By this article the Holy See was excluded from all peace negotiations. Behind it lay the traditional anticlericalism of the Freemasonic *Risorgimento* and the fear that otherwise the "Roman Question" could be referred to an international conference. Attempts in 1918 to change this article failed.

The legal and practical consequences for the Holy See at an outbreak of the state of war in Italy were after 1870 governed neither by international nor by Italian law. Hence the government of the Kingdom had theoretically a free hand. The diplomatic representatives accredited to the Holy See by Austria-Hungary and Germany withdrew immediately to Switzerland on 24 May 1915, after the Secretariat of State had refused to accommodate them in the Vatican. In other respects the Italian government observed its unilateral obligations according to the Law of Guarantees of 1871 throughout the war and showed itself generous in some matters not regulated by that law. The Holy See's freedom of movement was, it is true, limited by the Italian state of war; for example, *Osservatore Romano* was bound by the Italian rules of censorship. But on the whole the Vatican had to deal with fewer difficulties than had been previously feared. Even during the war the Curia was able to operate as the center of the Universal Church, and the Pope could continue his foreign policy. In this field his prestige even increased: in 1915 the Netherlands and Great Britain undertook diplomatic relations with the Holy See and sent their representatives to the Vatican. Formal relations with France did not yet materialize, it is true, and in Vatican-Italian relations there persisted the coexistence traditional since 1870 of legal nonrecognition and in practice the possibility of a many-sided contact. At the beginning of the First World War there were fourteen diplomatic missions of states at the Holy See, and at the end seventeen.

After Italy's entry into the war papal foreign policy strove ceaselessly to support whatever could offer a certain prospect of bringing the warring nations to the negotiating table. In this connection the Vatican also followed unconventional routes. Thus from May 1915 to May 1916 it accepted offers of contact from Jewish personalities of France, from whom it apparently expected influence on the Jewish organizations in the Western nations and thereby again on the foreign policy of the Entente Powers.

While, except in eastern Central Europe, the Catholics of all the warring countries very unselfishly carried out their duties as citizens, the Pope continued to be abstract in his frequent public expressions on peace and war, though individual concrete statements positively impressed themselves on the memory, as from his address of 28 July 1915 the formula "that the nations not die." On the other hand the "Peace Appeal" of 1 August 1917 to the heads of the warring nations contains declarations of concrete content.

The beginning of this diplomatic action went back to the turn of the year 1916–1917. It assumed concrete forms when the new nuncio at Munich, Eugenio Pacelli, on 13 June 1917 received instructions for personal soundings in Berlin. He discussed this on 26 June with Imperial Chancellor Bethmann Hollweg and Secretary of State Zimmermann. The pivot was Belgium. Bethmann had earlier offered the restoration of the nation only among "real guarantees" for Germany; now he promised "complete independence" of all three great powers — a fundamental concession, for which he had not yet internal agreement. A meeting of Pacelli with Austrian Emperor Charles I on 30 June showed that the Hapsburg Monarchy apparently still maintained its readiness of May 1915 for concessions to Italy. These verbal promises of Berlin and Vienna were materially so important that the Vatican could go further with them. Belgium should be the starting point.

It was precisely on this point that the papal action become jammed. The fall of Bethmann Hollweg on 13 July 1917 contributed to this. His successor Michaelis was not prepared for domestic policy promises that had not been assured. The Curia could not know this, and overestimated the actual chances of success, but apparently placed itself under a portentous time pressure, because it seemingly wanted to publish it unconditionally on 1 August, the beginning of the fourth year of the war. Nevertheless the new Center-Left majority of the Reichstag on 19 July rejected the celebrated peace resolution which came close to the Vatican program and had been accepted by the new imperial chancellor.

Before the Pope turned to all the powers, the concrete formulations with Berlin had to be unambiguously agreed to. To this end Pacelli on 24 July submitted in Berlin the so-called "Pacelli Punctation" that had been elaborated in Rome at the beginning of July. This was a memorandum in seven points, the first four of which described concrete material regulations — freedom of the seas; limitation of arms; international arbitration; German withdrawal from France, restoration of the complete political, military, and economic independence of Belgium with regard to Germany, England, and France, and on the other hand the return of the German colonies by England — while the last three enumerated the other subjects to be treated at the peace conference — economic questions; Austrian-Italian and German-French boundaries; Poland, Serbia, Rumania, Montenegro.

This memorandum corresponded to the status as of 26 June. But now Berlin at once raised objections, especially in relation to Belgium, where again there was talk of "guarantees." The written reply, the German counterstatement, was not presented until 12 August. The Vatican did not wait for it before drawing up and delivering the papal peace appeal.

The "peace appeal" is a document of Benedict XV, backdated 1 August, to the heads of state of the warring nations, which the cardinal secretary of state officially delivered to the powers on 9 August. The note consists of three parts: a review and recalling of the papal admonitions to peace, previously made, but in vain; a summons to the governments to reach an understanding on the points sketched in what followed as the basis of a just and lasting peace; a moving closing appeal to put an end to the more and more "useless carnage" through negotiations. The crucial second part corresponded in content to the Pacelli Punctation with regard to the verbal German replies of 24 July, except for the point of Belgium.

It could not be proved at the time which prospects the Pope had assigned to his step. If one starts with the probably compelling assumption that he had reckoned on the chances of success, then one must presume that, despite the replies of 24 July, he had estimated Bethmann's promise of 26 June as capable of being revived. This would have — thus, for example, may one understand the Vatican's assessment — released so much political leverage that the Entente could scarcely have avoided serious negotiations resulting from it, step for step. Hence, because the stone which the avalanche would set in motion was the German promise of 26 June concerning Belgium, the reply of Germany to the papal peace appeal acquired special importance. It consisted formally of a note from the imperial chancellor to the cardinal secretary of state of 19 September, which was followed by a confidential letter of Michaelis to Pacelli of 24 September.

The note of 19 September contains various civilities but no clear acceptance of the matter of the statements of the peace appeal. An evasion of this sort, especially in regard to Belgium, had been suspected by the Curia at the latest since 12 August. Thereafter Vatican diplomacy sought persistently and ingeniously somehow to obtain, vis-à-vis the Entente, a usable German declaration of renunciation of Belgium. This policy of delimitation culminated in a letter from Pacelli to Michaelis of 30 August which, with the adding of the English interim reply of 21 August to the papal note, demanded precise statements on Belgium as a presupposition "to further progress of the negotiations." Michaelis rejected such a declaration on Belgium on 24 September, since "certain preconditions" were still "not sufficiently explained." His letter was a provisional decree: the door was not slammed shut. But the papal effort at mediation had come to a halt: the precise German declaration did not come later either, so that the Curia could never again take up the thread.

The already mentioned notes of 21 and 30 August and of 24 September were published by the Germans at the end of July 1919 and were long the subject of passionate controversies, which in the meantime cleared the way for more quiet and painstaking investigations. It is firmly held today that Berlin with the German replies of September 1917 had wasted no unconditionally certain opportunities for peace. It is likewise established that Michaelis had not let himself be influenced in his treatment of the peace note by Protestant prejudices against Pope and Church. But there is today still not complete agreement on the bases and the consequences of the German decisions in September. Of course, it is known that Michaelis aligned himself in foreign policy alongside Secretary of State Kühlmann, and the latter, like Bethmann Hollweg, wanted to give Belgium complete independence. For reasons of negotiating tactics in foreign policy and perhaps also from domestic policy considerations, Kühlmann, however, was willing to use the Vatican's mediation only at the end of a three-phased plan. First he envisaged private probings through the Spanish diplomat Villalobar in England with a declaration of German concessions on Belgium; this should be followed by German-British preliminary peace negotiations and then more formal peace negotiations mediated by the Vatican with a definitive declaration of the renunciation of Belgium. This oversubtle concept foundered in Madrid and in London. Important, however, in this context is the attitude of the other powers to the peace appeal.

The three other Central Powers likewise replied formally to the Pope and in fact did not depart substantially from the German line; Russia, France, and Italy, on the contrary, chose one of the more rude types of rejection by not replying. The answer of the United States, on 27 August, was mainly conditioned by domestic policy. Wilson declared an Imperial Germany incapable of peace negotiations. British policy did not conform to this denial. The English envoy at the Vatican was instructed on 21 August to give an interim answer, which "to a certain degree conformed to the papal action" (W. Steglich). For reasons not clearly determinable, Paris at first attached itself to this step, and London communicated this to Rome on 23 August. The London instructions of 21 and 23 August led to the Vatican's overestimating France's readiness for negotiations completely and England's considerably. On 26 August France made an about-face in regard to England and pressed for aloofness. To what extent London agreed is controverted. England's actual readiness for negotiations from 30 August was probably described most precisely by Steglich, who thinks that London "wanted to defer the definitive stand until clarity had been obtained in regard to the willingness of the Central Powers to make concessions."

From these relations it becomes clear how very much Pacelli had to believe at the end of August that with a German renunciation of Belgium the open sea of the peace negotiations had been reached, but also that at the end of August such a declaration would in no way have guaranteed surer success. How London would have decided if it had resulted cannot be said. Historically it must be held that the German silence on Belgium on 19 and 24 September spared the English government from finding a political reply to Germany, which it could have stuck to internally and could have subscribed to externally.

The failure of the action of 1 August 1917 did not induce the Pope to a fundamental correcting of his readiness to mediate. But Benedict XV no longer expressed himself publicly in the further course of the war on concrete problems of peace.

The Pope did not need to observe this discretion during the Paris peace negotiations. He could, of course, exercise no influence on the content of the treaties, since he was excluded from the congress as well as from the League of Nations. Nevertheless, the secretary of the Vatican Congregation for Extraordinary Ecclesiastical Affairs, Bonaventura Cerretti, stayed for some time in 1919 at the congress as the Pope's secret representative. In this way he established numerous contacts which led to the assuming of diplomatic relations with the new eastern central European nations and constituted the point of departure for the concluding of many concordats. Altogether the Vatican foreign policy worked for the most extensive possible international presence and for contractual accommodation with all nations, in connection with which it was shown to be quite prepared for concessions. A great success of the Vatican's desire for reconciliation was the resumption of diplomatic relations with France in 1921. When Benedict XV unexpectedly died on 22 January 1922, the foreign policy prestige of the Holy See, as measured against 1914, had risen remarkably. That the number of diplomatic representatives at the Vatican had more than doubled was a clear indication of this.

Between the Two World Wars: Pius XI

The Lateran Treaties of 1929

The "Roman Question" to 1926.   Also for the election of Pius XI on 6 February 1922, not primarily political but inner ecclesiastical reasons were decisive. At this moment no one could know that this political novice, who had spent his life among books and manuscripts until 1918, would conclude the Lateran Treaty and thereby bring about the most important foreign policy decision of the papacy since 1870. The agreements of 11 February 1929 sealed the end of the more than millennial history of the Papal State: at the same time they did away with the "Roman Question" that the Holy See had left open since 1870.

In the decades since 1870 there had been no dearth of deliberations, proposals, and exertions for the elimination of the "Roman Question" by reconciliation. But nothing had been achieved in principle. Hence even Pius XI, in his first encyclical, *Ubi Arcano Dei,* of 23 December 1922, though in a conciliatory form, repeated the legal reservation of his predecessors against the occupation of the Papal State, which had made the Pope the "Prisoner of the Vatican," and against the Italian "Law of Guarantees" of 13 May 1871.

Meanwhile, the "Roman Question" had lost its first-class significance for Italian domestic policy. This facilitated an accommodation for the Kingdom. In addition, the liberal governments had become increasingly dependent on the Catholic voters. Out of reasons of principle and tactics the leading politician of the period before 1914, Giolitti, had already substituted for Cavour's old formula of the "Free Church in a Free State" of 27 March 1861 the new view of 30 May 1904, that of "Two Parallel Lines" which never meet in a contractual arrangement but also can never collide in conflict. Under Pius X a *conciliazione* policy on this basis was not timely.

It was otherwise under Benedict XV. In an interview of 28 June that became renowned, Secretary of State Gasparri broke with the tradition of the inflexible policy of revindication and a little later let the powers know by diplomatic means that the Vatican sought a compromise with Italy not through political pressure but through negotiation and compromise. So long as the war lasted, there was no prospect of this, and even afterwards the exclusion of the Holy See from the peace discussions made the including of Italian-Vatican negotiations among the business of the other states impossible. However, on the periphery of the Paris conference there occurred on 1 June 1919 discussions between Cerretti and Italian premier Emmanuele Orlando on a text which Gasparri had composed. It must have included: first, the demand for a material revision of the Italian Law of Guarantees of 1871; second, the renunciation of formal internationalization of the Roman Question, but assurance of the outcome or negotiations on the part of the other states through the entry of the Vatican State into the League of Nations; third, agreement of the Kingdom with the Papacy through Italian recognition of a sovereign Vatican State with an expanded territory. Differing from the arrangements of 1929, Gasparri's *appunto* certainly did not contain the demand for a simultaneous financial compensation and probably not a concordat that was to be signed at the same time. Orlando accepted Gasparri's plan but could not obtain the approval of the King of Italy for it. After Orlando's fall on 19 June 1919 contacts in this affair were not broken off, but the new minister-president, Nitti, probably again ran aground on King Victor Emmanuel III.

In these first postwar years there appeared many sorts of indications of the Vatican's readiness for negotiations. It was waiting, as Gasparri made clear in an interview of 29 September 1921, for a statesman with whom there could be discussion of the matter. The program of the Catholic Popular Party, *Partito popolare italiano,* founded on 18 January 1919, contained no direct allusion to a definitive contractual settlement of the "Roman Question" as an immediate aim, while the atheistic Fascist leader, Benito Mussolini, had departed in a famed speech in parliament on 21 June 1921 from his previous antiecclesiastical expressions and had signaled his readiness for reconciliation with the papacy. Thus matters stood when Benedict XV died.

The change of pontificate meant no alteration of the direction of Vatican foreign policy. This already appeared in the fact that Pius XI, contrary to tradition, left the cardinal secretary of state in office. To stress the significance of this continuity of personnel does not mean to imply that Pius XI was to a degree dominated by his bureaucracy. On the contrary, while Achille Ratti was an outsider to the Curia, he was a strong personality with a pronounced talent for independent judgment, quick grasp, and energetic action. And so the Lateran Treaties are historically his work, especially as he took a personal share in the origin of the treaty to the smallest formulation. Still, his treaty policy was completely in continuation of that of Benedict XV. Likewise, the replacing of Gasparri by Pacelli on 9 February 1930 meant no change of direction. The actual motives of the Pope for this change, over which there has been much speculation, cannot be determined.

Mussolini's rule — he became minister-president on 30 October 1922 — offered from the first a very confusing picture. Measures friendly to the Church stood alongside shock-troop violence. At first the Vatican reacted with a policy of the most extreme caution. No understanding on principles was sought, but on timely individual questions. This was apparently the result of a secret meeting of Mussolini with Gasparri on 19 or 20 January 1923 in the residence of the president of the Banco di Roma, Carlo Santucci. In this interview there was presumably question especially of this Vatican-controlled bank, which had fallen into difficulties. Its failure, which could only mean catastrophic consequences for Italian Catholicism, could not be averted without state help. Moreover, the two sides felt each other out and presumably agreed here to use the Jesuit Pietro Tacchi-Venturi for the future as go-between; his first intervention with Mussolini is demonstrable on 9 February 1923.

The Vatican's cautious reserve probably sprang first of all from the desire to avoid a frontal collision with Fascism, apparently especially because of the feared reaction on the Catholic organizational system. Only for a certain time, to the end of May 1923, and not beyond a certain limit was the Popular Party defended by the Vatican. Between the end of July 1923 and the end of October 1924 the Holy See by stages removed its founder, Don Luigi Sturzo (1871–1959), from political life. So long as the Vatican documents on these problematic proceedings are not accessible, it is difficult to make a correct judgment. In the election campaign of 1924 the Vatican prudently acted with reserve while clearly denouncing Fascist violence. On 9 September 1924 the Pope personally and publicly condemned a Popular Party coalition with the Socialists loyal to the constitution. When Mussolini had successfully weathered the Matteotti crisis on 3 January 1925, there began the real construction of the Fascist regime, which lasted until 1943. It was essentially characterized by repression of revolutionary radical, properly Fascist elements and by concessions of Mussolini to the more conservative forces and groups that supported him, hence, in a certain sense, moderates. It was firmly established with the November decrees of 1926.

At this time there began, on Italy's part, the policy which led to the Lateran Treaties. At the beginning of 1925 the government convoked a commission for a revision of the law of Church and state; it engaged in the work of amending from February to December. A former deputy of the Popular Party's center-right wing occupied the chair, and with papal permission, three canons of the Roman major basilicas belonged to the commission. The commission's final report was unanimously adopted. It made many concessions to the Church. The Italian episcopate reacted altogether positively toward it. As regards substance, the outcome of these consultations was already a piece of the Lateran Concordat of 1929. But the Pope rejected it, first orally on 26 December 1925 and then definitively by a letter of 18 February 1926 to Cardinal Secretary of State Gasparri and thus produced a linking between this work of amendment and a contractual regulating of the Roman Question.

This attitude seems the more astounding since at that time there were present agreeing views on the Roman Question on both sides of the Tiber, as the Vatican knew fully. In the spring of 1925 Carlo Santucci, acting in a private capacity, had elaborated a "project" on the regulating of the Roman Question. It treated the individual problems in general along the line of the Gasparri program of 1919, but deviated from it in two significant points: Santucci went into the financial problems passed over in 1919 and had misgivings in regard to the internationalization of the Roman Question. Santucci envisaged as the method of procedure an agreement of Italy with the Holy See on the material content but a formal regulation by a unilateral amending by the state of the law of 1871. On this point the Italian minister of justice was of another mind. He held that a regular treaty should be negotiated and included in Italian legislation and announced to the foreign governments. This was an overly clear offer of negotiations. The Pope, as Santucci later experienced, is said to have expressed the view that this sort of regulation of difficult matters had probably better be left to his successor.

Hence in the summer of 1925 the Holy See dropped Santucci's project and in the winter of 1925–26 rejected the acceptance of "unilateral" state legal reform. The reasons for these can be stated only hypothetically. It is certain that the Curia took its time, because so much was at stake for the Church's future. The negotiations which led to the Lateran Treaties began on 5 August 1926.

The Route to the Lateran Treaties (1926–29). The secret negotiations on the Lateran Treaties lasted two and one-half years, from 5 August 1926 to 10 February 1929, even though not continuously. Discretion was facilitated by the hardly exalted rank of the negotiators. On the Vatican side this was Francesco Pacelli, a layman, jurist in Vatican service, and brother of Eugenio Pacelli. For the discussion of the material of the concordat Prelate Borgongini Duca of the Secretariat of State was also involved. The Italian negotiator was, until his death on 4 January 1929, the state councilor Domenico Barone. Thereafter Mussolini himself, supported at the conclusion by high government officials, conducted the negotiations. The signing of the treaties and of the documents of ratification on 7 June 1929 was done on the Italian side by Mussolini, on that of the Vatican by Gasparri. The content of the negotiations was allotted to three treaties: the Lateran Treaty proper, which politically settled the "Roman Question," to which was added as Appendix IV a "Financial Agreement," and the Concordat.

The route was from the start determined by the fact that both sides had, even before entering upon the official preliminary negotiations, discussed their minimum demands and had reached agreement on the essential points of the Lateran Treaty proper: Mussolini's sole condition, that the Holy See recognize the regulating of the Roman Question as definitive and thereby say "yes" to 1870, was accepted by the Pope. Conversely, Italy had absolutely admitted the sovereignty of the Vatican, even though the important expression *Stato* for Vatican City was not conceded by Italy until 22 January 1929. In principle the Kingdom had recognized its debts to the Holy See from ARTICLE 3 of the Law of Guarantees of 13 May 1871.

The final great material difficulties and ceaselessly numerous small detailed questions of the form of the text were settled in January and February 1929. In the school questions Italy countered a Vatican maximal program — in a draft concordat of 5 December 1926 — with its own minimal program of 22 February 1927. The final compromise in ARTICLE 36 meant, it is true, a very solemn affirmation of the Church's principles, but drew from them only very limited consequences. And so in substance there was no agreement through a compromise. Similarly, even if it was much more favorable for the Vatican side, an agreement was reached in the complex of marriage law: when on 19 January 1929 the Italian minister of justice stated that, by the adopting of the canon law of marriage by the state, the Italian civil law was turned upside down — the Pope on 20 January declared any concession in the substance of this point to be unacceptable; rather should *conciliazione* founder. He thereby got his way. He was able to be so firm at this time also because he had immediately before lowered the financial demands already accepted by Mussolini on 14 January from 2 to 1.75 billion lire, whereby methods of payment tolerable for Italy had been worked out.

If one inquires into the historical and political importance of the treaties, it is undisputed that their signing meant for Mussolini a "great, undoubted success," according to the judgment of his competent biographer, "one of the greatest which he ever gained," in which there is no doubt that the "reconciliation" of 1929 had for him only the character of a tool and was purely tactically conditioned. The significance of the treaties for the Holy See, on the other hand, is very much disputed, so that there can certainly be no talk of a "success" without limitations, even if details that can be criticized are disregarded. One must proceed from the self-understanding of the modern Church, which wants to be a pastoral Church, and from the great aims of the Pope, whose whole activity here, as also elsewhere, was apparently not determined primarily by political goals but by the desire to create better and more effective possibilities for the care of souls. Under this aspect the short-term and the long-term must be separated.

From the short-term the Lateran Treaties offered the Church undeniable advantages. The intervening of the state into the Italian Church and Church administration was ended. The Vatican could cast off historically obsolete ballast and finally place the central government of the Universal Church economically on its own feet again — an advantage for the essential independence of the papacy that must be very highly evaluated. Furthermore, through the article of the concordat on the protections of associations — ARTICLE 43, par. 1 — the Church obtained a powerful legal position for the defense of the Catholic organizational system. This assured their presence in the Italian world, far beyond the limits of clergy and episcopate, over which the state now lost its most extensive personal political influence. Besides, the general jubilation in the country on the sudden report of the concluding of the treaty speaks for itself. So authentic a Catholic and a democrat as Alcide de Gasperi (1881–1954), the last secretary of the meanwhile forbidden Popular Party, thought, under the immediate impression of the signing, that even Don Sturzo, if he were Pope, would have had to sign this treaty, which definitively freed the head of the Church from the burden of *temporalia*. Of course, the Lateran Treaties strengthened the regime and hence the dictatorship: but this would pass. For the future, in any case, the Church should no longer be, as hitherto, constantly in search of unsuitable concessions for a solution of the Roman Question, and the solution should be obtained without the complication of an international guarantee. This outweighed all else. Problematic for the future was rather the concordat policy.

With this the second aspect is reached — long-term consequences. Precisely here opinions have been very much in conflict until today. Decisive is the question whether the Church, while letting itself be embraced by Mussolini's regime, jeopardized or sacrificed its own proper self. This did not happen. If Pius XI in the first weeks after the signing of the treaty, in favor of which he said little, hoped that Italy would now again become a "Catholic state" — in the sense of the pre-liberal epoch — Mussolini's arguments in May in the parliamentary debates on ratification unmistakably taught him otherwise. Two and one-half months after the signing the differences were so great that on 6 June it was still entirely unclear whether the treaties would become effective on the seventh. Ratification became possible only when both parties joined in a dilatory formal compromise which concealed the disagreement over principle.

In the next years Mussolini could not but recognize that the Church never unconditionally supported him — not in domestic policy and not at all in foreign policy. On the contrary, Catholic Action received a lift, especially the youth and student groups. This meant a serious hindrance to the penetrating of all of Italian society with Fascist tendencies, as Mussolini gradually became aware. Thus matters arrived at the great crisis of 1931, in the course of which the papal foreign policy advanced to the limits of its possibilities and finally had to accept a severe setback.

After the Lateran Treaties: The Crises of 1931 and 1938.

Mussolini produced the crisis of 1931, chiefly from domestic policy considerations. Catholic Action had gained too much ground for him. The great confrontation began in March with the accusations in the Fascist trade-union press that Catholic Action was overstepping its competence and interfering in the political-social sphere. In the background of the Fascist-Catholic journalistic polemic that now began, the government in April made demands through the diplomatic route which the Holy See rejected. At stake were two problems: the essential question of where the boundary ran between "ecclesiastical" and "extraecclesiastical," and the political question of who was to define the courses of this boundary. In the second question the Church claimed an unlimited autonomous competence. In the first question it demanded the right to have not only purely religiously oriented organizations, such as the liturgy and the administration of the sacraments, but also to be able to include the field of social Catholicism. In the Concordat Italy had recognized Catholic Action and its organizations as subject to ecclesiastical direction, so far as they "displayed their activity outside every political party for the spread and implementation of Catholic basic principles" (ARTICLE 43, par. 1).

From 19 April Pius XI publicly intervened in these confrontations. He placed himself before the "social" Catholic organizations, which are "legitimate,... necessary," and "irreplaceable," and in an open letter of 26 April to Cardinal Schuster of Milan he bitterly assailed the Fascist education of youth, oriented to hate and irreverence. In these circumstances the grandly staged ecclesiastical demonstrations gained more special political emphasis in mid-May. On 29 May Mussolini dissolved all Catholic youth and student groups by administrative measures.

After useless protests and exchanges of notes, the Pope turned against this police action with the encyclical *Non abbiamo bisogno* of 29 June 1931. The choice of this method of fighting was a political challenge of the first rank. In long and bitter passages the encyclical condemned the Fascist attack as clearly an injustice hostile to the Church. Mussolini's monopoly of the education of children and youth was founded on a "world of ideas which led professedly to a true and authentic deification of the state, which stands in full opposition, no less to the natural rights of the family than to the supernatural rights of the Church." The Fascist "notion of the state, which" claims "for it the young generation entirely and without exception," is "for a Catholic not compatible with Catholic teaching." The oath required of the members of Fascist organizations is "therefore, as its exists, not permitted," and hence at the least it must be taken with a *reservatio mentalis.* But the encyclical did not amount to a definitive break with the regime. It emphasized that the Pope had hitherto refrained from a "formal and express condemnation" and here too "in no sense" condemned "the Fascist Party as such." Rejected and condemned were only that part of its program and practice which are "irreconcilable with the name and profession of a Catholic."

And so the encyclical bore a contrary character: it could signify defining and signal readiness for negotiation. This ambivalence was perhaps the result of an inner-Vatican compromise between two groups with distinct notions in regard to the actual conflict. In any event, as early as 23 July the Pope had entered into compromise discussions with Mussolini, which led in September to a written agreement that ended the strife and — with reference to the *conciliazione* of 1929 — is frequently termed the *reconciliazione.*

The September Agreement was, of course, not a compromise without victors and vanquished, but a clear success for Mussolini. The agreement described the organization and functions of the associations protected by concordat and hence meant a renunciation of autonomous ecclesiastical regulation and, with this, a definition in principle unfavorable to the Church. As regards substance, in most points the state had carried the day. Italian Catholic Action was parceled into 250 diocesan units independent of one another and had to accept a sort of prohibition of former members of the Popular Party for its leadership. Trade-union and quasi-trade-union functions were in general forbidden to it, and in its work of social formation it was virtually bound to a support of the idea of the Fascist corporate system, a few months after *Quadragesimo anno.* Nothing was said of the suppression of the objectionable Fascist oath. The counterconcession was that the youth groups could again exist under a new name, now patterned to purely religious aims, and with the explicit prohibition of pursuing sports — which meant renunciation of an essential part of modern education of youth.

The reason for these papal concessions was presumably that no better alternative was at hand. From 9 July the provincial prefects reported to Mussolini that the encyclical did not go over well among the people, not even the clergy; agreement and peace were desired. The capacity of the clergy for a long fight with the state on the question of the Catholic system of associations was clearly slight. The ecclesiastical leadership could not ignore this. On 2 September it contented itself with the part of the education of youth which was permitted to it. It was much less than it wanted. But this little it had to accept, if the alternative was "still less."

The long-range political expectations which in 1929 could have been attached to Catholic Action became largely illusionary through the events of 1931. It was eliminated as politically dangerous opposition for Mussolini. Whether the successful preservation of the organizational framework of Catholic Action, especially of the youth and student groups, which as late as 1933 were joined by an academic organization, would alone have sufficed to prevent the advancing loss of the political importance and identity of Catholicism vis-à-vis Fascism is questionable.

The crisis of 1938 took place under changed political conditions; it was part and sequel of the gradually more open confrontation of Church and regime after the radical wing of Fascism had gained ground remarkably since the foreign policy rapprochement of Italy to Germany since 1936. The partial imitation of the anti-Jewish German policy by Mussolini aroused a spontaneous resistance among churchmen, to whom the Pope made it unmistakably clear that National Socialist notions of race stood in an irreconcilable opposition to the Catholic faith. Open conflict erupted in the fall, when the government amended the Italian marriage law in accord with "racial" viewpoints in a law of 17 November 1938. This meant that a marriage entered into in the Church between a baptized or unbaptized Jew and a Catholic lost its effect in civil law, which had been agreed to in Art. 34, para. 1 of the Lateran Concordat. As soon as the Holy See learned of these aims, it made use of its diplomatic means to prevent the introduction of these new forms or to modify their implementation. Seemingly in this there was question "only" of a peripheral problem, for in Italy in that year that there were about three hundred thousand marriages performed in the Church in comparison to a few dozen marriages which were affected by the amendment. But for the Church there were here at stake the validity and binding force of its sacramental law and its general mandate to the human race. Hence no one displayed any readiness for concession *in principiis.* The Vatican's protest notes did not, of course, prevent the Italian amendment from going into effect. To this extent the Holy See suffered another foreign policy defeat. But in regard to its intransigence it had churchmen on its side. In the long run this was a perhaps more important political event.

The Holy See did not exploit the 1938 violation of the Concordat to put entirely in question the treaty work of 1929. For twenty years the framework was maintained. On the tenth anniversary of the Lateran Treaty Pius XI would have risked a break in a public accounting with Mussolini if death had not meanwhile overtaken him. The outline of the text of the papal address, published in 1959, has pulled the rug from under this supposition. Pius XI intended before the entire assembled Italian episcopate to complain and to accuse the regime, but not to break with it. Hence the change of pontificate in 1939 meant in principle no alteration of course in Vatican foreign policy, even if a new handwriting and another political style are unmistakable. In fact, little changed — little was able to change: As the crisis of 1938 shows, the government of the Church, as soon as the sphere of the doctrinal and moral teaching was touched, could make no real concessions, even not with a dictatorship equipped with the twentieth century's techniques of power. The Church may be incapable of bringing the state or the prevailing regime to observance of the norms represented by it (which holds not only for our century), but it must insist on the validity of these norms.

Pius XI and the Totalitarian Systems

Opposition between the normative bases of a state and the teaching of the Church did not mean compulsion to renounce Vatican foreign policy with this state. So long as Catholic norms were not thereby sacrificed, the question of the beginning, continuing, or ending of the foreign policy activity of the Church with any state or regime was a question of expediency, in which the advancement of the possibilities of pastoral care represented the ultimate goal. In this way the lack of means of power and often the difficulty of gauging the consequences and side effects for the entire Church constituted the characteristic dilemma of papal foreign policy with reference to normative and/or *in praxi* hostile states. This dilemma appeared especially in relation to the really totalitarian systems of our epoch:

Bolshevik-dominated Russia and National Socialist–ruled Germany. In this connection "totalitarian" means the claim to dispose, without limit and exclusively,
of the totality of human existence, even in the sphere of conscience.

Pius XI and the Soviet Union.   At the Vatican there was never any question that
the old ecclesiastical delimitations vis-à-vis socialism were true to a still greater
degree in regard to the communism recognized as totalitarian — not yet according
to the idea, but in fact. If, nevertheless, between 1921 and 1927 the Holy See three
times seriously explored whether and under what conditions formal, perhaps
even diplomatic, relations could be established with the Soviet Union, it let itself
be guided by the same principles which in an entirely different context Pius XI
expressed on 14 May 1929 in the pointed statement: "If there would be a question
of saving a single soul, of warding off a greater harm from souls, then We would
have the courage to treat with the Devil in person." The details of these Vatican-
Soviet conversations and negotiations are knowable only in outline in the present
state of research; but the aims pursued in them by the Holy See and the reasons
for the failure can be described sufficiently clearly.

The starting point of the first attempt was the frightful famines following the
Russian civil war, which in 1921 led to extensive internationally organized acts
of assistance. Because of an Italian protest the Holy See could not take part in
these directly and had to organize its own activity, which called for contact with
Russian authorities. In this connection there appeared in Rome on 18 December
1921 a sketch signed by Pizzardo of a Vatican-Russian agreement which went far
beyond the technical problems of the distribution of charitable measures. In it
the agents to be sent by the Holy See were designated as *missionaires,* to whom
every sort of political action and propaganda was to be forbidden, but they were
allowed by treaty to set up schools and provide religious instruction. To permit
such beginnings of pastoral care and mission was an impossibility to the Bolshevik
ecclesiastical policy of the time. Accordingly, the definitive agreement, signed
at the Vatican on 12 March 1922, strictly limited the papal mission of assistance
to distributing food to the starving population and spoke of mere "agents." On
the basis of this agreement, from July 1922 to September 1924 a Vatican mission
composed of thirteen priests from various orders was active in several Russian
cities. Although the regime had on 26 February 1922 just taken a new step in the
persecution of the Church by the expropriation of liturgical vessels of the churches,
the Curia apparently tried to utilize even the slightest opportunities to counteract
the oppression and suppression of pastoral care in Russia.

This goal becomes still clearer in the second action which occurred on the
borders of the World Economic Conference of Geneva from 16 April to 19 May
1922. For the first time the new Russia had been invited again into the society of
nations. The Holy See used this as an occasion to formulate in a memorandum
addressed to the conference general conditions to which Russia should be bound
as condition of "reentry into the circle of civilized powers": full freedom of conscience, freedom of the private and public exercise of religion and worship, as
well as restoration of expropriated property to the "religious corporations." What
was important in this demarche, which the collapse of the conference deprived

from the outside of any prospects, was not least of all its universal concern: the Vatican demands affected all religious communities, not only the Christian.

In the third attempt, which was drawn out from the winter of 1923–24 to December 1927, at stake was the concrete question of what returns the Soviet Union offered if the Vatican changed the de facto into a de jure recognition. Since the Soviet Union was then very much concerned for legal recognition by the rest of the world, the presence of a papal nuncio at Moscow would have been a great Russian success. The Vatican had, apparently from tactical reasons of negotiations, brought up the question, not of a nunciature, but of merely an apostolic delegation, hence a representative without diplomatic character. The negotiations became jammed on the question of whether the Vatican conditions of 21 February 1924 should be the presuppositions for the erecting of a delegation or the subject of negotiations with the future delegate in Moscow. For unknown reasons the discussions were now transferred to Berlin and there continued by Pacelli. In February 1925 he negotiated with the Russian envoy Nikolai Krestinski about two Russian outlines — "theses" — both of which were unacceptable to the Pope, because they implied unilateral Vatican advance concessions. In place of this, Pacelli in a note of 7 September 1925 apparently designated two points as *conditio sine qua non:* appointment of bishops and freedom of religious instruction for youth within church buildings. It was only on 11 September 1926 that the Russian government replied, offering not a reciprocal agreement but a unilateral one, hence an internal right of religion revocable by the state at any time. Pacelli discussed this on 14 June 1927 with the Russian Foreign Minister Čičerin in Berlin, again unsuccessfully, because the Soviet Union would not concede religious instruction. The Pope apparently wanted now to cancel the negotiations, but was induced by the nuncio in Berlin and Gasparri to one last, clearly doubtful attempt. It is contained in a communication from Pacelli of 5 October 1927. Thereafter the Holy See would have been prepared, in the event that seminaries were opened and ecclesiastics could be sent from the Vatican, to appoint only such bishops and send only ecclesiastics who would be acceptable to the Bolshevik regime. Here it can be seen that there was a question of the absolute minimum possibility in pastoral care. But Moscow apparently rejected this too. Thereupon, on 16 December 1927 Pius XI directed that further discussions be stopped, so long as the persecution of the Churches lasted. And there things remained. The breaking off of the negotiations with the Soviet Union by the Curia in December 1927 clearly denoted the hopelessness of a situation. Basically this was the same problem that was included in Hitler's long-range goals.

Pius XI and National Socialist Germany

The Way to the Concordat with the Reich (April–July 1933).   Pius XI's foreign policy related to Hitler is marked in its first phase by the concluding of the concordat with the Reich. Next to the Lateran Treaties, it attracted contemporary attention as did no other concordat of the period between the wars. Its significance has again been much debated since the historical-political discussion in the early 1960s of the attitude of German Catholicism to Hitler's seizure of power.

The Holy See exercised no influence on Hitler's gaining of powers in the spring of 1933. The naming of Hitler as chancellor on 30 January, the Emergency Decree of 28 February, and the Reichstag elections on 5 March were never in question. A future concordat played no role in the yes of the Center on 23 March. Likewise, an exact analysis of the origin of the bishops' statement of 28 March, with which, conditionally, the prohibitions of National Socialism, lasting for years, were annulled, shows that neither the Vatican nor the Berlin nunciature had exercised any influence on it. Conversely, however, it is probably true that Hitler's declaration on 23 March of his government's friendliness toward Christianity and the Church, the subsequent yes of the Center to the Enabling Act, and the canceling of the earlier episcopal prohibitions of National Socialism on 28 May compelled the Vatican to act when the Catholic vice-chancellor, Franz von Papen, appeared on 10 April at the office of the cardinal secretary of state with the offer of concluding a concordat with the Reich and from the outset, among other items, offered in the law of education what the Curia had been unable to obtain in its negotiations since 1920 with the Weimar government.

For the Holy See there was obviously no question that it could not disregard this offer of negotiations. Pius XI had in the spring of 1933 thought for a brief time that in Hitler he could perhaps find an anti-Communist defense agent. This consideration was no longer present publicly on 19 May, when the bishop of Osnabrück visited him; he now fluctuated over the judgment of the internal German situation, in which pessimism apparently prevailed. At the end of August he condemned the persecution of Jews in Germany in very strong words as an affront "not only to morality but also to civilization."

Decisive for the Vatican's readiness for negotiations was the new dimension of danger in Germany. With the Emergency Decree of 28 February and the Enabling Act of 24 March the two "fundamental laws of the National Socialist state coming into being" (Volk) were created. Now in case of need the government could itself decide whether it intended to deviate from the constitution; this deprived the Catholic Church in Germany of all previous legal protection. Hence to a hitherto unknown degree it was "in need of a concordat"; for if the previous legal assurances were refused, it had to look for others, if possible. Thus the concordat with the Reich was understood by the Holy See as a defensive weapon from the negotiations in 1933 — in contrast to the Lateran Treaties.

The external course of the negotiations for the concordat with the Reich is not very involved. Von Papen conducted discussions in Rome from 10 to 18 April. In these was reached a preliminary draft on the part of the Church, which led on 20 April, out of consideration for changes in the Pope's wishes, to a sketch called "Kaas I." This was replaced on 11 May, not essentially altered, by the draft "Kaas II," which went both to Berlin and to the Fulda Episcopal Conference on 31 May. The desired changes of the episcopate were communicated to the government in mid-June. On 28 June Von Papen again took up his own negotiations on the Tiber, whereas he had entrusted the business of the concordat since 18 April to Prelate Ludwig Kaas, who was staying in Rome. Von Papen brought along a new text outline. From 30 June to 2 July the negotiations were in the Vatican, from 1 July including Archbishop Gröber of Freiburg. On 2 July agreement was reached on a text ready for initialing, which the Pope approved the same evening, but Hitler did not. The latter sought to gain time, then brought in the really appropriate Interior

Ministry of the Reich, and on 5 July sent the director of the ministry, Buttmann, as a new, supplementary negotiator to Rome. On 8 July, after further negotiations, the text ready for initialing was achieved and the *Reichskabinett* approved it on 14 July, so that Pacelli and von Papen could sign in the Vatican on 20 July.

The politically disruptive points during the three months of negotiations were until 1 July the depoliticization of the clergy (ARTICLE 32), then the protection of Catholic organizations (ART. 31). The German initial demand for a general prohibition of all partisan political activity by the clergy had been parried by Kaas in April by an extraordinarily clever counterproposal. It amounted, in a corresponding good conduct by the state, to promising by treaty a certain numerical reduction of the politically active pastoral clergy by canonical measures and actually meant "little more than nothing" (K. Repgen). But at the end of June the political scene in Germany had completely changed. Like the other parties, so too the Center was no more. Its dissolution was directly at hand. When this was once accomplished, ART. 32 was no longer a real concession of the Church, but on the contrary a "protection of the Church against a Nazi invasion of the clergy," as Leiber's *votum* on 29 June explicitly stated. When on 1 and 2 July the Vatican conceded ART. 32, scarcely anything was therefore really "sacrificed," but perhaps the opportunity to save Catholic organizations was seen. The concrete alternative to negotiations was narrowed to the concordat with the Reich — or renunciation of the organizations.

As early as April 1933 the German Catholic associations, in existence since the nineteenth century, and a greatly admired network of organizations strong in membership, were considered in jeopardy. True, they survived more intact during the following months than, for example, did the trade unions or the parties, since they were not exposed in the same degree to direct Nazi attacks and displayed a stronger willingness to assert themselves and to stay autonomous. But danger threatened them also from without. The sketch "Kaas I" had, therefore, envisaged a general article of protection for the Catholic societies, and then the Fulda Episcopal Conference had both expanded it and made it more concrete. On the other hand, according to the government's draft of the end of June a significant part of the doubtful organizations was to remain unprotected by concordat. This signified the worst, because it had meanwhile become apparent, through waves of political elimination of the opposition and police action, that now in Germany in this area also definitive facts were to be settled by force. The greatest part of the politically relevant Catholic associations were already dissolved or quite directly threatened by incorporation into Nazi units when the meetings at the negotiating table began in Rome.

And so, in this situation there was presented to the Holy See the basic question of whether there could be any negotiations at all. The issue was apparently decided by Gröber, the representative of the German bishops. On 1 July he saw only the alternative of allowing everything to collapse or, "at least temporarily," to recover the *status quo ante.* On 2 July he more reflectively posed the condition that the government publicly disavow its most recent police action — of 1 July — and offer guarantees for the future. This route was followed. At the moment of initialing Hitler publicly withdrew most of the measures of 1 July against the organizations and their heads and forbade a repetition. In contrast to the trade unions and the parties, therefore, the Catholic organizations continued, with some exceptions, in the summer of 1933, but of course not unassailed and also only for a while. For them the concordat with the Reich implied no concluding of peace but a pause in the struggle.

This is connected with the entangled story of the origin of ART. 31. The definitive formulation contained an unconditional guarantee for the Catholic associations which served exclusively religious and purely cultural and charitable ends (para. 1); the others enjoyed this guarantee, according to para. 2, only under definite preconditions. Paragraph 3 defined that the clarification of which societies should enjoy the protection of the concordat was to be regulated between the government of the Reich and the German episcopate. The concordat contained no explicit definition of the criteria and competence for this regulating. The fact that, nevertheless, the Holy See signed on 20 July was characterized by the competent expert in the Interior Ministry of the Reich as perhaps the "worst tactical blunder" of the Curia in the concordat. He cannot be contradicted. Immediately after the treaty took effect the state exploited the holes and claimed the decisive competence for establishing the principles and the drawing up of the protected list. The Vatican did not accept this. The (for the Church) unsuccessful struggle over the "principles of interpretation" and over the list of protected societies constituted a substantial part of Vatican-German relations after the concluding of the concordat with the Reich.

Perhaps the Church could still have settled the unresolved problems of ART. 31 if it had made ratification dependent on this. This did not occur because the German bishops at Fulda from 29 to 31 August were of the opinion "the sooner, the better." Urging this on the one hand was anxiety lest Hitler lose interest in the concordat, while on the other hand it was expected that one could make better headway with a treaty binding in law against the continuing anti-Catholic actions. The Holy See treated lightly some hesitations in regard to the desire of the German episcopate and on 10 September the ratification took place — that of the secret appendix on 2 November.

As in the case of the Lateran Treaties, the historical significance of the concordat with the Reich can be understood only if one distinguishes between short-range and long-range consequences. Incontestably Hitler gained prestige; his propaganda interpreted the signature of the cardinal secretary of state as papal legitimation of National Socialism. This was actually false, but politically inevitable. Of course, this propaganda operated in various ways. The concrete foreign policy of the other nations was hardly affected by it. "The concluding of the concordat implied very little sympathy of the Vatican for the Nazi regime in Germany," maintained the British envoy at the Vatican in retrospect at the end of the year. Equally slight was the impact on European Catholics outside Germany, somewhat stronger perhaps in Latin America, where, however, other factors were more important. More powerful was the effect on the German Catholics, even if here one must be careful of exaggeration. It was not established that by this agreement "the power of resistance of the German Catholics to a criminal regime had been broken," as was claimed on the political side in the 1950s and was repeated in the following decade by a too biased historiography. The concordat with the Reich probably offered a starting point to a series of Catholic journalists, who then came forward for the easing of tensions by the building of bridges to Nazism.

Meanwhile this small portion of German Catholics — in contrast to a not inconsiderable proportion of German Protestantism — sacrificed nothing of the content of faith, insisted on the Church's share in the right to issue rules in *res mixtae,* and furthermore claimed autonomy for the Catholic associations. Hence persons based on the illusory premise the expectation that the other side was ready for substantial restrictions of its totalitarian claim. This promise very quickly proved to be false. The Catholic attempts at bridge-building came to an end, with a few exceptions, in the winter of 1933–34 and at the latest in the summer of 1934.

On the other hand, in the short view the concordat meant a great success for the Church. The catastrophe of the Catholic associations was literally prevented at the last minute. One who stresses the negotiating blunders in ART. 31 must also emphasize this achievement. Precisely in the period immediately after the ratification the concordat with the Reich was, for the most endangered groups, an irreplaceable help in the struggle for self-assertion. In contrast to German Protestantism, the Catholic Church in Germany could at first remain for some time what it had hitherto been. This was attentively recorded on the part of ecumenism. "The position of the Roman Catholic Church in Germany was never so strong as now," wrote its probably best expert in Germany (A. Koechlin) on 30 September 1933. "It stands on its principles, which were guaranteed in the concordat. Priests are free to teach old and young in their churches what they [spacing of the author] wish without encountering the possibility of any secular interference" (Elly Heuss-Knapp).

In the long run, on the other hand, the concordat brought Hitler little, in fact no advantage at all. It did not, as was later said, get the German bishops back into line, but was, on the contrary, experienced by Hitler as an irksome fetter. Precisely for this reason he had it more and more disregarded, when and to what extent this seemed fitting to him, and this was not unexpected at the Vatican. But not all the rules were broken at once, and with the existence of the concordat the Church was given the possibility of complaining about and denouncing every violation. The concordat was an outstanding defense line — the cardinal secretary of state prophesied this in August 1933 and, now as Pope, was able to repeat it as a historical fact on 2 June 1945. For the concordat with the Reich essentially helped the Church in Germany to achieve the not self-evident accomplishment of maintaining its autonomy despite Hitler's rule to such a degree that the bishops and the clergy could proclaim the doctrine of faith and morals undiminished and administer the sacraments. That German Catholicism survived the Third Reich essentially more intact than almost all other comparable large bodies was, therefore, also a long-range effect of the agreement of 20 July 1933. It "created with its guarantees the legal basis by which resistance to totalitarianism could be and was realized" (K. Gotto).

Between the Concordat and the Encyclical Mit brennender Sorge *(1933–37).*   To maintain the administration of the sacraments and the proclamation of the faith in Germany remained, after the signing of the concordat, the chief goal of papal foreign policy. This becomes evident in the long quarrel over the "principles of interpretation" and the list of protected associations according to ART. 31. The Holy See went to great pains to make up here for the failures of July 1933. It did not succeed in this, but it contributed significantly to seeing that the concluding of agreements which would have been still more unfavorable for the Church than the situation without an agreement was prevented. At the beginning of 1935 the negotiations were practically wrecked because of Nazi intransigence, even though they were not formally declared to be ended by either party. The Ecclesiastical Ministry of the Reich, established in July 1935, in September 1935 once more asked for episcopal proposals and then conducted oral and written discussions. These were tacitly interrupted by the state in the spring of 1936. The resumption on 10 December 1936 was explicitly designated as "superfluous," because a new situation had arisen. The bishops would have been as ready in principle for further discussions, as was also the Vatican — but only to supply no pretext to the other side for easily disavowing the obligations of the concordat.

At stake in these exhausting negotiations was whether the Church could act beyond the walls of the sacristy or not. Every ecclesiastical concession extended totalitarian rule, every intransigence raised up obstacles to the Church. In this respect the question was where to draw the line — to a certain degree a problem of judgment. In general the Curia avoided letting the German bishops have a voice in this point. Its apodictic "no" to a draft agreed to in June 1934 by the episcopal delegation was an exception, scarcely to be overestimated in its importance, in which the Vatican of course knew that the affected societies in Germany were entirely behind it and with its protest strengthened their position vis-à-vis the bishops. Seen in its totality, the defense line of the Catholic societies was sought relatively far to the front, although this principle constantly encountered reductions in concrete details. For example, the Holy See consistently claimed only "partisan political" activity was forbidden to the associations, as the text of the treaty said; on the other hand, the Curia insisted on a general political right of activity for the organizations, hence on involvement with basic problems of political and social life. As a consequence the assertion of rights which the Church had negotiated for itself in the concordat created a dam against the totalitarian flood. While the Church was defending its own position with the means appropriate to it, it was at the same time a general antitotalitarian factor of importance.

On another plane a like function was performed by the thick exchange of notes of the Holy See with the German government, which began on the Vatican's initiative immediately after the ratification of the concordat. "Soul and mover" — such are the words of D. Albrecht — of this exchange of notes was the cardinal secretary of state with the intimate cooperation of the Pope. In almost wearisome repetition "again and again the brutal discrepancy" of the government "from law in accord with the concordat and activity hostile to the concordat" was brought up. In this connection Pacelli proceeded from the Church's Leonine neutrality in regard to all types of states. He used this start in order to define the moral minimal conditions which every form of state must realize, by which principles of natural law served as the rule of conduct. In statements of principle of great strength the notes registered charges against rule by force. "There is no regulation of the concordat which could oblige the Church to recognize state laws as binding on its members which were lacking in the requisite of morally obligatory state laws, that is, conformity with the divine law." A basic principle of National Socialism was sharply rejected: "Human norm is unthinkable without anchoring in the divine. This ultimate mooring cannot lie in an arbitrary 'divinity' of race. Not in the absolutizing of the nation. Such a 'God' of blood and race would be nothing other than the self-made reflection of one's own narrowness and tightness." The editor of these documents has correctly established in summary that here, on the basis of the concordat, the "painful truth was for years spoken directly into the face" of the government of the Reich, "as those could not do who would also have wanted to do, and those did not do who otherwise could have done."

On the other hand, it is objected that a real giving of witness would have demanded publicity "with ultimate personal risk," and this in fact was not the case in regard to statements of principle, but remained in the diplomatically internal official documents. In this view the goal which the notes pursued was not entirely known. They were not only diplomatic documents of a confidential nature. The most important pieces in the exchange of notes were printed by the Holy See in three issues in 1934 and 1936 as a white paper. The government of the Reich had a suspicion of this. It had to include the constantly threatening publication of these documents in its political calculations. It was still more significant that the white papers had been transmitted to the German bishops each time, and described the line of the Vatican's formation of view and will to the German episcopate; in this way they became an essentially inner-ecclesiastical instrument of government. In addition, in 1935 the contents of two very clear notes were published in *Osservatore Romano* and from there were taken into the official ecclesiastical newspapers of the German sees. This was already "publicity," if only officially. Entirely public and official was finally the encyclical *Mit brennender Sorge*. Concordat — exchange of notes — encyclical were logical steps of a uniform defensive struggle by the Church.

From the Encyclical Mit brennender Sorge *to the End of the Pontificate (1937– 39).* The encyclical *Mit brennender Sorge,* dated 14 March 1937, was read in the Catholic churches of Germany on 21 March, Palm Sunday, and was immediately distributed in print in an extensive issue. It is the best known papal document of the Catholic Church's struggle with Hitler. The German bishops had given the official impetus in the traditional letter of homage of the Fulda Episcopal Conference on 18 August 1936. Five of the bishops were invited to Rome for January 1936 to deliver a report: the three cardinals and two of the youngest: Clemens August von Galen of Münster and Konrad von Preysing of Berlin, who belonged to the "hard" wing of the Episcopal Conference. Several discussions produced unanimity to adhere to the Concordat as far as possible; although it was disputed whether a papal encyclical would jeopardize the concordat, there was agreement that such a pastoral letter was desirable. In addition, in strict secrecy Faulhaber prepared a first draft for Pacelli on 21 January 1937. Then, until 10 March, the cardinal secretary of state composed the definitive text, presumably with the collaboration of Kaas, demonstrably under the personal supervision of the Pope.

Faulhaber was an important preacher. He intended his draft as a homily. It described the most serious present dangers for the Catholic faith, proceeding first from the positive — "pure" divine faith, "pure" faith in Christ, "pure" faith in the Church, "pure" faith in the papal primacy; then, in a polemical defense against Nazi premises and methods, it warned against what would today be called "remodeling" ("no novel interpretation of holy values"). There followed an exhortation to the young as well as to the priests and the "loyal," especially the members of the associations and Catholic parents — struggle over the denominational schools.

The Faulhaber draft was a "letter for teaching and encouraging," says Volk. Pacelli added a third leitmotif. The persecution of the Catholic Church in the Third Reich was not only described by him as a fact but it was brought back to its political bases and aims. This gave the encyclical its timely sharpness. The other side, said the Pope, has "made the reinterpretation of the treaty, the undermining of the treaty, finally the more or less public violation of the treaty the unwritten law of operation." The "visual instruction of past years" reveals "machinations which from the first knew no other goal than a war of annihilation." That this war of annihilation had its cause in the irreconcilability of Catholic faith and National Socialist principles of government is worked out in copious detail. "Whoever dissociates race or the people or the state or the type of state, the executors of political power, or other basic values of the organization of the human community — which claim an essential and honorable place within the earthly order — from this secular value scale of theirs, makes them the highest norm of all, even of religious values, and deifies them with an idolatrous worship, overturns and falsities the divinely created and divinely commanded order of things." Ideas of race, the Führer principle, and totalitarianism were thus repudiated by faith. Man has "as a personality God-given rights," which "must remain immune" to any "interference on the part of the community"; in the context of school registration there was mention of the "condition of notorious absence of freedom." In contrast to *Non abbiamo bisogno,* the encyclical of 1937 is incomparably harsher. But, as in 1931, here too the Pope did not want to burn all bridges.

The impact of the encyclical can be described only in connection with its aims. The papal pastoral letter was intended as "a word of truth and of pastoral support." In groups loyal to the Church, which were amenable to the intellectual level of the encyclical, it presumably had this limiting effect to an optimal degree. In other groups, which could hardly receive the ingenious sentence structure of this text without assistance, the theoretical understanding may have been slight, but not the solidifying effect. The individual distinctions and conclusions were indeed far less important than the unprecedented fact that the Pope proclaimed publicly to the world: The Church in Germany is fighting for life and death; you German Catholics, you who are persecuted, are in the right; do not be confused; I am standing behind you.

Corresponding to the direct impact of the encyclical was the reaction of the other side, which had only learned of the imminent reading at the last minute. The Nazi leadership did not make the risky attempt to suppress the reading on 21 March in the 11,500 parish churches; instead, it exerted itself for the drastic stopping of further distribution and took up massive measures of retaliation. Of these the most spectacular was a barrage of propaganda. On 6 April Hitler ordered the immediate resumption of the trials on morals charges against Catholic religious and priests which had been halted the previous year. Thereby was inaugurated a propaganda action of unusual perfection and radical nature, the aim of which was to destroy the bonds linking the faithful to their clerical leadership. Not without a very active counterdefense by the bishops and clergy did the loyalty of German Catholics endure this ordeal.

Meanwhile, the government, taking up considerations from the period before the encyclical, prepared to give notice of denouncing the concordat. Into these plans there burst on 19 May a report which even further embittered German-Vatican relations. Because of an indiscretion of the press it was learned that the cardinal of Chicago, George William Mundelein, in the presence of five hundred priests of his diocese, had condemned the Nazi regime and had characterized Adolf Hitler as "an Austrian paperhanger, and a poor one at that." German policy made an issue of this. It let its minister at the Holy See go ostentatiously on leave and on 29 May delivered a testy note, which demanded "redress." The war of nerves against the Church was now pushed to its climax in Germany, but apparently this did not greatly impress the Vatican. Its reply of 24 June contained no apologies or weakening, but turned the tables and on its part again rejected the German policy. Furthermore, the Curia continued the war of notes in the previous form until in the summer of 1938 it was in practice called off, for reasons thus far unknown.

Berlin's plans for denouncing the concordat were put aside, unrealized, in the fall of 1937, without the relevant motives being clearly known. Presumably Hitler, as he was about to enter upon immediate preparations for his expansionist policy, desired relative peace on the domestic policy scene, in any case not an added burden because of this action.

Until the Pope's death the situation of the Church in Germany did not improve. Quite the contrary: the prohibition of youth associations and the abolition of denominational schools were now implemented by the state. At the same time there appeared areas not covered by the concordat: Austria after the *Anschluss* of 13 March 1938 and the Sudetenland from 1 October 1938. The German government refused, using legal arguments, to extend the validity of the concordat to these areas, and also rejected new agreements. The positive results of the concordat in the "Old Reich," despite serious inroads precisely in 1938 and 1939, here became well known. The Holy See, like many other powers, most of which were economically affected, did not lodge a diplomatic protest against the German Jewish pogrom in November 1938, whereas in the same days it pushed to its climax its conflict with Mussolini's "race legislation." In the long run the encyclical accomplished nothing, in so far as the actual relations thereafter became, not better, but worse.

It likewise meant no turn in the ecclesiastical battle tactics of the Fulda Episcopal Conference. Preysing and Galen apparently desired this. They felt that permanent mobilization of publicity against violations of rights was a more effective method than Bertram's previous "petition policy." The majority of the Episcopal Conference did not agree. Hence the putting to the test did not occur. The chances of such an attempt could be assessed with difficulty because it could not be said how long the episcopate, considering corresponding countermeasures of Hitler, could have kept the faithful on a permanent collision course. The Holy See did not meddle in these confrontations over the better defense tactics, although Pacelli would probably have been glad to see if Galen and Preysing were to be followed. Hence to this extent the encyclical was "not a caesura" (L. Volk).

On the other hand it incontestably produced a clarification whose long-term consequences must not be underestimated. Not only for foreign lands was it declared that the Catholic Church was in fact persecuted in Germany and that between Hitler and the Pope there existed an unbridgeable opposition: this clarification was of the utmost importance for the clergy and faithful in Germany. They found authentically marked here the route and the direction and indeed in the genuine ecclesiastical sphere of faith and morals, hence in an area in which the claim to obedient hearing was then undisputed. Exactly because the encyclical did not directly argue politically was it so demanding. The Church defended not its "influence" in the "world" but its *proprium.* No one could seriously challenge the legitimacy of this position. But by defending what was its own and by persevering in what was its own, it showed that it did not fit into Hitler's totalitarian system.

When the foreign policy of Pius XI vis-à-vis Hitler is surveyed from the beginning to his death, the absence of genuine alternatives becomes obvious. What would have happened if Hitler had not unloosed the Second World War and lost no one can positively say. Everything suggests that the Catholic Church in his sphere of rule would then have fallen into a situation without hope of escape, similar to that in Stalin's Russia.

The Second World War: Pius XII

More than in 1914 and 1922, political reasons, in addition to ecclesiastical, may have been decisive in the election of Pius XII on 2 March 1939. Anything more precise is unknown. The Second World War, which had already cast its shadows, by which it could be gauged that it would cause much greater spiritual and material damage than in 1914–18, brought the papacy far more difficult tasks than the first. This was very well known to the Pope, who had had experience in important political posts in the First World War. It was depressing for this austere observer that, despite the entirely correct insight, he could change so little in the course of things.

Most of Pacelli's contemporaries were of the opinion that he endured this ordeal magnificently. Apart from coarse Communist polemic, after 1945 a vast increase in the prestige of the Holy See was testified to by the Protestant and also by the liberal side and was referred essentially to the demonstration of the high, statesmanlike qualities of the Pope in the Second World War: "At no time since 1848 has the papacy had so good an international press as today" (K. Salvatorelli). Correspondingly it could be written at the Pope's death in 1958 that Pius XII had "brilliantly" discharged the heavy task of leading the Church through the Second World War. "In this epoch of raw force, of hatred, and of murder, the Church only gained in prestige, trust, and possibilities of effectiveness" (Leiber). Five years later a play by the hitherto unknown German poet Hochhuth, with its serious charges against Pius XII, evoked a uniquely passionate debate in the Western world, with numerous discussions, seventy-five hundred letters to editors, and so forth. The hitherto almost universal high esteem now changed in many to the opposite, even to scorn and hatred. Even a part of the literature appearing at the time and making a claim to scholarship did not hold itself far aloof from emotions, posing of problem questions, and even clear errors in method. This "Hochhuth Debate" produced for scholarship a substantial profit to the extent that the Holy See at the turn of the years 1964–65 gave to a group of internationally recognized historians of the Society of Jesus the task of publishing its acts and documents for the history of the Second World War. Research then had firm ground under its feet.

As with Benedict XV, the foreign policy of Pius XII is summarized from three points of view: neutrality — exertions for peace — humanitarian measures of assistance. To these is added as a fourth the problem of his "silence."

Neutrality

The reasons which had persuaded Benedict XV to opt for neutrality persisted in the Second World War. Two more were added. One was founded in Pacelli's personality. Pius XII, whom a bon mot characterized as the complete "diplomate de l'ancien régime," was by background, nature, self-evaluation, and experience an outspoken man of peace — but not at the cost of evil compromise. International law provided the other reason. In the Lateran Treaty the Holy See had assumed the obligation of holding itself aloof from the properly political problems of international politics (ARTICLE 24). This principle was, however, limited by two provisos: first, the Pope reserved the right to mediate peace in the event that both parties requested it, and, second, it had reserved the right to vindicate the moral and the ideal in every case. Tradition, circumstances, and legal situation converged in the Holy See's neutrality.

For this neutrality Pius XII, who was accustomed to think and to speak in very distinct ways, preferred the term "impartiality." In this manner the political facts should be removed from the moral circumstances. "Neutrality," Pius XII declared to the cardinal of Munich, "could be understood in the sense of a passive indifference," which in a period of war such as this "was unbecoming" to the head of the Church. "Impartiality means for us judgment of things in accord with truth and justice," by which, however, in public announcements he granted "to the situation of the Church in the individual countries every possible consideration in order to spare the Catholics there hardships that could be avoided." In other respects, like his predecessor Benedict XV, he declared: The Church "does not have the function of intervening and taking sides in purely earthly affairs. She is a mother. Do not ask a mother to favor or to oppose the part of one or the other of her children."

The consequences of such a neutrality were observed by Pius XII "almost rigoristically," according to J. Becker. It was certainly his view even before 1944 that a war of aggression is not a morally and legally legitimate means of politics. With regard to his obligations of international law, before the outbreak of the war and during the war he refrained with difficulty from any explicit condemnation of many acts of aggression on the part of Germany, Italy, the Soviet Union, the Allies, and Japan, and made only a much pondered exception in regard to the Benelux countries on 10 May 1940. He was likewise careful to see that the Vatican did not become entangled in any crusade propaganda of one of the warring sides — neither from 1939 to 1941 against Hitler and Stalin nor, from 1941, when both the anti-Communist and the anti-Nazi crusade would have liked to appeal to a papal support. Even the term "communism" disappeared from the vocabulary of the Holy See, and the idea of "West" was pretty much avoided from this period. The maintaining of such an impartiality was very much more difficult in comparison to the First World War. It required "almost superhuman exertions" in order "to keep" the Holy See "above the strife of parties," the Pope confided to the archbishop of Cologne. In this connection the integrity of the Vatican State represented the lesser, even if not a slight, problem.

The Lateran Treaty had guaranteed to the Holy See perfect independence and the possibility of communication with the rest of the world even in the event of a renewed state of war in Italy. These contractual decisions were not fully observed, but still, by and large, certain limits of flagrant violations of rights were not exceeded. The actual state of affairs depended on the general situation. Since Italy did not enter the war until 10 June 1940, the Vatican had to put up with relatively few restrictions until the beginning of the German campaign against France on 10 May 1940. Now matters underwent a change. Not only did measures such as blackouts and various other war-economy restrictions have to observed; Italy exerted strong pressures for the limiting of the Vatican's propaganda possibilities. The possibilities of communications by press (*Osservatore Romano*) and radio (*Radio Vaticana*) were thereupon curtailed; from the end of April 1941 *Radio Vaticana* discontinued its broadcasts on the status of the Church in Germany. On the other hand, direct diplomatic contact with the powers hostile to Italy was maintained even after June 1940. When, contrary to the treaty, Mussolini withdrew their extraterritoriality, the Pope did not have them withdraw, as in 1915, to Switzerland, but gave them cramped quarters in the Vatican State, where finally a dozen representatives were lodged. Their contact with the Curia was thereby facilitated, and they were not entirely cut off from their governments; there remained radio communication and the possibilities of travel. Roosevelt's deputy, Myron C. Taylor, went to Rome seven times for brief and long stays up to 1944; the English representative, Osborne, was able to journey to London and back for some time in the spring of 1943, and Archbishop Spellman of New York spent a few days in Rome. Conversely, in 1944, when Rome obtained an Allied garrison, the Holy See sheltered the diplomatic representatives of Germany, Japan, Hungary, and so forth. True, their possibilities of working were limited, but they were preserved in substance.

Hence during the entire Second World War the central authority in the Universal Church could continue to operate essentially intact and keep contact with its nuncios and the episcopate to the extent that this was not regionally and locally restricted and paralyzed, especially in the areas under German and Russian rule. This was not self-evident. From the spring of 1941 the Curia reckoned with the possibility of a German occupation of Vatican City and the forcible withdrawal of the Pope; it made preparations in case the central authority should no longer be capable of functioning. These measures reached their climax before and after the fall of Mussolini on 25 July 1943, which was followed on 8 September by the occupation of Rome by German troops and police. Then the foreign diplomats at the Vatican burned their papers; the Pope had a part of his documents hidden in his palace, and microfilm photographs of others sent to Washington in order to save them. The extraterritoriality of the Holy See was violated in December 1943 and February 1944 by police raids on political and racial refugees in papal buildings outside Vatican City. But the Vatican state remained outside Hitler's direct clutches. The reasons for this are not evident. But it is indisputable that the Pope and his collaborators had to take this possibility into consideration on the basis of their information since 1941, and they were delivered from this anxiety only by the Allied occupation of Rome on 5 June 1944, although many restrictions and limitations were still protracted beyond the war.

Also the considerable, altogether rather successful exertions of papal policy to keep Rome as a city out of the events of the war were not only conditioned by humanitarian reasons; at the same time they aimed at preserving the neutral independence of the papacy, not only for reasons of international law but still more from ecclesiastical motives. To the Pope belonged as a principal task of his office, in accord with the Church's understanding of itself, the preservation of the Church's unity. This presupposed unconditional loyalty of all Catholics, behind whichever warring front they stood, to the common Supreme Head of the Church, which could only be maintained if people knew that the Pope's independence guaranteed his impartiality. If Rome were involved in the direct action of the war, it was not to be expected that the Vatican's walls would thereafter protect its independence. Hence, as he himself wrote to the bishop of Berlin, the "further involvement of Rome in the war intensified to the intolerable" the excessive dangers to Church unity. This trial was spared the Church. Just as Benedict XV, Pius XII was therefore able to carry out a humanitarian, charitable activity and promote peace initiatives. In these two fields much was attempted but much or little was achieved in different ways.

Efforts for Peace

The Pope's exertions for peace began immediately after his election and were continued to the end of the war with undiminished readiness. They took place on two different planes, in the area of teaching and in that of practical politics. In both fields the difference between the pontificates of Benedict XV and Pius XII became obvious.

Benedict XV developed no real doctrine of peace, no coherent system of detailed expressions on theoretical bases and aims, on practical assumptions and possibilities of a domestic and international order of peace. He had been content to admonish abstractly to peace in his public statements and put the rest aside for negotiations which should lead to a compromise. It was different with his successor in the Second World War. Already his first public announcement as Pope on 3 March 1939 contained the keywords of a universal program for peace. He again took up these points in his Easter homily of 1939, further pursued it in his first encyclical, *Summi Pontificatus* (20 October 1939), and put it in the center of his Christmas address of 1939, in which the five basic conditions of a lasting international peace were discussed. All subsequent Christmas addresses, which were likewise planned with a view to the greatest possible publicity, treated pretty much in detail, and sometimes exclusively, problems of the ethics of peace — in 1940 the moral assumptions of a peaceful international order; in 1941 the bases of a new international order; in 1942 the basic elements of national and international community life; in 1943 the moral presuppositions for a world peace among victors and vanquished; in 1944 the bases of a true democracy; in 1945 the Universal

Church and universal peace. On other public occasions, especially regularly on 2 June, he constantly returned to it.

The Pope's concern was to develop the conditions, not for just any peace, but for a just and hence lasting peace. On the basis of natural law he displayed the ideal of an international order which should guarantee security and existence equally to all nations and national minorities, as the personal dignity of the individual human being demanded. His view was not restricted to the legal but was directed to the economic order — distribution of wealth — and to society. Special attention was applied to the problems of disarmament. Decisively but also prudently were treated the bases of the law of treaties, by which treaties were to be maintained or, if necessary, to be revised — a recalling of the Treaty of Versailles. Not least, the creating of supranational institutions with real competence was indispensable.

These instructive discussions by the Pope, in which actual everyday cases and principles were blended, clearly had a threefold aim. In the rather long run, material should here be circulated which would be further debated by the Church's social doctrine, by practical philosophy, and by the juristic disciplines. Thereby Pius XII intended to provide guiding principles to the political thought of the faithful and at the same time influence concrete political decisions to the degree this should be possible. The fact that between his concepts and the peace aims of Hitler or Stalin there ran insurmountable abysses was beside the point. But there were also important differences and contradictions relative to the guiding ideas of the Western democracies. While he had little influence on the postwar planning of the victorious powers, he did perhaps on the political development after 1945. To this degree it was not in vain.

On the other hand, with his exertions to prevent the outbreak of war and then Italy's entry into it and thereafter to bring about the ending of the conflict, Pius XII had as little success as Benedict XV, although the experience of 1914–18 must have been constantly present to the Pope, and he strove to avoid the mistakes of that period.

Three actions before the outbreak of the war must be mentioned: First, at the beginning of May 1939, probings for a five-power conference for discussion and regulation of the present German-Polish and French-Italian oppositions. They found rejection among all those addressed and were canceled on 10 May. Next, in close agreement with the English government, an extremely urgently formulated public appeal to reason and negotiation was presented on the evening of 24 August. The essential statement came from a preliminary draft by the future Pope Paul VI and read: "Nothing is lost with peace. All can be lost with war." Finally, on 30 August, there was the desperate attempt to gain Poland at the last minute for concessions to Germany, which originated with Mussolini and was supported by England, as well as, on 31 August, a plea to the powers for a just and peaceful solution of the conflict. In a declaration personally originating with the Pope, *Osservatore Romano* on 13 September 1939 remarked that the Holy See had "exhausted all possibilities which" had offered "in any way still some hope for the preservation of peace or at least the excluding of the immediate danger of war." This view was shared by the British government. The collapse of the papal efforts for maintaining peace was mostly caused by the policy of Hitler, who was unimpressed by reasonable motives in the framework of a possible revision of the Treaty of Versailles. Polish intransigence in August 1939 made the German dictator's game easier.

Meanwhile, on 1 September 1939 Italy proclaimed itself "not at war." The Curia had gone to great pains to nail Mussolini down to this and for this purpose assured itself of the support of Roosevelt, who at Christmas 1939 had entered into diplomatic relations with the Pope. The Vatican's internal demarches, strengthened by spectacular public happenings — on 21 December the visit of the King of Italy to the Pope; on 28 December, the return visit of the Pope to the King; on 5 May 1940, the Pope's homily at Santa Maria sopra Minerva — and a personal letter from the Pope to Mussolini on 24 April 1940 were unable to keep the Italian dictator aloof from the suggestion which the victorious march of the German armies in France exercised in the way of anticipation. Italy's declaration of war on 10 June 1940 confirmed the dread that had been pervading the Vatican for months.

Immediately after the French armistice of 25 June 1940 the Pope formally made preliminary soundings in England, Germany, and Italy in regard to possible negotiations for a "just and honorable peace." Behind these stood the wish at least to preserve England intact, before it could be overrun by a German invasion, as a European counterweight to German hegemony. When this preliminary probing found consent in none of those concerned, the diplomatic possibilities of the Vatican were at first exhausted. Whether in May and June 1940 the West had lost only a battle, as Churchill and de Gaulle said, or the war, as Mussolini felt, or whether this question could not yet be answered, as presumably Pétain and Franco thought, was unclear. How the Pope evaluated the views cannot be known in detail, because on that point there are hardly any sources. The editors of the papal acts warn, not by chance, that one must be cautious with judgments concerning the secret considerations of the Pope. In the period between the end of the war in France and the beginning of the war in Russia he presumably placed his hopes rather on a change in domestic politics in Germany than on a military victory of England over Hitler.

With the German attack on Russia on 22 June 1941 and the Japanese attack on the United States on 7 December 1941, the acts of war expanded into a global world war. At first there were no diplomatic possibilities of peace. Politically significant was a papal decision in September 1941 which, giving a theologically not unproblematic interpretation to Pius XI's communism encyclical *Divini Redemptoris* of 19 March 1937, made it possible to overcome the hesitations of conscience of North American Catholics in regard to military support of the Soviet Union. The Curia did not share the illusions in regard to Russian policy which underlay later American planning for peace. Neither Hitler nor Stalin could be peaceable, satisfied members of the European family of nations. In the smaller states, situated diagonally along the war fronts, people shared the Curia's anxieties since the German defeat at Stalingrad in the winter of 1942–43 and would have been glad to steer toward a compromise peace under papal mediation before Russia became overmighty. The Secretariat of State saw no concrete hopes for this in the spring of 1943 and had to be content with opposing Allied appeasement in regard to Russia with the facts known to it and the cares derived therefrom, which were proved later to be correct. This did not mean relying instead on Hitler's Germany, which since 22 June 1942 rejected the Holy See as a partner in discussions and negotiations for the area outside the "Old Reich," after it had not recognized the German annexations as definitive. Apart from other weighty reasons, such an attitude was forbidden as a result of the persecution of the Catholic Church in Hitler's entire sphere of dominion, worst of all in Poland. Only if the Second World War eliminated both dangers could the future Europe find peace. If either of them survives the war, "a peaceful and ordered coexistence of European nations" would be "impossible," and in the not distant future a new, still worse war would be faced.

The Vatican could not translate this insight into direct foreign policy because it lacked the means for putting it into effect and the preserving of the principle of impartiality and noninterference in domestic political problems became ever more difficult. This also determined the attitude of the Holy See toward Italy. It was able to avoid becoming involved in the preparations for the fall of Mussolini, who on 12 May 1943 completely shut his eyes to a very clear papal hint. The Holy See participated only on the periphery in the negotiating of the Allied armistice with Italy.

It is all the more astounding to "assess the extraordinary readiness of the Pope to incur risks" as J. Becker expresses it; in the winter of 1939 he was in intimate contact with the German military opposition, whose ideas he sent on to England, and functioned as connecting link. In 1944 also he still had contacts with this part of the German opposition. Perhaps toward the turn of the years 1943–44 the Pope's expectation was based on this, that perhaps "after not too long a time" the responsible statesmen would listen to the peace proposal of his 1943 Christmas address, "which then, God willing, would grow into a peace mediation." This did not happen, for the opposition was unable to topple Hitler. But "another Germany" was a presupposition that could not be waived for a realization of the papal peace idea by means of concrete politics in the last years of the war, although the individual details for 1944–45 are still secret until the publication of the acts of this period.

Papal Measures of Assistance

The cruelties of the Second World War, not restricted to the military conduct of the war, by far surpassed the horizon of ideas originating in 1914–18. The Pope understood this as a challenge, which must not be evaded. The question was not *whether* one should help, but *how* one could. In this regard, no role was played, as also under Benedict XV, by the religious, ethnic, or national background of those concerned, and the Vatican began, it goes without saying, from its experiences with the organization of measures of help of the First World War. However, there appeared entirely new forms and types of needs of gigantic proportions, in regard to which nothing could be achieved with the hitherto customary means. Time after time this forced an effort to achieve something in new and different ways. There was no lack of readiness to assist. But there survived an oppressive difference between being willing and being able as an historical experience from this epoch, in which aid for the politically and racially persecuted became necessary as a new problem for the Western world; for it there were no regulations of international law and no precedent by which to orient oneself.

The territorial war order of The Hague of 18 October 1907, supplemented in the Geneva Agreement on 29 July 1929, had fixed clear norms for the treatment of prisoners of war and had entrusted the implementation to the International Red Cross, but this did not exclude supplementary actions of other institutions. As in the First World War, from the start the Vatican would have gladly participated in the search for the missing and in the transmission of news about prisoners of war and civilian internees to their families. Under the responsibility of the later Pope Paul VI, who was then *Sostituto,* an "information bureau" was set up in Section II of the Secretariat of State in 1939. However, its possibilities of action were limited; for Germany and Russia refused and thwarted all cooperation. And so the "information bureau" had to limit its activity to the prisoners of states allied with Germany, which observed the traditional rules of war — Italy, Slovakia, Hungary, Rumania — and also, even though here not continuously accepted, of the Western Allies and Japan. Corresponding to the course of the war, it developed its chief activity, whose happy impact on those affected can scarcely be overestimated, after 1943.

Furthermore, there was erected in November 1941, likewise under Montini's responsibility, an "Assistance Commission" within Section II of the Secretariat of State. It was competent for the properly charitable measures, and this forced it to ever new improvisation and work techniques. In other respects, the entire well-coordinated apparatus, which the Curia and especially the Secretariat of State displayed, was requisitioned for these measures of assistance, so far as they were appropriate in individual cases. The documents published in recent years, for the period to the end of 1943, make it impressively clear that a very considerable part of the diplomatic activities of the Vatican in the Second World War, despite all the daily failures, was unflinchingly put at the selfless service of these charitable exertions. The Pope intentionally insisted on it as little as possible from without, because in most cases — in contrast, for example, to the present-day possibilities of effectiveness by Amnesty International — publicity impaired or even destroyed the chances of success. This affected especially those most in need of help — the Jews. If in the official sphere of activity of the Holy See for 1939 there was still mention of Vatican aid for "persons" who "were regarded as racially non-Aryan and hence were punished by laws of certain nations," this ceased for the succeeding years, after the German ambassador at the Vatican had called Berlin's attention to it in January 1940. The more Hitler's murderous grip closed on the Jews, the more laconic became the particulars from the Secretariat of State. "The Holy See did, does, and will do all that is within its power" was the stereotyped information from the Secretariat of State. This was not an alibi for indifference or inactivity but the indispensable presupposition for the efforts, renewed every day and perseveringly undertaken, to bring help whenever even only the slightest opportunities presented themselves. The number of cases is legion. Here only some outlines can be indicated.

The attempts to help the politically and racially persecuted in Germany and Italy went back to the days of Pius XI. They were continued under the new Pope. Once there was a question of not quite one thousand individual cases. In addition, help for those wishing to emigrate required great pains, in which the German *Sankt Raphaelsverein* in Hamburg played a substantial role until its forcible dissolution on 26 June 1941. Not least of all, there was a question of the effort to impede the "racial" legislation of states in the German sphere of influence or, if that was not possible, to effect modifications in the practical enforcement. In Germany, of course, influence was without prospects, but not in Italy. The presence of the Holy See contributed to the fact that the Italian Jewish policy throughout the war was in very favorable contrast to the German: up to his downfall, Mussolini did not release any Jews for deportation to the extermination camps of the S.S., and the Social Republic of Salò, to the extent that it could function, preserved this orientation in principle. In Rumania, supported by the stipulations of the concordat, relatively much was accomplished; Hungary, despite racial legislation, treated the Jews the least inhumanely; in Slovakia the Vatican chargé d'affaires had at first to limit himself to observing. The curial policy had especially in view the situation of baptized Jews or of Jews married to Catholics, since they were the farthest excluded from the aid given by the organizations of believing Jews.

After the outbreak of war the worst fate first affected the Poles, not only in the German-occupied area: in the Russian-occupied part the situation was scarcely less horrible. However, this area was almost hermetically sealed off from the rest of the world. News hardly got through, and Vatican help was completely impossible. The Curia did not succeed in learning anything substantial of the fate of those deported from there — one reckons with about 2 million — not even with the aid of the diplomatic representatives of other powers in Moscow.

In spite of ceaseless difficulties, the intelligence connections with the German-occupied part of Poland were better. In the winter of 1939–40 the Curia hoped to be able to help with food and clothing; but at the end of 1940 the Secretariat of State had to admit that the German authorities had intentionally and successfully boycotted the papal initiatives. Matters were otherwise in relation to the Polish refugees in other countries. In Hungary, Rumania, France, and Italy the Vatican, with the financial aid of American Catholics, could at first do something, but in Germany, on the contrary, it could do little. Even in Spain, basically amenable to Vatican requests, it required very much effort and patience to assist the Polish refugees.

The year 1941, in which the war essentially altered its countenance, also signified a caesura for the assistance measures of the Holy See. The restricted possibilities of emigration from Europe almost entirely ceased. Vatican exertions for aid from overseas for the hungry civilian populations of Belgium and Greece were wrecked on the English blockade. "Deportation" of Jews now became a new catchword of papal anxieties. To prevent it or at least to limit and restrict its volume became a chief item of papal assistance efforts, even where there was still no information on the mass-produced organized murders in the extermination camps.

In the present state of knowledge what was thereby accomplished cannot be put in precise figures, and in consideration of the situation of the sources will perhaps never be possible. One may proceed, in regard to a total number of victims, to a high of about 5 million. In addition, some nine hundred fifty thousand are said to have survived. The individual numbers from which this total sum is arrived at may be open to criticism, but hardly the order of magnitude. If it is estimated that, of the nine hundred fifty thousand saved, some 70 to 90 percent owed their life to measures taken by the Catholic Church, as the specific numbers are also subject to discussion in this case, on the whole, however, this result must be striking. In view of the number of murdered, the number of the saved is depressingly small. But behind it stands a desire of the Catholic Church under Pius XII to stand up for every individual human life, which cannot be minimized.

In individual cases the measures differed from country to country and also changed in the course of time. On the whole it can be said that the success of the papal rescue exertions was the greater the more the political influence of the Holy See continued on the government of the territory concerned; in other words: the less direct the possibilities of Hitler's grasp were, so much the more could the Pope accomplish. In Slovakia, Hungary, Rumania, Croatia, and especially in Italy relatively much succeeded.

In summary, today it may be held that the papal measures of assistance of the Second World War, accomplished under entirely different difficulties, need not at all fear comparison with the time of Benedict XV.

The Pope's "Silence"

In the debate of the 1960s over the Pope's conduct in the Second World War there was a question of his alleged silence at the extermination of millions of Jews. In this connection the expression "silence" was supposed to suggest a reprehensible omission of possible and/or necessary actions, while the opposite — "to speak, "to say," "to protest" — referred to morally mandated sympathy, signified willingness to help, or even stood symbolically for "help." This terminology is not suited to characterize the real problem to which the Hochhuth debate, in which the picture of Pius XII was distorted into caricature, can point: It is the question in what manner a Pope is bound, by virtue of his office, to bear witness against the violation of elementary human rights, such as the genocide of the Second World War. This question was itself posed at that time; he was confronted with it by others as well; and even in war he knew it had to be settled "with painful difficulty." The decisions of the Pope were taken neither blindly nor easily, but were pondered responsibly. For him the alternatives were not simply "to speak or keep silent." The question amounted to much more: how clear *must* be the word which was offered by virtue of office, how concrete *may* it be if the consequences are taken into account.

It was a curial tradition to speak, not of the erring, but of the errors, not of people, but of the mistakes of people. Pacelli's theological conception was in accord with this tradition. It amounted to this, that the Pope had to formulate the general and the fundamental, while it pertained to the bishops to translate the principle into the concrete, on the spot, with regard for all circumstances. This suggested to the Pope to condemn the false ideological directions and the violations of rights without "directly naming their proponents or perpetrators," according to J. Becker. This was the line which Pius XII followed in his many public utterances — every expression about peace was linked with these themes.

How strong his anxiety was about whether in view of the unleashed terror he was satisfying the duties of office by this behavior can be known from that fact that he several times clearly considered proceeding beyond the general condemnations. I must utter real "words of fire" on "the frightful things which are occurring in Poland," he hurled at the Italian ambassador on 13 May 1940. Only the knowledge that the fate of the unhappy Poles would then become still worse held him back from doing so. The intention of preventing worse was "one of the reasons why

We impose restrictions on Ourselves in Our utterances," he wrote to the bishop of Berlin on 30 April 1943. The Pope and his collaborators were, on the basis of their experiences with National Socialism, firmly convinced that a flaming papal protest would not put a stop to the murders but would increase their tempo and magnitude and at the same time destroy the remaining possibilities of diplomatic action in favor of the Jews in states such as Hungary and Rumania.

In this regard, the Secretariat of State was informed relatively early of the manner in which the murder of the Jews was organized and, in contrast to many others, trusted these reports. Communications from Jewish sources that the deportation meant for many of those affected a sure death sentence were obtained from Pressburg and Budapest in the spring of 1942. In December the Polish ambassador-in-exile at the Vatican correctly concluded from the fact that the aged, sick, women, and children were deported that the aim of deportation was not "workers' camps" — whatever persons might mean by that — but places erected especially for the "killing of persons in various ways." On 7 March 1943 the Vatican chargé d'affaires at Pressburg finally sent the report of a parish priest, who had credibly learned that deported Jews were killed by gassing; the corpses were used for making soap. Perhaps this report was already on hand when the Secretariat of State on 3 April 1943 laconically telegraphed to the apostolic delegate in Washington: "The Holy See continues its exertions for the Jews," after the delegate had been asked by three rabbis to induce the Pope to a "public appeal" which might put a halt to the systematic extermination of the Jews. Privately the Secretariat of State thought of this: "A public appeal would be inappropriate"; Germany had to be prevented from taking it as an occasion "to carry out even more rigorously the anti-Jewish measures in the areas occupied by it and exercise new, stronger pressures" on the Jewish policy of the satellite nations. On 5 May 1943 an entry in the documents of the Secretariat of State spoke of the "frightful situation" of the Jews in Poland and mentioned "gas chambers."

Against this background must be understood the sharp and impressively composed Christmas address of 1942, which proclaimed a catalogue of the inalienable basic rights of every person and thought explicitly of the "hundred thousands of persons," who, "with no guilt of their own, partly only because of their nationality or race" were delivered up "to quick or slow death." Privately the Pope thus characterized the purpose and reaction of this word on the extermination of the Jews: "It was brief but it was well understood." In the address of 2 June 1943 he repeated his condemnation with a quite similar formulation.

Hence the Pope also "spoke," but the "speaking" was not his chief or exclusive means in the struggle against Hitler's Jewish policy. After clear condemnation he followed the ethical demand of conscience, but predominant for him was the ethically responsible aspect that he must avoid choosing a form of provocation which would not bring a halt to *the* evil but would increase the evils: The extermination of the Jews could not be undone by a public appeal, but perhaps drastic retaliation against Jews, Catholics, and the Church lay in the logic of the Nazi system of government. Conversely, the papal policy preserved for the Holy See the opportunity to save the Jews in the future. As proof that this opportunity was effectively used, "the warmest recognition of his saving work" was at the time "expressed by the Jewish chief centers" to the Pope.

CHAPTER 86

The Second Vatican Council

John XXIII: Summoning and Preparation for the Council

The convoking of the Second Vatican Council was the action of Pope John XXIII. His election, after a brief conclave (25–28 October 1958), seemed at first the solution of a transition or at least of a perplexity. But it soon became evident that it was a decisive turning point in the history of the Church.

Angelo Giuseppe Roncalli was born in Sotto il Monte (Province of Bergamo) on 25 November 1881, the fourth of fourteen children of the farmer Battista (d. 1935) and his wife Marianna Mazzola (d. 1939), and was baptized the same day by the parish priest Rebuzzini; his godfather was his devout great-uncle Zaverio. After attending the minor and the major seminaries at Bergamo from 1892 to 1900, he continued his theological studies at the Roman Seminary of Sant'Apollinare from 1901 to 1905, interrupted by one year of military service at Bergamo, "un vero purgatorio," as he wrote to the rector of the seminary, V. Bugarini. From his professor of church history, Benigni, he received the advice, "Read little but well"; of his superiors, the vice-rector Spolverini was closest to him. His Roman studies were crowned by the doctorate in theology on 13 July 1904 and ordination to the priesthood on 10 August 1904. After the completing of his studies, he participated in the fall of 1905 in a pilgrimage to the Holy Land. Then Giacomo Maria Radini Tedeschi, appointed bishop of Bergamo, took him along as secretary to his home diocese of Bergamo, where from October 1906 he also lectured on church history in the seminary and later on patrology and apologetics and edited the ecclesiastical journal. *La vita diocesana.* At that time he began the editing of the visitation documents of Saint Charles Borromeo in the diocese of Bergamo, the last volume of which could, however, not appear until 1957.

After the death in 1914 of Radini Tedeschi, who as no other had formed his first priestly years, he wrote his biography. During the war (1915–18) he served as a military chaplain; it was probably the experiences then gained which induced the bishop to entrust to him, as chaplain of the seminary, the spiritual direction of the theologians returning from the field (1918–20). Then he went back to Rome for four years as president of the Italian work of the Propagation of the Faith. On 3 March 1925 he became apostolic visitor in Bulgaria and on 19 March was ordained as titular archbishop of Areopolis in San Carlo al Corso; as his motto he selected "Obedientia et Pax," Baronius's motto.

The position of the visitor at Sofia was in several respects not easy: the Queen was a daughter of the King of Italy, and hence a Catholic; the King was Greek Orthodox; the authority of the visitor over the approximately fifty thousand Catholics was not sharply defined. He saw himself reduced to an eremitical life, which did not gratify his need for activity, and he complained of "acute, intime sofferenze." After ten difficult years he was, on 24 November 1934, named apostolic delegate in Turkey and Greece and at the same time administrator of the vicariate apostolic of Istanbul; he thereby obtained greater pastoral duties. The delegate paid a visit to the ecumenical patriarch on 27 May 1939, spent a rather long time at Athens, especially after Greece was afflicted by war, and visited Syria and Palestine.

When, after the retreat of the German troops from France and the victory of the Allies, General de Gaulle demanded the removal of thirty-three bishops who had been adherents of the Vichy regime, Roncalli was made nuncio to France on 22 December 1944. He achieved a compromise. After the concluding of the armistice he instituted at Chartres theological courses for German theological students who were prisoners of war. Made cardinal on 12 January 1953 and three days later named patriarch of Venice, he felt fortunate to be able to live completely his episcopal-pastoral duties. The small area of the diocese permitted him frequent journeys, including visits to the Marian pilgrimage sites of Lourdes, Einsiedeln, Mariazell, Fátima, and Czestochowa.

The new Pope's personality was stamped by his ancestral home and his spiritual instructors, Rebuzzini, Spolverini, and Radini Tedeschi; his spirituality was thoroughly traditionally Catholic. His spiritual diary indicates that he frequently read *The Imitation of Christ* and regularly made the Ignatian exercises. The rosary was a fixed ingredient of his strictly regulated order of the day: praying of the breviary, Mass, a half-hour's meditation, weekly confession. His spiritual models were Francis de Sales and Philip Neri and, as a pastor, Charles Borromeo: as regards the otherwise highly venerated Baronius, it struck him that he never laughed. The craftiness of the peasant was in him united to the humor of the peasant; of no Pope since Benedict XIV have so many anecdotes been handed down. The young professor of church history unambiguously held himself aloof from modernism, but he still did not thereby escape the suspicion expressed concerning him in the Benigni circle and remained convinced that positive theology must be more intensively pursued than was then usual in Italy. Different from that of Pius X, whom he revered in his lifetime as a model pastor, his outlook for the task of the mission and for union was broadened by activity in the work of the propagation of the faith and the two decades in the Middle East. The other task of the Church, to work for a "better world," was for him not an item of a program but a foregone conclusion resulting from his simple origin. "I am one of you," he exclaimed to the faithful of a Roman suburban community; to his brothers and sisters he gave the advice, "You do well in living even more frugally," and he himself wanted "to be born poor and to die poor." Throughout his life bound to his Bergamo homeland, as nuncio he obtained the family's original fifteenth-century house as a place of holiday and rest.

Although in his youth Pope John had lived at Rome a rather long time and had then been active in the service of the Curia for almost three decades, he was no "curialist." He never regarded himself as a curial official, and constantly desired to be only a "good shepherd"; it was no accident that in the first year of his pontificate, on 1 August 1959, he devoted an encyclical to the Curé d'Ars, to him the "imago sacerdotis." As a church historian, familiar with the historical change of the Church in a constantly changing world, Pope John was convinced that the Church must adapt its preaching, organization, and pastoral methods to the fundamentally changed world, and for this he coined the much disputed notion of *aggiornamento.* In an effort to realize it, he convoked the Council.

In the presence of the cardinals gathered for the stational Mass in San Paolo fuori le mura on 25 January 1959 he announced a Roman diocesan synod and an ecumenical council. This announcement was certainly prepared for by his development, but in no sense was its result. Both in private conversations and in the opening address of the Roman diocesan synod on 24 January 1960 he understood it as the challenge of God, *divinum incitamentum,* but in no way was it the implementation of a long-prepared plan.

The announcement of an ecumenical council operated as a blare of trumpets, within and almost even more powerfully outside the Church. It was forgotten that, in Catholic usage and also in canon law, "Concilium oecumenicum" was the designation of the general councils embracing the whole Church; the Pope intended to convoke a general council of the Catholic Church, but from the start, and at the beginning more decidedly than in later stages, there moved before his view a participation, somehow constituted, of the Christians separated from Rome as a first step toward Church unity; he could hardly have been thinking of a great union-council of representatives of all Christian Churches and ecclesial communities. That there was no thought of a formal invitation to the separated Churches to full participation first appeared definitively from a press conference held by Cardinal Secretary of State Tardini on 30 October 1959; in it there came forth for the first time the plan of inviting the separated Churches to send official observers.

Meanwhile, the Pope had set for the future council its task of renewal within the Church. In the first session of the Antepreparatory Commission, established on 17 May 1959, he declared on 30 June 1959 that the Church strives, "loyal to the holy principles on which it is built and the unchangeable doctrine which the Divine Founder entrusted to it . . . with courageous energy to strengthen again its life and its unity, even with regard to all circumstances and demands of the day," hence both inner renewal and entry into the problems of the age. At the same time he announced in the encyclical *Ad Petri cathedram* the revision of canon law; the goal of his pontificate was the proclaiming of the truth, peace among peoples, and the unity of the Church in doctrine, government, and worship.

The preparation of the council began when the bishops — all together 2,594 — and 156 superiors of religious institutes and also the Catholic universities and faculties were called upon by Secretary of State Tardini on 18 June 1959 to submit suggestions for the program of consultation. The 2,812 *postulate* thereupon sent in were sifted by the Antepreparatory Commission and turned over to the competent curial offices, which for their part composed the suggestions and admonitions. After the sifting of the material was completed, the motu proprio *Superno Dei nutu* of 5 June 1960 introduced the proximate preparation.

The motu proprio determined for the first time the name of the future council: The Second Vatican Council. Then ten "preparatory commissions" were formed to work out the draft of decrees to be laid before the council. Nine of these were modeled, in accord with their defined purpose, but also in organization, on existing central offices of the Roman Curia: the Theological Commission was competent for all questions of the teaching office, which pertained to the competence of the Holy Office; the Commission for the Bishops and the Government of Dioceses corresponded to the Consistorial Congregation; the Commission for the Discipline of the Clergy and the Christian People, to the Congregation of the Council. The Commissions for the Discipline of the Sacraments, (ecclesiastical) Studies and

Seminaries, the Sacred Liturgy, the Eastern Churches, and the Missions received essentially the same tasks as the corresponding central offices, whose heads were at the same time the chairmen of the related commissions. Only the Commission for the Apostolate of the Laity was not modeled on any congregation, because none such existed.

If these preparatory commissions are compared with the five of the First Vatican Council, important differences appear: through their chairmen and their composition they were more closely bound than the earlier ones with the central offices in which the tradition of the Curia is incarnate; they were not composed, like the earlier ones, almost exclusively of theologians and canonists, that is, *periti* who had no right to vote in the council, but included up to about one-half bishops and religious superiors, hence future council fathers with a right to vote. The first measure subjected the preparatory commissions to the strong influence of the curial official mechanism, the second enhanced its power in so far as the participation of the future council fathers made these latter familiar with the themes presumably to be discussed at the council and seemed from the start to recommend them to the *periti* for the conciliar commissions to be set up later. On an equality with the ten commissions in respect to the preparation of the schemata, as an agency of contact with the churches not united with Rome, but going beyond their competence, was the Secretariat for Promoting Christian Unity under the direction of Augustin Bea, S.J., rector of the Pontifical Biblical Institute, named a cardinal on 14 December 1959.

The examining and coordinating of the drafts prepared in this manner was incumbent on the Central Commission, set up on 16 June 1960, to which belonged, in addition to the presidents of the commissions, the chairmen of national and regional episcopal conferences; their number rose finally to 102 members and 29 consultants. Since the commissions were continually expanded by the naming of new members, their total number increased at the end of 1961 to 827, two-thirds of them Europeans.

The work of the preparatory commissions in the almost two years from the fall of 1960 to the summer of 1962 suffered from the fact that no directives had been given them for the constituting of centers of gravity. It was undoubtedly an advantage that they were free in the choice and elaboration of the themes, but on the other hand it worked in favor of the strong influence of the Curia, of the Roman universities, and of the central authorities of religious institutes in the tendency that the sixty-nine schemata submitted by them to the Central Commission were rather a summary of papal statements during the last decades or, respectively, an inventory of the theology and practice prevailing in Rome rather than the hoped for advance into new areas. The Central Commission first met on 12 June 1961; this session was followed by six more. In addition to the schemata submitted to it, it also drew up the rules of procedure.

If it was possible to hear during the period of preparation that the Second Vatican Council would be the best prepared council in the history of the Church, it soon became evident that the material collected in overwhelming mass was chosen unilaterally and did not satisfy the council. Of the seventeen schemata which had been worked out by the Commission for the Discipline of the Clergy and the Christian People under Cardinal Ciriaci, not a single one was approved in this form by the council; of the six texts of the Theological Commission under Cardinal Ottaviani, after complete revision only two; of the nine of the Commission for the Discipline of the Sacraments, not even one obtained the acceptance of the council. Only the Commissions for the Sacred Liturgy, Religious, and the Apostolate of the Laity submitted each only one document, which constituted the point of departure of the corresponding conciliar decrees. Out of the five texts prepared by the Commission for Studies and Seminaries there originated through concentration and revision two conciliar decrees on the formation of priests and Christian education; the four schemata worked out by Bea's secretariat went, after amalgamation with related material of the Theological Commission and the Commission for the Eastern Churches, into the Decree on Ecumenism, and the declarations on religious freedom and non-Christian religions. Nevertheless, the work of the preparatory commissions was not in vain: it furnished a voluminous collection of material, few new viewpoints. Only at the council did these break through.

The preparatory work was kept strictly secret, so that only a small part of it leaked to the public. Thus it could hardly fail to happen that during the long waiting period a certain disappointment began to spread, especially since the Roman Diocesan Synod, which the Pope himself had opened on 24 January 1960, moved in the traditional routes and gave little notice of the desire for bold reforms and large-scale ecumenism, which appeared in numerous books and articles of theologians and lay persons. The expectations had been strained too tightly, it had not been made sufficiently clear that councils had never been revolutionary, but instead the necessary new elements had to be consciously linked with the proven old elements. But even during the years of preparation unmistakable were the voices from the episcopate that "all problems posed by the development of the world" must concern the council, that the Church must be universal in the true meaning of the word, that a decentralization and a deeper and broader ecumenical understanding were necessary. In February 1962 Cardinal Montini of Milan demanded a discussion of the nature and function of the episcopate in unison with the Roman Pope; a deepened self-awareness, he said, would enable the Church to adapt itself to the needs of the age. But he warned against seeing in a council a healing means of miraculous and immediate effect.

Earlier than anticipated, on 25 December 1961, the council was summoned to Rome for the next year by the constitution *Humane salutis,* but still without indication of the opening date; the motu proprio *Concilium diu* of 2 February 1962 appointed 11 October of the same year as the opening day. In these documents the tasks of the council were again sketched only in very general outlines. The promulgation, surrounded with unusual solemnity, of the constitution *Veterum sapientia* on 22 February 1962, whereby Latin was imposed as the language of ecclesiastical speech and theological instruction, was in opposition to the wishes prevalent in the Preparatory Commission for Studies and Seminaries and strengthened the impression that everything would continue as before. The paving of the way for church unity was not expressly mentioned, but a step was taken in this direction when the churches and ecclesial communities not united with Rome were invited through the Secretariat for the Promotion of the Unity of Christians to send official observers to the council. The invitation met a better reception among Protestants than among the Eastern Churches. The Anglican Church, whose head, Archbishop

Fisher of Canterbury, had paid a visit to the Pope on 2 December 1960, sent three representatives; the Evangelical Church of Germany sent the Heidelberg professor Schlink; the Lutheran Reformed World Union and the Ecumenical Assembly in Geneva acceded to the invitation; on the other hand, the Orthodox patriarchs of the East reacted with hesitation. The patriarchate of Moscow agitated powerfully against the "sirens" from the Vatican. All the greater was the surprise when, on the eve of the opening of the council, it became known that two representatives of Patriarch Alexius were en route to Rome. This about-face was due to a visit to Moscow of the closest collaborator of Cardinal Bea in the Secretariat for the Promotion of the Unity of Christians, his eventual successor, Johannes Willebrands. The other dissident patriarchates later followed the Russian example.

By means of the motu proprio *Appropinquante concilio* of 6 August 1962 the Pope gave the council its agenda, the *Ordo Concilii Oecumenici Vaticani II celebrandi.* It had been worked out by a subcommission of the Preparatory Central Commission under the presidency of Cardinal Roberti and his secretary, Vincenzo Carbone, and in seventy articles defined, first, the rights and duties of those participating in the council and, second, the general, and, third, the special norms for the order of business.

As at Trent and the First Vatican Council and in conformity with Canon 223, paragraph 1, of the Code of Canon Law, the right of deciding on proposals pertained only to the plenary session of the council fathers qualified to vote in the general congregations and sessions. The direction of the discussions was entrusted to the presidency of ten cardinals appointed by the Pope. It devolved on the ten permanent conciliar commissions to draw up the drafts of decrees (schemata) to be submitted to the council and to modify them, having regard for the motions offered by the council fathers; of its twenty-four members, two-thirds were to be elected by the council, one-third and the chairman were named by the Pope. To the full members entitled to vote were added *periti,* summoned by the Pope, without the right to vote; among them were laymen; at the beginning of the fourth session they numbered 106. An entirely new category was constituted by the observers sent by the churches and ecclesial communities not in communion with the Holy See; all texts were delivered to them and, like the *periti,* they were entitled to participate in the general congregations. Not yet envisaged in the agenda were the "hearers" who were permitted in the *aula* of the council from the second session, and who from the third session also included women. At the head of the official machinery of the council stood the secretary-general named by the Pope; to him were allotted several undersecretaries.

The routine was as follows: The drafts submitted by the presidency were explained by one or more commentators; the general debate on the schema as a whole was followed by special debate on its individual parts. For the adoption of a text a two-thirds majority was required. Out of regard for the number of council fathers, oral intervention in the general congregations was made dependent on previous written notice and its length was restricted to ten, finally eight, minutes; the council fathers had the right to present written suggestions for changes, which were to be submitted to the commissions. The process was continued until a two-thirds majority was achieved, and the promulgating of the text could take place in the solemn session.

In the course of the very first session of the council it appeared that the *Ordo* in its existing form was inadequate to achieve concrete results in a reasonable period of time. And so it was revised on 13 September 1963, with regard for various modifying motions made by, among others, Cardinals Döpfner and Spellman: The direction of the general congregations was turned over to four moderators, again named by the Pope, and, together with the presidency, now expanded to twelve members, they constituted the Presidential Council. For the rejecting of a proposed schema now a simple majority of those present sufficed; fifty fathers could submit a new draft to the moderator, who could bring about the close of the debate by a simple majority decision; the minority in the case was protected by this, that it might have its viewpoint set forth by three speakers. The same end was served by changes in the composition and procedure of the conciliar commissions. By the side of the chairmen were two vice-presidents, who were to be named with the consent of the commission; they together determined the commentator or commentators.

A second modification of the *Ordo,* of 2 July 1964, went into effect during the third session. Speakers who acted in the name of at least seventy council fathers received certain privileges; the distributing of propaganda material in the *aula* and nearby required the approval of the Presidential Council.

Even in this altered form, the *Ordo* could not eliminate all defects and confusion from the routine. The relationship of the Pope to the council, severely burdened by history, led to tensions also at the Second Vatican Council. As head of the council, the Pope had the right to intervene in the procedure, and both Popes of this council made use of this right when unexpected difficulties arose. He could approve the decrees and promulgate them, but he could also refuse his assent. It was not foreseen in the *Ordo* in what form he, as a member of the council, which he was, could make known his view to the council in the course of the deliberations. Also unclarified was the question of whether a vote was necessary at the end of the general debate.

As regards the form of the conciliar decrees, in conformity with Pope John's wish but different from all earlier councils, the council refrained from condemning errors by means of canons with a subjoined *anathema.* The texts approved by it bear three different signs in which their authority is graduated: at the head are four constitutions — on the liturgy, the Church, divine revelation, and the Church in today's world; then follow nine decrees and three declarations.

An actual change of the procedure was under way toward the end of the council in this regard, that the real work of the council was transferred more and more to the commissions, and the general congregations were more and more filled with voting, which could be carried out far more quickly with the aid of a punch-card system than at the First Vatican Council. Still other technical contrivances contributed to overcoming the problem of sheer numbers.

The First Session and the Change of Pontificate

The opening session on 11 October 1962 by far surpassed in grandeur that of the First Vatican Council. Two thousand five hundred forty council fathers with the right to vote took part in it, a number not even remotely reached at any previous council. The Pope was borne through the bronze door to the entrance of Saint Peter's on the *sedia gestatoria,* but then he left it and walked through the ranks of the council fathers; the fact that on this occasion he wore, not the tiara, but the miter, had symbolic value. The rite was basically that usual since the Council of Vienne: *Veni Creator* and Mass of the Holy Spirit, celebrated by Cardinal Tisserant; enthroning of the gospel on the council altar erected in front of the presidents' table; making of the profession of faith; the conciliar prayer, *Adsumus;* singing of the gospel (Matt. 28:18–20 and 16:13–18) in Latin, Greek, Old Church Slavonic, and Arabic.

In his opening talk the Pope repeated the conviction that the summoning of the council followed an inspiration from above and indicated to the council its direction: to bring to mankind the sacred wealth of tradition in the most effective way, with regard for changed conditions of life and social structures; not to condemn errors but "fully to declare the strength of the Church's life." The council was charged to move nearer to the unity willed by Christ in the truth. Overcome by the magnitude of the moment, the Pope ended with a prayer for divine assistance.

The council assembled in the nave of Saint Peter's was the most universal in church history. Not only in accord with its mandate and claim, but in fact the Church of the twentieth century was a Universal Church. All five continents were present in their episcopates. Europe, which at the medieval councils was virtually the only continent represented, sent only a mere half of those qualified to vote — 1,041; America, which was not at all represented at Trent and only weakly at the First Vatican Council, sent 956 bishops, Asia more than 300, Africa 279. The numerical superiority of Italians, which had led to voting by nations at Constance and even at Trent had produced tensions, was ended: the 379 Italian bishops made up less than one-fifth of the council fathers, but just the same the Italian curial cardinals and high curial officials exerted an additional strong influence.

The order of seating was more than a formality. The presidents, and later also the moderators, had places in front of the *confessio;* on the platforms to their right sat the cardinals, to their left the patriarchs of the Uniate Eastern Churches; then followed, on both sides, first the archbishops, then the bishops according to the date of their nomination. The generals of religious institutes had places on the front balconies, the *periti* on the others. For the observers a platform was designated to the left of the presidency; for the later admitted *auditores* platforms on the other sides of the high altar. Each general congregation was opened with Mass, frequently in an Oriental or the Slavonic rite.

That the council was esteemed as a world happening appeared from the presence of almost one thousand reporters sent by the press and the mass media. During the first session they almost entirely referred to indiscretions, only from the second session were its members permitted in the *aula,* and the press office was no longer subject to the secretary-general but to a conciliar commission. Thereafter the official reports were fuller in content, and the still valid rule of silence was in practice relaxed.

Although the superficial facts are better known than in any previous council, there were also many enigmatic incidents in this council that are either unknown or demonstrable only with difficulty. What follows is not a history of the council, but only a report in which should be noted what Oscar Cullmann said: that this council must be evaluated not only from the texts approved by it, but the total council event must be considered, for its impulses are as effective as the texts. These proceeded from a tension-filled struggle between "intransigent" and "progressive" forces. The former, numerically weaker group had its firm prop in the Roman Curia, the latter was composed, in addition to bishops from central and western Europe and North America, surprisingly also of council fathers from so-called mission countries. Of great significance were the national and regional Episcopal Conferences, partly constituted only at the beginning of the council.

In the first general congregation on 13 October the election of the conciliar commissions was on the agenda. In addition to the ten ballots, on each of which sixteen names were entered, the lists of those qualified to vote who had belonged to the preparatory commissions — and a majority of them were candidates of the Curia — were given to the council fathers. Against this procedure misgivings were first expressed by Cardinal Liénart of Lille, then in more detail by Cardinal Frings of Cologne: In view of the importance of these elections it is necessary to prepare them carefully; they should be postponed for a few days. The motion was passed with overwhelming approval and became a decree.

In the next days the Episcopal Conferences caucused and drew up their own election lists. The most successful among them proved to be that prepared by the cardinals of central Europe and France, because it took into consideration distinguished experts from all parts of the world.

The general congregations of 13 and 16 October were the "starting point" of the council. In them it made known its wish to make its decisions according to its own judgment and conscience, not merely to approve what was suggested to or submitted to it. This self-will of the episcopate became still more clearly visible in the debate on the liturgy schema, which began on 22 October and lasted to 14 November. Previously, on 20 October, the council issued a proclamation to the world, to the effect that "the message of salvation, love, and peace which Jesus Christ brought to the world and entrusted to the Church" was announced to all mankind.

The liturgy schema drafted by the Preparatory Commission had adopted the basic notion of the liturgical movement, that the Christian people should not passively attend the worship of God but actively participate in it, not only hear but pray and act together; as a consequence it recommended an extensive introduction, to be determined in detail by the respective episcopal conferences, of the vernacular in the Liturgy of the Word at Mass and in the administration of the sacraments and envisaged a reform of the liturgical books and, on specific occasions, the reintroduction of Communion *sub utraque specie.* On these questions there was enkindled the opposition between traditionalists and progressives which, in changing groupings, was to put its stamp on the council throughout its duration. For the schema were especially cardinals and bishops of countries in which the liturgical movement had spread, at their head Cardinals Frings, Döpfner, Feltin, Lercaro, Montini, and Ritter; the opponents of the draft fought the substitution of Latin by the vernacular and the intervention of the episcopal conferences in its introduction.

And so the surprise of the first general congregation was repeated: the bishops of Latin America, Asia, and Africa, although they were in great part trained at Rome, turned out to be, in the majority, thoroughly noncurialist and nontraditionalist; their pastoral experiences drove them to the side of the "progressives." What could be foreseen only with difficulty was that the "pastoral" goal which Pope John had set for the council was accepted by the majority of the council fathers.

In the course of the debate on the liturgy many requests were presented which had long ago been discussed in the pale of the Liturgical Movement: the adapting of the Divine Office to the spirituality of the diocesan clergy; the better choice and distribution of the scriptural readings; in the ecclesiastical calendar the deemphasizing of celebrations of the saints in favor of the Christocentric Church year; a reform of the calendar with a fixed date of Easter; ecclesiastical music and Christian art. The vote on 14 November produced a large majority — 2,162 to 46, with 7 abstentions — for the further revision of the schema, with consideration of the suggestions for change brought forward in the debate by the standing conciliar commission under the direction of Cardinal Larraona, of whose sixteen elected members twelve were on the central European list. Even before the council dispersed, on 7 December, the new first part, composed by the commission, was approved, but with 180 reservations.

Not so clear was the outcome of the debate begun on 14 November on the schema worked out by the Theological Commission under the centralized control of its Jesuit secretary, Tromp, on the sources of divine revelation. It obtained its pungency first through the fact that the text submitted sought to exclude the interpretation of the Tridentine decree defended by the Tübingen theologian Geiselmann — "tradition" means that the Bible is to be interpreted by the Church, but does not represent, beside it, a second independent source of revelation — and through this intensified condemnation of the Protestant scriptural principle affected the ecumenical rapprochement. In addition, the draft was directed to damming up the penetration of modern biblical criticism into Catholic exegesis, over which a powerful controversy had erupted between professors of the Papal Lateran University and members of the Biblical Institute. In contrast to the "progressive" liturgy schema, which had evoked the resistance of the "traditionalists," now the "progressives" were the aggressors. Many fathers, including Cardinals Frings, Döpfner, König, and Alfrink, rejected the schema totally and had already prepared a new one; others, such as Cardinals Suenens and Bea and Bishop De Smedt of Bruges, demanded a complete revision and presented the principles to be taken into account. A vote on the schema as a whole, contrived on 20 November — the first of its kind — led to the result — probably as a consequence of the motion, which required a "yes" *for* the ending of the debate — that 1,368 council fathers voted *placet,* 822 voted *non placet;* hence the opponents of the draft did not obtain the two-thirds majority. On the other hand, it had become obvious that it could never count on adoption in its current form.

The Pope resolved the existing situation, not envisaged in the agenda, by setting up a mixed commission under the chairmanship of Cardinals Ottaviani and Bea for the further revision of the schema; in it both tendencies were represented equally. This measure, at first accepted with great skepticism, proved to be the right one: in protracted discussions a middle road was found.

In the debates over the schemata on the liturgy and revelation, the oppositions had collided harshly. Now a certain relaxing of tension showed itself in the fact that a proposal prepared by the Secretariat for the Means of Social Communications and treating the mass media — press, cinema, radio, television — was submitted on 23 November. It essentially restricted itself to a fundamentally positive stance of the Church toward them, the possibilities of using them for the apostolate, and the dangers to be encountered. The schema had been only in the next to last place among the drafts sent to the council fathers in August 1962. Although the chairman of the conciliar commission, Cardinal Cento, and the commentator, Archbishop Stourm of Sens, had recommended the adoption of the text, in the debate from 23 to 26 November it encountered opposition because it one-sidedly stressed the Church's right to the modern means of communication and too little the right of persons to appropriate and correct information and did not condemn sharply enough the misuse of the mass media. On 27 November the council by a great majority — 2,138 to 15 — approved the substance of the schema, but demanded its abbreviation and limitation to instructional principles and pastoral guidelines.

In the treatment of the schema submitted on 26 November on the Eastern Churches it became clear how inadequately the preparatory work had been co-ordinated. The first part of the schema, which treated of the unity of the Church under one Supreme Shepherd, contained passages which, as was remarked in the debate by Patriarch Maximos IV and others, were suited rather to upset the Orthodox than to gain them. Cardinal Bea proposed that the draft be reworked with that of his Secretariat for Promoting Christian Unity and merged with a third, which originated with the Theological Commission. On 1 December the council decided, 2,068 to 36, to send it back with this version to the commission.

As early as this debate it had been said by Archbishop Heenan of Liverpool that the difference between the Roman Catholic Church and the separated Eastern Churches lay less in a discrepancy of the doctrine of salvation than in the concept of the structure of the Church.

Nature and structure of the Church were the central theme of the schema *De ecclesia,* which the chairman of the Theological Commission, Cardinal Otta-viani, and Bishop Franič of Split, as *relator,* explained on 1 December. To no other theme were so many *postulate* appended, and no other would be so powerfully contested as this one. The draft occupying 123 printed pages linked the view of the Church, prevailing since Bellarmine, as an institution with ideas from the en-cyclical of Pius XII on the Church. Its twelve chapters were, as Cardinal Montini remarked in the course of the debate (1–7 December), placed side by side, not developed separately, and the doctrine of the Episcopal College was present only as a start. Thus were the signposts for the further reworking set up, which, without a formal decree, was entrusted to the conciliar commission.

When on 8 December the Pope dismissed the council for the time being, none of the five discussed proposals was ready for publication. He comforted the fa-thers: "It is easy to understand that in a so broadly planned gathering a great deal of time must be devoted to achieving agreement." The public displayed disap-pointment over the absence of concrete results, many Catholics took offense at the "lack of unity" of the council fathers, which was in reality only the struggle, necessary in all councils, concerning the true and the right. One important result was achieved: The episcopate had learned to feel as a unity, had understood the council as its own affair and testified to its desire actively to form its decisions itself. Even if the council had not been continued, it would have left behind its mark on church history. But if it wanted to realize concrete results, priorities had to be established, the mass of current schemata had to be reduced, they had to be combined and abbreviated. The Secretariat for Extraordinary Affairs, set up in the procedure (ARTICLE 7, par. 2), had not sufficient authority for this. Such authority was given to a Coordinating Commission established by the Pope on 6 December. To it belonged: as chairman, Cardinal Cicognani, since 12 August 1961 successor of the deceased Cardinal Tardini as secretary of state, as well as Cardinals Confalonieri, Döpfner, Liénart, Spellman, Suenens, and Urbani. The Coordinating Commission was also instructed to turn over all details relative to the revision of canon law and the regulations for implementing the conciliar decrees to the postconciliar commissions. It acquitted itself of its mandate in close cooperation with the conciliar secretariat and the conciliar commissions, but also in constant contact with the whole body of council fathers, whom the Pope in a letter of 2 January 1963, not published until 8 February, had called upon for cooperation. The drafts newly formulated in this manner, which at the beginning of May were sent to the council fathers, showed almost entirely another face than the drafts of the preparatory commissions. The will for renewal of the conciliar majority carried the day: the proponents came from the previous opponents. Only now was the direction of the council definitely decided. The resumption of the discussions was proposed for 8 September 1963. Pope John was not destined to witness them. Only with great effort had he, already marked by death, continued the usual reception of the Episcopal Conferences. On 3 June 1963 he died, mourned by the whole world, almost more outside than inside the Church.

In his brief pontificate John XXIII, parallel with the council and supplementing it, had in several encyclicals shown the Church new routes and again taken up some earlier trodden. The mission encyclical *Princeps pastorum* of 28 November 1959 came out for a native clergy and the lay apostolate in the missions and approved the accommodation to non-European cultures. *Mater et magistra* of 15 May 1961 aimed to continue the tradition of the great social encyclicals since Leo XIII, but with some new emphases. The Pope regarded as his legacy the encyclical on peace, *Pacem in terris*, of 11 April 1963. Cutting deeply into the traditions of the Roman Curia were the Pope's arrangements in regard to the College of Cardinals: The suburbicarian sees received residential bishops with full authority, while their former occupants, the cardinal-bishops, retained only the title. The cardinal-deacons also received episcopal ordination: on Holy Thursday 1962 the Pope personally ordained them. In five consistories the Pope created fifty-two new cardinals and thereby definitively and basically exceeded the guiding number of seventy established by Sixtus V. The question was already raised of whether the College of Cardinals should retain the exclusive right to elect the Pope.

In accord with the prevailing canon law, the council was suspended by the death of the Pope. But Giovanni Battista Montini, archbishop of Milan, elected Pope on 21 June 1963 after a conclave of only two days, from the outset allowed no doubt to arise that he was determined to continue the council.

Paul VI (1963–78) was, by background, spiritual makeup, and the course of his education and his life, as different as possible from his predecessor. His father Giorgio (d. 1943) was a well-to-do publisher at Brescia and had been a member of the Popular Party and deputy in parliament. The son, born 26 September 1897, had in 1916 finished his schooling at the Liceo Arnaldo da Brescia, a public school, then attended the lectures in the seminary at Brescia, after ordination to the priesthood on 29 May 1920 studied canon law at the Gregoriana in Rome, then from 1922 prepared in the Accademia dei Nobili for an ecclesiastical diplomatic career, for which a short stay at the nunciature in Warsaw in 1923 could count as his first practical introduction. From 1924 he was active for almost three decades in the papal Secretariat of State, from 13 December 1937 as undersecretary (*sostituto*). After the death of Secretary of State Maglione in 1944, he remained, together with Tardini, secretary for extraordinary affairs, the closest collaborator of Pius XII. Parallel with his activity in the Secretariat of State proceeded zealous work in the pastoral care of students and academics. He first entered upon the normal pastoral care after his surprising nomination as archbishop of Milan on 1 November 1954, where he succeeded Cardinal Schuster. From the outset he gave social impulses. At the council he was very reserved and intervened only twice; next to the outspokenly progressive Cardinal Lercaro of Bologna, he ranked as a moderate progressive, and it was as such that he was elected. He approved the course of his predecessor, but differing from him he controlled the keyboard of the Roman Curia and knew the opposition which had come out against the new course during the first session.

As early as the day after his election Paul VI announced in a radio message that he intended to continue the council and appointed 29 September as the beginning of the deliberations. On the solemnity of Peter and Paul he received about one thousand journalists and promised to improve their possibilities of information at the council. On 1 July, in a speech to the diplomatic missions that had come for the coronation on 30 June in the piazza of Saint Peter's, he took up the theme of the "Church in today's world." He showed his ecumenical attitude by sending a representative to the celebration of the Golden Episcopal Jubilee of Patriarch Alexius of Moscow. In a letter of 12 September to Cardinal Tisserant he expressed the wish that in the future more lay persons should be used as *periti* at the council and introduced a new category of participants, the *auditores.* On 14 September he appointed for the directing of the general congregations four moderators, not legates, as was originally considered: Cardinals Agagianian, Döpfner, Lercaro, and Suenens. In a speech to the members of the Roman Curia on 21 September he adhered to the principle already represented by the Popes of the Council of Trent, that the reform of the Curia was the concern of the Pope, not of the council, but at the same time demanded strict obedience from the members of the Curia. The warning was unmistakable.

Second Session (1963) and First Results

In his opening address on 29 September the Pope appointed, more precisely than his predecessor had ever done, four tasks for the council: a doctrinal presentation of the nature of the Church — whereby he advanced the schema *De ecclesia* to first place — its inner renewal, the promoting of the unity of Christians, and — in this form again new — the dialogue of the Church with today's world. For the first and now the chief task a guideline was given in the statement: "Without prejudice to the dogmatic declarations of the First Vatican Council on the Roman Pope, the doctrine of the episcopate, its tasks, and its necessary union with Peter, is to be investigated. From this will result for Us also guidelines from which, in the exercise of Our apostolic mission, We will derive theoretical and practical advantage." The collaboration of the bishops in the exercise of the primatial authority, which he designated as desirable, already pointed to the future establishment of the Synod of Bishops. The inner renewal of the Church, the Pope continued, must orient it to Christ, but not as though it had abandoned him so that its traditions would have to be broken up and its life completely reorganized. In the ecumenical area another statement created a great sensation: "If any guilt in the separation is Ours, We humbly ask God's pardon and also seek forgiveness from the brethren who should have felt themselves separated from Us; for Our part, We are prepared to forgive the wrongs which have been done to the Catholic Church." This was no unconditional confession of guilt, such as that of Pope Hadrian VI of 3 January 1523, but the avowal that the causes of the ecclesiastical division lay not only on *one* side. The still existing great obstacles to union must not stifle the hope for it. The Pope greeted the observers present and then turned to those holding themselves aloof — adherents of non-Christian religions and atheists — and made mention of those persecuted for the sake of their belief.

The revised schema on the Church, which was explained on 30 September by Cardinals Ottaviani and Browne — the latter had been general of the Dominicans — was divided into four chapters: The Church as *mysterium,* its hierarchical structure, the People of God and the Laity, holiness of the Church. On the very first day of the debate Cardinal Frings moved to place the concept of "People of God" at the beginning, because hierarchy and laity together constitute the Church; furthermore, he recommended the adding of a chapter on the eschatological character of the Church and the incorporating of the text on the Mother of God into the schema.

A vote arranged for 1 October on the schema as a whole produced an overwhelming majority, 2,231 to 43, for further discussion. In the special debate, which was protracted throughout October, Cardinal Lercaro referred to the fact that *Corpus Christi mysticum* and "Visible Church" are not identical, because all the baptized belong in some way to the mystical body of Christ without their necessarily being members of the visible Catholic Church. But this very important question in the ecumenical view was soon eclipsed by the opposition which erupted in the debate on the second chapter, the hierarchical structure of the Church. It lasted from 4 to 16 October, and 127 speakers managed to be heard. The bone of contention for a minority, consisting especially but not exclusively of members of the Curia, was the doctrine that the College of Bishops, into which the individual is admitted by episcopal ordination, together with its head, the Pope, authority and responsibility for the whole Church.

A second, if not so strongly contested question was the restoration of the permanent diaconate. Since the Council of Trent the diaconate had been considered as a transitional stage to the priesthood. Now the lack of priests prevailing in many countries suggested the notion of gaining in deacons helpers for the steadily growing pastoral and charitable services. But since there was also consideration of freeing them from the law of celibacy, the proposal encountered powerful resistance, not only among clear traditionalists, so that in this question the factions were not identical with those in regard to collegiality.

The debate on the third chapter — People of God and Laity — offered the opportunity to refer to the coresponsibility of the laity, rooted in the universal priesthood and often claimed on the part of the Church and the necessary overcoming of clericalism. There were not lacking voices which warned against an obliteration of the distinction between the general priesthood and the official priesthood of orders and saw in the "higher evaluation" of the laity a danger to ecclesiastical authority.

In the fourth chapter — the holiness of the Church — there was discussed, even if not yet in a gratifying manner, the call of all the baptized to sanctity, then the religious state and the evangelical counsels were treated in particular. There was so section on the diocesan priesthood and nothing about its goal, except perhaps in the different means of the way of holiness of religious and lay persons. Also the total picture of the church drafted in the schema appeared unrealistic to Cardinal Bea; it did not accord with the reality of the Pilgrim Church.

The debate on the schema on the Church lasted an entire month. The question was: Which of the proposals of change should the commission adopt for the revision? Which corresponded to the will of the majority of the council? To produce clarity, Cardinal Suenens, as moderator in the general congregation of 15 October, had announced a preliminary vote on four controverted items. It did not take place. On 23 October the Presidential Council, on the motion of the moderators, decided with a bare majority the proposal of five, not four, questions: (1) Whether episcopal ordination has a sacramental character; (2) Whether the bishop ordained in communion with the Pope and the bishops becomes thereby a member of the *Corpus episcoporum;* (3) Whether the College of Bishops is the successor of the College of Apostles and, with its head, the Pope, and never without him, possesses the highest authority over the entire Church; (4) Whether this power is based on divine right; (5) Whether it is fitting, in each case in accord with the needs of the Church in certain areas, to reinstitute the diaconate as a special and permanent degree of orders. The five questions did not have the character of final votes, but were related only to the future formulation of the schema by the commission.

Again a week elapsed until the five questions were submitted. The dissension was further increased by the fact that a powerful propaganda had been unleashed against the insertion, decided on 29 October with a simple majority, of the text on the Mother of God into the schema on the Church by broadsheets which were distributed in front of the conciliar *aula* or sent by mail, without any steps having been taken against their authors. Only on 30 October was there a vote on the five questions. Questions 1 and 2 were approved by a large majority, but in the case of the next three questions the number of "no" votes increased: 1,808 to 336; 1,717 to 408; 1,588 to 525. Although the opponents of collegiality and of the permanent diaconate urged that the vote was not binding, their future acceptance by a two-thirds majority now seemed as good as assured. The "October Crisis" was thereby overcome, and the general congregation of 30 October 1963 was a second climax of the council after that of 13 October of the previous year.

The confrontation over the structure of the Church naturally influenced the discussion of the schema on the pastoral office of bishops and the government of dioceses, which claimed nine general congregations from 5 to 15 November. The schema had originated in the combining of five texts of the Preparatory Commission and was submitted to the council fathers at the end of April. It was still restricted to the bishops' tasks of governing: their relation to the Roman central departments, the position of auxiliary bishops, the episcopal conferences, the boundaries of sees, and the administration of parishes; hence it proceeded from above to below, not from the local church. After its presentation it was accepted after a brief general debate, against 477 "no" votes, as the basis for the special debate. While some demanded that in the first chapter the outcome of the votes on collegiality be taken into consideration, its opponents — Ottaviani, Carli — contested the binding nature of the vote of 30 October. The chief problems were picked out: the reorganization of the Curia, the composition and rights of the episcopal conferences, the position of auxiliary bishops, and the question of an age limit for residential bishops.

Although the great majority was clear in regard to the desire that the request for reform of the Curia could be fulfilled only by the Pope, not by the council, far-reaching wishes were expressed: an episcopal council should be established in order to exercise the collegial direction of the Church (Cardinal Alfrink), and to it, so some thought, instead of to the College of Cardinals, could be entrusted the right of papal election. Many speakers indulged in complaints about the curial bureaucracy without taking into account its great importance as bearer of many centuries of traditions and experiences. There had been regularly meeting episcopal conferences in Germany since 1848, and they had become usual in some other countries later, but plenary conferences of the bishops of France and Italy only very recently. The nine African episcopal conferences were constituted with a central secretariat under the leadership of Cardinal Rugambwa only at the council. Their structure and their authority had to be more precisely determined, because greater competence, for example, in the sphere of liturgy, needed to be given to them, especially the right to issue decrees binding on the members. In Germany and the United States they had hitherto got along without such a right, but it was to be expected that just this right was necessary to prevent dissension and even ruptures in certain areas, for example, the school system and trade unionism, and in dangerous situations of ecclesiastical politics.

Supported by the doctrine approved by the majority in the debate on the Church, that one becomes a member of the College of Bishops by means of ordination, the auxiliary bishops demanded an improvement in their legal position. African bishops spoke out against the naming of auxiliary bishops, because these latter jeopardized the unity of direction; also criticized was the naming of titular bishops for the sake of personal distinction. If the residential bishop is shepherd and teacher of his diocese, then would it not be desirable that, through establishing an age limit — in one comment the seventy-fifth year was given — the superannuation of the bishop could be prevented? It was easy to cite examples that a superannuated or sick bishop stubbornly refused to step down; but had not the council's Pope John been elected at the age of almost seventy-seven, and were there not men of more than eighty years among the most active and fertile in ideas among the council fathers? The list of problems touched on extended even to the complaint over the many tiny dioceses not capable of surviving by themselves and the dioceses that had become too large and tortuous around great cities and in high-population-density areas, over friction with the personal dioceses of Eastern Rites and with the military ordinariate, and finally over the lack of priests in Latin America. One hundred fifty-eight fathers had spoken when the debate was closed on 15 November without a vote and the schema was referred back to the commission for further revision. Even before the session ended, the apostolic letter *Pastorale munus* of 30 November 1963 conferred on diocesan bishops forty powers of office and on all bishops, including titular bishops, a series of privileges by which the episcopal office was revaluated vis-à-vis the papal central authority and at least partly restored to its original extent.

The schema *De oecumenismo,* debated from 18 November to 2 December, was, on the basis of the conciliar decree of 1 December 1962, revised and abridged by a mixed commission of members of the Secretariat for Promoting Christian Unity and of the Commission for the Eastern Churches. It treated the principles of Catholic ecumenism (Chap. 1), its actual state (Chap. 2), the relations with the Eastern and, of course only briefly, with the Protestant churches (Chap. 3), the position of the Jewish religion in the history of salvation (Chap. 4), and the principle of religious liberty (Chap. 5). Whereas the first commentator, Cardinal Cicognani, claimed to understand the ecumenical efforts of the council merely as a continuation of the tendency "of almost all councils" to restore peace and unity, the second one, Archbishop Martin of Rouen, designated it as entirely new; the third, Coadjutor Archbishop Bukatko of Belgrade, who spoke for the Eastern Churches, took a stand for improvements. In the course of the debate the question was posed: Just what is "Catholic Ecumenism"? Must the Church not seek union with the powerfully strengthened ecumenical movement? Does the Roman Catholic Church surrender its claim to be the true Church if it designates the separated ecclesial communities simply as "churches"?

The presentation of the common elements, just as that of the differences, in Chapter 3 satisfied neither the representatives of the Eastern Churches nor the Protestant observers. There was agreement only on this, that it was meaningless, as happened before the First Vatican Council, to invite to a return to the Catholic Church and to accentuate the existing differences, but that it was also not right to gloss over the existing doctrinal differences. The schema turned to Catholics with the invitation to make their Church a model by striving for Christian perfection; it recommended a mutual getting acquainted and dialogue, common prayer for unity but not common celebration of the Eucharist; it warned against any injury to love in the interchange. It was above all Cardinal Bea and Archbishop Jaeger of Paderborn — the latter well-known for his ecumenical work in Germany — who supplied as the guiding idea for the third chapter the stressing of the uniting elements in doctrine, piety, and Christian fulfillment. They found support from bishops from all parts of the world, for example, even from Spain, but of course also contradiction from those who already glimpsed a danger in the word "ecumenism." It remained controversial how far the collaboration of the denominations might and should go in the charitable and social sphere. The question of mixed marriages only appeared on the edges.

Despite many still unresolved problems, whose existence Cardinal Bea did not dispute, the debate left the impression that a genuine breakthrough to ecumenical thought had taken place. Strongly disputed, on the other hand, were the last two chapters of the draft, on the Jews and on religious liberty. The former seemed required by the unique position of Judaism in the history of salvation, but also operating was the motive of opposing to modern anti-Semitism a basic declaration that would correct earlier failings in the Church's behavior. Against it was raised opposition especially from bishops from Arab states, who feared from such a declaration, which would be interpreted as taking a position in favor of the State of Israel, a deterioration of their own already difficult situation and as a compromise wanted a word on Islam added.

The chapter on religious liberty had to be defended by its commentator, Bishop De Smedt of Bruges, against objections chiefly of a theological sort: that it equated truth with error. In many fathers there emerged doubts whether the last two chapters were in their right place at all. These doubts and the opposition from the Arab world declared that, although the schema as a whole had been accepted in the general voting of 21 November by a great majority, 1,966 to 86, as a working basis, there was no longer harmony on these two chapters. They continued in suspense; still powerful confrontations were imminent over both, not only their content but also their position.

In the drafts on the Church and ecumenism the council had laid hold of decisive problems of the Church's self-awareness without being able satisfactorily to solve them. Nevertheless, at the close of this second session, in *Sessio III* of 4 December 1963, two texts were adopted by vote: the Constitution on the Sacred Liturgy and the Decree on the Media of Social Communication.

The voting was done by chapters on the schema on the liturgy, which had been once more basically revised by the conciliar commission in the spring, from 23 April to 10 May 1963; the voting took place during the debate on the schema on the Church. In regard to Chapters 2 and 3 on the Mass and the sacraments — so many reservations, 781 and 1,054 respectively, were made on 13 and 18 October that they had to be reworked. Not until the final vote on the constitution as a whole on 22 November did an overwhelming majority appear: 2,158 to 19. And so it could be confirmed and proclaimed by the Pope in *Sessio III* on 4 December. Its basic idea is the "full and active participation of all the people" in the Easter Mystery, the fundamental concept of the liturgical movement. Subordinate to it was the authority conceded to the episcopal conferences to permit great parts of the Liturgy of the Word at Mass, especially the scriptural readings and the Universal Prayer before the preparation of the gifts, to be performed in the vernacular and *only* in it, hence not *also* in Latin. Latin was by no means abolished as the liturgical language of the Western Church; on the contrary, "The use of the Latin language," it is said in Article 36, par. 1, "should be maintained in the Latin Rite to the extent that special rights do not oppose this." Enhanced significance was granted to the texts of Holy Scripture and the homily that explained them, and concern for congregational singing was recommended. For special occasions the concelebration of Mass by several priests was permitted.

At the end of the Constitution on the Sacred Liturgy the formula of approval and promulgation, issuing from long consultations with *periti,* was first used. It was based on the Church's understanding that had been gained at the council: "What is expressed in this constitution, as a whole and in particulars, has obtained the assent of the fathers. And We, by virtue of the apostolic authority entrusted to Us by Christ, approve, decree, and enact it together with the venerable fathers in the Holy Spirit and command to the honor of God the publication of what has been ordered by the council."

The rules for implementation were left to the episcopal conferences dependent on confirmation by the Holy See; the reform of the liturgical books, especially of the missal and the breviary, was entrusted to a postconciliar commission which was instituted by the Pope on 25 January 1964, shortly after the end of this session; it established numerous special commissions. The reform of the liturgy, thus introduced, broke with the rubricist rigidity of the last centuries: whether it would produce an organic further development of the liturgical heritage without substantial loss could not yet be foreseen.

Not so close to unanimity as in the case of the Constitution on the Sacred Liturgy was the assent of the council fathers to the Decree on the Media of Social Communication, greatly abbreviated by the conciliar commission, on 14 November. The new text defined the attitude of the Church to the press, theater, cinema, radio, and television, but still without seeking a theological and sociological deepening; especially missed was the elaboration of persons' *right* to information and the *duty* of state and Church to provide it. This opposition explains the fact that in the final vote on 25 November a relatively large number of "no" votes (503) was cast against the 1,598 "yes" votes, so that for a moment it was doubtful whether the decree would be approved. But since a supplementary instruction was taken into consideration, for the working out of which more lay experts than previously were to be employed, in the session the "no" votes dropped to 164. It was noted that preconciliar vision of the Church was at the basis of this decree; but if it is pondered how negatively for a long time the mass media were evaluated in ecclesiastical circles, it was certainly a forward step, even if it remains true that it did not yet take account of the current importance of the mass media.

In his closing address the Pope admitted that the outcome of this session did not indeed correspond to all expectations, and still many tasks had to be accomplished. He indicated, alluding to the establishing of the Synod of Bishops and the reorganization of the Curia, that the "share of the bishops in the service of the Universal Church" would be made "still more effective." With satisfaction he stated: "We have mutually gotten to know ourselves better and learned to exchange ideas"; two important decrees had been passed. But the Pope warned against interpreting the Constitution on the Sacred Liturgy arbitrarily before the necessary norms had been laid down. At the end of his talk, the Pope announced, to the great surprise of most, a pilgrimage to Jerusalem, during which a meeting with Ecumenical Patriarch Athenagoras was envisaged. It took place from 4 to 6 January 1964, followed by the world public with great attention. More than words could do, this act strengthened the ecumenical orientation of the council.

Third Session: Crisis of November and Constitution on the Church

The third session, which was opened on 14 September 1964 with a Mass celebrated by twenty-four council fathers, the first concelebration at the council, brought the climax of the council but also its most serious crisis. The commission work directed by the Coordinating Commission had in the meantime so broadly expedited six schemata than on 7 July there could be indicated to the bishops as program points of the coming deliberations: the Church, the episcopal office, ecumenism — hence the three chief subjects of the second session — revelation, discussed in the first session but tabled, the lay apostolate, and the Church in the world of today. The last-mentioned concern, the "Dialogue with the World," was touched by the Pope in the encyclical *Ecclesiam suam* of 6 August 1964, and thereby the catchword given by his predecessor, *aggiornamento,* had been made concrete; on the other hand, the Pope had warned against novelties, according to the view of which the Church must break radically with its traditions and find entirely new forms of its life. The stand against atheistic communism and the mention of the Jewish religion and of Islam as partners in the dialogue seemed to broaden the council's program.

The Pope's opening address on 15 September, however, made it clear that he, now as earlier, considered the schema on the Church as the most important subject of deliberation, and if he indicated that the nature and function of the episcopate as complement of the doctrine of the primacy must be clarified, this was an unmistakable sign to the opponents of collegiality to abandon their opposition, but at the same time to its adherents that there must be no undermining of the papal primacy in the extent defined in the First Vatican Council. On the basis of the preliminary votes on 30 October 1963, the commission had given to the schema on the Church a new arrangement and form. To the schema, divided into six chapters, were added a seventh on the eschatological character of the Church and an eighth on Mariology. They still had to be debated from 15 to 18 September, and at the same time began the voting, without debate, on the first six chapters. The first two — Chapter 1: "The Mystery of the Church" and Chapter 2: "The People of God" — passed without serious opposition. But Chapter 3 "The Hierarchical Structure of the Church and the Episcopate in Particular" — was vigorously disputed. It was divided into thirty-nine sections for the voting from 21 to 30 September; on each of these the vote had to be *placet* or *non placet.* As regards the sections on the College of Bishops, the "no" votes mounted to more than 300: it was the influential group, which saw the papal primacy endangered in these statements. Far more numerous but differently made up were the 629 "no" votes against the conceding of the diaconal order to older married men; the concession to young men without the obligation of celibacy was rejected with 1,364 "no" votes. Although the opponents of collegiality had not by far mustered the necessary one-third for rejection, they sought in the final vote on Chapter 3, in which *placet iuxta modum* was permitted, still to put their views into the text. They may have constituted the great majority of the 572 votes with reservation, in addition to 42 "no" votes, cast on 30 September on the first part of Chapter 3. The curial opposition began to crumble, but it did not yet admit defeat. Chapter 4 on the laity was well received, as were Chapter 5 on the vocation to holiness and Chapter 6 on religious. Chapter 7, "The Eschatological Nature of the Pilgrim Church and its Union with the Church in Heaven," drafted by Cardinal Larraona, could be substantially improved because of the debate of 15 and 16 September: the time between the Lord's Ascension and the Parousia was emphasized as the Age of the Holy Spirit, the Christocentric cult of the saints was approved. Greater resistance was evoked in the debate, from 16 to 18 September, on Chapter 8: "The Blessed Virgin Mary, Mother of God, in the Mystery of Christ and of the Church," the including of which in the schema on the Church had encountered powerful opposition and appeared to some zealous devotees of Mary to be minimalistic. The primate of Poland and some Spanish and Italian bishops desired a solemn consecration of the world to the Mother of God, some recommended the adoption of titles such as "Mother of the Church" and "Mediatrix" into the text, but Cardinals Bea and Frings raised scruples against this: One should stay on strongly dogmatic ground.

Before it came to a vote on these last chapters the opposing views collided again more severely on the second schema, which was in the program as: "On the Pastoral Office of Bishops in the Church." The submitted text had originated through the curtailing of the draft debated in the second session on the episcopal office and its combination with a draft on the form of pastoral care in March 1964, and hence, because it had been greatly altered, it had to be discussed anew, from 18 to 22 September. The schema revised by the commission was once again opened up for debate, from 4 to 6 November, but so many *modi* were submitted on the first two chapters — 852 on Chapter 1, 889 on Chapter 2 — that the revised text could not again be presented until the close of this session.

Tensions became even sharper when on 23 September religious freedom and on 25 September the declaration on the Jews came up on the agenda; originally they had been linked, as Chapters 4 and 5, to the schema on ecumenism. Proceeding from the natural dignity of humans, the decree protected freedom of conscience in the civil sphere, even if the conscience is in error. The opponents quite rightly felt that this concept broke decisively with the medieval legal order, which required the proscription of heretics by common action of Church and state. In the debate, 25 to 29 September, Cardinal Ruffini posed the question: How can the Catholic Church, which is the true Church and bearer of the truth, abandon the fostering of this faith, wherever possible, even with the help of the state? Toleration — yes; freedom — no! Cardinal Ottaviani raised the question: Will not the concordats concluded by the Holy See, for example, with Italy and Spain, which allow to the Catholic Church a privileged position, come to nothing through this declaration?

The draft found firm defenders above all in the American episcopate, through Cardinals Meyer and Ritter, and also in the Polish through Archbishop Wojtyla of Cracow, eventually Pope John Paul II, who understood its worth vis-à-vis Communist totalitarianism. It was perceived that the motivation and the sphere where religious freedom prevailed must be more keenly grasped in order to meet the objection that truth and error as such — not the people who defend them — are equated. The debate ended without a vote, and the text was turned over to five members of the Theological Commission for appraisal, while the Secretariat for Unity undertook the further revision.

In comparison with the "Declaration on the Jews," submitted in the second session as Chapter 4 of the schema on ecumenism, but not discussed, the text introduced by Cardinal Bea on 25 September was planned with a view to appeasing its Arab opponents. In this regard, Islam was expressly mentioned; in the opinion of its champions the text was diluted, because only the Jews now alive, not the people as a historical unit, were absolved from the charge of "deicide," which in the past had been raised by Christian polemicists; twenty-one fathers demanded a return to the earlier wording. Other critics desired the deepening of the accomplishment of the history of salvation and the taking of other monotheistic religions into account. The chief difficulty was and remained the political misunderstanding. The Arabic countries interpreted the "Declaration on the Jews" as taking a stand for the State of Israel and exerted strong pressure on the bishops of their countries and by way of diplomacy; Patriarch Maximos IV had the presumption to charge that the authors of the text were "bought." This explains why the secretary-general of the council in a letter of 8 October invited Cardinal Bea to have the text still once more examined by a group composed of three members each from the Secretariat for Promoting Christian Unity and the Theological Commission; the effort to insert it into the Constitution on the Church and thereby to take it entirely away from the Secretariat for Promoting Christian Unity misfired.

Surprisingly calmly proceeded the debate, from 30 September to 6 October, on the schema on revelation, tabled two years previously, which had received a new text from a subcommittee, on which Philips, Ratzinger, Congar, K. Rahner, and other leading theologians had collaborated. As Bishop Franič, the second commentator, expressed it, it was not in accord with the notion of a minority of the commission, which saw in it a departure from the Tridentine decree on Scripture and tradition. In reality, it constituted its completion, gained from the deepening of the ideas "Scripture, "Tradition," and "Teaching Office," which are intimately linked and can exist only together; the theological discussion on the interpretation of the Tridentine decree was purposely left in suspense. Other disputed points were the inerrancy of Scripture and the historicity of the Gospels. As in the votes on the schema on the Church and in the debate over religious liberty, so too in this on the schema on revelation it was apparent that the great majority of the council concurred with the aims set by Popes John and Paul, and that the group which held stubbornly to the views hitherto represented at Rome was influential, numerous, but weak.

From this procedure of the council's majority resulted the fate of the nine texts which were submitted to the council between 7 October and 20 November. Two of them were sent back to the relevant commissions: on 14 October the schema, consisting of only twelve basic points, on the life and ministry of priests, and on 9 November the schema on the missions, even though on 6 November the Pope had appeared personally in the *aula* and recommended its adoption. The schema on the lay apostolate escaped this fate in the debate of 7 to 13 October, but exception was taken to the fact that it did not draw the necessary conclusions from the doctrine of the People of God; it did not adequately elaborate the proper rights of laity or also their proper responsibility and specific spirituality; for the first time a layman, P. Keegan, spoke on the matter.

The basic principles on the renewal of the life of religious, debated 10 to 12 November, and on Christian education, 17 to 19 November, seemed to many fathers to be too abstract, but capable of being developed. Better received were the twenty-two basic principles on the formation of priests, which entrusted to the episcopal conferences the creation of plans of studies and thereby the accommodation to the regional circumstances; only on the question of what authority Thomas Aquinas had to occupy in the system of teaching philosophy and theology was there a separating of minds.

The text "On the Church in the Modern World," debated from 20 October to 9 November, at first schema 17 in the original sequence in the list of drafts, later schema 13, was drawn up by a working group which had met in February 1964 at Zurich — hence it was dubbed the "Zurich Text." It had been preceded by a "Roman" draft, composed in the spring of 1963, and a "Mechlin" text in French, conceived by Belgian and French theologians in September 1963 at the suggestion of Cardinal Suenens. The Zurich draft, in which the Redemptorist Bernhard Häring had a powerful share, discussed in accord with a theological foundation the ministry of the Church to the world (Chapter 2), poverty, overpopulation, and war (Chapters 3 and 4). In the course of the general debate, opened by the comments of Bishop Guano of Livorno, Cardinal Meyer demanded the deepening of the theological bases; however, the text was accepted by a large majority, 1,576 to 296, as the basis for the special debate. In it Cardinal Lercaro moved a decision on the problem "Church and Cultures," and on 9 November the layman James J. Norris submitted copious material on the questions raised. Taken into account was the fact that this document, appearing for the first time in the history of the councils, had to mature slowly so that it could correspond to the expectation of people. The encyclical *Ecclesiam suam* of 8 December 1964, which in its third part treated the dialogue of the Church with the world, encouraged further work.

A schema on the sacrament of matrimony, worked out by the Commission for the Discipline of the Sacraments with the aid of members of the Theological Commission and of the Secretariat for Promoting Christian Unity, treated in five chapters of the impediments, mixed marriages, matrimonial consent, the form, and matrimonial processes, but at the direction of the Coordinating Commission was reduced to a *votum,* which limited itself to listing the guidelines for a reform of the law of marriage. Introduced by Archbishop Schneider of Bamberg, it was discussed on 19 and 20 November in the *aula,* but at the end of the general congregation of 20 November Cardinal Döpfner, as moderator, proposed, with regard to the law on mixed marriages, which in denominationally mixed countries was felt to be a great hindrance to the rapprochement of the denominations, to turn over the *votum* to the Pope in order to assure as quick a regulation as possible. The Council understood that so difficult a juridical and pastoral problem could hardly benefit in the plenary session, and a fortiori could not be solved, because the circumstances in the various countries were all too different. This expedient was declared for by 1,592 fathers, 427 declaring against it.

Of the nine texts debated in October and November, only one accomplished its purpose after a brief debate, 16 to 20 October — the schema on the Eastern Churches, which was promulgated in the fifth *sessio.* While the Council, seen from without, moved ahead uninterruptedly, within it the tensions had increased. On 11 October seventeen cardinals from central and western Europe and the United States, by means of a letter to the Pope, thwarted the attempt to send the two controversial declarations on religious liberty and the Jews, by outflanking the council through appeal to an alleged desire of the Pope, to new mixed commissions, from whose planned makeup the aim of the minority to alter the text in its sense was recognizable. The appeal to the Pope was successful, but the opposing faction did not admit defeat.

Chapter 3 of the Dogmatic Constitution on the Church also encountered the stubborn resistance of the most active and influential minority in the Vatican. When on 14 November a thick book with proposals for changes in Chapters 3 to 8 together with the replies of the Theological Commission was handed to the council fathers, it was preceded by a *nota explicativa praevia,* which was supposed to exclude every encroachment on the doctrine of primacy by the doctrine of the College of Bishops developed in Chapter 3. It had, to be sure, been submitted to the Theological Commission, but, as the secretary-general communicated, came from a "higher authority," hence from the Pope personally. It was supposed to reconcile with the text the minority, whose *modi* that altered the meaning were not accepted by the commission, and assure its acceptance with moral unanimity. Twice, on 16 and 19 November — the latter was the day before the final vote — the secretary general declared that the *nota* was, it is true, not an element of the text, but the text had to be interpreted in its sense.

The aim underlying the *nota* was achieved: the "no" votes to Chapter 3 dropped to forty-six on 17 November, including no doubt such of the defenders of collegiality who suspected an injury to or a weakening of this doctrine; in the *sessio* only five fathers still voted *non placet.* The Pope had, therefore, achieved his purpose. The question was: Did the *nota* alter the value of the statement of the text?

One who lays both side by side impartially will answer in the negative. The *nota* strengthened the adherence to the doctrine of the First Vatican Council on the primacy, but it did not subsequently strike out anything from the direct divine origin of the episcopal office and its function and the responsibility of the College of Bishops for the Universal Church. In any case, the minority abandoned its scruples and gave up its resistance. What was doubtful was less the content than the form in which the *nota* preceded the conciliar text. But had not the Pope, as head of the council, the right to make his consent dependent on an interpretation determined in advance?

The agitation over the *nota* had not yet subsided when on "Black Thursday," 19 November, the vote published on the previous day on the Declaration on Religious Freedom was canceled by the ranking member of the presidency, Cardinal Tisserant. This was preceded by a petition to the presidency from 200 Spanish and Italian bishops, which, appealing to ART. 30, par. 2, and ART. 35 of the order of procedure, demanded more time for study of the actually significantly altered draft and the postponement of the vote. If voting took place, there could be scarcely a doubt as to its outcome: the great majority would give the draft the green light, even if it did not fully satisfy the defenders of religious freedom. When shortly after eleven o'clock the vote was to take place, Tisserant, after a conference with other members of the presidency, announced that it was prorogued — and that meant that the declaration could no longer be passed in this session. Was the council's freedom endangered? After the close of the general congregation, Cardinals Meyer, Ritter, and Léger went to the Pope, but received only the assurance that the declaration would come as the first point on the program of the fourth session; this assurance was repeated the next day by Cardinal Tisserant.

The stormy general congregation of 19 November produced yet another surprise. The text of the Decree on Ecumenism, formulated by the commission and explained on 5 October by the commentators Martin, Helmsing, Hermaniuk, and Heenan, was, it is true, rejected by only a few fathers but almost two thousand *modi* were introduced, which had to be sifted and compiled. The fathers waited in vain for the printed definitive text, on which there was supposed to be a vote on 20 November. Then the secretary general announced that it was not yet ready, because some changes had been made; he read these changes, nineteen altogether, with the additions; they went back to a "higher authority." The Pope had sent forty suggestions for changes to the chairman of the Secretariat for Promoting Christian Unity, which because of lack of time Cardinal Bea could submit to only a few members from his closest associates, with the result that the nineteen mentioned had been worked into the text. Some were only stylistic, but others changed the sense. Only the form was strange: that a text produced with great care by a council and its competent organ, in this case the Secretariat for Promoting Christian Unity, had at the last moment been altered, not entirely over its head but still not in a form in keeping with the order of procedure. Among the sixty-four fathers who on the next day voted *non placet* not a few declared their disillusionment in this way; in the *sessio* of 21 November the "no" votes dropped to eleven.

In the fifth *sessio* of 21 November 1964, with which the third session ended, three texts could be adopted and promulgated. The constitution *Lumen gentium* is in two respects the climax and center of the conciliar decrees. Historically considered, it is the climax, for it ended the Church's quest for its self-understanding which had begun at the end of the thirteenth century, had led to the reform councils of the fifteenth century and at Trent to serious collisions, and had not been brought to an end at the First Vatican Council. It is the center of the conciliar decrees, for almost all other decrees of the council must be interpreted in its light. As the Theological Commission had declared on 6 March 1964 with regard to all doctrinal statements of the council, it does not claim infallibility but demands acceptance in faith in accord with the measure of the subject and the form of statement. The definition of the Church as "People of God" broke with the one-sided juridical concept of an institution and the notion which practically identified it with the clergy and forced a passive role on the laity. It ended the confrontation over the relation of the papal primacy to the episcopate in the sense of an organic union of both: the College of Bishops, into which the individual bishop is admitted by sacramental ordination and receives the charisms and full authority to exercise the apostolic office, possesses, by virtue of divine right as successor of "The Twelve," power over and responsibility for the Universal Church, but only in communion with the Pope, who is its member and its head. The successor of Peter regulates the exercise of the full authority given by God by the entrusting of a specific territory to the bishop, which can be refused or taken away. The bishop thus appointed rules the local church with full authority and responsibility, by virtue of *potestas propria, ordinaria et immediata.* The College of Bishops is a spiritual community (*communio*), not a college in the sense of Roman law. It can exercise its authority continually only in union with its head, and here it is left undecided in which form, without possessing the right of corule (*ius congubernii*), it can be given a share in the government of the Universal Church by the Pope, but equally also whether the Pope is the source of all and every actual power of government in the Church or may intervene only subsidiarily in the interest of Church unity.

The diaconate was reinstated as a state of life. All Christians are called to holiness, but the way to it in the religious state, which complies with the evangelical counsels, is different from the way of persons living in the world. The Church feels itself less as "fighting" and still less as "triumphing," but as being on pilgrimage, looking forward impatiently to its eschatological fulfillment. The Mother of the Lord stands also in a unique relationship to the Church by virtue of her singular position in the history of salvation; she is "our Mother," but is not called "Mediatrix of salvation": the chapter on Mariology suited neither the maximalists nor the minimalists.

If the constitution *Lumen gentium* is by far the most important outcome of the council because it articulates the Church's self-awareness, it is followed at a short interval by the Decree on Ecumenism, which regulated anew the relations with other Christian Churches and ecclesial communities. It proceeds from this, that there can be and is only *one* Church of Christ, but that in the Churches separated from the Roman Catholic Church, not without fault on both sides, "non sine hominum utriusque partis culpa," the written Word of God, the life of grace, faith, hope, and charity, and other interior gifts of the Holy Spirit" are operative. The Decree on Ecumenism ended the stressing, necessary in its day at Trent, of denominational opposition by throwing into relief what is common, opening the door to mutual knowledge and understanding, and by the invitation to common prayer evoked the power which can make possible the apparently impossible, the reunion of the Christian Churches. The separating differences in doctrine and piety, more numerous in the Churches of the Protestant Reformation than among the Eastern Churches, are not denied out of a false irenicism but must be discussed in the spirit of love, as occurred in the ongoing dialogue of the observers with the Secretariat for Unity during the council. Persons were thoroughly aware that in this field a greater distance still had to be covered.

The third decree promulgated in the fifth *sessio,* the Decree on the Oriental Catholic Churches, declared solemnly in ART. 5: "The Churches of the East, like that of the West, have the full right and duty always to be governed according to their proper principles, which are recommended by their venerable antiquity, correspond better to the customs of their faithful, and appear more adapted to care for the salvation of souls." *Orientalium ecclesiarum instituta* regulates especially practical questions of ecclesiastical communities — liturgy, administration of the sacraments, here for example the abolition of the obligation of the form in mixed marriages — but it disappointed the representatives of the Eastern Churches in ARTS. 7 to 9 on the patriarchates, the "pivot of the entire Eastern question," according to Abbot Hoeck.

Fourth Session and Closing

On 4 January 1965 the Pope, who at the beginning of December had taken part in the eucharistic congress at Bombay, appointed 14 September as the beginning of the fourth session. Meanwhile, the commissions worked more intensively than ever before on the already discussed eleven texts, five of which were sent to the council fathers at the end of May. If the November Crisis had left the impression that the Pope feared a diminution of the Petrine office, the following statements and measures showed that he still unerringly pursued the line drawn by him at the beginning of his pontificate. In an address to the College of Cardinals on 24 June 1965 he held out the prospect of the reform of the Curia and the revision of the canon law, but also the alteration, turned over to him by the council, of the law on mixed marriages and the study of birth control. In the encyclical *Mysterium fidei* of 11 September 1965 he repudiated the effort to weaken the dogma of the Eucharistic transubstantiation and stressed on various occasions that the Church has no cause to abandon good and proven traditions. "We have a Pope," was one radio commentator's summary of his impression.

On the day of the opening of the fourth session, 14 September 1965, Paul VI surprised the council by the announcement that he would summon a Synod of Bishops, through which the episcopate could work together for the welfare of the Universal Church. From the motu proprio *Apostolica sollicitudo* of 15 September it appeared that the majority of the members of the Synod of Bishops was to be elected by the episcopal conferences, whereby a general representation of the bishops, not of the College of Bishops as such, was assured. The Synod of Bishops is convoked, prepared, and guided by the Pope. It is "a permanent synod of bishops for the entire Church, which is directly and immediately subject to Our power," and hence not a "little council" with its own deciding power.

The fourth session differed from all the earlier ones in this, that the work of the commissions in refining the texts was in the foreground, the general congregations were to a great extent taken up with voting and were several times interrupted by rather long pauses. The council was under the pressure of time, for this session was to be the last. Without a break the still outstanding decrees were brought to a conclusion.

At the beginning of the renewed debate on religious freedom, on 15 September, the commentator, De Smedt, once again made it clear that the text did not equate truth and error and that it did not release the individual from the moral obligation of seeking and embracing the truth but merely contained freedom from religious compulsion in the civil sphere. A newly inserted passage left open the possibility of allowing to the Church a privileged position in states with an overwhelmingly Catholic population and thereby reconciled a part of the Italians, such as Cardinal Urbani of Venice, but not all opponents: In the final vote on 21 September, 224 fathers voted *non placet*. After repeated clarification of the text on the basis of *modi* submitted, the number of "no" votes on 19 November even rose to 249. In the preceding debate the Polish Cardinal Wyszyński and the Czech Cardinal Beran, only released in the spring, had indicated the importance of the declaration for the Church behind the Iron Curtain: acts of conscience could be neither commanded nor prevented by a purely human power. The Church claims for itself, as a "spiritual authority established by Christ the Lord," the freedom to proclaim the Gospel to all creatures. It renounces the notion that the secular power is justified and obliged to support the Church's saving work by compulsory means; it notes that the modern state is no longer Christian, but neutral; modern society is no longer monistic, but pluralist; but it limits their rights through the natural right of the individual not to be impeded by the civil power in the following of conscience. The burning of a Hus, the principle "Cuius regio, eius et religio" are henceforth not only historically outdated according to the teaching of the Church but are basically repudiated. The impact of this decision explains why the Declaration on Religious Liberty was only ready for publication in the last session.

On the other hand, from the end of September to the end of October the five decrees which were approved and proclaimed in the seventh *sessio* on 28 October 1965 moved quickly and without great objection across the stage of the council. The Decree on the Pastoral Office of Bishops assumed the doctrine of the episcopal office explained in the Dogmatic Constitution on the Church and was oriented to practice. The curial offices and tribunals are "to be more strongly adapted to the needs of the time, the regions, and the rites," and more foreign bishops, "ex diversis ecclesiae regionibus," are to be brought into them for permanent cooperation. The right was given to the episcopal conferences to issue statutes for themselves and to make legally binding decrees with a two-thirds majority. A redrawing of episcopal sees and ecclesiastical provinces was envisaged. Bishops were authorized to appoint episcopal vicars with material or territorial competence. Fruitful, even if also difficult to realize in large dioceses, was the idea of the *presbyterium* united with the bishop as father — ART. 28: "unum constituunt presbyterium atque unam familiam cuius pater est episcopus." The final vote on 6 October yielded almost unanimity — 2,161 to 14, and only two "no" votes in the *sessio*. The decree "interlocked more powerfully than any other conciliar document in the juridical order of the Church," says Mörsdorf; it would only achieve its full impact in the course of the reform of canon law.

The schema on the renewal of religious life had, in the debate of the third session, 10 to 12 November 1964, incurred the opposition of several bishops, for example, Cardinals Döpfner and Suenens, but especially of the religious institutes — 882 *non placet* at the close of the general debate — and so in the spring of 1965 it was again revised by three subcommissions with such success that in the final vote on 11 October there were only thirteen negative votes, and in the *sessio* only four. It proceeded from the ideal of perfection developed in Chapter 6 of the Dogmatic Constitution on the Church; in its practical part it is, like the Tridentine reform decree, a law providing a framework which did not encroach on the differences and the proper life of the orders and other religious communities, but obliged them to sift from the order's tradition what was original and essential, to improve the formation of the young members, to give them the salutary measure of freedom, to understand the, now as earlier, necessary obedience not as renunciation of their own responsibility to live for God but likewise for people. Of course it happened, as Cardinal Ruffini had already said, that this decree would evoke "extravagant" desires for reform.

The text on the formation of priests, expanded again from a principle to a decree, explained by Bishop Carraro of Verona, found so favorable a reception in the third session that only a few controverted points were left. The revision submitted on 11 October was accepted almost unanimously — 2,196 to 15. The decree *Optatam totius Ecclesiae renovationem* designated the family as "a sort of first seminary" for the vocation to the priesthood and left the preparation to the Tridentine seminary, but attached importance to the improvement of biblical and liturgical studies and of the practical pastoral instruction that was neglected in some countries. The natural virtues, *sinceritas, urbanitas, modestia,* were to be cultivated. The episcopal conferences were instructed to set up programs of study which were adapted to the intellectual and religious level of the country. A debate suggested by Latin American bishops on the law of celibacy was rejected by the Pope as "inopportune" in a letter of 11 October 1965 to Cardinal Tisserant but it invited the council fathers to express their views in writing. Shortly before, the intervention of a Brazilian bishop of Dutch descent on the eliminating of the lack of priests by ordaining laymen who had been married for five years for pastoral work in smaller congregations had been rejected by the moderators.

The Declaration on Christian Education, *Gravissimum educationis momentum,* was the eighth version of a text elaborated by the Commission for Studies, which after a temporary reduction to seventeen basic principles in March 1964, was again expanded and explained by Bishop Daem of Antwerp and in the debate of the third session, 17 to 19 November, ran into heavy criticism and obtained 419 "no" votes. Thereupon Archbishop Coadjutor Elchinger of Strasbourg had directed attention to the importance of the formation of teachers and pointed out the danger that the state might force its own ideology on the children in its schools. Not only was there a vote on the new version on 13 and 14 October 1965: the final vote turned out to be 1,912 to 183. In twelve principles the declaration developed the right of the individual to education, the right of parents, the desirability of denominational schools and Catholic universities, but it intimated that both, especially the last, urgently needed coordination and consolidation. Of the fact that the great majority of Catholic students attended neutral universities and that many Catholic professors taught at these, the declaration took note only in passing, in ART. 7.

The Declaration on the Relationship of the Church to Non-Christian Religions, frequently called the "Declaration on the Jews" because of its principal item, was not yet able in its new form, in comparison with the earlier diluted form, to satisfy all its opponents. Then the reaction had been so strong that publication had been abandoned. The bishops of Arab countries, such as Jacobite Patriarch Jacob III, intimidated by the threats of the Arab states but supported by members of *Coetus Internationalis,* continued their resistance, and anti-Semitic pamphlets against the alleged "Jewish-Freemason Conspiracy" were distributed; on the other hand German Catholics in a petition to the Pope had intervened in favor of promulgation. The form now presented for a vote endeavored to remove misunderstandings and also to gain the opponents. Their number remained mostly under 200 in the special votes on 14 and 15 October, but in the vote on the whole rose to 250; in the *sessio* it dropped to 88. The disputed expression "deicide" was dropped, but it was stated clearly that the guilt for the passion and death of Jesus must be laid neither on the Jews of today nor "on all Jews living at that time, without distinction." Urged not by political motives but by the love of Christ, the Church "deplores" anti-Semitism and "rejects every discrimination against a person, every deed of violence against him because of his race, his color, his status, or his religion." By means of this closing statement the condemnation of anti-Semitism was placed on a broader basis and made applicable to every racial discrimination. It was to become the maxim of Catholics in the approaching period of racial strife.

The far less controverted central part of the declaration applied the basic attitude of the Decree on Ecumenism, with which it had been originally united, to Islam, Hinduism, and Buddhism. Monotheism was recognized as obligatory in Islam, and in a reference to the crusades, in which Muslims had been fought with the sword as "heathens," the wish was expressed that the past be forgotten. In Hinduism the liberating "contemplation of the mystery of God" was positively evaluated; in Buddhism, the effort to become free, by means of asceticism, from this passing world. For all the world religions the principle was valid: "The Catholic Church rejects nothing that is true and holy in these religions"; it is often "the reflection of the ray of that truth which enlightens all people," where the fullness of life is to be found: in Christ. For the confrontation with non-Christian religions the declaration has no less significance than the Decree on Ecumenism for the relations with the separated Churches.

In his homily the Pope, alluding to the five promulgated texts, exclaimed: "The Church lives!" It has not grown old, but young; it does not let itself be sucked into the whirlpool of historical change, but remains constant; it speaks, prays, watches, rebuilds itself. The council convoked by Pope John "represents the entire Church," *totam repraesentat.* At the end the Pope recalled the persecuted Church, whose representatives were concelebrating with him.

After the October meeting the last snags were quickly overcome. The Dogmatic Constitution on Divine Revelation still had to contend with the opposition of a minority, which based itself on Trent. It only crumbled when, at the personal desire of the Pope in a letter of 18 October 1965 to Cardinal Ottaviani, the inerrancy of Holy Scripture was more precisely defined and the relations of Scripture and tradition were newly formulated: "The Church does not derive assurance on all the truths of revelation from Scripture alone"; "tradition" is the living teaching office of the Church, which authoritatively interprets and complements Scripture. This formulation left to the theological schools the liberty of defining more in detail the mutual relations of the two. The doctrine of inspiration — "God speaks through men in a human way" — and the historical character of the Gospels were expressly affirmed. The study of the books of the Bible in the original languages and the ancient translations, as well as of the ancient commentaries and liturgies, and the reading of biblical translations in the vernacular were recommended. In the voting on the individual parts of the constitution on 29 October, only the passage on the relationship of Scripture and tradition got 55 *non placet;* the vote on the whole was 2,081 to 27, and in the *sessio* the "no" votes dropped to 6.

After 29 October the general congregations were interrupted for ten days in order to allow time to the commissions for working on the *modi.* The Decree on the Apostolate of the Laity, explained on 9 November by Bishop Hengsbach of Essen, had assimilated the proposals for change submitted in the voting of 23 to 27 September, as were also those presented personally by the Pope. It received a virtually unanimous approval on 10 November. If Trent had defended the priesthood of ordination, so too in the justification of the lay apostolate the general priesthood of the faithful came into its own. "In the Church there are various ministries but only one mission"; no member of the Church is only passive; all are called to cooperate actively in the building of the Body of the Church as witnesses of faith and love, in the family, in charity, in the missions — everything under the direction of the ecclesiastical hierarchy, as the authority established and ordered by God, but not intended to patronize. The council itself gave an example by the fact that it employed lay persons as *periti* on the commissions in an increased measure.

A schema *De Indulgentiis recognoscendis,* drawn up not by a conciliar commission but by the Congregation of Rites, was felt almost by all to be a disaster when it was explained by Grand Penitentiary Cento and the regent of the *Poenitentiaria* on 9 November. The text envisaged certain simplifications in the practice of indulgences, for example, that only *one* plenary indulgence could be gained in one year, the time references in partial indulgences were suppressed, but it did not grasp the theological problem of the indulgence in its depth and was withdrawn on 13 November because of the keen criticism which it encountered from the episcopal conferences which had been questioned about it.

The Dogmatic Constitution on Divine Revelation and the Decree on the Apostolate of the Laity were proclaimed in the eighth *sessio* on 18 November 1965. In his talk the Pope tried to dissipate the hesitations concerning the now imminent ending of the council's work by reference to the establishing of postconciliar agencies: the *consilia* for the liturgy, for the revision of canon law, and for the mass media; the already existing Secretariat for Promoting Christian Unity would be complemented by one secretariat each for non-Christian religions and for unbelievers; the first meeting of the Synod of Bishops was held out in prospect for 1967. By far most important of all was the renewal of Christian life.

Until the close of the council three problem children still had to be examined: The Decree on the Missionary Activity of the Church, the Decree on the Ministry and Life of Priests, and Schema 13.

The general of the Divine Word Missionaries, Johannes Schütte, named by the chairman, Cardinal Agagianian, as vice-chairman of the Commission for the Missions, succeeded, with the assistance of newly added *periti* — Congar, Ratzinger, Seumois — at a private meeting at Nemi in the Alban Hills in drafting a wholly new schema, which was based on a theological foundation corresponding to modern mission scholarship and, in that respect, from a backward-looking had become a forward-looking document. In the debate, 7 to 12 October, Cardinal Frings had come out for the retaining of the old "classical" idea of the mission, but the Jesuit General Arrupe harshly criticized the practice of the past. There was no dearth of unresolved problems: the relations of the orders, which till now were the chief agents of missionary work, to the native clergy and of both to the Congregation for the Propagation of the Faith; financing; competition with non-Catholic missions. When the vote was taken on the refined text, 712 fathers — most all from mission lands — expressed in their *modi* to Chapter 5 that the missionaries active on the spot should have to collaborate in the decisions of the central offices. Thereupon the contested passage was revised, so that "elected representatives" of the missionary episcopate and of the missionary orders had to be summoned to the Propaganda with a decisive vote, hence not merely as advisers.

In the third session the council had also sent back to the competent commission the schema on the priesthood. At that time there prevailed the impression that priests, compared, for example, with bishops and religious, would be unduly neglected by the contracting of the schema into guiding principles. The commission worked out a new schema, which was submitted at the end of the third session and was again revised, better organized, and stylistically polished at the beginning of 1965 on the basis of 157 suggestions for change, presented in writing. Archbishop Marry of Rheims introduced it on 13 October; on 16 October the council decided to have the proposals for changes presented by Cardinals Döpfner and Léger and other speakers reworked by the commission. The vote by parts on 12 and 13 November, however, produced so large a number of *modi* — 1,331 on celibacy alone — that still another revision became necessary, and on 2 December it was approved by a great majority, 2,243 to 11.

Nevertheless, the decree *Presbyterorum ordinis* had by no means fulfilled all expectations. With reference to the pertinent parts of the constitutions on the liturgy and on the Church, it treated the mission of the priest, his threefold ministry, the relation of priests to the bishops, to one another, and to the laity. "Every priestly ministry shares in the worldwide mission which Christ entrusted to the Apostles"; the priest should be prepared to work in other dioceses with too few priests. Celibacy is "not demanded by the nature of the priesthood," as the practice of the Eastern Churches proved, but is "in many respects appropriate to the priesthood." The law of celibacy was approved and confirmed. "And so the council admonishes all priests who have taken celibacy upon themselves with confidence in God's grace in a free decision according to the model of Christ, to remain faithful to it generously and with the entire heart and to persevere loyally in this state." (ART. 16).

Schema 13 evoked by far the greatest concern. For even the new draft, produced between the third and fourth sessions at Ariccia, Paris, and Louvain, upon which Archbishop Garrone of Toulouse gave the report, ran into varied criticism in the debate from 21 September to 8 October — the fourteenth general congregation — because of the superabundance of general claims which it contained (Elchinger), because of the language, unclear in many passages (Frings), because of its all too optimistic evaluation of the "world" and its confidence of progress (Höffner), but especially because it said only a little on what the Church of today has to give to the world (Bishop Volk of Mainz). Cardinal König and others noted the absence of a confrontation with atheism, especially with atheistic communism, whose express condemnation was demanded by 450 fathers in a petition to the presidency. A fortiori views were juxtaposed in the concrete problems: total war, atomic weapons, disarmament, refusal of military service, assurance of peace. The council was naturally in no position to give a clear answer to these pressing questions. The appearance of the Pope before the United Nations in New York on 4 October was, it is true, suited to make visible the Church's involvement in today's world; in the structurally conditioned problems of this organization it changed nothing.

In feverish work the commission, which had divided itself into ten subcommissions, strove to incorporate into the text the more than three thousand proposals for changes for the votes on 15 to 17 November. Even the tide "Pastoral Constitution" was challenged — 541 *non placet*. The most "no" votes (140) were cast on ARTS. 54 to 56 (marriage, birth control) and the section on war and peace (144). The final vote on 6 December produced, just the same, a respectable majority: 2,111 to 251.

The pastoral constitution *Gaudium et spes,* the most voluminous text of the council, was placed, as the "heart of the council," at the side of the three other constitutions. It aimed to be "a fundamental new definition of the relation of the Church to the world" and thereby to orient the Church to the world, and that meant to the spirit of the new epoch, from which it had held itself aloof since a century earlier in the Syllabus. This constitution was greeted with enthusiasm, but history has already proved that at that time its significance was greatly overestimated and there was hardly a suspicion of how deeply that "world" which people wanted to win for Christ would penetrate the Church. Only too confident of progress, it remained self-consciously in a static manner of contemplation without being able to give clear answers to such urgent problems as birth control and the prevention of war; entirely inadequate is ART. 58 on the relation of the Church to the cultures. Perhaps a brief "declaration," in which the Church turned *ad extra,* would have made a deeper impression than this diffuse treatise.

When the secretary-general announced in the general congregation of 6 December that this, the one hundred and sixty-eighth, was the last of this council, stormy applause thundered through the halls of Saint Peter's. The council had done its work. In the ninth *sessio* on 7 December, in addition to *Gaudium et spes,* the decrees on the mission and the priesthood and the Declaration on Religious Freedom were approved and proclaimed. Once again the ecumenical orientation of the council was confirmed. In a common declaration the Pope and the ecumenical patriarch canceled the mutual excommunications of 1054. In his homily during the Mass celebrated by twenty-four fathers, the Pope admitted that "not a few questions which were taken up during the council still awaited a satisfactory solution"; nevertheless, it might be said that the council had corresponded to the goal set by Pope John. The Church had not been concerned to admire itself but to serve people, *ut homini serviat.*

On the next day, 8 December, the council was declared ended in a closing celebration arranged in the piazza of Saint Peter's. There were messages in French directed to political leaders, scholars and artists, women, the poor and suffering, workers and youth, delivered by representatives of these groups. The Pope had said good-bye to the observers in an hour of devotion which deeply impressed all the participants in the basilica of San Paolo on 4 December.

The Second Vatican Council was a world event. Was it an event of world history? A reply to this question would assume that one could in some way take in its effects at a glance.

Impact

In an interval of only a decade the impact of the Second Vatican Council cannot be decisively determined, but its effects can be observed. It is now established that it penetrated more deeply into the history of the Church than the First Vatican Council; in any event, its effects are comparable to those of Trent. The first historians of Trent, Sarpi and Pallavicino, were not able to give a historical orientation, although they wrote more than half a century after the event: for them the council was still an object of strife, not history. It is tempting to say something similar about the Second Vatican Council. Of course, it can hardly be disputed that it represented a turning point in the history of the Church. Much began to move in it, its internal structure was loosened up, it opened itself up ecumenically and to the world. Was this movement for the business of Jesus Christ on earth gain or loss?

The verdicts differ widely. The original enthusiasm with which the council was greeted yielded to harsh criticism. The critics pointed to the perplexity in the faith which "pluralism" in theology and preaching had caused; to the constantly declining participation of the faithful in Mass; the sharply increasing number of priests and religious who abandoned their vocation; the bewildering number of "councils" which were supposed to promote the "democratization" of the Church; the weakening authority of the Pope and the bishops; the increase of mixed marriages; the "earthly messianism," to use Ratzinger's term, which throws man back to the feasible; to the new sexual morality: the influence of the Church on the world has not increased but dissipated. The fact is incontrovertible.

The "progressives," on the contrary, have to reflect that an inner process of fermentation was necessary in order to realize Pope John's *aggiornamento*. They do not deny that the new liturgy is experiencing its "childhood illnesses," but claim that, thanks to the vernacular, the faithful participate in it more actively than previously. "Declericalization" and "democratization" are consequences of the doctrine of the People of God: a far-reaching cooperation, even having a voice, by the laity is necessary if the Church is to fulfill its mission in today's world. Finally, the ecumenical stance has reduced denominational strife and brought about the "end of the Counter-Reformation." The positive assessment of the religious and ethical content of the ancient world religions offers to the mission positive starting points, and Europeanism has long been outdated. They rightly affirm that the undoubtedly present phenomena of dissolution are, at least partly, not to be referred to the council but to the upheavals within industrial society and in the Third World, and hence in the long run have struck root in the turn in world history in which we stand. In an intermediate stage, which is full of uncertainty but also full of honest struggling and full of hope, there are movements and beginnings which promise new possibilities; a search for the mean appears, which gives the lie to the diagnosis of the end of the religious and paves from faith ways of new life, in which the unexhausted fertility of the Church's faith again proves itself, as Ratzinger says.

An accommodation of the opposing views is not yet in sight. It can be found only if one adheres to this: that the council, the highest authority in faith and morals, had set up binding norms, behind which one must not fall back, which one must also not go beyond or even disregard. There is no retreat back behind the council, but even less is this only an initial kindling for a total adaptation of the Church in faith, morals, and structure. Only if one holds fast to the council itself can the compromise between tradition and progress be found, the identity of the Church in a changing world be preserved.

After the close of the Council of Trent a deputation of cardinals was instituted for the interpretation of the decrees, which later undertook the added task of promoting and supervising their implementation. The Second Vatican Council, differently from Trent, did not enact any decrees directly to be admitted to the canon law; this task was given to the Commission for the Revision of the Code, set up during the council. For the interpretation of the decrees for the period from 3 January 1966 to 11 July 1967 the Coordinating Commission of the council was still competent, but on 11 July 1967 a special commission for interpretation was instituted, the *Pontificia Commissio decretis concilii Vaticani II interpretandis.* It does not have the same authority as did in its day the Congregation of the Council, expanded into an office.

The council itself had in several places referred to the still to be issued rules of implementation (directories) and turned over other tasks — celibacy, indulgences, mixed marriages — especially the reform of the Roman Curia, to the Pope.

For the implementation of the council, on 3 January 1966, to the three post-conciliar commissions set up during the council, five others were added, whose chairmen and members were identical with those of the corresponding conciliar commission: (1) for bishops and the government of dioceses; (2) for religious; (3) for the missions; (4) for Christian education; and (5) for the lay apostolate. The Secretariat for Promoting Christian Unity and the Secretariats for Non-Christian Religions and for Unbelievers were confirmed.

The reform of the curial offices was begun after the Council of Trent by Pius IV and Pius V but only completed by Sixtus V. After the Second Vatican Council the reconstruction of the Roman Curia, demanded during the debate on the Decree on the Pastoral Office of Bishops and promised by the Pope, had to wait only a year and a half. In the constitution *Regimini Ecclesiae universalis* of 15 August 1967 the work hitherto performed by the Curia received high praise, *egregia laude digna.* The Secretariat of State obtained the competence to coordinate the work of the congregations. Even the hitherto "Suprema," the Holy Office, was subordinated to it, obtained the name of *Congregatio de doctrina fidei,* and was instructed to declare the prohibition of books only after hearing the author, *audito auctore,* and reaching an understanding with the competent ordinary, *praemonito ordinario.* The former Congregation of the Council received the name of *Congregatio pro clericis:* the Congregation *De Propaganda fide,* the name of *Pro gentium evangelizatione seu De Propaganda fide.* The divisions at first acting as sections of the Congregation of Rites for the liturgy (*de cultu*) and canonizations (*de causis servorum Dei*) soon became independent. Entirely new was the Council on the Laity, *consilium de laicis.* The composition of the congregations was changed by the fact that seven residential bishops were assigned to each as ordinary members.

The three tribunals — the Apostolic Signatura, the Rota, and the Sacred Penitentiary — the Apostolic Chancery, and the Apostolic Camera remained in existence, but the entire economic sphere was reorganized by the establishing of a finance ministry, *Praefectura rerum oeconomicarum S. Sedis,* and of a central administration of property, *Administratio Patrimonii S. Sedis,* beside which the Prefecture of the Apostolic Palace took its place; also new was the Office of Statistics.

Three years after this reorganization of the Curia came the motu proprio *Ingravescentem aetatem,* which deprived cardinals after the completing of the eightieth year of age of the right to participate in a papal election, but the right to elect the Pope remained as such in the College of Cardinals.

It far exceeds the possibilities of space here to offer even only a fleeting glance at the activity of the individual curial departments. New is that at their side, not subordinate to them, appeared the Synod of Bishops. So far it has had three regular sessions and one extraordinary session. The theme of the first regular session of 29 September to 28 October 1967, in which 199 synodalists took part, was: principles for the revision of the code; dangerous doctrinal opinions; seminaries; mixed marriages; liturgy. The newly composed profession of faith was published. The extraordinary session of 11 to 27 October 1969 took up the collaboration between the Holy See and the episcopal conferences and of these conferences among themselves. It was significant that at the opening of the Synod of Bishops the Pope referred the episcopal conferences and the summoning of residential bishops to the congregations to the principle of collegiality.

The second regular session of 30 September to 6 November 1971 took up in thirty-seven meetings the problems of the priestly office and of justice in the world. The third session of 27 September to 26 October 1974, in which 207 synodalists participated, dealt with the "evangelization of the world of today." It probably corresponded best to the meaning of the institution in so far as during it a survey was given of the status of the Church in Africa, Latin and North America, and Asia, as well as in the Second World behind the Iron Curtain. Continuity was assured by the Permanent Secretariat under the Pole Rubin, whose competence was significantly expanded in the course of time. There is no doubt that this typical fruit of the Second Vatican Council, a new thing in church history, still needs further development.

Pope Paul VI continued the form of apostolic proclamation by means of doctrinal writings, as cultivated by his predecessors. In the encyclical *Populorum progressio* of 26 March 1967 he took a stand in favor of the Third World; in the Encyclical *Humanae vitae* of 25 July 1968 he again inculcated Christian principles for the reproduction of human life. He utilized the Holy Year 1975, proclaimed by him, to make stronger the union of the local churches with Rome and to inspire the pilgrims arriving in unexpectedly great numbers. For the more the idea was put across that the Universal Church lives in the member and local churches, the more urgent became their internal and external problems for the Church as a whole; the *communio ecclesiarum* is more demanding than any legal order. This structure of the Church, which can appeal to *Lumen gentium,* also sets new tasks for Church history. The national and regional episcopal conferences have acquired a previously undreamed of importance. The postconciliar synods organized by them give reason for a variety in ecclesiastical life which on occasion threatens its unity. Guarantor of this unity is the Petrine Office. It would be fatal to aim to prune it back to its functions in the ancient Church, and just as fatal to maintain certain claims raised in the high and late Middle Ages. The world Church of the twentieth century, in which all continents and races are on an equal footing, cannot be governed in a centralized way, as was the Church of the nineteenth century. However, it is just as certain that the centrifugal tendencies, becoming inexorably stronger, can be met only by a strong central power; an honorary precedence is inadequate for this, quite apart from the fact that it withdraws behind the dogma of the primacy. The modern means of news and communication give the Apostolic See the possibility of being abreast of all happenings in the world Church and, where necessary, of intervening in them to preserve the unity of the Church without reestablishing uniformity. The relaxing of centralization is demanded by the mission of the Church in our time; the Petrine Office further preserves the unity.

The Council of Trent would never have been able to exert its impact if it had not been carried by a wave of holiness. The impact of the Second Vatican Council will also depend on whether the Church of the twentieth century renews itself in the spirit of Jesus Christ. "The definitive decision on the historical worth of the Second Vatican Council depends on whether people realize in themselves the drama of the testing of chaff and wheat"; "whether at the end it will be reckoned among the luminous moments of Church history depends on the people who transfer it into life," says Ratzinger.

CHAPTER 87

The Code of Canon Law and the Development of Canon Law to 1974

From the Promulgation of the Code to the Second Vatican Council

The Codification of Canon Law

The codification of the canon law of the Latin Church is due to the energy and initiative of Pius X. In the motu proprio *Arduum sane munus* of 19 March 1904 the Pope had made known his intention of assembling in one uniform codification the valid canon law of the Latin Church, which lay scattered in many sources of the law. The task was courageously undertaken and energetically pursued under the direction of Pietro Gasparri. The bishops of the world and consultors from the most important countries took part in the work. In the secret consistory of 4 December 1916 Benedict XV announced the completion of the project. On 27 May 1917 the Pope issued the law in which the Code of Canon Law obtained ratification — the apostolic constitution *Providentissima Mater Ecclesia.* The Code of Canon Law was promulgated on 28 June 1917 and took effect on 19 May 1918. The intended aim — to unify the fragmented law in the great and important questions of ecclesiastical life — was accomplished. The Code of Canon Law is a codification, complete in itself, of the common law of the Church of the Latin Rite. But it refers to earlier laws which retain their validity because and in so far as it mentions them (Canon 6). The Code of Canon Law is the law book of the Church of the Latin Rite, but to a certain extent it is also valid for the congregations of the Eastern Rites (Canon 1). The codification was stamped by the principles of the greatest possible retention of the traditional and by prudent adaptation. The code thus contains no radical novelties, but only modifications suited to the age. Some archaic elements were dragged along, and certain newer developments, for example, in the sphere of the law of property and benefices, were not considered. The code accepted in the widest scope the proposals made by the fathers of the First Vatican Council and the bishops employed for consultation. It built also, in many ways, on the ideas and guidelines given by Leo XIII. Finally, some elements from the law of concordats entered the code, for example, in regard to the privileges of the clergy. The thinning, reworking, and modernizing of the vast matter of traditional norms represent an important legislative achievement. The code is the climax and conclusion of the development begun in the nineteenth century, which the Church aimed also to make through strict uniform discipline and close union with the Apostolic See into a fit tool of the Christian penetration of the earth. It is an achievement due preeminently to the work of the Catholic Church in Europe. It stands in the tradition of medieval canon law and draws upon the lines begun by Trent.

The Code of Canon Law is divided into five books; to it were attached eight older documents which, as regards content, had not been adopted into it. It is introduced by the *Professio catholicae fidei*. Its principles of classification are not satisfactory in every respect. For example, the law on ecclesiastical offices is dismembered and divided between two different books. The code aimed to be basically only an internal law book of the Church and hence omits from the codification the regulation of the relations of Church and state. It thereby considerably facilitated its implementation. The language of the code is succinct and clear, but it suffers from uncertainty in terminology. In regard to new elements in the content, the following examples are illustrative. The position of the bishops was strengthened. The inclination existing since the Middle Ages to curtail the power of the hierarchical courts between Pope and bishops is expressed in the insignificance of the metropolitans (Canon 274). The bishops are freely named by the Pope (Canon 329, paragraph 2), and in this matter he makes ever more use of the lists submitted by the bishops. For the first time, the office of the bishop's vicar general was regulated by the common law (Canons 366–71). Trent's law on the contracting of marriage was made binding on the whole Church, and the exceptions for Germany and Hungary were abolished (Canon 1094).

The code was accepted by Catholics in general with joy and gratitude; they showed themselves overwhelmingly convinced of the advantage of the reform. The enacting of the code actually strengthened the inner order of the Church. The states accepted the codification at least without delays. The upheavals after 1918 assisted the introduction of the code to a great degree. A considerable part of the Church-state law, which chained and limited the Church, broke apart. Numerous conditions based on concordat, privilege, or indult disappeared as a consequence of the cessation of states or favored subjects. More open regulations were often found in the building and rebuilding. The other religious congregations, apart from some German Protestants, raised hardly any objections to the code.

In an effort to assure the legal unity effected by the codification, Benedict XV on 15 September 1917, through the motu proprio *Cum iuris,* set up a Commission of Cardinals and gave it the task of authentically interpreting the code and incorporating in it modifications that had become necessary. It fulfilled the first part of its office, but, apart from two exceptions, it did not take up the second. At the same time the Pope decreed that the congregations of the Roman Curia should issue no new *decreta* without urgent cause, but should limit themselves to *instructiones*.

The Development of the Law from 1918 to 1958

It soon became clear that it was not to be supposed that scholarship and practice could get along essentially with the code. The law formulated in the code required implementation and completion by further norms. Codification did not halt the development of the law, but fostered it. The law of the code developed further powerfully, especially through the numerous authentic declarations of the Commission for Interpretation, but also through the legislation of the Popes, especially Pius XI and Pius XII and the Congregations of Cardinals. The last mentioned issued their norms under the title of *instructiones, decreta, normae, indices,* and *formulae.* The judgments of the Roman Rota, published annually from 1912, and the decisions of the congregations in individual cases likewise contributed to the interpretation and further growth of the law, especially that of marriage. And the letters of admonition and of teaching of the Holy See were also of great significance for the implementation and growth of the law.

The law of the code, so far as this can be observed, on the whole made its way relatively successfully. However, it was not possible to convert all prescriptions of the code into actuality. The code left untouched the treaties made by the Apostolic See with countries and hence to that extent renounced any claim to enforce them (Canon 3). Likewise, acquired rights as well as privileges and indults granted by the Apostolic See remained basically valid (Canon 4). Hence law that was compatible and recognized by the Holy See constituted a limit for the expansion of the new law. In view of the extensive sphere of validity of the code, one must reckon with a still stronger separation between formal and actual validity than with other codifications. New particular law, which supplemented or modified the code, was created especially by concordats. And in the enforcing of the code the bishops displayed an abundant activity at diocesan synods through the adapting and collecting of diocesan law.

Benedict XV. The remaining years of the pontificate of Benedict XV stood under the standard of the imposing, the constructing, and the maintaining of the situation of legal unity that had been achieved. The manner of appointing to episcopal sees in the United States that had been set by the decree *Ratio iuris* of the Consistorial Congregation on 25 July 1916 was extended with insignificant changes to a number of other countries. The Pope undertook important changes in the constitution of the missions. In view of certain radical movements in Czechoslovakia and Hungary, he several times declared, most clearly in the letter of 3 January 1920 to the archbishop of Prague, that the Holy See would never grant the abolition or modification of the law of celibacy.

Pius XI. Pius XI did the chief work in legislation for the enforcing of the Code of Canon Law. Nevertheless he permitted no profound changes in the code. The norms issued by him were thoroughly worked out and adjusted to practice. A special characteristic of Pius XI's legislation was the comprehensive establishing of norms for concordats.

In 1929 the Pope introduced the codification of the canon law of the Eastern Churches, establishing a Commission of Cardinals under the chairmanship of

Pietro Gasparri. To two other commissions, which were set up in 1930, he confided the task of collecting the sources of Eastern canon law and elaborating drafts for the codification. The second commission was changed on 17 July 1935 into the *Pontificia Commissio ad redigendum "Codicem Iuris Canonici orientalis."* From the codification of the Eastern canon law it was expected that it would consolidate the bonds among the Eastern Rite congregations on the one hand and that of these with the Latin Church on the other and produce adaptations of law suited to the day. In two decrees some canons of the code were extended also to the Eastern rite communities. The motu proprio *Sancta Dei Ecclesia* of 25 March 1938 subjected also the Latin rite Catholics living in the Middle East to the Congregation for the Eastern Church.

The delayed arrival of three American cardinals on the occasion of the papal election of 1922 was utilized by Pius XI as an opportunity to modify in the motu proprio *Cum proxime* of 1 March 1922 the regulation of the conclave by Pius X on 25 December 1904. According to it the legal interval for the beginning of the conclave was lengthened from ten to fifteen days, to which, by decision of the College of Cardinals, three more days at the most might be added. The motu proprio was adopted into the appendix of documents of the code. Many decrees of the Pope affected the organization and the order of the competence and of the procedure of the departments of the Roman Curia. The congregations were strongly meshed in personnel. Through the constitution *Quae divinitus* of 27 March 1935 the *Sacra Poenitentiaria* obtained a new organization; on 29 July 1934 the *Sacra Romana Rota* underwent a reorganization of its constitution and its procedure. In the carrying out of Canon 328 there appeared on 15 August 1934 the constitution *Ad incrementum* on the prelates of the Roman Curia. For the quinquennial faculties of residential bishops, reintroduced on 17 March 1922, the motu proprio *Post Datam* of 20 April 1923 created a uniform formula, which was issued by the Consistorial Congregation. For carrying out Canon 296 the Congregation for the Propagation of the Faith on 8 December 1929 issued the important instruction *Quum huic Sacrae* on the relations between missionary bishops and religious superiors. In order to bring the statutes of cathedral and collegiate chapters into conformity with the law of the code, the Congregation of the Council on 25 July 1923 directed the bishops to allow the chapters an interval of six months for the adjustment of their statutes; if nothing should be done during this period, they should themselves carry out the revision. The discipline of the clergy was strictly inculcated or regulated by a considerable number of complexes of norms; in the encyclical *Ad catholici sacerdotii* of 20 December 1935 the Pope had called the clergy's attention to the dignity and importance of its mission. The constitution *Deus scientiarum Dominus* of 24 May 1931, with the *ordinationes* of the Congregation for Studies of 12 June 1931 on Catholic universities and faculties represented a sort of fundamental law of the Catholic system of higher education. It demanded an increase of ecclesiastical faculties and the raising of the scholarly requirements for promotions as well as the improvement of the teaching profession and the means of instruction. The Congregation of Seminaries and Universities was stripped of the right of promotion granted in Canon 256, par. 1. Under the name "Catholic Action," Pius XI called into being a lay movement united to the apostolate of the hierarchy. On 7 May 1923 appeared the decree of the Congregation of the Sacraments, *Catholica doctrina,* which in the appended bylaw exhaustively regulated the procedure in the dissolving of marriage *ratum sed non consummatum.* The instruction of the Congregation of the Sacraments of 27 December 1930 on the ordination *scrutinia* set up a detailed method for examining candidates for orders in an effort to keep out of the priesthood unsuitable or unworthy persons. The instruction of the Congregation of the Sacraments of 15 August 1936 brought, in 240 articles, detailed norms on the conducting of the annulment of marriages in the diocesan tribunals, which further developed the law of the code.

Pius XII. Pope Pius XII displayed a voluminous legislative activity in all areas. He intervened considerably more deeply into the body of the Code of Canon Law than had his predecessor. Pius XII was himself a learned canonist, who knew the history, system, and spirit of canon law. Together with his delight in responsibility and decisiveness, as well as with his gift for choosing the right collaborators, he was in a sense created to be a legislator. The legislation of Pius XII was throughout determined by the intention of coming to the aid of pastoral necessities. It was dedicated to doing justice to all realities conditioned by time and locally circumscribed. The Pope courageously faced changed conditions and took into account new insights. He carefully put his laws in the right way for legal reality. Modified norms for the Universal Church were often prepared and tested by indults for specific areas. Then they were introduced in gradual steps. The basic features of this legislation were prudent adjustment to new situations, openness to developments, foresight in changes, firmness in the fundamental, and flexibility in questions of procedure. Although the legislation of Pius XII partly involved deeply incisive changes of ecclesiastical discipline, at no time did there exist in clergy or faithful a feeling of insecurity or of helplessness. There never was even the appearance that the Pope was pushed or subject to pressure. At all stages he remained sovereignly the master of the situation.

In the encyclical *Mystici Corporis* of 29 June 1943 Pius XII treated the fundamental relation of Church and canon law. In a happy synthesis he sketched the correlation and distinction of legal structure and supernatural life in the Church. The encyclical was a landmark for the doctrine of Church membership. On 8 December 1945 he issued the constitution *Vacantis Apostolicae Sedis.* In content it adhered essentially to the constitution *Vacante Sede Apostolica* of Pius X of 25 December 1904, but added the modification that in the future for the papal election one further vote beyond the two-thirds majority was required. Above all, Pius XII became the great legislator in the field of the law of the sacraments. In the constitution *Episcopalis consecrationis* of 30 November 1944 he clarified the role of the two coconsecrators in episcopal ordination; in the constitution *Sacramentum Ordinis* of 30 November 1947, the matter and form of the ordination of deacon, priest, and bishop. By the decree *Spiritus Sancti munera* of 14 September 1946 parish priests obtained the authorization to administer the sacrament of confirmation, in the territory of their parish, to the faithful who as a result of a serious illness are in danger of death. The encyclical *Mediator Dei* of 20 November 1947 is important for the law of the sacrament-sacrifice of the Eucharist and of the liturgy in general. The constitution *Christus Dominus* and the appended instruction of 6 January 1953 reorganized the precept of the Eucharistic fast and granted to local ordinaries the power to permit the celebration of evening Mass. The motu proprio *Sacram Communionem* of 19 March 1957 brought further mitigations of the Eucharistic fast and the extension of the faculty to permit evening Mass. Many legislative acts of the Pope and his assisting agencies applied to matrimony. The premarital investigations were minutely regulated in 1941, the order of precedence of the ends of marriage was clarified in 1944, artificial insemination, apart from the permissible *adiuvatio naturae,* was rejected in 1949 and 1956. Liturgical law was permanently developed by Pius XII. The Solemn Easter Vigil was restored in 1951, the liturgy of Holy Week was reorganized in 1955, the reform of the missal and breviary was taken up in 1955. Church music obtained guidance in the encyclical *Musicae sacrae disciplina* of 25 December 1955 and in the instruction *De Musica sacrae* of 3 September 1958. The constitution *Provida Mater Ecclesia* of 2 February 1947 is in a sense the founding charter of secular institutes. To the already existing three forms of the state of perfection a fourth was added. The constitution *Sponsa Christi* of 21 November 1950 and the related instruction *Inter praeclara* of 23 November 1950 brought about an adaptation of the enclosure of nuns to the times without sacrificing anything essential of the life of virginity and contemplation. The constitution *Exsul Familia* of 2 August 1952 introduced an exhaustive ordering of the pastoral care of refugees, exiles, and emigrants. Under Pius XII the codification of the canon law of the Eastern Churches reached its maturity. The following parts were promulgated: on 22 January 1949 the law of marriage; on 6 January 1950 the law of trials; on 9 February 1952 the law of religious institutes and of property as well as the stipulating of specified concepts; on 2 June 1957 the constitutional law. That this law of the diversity of the communities of the Eastern rites was adequate in every respect is not claimed. But a certain simplification was necessary. Nevertheless, it is questionable to what extent the codified law has been put into practice.

From the Convocation of the Second Vatican Council

The Second Vatican Council was an event of the greatest significance for canon law. Let merely this be remarked: the greatest part of the declarations and directions of the council was not directly oriented to the individual law in force, but, so far as there was question at all of legally relevant texts, a sort of legislative program or stating of principles, which had in view the ecclesiastical legislators. They were called upon to undertake a modification of canon law in accord with the spirit and the letter of the conciliar texts.

John XXIII

On 25 January 1959 Pope John XXIII announced a revision of the Code of Canon Law. On 28 March 1963 he instituted a Commission for the Reform of the Code. At first the chairman was Cardinal Pietro Ciriaci. In view of the short duration of the pontificate no results could be expected from the work of the commission, especially since all the personnel were monopolized by the preparation and implementation of the council. Under John XXIII the legislation of the Holy See bore thoroughly traditional characteristics. No single decree of the Pope or of the Holy See abandons the line of continuity and of cautious change. That the genial but indecisive impulses of the Pope had intended extensive changes is at least doubtful, considering his conservative outlook. Nevertheless, this legislation has no uniform character; it lacks planning and a dominating guidance. The Synod of the Diocese of Rome, held by John XXIII from 24 to 31 January 1960, proceeded in expressly traditional paths. It seemed to wish to impose once more the traditional church discipline firmly and sharply. The law, already challenged from 1910 to 1915, of the suburbicarian sees underwent new modifications through the motu proprio *Ad Suburbicarias* of 10 March 1961, which abolished the cardinals' right of option to the suburbicarian sees, and especially by the motu proprio *Suburbicariis sedibus* of 11 April 1962. Thereafter the cardinal bishops no longer have any jurisdiction in the see whose title they bear. It is governed rather by a residential bishop. The cardinal deacons, for whom the code already required priestly ordination (Canon 232, par. 1), in the future had to be bishops, in accord with the motu proprio *Cum gravissima* of 15 April 1962. To this higher valuation of the College of Cardinals scarcely corresponded the increase in the number of cardinals carried out by John XXIII. In the creation of 15 December 1958 the Pope for the first time exceeded the maximum number set by Sixtus V. The motu proprio *Summi Pontificis Electio* of 5 September 1962 supplemented the constitution *Vacantis Apostolicae Sedis* and changed the law of the papal election in the sense that he is elected who obtains two-thirds of the valid votes. Only in the event that the number of cardinals present is not divisible by three is a further ballot required. The turning of the Pope to the separated Christians began to appear in law. On 17 July 1961 the graduation of non-Catholics was conceded to ecclesiastical faculties.

Paul VI

Organs. Naturally, the chief role in the implementation of the Second Vatican Council devolved upon the Holy See. In numerous apostolic constitutions, motu proprio, decrees, instructions, directories, encyclicals, norms, and proclamations an exhaustive material in norms of varied obligatory force was spread through the Church, claiming to serve the carrying out of the Second Vatican Council. The centralized control lies regularly in the Congregations of Cardinals. The Secretariat for Promoting Christian Unity and at first the Commission for the Implementation of the Constitution on the Liturgy also had an important share. The episcopal conferences and the Synod of Bishops exercise a powerful influence on the shaping of papal law. By the motu proprio *Finis Concilio* of 3 January 1966 Paul VI called into being the postconciliar commissions. The authentic interpretation of the conciliar decrees was entrusted to the Central Commission. Its place was taken in 1967 by the *Pontificia Commissio decretis Concilii Vaticani II interpretandis*. However, this commission interprets not only documents of the council, but also the decrees issued for their execution. But other congregations likewise care for the interpretation of the conciliar decrees and the norms pertaining to them for their sphere.

The legislative acts of the Holy See in turn call forth numerous rules of implementation from episcopal conferences and from bishops. In several countries diocesan synods or synods of a new sort were held for the enforcement of the council. As the first, the Catholic Church in the Netherlands organized a so-called Pastoral Council at Noordwijkerhout from 1966 to 1970. The bishops of the country, priests, and laity took part in it, and non-Catholic observers played an important role. The legal nature of the meeting remained undefined. The binding force of the decrees passed by it must not have gone beyond the character of recommendations. This new type of synod aspired to show, as the first after the close of the Second Vatican Council, how to realize and concretize the decrees and initiatives of the council in a particular Church. Its chief goal, however, was probably the creating of a changed awareness among the Dutch Catholics. Voluminous texts were enacted in six sessions, and their range extended from the concepts of authority to the Jewish question. However, they are very frequently conceptually ambiguous and theologically inadequate as well as to a great extent determined by the ideology of democracy and of hostility to canon law. Opposed to individual positive regulations was an abundance of misleading and erroneous assertions. At the synod the spirit of a radical reformism was predominant, and neither the common law of the Church nor the binding teaching of the Church was a barrier against it. Experiments were unscrupulously advocated, regardless of the possible consequences. Many novelties were introduced without regard to the Universal Church. Decisive statements of faith were obfuscated or disregarded. A binding profession of faith seemed not to exist for the synod's majority. The concept of God and revelation were reinterpreted. Holy Scripture was in many passages improperly interpreted. The idea of the Church was completely deformed. Heretics and unbelievers also have a place in the "Church" described by the Pastoral Council. The sacramental and hierarchical structure of the Church was denied. The primacy was leveled, the ecclesiastical teaching office eliminated, jurisdiction reduced. The Church was sociologized and humanized. Unequivocal moral norms disappeared. Pope Paul VI in his letter of 24 December 1969 to Cardinal Alfrink displayed anxiety over the direction taken by the Pastoral Council. The bishops, however, who took part in it were in general silent in regard to the statements that were contrary to the faith. Nevertheless, the episcopate wanted to avoid a break with the Pope. The Dutch Pastoral Council was at the same time the expression and cause of the crisis in which the Catholic Church in the Netherlands finds itself. As far as putting the Second Vatican Council into practice it accomplished hardly anything. In Germany, following individual diocesan synods — Hildesheim, Meissen — the so-called Common Synod of the bishoprics in the Federal Republic of Germany and then the so-called Pastoral Synod of the German Democratic Republic were convoked. They met in several sessions from 1971 or 1973 respectively to 1975. The first meeting of the Common Synod suffered from serious structural defects. Its statutes overlooked the fact, first, that the episcopal conference possessed no general competence to legislate for all ecclesiastical matters, but only for those concerning which such competence was given it by the Apostolic See. In the area of local ecclesiastical legislation, for which the episcopal conference had no competence, the synod was instructed to have the individual residential bishops adopt the synodal material as their own. No however great majority of the members of the episcopal conference could oblige them to this. The synod was erroneously conceived. The roles within the commission were not properly distributed. The synod gave priests and lay persons a share in legislation and hence obscured the fact that legislation in the Church pertains only to the bishops by right and that priests and lay persons are restricted to advising. More satisfactory was the structure of the Pastoral Synod of the jurisdictional area of the German Democratic Republic. In it the members of the Conference of Ordinaries did not partake in the voting, according to the statute. In this way the fundamental distinction between shepherds and subjects, as well as that between legislating and advising, persisted.

The Common Synod issued numerous documents on the share of the laity in preaching, on the duties and goals of religious instruction, on the administering and receiving of the sacraments, on the importance and form of the liturgy, on the aims of youth work, on the obligation of the Church vis-à-vis foreign workers, on the Church's duties in the sphere of education, on the position of religious communities in the Church, on structures and services of pastoral care, on the protection of the personal rights of the individual within the Church, and on the coresponsibility of all the faithful for the Church's mission. In the main, they have declamatory value, but to a degree they penetrate deep into the structure of the congregations.

In Austria most bishoprics held diocesan synods. The Holy See granted the admission of lay persons under the proviso that the priests had at least an absolute majority on the commissions and in the plenary assembly. All dioceses of the country met in the "Austrian Synodal Proceeding," which, despite extensive borrowing from the statute and routine of the German synod, did not constitute a synod. The decrees of the meeting represented only recommendations to the episcopal conference. In Switzerland meetings of diocesan synods alternated with those of the Swiss Plenary Assembly.

General Character. The task of implementing the Second Vatican Council was given to Paul VI, the episcopal conferences, and the individual bishops. However, several obstacles presented themselves to the converting of the directions and efforts of the council into practicable norms. First, many statements of the council were not clear as a consequence of the "pastoral" style and hence were controverted. On the other hand, the development in the Church had already actually gone on ahead of the council in many respects. Finally, a uniform desire, such as is indispensable for a harmonious legislation, was usually absent. The Church was in a leadership crisis, which adversely affected legislation to a serious degree. And so the development of the law since the Second Vatican Council is basically different from the earlier. The traditional reserve and discretion of the changes were abandoned. Incisive, even radical changes took place rapidly and without preparation, often in homely dress. The haste with which norms were produced in the postconciliar period was favorable to neither their quality nor their content. Contradictions in one and the same law, to the law of a higher legislator, or in laws rapidly succeeding one another were not rare. Mistakes and omissions made improvements necessary. Changes in the law increased so that a growing insecurity seized upon members of the Church. Legal material grew enormously and even for the expert was not always easy to master. The voluminous production of norms was, to be sure, not only an effect of the Second Vatican Council but also a symptom of critical phenomena appearing in the Church in almost all spheres and in most countries. The trend of the legislation was regularly to adaptation and relief, adaptation not so much to changed circumstances, whose form was not subject to the power of the Church, but rather to a changed mentality, for example, to the ideology of equality and the wave of democratization, and relief not from burdens which could no longer be borne, but from obligations whose fulfilling demanded moral effort and strength of self-control, for example, in regard to the Eucharistic fast or the carrying out of the obligation of attending Mass on holy days. The trust of the legislator in the strength of men's self-determination had grown, and greater responsibility was laid on the individual. Ecclesiastical standardization withdrew from some subjects; it became grandiose. Lower courts were empowered to a great extent to deal with business hitherto reserved to higher. Full authority was ever more generously imparted to bishops and pastors, and even to chaplains. In increasing measure power of jurisdiction was turned over to lay persons. Legislation was not rarely determined by external motives, not those inherent in the matter, especially with the aim of letting powerful groups do their will. In an effort to relieve the pressure on the bishops, made aware of their importance at the council, Paul VI, long before the issuing of the Decree on Bishops, granted them new faculties in the motu proprio *Pastorale munus* of 30 November 1963. The standardization of the valid dispensations from the precept of the Eucharistic fast was made known orally by the secretary-general of the Second Vatican Council on 21 November 1964. In not a few cases modifications of the law were regularly extorted. Proceeding from the statements of specific theologians, certain circles of clerics and lay persons introduced practices and texts desired by them and placed the bishops before faits accomplis. This procedure was practiced especially in the sphere of liturgy. The bishops, sometimes after trivial resistance, gave in, and the arbitrarily introduced methods of acting and texts were made law or permitted by the Holy See to become law. A further characteristic of this legislation was the intention of meeting the wishes or the pressure of non-Catholics. The ecumenism proclaimed by the council had turned out to be a fertile motive of many alterations of law, for example, in regard to mixed marriages, *communio in sacris,* and the reception of the sacraments. The connivance with Protestantism in the area of liturgy and sacramental law, whereby the innermost sphere of ecclesiastical life was affected, became serious. The claim for many postconciliar documents of compliance with the directions of the council could not be verified after exact examination, because either the programmatic declarations of the council were observed too imprecisely or the postconciliar norms did not remain within the clearly discernible will of the council. Thus, for example, as regards the system of government by councils, which was set up in the German dioceses, it was demonstrated from many sides that it was in opposition to the conciliar directives.

The particular synods sought to introduce into the life of the Church by way of legislation in the local churches all the matters which had no prospect of being taken up at the Second Vatican Council. The following examples may be cited. Confirmation should be administered to a greater degree by nonbishops. The penitential devotion should acquire a sacramental character. Remarried divorced persons should be admitted to receive Communion. The matrimonial impediment of disparity of cult and the obligation to the canonical form in contracting marriage should be abolished. The participation of Catholics in the Protestant Lord's Supper should be made possible. Also demanded were the admission of married men to the priesthood, the reinstatement of married priests in the priestly ministry, and the investigation of the possibility of granting priestly ordination to women. In the question of contraception there even appeared in the synodal statements a deviation from the Church's binding moral teaching. In the light of these aberrations and numerous other serious flaws, the verdict on the synods in the German-speaking lands can only be that they increased the perplexity in the Church. The critical and most urgent task of confirming the faith and intensifying devotion was not even approached by them, let alone implemented. Many decrees of the synods did not promote the carrying out of the council but worked against it or disregarded it. To the extent that they aimed to implement the council, they partly skipped over the middle portion of the still existing regulations for total church implementation. In any event the synodal assemblies encroached upon the law of the revised code. In the question of lay preaching the offense against the common law was later censured by the Holy See. But this was precisely the matter which, after the Holy See had given in, became the first to be put in force. Presumably the intention was to present a fait accompli which the universal legislator could not disregard. The chief significance of the synods lies in the fact that they acted as opinion-forming agents, and indeed in the demolition of dogmatic, moral, and legal ties. Practice already closely followed the perspectives which appeared at the synods, regardless of contrary law. The so-called pastoral character of many documents, which claimed to be practicable norms, frequently obscured their normative value and thereby paved the way for a dangerous legal uncertainty. Many of the *vota* issued at the synods just mentioned were useless for the further developments of ecclesiastical law because they either were too vague or bypassed reality.

Of the greatest significance for the development of canon law, then, was the raising of the episcopal conferences to a real hierarchical tribunal between the individual bishop and the Apostolic See by the Second Vatican Council. Their legislative competence was constantly growing. In this way the process of centralizing and standardizing the law by the Holy See, to be observed in the nineteenth century and the first half of the twentieth, was halted and gave place to a countermovement. The particularizing of the law increased. Peculiarities of national Churches gained greater weight, in fact were to a degree consciously promoted. The inserting of ever broader circles of persons into the process of legislation showed the enactment of norms and well-nigh leveled every legislative project. The actual incompetence of most members of synods of the new type for the treating of the questions posed is notorious. The assignment of competence and the precedence of the norms were especially not often observed by the particular legislators. The synods mentioned considered themselves competent for almost all areas of church life and interfered illicitly in the sphere of the Universal Church.

Individual Legislative Actions. The Second Vatican Council was under the aegis of a revalorization of the episcopal office. The lever for this undertaking was the principle of collegiality. According to it, the holders of the highest power in the Universal Church are not only the Pope but also the College of Bishops acting in agreement with the Pope. The episcopate logically claimed to share in the rule of the entire Church even outside the general councils. The Pope had regard for this desire in a twofold respect. First, he announced to the surprised fathers at the opening of the fourth session of the Second Vatican Council on 14 September 1965 the establishing of a Synod of Bishops. On the next day the motu proprio *Apostolica sollicitudo* was published in the council *aula.* The Synod of Bishops is a central ecclesiastical institution, which represents the episcopate of the world. In accord with its nature, it is a permanent institution, but meets only on special invitation. The Synod of Bishops has fundamentally only an advisory function, but can, if the Pope allows, also issue decrees; its decrees are subject to papal confirmation. It should foster the union and cooperation between Pope and bishops, put information at disposal, bring about uniformity in questions of doctrine and in procedure within the Church as well as advise in regard to the subjects which from time to time are to be placed on the agenda. Convocation, approval of elected members, drawing up of the list of *tractanda,* and issuance of the agenda, as well as the chairmanship, belong to the Pope. Representatives of the episcopal conferences constitute the greatest part of the members. In addition, there are the Eastern patriarchs, religious, heads of the departments of the Roman Curia, and bishops, clerics, or religious nominated by the Pope for this case. Then the motu proprio *Pro comperto sane* of 6 August 1967 prescribed the admittance of seven residential bishops as full members into each of the congregations of the Roman Curia. They took part in their plenary sessions. Together with the motu proprio *De Episcoporum muneribus,* issued on 15 June 1966 to implement the decree *Christus Dominus* on the pastoral duty of bishops, which gave bishops the faculty basically to dispense in individual cases from all general laws of the Church, as well as with the abolition of the fundamental irremovability of pastors by the motu proprio *Ecclesiae Sanctae* (no. 20), the aims of the bishops for the mentioned changes seemed to have been satisfied.

In connection with the stressing of the collegiality of the bishops was the diminution of privileges of the College of Cardinals. The dignity of cardinal-protector of monastic congregations was abolished as early as 28 April 1964. In order to take into account the special position and the sensibilities of the Eastern patriarchs, Paul VI in the motu proprio *Ad Purpuratorum Patrum* of 11 February 1965 decreed that at their admission into the College of Cardinals these should be assigned to the *Ordo episcopalis.* The motu proprio *Sacro Cardinalium consilio* of 26 February 1965 allowed the election of the dean and subdean of the Sacred College only from among the suburbicarian bishops. The motu proprio *Ingravescentem aetatem* of 21 November 1970 dealt a severe blow to the Sacred College. It decreed that cardinals who had completed their eightieth year without more ado lost their curial offices as well as the right to elect the Pope.

The Pope began the reform of the Roman Curia, desired by the council, with the Holy Office. He sought to counter the attacks on this congregation, which were made to some extent even in the conciliar *aula,* first with the change of name and of sphere of competence, prescribed in the motu proprio *Integrae servandae* of 7 December 1965, as well as the reorganization of the procedure of the department, also held out in prospect in the same document. Further steps followed. On 14 June and 15 November 1966 respectively, the *Index librorum prohibitorum* and the prohibition of books by law as prescribed in Canon 1399 were declared abolished. A little later a Commission of Theologians from the various countries was set up beside the Congregation for the Doctrine of the Faith. On 15 August 1967 the constitution *Regimini Ecclesiae Universae* effected the reorganization of the Roman Curia demanded by the council. According to it, the Curia remains the representative and assisting agency of the Pope and is in no relationship of subordination to the episcopate, as some bishops desired. In the structure and activity of the Curia, however, a series of changes is found. Henceforth the Pope is no longer the prefect of some congregations; he is no longer also in them, but only above them. The position of the cardinal secretary of state was strengthened, and a better communication and coordination of the individual congregations was provided for. The Secretariat of State had to assure the close union of the offices of the Roman Curia with the Pope and among themselves. The cardinals who presided over the departments of the Curia could be summoned by the cardinal secretary of state to a common meeting. A number of offices were newly instituted or confirmed respectively, especially the Secretariat for non-Catholic Christians, non-Christian religions, and unbelievers, as well as an Office of Statistics. The *Dataria* was abolished. The "Council for the Public Affairs of the Church" is competent for relations between the Church and state governments. All members of the congregations are for the future appointed for only five years, and after the lapse of this period must be again appointed, which, of course, hardly works to the benefit of willingness to accept responsibility and independence of judgment. The members of the Curia are selected from the various peoples, in each case in accord with knowledge and pastoral experience. Contact with the bishops should be maintained and their views taken into consideration. A detailed *regolamento* regulates the routine of the Curia. But the organization of the Roman Curia created by the constitution *Regimini Ecclesiae* soon underwent new changes. By the constitution *Sacra Rituum Congregatio* of 8 May 1969 the Congregation of Rites was divided and a new Congregation for Divine Worship was established. The constitution *Constans nobis studium* of 11 July 1975 abolished it again and joined it with the Congregation of the Sacraments as the new "Congregation for the Sacraments and Divine Worship." The motu proprio *Quo aptius* of 27 February 1973 put an end to the Apostolic Chancery and transferred its duties to the Secretariat of State. The instruction of the cardinal secretary of state of 4 February 1974 on the obligation of secrecy in regard to the proceedings of the Holy See, which arose from an actual incident, made known that the critical procedures in the Church did not stop at the Roman Curia.

The motu proprio *Sollicitudo omnium Ecclesiarum* of 24 June 1969 again defined the duties of papal envoys. The law produced a stronger differentiation of the Holy See's diplomatic representations and made provision for extraordinary circumstances in nations. The duty of legates to promote the union of the bishops with the Pope was put at the head of their obligations. On 25 March 1972 the Council for the Public Affairs of the Church issued a directive for the determining and naming of candidates for the episcopal office in the Latin Church.

In taking up relatively vague statements of the Second Vatican Council a comprehensive apparatus of councils on all levels of ecclesiastical activity, from the parish to the episcopal conference, was constructed, above all in the German-speaking countries. These bodies moved beside, and in the parochial sphere partly over, the ordained shepherds. No longer the cathedral chapter, but the

Priests' Council is, according to a declaration of the Congregation for the Clergy, the bishop's senate for the future. Many decrees aimed to promote the renewal of religious institutes or sought to master the critical conditions in them. Comprehensive complexes of norms were issued for the implementation of the Second Vatican Council's Constitution on the Liturgy, beginning with the motu proprio *Sacram Liturgiam* of 25 January 1964 through the instructions of 26 September 1964, 23 November 1965, 4 May 1967, 25 May 1967, 29 May 1969, and 5 September 1970, and numerous decrees and norms, up to the encyclical on the Eucharistic Prayers of 27 April 1973, without there being an end to this production of norms in prospect. New texts were published for the Mass, new *ordines* for the administration of the sacraments. The constitution *Missale Romanum* of 3 April 1969 promulgated the changed Roman Mass book. From 1965 the fulfilling of the Sunday obligation of attending Mass was already granted for the preceding evening. Concelebration and Communion *sub utraque* became more and more widespread. The instruction from the Congregation of the Sacraments, *Immensae caritatis* of 29 January 1973, granted the faculty of permitting lay persons to administer Communion, increased the number of cases in which Communion could be received twice on the same day, and further modified the Eucharistic fast. Under specified conditions, according to the instruction of the Secretariat for Promoting Christian Unity of 1 June 1972, non-Catholic Christians can be permitted to receive Communion in the Catholic Church. The motu proprio *Firma in traditione* of 13 June 1974 brought a new regulation of the system of Mass stipends. The motu proprio *Sacrum Diaconatus Ordinem* of 18 June 1967 created the canonical basis for the reintroduction of the permanent diaconate in the Latin Church. Because it was intended to ordain married men of mature age as deacons, there resulted the first breakthrough in the law of celibacy. The minor orders and the subdiaconate were abolished by the motu proprio *Ministeria quaedam* of 15 August 1972. Their place was taken by the ministries of reader and acolyte, which could also be bestowed on laymen who had no intention of entering the ecclesiastical state. The motu proprio *Ad pascendum* of 15 August 1972 joined entry into the clerical state with the reception of the Order of Deacon. On 17 February 1966 appeared the constitution *Paenitemini.* The penitential discipline, especially fasting, was considerably mitigated by it. A decree of the Congregation for Divine Worship of 2 December 1973 prescribed a new *ordo* of penance. The constitution *Sacram Unctionera Infirmorum* of 30 November 1973 regulated the Sacrament of the Anointing of Sick anew. The law on mixed marriage had already been mitigated in the instruction *Matrimonii sacramentum* of 18 March 1966. The decree *Crescens matrimoniorum* of 22 February 1967 eliminated the sanction of invalidity for the nonobservance of the obligatory form in the contracting of marriage between Catholics and Eastern non-Catholics. The motu proprio *Matrimonia mixta* of 31 March 1970 was a new retreat before Protestant pressures and for the first time in the history of papal regulation of mixed marriages abandoned the assuring of the Catholic upbringing of the children in mixed marriages. In issuing this law, the Pope was standing, as was remarked, under "progress compulsion." The instruction of the Holy Office of 5 July 1963 basically allowed cremation to Catholics. The motu proprio *Pastoralis migratorum cura* of August 1969 reorganized the pastoral care of emigrants.

Numerous rules of procedure were revised or issued anew. The motu proprio

Sanctitas clarior of 19 March 1969 rearranged the process of beatification and canonization. In view of the more and more public celibacy crisis Paul VI reasserted the celibacy of priests in the encyclical *Sacerdotalis Caelibatus* of 24 June 1967. The growing number of laicizations of priests induced the Congregation for the Doctrine of the Faith on 13 January 1971 to issue new norms for the implementing of the procedure of reducing men in major orders to the lay state. In implementing the motu proprio *Integrae servandae* the Congregation for the Doctrine of the Faith on 15 January 1971 issued an order for the procedure in the examination of doctrinal opinions. The motu proprio *Causas matrimoniales* of 28 March 1971 provided norms for the expediting of marriage cases in the Latin Church; the motu proprio *Cum matrimonialium* of 8 September 1973, in the Eastern Churches. The instruction of the Congregation of the Sacraments of 7 March 1972 improved the rules of processes for establishing the nonconsummation of marriage. The decree of the Congregation for the Doctrine of the Faith of 19 March 1975 reorganized the previous censorship of books. Henceforth only editions and translations of Holy Scripture, liturgical books and their translations, catechisms and theology texts are subject to it. Nevertheless, it was urgently recommended to diocesan clerics and members of the state of perfection to obtain the permission of their local ordinary or higher superior respectively for books which are related to religion and moral teaching.

More and more often was the instituting of an ecclesiastical jurisdiction over acts of administration requested. The Holy See sought to take this concern into account in a twofold way. In the process of reform of the Curia the tasks of an ecclesiastical law court for administration were assigned to the Church's supreme tribunal, the Apostolic Signatura. They are cared for by the newly formed Second Section. Recourse can be had to this if the contested administrative act was issued by a department of the Roman Curia and a law was transgressed by it. The Apostolic Signatura grants no legal protection against measures of lower ecclesiastical organs. Two drafts were elaborated in 1970 and 1972 for the establishing of a court for administrative acts on the other ecclesiastical levels. While the first draft envisaged three types of legal devices against burdensome acts of administration — recourse to the hierarchical superior, recourse to the court of administration, complaint to the regular court — the second draft proceeded from the possibility of complaint before the regular court. The promulgation of a corresponding motu proprio is still to come.

On 1 October 1975 Paul VI published the apostolic constitution *Romano Pontifici Eligendo,* the new regulation of the papal election. On 5 December 1973 the Pope had posed the question of whether it was not fitting to expand the group of electors for the choosing of the Pope and to add to the College of Cardinals the patriarchs of the Eastern Churches and the members of the Council of the General Secretariat of the Synod of Bishops. Nevertheless, the above-mentioned constitution, for the sake of the freedom and independence of the proceedings, retained the election of the Pope by the cardinals, but including only a maximum of 120 (no. 33). Likewise, the conclave and the three forms of election procedure were retained. Difficulties in achieving the prescribed majority of two-thirds plus one, which are to be anticipated in view of the increasing pluralism in the Church, permit the cardinals, under specified presuppositions, to be satisfied with an absolute majority plus one or with a final ballot between the two candidates with the most votes (no. 76). With his acceptance of the election, the one chosen, if he has already received episcopal ordination, is immediately bishop of the Church of Rome and at the same time Pope and head of the College of Bishops with complete and supreme power over the Universal Church (no. 88).

Revision of the Code and of the Canon Law of the Eastern Church. The revision of the Code of Canon Law could be seriously taken up only after the close of the Council. On 20 November 1965 the *Pontificia Commissio Codici Iuris Canonici recognoscendo* began its work. It worked in constant contact with the Synod of Bishops, the episcopal conferences, and the individual bishops. In 1974 the commission was enlarged to fifty cardinals from twenty-five nations. Ten, later thirteen subcommissions of consultors prepare the drafts of the revised code, which are then submitted to the commission, and this in turn sends them to the bishops. Following the revision of the drafts in accord with the bishops' remarks, the individual partial codifications are presumably to be promulgated by the Pope *ad experimentum*. Since 1969 the periodical *Communicationes* has reported the aims and progress of the work. The new law book is supposed to be in keeping with the intellectual outlook of the Second Vatican Council and oriented more strongly than the code to pastoral requirements, but to retain its legal character and not be a sort of rule of faith or morals. In jurisdiction and administration the subjective rights of physical and juridical persons are to obtain an effective protection. Sanctions are reduced to a minimum. The principle of subsidiarity is to be utilized to a greater degree. The new code should be restricted to the codification of canon law indispensable and feasible for all parts of the Church. It is the duty of the regional legislative tribunals to create norms for the respective territories. The position of the bishops is to be further strengthened. A common legal status is to be granted to all Christians, on which then are based the rights and obligations which are united with specific ecclesiastical offices and functions. The strict territorial principle of ecclesiastical organization should be modified. In the law relating to the sacraments and to penalties a better coordination of *forum externum* and *forum internum* should be undertaken. The Synod of Bishops, meeting from 30 September to 29 October 1967, expressed itself in favor of the ten principles of renewal of the canon law.

The current drafts for individual books of the revised code make it obvious that the revision will be, not a new edition of the Code of Canon Law, but a new law book. The changed canon law will presumably carry to a considerable extent the marks which were presented above in their general characterization. For the canonical changes of the postconciliar period are ordinarily adopted into the revised code little or not at all modified. Tense expectations which were set for the new law must be disappointed. For example, the draft of the penal law, submitted in 1973, suffers from many, partly serious defects. The schema aims to abbreviate the penal law, to unify it, and to avoid the confusion of the external and the internal *fora*. Baptized non-Catholics are basically excepted from ecclesiastical penal sanctions. However, the practicability of the penal law which the schema envisages is doubtful, among other reasons because of the excessive extension of the competence of particular law and of the enormous number of mere authorizations of penalties. As in the code, the penal criminal law is again mixed with the law of disciplinary penalties. In addition to the technical, the draft also displays serious theological flaws.

The draft of the new ecclesiastical law of marriage, sent to the bishops in 1975, must, on the contrary, despite certain weaknesses, rather measure up to the claims which must be set for a codification of this material that is theologically and canonically unobjectionable. It leaves the structure of the matrimonial law of the code untouched and in general proceeds cautiously with the integration of the law's development since 1918. The legislative competence of the episcopal conferences and the faculties of the bishops are extended, of course, to a tolerable degree. The notion and precedence of the "ends of marriage" are, however, abandoned to the detriment of the matter. The impediments to contracting marriage are strictly limited. The will to marry is again defined, the defects in knowledge are thoroughly discussed, the idea of cunning deception is reintroduced. The ability to contract marriage is treated on a grand scale. The circle of persons bound to the canonical form is drawn considerably more narrowly than before. Catholics who have separated themselves formally or publicly from the Church are no longer to be bound to the canonical form of marriage (Canon 319, par. 1).

Since the death of Pius XII and in consequence of the development then getting under way the codification of the Eastern Canon Law came to a standstill. The opposition of certain hierarchs to some tendencies of the codification, the decay of discipline in the Church, the widespread hostility to law, and the effects of the Second Vatican Council were not favorable to the continuation of the codification. Account had to be taken of the new trends coming to light. And so on 10 June 1972 Paul VI set up a new Commission for the Revision of the Eastern Canon Law — *Pontificia Commissio Codici Iuris Canonici Orientalis recognoscendo* — with Cardinal Joseph Parecattil, archbishop of Ernakulam, India, for the Syro-Malabar Christians, at its head. It had to revise the parts of the Eastern Canon Law that were already in force as well as those not yet published. On 18 March 1974 the Pope set two goals for the commission: to bring the Eastern Canon Law into harmony with the decrees of the Second Vatican Council and to preserve fidelity to the tradition of the Eastern Churches. The commission publishes *Nuntia* as its organ of communication.

From the Second Vatican Council the project of a constitutional law of the Church, a *Lex Ecclesiae Fundamentalis,* was championed by bishops and theologians. On 20 November 1965 Paul VI referred to it in an inquiry. Now, from the very beginning the Church has had a constitution in the material sense, the norms of which are scattered through the various sources of law, especially the code. A constitution in the formal sense, that is, a constitutional law, would have to assemble the norms essential and characteristic for the fundamental legal organization of the Church and prescribe the degree and limits of the legislation of each particular church. Such a constitutional law, in view of the increasing particularization of canon law, is an imperative necessity to guarantee the integration of the parts into the whole, especially to facilitate the verification of particular legislation for its compatibility with the law of the Universal Church. In 1971 the frequently improved draft of a *Lex Ecclesiae Fundamentalis* was officially submitted by the Commission for the Revision of the Code to the bishops. Of 1,306 bishops who gave

an opinion on it, 593 replied *placet,* 462 *placet iuxta modum,* and 251 *non placet.*
The draft fulfilled the demands to remain within the spirit and letter of the Second
Vatican Council, to unite theology and law, and to speak in a pastoral manner. In
the ninety-five canons formulations in more than three hundred passages were
adopted from the texts of the Second Vatican Council. And for the first time the
draft codified basic laws of Catholics. Nevertheless, it found criticism chiefly from
three areas. Some approved it basically, but wanted to see it improved in content
and in legal techniques. The difficulty of examining theological statements as to
their legal power to bind, or respectively, to convert them into norms, explains
the variety of the proposals for correction made by members of this group. Others
assented, in itself, to the notion of a *Lex Ecclesiae Fundamentalis,* but repudiated
the submitted draft as impracticable. They saw in it an obstacle for developments
that were under way in the Church, especially the ecumenical strivings. A third
group came out against any codification of the constitutional law of the Church.
Their criticism was aimed, to a considerable degree, not only against the draft,
but against the hierarchical, in fact the legal structure of the Church in general.
As a matter of fact, the draft of the *Lex Ecclesiae Fundamentalis* stands clearly
in ecclesiastical tradition and checks all promiscuity and arbitrariness. If the one
Church of Christ is the Roman Catholic Church (Canon 2, par. 1), then there is
no possibility of labeling non-Catholic ecclesial communities unequivocally as
Churches. If the Pope possesses the supreme and immediate power over the Universal Church (Canon 34, par. 1), then it is inadmissible to lower his position to that
of a secretary-general. If the bishop is the sole legislator in his diocese (Canon 81,
par. 2), then synodal committees of priests and laity cannot issue norms. If every
believer in Christ had a right to this, that the liturgy be celebrated according to the
prescriptions of his rite (Canon 15), then the foundation is removed from under
liturgical experimentation and manipulation. Although the arguments of the opponents of the *Lex Ecclesiae Fundamentalis* are frequently at variance with one
another, Paul VI showed himself to be impressed by the resistance. He had the
draft withdrawn and turned over to the commission for revision.

The revised form of the *Lex Ecclesiae Fundamentalis* will presumably, in conformity with the wishes of many bishops, contain hardly any basically theological
statements. The juristic character of the law should stand out more prominently,
especially its binding effect in relation to the total subordinate legislation. The
enumeration of the basic rights of the faithful should become more complete.
The ecclesiastical organs of the Universal Church and of the particular Churches,
hence also the councils, should be mentioned.

The manuscript of this chapter was ready at the end of 1974. The subsequent
development could be added only to a slight extent.

CHAPTER 88

The Holy See's Policy of Concordats from 1918 to 1974

Era of Concordats under Pius XI and Pius XII

To the Beginning of the Second World War

Point of Departure, Motives, and General Character. The First World War ended with a profound convulsion of the structure of states and peoples. The peace treaties in the years from 1918 produced no secure peace among nations, because too little justice and wisdom were inherent in them. The drawing of boundaries frequently did not agree with the ethnographical realities. Minorities were further suppressed. In the interior of many countries fermentation and unrest became chronic. In most states of Europe which began as parliamentary democracies after the First World War authoritarian regimes soon came to power. The attitude toward the Church was generally in danger in the former because of instability, in the latter because of caprice. The Church was ordinarily in a difficult position and was left to the good will of the civil partner. The constitutions of almost all countries contained a guarantee of freedom of denomination and of the practice of religion. But the text of the constitution did not ordinarily indicate as a matter of course how the relations of Church and state appeared in practice. Too much depended on its interpretation and application, on the ecclesiastical personnel, and especially on the religious feeling of the people and the spiritual power of the Church in the country in question. The legal ordering of the relations of Church and state is only one facet of the reality of this relationship. It made models and standards obligatory, according to which the mutual outlook of Church and state was to be fashioned, and only to the extent that this occurred was the relation of Church and state a legal relationship. The situation of Church-state policies must not be regarded as the legal Church-state situation. The constitution ordinarily permitted different forms of the relations of Church and state within a specific framework. Thus the constitutionally legal security of religious freedom was in many countries in sharp contrast to the legal reality. In some countries it was not taken for granted even as a private legal freedom. In so far as it was a matter of states governed by law, the Church had no interest in the surrender of a moderate involvement in the state because this assured it of favorable possibilities of acting in society. The quality of a corporation of public law seemed to the Church as the relatively best suited manner of fulfilling its mission in the sphere of state law. A number of countries decided for the constitutionally legal separation of Church and state. However, the implementation of this was subject to the greatest differences. The concept "separation of Church and state" is ambiguous and hence impracticable in a country without an interpretive addition to the description of the relation in the sphere of canon law. Separation can be recommended in order to free the Church from the pressure of the state, but also in order to weaken it as the agent of religion. Separation which a state ruled by law undertakes seeks, of course, to end the relations to religious societies as far as possible but does not forbid their effectiveness; it does not even exclude the formal legal recognition of one or several Churches as well as the making of treaties with them. The separation legislation of many countries, it is true, consciously or unconsciously took as model the French law of 9 December 1905, which was not, of course, motivated by benevolence toward the Catholic Church. On the other hand, a system of union of Church and state can be a heavy burden for a Church, compromise it, even cripple it. Even a concordat, which in itself serves the adjustment between ecclesiastical and secular interests as well as the production or promotion of a harmonious cooperation of Church and state, must operate not without conditions in favor of the Church's life. It depends too much on the manifold organizational powers and power factors within a country whether a legal relationship between Church and state brings benefit or injury to religion. The Code of Canon Law basically does not treat the relations of Church and state and touches on them only occasionally in consequence of objective connections. Law agreeable to states, even that which contradicted the Code of Canon Law, was to be maintained (Canon 3). Relations in the religiously neutral countries, for example, in regard to marriage, were taken into account to a certain extent.

The reorganization of ecclesiastical relations was an imperative necessity in many countries after the First World War. The map of Europe had been, especially in the east and southeast, profoundly altered. From the bankruptcy of tsarist Russia and of the Dual Monarchy of Austria-Hungary had arisen a large number of new states. In other countries territorial changes and alterations of state forms took place. Inflation had serious financial restratifications as a consequence. The Apostolic See sought to control the circumstances especially through the establishing of diplomatic relations with the states and the conclusion of agreements with them. In the address in the consistory of 21 November 1921 Pope Benedict XV (1914–22) declared that many older concordats had lost their force and practicability because of the political changes of the last years. A concordat had to be regraded as null when the legal personality of a state was no longer identical with the partner which had concluded it with the Holy See. But, he said, the Church was ready to enter into negotiations with the governments, of course without prejudice to its dignity and liberty. In this manner the Pope indicated his readiness to conclude new concordats which would take account of altered circumstances. As a matter of fact, Benedict XV's talk released a wave of concordats and other treaties, so that it is correct to speak of an Era of Concordats between the two world wars and beyond. In concluding concordats the Holy See principally aimed to assure the freedom of religious life and of the Church in general by legally binding the state. It was also concerned that the state recognize the position of the Church and its organization. The law of the code had to be circulated and implemented. This was not possible without a tolerant attitude on the part of states. Likewise, a satisfactory arrangement of *res mixtae,* such as schools, religious instruction, marriage, the system of associations and institutes, as well as property could be realized only in harmony with the state. Of primary importance to the Holy See in this regard was the assuring of the religious instruction of children, especially through the guarantee of the erecting of Catholic schools. Then the ecclesiastical circumscription and organization had to be adapted to the changed political and legal circumstances. The drawing of boundaries in the peace treaties had, moreover, created numerous new problems of minorities, which included for the Church in these countries the danger of serious conflicts with the nationalistic-minded popular majorities that dominated the state. Hence, not a few concordats of the postwar period saw to the religious protection of these minorities. The Holy See regularly tried to translate the attempts and desires of governments relating to stipulations in individual points in negotiations for a concordat as comprehensive as possible. Even if the arrangement worked out was frequently not satisfactory or the content of a treaty was meager, the mere fact that it had achieved the concluding of an agreement with a state seemed to the Holy See to be a gain. For in fact in not a few countries there was a fundamental antipathy to any making of a treaty with the Church. Under favorable circumstances there could be further building on the position reached.

On the other hand, new states endeavored to consolidate and exalt their newly won existence by means of treaties with the oldest sovereign of Europe. The esteem for the Holy See was not only not affected since the loss of the Papal State but had even increased because of the effectiveness of important Popes. Also, the Holy See wanted to help strengthen the new states with its means and hoped thereby to serve the cause of peace. The liturgical prayer for the country, for example, corroborated the union of Church and state and testified to the Church's concern for its welfare. Further, the states were interested in a visible and enduring organization of the Catholic Church in their territory, in the coinciding of the ecclesiastical circumscriptions with the national boundaries, in the appointing of loyal bishops, and in the formation of a clergy reliable in regard to the nation. The new states especially placed great value on this, that no territories or monasteries in their country should be or remain subject to foreign bishops or superiors. The Code of Canon Law, as a clearly arranged, precise source of the law of the Church, made it easy for the states to take part in the concluding of treaties with the Church. They knew to what they were obliging themselves, and the interpretation and implementation of the concordat norms were considerably facilitated.

Concordats are systems of mutual concessions by Church and state. In the majority of cases the Church is the receiving party to a greater extent than the state. Hence, after the First World War the nations whose principle of separation proceeded from an ideology hostile to the Church generally avoided the concluding of concordats. They were ordinarily made by states which conceded to the Church a position in public law.

The norms contained in the concordats are, each looked at separately, particular canon law, but, seen in context, they constitute, because of their repetition, the substratum of a common law, of the *ius concordatarium* on specific subjects. The law of concordats between the two world wars was relatively homogeneous; the legal forms and legal institutions utilized by it displayed an extensive agreement. This similarity was derived from two roots. First, in the negotiations the Church proceeded from canon law, which had fortunately just been codified, and so it constantly had basically the same point of departure. Then the effect of precedence was greatly developed in the concluding of concordats. Usually, previous concordats served to a greater or lesser degree as models for later ones.

In individual cases the Church aspired to assure, by means of concordats, a minimum of those guarantees and prerogatives which belonged to it by canon law. And so, treaties frequently repeated principles and assurances which were already expressed in the constitution of the country in question. The Church set critical importance on independence from the state in the filling of its offices. Numerous concordats logically stipulated the free nomination of the bishops by the Pope (Canon 329, par. 2). The government of the state concerned was ordinarily permitted the right, partly in place of an earlier right of nomination, to make known misgivings of a general political nature — the so-called political proviso — before the appointment of residential bishops and of coadjutor bishops with the right of succession. Then, the concordats of Pius XI as a rule contained regulations on appointments to canonries and parishes, schools and theological faculties, the supervision by the bishops of the religious and moral instruction of youth, and the liberties and legal rights of religious institutes. Teaching in the name of the Church was made dependent on the possession of the *missio canonica.* A special legal protection was assured to clerics in the exercise of their office. Pastoral viewpoints induced the Holy See in some cases to agree to the prohibition of partisan political activities by clerics. The right of minorities to religious instruction in their vernacular was assured. In many concordats the legal competence of ecclesiastical legal persons to acquire, possess, and administer property was recognized. In some cases concordats referred to individual canons of the code or other ecclesiastical norms explicitly named. In the main, however, reference was made to the prescriptions of the code or of ecclesiastical law or ecclesiastical principles in general, for example, in the sense that questions pertaining to ecclesiastical persons or things and not expressly treated in the concordat should be regulated according to canon law. Finally, the rule was often adopted into the treaties that both parties, in the event of differences of interpretation, will effect an amicable solution in a common agreement. In this way, repudiation and break were made difficult and at the same time the door to new negotiations was kept open.

One can say that after the First World War the concordat was found in an increasing measure to be the suitable form for ordering the relations of Church and state. The territorial episcopate was regularly consulted by the Holy See in the negotiations, and its ideas and wishes were as far as possible taken into consideration. Elected representatives of the episcopate played a direct role in the negotiations. The Holy See regularly aspired to have the ratification of completed concordats take place in the Vatican.

In retrospect it must be admitted that the concordats achieved their goal only inadequately. The circumstances and the development were not to a great extent favorable to their existence and their implementation. Most were ruined by the Second World War and its sequel. In concluding them, the Holy See in general showed itself to be well informed about the situation in the individual countries. However, occasionally it seemed to have overestimated the power of the forces prepared for cooperation. Nevertheless, the concordat policy was right and necessary. By it the Holy See went on record that in its relations with nations it did not champion the view of all or nothing but in recognizing realities was ready for compromise solutions. The concluding of a treaty as such testified before the whole world to the claim and the right of the Holy See to represent the Catholic Church uppermost and definitively. The concordats also strengthened the self-awareness of the Catholics, who saw themselves cared for and protected by the supreme head of the Church and for the first time mentioned by the government of the nation. They set up signs which could not be obliterated; they created an incontestable legal basis for the Church and in many cases prevented worse. The separation legislation of states and the concordat policy of the Holy See over-came, from different points of departure, the system of state Churches and of state supremacy over the Church and provided the Church with the autonomy for the regulating of which the Code of Canon Law stood, seen in its entirety, as one excellent instrument at its disposal.

Individual Concordats

With the New States.   A majority of the new nations in the east and the southeast of Europe were ready for agreements with the Apostolic See for reasons of for-eign and domestic policy. Nevertheless, there were also usually obstacles to the concluding of treaties, namely, laicism, exaggerated nationalism, and the negative attitude of non-Catholic religious groups, especially the Orthodox. On 30 May 1922 Pius XI concluded a concordat with predominantly non-Catholic Latvia, at first for three years but with the implied prolongation from year to year on a six-months' notice. An exempt archbishopric was established at Riga. An oath of loyalty, to be made on entering office, was prescribed for the archbishop, a stipulation that was to be repeated in the following concordats.

In Poland, where the territorial boundaries were disputed until the end of 1924, the constitutional mandate to regulate the future relations of Church and state in a concordat with the Holy See could not be carried out until 10 February 1925. The Polish concordat reorganized the Church in this country — five provinces of the Latin Rite with twenty-one sees, one province of the Byzantine Rite, and one archdiocese of the Armenian Rite — and especially arranged questions of the filling of offices, of religious instruction, and of Church property. In regard to Poland the Holy See showed especially generous willingness to cooperate. ARTICLE 19, Section 2, page 2 of the concordat excluded from the office of pastor all clerics whose activity jeopardized the safety of the state. Thereby an at the time unrivaled right in the nomination of pastors was conceded to the Polish government.

On 10 May 1927 a concordat with Rumania was concluded, which was not ratified until 1929 because of the opposition of Orthodox circles. The Catholic Church in the nation was to be organized in one province each for the Greek and the Latin Rites, with four auxiliary sees each, as well as a spiritual head for the Armenians. As in Poland, here too the state laid special importance on the national reliability of the pastors (ART. XII, par. 2). The two contracting parties reserved to themselves, by way of exception, the right to repudiate the concordat after a preliminary notification of six months (ART. XXIII, Section 2). On 27 September 1927 Lithuania made a treaty with the Holy See. It gave the Church extensive rights in the school system, entrusted to ecclesiastics the direction of the register of births, deaths, and burials, and gave civil effects to the canonical form of marriage. The pastoral care of the faithful in their vernacular was assured. But there was constant friction over the interpretation of the concordat.

The government of Czechoslovakia usually showed itself to be unfriendly to-ward the Catholic Church and pursued a policy of petty annoyances against it. The

Hus Celebration of 1925 almost led to the breaking off of diplomatic relations. On 2 February 1928 a meager modus vivendi was arrived at. It was concerned with the circumscription of dioceses and the naming of bishops. The agreement eliminated a group of points of difference and envisaged negotiations for the future. The carrying out of the regulations of the modus vivendi encountered considerable difficulties. Not until seven years after its signing did the government fulfill the chief condition whereby the Holy See had made the defining of dioceses (ART. 1) dependent on the restoration of the church property in Slovakia. Nothing further could be achieved before the collapse of the state in 1938–39.

On the other hand, the concordat of 5 June 1933 with Austria involved a comprehensive regulation. ARTICLE 30, Section 3 of the federal constitution raised specific articles of the concordat to constituent parts of the constitution and thereby gave them a constitutional character. It partly corresponded to the concordat concluded soon after with the Third Reich. The concordat promised the erecting of the bishopric of Innsbruck-Feldkirch and of the prelacy *nullius* of Burgenland (ART. III, Par. 2) and endeavored, through prudent fostering and the promise of financial support for free Catholic schools, to create the presuppositions for the development of public Catholic schools (ART. III, Pars. 3–4). However, the government lacked the majority and the power to implement the stipulations agreed to. Above all, the subordination of marriages contracted in Church to the canon law (ART. VII) evoked the united bitter resistance of liberalism, Marxism, and National Socialism.

Tedious negotiations led in 1935 to the concluding of a comprehensive concordat with Yugoslavia. But the resistance of the Orthodox Serbs was so strong that it caused the fall of the government after the chamber had accepted it, because it agreed not to bring it before the Senate. In it were the important stipulations that, when the concordat became effective, contrary norms of the Kingdom of Yugoslavia should become null (ART. XXXV) and that subjects not treated in the concordat should be handled in accord with the pertinent canon law (ART. XXXVII, Sec. 1).

With the "Separation Countries" of Europe.   As a consequence of the ideology of separation there ordinarily occurred in the "separation countries" of Europe an agreement with the Holy See only if governments of a different political orientation came to power in them. In regard to France, from the beginning of the pontificate of Benedict XV the Holy See pursued a policy of yielding and of concession, which in a certain respect prevailed over the separation regime. The Law of Separation had also proved to be impracticable. From the end of the First World War the élan of laicism diminished. From the resumption of diplomatic relations in 1920 the Holy See inquired of the French government before the appointing of a bishop whether there were any political objections to the candidate. In the corresponding declarations of the French Council of State of 13 December 1923 and Pius XI's encyclical *Maximam gravissimamque* of 18 January 1924 on diocesan associations could be seen a tacit agreement on the thorny problem of the administration of church property. The Council of State declared on 3 February 1925 that the French government and the Holy See were in agreement on maintaining the concordat of 1801 in Alsace and Lorraine. In 1926 were concluded two accords with France, insignificant in content but important for the atmosphere. In them were determined the liturgical privileges which belonged to the representatives of France in the countries where France still occupied the religious protectorate or in which this had been recently abolished.

In Portugal, which had again established diplomatic relations with the Apostolic See in 1918, there began under the dictatorship of Carmona a rapprochement of Church and state. The decree of 18 July 1926 annulled some of the most odious provisions of the Law of Separation of 1911. The constitution of 19 March 1933 was strongly influenced by Catholic ideology. In one and the same article it proclaimed the Catholic religion as the religion of the state, the principle of religious liberty, the principle of separation, and the maintaining of diplomatic relations with the Holy See (ART. 46). Thus no serious obstacle prevented the concluding of treaties with the Holy See. The accord of 15 April 1928 reorganized the hierarchy in Portuguese India and solved the question of the patronate that as of 11 April 1929 regulated the situation in the diocese of Meliapôr.

Ever since its unification, Italy had more and more became a nation with a hostile separation of Church and state: state schools without religious instruction, abolition of theological faculties at the state universities, compulsory civil marriage. However, after the end of the First World War a slow rapprochement between the nation and the Holy See made progress. In January 1919 a Catholic party was formed with the toleration of the Holy See; in this way the principle of the "Non expedit" was canceled. In the encyclical *Pacem Dei munus* on 23 May 1920 Benedict XV abandoned the prohibition, applying to Catholic heads of states, of making an official visit to the Quirinal. The Fascist regime recommended itself to the Church through many laws and measures that were friendly to the Church in relation to school and marriage, clergy, and ecclesiastical property. Thus was the way opened for a comprehensive clearing out of the matter of conflict between Church and state. In 1929 occurred the solution of the Roman Question in the Lateran Treaties. On 11 February 1929 three agreements were signed: the political treaty, the financial settlement (as Appendix IV of the political treaty), and the concordat. On 27 May 1929 they were transformed into internal state law. In the political treaty the Italian state recognized the Catholic religion as the "sole religion of the state" (ART. 1). Likewise, the sovereignty of the Holy See was confirmed (ART. 2) and a territory of its own, Vatican City, was guaranteed (ART. 3). The neutrality of Vatican City was established (ART. 24). The person of the Pope is sacred and inviolable (ART. 8). The Holy See's active and passive diplomatic right was acknowledged (ART. 12). The Holy see declared the Roman Question definitively and irrevocably settled and recognized the Kingdom of Italy with Rome as capital (ART. 26). In the financial settlement the payment of compensation for the losses which had befallen the Pope through the events of 1870 was agreed to. The concordat complemented the treaty and brought a detailed regulation of affairs touching Church and state (45 articles). The state guaranteed to the Catholic Church its special position in Italy and the rights pertaining to this. To the Church was assured the free exercise of spiritual power, of public worship, and of jurisdiction in ecclesiastical affairs. The sacred character of Rome was acknowledged and protected (ART. 1, Sec. 1). The freedom of the filling of episcopal sees and of other offices was restored (ARTS. 19, 24, 25). No cleric could acquire or

retain a post or an office in the Italian state or in a public institution or corporation dependent on it without the approval of the local ordinary. Apostate priests
or those under censure must under no circumstances be employed in education
or in an office or post in which they came directly into contact with the public
(ART. 5). The civil effects were recognized in the sacrament of matrimony, which
was regulated by the canon law. Cases of invalid marriages and the dispensation from nonconsummated marriages continued to be reserved to ecclesiastical
courts and officials. Only the procedure in the separation from bed and board was
conducted by the civil courts (ART. 34). Instruction in the Catholic religion was designated as the "basis and crown" of public instruction and was now envisaged
also for the universities (ART. 36). The state promised a change in its legislation in
order to bring it into harmony with the Lateran Treaties (ART. 29). For its part, the
Church made considerable concessions. A revision of the boundaries of dioceses
and their decrease in number were envisaged (ARTS. 16 and 17). In connection
with the appointment of bishops the government had the right to adduce political
memories (ART. 19). In the naming of pastors its right to express reservations was
allowed. Especially far-reaching appeared the power likewise conceded to it, in
relation to the emergence of reasons which made it seem harmful for a pastor to
continue in his position, to inform the local ordinary, who had to take appropriate
measures in accord with the government within three months (ART. 21). Partisan political activity was forbidden to all ecclesiastics (ART. 43 Sec. 7). The Holy
See obliged itself to a condonation in regard to all possessors of church property
(ART. 28). Noteworthy is the concession that the state, in the case of unfit administration of property, may proceed, in agreement with the ecclesiastical authority,
to the sequestration of the temporalities of the benefice (ART. 26, Sec. 2).

The Lateran Treaties ended the decades-long opposition of the Church to a
united Italy and were for both parties an honorable peace treaty. They satisfied
the national will of the people and assured the Church's possibility of effectiveness. The treaties produced a solution which, as is said in the preamble of the
treaty, corresponded to the justice and dignity of both sides. They were in general
balanced, took account of the Catholic tradition of the people without violating
the rights of the state or of other religious communities, and fulfilled the political claims without treading too near the freedom of the Church. The Holy See
sought not a restoration but a new start. In it it saw the guarantee of permanence.
It accommodated itself in the renunciation of the Papal State, which was overdue, and set resolutely about carrying out its universal mission from the area of
a diminutive state. This was the only remaining possibility of assuring, at least
in normal circumstances, the independence required for the fulfilling of its task.
Of course, in the sequel there were some collisions between Church and state,
which usually had their cause in the interference and usurpation of the Fascist
regime. Nevertheless, Mussolini did not permit a prolonged conflict to occur, but
strove constantly for an adjustment acceptable to both sides.

With the Latin American States.   The economic and social grievances as well
as the unstable political conditions in most countries made Latin America for a
considerable time the object of special concern of the Holy See. The ordinarily
traditionally Catholic people often could not assert themselves against the Freema-

sonic oligarchies that were hostile to the Church. Thus is explained the surprising fact that relatively rarely did the conclusion of satisfactory agreements of the Holy See with Latin American nations succeed, which would either have established a system of concordats or have continued the concordats made in the past century. Only Colombia was an exception: with it, between 1918 and 1928, several treaties, the most important being the mission accord of 5 May 1928, were concluded. Only the agreement of 1928 put an end to the uninterrupted *Kulturkampf* in Guatemala. Likewise in 1928 there came about an agreement with Peru over the naming of the bishops. With Ecuador, following the decrees of the 1920s, hostile to the Church, a modus vivendi was achieved on 24 July 1937. The government guaranteed freedom of instruction. State and Church joined to evangelize the Indians and to encourage them in every respect. Any political activity was forbidden to the clergy.

Germany.   The German Reich had to pay for the First World War with serious territorial losses. Through the Treaty of Versailles the Catholic Church in Germany lost the bishoprics of Strasbourg and Metz, the greatest part of Gnesen-Posen and Kulm, and a considerable part of Breslau. In the Free City of Danzig, separated from Germany, an Apostolic Administration was created in 1922, an exempt see in 1925. The German Reich changed from constitutional monarchy to parliamentary democracy. On 11 August 1919 the constitution decided upon by the National Assembly at Weimar went into force. In contrast to the situation in the German Empire of 1871 it established the competence of the state as a whole for the regulation of the relations of Church and state and of Church and school (ART. 10, nos. 1 and 2). The basic legislation of the Reich on Church and school assured to the Church for all of Germany a specific degree of freedom and potential efficacy. The ecclesio-political system of the Weimar Republic was that of an organizational separation with mutual cooperation of Church and state. The foundation of the position of religious society in the Weimar constitution was religious freedom (ARTS. 135, 136, 137, 140, 141). ARTICLE 137, Secs. 1 and 7, contains the idea of separation; ART. 138, Sec. 1, is in accord with it. ARTICLE 137, Sec 1, declares that no "state Church" exists. Thereby the Protestant territorial church system was once and for all abolished, but at the same time the fundamental secularism, neutrality, and equality of the state were expressed. The Weimar Republic looked at the principle of separation as an institutional guarantee for the protection of the state from the power of the Church and of the Church from interference by the state and saw in it the means of restoring a liberal arrangement of the compromise. Nevertheless, the Churches continued to be corporations of public law, and this status could be bestowed on other religious congregations (ART. 137, Sec. 5). In this way the importance of Churches and religious groups for the life of the people was recognized and the ability was granted them to be bearers of public competencies and rights. The granting of the right of self-determination to religious societies (ART. 137, Sec. 3) protected the liberty of the whole of ecclesiastical activity in the world, to the extent that it was regarded by the Church as necessary for "its affairs." ARTICLE 137, Sec. 3, assured to religious groups a sphere of freedom within which they could establish an independent legal power, for example, ecclesiastical power, and by means of them an independent legal order.

With the system of the relations of state and Church created by the Weimar constitution the state's sovereignty over the Churches was no longer compatible, but of course it was still practiced by the government and administration of some states. The public denominational school, which was regarded by the German Catholics as a vital question, was basically guaranteed (ART. 146). Religious instruction continued in all public schools, except the nondenominational, to be a regular subject (ART. 149).

The ecclesiastical articles of the Weimar Constitution were the best that could be obtained in view of the political power situation. However, during the entire epoch of the Weimar Republic the reciprocal alienation of Church and state could not be overcome. Still, in 1920 an embassy of the German Reich was established at the Holy See in place of the previous Prussian legation. The German Catholics set great hopes on it. The legal binding force of the concordats and conventions with the Holy See surviving from the nineteenth century had become uncertain. The territorial alterations following the peace treaty necessitated an adaptation of diocesan boundaries. For these reasons, in order to exhaust the possibilities supplied by the Weimar Constitution and convert them into concrete assurances, in regard to which the concern for the Catholic denominational school was predominant, the Church endeavored to conclude a concordat with the Reich. The Weimar Republic was also basically interested in this. The Reich sought from the Holy See moral and political support against the front of the victorious powers. From time to time in 1921 the Reich government promised itself from a concordat a stabilizing influence on the German boundaries, threatened by desires for annexation in the east and desires for separation in the west. But the party constellation in the Reichstag did not go beyond drafts of a concordat. The liberal and Protestant forces, like the elements in the Social Democratic Party that were hostile to the Church, refused the conclusion of a treaty. In particular, the hurdle of the Reich School Law, that was first to be enacted, could not be overcome.

However, in view of this situation, the Holy See did not give up. Instead, it utilized the tension between the Reich and the states, produced by the federalist construction of the state, to pursue a multitrack concordat policy. The extensive independence of the states in cultural policy even gave to concordats with the states a precedence over a concordat with the Reich. From the standpoint of the Church as well as of the state Bavaria was especially suited to be the pacemaker for such agreements. The Holy See wanted to come to an accommodation with Bavaria first, because here it could most easily expect a relatively favorable concordat, which should then serve as model for the other German states. The Free State of Bavaria saw in the conclusion of a concordat a means of stressing emphatically its threatened political independence. On 24 March 1924 the concordat with Bavaria, advantageous to the Church, was concluded. However, particularly because of the state's concessions in the school question it had a chilling effect on public opinion.

A concordat with Prussia of 14 June 1929 was, as far as concerns the meager content, a casualty because in it there was no agreement on school, marriage, and religious institutes. Indicative of the atmosphere heated up by the Protestant side is the fact that in the negotiations and the wording of the text the term "concordatum" was purposely avoided. Nevertheless, the Prussian concordat was of importance as a political event.

In 1932 two treaties were made with the Free State or Anhalt, and a concordat was concluded with Baden on 12 October 1932. Although in Baden everything except a maximum program for the Church could be negotiated, the concordat obtained only a perceptibly weak parliamentary majority.

The other German states did not make concordats with the Holy See. In them the relations of state and Church were regulated according to legal decisions, for example, in Württemberg by the comprehensive law of 3 March 1924.

The three state concordats sought especially to create a new order in their territories, which were affected by the alteration of boundaries, of the form of government and of the constitution, as well as by the codification of canon law. They guaranteed the claims of the Church going back to older legal titles — endowment of sees, establishing of new sees and parishes — and the interests of the state in specific presuppositions for ecclesiastical officeholders — state citizenship, triennium — as well as the appointment to episcopal sees and cathedral chapters. Except for Bavaria, the cathedral chapters' right to elect the bishops was maintained in the German states, but was limited to a proposal of three names by the Holy See. The cooperation of the Church in the appointing of professors on Catholic theological faculties of the state universities and of posts for the teaching of religion was minutely regulated. Only the Bavarian concordat contained greater concessions to the Church in the guarantee of denominational public schools and teacher training (ARTS. 5 and 6) as well as in the awarding of the right to religious orders, eventually as publicly recognized, to maintain private schools (ART. 9). Contrary to the wishes of the Church, no settlement of the school question was included in the concordats with Baden and Prussia, but just the same in an appendix or, respectively, an exchange of letters pertaining to the work of the treaty, the observance and implementation of the stipulations of the constitution of the Reich relevant to the school and religious instruction were promised. In Prussia, in addition to that of Cologne, the provinces of Paderborn and Breslau (Wroclaw) were created, and the sees of Aachen and Berlin and the prelacy *nullius* of Schneidemühl were newly established. The concordats with Bavaria, Prussia, and Baden followed, as regards content, similarly shaped treaties with the Protestant Churches. Concordats and ecclesiastical treaties assured the public status of the Churches by contract, thereby set them off from the group of other religious congregations of public law, and laid the foundation for a relationship of coordination of Church and state. Thus there appeared in Germany a new type of relation of Church and state, that of the "autonomous separate Church guaranteed by treaty or concordat," to quote Ulrich Stutz.

A new phase of ecclesiastical policies began when on 30 January 1933 Adolf Hitler became chancellor of the Reich. In his government's statement of 23 March 1933 he labeled the two denominations as "most weighty factors for the preservation of our nationhood" and bound himself to respect the treaties concluded with them and not to attack their rights. Most especially he promised that he intended to "allow and assure" to the Christian denominations "the influence pertaining to them" in school and education. Hitler at once made known his intention of reaching an agreement with the Catholic Church. With recourse to the preliminary work since 1920 and 1921, the concordat with the Reich was signed in Vatican City on 20 July 1933. On 10 September 1933 the documents of ratification were exchanged. By the law of 12 September 1933 the Reich's minister of the interior was empowered to issue legal and administrative regulations required for the implementation of the concordat. They were never issued.

The concordat with the Reich let those with Bavaria, Prussia, and Baden continue and complemented them, but in addition it applied also to those German states in which there was previously no agreement (ART. 2). And so certain assurances were given by the Reich to those Catholics who were in a hopeless minority position. The assurances of the Weimar Constitution for the freedom of denomination and worship, as for the autonomy of the Churches, were now established by treaty (ART. 1). The exercise of the spiritual functions of priests was placed under special protection (ARTS. 5 and 6). Pastoral care in public institutions was assured (ART. 28). Catholic societies were protected in a defined framework (ART. 31). The German episcopate was named in ART. 31, Sec. 3, as a partner of a definitive agreement with the government of the Reich. In this manner was taken a route heavy with consequences for the future. Nevertheless, the opportunity was neglected of making the principles of interpretation agreed to between the German bishops and the government concerning this article an integral item of the treaty in an incontrovertible manner. The decisive concessions of the state lie in ARTS. 21 to 25, in which the Church's demands in regard to religious instruction and denominational and private schools were essentially met. Religious instruction was to be a regular subject of instruction in the public schools, including the professional schools (ART. 21). The maintenance and establishment of Catholic denominational schools was assured under certain conditions (ART. 23). Equality of rights was promised to the private schools of the orders (ART. 25). The Holy See for its part held out the prospect, "on the ground of the special circumstances existing in Germany" and in view of the guarantees contained in the concordat with the Reich, of issuing decrees which forbade clerics and religious from participating in party politics (ART. 32). The "Depoliticization Article" was the *conditio sine qua non* of the government for the conclusion of the concordat. Hitler's goal was the depoliticization of the clergy in order thereby to destroy political Catholicism. It coincided with the intention of the Holy See to keep pastors out of political party involvement for pastoral reasons. Matters of ecclesiastical competence which were not dealt with in the treaty were regulated "for the ecclesiastical sphere" in accord with the prevailing canon law (ART. 33, Sec. 1). In regard to the law of marriage, the German government was not ready to make any concession (ART. 26).

On the whole, with the concordat with the Reich there came into being a moderate and durable system of accommodation and cooperation between Church and state. In its essential prescriptions it was modeled on the democratic state constitution of the Weimar Republic. Only a few regulations resulted from the development toward the totalitarian one-party system, in which the German Reich found itself (ARTS. 16, 31, 32). The Holy See strove to bring the concordat with the Reich as close as possible to the most recent ecclesiastical treaties — with Italy and Austria — and thereby to achieve a type of concordat that was uniform in its fundamental lines. The drawback of the German concordat lay in the fact that it was perhaps not honestly meant by the leading statesman and in any event was not taken seriously. The treaty, just like the state concordats, was from the beginning and to an increasing degree circumvented, reinterpreted, violated, and broken. The rights which were guaranteed to the Church by constitution and concordat were extensively undermined; in this matter the procedure was rather by way of decree and administrative practice than by means of legislation. The freedom of the Church's activity was severely impaired. The aim was a state corresponding to the National Socialist ideology. If at this time matters did not go so far as an annulment of the concordat, at times pushed by the minister for the churches, Hanns Kerrl, and to a full separation of Church and state, still the reasons were suited for the regime effectively to be able to effect a supervision of the Church under the existing system, and it meant to take still more certain domestic and foreign policy motives into consideration.

Things moved forward with similar, partly far worse measures of persecution in the occupied and annexed territories. In the part of Poland occupied by Germany, the so-called Government General, there occurred a furious persecution of the Church, which decimated the clergy. The Polish concordat, the Austrian concordat, the modus vivendi with Czechoslovakia, and the Napoleonic concordat in Alsace-Lorraine were considered abolished. In regard to Austria, the government of the Reich adopted the view that the Austrian concordat had been ended by the annexation of Austria to the German Reich, because the country had perished as an independent state and had lost its position as a subject of international law. In Austria there now prevailed "a situation without concordat" (K. Scholder). In the Wartheland District the Church was treated as a private association. An extension of the concordat with the Reich to the newly acquired territories was rejected.

The Holy See tried to influence the Nazi regime by the diplomatic route, but, when the exchange of notes remained without effect, turned to publicity. In the encyclical *Mit brennender Sorge* of 4 March 1937 Pius XI stigmatized the interference and usurpations by the state. Despite the just described hostile measures, the concordats were not entirely useless. Their existence acted, in some respects, as a restraint on the pressures, preserved for the Church one or another position for the proclamation of the Gospel, even though curtailed, and even exercised a certain influence in the concentration camps. The binding of the state to the concordats made, on the one hand, its measures of oppression visible even on the plane of international law and induced it to certain considerations, and on the other hand offered the Holy See the basis for interventions. The fact that the Holy See had, by the concluding of the concordat, recognized the Nazi government as a treaty partner could no longer be annulled. By concluding the concordat the government of the Reich had acknowledged the competence of the Holy See over the Catholic Church in Germany as legitimate in an agreement of international law. Every violation of the concordat injured the credibility of the Nazi regime.

During the Second World War

The approaching Second World War naturally interrupted the conclusion of concordats with the warring nations. Only with countries which lay on the lee side of world politics or could keep themselves aloof from the power struggle were a few treaties made.

In Salazar's Portugal the Church was cautiously encouraged. On 7 May 1940 the country concluded with the Holy See a significant concordat and a mission treaty, which Salazar termed a "concordat of the separation of state and Church." The concordat extended the existing system of the demarcation and collaboration of Church and state in free agreement and mutual respect. The legal personality of the Catholic Church was recognized, the maintenance of diplomatic relations was agreed (ARTICLE 1). A series of guarantees assured the activity and the property of the Church (ARTS. II–VII). Clerics enjoyed special protection and certain immunities (ARTS. XI–XV). Religious instruction was an obligatory subject in the country's public schools, and their entire teaching had to be oriented to the principles of the Christian faith (ART. XXI). Private schools could be erected by the Church (ART. XX). The law of marriage was governed by the principle of optional civil marriage (ARTS. XXII–XXV). The state supported the missions in the overseas territories (ARTS. XXXVII–XXVIII). The mission treaty envisaged the admittance of foreign missionaries to Portuguese colonies (ART. 2). Mission societies were supported by the government (ARTS. 9–14). The free operation of the missions was assured (ART. 15). With these two agreements, peace and cooperation between Church and state in Portugal and its overseas possessions seemed assured for a long time. The effects of the Second World War could not be foreseen at the time of their signing. The conclusion of the concordat of 1940 led to the revision of the present ART. 45 of the constitution on 11 June 1951.

In the 1930s the Church experienced difficult times in Spain. The republican constitution of 9 December 1931 adopted a hostile attitude toward religion and Church. In the following years there erupted a full-scale war against the Church. In 1933 the Spanish government declared it regarded the concordat of 1851 as ended. Parts of the army rose against maladministration and terror, and for several years a bitter civil war raged. Chief of State Franco sought to restore the Catholic character of the nation. Laws and measures hostile to the Church were annulled. On 7 June 1941 the Spanish government concluded with the Holy See an agreement on the exercise of the privilege of nomination in the appointment to episcopal sees. According to it, the apostolic nuncio, after an understanding with the government, draws up a list of six qualified persons and transmits it to the Holy See. This submits to the government a proposal of three names, with regard for the list but without being restricted to it. From this the chief of state names a candidate, so far as he raises no objections of a general political nature. A concordat was envisaged.

A treaty going into the greatest detail on questions of church property came into existence with Haiti on 25 January 1940. The Holy See concluded an agreement with Colombia on 22 April 1942. The greatest part consisted of the regulation of questions of marriage law (ARTS. 4–10), which were largely in accord with canon law. The civil registrar of marriages was present at the church wedding, without his presence being an indispensable condition for the recognition of the civil effects. The government's right of proposal in the naming of the bishops was replaced by the right to express reservations "of a political nature" (ART. 1). Thereby the traditional *patronate* was done away with.

In the Postwar Period

The effects of the Second World War were much more comprehensive and profound than those of the First World War. The map of Europe was again considerably altered. In Asia and Africa the colonial epoch ended. Within many states there proceeded considerable changes, which also concerned religious law. The close union between Church and state was dissolved or at least loosened in many countries. The number of countries with a system of union of Church and state progressively declined. This was especially the case with nations having a predominantly Christian population. The order established by concordat in Eastern Europe completely broke up. The Church's concordat policy entered a new phase.

Fate of Concordats in Socialist Countries. For religion and the Church the most fateful effect of the Second World War was the advance of the Soviet Union dominated by the Bolshevik Party, the strongest military power of Eurasia, as far as the Elbe, and the establishing of a Communist regime in China, the most populous nation on earth. For communism religion is a scientifically untenable prejudice. The ecclesiastical policy of the Socialist states is in accord with this notion. It has the chief goal of hastening the death of religion, viewed as inevitable, by restricting or neutralizing the Church's possibilities for influence. In the final analysis the Socialist regimes aimed to exclude the Church little by little as guardian of religious faith but also as guarantor of civil liberty. The state bureaucracy moved openly or secretly into the service of the antireligious and antiecclesiastical strivings of the Communist Party. It made use of two means: tempting offers on the one hand, obstacles, prohibitions, force, and terror on the other. A failing off of the suppression or persecution always sprang only from tactical viewpoints and was caused by pressure from without or unrest within. The difference between constitutional law and constitutional reality is nowhere greater than in Socialist lands. It is not the constitution that is inviolable but the historical process of development. The constitution describes only the state of development of the revolution achieved at the time of its adoption. Basic rights in our sense are impossible systems in Soviet ideology.

There were differences in the manner and rapidity of the advance among the individual Socialist countries. In general it is to be noted that the area of freedom left to the Church is the greater, the nearer the states in question are to the free West. Relatively the greatest degree of freedom of movement is possessed — or assumed — by the Catholic Church in Poland and is permitted to the Orthodox Church in Rumania and Bulgaria. Hopeless, on the other hand, is the situation in Czechoslovakia. The "Marxist Josephinism" of this country allows the Church only a narrow living space and trivial freedom of organization. Not much more favorable is the situation in Hungary. The model for the Socialist countries even in ecclesiastical policy is basically the Soviet Union. Since 1918 the hostile separation of the Church from the state and of the school from the Church has existed there. The Church's sphere of activity is limited to worship. Correspondingly, the constitutions of the so-called People's Democracies of Rumania, Bulgaria, Hungary, Czechoslovakia, Albania, and Yugoslavia carried out the separation of Church and state. It happened regularly in conscious opposition to the still considerably popular ecclesiastical situation of religion in these nations. The principle of freedom of religion and conscience, proclaimed with the separation of Church and state, nowhere benefited the Catholic Church. It was often more severely persecuted than all other religious communities. The Church lost its status in public law and as far as possible was completely excluded from public life. Everywhere there was an effort to restrict it to undertaking cult functions and to prevent every other influence on people, especially on youth. At the same time the Church was to a very great degree subjected to control. In all Socialist states there are offices for ecclesiastical affairs, which to an enormous extent interfere in the filling of ecclesiastical offices, supervise the formation of the clergy, and determine the number and capacity of the places of this formation. Where several religious groups face one another, the government tries to play them off against one another, but in every case the chief opponent is seen in the Catholic Church. In the individual Church it strives to provoke various groups against one another, in this way to introduce schism into the Church, and thus to maintain its influence over it the more effectively.

The union of the bishops with the Holy See was either thwarted or subject to control, diplomatic relations were severed, and concordats were repudiated, that with Lithuania on 1 July 1940, with Poland on 12 September 1945, with Rumania on 17 July 1948. Without any official repudiation, Czechoslovakia disregarded the modus vivendi and in 1950 broke off diplomatic relations with the Holy See, as did Yugoslavia in 1952. So long as religion was not yet extirpated, communism tried to make use of its adherents, especially its clergy and its institutions for its own ends. For the sake of this advantage it was even ready to aid the Churches to a certain extent. Although the Socialist states almost everywhere have the means of power to carry through almost any desired measure against the Church, they were anxious for the assent, even if extorted, of the Church to their regulations. The Communists know that the most secure route to a gaining of the Catholics of a country is through Rome. Furthermore, they anticipate from the concluding of a concordat that they can win the sympathy of some Catholic circles outside the country. In case they have no success in reaching an agreement with the Holy See, they turn to the bishops. If these refuse, they approach the priests. Thus are explained not only the repeated attempts to come to an understanding with the Holy See, but also the series of agreements with the episcopate in the 1950s. The governments of Czechoslovakia and Yugoslavia sent out feelers in the direction of a concordat in 1949 and 1952 respectively. The Holy See rejected them in the case of Czechoslovakia because it regarded any agreement as hopeless, considering the situation, but it showed itself accommodating toward Yugoslavia. However, the contacts did not lead to the signing of a treaty, because Yugoslavia was not prepared to acquiesce in the Church's minimum demands. The Polish government was unwilling to apply to the Holy See. It expected the attainment of its goals from negotiations with the nation's episcopate. On 14 April 1950 and 8 December 1956 it made an agreement with the Polish bishops. These treaties were not concordats but administrative agreements on the plane of domestic public law. Their content differed greatly from that of the concordats which were concluded before the appearance of socialism. In them the state endeavored to put the Church at the service of its political and economic aims. The bishops manifested a broad accommodation in order to promote the desired relaxation of tensions. But the government did not adhere to even trivial promises. Especially in the school system all concessions promised or made were again revoked. The agreements reached in Hungary, Rumania, and Czechoslovakia were considerably more unfavorable to the Church than the Polish. In Hungary the episcopate made great concessions in the agreement of 30 August 1950. It bound itself to support the policies of the government, which promised to supply subsidies to the Church for a period of eighteen years. The signing of the agreement could not prevent the further disorganization of ecclesiastical life. In Rumania an assembly of progressive clerics signed the agreement of 15 March 1951 submitted by the government. In Czechoslovakia a part of the clergy accepted the law of 14 October 1949, which unilaterally regulated the situation of the Church.

Concordats with Free Countries. The situation of the Holy See with regard to the free nations was, in general, not unfavorable after the Second World War. In the postwar period the Holy See entered into diplomatic relations with a considerable number of states, especially in Africa and Asia. On the other hand, it did not succeed in inaugurating with them an era of concordats like that after the First World War. In many countries material reconstruction following the devastation of the war occupied the foreground. In the new states of Africa and Asia Catholics were ordinarily too weak to be able to effect the conclusion of an agreement with the Holy See, apart from the inner chaos and necessities of existence of many of these areas. The raw nationalism and the sensitive self-esteem of the young African states opposed the solving of occurring questions between Church and state by means of agreements and insisted on their unilateral regulation by law. Most states exercised strict control over the external affairs of the Church. The state reserved to itself the ultimate competence for decision in mixed matters. The majority of these countries have hitherto not developed their own legal system regulating Church-state relations. The relations of the religious groups to the state were still based extensively on improvisation. The instability and uncertainty of the political situation recommended to both parties, Church and state, that they avoid the conclusion of treaties, whose binding force confronted the often abrupt changes and hence could evoke tensions and conflicts. It was enough to assume diplomatic relations whereby occurring questions could be solved quickly and without complication. In other countries the traditional reasons that did not permit a concordat with the Holy See persisted. Still, where concordats were concluded, they displayed a stronger individualism than those earlier entered into.

The Catholic nations of southern Europe — Italy, Spain, and Portugal — had, after bitter struggles, restored the traditional close union between Church and state. In Italy the Lateran Treaties held good after the war's end. They survived the overthrow of Fascism and of the Kingdom and were confirmed by ARTICLE 7 of the republican constitution of 27 December 1947. They thereby obtained a direct constitutional guarantee. The Holy See entered into an accord with Portugal on 18 July 1950 in regard to the filling of episcopal sees in Portuguese India. In it the government renounced the privilege of presentation belonging to the president and freed the Holy See from the obligation of appointing bishops of Portuguese nationality for specified sees. Here was introduced a development which was continued by the Second Vatican Council.

The development in Spain tended toward a climax in the matter of concordats. The constitutional law of 17 July 1945 placed the profession and practice of the Catholic religion as the religion of the state under official protection (Article 6, Section 1). The private practice of worship was permitted to non-Catholic religious groups (Art. 6, Sec. 2). With this arrangement Spain returned to unity of nation and religion, which was in accord with its tradition. In Spain the Catholic religion is a part of the culture. The activity of the Protestant religious groups was logically usually opposed to both. And so the government regarded itself as justified in hindering any agitation by them. Thereby the road was staked out for the contemplated concordat. The accord of 16 July 1946 regulated the filling of nonconsistorial benefices. According to it, half the dignitaries of the chapters, after nomination by the chief of state, were filled from a list of three names presented by the appropriate bishop. Before the appointing of pastors the government had the right to raise objections of a general political nature. On 5 August 1950 a convention on the pastoral care of the military was signed. But these and other smaller treaties were only the introduction to the great concordat of 27 August 1953. It was the climax of Pius XII's concordat policy. According to the concordat, the Catholic religion remained "the sole religion of the Spanish nation," with all the rights pertaining to it in keeping with divine and canon law (Article I). The prescriptions of the agreement of 7 June 1941 continued in force for the naming of residential and coadjutor bishops (Art. VII). The immune legal status of the clergy was recognized with certain modifications (Art. XVI). The state obliged itself to important financial donations to the Church (Art. XIX). Marriage contracted in accord with the prescriptions of canon law had full validity in the civil sphere (Art. XXIII). Questions of nullity and separation were the responsibility of ecclesiastical courts (Art. XXIV). In all schools the instruction was to be given in harmony with Catholic doctrine (Art. XXVI). Catholic religious instruction was an obligatory subject in the schools of every rank (Art. XXVII). In the agencies for the formation of public opinion room was assured to the Church for the presentation and defense of religious truth (Art. XXIX). The freedom of ecclesiastical universities and academies as well as the possibility of erecting schools of every kind were guaranteed (Arts. XXX and XXXI).

By means of the concordat the Church in Spain obtained a position of imposing compactness. The Spanish concordat once again took into account the Catholic tradition of the Spanish people and created a system of the relations of Church and state in a Catholic country that must be termed, theoretically, almost ideal. A more far-reaching favoring of the Catholic Church and a more intensive collaboration of the state with it was scarcely conceivable. Nevertheless, in Spain one can speak of a system of state Church only with restrictions. For the concordat did indeed proclaim the Catholic religion as the religion of the state, but not a state Church. Even more, the free exercise of its sovereignty was expressly guaranteed to the Catholic Church (Art. II). Its independence in Spain is incomparably greater than that of Protestantism in the Scandinavian countries. In addition, the concordat did not essentially impair the individual's freedom of denomination. The concordat did not represent a capitulation of the state to the Church but the attempt, undertaken in the interests of both parties, to realize the closest possible union between Church and state. The Spanish system of the relations of Church and state, as constructed by the concordat, was based on the principle that the Catholic religion, as the sole true one, alone possessed an objective right to existence and social liberty and that consequently the adherents of the other religions had only a claim to the protection of their erroneous conscience. On the other hand, the propagation of error implied a danger for the faith of the Catholics and for public morality and hence was to be thwarted. The state has the duty of protecting and supporting the Catholic Church as guardian and proclaimer of the truth. The concordat strove to create for the Church the legal and economic presuppositions necessary or useful for the exercise of its mission. The example of the Islamic states with their system of unity was as effective in the conclusion of the concordat as was the memory of the civil war, which, in view of the reign of terror in the republican part of Spain and the atrocities of the Republicans against the Church, had here and there assumed the character of a crusade. The de-Catholicizing of the country, which the republican regime had sought, ranked as treason to the national tradition.

For the conclusion of the concordat some deliberations were decisive, which proved later to be miscalculations. The two contracting parties were not, it is true, mistaken as to the religious situation among the Spanish people. They knew of the spread of Socialist, Communist, and anarchist ideologies; they knew the religious lethargy and antipathy of broad groups. They did not fail to see that in Spain there was a considerable number of persons who were or wanted to be at the same time Catholic and anticlerical, and that the liberalism disseminated especially at the universities was not pleased with a powerful position for the Church. If they nevertheless could not be deterred from allowing the Catholic religion and Church so outstanding a position, then this happened because they had confidence in the power of the Church to bring its mission convincingly and enticingly to development if only the external presuppositions for this were created for it. But they did not foresee that a decade would suffice to weaken the Church critically, and, in fact, from within, not from without. They counted on the stability of the Church and its stabilizing function for society and state. They did not suspect that this stability was based to a considerable extent on factors which could be swept away with a change of pontificate. The contracting parties also probably underestimated the publicity strength of Protestantism, which, despite numerically insignificant circumstances, was employed to the fullest extent, the mood of so-called world publicity, which was decisively determined by Protestantism, and the inclination of many states with a Protestant majority, especially the United States, to intervene on behalf of their coreligionists in Catholic lands. The concordat became the occasion for isolating Spain economically, culturally, and politically. The untiring attacks of world Protestantism against the concordat could not be without effect in the long run. They could not but gradually undermine also the power of resistance of some politicians and bishops, for whom the defense of the concordat was an obligatory responsibility. Finally, it appeared that the hope linked with the conclusion of the Spanish concordat that it could serve as model for the other Catholic countries was unfulfilled. With one exception, now to be mentioned, it remained a unique case.

With the Latin American states, to which Pius XII constantly brought his increasing care, the conclusion of treaties occurred in three cases. On 29 January 1953 a mission agreement was signed with Colombia. The government granted to the mission protection and support, among other reasons for the formation of a native clergy (ARTICLE 7). On 16 June 1954 the Dominican Republic signed with the Holy See a comprehensive concordat, which borrowed extensively from that with Spain. The Catholic religion remains the religion of the state (ART. I). The patronate was abandoned (ART. V). The activity of foreign clerics and religious in the country is assured (ART. X). Until the present (1974) this was supposed to be the ultimate treaty, basically regulating all questions of common interest. On 21 January 1958 there followed, in accord with ART. XVII of the concordat, an agreement on the pastoral care of the military. With Bolivia a mission agreement was reached on 4 December 1957, a treaty on the pastoral care of the military on 29 November 1958. On the missionaries was laid, besides the work of evangelizing, also care for the promotion of the temporal welfare of the natives (ART. VII). In the agreements with the Dominican Republic (ART. XIX) and with Bolivia of 4 December 1957 (ART. XIV) the Church's charitable activity was taken into consideration, which was something new. In Peru the mandate of the constitution of 9 April 1933 and that of 5 September 1940 did not permit the conclusion of a concordat with the Holy See (ART. 234). Finally, a long cherished desire of Pius XII was fulfilled in Germany. The successor states of Prussia in the Federal Republic proceeded after the war, even if partly after long hesitation, on the basis of the continuing validity of the Prussian concordat. Likewise, Bavaria and Baden-Württemberg adhered to the continuing validity of the respective concordats. To supplement the Prussian concordat, the state of Nordrhein-Westfalen and the Holy See made a treaty for the erection of the see of Essen on 19 December 1956. In this way, the care of souls in the Ruhr district was united and uniformly directed.

The Agreements under John XXIII and Paul VI

The Significance of the Second Vatican Council for the Legal Relationship of Church and State

The death of Pius XII meant the end of an epoch in the government and politics of the Church. The most momentous happening in the pontificate of John XXIII was without any doubt the convocation of a General Council. The Second Vatican Council had a heavy impact, not only on the relations of Church and state in general but on the policy of the Holy See especially. Here let reference be made to only three decisive statements of the council. The declaration *Dignitatis humanae* on religious liberty demanded the freedom of religion of the individual and of groups in the state without regard to the question of truth. According to it, religious freedom is a basic human right, derived from human dignity, the striving proper to human nature for a knowledge of the truth, the different task of Church and state, as well as the goal of the state to serve the common good. The legal order must make this human right a civil right (ARTICLES 2 and 3). Hence, fundamentally the state must guarantee free possibility of activity to all religions. The only restriction on this liberty is the endangering of public order ART. 4; ART. 2; also ART. 7. The declaration takes note of the system of a state religion only as a fact based on special circumstances, without recommending it. In case it is introduced, the right of all citizens and groups to religious liberty must be recognized and preserved (ART. 6). Thus the ideal of the Catholic state seemed to have been abolished. True, in ART. 1 of the cited declaration occurs the *clausula salvatoria:* that the traditional doctrine on the moral obligation of persons and of groups vis-à-vis the true religion and the One Church of Christ remains unaffected. But this abstract allusion to a doctrine which is itself not expounded cannot prevail against the concrete statements of the articles mentioned. They became of great importance for the relationship of legal proximity of Church and state existing in some countries.

The pastoral constitution *Gaudium et spes* on the Church in today's world stressed that the Church is tied to no political system but is basically prepared for cooperation with each one. While it makes use of the temporal to the extent that its mission requires, it does not place its hope on privileges offered to it by the state authority. It would even renounce the exercise of certain legitimately acquired rights if it is established that their use jeopardizes the credibility of its witness or changed conditions of life demand another arrangement (ART. 76). These statements, which are in themselves self-evident, corresponded to a wide-spread mentality which saw in the depriving of the Church of earthly assurances and temporal means an opportunity for the better propagation of the faith. They supplied the signal for a movement under way in many countries, which antici-pated from the sacrifice of legal positions a deepening and greater effectiveness of the Church's ministry.

The decree *Christus Dominus* on the pastoral office of bishops finally expressed the wish that in the future no more rights or privileges be conceded to heads of state to select, appoint, suggest, or designate bishops. Heads of state were asked to renounce, in agreement with the Holy See, these rights, just mentioned, which they possessed at present by virtue of a treaty or through custom (ART. 20). With this invitation was continued a development which had begun long before the council, but which had been sensationally infringed in Spain because of the special circumstances.

As important as the above mentioned and other pertinent expressions and directions of the Second Vatican Council were for the relations of Church and state, all the more must one not overlook, for the understanding of the changes which have taken place in this area since the council, the development which proceeded in the Catholic Church itself from about the beginning of the 1960s. For the unity, the vitality, and the missionary élan of the Church determined its radiation to society and thereby regularly decided its influence on the state and its work. Particularly in the democratic state is the Church left to influence its mem-bers in the state to grant it freedom to move and support, which it needs for a wholesome activity. The importance of the Church in the pluralistic democratic state depends to a decisive degree on the spiritual substance, the inner strength, and the credibility which it is able to display and radiate. But the just mentioned qualities of the Catholic Church are in a state of constant and rapid retreat. The faith, the foundation of the Church and of all its activity, has been attacked and questioned for years from its own ranks. As a consequence countless Catholics are insecure, devoid of a vital conviction of the faith, and unfitted for an effec-tive witness to the faith. The authority of Pope and bishops is gravely weakened.

The clergy is to a great extent disoriented and divided. Discipline in the Church has seriously declined. Ecclesiastical laws are unashamedly transgressed and liquidated as a result of mounting disobedience. In extensive Catholic circles this worldliness and antihierarchical sentiment are widespread. In the name of pluralism the most contrary views on almost all subjects establish themselves in the Church. The holders of the teaching office contradict one another in important points. Many theologians ignore the Church's authentic doctrine. The release of diversity of opinion among Catholics by the Second Vatican Council — ART. 43 of the pastoral constitution *Gaudium et spes* — scarcely permitted any further unity of public activity of Catholics and also raised questions about the capability of function of ecclesiastical authority in the realm of politics. Subjects in which the Church appeared united grew steadily fewer. A gathering of the strengths of the Church became ever more difficult. In consequence of the enervation and disunity within the Church the influence of Catholics on society noticeably and constantly declined. The evidences of decay within make the Church an even weaker pole in the partnership relations with the state. They make it easy for forces which abhor the Church to ignore it or to play off hierarchy and theologians against one another. On the other hand, the well-intentioned governments show their concern whether the Church is able henceforth to measure up to its task in the forming of morals and in the education of persons. Following the example of other Christian religious groups, especially of German Protestantism and Russian Orthodoxy, in the most recent period certain elements of the hierarchy have taken part in politics, often with notable partiality. Among the members of the Church appear fanatical associations which attack the intimacy with the "authoritarian" or "capitalistic" state, but at the same time advocate the surrender of the Church to the Socialist state, unite with Socialist and Communist cadres, and support real or alleged freedom movements in European and non-European countries. Some groups in a sectarian spiritualism question all connections between Church and state and demand the repudiation of valid concordats. The political disunity of Catholics increases, and this condemns the Catholics in lands where they represent a minority to a status of no influence. Christian politicians to a great extent no longer have clear directions of the Church at their disposal. All in all, it must be noted that the strength of the Catholic Church has strongly declined in the last few years. The phenomena described are suited to jeopardize from within the current legal positions of the Church. A Church which no longer corresponds to the claims which are made on it and to the promises which proceeded from it loses in the eyes of citizens who measure by democratic rules the justification of occupying an outstanding position in the structure of society.

It has been correctly stated by Hans Maier "that in a democracy every right becomes obsolete if it is not maintained and renewed by vital political forces." Where the spiritual power of Christians yields, experience teaches that sooner or later constitutional.guarantees for the Church break up. The Church is an essentially public power with demands on the state that cannot be renounced. But the more the strength of the faith and the moral level in the Church decline, the more the number of practicing Catholics drops, so much the less understanding do its "privileges" find in the sphere of public law. The state will be equally prepared for treaties in the long run only with a society which fulfills a significant function in the life of the people. Hence, for the concluding of concordats there are no favorable assumptions now and for an unforeseeable future. In this regard the situation in the free nations and the Socialist states is not very different. Concordats are basically agreements made to last between Church and state. The present is not favorable to this permanence. Most free countries show in increasing measure critical phenomena, experience a continuing rapid change of law and partly even of institutions, and look insecurely to the future. Considering this instability there exists for the civil partner an understandable aversion to tie itself down for a somewhat long time or soon to consider new negotiations. In case of real necessity to reach an agreement, people are usually content with individual understandings, which contain a minimum of regulating content. In place of concordats there are new possibilities of collaboration of Church and state, for example, through permanent contacts or those agreed to as occasion suggests. The striving for an institutionalization of the relations of state and Church yields to a certain extent to the contentment with a functional relation. In place of the assignment and definition of rights and competencies there comes to a great extent the cooperation agreed to for a short to a moderately long period. The Socialist states do not necessarily intend to have a comprehensive agreement with a structure condemned to extinction, as in their view the Church is. What they are in any event prepared for is the contractual regulating of particular questions, from which they promise themselves a tactical advantage. The hopes of a gradual dying out of hostility to religion in the Socialist countries have so far not been realized. Aleksandr Solzhenitsyn says, "The furious hostility against religion is what is most permanent in Marxism." To be sure, now as earlier, the Holy See ordinarily puts the greatest value on the realization of accords with the states and in this connection displays its proved flexibility. It even concludes agreements with states that are atheistic or non-Christian and is ready to enter into accords of slight range of content. The pluralistic structure of the constitutional democracies is recognized without reservation. Nevertheless, there exists, at least in parts of the Church, a widespread weariness of concordats. The enhanced self-confidence of the bishops finds expression in the demand raised in some circles that, in the future, in place of concordats should come easily repudiated particular accords, which are negotiated by the bishops and, if need be, submitted to the Holy See for confirmation.

The Individual Agreements

The "Protocols" with Socialist States.   Since John XXIII Vatican diplomacy has sought to prepare an accommodation with the Socialist states, especially those of Eastern Europe, at the cost of heavy sacrifices and considerable advance concessions. Talks were agreed upon by means of preliminary contacts on the occasion of international meetings, and it was anticipated that they would result in the contractual solution of this or that question of the Church's life. On the other side, with the Second Vatican Council and Montini's election as Pope, the Socialist governments sought contact with the Holy See in order thereby to gain influence over the Church and the more easily to tie the Catholics in their sphere of power to their course. On 15 September 1964 there first came into existence a "protocol" between a Socialist state, Hungary, and the Holy See. In it the political condition and the oath of loyalty of the bishops were granted to the government. On 25 June 1966 there followed a "protocol" with Yugoslavia. In it the government acknowledged the competence of the Holy See to exercise its jurisdiction over the Catholic Church in Yugoslavia in spiritual, ecclesiastical, and religious questions, without prejudice to the internal order of the nation. The Holy See guaranteed the restricting of the activity of clerics to the religious ecclesiastical sphere and disapproved every type of political violence. The secular side intended by these stipulations to keep the Croatian clergy apart from the national aspirations of the people and to gain the Holy See as a confederate against the protesting Croats. Also in the "protocol" the exchange of an envoy to the Holy See and of an apostolic delegate — not of a nuncio — in Yugoslavia was agreed upon; but, going beyond Canon 267, par. 2, to the delegate pertained the duty of fostering contact with the government. However. in 1970 Yugoslavia resumed diplomatic relations with the Holy See. These "protocols" represent agreements at the lowest stage of diplomatic activity and of minimum content. They were the first fumbling steps on an uncertain road. The situation of the Church within the country scarcely improved in Hungary by the signing, and in Yugoslavia only insignificantly, and the alleviations obtained are constantly threatened by a change of course.

The Holy See's contacts with other Socialist nations have not yet advanced to the signing of "protocols." In Poland the government is keenly interested in an arrangement with the Holy See, whereby it expects to play down the irksome primate, Cardinal Wyszyński, and to be able to bring him to submission. Nevertheless, the Polish bishops want no arrangement with the government purchased by precipitate concessions. Without the concluding of a treaty but in accord with the state, Paul VI in the apostolic constitution *Episcoporum Poloniae* of 28 June 1972 organized the Catholic Church in the area beyond the Oder-Neisse line. Four dioceses — Opole, Govzow-Wielkopolski, Szczecin-Kamien, and Koszalin-Kolobrzeg — were erected, the see of Ermland was incorporated into the ecclesiastical province of Warsaw, and that of Gdansk into the province of Gniezno. On the basis of prolonged and often interrupted negotiations, four new bishops were ordained in Prague at the end of February 1973. A written agreement was not published. In May 1973 the Holy See declined when the government of Czechoslovakia offered new talks, because they appeared to be without prospects. The predominant power of the Socialist nations, the Soviet Union, now as earlier, rejected institutional relations with the Holy See because it wants to conduct its religious policy according to its own discretion.

The "Modus vivendi" with Tunisia.   On 27 June 1964 there came into being for the first time a treaty between the Holy See and a country where Islam is the state religion (ART. 1 of the constitution of 25 July 1957), the "Modus vivendi" with Tunisia. The treaty aims to guarantee to Catholics the practice of their faith. However, the public performance of the liturgy and preaching in public are not allowed. The Church is subjected to a strict police regime. Whether the treaty, with its humiliating conditions — suppression of the archbishopric of Carthage — and the great sacrifices which the Catholic Church accepted in it, can be of future significance for similar agreements with other Afro-Asian states is unclear.

The Changes in Concordats in States Giving Preferential Status to the Catholic Church.   The unity of the state-Church system is today more or less shaken or jeopardized everywhere in Europe. Secularism and pluralism undermined the foundations on which state religions and state churches rested. The number of countries with coordination and separation systems is increasing. The existence of a state Church now ordinarily presupposes a religiously homogeneous population with a pervasively positive attitude to religion and Church. Today this assumption is no longer present for any Church of the so-called Western World. Its members are, in a considerable number, no longer rooted in it by virtue of conviction. As a result of serious opposing views in theology and faith, its theologians and clergy are no longer united. The religious foundation of the state-Church system is, it is true, broader and more stable in the Catholic countries of southern Europe than in the Protestant nations of Scandinavia, but it displays dangerous cracks and is constantly further undermined by the development of the Church since the council. It is unlikely that this system can still be maintained in the long run by constitutional legal means. Violent changes through rapidly erupting passions are not to be excluded in some countries.

Paul VI's policy seeks a loosening of the bonds which exist, especially in the Iberian Peninsula, between Church and state, and the sacrifice of those privileges of the Church which find growing criticism. It agrees with the urging of the majority of the Spanish bishops for a revision of the concordat. The state has reluctantly yielded to the desire and entered into negotiations with the Holy See. The revision of the concordat should assure "independence of each other, mutual respect, and the necessary cooperation." In particular, the Church should renounce its right of nomination in the appointment of bishops in the Council of State, and in the Council of the Kingdom, as well as the privileged position of the clergy in penal law; the government should renounce its right of nomination in the appointment of bishops. The Spanish government yielded quickly to what is regarded as an expression of the will of the Second Vatican Council. On 10 January 1967 ART. 6, Sec. 2, of the Charter of the Spaniards was changed and the principle of religious liberty was proclaimed in a word-for-word borrowing from the declaration *Dignitatis humanae.* On 26 June 1967 the law on religious liberty was adopted. On 28 July 1976, after the death of General Franco, there was signed a treaty in which Spain renounced the right of presentation of the chief of state (or king) in the filling of bishoprics, and the Holy See renounced the criminal-law privilege of the clergy (ART. XVI of the concordat of 1953). The negotiations for the revision of the concordat were quickly continued.

A development similar to that in Spain proceeded in Portugal. The law on religious liberty of 21 August 1971 and ART. 45 of the constitution revised on 23 August 1971 conceded legal equality to all religious groups. The concordat and the missionary agreement were discussed. The toppling of the authoritarian state in 1974 introduced a development which certainly intended to weaken the position of the Catholic Church. In the agreement of 15 February 1975 the Holy See, by changing ART. XXIV of the concordat of 7 May 1940, sacrificed the principle of the civil indissolubility of marriages contracted in church.

In Italy negotiations on the revision of some articles of the concordat have long been under way. Without consultation with the Holy See, contrary to ART. 34

of the concordat, civil divorce was introduced in 1970. The popular referendum against it produced a serious defeat for the Catholics. At the end of 1976 the Italian government and the Holy See agreed on a document which aimed to adapt the concordat to Italian constitutional reality and the spirit of the Second Vatican Council. The Catholic religion was thereafter no longer to be the religion of the state. The restrictive stipulations against apostate priests were to be dropped. The obligations which encumbered the state because of Rome's sacred character were to be abolished.

In Ireland (Eire), whose relations with the Church posed no problem and needed no guarantee by concordat, the deletion of the so-called Church Clause from the Irish constitution (ART. 44), which granted to the Catholic Church a special status as "Custodian of the Faith which the majority of the population professed," was decided by popular vote in 1972.

Latest Concordats and Agreements with Free Countries.   In the most recent period the Holy See has also signed treaties with many states. However, most of them deal only with particular questions, and not one provides a comprehensive regulation of the total complex of subjects affecting Church and state. In many agreements existing treaties were altered or expanded, in which case the adjustment meant in most cases a diminution of the Church's legal position, which had been gained through previous concordats. In some agreements references to the Second Vatican Council appear. In place of institutional guarantees there are in increasing measure guarantees of religious liberty for individuals and groups. One of the most difficult questions which confronted, now as previously, the nations of central and Western Europe in connection with the ordering of the relations of Church and state is usually the regulation of the school system, in particular the assurance of the establishment of free, nonstate, private schools. The council saw as the optimal type of school — in the declaration *Gravissimum educationis* on Christian education, ART. 9 — the free Catholic school, endowed with public legal position and supported by public means. Accordingly, the Holy See strove to have the justification of the Church's maintaining its own schools and the financing of them by the state assured by treaty.

The Austrian concordat of 5 June 1933, whose further validity had at first been challenged, especially by the Socialists, was continued by a series of treaties, of which especially noteworthy are those which led to the erecting of the two new dioceses of Burgenland in 1960 and Feldkirch in 1964 and gave the ecclesiastical school system financial security in 1962 and 1972. In the treaty of 5 April 1962 Spain expressed a generous recognition of nontheological studies at ecclesiastical universities. On 26 November 1960 the Holy See concluded with Paraguay a convention on the establishment of a military vicariate. The convention with Venezuela of 6 March 1964 moved generally in traditional paths. But, as earlier in the concordats with Latvia (ART. XII) and the Dominican Republic (ART. X), so also in this agreement attention was given to the activity of foreign priests and lay persons in the care of souls and in social services (ART. XIII). The patronate for the naming of bishops (ART. VI) and for the filling of capitular and parochial benefices (ARTS. VIII–X) was abolished, but in regard to the bishops, in contrast to other countries, the state's right of veto in the procedure was confirmed in accord with the political proviso. The "protocol" with Haiti of 15 August 1966 confirmed, after preliminary conflicts, the intention of the government especially to protect the Catholic Church in accord with ART. 1 of the concordat of 1860 and to guarantee its free exercise of its pastoral care in conformity with the concordat, canon law, and the Second Vatican Council. Similarly, the treaty with Argentina of 10 October 1966 referred in the preamble to the principles of the Second Vatican Council. It gave the Church freedom to alter the diocesan organization in the country (ART. II) and abolished the state's right of nomination to episcopal sees (ART. III). The agreement of 24 July 1968 with Switzerland led to the long desired establishment of the see of Lugano for the canton of Ticino.

A new concordat with Colombia was concluded on 12 July 1973 and ratified on 2 July 1975. This is a typical postconciliar concordat with a Catholic country. In it the humane and social aspect of the Church's activity comes strongly to the fore. The ministry of the Church to the human person is expressly mentioned (ART. V). The Catholic religion is recognized only as the "basic element of the common good and of the total development of the nation," and the Church's freedom is assured in the framework of the religious freedom of the other denominations (ART. I). The independence of Church and state is strongly emphasized (ARTS. II and III). The ministry of the Church and its cooperation with the state in the area of the educational and social systems is especially stressed (ARTS. V and VI). The canonically contracted marriage remains basically subject to the Church alone, except for separation from bed and board (ARTS. VII-IX). The Church's activity in instruction and education is regulated in detail (ARTS. X XIII). The naming of the bishops is done freely by the Pope, but in this matter there is conceded to the president of the republic a right to express reservations "of civil or political character" (ART. XIV). The immunity of clerics and religious is retained in modern form (ARTS. XVIII–XX). The Church's property is protected with noteworthy adaptations to today's circumstances (ARTS. XXIII–XXVI).

With regard to comparative law the state-Church law of the Federal Republic of Germany occupies a special place. The Second World War ended with the occupation of the country by the victorious Allies. The Western occupation powers in general assured the Churches freedom of action. Immediately after the ending of the war, which the Churches had survived as intact organizations, these were sought and recognized as guarantors of a civil law order. Their position in public life seemed to be consolidated and to prepare for a new alliance of Church and state. The Churches were first restored to their former rights, but in some states with marked restrictions, particularly in the school system. In the positive law of the state Church the experiences of the period of Nazi domination were expressed in only a relatively modest measure. A fundamental new ecclesio-political orientation was either prevented or made difficult both in the Federal Republic and also in many federal states because of the resistance of the Socialists and liberals. In the federation, just as in the states, a beginning was made basically with the state-Church law of the Weimar Constitution, which was modified only in details. Even the capability for compromise of the Weimar solution of the relations of state and Church proved to be realistic and lasting. The Basic Law for the German Federal Republic of 23 May 1949 adopted word for word ARTS. 136–39 and 141 of the Weimar Constitution and in ART. 4 guaranteed freedom of denomination and of worship and in ART. 7 religious instruction. The constitutions of the states proceeded in a similar fashion. In this matter, in each state according to the partisan political composition of the state conventions that drew up the constitutions, certain changes and supplements were included. On the whole the states with a predominantly Catholic population granted the Church a more favorable position than did those with a Protestant majority population. In contradistinction to the Weimar Constitution, the federation no longer has any principle of legislative competence in ecclesio-political questions. However, it retains a series of legislative competencies, because the constitutional legal bases of the relations of Church and state are, now as before, federal law (ART. 140 GG). In view of this legal situation it was principally the business of the states to take the initiative in the construction and completion of the arrangement between Church and state.

If there can be no question of a fundamentally new order of the relations of state and Church, there can still be the question of a new manner of interpretation of the traditional formulas. As a consequence of the different legal constitutional framework of the Weimar Constitution, the stipulations on religious groups have experienced a change of meaning. This can be briefly summarized in the two poles: end of the state-Church sovereignty and recognition of a full public status of the Churches. The ecclesiastical treaties with the Protestant state Churches in Lower Saxony (1955), Schleswig-Holstein (1957), and Hesse (1960) accepted, recognized, and legally concretized the new interpretation of the relations between Church and state in legal theory. The claim and the task of the Churches are positively evaluated by the state and regarded as basically worthy of assistance. The coresponsibility of the Churches for the shaping of public order, even for the fate of state and society, is accepted. The achievements of the Churches for the maintenance of the moral foundations of human life, their struggle for freedom and human dignity, as well as their stabilizing function have led to the recognition of their qualification basically to take a stand on all questions of the life of the people. The assertion of overly positive rights antecedent to the state in the Basic Law forbids state interference in ecclesiastical affairs, just as it even seemed possible according to the Weimar Constitution, and gives the Church an independence such as, with this clarity, the Weimar Constitution did not. The state's traditional powers of supervision and collaboration are almost entirely abolished or placed on a contractual basis. But the state does no longer wish regularly to drop mere ties, but rather to free the Church for the carrying out of its tasks. Its position in public law is confirmed by treaty.

The relationship between Church and state existing since 1945 is, according to the prevailing view, that of coordination. Church and state face each other as independent partners in their own right, which, because of their common responsibility, regulate in fundamental harmony questions affecting each other. True, the state is not obliged by a treaty with the Church to arrange common matters. But the treaty is the adequate means in a constitutional system that expresses the independence of the Church and the secular nature of the state. Besides, the modern socially active state has created or reemphasized many relationships with the Church. Hence the number of treaties concluded with the Churches in the years since the end of the war is very high. Most of the agreements were made between the federal states on the one hand and the Protestant state Churches or the Holy

See respectively, or the bishops of a state, on the other, and relatively few by the federation with the groups of Churches. In regard to the treaties, the two groups of fundamental agreements determining status and regulating individual questions must be distinguished. The number of administrative agreements with bishops is considerable, for example, for regulating the appointment of teachers of religion or of questions of property. For the first time in the history of German ecclesiastical law, after the Second World War the initiative for treaties between Church and state in the various federal states proceeded from German Protestantism. In double contrast to the practice in the period of the Weimar Republic, the treaties with the Protestant Churches were, first, not mere equalizing complements of Catholic concordats, but independent agreements developed from Protestant ideas and exigencies, and, second, they were not followed by any, or by any adequate, agreements with the Catholic Church that took into account principles of parity. All the more noteworthy is the fact that in some of these treaties, likewise for the first time in the history of German ecclesiastical law, there appear express provisos of parity, which guarantee to Protestantism equal treatment with Catholicism.

The Catholic Church was at first hindered in the conclusion of new agreements because of its clinging to the concordat with the Reich, whose existence with legal effect and whose continued validity were challenged by leftist groups, and especially by its insistence on the school articles, which were annoying to some state partners. In several federal states there were long-lasting conflicts over the school regulations. The state of Lower Saxony enacted a school law which, in the Church's view and that of the federal government, was in opposition to ART. 23 of the concordat with the Reich. The conflict was brought before the Federal Constitutional Court by the federal government. This was supposed to decide the question whether the state of Lower Saxony was obliged, vis-à-vis the federation, to observe the stipulations of the concordat with the Reich in fashioning its school law. In its verdict of 26 March 1957 the Federal Constitutional Court accepted both the legally effective existence and the continued validity of the concordat with the Reich, but denied the authority of the federation to hold the states to the observance of those obligations of it whose object, according to the Basic Law, falls under the exclusive competence of the states. This decision granted to the states, with regard to their exclusive legislative competence in questions of the educational system, the legal constitutional freedom arbitrarily to exempt themselves from international law ties. By it the concordat with the Reich was annulled in essential parts. Nevertheless, the Lower Saxon school controversy became the occasion to seek a contractual solution of the open questions and to restore, to a certain extent, the equality in Lower Saxony, which was no longer protected by the Loccum Treaty of 19 March 1955, very favorable to the Protestant state Church. After prolonged discussions, which were accompanied by a passionate anti-Catholic campaign in the state, there occurred on 1 July 1965 the conclusion of the first and only concordat with a state of the German Federal Republic, Lower Saxony. It continued the Prussian concordat of 1929, but went considerably beyond it in topics and statements. The treaty eliminated the splintering of the state-Church law in the state and ended the conflict between Church and state over the organization of the school system. The state guaranteed under certain conditions the maintaining and erecting of public Catholic denominational schools. The Church recognized the nondenominational school as the regular school, the denominational school as a school by request (Art. 6). In the matter of a substantial altering of the structure of the public school system, the opening of discussions in the spirit of the treaty was envisaged (Art. 19, Sec. 2). The encouragement of Catholic adult education by the state was promised (Art. 9). The interests of the Church in broadcasting were taken into consideration (Art. 10). With these two regulations the attempt was made to introduce newer developments into the usual matter of concordats. The agreement went beyond the traditional friendship clauses to establish "continuing contact" on all questions of the mutual relationship (Art. 19, Sec. 1).

The Lower Saxon concordat did not give rise to other similar treaties. Other states, like Hesse and Rhineland-Palatinate, were prepared only to conclude agreements with the bishops of the state. Today there is no favorable set of circumstances in the Federal Republic for the signing of concordats. The erecting of new theological faculties at Bochum, Regensburg, Augsburg, and Passau or, respectively, of technical disciplines at Osnabrück and professional chairs at Saarbrücken at the state universities, as well as the extensive elimination of the denominational character of the public elementary schools and of teacher education made necessary a number of treaties of individual federal states — Bavaria, Rhineland-Palatinate, North Rhine-Westphalia, Saarland, Lower Saxony — with the Holy See. The tendency to push the denominational schools and teacher education conformable to the creed to the private level is unmistakable. Articles 23 and 24 of the concordat with the Reich became entirely obsolete through this development. Still, some states have been found ready for extensive support of Catholic private schools. The treaty with Bavaria of 4 September 1974 confirmed the possibility, already agreed to on 7 October 1968, of forming in the public elementary schools, under certain conditions, classes and instruction groups for pupils of the Catholic faith; in these the instruction and training would be governed by the special principles of the Catholic denomination (Art. 6, pars. 2 and 3). The state of Bavaria bound itself to grant financial and personnel assistance to the schools of Catholics "in the framework of the general encouragement of private schools" (Art. 8, par. 1). To the private Catholic elementary and special schools was promised, with certain restrictions, the repayment of the necessary expenditure and building costs (Art. 8, pars. 2 and 3). The accord of 15 May 1973 with Rhineland-Palatinate also assured the establishment and financing of Catholic private schools. The treaty contains generous promises of state contributions for the expenditures for building projects of Catholic schools (Art. 7) and for the assignment of state teachers to Catholic private schools (Art. 10). Essentially similar is the agreement reached on 21 February 1975 between the Holy See and the Saarland on the same subjects.

In the most recent period a new phase of the relations of Church and state in the Federal Republic seems to be under way. The Church fell into strong dependence on the movements in society. The changed public attitude reacts upon the interpretation of the norms, but now in a sense increasingly more unfavorable to the Churches. The interpretation of the rules of the ecclesiastical law is, to a great degree, dependent on the political and ideological tendencies in public life prevailing at the moment and occasionally rapidly changing. For example, since the close of the Second Vatican Council the public position, as well as the political, social, and cultural influence of the Churches in the Federal Republic, are in increasing measure questioned by teachers, party politicians, and certain organizations. The process of secularization moves after the trauma of the lost war and the "shock of the first postwar period," as Siegfried Grundmann expresses it, with new intensity. An influential movement sees the Churches to an increasing degree in relation to other social forces and includes them in the associations and interest groups. This view does not let the nature of the Churches be given adequate recognition any more. The institutional relations between Church and state become weaker; they are abandoned in favor of a stronger social orientation of the two powers. The Church must engage in the process of forming the state's will less as an institution than through the presence of its faithful in society. In the administration of justice there partly exists the tendency to overstress the negative side of religious freedom, that is, less to protect liberty in the practice of religion and rather much more to assure the right of dissidents to the nonexercise of religious acts. In the course of this development religious practice is threatened with being restricted to the church building and the family sphere.

Quite differently from the situation with the Western occupation zones, or the German Federal Republic, proceeded the development of the relations of Church and state in the Soviet occupation zone, or the German Democratic Republic. At first the Soviet occupying power refrained from interference in the inner ecclesiastical sphere. The constitution of the German Democratic Republic of 7 October 1949 in ARTS. 41–49 adopted in great part formulas of ARTS. 135–41 of the Weimar Constitution. But these regulations were essentially modified by the intensified principle of the separation of Church and state. The constitution guaranteed religious freedom (ART. 41) and guaranteed to religious groups the character of corporations of public law with the traditional right to raise money (ART. 43, Secs. 3 and 4). Religious instruction might be given by them in school buildings (ARTS. 40 and 44). But the educational system was subject exclusively to the control of the state (ARTS. 34–40). More unfavorable than the constitutional law was the constitutional reality. By means of laws and directives, as well as through administrative measures, the Church's sphere of action was ever more strictly limited and the de-Christianization of the people was pressed as planned. A relatively more trustworthy expression of the present status of the relations of Church and state is the constitution of the German Democratic Republic of 6 April 1968. It guarantees liberty of conscience and of belief and equality of rights of all citizens without regard to religious denomination (ART. 20, Sec. 1), as well as freedom of denomination and of the practice of religion (ART. 39, Sec. 1). The arranging of the affairs of the Churches and religious groups and the exercise of their activity are subject to the reservation of the constitution and of the law (ART. 39, Sec. 2). The independence of the Churches in the arrangement and administration of their affairs is no longer guaranteed. There is no longer any constitutional protection against interference in their inner sphere. There is no more word of any rights of the Churches. Ecclesiastical activity is handed over to the arbitrarily manipulable "legal decisions" of the German Democratic Republic. Churches and religious groups are, according to the 1968 constitution, no longer corporations of public law. Hence, from now on they move only in the area of private law and have lost the capacity to employ any disciplinary power. In the other fields of law also, for example, in penal law, the prerogatives accruing to the Church from its public position are eliminated. A guarantee of religious instruction is absent, just as is the assurance of pastoral care in public institutions. No constitutional guarantee of ecclesiastical property exists any longer. The right of the Church to raise money has come to nothing. The public achievements are no longer mentioned. The 1968 constitution of the German Democratic Republic does, however, mention, as the sole constitution of a Socialist country, the agreements as means for regulating the relations of state and Church (ART. 39, Sec. 2). It thereby makes known that it is aware of the independence of the Churches. Apparently, the leadership of the German Democratic Republic has grasped that treaties can be a useful means of Socialist ecclesiastical policy. The German Democratic Republic especially has some desires relating to the Catholic Church, the fulfilling of which can be obtained only from the Holy See, for example, a new arrangement of diocesan boundaries. First contacts with the Holy See have been made. However, a concordat with substantive guarantees of the Church's activity is presumably not sought by the German Democratic Republic. It treats as nonexistent the concordats with Prussia and with the Reich. The appointment of apostolic administrators in the German Democratic Republic on 23 July 1973 took place without a treaty.

Section Two

The Diversity of the Inner Life
of the Universal Church

Chap. 89: Wilhelm Weber; Chap. 90: Leo Scheffczyk
Chaps. 91, 97: Erwin Iserloh; Chap. 92: Norbert Trippen
Chap. 93: Viktor Dammertz; Chap. 94: Paul Ludwig Weinacht
Chap. 95: Michael Schmolke; Chap. 96: Erwin Gatz

C H A P T E R   8 9

Society and State as a Problem for the Church

The period since the outbreak of the First World War (1914–18), the start of which is marked within the Church by the change in the See of Peter from Pius X (1903–14) to Benedict XV (1914–22), presents itself as an epoch of socio-political crises and a global inability to establish peace. During the very war itself the Bolshevik Revolution — the "October Revolution" of 1917 — under Lenin was victorious in Russia. Five years later Mussolini inaugurated the Fascist era in Italy with his "March on Rome" of 28 October 1922. On 30 January 1933 there followed the subjection of Germany to the dictatorship of National Socialism through Hitler's so-called "seizure of power."

The three revolutionary movements with more or less monistic ideologies ended politically in totalitarian dictatorships of nationalistic style, but with claims beyond their own national frontiers — Bolshevism: "Socialist World Revolution"; Fascism: "Mare Nostro," with claims of hegemony around the Mediterranean; National Socialism: "Living Space for the German People" in the east. In this way, as also by means of the continuing nationalism of the nontotalitarian states, all good starts for a global understanding of peoples — the League of Nations — or at least for a European understanding between the former opponents in the war — Briand/Stresemann — were finally condemned to failure. The world economic crisis of 1930 led with its army of millions of unemployed to a complete disorganization of world commerce and to serious social upheavals in the industrial nations, which finally helped to smooth Hitler's route to power in Germany. The world economic crisis marks the end of the era of liberal economics and the beginning of a national state policy of controlling and standardizing. The hectic fever with which the individual nations reacted to the severe depression by ever new restrictive measures consolidated the crisis. "The cyclical crisis produced a structural crisis of the world economy. The crisis *in* the system became a crisis *of* the system" (A. Predöhl). The crisis led to the injury especially of the small and middle independent livelihoods, to a further concentration in the economy — financial capitalism — and thereby to a serious derangement of the world political and inner social equilibrium.

After the Second World War (1939–45) thinking in terms of political blocs (NATO, the Warsaw Pact), problems of conventional and nuclear rearmament, of the Cold War, and locally restricted warlike confrontations were increasingly prominent, partly in connection with the West-East conflict (Korea and Vietnam), partly in connection with the elimination of the former European colonial rule (Algeria and Angola), partly from very dissimilar motives (Hungarian revolt, suppression of the reform socialism of Prague, the Middle East conflict). Alongside the West-East conflict the North-South problem emerged more clearly, namely, the tensions from the imbalance between the developed industrial nations of the northern hemisphere — "First" and "Second World" — and the populous but economically undeveloped and hence poor and partly hungry countries of the so-called "Third World."

However, the picture would be incorrect if note were not taken also of positive starts and developments, even if not all or only few were actually developed. To be named here would be the above-mentioned idea of Europe, the activity of the International Worker's Organization (ILO) at Geneva, which was founded in 1919 and since then has displayed a comprehensive and beneficial activity, the development of labor and social law, especially in Germany in the period between the wars, the beginnings of a new international order of law and peace, such as the establishing of the United Nations with its subsidiary and/or successor organizations — UNESCO, FAO, UNICEF, etc. — toward and after the end of the Second World War, the "Declaration of the Rights of Man" by the United Nations of 10 December 1948, and the founding of the European Community, to name only a few of the most important happenings.

The newer Catholic social doctrine, called into being since Leo XIII (1878–1903), experienced in the period after the two world wars, especially since the encyclical *Quadragesimo anno* of 1931, a vast further development and acquired the contour of a "system," if one understands by a social doctrinal system logically arranged and coherent propositions on the structural principles underlying society. Simultaneously there grew also reflexively the Church's self-consciousness of possessing its own social teaching and of having to present it as obligatory. In his encyclical *Mater et Magistra* of 1961, John XXIII thus expressed this self-awareness: "We especially point to the fact that the social teaching of the Catholic Church is an integrating component of the Christian doctrine of mankind." "For this reason it is especially important that Our children not only know the principles of the social doctrine but also be formed according to them."

The most important questions and problems with which the social message of the Church had to do were proposed to it through the development indicated earlier. They constitute the "life-centered problems" of the most recent phase in the development of Catholic social teaching.

Thus Pius XI (1922–39) had to deal with the totalitarian ideologies and dictatorship movements of socialism/communism, of Fascism, and of National Socialism. To each of the three he devoted a special encyclical. In the world economic crisis, which announced the breakdown and end of the era of liberal economics with the social ills appearing in its wake, appeared the second great social encyclical in the strict sense, *Quadragesimo Anno,* which, as a follow-up of the encyclical *Rerum novarum* of 1891, which dealt almost exclusively with the classic social question of the nineteenth century, namely, with the labor problem, had as its subject the disorganization of society. The experiences with the totalitarian dictatorships, especially with National Socialism, made Pius XII (1939–58) the herald of the rights of the human person. Under him there emerged in a stupendous abundance of proclamations of the most varied sort (although he did not compose a social encyclical of his own in the strict sense), the ever clearer outlines of what can be termed Christian "personalism" and "solidarity." Thus is explained his almost obstinate insistence on the principle of subsidiarity. To Pius XII we owe remarkable and penetrating ideas on the problem of democracy, of toleration, and of public opinion. In his range of ideas, that of the underdeveloped countries appears early on. The universal or world common welfare led him to make the notion of a family of mankind again and again the subject of doctrinal expressions and proclaim the vision of a "world state" on the basis of federation. The era of John XXIII (1958–63) was marked by two important social encyclicals which in their statements on the one hand continued the tradition of the Church's social teaching and on the other hand gave important impulses to the following council. *Mater et Magistra* has already been mentioned. The encyclical *Pacem in terris* of 1963 was experienced in both the West and East as a sensation. It constituted, as has rightly been said, the Pope's last will. In both encyclicals he extensively synchronized the social thought of the Church with the exigencies or, as John XXIII especially liked to express it, with the "signs of the time," or, as the same Pope demanded in his opening address to the Second Vatican Council on 11 October 1962, brought the Church an essential step nearer to *aggiornamento.* He sought to secure for the striving of mankind for justice and peace, by employing its own manner of speaking, the most profound and ultimate impulses from the Christian view of mankind and of society.

The Social Claim to Educate and Its Bases:
Natural Law and Revelation ("Question of Competence")

In *Rerum novarum* Leo XIII had already laid claim to the social doctrine to teach. "With full confidence We approach this task and in the awareness that the word belongs to Us" (13). Pius XI energetically repeated this claim in *Quadragesimo anno* and at the same time made it more precise against possible misinterpretations. "The deposit of truth entrusted to Us by God and the holy duty committed to Us by God to proclaim the moral law in its entire compass, to declare, and, whether or not he desires it, to press for its observance subject on this side both the social and the economic sphere without reservation to Our supreme judgment" (41).

Three considerations simultaneously justify and limit the Church's claim: (1) Society and economics cannot be considered apart from the moral law;

(2) under this exclusive respect — "not in questions of a technical sort for which [the Church] neither disposes of the suitable means nor has received a mission, but in everything which is related to the moral law" (41) — a sovereign authority belongs to the Church or, respectively, the ecclesiastical teaching office; (3) this has nothing to do with unjust claims to power, as they are often imputed to the Church.

Pius XII not only frequently confirmed this claim of his predecessors, but regarded as a legitimation of the Church's claim the ontological fact of the "intrinsic involvement," as G. Gundlach calls it, of the Church with society and expressed this state of affairs in the controversial formula of the Church as the "vital principle of human society." John XXIII unmistakably made the same claim when he had his first social encyclical begin, almost as with a roll of drums, with the words: "Mother and teacher of peoples is the Catholic Church" (*Mater et Magistra,* 1).

Pius XII, with appeal to Leo XIII, characterized as the "undeniable sphere of the Church" the judgment on those principles "of the eternally valid order...which God, the Creator and Redeemer, has made known through natural law and revelation." His essential statement in this question is: "Rightly: for the principles of natural law and the truths of revelation both have, as two in no way opposite but parallel water courses, their common source in God" (*UG,* 498).

The idea of natural law, undoubtedly dominant in the newer Catholic social doctrine since Leo XIII, experienced under Pius XII an important further development. The "authenticity of natural law," still always a problem in a developed dynamic society, was appealed to by Pius XI in connection with the right of property, which, as "history shows, . . . is not immutable" (*Quadragesimo anno,* 49). But while in tradition an authenticity or "mutability" of natural law was derived rather *ab extra,* that is, from the changes of external circumstances or conditions (*circumstantiae*), for Pius XII there ensues from the study of the history of the development of law the fact that, under special conditions, specific rights can change *ab intra,* from their content. Of course, there is an unchangeable nucleus in natural law.

Pius XII developed this idea in greater detail in one of his most noted addresses, which he gave on 13 October 1955 to the *Centro Italiano per la Riconciliazione Internazionale.* Because the matter is sufficiently important, the decisive sentences are repeated here verbatim: "The study of history and of legal development from remote times teaches that, on the one hand, a change in economic and social (and often also in political) situations demands new forms of those postulates of natural law to which the systems hitherto prevailing can no longer do justice; but, on the other hand, that in connection with these changes the fundamental demands of nature always recur and pass themselves on, with greater or lesser urgency, from one generation to the others."

In his address of 7 September 1955 to the participants of the Tenth International Congress of Historians Pius XII had already formulated for the Church the claim, as "historical power," as "living organism," regularly to intervene in the sphere of public life "in order to assure the correct balance between duties and obligations on the one side and rights and freedoms on the other."

Also with Pius XII we still find the problem, drawn along from tradition, especially by Leo XIII, of defining the relations of natural law, truth, and the discovery of truth. True, there is expounded by him in connection with the discussion of democracy the essential function of public opinion for a democratic commonwealth. In the complete absence of public opinion must be seen "a lack, a weakness, a sickness of social life." But the truth, also the true perception of the norms of natural law as possessed "objective" truth, is claimed for the Church and the teaching office in such a manner that all other tribunals, even public opinion, must stand almost rather as hearers, as receivers of the second rank.

In this context one can now — in contrast to almost all other statements in which there is incorrectly mention of a "turn" in thought — ascertain in John XXIII a genuine breakthrough to new shores. If he speaks of truth or of the rights bestowed by God on mankind in its very nature, then he presupposes the entire traditional theology of these rights, in regard to which, however, Leo XIII, Pius XI, and also to a great extent even Pius XII had basically come to a standstill. But this did not satisfy John XXIII. To him it was not a question, in an encyclical, moreover, that was oriented to the whole pluralistic world, only of the absolute, eternal, changeless truth, which, furthermore, is not capable of being imposed by the teaching office in an ideologically dismembered world. For him the truth was concretized, knowledge of truth grows in the "veracity" of mutual human relationships. Supported on the hope of rational understanding and love among people, the optimistic Pope believed in the realization of veracity in human relationships as the basis of the feasibility of every knowledge of truth. Truth is no longer a merely possessed, guarded, and authoritatively interpreted objective *Depositum:* truth occurs rather in the freedom of mankind as a social process of truth-finding. Here is present a gifted understanding of the so powerfully fatigued formula of the identity of "theory and practice."

Because of the importance of the matter, the central statements of the Pope will again be presented here verbatim: The "happening of truth" lives by this, "that people mutually exchange their perceptions in the bright light of truth, that they are put in the position of making use of their rights and fulfilling their duties, that they are incited to strive for spiritual goods, that from every honorable thing they ... gain an occasion for common honest joy, that they seek in tireless desire to share among themselves and receive from one another the best they have. These values affect and control everything that is related to scholarship, economics, social institutions, development and organization of the state, legislation, and finally to all other things that constitute externally human coexistence and develop in constant progress." In order that truth "may function" in this way, the right to free expression of opinion and to information in conformity with truth must be respected: "From nature people have ... the right ... to seek the truth freely and to express their opinion while respecting the moral order and the common good, to disseminate it, and to exercise any profession; finally, to be informed of public events in accord with the truth." "The truth further commands that a person let himself be guided in the use of the manifold possibilities which were created by the progress of modern means of publication and by which the mutual understanding of peoples is promoted by the highest objectivity."

In these sentences can rightly be seen the fundamental ethical justification of democracy and at the same time of an ethics of public communication in accord with the times. In the climate of the encyclical *Pacem in terris,* Paul VI was then able during the council in his own first encyclical *Ecclesiam suam* of

6 August 1964 to proclaim the dialogue with the world in keeping with the new model of ecclesiastical communications, and the Second Vatican Council was able to acknowledge what in the understanding of the truth the Church owes to the world and its striving for truth. "The experience of the historical past, the progress of scholarship, the riches which lie in the various forms of human culture, through which human nature comes ever more clearly to manifestation and new ways to the truth are opened redound also to the Church's good."

Social Principles: Personality, Subsidiarity, Solidarity, Common Good, Universal Common Good

At the beginning of his encyclical on peace John XXIII puts the central principle of all human social organization: "At the basis of any human coexistence that should be well ordered and fruitful must lie the principle that every human being is by essence a person" (*Pacem in terris,* 9). "If we consider the dignity of the human person according to revealed truths, we must value it even much more highly" (*Pacem in terris,* 10).

1. Pius XI and especially Pius XII had already established the social doctrine of the Church definitively and unmistakably as "personalism." Everything social is related to the person and must promote its perfection. In other words, society has no end in itself, it is no domineering superego but has a ministerial character. The state has to promote the security of the person by guaranteeing the rights of the person as rights implanted in its nature by God. However, at times other social conditions require other emphases. Thus Leo XIII had primarily to defend the existing social order in its basic structure — state, state authority, private property — against anarchist and Marxist strivings, while the experiences with totalitarian states or movements — persecution of Catholics in Russia, Mexico, Spain, Fascism, National Socialism — caused Pius XI to speak again and again for the protection of human freedom and dignity and for the defense of the rights of the Church. But then Pius XII became especially the herald of human liberty and of the dignity of the human person.

To avert from the start any charge of individualism, Pius XII stressed that human rights are not by chance proclaimed as inviolable and inalienable against the state, but that they belong precisely to the "most precious in the common good" (*UG,* 213), for which the state has to stand up. And so "they can never be sacrificed to the common good, precisely because they are essential ingredients of it" (*UG,* 213). This truth is so central for Pius XII that he emphatically exclaimed: "This is the Catholic worldview!" (*UG,* 213).

To become politically effective, the rights of the person need a foundation in positive law, a demand which Pius XII had made and which was taken over verbatim by John XXIII from his predecessor. "To the human person also belongs the legal protection of its rights, which must be effective and impartial in harmony with the true norms of justice, as Our predecessor of happy memory, Pius XII, admonishes: 'From the divinely established legal order results the inalienable right of the human being to legal security and with it to a tangible legal sphere, which is protected against every attack of caprice' " (*Pacem in terris,* 27).

2. All other principles of Catholic social doctrine, especially the principle of "Catholic" subsidiarity that has entered into general linguistic use, follow from the principle of the person with logical cogency. Already long evident in accord with its essential content in its beginnings, in Leo XIII especially established in connection with the preeminence of the family over the state — cf. *Rerum novarum,* 10: "Since domestic common life, according to both the notion and the reality, is earlier than the civic community, so too its rights and duties have precedence, because they are closer to nature"; cf. also *Rerum novarum,* 38, in relation to free social unions and their relation to the state — it finds its classic definition in *Quadragesimo anno:* "Just as whatever the individual man can accomplish on his own initiative and with his own abilities must not be taken from him and allotted to the activity of society, so it is contrary to justice to claim for the wider and higher community whatever the smaller and subordinate communities can achieve and lead to a good end; at the same time it is entirely injurious and confuses the entire social order. *Every activity of society is subsidiary in conformity to its nature and concept:* it should support the members of the body social but must never destroy or absorb them.... The better the hierarchical order of the various socializations is maintained through strict observance of the principle of subsidiarity, the more social authority and social effectiveness stand out and the better and more fortunately is the state administered" (*Quadragesimo anno,* 79–80).

The principle of subsidiarity finds its justification as much in the liberty of the person as also in the structure of the smaller life groups, whose rights to life must not be curtailed by encroachments of more extensive social organizations ("statism"). On the one hand it protects the identity and privacy of the person and of the intermediate groups and institutions between the individual and the state — "defensive" function — and on the other hand it demands, according to the original meaning of the word, "help [*subsidium*] from above to below," if the individual or the smaller life groups, for example, the family, fail in their task of educating, with or without guilt — "responsible" function. It goes without saying that Pius XII as a determined defender of the rights of mankind especially stressed the "defensive" function of the principle of subsidiarity. Other situations demand other accentuations of the principle.

Pius XI characterized the principle as "gravissimum illud principium" (*Quadragesimo anno,* 79), which, with regard to the importance of the principles of solidarity and of the common good, must probably be translated as "extremely significant principle." Pius XII calls the principle a "principle constantly defended by the social doctrine of the Church," and emphasized its validity "even for the life of the Church, without prejudice to its hierarchical structure."

With John XXIII we find the principle of subsidiarity frequently referred to in *Mater et Magistra* directly (53) and indirectly (for example, 165), less in its defensive function than in its positive function of the support of society in regard to the weaker. In *Pacem in terris* the Pope also directly considers the principle (140). Here he especially stresses the right of the smaller life groups, of the *corps intermédiaires* within the political community (cf. *Pacem in terris,* 24).

3. In the human person identity — singularity, individuality — and being part of society — socialization, mutual dependence, and need for society as a reference point — are intertwined. Person is "identity in the rational subject." From this

state of being flows the principle of solidarity, by which all individualism and all collectivism is rejected. On the basis of these considerations the personalism of Catholic social doctrine is presented under the aspect of "solidarism." This name not only aims to express an ethical attitude of solidarity but to express a state of being, namely, the fact that all people in their respective social relations — individuals among themselves, in the union of the family, in the intermediate groups, in the state, in the community of nations — stand in an ontological union and reciprocal obligation to one another. This union demands social and legal organization in the sense of the principle of subsidiarity, by which the uniting of the two principles takes place. The Popes have not employed the concept of solidarism, but have argued, especially Pius XII, essentially in the sense of solidarism. More frequently, on the contrary, is the "principle of fraternal solidarity" affirmed, both as an ontological as well as an ethical principle of action.

4. The service function of society and of the state lies in promoting the common good. This does not consist, as corresponding to the individualistic concept, in the sum total of individual goods but has its own quality. It also does not oppose the just claims and expectations of individuals, but, as Pius XII said, the rights of the person pertain to the "most precious in the common good" (*UG,* 359). But it is the task of the state to reduce the often egoistic claims to one measure to be expected of and tolerable to all. To this extent the idea and realization of the common good stand against the pure standpoint of interest and power.

There have been controversies as to whether the common good is to be defined in the sense of *bona communia,* hence primarily in regard to content, or whether rather it aims at the making possible of *bene vivere in communitate,* that is, at the organizational side of society. The question is not only of academic interest, since in a pluralistic society a consensus as to the content of the common good, apart perhaps from the *minima moralia,* may be difficult to reach and besides in an ideologically colored dictatorship the content of the common good can be decreed in a totalitarian fashion — common good = good of the German people = good of the Aryan race. Both Pius XII and John XXIII stressed the primarily organizational function of the common good. This appears clearly from the descriptive definition which John XXIII gives in *Mater et Magistra.* According to the "correct notion of the common good," this embraces "the aggregate of those social presuppositions which make possible or easier to people the full development of their values" (*Mater et Magistra,* 65). From this definition it follows that the content or "values" do not belong primarily to the common good, that this rather presupposes them and should make possible and promote their development. Exactly in this sense had G. Gundlach, the adviser of Pius XII of long standing, already interpreted the common good in his commentary on Pius XII's Christmas address of 24 December 1942, when, characterizing the common good as "organizing element," he declared it to be impossible "that the organizing element as such determines that which is to be organized, which ideally presupposes it, namely, the inner structure of social life with the objective 'common goods' (the person with the cultural and religious values)."

Thus the circle again ends with the individual, whose development ultimately serves the common good. Thus the common good is the correct organizing principle — in the sense of becoming — or, respectively, as the correct organization —

in the sense of being — of society, a view which is possible only with regard to society's subsidiary and solidarist character. Thereby all principles of the Catholic social doctrine culminate in the common good.

5. There is no encyclical in which the common good is so often and in such diverse connections appreciated and stipulated for a wholesome common life as in *Mater et Magistra*. However, after it had been regarded in the past predominantly under the aspect of the national state — the state as primary guarantor of the common good — after the early peace efforts of Benedict XV and Pius XI, under the growing impression of the "unification of the world," the threat of a nuclear catastrophe, and the problem of underdeveloped countries, the idea of a world common good more and more gained ground. Pius XII saw in the relations to the other states an integrating part of the internal common good. "Serve," he said to journalists, "it [your people and state], however, in the conviction that its good relations to other nations, the understanding of their peculiarity, and the respect for their rights belong equally to the *bonum commune* of your own people and more effectively prepare for and consolidate peace as many another means." Finally, John XXIII speaks clearly of the "universal common good" (*Pacem in terris,* 132ff.), from which he deduces the necessity of a world state with "universal political power" (*Pacem in terris,* 137). But even on this high plane the human person must remain the ultimate goal of all social life. "Just as the common good of individual states cannot be defined without regard to the human person, so also not the universal common good of all nations together" (*Pacem in terris,* 139). Thereby, once again the personalist character of Catholic social doctrine is proclaimed in unmistakable clarity.

State and State Power — Democracy

The most important theological principles concerning state, state power, and common good as the goal of the state had been elaborated in a long tradition to the end of the pontificate of Leo XIII in their basic features. To these belong especially the tracing back of state and state power to God as the Creator of socially oriented humanity and the binding of state power in regard to the maintenance of the common good to the natural law as expression of the *Lex aeterna.* Questions about the best form of state and government could play a subordinate role in a simple theoretical structural grid that confined itself more to principle.

The Popes since Benedict XV could assume all this as known in essentials and as the certain doctrine of the Church. A brief recapitulation in the appropriate context was sufficient. But meanwhile the new and pressing questions had to do with a detailed specialization of the tasks of the state in view of the totalitarian developments since the First World War, a nuanced justification of state power under the presuppositions of a modern democracy, the question of the functional conditions of democracy in general, and finally the problem of moral norms in a pluralistic democratic society. Thus were the essential themes of the Church's political doctrine designated in the first half of the twentieth century.

1. As regards the end of the state, it was defined by all Popes since Pius XI unambiguously in the light of the social principles further developed above. Es-

pecially in connection with the totalitarian movements Pius XI underlined the instrumental character of the state as well as of society in general in relation to the human person. This is nothing else than "a natural means which one can and should use to achieve his goal; for human society exists for people and not vice versa." Pius XII more precisely stated the task of the state in enjoining on it the protection of the rights of the human person (*UG*, 3455). In this sense the state is primarily a state of law for the guaranteeing of the areas of personal freedom of the citizens. It is at the same time a welfare state, without, however, having to be a state affording total relief; for law and justice oblige it to undertake all political and socio-political measures only with consideration of private initiative, that is, in accord with the principle of subsidiarity. Pius XII warned against the relief state ("Etat-Providence"), "which should grant to each of its citizens for all the vicissitudes of life claims to achievements that are ultimately unrealizable" (*UG*, 3270). Pius XII also regarded the state only as a means — it is "subordinate to the person and has the sense of a means" (*UG*, 3763) — and rejected all state planning (*UG*, 6120). But these considerations in no way exclude the acknowledgment of the necessity of a state authority capable of functioning and equipped with power. In an address to a group of the Youth Union of the Christian Democratic Union of West Berlin on 28 May 1957 Pius XII characterized this acknowledgment precisely as an expression of a "Christian" concept of politics. "The state is not an ultimate, and there is no state omnipotence, but only a state power, and 'Christian politics' has a strong feeling for it. For without power the state cannot accomplish its goal of assuring and promoting the common good by means of a legal and social order adhered to by all" (*UG*, 6250).

John XXIII, who, as noted earlier, stressed the principle of subsidiarity more from its "positive" side — "help from above to below" — expressly says that the state must intervene in the economy "today to a more comprehensive degree than before" (*Mater et Magistra*, 103), that it "more and more penetrates areas which pertain to the most personal concerns of mankind and" are "therefore of the greatest importance" (*Mater et Magistra*, 60). But at the same time the limits of its competence are imposed on the state. They lie, to give a few examples, in the common good (*Mater et Magistra*, 65, 147, 151), in the fundamental rights of the person and the autonomy of the free social groups (*Mater et Magistra*, 52, 65), in the principle of subsidiarity — or, respectively, in its "defensive" function (*Mater et Magistra*, 53, 117, 152) — in the God-given arrangement and obligation of values (*Mater et Magistra*, 205ff.). In order that the state may remain a state of law under modern conditions, which is expressly to be emphasized, John XXIII regards the separation of powers — "that threefold classification of offices" — as "appropriate to human nature" (*Pacem in terris*, 68). This is the first time that the separation of powers was expressly mentioned in papal social teaching.

2. As regards the legitimization of the concrete agents of state power at a given time, over and above the theological and natural law derivation of the state's authority in general, Leo XIII in his encyclical *Diuturnum illud* strongly repudiated the liberal thesis that "all power proceeds from the people." What Leo intended to strike at is clear, namely, the "Contract Thesis," according to which — without any reference to God as the Creator of mankind and its society — the autonomous individuals creatively produce the state, as though in a quasi-contract (Rousseau's

contrat social), and hence naturally possess also the absolute right in relation to the appointment of the holder of state power.

Since the republican problem was now in hand because of his *Ralliément* policy, Leo XIII sought to aid himself with the construction in order that the people of the state might indeed have the possibility of "designating" — the "Designation Theory" — the actual holders of state power but not of appointing and commissioning them — the "Delegation Theory" — in order that the real investiture might follow, as it were, rather from God as Creator of the state. In this way the possibility of a compromise between the republican type of state on the one hand and the connection of state power to its divine origin on the other hand seemed to be maintained. Despite this compromise, whose difficult theological background considerations could not, of course, be comprehended by the theologically less trained wider public, there remained until today a strong mistrust of Leo XIII's attitude to the republic and to democracy. In this context the old Scholastic doctrine, of Thomas Aquinas in its beginnings and fully developed by Francisco Suárez, of the sovereignty of the people unified in the state would have offered itself spontaneously. Pius XII mentions the doctrine, though only *en passant,* when he speaks of the "thesis which outstanding Christian thinkers at all times have championed," the "principal thesis of democracy," that "the original agent of the political power coming from God [is] the people, not the 'mass' " (*UG,* 2715).

3. This raises the question of democracy in the Church's social doctrine. As late as the time of John XXIII the basic principle was repeated that it cannot "be decided once and for all which type of state is the more suitable or which is the most appropriate manner in which the state power fulfills its task" (*Pacem in terris,* 67); for the "necessities of life of any sound community ... are fulfilled or at least can be fulfilled under the same conditions as in other [than democratic] types of government conformable to law" (*UG,* 2713). Apart from this traditional principle, Pius XII testified to a clear sympathy for peoples who require "a system of government that is more in harmony with the dignity and liberty of the citizens" (*UG,* 3469).

For Pius XII it especially mattered to ask which assumptions must be realized for the functioning of democracy. He saw before him the empty appearance of a purely formal democracy, which "serves only as a disguise for something wholly undemocratic" (*UG,* 3482). It must be noted that Pius XII stressed this in the radio address for the last Christmas of the war in 1944, hence on the eve of the foreseeable end of two dictatorships — Fascism and National Socialism — and of the possibility thereby being sketched of a democratic state constitution for the nations concerned after the war's end. The state, including the democratic, "does not mechanically contain and unite in itself a formless aggregation of individuals in a defined territory, it is and must be an organized and organizing unity of an actual people" (*UG,* 3475). This was said against the individualistic notion of democracy, according to which faceless abstract individuals join together politically. Pius calls it more often "mass" in contrast to "people." For him the state citizen as a person is always *personne située,* that is, a person to be seen in different social contexts.

Pius XII thereby recalls the fact especially annoying today that people are unequal for the most diverse reasons. But this in no way injures "the civic equality of rights"; it gives to each, "vis-à-vis the state, the right ... to lead his own personal life in honor" (*UG,* 3478). In other words, the freedom of the person gives him the right to be "different" while maintaining intact the civic political equality of rights. That the continuation of such tension between the poles of freedom and equality needs, of course, the "genuine spirit of community and fraternity" (ibid.) Pius knows and he thereby makes known that he does not overlook one of the three ideals of democracy which has meanwhile fallen into oblivion, namely, the "principle of fraternity." The Christmas address of 1944 is thus a real comprehensive hermeneutic interpretation of the ideals of "Liberty, Equality, and Fraternity" (cf. especially *UG,* 3478).

4. Leo XIII and Pius XI had already deduced, arguing from the fact that people are by nature unequal, that the state must be an organic functional structure in which a large plurality of various groups and institutions in their own right seek to realize the common good by means of the enclosing function of the state. Neither an antagonistic class society nor a faceless, classless society corresponds to this "organic" concept. In this context must be viewed the Pope's insistence on family and private property as areas of freedom of the person within the state, and also on the much abused "corporate order," which is better designated as "meritocracy." Pius XI contrasted the idea of the meritocracy to the economic social chaos into which liberalism had plunged society. Since G. Gundlach had evidently already decisively assisted in preparing the idea for *Quadragesimo anno* and strongly favored it until his death in 1963, it becomes clear why Pius XII also came back to it so frequently, while in *Mater et Magistra* John XXIII no longer spoke of it directly. However, he considered the plural diversity of social life and political compromise among groups as very necessary. But his allusion to the "present day" (*Mater et Magistra,* 66) should probably mean that there can be no permanently obligatory ideal solution. John thereby abandons the concrete model but not the fundamental idea of the "corporate order" when he demands that the social systems lead their own life and be able "really to develop by virtue of their own right" (*Mater et Magistra,* 65).

5. Only in outline can still other important presuppositions for the progress of democracy from the view of papal social teaching be mentioned: Democracy cannot rely exclusively on legal assurances, otherwise it is condemned to fall. It depends "on the moral character of the citizens" (*UG,* 4393). From this it also follows — Pius XII thus addresses the problem of an elite for democracy — that precisely in a democracy high moral demands must be made on the holders of state power. Of course, those people "whose spiritual and moral predisposition is sufficiently sound and fruitful [will find] in themselves the spokesmen and overseers of democracy . . . men who personally live from those predispositions and understand how to transform themselves in fact" (*UG,* 3486). Also important is the political education of the citizens, not only the instruction on the manner of operation of democratic institutions but especially the introduction "to the protection of their true interests and especially of their conscience" (*UG,* 1779). Pius XII very urgently admonishes Christians to exercise the right to vote and elect, the neglect of which means a danger for democracy (*UG,* 4305). Not least is it required that the Christian in a democracy make himself available for the construction of an enduring order of law and peace both within and without (*UG,* 180).

6. As regards the relations of Church and state, Benedict XV in his address

on the occasion of the secret consistory of 21 November 1921 had proclaimed the inalienable right of the Church to freedom from all state interference. Pius XI demanded, vis-à-vis the totalitarian states, the right of the citizens to free exercise of their faith and the right of the Church to proclaim its message and to form consciences. Pius XII spoke of a "legitimate laicism of the state" (*UG,* 4555), which was always a principle of the Church. Nevertheless between Church and state there must not prevail a cool and separating atmosphere. A "complete" separation of the two cannot be approved (*UG,* 3985). In other respects Pius XII does not tire of presenting the fortunate impact of the Church on the state (for example, *UG,* 4103f, 3450f.)

The Church and the Social Errors of the Age

Socialism-Communism

In the nineteenth century socialism became the chief adversary of the Church and of social Catholicism in the social sphere. While Leo XIII had had to deal essentially with a complete Marxist ideology, which moreover had not yet acquired any political relevance of great importance, Pius XI could attest for socialism a development which he concisely sketched as follows: "If in Leo's time socialism was chiefly at least a homogeneous structure with a definitely complete doctrinal system, today it has developed in two sharply opposed and violently contending main trends, without, of course, having forsaken the anti-Christian basis common to all socialism." Pius XI spoke of "socialism become communism" and of the "more moderate direction which today the designation 'socialism' still retains."

In *Quadragesimo anno* the Pope did not employ many words in the criticism of communism, probably because among Christians and Catholics doubts in regard to it are scarcely possible. What especially characterizes communism in the Pope's view is, first, the open and ruthless force with which it seeks its goal, then its hostility to God and Church. However, what concerned the Pope was the warning against the heedlessness of those "who, regardless of the danger threatening from this side, look on calmly as the exertions of a violent and bloody revolution are borne into the whole world" (*Quadragesimo anno,* 112). Just as he did to the two other totalitarian ideologies of his day, Fascism and National Socialism, Pius XI also devoted to "atheistic communism" a special encyclical, which appeared on 19 March 1937 and began with the words *Divini Redemptoris.* In it the Pope provided evidence that the Marxist doctrine at the basis of communism experienced an expressly atheistic interpretation in dialectical materialism. In this way mankind was robbed of its freedom, the spiritual foundation of its human way of life and its dignity.

Pius XII also adhered clearly and unambiguously to his predecessor's express condemnation of the social system and the ideology of communism. By means of decrees of the Holy Office of 1 July 1949 and 28 July 1950 not only membership in the Communist Party but even its promotion was threatened with excommunication. The Pope could not conceive of the hope of "peaceful coexistence" with the Communist systems as a compromise but only as "coexistence in truth." Blows against the rights of the Church, for the most part connected with persecution and imprisonment of leading bishops, were answered by the Pope with the excommunication of those responsible, as in the cases of the Yugoslav Archbishop Stepinac on 14 October 1946, the Hungarian Cardinal Mindszenty on 28 December 1948 and on 12 February 1949, of the Czech Cardinal Beran on 17 March 1951, and of the Polish Cardinal Wyszyński on 30 September 1953.

John XXIII put the accents differently. Not only that in the spring of 1963 he received in audience the son-in-law of the then first secretary of the Central Committee of the Communist Party, Nikita Khrushchev, and that he sent Cardinal König of Vienna and an official of the Secretariat of State to Budapest and thereby took the first steps in the direction of a new Vatican "Eastern Policy"; in doctrinal evaluation he also sought cautious nuances. In his encyclical *Pacem in terris* he believed he could distinguish between the ideology of Marxism-socialism on the one hand and certain humane concerns on the other. He wrote: [It is] "entirely appropriate to distinguish specific movements which deal with economic, social, cultural questions or policy from false philosophical doctrinal views on the nature, origin, and end of the world and of mankind, even if these movements originated in such doctrinal views and are stirred up by them."

The years of the "Dialogue between Christianity and Marxism" starting after John XXIII, the breaches in the dike, which occurred in various parts of the world in the form of a "Theology of Revolution," "Liberation Theology" on a Marxist basis, led Paul VI, in order to round out the picture, to warn of a confusion of Christianity and Marxism. And so he wrote in his apostolic letter *Octogesima adveniens* of 17 May 1971 — the eightieth anniversary *of Rerum novarum:* — "If in Marxism as it is concretely lived these different facets and questions can be distinguished which present themselves positively for the reflection and action of Christians, it would be foolish and dangerous to reach the point where one forgets the inner bond which basically joins them together, that one adopts the elements of the Marxist analysis without recognizing its relations with the ideology and participates in the class struggle and appropriates its Marxist interpretation while neglecting to perceive the type of totalitarian and brutal society to which this method of proceeding leads."

Quite different and more difficult for the discussion within the Church was the prolonged confrontation with what Pius XI in *Quadragesimo anno* had termed the "moderate trend" in socialism. Again and again the discussion was enkindled by two central statements of the Pope: "Socialism, no matter whether as doctrine, as historical phenomenon, or as movement... is always irreconcilable with the doctrine of the Catholic Church — for then it would have to cease to be socialism: the opposition between Socialist and Christian notions of society is irreconcilable." "If socialism, like any error, also contains something right, which the Popes have never denied, still at its foundation lies a concept of society which is proper to it but stands in opposition to the authentic Christian concept. Religious socialism and Christian socialism are contradictions in themselves; it is impossible to be simultaneously a good Catholic and a real Socialist."

That the discussion, especially in Germany, did not get more strongly under way until after 1945 and then especially since the "Godesberg Program" of the Social Democratic Party of Germany is explained, first, by the fact that during the period of National Socialism public discussion was not possible, and, second, by the fact that the Social Democratic Party, in its effort to change from a class party to a popular party with its program of 1959, especially had to assure the Catholic part of the population that the socialism which Pius XI had meant in *Quadragesimo anno* had nothing in common with the Social Democratic Party after the Second World War.

The just quoted verdict of Pius XI against socialism appeared with the claim of being able to say with certainty what socialism really is. According to Pius XI the special ideological nucleus of socialism, which makes it what it is, is not Marxism or class conflict, but, as it is put tersely in the just quoted passage from *Quadragesimo anno,* "a concept of society... which is proper to it but stands in opposition to the authentic Christian concept." The unmistakably proper basic axioms as regards the Christian notion of society are according to *Quadragesimo anno,* 118f.: the human being was created by God as a person with his social nature, in his own image; also the necessary social authority is based ultimately in God, the Creator of mankind and final end of all things. Also, the commentary of the encyclical: "Of all this, socialism knows nothing; completely unfamiliar and indifferent to it is this exalted definition of both mankind and society; it sees in society solely a useful institution."

The claim to know what socialism is and to repudiate it as such was accordingly based by Pius XI on the incontestable fact that socialism was indebted to an ideological liberalism which withdrew mankind and its sociability from its origin and reference to God and thereby drove it to a road which the Christian could no longer accept. O. von Nell-Breuning expressed it thus: "With good reason socialism is called 'the natural child of liberalism' " or, respectively, "proletarian liberalism."

Pius XII said nothing on the theme of "moderate" or "liberal" socialism which went beyond Pius XI. In regard to him it can be admitted that from his viewpoint he had to add nothing essential to the verdict of *Quadragesimo anno.*

In the years around the death of Pius XII (1958–59) falls a period of heightened discussions of the relations of Christianity and socialism, especially of the Catholic Church and liberal socialism. The meeting of the Catholic Academy in Bavaria on "Christianity and Democratic Socialism" in January 1958 became a much noticed event in the political life of the Federal Republic of Germany: at it for the first time representatives of the Social Democratic Party and of German social Catholicism met to undertake the effort to demolish the traditional oppositions which were not for the last time still determined by the verdict of *Quadragesimo anno.* The leader on the Catholic side at this meeting was the adviser of Pius XII, the German Jesuit Gustav Gundlach, lecturer at the Gregoriana in Rome. He obtained such great attention because, to the general amazement, he came to terms in much greater detail with the rationalism in socialism, and even in liberal socialism, than with Marxism, so that, as the *Süddeutsche Zeitung* then reported dumbfoundedly, he "scarcely mentioned Marx's name, but instead all the more took offense at the liberal element in social democracy."

But in this way the chief item of criticism was identical with what *Quadragesimo Anno* had also criticized, and the burden of proof that this criticism was wrong lay with the Social Democrats and those Catholics who exerted themselves to build bridges.

In two documents addressed to the German Catholics an attempt was made to effect for the socialism of the Godesberg Program a Catholic approval and a revision of the harsh "no" of the encyclical *Quadragesimo anno.* Naturally, the manner of argumentation was criticized. All unsuitable passages were omitted as clearly disturbing, especially the central text in 118 on the picture of mankind, on the *humanum* as the normative force of all politics.

The leading Catholic social theologians of the day, G. Gundlach and O. von Nell-Breuning, were in agreement in their estimation of the Godesberg Program. The latter stressed the fundamental differentiation from the Christian beginning when in 1960 he unmistakably declared in the first of the two above mentioned brochures of the Social Democratic Party: "Much, it may be said, very much is common, but still not everything.... It is especially to be asked — and here our 'but' is inserted.... May one, while reading the encyclical, end with Number 120 and pass over the subsequent paragraphs as not present?" (Numbers 118 and 119 on the Christian view of mankind had also been disregarded.) "Nevertheless," continues von Nell-Breuning, "the title to Numbers 121–22, 'Cultural Socialism,' should catch the eye ... and the concluding words of 122: 'At the beginning of this cultural socialism stands cultural liberalism; at its end stands cultural Bolshevism.' " Accordingly the answer to the quest for a Catholic approval can logically only fail: "But in the cultural area — and ultimately society and economy are cultural affairs — liberal democratic socialism must first rid itself of its liberal [liberalistic] legacy." A "new edition will then be able to bring that decisively important element which not by chance is apparently lacking in the present one, but in accord with the situation of affairs must unfortunately be lacking." However, the document of 1962 did not bring, in this regard, the "decisively important element," namely, the renunciation of the "liberalistic legacy," and so up to the present for many it is not clear that the "no" of *Quadragesimo anno* to ideological socialism could be overcome in the form of cultural socialism.

Also the encyclical *Mater et Magistra* of 1961 brought no essentially new aspects for the further discussion and hence no alleviation for the discussion. At first John XXIII adopted the repudiating attitude of *Quadragesimo anno* to the "more moderate," revisionist socialism (*Mater et Magistra,* 34). Later he spoke of "ideologies" which aim to eliminate inner social and international tensions with inadequate means and on false routes, because they possess no correct picture of mankind. And so the discussion of the Church and liberal socialism remained for the future on the agenda beyond John XXIII and the council.

Fascism-National Socialism

Whereas communism and socialism not only still exist but have experienced a powerful expansion in the whole world and have penetrated with their ideology even into theology and partly into the Church, Italian Fascism and National Socialism, with which Pius XI had to deal, did not survive the end of the Second World War.

Italian Fascism under the leadership of the "Duce" Mussolini never assumed so rigid and ideologically monistic a position as did its counterpart in Germany and its opponent in Russia. Nevertheless, one can designate as its ideological nucleus, under the influence of Hegel and of his Fascist interpreter, Giovanni Gentile (d. 1944), who was minister of education from 1922 to 1925 and in 1923 was responsible for the Fascist reform of education, the Hegelian doctrine of the total state. "La nazione" became the key idea. This involved internally a strong, antiliberal, collectivist policy, and externally imperial claims around the Mediterranean — "Mare nostro": annexation of Libya and Ethiopia and occupation of Albania and Greece during the Second World War. The "Dottrina del Fascismo" culminated in the profession of a national imperialism.

The preindividualistic, preliberal, and pre-Fascist values of the family, the people, and the Church, or religion, respectively, worked to consolidate the national idea in the interior sphere. And so Fascism's attitude toward the Church was at first entirely friendly, and Mussolini esteemed it as especially a national cultural agent. And so, following two and one-half years of discussions there occurred the solution of the so-called "Roman Question" and a concordat in the Lateran Treaties of 11 February 1929. The Catholic religion was confirmed as the religion of the Italian state. Nevertheless, there ensued strong tensions, because the total "ethical state" claimed for itself exclusively all rights in the area of education and of youth work and hence curtailed the Church's influence. Only a few months after the conclusion of the Lateran Treaties Pius XI, in a letter of 30 May 1929 to Cardinal Secretary of State Gasparri, attacked the totalitarian interpretation of the treaties by the Fascist state. In the winter of 1930 began Fascism's struggle against "Catholic Action" and in March 1931 open war broke out over the autonomy of the Catholic youth organizations. This produced the encyclical *Non abbiamo bisogno* of 29 June 1931, in which the Pope spelled out his fiery protest against the limiting of ecclesiastical activities in public life and against the unilateral interpretation of the Lateran Treaties. The reaction on the part of Fascism was marked by deep emotions against the Church. After the dust which had been raised by the encyclical had settled, there came about on 2 September 1931 an agreement whereby the Catholic youth organizations were restricted to religious and educational tasks.

In *Quadragesimo anno* Pius XI attacked Fascist corporatism, the politically monopolistic compulsory organization of employers and employees.

A still more dangerous opponent of the Church sprang up in Germany with the seizure of power by National Socialism in 1933. In contradistinction to Italian Fascism, which essentially disavowed a political theology of its own, National Socialism understood itself as a doctrine of salvation of racist and nationalist style, which raised a total claim to the soul of the German person.

Although in the effort soon to realize a first very important foreign policy success Hitler was able to reach a concordat with the Holy See on 20 July 1933, confrontations were not slow in coming. In addition to the malicious struggle against the Christian faith with all the means of propaganda and of administration, there was especially the "neo-pagan" doctrine, there were the scientifically totally unqualified expositions of revealed religion and its origins in the Old Testament — Cardinal Faulhaber of Munich-Freising: *Judentum-Christentum-Germanentum* — which provoked the Church to resistance. On 14 March 1937, five days before the encyclical *Divini Redemptoris* against atheistic communism — a timely coincidence in which can be seen a clever, tactical move — the Pope published in German the encyclical *Mit brennender Sorge,* in whose first, ecclesio-political

part he protested against the "treaty reinterpretation, treaty evasion, treaty undermining, and treaty violation" in relation to the concordat, while in the second,
religious part he expressly took to task the teachings of National Socialism: racial
delusion, myth of "blood and soil," the principle that "that is right which benefits
the [German] people," the effort to create a German national Church not bound
to Rome. A quite mild protest by the German ambassador at the Holy See, Diego
von Bergen, was rejected by the cardinal secretary of state.

With the encyclical *Mit brennender Sorge,* Pius XI thought he had taken only a
first step in the confrontation with racism. Racism appeared to him as an especially
virulent ideology against the religiously based unity of the human species. Thus
it was made known through a sensational publication from the pen of Thomas
Breslin in *The National Catholic Reporter* of 15 December 1972 and 19 January
1973 to a wide public that Pius XI had on 22 June 1938 commissioned an encyclical,
the outline of which was supplied by the American Jesuit John LaFarge and by
Gustav Gundlach under the title "Societatis Unio." Because of the change in the
See of Peter in March 1939 this encyclical was never published.

In his address to the College of Cardinals of 2 June 1945 Pius XII dealt in detail with National Socialism and its consequences for the future. His repeatedly
presented appeals toward the end of the war not to impose the war released by
Fascism and National Socialism and the crimes perpetrated by them as a moral
burden on entire peoples — the "collective guilt thesis" — attracted notice. He
thereby already led across to the theme of the understanding of peoples after
the war.

Understanding of Peoples: "World State"

In his exertions for peace after the outbreak of the First World War, Benedict XV had
again and again referred to the moral force of law vis-à-vis the power of weapons.
He was especially concerned further to develop international law on the basis
of moral norms and also to inculcate international institutional provisions for a
lasting order of peace.

Although the pontificate of Pius XI was not troubled by a world war, still the
Pope suffered severely from the consequences of the First World War and the
preparedness for war, by no means eliminated from the world but on the contrary
renewing itself, with the prospect of an even more terrible war. For this reason
he based both his election motto "Pax Christi in Regno Christi" and his first encyclical *Ubi arcano* of 23 December 1922 entirely on the idea of peace and of
the understanding of nations. The Pope complained that there was "no human
tribunal which could oblige all nations to an international law code in accord
with the time." The Pope discreetly offered the aid of the Church, which could be
understood entirely in the sense of arbitration function.

After all the efforts to arrive at an understanding by means of the League of
Nations and the Pan-European movement had foundered, after a catastrophic Second World War had afflicted humanity in extensive parts of the world, the Popes of
the war and postwar periods saw one of their chief tasks in taking a stand with their
means and possibilities for the understanding of peoples. Pius XII considered it as

the "special mission" of his pontificate "to contribute in patient and almost grind-
ing activity to leading humanity back to the paths of Peace." The Pope demanded
an organization of the community of nations with the character of a federation. Into
this community must be inserted the sovereign rights of the individual nations "in
the framework of international law." Hence, to be repudiated is a principle of the
national state which "consists [in] the confusing of national life with nationalistic
policy"; for "the national life [is] something nonpolitical . . . which only then [be-
came] the principle of the dissolution of the community of nations when people
began to exploit it as a means to political ends."

The community of nations presupposes another concept of sovereignty than
that of nationalism. The individual state is no longer "sovereign" in the sense of
absolute absence of restraints. It is subordinate to international law but not to
the extent that it thereby completely loses its independence. Pius XII emphasized
that even international law is subject to natural law. Corresponding to his ontological, natural law beginning, questions of national statehood, of sovereignty and
its limits, of international association, are not left to the good pleasure of peoples
but are determined by the "nature of the thing" in the historical context of the
moment. Hence, agreements among states, though belonging formally to positive law, oblige by virtue of natural law if "they contain nothing which would be
contrary to sound morality." Pius XII regarded the present organization of nations,
the United Nations, in its early stage as not yet ideal, since it had come into being
on a "war solidarity" rather than on a true solidarity. However he said it was an
expression of the wish of peoples for a more jointly responsible cooperation, it is
a possibility "of speaking to the world conscience from an elevated spot."

Pius XII followed with special sympathy the efforts for unification in Europe,
in fact he saw in the unification of Europe "one of the concrete demands of the
hour, one of the means of assuring peace to the entire world." He spoke of the
"risk" of Europe and stressed that it "is a question of a necessary risk, of a risk,
however, which is in accord with current possibilities, of a reasonable risk." As
early as 1940 the Pope had seen in a new, united Europe a model for the unity of
the family of nations, the possible "start of a new world epoch."

If Pius XII had already again and again implored solidarity for a beneficial
international order of peace, John XXIII energetically carried this idea further,
especially in his encyclical *Pacem in terris.* "Since the reciprocal relations of states
should be regulated in conformity with truth and justice, they must be especially
promoted by energetic solidarity. . . . With reference to this, we must keep before
our eyes that the state's power was instituted, by its very nature, not to force people
into the limits of the existing political community, but especially to look out for the
common welfare of the state, which can certainly not be separated from that of
the entire human family" (*Pacem in terris,* 98).

The Pope was convinced that "considering the present state of human society,
both the political organization as also the influence of which the individual state
power disposes in relation to all other nations of the world [are] to be regarded
as inadequate to foster the common good of all peoples" (*Pacem in terris,* 135).
From this "there follows conclusively for the sake of the moral order that a universal political power must be instituted" (*Pacem in terris,* 137), in other words,
that mankind must come to a sort of world state. But the Pope knew that such a

general political power, which should lead to a "universal common good" must "be based on the agreement of all peoples and not be imposed by force" (*Pacem in terris,* 138). And for such a "world state" the principle of subsidiarity must hold good, by which "those relationships are regulated which exist between the authority of the universal political power and the state power of individual nations" (*Pacem in terris,* 140).

The Pope regarded as important steps, even if not without criticism, the founding of the United Nations and the Universal Declaration of Human Rights of 10 December 1948 (*Pacem in terris,* 142f.). In an effort to manifest the Holy See's active interest in an international order of peace, even on the institutional side, he maintained representatives, usually through so-called permanent observers, at many international organizations, including the United Nations and UNESCO, to which, during his time as nuncio at Paris, John XXIII had been assigned as the first permanent observer.

The problem of the underdeveloped countries, which came more clearly in view under Pius XII, experienced under John XXIII a special attention in his two social encyclicals, *Mater et Magistra* and *Pacem in terris.* Finally, Paul VI expressed the thorny problem in the concise formula: "Development, the new name for peace."

CHAPTER 90

Main Lines of the Development of Theology between the First World War and the Second Vatican Council

The Departure from Neo-Scholasticism in Systematic Theology

Temporal and Intellectual Presuppositions

The end of the First World War did not produce for Catholic theology that epochal radical change that occurred on the Protestant side, especially in Germany, and became visible as a radical turning from liberal to dialectical theology, from cultural Protestantism to neoorthodoxy. In accord with the stronger forces of continuity in Catholicism, which had grown further through the defense against modernism, here the further development took place not in dialectical leaps but in a continuous development and in positive progress. Hence at the beginning of this period the effects of the First Vatican Council and the not always positive result of the modernist controversy became still more clearly discernible. As regards the negative consequences of the suppression of modernism for Catholic theology, the verdict of R. Aubert must be noted, that "the total balance . . . was less negative than has often been claimed." This applies especially to German theology, which around the turn of the century, it is true, discussed problems raised with the so-called Reform Catholicism, but was not seized by the highest waves of this crisis. The position and the general assessment of this theology, represented especially by the university faculties, in the awareness of the age can be characterized by the fact, that in connection with an inquiry internally organized at some universities in regard to the elimination or retention of the theological faculties the overwhelming majority of professors of the profane disciplines expressed themselves for retention.

Of course, this vote was and is not actually to be evaluated as a judgment on the distinguished state of Catholic theology, especially not in respect to *all* its disciplines. For Germany the cheerful promise of J. I. Döllinger (d. 1890) at the Munich Assembly of Scholars in 1863, according to which the homeland of Catholic theology would lie here for the future, was not fulfilled, especially not for systematic theology (dogmatic theology), which advanced further in the paths of a still moderate Neo-Scholasticism. On this road it at first admitted neither the stimulation coming from M. J. Scheeben, the "most precious flower of Neo-Scholasticism," according to K. Eschweiler, for the intellectual deepening and organized grasping of the rational Neo-Scholastic system nor even the fruitful knowledge, coming from France, of Neo-Thomism, which, with P. Rousselot (d. 1915) and J. Maréchal (d. 1944), tried to establish a synthesis between genuine Thomism and modern philosophy. In this it was followed by systematic theology in the Romance countries, which, in keeping with its self-evaluation of a didactically moderate "school theology," assumed a superiority only in individual cases over the traditional Neo-Scholastic statement of problems and its answers.

The melting down of this hardness and a revival occurred through forces and impulses which lay outside the narrow bounds of systematic theological specialists and was rooted in the area of the general awareness of the age like a new philosophical thought. The temper of Catholic life and the consciousness of the faith in the period after the First World War made it possible to admit these tendencies and to integrate them in a manner which gave to Catholicism not only inner drive but also a certain radiation to the surrounding world. While a not unimportant basic tendency drew from the political and cultural crisis situation on the basis of a biologically determinist thought the conclusion concerning the "Decline of the West," in the Catholic sphere, especially in Germany, there was awake the conviction of the capability of regeneration on the part of the Church and the culture from the forces of the spirit, which of course was the spirit of traditional Christian humanist culture and of the Catholic faith. At that time there appeared simultaneously the programmatic formulations of *The Awakening of the Church in Souls* by Romano Guardini in 1921 and of the establishing of a "New West," the title of a periodical of Catholic intellectuals that appeared between 1926 and 1930. The concerns expressed in them were further accentuated in the generally prevalent notions of the "living," the "organic" "and "authentic," the "emotional," and of "history," of "personality," and of "appreciation of value."

These ideas proceeding from a new temper of life were taken up by corresponding "life movements" and reflected in diverse ways, such as the youth movement, going back to the period before the First World War, the rising liturgical movement, and also the Bible movement, which, of course, because of its being restricted to smaller groups cannot be equated with the first two movements mentioned. The idealistic ardor which belonged to these movements, supported especially by lay persons, and which of course became useful only to a degree to the "hierarchical apostolate of the Church" in the Catholic Action of Pius XI, was certainly not free from restorative tendencies.

This can clarify a view of the philosophical undercurrents on which these movements were based and which, indirectly by way of a prescientific discussion, also influenced the new starts in Catholic theology. It was a partly surprising, but partly obvious turn on account of the paradoxes of Kantianism as well as of Neo-Kantianism, which occurred after the First World War and was denoted by the catchword or slogan of the "resurrection of metaphysics." In accord with its objective content, however, it was a question here, not of a mechanical renewal of Aristotelianism or of Wolffianism as of the less vital Neo-Thomism in Germany, in contrast to the France of A. G. Sertillanges, É. Gilson, and J. Maritain, and despite Pius XI's encyclical *Studiorum ducem* of 1923 on the sixth centenary of the canonization of Thomas Aquinas, but of an investigation of being that had become more critical, which was influenced both by the new unspeculative ontology of N. Hartmann (d. 1950) and by the doctrine of reality of H. Driesch (d. 1943), but especially received stimulation from the "view of reality" of the phenomenology of E. Husserl and M. Scheler and its philosophy of value, represented by J. Hessen and D. von Hildebrand. Thereby attention was also powerfully directed to the other basic current of Western Christian intellectualism, namely, to the Augustinian-Franciscan thought in philosophy and theology. This new doctrine of knowledge and being, which did not understand metaphysics as a search for an abstract posterior world and ventured upon the new draft of a "Christian philosophy" as embodiment of a *philosophia perennis,* itself remained open to the philosophy of life of W. Dilthey (d. 1911), even if it repudiated the elements of historicist relativism present in it.

However, the most persistent influence in the 1920s and 1930s on the consciousness of the faith that was rearticulating itself was exercised by the philosophy of life and phenomenology, the latter not without the mediating role of the gifted M. Scheler (d. 1928), whose lot in life, of course, reflected the imbalances, tensions, and situation of the groping attempts in the Catholic intellectual life of the time. Only in regard to the rising existentialism of M. Heidegger and the philosophy of existence of K. Jaspers was the reaction generally negative, despite the mediating efforts from France of Gabriel Marcel, but this was partly based on the obscurity and individuality of this thought and its language.

The Turning of Dogma from "Reason" to "Living"

The turning of the dogmatic method of reflection to the "living" and to "religious value," also partly inspired by the suggestions of the philosophy of religion, for example, by *Das Heilige* (1917) of R. Otto, at first made its appearance only sparingly. But the formulations, appearing in various forms, of the theme "Dogma and Life," the efforts to disclose the life value of dogma — and even if at first it was only in corollaries at the end of the positive presentation — the connection between theology and spirituality in the works of Columba Marmion (d. 1923) and A. Gardeil, O.P., created an atmosphere which could not entirely refuse to have anything to do with Scholastic dogma for long, although the texts and manuals that had meanwhile become standardized were still kept in Neo-Scholastic strictness. Of course, this experienced a pleasing relaxation through the admission of newer problems in Pohle-Gierens (9th ed. [1936]), and through the regard for the history of dogma in F. Diekamp (7th ed. [1934]).

It was only consistent and a proof of the accuracy of the systematic work when thereupon the question of method and the problem of the way of systematic theology was again taken up by it. The most basic and stimulating effort in this regard, that of K. Eschweiler (d. 1936) in the German area, determined the point of departure of theological thought, following M. J. Scheeben and against G. Hermes, not from a neutral reason but from faith and the reasonableness inherent in it, which was to be developed by theology in accord with the method of intellectual scientific knowledge. In this way theology was, on the one hand, anchored in the supernatural basic faith essential to it, but, on the other hand, it was confirmed as a theoretical science. Hence a special significance belonged to the last named factor, because at about the same time other theological basic concepts came under discussion: the affective-charismatic concept of T. Soiron, O.F.M., based on the Franciscan tradition, the mystical devotional type of A. Stolz, O.S.B. (d. 1942), derived from patristics, which was inspired by the studies on the spiritual life, cultivated especially in France by H. Bremond, R. Garrigou-Lagrange, and the periodical *La vie spirituelle,* and a "kerygmatic" type which appeared under the name of "Proclamation Theology."

The theology of a living proclamation, intended especially by the Innsbruck theologians, J. A. Jungmann, F. Dander, F. Lakner, H. Rahner, and others, was supposed to present its own way and field of work in addition to the theoretical essential dogma and direct revealed truths directly to the listener in the language of kerygma. Although this attempt cannot simply be designated as "stillborn" because of the further operation of its intention, yet it could not be realized in method and would also have been a disadvantage for the still sought unity of theology.

Previously the aim of approximating dogmatic theology to the modern temper of life and of making it fruitful for the living faith had been realized in a more convincing way by Karl Adam (d. 1966) in his *Das Wesen des Katholizismus* (1924; 12th ed. [1949]), which, taking as a basis the phenomenological view of essence, the psychology of religion, and the scriptural concept of the Body of Christ, revealed a mystical understanding of the essence of Catholic Christianity and of the Church. Here the theme of the Church, especially questioned in those years, which had hitherto had a place only in apologetics, was made a subject of dogma and thereafter more richly developed from the dogmatic viewpoint.

This occurred emphatically in the *Dogmatik* of M. Schmaus (1938, 6th ed. [1964]), in which the religious and existential, as well as the scientific motives of the period before the beginning of the Second World War, received an authentic summary. Taking up the affirmative of the kerygmatic concern of an easing of the tension between scientific faith and living faith, but without sacrificing the scientific way of knowledge, the attempt was here undertaken to derive dogma from the sources of Scripture and genuine patristic tradition, both of which came up for detailed discussion and were no longer presented only in *dicta probantia,* and to disclose it to the understanding of an age which was influenced by Nietzsche's philosophy of life and by Heidegger's and Jasper's philosophy of existence that were gaining influence.

To be sure, the unique character and importance of this work, which was also the first to make use, for scriptural argumentation, of Kittel's *Wörterbuch zum Neuen Testament,* otherwise still held in suspicion in Catholic theology, can only be fully understood if the developments that had in the meantime taken place in historical as well as biblical theology are assessed and the fact of the opening up of dogma with respect to the influences from both areas. For historical theology this influencing goes without saying, since the representatives of the system almost without exception had gone through the school of historical theological investigation, which was then concentrated especially on the Middle Ages, with C. Bäumker, M. Grabmann, A. Landgraf, É. Gilson, M. de Wulf, J. de Ghellinck, J. Koch, B. Geyer (d. 1974), and others. Retrospectively it may also be established that these entirely solid investigations really required the chief energies of the theologians active in systematic theology, so that, apart from the exceptions mentioned, a stronger actualization of the Catholic world of faith and of dogma lying in the sphere of the possible did not occur. In this regard it was due to a preference for detailed research and to the deemphasis on summary presentations of theology and of the history of dogma that the knowledge from history was not used to its full extent for the historical understanding of dogma. A really historical understanding of dogma, as developed, of course with a one-sided aim, on the Protestant side by the triple constellation Harnack-Loofs-Seeberg, had not yet started in the Catholic theology of the 1930s. Nevertheless, the beginnings in this direction, which were made as early as the First World War with J. Tixeron and were carried further in a continuing succession, must not be overlooked. Historical awareness, becoming stronger, and interest in the development of dogma are especially attested by the then notable effort of the Spaniard, F. Marín-Sola, O.P. (d. 1932), concerning the homogeneous development of dogma, in which, to be sure, it was not the history of dogma as such that was pursued but instead a fully worthwhile theory of the development of dogma was demonstrated with the aid of historical facts that were not always interpreted in a manner free of doubt. Questions in the history of dogma were to experience a further stimulus on the eve of the definition of Mary's Assumption in 1950, when it was shown that the problem of the relation of revelation and history still needed some intellectual work within Catholic theology.

On one point the fecundity of the encounter of historical research and interest in systematic theology appeared clearly in the period before the First World War, and also afterwards, namely, in the *mysterium* theory conceived by Odo Casel, O.S.B. (d. 1948), which pushed the theme of sacramental theology, then as highly regarded as the theme of the Church, into the foreground in an original way and gave occasion to a discussion of considerable intensity. The Maria Laach Benedictine, proceeding from the history of religion and literature, who felt obliged to the liturgical movement and its progress toward the originality and authenticity of liturgical life, interpreted the sacramental acts of the Church, especially the Eucharist, no longer in the sense of the Scholastic theory of *effectus,* according to which the believer received only effects from the saving deeds. Instead, the saving act should make itself present, according to the new interpretation, which, however, sought support in Greek patristics, as such and in its being, of course *in mysterio,* that is, under the veil of symbols. Although this theory did not establish itself in its entirety because of the historical as well as the objective problems inherent in it, nevertheless it certainly contributed to the deepening of the Catholic understanding of the sacraments. This contribution, still critically evaluated by Pius XII, but, on the contrary, regarded benevolently in its main features by the Second Vatican Council, also offered certain points of departure for the ecumenical dialogue, which was at that time accepted only with hesitation by systematic Catholic theology.

In spite of this not lifeless or even stagnating condition of dogmatic theology before and immediately after the First World War, in contrast to modern pluralism it still supplied the image of inner compactness, which results not least from its unquestioned anchoring in the faith and from its positively understood ecclesiastical essence. In comparison, the new starts may be regarded as less radical and relatively trivial, and the connection with tradition may be found fault with. Nevertheless, it must be considered that especially the German theology and Church could oppose the dangers of Nazism in this basic outlook, which was also true especially of the threatened faculties of the Catholic universities. The picture supplied by the Protestant faculties was, with a few exceptions, much less favorable in this matter.

Many of these positive developments toward a more vital grasp of dogma and its interpretation in regard to salvation were, especially in Germany, interrupted or ended by the catastrophe of the Second World War. A new beginning took place especially in France, where the characteristic spirituality and the speculative strength had already been concerned with questions of the basic position of systematic theology and in this connection had come to a criticism of the scientific deductive theology of the past. These tendencies took shape in the works of a group of theologians, to which belonged, among others, H. Bouillard, H. de Lubac, J. Daniélou, and Y. Congar, all lumped together under the pretty colorless designation of the "Nouvelle Théologie." What was characteristic of these efforts did not appear prominently under this label, namely, the attempt to orient theology again more definitely to the biblical-patristic tradition, but in the horizon of modern thought and its *desiderata.* Thus the origin of this trend of theological interest was connected not coincidentally with the appearance of a new edition of the Church Fathers, *Sources chrétiennes,* which intended to make fruitful for modern thought the ancient wealth of the tradition of the faith and thereby, contrary to the narrowly oriented Scholastic theology, to emphasize again Augustinian theology and the Greek universalism of salvation of Origen, using the paradigmatic guiding principle of H. Bouillard: "A theology which would not be timely would be a false theology." The means employed in this regard of a spiritual exegesis, a personalist concept of the truth of faith and its "historical" interpretation, and an option for a certain diversity in theology must have seemed dangerous to the representatives of a strictly oriented Thomistic theology of essence. In their not always entirely objective criticism they dealt more with the ever present possibilities for false conclusions, for example, a making of grace immanent, a raising of dogma to evolution, a relativism of the knowledge of truth, than with really present failings and distortions. Hence the suspicion of a resurgence of modernism was unjusti-fied. Nevertheless, Pius XII was induced in the encyclical *Humani generis* of 1950, without mentioning this theological trend, to point to the mistaken tendencies which were found not so much in the original initiators of this movement as in some of its one-sided interpreters. The encyclical neither intended nor produced a limiting of theological research or a stagnation of theological development. But it exposed a process of theological ferment, which, because of the concentration of dogmatic theology on Mariology in the years before and after the definition of Mary's Assumption in 1950, had not yet entered the general awareness. This pro-cess was marked by a deeper reflection of systematic theology on the authenticity of mankind, the Church, and theology, on the related problems of hermeneutics, on the doctrine of evolution just brought to light by Teilhard de Chardin (d. 1955) and his writings, hitherto known only fragmentarily, as well as on the urgency of ecumenical efforts and the problems of the concern with a secularized world at the "end of the new age." The results of the posing of these critical questions were entirely positive in the material as well as in the formal senses: historical thought dared to draw near to outlines of salvation history and history of theology; the long treated theme of the Church, which had been discussed in the encyclical *Mystici Corporis* especially under the mystical-organological and hierarchical as-pect, was expanded into the dimension of the communitarian, in which also the lay element played a stronger role; in Christology, which was stimulated and en-riched by the confrontation with Déodat de Basly's (d. 1937) doctrine oriented in Scotism, the interest in the manhood and the humanity, the *psychologia,* of Christ was prominent. A special significance, which until the present has experienced no diminution, was gained by the theme of the relations of "nature and grace," again brought into discussion by H. de Lubac; in its solution the concept of the unity of creation and redemption, of the worldly and the Christian, of the immanence and the transcendence of the divine, must be distinguished.

All these profound problems of systematic theology were discussed with a sharpened consciousness and answered throughout in the sense less of "supra-naturalistic" and "extrinsic" ideas and models. Hence it probably did not entirely do the situation justice when, around the mid-1950s, it was said that "the dogma of today [is] very orthodox but not very alive." But perhaps at the basis of this verdict lay the right instinct that a thorough basic concept and a comprehensive systematic overview were missing from the deepened posing of questions and intellectual efforts. And so K. Rahner outlined at this time the new program of a dogmatic theology of salvation history, the implementation of which, of course, was taken up only later. But as regards this theology's claim to orthodoxy, it hit upon a positive state of affairs in so far as theology after the Second World War, despite the totally different kinds of beginnings and trends of interest, still worked from a strongly developed awareness of the obligation to the common tradition and its inalienable content. This appeared especially clearly in connection with the confrontation and adaptation of the program of demythologizing developed by R. Bultmann, which especially affected Christology. The reply, given to this pro-gram, for example, by J. R. Geiselmann in his book on Christ, was established by a profoundly biblical as well as by a hermeneutically acute historical thought, which, however, was not subject to a philosophical option of "authenticity," in which the objective salvation history was condensed with its alleged meaning to the *puncture mathematicum* of the existential faith decision and of the subjectivistic *pro me*. Here "authenticity" was understood not without the reality of real history and its transmission in the tradition of the Church. Characteristically, in theology on the eve of the Second Vatican Council the theme "Scripture and Tradition" was again taken up and, with the abandonment of the unorganic "Two-Sources Theory," led toward a unified concept, which was thus adopted by the council. Only in this state of affairs can it be considered that the council was determined by the spirit and content of the theology preceding it. Therefore, in relation to the dogmatic motive, the question "Who determined the theology of the council?" can be answered by a competent representative of the theology following the First World War: "An intensive work . . . for a good thirty years." But it may also be added that in dogma the council neither would nor could go beyond the results of this work.

The "Theological" Deepening of Moral Theology

The intellectual movements appearing after the First World War also changed the figure of moral theology, even if the development here proceeded only slowly, which had its reason in the fact that the appearing Catholic moral teaching, especially exposed to modern philosophical ethics and to pugnacious cultural Protestantism, had more strongly to guard against attacks which were forcing it to tenacity and determined it to a certain integralist attitude. Characteristic of the situation at the beginning of the century were the attacks of the Marburg Protestant systematizer, W. Herrmann (d. 1922), R. Bultmann's teacher, against the inflexible Catholic precept morality, which allegedly stifled the moral sentiment, and the Catholic reply from the pen of the Lucerne theologian A. Meyenberg (d. 1934), entitled *Die katholische Moral als Angeklagte* ("Catholic Morality as the Accused"). Thus it goes without saying that the presentations of moral theology partly assumed an apologetic character and in spite of their solidity and intellectual clarity — as seen for example in J. Mausbach's repeatedly published *Die katholische Moraltheologie und ihre Gegner* ("Catholic Moral Theology and Its Opponents") — were unable to achieve a positive adjustment to the spirit of the age. Still, at this time individual representatives of this field took the podium to promote a new orientation of their science with a disregard for its legalistic and casuistic traits. In favor of the still present awareness of the unity of ethical and dogmatic theology was especially the proposal of A. Müller, who, following M. J. Scheeben's idea of grace, pleaded for a "theological morality" which should be based on the mystery of the faith and on the reality of grace. J. Mausbach, in an opinion significant for the history of the time, sought to reduce, around the turn of the century, the tensions arising in regard to the reform of moral theology: in it was even sounded the demand that "the moral norm must accommodate [itself] in accord with nature to the essential changes which the development of humanity and of nature bring." Of course, this should take place only with the means supplied by Thomistic philosophy and the *philosophia perennis*. Nevertheless, the *Catholic Moral Theology* conceived by him was a progressive step in the sense that it did not develop a pure teaching of precepts but a doctrine of virtue which was directed to the loftiest principle of the honor of God and to the principle of the perfection of being.

True, the speculative orientation and penetration also sought stronger support in biblical doctrine, without, however, more deeply fathoming this, in accord with the contemporary situation of the use of the Bible in systematic theology.

There also came to light in O. Schilling, professor at Tübingen, and his *Moraltheologie,* not without influence from the Tübingen tradition, the endeavor to develop moral theology from a supernatural beginning, which he found in the principle of *caritas.* However, in regard to content he remained extensively indebted to Thomas Aquinas and Alphonsus Liguori. On the other hand, the strong regard for the socioethical aspect presented something relatively new.

The fact is that these new starts from the German sphere, in which as early as the nineteenth century a relatively unique "German type" of presenting moral theology had been developed by J. M. Sailer and J. B. Hirscher, were at first not further elaborated, and dominance lay in the still existing preponderance of the "Roman type" of moral theology, which in the manuals and texts of H. Noldin, B. Merkelbach, D. M. Prümmer, and others asserted its influence in the direction of a doctrine of duties, often oriented to the Decalogue, with a strongly juridical and casuistic element. Since these works were widespread in the French area, despite the different method of Saint-Sulpice, directed more to practical use in pastoral care, and in the Anglo-Saxon linguistic sphere, the renewal trends could be established only with difficulty. The additional pragmatic viewpoint in this sphere was especially prominent in the moral manual of T. Slater (d. 1928), who declared in the introduction: "Manuals of moral theology are technical works . . . just as the texts of the lawyer and the physician. . . . They deal with what is duty under penalty of sin. They are books of moral pathology."

In view of such lack of appreciation, of course not to generalize too far, of the deeper concern of moral theology, it goes without saying that in the 1930s the call for a new basis of the "theological character" of moral theology became ever stronger. The affirmative answer which now was offered to it was inspired by the spirit of recent biblical thought, which at that time created in moral theology an even more vigorous expression than in contemporary dogmatic theology. This changed attitude underwent an imposing formation in the five-volume *Handbuch der Katholischen Sittenlehre* of F. Tillmann, which had its center in the "idea of the imitation of Christ" (Vol. III) and its "realization" (Vol. IV). By means of an extensive abandonment of casuistic and practical applications, which Tillmann assigned as legitimate functions to the texts of casuistic moral theology, there succeeded here a new type of supernatural foundation of Christian morality on the ethos of love and its being made concrete in the Sermon on the Mount. Not an excessive natural-material morality, but a supernatural motivation of Christian life on the person and work of Jesus stood here in the center of ethics, which thus advanced from the position of a morality of commands and prohibitions to one of a direction inspiring and forming life. Even if Tillmann did not succeed, in a more flat view and estimation of the evidence of Scripture, in taking soundings of the full depths and problems of the testimony of Scripture, still the theological fecundity of this effort cannot be doubted. Despite occasional criticism, such as that of O. Schilling, this draft was considerably acknowledged as a directional work, which, "as no other . . . contributed to extricating Catholic moral theology as a science from a centuries-old rigidity." The basing of moral theology on a biblical-theological foundation was also decisive for other efforts around this time, such as for F. Jürgensmeier and E. Mersch, who oriented the Christian ethos on the concept of the "Mystical Body." The theological deepening and intensification of the Christian ethos, which was achieved here through the tying of moral theology to exegesis, to ascetical, and to dogmatic theology, and which continued long after in the striving for a rightly understood "dogmatic moral theology" (R. Egenter), was characteristically no hindrance to a widening of moral theology and its extension into the areas of the humanities. Tillmann's work had also laid the ground for this extension corresponding to the relation of moral theology to life and had supplied further stimulation; for here not only "the philosophical foundation of Catholic moral teaching" (T. Steinbüchel) was offered, but the "psychological bases" (T. Steinbüchel) were reflected and the "sociological bases"(W. Schöllgen) were considered. In T. Müncker's moral-psychological contribution the results of psychoanalysis, hitherto still suspect in Catholic circles, were also included. The stronger relationship thereby reached with the "bordering questions," as W. Schöllgen puts it, and with the humanities was further developed after the Second World War by French, Dutch, and German theologians — M. Oraison, A. Snoeck, W. Heinen, R. Egenter — and promoted in newly appearing periodicals (*Arzt und Christ* [1954]). In addition, the orientation, always to be made more profound, to revelation was not forgotten and, among other things, was fostered by the original attempt of J. Stelzenberger (d. 1972) to develop moral theology, with reference to J. B. Hirscher, as "the moral doctrine of the Kingship of God." Noteworthy, however, was the continuing impact of Mausbach's more speculatively interested sketch, which G. Ermecke completed in a new edition as a "Christological synthesis." A certain definitive bringing together of the various basic concepts was accomplished by B. Häring in his work, *Das Gesetz Christi,* which succeeded in uniting the three normative principles — imitation of Christ, *caritas,* rule of God — in an excellent manner. Meanwhile, interest in the working out of the history of moral theology and its problems was reawakened and documented in publications rich in content.

In view of the thoroughly positive state which moral theology achieved, by overcoming considerable resistance and a still thoroughly disunited situation in the 1930s, it may seem astonishing that in the 1950s there also was heard talk of the "crisis of moral theology," which threatened to jeopardize again the firm position that had been obtained. J. Leclerc especially reproached the current moral doctrine and instruction with a lack of dynamism and enthusiastic force, too little regard for philosophy, failure to consider the world situation of Christianity, and no understanding of progress. Here was evident something of that artificially nourished disquiet which, with the demand for a "complete transformation" of moral theology and a new beginning at zero, served an organic progress less. It thus happened that moral theology in the years before the Second Vatican Council became more eager for discussion and more stimulated by the resumption of the question of the principle of morality, by the questionable experiments of an existential and situation ethics, against which the teaching authority had taken a stand in 1952 and 1956, but not unconditionally more fruitful. The council itself had not accepted such experimenting considerations, but had regard for the fundamental results of modern moral theology, as, for example, in relation to religious freedom, the relative autonomy of secular matters, the importance of service to the world, the organic articulation of the ends of marriage and a personal notion of marriage, which, however, partly in the question of methods of birth regulation did not disavow tradition and gave no room to subjectivism.

In the total view of the process of development of moral theology in the period after the First World War the fact of the dissociation and autonomy of two new partial disciplines from the whole body must not remain unnoticed: the science of *caritas,* which of course grew out of practical theology, and that of Christian social doctrine and sociology. Above all, in the wake of the pioneering social encyclicals since Leo XIII, Christian social doctrine has won an increasing importance, which is borne by research now lasting more than one generation. Of course, considering the youthful status of this science and also the involvement of natural and supernatural rules in it, it cannot cause surprise that the questions of the proper subject and the function of Christian social teaching are still under discussion. The ideas are still confronted by a preeminently philosophical discipline, which makes use of faith only as a clarifying auxiliary function, and a properly theological discipline, which proceeds from faith. And so "the dialogue on how the dignity of mankind, social justice, and ecclesiastical ministry *sub luce Evangelii* maintain and receive their claim, is certainly not at an end" (R. Henning).

From "Apologetics" to "Fundamental Theology"

The modern striving for a deeper accessibility of the living, organic, and personal in the faith as well as in the understanding of the Church led also in the traditional apologetics to new accentuations, which ensued especially from the discussion of the different ways and methods of this relatively young theological discipline. A. Gardeil (d. 1931) declared that it was a "badly defined doctrine [whose] subject and method [presented] a problem for theologians."

The development of this branch of theology in the twentieth century may best be understood if it is seen under the aspect of the religio-existential as well as of the theoretical scientific search for the more exact definition of the specific subject of this discipline and its total presentation.

While the impulses for the founding of fundamental theology came especially from Germany in the nineteenth century, with J. S. von Drey in 1853, the new orientation in the twentieth century was first suggested by French theologians, who sought to put the "proof of the credibility of Christianity" proper to this field on a new basis with reference to the increasingly more comprehensive modern experience of life. The traditional, purely objective, and "externally" arguing *demonstratio christiana* and *catholica* could no longer satisfy a foundation of faith that took into account the totality of the modern social, moral, and philosophical question.

Already at the end of the nineteenth century attempts were made to establish the so-called "Apologetics of Immanence" by F. Brunetière, L. Ollé-Laprune, and G. P. Fonsegrive, but M. Blondel (d. 1949) first enabled it to achieve a real breakthrough. Without wishing to deny the merits and importance of classical apologetics, Blondel aimed to deepen the inadequacy of a purely rational and positivist argumentation by attending to the subjectivity and transcendentality of human fulfillment (*L'action* [1893]). This incentive to an "inner" apologetic involving subjective factors led, despite a first considerably disavowing attitude, to a spread of the scope of apologetics, to which A. Gardeil attributed, in addition to the strongly scientific proof of the credibility of the faith, a subjective practical foundation of faith. In addition, Gardeil called for an "apologetic theology," which should be developed as a self-reflection of supernatural theology on its epistemological bases. If the concept, which was again discussed in Germany also in a somewhat modified form in the 1950s, ultimately did not establish itself, still it consolidated the rising tendencies to the integration of "external" and "internal" apologetics and promoted the unity of rational credibility and the awaking of the inner willingness to believe. Later in Germany A. Lang especially followed this aim. With the last mentioned element the importance of the supernatural, grace-filled motivation of faith moved to the foreground, as, parallel to the total concept of theology recommended in Germany by K. Eschweiler, the effort became noticeable to develop fundamental theology, or apologetics, also from a standpoint inside the faith, which of course brought it close to dogma and to a degree threatened to jeopardize its autonomy. Even authors coming from the older rational objectivating school concept, such as R. Garrigou-Lagrange and J. Brinktrine, felt an obligation to this tendency. But in them the separation between the supernatural motive of faith and natural credibility was so sharply marked that the strict demonstrability of natural credibility, and thereby of the rational scientific character of apologetics, was maintained, but an underground dualism continued.

M. Masure, building on the thought of R. Rousselot (d. 1915), opposed to this option, somewhat objectivistic and inclined to disintegration, an "inductive procedure," in which the external signs of credibility were to be opened up as a result of their invisible importance and their supernatural value. In this regard the moral disposition of the subject and the influence of grace are appraised with full importance for the origin of the assent to faith, which in this "Apologetics of the Sign" was also made powerfully dependent on the community of faith, as well as of believers, that is, on a social character.

These "stimuli" to the development of an "integral apologetics" and its orientation to the personal reality of mankind by B. Welte enjoyed in Germany general assent and only occasionally encountered criticism. Nevertheless in the textbook literature of T. Specht, H. Dieckmann, J. Brunsmann, and H. Straubinger the old outlines retained the upper hand; they were more obliged to the "Romance form" of apologetics, as opposed to the "German form," which also had regard for the philosophy of religion. Thus at first the new impulses made an impact rather in individual presentations, which appealed, among other things, to the act of faith and the miracle, both of which were more strictly involved in the sphere of influence of the grace of faith. This tendency, as already indicated, approached the apologetics of dogma and its method, but also evoked new attempts to define the place and proper justification of this discipline.

These exertions became even more prominent in Germany after the Second World War. They were, first, conditioned by the crisis of faith, coming more sharply into awareness, and the "new profile of the unbeliever" (A. Kolping), on which especially fundamental theology had to take a stand; but they were also caused by a deeper scientific theoretical awareness of the problem, which was likewise made keener by the situation of the times. Here they first led to a sharper theoretical differentiation within this discipline, which was expressed in the distinction between "apologetics" and "fundamental theology." The term "fundamental theology," ever more establishing itself in place of the defensive-appearing term "apologetics," was to be understood as a self-reflection, immanent in the faith, on the motive of one's own faith, according to H. Lais, and separated from the "apologetics" directed to the unbelievers and proving the "credibility of faith." But at the same time the idea of "fundamental" experienced a new orientation in the progress of modern reliance on science, while it was brought to the meaning of an investigation of foundations, a theological methodology or epistemology. Thus "fundamental theology" was conceived as "theological basic science" after a sort of theological doctrine of principles, which should elaborate and reflect the material as well as the formal principles of theology. A still greater expansion was experienced by the concept of "fundamental," and hence the assigning of the functions of fundamental theology, in K. Rahner, who joined "fundamental theology" with a previous "formal" theology and sought to develop the former as the phenomenology of religions and of Christianity with its culmination in a theory on the "approach of the single to the true religion." But in such an expansion the unity of the subject threatened to be lost again, for such a fundamental theology had the theological scientific theoretical concern common to all theological disciplines, whereas in content it had to be in conflict, as "philosophy of faith," with the philosophy of religion. Therefore these efforts were subject to a not unjustified criticism with regard to the distinction which existed between the foundation of faith and that of theology as a science, and which could be overlooked only to the injury of the clarity and stringency of this discipline. Thus, basically the idea could not be refuted that the task of fundamental theology lay first in the foundation of the act of faith and in the motive of credibility.

This basic discussion, which was related also to the recently defined relationship of fundamental theology and apologetics, would then as today, where the discussion has still not ended, have been able to awaken the impression that this discipline is in a crisis which affects its existence. However, it must not be overlooked that fundamental theology, despite this uncertainty, did not actually avoid the function of laying the foundation of faith and in this regard involved an abundance of new questions, which were proposed to it by the modern intellectual development. To these belonged, among others, the problems of hermeneutics, of the authenticity of revelation, of existential and transcendental philosophy, but also questions of ecumenism. The Second Vatican Council especially took up what remained of these exertions and sanctioned them in its historical concept of revelation and of its relation to mankind, without thereby legitimizing the excessive tendencies of the "anthropocentric."

The Evolution of Historical Theology
with the Aid of the Historicocritical Method

The Progress of Church History

Catholic church history, as research and teaching, achieved a high status already in the course of the nineteenth century and did not fall behind it in the twentieth. As early as the beginning of this century it became clear that the historicocritical method would be maintained still freer and more decisively than before. In this it was inevitable that the judgments on the ecclesiastical past were more strictly adapted to the assumptions of natural history and that they thereby became also more sober and severe. Symptomatic of this new beginning in the twentieth century can be considered L. Duchesne's (d. 1922) *Histoire ancienne de Église,* which, because of his method and presentation, strictly in keeping with the history of religion, of the history of the origin of Christianity was put on the Index in 1912. The extremely positive verdict of A. von Harnack on this work proves that Catholic Church historical investigation was no longer inferior to the Protestant in form but probably permitted the conclusion that in this case it had not yet surely taken the "theological" direction. The attitude of the thoroughly critical S. Merkle (d. 1945) is to be characterized here as more appropriate; it appeared, for example, in its different evaluation of the Enlightenment philosophy, although at that time this did not find general acceptance in the Catholic world. Such expressions of a critical awareness were as little to be attributed to modernism as the initiatives of A. Ehrhard (d. 1940), working in all areas of church history, who gave to this discipline some stimulation toward its actual and cultural-determinant interpretation. Thus it happened not by chance that out of this historical thought flowed also impulses for the new shape of the Church in modern times, which appeared, among other places, in the much discussed *Catholicism and the Twentieth Century in the Light of the Church's Development in the New Age* (1901). The perspectives offered here for a meeting of Church and secular world could still be termed modern today, but of course they also display the limits set for all concepts and prognoses gathered from history; for, of the two conditions there named for a meeting between Church and world — turning of *modern thought* away from anti-Christian prejudices, turning of *the Church* from an absolutizing of the Middle Ages — the second has indeed been fulfilled in a not always easy development, but not the first, as the appearance of the great movements of apostasy in the first third of the twentieth century shows.

The élan and the interest in intellectual and cultural history which a church history thus oriented showed at the beginning of the century in its representatives, was, it is true, slowed but not entirely suppressed by the modernist controversy and the catastrophe of the First World War, which brought disillusionment to optimistic cultural thought. It was only natural that after the end of the war the perspectives in ideas should be deemphasized and a calm research should appear predominant, with historians of all nations participating. It included and expanded all areas of church historiography: archeology, with J. Wilpert (d. 1940) and J. P. Kirsch (d. 1941); ancient church history and patrology, with F. J. Dölger (d. 1940) and B. Altaner (d. 1958); the Middle Ages, modern times, and hagiography, with

H. Delehaye (d. 1941) and P. Peeters (d. 1950); the new history of the missions, with J. Schmidlin (d. 1944); and the especially assiduously cultivated history of the Popes, which, with L. von Pastor (d. 1928), J. Schmidlin, and F. X. Seppelt (d. 1956), posed an equivalent counterweight in this field to Protestant research. A special significance because of its affinity to a deeply felt concern of the age was acquired by the investigations of A. Baumstark (d. 1948) and C. Mohlberg (d. 1963) in the history of liturgy, the results of which indicated the way to the liturgical movement.

The intensification of the work of research could not remain without an impact on the exterior organization of the research profession. And so in the course of this widespread activity there came about a recent specialization and separation of individual fields, such as iconography and folklore. On university faculties there resulted, for the same reasons, a dichotomy of the spheres of work and the professorial chairs — ancient church history/patrology, history of the Middle Ages and of modern times — which after the Second World War was followed in some places by still further divisions, such as the church history of a nation.

The works mentioned extended not only to the fundamental investigation of the sources and their editing, in regard to which Catholic researchers in a masterful fashion made their own the precision of the historical method, as, for example, H. Denifle (d. 1905), F. Ehrle (d. 1934), and F. Stegmüller; they proceeded likewise to a comprehensive opening up of new auxiliary means through encyclopedias, lexica, and publication agencies, such as T. Klauser's *Reallexikon für Antike und Christentum* and Hefele-Leclercq's *Dictionnaire d'archéologie chrétienne et de liturgie* (1924–53); but they also produced new total presentations of church history and likewise more detailed particular presentations elaborated with a new type of hermeneutical understanding. This is true especially of the research in the German sphere, which was still in touch with the roots of historical thought in the nineteenth century. Hence its interests went also to the working out of the historical details, of the specific and organic, while the work in the Latin countries sphere was still interested chiefly in emphasizing the general and the universal. Thus are explained, among other things, the origin of work which revealed the deeper understanding of original Christianity in its specific peculiarity by F. J. Dölger (d. 1940), a new view of the history of the Reformation by J. Lortz, a deeper penetration of the history of the councils by G. Dumeige, H. Bacht, and H. Jedin, and the attempt at a presentation of church history according to the history of ideas. These and like achievements, which had to have an impact on the teaching profession, produced for church history in the German university faculties a leading position which for a time seemed to surpass dogmatic theology, especially when this was taught according to the Neo-Scholastic textbooks. Thus in retrospect it can be ascertained that Catholic church history not only exploited the favor of the spirit of the age, which was unlocked for historical thought, but, conversely, promoted and positively determined this inclination. In this connection, this discipline, which at the beginning of the century had still awakened the suspicions of the ecclesiastical *magisterium,* proved itself, in its solidarity and objectivity, more and more to be the support of Catholic thought.

On the whole, even after the Second World War church history retained this positive upward development. The tensions which appeared in the course of the preparation for the dogma of Mary's Assumption between positively oriented history and the different procedure of the justification of the faith resulted from the nature of the matter and were overcome without false dramatizing. In the course of the methodical self-reflection of theology the discussion of the theological character of church history was again taken up and understood by an emphatically theological idea in a salvation-history sense. Nevertheless, it was to be perceived since the 1950s in the stage when "history" dissolved into "authenticity" and the intellectual orientation was preeminently to the present and future, that historical thought was pushed to the defensive.

Overcoming Resistance to the Historical Method in Biblical Scholarship

While in church history the historicocritical method ever more established itself from the beginning of the century and could be managed without hindrance in this field, clear limitations ensued for exegesis. In this regard the points of departure for a rise of this discipline were not the worst at the end of the nineteenth century, a situation to which especially the founding of the École biblique in Jerusalem by M. J. Lagrange in 1890 and the works published in the *Revue biblique* since 1892 and in *Études bibliques* since 1900 contributed decisively. The establishment of Catholic biblical criticism undertaken by Lagrange was taken note of even in Germany, where it led, among other things, to the conception by F. von Hummelauer, S.J. (d. 1914), of the idea of an organic notion of inspiration ("economy of salvation") and to the generic historical classification of biblical primitive history, the "vision hypothesis." The *Biblische Zeitschrift,* edited by J. Goettsberger and J. Sickenberger since 1903, worked also in the direction of this thoroughly moderate criticism. But a strongly conservative faction represented by L. Méchineau and L. Fonck opposed this *école large;* this group sought especially to emphasize the principle of fidelity to tradition in scriptural work. A mediation between the opposing forces was hindered by the condemnation of modernism and of the liberalizing tendencies in the decrees against these emanating from the Biblical Commission in 1903. Although this ecclesiastical agency, like the Biblical Institute, also founded by Pius X in 1909, was intended per se for the positive advancement of scientific scriptural studies, at first they displayed a retarding influence on exegetical research within the Church, which thereupon turned partly to safe peripheral areas, such as textual criticism.

Thus it was not possible for Catholic exegesis to adopt without restriction the results of Protestant scriptural scholarship and the methods of literary criticism, of the comparative science of religion, of the history of tradition and form which lay at its basis. To be sure, it was in this way also spared the mistakes, appearing ever more clearly today, which pertained to the employment of this method, especially in the beginning, and its extreme use. Much as one may occasionally complain that Loisy's (d. 1940) suggestions for the use of the historicocritical method were too seldom applied to Holy Scripture, still M. Blondel, here amazingly farsighted, recognized in his confrontation with Loisy that the historical absolutizing of this method could not do justice to Christianity, especially in the form of Catholic dogma, because it threatened finally to lead to a reduction of the whole natural-supernatural reality to the plane of naturalism and positivism.

The tension here showing itself between history and dogmatic faith and the

task implicit in it of mediating between exegesis and dogma, which would thereafter prove to be an essential motive force of Catholic theology in the first half
of the twentieth century, could not yet be absorbed after the First World War
by Catholic exegesis. Nevertheless, it by no means refused to have anything to
do with the knowledge coming from Protestant scriptural scholarship, although
the biblical encyclical *Spiritus Paraclitus* of Benedict XV in 1920 warned against
"the novel methods of profane science." True, this opening of exegesis occurred
in a cautious way, which especially bore fruit in the preferred fields of work of
research into the history of the text and literary criticism. But the results found
expression also in the respectable work of "introduction" to both the Old and the
New Testament, which appeared, among other places, in the prudent adoption
of the results of the criticism of the Pentateuch, of the clarification of the sources
by J. Wellhausen (d. 1918) as well as in the genre research of H. Gunkel (d. 1932),
but also in the Two-Sources Theory relating to the synoptic question. Also the
understanding of the history of the form of the Gospels, brought to light by K. L.
Schmidt, M. Dibelius, and R. Bultmann around the turn from the second to the
third decade, was recognized by Catholic exegesis — H. J. Vogels, M. Meinertz,
J. Sickenberger, P. Benoit — in its positive aims and critically adopted.

If no real originality belonged to Catholic exegesis between the two world wars,
in comparison to the Protestant, and its strength lay rather in historical-philological
precision than in total theological plan, it in no way remained preoccupied in
literary-critical and philological explanation. The exertion for a deepened and total view of Holy Scripture led also to first sketches of the genre, long cultivated
in Protestantism, of "biblical theology," by F. Ceuppens, P. Heinisch, A. Lemonyer,
F. Maier, O. Kuss, and F. Prat, even if these outlines at first, as a consequence
of their attachment to the dogmatic tradition, preferred the systematic collective
view to historical analysis and its problems. Teaching on the university faculties
and also work on the newly appearing biblical commentaries profited from this
deeper theological penetration into the spirit and content of Holy Scripture. In addition to the strictly scientific and detailed commentaries, whose prototype was in
France the commentary founded by M. J. Lagrange in *Études bibliques* from 1903
and in Germany the never completed *Handbuch zum Alten Testament*, edited
by J. Nikel and A. Schulz from 1911 to 1933, there arose a relatively new genre
of exegetical work in the form of the biblical explanations extending beyond the
world of specialists, which were directed to a broader circle of readers and to
the religiously educated laity. These efforts were pushed further and made available even for practical preaching through biblical homiletic works — "Keppler
School," F. Tillmann — to which, of course, the corresponding understanding was
not offered among the parish clergy.

Still, these efforts remained precisely a proof of the interest in the Bible newly
awakened by exegesis, as did also the Bible movement, which, recommended by
the Popes since Pius X, gained influence in various forms in all European countries.

It was probably a fruit of this positive development of the understanding of
Scripture in Catholicism and of the method cultivated in the Pontifical Biblical
Institute by Augustine Bea that the *magisterium* through Pius XII in the biblical
encyclical *Divino afflante Spiritu* of 1943 proposed caution in regard to modern
scriptural scientific methods and recommended to the exegetes to use "pru-

dently" the auxiliary means offered by the modern sciences and to define precisely the literary genres. This official doctrinal pronouncement of the "Liberating Encyclical," often regarded as a breakthrough, was followed by similarly directed official pronouncements in the letter of the Biblical Commission to Cardinal Suhard in 1948 down to the instruction of the Papal Biblical Commission on "the historical truth of the Gospels" 1964, which on the one hand insisted on the "historical truth" of the Gospels, but on the other hand warned against the influx of philosophical and ideological prejudices in the operation of the historical method. At the same time it gave reason to think that the exegete must pursue his work not only as a responsible investigator but also as a believing theologian of the Church.

Exegesis used this freedom just granted to it with great élan, which found expression in newly conceived commentaries, such as the *Herder-Kommentar,* in fundamental investigations in biblical theology, as also in the "biblical dictionaries" indispensable for the deeper, comprehensive grasp of the deep layers — *Bibellexikon* of 1951, *Bibeltheologisches Wörterbuch* of 1950. Even if here and in general the breadth and originality of Protestant biblical scholarship, with its richer tradition, naturally could not be equalled, still a closing of the gap and an approximation to its format became evident. Thereby biblical scholarship also within Catholic theology advanced to a similar position, as befitted it in the sphere of Protestant theology. This resulted, for obvious reasons, in a stronger influence on the systematic disciplines, in relation to which exegesis gained a certain superiority after the Second World War.

For the relations of this discipline to dogma, as in general for its ecclesiastical and faith status, some problems had to ensue, which in the 1950s had not yet made an appearance. Thus it is noteworthy that Catholic biblical scholarship at this time exercised caution, for example, in the effort to justify the new Marian dogma, but also did not deny the ecclesiastical position (consult, for example, the problem of the *ultimum fundamentum* of this doctrine in Scripture). Even more attempted at this time was the building of a bridge to dogmatic theology and to the dogma proceeding from Scripture, as when, for example, the route from the New Testament to the doctrine of Chalcedon was shown to be legitimate, a point of departure for the later dogma of original sin was acknowledged in Romans 5:12–19, and in the New Testament precursors of ecclesiastical dogma were found in the presymbols.

From this basic attitude must probably also be explained the fact that Catholic exegesis in the debate, advancing like an avalanche, over R. Bultmann's thesis on demythologization, did not abandon itself to the fashionable trend, but exercised a sensible and firmly fundamental criticism, which still did not underestimate what was positive in Bultmann's concern. The Second Vatican Council recognized intact the results of the epochal upward development of Catholic exegesis since the Second World War and confirmed to this discipline its leading role within theological scholarship in a series of significant statements, as when it approved the application of literary criticism and the rules of modern hermeneutics, when it placed the ecclesiastical *magisterium* as a ministerial function below the Word of God in Scripture, and evaluated all of Scripture and its study as "soul of all theology." Of course, the council also expressed the obligation of ecclesiastical scholarship to cling to the theological basis of exegesis according to faith, in the doctrine of inspiration, the identification of Scripture and God's Word, and in the emphasis on tradition and Church as the ultimately binding courts of interpretation. Of course these positive statements of the council could not completely develop and clarify the problem involved in them for the self-understanding of exegesis.

The Rise of Pastoral Theology to a Scientific Theological Discipline

The Increased Significance of General (Fundamental) Pastoral Theology

The initiatives, which proceeded from the theology oriented to preaching and from the Bible and liturgical movements, could not remain without effect in the "pastoral care science," especially since these had come into prominence as early as the end of the nineteenth century through a certain flexibility and capacity for accommodation. As a visible sign of this may be regarded the differentiation, beginning around the turn of the century, of pastoral theology into homiletics, catechetics, and liturgy, oriented to the Three Offices Doctrine. Of course, this specialization was purchased with the disadvantage that now there was left for general pastoral theology only a relatively meager space, which, provided with the colorless designation of "hodegetics," was filled out as regards content with a professional instruction for the pastor which engaged especially in practical directions for its official exercise. Such a "clerical" formal object not only excluded the relation to the entire community but even formally hindered a really scientific elaboration of this subject. And so it was actually taught more·in the manner of a technique which should be practiced by the individual pastor on the individual believer than in the manner of a theological reflection. It required a long way until this "remnant" of a pastoral theology again developed to full stature, gained scholarly features, and also again displayed its integrating function relative to the separated partial disciplines.

In fact, the rise of pastoral theology from a practical instruction for the pastor for the individual care of his charges to a scientific theological discipline is one of the most positive advances of the history of theology in the first half of the twentieth century. It is self-evident that this progress was completed not uninfluenced by external factors — negative: pastoral and social distress of proletarianization, departure of the masses from the Church; positive: youth, Bible, and liturgical movements — but it still had its own origin in an inner theological area, namely, in the understanding of the significance of Church and community for the self-realization of the Christian in a world which was ever more alienated from the Christian faith.

The actions initiated in the nonscientific area — Pius XI's Catholic Action in 1925; Workers' Movement of J. Cardijn in 1912 and H. Godin in 1943; Young Christian Workers, and so forth — were first expressed only sparingly in scholarly work, as, for example, V. Lithard's *Précis de Théologie Pastorale* with its emphasis on Catholic Action, in G. Stocchiero's *Pratica Pastorale* with its summons to the Church to turn to the world, and in C. Noppel's *Aedificatio Corporis Christi* with the tendency to the inclusion of the laity into the hierarchical apostolate of the Church and to the notion of a care of souls supported by the community.

These impulses were increasingly accepted and scientifically investigated by L. Bopp in his *Zwischen Pastoraltheologie und Seelsorgewissenschaft,* which also included the still suspect results of psychoanalysis in the circle of its reflections on pastoral theology. To a greater degree the knowledge of the human sciences, especially psychology and medicine, was included in this phase of development of the research into pastoral theology, just as in moral theology.

But a really theological basic concept only established itself since the 1940s, when, not least on the basis of the utilization of historical knowledge rather than the previous route of pastoral scholarship since the Enlightenment, the proper goal of this science was recognized by F. X. Arnold as "the theological understanding of the pastorally operating Church and its types of activity." The basic theological idea, which C. Noppel had found in the then quite attractive concept of the Body of Christ, was here concretized into the "God-Man Principle." The deeper-lying intention went, on the one hand, to a departure from the anthropocentric narrowness of the pastoral theology of the Enlightenment, on the other hand to the pushing back of the guiding idea, felt as illegitimate, of the salvation-mediating Church, in contrast to which, with the "God-Man Principle" the "Divine Incommunicability" and direct relationship of all the work of salvation moved into the foreground, while only the character of a tool, of a personal sort, was acknowledged for the Church itself. In this definition of aim was really found a very fortunate synthesis of the contemporary concerns and movements in dogma, scriptural theology, liturgy, and history. The "unity of theology" here found once again a clear expression that could hardly have been achieved better later.

In favor of the religious theological content of this basic pastoral start there speaks, among other things, the demand then appearing, for a "care of souls from the altar," as J. Pascher calls it, which indeed set up a high ideal, but nevertheless was not perceived as a slogan and became quite effective in union with the liturgical incentives of the epoch.

Immediately before the beginning of the Second Vatican Council the scientific elaboration of fundamental pastoral theology achieved new progress with the publication of the *Handbuch der Pastoraltheologie.* In it this discipline was emphatically developed out of the nature of the Church and the "theological analytics of the situation of the Church," to quote K. Rahner, was defined as its basis. This ecclesiological concept appeared more comprehensive than the previously prevailing "God-Man" or personological foundation. It anticipated in much the results of the "Pastoral Council," as the Second Vatican understood itself, as, on the other hand, the council also sanctioned these results. Hence it is comprehensible if thereafter pastoral theology, borrowing an idea from Schleiermacher, understood itself as the "crown" of theological scholarship. However, the postconciliar development seems to show also the dangers of this claim to exclusiveness, which are contained in it, namely, that theology as a whole is subject to practical ends.

The Catechetical Renewal

The new *theological* orientation with the utilization of general scholarly knowledge made itself especially noticeable positively also in the partial discipline of catechetics, which naturally had to find special attention in the age of a general awakening of youth and its own psychological assessment. To be sure, in catechetics the textual analytical, deductive method of the improved Deharbe Catechism and its preference for the abstract rational presentation as well as its basically apologetic outlook still remained predominant. As an example the *Catechismus Catholicus* published by Cardinal Gasparri in 1930 can serve: in its narrow, theoretically doctrinally conceived manner it did not correspond to the new pedagogical, didactic, and religious psychological demands. Only in the 1930s, especially in Germany and France, did there begin a turning to the kerygmatic direction of presentation, which, following models of a period before Neo-Scholasticism — J. B. Hirscher and his "salvation history" orientation — after a not unproductive "controversy on method," sought a renewal on the bases of the newer theology, the Bible, preaching, and pedagogical understanding.

Here also the inspiring principle consisted in the synthesis of "religion and life," which could counteract the previous separation of teaching and life and the intellectualistic orientation of instruction. The "Munich Catechetical Method" of textual development in three formal stages — presentation, explanation, stimulation — defined by H. Stieglitz (d. 1920), following O. Willmann, found, after initial resistance, acceptance in Germany as in most other European countries. But it was also fostered by stimulation from other areas, as by the Work School Principle, according to G. Kerschensteiner (d. 1932), which activated in a new way the peculiar activity of students and group instruction. By means of psychology and the philosophy of value the "principle of experience" also more strongly found admission into catechetical instruction, whereupon the format stages were modified to the triad of value experience, value exposition, and value realization.

Also very significant were the initiatives which proceeded from Austria, specially interested in practical theology since the Josephinist reform. The *Religionsbüchlein* published by J. Pichler as early as 1913, with its wide extension into more than fifty languages, intended the turning away from the theoretical doctrine following in the wake of Neo-Scholasticism to personal proclamation of salvation and address. These efforts did not accomplish a formal breakthrough until the 1930s, when, following general pastoral theology, the establishing of a proper material kerygmatic and of a material-kerygmatic method occurred with M. Pfliegler and J. A. Jungmann. Here Christocentrism and the biblical foundation were elaborated in a new way to structural elements of religious instruction and of a "thematic didactic play method," which also facilitated a more intimate union between catechesis and biblical instruction. On the whole, in the course of this development catechetics reached the status of a special form of preaching, which not only proved the theological depth of this movement, but also gave evidence of the unbroken strength of the awareness of faith to introduce the aim of kerygmatics among school-pedagogical conditions.

Of course, this development would not have been thinkable without the stimulus coming from France, where since the separation of Church and state the necessity of the external as well as of the internal reform of religious instruction was especially pressing. But the realization of these aims did not occur until after the First World War — pastoral letter of Bishop A. Landrieux of Dijon in 1922 — when the "Munich Method" was also accepted there, and the historicobiblical and salvation history orientation was then definitely set in motion. The *Catéchisme a l'usage des Diocèses de France* (1940, 2d ed. 1947), constructed on these foundations, first developed the types of a specific didactic play catechism with clear founding in Holy Scripture, with inclusion of the church year, with consideration of elements of a work of instruction, and with the purposeful orientation to the inner participation in prayer and in religious practice. The model work supplied decisive stimuli to the *Katholischer Katechismus der Bistümer Deutschlands,* which after seventeen years of preparation was published in 1955 and by being translated into some thirty languages had a worldwide effect. Of course, soon after the Second Vatican Council it was regarded as no longer suited to the times, which could be less a judgment of its absent qualities than a sign of the quickly changing situation of the age, which catechetics was hardly able to follow with its outlines.

And so, after the Second Vatican Council there again broke out the controversy over method, ignited at the beginning of the century, in the wake of the manifold strivings for adaptation, but also with the rise of the principle of pluralism, which put the unity of catechetics as a science to the test. The move to existential anthropology, becoming effective thereafter, brought about not only a certain turning away from the kerygmatic and biblical orientation, considered as fundamentalist and biblicist, but also produced the danger of leveling catechetics as a kerygmatic communication of the truth of faith in favor of a purely school history of religious information and of a religious and moral offering. True, the Second Vatican Council acknowledged catechetical instruction as the first means of help in the Church's task of educating, but it also clearly placed it in the "service of the Word," and did not inaugurate its narrowly existential or informative direction.

The Turning of Homiletics to Kerygmatics

Following the rise of catechetics and in a certain parallelism to it, there also took place in homiletics an upward movement, which benefited from the stimulation of historical, biblical, and liturgical theology. The difficulties and problems of this ecclesiastical service to people of the mass-epoch and modern industrial society could not but be especially dramatically prominent in the Church's preaching ministry. The disparity between the expenditure of work here occurring and the visible success spread the impression of a "collapse" of preaching, which Benedict XV's encyclical on preaching, *Humani generis* (1917), appearing during the First World War, complained of without being able to oppose anything substantial to it. This lay not only in the unfavorable state of the times, which prevented a stronger echo of the papal doctrinal letter, but even more in the missing theological foundation of homiletics, which was more and more strongly dependent on the idea of a "theory of spiritual eloquence." In this connection interest in preaching and the effort for its greater efficacy were not slight, as the growth of special periodicals, of systematic instruction, of practical means of assistance, but also of more profound theological and spiritual guides prove. The putting of these exertions into practice was done by a series of impressive preaching figures, such as Bishop P. W. Keppler (d. 1926), A. Donders (d. 1944), Cardinal Faulhaber (d. 1952), R. Guardini (d. 1968), and others, whose activity, especially in the Germany of the Nazi era, did not remain without echo. If it also appears somewhat exaggerated to speak of this epoch beginning after the First World War as of an "age of homiletics," still on the whole a suitable estimation of the effort of this period is thereby given.

The novelty and central point of this effort is only appreciated, however, if one points to the biblical-theological foundation. Compared with the previous exertions of homiletics in regard to preaching, which were of a predominantly formal-rhetorical sort, though not without regard for the religious subject, there occurred at the end of the first third of this century in the framework of the development of fundamental pastoral theology also an application of the kerygmatic to preaching as its material and formal principle. From this principle was derived the joining of the content of preaching to Scripture, which led in practice to the rediscovery of the homily as the form directly modeled on the reading and interpretation of Scripture, but from it also derived in the formal realm the personal character of address, the authority of Christ lying in the Word, and the conviction of the quasi-sacramental efficacy of this Word in the believing hearer. In the theoretical elaboration of these theological bases the works of J. A. Jungmann and others showed the way. In the practical application of these principles the explanations of preaching by F. Tillmann, which were on a high level, accomplished much that was significant.

After the Second World War the theological basis of kerygmatics experienced also from the side of dogma a broad support and deepening in the development of a "Theology of the Word," which was conceived not without stimulation by the Protestant theology of the Word. Also this meeting of homiletics and dogma may be regarded as an example for the awareness of unity of the theological disciplines, which was significant for the state of all of contemporary theology.

Of course, after the Second World War the inadequacies of this kerygmatic were felt, with the emergence of the notion of "radical authenticity" into theological thought — demythologizing — with the turn to philosophical-theological existentialism, and with the appearance of reflection on the phenomenon of secularization. They concerned not only the precritical, somewhat unhistorical previous exegetical justification — but also the authoritative address of this "kerygmatic" and its defective adaptation of the message to the one "addressed," who was no longer to be seen only as "object" of the address and also rather to be "met" in his secularized environment. But contrary to these critical objections, which became still stronger after the Second Vatican Council, although the council accepted and gathered together all these impulses in its sober attitude, it must be considered that the problems touched on in them were articulated but not solved. It even seems that the radical solutions — preaching as "information"; preaching as a form of a "political" theology — on the whole approximated rather a step back and a withdrawal from the center. All together, a glance backward to the homiletic and pastoral theological efforts of the period before the council could establish what generally holds good for the development of theology: the building of a bridge to the contemporary believer. Overall the mediation to the spirit of the age succeeded not badly and perhaps better than that of modern theology in its too pronounced and intentional striving for modernity and accommodation to the spirit of the time. As historical experience can teach, theological scholarship must not merely "straggle behind," it must also, to a certain extent, lead.

The Reestablishment of Liturgy as "Theology of Worship"

Unquestionably the liturgy had the most extraordinary and for the outside observer the most visible rise in the first half of this century. It developed in this period from a peripheral theological science, which was still included by the constitution *Deus scientiarum Dominus* of 1931 among the auxiliary disciplines of theology, to that of a necessary and important "principal subject," a position attributed to it by the Second Vatican Council. In this connection the original incentives and impulses for this development characterizing modern Catholicism lay at first not in the purely scholarly sphere, even if scholarship after a certain starting time opened itself to the new awakened forces, regulated them, and influenced them in turn.

Stimulated by the liturgical movement, liturgical scholarship also displayed an activity of a new type, which now had as its subject no longer only historical work on the sources, which had been intensively under way since the turn of the century in the course of the growing interest in history. Now ensued the widening and deepening of the work to a sort of "theology of worship," which was accomplished with the acceptance of the equally vigorous ecclesiological and sacramental thought in this period by the theological foundation of the pastoral-practical movement. Its aim was directed to raising the theological stock of ideas from the liturgical sources to the goal of their more profound exploration, but also to the fructification of the entire life of faith. Pius XII later gave to this aim the motto taken from tradition of the *lex supplicandi,* which is to determine the *lex credendi.* In the course of this orientation there occurred considerations, pressing to the essential, on the "spirit of the liturgy," on the connection between "liturgy and the kingdom of God," on the meaning of the Eucharist," as well of the sacraments, all of which contributed to the enrichment of dogmatic theology. Again the greatest significance for this intellectual foundation-laying was gained by the *mysterium* theory of O. Casel (d. 1948), in the discussion of which the work was altogether motivated to the theological clarification of the Sacrifice of the Mass and of sacramental reality. It was not least of all the process of theological deepening which obstructed an externalization of the aims, lying within the area of the possible, and which finally also paralyzed the fears and resistances to this movement, that occasionally increased enormously. A clarification to be understood in the affirmative sense was finally produced by Pius XII's encyclical on the liturgy, *Mediator Dei* (1947), which by way of suggestion already made known the desire for reforms in liturgy, whereas the hitherto practical efforts in regard, for example, to Gregorian chant and church music, had operated rather in the sense of a restoration. The Pope introduced some significant reforms, including the approval of numerous rituals with vernacular texts and songs, the introduction of a new translation of the psalms, the *Psalterium Pianum,* but especially the renewal of the Holy Week and Easter Vigil liturgies. The fact that these reforms were either prepared or accompanied by research, ever more intensified after the Second World War, as well as by the work of the newly founded Liturgical Institute and the liturgical congresses produced for liturgical scholarship a theological importance which was highly esteemed by the Second Vatican Council. The council itself had multiplied the tasks of this discipline with its reforms, carried out or announced. But it could not be foreseen that it would be necessary for the liturgy in the era beginning after the council, when the liturgical movement branched out and an at times excessive wave of experimenting and adapting followed it, to look back again rather at the "spirit of the liturgy," as R. Guardini expressed it, and the theological bases of its work as Opus Dei.

The formation and growth of liturgical scholarship, which was intentionally placed here at the end of the first phase of the history of theology in the first half of the twentieth century, can, it is true not be taken as the supreme value for reaching a verdict on the total development of the theology of this period, because naturally a development does not proceed in all departments of knowledge in the same way. Hence the entire verdict on this theological period must also be more cautious. Nevertheless, it cannot be expressed negatively: Measured by the standard of scholarship, the accomplishments of the historicocritical work of theology stand on no low stage; in the systematic sphere the effort for a more vital grasping and stating of the truths of faith was not to be underestimated, even if great syntheses remained rare. As regards the claim of this theology on the Church, it felt itself on the whole to be rather the serving agent of the body of teachers and believers than as a critical tribunal. And so its calls for reform were moderate and restrained, although it was precisely in this moderation that they had their effect in the Church and did not leave the faithful uninfluenced. As regards this theology's ecumenical and world relations, the total attitude may often seem to the modern observer to be strongly introverted, too self-centered, and too little open. True, the "bringing back of the world" (O. Bauhofer) was also its concern, which it intended to realize not by means of external activities and proclamations but by the interior way of penetration into the *mysterium* of salvation, which remained the real object of its work. Surely there resulted from this the danger of an imbalance of the "sapiential, contemplative" factor to the detriment of direct and world-related action, the limits of which it recognized in a certain sobriety. Here it was more realistic than the enthusiastic optimism of an A. Ehrhard at the beginning of the century, and under the impression of the powers of wickedness that burst forth in two world wars it could rightly be convinced that the modern world would never abandon its aversion to Christianity. Nevertheless, this theology, with all its limitations and boundaries, prepared the council of the "Church's opening up to the world" and paved the way for it.

CHAPTER 91

Movements within the Church and Their Spirituality

In the years following the First World War there ensued a series of new starts, indeed an extensive and profound renewal of religious and ecclesiastical life in Central Europe. The reasons for this are many-layered: first of all, the concentration and consolidation of church life in the nineteenth century under the guidance of Popes such as Pius IX, Leo XIII, and Pius X produced their fruit. Very different in character, style of leadership, and determination of goals, these Popes made their contribution each in his own way. What had long been regarded as dead proved to be alive. The experience of the war and of the collapse of a liberal, individualistic culture that believed in progress created a new openness to transcendence and the predetermined truths of revelation, as well as to the form of religious life in the ecclesial community. The philosopher Peter Wust (1884–1940) indicated the keyword, applicable also to other fields, with titles such as "resurrection of metaphysics" (1920) and "the return of German Catholicism from exile" (1924). The call of the age for the "spirit of the whole," as expressed by Julius Langbehn, the demand for the organically grown, for life as the genuinely real and creative against intellectualism and materialism, against isolation and uprooting, the turning to the original, to the sources, away from the manufactured, derived, and merely imagined were united with the new self-consciousness of awakened religious forces. These were expressed especially in the liturgical movement, the Bible movement, and the lay movement supported by a new awareness of the Church. But these were not currents moving parallel and to be separated from one another; rather, they influenced one another and supported one another. At first they affected smaller circles of academicians and youth in the associations of the Catholic youth movement, whereas the broad strata of the communities were further supported in their religious life by the forms of devotion characteristic of the nineteenth century: devotion to the Blessed Sacrament, to the Sacred Heart of Jesus, and to the Virgin-Mother Mary. But the development of the decades from 1920 to 1950 was noted for the fact that these more traditional forms of devotion were also affected by reflection on Holy Scripture, the theology of the Fathers, and the liturgy of the Church and the Christocentrism contained in it.

The Liturgical Movement

The beginnings of the liturgical movement extend into the nineteenth century; they are related to the renewal of Benedictine monasticism. The Belgian abbey of Maredsous, founded in 1872 from Beuron, which had been established in 1863, in 1882 published a people's missal, the *Missel des Fidèles.* Anselm Schott (1845–96), who had lived at Maredsous during the temporary suppression of Beuron in the *Kulturkampf,* followed this example in 1884. By means of his *Mass Book* he aimed, as he said in the foreword, "to contribute a little so that the Church's rich treasure of prayer, which is set down in its sacred liturgy, may become more and more accessible and familiar to the faithful."

The impetus to the liturgical movement as a breakthrough of the laity to active participation in the Church's liturgy proceeded from Belgium. It had been preceded by the decrees of Pius X of 1903 and 1904 on the chant and of 1905 on frequent and early Communion. In keeping with his motto, "To unite all things in Christ," the Pope aspired to the renewal and consolidation of the Christian spirit of the faithful. "The first and indispensable source from which this spirit is drawn," so Pius X stressed in the motu proprio of 1903, "is the active participation of the faithful in the sacred mysteries and the public and solemn prayer of the Church." A Benedictine of Mont César, Lambert Beauduin (d. 1960), was deeply affected by these ideas of the Pope. Before his entry into the monastery — he was professed in 1907 — he had been a diocesan priest at Liège and had belonged to the "Labor Chaplains," a community of worker-priests. Accordingly, also as a monk he strove to work among the people by means of the liturgy, that is, to move out of the narrow framework of academic circles into the congregations. At the National Congress of Catholic Works, inaugurated by Cardinal Mercier, he demanded at Mechelen in 1909 that the missal itself should be disseminated as the prayerbook but at least that the complete text of the Mass and of Sunday vespers should be made available to the people in a vernacular translation. This congress became the "Mechelen Happening" through the enthusiastic talk of a layman, the history professor Godefroid Kurth (d. 1916). In it he traced religious ignorance back to the still greater ignorance of the liturgy. He concluded thus: "Give to the faithful an understanding and, as a consequence, a love for the mysteries which they celebrate, give them the missal to use, and with it replace the many mediocre prayerbooks." An enthusiastic assent of the congress was given. A few weeks later there appeared in a large printing for Advent the first fascicle of *La vie liturgique,* a small booklet which provided the liturgical texts with the corresponding explanations.

In Germany the liturgical movement at first remained confined to academic circles. The spiritual leadership belonged to the abbey of Maria Laach under Abbot Ildefons Herwegen (1874–1946). In 1913 he celebrated Holy Week with a group of academicians — among them men such as the future Chancellor Heinrich Brüning and French Foreign Minister Robert Schuman — and revealed to them the liturgy as source of piety. At Maria Laach in 1918 the first "community Mass" was celebrated as *Missa recitata* or, preferably, *dialogata.*

The Catholic youth, affected by the general German youth movement, first the Fountain of Youth under Romano Guardini, then the student movement New Germany, and finally the Association of Young Men and the Storm Band under Ludwig Wolker (1871–1955), enthusiastically adopted the new manner of celebrating the liturgy. In the liturgy these youth found a realization of their longing for community, for essential and authentic form, and for the embodiment of religion in "sacred signs." For their part they promoted the liturgical movement with their untroubled enthusiasm to victory against resistance and abuses as well as against theological hesitations. The spontaneously growing new liturgical practice was from the start accompanied and clarified by a theology which united strictly scientific, even historicoarchaeological investigation with proclamation and piety. Especially effective in the area of liturgical formation was Romano Guardini (1885–1968) with his *Vom Geist der Liturgie* (1918), *Liturgische Bildung* (1923), *Von heiligen Zeichen* (1927), and his scriptural-theological introduction, *Der Herr* (1937). He led to reading and reflection on Holy Scripture, but also encouraged that the world should be taken seriously and interpreted with the eyes of faith. From 1923 professor in Berlin of Philosophy of Religion and Catholic Worldview, he understood these as "the unity of that view which embraces the living reality of the world by faith."

The texts of the Ordinary of the Mass, published by the three communities mentioned for common prayer in the "Community Mass," give a picture of the growing liturgical and religious and pedagogical experience: The *Gemeinschaftliche Andacht zur Feier der heiligen Messe,* published by Guardini in 1920, provided the text of the Mass only with paraphrasing interpretive additions. The *Missa* composed in 1924 by Father Joseph Kramp (1886–1940) for the "Union of New Germany" led to the praying aloud of the entire Mass from the prayers at the foot of the altar to the Last Gospel except for the canon, without making any distinction between the public prayers of the priest and the congregation and the private prayers of the priest. This booklet was an expression of the first excess of zeal in which people felt that the community nature of the Mass was expressed by the fact that all prayed everything, which threatened to lead to an empty, loud operation and supplied welcome material to critics. The *Kirchengebet* published in 1928 by Ludwig Wolker made the newer knowledge its own, especially in the later issues, and, in accord with the "High Mass Rule," asked which prayers belonged to the priest, the reader, and the congregation respectively and which were to be prayed quietly. The translations of the *Kirchengebet,* which had a circulation of several million, were transformed into new editions of diocesan prayerbooks.

This route of the liturgical movement into the congregations was first taken in the German language area by the "Popular Liturgical Apostolate" of Klosterneuburg near Vienna under Pius Parsch (1884–1954). In his own publishing establishment he published the texts of the Sunday liturgy — 25 million down to 1930 — in order to "bring the Church's worship to the simple folk." He revealed the meaning of the liturgy for a new biblical piety in books such as *The Church's Year of Grace* (1923, 14th ed. 1952–58) in three volumes, *Lernt die Messe verstehen* (1931), and in the periodicals *Bibel und Liturgie* (1926ff.) and *Lebe mit der Kirche* (1928ff.).

"Popular liturgy and pastoral care" were also the supporting elements of the parish work of city pastors such as Georg Heinrich Hörle (1889–1942) at Frankfurt, Konrad Jacobs (1874–1931) at Mühlheim in the Ruhr, Joseph Könn (1876–1960) at Cologne, and of the Oratory of Saint Philip Neri, founded at Leipzig in 1930. Starting with the axiom that all participation has to take place in accord with the capabilities of the participant, there was sought a celebration of Mass and of the Liturgy of the Hours that would do justice to both the liturgy and the congregation. Thus there came about the "Prayed Sung Mass" and the "German High Mass," in which the texts were sung in melodies adapted to the German language, and priest, servers, choir, and congregation performed the parts of the liturgy proper to them.

With such a distribution of roles the danger of an activist industry was banned; in the liturgical happening there were periods when the individual priest or member of the congregation listened quietly or silently sought union with the common action or assented to the effecting word of the priest. If liturgical piety meant extension of often narrow and egoistic prayer to the concerns of the Church, immersion in the movement through Christ in the Holy Spirit to the Father, it is still not a substitute for prayer in the "private room," that is, for the intimate encounter of the individual with God. Community prayer demanded that reflective "personal" prayer should not become a soulless idling. This integration of the public congregational prayer and the prayer of the individual has still not been fully achieved. This shows the difficulty of terminology. For the latter must not be "private," and the former must not be impersonal. It is not enough that one praying liturgically should lend only his lips to the Church for the praise of God. In the 1930s there were violent confrontations over this.

Exaggerations, narrow-mindedness, and willfulness of overzealous circles from the liturgical movement led to anxious and passionate criticism, among other places, in the lively book of the popular missionary M. Kassiepe, *Irrwege und Umwege im Frömmigkeitsleben der Gegenwart* (1939), and in A. Doerner's *Sentire cum Ecclesia* (1941). But there was no "official short circuit," against which R. Guardini had warned in 1940 in his "Word on the Liturgical Question," a letter to Bishop Stohr. Instead, the conflicts led to the German bishops' taking up the liturgical efforts, and so the liturgical movement became the liturgical renewal directed by the Church's authority. In 1940 the Episcopal Conference formed the Liturgical Section under Bishops Albert Stohr and Simon Konrad Landersdorfer and a Liturgical Commission of experts in theory and practice. Their work led to the 1942 "Guidelines for the liturgical structure of the parochial liturgy."

A memorandum of Archbishop Konrad Gröber of Freiburg, which he submitted on 18 January 1943 to the Curia and his fellow-bishops, threatened to lead to a new crisis. The seventeen points "giving occasion for uneasiness" were, among others: the imminent schism in the clergy, an "alarmingly flourishing mysticism of Christ" as a consequence of an exaggerated interpretation of the doctrine of the *Corpus Christi Mysticum*, the overstressing of the doctrine of the general priesthood, the "thesis of Meal-Sacrifice and Sacrificial Meal," the "overemphasis of the liturgical," the effort to make the congregational Mass obligatory, and the use of German in the Mass. "Can we German bishops," thus concluded Conrad Gröber, "and can Rome still keep silent?" This memorandum crossed a letter of Cardinal Secretary of State Maglione, which the chairman of the Episcopal Conference, Cardinal Bertram, received on 11 January 1943. In it there was complaint against encroachments by radical representatives of the liturgical movement, a report on them was demanded, and a series of proposals was made as to how the good in it could be fostered.

In the opinion of the West German bishops of 8 April 1943 to the Roman inquiry there was expressed how very much the celebration of the liturgy had become a source of strength in the age of National Socialism and of the war. "German Catholicism has been for ten years in abnormal circumstances. An activist young clergy and an equally activist Catholic youth that is enthusiastic for the faith see themselves more and more abruptly repressed on all sides.... Add to this, that it is of great importance to zealous young priests to give at least to the youth in the Church an awareness and experience of community, to bind them to the Church, and thereby to deepen and consolidate them in the faith."

On 10 April 1943 Cardinal Bertram gave to Rome a comprehensive report on the origin of the liturgical movement, on the forms of congregational participation in Mass, including the German High Mass as a "sung Mass, joined with popular singing in German," and on the "defects and mistakes of the liturgical movement." An indirect position on the controverted questions was indicated as early as Pius XII's encyclical *Mystici corporis,* because in it the Pope acknowledged the understanding of the Church by the liturgical movement and termed the new understanding of the sacred liturgy the cause of a deeper consideration of the riches of Christ in the Church.

On 24 December 1943 Maglione made known the Roman decision to Cardinal Bertram. In it the religious and pastoral fruits of the liturgical movement were praised but a warning was lodged against arbitrary innovations, the desires made known by Bertram relative to the forms of Mass were granted, and work on a German ritual was encouraged. Finally, it was suggested to the bishops to take the leadership in hand. The final point of the Roman examination and the point of departure for the liturgical reform pursued by the Curia came in the encyclical on the sacred liturgy, *Mediator Dei,* of 20 November 1947. In it Pius XII made use of the keyword of "active and personal participation." The liturgy is "the public worship which our Redeemer, the Head of the Church, gives to the heavenly Father and which the community of believers offers to its Founder and through him to the eternal Father. . . . It displays the total public worship of the Mystical Body of Jesus Christ, namely, the Head and his members."

A Roman commission was established in 1946–47 for the reform of the liturgical books. In the "Liturgical Institute" the German bishops created a work center at Trier. Corresponding institutions arose in other countries, such as the *Centre de pastorale liturgique* at Paris. In addition to liturgical congresses at Frankfurt in 1950, Munich in 1955, and Assisi in 1956, international study meetings took place. The Congregation of Rites approved the German ritual in 1950, in 1951 occurred the restoration of the Easter Vigil, and in 1955 the renewal of all of Holy Week. The precept of the Eucharistic fast was greatly mitigated in 1953 and 1957 and thereby the way for the general permission for evening Mass was opened. Even after the announcement of the council and although the general reform of the liturgy was reserved to it, in 1960 a reform of the rubrics of breviary and Mass was decreed. It produced a simplification and served the real and meaningful performance of the rites and prayers. All these preliminary activities make it understandable that at the council the "Constitution on the Sacred Liturgy" (1963) was the first item ready for a decree and also that the postconciliar reorganization of the liturgy could proceed quickly. The council made the active participation of the congregation, called for by Popes Pius X, Pius XI, and Pius XII, possible in a way that no one could have expected and thereby took up the aims of the liturgical movement for the Universal Church. Meanwhile, it had spread to other European countries — for example, to the abbey of Silos in Spain — and to America — to Saint John's Abbey in Collegeville — where it obtained a social and ethical character.

New Awareness of the Church and the Scriptural Movement

The liturgical movement was an expression of a new awareness of the Church, just as, conversely, the celebration of the liturgy permitted an entirely new experience of the Church as community. Against religious individualism and subjectivism Guardini showed: "The religious life no longer proceeds only from the I, but at the same time awakens in the opposite pole, in the objective, formed community."

It could be expected that youth which, in the name of truthfulness and personal responsibility, stood up against convention and the claims to authority on the part of civil society would have rejected the Church with its foreign legality and its rigid institutions. On the contrary: In the Church's liturgy wide circles of youth found a vital expression and a corroboration of their longing for community and at the same time correction and support in their predetermined and established position. Church was experienced not so much as institution, as agent of salvation, but as fruit of salvation, of community of life and love, whose center and foundation is Christ himself. "Christ the Lord is the real I of the Church" (Karl Adam). He is the head, and Christians have life and salvation as members of his body. Church was seen preeminently as *Corpus Christi mysticum*. If hitherto, especially in the nineteenth century, the Catholic had understood the Church as something like a collective person, to which he belonged, whose adherent or child he was, which he defended and loved, and in which he believed, so now there is question of a community, which he believes and whose member he is. The Christian does not stand facing the Church, but in it: "We are the Church," is said in many addresses and professions. Submission to the Church or, better, into the Church does not mean self-alienation but self-discovery: "To that extent I am a Christian personality, when I am a member of the Church and the Church is living in me. If I speak to it, then I say, in a fully profound understanding, not 'you' but 'I' " (Karl Adam).

Thus the Church could be understood, in fact experienced, as a principle of life, not so much as a legislator but as the source of strength and in the effort for the neighbor as the motive of moral and ascetical exertion. Books such as *Der mystische Leib Christi als Grundprinzip der Askese* (1936) by F. Jürgensmeier or *Morale et Corps mystique* (1937) by E. Mersch are characteristic of this. Altogether people wanted to move away from a casuistic and individualistic doctrine of sin to a doctrine of virtue as the message of the imitation of Christ. This was the direction taken by the *Handbuch der katholischen Sittenlehre* (1931–37) of the former exegete, Fritz Tillmann (1874–1935), with the volumes *Idee der Nachfolge Christi* and *Die Verwirklichung der Nachfolge Christi*.

The scriptural movement had made it possible to get to know this Christ, to meet him not in the rarefaction of Neo-Scholastic theology or of catechisms, but directly in Holy Scripture. Christocentric piety was awakened and deepened by means of the text of the New Testament itself in good vernacular translations and a series of scientifically based books on the life of Jesus, such as M. J. Lagrange, *L'Évangile de Jésus-Christ* (1928); L. de Grandmaison, *Jésus-Christ, sa personne, son message* (1928); J. Lebreton, *La vie et l'enseignement de Jésus-Christ, notre Seigneur* (1931); F. M. Willam, *Das Leben Jesu im Lank und Volke Israel (1933);* K. Adam, *Christus unser Bruder* (1926) *and Jesus Christus* (1933); R. Guardini, *Der Herr* (1937); and others. The program of Catholic youth read: "Life formation in

Christ." Jesus, undiminished Man in his divinity, became the model, and the "Christus totus," Christ continuing to live as the Church, was seen as the basis of one's own life and of love of neighbor. Untroubled by an opposition between the historical Jesus and the Christ of faith, people directly took up the text of the Gospels in private reading of Scripture or in "Bible Groups," sought to make present, in the style of the *Spiritual Exercises* of Saint Ignatius Loyola, the scenes, situations, and figures described there, and to find the "application" to their personal life. Characteristic of this sort of biblical work is the book by Martin Manuwald, S.J., *Christuskreis. Der Jugend und ihren Führern.*

Catholic Action

Corresponding to the new awareness of the Church in broad circles of the laity and their understanding that a person could be a living member in the body of Christ only if the life stream is passed on, was the summons by the Popes to the lay apostolate, to Catholic Action. At the beginning of his pontificate, which was put under the motto "The Peace of Christ in the Kingdom of Christ," Pius XI, alluding to the general priesthood of all believers, summoned to "active work for the spread and renewal of the Kingdom of Christ." In a letter of 13 November 1928 to Cardinal Bertram and elsewhere, the Pope several times defined *Actio catholica* as the "participation of the laity in the apostolate of the hierarchy." It is a "social movement" with the aim "of advancing the Kingdom of our Lord Jesus Christ and thereby communicating to human society the highest of all goods." Catholics, in their sharing in the hierarchy's apostolate, should be put in the position "of spreading everywhere the principles of the Christian faith and of Christian doctrine, defending them energetically, and giving effect to them in private and in public life." The Pope saw the Church preeminently as the kingdom of God on earth. In conformity with this was the institution of the solemnity of Christ the King in the jubilee year 1925. Christ's royal dominion was based on the innate right of his divine and human natures as well as on the acquired right of his work of redemption. Only in the recognition of his Kingship in private and public life can a world without peace help find peace. "The plague of our age," stressed the Pope in the encyclical *Quas primas* on the institution of the solemnity of Christ the King, "is the so-called laicism, with its errors and godless aims." Catholics have "neither that social position nor that influence . . . which those really should have who hold high the torch of truth." The Pope attributes this deplorable state of affairs "to the indifference and timidity of the good, who withdraw from the fight or make only a weak resistance. . . . But if only all the faithful understand that they must fight under the standard of Christ the King with courage and perseverance, then they will strive with apostolic zeal to lead the alienated and ignorant souls back to the Lord, and they will exert themselves to maintain his rights inviolate."

The organization of Catholic Action under strict guidance of the hierarchy was strongly determined by the situation of the Church in Italy under the Fascist regime, which wanted to assure the Church only a meager freedom of movement for its impact in the world and which especially claimed for itself the education of the young. A crisis arose even after the Lateran Treaties as a consequence of the totalitarian claims of Fascism. In the sharp encyclical *Non abbiamo bisogno* on 29 June 1931 Pius XI warded off the attacks on Catholic Action, whose nonpolitical character had been established in ARTICLE 43 of the concordat and himself attacked the absolutizing of the state. On 2 September 1931 an agreement was reached whereby the Catholic Youth Associations were incorporated into the state organization, Balilla, in which their own chaplains should provide religious instruction. Catholic Action, on the contrary, was to be able to work freely and independently. Its purely religious character and its direct dependence on the hierarchy were to be assured by its organization according to parishes and dioceses and a rearrangement according to "natural states" and not according to professions.

This model could not be realized or encountered opposition in countries like Germany, where for decades in the free sphere of the Church a series of associations related to various professions had been established, which, indeed, saw in the apostolate an essential element of their work, but in relative independence of the bishops were able to undertake functions and make decisions which did not pertain to the direct mandate of the bishops. They incorporated the idea of *Actio catholica* and of the apostolate as work for the Kingdom of Christ the King into their program and their work, without making essential changes in the structure of these societies.

In Belgium and France Catholic Action gained a special position as a "specialized" organization, that is, oriented to defined professions, such as working youth, rural youth, and students. In Belgium there was established in 1924–25, as a continuation of the *existing Jeunesse syndicaliste* founded by the priest Joseph Cardijn (1882–1967, a cardinal in 1965), the *Jeunesse Oeuvrière Chrétienne* (JOC), which was approved by Pius XI in 1925, adopted in France on the Belgian model in 1926, and then, especially after 1945, spread throughout the world. In West Germany after the Second World War there was at first no agreement as to whether the workers' unions — as was compulsory in the Nazi period — should be further established on the basis of parishes according to states of life and nature — male and female youth, men and women — or be again distinct according to profession — workers' unions, journeymen's unions, rural people, New Germany, academic associations, and so forth. The decision was again overwhelming for the latter form. The Young Christian Workers (CAJ) was basically the only new foundation as regards organization and method of work. It was called into being in 1947 and operated like the JOC, separated into male and female youth. The training took place according to the principle "see, judge, act." The young worker was to be led to see the concrete reality of his life, to evaluate and form it in the light of the Catholic faith. It especially mattered to the CAJ to fill a firm nucleus of "protagonists" with a missionary spirit by retreats and social and political study meetings. Correspondingly there arose for student youth *the Jeunesse étudiante chrétienne* (JEC) and for rural youth the *Jeunesse agricole chrétienne* (JAC).

In view of the numerous forms of the lay apostolate, differing in directness, intensity, and the structure required by the situation, Pius XII was moved to expand the concept of Catholic Action and to distinguish various forms of the organization and gradations of dependence on the hierarchy. Concerning the Marian congregations he declared in the apostolic constitution *Bis saeculari* of 27 September 1948 that they could be termed "with full right Catholic Action under the guidance and support of the Blessed Virgin Mary." If Pius XI spoke of the participation of the laity in the hierarchical apostolate, Pius XII preferred to speak of collaboration or help. According to the encyclical *Mystici corporis* of 29 June 1943, Christ requires the help of his members. "A really awesome mystery . . . that the salvation of many is dependent . . . on the cooperation which the shepherds and the faithful . . . have to provide."

In his address to the First World Congress of the Catholic Lay Apostolate on 14 October 1951, the Pope stressed that dependence of the lay apostolate on the hierarchy admitted gradations; the nearest was that for Catholic Action: "It is a tool in the hand of the hierarchy and should be, as it were, the extension of its arm. Hence, by its nature it is subordinate to the chief shepherds of the Church. Other organized or unorganized works of the lay apostolate can relinquish their free initiative to a greater degree, each as its aims require." As the Pope emphasized at the Second Congress for the Lay Apostolate in 1957, Catholic Action can — understood as an organization — claim no monopoly for itself. It bears well the character of an official lay apostolate. The apostolate of prayer, of vocation, and of life witness can be termed lay apostolate in the broader sense. Further there is the "free apostolate" of individuals and groups that put themselves at the disposal of the hierarchy and let themselves be assigned tasks by it for a limited or indefinite time. There remained the danger that the lay apostolate would be restricted to the tasks which take place in the Church itself or which are worked out by the laity as the "elongated arm of the hierarchy" and came from the field of vision of the strictly lay functions of interpretation of the world, guidance of the world, and sanctification of the world. The conciliar decree "On the Apostolate of the Laity" seeks to meet this danger by stressing, among other things, that the laity "exercise their apostolate in the Church as in the world, in the spiritual as in the secular order" (ART. 5). According to the "pastoral constitution on the Church in the world of today" there must be made a "clear distinction between what Christians as individuals or as a group do in their own name as citizens who are directed by their Christian conscience and what they do in the name of the Church together with the shepherds."

The Spiritual Exercises Movement

If in the mind of Pius XI the first goal of Catholic Action is to form the conscience of Christians in so powerfully Christian a way that at any time and in any situation of private and public life they are in a position to find the Christian solution of the many problems that arise, then the Ignatian *Spiritual Exercises* were a valuable help in this. It was their aim to lead to the personal sanctification required as the basis of apostolic spirit and life as a preliminary to the sanctification of others. The number of participants in the Exercises grew by leaps and bounds in the 1920s. If into the nineteenth century they were conducted almost exclusively by Jesuits, now other orders also took part, to a degree in a form corresponding to their special spirituality. Since the Exercises Convention at Innsbruck in 1922 and Pius XI's constitution *Summorum Pontificum* of 25 July 1922 and his encyclical on the promoting of the *Spiritual Exercises* of 20 December 1929, it is possible to speak of an Exercise Movement. Pius XI named as the worst sickness of the day the "continuous passionate devotion to the external world" and the "insatiable greed for wealth and pleasure," which no longer let people think of eternal truths and of God, the first cause and last end. The Exercises should provide place, time, and quiet for this. The sharing by groups of Catholic Action in the Exercises especially gladdened the Pope. "Many take part in them, the better to equip themselves and to keep themselves ready for the Lord's battles. Thus they find not only prop and support perfectly to develop in themselves the ideal of the Christian life; not rarely they also find in their heart a mysterious call from God, who invites them to the holy service and the fostering of the good of the neighbor's soul and this incites them to the exercise of a full apostolate." In 1936 the Jesuits alone gave 16,043 courses with 680,788 taking part. Add to this in the missionary areas 631 courses with 24,225 participants. In Germany 109,000 men, women, and youths made the Exercises in 1955. After the Second World War they became part of the extraordinary care of souls, systematically promoted and attended by pastoral officials.

If the Exercises, in accord with their origin, aimed rather at conversion of life, the "great decision" of the adult, as H. Rahner expresses it, then the pastoral care of the young developed in religious days of recollection ("retreat days, free times") forms of training in the spiritual life and of a deepening of faith suited to the mentality and situation of the young and students. According to Ludwig Esch, S.J. (1883–1956), who in the years 1919 to 1951 gave the Exercises for 54,884 pupils, students, and priests, these provided "a new setting on the right road, a growth in the setting of goals, a clarifying in regard to self and the entire world of the faith, but thereby also a profound joy."

Eucharistic Piety in Transition

The liturgical movement and the reflection on the Bible were at first matters for circles of youth and academicians. Parish congregations were first affected by them after 1930. The broad mass of the Catholic people was still supported by the great currents of the traditional piety of the nineteenth century, which lived and found expression in the worship of the Eucharist, devotion to the Sacred Heart of Jesus, and the veneration of Mary and the saints. But it is characteristic of the situation that the old was gradually permeated by the new and thereby experienced a deepening and return to essence and center. This becomes especially clear in the Eucharistic piety, which until the end of the nineteenth century was almost exclusively a worship of adoration, then as the Eucharistic movement led to frequent Communion, and only after uniting with the liturgical movement again understood the Eucharist as a sacrifice of thanksgiving, which the Lord celebrates with his Church and into which the Christian enters fully by sharing in the sacrificial meal.

Dogmatic theology used to treat the Sacrament of the Altar in three sections, which were isolated from one another: (1) the Real Presence of Christ in the Eucharist, which had as a consequence the merit of adoration; (2) the Eucharist as sacrament, that is, as Communion; (3) the Eucharist as sacrifice. For devotion the deciding factor was the presence of Christ in the tabernacle or in the monstrance. The Mass was seen predominantly as the means for "confecting" the sacramental presence, and therefore attention was focused on the moment of transubstantiation. But even this happening was covered over, because the Mass was often celebrated, for the sake of special solemnity, before the Blessed Sacrament exposed on the altar, and from the start this presence had to be venerated by, among other things, kneeling, before the Lord offering himself became present under the appearances of bread and wine and the congregation could go through him and with him and in him before the Father.

Although Pius X had demanded in 1903 that the faithful should draw the Christian spirit "from the first and real source, namely, from active participation in the holy mysteries and the public and official prayer of the Church," whereby he gave the keyword for the later liturgical movement, he did not himself, in the decree *Sacra Tridentina synodus* on daily Communion of 1905 and in the First Communion decree *Quam singulari* of 1910, go into the connection of Mass and Communion and treated the value and the significance of frequent and early Communion by itself in isolation. The "Eucharistic movement" inaugurated by him thus became the "Communion movement" in its own development, independent of the liturgical movement, in fact in some respects retarding it. It did not produce the breakthrough to a common view of Mass and Communion. The fostering of frequent, even daily Communion brought about that — in accord with the Pope's desire — the worship of adoration no longer occupied the first place within Eucharistic piety and relaxed that only too close connection of confession and Communion. However, from now on Communion was seen in isolation: isolated from what happened at Mass, but also isolated in so far as the understanding of Communion saw only the union of the individual soul with Christ but not the community of those communicating; characteristically in the decree *Sacra Tridentina synodus* there was no reference to *Communio* as community in the body of Christ.

It was in keeping with this isolated understanding of Communion that the real happening at Mass was completely overlapped and concealed by the preparation for the reception of Communion and by the thanksgiving and that one prayed one's own Communion devotions. To obtain time for the thanksgiving, Communion was often distributed before Mass or after Mass in order not to detain long those not communicating. The Eucharist was especially at the service of the religious and moral character formation of the individual; it was regarded as "countermeans for the freeing from daily sins and reservation from mortal sins."

Even after the First World War the situation seemed not essentially different, and as late as 1928 it could be said in a lecture at the Second Catechetical Congress at Munich: "Holy Communion . . . in spite of Pius X's decrees on Communion still has not always in the awareness of the people the significance proper to it in the liturgy." Only the encounter and connection with the liturgical movement at the beginning of the 1930s assisted the Eucharistic movement to the correct theological self-understanding and to an effective breakthrough in the following period. With its efforts for as active a participation as possible by all in the celebration of Mass, the liturgical movement led to Communion as a sacrificial meal being organically added to conscious and active participation in the action of sacrifice and forming a whole with it. In the course of this development to an "organic' "understanding of the Mass the preparation for Communion was increasingly seen in the celebrating of the Sacrifice of the Mass itself and no longer relegated to the

Communion devotion that ignored what happened at Mass. Assiduous ascetical exertions, characterized by concern for the worthiest possible Communion, gradually gave way to a more uncomplicated and more joyful Communion and Mass piety, by which were increasingly created more favorable presuppositions for the early and frequent reception of Communion.

No longer the consummated sacrament, that is, the sacramental presence of the Lord under the species of bread and the adoration of his divinity, stood in the foreground, but the process, the celebration in which with thanksgiving the surrender of the Lord to the Father, his sacrifice, becomes present and he, as Mediator, leads us to the Father. The only too static notion of the Eucharist was overcome, and the Eucharist as an action was more strongly stressed, for example, the abolition of exposition during Mass, which was in any event contrary to the Church's decrees, and the custom, twice recommended by Pius XII in *Mediator Dei* (1947), of giving Holy Communion with Hosts consecrated during the same Mass.

The new understanding of Communion and Mass only slowly acquired influence on the organization of Eucharistic congresses. Before and after, here the worship of adoration was in the foreground, joined to a powerful demonstration of faith, so that the procession, arranged with great display, appeared as the climax of each congress. The growing internationalizing of the congresses, at whose head stood a papal legate from 1906 on, gave these meetings the character of a "World Corpus Christi."

After the First World War the series of congresses began again at Rome in 1922. The world's disunion experienced in the war evoked for this and the succeeding congresses a new accentuation: the Host was honored as the symbol of the unity among peoples and asserted as the sole means of leading people together to lasting union. At Rome's desire there followed congresses at intervals of two years: in 1926 at Chicago, in 1928 at Sydney, in 1930 at Carthage, in 1932 at Dublin. Latin America was first added in 1933 at Buenos Aires. There followed those at Madrid in 1936 and Budapest in 1938. Once again war interrupted the series of congresses, which was not continued until 1952 at Barcelona. In the organization of this congress the growing together of the liturgical and the Eucharistic movements found clear expression: the closing procession no longer constituted the climax, beside which, more or less without visible connection, Masses and the distribution of Communion took place, but the common celebration of the Eucharist was moved directly into the center.

The complete elaboration of this new accentuation took place at the Munich Congress in 1960, for which Josef Andreas Jungmann had awakened to new life the idea of the *statio.* As early as 1930, on the occasion of the Eucharistic Congress at Carthage, Jungmann had called attention to the custom, frequently attested in the ancient Church but acquiring a special form in the Roman Church of the Middle Ages, whereby the bishop on specific Sundays and Feasts of the year, but especially in Lent, celebrated a migratory Mass in the most important churches in order to make visible the notion of the unity of bishop, clergy, and people.

This *Statio Urbis,* as Jungmann said, could serve as model for a *Statio Orbis,* the experience of the community of the Church in the common Eucharistic celebration as the climax of the Eucharistic Congress. Jungmann's suggestion, hardly noticed in 1930, was adopted in the episcopal pastoral letter for the Munich Congress of 1960. Thus the community Eucharistic celebration, in which the Universal Church became experienced and visible as the Mystical Body of Christ, gave to this congress a special character and emphasized with incomparable clarity the preeminence of the sacrificial event in union with the sacrificial meal as contrasted with the adoring gaze. The notion of the *Statio Orbis* deprived this congress of the character of a triumphalist stressed self-celebration; the stress lay not on demonstration but on the daily accomplishment of the sacrifice.

The organization of the Munich World Congress in accord with the concept of the *Statio Orbis* allowed the spirit of the liturgical renewal to acquire a quite visible form and thereby facilitated the preparation of new liturgical arrangements by the Council.

Devotion to the Sacred Heart of Jesus

Devotion to the Sacred Heart of Jesus, which achieved a high rank in the nineteenth century because of papal encouragement, occupied also in the twentieth century a broad area in popular piety; very widespread was the observance of the first Friday of the month as Sacred Heart Friday, joined with Communion and prayer for an intention determined each month by the Pope. The effort for a solid theological foundation of this devotion by recourse especially to biblical statements, but also to patristic theology, marked both the work of theologians and expressions of the *magisterium:* this work was all the more urgent, as trashy, sentimental distortions were a great danger in this devotion that appealed to the affective-emotional classes.

In the encyclical *Miserentissimus Redemptor* of 1928 Pius XI gave the feast of the Sacred Heart the highest liturgical rank, with a new Mass formulary and office. In view of the needs of the day, the encyclical called for penance and expiation, which occupy "always the first and foremost position in the honoring of the most Sacred Heart of Jesus" (no. 135). Through the papal regulations the devotion to the Heart of Jesus and its incorporation into the liturgy achieved a first goal; the theological foundation also here reached an important stage as the attempt was made to join the Heart of Jesus mysticism with the theology of the Fathers and to consolidate the devotion to the Sacred Heart in the central mysteries of salvation.

The world crisis of the 1930s again afforded the Pope the occasion to recommend the devotion to the Sacred Heart as a means of salvation in the encyclical *Caritate Christi compulsi* of 3 May 1932. Considering the misery of the period, the godlessness, and the hatred of every religion, joined in socialism with the struggle for one's daily bread, the Pope commanded the holding of public Masses of atonement on the solemnity of the Sacred Heart.

Under Pius XII, who in his first encyclical had referred to the consecration of the human race to the Sacred Heart, exertions in regard to the devotion to the Heart of Jesus reached a climax, especially in regard to theology. True, at this time doubts and objections were also heard, for example, that the devotion to the Sacred Heart fostered a purely individualistic piety, which in view of the growing awareness of community in the sphere of the Church could not but evoke grave hesitations. To others some vivid presentations and devotional forms seemed rather repulsive; others again attributed to the devotion to the Sacred Heart a historical right, it is true, as a reaction to the sentiment-destroying and rigoristic Jansenism and as a Christianization of subjectivism in the nineteenth century, but they were inclined to deny the importance of this cult for the twentieth century and the tasks allotted to it. And some raised the reproach of particularism: one element, the heart, would be dissociated from the person of the Redeemer and hence a total view would be made more difficult.

An intensive theological work, especially in the 1950s, sought to take into account the doubts that were becoming loud and the difficulties by undertaking to clarify the heart in its total character, the physical as well as the spiritual included, from biblical expressions of the Old and New Testaments.

"Heart is," as Guardini writes, following Blaise Pascal, "the spirit in so far as it is in contact with blood.... Heart is the spirit made hot and sensitive by blood, but at the same time spirit elevated by the clarity of contemplation, by the distinctness of character, by the precision of judgment. Heart is the organ of love.... It is that which is experienced in the heart." Thus the Heart of Jesus is the symbol of the love of the Redeemer, as love of the Father and of mankind. Devotion to the Heart of Jesus means to let oneself be embraced by this love of Jesus. It must be expressed in a serving apostolic life.

The fruit as well as the point of departure of such exertions for a theological justification of devotion to the Sacred Heart in accord with the time were the statements of Pius XII in his encyclical *Haurietis aquas* of 15 May 1956. This document took issue with the most varied misunderstandings and errors and sought — contrary to the minimizing of this cult as based on a private revelation — to make clear that the devotion to the Sacred Heart "can look back to an advanced age in the Church and has in the Gospels themselves a solid foundation, so that tradition and liturgy clearly favor it." The reason for this cult, which is distinguished as the "most effective school of the love of God," is twofold: the first consists in this, that Christ's heart, "the noblest part of human nature, is hypostatically united with the person of the divine Word; hence to it must be paid the same worship of adoration by which the Church honors the person of the incarnate Son of God.... The second reason results from this, that his heart, more than all other members of his body, is a natural indication or symbol of his unending love for the human race."

The Pope's explanations, which apply in detail especially to biblical statements, end in the admonition that in the devotion to the Sacred Heart there is "no question about just any traditional form of piety, which may, according to the preference of each, be treated lightly or underestimated in relation to other forms, but of a practice of divine adoration, which, like no other, is able to lead to Christian perfection.... Everyone who then has a slight estimation of this great gift of Jesus Christ to the Church is pursuing a dangerous and unholy matter and is offending God himself."

Despite the encouragement of and propaganda for the devotion to the Sacred Heart by the official *magisterium,* it seems to be fading more and more from the awareness and life of piety of the members of the Church. This probably has less theological than spiritual-historical reasons. An age like ours, which sees so strongly in Jesus the "Man for us," would have to have in it understanding for love that is self-sacrificing and consumed for the neighbor; but to see and honor this represented in the bleeding Heart of Jesus — for this there is lacking today the sense of the symbol.

Devotion to Mary and Mariology

The growth of the Marian movement from the second third of the nineteenth century continued on into the twentieth. Pius XI and Pius XII continued the line of their predecessors in the promoting of devotion to Mary. Among believers it received impetus from appearances of Mary, especially from that at Fátima in Portugal, which was made to three Portuguese children in 1917. It and also the appearances in the Belgian localities of Beauraing in 1932–33 and Banneux in 1933 obtained ecclesiastical approbation. They led to a brisk pilgrimage. At Fátima Mary demanded especially the praying of the rosary for the peace of the world, the consecration of Russia to her immaculate heart, and Communion of reparation on the first Saturday of each month. Pope Pius XII, whose episcopal ordination occurred at Rome on 13 May 1917, the day of the first appearance of Mary at Fátima, regarded himself throughout his life as bound to the aims of Fátima in a special way. On 8 December 1942 he performed the consecration of the entire human race to the Immaculate Heart of Mary. On 7 July 1952 he finally addressed to all the people of Russia an encyclical in which they were dedicated to the Immaculate Heart of Mary. To spread the aims of Fátima there was established, at the urging of the Canadian Bishop Dignan, a "Rosary Crusade," which had a worldwide expansion. In 1947 there arose in Vienna, under Franciscan leadership, the Rosary Atonement Crusade.

The Marian piety and the lay apostolate were now in close connection. Thus in the lay organization, the "Legion of Mary," which was founded by Frank Duff in Dublin in 1921 and spread rapidly on all the continents, especially in mission countries. With an aggressive tone like that of the Legion of Mary, there appeared also the Militia of the Immaculate Conception, founded in 1917 by Father Maximilian Kolbe (1894–1941), who later died in a concentration camp, and also the Blue Army of Mary, called into being in 1947 by Harold Colgan. The last named sees its task principally as the spreading of the message of Fátima.

The lay apostolate of the Marian congregation, which are called "Marian" not only "because they take their title from the Mother of God, but especially because the individual members promise an especially interior veneration of the Mother of God and give themselves to her through a complete surrender of consecration, received encouragement and impetus from Pius XII's apostolic constitution *Bis saeculari* of 1948. In 1953 was founded the World Association of Marian Congregations, which since 1956 is a member of the Conference of International Catholic Organizations. From the spirit of the Marian congregations proceeded, at first depending on the Pallottines, the Schönstatt Movement, building on the educational work of Father Josef Kentenich (1885–1968); Marian sisters, Marian brothers, and Schönstatt priests are the agents of the work.

In encyclicals Pius XI and Pius XII several times expressed their views on problems of Mariology and devotion to Mary and gave new impulses or took up such.

Thus in 1937 Pius XI in the encyclical *Ingravescentibus malis* recommended the rosary, with clear allusion to Fascism and communism, in view of the threatening world situation. A series of new Marian feasts was introduced: in 1931, on the occasion of the fifteenth centenary of the Council of Ephesus, of the feast of the Maternity of the Blessed Virgin Mary on 11 October, in 1944 the Feast of the Immaculate Heart of the Blessed Virgin Mary on 22 August, and finally in 1954 the Feast of Mary our Queen on 31 May. The climax of the papal initiatives came with the proclamation of the dogma of the bodily Assumption of Mary into heaven on 1 November 1950. The proclamation was preceded by a survey of the episcopate of the world. This confirmed that the bodily Assumption of Mary was a firm conviction of faith of the members of the Church and almost unanimously agreed to the opportuneness of the definition. According to the dogmatic bull *Munificentissimus Deus*, Mary, who was already a sharer in the full redemption, is a sign for mankind, threatened in a secularistic world of materialism; mankind should recognize in Mary that human fulfillment is to be found only in God: it is to be hoped, said the Pope, "that through the contemplation of the glorious example of Mary there may grow ever stronger the insight into what high value human life has, when it is used to carry out the will of the heavenly Father and to act for the welfare of the fellow man. And it can also be . . . expected that the truth of Mary's Assumption may show to all clearly to what noble end we are destined in body and soul. Finally, faith in the bodily Assumption of Mary into heaven will strengthen faith also in our resurrection and lead to energetic activity."

Marian literature, powerfully increased in the twentieth century, reached its climax in the 1950s in regard to mere number of publications: thus, between 1948 and 1957 about one thousand titles per year appeared. Not rarely these works contained exaggerations which went far beyond the measure found in the dogma and liturgy of the Church. All the more, theologians such as Otto Semmelroth, Hugo and Karl Rahner, Michael Schmaus, and others, sought to open up the biblical and patristic sources of Mariology and to consider the ecumenical problem. Inspired by the works of early Christian tradition, which had treated Mary not for her own sake but in the framework of the divine economy of salvation, theologians of the 1940s and 1950s dealt with Mary and her privileges no longer as isolated, but with a view to the entire doctrine of salvation: thus Mariology was seen in its relations to Christology, ecclesiology, and eschatology. Mary was no longer the object of a merely individual cult — just as also the individualistic understanding of the Church in these years yielded to a more community-related view — but she was seen in the framework of the theology of salvation, hence in connection with redemption, humanity, Church, and perfection: Mary, prototype or type of the Church.

Also concerned for a new basis for devotion to Mary were the Marian congresses, which took place on regional, national, and international levels. Further, there were formed societies for Marian studies, and in 1950 an international Marian Academy was founded. In Germany must be mentioned the Mariological Workers Community of German theologians; in France the Institut Catholique at Paris received a special Mariological chair; and at Rome the Mariological Academy was made a papal academy by a motu proprio of John XXIII of 8 December 1959. Institutes, academies, societies, and working communities published the results of their individual investigations and meetings in numerous periodicals and cooperative works. With the end of the pontificate of Pius XII, as whose Marian climaxes must be given the years 1950, 1954 (the Marian Year), and 1958 (centenary of Mary's appearance at Lourdes), there began a slackening of enthusiasm in devotion to Mary and Mariology, a tendency which even the suggestions of the Second Vatican Council could not stop and which lasts till today. The council composed no Marian schema of its own, but dealt with Mary within the schema on the Church. Here Mary appears expressly as "type of the Church with respect to faith, love, and perfect unity with Christ." For the rest, the Second Vatican Council imposed on itself with regard to Mariology an intentional caution; it had "no intention of proposing a complete doctrine of Mary or to decide questions which were not yet fully clarified by the work of theologians." The constitution presented Mary's position in Christ's salvific work but avoided the term "Coredemptrix," which since the beginning of the twentieth century quite often stood in the center of the discussion and had even been used by the Popes, but had given occasion to misunderstandings.

In regard to the fear that, because of the devotion to Mary and the emphasis on the cooperation of the Mother of God in the work of redemption, the image of Christ would be obscured, the council made it clear that "in the honoring of the Mother, the Son, on account of whom everything is ... is correctly known, loved, and glorified, and his commandments are observed." But in the veneration of Mary the correct measure must be maintained. Thus the council admonishes "to promote generously the veneration, especially the liturgical, of the Blessed Virgin" and thereby "also to hold carefully aloof from every false exaggeration as well as from too summary an attitude in contemplating the unique dignity of the Mother of God."

The Spiritual Development of the Orders

The continuing growth since the second half of the nineteenth century of the number of members of the orders and congregations as well as of the number of their foundations was at first maintained in the twentieth century. More or less clear variations within the development can be explained by a parallel reflection on the history of the period and to a great extent referred to external factors.

Whereas, following the recovery from the losses of the First World War, a "monastic spring" was clearly to be recorded in Germany, there appeared toward the end of the 1920s a noticeable slackening of the growth, which found expression in 1936 in the orders of sisters in a slight decline in the number of recruits; this was in part the effect of the low birthrate of the years between 1914 and 1920 but must also especially be regarded for the following period under the aspect of the propaganda of the National Socialist regime. Its measures hostile to the orders reached their climax in the decree by Rudolf Hess of 19 November 1940 whereby entrance into monasteries was stopped. After the end of the Second World War, it is true, the number of members of the orders was stabilized in a thereafter slight growth, but the number of novices reached only little more than half of the prewar recruits. Also to be coped with were the severe damages done to the religious life because of members killed in the war, a considerable migration movement, and the loss of houses and schools of the orders. If after the war the orders could again attend to their tasks in the schools, then this meant additional deficiencies in the charitable work, in which meanwhile the sisters had found a field of activity. In part, the losses were compensated by the religious expelled from Eastern countries.

If the development of the religious clergy is compared with that of the diocesan clergy, it must be stated, at least for Germany and its Western neighbor nations, that during the postwar years the religious clergy could record a relatively larger growth than the diocesan clergy. The reasons for this were the readiness for radical response after the experiences of the war and the collapse and the demand for stability and security, which were promised by the *vita communis* of the religious community. In mission lands the stronger increase in native religious priests must also be attributed to the fact that missionary work was almost exclusively in the hands of the orders and the model of the diocesan priest was absent.

As regards the distribution of the recruits among the various orders, a "change of tendency" must be noted: While from the beginning of the century the recruits applied chiefly to the "active" communities and among these the more recent congregations and those more adapted to the needs of the time had on an average a larger growth than the ancient types of orders, from the 1950s especially the number and spread of the contemplative communities increased.

Raymond Hostie specified alongside numerical growth as a mark of all religious communities in the twentieth century, "stability of the organizational structure" and a certain "immobility." The latter appeared in a certain rigidity in the interpretation of the rule and a concealing of the basic uniformity of communities by emphasizing originality in unessential externals and in an isolation of the monasteries from the general cultural development. It was no accident that, in the renewal movement within the Church of our century, monasteries such as Solesmes, Subiaco, Beuron, Maria Laach, and others took part: by recourse to monastic origins they gained a clear ideal and hence were in a position to supply new impulses. Against this background must be understood the efforts of the Popes to bring the orders back to the essential by reflection on the spirit of the respective founders and law which inspired them and thereby to free them for the tasks of the day.

After Pius XI (1922–39) had worked successfully for an adjustment between the liturgical reform movement of the Benedictines and the tradition of the exercises and of devotion to the Sacred Heart of the Jesuits, the exertions for a reform of the orders achieved its climax in many pronouncements of Pius XII (1939–58). The prelude to the accommodation of the orders to the time and its needs, as desired by the Pope, was given in an article, inspired by his ideas, by the Jesuit Riccardo Lombardi in *Civiltà Cattolica*. Although religious were admonished in it not to be "adventurers" in order that "the conservative viewpoint may always retain its validity alongside the mood for innovation," still they should as "the highly motivated avant-garde in an anxious hour give to reform the example of the greatest preparedness in relation to the new positions demanded by the welfare of humanity." "Avoid," Lombardi called upon the religious, "a stagnating rigidity which would remove you from the course of life; on the other hand, be unchanging, as a river is unchanging, which is fed from an everlasting source but constantly renews itself in the stream!"

This impulse found its continuation at the First International Congress of Religious at Rome in 1950, which was under the slogan determined by the Sacred Congregation for Religious: "The renewal of the states of perfection adapted to the present day and its circumstances." In his addresss to some five hundred representatives of the orders and secular institutes the Pope called upon the religious: Motivated by the conviction that the Catholic faith is able to form every age, "pay attention to the opinion, judgment, and morals of your environment and accept what you find good and just in it as valuable indications; otherwise you cannot be advisers, help, support, and light to your fellow human beings.... There are areas, indeed very many, in which you may, in fact must, adapt yourselves to the style and needs of the time and the people...."

Especially for the contemplative orders of women the Pope derived from this the duty to "reasonable modernization," which should find its expression not least in a "moderate participation in the apostolate." The apostolic constitution *Sponsa Christi* of 21 November 1950, decisive in this context, accordingly supplemented, among other things, the strict prescriptions of enclosure for monasteries of nuns with the modified form of the so-called "little papal enclosure." In ARTICLE 8 of the constitution, with reference to the economic security of the orders, there was imposed on the nuns the obligation to a suitable work, which was consistent "not only with the law of nature but equally with a duty of penance and expiation." In a glance at the lack of recruits the Pope in 1952 repeated his plea to the superiors of orders: "Pay attention, especially in this age of a vocation crisis, to this, that the behavior, manner of life, and asceticism in your religious families not become hindrances or reasons for refusal.... Adapt yourselves in all things which are not essential, so far as reason and regulated charity permit." Pius XII's special concern was for the formation of the recruits. He demanded a uniform formation of the young religious by "proved and selected personalities."

A further effort to lead the monasteries out of their isolation went in the direction of a greater cooperation, both through "coordinating of the diocesan clergy and the religious clergy" and through stronger contact of the individual religious communities with the competent bishops as with Rome, and finally through cooperation or, respectively, even merger of monasteries. Results appeared in the form of unions, chiefly of monasteries of women, and in an improved organization and coordination of the efforts of the orders from Rome as the center. In spite of some very promising new starts, however, the reform efforts led on the whole — as also hints of the Pope in his talk at the Second International Congress of Religious at Rome in 1957 confirmed — to further difficulties, among others in the interpretation of the vow of obedience, rather than to fruitful renewal. The chief problems seemed to be the form and exercise of authority, the common life with experiments of small communities, uncertainty in regard to function, the age structure, and so forth.

It was damaging for religious that they were scarcely supported by the believing awareness of the community, let alone that of the broader public. Their services were expected, there were protests when communities closed houses because of lack of recruits, but there was no effort to offer a solution in prayer, meditation, and concern to the problems of the life and recruitment of the orders.

In this situation there occurred new types of attempts at a uniting of the monastic ideal with the demands of the apostolate through an extensive breaking away from the framework of the old orders and congregations. As an example may be mentioned the Little Brothers of Jesus, which, as a continuation of the work of Charles de Foucauld (1858–1916), realized a new type of apostolate "in the midst of the world." With complete abandonment of inclosure, they live together in communities of about four members and separately pursue a secular calling. As their founder tried, by an exemplary life, to bring the Gospel to the tribes in the Sahara, so his brotherhoods pursued the same goal in the non-Christian and, for evangelization, very accessible "desert" of our modern secularized civilization. Out of the strength of the love and imitation of Christ, they seek through the simplicity of their life-style and hospitality to be open to the encounter with the Lord in people. And so the Eucharist and Holy Scripture constitute the support of their community. "Work for the sanctification of the world," Charles de Foucauld has the Lord say and thereby expresses the essential element of his vocation, "work for it as my Mother, wordless, silent, build your retreats in the midst of those who do not know me, carry me into their midst by erecting there an altar, a tabernacle, and bring there the Gospel, not by mouth but by example, not by preaching it but by living it" (H. Urs von Balthasar). By 1960 the number of brotherhoods grew to forty-five in twenty countries with a total of 216 brothers. Since 1939 there has been a female branch of the Little Sisters of Jesus with like aims.

The Secular Institutes

Whereas the new impulses for a reform and adaptation of the orders and congregations to the needs of the time proceeded essentially from the Holy See, there was active around the middle of the twentieth century in the "secular institutes" a form of striving for Christian perfection which had developed without the cooperation and to a degree under the skeptical observation and repudiating reactions of the official ecclesiastical offices. The members of these new communities, whose beginning extend back to the early nineteenth century, strove to realize the life of the evangelical counsels as individuals or in small groups in the midst of the world; without public vows and without being bound to a strictly organized community life, they felt themselves entirely bound to the apostolate in the milieu of the moment, especially of a secular calling.

Soon these communities turned out to be as necessary as they were suited to the apostolic permeation of the secularized world. The number of *Instituta saecularia* grew. The initial opposition on the part of theologians and the Curia was to a great extent based on the traditional teaching of the inseparability of the state of perfection and solemn profession. But the then ensuing papal approval, at first only in individual cases, was all the more possible when Leo XIII in the constitution *Conditae a Christo* of 8 December 1900 had recognized the congregations that had already reached flowering as communities of religious and as a state of perfection.

Protracted preliminary work by ecclesiastical commissions and consultations by the Congregation of the Council in union with the Holy Office and the Congregation of Religious paved the way for the recognition of secular institutes as a "third state of perfection" by Pius XII's apostolic constitution *Provida Mater Ecclesia* of 2 February 1947. The norms of this constitution applied to "communities, both of clerics and of lay persons, whose members observe the evangelical counsels in the world for reaching Christian perfection for the complete fulfillment of their apostolate." The Church recognizes the dedication of life of the members of secular institutes and their vows or promises but does not grant either the public nature of these vows in the form of a solemn profession or make obligatory their "common life or living under the same roof"; "one or several common houses" are, however, desired as centers of formation and meeting, as dwelling places of the leaders of the union, and for the reception of individual members for reasons of health or other considerations. The connection between the institute and its members is a "perpetual or temporary" one, as well as a "mutual and perfect" one. The right to found "secular institutes" pertains to the bishop, with the obligation of consulting the Congregation of Religious and reporting to it.

A year after *Provida Mater Ecclesia,* Pius XII on 13 February 1948 issued the motu proprio *Primo feliciter anno,* in which the "secular institutes" were expressly praised and confirmed. In it the Pope expressed gratitude for the "help which brought to the Catholic apostolate in extremely great providential wisdom consolidation in our evil age that has fallen to pieces. The stressing of the striving for perfection, which should "be adapted to life in the world in all things and brought into harmony with them," as well as the emphasis on the apostolic activity of the "secular institutes," which should be carried out "not only in the midst of the world, but, so to speak, out of the world," make clear the change which the notion of "secular institutes" has gone through since their origin: Whereas it originally was meant in the sense of a purely negative limitation in relation to the religious state, and in the preparations for *Provida Mater Ecclesia* there was still consideration of including the new societies in the concept of "religious state," now with the stressing of the "worldly" character of the secular institutes the qualitative distinction to the orders appeared in a manner which assisted the notion of "secular institutes" to an independent development and a positively filled autonomy. The new departure, which was rather hindered than encouraged by tendencies to "claustration," through the making aware of the general vocation released forces for sanctification which opposed the increasing clericalization of the orders and in general the tension between clergy and laity. Areas not yet reached or attainable — especially in the missions — could be opened up for apostolic penetration.

The number of secular institutes grew by 1962 to fifteen communities of papal right, about sixty of diocesan right, and a still greater number of unions which were just seeking ecclesiastical approbation. In the great majority these were communities of women, and strikingly enough many of them in Latin countries.

Because of the considerable number of existing "secular institutes" and the great diversity of their tasks, here only a few of the most important can be mentioned as representative: As "the authentic model of the secular institute" the Opus Dei is designated in the papal charter of approbation. It is one of the most widespread, numerically strongest, and, on account of the professional excellence of its members, most influential "secular institutes." The community was founded at Madrid for lay persons and priests by the young priest José María Escrivá de Balaguer (1902–75) under the name of *Sociedad Sacerdotal de la Santa Cruz y Opus Dei* and, as the first of the "secular institutes," obtained papal approval on 24 February 1947. At the beginning of the 1960s it already comprised around fifty thousand members from sixty-five nations and virtually all classes and professions, including some 2 percent priests.

An essential center of gravity of the activities of the institute lies in the field of the religioideological and scholarly formation and training of the academic recruits. This was seen in the founding in 1952 of its own university, recognized by the Holy See in 1960, in the Basque provincial capital, Pamplona, as a first step to other foundations of schools in many countries. But the stressing of the profession as the chief means of personal sanctification and of the apostolate became the occasion for the forming of centers *of Opus Dei* in the worker's quarters of large cities, whereby the chief stress lay on the erecting of places of formation and of pastoral care in the milieu of the workers' calling. Members of Opus Dei also put themselves at the disposal of the missions, and thereby they joined apostolic activity with professionally qualified work of development. In Peru Opus Dei undertook one of the most difficult missionary areas of Latin America. Finally, a series of literary and publicity activities in periodicals and publishing must be mentioned.

Likewise of papal right is the institute of the *Prêtres du Prado,* which is restricted to French members but is typical of many communities of a like orientation. It was founded in the nineteenth century as purely a community of priests by Father Chevrier (1826–79), who was closely linked to the Curé d' Ars, Saint Jean Baptiste Marie Vianney. In accord with the aim fixed at that time, the members aspire, even today, to make the Gospel credible to the poor through personal poverty. While the work threatened to fail in Chevrier's lifetime, the number of members increased in the present century from 32 in 1922 to 610 priests in 1960, as well as 202 sisters, whose sphere of activity extends far beyond France to Africa, Japan, Chile, and elsewhere. The members see the sphere of their apostolate especially in parochial care of souls, but also work as catechists and pastors among the workers and the working youth.

The most important German contribution to the development of the secular institutes is the multibranched Schönstatt Work with its international expansion. It was called into being in 1914 by Father Josef Kentenich (1885–1968). To this work belonged a group of Marian apostolate lay communities as well as several secular institutes, of which first the "Schönstatt Marian Sisters" obtained in 1948 the papal *Prodecretum laudis,* a step toward definitive recognition, which came on 8 December 1976. The long-range goal consists in the "Marian formation of the world to Christ." In conformity with the spirituality of "working-day sanctity," a "dynamic relation to the world" should make it possible for the institute, in the most suitable form of the moment, whether as individuals or in the group, to carry out the tasks in Church and world. The male branch includes, besides the institute of the "Schönstatt Fathers," who are chiefly professionally active for the Schönstatt Work, the "Schönstatt Priests" as a community of diocesan priests and the less strong "Schönstatt Marian Brothers." The members of the community of the "Ladies of Schönstatt" remained in their lay calling and frequently devoted themselves secondarily to various apostolic tasks in the Church's pastoral care and *caritas.* A two-year novitiate and two tertiarates should consolidate and deepen the religious life of the members by means of further religious formation and introduction to study. Due to the unobtrusiveness of their dress and life-style many of the women were able to continue their apostolic work to an astonishing degree even during the Nazi period. Around 1976 the "Schönstatt Marian Sisters," with more than twenty-eight hundred members from almost thirty nations, were the largest female secular community in Germany. Since 1933 they have expanded outside, among other places to South Africa, Brazil, Argentina, Uruguay, Chile, the United States, Australia, and Switzerland. During the period of the war and persecution the institute undertook tasks in some Slavic countries. The centers of gravity of its efforts lie in the fields of education and *caritas.* Community experiences in this branch of the Schönstatt Work set forth a very intensive emphasis: One who desires to enter leaves his former group in life and places himself entirely at the disposal of the institute. The members are prepared for the tasks of their calling by an intensive schooling of eight and one-half years. After the completion of their training they are divided into intern members, who live with uniform dress in the home community, and extern members at individual posts in religious or secular dress, as well as the Sisters of Adoration.

Through its many-faceted apostolic commitment, the new form of life of the "secular institutes" had a favorable impact on the pastoral attitude of the old orders and on making aware the close connection of the contemplative ideal with the apostolate. Hans Urs von Balthasar also points to the importance of the "secular institutes" for the choice of a state of life by the unmarried woman. If she sees herself not called to the religious state, then, since admittance to the priesthood is denied her, she can easily incur the tension of an unclear intermediate stage between the simple "unmarried life" and virginity undertaken from religious motives. Here membership in a "secular institute" can offer a function in life and support.

While the "secular institutes" in their adaptation to the needs of the time also supplement the old orders and congregations in many ways with the élan of a new departure, for their part they are supported by the spirituality living in these orders, so that, in the continuity of the Christian striving for perfection, no break but an enrichment pointing to the future may occur.

Worker-Priests

The ecclesiastical authority also directed to secular institutes the groups of dedicated pastoral workers who, searching for new ways to regain for the faith the workers alienated from the Church, were willing to share their daily work, their manner of life, and their environment. A highly motivated experiment became in its beginnings the "scandal of the twentieth century and the drama of the worker priests." In 1943 Fathers Henri Godin (1906–44) and Yvan Daniel had issued a report on the Christian conquest of the proletarian classes under the title *Is France a Mission Land?* The work, which courageously expressed what had long been known but not admitted, proceeded from the observation that, for the proletariat alienated from the Church, the traditional parish was entirely inaccessible, because it required of it the changing of its mentality and way of life, and conversely the parochial care of souls scarcely penetrated into the modern pagan world. Loyal to the model of Gregory the Great in regard to the Anglo-Saxons and to the efforts of the mission in remote lands for native priests and a preaching adapted to the manner of thinking and intelligence of the natives, one should bring to the workers' world a pure religion purged of human additions which enclose a civilization. Was not Saint Paul a pagan with the pagans and a Jew with the Jews? A year previously, on 5 October 1942, on the initiative of the Assembly of the Cardinals and Archbishops of France at Lisieux, the priestly seminary of the *Mission de France* had been opened. It was supposed to attract to the de-Christianized areas suffering from a lack of priests those who were capable of entering into the mentality of the outsiders. Cardinal Suhard (1874–1949) of Paris, who had approved Godin's report before its appearance, formed in 1944, under the name of *Mission de Paris,* a group of priests who, freed from ordinary parochial ministry, were to seek and go into new ways of the apostolate. They proposed to "hold up the Catholic priesthood as a model in a missionary manner, beginning with the dependent, deprived, collective life of the poor of this day, through the same living conditions, ... through the clear intention of belonging to a given social class and of living on the level of the best of its members."

The designation "worker-priest," *prêtre-ouvrier,* for a priest who worked a full day at a job, was not distinguishable externally from a worker, and was not at first known as a priest in his closest environment, came into use through the *Diary of a Worker-Priest* by Henri Perrin, S.J. The book told of the activity of French priests among their countrymen who were prisoners of war or those bound to work in Germany. The access into the life-style of the working world here offered by the situation was experienced as an effective apostolic possibility and after the war was continued by priests, including members of the Mission de Paris, Lyon, and other industrial towns. It was less concerned, after the example of Saint Paul (1 Cor. 9:15–18), to earn one's livelihood by one's own work; rather, according to Cardinal Suhard, the work of these priests was "the act of naturalization of the priests among people to whom he was hitherto only a foreigner; suffering and ready for penance, he shares in human existence." In his 1947 pastoral letter "Growth or Decline of the Church," which obtained worldwide attention, the cardinal had demanded an apostolate of incarnation in the overcoming of modernism and integralism. "Adaptation means not compromises, not systematic substitution of the old by the new, a fortiori not mutilation of the Gospel but only integral and intelligent incorporation of this Gospel into that which is to be converted. ... To be an Apostle means to undertake in so far as it can be properly undertaken all of the human and of the world which man had fashioned for himself, to permeate all. All, which means, apart from sin, all values, even those hitherto foreign to the Christian, in so far as it is not simply a question of mankind's own mad ideas."

The boundaries indicated by the cardinal between the required adaptation to the world and becoming uniform with the world (Rom. 12:2), the falling victim to the world, cannot easily be carried through in daily life and demands great religious strength and a considerable gift of discernment. This and a basic philosophical and theological formation for the confrontation with the ideology of Marxism have not rarely been lacking. Solidarity with the workers and this included sharing in struggles over wages and strikes in a front with the Communists brought the worker-priests into the twilight. And at the Curia there was concern for their spiritual life and the preeminence of the priesthood proper and pastoral care. On 23 September 1953 there was issued through Nuncio Marella to twenty-six bishops and religious superiors the request to break off the experiment.

Meanwhile, public opinion had been attracted in a sensational way to the worker-priests through the press and Gilbert Cesbron's novel that appeared in 1952, *The Saints Go to Hell,* which obtained a circulation of more than two hundred thousand copies and many translations. Secrecy about the measures of the Curia, as was demanded, was impossible. Millions of Frenchmen had gained a great sympathy for the worker-priests and were indignant. In difficult discussions among Rome, the bishops, and the worker-priests possibilities were sought for continuing the apostolate under other conditions — only three hours work per day, life in a community of priests. Not all the approximately one hundred priests followed the directions of the bishops. Others, in an understanding with the bishops, quietly made new efforts. In March 1957 the Assembly of the Cardinals and Archbishops of France founded the Mission Ouvrière in an effort to make possible in modified form the presence of the priest in the workers' milieu. On the occasion of his first visit, in June 1959, to John XXIII, from whom as the former nuncio at Paris a special understanding was anticipated, Cardinal Feltin, archbishop of Paris, made a report on the matter. To his request that in special cases worker-priests might again be appointed as full-time workers, there was made known to him on 3 July the decision of the Holy Office that for the future every sort of factory work should be forbidden to priests. "The Holy See," said the decision of the Holy Office, "is of the opinion that for the apostolate in workers' environments it is not essential to send priests into the workers' milieu and that it is not possible to sacrifice to this end the traditional notion of the priesthood, even if the Church sees in this apostolate one of its dearest tasks. . . . It is true that the priest, like the Apostles, is a witness (cf. Acts 1:8) but a witness of the resurrection of Christ (cf. Acts 1:22), as of his divine and redeeming mission. He gives this witness especially by the word and not by manual labor among factory workers, as if he were one of them." Factory work makes it impossible to pursue the priestly duty of prayer. Even if some accomplish this, they should devote their time better to their priestly office than to manual work. "Did not the Apostles institute the diaconate precisely in order to free themselves from temporal affairs . . . ? (Cf. Acts 6:2, 4)." The bishops should reflect whether it is not the time to establish for the apostolate in workers' environments secular institutes whose members could be taken from priests and lay persons, of whom the latter could pursue the apostolate of work without temporal limits. The priests give their lay brothers a basic instruction and spiritual formation adapted to the workers' life, advise them in their problems, and support them in their difficulties.

The community called "of the Prado" after one of the former amusement sites purchased by the founder in a slum quarter of Lyon, worked with mission teams, three to five strong, of priests and lay brothers, who settled in the midst of workers' areas and earned their own livelihood. Auxiliary Bishop Alfred Arcel pursued a cobbler's trade in Lyon-Gerland as head of a team in homework until 1959. He had to give up this activity but remained superior of the "Prado" and, as auxiliary bishop, collaborator with Cardinal Gerlier.

The basic feature common to the religious movements here discussed, the spirituality from which they arose or by which they were stamped in their course, is difficult to pinpoint. The spirituality of these decades seems most clearly characterized by a Christocentrism that is oriented to the apostolate. The historical

Jesus, "Christ our Brother," came alive again: Jesus assumed our concrete life and fulfilled it in his death and resurrection. In his passage, *Pascha,* through death to glory he expanded his existence — limited to him as an individual during his earthly life — to the "mystical Christ," who has us participate by baptism in his destiny and his divine life. This is accomplished in the Church, which is the body of Christ mysteriously united to it in a living unity. The new life of the child of God, Christ in us and we in Christ, is a task for the Christian. He should form his life and the world in Christ to the honor of God the Father. But Christocentrism means not a spiritualistic reversion to individualistic interiority or flight from the world, but, on the contrary, the stressing of the fully human and of the world, which is included in the spiritual life.

If in Jesus Christ divinity and humanity have become a personal unity, without admixture or separation, then the "yes" to Christ means also a "yes" to people and to his earthly creation. The human is not annihilated in him but confirmed and surrendered. "If the human and earthly, nature and culture, are to be accepted, then this happens on the highest and purest level in Christ's human nature." "The miracle, the shocking, does not lie in a man's becoming God but in the incarnation of God. This makes the Christian exult" (Karl Adam).

Like theology, so also spirituality stands under the sign of a turning to the world: the taking seriously of one's own worth and one's own destiny in the light of the mystery of the incarnation of God. Creation and incarnation are seen in intimate connection. The Logos, in whom everything was created, became Man in order to lead everything back to God. The incarnation is not intended first with reference to redemption from sin; it is the goal and crown of creation and would have happened even without the fall into sin. "Through him and by him everything was created" (Col. 1:16). God's "yes" to the world in creation finds its confirmation and fulfillment in the incarnation. From here on one strives to refute by word and deed Nietzsche's charge and that of the Marxists, that Christ misused the world for a beyond, that Christianity is far from people and their problems.

The salvation history line — creation, incarnation, Parousia — makes one think of Jean Daniélou's *Secret of History* (1953), and of Hans Urs von Balthasar's *Theology of History* (1950), but again makes one aware of the eschatological feature of Christianity in contrast to an often too optimistic incarnational theology.

In asceticism the active virtues were more strongly stressed. It was explained that the Christian can only assure his own salvation if he is concerned for the salvation of the others. The diversity of Christian manifestation in a rapidly changing political, economic, and social environment became clear and with it the necessity of again preparing for it. This required a greater measure of personal responsibility and gave to the spiritual and moral life an unequally greater dynamism. It penetrated more strongly into the awareness that not only the human acts directly related to God — prayer, meditation, and liturgy — are religious, but everything that is done for the honor of God, in accord with Paul's statement: "Whether you eat or drink or whatever else you do, do all for the glory of God" (1 Cor. 10:31). Thus it is significant that on the four-hundredth anniversary of the death of Saint Ignatius (d. 1556) "in actione contemplativus" or the "to find God in all things" was stressed as the message of the saint for our day. It corresponds to this, that "working-day sanctity" became the characteristic slogan for the spirituality of religious movements, and the "little way" of Thérèse of Lisieux obtained new luster. In contrast to the disillusioned and self-centered Christocentrism of the *Devotio moderna,* for the "little" Thérèse it meant to love Jesus above all, to save souls for him, in order that he might be loved more.

CHAPTER 92

Developments in the Clergy since 1914

The Swiss theologian Hans Urs von Balthasar, on the occasion of the Third Synod of Bishops at Rome in 1971, expressed the conviction that the clergy is today "the clear trouble spot of the Church." In this connection he had in mind the role of priests within the postconciliar development, especially within the reform of the liturgy just as much as the alarming tendencies in the clergy itself and its relations to the episcopate.

The most recent "priestly crisis" cannot be understood and properly explained against the background of the immediately preceding decades. Its roots go deeper. At the beginning of our century individual priests and groups of priests had taken an interest in bridging the chasm between Church and theology on the one side and the modern world and its temper on the other side, and hence had demanded reforms within the Church. Even then there was question of the language of the liturgy, of church discipline, of the Church's stance in the social question, as well as of problems of the clerical state, for example, the obligation to celibacy, the relations between priests and bishops, and the form of clerical education. As widespread as the aims of such priestly groups were their motivation and character.

All these initiatives in the clergy, effected independently of the episcopate and directed to inner church reform goals, fell under Pius X's suspicion of modernism and were suppressed in this Pope's struggle against the heresy assumed by him to be everywhere. The encyclical on modernism, *Pascendi,* of 8 September 1907, again forbade priests to take the editorship of newspapers and periodicals without the previous permission of the bishops, who were moreover obliged to supervise the activity of priests as reporters or collaborators on such publications. The bishops should permit congresses of priests only in very rare cases. At the same time the Scholastic orientation of theological studies and strict rules for the education of priests in seminaries were decreed, so that the suppression of these reform groups in the clergy succeeded, especially since the First World War and the subsequent upheavals left no room for a further confrontation with modernism that was not desired by Benedict XV.

Between the two world wars there appeared or developed a few associations of priests, which pursued, however, purely religious and ascetical or legal and economic aims. There were no tensions worthy of mention between episcopate and clergy. The system of the strictly secluded seminary training functioned, even if it was already regarded as antiquated and occasionally smiled at by more far-sighted academic teachers and numerous students. However, there was no thought of a fundamental reform but of assisting in a mild practical application of the existing order. Exegetes, dogmaticians, and church historians, especially in the state academic chairs in Germany, were able to distinguish between research hypotheses and results and what might have been publicly represented and published.

A limited field of activity for autonomous reform tendencies of the younger clergy that were not always familiar to and approved by the episcopate was supplied especially in Germany by the youth movement and, in connection with it, the liturgical movement in the 1920s and 1930s. The introduction of the "community Mass" with the recitation of the vernacular translation parallel to the Latin Mass texts occurred not without tensions between liturgically active circles of youthful priests and the older pastors or the episcopate. Also the beginnings of the ecumenical movement were in no way under the encouraging benevolence of all bishops. Nevertheless there prevailed among the diocesan clergy a relationship of serene loyalty between priests and bishops.

The worker-priests in France can be regarded as a first movement in the clergy in which postconciliar points of discussion on the priestly state and priestly life seemed to be anticipated. It is characteristic of its starting situation in the early 1940s that this movement was begun by the French episcopate: When during the war several thousand French seminarians and members of Catholic Action were forced to work in German factories, the bishops of France founded a secret pastoral work to take care of them. Twenty-five priests put themselves at their disposal. The experience of this enterprise with an entirely different priestly activity and life-style constituted the basis for the *Mission de Paris* after 1946. Renouncing the middle-class manner of life, priests sought to live as workers among the workers. However, it soon appeared that, because of the solidarity with the working class and its social and political goals, conflicts with the ecclesiastical authorities could not be avoided. The relations of the worker-priests to the parish priests were increasingly strained. The bishops of France were partly concerned for the social position of the worker-priests, the Roman Curia rather for their spiritual life. In 1953–54 the experiment was interrupted at Rome's direction.

The Second Vatican Council expressed itself in two decrees on the formation and on the ministry and life of priests, but the question of priests did not supply any of the council's central subjects. For the succeeding unrest among priests quite other statements of the council were of indirect but all the more persistent effectiveness, above all the dogmatic constitution *Lumen gentium,* with its new self-understanding of the Church as the pilgrim "People of God," but also the higher valuation of the general priesthood of the faithful and the opening to the world in the pastoral constitution *Gaudium et spes.*

With the end of the council there began in Europe and America a theological discussion on the raison d'être of a priesthood based on a sacramental ordination and undertaken for life. Do the beginnings in the New Testament offer a dogmatically satisfactory justification? it was asked. The lack of priests, the permanent diaconate restored by the council, and the higher valuation of the general priesthood of the faithful as well as their being entrusted with pastoral services hitherto reserved to priests made unavoidable the question in what did the *differentia specifica* of the ordained priest consist in contrast to other believers active in the pastoral ministry. If the priesthood as a special state, in contrast to the rest of the faithful, came under discussion in relation to theology and the inner structure of the Church, the decline of authority during those years in the Western democracies went out of the way to make acute the question of the self-understanding and role of the priest in Church and society. Just as in the secular sphere only authority based on objective competence and transmitted for a limited time would be tolerated, so too priests and their "solidarity groups" that were being established demanded that the official priestly ministry be justified, no longer sacramentally (vertically) but functionally, that is, by service to the congregation (horizontally); it had to be bestowed for a time and, depending on the circumstances, could be exercised in a secondary occupation.

Younger priests especially were affected by these considerations. At first, these considerations led to their demanding the abandonment of priestly dress and class privileges. For many there lay here the profession that sacramental ordination did not essentially distinguish the priest from the other members of the People of God.

Parallel to the discussion over the office and function of the priest and in inner dependence on it was a confrontation over the obligation of priests to celibacy. At the council there had been widely opposed standpoints and motions on the extension of this obligation and its theological justification within the Decree on the Ministry and Life of Priests. Pope Paul VI had finally rendered the discussion harmless when on 10 October 1965 he sent a letter to the president of the Conciliar Praesidium, Cardinal Tisserant, in which he requested that the question of celibacy not be discussed in full council and announced a statement to the clergy on priestly celibacy. This letter determined the further decisions of the council fathers. In number 16 of the Decree on the Ministry and Life of Priests it was recognized that celibacy is "not demanded by the very essence of the priesthood, as the practice of the Ancient Church and the tradition of the Eastern Churches show. . . . But celibacy is in many respects proper to the priesthood." As justification were cited the identification of the priest with Christ and the greater availability for the priestly ministry.

If it is hardly possible to obtain exact figures on the number of those who abandoned the official priesthood, still the research of the Swiss Pastoral Sociological Institute must have come close to reality when it reckoned between 1963 and 1970 from twenty-two to twenty-five thousand resignations in the diocesan clergy, corresponding to 5 percent of the clergy. Especially alarming is the preponderance of younger priests among those leaving. This trend converged with the shockingly declining number of candidates for the priesthood and especially of priestly ordinations.

This distressing development may have induced Paul VI very soon to redeem the promise to the council fathers of a statement on priestly celibacy. The encyclical *Sacerdotalis caelibatus* of 24 June 1967 did not, however, contribute to relaxing the tensions over the celibacy discussion but rather made them more acute. The Pope adopted the essential statements of the conciliar decree on the celibacy of priests, but continued in the justification of celibacy, in the retaining of the union of the priestly vocation and the obligation of celibacy as well as in the estimation of those who abandoned the priesthood as "pitiable deserters" in the traditional ideas and arguments.

The dissatisfaction with the celibacy encyclical must have been one of the determining events for the founding, still in preparation, of the solidarity groups of priests in various European countries. Thus the meetings and publication organs of these groups were then also the forum in which the demands and expectations in regard to the celibacy question were articulated not as representing the entire clergy — the groups included only a very small percentage of priests — but still for an active stratum of younger priests in the Western hemisphere. It was again and again stressed that it was not a question of suppressing celibacy as a freely accepted charism but of ending the legal obligation of celibacy for all priests of the Latin Church. Even more strongly was it demanded that tried men in the married state, *viri probati,* be admitted to priestly ordination — a demand that had already been rejected by the council — and married priests allowed to exercise their office further.

The effort to represent such demands, especially the specifically professional, more effectively, to find solidarity for episcopally disapproved experiments in liturgy and pastoral care, or even to effect changes of awareness in favor of ecclesiastical or political reforms, was the basis on which, from the beginning of 1968, priest groups appeared in various European countries. To be sure, in ARTICLE 7 of the decree on priests the council had obliged the bishops to establish a Priests' Senate, representing the *presbyterium* of the diocese, and in many countries this directive of the council had already been complied with. But the Priests' Senates found their place and field of activity only slowly among the existing and canonically firmly established advisory bodies of the dioceses. In any event, they proved to be unsuited to parry and overcome the unrest in the clergy. With surprising rapidity there arose organized associations and principle papers on the diocesan level, but also supranational contacts.

The priest groups in the various European nations had a different orientation conditioned by the political and inner-ecclesiastical situation. The German SOG groups developed an overwhelmingly professionally specified goal, which was critical of the hierarchy. The Netherlands group *Septuagint* occupied an influential position in the contemporary development process of the Dutch Church. It was supported by broad strata of the clergy and faithful and had continuous contact with the Dutch bishops. The French groups, *Concertation* and especially *Échanges et Dialogue,* stood in an extraordinarily tense relation with the hierarchy.

The very differently structured and oriented European priest groups reached the apogee of their importance in 1969 when they met, so to speak, as a contrasting program to the contemporary episcopal symposium, at Chur from 5 to 10 July, and, parallel to the Second Synod of Bishops, from 10 to 16 October at Rome, for a "Conference of Delegates of European Priest Groups." On these occasions, the groups, their aims, and their style of procedure in regard to the bishops, going beyond all the usual amenities, became familiar to the public. At Chur the delegates demanded admittance to the episcopal symposium, which had chosen as its theme "The function of the priest today." But the bishops refused to admit the priests' representatives; there were indeed contacts on the periphery, some informal talks between individual bishops and delegates of the priests.

The Conference of Delegates of Priest Groups at Chur passed several resolutions, which were put together by the sharply antihierarchical French group, *Échanges et Dialogue:* the "Resolution on Work, Resolution on Celibacy," "Resolution on the Commitment of Priests." In addition there were a text on "The Permanent and the Changing in the Episcopal Office in the Church," which presented a reply to the talk of Cardinal Döpfner on the same subject to the episcopal symposium, and a letter "To our Brother in Peter's Office, Paul VI."

Three months later in Rome the next conference of delegates, on the occasion of the Synod of Bishops, wanted to be received by Paul VI, but the Pope refused. The conference, in the rooms of the Waldensian faculty, worked for a theological elaboration of the priests' insecurity as to role but was under stronger internal tensions than the meeting at Chur. There appeared only "study documents" of which it was said: "The texts are not accepted in all individual formulations, they are not regarded as definitive statements but as the point of departure for new reflections." The themes were: "On the Local Church" "On the Bishop," "On the Petrine Ministry," "A Church for the World," "Ministry of the Priest."

It seems that with these two large conferences of 1969 the Priest-Group Movement had already exceeded its high point. The European groups were themselves aware that they had got themselves too much entangled in a — partly only due to prevailing circumstances — class problem. The radical attempts at a public overcoming of these problems aroused only in passing the interest of the ecclesiastical and nonecclesiastical public, did not further assist those immediately concerned, and at times gave the impression of a new "left" clericalism. And so the organizers of the "Congress of Priestly Solidarity" at Amsterdam from 28 September to 3 October 1970 sought for ways to a new contact with the people and the world. The meeting had as its theme "Church in Society," and non-European, especially South American, priest groups were also invited. But the course of the congress revealed an internal discord and a considerable difference of opinion between the European groups, hitherto predominantly concerned with questions of class, and the Latin Americans, arguing from a political revolutionary standpoint. And there was disappointment over the slight public interest. The priest groups and their publication organs either disbanded expressly on their own or they quietly discontinued their work. Some still vegetated for a while without attracting attention. More enduring than these progressive groups were the traditionalist priest groups that arose or revived as a reaction, for example, the "Movement for Pope and Church," which found its adherents predominantly in the middle and older generations of the clergy.

The bishops met the inner insecurity and external solidarity in the clergy totally unprepared. How did the papacy and the territorial episcopates react? The gamut extended, at first, from surprised nervousness by way of helplessly watching patience to the attempt at open dialogue with the priests on the edges of the conferences at Chur and Rome.

The German bishops made a very early theological contribution of high quality to the overcoming of the priests' crisis by the doctrinal letter on the priestly office issued at their plenary meeting on 11 November 1969. In a biblical and dogmatic consideration the bishops sought to clarify what had become unsure: the understanding of the office of priest based on the New Testament and developed in the history of the Church. This document of the German bishops was of importance for the choice of themes and the course of the Third Synod of Bishops at Rome in 1971. "The Priestly Ministry" was one of its chief themes. The document issued by this Synod, "The Office of Priest," was decisively stamped by Cardinal Höffner and Hans Urs von Balthasar. It led beyond the biblical-dogmatic consideration to a statement on the basic questions of priestly ministry and priestly life.

Parallel to these exertions for a theological and spiritual mastering of the crisis of the priesthood proceeded the attempt at an inventory carried out by sociological methods. Even if the priest groups with their radical programs represented only a minority, in the years after the close of the Second Vatican Council it became in general ever clearer that the clergy no longer constituted a closed unity among themselves and with the bishops. The uncertainty in regard to this phenomenon offered to some territorial episcopates the occasion to permit or even to commission surveys or inquiries among their priests by scholarly institutes employing the methods of the public-opinion poll. From 1969 to 1972 such inquiries, more or less simultaneously but independent of one another, took place in the Netherlands, the German Federal Republic, Italy, Austria, Switzerland, Spain, and the United States. Not counting the Netherlands, about 43 percent of the Catholic priests of the world were affected by this wave of interrogation. Definite common tendencies and also regional differences are clearly visible.

The questions which were submitted to the priests referred first to the background, development, and living conditions of priests. Precisely in this area considerable differences appeared among the individual countries. A second series of questions dealt with the functions of the priest and the difficulties connected with them. Understanding of function and calling, spiritual life, and celibacy constituted a third complex, with which finally was closely associated the relationship of the priests to the Church and the authorities. The outcome of the interrogations operated on the one hand in a sobering and at the same time calming manner after the shocking rise of the priest groups. There could no longer be overlooked what people had long not been ready to admit: "The priesthood is not monolithic, a broad spectrum of pastoral and theological positions is recognizable, and hence an inner-ecclesiastical tension, which appears to some as fatal, to others as a sign of hope. There is hardly a question of fundamental importance any more on which priests would be of one opinion and on which they would not express themselves very clearly in one sense or another" (Schmidtchen). An increasing stratum of younger priests in Europe and the United States is critical of the "vertical" understanding of the priestly office and bases the priestly ministry not so much in relation to sacramental priestly ordination as a result of preaching and the administration of the sacraments, as rather "horizontal-functional" in the sense of a service to mankind and to the unity of the congregation. With this understanding of the office is united the rejection of a special priestly state, clerical dress, and the joining of the priestly office and obligatory celibacy, which is found to be not adequately based theologically and burdensome. Even more definitely than the demand for the "uncoupling" of priesthood and obligatory celibacy was the demand for the admission of proved married men to the priesthood. With this notion of the office and of the appropriate manner of life of the priest there was joined in the younger clergy a critical attitude toward ecclesiastical authority and its carrying out of its office, the demand that priests and lay persons take part in the calling of the holders of office, just as an extensive collaboration in pastoral work and the leading of the community be intended for the laity in general.

In an inquiry among the German priesthood candidates in 1974, "in their open, partly critical attitude the priesthood candidates are much like the young priests — in general, they entirely resemble them rather than the older ones. But then the new must be noticed: a different, perhaps strengthened drive toward spirituality. Among the authenticating ideas of the candidates there are clearly prominent the concepts of being borne by Christ's commission and of the personal relation to God" (Schmidtchen).

With this a last and decisive effect of the crisis of the priesthood is touched: the insecurity and decimation of the recruits for the priesthood. Parallel to the forming of solidarity groups of younger priests there occurred in European and American countries a convulsion of the previous system of seminary education and theological studies. Everywhere the number of priesthood candidates dropped strongly, so that not a few diocesan seminaries and religious houses of studies had to close. In particular, the strictly isolated manner of life of the seminaries could not be maintained. Seminarians demanded the possibility of being permitted to live individually or in groups in the midst of the other students in their places of study. The previous curriculum of theological studies, the narrow Neo-Scholastic dogmatic theology, the unconnected juxtaposition of theological disciplines in the program of studies, the unsatisfactory inclusion of didactic-pedagogical and pastoral-practical disciplines, were perceived as inadequate for the preparation for priestly and other pastoral ministries, especially as soon the number of students, even of females, increased, who began a study of theology without the intention of becoming priests. The education of such students in Germany, for a chiefly professional career as teachers of religion, demanded the development of corresponding programs of study and organization of examinations, which were included in the framework of the formation of other teachers.

The concern for a reorganization of the seminary education of priests and of theological studies had already occupied the Second Vatican Council. The decree *Optatam totius* on the formation of priests, of 28 October 1965, was characterized by some, chiefly the Protestant observers at the council, as one of the most productive and important conciliar texts. In balanced instructions the way was pointed to a reform of priestly formation and, for the first time with this clarity, the value of human maturity and the properties of character esteemed by people in prospective priests was stressed. In the discussions it became clear that the demands for a reform of priestly education were very different in the several continents and countries. And so the council decided on an incisive shifting of competencies in the area of priestly formation: no longer the curial Congregation of Studies and Seminaries, but the episcopal conferences should in the future have the legislative competence for this sphere.

In 1966–67 Cardinal Garrone, prefect of the Congregation of Studies and Seminaries, in four circulars admonished the chairmen of the episcopal conferences to carry out this mandate quickly. However, many episcopal conferences were taken unawares by the reorganization in the training of priests and were in no position to achieve a required reorganization in the brief time, so that it was possible only to attempt national educational organizations. Hence on the occasion of the First Synod of Bishops in 1967 Cardinal Garrone arranged for a *Ratio Fundamentalis*, a framework for the education of priests throughout the world. In it lay the danger that the Congregation of Studies and Seminaries would again take over the competence which the council had just granted to the episcopal conferences. However, the *Ratio Fundamentalis Institutionis Sacerdotalis* of 6 January 1970 avoided this danger. It produced an orientation framework for the legislation of the episcopal conferences with a proposal in examples and preformulations, which took none of their competence from the bishops. When the reform of priestly formation was perceived as urgent under the pressure of contemporary circumstances, the determination showed that the episcopal conferences within a year should draw up a *Ratio Nationalis* and submit it to the congregation for approval.

With all the imperfections and the marks of haste which adhere to the *Ratio Fundamentalis*, it must as a whole be regarded as a positive framework for priestly education outlined against the background of the situation existing in many countries. In content it follows the *schema* of the decree *Optatam totius* and is concerned with the pastoral theology of the clerical vocation, seminaries and their direction. the candidates for the priesthood, their human, spiritual, scholarly, and pastoral formation, as well as with the continuing education of the priests after their seminary days. The necessity of some continuing professional training was at this time definitely demanded in the survey of priests by priests of Latin countries, formed in a narrow Neo-Scholasticism and exclusively educated in isolated seminaries, and it constituted one of the central points of the program of the priest groups of Europe and South America. The delay of a year, determined in the *Ratio Fundamentalis*, for the setting up of regional or territorial organizations of priestly formation was not to be observed for the reason that not only the territorial episcopates but also others who were to take part — regents, directors of boarding schools, professors — had to prepare for a cooperation and finally for an agreement. The work on the *Rationes Nationales* was not finished in a moment. The acute crisis seemed to be followed by a phase of sober seeking. It would be a fallacy to assume that the development would quickly lead back to the interior and exterior uniformity characteristic of the clergy in the first half of this century.

This insight must have been the occasion for the traditionalist groups in the clergy, especially for the movement around the former missionary Bishop Marcel Lefebvre, to forcibly bring about this uniformity in the education, theology, spirituality, and discipline of priests by a return to old forms and with radical means. In this connection Lefebvre appeals, not without reason, to Pius X and the struggle of this Pope against the dangers of modernism and its reform efforts.

CHAPTER 93

Religious Communities and Secular Institutes

The Orders between Persistence and Change

The history of religious institutes of the nineteenth century was characterized by the unanticipated resurgence of the old orders and the founding of many new congregations. When the First World War broke out, this period drew to a close. Most religious institutes had been consolidated and found their manner of life and field of action, and there began for them a period of unforeseen growth. In the years 1920–60 almost all religious communities experienced a hitherto unprecedented influx of novices. This extraordinarily strong accumulation was certainly conditioned also by external factors — the world economic crisis with massive unemployment; inadequate possibilities for education and professional goals outside the monastery, especially for women. Nevertheless, in the case of most of the young people who decided for the religious life, this choice was based on religious motives. Readiness for commitment to the Church and for service to people, as well as concern for the salvation of one's soul, were an effective motive in the decision for the religious vocation.

The end of the First World War presented the communities with a new situation: the peace treaties altered the map of Europe. Because of this, the institutes were compelled to adapt their own structures to the new boundaries; in particular, the national states just established were not pleased that their religious should be directly subject to foreign tribunals. On the other hand, the events of the war contributed to a destruction of the state-Church system and of some laws hostile to the Church, so that now also for the orders previously existing legal restrictions and state regulations disappeared. The great misery which the First World War left and which was intensified by the subsequent economic crisis meant a challenge for the institutes, especially in the social and charitable sphere.

Within the Church the new Code of Canon Law meant some significant changes for the religious institutes. They not only aimed at a generally welcomed simplification, at greater clarity and legal security, but they bore an especially emphatic pastoral, spiritual accent. The legislator had obviously striven to create a legal order which should facilitate an authentic religious life. Of course, this all-inclusive codification of the canons for religious also involved negative consequences. The prescriptions of the canons for religious, partly going into great detail, attempted, it is true, through repeated references to the particular law of the individual institutes, to take account of the variety of religious life, but nevertheless promoted a considerable thrust toward uniformity and the leveling of the religious life. Since Canon 489 annulled all regulations of rules and statutes which were contrary to the norms of the code, the institutes were asked to adapt their constitutions to the new code, and, in making the necessary changes, to employ where possible the words of the code itself. On 6 March 1921 the Congregation of Religious published norms for the formulation of the statutes of the new congregations.

All these prescriptions confirmed the tendency already discernible under Leo XIII to centralize the structure of the religious life; in particular, the institutes of papal right should be united more closely to Rome. The prescription proved to be especially harmful in the long run which required that the constitutions must contain neither historical references nor quotations from Scripture, the councils, the Fathers, or the works of other authors, and a fortiori no rather long ascetical directions, detailed spiritual admonitions, or mystical reflections. They should be confined instead to the canonical decisions on the special character of the respective institute, its aims and functions, on the essential content of the vows, on the acquiring and loss of membership, on the life-style of the religious, as well as on the government of the institute. If brief spiritual texts were tolerated, this narrowing of the fundamental document of each institute favored a lasting codification of the institute's life, especially as it was no longer clear that the canonical decrees on the structure of religious life were derived from spiritual foundations. Also it could not fail to happen that the new statutes of many institutes in their structure and content looked very much alike and so the character of the individual institutes threatened more and more to disappear.

Still, many of the young people who entered the monastery found spiritual and religious security in the existing strict organization. Incorporation was facilitated for them by the patterns of religious life which were given to them. In the instructions of the novitiate more was said about constancy and submission, sacrifice and renunciation, obedience and confidence in the superiors than about innovation, self-development, and personal initiative, just as the Church itself proved to be very much an unshakable institution and guarantor of order and security in the breakdown of the period between the wars.

But developments in Church and society were not without their effects on monasteries. The liturgical movement and the striving for a piety nourished on Holy Scripture evoked disgust among religious with the prayer formulas and devotional exercises of some communities, as well as with the often very petty directives of a moral and ascetical character which governed the everyday life, even in details, and left little room for personal responsibility. More and more the lack of a religious life directly oriented to the Bible was felt. Besides, religious in many countries saw themselves challenged by a growing secularization of public life and the alienation of many from the Church. Measures hostile to the Church, suppressions of monasteries, and open persecution presented existentially to the religious affected by them the question of their vocation. Religious often found themselves inadequately equipped for an intellectual confrontation with an environment which faced the Christian faith with indifference, rejection, or even hostility.

The Second World War and its consequences tore many institutes of men and women from their traditional organization and transplanted them to situations in which they had to come to independent decisions and prove themselves in their spiritual vocation without being able to count on leadership and guidance "from above."

The Rise of New Types of Communities

Against this background must be viewed the origin of new kinds of communities. As early as the turn of the century Charles de Foucauld (1858–1916) planned to establish a community of Little Brothers of Jesus that departed from the traditional structures. In the following years he sketched several rules but at his violent death he left behind no disciples. The seed he had scattered sprang up only later. In 1933 René Voillaume and some followers founded at El-Abiodh-Sidi-Cheikh on the edge of the Sahara the community of the Little Brothers of Jesus, which was recognized as a congregation of episcopal right in 1936 and in 1968 obtained a papal decree of approbation. The Little Brothers of Jesus live in brotherhoods of usually three to five members, preferably in environments which are not accessible to the Christian message or are entirely alienated from it. They want to attest the love of God less through preaching than through solidarity with the people among whom they live. Their model is Jesus, the worker of Nazareth. Their effort is to shun all division. And so they make themselves with their work a part of the occupational world of their neighborhood, live in small dwellings which are in keeping with the milieu, and extensively adjust themselves to their environment in the externals of life. Their spirituality is characterized by a piety which is nourished especially on the cult of the Eucharist and reflection on Scripture. Every brotherhood is directed by a "responsible person," and the entire congregation is subject to the superior general. In the same spirit there arose in 1939 at Touggourt in the Sahara the community of the Little Sisters of Jesus, which was erected as a congregation of episcopal right in 1947 and in 1964 obtained a papal decree of commendation. To it belong 990 sisters in 212 communities. These religious communities inspired by Foucauld's spirit differ from the traditional institutes especially through a strong emphasis on brotherhood, which should be experienced in the small community, the team, through a new interpretation and realization of poverty, which is understood as wholehearted common destiny with the strata of population oppressed by poverty with all their insecurity and lack of protection, and through their unobtrusive presence "in the heart of the masses" "in the midst of the world," where they intend to influence through nothing other than their exemplary Christian life. Later arose other communities, which likewise were oriented to Charles de Foucauld, as in 1956 the fraternity of the Brothers of the Virgin of the Poor, to whom the model for their contemplative life is Jesus, praying and doing penance in the desert, and the community of Little Brothers of the Gospel, erected as a congregation of episcopal right in 1968, who also wish to live among the poorest, not only to share their poverty in solidarity, but to preach the Gospel to these poor.

To live in the midst of the world is also the motto of the secular institutes, which in part already had existed for a long time as "pious unions" or without any ecclesiastical approval, but only found their recognition as a canonical state of perfection through the apostolic constitution *Provida Mater* of Pius XII of 2 February 1947. It is proper to the secular institutes that their members live on principle in the midst of the world. By the *character saecularis* they are essentially distinguished from the religious state, the *status religiosus,* with which, however, the striving for perfection unites them in a form approved by the Church. The wearing of a religious habit, common life in community after the manner of the orders, and in general any approximation to the life-style of the religious communities, are not in accord with the essence of a secular institute.

Meanwhile, there are many secular institutes which were established by the bishops with Rome's *Nihil obstat:* six institutes of men and twenty-one of women have so far become of papal right. The best known and most influential of them is the Opus Dei. Its male branch was founded in Spain in 1928 by the priest J. M. Escrivá de Balaguer (1902–75); on 24 February 1947, a few weeks after the appearance of *Provida Mater,* it was the first secular institute to obtain the papal decree of approval, and in 1950 it obtained definitive confirmation. This branch includes priests, who are united within the institute in the *Societas Sacerdotalis Sanctae Crucis,* and laymen, who, in accord with the statutes, must constitute the majority. The ordinary members, who must have had a complete theological program, if possible with a doctoral degree, and a broader, likewise complete training in another academic profession, as well as the "Oblates," in regard to whose education not such high claims are made, bind themselves by vows to a life according to the evangelical counsels. Even married men can be admitted as extraordinary members, who seek to realize the spirit of the evangelical counsels in a manner of life corresponding to their situation. For the rest, the members pursue their professions and exert themselves for the Christian permeation of the families, the working world, and public life. In general they are not to be known as members of the Opus Dei; usually they appear not as a group, but each works in his place in the sense of the institute, in regard to which a characteristic élite-awareness unites them. However, the institute also appears as performer of common tasks. Thus, it is responsible for the Catholic University of Navarre at Pamplona, founded in 1952 and erected by the Holy See in 1960; with its thirteen faculties and scholarly institutes it ranks as one of the best universities in Spain; a majority of professors belong to Opus Dei. Further, the institute supports centers of study and student homes in many university cities. Outside Spain, Opus Dei has spread to about fifty other countries, especially Italy, France, and Latin America. The prelature *nullius* of Yauyos in Peru is entrusted to the community of Priests of the Holy Cross. In admitting members, the institute makes no distinctions of class, but it appeals especially to intellectuals, and it is well known that members of Opus Dei occupy many important posts of the political, economic, and cultural life of Spain. The ensuing involvement in the affairs of daily politics, joined to a certain secretiveness, has led to serious attacks on the institute. In addition to the male branch, in 1930 a female branch, marked by the same spirit, was founded, which meanwhile has also obtained papal confirmation. It forms a special secular institute with independent organs of government, but is, however, subject to the president general.

The Acclimatization of the Orders in Mission Lands

New routes were also traveled in mission lands. In his encyclical *Rerum Ecclesiae* of 28 February 1926, Pope Pius XI appealed to missionaries to devote themselves more strongly to the Church's intimate relationship with these countries. He pushed not only for the training of native priests and catechists but also for the establishing of communities of male and female religious. True, he regarded it as legitimate for missionaries to admit candidates from mission lands into their own communities, but admonished the mission superiors: "Reflect...whether it would not be better to establish new religious communities which were more in accord with the concerns and interests of the natives as well as the local situation and special circumstances." He especially urged the founding of contemplative monasteries. The missionary decree of the Second Vatican Council again underscored this instruction and pointed to the necessity of making the religious life indigenous in a form suited to the respective culture and circumstances of individual peoples (ARTICLE 18).

Even if there were previously, especially in Asia, several congregations of native sisters, their number increased quickly after the appearance of the mission encyclical. It grew in Africa between 1920 and 1960 from nine to seventy-nine, although here at first great obstacles rooted in the tribal idea had to be overcome. For the ideal of the celibate life was at first totally foreign to the African mentality: a woman and her dowry were regarded as part of the wealth of her tribe, and the tribe to which she was turned over on the occasion of the marriage treasured her especially as mother of the children which she bore for the tribe. Only slowly did an understanding of the ideal of the religious life for the woman grow. The low educational status of many girls, due to the nonexistent school system, meant further impediment, especially in view of the independence of these African communities. In Asia, however, the presuppositions were much more favorable. In regard to the native applicants for the priesthood the missionaries in Asia generally preferred an integration into their own community. The cultural level of these countries facilitated such a common life.

The appeal of Pius XI for the founding of contemplative monasteries at first found no very loud echo. The mission superiors were especially concerned to gain native collaborators in the pastoral, social and charitable, and educational sphere. Only after the Second World War and especially after the Second Vatican Council did the number of contemplative foundations greatly increase. For the support and promotion of the Benedictine foundations in the Third World there arose at Vanves near Paris the *Secrétariat de l'aide à l'implantation monastique* (A.I.M.).

The strivings to make the religious life indigenous in these lands and to accommodate it to the local situations proved to be difficult. The first experiments in this area were planned and implemented by Europeans. Only the native religious succeeded by patient work in discovering an organic and enduring adaptation in fidelity both to the essential elements of the Christian religious life as well as to the cultural heritage of their own people.

Religious Reform under Pius XII

In the congregations of the new type and the secular institutes it was believed that the goal sought could not be realized in the traditional structures of religious life. New routes were sought for shaping life in accord with the evangelical counsels in a contemporary form. Meanwhile, however, there was no lack of reform plans and desires in the existing orders. However, it was in accord with reality that these were discussed in small groups of members of the orders and were not given wide publicity. It was Pope Pius XII, who as early as the first months of his pontificate, but especially from the end of the Second World War, made the *accommodata renovatio,* the renewal in accord with the times, of religious life an essential point of the program of his pontificate. This renewal should likewise be marked by fidelity to the traditional heritage as well as by courage for wise adaptation. In his talks and letters to individual religious communities he returned again and again to this great concern. The papal directives make clear that they aimed to regulate a process of fermentation which was meanwhile under way in many religious communities and was especially spelled out in some general chapters. The Pope strongly emphasized the obligation not to attack the essentials of religious life and of the particular institute and not to be unduly influenced by the current views and opinions.

The Roman Congregation of Religious took up the aim of renewal of religious life in accord with the time when, for the first time in history, in the Holy Year 1950 it convened at Rome an International Congress for (male) Religious, which dealt in many lectures and reports with the *accommodata renovatio statuum perfectionis.* This general theme was discussed in three subdivisions in regard to the life and claustral discipline of religious, their formation and instruction, and their apostolic work. Two years later a Congress of Superioresses General took place at Rome, which also treated of the question of reform of the institutes, as did the "Second General Congress on the Timely Renewal of the States of Perfection," which the Congregation of Religious summoned to Rome in 1957.

From these large congresses proceeded the stimulus for a closer collaboration of the orders, whether on the national or the international plane. In many countries appeared conferences of superiors of the male and the female institutes, which were officially recognized by the Holy See and erected as institutions of papal right. On the international level were held the *Unio Superiorum generalium* (USG) for male religious in 1957 and the *Unio internationalis Superiorissarum generalium* (UISG) for female religious in 1965, both of which took place at Rome.

Even before the first international congress met, the Pope undertook a partial reform. On 21 November 1950 he published the apostolic constitution *Sponsa Christi* on nuns, which was followed two days later by directives for its implementation from the Congregation of Religious. Entirely in the spirit of the papal reform program, these documents first underscored the unalterability of the contemplative life, the propriety of solemn vows, and the unrenounceable papal enclosure for all nuns. However, in adaptation to new requirements the rules on enclosure were modified, namely, by the creation of the so-called little papal enclosure, which permitted a meeting of nuns and outsiders in an area of the enclosure that was intended for work directed to the outside. The obligation to a proper, productive work was stressed. A broader area which stood in need of reform was that of the formation and instruction of candidates for the priesthood in religious communities. As early as 1924 in an apostolic letter to the superiors of orders Pope Pius XI had indicated the necessity of a solid education of religious clerics, oriented to the heritage of Saint Thomas. Pope Pius XII also, throughout his pontificate, was concerned for a good formation of religious, especially of the priests, through which they should be equipped for the manifold tasks which were imposed on them in the period of the upheaval that was becoming ever more clearly outlined. Finally, on 31 May 1956 appeared the apostolic constitution *Sedes Sapientiae,* followed on 7 July by general statutes of the Congregation of Religious in the form of directives for implementation. These documents treated not only the forming of candidates for orders of males and for the priesthood, but attributed great importance to their education in pastoral theology as good shepherds of souls. As something new, they prescribed by common law after the completion of the study of philosophy and theology, oriented to the care of souls but more theoretically presented, and the reception of ordination, one additional year devoted to pastoral introduction and practice. And it was urged on all religious institutes to oblige the young fathers, after several years of work, to a year of probation, a sort of second novitiate.

However, Rome's concern was not only for the education of religious priests. In an effort to equip orders of women for their tasks that were becoming more difficult, the Congregation of Religious on 31 May 1955 erected the papal institute Regina Mundi at Rome, which was associated with the theological faculty of the papal Gregorian University. In it women religious were to be prepared in a three-year theological course both for the tasks of directing the members of their institute and for pastoral charges, especially in the area of schooling and education. Rome thereby took up a burning concern of the Congress of Superioresses General of 1952.

The Second Vatican Council and Its Effects

At this stage of the process of a prudent, even timid "timely renewal" came the announcement of the Second Vatican Council, which, with its program of *aggiornamento,* aroused in wide circles of the Church, even among religious, great and partly also utopian hopes for a comprehensive reform and a profound renovation. The first schema on religious, which had been worked out by the preparatory commission, hardly went beyond what had been planned in reforms under Pius XII and had been in part introduced or implemented. It was understood as a rectilinear continuation of the Pian reform of the institutes. Hence it did not correspond to the expectations which had been placed in this conciliar document on many sides. After tenacious work in the conciliar commissions and lively debate on the place and mandate of the institutes in the Church, at the close of the council there were on hand two important texts, which were expressly concerned with the religious state. Chapter 6 of the Dogmatic Constitution on the Church (ARTICLES 43–47) aimed to define the theological place of the orders in the Church. Advisedly, the chapter on the general vocation to sanctity in the Church preceded it. The Decree on the Appropriate Renewal of the Religious Life presupposes these statements and is concerned more in detail with the principles and with particular points of the reform of religious. It is the only one of the documents issued by the council that adopted the program of *aggiornamento* in the heading, in connection with which, of course, it could refer to the formula of *accommodata renovatio* coined under Plus XII. The desired timely renewal is defined in the key statement of this decree; it mentions "constant return to the sources of every Christian life and to the spirit of the origin of the individual institutes, but at the same time their adaptation to the changed conditions of the times" (ART. 2).

The reform program which is presented in the decree on the religious life and in the directives issued for its implementation differs essentially in its presuppositions from all preceding efforts in this direction. The reform of the orders under Plus XII was effected by the Holy See and centrally directed. Little latitude was given to the individual institutes for independent decisions. The directives for implementation of the decree on religious now declares: "The religious communities have themselves above all to implement a suitable renewal of the religious life and indeed mainly by means of general chapters" (no. 1). To a special general chapter to be convoked in from two to three years was given full authority to modify particular prescriptions of the constitutions by way of experiment in so far as neither the essence nor the character of the institute was affected; they were promised that experiments contrary to the current general canon law would gladly be permitted by the Holy See, but of course it was required that they must be implemented wisely. The stage of experimentation could be extended, in accord with these guidelines, to as long as fifteen years (no. 6). In the preparation for this reform chapter all members should be involved in a suitable manner through a comprehensive and open survey (no. 4). Together with this decentralization of the reform there occurred a further revision: each institute should strive to preserve or recover its own image, because in this diversity of religious life lay a genuine advantage for the Church. The institutes should investigate the spirit and the original intentions of the founders and the proper healthy traditions and loyally maintain this special legacy in each institute. Finally, again in contrast to the prescriptions issued after the appearance of the Code of Canon Law, it was ordered that the constitutions must consist not only of canonical directives on the nature, goals, and organs of the institute, but must also contain the scriptural and theological principles of the religious life and statements on its relation to the Church and the heritage proper to the particular institutes. The spiritual and the juridical elements must constitute a unity in the constitutions. Clearly these regulations wanted to eliminate the defects which, five decades earlier, after the appearance of the Code of Canon Law, had shown up because of an excessive centralization, leveling, and legalization.

Three guiding principles were given to the reform chapters as a standard for their decrees: renewal had to take place in fidelity to the spirit of the founder and the sound traditions of the institute, in obedience to the directions of the council, and in receptiveness to the signs of the time. Now the proposed renewal of religious life is primarily a spiritual event; hence it is difficult to grasp and to measure. However, in general it can be said that the religious institutes worked in the preparation of their reform chapter and in the discussions and decrees of this chapter in the light of the documents of the Second Vatican Council for a deepened view of the religious life and an up-to-date organization, and rethought the position and mission of their institute in the Church and the world of today. Of course, the lack of clear statements of aim, approved by all, often led to tensions even within individual communities, and made difficult the discovery of jointly decided solutions. In a partly irksome learning process most reform chapters adopted a middle way. The relation to the world stood in the focus of the discussion. At stake was the answer of the institutes to secularization, their openness to the world, their responsibility for the world. Discussion was accompanied by experiment. The general chapters for the most part made vigorous use of the possibilities granted to them. Usually the desires for adaptation regarded as necessary did not break up the framework of the institute's traditional life. However, some experiments exceeded the lines laid down or slipped out of the hands of the orders' superiors. Especially the small communities, which sprouted up in some places, in particular in Holland and the United States, were and are a favorable field of experimentation for more or less radical innovations. These "communes" are obviously inspired by the life-style of the Little Brothers and Little Sisters of Jesus. If many of them proved not to be viable and soon fell apart again, this lay not least in the fact that they lacked the spiritual depth of the communities of Father de Foucauld. On the other hand, there were undoubtedly also uncontrolled growth and signs of decay. To ward off these errors and debasements was the Pope's aim when on 29 June 1971 he sent to religious the apostolic doctrinal letter *Evangelica testificatio* on the renewal of the religious life in accord with the Second Vatican Council.

The most critical and lamentable phenomenon of the recent period is the many departures from religious communities, which, together with the lack of recruits, have led to a strong rise in the ratio of the old to the total population of the houses and forced the institutes to a drastic reduction of their work in Church and society. Unfortunately, because of the absence of reliable evidence, no exact picture can be gained for the entire Church. However, spot-checks can make the trend clear. Thus in Germany the number of religious priests doubled between 1915 and 1932 from 2,015 to 4,024 and up to 1941 increased further to 5,282. This upward development continued in the postwar years and reached its climax in 1971 with 6,825 religious priests. Thereafter an at first still slow drop-off began, which however soon accelerated because of the age structure.

A similar picture is sketched in the statistics published by individual religious institutes.

The reasons for this falling-off of religious vocations in the last fifteen years are many-layered. As especially the look at the novitiate shows, the council did not cause the crisis of recruits — it was already present — it could not, however, eliminate it but rather accelerated it. Especially to be mentioned as reasons are the general insecurity, especially of young people, following the upheaval in society and Church, the uncertainty of role, conditioned by this, of many religious, the polarization of opinions becoming evident in religious communities, also a narrow presentation of marriage and sex and their significance for the autonomous development of persons, an at times unrestrained criticism of every form of authority, and the influence of the welfare and consumer society on the thought and attitude of youth in the industrialized countries. But on the other hand another circumstance must not be overlooked. The family of many children has become a rarity today, especially in the country, and so this source for religious vocations is to a great extent exhausted. Besides, today in the industrialized nations educational opportunities and professions are available to all girls, whereas earlier they were accessible almost exclusively to religious women.

The enhanced collaboration of male and female religious superiors on the national and international level since the council became of great importance. The conferences of superiors, urged as early as the Congress of Orders in 1950, were now set up in almost all countries, to the extent that they did not exist before the council. The Roman unions of superiors general and of superioresses general acquired a new importance because in a much greater degree they were invited by the congregations of the Curia for consultations and exchange of experiences. Similarly the contact of the superiors and superioresses general of missionary institutes was established with the Congregation for the Evangelization of Peoples. The "Council of Eighteen" meets several times a year with the authoritative officials of that congregation. Also outside this organizational framework the efforts of the congregations of the Curia for increased contact with the religious communities are unmistakable. The exchange of experience, which is thereby facilitated, has a very positive impact.

The Orders in the Field of Tension between Church and State

The religious institutes were especially exposed in the field of tension between Church and state. They were for the most part extraordinarily severely affected by the anti-Church measures of a government. The laws of the *Kulturkampf* had an aftereffect on the orders, partly even far into this century. In Germany the "Jesuit Law" of 1872 was not entirely repealed until 1917. Norway abolished the prohibition of Jesuits, which was incorporated into the constitution, in 1956, and in Switzerland the article on denominational exceptions in the constitution of the federation, which forbade the Society of Jesus and the "societies affiliated" with it and prohibited new foundations of all institutes, did not come to an end until after a majority of only some 55 percent of the citizens had expressed themselves in favor of its abolition in a referendum in 1973.

Hence it goes without saying that the Church, wherever there was question of negotiations for a concordat with a government, exerted itself to secure by treaty the legal situation of the institutes, their right to erect new houses, and the free exercise of the activities proper to them. In countries with a sufficient number of native religious the Church was usually prepared for the compromise that the higher superiors of the institute must have corresponding citizenship in the nation. Of course, this protection by concordats was to prove to be of little effect in many nations in the succeeding decades.

In Mexico the conflict between Church and state, going far back into the nineteenth century, reached a climax in the first decades of this century. In 1917 the country obtained a new constitution, which, among other things, forbade celibacy, religious vows, and the religious state. Religious were expelled from their houses, their schools and other institutions were closed. After two years these regulations were somewhat modified, but in 1926 they were again put into effect in full severity. Their transgression was strictly punished.

A republic was proclaimed in Spain in 1931 and a constitution put into force which had as its aim a radical separation of Church and state and hit hard at the religious institutes, since it not only subjected them to state supervision but also supplied the legal basis for the expropriation of all property of religious. The Society of Jesus was dissolved and its property was confiscated by the state. If the riots of 1931 against the Church were still locally restricted, the storm broke out furiously against the monasteries during the three-year civil war, which followed General Franco's coup d'état of 1936.

In Germany at first National Socialism found sympathizers among a certain segment of the Catholics as well as among some of the religious. An especially unfortunate role was played by an outsider, Abbot Alban Schachleiter (1861–1937), who had been expelled from his abbey, Sankt Emaus at Prague, in 1918 and had lived in Bavaria since 1921; he expected from Hitler the realization of his own German national ideas, and so from 1922 he recruited for him and his movement in talks and appeals and let himself be misused as a pretense. Energetic rebukes and even penal measures of the archiepiscopal ordinariate of Munich and of the superiors of the order could not make the aging abbot change his tune. After the seizure of power the Nazi government in ARTICLE 15 of the concordat guaranteed the freedom of religious communities and the unimpeded exercise of their activities both in the pastoral and in the educational and social and charitable sphere; the private schools of the orders were even dealt with in a special article (ART. 25). But the orders were soon able to experience the true aims of the new holders of power. This began with annoying searches of the houses and interrogations. In 1935–36 a series of show-trials was conducted, chiefly against religious because of transgressions against rules on foreign exchange; heavy sentences of imprisonment were decreed against the accused. While the trials on foreign exchange were still in progress, preparations were being made for a second series of trials against religious and priests. From the end of 1935, but especially in 1936 and 1937, the Gestapo searched in monasteries and in boarding schools and nursing homes conducted by monasteries for evidence of moral failings in order to be able to denounce the monasteries as hotbeds of immorality. The intensity of the searches, the methods employed in the inquiries, the fixing of the dates of the proceedings, ordered by the executive, as well as the carefully prepared and centrally directed evaluation for propaganda purposes make clear that the authorities were not mainly concerned for the punishment and elimination of evil situations. Instead, here the orders were to be affected in their entirety. Not by accident did the chief trials reach their climax in the months following publication of the encyclical *Mit brennender Sorge* of 14 March 1937. But above all these trials were steps toward a still more comprehensive goal that was thus formulated in a secret instruction of the Ministry for Security of 15 February 1938: "The orders are the militant arm of the Catholic Church. Hence they must be forced out of their spheres of influence, curtailed, and finally annihilated." On the most varied pretexts, but often without any justification, many religious houses were confiscated between the fall of 1940 and the spring of 1941 and the religious expelled from the monasteries or even from the very districts of their former residences, as long as they were not required for the continuance of farm work or made liable to service. These measures were stopped at the beginning of the Russian campaign, and the total annihilation of the orders was put off until the postwar period in order not to evoke further unrest among the Catholic population. Of course, these measures extended also to the countries and territories incorporated into the Reich and to the occupied areas. There they were carried out more severely and ruthlessly because no concordatal restrictions existed.

The persecution of the Church which broke out in Russia after the Bolshevik

October Revolution affected chiefly the Orthodox monasteries; however, the few Catholic religious houses were not spared. Only after the victory over Poland and when, after the Second World War, the Baltic countries and eastern Poland were definitively annexed to the Soviet Union did Catholic religious houses in large numbers fall into the Communist power sphere. In Latvia and the formerly Polish part of the Ukraine religious men and women were expelled from their houses and forced to return to civilian life; their houses fell to the state. In Lithuania, where about 80 percent of the population professed the Roman Catholic faith, such severe measures were at first not feasible. At first the government was content with a strict supervision and spying on the monasteries, but after 1944 all religious houses here were suppressed.

In the countries in which the Communists seized power after the Second World War, regard for the denominational situation likewise obviously played an important role in the proceedings. The harshest measures occurred everywhere in the years before 1956. In Albania the orders were entirely extirpated. The foreign religious were expelled, the Albanians were forced to put aside their habit and become part of the economic process. Something similar was true of Bulgaria. In Czechoslovakia all religious houses were occupied by the militia in April 1950 after a highly publicized show-trial of ten religious had taken place in Prague on the allegation of high treason. Religious of various communities were crowded into "concentration monasteries," the male and female religious still capable of work were requisitioned for places in farming and in factories. Some sisters were allowed to continue caring for the aged, the sick, and the invalids because of the lack of other personnel. "At the end of 1951 there was in all Czechoslovakia not a single religious house apart from the concentration convents, which were in reality compulsory labor camps" (A. Galter). The mitigations and relaxations of the Dubček era were again annulled, step by step. Of the 160 religious houses which there were in Rumania in 1945, only 25 still existed in 1953. The Hungarian minister for popular education, József Révai, explained in a speech delivered at the beginning of June 1950: "In the people's democracy religious are no longer needed because they no longer correspond to their vocation, indeed they sabotage the tasks of democracy. Hence it is necessary that as soon as possible it be made impossible for them further to harm the interests of democracy." Shortly thereafter began a wave of deportations of religious. The Hungarian episcopate tried to avert the worst and on 30 August 1950 signed a treaty, which, among other things, provided that eight Catholic schools — six for boys, two for girls — might again be opened and the religious needed for the administration of their schools continue in this function. A *numerus clausus* was imposed on these communities in regard to the acceptance of new members. All other religious communities were suppressed in September 1950 against the protest of the episcopate, and the approximately ten thousand male and female religious were ordered to leave their houses within three months, to discard the habit, and to take up a secular occupation.

In Yugoslavia the situation of the orders in the first ten years of Communist rule was no less miserable. In Bosnia-Herzegovina and Slovenia all religious houses were suppressed and many religious were arrested and killed. In the mid-1950s there occurred a relaxation of tension, which had as a consequence an amazing revival of the orders, especially in the republics of Slovenia and Croatia, where the number of members of the orders has risen considerably since 1958.

A similar picture results for Poland. Here at first there were years of misery and distress. Religious were removed from schools, hospitals, and other institutions. Up to 1953, 54 religious had been killed, 200 deported, 170 thrown into prison. On 14 April 1950 an agreement was reached between the government and the Polish episcopate, which in ARTICLE 19 contains the guarantee: "Orders and congregations of religious will have full freedom of action in the framework of their calling and the laws in force." Nevertheless, at first there occurred further imprisonments. Not until the mid-1950s did the situation calm down, and the number of religious has since then grown significantly, both in the male and the female institutes.

In China and North Korea there are no more religious houses. The foreign missionaries were expelled, the not inconsiderable number of native religious were sent home in so far as they did not perish.

The glance at the last six decades of church history shows how very much the orders live in and with the Church. Periods in which ecclesiastical life flourished were for the orders times of interior and exterior growth and vitality; in ages of crisis, on the contrary, they proved to be especially vulnerable. This dependence on the total ecclesiastical climate, however, must not cause the orders to forget that in all generations healing influences and impulses are expected from them.

CHAPTER 94

Educational System, Education, and Instruction

Church and Society in Their Relation to the Educational System

The influence which the Church can exert on the educational system of our time is dependent on its position in the social and political system of the moment, the legal, moral, and material conditions prevailing in it, the relations of the Church's educational mission to the expectations of the population or, respectively, the aims of the government — and all this is often dependent on the history in which and out of which the Church's educational efforts have acquired their national character. The influence thus depends also on the Church itself: from its understanding of its function and from the ideas and energies which it proclaims in favor of its educational mission and which can apply to the apostolic mission in the stricter sense and to the service of the world in the broader sense.

In Europe the educational system, earlier established by the Church and for a long time determined by it, lost much ground after the introduction of the general obligation of going to school, the taking over of schools and universities by the state, the emphasizing of science and of the secular in instruction, and the rapid increase of voluntary school attendance — *explosion scholaire.* Educational systems with overwhelmingly Catholic — for example, in Belgium — or at least nonstate educational institutions — for example, the Netherlands — are the exception. In the United States the Catholic educational system has powerfully gained in substance in the course of this century and has reached a point where further increases scarcely seem any longer possible, and the distinction in regard to the education and formation imparted in non-Catholic institutions is beginning to decrease. In the Latin American nations there is, it is true, a stability in Catholic educational institutions, but the great task of mass education which cannot be accomplished by them reduces their earlier importance. In the missions of the nations of the Third World the situation is determined by the form of decolonization, "nation building," and socio-economic development; Socialist regimes which are modeled on the protecting powers of the Communist camp, whether dominated by Moscow or Peking, are hostile to the Church's educational mission; the same is true where a non-Christian religion, such as Islam, is the state religion. More favorable are the circumstances in countries supported by Western powers. In the Communist states of Europe and Asia the Church was radically excluded from the educational system.

On the whole few generalizations can be made on the present state of the educational system established or determined by the Church or oriented to it. The generalization according to which the impact of the religious factor in instruction and education slackens and the Church is either excluded from the educational system or withdraws from it is surely too sweeping. For it mistakes the new type of exchange relations between Church and society as they were expressed and urged in the pastoral constitution *Gaudium et spes* and introduced a turning in Catholic school policy.

While before the Second Vatican Council the Catholic Church understood education as an integrating element of an educational process of the faithful to be religiously founded and forming part of the Church's responsibility, and accordingly placed the greatest value on the institutionalization of the "Catholic school," the Protestant Church, at least in Germany, had given up such ideas since the 1950s. In its 1958 declaration of the school question the Protestant Church in Germany made known that it understood itself not first of all as an educational power struggling for influence but as the custodian of liberty. In this was expressed the Lutheran conviction, preserved in Protestantism, of the necessity of a "strictly secular government." Here school no longer meant — a few years before the pastoral constitution *Gaudium et spes* — an innate function of the Church but an objective task which could be provided for in a worldly and sensible way, even in collaboration with non-Christians.

The educational system is not only the means and addressee of ecclesiastical influence; it also has an impact of its own on the Church. Such repercussions occur over the conditions of formation of the ecclesiastical recruits — state reforms of education, in Germany: the altered status of humanistic programs, and so forth — over changes in the curriculum and of the conditions of scholarship in which theology is expressed, over the type of teaching in religious instruction — the didactics of religious instruction — and not least over the expansion of the hitherto charitably restricted services in the field of school and nursing through the professionalization of the teaching personnel. These changes got under way on a broad front without its being already discernible which formula — rationalization of the *mysterium,* adaptation to the world, loss of the *philosophia perennis,* dissolution of unity or viable diversity, dialogue, new catholicity, and so forth — is suited conclusively to describe the direction of the process.

Catholic Educational and School Doctrine

The doctrinal expressions of the Popes on the educational system must be understood as concretizations, relevant to the occasion and the time, of the apostolic task of the Church to proclaim and attest the message of Jesus Christ, to assure the conditions for the realization of this apostolate against encroachments and decay and constantly to improve it and in this regard to express ever more strongly the personal importance of education and solidarity with those who, like UNESCO since 1946, have also set as their goal the education and training of all peoples.

In the first half of the twentieth century the Church was interested in retaining Christian education intact as an integral element of formation in and spreading of the faith. The Holy See exerted itself in the reorganization of the educational system in Europe after the First World War to assure the Church's interests by diplomatic means — the concordat policy — by the encouraging of ecclesiastical educational institutions, for example, the recognition of universities as "papal universities," by establishing a Christian educational system independent of the state, and by support of the missions, especially under Pius XI, to promote the spread of the faith through educational institutions. At the same time, that is, from the end of the First World War, the Popes, beginning with Benedict XV's letter of 19 April 1919, *Communes litteras,* formulated a relatively complete "Catholic educational and school doctrine," which on the basis of biblical and theological statements, of traditional ecclesiastical ideas on education, *paedagogia perennis,* as well as of pertinent articles from the Code of Canon Law (Canons 1372–83), contained doctrinal propositions on education and school under compulsory aspects and determined the epoch down to the Second Vatican Council. In addition to the letter *Communes litteras,* its standard document is Pius XI's encyclical *Divini illius Magistri* of 31 December 1929; also to be mentioned are the messages of Pius XII — address to the Youth of the A.C.I., to the Fathers of Families of France of September 1951 — the message of John XXIII of 30 December 1959 on the thirtieth anniversary of the appearance of Pius XI's encyclical on education as well as passages of the encyclical *Mater et Magistra* of 15 May 1961.

All the expressions were based on the twofold right of the Church, which, first, by virtue of its teaching function, has to educate its members for full citizenship in the kingdom of God, and, second, by virtue of its supernatural motherhood, brings forth, nourishes, and trains souls for the divine life of grace, according to the encyclical *Divini illius Magistri* nos. 16 and 17. Against the background of a really centennial loss of the Church's power to regulate education and in view of the threat to Christian cultural values from liberalism and modernism in Europe and North America, the Popes raised the demand for the material catholicity of the educational world of its members, that is, either educational institutions must stand under Catholic auspices and responsibility or state and other educational institutions must be permeated by the Catholic spirit. These demands were pinpointed from two sides: Catholic Christians were obliged in conscience to send their children to Catholic schools; non-Church, mixed, or neutral schools were forbidden to them in Canon 1374 and the encyclical *Divini illius Magistri,* no. 79; the Church itself claimed an all-embracing right of supervision of the schools, guaranteed only fragmentarily by concordat.

Within the papal teaching the role of the state was defined to the effect that it has a right to educate and must exercise it, not immoderately by a school monopoly but according to the principle of subsidiarity, with regard for the parents' right. Its tasks lay especially in the spheres of training state officials and education in citizenship. In the papal teaching the parents always ranked as the innate and professional educators of their children. However, their right of education was not "autonomous" but one participating in the mandate of salvation and the Church's *magisterium* and pastoral office. The vigorous defense of this denominational right of parents by the Church was marked characteristically by the obligation of the parents to exercise their right in accord with their duties as Catholic parents — baptism, Catholic training of the children. In the concrete this could mean that they had to vote for Catholic denominational schools, if possibilities of voting were available and corresponding ecclesiastical directives were at hand.

The Catholic educational and school doctrine assumed as a condition of its effectiveness that traditional ecclesiastical authority, the structure of social institutions, and a certain "Catholic milieu" were intact. On such a basis it was possible that a few simple so-called "Catholic educational principles" were respected: the right of parents, family and school instruction in accord with the denomination, rejection of coeducation, and care for an instruction proper to each sex. They could easily be integrated into the system of Church doctrine and canon law and possessed the character of commandments.

The Second Vatican Council and the Postconciliar Period

After the Second World War there appeared throughout the world new situations in the sphere of education which could not but convulse the Catholic educational and school doctrine. Education was assigned social functions and became, especially in the countries of the Third World, but also in the industrialized nations, a strategic point of social development. The road of separate and particular cultures to a modern, Western, secular, and dynamic educational society, concerned with economic growth and the growth of information, seemed to indicate the direction of general progress.

From the viewpoint of the Catholic educational system there were various problems: the problem of the quality and of the comparable standards relative to the developed non-Catholic educational institutions; the problem of quantity in view of newly appearing needs in accord with the degrees of education — basic education, eradication of illiteracy; the problem of subsistence in view of rising building and maintenance costs; the problem of spirituality in view of the reduced number of clerical teachers or political exactions on the part of the governments of the moment — thus in Pakistan and Egypt religious instruction in Islam must be given; finally, the problem of self-understanding: as agent of the spreading of the faith or as a regular school for children of Catholic families or as an offer by Catholics to all, that is, as an instrument of Christian service to the world.

In its "Declaration on Christian Education" the council confirmed the basic features of the traditional Catholic school doctrine in the question of the function of education, of those qualified to educate — "first and preferably" the parents, subsidiarily the state, in a specific way the Church — of the natural law character of the parents' right and its confirmation in the question of the "choice of school" for the child; it also affirmed the assumption of the rights of education by means of the "child's right," which is not applied without distinction but must be seen by means of the child's natural abilities and his supernatural goal lying in the coresponsibility of the Church.

Traditionally the means suited to this goal and hence obligatory were seen in institutions of material catholicity. In this point the council proved to be more realistic and open: Since it happens that an ever larger area of education is fact-oriented, which neither positively nor negatively touches upon the meaning of Christian existence, it all amounts to the *formatio christiana* keeping in step with the *formatio profana*. And since it likewise happens that Catholic Christians are ever more frequently educated in mixed or neutral schools, where the Christian development of the school is institutionally not possible, the religious instruction remains possible, and — in the event that it does not take place in the school — at least the moral and character formation is guaranteed by the Christian spirit. Here the council puts great hope on the personal model of Christian teachers and fellow students, and it refers to the necessity of spiritual help even when this cannot result from within the school district.

With these adaptations to current conditions of Christian existence in the world, a giving up of institution and program bound to the *schola catholica* is not necessary, even if precisely here in the postconciliar period differences of opinion emerge. In the declaration itself the "Catholic school" is claimed for the educational mandate of the Church against all monopolizing tendencies of the state. Catholic school — this is principally the nonstate school under ecclesiastical or free auspices of a Catholic spirit. In the mission lands it is the first source of divine life and bearer of human culture with a strong apostolic content. As a program it means the exhibition of the "presence of the Church in the modern world," as demanded in the pastoral constitution *Gaudium et spes;* its function is the apostolate, that is, education and formation must serve the spread of God's Kingdom and, along with that, the welfare of the earthly community and its eternal salvation. The character of the educational apostolate defines also the function and position of the teacher in Catholic schools: it depends on him to what extent the aims and initiatives of Catholic schools are realized. Hence he needs a fundamental and constantly renewed formation in the profane and the religious areas and in teaching methods. He should be in a dialogue with his pupils — inspired by the Christian spirit and extending beyond the school-day, and work intimately with the parents. In this place, hence in part of the program referring to the teacher in the Declaration on Christian Education, occurs the traditional reminder that

Catholic parents have the duty "of entrusting their children, when and where this is possible, to Catholic schools, to support these in accord with their means, and to cooperate with them for the good of their children" (ARTICLE 9).

The program of the *schola catholica* extends over the total grade structure of the educational system, beginning with schools of the elementary and secondary grades, which "lay the foundation of education," for the professional schools, the institutes for adult education and for social professions, special schools, and institutions for the education of teachers and catechists.

On the universities the declaration expresses itself in a triple aim; it expects from them the training of the national leaders, scholarly contributions to the discovery of truth and to the problems of the modern world — undernourishment, sickness, unjust distribution, and so forth — and finally it expects the institutionalizing of religious and scientific faculties or at least institutes and, from these, contributions to the dialogue between faith and reason, which, if they conscientiously observe one another's conformity with law and competence, can come together in the one truth. These expectations set the framework for "Catholic universities": they deserve encouragement, but so that they stand out, not by their number, but by their scholarly achievement (ART. 10). The statements of the council on the university system remain throughout in the framework of the papal pronouncements of Pius XII, John XXIII, and Paul VI.

The postconciliar period is determined by a partly violent difference of opinion on the existence and range of a Catholic theory of education. Between conservative and progressive theoreticians various passages from conciliar documents were offered as proof of the ecclesiastical nature of their respective ideas. According to the selected theological or ideological relationship in each case there stood out in the Catholic school doctrine long familiar or entirely new features. The newer ones appealed to the Pastoral Constitution as "Magna Carta of the Christian World Understanding and World Mission" and sought to "rethink" the Catholic educational and school doctrine in its light. What is Catholic is understood, not as the culture-determining, religious content, but as form of solidarity, world responsibility, and condition of cooperation with all persons of good will: What must be done concretely is not different for the Catholic from what everyone can aspire to and understand. The Christian faith provides, as regards content, no new insights for the organization of the world and of humans living together; in fact, Catholics would not even have the right to a culture of their own. Since the Church makes its own general human demands and stands up for them, "Catholic schools" must not be understood as special institutions of Catholics for Catholics, but as integrating elements in "front of all of goodwill" under the idea "of creating in common with them a world in humanity, justice, and freedom" (W. Seibel).

Similar results are reached by whoever takes as a guiding principle the new nonmetaphysical anthropology of the pastoral constitution, according to which the human being is "defined by his responsibility toward his fellows and toward history." Responsibility toward history is then understood as the obligation to participate in scholarly progress in all varieties and as the abandonment of that older Augustinian outlook, whereby education has meaning for the Christian only where it ceases to be empty curiosity (*curiositas*) and assumes a relation to eternal salvation. The council simply makes progress and knowledge a duty because in the anthropological view, which corresponds to the situation of today's world, work in it must be understood as a form of fraternity, of humanity, of responsibility, hence in the last analysis as an overflow of the Christian commandment of love. In such a context it is the conscientious duty of Christian parents, in choosing the school for their children, to give the preference to the "Catholic school," seen and justified as the criterion of social liberty. The pluralism of society, hence not a metaphysical but a political principle, justifies the institution "Catholic school." But then may it, as such, be made a conscientious duty for Catholics? Three restrictive considerations are named: (1) the Declaration on Religious Freedom intends that only one who believes of his own accord can be bound in conscience; (2) the pastoral constitution binds the secular discipline to its respective subject matter, hence also the Catholic school to the modern demands on "school"; (3) the Declaration on Christian Education demands that a Catholic school must be Catholic not only formally but materially.

Only if all three factors are present can there exist an obligation in conscience for the parents to exercise their right to the free choice of a school in favor of the Catholic school.

In the postconciliar period further decisions were added to the Catholic educational and school doctrine by the Holy See as well as by regional episcopal conferences and other bodies, such as synods. They begin with the commentary of Bishop D. Pohlschneider on the German translation of the Declaration on Christian Education, which especially emphasizes the principle of the "apostolate" and attaches it to many conciliar texts. The notion of the Church's mission of salvation in the educational system — not only its solidarity with "all people of good will" — is the "dominant guiding idea of the declaration."

If one surveys the messages of the Holy See published since then, the impression can arise that the reference to the Declaration served rather the inner Church dialogue, since in it the interests of institutions under Catholic or ecclesiastical auspices are especially well expressed and justified; on the other hand, the pastoral constitution or the encyclical *Populorum progressio* are readily quoted when solidarity with extraecclesiastical organizations should be expressed, whether on the occasion of the anniversary of the eradication of illiteracy campaign of UNESCO or of the twenty-fifth anniversary of the founding of UNESCO.

The Latin American Church placed its resolutions on education entirely under the idea, urged by *Gaudium et spes,* of the coresponsibility for the process of transformation of the Latin American peoples and their liberation. Clear postponing of accent vis-à-vis Western European and North American philosophy and theology were discernible. The promise for the problems of Latin America lies not in the industrialized countries of the First World, but in Latin America itself. The task for education consists in enabling the Latin American illiterates "to develop a cultural world themselves, as creators of their own progress, in a creative and original way."

The line which the Holy See pursues in the assuring and promoting of ecclesiastical interests in the educational system of the European states is not different from the preconciliar line: by means of treaties between the respective nations and the Holy See prescriptions of concordats in force are extrapolated or supplemented. More powerfully than in the preconciliar phase, the pronouncements of the council and of the Popes are placed in close contact with declarations of other sovereign political bodies, and the unity of all peoples of good will in the one goal is stressed. The Declaration on Christian Education in Art. 12 had already pointed in this direction, that people must strive with all their means that "an appropriate coordination may come into being among Catholic schools, and between them and the other schools that cooperation may be fostered which the welfare of all human society demands." Coordination and cooperation were realized in the inner Catholic sphere by a liaison office for the national school bureaus and societies in Brussels, the *Office International de l'Enseignement Catholique* (OIEC); active in relation to UNESCO in Paris is the *Centre Catholique International de Coordination auprès de l'UNESCO* (CCIC).

C H A P T E R   9 5

Information and the Mass Media

Among those social changes which affected the Church's activity in essential points in the twentieth century were the developments in the field of mass communication. True, the Church and journalism always stood in certain reciprocal relations, and the critical confrontation with the press as it was becoming free had already started in the first decades of the nineteenth century. However, the twentieth century first produced that full development of those "instruments of social communication" — the Vatican linguistic usage since 1963 — which are summarized under the notion of mass media or means of mass communication: to the modern press in its forms as informing and opinion-making daily and weekly with a large circulation, recreational press, and specialist press have been added the cinema, radio, and television. Their technical development, as in general the industrialization of publicity production, evoked also the development of new agents of public communications offerings which caused new markets to appear: phonograph records, recording tape, eight-millimeter film, video disk, and, not to be forgotten, the paperback, which is changing the book market.

Since the turn of the century the Church saw or sees itself facing essentially five important phenomena and developments in mass communication with which it must come to terms; for changes in the mass communication system of particular nations, of entire cultural groups, and in individual cases even of "world society" affect the activity of the Church, especially in its mandate to preach and in its pastoral commission. These five points are: (1) the decline, in some countries the disappearance, of the "opinion press"; (2) the new, so-called audiovisual media — cinema, radio, television; (3) the grasping of totalitarian political systems for the publicity institutions in various countries; (4) the completely new tasks and opportunities which result for the use of communications means in the underdeveloped countries; and (5) the disintegration of the "Catholic public" in countries or cultural groups where this concept of practical journalism, but also of pastoral work, had been used for decades with some justification. As a sixth point, which however arose not against the Church but from the Church as a reaction to the journalistic opposition, the organizational and, recently, theoretical confrontation of the Church with mass communication deserves special notice.

The Catholic Claim and the "Colorless Press"

If the Catholic discussion of journalism in the nineteenth century was predominantly determined by the struggle against the "bad press" — *mauvaise presse, stampa perversa, stampa negativa* — the early twentieth century brought a new enemy: more correctly, the knowledge that, in addition to the "bad," that is, the liberal, Socialist, and occasionally even Protestant press, a new form of newspaper had appeared — the "colorless press." The Catholic press, as the only "good press," was, to be sure, respected by many Catholic critics only as the lesser evil, but it still had gained some noteworthy initial successes in the last third of the century that was ending. Proud of enterprises such as *De Tijd* (1845), *Kölnische Blätter* (1860; from 1869 *Kölnische Volkszeitung*), *Germania* (1871), or *La Croix* (from 1883 as a daily), for some time it was overlooked that meanwhile a new type of newspaper had appeared — the informative newspaper, *presse d'information,* which, differing from the classical type of the nineteenth century, the "opinion newspaper," abandoned partisanship or clear ideological lines. The Catholic press, on the contrary, was conceivable only as an "opinion press"; also the many small papers, which the statistics of founding of Catholic newspapers show to have increased during the *Kulturkampf* or a little later as foundations of local or regional "press associations," especially in Bavaria and Austria, took care of further growth, were, despite their character as local papers, opinion newspapers. In the United States (*The Sun,* 1833; *The New York Herald,* 1835), in France (*La Presse* and *Le Siècle,* 1836), and in England (*Daily Telegraph and Courier,* 1855), newspapers "for all," which in order to achieve the widest possible circulation not only lowered their price but also renounced partisanship, had existed the longest. In Germany the first newspapers of this sort occasionally appeared from 1871, using the title, or element in the title, of "general advertiser." The idea soon had an unpleasant connotation. The general advertising press lacked staunchness, and this is what constituted its "colorlessness." The fact that the "colorless press" was a publishing success, that, in regard to the issues, only with it did the age of the mass press begin, only made it more suspect.

The general advertisers were the "bad press" of a new sort, which were regularly condemned in Germany from 1889 at the general Catholic meetings. Especially typical of this phase of the "press apostles" are the books of Joseph Eberle (*Grossmacht Presse*) and Giuseppe Chiaudano (*Il Giornalismo Cattolico*). While Eberle chiefly denounced the general non-Catholic press, Chiaudano made clear all that the Catholic press must not do, but which north of the Alps it had long presumed to do, for example, in the discussion of *dubia* or the criticism of ecclesiastical decisions, in opposition to the Jesuit father's statements on the "necessità dello spirito di disciplina e di obbedienza." And the Code of Canon Law summarizes in Title XXIII the rules of censorship and prohibition, which, in consequence of a strict observance, had made almost impossible to Catholics a normal participation in the journalism of the time, active and passive. Where they took part in social communication as publishers, journalists, and readers, they could never entirely do this, if they were conscientious, without a bad conscience. The broken relationship of the Church to journalism had by no means been overcome when the age of the "new media" began.

Film and Radio in the Early Phase

Shortly before the turn of the century film presentations, at first as *varieté* attractions, and since 1920 the radio were ready for the use of the public. The early history of the Church's confrontation with these new media has as yet hardly been investigated. It can be taken as certain that at first it was not recognized as a publicity medium of general social and political relevance. Popular education and art were the spheres to which the cinema and the radio were assigned. With the catchword "educational functions" people noticed them quite early, at least in Central Europe, while in the United States, which quickly developed into the motherland of the great film industry, ecclesiastical attention was focused more strongly on the excesses of the content of the moving picture. For example, at the general assemblies of the Catholics of Germany there was criticism of the "poisoned abuses of the cinema," but at Aachen in 1912 in *Kino-Reform-Anträgen* there was adherence to the goal of the "positive reform work." Today it is almost forgotten that as early as 1910, in the framework of the Popular Association for Catholic Germany at Mönchen-Gladbach, there was founded the "Photographic Society with Limited Liability," which provided, loaned, or supplied together with the necessary equipment slide series and soon didactic films. A series of writings, *Lichtbühnen-Bibliothek* and the technical periodical *Bild und Film* (from 1912), supplemented the offering until the First World War ended these constructive efforts. After the war the film work and the Catholic radio work, at first pursued by free initiative, settled in special workers' groups in the Central Educational Committee of the Catholic Associations of Germany (ZBA), founded in 1919.

Of course, both the ZBA and the Fulda Episcopal Conference at first hesitated when, after the official beginning of public radio broadcasting in Germany in October 1923, possibilities resulted for ecclesiastical collaboration in the organizing of broadcasting. The broadcasting of liturgical actions, a problem which has not been thoroughly discussed even today, caused anxiety, while access under the titles of art and popular education was less problematic. More eagerness for risks was present in the movie: with its own production firms — Leo-Film of Munich in 1927, Eidophon of Berlin — a Catholic share in moving picture offerings could be financed. But the enterprise was a failure. Film work as an educational function and increasingly as a function of a protecting pastoral theology was, however, able to consolidate itself. The American example of the Legion of Decency, founded in 1933, and its growing influence on American film production made a powerful impression. Also the collaboration in radio was permanently established.

This first phase of the Church's concern with film and radio found a certain conclusion in the establishing of international organizations: In April 1928 the *Office Catholique International du Cinéma* (OCIC) was founded at The Hague, and also in 1928 there appeared, following the Cologne international press exhibition *Pressa*, the *Bureau International de la Radiophonie Catholique* — after World War II, UNDA. However, in the succeeding years the American model of the Legion of Decency acted as a standard, that is, the practice based on "moral codes," rather amounting to a censorship-like pastoral care of protection, established itself. It found the respect of the American film producers and the approval of the Pope: Pius XI was moved by the work of the legion to issue the film encyclical *Vigilanti cura* in 1936: for the future moral evaluation listings of films were to be issued in all countries and made known to the faithful.

The Development of the Catholic Press in the International Survey

The origin of a distinctively Catholic press seems to be promoted by definite social structures but impeded by others: Extreme diaspora situations permit Catholic periodicals to appear only marginally, as the examples of England or of the Scandinavian countries show; but even traditionally purely Catholic societies, wherever possible still with the state-Church character of the Catholic denomination, are not unconditionally favorable to the distinction, for example, Spain and Italy. This changes the moment when strong laicizing or anti-Church movements appear, for example, in France and recently in Poland. Also operating favorably are the existence of approximately equally strong and large denominational groups, the polarization in fashion-setting Christian or Socialist-liberal political parties, or also the denominational underpinning of a pluralistic society; to this extent Germany, Austria, Switzerland, and the Netherlands are classic Catholic press countries, and even the United States has produced a varied Catholic press system. Growing prosperity and comprehensive, varied, and politically unhindered assistance with communications offerings seem to weaken the denominational press, as also the party press, whereas political communications pressure — control of the press, bringing the press into line — to the extent that it does not completely eliminate denominational publication, consolidates the remaining agencies. The conditions mentioned here have determined the history of the Catholic press in the twentieth century — naturally, different in the various social and political organizations. For the German-speaking countries of Europe and the Netherlands a similar development has resulted in this connection in so far as the Catholic press usually moves closer to the Catholic parties or supports these parties without its thereby becoming, apart from some exceptions, a strictly regulated party organ, as is the case, for example, with the Communist and Social Democratic Parties as well as the NSDAP. The party relationship developed before the First World War, whereas since the end of the Second World War a growing aloofness becomes discernible.

In Germany until 1933 Catholic press and Center press were de facto identified, despite numerous discussions of differences. Resulting from the *Kulturkampf,* this press reached the quantitative climax of its development shortly before the First World War.

The general customary relation to the Center Party caused the Catholic daily press, after the Nazi seizure of power in 1933 or at the latest after the self-dissolution of the Center, to fall into the category of the "civic" press controlled by the Nazi press. This meant merely that it was not at once eliminated, as was the press of the KPD and SPD by means of the decree for the "Protection of People and State" of 28 February 1933. The formerly Catholic among them were, even if at first direct prohibitions were rare, exposed to all the measures of confor-mity of the Nazi press policy. In 1934–35 occurred the spectacular throttling of the *Rhein-Mainische Volkszeitung,* which in the last years of the Weimar Republic had, alongside *Germania* and the *Kölnische Volkszeitung,* acquired a supraregional stamp of a progressive Catholic type. The *Kölnische Volkszeitung,* which in 1932 had just fallen into an economic crisis affecting its existence, or the *Germania,* were able to survive, but the Catholic legal line of the *Germania* (close to Hitler's first vice chancellor, Franz von Papen) did not always meet with the approval of its public: not suppressed literally but deserted by its own readers, it suspended publication on 31 December 1938. The remaining, mostly smaller, daily press was exposed to various concentration procedures, which were for the most part as-sisted by Nazi measures. Their aim was to bring as many as possible of former Catholic papers into one of the Nazi collective publishing companies. It was oblig-atory to sell to them if, for example, a publisher could no longer publish because of exclusion from the compulsory professional organization of the Reich press office.

In the same Reich press office, on the other hand, the Catholic newspaper press, as a "professional organization Catholic Church press," could create for itself something almost like a reservation; until 1936 it was granted, among other things, by utilization of the idea, unclear in the concordat, of the "official diocesan papers," as the only kind of press brought under the protection of the 1933 concordat, relatively extensive and, after 1936, still some protection. Not until 1936 did those measures begin which, before the general shutting down of papers in 1941, caused almost three-fourths of the 416 titles of 1936 to disappear, but which also gained by force the kind of "diocesan paper" that thereafter determined the structure of the Catholic press in Germany and Austria: in each diocese there was now to be only one diocesan paper, to be decided and authorized by the bishop.

The Second World War also meant a clear determining boundary line for the Catholic press in many other countries of Europe. For Germany and a little later for Austria it appeared earlier than for the Netherlands, Belgium, Poland, or France. In all these nations in the two decades of 1920–40 the Catholic press displayed a certain stability, although tending rather to concentration than to expansion. An overview, already in the shadow of the approaching catastrophe, was supplied by the "World Exposition of the Catholic Press," which was held at Vatican City from 12 May 1936 to 31 May 1937 with strong international participation — sixty-three exhibitors, mostly of countries or groups of countries from all the continents. The volume of reports is not only one of the few comprehensive sources for the status of the Catholic press in the 1930s, it also makes known the European situation: Germany was represented by a total of two and one-half printed pages — France by thirty-four, while Italy and Austria were tersely represented with lists of their still voluminous stocks, although the volume of reports did not appear until 1939.

The Catholic press of the Austrian lands was supported by the "Catholic Press Associations," founded everywhere toward the end of the nineteenth century. Their tradition proved to be so strong even after the end of the Second World War that the publishing enterprises proceeding from them, mostly medium-sized, could provide the foundation of the new diocesan papers as well as of those newspapers which were Christian-oriented and supported the Austrian People's Party.

In Vienna there was after 1945 no recourse to the tradition of the Catholic daily of the *Reichspost;* the weekly *Die Furche* understood itself as the agent of tradition. In addition to the Innsbruck *Volksboten* (since 1973 *Präsent),* it represents the type of weekly newspaper for the intellectual Catholic reading public.

The Catholic press in Switzerland goes back, with some important organs, to the same period when in Germany the *Kulturkampf* brought about the rise of Catholic papers: *La Liberté* of Fribourg and *Vaterland* of Lucerne were founded in 1871, the *Basler Volksblatt* in 1872, and the *Ostschweiz* of Sankt Gallen in 1874. The most recently founded, the *Neue Zürcher Nachrichten* (1896 as an association paper, 1904 as a daily), developed not only in competition with the *Neue Zürcher Zeitung* but became the best known Catholic paper of a large Swiss city, while the *Vaterland,* as the "conservative central organ for German Switzerland," still functions not only to form opinion but also to effect economic stability. For the Swiss press also attempts to assure its existence by concentration measures, which have recently led to intensive cooperation with the calming poles *Vaterland* and *Ostschweiz* and have brought about some changes in the news press.

The activity of the English Catholics found journalistic expression in the founding of only a few important newspapers: *The Tablet* (1840), *The Universe* (1860), *The Catholic Herald* (1884), and *The Month,* founded by Jesuits in 1864, look back to noteworthy traditions. France, on the other hand, now as earlier is counted among the important countries for the Catholic press. The publicity activities of the nineteenth century, rich in number and in conflict, found a concluding climax in the establishing of the Maison de la Bonne Presse by the Assumptionists. That Catholic publicity center in the Rue Bayard at Paris, which adopted the "good press" as a program into the title of the firm, proceeded from the founding of two periodicals, which were then for decades essential voices of the Catholic publicity of France: in 1872–73. Bally began with *Le Pèlerin,* founded originally as a monthly organ of the *Conseil Général des Pèlerinages,* but in 1877 transformed into a popular illustrated peridocal. In 1880 a monthly periodical, *La Croix,* was added; in 1883, changed into a daily paper, *La Croix* developed into the "Quotidien catholique par excellence." The Catholic daily press of France shrank between 1958 and 1964 from nine to four independent papers, among which only *La Croix* was of importance, but the periodical press lived on the rich diversity to which it had developed in the nineteenth century and the first third of the twentieth century. In the mid-1960s it was believed that, after the disappearance of the parish papers, one could still speak of about one thousand titles. Besides the Bonne Presse, the most important publishers are the Union des Oeuvres Catholiques de France, founded in 1871, and, since 1945, the publisher of the illustrated *La Vie*

[*Catholique Illustrée*]. The Sunday press is powerfully represented in the chain of the various *Croix-Dimanche* editions (in 1964 in fifteen *départements*), begun in 1889 under the title of *La Croix du Dimanche,* the political appendix to the *Pèlerin.* The supraregional weekly press with intellectual pretensions exhibited for a long time a wing-formation, like comparable media in Germany: *La France Catholique,* founded in 1925, was classified as conservative, *Témoinage-Chrétien,* founded in 1941, as progressive.

The development of the Catholic press of France took place on the whole independently of the official Church. The independent Catholic press was united in two associations in 1951 and 1952, the *Association Nationale des Périodiques Catholiques de Provence* (ANPCP) and the *Centre National Catholique de Presse* (CNPC). "The registration of a periodical or newspaper in one of these associations amounted to a clear indication of the membership of these publications in the Catholic press" (A. Montero).

In Spain "it would not be false to maintain that all daily newspapers which . . . appear today regard themselves as in some sense Catholic. However, not all rightly deserve this designation." The problem of the Catholic press after the end of the civil war was so to adapt itself under a government that was officially friendly to the Church in a nonliberal democratic system that a specifically Catholic profile could again be discernible. The press law of 22 April 1938 left little latitude for this, and the new, more generous press law of 18 May 1966 was altered by restrictions in 1968. A Catholic profile was sought in three ways: (1) as regards the daily press, through collaboration in groups, of which the *Editorial Católica* and the newspaper chain of Opus Dei could each be found, in second or third place behind the Cadena del Movimiento; (2) as regards the periodicals, through a more or less clear attitude of opposition, which, as in the case of *Signo* in 1967, could run the risk of their existence; (3) in the training of journalists, to which special attention was paid by the Catholic side. Internationally noteworthy and in Spain not only recognized by the state but meanwhile standard-setting, is the journalism curriculum founded as the institute for journalism in 1958 on the Facultad de Ciencias de la Información of the Opus Dei University of Navarre at Pamplona.

The growth of the Catholic press of Italy was determined into the twentieth century by the conflict between the Italian state and the Papal state. For decades the nationally minded press could be sure to conform to the official view. The Catholic press of the entirely Catholic country was, on the other hand, from the beginning politically in a defensive posture. *L'Osservatore Romano* began to appear on 1 July 1861 as "giornale politico-morale"; while it was under the control and encouragement of the Interior Ministry of the Papal State (but in the beginning, outside of it) and appeared, together with the official *Giornale di Roma* of 1849–70, as a quasi-private political newspaper, the expression used by Montini did not yet apply to it: "Non per nulla, come si dice, è 'il giornale del Papa.'" The purpose of the new paper was defense: "'to unmask calumnies' and, as was later added, 'to refute what was hurled against Rome and the Roman papacy.'"

The succeeding fifteen years saw *L'Osservatore Romano,* like the rest of Italy's Catholic press, in a difficult position. However, there were direct encroachments only after Italy's entry into the Second World War. Besides occasional prohibitions of its sale in Italy — "now [at the beginning of 1940] the Catholic paper of Vatican

City has too many readers, who must be carefully supervised!" — on 13 June 1940 was suppressed *L'Osservatore Romano's* custom of printing the armed forces reports of the warring powers. Still, the circulation in the war years is said to have risen to more than 300,000 copies.

After the Second World War *L'Osservatore Romano* so developed "officially, as regards the announcements coming from the Vatican and semiofficially as regards the rest," that it evoked conflicting evaluations: on the one hand, for example, addressed by *The Times* as belonging to the "world press,"as on the other hand, it was criticized even by Catholic journalists because of the various dependencies of its editorship and its hardly justified journalistic work. In view of the poor working conditions, however, the intentional international expansion was noteworthy, despite the modest circulation, about 70,000, of the branch editions.

For the rest, the Catholic press of Italy, like that in other countries of Western Europe, was subject to increasing concentration pressure after the Second World War. Of its not very numerous daily newspapers *L'Avvenire d'Italia* of Bologna, founded in 1896 and rich in tradition, had to combine, for economic reasons but also for the sake of a progressive outlook, with *L'Italia* of Milan, founded in 1912; their new title is *Avvenire.*

Dissolution of Catholic journalistic unions seems, on the other hand, to mark a decisive turn in that country which can be described as the sociologically and sociohistorically most productive field of historical investigation of the Catholic press: the Netherlands. Catholic journalists and also their public were bored, at the latest since the Second Vatican Council, with "columnization" (*verzuiling*) as the special form for expressing pluralism in the Netherlands. Of the continually relatively strong Catholic daily press since the apologetically struggling nineteenth century — in 1937 there were thirty-two Catholic daily newspapers out of a total of seventy-nine — that paper proved to be the most vital which displayed itself after the Second World War as a *journal d'information* with a political Catholic policy of socially oriented progressivism without especially hiding its Catholicity: *De Volkskrant* of Amsterdam could raise its circulation from 150,000 in 1947 to 206,000 in 1974, and also a Catholic-oriented local press acquired a considerable share of circulation. All together, the share of at least the Netherlands press that followed Catholic traditions remained quite high. Something similar is true also for neighboring Belgium, whose Catholics achieved a stable political and journalistic position still earlier. Among the great papers of Belgium Catholic titles in French — *La Libre Belgique* since 1883 — as well as in Flemish — *De Standaard* since 1914 were able to maintain good positions — in 1968 their respective circulations were 170,000 and 290,000. Unique, at best only comparable to *L'Osservatore Romano*, is the role played by the *Luxemburger Wort* in the little Benelux nation: the largest newspaper of the country with an uninterrupted tradition since 1848 and a stable circulation of 73,000.

Hence while in most countries of Europe worthy of mention in connection with the Catholic press Catholic duties were able to continue to a certain degree beyond the Second World War, this turning-point meant for Germany and those nations which were thereafter reckoned as Socialist, including Catholic Poland, the end of the Catholic daily press. The licensing policy of the Allied occupying powers and the founding of the Christian-Democratic Union that intentionally went beyond denominations prevented the reestablishing or establishing of dailies. Only one newspaper was authorized as a bearer of the tradition of the Weimar period, Johann Wilhelm Naumann's *Augsburger Tagespost* on 28 August 1948, from which emerged the supraregional *Deutsche Tagespost* of a strictly conservative Catholic outlook but weak in circulation — less than 30,000. When, after the abolition of the compulsory licensing in September 1949, the "Old Publishers" tried to reestablish the traditional titles or their continuations, some Catholic publishing companies also took part. However, most of these foundations again disappeared from the market.

Quickly and stably twenty-two diocesan newspapers were reestablished and in part newly founded in the Western Zone and two in the Soviet Zone. Besides them there appeared in the West a richly developed press for associations, youth, and religious institutes. (In 1949 publishers and editors united in the Arbeitsgemeinschaft Katholische Presse e.V. and Catholic publicists of all the media in 1948 in the Gesellschaft katholischer Publizisten Deutschlands.) Recreational periodicals could develop only modestly; cultural periodicals suffered, except for the *Stimmen der Zeit,* from deconfessionalization; finally political weeklies confronted a quantitatively not adequate target group and could not go beyond the circulation minimum that assured existence. Even the circulation, stable for years and oscillating from 50,000 to 60,000, of the *Rheinischer Merkur* of Cologne and Koblenz, founded in 1946, regarded as Catholic and close to the Christian Democratic Union but politically and as a publishing enterprise independent, could not, in view of increasing production costs, retain its economic independence; in 1974 the paper passed into ecclesiastical majority ownership. At that time the Catholic press had long left behind the climax of its postwar development. The twenty-two diocesan papers — in 1963 they had a total circulation of 2.45 million — had lost, apart from some exceptions, portions of their readership year by year — in 1974 they had fewer than 2 million readers. The Catholic youth press died out. While the first postconciliar phase in Germany generally gave the impression of an intellectually strengthened Church, the decline of the publicity potential began to cause anxiety.

Catholic News Agencies

A need to provide the Catholic press with special information material, by means of press or news agencies, was understood before the turn of the century. From this there occurred in Germany the founding in 1879 of the *Centrums-Parlaments-Correspondenz* (CPC) to serve Catholic political ends, an initiative not of the Center Party but of the *Augustinusverein zur Pflege der katholischen Presse.* It and its succeeding institutions — supplied Catholic newspapers more poorly than correctly with information from the parliamentary activities of the Center — down to its dissolution of the ZPK in 1922. Catholic press agencies in the strict sense only appeared in the First World War: in 1917 at Fribourg in Switzerland the KIPA (Catholic International Press Agency); the American National Catholic News Service of Washington also goes back to 1917. It grew out of the press department of the National Catholic War Council, founded in 1917, and later renamed the National Catholic Welfare Conference, and today the United States Catholic Conference.

The third, for Catholic concerns, "great" agency is the KNA (Catholic News Agency of Bonn and Munich), emerging in 1952 from its precursors, the KND and CND. Besides its current service, it has developed a whole division of special services, has at its disposal a European and overseas net of correspondents, and was one of the driving forces in the collaboration of Catholic news agencies beginning at Rome with the Second Vatican Council: in 1971 it found a definite form in an international union of Catholic news agencies, in which KNA, KIPA, Kathpress of Austria, CIP of Belgium, and KNP of the Netherlands maintain joint editorship under the designation CIC (*Centrum Informationis Catholicum*).

In 1936 there were Catholic agencies or similar institutions in sixteen countries, in 1971 in twenty-one.

Radio and Television under the Restrictions of Commercial or of Public Control

Since the radio became a public medium in 1922, three forms of organization have developed: radio as a state industry, radio as a public law institution, and radio as a private economic undertaking, which sells its broadcast time partly to a third party and from the net proceeds draws not only subsistence but a profit. The first two types are predominantly based on financing by the fees of participants and are characterized by the mark of public control, in part directly by the state, in part by special social control bodies, for example, in Germany the *Rundfunkräte*, in Austria the *Kuratorium* of the ORF.

In accord with the respective "radio constitution" of each nation the Church has various favorable opportunities of participating in or at least of influencing radio and television. Only state radio systems in countries fundamentally hostile to the Church completely exclude its cooperation.

To give a comparative international description of the entire development is impossible because of lack of space. In general it can be said that the Church makes use of all types of possibilities available, but often has by no means exaggerated them. The private economic pattern provides two opportunities in those countries where it is followed, hence especially in the United States and in the countries of Latin America and Asia that are influenced by the United States: (a) the sale of broadcast time for church broadcasting, practiced, for example, in the United States and Japan, and (b) the establishing of private broadcasting facilities, for the countries here mentioned are rather liberal in the granting of radio concessions. The second method was followed successfully especially by international Protestant agencies. Comparable on the Catholic side would be the enterprise Radio Veritas, established with German aid at Manila/Quezon City, which started its operation in 1968 and had to struggle with many difficulties presented by the state, and the Federation of Catholic Broadcasters, also active in the Philippines, with headquarters at Manila. In countries with public law or similar broadcasting systems, the Church shares in the social control of broadcasting institutions, for example, through radio councils, in the framework of the legal possibilities on the one hand, while on the other hand, it employs the possibilities of forming its own preaching broadcasts, for example, conveying the Mass, and of cooperating in the broadcasting of sections appropriate for Church and religion, by constituting them or advising. These distributions of competition are clearly marked, especially in the German Federal Republic, and in Austria. In the course of the ideological "columnization," the broadcast system of the Netherlands developed fully. While the Nederlandse Omroep Stichting is the sponsor of the entire broadcasting system, the program is produced by several, mostly ideologically oriented operating enterprises, the position of which depends on the number of participants acknowledging them. Since 1925 the Katholieke Radio Omroep (KRO, Hilversum) handles the Catholic role. While foreign observers not rarely regard the Dutch system as the ideal realization of pluralistic broadcasting work, there are in the Netherlands also many critical voices.

In 1931 the Vatican established its own radio station under the name Radio Vatican; at first its broadcasting techniques operated with very modest means. Since the construction in 1952–57 of Santa Maria in Galeria on a tract outside Vatican City, twenty-five kilometers north of Rome, Radio Vatican beams broadcasts on medium wave, shortwave, and ultra shortwave to the whole world in some thirty languages.

Church Journalism in the Third World

In many countries of the Third World the ecclesiastical journalism of the present is based on foundations laid in the colonial period by missionary work. In this regard, two different centers of gravity can be determined: In some countries of Asia, but especially in Africa, it began early with Christian press work; in Latin America, on the contrary, there developed from modest beginnings a fruitful field of Catholic radio work, especially in the area of educational radio. Catholic "radio schools" and comparable institutions or program offerings appeared after the Second World War in, among other places, Bolivia, Brazil, Chile, the Dominican Republic, Ecuador, Colombia, and Peru. Catholic broadcasters were, in this connection, not oriented only to the aim of teaching, but especially developed systems of social communication that served the rural population, to move up in these occasionally newspaperlike information sheets to radio programs and school courses, as in the internationally well known radio school project, Radio Sutatenza in Colombia, the weekly newspaper *El Campesino* with a circulation of 70,000. The enterprise supported since 1949 by the *Acción Cultural Popular* (ACPO), founded in 1947 by the chaplain José Joaquín Salcedo, was able to lower considerably the number of Colombia's illiterates and make important contributions to village development.

In general church journalism in the Third World in the decade after 1960 came ever more under the idea of the promotion of development. This is a new emphasis in contrast to the missionary and pastoral motivation which for decades long determined Catholic press activity in many African and some Asiatic countries, such as India. The more African states became independent, the more frequently Catholic newspapers and periodicals fell into difficult situations: On the one hand, they were the politically less burdened representatives of a journalistic expertise which was lacking in many of the young states, on the other hand they came into conflict with politically prejudiced systems but also into economic difficulties, which caused the Union Catholique Internationale de la Presse to ask anxiously: "La presse catholique d'Afrique est-elle condamnée?" Many Catholic papers, rich in tradition, had to stop publication for a time or permanently; others remained alive. Political prohibitions or hindrances came from totally different directions: in Zaire the entire Catholic press was suspended in 1973, in "white" Rhodesia the critical attention of the government was concentrated on the products of the Catholic publisher, Mambo Press (Gwelo).

Despite manifold dangers and economic straits there exists in Africa and Asia a Catholic press of modest dimensions but of astonishing diversity. In this regard the founders and editors, mostly members of missionary orders or companies, attempted early to publish in the national vernaculars. This is true also of the journalistic opening up of very remote areas, for example, Oceania, and obviously in general for broadcasting work in all missionary lands.

To promote an understanding of the problems of the missions and today of the underdeveloped countries — such is the goal set for itself by the quite strongly developed mission press in the United States and many countries of Europe. Its beginnings, marked in Germany by the founding of the periodical *Die katholischen Missionen* in 1873, extend back into the nineteenth century. For a long time the popular periodicals were welcome reading material as recompense for sacrifice for the sake of the mission. The changed relationship to the Third World — aid for development, encouraging of structure, the new auxiliary works *Misereor, Adveniat,* and so forth — caused interest to go back to the classical mission journalism; the circulations of many papers declined, and there appeared, proceeding from the first freely initiated concentration procedures in the Catholic press market, a new type of mission magazine, which was at times published in common by several religious communities active in the mission: in Germany *Kontinente,* since 1966, at first twelve, later twenty-five representatives; in the Netherlands *Bijeen* (1968), with seventeen representatives; in Spain *Tercer Mundo* (1970), with six representatives; in France, less successful, *Peuples du Monde* (1965). In addition, a few individual titles, some of them of strong circulation, could continue, whose steadfastness rests on the combination of family entertainment and mission aims.

Church and Mass Communication in Theory and Organization

The rather negative relation of the Church to the journalistic media since the Reformation evoked as early as the nineteenth but especially in the twentieth century a large number of papal and episcopal decisions, whose basic tone was condemning to rejecting, only occasionally encouraging the "good" (Catholic) press. Meanwhile, they fill their own professionally specialized source collections. A change began with the first really mass-media encyclical, the film encyclical *Vigilanti cura* of Pius XI in 1936. As regards content, this encyclical introduced binding control institutions: On the model of the American Legion of Decency there arose in many countries Catholic offices for evaluating films, as after the Second World War in Germany, Austria, and Switzerland Catholic film commissions, whose activity was very beneficent in their informative ingredient but meanwhile was out-of-date in their aim of moral guidance. The pacemaker function of *Vigilanti cura* was the fact that there was now a media encyclical at all. It was followed in 1957 by *Miranda prorsus,* a second encyclical, which treated of the audio-visual media, and in 1963 by the decree *Inter mirifica* of the Second Vatican Council. Actual progress in the — in the real sense — theoretical confrontation of the Church with the mass media was produced by an address of Pius XII in 1950 to the Third International Congress of the Catholic Press at Rome, and the pastoral instruction *Communio et Progressio,* brought about by the just mentioned conciliar decree but only prepared in 1971. Pius XII recognized and described mass communication as a social function in presenting public opinion — "natural echo," "common response" — as unalterable by natural law for the functioning of society. Unfortunately, then the decree *Inter mirifica,* which especially stressed the Church's right to possess and use the mass media as well as the morally "right employment of these instruments," remained "considerably behind the doctrine developed by Pius XII" (O. B. Roegele). On the other hand, *Communio et Progressio* produced not only important results of modern journalistic and communications science, but presented generally relevant social principles: the function of the media as communications institutions, which gather "contemporaries around a round table, as it were," the right to information and free choice of information, freedom of communications, necessity of media pedagogy (instead of censorship and Index), acknowledgment of the untrammeled individuality of journalistic work, the claim of Catholic journalists, communications institutions, and the Catholic public to the helping partnership of the Church. Without abandoning standards — common welfare, human dignity, objectivity — the withdrawal from the "defense principle" and from the moralizing discrimination between "good" and "bad" press becomes pleasantly clear.

The instruction also points, by suggestions, to the absence of a journalistic organization, as it can be established in the Churches of many countries. Comprehensive tasks are attributed to the already existing international journalistic associations, while in reality these organizations, despite historical and national unifying merits, today can do justice to their very narrow determining of functions often only with difficulty. In this connection there is question of the *Union Catholique Internationale de la Presse* (UCIP), founded in 1927 — its precursor in 1923 — UNDA (*Association Catholique Internationale pour la Radiodiffusion et la Télévision*) proceeding from the *Bureau International de la Radiophonie Catholique,* founded in 1928, and the *Office Catholique International du Cinéma* (OCIC). The UCIP, divided professionally into five federations — newspaper and periodical publishers, news agencies, journalists, journalist science, and ecclesiastical press — and regionally into several continental subassociations, acting as international representative in appearance with world congresses of the Catholic press, sees its general aim in the fostering, organizing, and representing of the work of Catholic journalists and press associations on an international plane, especially in the spheres of activity of professional ethics and theology of mass communication, promotion of Catholic journalism in underdeveloped countries, and representation in international organizations (United Nations, UNESCO). UNDA, which owes essential impulses to the first and second International Catholic Radio Congress at Munich in 1929 and Prague in 1936, has likewise built continental subgroups in South America, Asia, and Africa, and takes care of the international cooperation as well as the interdenominational with the World Association for Christian Communication (WACC). UNDA and OCIC give international radio and film prizes respectively. The chief tasks of OCIC lie in the collaboration of about fifty national Catholic film bureaus, in the study of film art and economics in accord with Christian categories of values, in the initiating of new Catholic film movements, and in the effort for artistically and educationally worthwhile films.

For new international functions, namely, the advisory promotion of Catholic journalism in underdeveloped countries, the Catholic Media Council was founded on the basis of the cooperation of UCIP, UNDA, and OCIC at Aachen in 1969. Its tasks are the international exchange of experience, the coordinating and advising of planning, the utilization of scholarly results, and not least the professional preexamination of concrete promotional projects. The journalistic projects of supporting Catholic auxiliary and mission works are represented on the Board of Trustees. The CMC elaborates and advises projects, which are encouraged by the auxiliary works of Belgium, the Netherlands, Austria, Switzerland, England, Ireland, the United States, and Germany.

Concluding remark: The considerable theological, organizational, economic, and journalistic expense with which Catholic journalism, now as earlier, is carried out and also the (relatively late beginning) positive official teaching and pastoral attention to problems of mass communication cannot obscure the fact that at the latest since the Second Vatican Council a striking withering of integration is to be observed on the part of the "Catholic public," and especially in the "strongly" Catholic journalistic countries, in which Catholic media were not able to remain traditionally conservative, but had constantly to stand out with respect to non-Catholic groups of the population, hence especially clearly in the United States, the Netherlands, Switzerland, the German Federal Republic, but also in Austria. The fact that a growing part of the potential Catholic public avoids the specifically Catholic journalism, and the assured observation that this process is quantitatively similar to the decline of the numbers that attend Mass, will possibly be the characteristically basic feature of the history of Catholic journalism of the second half of the twentieth century. Documents of some postconciliar synods have sought to take this development into account, at least as a start.

C H A P T E R   9 6

Charity and Ecclesiastical Works of Assistance

Laying the Foundations in the Nineteenth Century

Caritas, as a turning to fellow believers and other persons who are in need, ranks alongside the proclaiming of the Good News as a basic function of the Church. Hence the intensity of charitable activity is always an indicator of its spiritual vitality. However, its present social-charitable activity differs in many respects from that of previous centuries. It proceeded entirely out of the charity movement of the nineteenth century, for then were developed those ideas and working methods which, spreading from Europe, have in timely fashion influenced almost all countries. And so a look at the nineteenth century is indispensable for the understanding of the present.

The numerous secularizations became a powerful and mostly overlooked precondition of the new surge of charity in the nineteenth century — not only in the France of the Revolution, with the nationalization of the Church's property in 1790, the suppression of the orders in 1792, the nationalization of hospitals in 1793, and in the German Reich with the Imperial Delegates Final Recess in 1803, but in most countries of the North Atlantic and Iberian world they withdrew the old social institutions from the Church's control. In this way the Church lost the traditional means of support of its care of the poor, but at the same time it was relieved of the often antiquated obligations of the foundations. Accordingly, the secularizations compelled new initiatives and they facilitated the appearance of that mobility and of that large-scale concept, which, in view of the increase of population and of all those miseries accompanying industrialization, were urgently necessary. And the Church had to devote its attention to the new social problems, if it would continue to be credible. European Catholicism, particularly in France and Germany, but also in Italy, thus undertook enormous social-charitable exertions in the course of the century. Only slowly did the idea establish itself that here only state intervention with the cooperation of free personnel could help. This was introduced in the German Empire by Bismarck's social legislation of 1883–89, while other states partly followed suit much later. From these originally modest beginnings there gradually developed comprehensive social security systems and large organizations that introduced a "fundamental change of the care for existence." They culminated in the concept of the "social state," which intervened in the social sphere by directing without degenerating into a total welfare state. It represented the reply to the Industrial Revolution and the restratifications in the wake of the great wars and economic crises. The aims of the state were expanded in the social state to social justice and the creating and maintaining of institutions for the protection of the individual in the various situations of life. The fact that state budgets in the industrialized countries today designate up to one-third of their total for social works is eloquent testimony.

This development deeply affected ecclesiastical charity, for in this way its center of gravity in the industrialized states increasingly shifted from economic to spiritual and personal help, without excluding the economic. For the rest the social-charitable personnel of the Church and the social agencies of the state cooperated to a considerable extent in almost all countries, even in those where Church and state were formally separated. The Church particularly brought to this teamwork its religiously motivated collaborators, while the state offices set aside partly considerable financial means for social institutions under the Church's auspices. The Church's financial contribution for this work was based, after the loss of the old foundations, partly on Church means of taxation but chiefly on gifts.

Concern for the whole person is characteristic of charity on the basis of its fitting into the care of souls. But since the Enlightenment growing secularization and alienation from the Church have incessantly and increasingly questioned its denominational method. The Church's personnel, who had long devoted themselves almost without competition to the charitable tasks of a homogeneous society, could no longer entirely measure up to the growing functions. Since the nineteenth century, therefore, other agents of free welfare work have pushed themselves beside the Church's charity; among them decided Christians collaborated, and they were partly inspired by Christian motives. To the secularization of society corresponded, with a certain reluctance, the secularization or laicization of social work. Today the Church is only one — even though of the utmost importance — of those social forces which are devoted to these tasks. For the rest, in opposition to an all-embracing state social and assistance policy there have not been lacking voices since the nineteenth century which claimed charity even under the changed circumstances as an unchangeable basic function of the Church, even if needing to be kept up-to-date. The demand for the unimpeded growth of the Church in the social sector also was derived from religious freedom. For this was taken from it only in totalitarian states, whereas, for example, in the German Federal Republic in 1961 precedence was accorded to the free representatives of social and youth assistance in accord with the principle of subsidiarity; recently, on the other hand, tendencies making for state management are again appearing.

During the nineteenth century synods and individual bishops repeatedly recommended the traditional care of the poor, but in reality official ecclesiastical initiatives in this area were isolated and locally restricted. The charity movement arose rather from its basis in the communities where it had always rested. Only in our century have an extensive and finally global view and corresponding organization established themselves.

From the nineteenth century charity was administered essentially by two groups. On the one hand, these were the various local charity groups, which at times operated without the cooperation of the clergy and often renounced any publicity. They found their classical form in the Conference of Saint Vincent de Paul, founded by Frédéric Ozanam at Paris in 1833, which became the model for similar establishments in many countries. Particularly in Germany, where the ecclesiastical association system was more strongly pronounced than elsewhere, there was formed, alongside the Saint Vincent Conferences and their female counterpart, the Saint Elizabeth Conferences, a large number of groups with social-charitable and often very specialized tasks. On the other hand, in recent times the parish first appeared as an institution qualified for charity, but of course the activity of the traditional societies was not supposed to be affected adversely by this.

In addition to these small groups, often merged into working communities and predominantly established on the local level, from the nineteenth century the many newly founded congregations assumed the chief burden of charitable work. The Daughters of Charity were, it is true, already represented before the Revolution in some European countries but began their global expansion only in the nineteenth century. For the rest, there then appeared those occasionally wildly growing large numbers of male and female congregations, which provided for social work a mainly professional personnel, thoroughly qualified by a professional code of ethics. In the territory of the German Reich, for example, there were scarcely several hundred at the beginning of the nineteenth century, but before the First World War 47,545 female religious and 1,963 male religious in 5,036 and 101 houses, respectively, were at work. In the other Catholic countries the growth was similar. The founding and expansion of these communities took place to a great extent without the directing intervention of church authorities. At that time there was coordination among them only in isolated cases.

Ecclesiastical charity, like its secular counterpart, was divided since the nineteenth century into an "open" and a "closed" sphere, a distinction which the legislation of the French Revolution made. To the open sphere belong those works of assistance that can scarcely be grasped statistically, particularly as they were performed in the communities. Beside them the institutions rapidly appearing from the mid-century, and with them the "closed" work, acquired growing importance. But the most fundamental change in ecclesiastical social work since the nineteenth century lies in the elimination of the traditional care of the poor, which was concentrated on the elementary livelihood of its protégés, by a differentiated and specialized care of people in their various needs. The professional formation of collaborators and the classification of the institutions in professional spheres were a self-evident consequence of this development. For the rest, educational and health assistance were not definitely separated. The religious and the ecclesiastical institutions not only accepted this development but supported it to a decisive degree in the industrialized nations. They not only supplied their personnel for it, but by opening up private sources of financing often first made possible the creating of such institutions. While the financing of institutions in countries with progressive social legislation is today to a great extent cared for by social security institutions or by the public, church personnel as well as other agents of free welfare in the countries of the Third World more and more finance this work largely out of their own means. The new types of social-charitable work outlined here grew in the traditionally Christian countries of Europe. In addition, an autonomous charity was able to develop also in the United States and Canada. Over and above this, the European methods of work were carried by the missionary institutes into all parts of the world, since the works of love have from time immemorial been counted as an integrating part of the missionary method.

National Organizations

The almost incalculable diversity of charitable efforts illustrates that there was at work not a planned procedure but a spontaneous movement. True, there was no lack of bishops interested in charitable and later also in social-political activities, but the Church leadership, despite its good will, stood aside and made scarcely any gestures to canalize the new breakthrough. In an age of increasing entanglements and of a more spacious thought, however, this fragmentation constituted a serious danger. Individual societies, as, for example, the Conferences of Saint Vincent de Paul, quite early combined, but a coordination involving all fields of charity was only attempted from the turn of the century. In this field Germany took the lead, although the Catholics themselves here lagged behind corresponding exertions of other welfare associations. The project was first realized by the brilliant organizer, Lorenz Werthmann (1858–1921). The Limburg priest went to Freiburg im Breisgau in 1886 as court chaplain of Archbishop Christian Roos (1886–98) and there became acquainted with the Church's social work. Important preliminary stages of the later organization were constituted by the founding of the periodical *Caritas* in 1895 as the first professional organ of this type in German and of a "Charity Committee" as the circle of promoters of the periodical. Werthmann edited the periodical personally until his death. From 1896 the "Committee," in which Werthmann set the tone, conducted annual study meetings — *Caritastage* — which likewise served the spread of the idea of charity. In February 1897 it called for the founding of a *Caritas Verband für das katholische Deutschland.* After initial hesitations on the part of the episcopal leadership of Cologne and Freiburg because of Werthmann's independence of action, there occurred on 9 November 1897 the planned founding, with headquarters at Freiburg, on the occasion of the second *Caritastag* at Cologne. Its aim was to be study and publication, the education of co-workers, professional charitable work, and coordination. While the organization made progress only with difficulty for two decades, despite the intensive efforts of the first president, Werthmann, the association achieved great successes in other fields. This was true also of the charity science developed at Freiburg, which in 1925 acquired a scholarly institute and a chair at the university — since 1964 it has been called *Institut für Caritaswissenschaft und Christliche Sozialarbeit.* In addition, before the founding of the *Karitasverband,* Werthmann organized a special library, which gradually grew into a study center unique in its kind. In the midst of the First World War the episcopal conference at Freiburg in 1915 and that at Fulda in 1916 recognized the Freiburg central office as a "legitimate gathering of the diocesan societies into one uniform organization." Thereby the early history of the association ended and its organizational rise was introduced.

The German example acted as a stimulus beyond the national boundaries. But the charitable organization became more important in the United States because of its order of magnitude. The initiative proceeded from the New York religious Barnabas of the Brothers of the Christian Schools. In youth work over the years he had felt the isolation of the individual charitable groups as a serious flaw, and in 1908 he proposed to Bishop Thomas J. Shahan, rector of the Catholic University, the convoking of a charity conference. An organizational committee then decided the establishing of a national conference, which met on 25–28 September 1910 at the Catholic University. Shahan became the first president (until 1925) and William J. Kerby the secretary of the newly established National Catholic Charities Conference (NCCC). Its functions, like those of the DCV, were to be the educating and informing of the members. This was effected by working-meetings, the establishing of places of formation, and the publication of the *Catholic Charities*

Review in 1916. During the first years the horizontal connection with the charitable religious institutes was inadequate, although these then carried out 75 percent of the total work. Hence, as secretary (1920–61), John O'Grady in 1920 inaugurated the founding of the National Conference of Religious on Catholic Charities as the organ representing the congregations with the NCCC.

The establishment of other national charity associations took place between the two world wars, especially in Europe — in Switzerland (1920), Hungary (1931), Luxemburg (1932), Belgium (1938), Ireland (1941), and Spain (1942), then in Poland and Yugoslavia and also in Syria, whereas France still held itself aloof.

International Cooperation

An international charity assistance, or at least one that extended beyond the frontiers of nations, was already included in the mission to the pagans and then with the care of emigrants of the late nineteenth century. Then it became a pressing need because of the misery attending wide circles of population in the countries affected by war. Alongside the national charity institutions, the Holy See, from the beginning of the war, also developed a vigorous war welfare care. This concentrated on the prisoners of war and the civilian population in the occupied countries. In addition, the Holy See helped many individuals through consultation and donations. Besides this, it directed requests for help to the Catholics of the countries not greatly affected by the war. Particularly in the United States considerable donations were thereupon made; the German-Americans' awareness of solidarity with their homeland was still great and was influential as a motive for making donations.

The foreign aid during and after the First World War had made the international cooperation of charitable works of assistance an urgent necessity. As early as 1918 Werthmann had pointed out that an international union was necessary, and in February 1920 the Catholic delegates at the congress of the Union Internationale des Secours aux Enfants at Geneva urged this desire. In this way the insight was put across that a "World Charity Society" should be founded. The Holy See approved the project. And so, on the occasion of the World Eucharistic Congress at Amsterdam in July 1924, at the invitation of the Preparatory International Charity Committee, sixty delegates from twenty-two nations met for a four-day conference. Here the establishment of a permanent "Charity Conference" with headquarters at Lucerne at the Swiss Central Office of Charity was decided. The preeminent tasks were to be the uniting of all charitable organizations as well as reciprocal information, while an international aid fund could not yet be realized. Then in 1926 the second conference at Lucerne stated as its aim the promotion of all charitable efforts, the exchange of information, the beginnings of cooperation, and finally the representation of charity in international welfare societies. It also decreed the founding of the sections *Iuventus, Migratio, Infirmitas, Paupertas, Sobrietas,* and *Literae.* In 1928 the conference constituted itself as a permanent organization with the name *Caritas Catholica,* as Pius XI had desired, in order to emphasize the religious motivation of the work here accomplished.

That collaboration beyond national boundaries even in the inner Catholic area was not without problems appeared when a congress of charity, planned for

Strasbourg in 1927, had to be canceled at the last moment because of strained German-French relations. Subsequently the delegates met repeatedly in Switzerland, but international cooperation was considerably impeded after 1933 under Nazi pressure and in 1937 it was stopped. Despite these setbacks, the first union of national charity associations had powerfully strengthened their solidarity. Above all, the effects of the exchange of experiences must not be lightly underestimated. Furthermore, *Caritas Catholica* caused the founding of new national charity associations.

Consolidation of Charity between the World Wars

After the First World War the charitable institutions in many countries were intensively consolidated. In this connection must be noted not only the improved organization but also the multiplication and the differentiation.

Activities varied according to country, from the differentiated institutions in industrialized states to the weakly developed structures in the Churches with Iberian backgrounds. In the missions also during this epoch European models were still the pattern. In the territories subject to the Congregation for the Propagation of the Faith there were institutions and personnel in the service of charity in 1930.

Charity in the Totalitarian State

Charity in the German Reich first came into conflict with a totalitarian state after 1933. Thereby the DCV suffered severe losses, but it still was able, under its capable tactician-president, Benedikt Kreutz (1921–49), to retain the greatest part of its substance and especially its ability to function. On the other hand, other free welfare associations were dissolved — in 1933 Welfare Work and Christian Workers' Aid — or incorporated into the National Socialist People's Welfare (NSV), founded in 1933, or brought into line — in 1933 the Equal Welfare Society, later actually also the German Red Cross. The concordat assured the continuation of the Church's social institutions (ARTICLE 31), and the bishops energetically exerted themselves for this. Nevertheless, after 1934, 1,200 kindergartens had to be closed or turned over to the NSV. The same fate befell 300 stations of the mobile care of the sick, 156 Travelers' Aid Societies, 136 employment exchange offices for the protection of girls, 35 seminaries for kindergarten teachers and female youth leaders, and 2 social schools for women. And in 1938 the Institute for Charity-Science at the University of Freiburg was suppressed. The Nazi state tried to limit charity as far as possible to the care of the physically or mentally handicapped. Another serious restriction was the limiting of charitable gatherings, which were of decisive significance for the funding of the work. Severe losses were also experienced by the charitable orders and congregations, which before the Second World War had more than 70,000 nursing personnel in Germany. In spite of the enormous need for the care of the wounded, entry into charitable communities was no longer granted after 1940, although a formal prohibition did not occur. Thereafter the number of members of institutes sharply declined in Germany. After the war's end this development was stopped for only a few years. During the Nazi epoch religious also had to leave many public institutions, where they were replaced by the rival establishments of the Nazi Sisters. *Caritas* President Kreutz for his part had in 1937 called into existence the *Caritas* sisterhood for sisters not bound by enclosure — in 1939 they had 5,000 members. Finally, the war offered opportunity for the confiscation of 1,871 institutions (the total was 3,971), and 1,358 were destroyed or severely damaged by war measures. Nevertheless, the DCV was able to save essential areas before the Nazi grasp and even to create new institutions for aid. Of 4,000 kindergartens, 70 percent remained under Church auspices, and the hospitals could also continue their activity. The DCV brought effective help to many persecuted by the Nazi regime. On the other hand, the risk for those handicapped threatened with murder was very difficult and often useless.

While charity was curtailed in so many ways, the difficult situation also compelled positive new starts. Among these were the activation of parish charity and personal acts of charity not measurable by statistics. And reflection on the founding and responsibilities (tasks) of the Church's social work was intensified in these years.

Assistance in Emergency and Catastrophe since the Second World War

The miserable condition of millions at the end of the war and the vast displacements of populations — 30 million refugees in Europe — evoked, as in 1919, a worldwide readiness to assist. The discrimination against Germans and the long period of strictly closed state boundaries of course created conditions different from those after the First World War. On the other hand, the great aid organizations had meanwhile been more strictly organized and thereby made more capable of achievements. The great misery also compelled charity to extraordinary exertions. Thus in 1944 Italy obtained a national charity organization in the Pontificia Opera di Assistenza. France followed in 1946 with the founding of the "Secours Catholique" by the Conference of Cardinals and Archbishops. At its head stood, as secretary-general, Jean Rodhain, who during the war had organized pastoral care for French prisoners of war and slave laborers in Germany. The French merger was oriented on the American and German model. In many countries appeared similar organizations, which originally were intended to alleviate actual misery but soon grew into permanent central offices. All other aid institutions were surpassed by those of the American Catholics. The War Relief Services (WRS), founded by the bishops in 1943, were incorporated into the National Catholic Welfare Conference (NCWC), and united the hitherto fragmented particular initiatives. They concentrated on direct help for refugees, prisoners of war, and all other victims of war. The assistance measures first beginning in Europe were soon extended to almost all countries devastated by the war. WRS worked in 1945 in sixty-two countries and throughout supported some missions, but it also claimed the cooperation of local institutions. Then when it was apparent that the organization produced by the war continued to be necessary for the future, the episcopate in 1955 renamed the WRS the Catholic Relief Services (CRS). Up to 1963 the assistance work distributed relief material (food, medicine, clothing) to a total amount of $1.25 billion overseas. The entire Catholic emergency help of the postwar period would not have been thinkable without the immense achievements of the 30 million American Catholics. These financed their activities exclusively by donations. In addition, since 1950 the American government put superfluous food at its disposal.

Even before the American aid, the help of the Vatican and of Switzerland began in Germany. When later the war misery disappeared in European countries, the activity of the existing assistance works was concentrated on help in catastrophes, which had never before occurred to such a degree, as well as on measures for other countries hurt by the war and on the always smouldering problem of refugees.

On the other hand, the Church's social work could not but endure considerable damage in Communist-ruled countries. In all the "People's Democracies" outside the German Democratic Republic the Church's social works and institutions were nationalized or withdrawn from the influence of Church direction — Poland, U.S.S.R. in 1949, China in 1950. The personnel of religious institutes were partly taken into the service of the state but had to renounce any pastoral activity. Besides, various waves of refugees from countries under Communist domination repeatedly made assistance measures necessary — in 1956, for example, 200,000 refugees from Hungary.

Caritas Internationalis

After the war the revival of *Caritas Catholica* was variously stimulated, but at the same time there appeared a tendency toward a dissolution of the Swiss central office and the creation of an independent bureau, perhaps also situated in Switzerland, which should cultivate contact with the non-Catholic welfare societies. Then in 1947 occurred, due to French initiative, the founding of an *Auxilium Catholicum Internationale,* with headquarters in Paris, for extraordinary assistance measures, which was regarded at Lucerne as an undesirable competition. The director of the Swiss *Caritas,* G. Crivelli, who was working for the continuation of *Caritas Catholica,* founded in 1924 and never dissolved, stressed on the contrary that other national societies would have to be established before an international merger. At the suggestion of the Holy See there then followed in 1950 the founding of an "International Charity Conference." On the occasion of the Holy Year, the president of the *Pontificia Commissione di Assistenza,* Ferdinando Baldelli, after consultation with the Papal Secretariat of State, had invited the national societies to a study meeting at Rome from 12 to 15 September 1950. At this appeared sixty delegates from twenty-two nations, including the directors of twelve national charity associations. The desire of the Secretariat of State was a stronger and more systematic organization on the international level. A central office should serve for coordination, information, and representation but the delegates expressed concerns in regard to the future autonomy of the national associations. Nevertheless, on the last day of the conference they united for the establishing of an "International Charity Conference" with headquarters at Rome. This should take care of the tasks mentioned but not attack the individuality and autonomy of its member organizations. The statutes, which the Holy See approved in 1951 *ad experimentum,* envisaged as organs the general assembly, an executive committee, a general secretariat, and delegations at international organizations. The national episcopates, informed by the Secretariat of State, approved the new foundation, except for the United States, where at first there were reservations. At the founding meeting on 12 and 13 September 1951, of the twelve delegations only two non-European, those from the United States and Canada, were represented. The meeting took the positions envisaged by the statutes, according to which it sought the greatest possible international distribution. In the executive committee the chief Catholic countries were represented — the United States, France, and Germany, also Italy and, as representatives of the smaller nations, the Netherlands, Canada, and Spain. The delegation at the United Nations was given to Switzerland. Baldelli of Italy became president, and O'Grady of the United States vice-president. Karl Bayer, a German hitherto active on the *Pontificia Commissione di Assistenza,* was elected secretary-general. The meeting confirmed Rome as headquarters of the conference, but expressly desired that the secretariat be accommodated outside Vatican City. Preeminent tasks were to be the gaining of other national societies, the making of contact with the United Nations, and the creating of an agency in New York. The budget for the first fiscal year, which was proportioned among the participating associations — United States 28 percent, Luxemburg 2 percent — was a quite modest twelve thousand United States dollars.

In spite of this restricted framework, the general secretariat displayed a vigorous activity. It established the connection with the national member organizations and divided, as had the earlier *Caritas Internationalis,* into particular professional groups. It placed special importance on information and the compiling of archives. The delegations in New York and Geneva promoted collaboration with international delegations and with agencies of the United Nations. The organization renamed in 1954 *Caritas Internationalis* quite early gained consultative status in the Economic and Social Council (ECOSOC), in the International Assistance Work for Children (UNICEF), and in the Food and Agricultural Organization (FAO) of the United Nations. *Caritas Internationalis* had considerable success also in the promoting of charity in those countries which hitherto had no corresponding organizations. Following a journey by Bayer through Latin America to gain information and recruits, many national associations appeared there in 1955–56. Corresponding foundations also occurred in Africa and Asia, and, while only twelve countries were represented at the first meeting in 1950, the number of members grew to eighty in 1972. Correspondingly the central service offices were completed. Over and above this, there took place in 1954 the coordination with the *Société de Saint-Vincent-de-Paul* at Paris and the *Association Internationale des Charités de Saint-Vincent-de-Paul* at Paris, and in 1958 that with the *Confédération Internationale Catholique des Institutions Hospitalières* of Nijmegen, which participated as permanent observers in the general assemblies and on the executive committee. To the earlier existing delegations was added in 1968 another at UNESCO in Paris. Further, *Caritas Internationalis* displayed a vigorous assistance in catastrophes, for example, in floods — in the Netherlands and Belgium in 1953 — earthquakes, and political complications, for example, in 1954 the care of refugees from Vietnam, in 1956 the care of refugees from Hungary, and in 1970 aid to Biafra.

Catholic Works of Assistance

From the middle of this century there appeared a completely new understanding of charity that was actually revolutionary because of the separation from preaching. This resulted from the insight, more and more penetrating into awareness, that the Church also must make a contribution to the development of the Third World. Ecclesiastical social work in its manifold specializations was from time immemorial bound up with the mission, and as late as 1962 T. Ohm emphatically demanded the inclusion of charity in evangelization. "A mission which disregards the really religious for the 'social gospel' is no mission." The population explosion and the spread of the industrial types of society led, however, in the Third World to a pauperism whose dimensions far exceeded the problems of the industrial society coming into being in the nineteenth century. The missionaries now had to show very impressive achievements in the social sector; education oriented to economic and technical progress, hence to self-development, had been, on the other hand, disregarded by them. Basically they did not question the colonial foundation. Even before most former colonies had obtained political independence, a new awareness of responsibility and a reorientation of social work for the countries of the Third World established themselves. Classical charity was not suspended by this fact but it was supplemented by "help for self-help," hence the encouragement of self-development. In motivation this is identical with its older sister but it must be clearly separated from preaching and no longer understands itself, as the former did, as an indirect mission. On the other hand there are also assistance works which accomplish decidedly pastoral works of development.

This new type of charitable activity has not been able to establish itself equally in all countries. The largest of the Catholic assistance organizations, CRS, began, for example, in 1960 with its own projects of help in development, but, then as earlier, stressed direct help. The new idea made itself most strikingly felt in the German Federal Republic. At the suggestion of Vicar General Josef Teusch of Cologne, who thereby took up the initiatives of various Catholic groups and societies, Cardinal Frings proposed to the German Episcopal Conference in 1958 the founding of the activity *Misereor* against hunger and sickness in the world. The business office was erected at Aachen, and in this way the intimate relationship with the German branch of the papal work of spreading the faith, *missio,* then located there, was expressed. Nevertheless, *Misereor* was supposed to be run not as a mission but as an enterprise for assisting development. The first collection on Palm Sunday 1959, with a yield of 33.4 million German marks, surpassed all expectations and contributed to the rapid consolidation of the new foundation. The donations of those attending Mass — up to 1973 they amounted to 786.7 million German marks — constitute the decisive source of revenue of the bishops' assistance work. The choice of project, which a professional committee decides, is concentrated not on direct aid for the signs of misery but tries to deal with the causes and to foster personal initiative. On the other hand, the aid of the German Catholics for catastrophes is directed by the DCV. The "Workers' Community for Development Aid," founded in 1959 by *Misereor* and other Catholic societies, serves also the enlisting, preparing, and informing of helpers in development — by 1974 there were some seventeen hundred.

In addition, the German bishops in 1961 established the activity *Adveniat* to support the pastoral tasks of the Church in Latin America. The activity, first conceived as a single collection for the education of priests, was finally continued as all-embracing aid for the carrying out of pastoral care in Latin America. Up to 1972 the German Catholics spent 621.1 million German marks for this end — the Christmas collection. That clear distinction and organizational separation of development and pastoral assistance which is practiced in the German Federal Republic, has not been imitated everywhere, for the aid works of other nations, which appeared partly at the same time or a little later, often unite other functions with development aid. Naturally, the desire to give development aid directly or indirectly to the foreign missions, especially in lands with an old mission tradition, is lively. Moreover, the implementation of many projects is referred to the missionary substructure and is carried out in a certain personal connection with the mission work. There were precursors of the later aid works in various countries — in England the Miss-A-Meal Movement, in Austria in 1958 family fast day — but the real wave of foundations began only with the Second Vatican Council, which confronted bishops and Catholicism with worldwide problems. Individual new foundations first concentrated on strictly defined projects, in which the former colonial ties played a role — Belgium in Zaire, France in its former African colonies. Since then the notion has increasingly expanded to become global.

The first stimuli for the cooperation of the national assistance works were expressed even before the council. In 1960 a small group of experts urged this concern on the occasion of the Eucharistic Congress at Munich. But the formal initiative for a foundation came only four years later, when on 5 November 1964, during the third session of the council, Cardinal Frings appealed to the episcopal conferences of all countries for the establishing of aid works against hunger, poverty, sickness, and illiteracy. Beyond this he suggested the international merger of already existing organizations. This impulse found a very positive echo among the council fathers. Other discussions of this question as well as the temporary founding of a workers' community with a view to the instituting of a center of information and coordination on 8 May 1965 went back to Frings's suggestion. The episcopal conferences represented in it — Belgium, German Federal Republic, France, Netherlands, Austria, Switzerland, United States — decreed on 18 November 1965, with the consent of the Holy See, the founding of a permanent workers' community and of a secretariat, which in 1966 took up its activity in Brussels. The national character and autonomy of the members of this *Cooperation Internationale pour le Développement Socio-Economique* (CIDSE) were thereby not touched. Its directing agency is the general assembly, which meets about every three years. It decides the principles and functions of the CIDSE. In addition there are an administrative committee ("Commission"), which determines the activity of the secretariat, and a managing board of directors. The secretary general is at the same time secretary of the general assembly, of the commission, and of the management committee and directs the secretariat.

The goal of CIDSE consisted from the first neither in the giving of their means by its members nor in the imparting of instructions, but in coordination, information, and consultation. Hence, among other things, all projects were registered at Brussels and a comprehensive card file of experts was compiled. In addition,

CIDSE stimulated the instituting of other assistance works, which meanwhile are no longer restricted to the industrialized nations, but have found admittance to the Third World. Such assistance works appeared in Malawi — in 1968 the Christian Service Committee of the Churches in Malawi — where the work overlaps the denominations, also in Canada, Thailand, Indonesia, Rhodesia, and finally Ireland, the Caribbean, the Nordic countries, and Spain. The Australian assistance work, on the contrary, disappeared because it cooperated more powerfully with *Caritas Internationalis.*

The working methods of the assistance works are varied and are not impaired in their respective characteristics. In this regard aid for the Third World is often united with measures inside the donor country. Naturally, this applies especially to the assistance works of the underdeveloped countries. While large assistance works, such as *Misereor,* can take into consideration extensive programs and greater projects, the smaller assistance works are restricted to partial programs or small projects.

The financing of aid activity is based primarily on donations (collections) of the faithful. In their differing amounts is without doubt expressed something of the vitality of Catholicism in the various countries. On the other hand, the statistics of CIDSE comprise, it is estimated, only a fourth of the aid-means for development produced by Catholics, for the accomplishments made by religious communities and particular groups or individuals appear in no list. The donation yield of assistance works related to CIDSE amounted in 1973 to 50.1 million United States dollars, not counting Spain, Ireland, and the United States. In the Netherlands, the German Federal Republic, Switzerland, and Canada the Church's aid projects for development were financed also out of state means. Despite initial hesitations this cooperation has not operated to the detriment of the Church's independence, since the donation occurred exclusively in accord with objective aspects. If regard is had, in addition, for the very large sums for aid from CRS, which of course to a great extent are made possible by the government because of the presence of superfluous food, which must not be regarded as real development help, as well as of the donation yield of *Adveniat,* which like *Caritas Internationalis,* is equally a consultative member of CIDSE, then the total value of help provided in 1973 by these organizations amounted to 248,342,155 United States dollars.

The functions of the papal commission *Iustitia et Pax,* founded in 1966, lie in the area of study and promotion, not of social action. And the council *Cor unum,* founded by Paul VI in 1971, is intended to further the more intensive cooperation of charity and development aid as well as agents in any way occupied with them.

There has never been any dearth of official church recommendations of the traditional care of the poor. But only the Second Vatican Council found, on the basis of experiences endured for a century, a new view and expressly approved and recommended the social-charitable activity as well as the ecclesiastical development aid meanwhile developed. True, there is no special conciliar document which is devoted to charity or development aid, but expressions on them are found in various contexts. According to these, charity is acknowledged as the Church's basic function and activity. This is true not only for the ethos of the turning to those suffering need but also for organized charitable activity, which is expressly, even in its branches extending beyond denominations, approved and recommended. Unambiguous also is the profession of development aid, for which clear norms are given in ARTICLE 86 of the pastoral constitution. Their aim is full human development — "plena perfectio humana" — which indeed refers to the aid of the industrial nations, but primarily challenges the capabilities and traditions of the Third World — "non solis opibus alienis, sed propriis plene explicandis necnon ingenio et traditione propria colendis." Thus were the principles originally formulated and practiced in the North Atlantic world accepted for the Universal Church.

CHAPTER 97

History of the Ecumenical Movement

The Development of the World Council of Churches and Its Route from Amsterdam (1948) to Nairobi (1976)

The beginnings of the ecumenical movement go back to the nineteenth century. Neither theology nor church leaders supplied the impetus to it, but rather the free groups of religious renewal, which were partly in conscious opposition both to the theology of the Enlightenment and to organized ecclesiastical systems. In addition to the Oxford Movement in the area of Anglicanism, there were above all associations of youth and of the Christian Student Movement. The Young Men's Christian Association (YMCA) and the Young Women's Christian Association (YWCA), founded in England in 1844 and 1854 respectively, soon spread to Europe and North America. Supranational and supradenominational and also organized in an emphatically evangelical and missionary context, they were referred from their own center to the *ecumene.* In contrast to the liberal theology of the time, persons were convinced that the unity of the Church could be found only on the basis of a clear creed. This was expressed in the Paris basic formula of the YMCA of 1855, which begins thus: "The Young Men's Christian Association has the aim of joining such young men together who acknowledge Jesus Christ, in accord with Scripture, as their God and Saviour." Here was unmistakably prepared the later basic formula of the World Council of Churches. At first the YMCA acquired importance for the founding of the Christian Students' World Union, which was joined at Vadstena in Sweden in 1895 by the student movements of many countries in the Protestant sphere. From it or the YMCA respectively proceeded the leaders of the ecumenical movement of the twentieth century, such as John R. Mott (1865–1955), Nathan Söderblom (1866–1931), and Willem A. Visser 't Hooft (b. 1900).

Mott had played a decisive role in the preparing and implementing of the World Mission Conference of Edinburgh in 1910, which was intended to bring the various mission societies to collaboration. This was first institutionally assured in a continuing committee (1910–20) and then in the International Mission Council, which from 1921 to 1942 was under Mott's chairmanship. From the World Mission Conference at Edinburgh proceeded the decisive impetus to the ecumenical movement. If, according to John 17:23, the credibility of the Christian message depends on the unity of Christians, then the disunion in the mission, with its numerous mission societies working alongside and in opposition to one another, could only be experienced with the greatest pain.

At Edinburgh questions of faith and of ecclesiastical organization were excluded, but no agreement on them was to be expected. On the basis of this procedure it was possible to gain the cooperation of the High Church branch of the Anglican Church. Catholics and Orthodox were not invited.

The practical experience expressed by the American missionary bishop from the Philippines, Charles Brent (1862–1929), that one could not stop at practical collaboration but must ask questions precisely about doctrinal differences for the sake of unity, gave the stimulus to the movement Faith and Order. At a preparatory conference in Geneva in 1920 the Protestant Churches of Germany and France were not represented. Those of Switzerland declined to participate officially because among them there was no assumption that faith in the divinity of Christ must be acknowledged as an essential dogmatic basis. A continuing committee took over the rest of the preparation until finally on 3 August 1927 the first World Conference for Faith and Order could meet at Lausanne. There were 385 men and 9 women representing 108 ecclesial communities. The reports of the work groups on the themes unity of the Church, its message, its nature, its creed, its function, its sacraments, and on the unity of Christianity and the separated Churches were not adopted, but only received for transmission to the Churches. The experience of the great difficulties which opposed unification produced a salutary sobriety. There was a willingness not to conceal contradictions but honestly to expose them. Above all, the Orthodox were concerned with stating their viewpoint clearly. With them and the Anglicans the Protestants came into contact with a strongly ecclesiological-sacramental mentality; on the other hand, the Lutherans' fear of everything institutional and hence of a concrete Church became obvious.

From the experience "Doctrine separates — service unites" the Life and Work movement sought to prepare on another route, namely, through practical work for peace and social work, on the international level of the *ecumene*. At the meeting of the World Union for the Work of the Friendship of the Churches in 1919 at Oud Wassenaer near The Hague and following its activity and the exertions of the International Conciliation Union, Bishop Nathan Söderblom (1866–1931) of Uppsala urged a world conference on questions of social ethics. Dogmatic questions were to be excluded. Progress resulted more quickly than in the case of Faith and Order. As early as 1925 the World Conference for Life and Work was able to meet at Stockholm. It was the first expressly ecumenical conference. Representatives of all the great ecclesial communities, except the Roman Catholic Church, were present. The importance of the conference lay, of course, more in the fact that it took place at all than in its content and outcome. Brilliant festive gatherings and worship services could not conceal the deep dissents. If some, chiefly the Anglo-Saxons, intended to bring about the Kingdom of God by a constituting of social conditions in accord with God's world plan, others believed, especially the German Lutherans, that they must stress the transcendence of God's kingdom and its eschatological character. The conference was carried further in a continuing committee with various working groups, which from 1930 on was active in Geneva as the World Conference for Life and Work.

The relationship of German Protestantism to the ecumenical movement was considerably disturbed between the two world wars. If after 1918 "ecumenical cooperation was immensely impeded" (A. Deissmann) by the thesis of the sole guilt of Germany for the outbreak of the world war in the Treaty of Versailles, the question of attitude toward the Nazi state was posed for ecumenical groups from 1933. This problem was especially delicate when two German groups, the "German Evangelical Church" and the "Confessing Church" exerted themselves for recognition and collaboration. The World Council for Life and Work expressed itself in support of the Confessing Church and in 1934 decided to discuss at the next world conference the theme "Church, State, and People." For, because of the rise of totalitarian states, this old theme had caught fire in a new, even more acute form. The continuing committee of Faith and Order declared, on the other hand, for the admission of representatives of the official German Evangelical Church. The difficulty was removed when the Nazi state made participation in the world conference impossible for both groups — as for German delegations in general. The suggestion of the World Conference for Life and Work at Oxford in July 1937 to combine the two movements into a corporation and establish a World Council obtained also the assent of the Conference for Faith and Order at Edinburgh in August 1937. A committee discussed the constituting of the World Council at Utrecht in 1938. But because of the outbreak of war a plenary meeting could no longer be convoked. Not until 1948 did there occur at Amsterdam the establishing of the World Council of Churches; Faith and Order was to continue as a committee of the council and deal with questions of doctrine.

The first plenary meeting of the World Council of Churches at Amsterdam from 22 August to 4 September 1948 stood under the theme: "The Confusion of the World and God's Plan of Salvation." The basic formula adopted at the start reads: "The World Council of Churches is a community of Churches which acknowledge our Lord Jesus Christ as God and Saviour." According to the constitution, not individuals or associations but only Churches can be members. For at stake is a community of autonomous Churches, not a "superchurch." The World Council may be a help to the member Churches in their efforts for unity and in matters which can be done in common. "But it is alien to the council to wish to seize upon any functions which belong to the member Churches or to control them or wish to enact laws for them."

At Amsterdam 147 Churches were represented by 351 delegates from 47 countries. Fundamentalist Protestant groups, for example, the Lutherans of the Missouri Synod of North America, had refused to join, because they missed a clear and solid dogmatic position and, a few days before the meeting of the plenary assembly, had founded the International Council of Christian Churches.

The Orthodox were represented chiefly through envoys of the ecumenical patriarch of Constantinople and of the Greek Church. A gathering of the heads of the autocephalous Churches under the direction of the Patriarch of Moscow had declined participation in the World Conference. The Roman Catholic Church also was not represented; only individual theologians had obtained permission from the Curia for private participation.

The plenary meeting at Amsterdam had the task of giving the World Council a constitution and, in view of the world torn apart and bled to death by the war, to gain clarity on the mandate of Christianity in and for the world. In Section 1, under the direction of Bishop Hanns Lilje and with the cooperation of Karl Barth, the unity of the Church and inner renewal were stressed under the theme "The Church in God's Plan of Salvation." In this connection it became obvious that the ideas of the unity of the Church differed very deeply.

There were serious conflicts in the "political" Sections 3 — "the Church and the disorder." Here the world political and ideological struggle between East and West entered. It was bluntly stated in the talks of the American John Foster Dulles (1888–1959) and of the Prague theology professor Joseph L. Hromadka (1889–1969). In opposition to the harsh rejection of atheistic and materialistic communism by Dulles, Hromadka offered an emotional criticism of the capitalistic West. The conference saw itself facing the task of upholding the Christian community despite all "Iron Curtains" and at the same time of standing up for human liberty and social justice. It was stressed that "Christianity must not be identified with any particular system" and there was a warning against a bringing of the Church into line with a totalitarian system. In Section 3 it was emphasized as a supplement that the preserving of their independence in the face of the conformity and conflicts of the world must not mean any world-alienating neutrality of the Churches.

Amsterdam was only a beginning. It aimed to clarify, deepen, and expand the theological range of the very generally held basic formula and to find the right working method of the World Council. If there was great caution in the programmatic claim, it was hoped all the more, thanks to the importance of the institution and the sharing in dialogue and in work, to create ecumenical facts, which would in time permit it to proceed more energetically to the question of truth. In the declaration of the Central Committee at Toronto in 1950, "The Church, the Churches, and the World Council," it was again emphasized: "The World Council of Churches is not and must never become a super church. It is not the 'World Church.' It is also not the 'Una Sancta,' of which there is mention in the creed.... Each Church reserves to itself, in accord with its constitution, the right to ratify or reject the statements or actions of the council.... Within the World Council there is room for the ecclesiology of every Church which is ready to share in the ecumenical dialogue.... From the membership it does not follow that every Church must see the other member Churches as Churches in the true and full meaning of the word."

This declaration was intended to make easy the admission of the Orthodox Churches into the World Council. In addition to individual small national Churches and the Russian Church-in-exile, only the ecumenical patriarch of Constantinople and the Church of Greece had become members of the World Council at Amsterdam in 1948. The patriarchs of Alexandria, Antioch, and Jerusalem had soon followed. Favored by the change of Moscow's foreign policy after the death of Stalin (1879–1953), efforts were made, especially by the Evangelical Church of Germany, for contacts with Russia. In August 1956 the Central Committee of the World Council met in Hungary. At the same time the patriarch of Constantinople,

Athenagoras I (1886–1972), worked for a collaboration of all Orthodox Churches, including that of Russia. This led to the Pan-Orthodox conferences on Rhodes since 1961 and to the entry of the Churches of Russia, Bulgaria, Rumania, and Poland into the World Council at New Delhi. Here on 19 November 1961 met the third plenary assembly of the World Council of Chutebeg under the slogan: "Jesus Christ — Light of the World." The second plenary assembly had taken place at Evanston on Lake Michigan in 1954. At New Delhi the International Council of the Mission was integrated into the World Council as an autonomous section, the Commission for World Mission and Evangelization.

The Orthodox stood up for giving the status of an autonomous section to Faith and Order, hitherto only a report of the division of studies, and thereby to give greater weight to the question of truth. Their demands and questions facilitated also the acceptance of the Trinitarian expansion of the Christological basic formula. It now reads: "The World Council of Churches is a community of Churches which confess the Lord Jesus Christ in accord with Holy Scripture as God and Saviour, and therefore try in common to fulfill that to which they are called, to the honor of God, the Father, Son, and Holy Spirit." Especially the "young Churches," whose importance the selection of the meeting place within the Asiatic world intended to stress, urged the early realization of visible unity of the Churches and intercommunion. The detailed report of Section 3, "Unity," took this into account; it was approved "whole and entire" by the plenary assembly and recommended to the churches for study. In emphasizing the necessity of *visible* unity it meant, according to Edmund Schlink, "a real progress on the way to overcoming an ecclesiological Docetism."

Meanwhile, 198 member Churches belonged to the World Council. At New Delhi for the first time an official Roman Catholic delegation was present at the plenary meeting of the World Council, with five representatives of the Secretariat for the Unity of Christians at Rome and two representatives of Cardinal Gracias of Bombay. The "World Responsibility of the Churches," since Amsterdam in 1948 the prevailing theme of the conferences of the World Council, came strongly to the foreground since 1966, the year of the change in the general secretariat from W. A. Visser 't Hooft to Eugene Carson Blake. The World Conference for Church and Society at Geneva in 1966, the third following Stockholm in 1925 and Oxford in 1937, which was predominantly occupied with social ethical questions, was supposed to give "the Christian reply to the technical and social revolution of our age." It was marked by a top-heaviness of laity and by an almost equally strong representation of the Churches of Africa, Asia, and Latin America as of those of Western Europe and North America. Experts and the disconcerted were supposed to speak to the Churches and there were discussions of their answer to the challenges of the revolutionary changes of the day.

Out of the conviction that the social responsibility of Christians must not be limited to the personal relations of the individual Christian to his neighbor, "Love through Structures" became a chief slogan of the conference and revolution theology a heated topic of discussion. In the message of the conference it was said: "As Christians we must stand up for change.... Today many of those who devote themselves to the service of Christ and their neighbor take a more radical and revolutionary position. They in no way deny the value of tradition and social order but they are in search of a new strategy, by the aid of which basic changes can be carried out in society without too great a loss of time.... At the present time it is important that we recognize the deeper mooring of this radical position in Christian tradition and give it a rightful place in the life of the Church.... "

The conference demanded active participation of the Christian Church in the struggle for racial equality. The World Council of Churches was supposed to establish, among other things, a secretariat for the elimination of racism. This change to social and political commitment determined the theme of the fourth plenary assembly, which met at Uppsala from 4 to 20 July 1968, under the scriptural text, "See, I make all things new," and saw as signs of the time "sensational steps into a new scientific land, the protest of rebel students, the alarm over political murder and hostile clashes." In view of the reports, emotionally delivered before 704 delegates, many guests, and journalists, on "Rich and Poor Nations," "Racism or World Community," "Christianity and Human Rights," "Work of the Church in a Revolutionary World," it became difficult to bring the "gospel of conversion" to accommodation with the "gospel of social responsibility." This tension, further sharpened since 1969 by the development of an ecumenical program for the fighting of racism and a call to the member Churches for donations for the support of liberation organizations, drove the World Council into the shattering test of a polarization. According to the resolution of the Central Committee at Addis Ababa in 1971 the money must not be used for military purposes. Further, a study on violent and nonviolent methods for causing social change was to be undertaken.

In 1972 with the choice of Philip Potter, a Methodist from Jamaica, a Christian of the Third World became secretary-general of the World Council of Churches. At the conference of the Commission for World Mission and Evangelization of the World Council at Bangkok from 29 December 1972 to 8 January 1973, with the theme "Salvation of the World — Today," the delegates from Africa, Asia, and blacks from the United States were in a majority. "Salvation" was understood with the strong stress on "liberation," the work of salvation seen as a fight against exploitation, political suppression, and alienation. The aloofness from the Western Churches because of their "membership in colonial power structures" went as far as the demand for a "moratorium": at least temporarily the Churches of the Western world should stop sending out persons and money.

The geographical proximity to the great Asiatic religions suggested dialogue with them as a particular section theme. Thereby was posed the question of the right of mission, and the danger of a syncretism became acute in connection with the demand for "contextualizing" of the Christian message or the making of Christianity indigenous in the cultures of the Third World.

To judge from the preparations, the accent at the fifth plenary meeting, which took place from 23 November to 10 December 1975 at Nairobi, Kenya, with the theme "Christ liberates and unites," should have been placed on internal world problems, such as racism, sexism, and education. The great majority of the 757 delegates from 271 member Churches (with observers, advisers, and journalists there were ca. 2,300 participants) decided, however, for the theological themes of Sections 1 ("confession of Jesus Christ") and 2 ("unity of the Church"), and rising opposition, especially from the delegates of Orthodoxy, thwarted a slipping into the horizontal. The One Church was understood as a conciliar community of congregations which profess the same faith, celebrate the same baptism and the same Lord's Supper, and recognize the spiritual officers of the others. It was obvious that the World Council of Churches is not this conciliar community but is to prepare it. Worship, scriptural work, and spirituality occupy a broad space. Thus Nairobi became a "spiritual happening." In a "spirituality for combat," or, better, a "spirituality of commitment" the effort was made to recover the positive uniting of the proclamation of Christ and of social responsibility. It was attempted to surround anti-racism with a large program for the realization of human rights. Thus there was compulsion also to deal with the situation in the Soviet Union. The denial there of religious liberty led to the harshest debates; as generally at Nairobi, however, the course in this question also stood for integration and compromise. But the World Council of Churches will not fulfill its task with a passage from a "conflict *ecumene*" to a "community *ecumene*," if, as Lortz says, this is an "*ecumene* without truth."

The Share of the Roman Catholic Church in the Ecumenical Movement

With the participation of Catholic delegates in the plenary assembly in New Delhi a deeply rooted hesitation of the Roman Curia vis-à-vis ecumenical meetings was overcome. Convinced that it, and in the full sense only it, visibly represented the one, holy, catholic, and apostolic Church founded by Jesus Christ, the Roman Catholic Church was concerned that this claim could be made relative if it sat down with other ecclesial communities at the conference table.

To the invitation from the Scandinavian Lutheran archbishops to Pope Benedict XV to send representatives to Uppsala for an ecumenical conference on 8 September 1918, Cardinal Secretary of State Gasparri asserted that everything would be agreeable to the Pope which operated for peace and Christian brotherhood, because it "smooths the path for what the Gospel expresses in the words: 'that there may be one flock and one shepherd.'" But there was no mention of a representation of the Pope at the proposed conference. Instead, on 4 July 1919 a decree of the Holy Office forbade any participation in congresses for the promotion of unity without the permission of the Holy See. As early as 16 May 1919 Benedict XV had given the decision to a delegation which brought him the invitation to the conference of Faith and Order: "The teaching and practice of the Roman Catholic Church in regard to the unity of the visible Church of Christ are well known to everyone, and so it is not possible for the Catholic Church to participate in a congress like the one proposed. However, His Holiness wishes under no circumstances to disapprove the congress in question for those who are not united with the See of Peter."

The lively interest of Pius XI in movements for unity applied especially to Orthodoxy. As a scholar, an apostolate of the spirit was in first place in his eyes. For this he in 1922 established the Oriental Institute at Rome and required also an intensive study of the theology and liturgy of the Eastern Churches. Here he saw a special task for the Benedictines. In addition to the abbey of Niederaltaich on the Danube, this call was heard by the priory founded at Amay-sur-Meuse in 1925 and transferred to Chevetogne, Belgium, in 1939. It celebrated the liturgy in

Eastern rites, cultivated the theology and spirituality of the East, and published the periodical *Irénicon.* In the Pope's view it is... "necessary for reunion especially that people know and love one another.... The separated parts of a gold-bearing rock are likewise gold-bearing."

This could have been used of relations with Protestants. Accordingly, in an address in the consistory of 24 March 1924, Pius XI asked for ecumenical efforts in regard to all separated Christians: "We will be obliged to all Catholics who strive, under the impulse of divine grace, to facilitate admittance to the true faith for their separated brothers, whoever these may be, by dispelling their prejudices, keeping in view unadulterated Catholic teaching, and especially making evident in themselves the feature of disciples of Christ, for there is love." In practice, however, the Pope occupied a rather reserved attitude in regard to Protestant ecumenism: in his view, that of historian and scholar, everything remained too much on the surface, that is, he missed the basic study of the sources, especially of the Church Fathers; as a churchman, he saw the danger of relativism and indifferentism. For some Catholics and many Protestants, especially for the participants in the conferences of Stockholm and Lausanne, it was a keen disappointment that the Catholic Church was absent. Archbishop Söderblom and with him others went so far as to conclude from this conduct that Rome thereby showed to the whole world its sectarian spirit and placed itself outside the totality of Christianity.

After Lausanne, Pius XI in the encyclical *Mortalium animos* of 6 January 1928 subjected the ecumenical movement, as it had thus far developed, to a sharp criticism: "Can we endure... that the truth, in fact the truth revealed by God, be made the object of negotiations?" In the Pope's view the Catholic Church took an interest in the ecumenical movement only so far as this meant a return to the sources of faith, to the Gospel and tradition.

Despite the official refusal, private observers were present, with papal and episcopal approval, at the World Conference for Life and Work in Stockholm in 1925 and at that for Faith and Order in Lausanne in 1927: from Germany Max Joseph Metzger (1887–1944) and Hermann Hoffmann (1878–1973). It can be said that in Germany the situation was in some respects favorable for the meeting of the denominations: Here the number of "denominations" was not so large as, for example, in the United States, and in the great Churches of the nation one had to deal with partners in dialogue who were to some extent committed to a creed. At the universities were Catholic and Protestant theological faculties which with the aid of the historicocritical method demolished some prejudices and exposed common foundations. The history of the Reformation and the life and work of Martin Luther were, especially after the appearance in 1939 of the *Reformation in Deutschland* by Joseph Lortz (1887–1975), presented more objectively and with more understanding of its religious motives, and the Catholic share in the guilt for the schism was candidly admitted. The threat to the Churches and to Christianity from National Socialism contributed substantially to the rapprochement of the denominations. Now what was important, beyond all differences, was to save the Christian substance. It worked in favor of the cooperation of the denominations that Protestantism, as "Confessing Church," thought better of its being as Church.

Among the pioneers of Catholic ecumenism in Germany were Arnold Rademacher (1873–1939), Max Pribilla (1874–1956), Robert Grosche (1888–1967), the founder of the periodical *Catholica* (1932), Matthias Laros (1882–1962), Joseph Lortz, Karl Adam (1876–1966), and Max Joseph Metzger. In 1938 the last named founded the brotherhood *Una Sancta,* with the aim of working for unity through prayer and fraternal meetings. Due to his initiative there took place larger meetings at Meitingen near Augsburg in 1939–40. Suspected by Nazi officials as an apostle of peace, spied on and often imprisoned, Metzger was executed on 17 April 1944.

In France ecumenical thought was roused by Paul Couturier (1881–1953), who spread and spiritually deepened the World Octave of Prayer for the Unity of Christians from 18 to 25 January, which had been suggested by Anglicans, and by M. Yves Congar, O.P. (born 1904). There was to be prayer for "the unity of all Christians, as Christ desired."

After the Second World War there arose in many places *Una Sancta* circles of lay persons and theologians as sites of productive encounter of Catholics and Protestants in prayer and discussion. Their spontaneity naturally declined, the clearer it became how long and difficult was the road to unity. The monitum *Cum compertum* of the Holy Office at Rome, issued on 5 June 1948 before the first plenary assembly of the World Council at Amsterdam, seemed to produce a setback. In it was inculcated, with reference to the regulations of canon law (Canon 1325, par. 3), that participation in discussions of faith with non-Catholics was allowed only with the previous permission of the Holy See. More positive in tone were the directives for its implementation in the instruction *De motione oecumenica* of 20 December 1949. In it the bishops were requested not only to bestow their attention on strivings for unity but to foster and direct them. Meetings and discussions with non-Catholics were regarded as a desired opportunity to make known to non-Catholics a knowledge of Catholic teaching. To the bishops was given for three years the faculty of granting the necessary permission of the Holy See for participation in ecumenical dialogues. "The very important work of reuniting all Christians in the one true faith and in the one true Church," so the instruction concluded, "must more and more become one of the preferred functions of all pastoral care and a chief concern of the urgent prayer of all believers to God."

After the Second World War the discussions of theologians received a strong stimulus. At the initiative of the archbishop of Paderborn, Lorenz Jaeger (1892–1975), and of the Lutheran bishop of Oldenburg, Wilhelm Stählin (1883–1975), theologians of both denominations met annually in Germany since 1946 to discuss common and separating doctrines. With the decisive participation of the Dutch professor of theology, Jan Willebrands (b. 1909), there was formed in 1952 the International Conference for Ecumenical Questions, whose work was incorporated into the Secretariat for Promoting Christian Unity established in 1960 by Pope John XXIII and directed by Cardinal Augustin Bea (1881–1968). In 1962 it obtained the official status of a conciliar commission and as such was able authoritatively to prepare the Decree on Ecumenism of the Second Vatican Council.

The council was to introduce a new epoch of the Ecumenical Movement within the Catholic Church. It professed ecumenism as a movement produced by the spirit, which is the task "of the whole Church, of the faithful as well as of the shepherds" (ARTICLE 5). It must be supported by the spirit of penance and inner renewal. The Catholic Church knows that it shares in the guilt for the split and it is aware that it has not always properly preached the truths of faith entrusted to it, so that it became difficult for people to find the truth. Thus it sees itself summoned to a "lasting reformation" (ART. 6). But if one can have access "only through the Catholic Church of Christ, which is the common means of salvation, to the entire fullness of the means of salvation," (ART. 3), there are still "many important elements or goods by all of which the Church is built up and acquires its life, even outside the visible limits of the Catholic Church" (ART. 3). The Holy Spirit uses the separated Churches and communities as "means of salvation." Catholics are asked "joyfully to acknowledge and highly to esteem the really Christian goods from the common heritage which are found among the separated brethren" (ART. 4).

Of course, the differences still existing despite all that was common could not be concealed. "Nothing is so alien to the ecumenical spirit as false irenicism." Doctrinal differences that cause separation had to deal especially with the nature of the Church and with its power, its office. Because of the absence of the sacrament of orders, Protestants have "not preserved the original and complete reality of the Eucharistic mystery" (ART. 22). Hence "the doctrine of the Lord's Supper . . . and of the ministerial offices of the Church [are especially] necessarily the subject of the dialogue" (ART. 22). This discussion is carried on in the field of tension of the common and the separating. But one must not rest content with dialogue. The council called to common prayer. In it the grace of unity must be asked for, but the community persisting despite the split must be attested. Further, the separated brothers must work together in service to the world. This practical work is possible, even if persons are of different views in the questions of principles of morals and of the relationship of Church and society. Without prejudice to some criticism — it was especially objected that in the decree the Catholic Church saw itself as the center around which the other Churches stood more or less close, like concentric circles — the decree was generally praised; it "opened new doors for ecumenical contacts" (W. A. Visser 't Hooft).

To implement the conciliar decree the Secretariat for Promoting Christian Unity at Rome published guidelines for practical collaboration and dialogue with the non-Catholic Churches in 1967 and 1970 in the *Ecumenical Directory*. If ecumenism is an affair not only of church leadership but of all Christians, then it is important to activate "ecumenism on the spot," that is, to bring Christians together on the level of the congregations for dialogue, prayer, and common ministry to the world. This will be aided by the Roman document on "Ecumenical Cooperation on the regional, national, and local level" of 7 July 1975. In 1973 the union of dioceses of the German Federal Republic joined the Working Community of the Christian Churches in Germany, founded in 1948 and similar to the Councils of Christians in other countries. Likewise the Catholic dioceses became members of the Working Community founded on the level of the German federal states.

Membership of the Catholic Church in the World Council of Churches is still subject, of course, to various kinds of difficulties. On the basis of the existing charter the weight of the Catholic Church, preponderant in members, would be too heavy. A "common working group" consisting of eight representatives of the World Council and of six of the Catholic Church was set up and undertook its work at Bossey near Geneva in June 1965. This was related to all questions for which the World Council itself was competent; in the first place, it was to gain information on the possibilities of dialogue and cooperation and eliminate sources of tension. The

Ecumenical Work Community for Justice, Peace, and Development (Sodepax), set up at first on a trial basis by the papal commission for development assistance, *Iustitia et Pax,* and by the World Council in 1968, aims to help all races, peoples, and religions in the struggle against misery and war. Since the fourth plenary assembly of the World Council at Uppsala in 1968 nine Roman Catholic theologians belong as full members to the Faith and Order commission, embracing 150 persons.

The doctrinal dialogue was and is conducted in various groups on the national and international level. Except for the dialogue in 1971 between the Roman Catholic Church, the Lutheran, and the Reformed World Union on "the theology of marriage and the problem of mixed marriages," these discussions are bilateral, that is, they are conducted by the Catholic Church with one denominational Church at a time on the international, regional, and national level. Contact talks with the Lutheran World Union (LWB) led to the establishing of the study commission "The Gospel and the Church," which held five sessions in 1967–71 and collected its "working results" in 1971 in the so-called *Malta Paper.* No complete agreement could be reached on function and intercommunion. The dialogue was continued by the Common Lutheran-Catholic Commission, newly constituted in 1975.

"The Eucharist" (1967) and "Eucharist and Office" (1970) have also been the chief themes of the Catholic-Lutheran dialogue in the United States since 1965. It became clear that the way to intercommunion lay only by way of harmony in the understanding of the Eucharist and a mutual recognition of ecclesiastical offices. On the basis of the talks the participants thought they could invite their respective Churches to acknowledge the validity of the offices of the other Church and the real presence of Jesus Christ in its Eucharistic celebrations. Then the commission in the United States turned to the question of the papal primacy. The inner consistency of this further step was perceived: "Our earlier discussions had concentrated on the ministry of office in the local communities. Now we concentrate on the unifying and organizing function of this office for the Universal Church — on the question of how a definite form of this office, that is, the papacy, has served the unity of the Universal Church in the past and how it can serve it in the future." There was a striving for a certain agreement on the necessity of a special office for the entire Church. Of course, the structure and exercise of the office had to be discussed in still more detail. The talks, which are still in progress, produced in 1974 the report "Office and Universal Church," which dealt with the primacy and not yet with the problem of infallibility.

The International Anglican-Roman Catholic Commission summoned in 1970 by the Pope and the archbishop of Canterbury, came in the so-called Windsor Statement of 1971 to an "essential agreement on the doctrine of the Eucharist" and in 1973 to a basic consensus on "Office and Ordination" in the "Canterbury Statement." In these, to be sure, the question of the Petrine office and of the recognition of Anglican orders was excluded and reserved for a later discussion. This was taken up in 1974. In 1976 it led in Venice to the acceptance of a declaration on "Authority in the Church." In connection with authority in questions of faith for the *koinonia* of local Churches there were also taken up the primacy of the Bishop of Rome and his special responsibility for faith and doctrine of the Universal Church. There was demanded an appropriate balance between the primatial, collegial, and synodal exercise of authority, but recognition of a special position of the Bishop of Rome in a reunited Church as a service to its unity and catholicity was underscored. "The only episcopal see which claims a universal primacy, which has also exercised and still exercises such an *episcope,* is the episcopal see of Rome, the city where Peter and Paul died. It seems fit that in any coming unity a universal primacy, such as we have described it, be exercised by this episcopal see."

Discussions with the Methodist World Union have shown remarkable agreement in the sphere of spirituality and piety. As a result, the Dialogue Commission of the United Methodist Churches and of the Roman Catholic Church in the United States published in January 1976 a statement "Holiness and Spirituality of Ecclesiastical Office."

The positive development of the relations of the Roman Catholic Church and the World Council of Churches found expression in the visit of Paul VI to the central office of the World Council at Geneva on 10 June 1969. But at the same time it became clear that the expectations expressed at Uppsala in 1968 of an imminent membership of Rome in the World Council prejudiced the development. "With all fraternal candor it is said: We are not of the opinion that the question of membership of the Catholic Church in the World Council is ready to the extent that one can or must give a positive answer to it" (Paul VI).

The Church in the Individual Countries

Chap. 98: Gabriel Adriányi; Chap. 99: Ludwig Volk
Chap. 100/I-II: André Tihon; Chap. 100/III: Johannes Bots
Chap. 101: Luigi Mezzardi and Franco Molinari
Chap. 102: Pierre Blet; Chap. 103/I: Quintín Aldea Vaquero
Chap. 103/II: Antonio da Silva; Chap. 104: Robert Trisco

C H A P T E R   9 8

The Church in
Northern, Eastern, and Southern Europe

The end of the First World War produced fundamental upheavals in northern, eastern, and southern Europe. On the ruins of the destroyed Habsburg and Romanov empires arose new or very different national states, which in their reorganization and the building of their new structure made use of the help of religious groups. In the overwhelmingly Catholic countries, such as Lithuania, Poland, and Hungary, therefore, Catholicism flourished, whereas in countries with a majority of Orthodox population, like Rumania, Yugoslavia, and Bulgaria, the independent Eastern Churches obtained a leading position. However, in these states, as also in Czechoslovakia, which represented a sort of special case, and in the Scandinavian and Baltic countries with a Protestant majority, the Catholic Church was able to develop freely, due to the middle-class democracies. Only the Soviet Union constituted an exception. For its Communist, strictly antireligious ideology led to an unprecedented anti-Church struggle, which, after the Second World War, in consequence of the Soviet seizure of power in eleven nations in all of eastern and southern Europe it was extended to almost 70 million Catholics. Only from the early 1960s did the situation begin to relax gradually in the course of international politics. The long-range method of the interior withering of the Church replaced the open struggle against it. But the changed international situation also made it possible for the Holy See, through a reoriented policy, to hasten to the aid of the oppressed Church in the East.

The Scandinavian Countries

In Denmark Catholicism could continue after the First World War its upsurge that had begun at the turn of the century. As a result of numerous and important conversions the number of the faithful grew within eighteen years from 3,000 to 15,000, and in 1938 to 22,000 in a Protestant population of 4.2 million. Due to the circumstances of domestic policy, the Church displayed a vigorous activity in pastoral care, charity, the press, and the care of youth. Thirty new churches, chapels, seven schools, and nine hospitals were built. The number of Catholics rose also on the Danish islands. In 1923 the Holy See established a prefecture apostolic in Iceland, which was raised to a vicariate apostolic in 1929. Great ecclesiastical celebrations and meetings made clear the strength and importance obtained by Danish Catholicism. The German occupation of Denmark from 1940 to 1945 brought trouble for the Church especially in economic respects. However, the Catholic renewal not only could maintain itself but continue its development. During and after the Second World War Denmark admitted for the time being some 250,000 refugees, including 24,000 Catholics, and this especially gave an impetus to charity. In keeping with the favorable development of the postwar years, Pius XII in 1953 made Copenhagen a diocese and placed it immediately under the Holy See. Since then Danish Catholicism has displayed a vigorous activity, especially in the care of souls, education, and social work.

Because of the powerful Lutheran state-Church system, the unfamiliarity of Catholicism, and the large diaspora, the Catholic mission in Sweden was able to develop less favorably. Through tireless missionary work, but especially through the immigration of ca. 20,000 Catholic refugees during and after the Second World War, especially from Eastern Europe, the situation of the Church gradually improved. In the process of the erecting of the autonomous Scandinavian hierarchy, Pius XII in 1953 also elevated the vicariate apostolic of Stockholm to a bishopric.

As in Sweden, the Catholic mission in Norway could acquire greater importance only in the most recent period because of immigration and conversions. Here the number of Catholics in a population of 3.6 million grew in 1974 to 9,127. Here too in 1953 Pius XII founded its own ecclesiastical organization: out of the vicariate apostolic erected in 1931 came the see of Oslo and two other vicariates apostolic. Of course, in Norway Catholics represent a very small minority in the diaspora, but their religious life is exemplary.

Like Sweden and Norway, the Catholic Church in Finland has only a small number of faithful — 2,959 in 1974 — who live dispersed among 4.6 million Protestants. Here in 1955 Pius XII organized its own hierarchy, the see of Helsinki, after the Finnish Catholics had in 1920 been separated from the archbishopric of Mogilev and obtained a vicariate of their own. In spite of some restrictions, the Church in Finland enjoys free activity.

The Baltic Countries

The Republic of Estonia, proclaimed on 2 April 1918 but only recognized in international law on 26 January 1921, embraced at its independence 47,549 square kilometers with a population of ca. 1.1 million, of whom 77.6 percent belonged to the Lutheran and only 2,327 — .2 percent — to the Catholic Church. In 1940 the latter were cared for in six parishes by eleven priests and about twenty religious of both sexes. Since the faithful had previously been subject to the Russian

archbishopric of Mogilev, a special apostolic administration, under a titular archbishop, was erected for them in 1925. The first Soviet occupation in 1940, then the
incorporation of Estonia after the end of the German occupation into the Soviet
Union in 1945, and the implementation of the Soviet religious policy completely
destroyed the organization and life of the Church in Estonia.

Like Estonia, the Republic of Latvia appeared on 18 November 1918 as a result
of the collapse of the Russian Empire, and, also like Estonia, it did not receive
recognition in international law until 26 January 1921. The new nation had a total
area of 65,791 square kilometers with a population of 1.8 million. The majority
of the population was Lutheran — 58 percent — but here the number of Catholics amounted to 450,210 souls — 23.69 percent — in 1930. For them the Holy
See restored the old see of Riga as early as 1918 and removed it from the earlier
diocesan union of Mogilev and Kaunas. Because of religious liberty and the accommodating policy of the state, the Church was able quickly to develop. There
appeared religious institutions, societies, seminaries, a Catholic theological faculty
and a considerable Catholic press. In order further to complete the ecclesiastical
organization and to clarify the relations of state and Church, Latvia conducted
discussions with the Holy See in 1920, which ended on 30 May 1922 with the concluding of a concordat. The concordat guaranteed the Church full possibility of
development and called into existence the archbishopric of Riga and the auxiliary bishopric of Kurland-Semgallen, with its seat at Liepaja. The outbreak of the
Second World War, the events of the war, the forcible annexation of the country
to the Soviet Union on 21 June 1940, and Soviet domination also made a quick
end of the flourishing life of the Church here too. All church organizations were
forbidden, and bishops were imprisoned. After 1963 the situation relaxed a bit.
Thus the one vicar general for the two sees of Riga and Liepaja could take part in
the Second Vatican Council and in 1964 receive episcopal ordination at Rome.

Lithuania declared its political sovereignty on 16 February 1918, but, after
Poland had occupied Lithuanian Vilna, and Lithuania the district of Memel that
was under Polish rule, it was recognized in international law only on 8 May 1924.
The republic covered 58,810 square kilometers with a population of 2.3 million, of
whom 1.7 million were Catholics. Although the overwhelming majority of the population was Catholic, and the Church had fostered the independence of Lithuania
with all its power in the most recent past, there occurred repeated conflicts between Lithuania and the Holy See because of the question of Vilna. When the
Polish concordat of 1925 left the see of Vilna with Poland, the diplomatic relations
assumed in 1920 between Lithuania and the Vatican were broken. On 4 April 1926
Pius XI created a Lithuanian ecclesiastical province by the bull *Lituanorum gente.*
He elevated Kaunas to an archbishopric and subjected to it four new dioceses and
a prelacy *nullius.* But since this took place without previous consultation with the
Lithuanian government, the government did not recognize the papal bull. Long
and difficult negotiations between the Holy See and Lithuania led on 10 December
1927 to the concluding of a concordat. It restored diplomatic relations between the
Vatican and the republic, guaranteed the complete freedom of the Church, and
confirmed the new Lithuanian ecclesiastical organization. Church life flourished.
Also the Catholic press and religious institutes renewed themselves energetically.
But the political conflicts from 1938 on, the Second World War, the invasion of

the Soviet army after a three-year occupation by the Germans (1941–44), and the incorporation of Lithuania into the Soviet Union on 3 August 1940 made a quick end of this development. The new rulers denounced the concordat in 1940 and introduced the same measures as in the two other Baltic nations. Also there occurred a mass deportation, which annihilated not only the entire hierarchy and a great part of the clergy but also a third of the Catholic population of Lithuania.

After 1963 the situation became a bit easier. In 1965 a Lithuanian vicar capitular could be ordained a bishop at Rome, in 1968 a Lithuanian priest in his own country, and in 1969 two other priests. In 1967 two bishops could journey to Rome.

The Soviet Union

When, on the collapse of the Empire of the Tsars, the Bolshevik Russian Socialist Federated Soviet Republic arose in 1918, then in 1922 the Union of Soviet Socialist Republics, there was in the new state only a shrinking Catholic minority. For the number of Roman and Uniate Catholics decreased as a consequence of the independence of Poland and of the Baltic nations from 15 to 1.6 million, who now lived among 78 million of other faiths, of whom 71 percent were Orthodox. The Catholics of the Roman Rite, mostly foreigners or non-Russians, were in Russia itself subject to the archbishopric of Mogilev and its four auxiliary sees and were all cared for by ca. 4,600 priests in 4,234 churches and 1,978 chapels. But the new frontiers of the state left only the archbishopric and two other dioceses and the vicariate apostolic for the Crimea, the Caucasus, and Siberia, the apostolic administration of the Armenian Rite, and the exarchate of the Slavonic Byzantine Rite in their former extent.

On 23 January 1918 the new rulers proclaimed separation of Church and state and began at once with the dissolving of the organization of the Catholic Church. By 1923 all bishops had been imprisoned, expelled, or shot. The normal church administration came to an end with the hierarchy. The number of priests dropped rapidly also through natural and violent deaths, deportations, imprisonment, and the preventing of reception of the priesthood by candidates. All seminaries and the important ecclesiastical academy at Petrograd were dissolved. Most churches and chapels were closed or profaned. Within a few years the external religious life of the Church had been completely destroyed.

In view of this situation, the Holy See left nothing untried to stop the destruction of the Church. But repeated diplomatic interventions achieved only the freeing and expelling of Archbishops Eduard von Ropp in 1920 and John Cieplak in 1923. The papal assistance mission in the Soviet Union, visited by famine, which was carried out with the cooperation of the Divine Word Missionaries and a donation of ca. 2 million dollars in 1922–24, did not realize the missionary expectations connected with the giving of aid. Now as earlier, the authorities kept any church activity away from works of charity.

Because of the serious ecclesiopolitical situation and the great upheavals in Eastern Europe, as early as 1917 Benedict XV established the Congregation for the Eastern Churches and in the same year the Institute of Oriental Studies. In the former a special "Commission for Russia" was formed, which worked as an independent office from 1925 to 1934. Since it was of interest to the new Soviet state to obtain recognition in international law, it had been ready to have a nuncio sent to Moscow, despite the retaining of its church policy. The negotiations foundered when Pius XI made the resumption of full diplomatic relations dependent on the attitude of the Soviet government to the Church.

Meanwhile diplomatic "feelers" were not ended. Thus Pius XI could in 1925 and 1926 authorize a member of the papal "Commission for Russia," the Jesuit Michel d'Herbigny, who was ordained a bishop, to arrange a new organization of church administration in the Soviet Union and send him to Moscow. There in 1926 he erected nine apostolic administrations and secretly ordained four bishops. However, this was soon discovered by the state. Monsignor d'Herbigny had to leave the country, and the new bishops were imprisoned. The reorganization of the Church collapsed thereby. Now the whole of ecclesiastical life was paralyzed. Only some fifty to sixty priests escaped the measures of terror, and their activity was strictly supervised. From 1933 a priest in the American Embassy at Moscow could function for the personnel and celebrate Mass in the church of Saint Louis.

After his predecessor had already in 1920 rejected the Communist ideology in the motu proprio *Bonum sana,* Pius XI condemned Bolshevism and its violence in numerous declarations, especially in the encyclicals *Miserentissimus Redemptor, Caritate Christi compulsi,* and *Divini Redemptoris.* And on 2 February 1930 he summoned all Christianity to prayer services against communism.

The events at the beginning of and during the Second World War, especially the annexation of eastern Poland, the Baltic nations, Bessarabia, and the Carpatho-Ukraine by the Soviet Union, and the Soviet military occupation of Eastern Europe, as well as the decision of the three-power conference at Yalta from 4 to 11 February 1945 to leave all of Eastern Europe under Soviet influence, had as a result a cruel way of the cross for some 70 million Catholics in eleven countries. The harshest blow, of course, fell on Catholics in the areas incorporated by the Soviet Union.

As early as 1939 the state had moved with all its means against the Uniate Armenians and Ukrainians (the Ruthenians) who lived in the archdiocese of Lvov and its auxiliary sees. Church property was confiscated, seminaries were closed, monasteries and churches were plundered. After the end of the German occupation and the second Soviet invasion, the persecution of the Church was resumed and the forcible reincorporation of the Uniates was carried through. The annexation to the Patriarchal Church of Moscow was enforced by an illegal synod on 8 March 1946 after the imprisonment of ten bishops and apostolic administrators. In this way the Catholic Church in the Ukraine was liquidated. In a similar fashion there occurred the return of the Uniates in Carpatho-Ukraine. After the bishop of Užhorod had been eliminated by a fatal automobile accident in 1949, the state's arbitrary measures climaxed on 15 August 1949 in the proclaiming of reunion with the Orthodoxy of Moscow. Meanwhile, 67 churches had been expropriated and 18 priests imprisoned.

In 1963 the Vatican's Eastern policy was able to effect the release from prison of the Ukrainian metropolitan of Lvov, Josyf Slipyi. However, the sad situation of the Church in the entire Soviet Union was unchanged.

Poland

Proclaimed by the Central Powers on 5 November 1916, the sovereign Polish state was restored in the Peace Treaty of Versailles on 28 June 1919 after more than a century of total partition. About the same political boundaries were reinstituted as after the second partition in 1793. In 1927 the Republic of Poland included, after some correcting of the frontiers, 385,030 square kilometers. In addition the new nation comprised a variety of national minorities, for the Poles constituted only ca. 78 percent of the population.

If Polish Catholicism was in modern times, especially however during the difficult period of the partition of the state, the unselfish bearer of national interests and the strongest promoter of the reestablishment of state sovereignty, it is not to be wondered at that, thanks to its unbounded popularity, it played a key role in the reconstruction of the state and in public life. Since the boundaries of the ecclesiastical provinces were often at variance with those of the state, the reorganization of the Church's structure took precedence for the episcopate in the reconstruction and standardization of church life. There began discussions between the papal nuncio, Achille Ratti (1919–21), the future Pope Pius XI, the episcopate and the government. They proved to be difficult, but were successful. After nine episcopal sees had been filled in 1919 and in 1920 the diocese of Lodz and in 1922 two apostolic administrations had been erected, there ensued on 10 February 1925 the signing of a concordat between Poland and the Holy See. On the one hand, the concordat guaranteed the complete liberty of the Church and granted the Curia influence on the organization of the Church in Poland, but on the other hand it took into account the national political wishes of the government. The new diocesan arrangement of Poland was agreed upon in ARTICLE 9; it resulted on 28 October 1925 in the bull *Vixdum Poloniae,* which in addition to the three existing archbishoprics — Gniezno, Lvov, Warsaw — established two new metropolitanates — Cracow and Vilna — and five more bishoprics.

Although, because of the stern state direction and some state encroachments, sometimes serious tensions existed between Church and government, ecclesiastical life was able to develop fully. The Church's greatest efficacy appeared especially in public life. Poland presented itself as an expressly Catholic country. But the inner life of the Church also flourished. Ecclesiastical congresses, great pilgrimages, Catholic associations and organizations, intensive parochial care of souls, new synodal laws, a greatly improved Catholic press, basic theological instruction in seminaries and on Catholic theological faculties, general Catholic education and the Catholic University of Lublin, founded in 1918, deepened the faith decisively. But this did not prevent the Polish episcopate from energetically Latinizing the strong Uniate Ukrainian Church.

On 1 September 1939 Poland was attacked by Germany and, seventeen days later, by the Soviet Union. Poland soon succumbed to superior strength and was again partitioned. Its western areas were for the most part allotted to Germany with 16.9 million Catholics — 80.8 percent of all the Catholics. The southern part and the remainder of Poland was made a sort of German colony as the *Gouvernement General,* while the Soviet Union incorporated the eastern areas of Poland, which in the course of the Second World War also came under German occupation from 1941 to 1944–45. The inclusion of the eastern parts of Poland in the Soviet Union (1939–41) produced a brutal persecution of the Church. But also in the areas occupied by Germany the fate of the Polish Catholics was unbearable. Nazi directives deprived the Church of its liberty and almost outlawed it, the clergy was decimated, a great part of the bishops and priests were arrested and taken to concentration camps, all associations and organizations were forbidden, and worship was restricted to a minimum. At the end of the war the Church in Poland had to lament the death of 4 bishops, 1,996 priests, including the Blessed Maximilian Kolbe, 113 clerics, and 238 female religious. A total of 3,647 priests, 389 clerics, 341 lay brothers, and 1,117 sisters were confined in concentration camps. The Holy See, which had very sharply condemned the partition of Poland and the oppression of the Polish Catholics, could not help the afflicted Church.

The restoration of the Polish state on 5 July 1945, in which Poland had been compensated for its eastern areas that had been annexed by the Soviet Union with the eastern areas of Germany as far as the Oder-Neisse line, brought the Church only a temporary relief. For soon there began also in Poland, with the aid of the Soviet occupation, the setting up of a Communist political system. On 16 September 1945 the new Polish government denounced the concordat. But first the Church had to tackle the rapid restoration of church administration and of religious life because of the vast losses in the war and the great territorial changes. This was facilitated by the fact that in 1945 Poland was reduced in size by about one-fifth, but the proportion of the Catholic populations — especially through the replacing of the expelled Germans, who were partly Protestants, by Catholic Poles from the eastern areas — grew to 97.8 percent. On 15 August 1945 Cardinal Primate August Hlond erected five apostolic administrations in the formerly German eastern areas. Religious life could again develop. However, the original religious toleration of the state was supplanted by a latent attitude of hostility to the Church. Between 1946 and 1948 the government tried to drive the Church's activity out of public life into the area of the sacred. Severe measures of curtailment affected especially Catholic education, the pastoral care of youth, and the Catholic cultural and educational system. Also an effort was undertaken to split the clergy by the creation of a national Church. The struggle against the Church erupted openly in 1951. An abundance of administrative measures affected the Church, such as the dissolution of all ecclesiastical organizations, except that of charity, the secularization of church schools, hospitals, and orphanages, and the expropriation of church property. The episcopate was forced to conclude an agreement with the government on 14 April 1950. While the Church renounced its land and promised its help in the integrating of the new western areas, the state guaranteed a minimum of church activity.

The state did not observe the agreement. The government placed men of its confidence as vicars capitular in the apostolic administrations, displayed a propaganda campaign, and further persecuted the Church. Many bishops, including Primate Stefan Wyszyński, and hundreds of priests were imprisoned, while the collaborating "patriotic priests" obtained key positions. A decisive ecclesiopolitical change did not occur until October 1956, when the Polish Communist Party abandoned the former Stalinist course and entrusted the direction of the state to the moderate Wladyslaw Gomulka. He ended the imprisonment of Wyszyńiski and the priests and on 7 December 1956 concluded a new agreement with the Church, which essentially guaranteed the Church activity agreed to in the previous treaty, even if still more curtailed. This time the government kept its word. New vicars general could be installed in the administrations, and church life could again develop, even if modestly. Renewed tensions between state and Church appeared only in isolation, as on the occasion of the message of reconciliation of the Polish episcopate to the German Catholics on 18 November 1965 and of the millennium celebration of the conversion of Poland in 1966.

Paul VI, who would have liked to visit Poland, accommodated Polish desires in the context of his Eastern policy. In 1971 he beatified Maximilian Kolbe, and, after the German Federal Republic had signed the Treaty of Warsaw on 7 December 1970, he took up the reorganization of Poland's western territories on 28 June 1972. The previous apostolic administrators became diocesan bishops, three new sees were erected, and German ecclesiastical jurisdictions, that is, dioceses, were separated from the Polish western territories. Thereby the Polish western lands became autonomous in canon law.

The contacts and negotiations between the Vatican and the Polish government were not thereafter interrupted. This all the more, because Polish Catholicism with its uncrushed vitality has remained an unmistakable element of the Polish people.

Czechoslovakia

When on 28 October 1918 the Republic of Czechoslovakia, with 140,546 square kilometers and 13.6 million inhabitants, of whom 95 percent were Catholics, was constituted out of territories of the crumbled Austro-Hungarian Monarchy, the situation of the Church in the new state began to appear quite complicated and difficult. A nationalistic and anticlerical Czech ruling class acquired power. The anti-Roman, nationalistic tendencies which for decades had grown in the Czech clergy under the direction of the Jednota society and now peaked in the powerful and, especially among Czech intellectuals, very popular Away-from-Rome movement, first led to serious conflicts within the Church, and then on 8 January 1920 the proclaiming of the Czech National Church. This and Protestant religious communities, as well as Orthodoxy in the Carpatho-Ukraine that belonged to the republic, soon experienced the widest spread through massive state support.

In addition, the government prepared to adapt the church organization, which now consisted of two archdioceses and ten bishoprics, to national interests and to approximate the diocesan boundaries to the national frontiers. In November 1918 Archbishop Count Paul Huyn had to leave Prague, and in 1919 four bishops in Slovakia had also to resign or were deported to Hungary. In order to put pressure on the Church, the state on 11 August 1919 sequestered 251,925 cadastral yokes (ca. 126,000 hectares) of church property in Slovakia. Various church schools were secularized, and especially by means of the Sokol Unions a massive nationalistic anticlerical propaganda was promoted.

The Holy See, which had taken up diplomatic relations with Czechoslovakia as early as October 1919, tried by all means to stop the exodus from the Church and to normalize the situation. In accord with the desires of both sides, there soon began diplomatic negotiations, which proved to be difficult. As a mark of his willingness to accommodate, on 16 December 1920 Benedict XV appointed three Slovaks to the local sees under the assumption that two of their predecessors, who had had to emigrate to Hungary, would be provided for by Czechoslovakia. Although the Czechoslovak ambassador to the Holy See, Kamill Krofia, guaranteed this in writing in the name of his government, the promise was not kept. This was the reason why the Vatican later, in the carrying out of the so-called *modus vivendi,* made its concessions dependent on the previous settlement of the material questions.

After long negotiations the apostolic administration of Trnava in Slovakia was erected and a titular bishop placed at its head. However, the see of Rožnava remained vacant from 1920, for the Czechoslovak government intended to dissolve it because of is Hungarian majority and integrate it into a new Slovak metropolitanate that was to be established. Relations between state and Church noticeably deteriorated. When, before the approaching parliamentary election, the Slovak bishops on 26 November 1924 in a common pastoral letter, with which the Czech bishops declared their solidarity, urged the faithful to hold themselves aloof from all parties that were hostile to the Church and religion and refused Communion to the members of radical parties, the state pressure increased. Trials were instituted against priests, Church feasts were abolished, new anticlerical laws were enacted, and on the occasion of the celebration to honor Hus in 1925 the nuncio was forced to leave. But the government soon had to yield because of the domestic and foreign policy conditions. In the summer of 1927 the government promised to permit the Catholic Popular Party, to restore Catholic schools, and to regularize the sequestered church property. The negotiations led on 17 December 1927 to a *modus vivendi.* In this were agreed: the imminent assimilation of diocesan boundaries with the political frontiers of the nation, the restitution and the administration of the sequestered Church property by an episcopal commission, the autonomy of the religious orders, and the free nomination of bishops by the Holy See, subject to the state's right of veto. And the interrupted diplomatic relations between the Vatican and Czechoslovakia were restored.

But the implementation of the *modus vivendi* foundered on the objections of Czechoslovakia to undertaking the restoration of church property before the rearrangement of diocesan boundaries. Thereupon the Hungarian government sequestered the property of the Slovak dioceses that lay in Hungary, and Cardinal Primate Jusztinián Serédi introduced a suit at the International Court at The Hague. This led again to further tensions in the relations between the Vatican and Prague, which were made worse by the forced resignation of Archbishop František Kordač. The nuncio Pietro Ciriaci was attacked, excluded from the discussions, and hence recalled in November 1933. But the government yielded again before the parliamentary elections of 1935. This time the negotiations led to the restitution of the sequestered church property, whereupon Pius XI issued the bull *Ad ecclesiastici regiminis* of 2 September 1937. The boundaries of the Slovak sees were assimilated to the national frontiers, the dioceses and the two administrations — Trnava of 1922 and Satu Mare of 1930 — were separated from the Hungarian diocesan organization and placed directly under the Holy See. Furthermore, the Pope promised the erecting of two new metropolitanates, one in Slovakia and one in Carpatho-Ukraine.

Meanwhile, the expansion of the Third Reich not only caused the destruction of Czechoslovakia, but led in the areas occupied by Germany to a real struggle against the Church. Ecclesiastical administration, press, and organizations were restricted, and hundreds of priests were imprisoned. Most sees remained vacant. The situation of the Church was normal only in the Slovak Republic, at whose head was the Catholic priest Josef Tiso. Here there were difficulties only with the Uniates of the dioceses of Prešov and Mukačevo, since, because of massive state pressure, their number greatly declined by 60,000 in favor of the Orthodox.

In spite of the political and economic difficulties, the lack of priests, and an antiecclesiastical propaganda, the Church was able to revive in Czechoslovakia in the postwar years, in many areas even develop anew. A vigorous renewal took place especially in the school system and the press and among the religious orders and associations. Great meetings, congresses, and celebrations strengthened Catholic self-consciousness.

On 9 May 1945, after the Second World War, there emerged with the support of the Soviet occupation the Czechoslovak People's Democratic Republic. The former political boundaries could be restored, apart from the Transcarpathian district, which was ceded to the Soviet Union. The country now included 127,869 square kilometers, with ca. 13 million inhabitants. On 25 February 1948 by means of a coup d'état the Communist Party obtained power, which began at once with the establishing of a Communist state system. The hierarchy, just established, and the reviving religious life, which had at first, however, suffered a harsh setback through the expulsion of hundreds of thousands of Catholics of German and Hungarian nationality, were paralyzed. The apostolic internuncio, Xaver Ritter, was expelled from the country. A series of administrative measures deprived the Church of its rights and its possibilities in the apostolate. Catholic schools, all seminaries and religious orders, organizations and societies, and the Catholic press were suppressed, religious instruction in the schools was ever more curtailed, the clergy was split by a pro-Communist Priests' Peace Movement, headed by Josef Plojhar, and the leading ecclesiastical personalities, bishops, including Josef Beran, were condemned in show trials to long prison terms. On 14 October 1949 the state Department of Churches assumed full control of the Church. On 28 April 1950 the Uniate see of Prešov was transferred to the obedience of the Orthodoxy of Moscow. However, neither the clergy nor the faithful complied with this return, but as soon as circumstances allowed the Uniate diocese was reestablished. It was again permitted (since 13 June 1968).

Negotiations between the Vatican and Czechoslovakia, which began in the course of the Church's new Eastern policy because of the changed political situation, led in the early 1960s to a slight relaxing of tension. In 1962–63 four bishops were able to take part in the Second Vatican Council, in 1965 Cardinal Beran was exiled, two seminaries could be opened, and, fostered by the political change of climate, several bishops and priests were reinstated. After the military occupation of Czechoslovakia by the Soviet Union and the states of the Eastern bloc on 21 August 1968, however, the situation of the Church significantly worsened. Neither new discussions nor new appointments of bishops in 1973 could stop this.

Hungary

The military defeat of the Central Powers and the collapse of the Austro-Hungarian Monarchy let loose an internal political chaos in Hungary at the end of October 1918, which climaxed on 16 November 1918 in the proclamation of the republic and on 21 March 1919 in the constituting of a Communist Soviet Republic. It opened a new chapter in the history of Hungary and its Church. On the basis of a new constitution, issued on the model of that of Soviet Russia, the state was separated from the Church. This meant the secularization of all Church property — 114,700,000 crowns in cash and 639,000 cadastral yokes, that is, ca. 320,000 hectares — and of the Catholic school system — almost 3,000 schools of every sort. A ruthless dictatorship pursued the openly proclaimed goal: the total annihilation of the Churches. Religious instruction was everywhere forbidden, most Church institutions, monasteries, and episcopal residences were confiscated and plundered, and seventeen of the faithful, including nine priests and one sister, were executed for their loyalty to the Church. When on 1 August 1919, after a reign of terror of 133 days, the Soviet Republic collapsed because of the invasion of Rumanian troops, bleeding Hungary, occupied by Serbs, Rumanians, and Czechs, except for a small remnant, could think only of a "Christian course" in its reconstruction.

The kingdom was restored, and all laws of the Soviet republic were annulled. The new Hungarian government was under the administration of the royal representative, Miklós Horthy (1920–44), on the basis of a constructive cooperation with the Christian religious communities, especially of the Catholic Church. A decree of the Council of Ministers renounced the exercise of the royal right of patronage, but later the government secured for itself the customary political right of veto. There existed between Church and state a very good relationship, which helped the Church to develop fully its efforts for renewal. The governments saw in the Church a dependable ally, and they were concerned for the Church's restoration and even for its growth. And in 1920 diplomatic relations were established between the Holy See and Hungary.

By the Treaty of Trianon of 4 June 1920, Hungary lost two-thirds of its earlier national territory and one-third of its own population. To the new state were left 92,963 square kilometers, with 7.6 million inhabitants, of whom 5.2 million (66.1 percent) were Catholics, 1.6 million (21 percent) Calvinists, 497,000 (6.2 percent) Lutherans, and 473,000 (5.9 percent) Jews. The new frontiers corresponded neither to the ethnographic nor the previous ecclesiastical boundaries. Of the twenty-six dioceses, not counting Croatia-Slovenia, only four remained entirely unimpaired. Six bishoprics retained their sees in Hungary, but lost a great part of their territories. Now the episcopal sees of seven bishoprics belonged to neighboring states, but still retained areas in Hungary. Nine dioceses were completely separated from Hungary. Because of the new territorial frontiers, the Hungarian Church lost almost half of all its property — ca. 336,100 hectares.

Because of the loss of church property, which had especially hurt the archbishopric of Esztergom, because of the impeding of the jurisdiction of Hungarian bishops in the parts detached from their dioceses, because of the removal of Hungarian bishops from their local offices, on account of the organizational ecclesiastical independence of the detached areas, and on account of the nationalistic policy of the successor states, there arose several controversies between the Hungarian episcopate and the neighboring states, which were settled in the diplomatic manner by means of the Vatican and the governments. The complicated ecclesio-political situation was still further complicated by the first and second Vienna awards of 2 November 1938 and 30 August 1940 as well as by the occupation of the Carpatho-Ukraine and northern Yugoslavia by Hungary, since areas earlier detached, with some 4.5 million Catholics, returned to Hungary. Hungary lost them again in 1944–1945.

In spite of its doubtful economic situation, the Church was able energetically to renew itself. Of course, politically this was conditioned by the preceding tragic years of war and revolution and the impact of the Treaty of Trianon, which produced the consolidation of the conservative forces and an alliance with the Church. Besides, in Hungary there was no Catholic answer to the Enlightenment, Josephinism, and liberalism. Thus the Catholic renewal came, long delayed, only after the turn of the century, but then, accelerated by external events, it was all the more stormy in appearance. Under the leadership of Cardinals-Primate János Csernoch (1912–27) and Jusztinián Serédi (1927–45) there appeared apostolic bishops — Gusztáv Majláth, Gyula Glattfelder, Tihamér Tóth, and others — among them the most outstanding personality of Hungarian Catholicism since Cardinal-Primate Péter Pázmány (d. 1637), Ottokár Prohászka (1858–1927). The imposing Catholic renaissance was connected with the revival of the religious orders, the origin of a notable Catholic press, the complete renewal of the Catholic intellectual life and of the Catholic school system, and the establishing of many important societies and organizations. The Hungarian Catholic Days, the anniversary celebration of Saint Emeric in 1930, and the Thirty-Fourth International Eucharistic Congress at Budapest in 1938 gave eloquent testimony to the inner renewal of Hungarian Catholicism.

However, the close relationship of the Church with the state proved to be detrimental when Hungary, in keeping with its revisionist policy, got caught in the wake of German National Socialism. It was hard for the Church to separate itself from the state. Hence it could only slowly display the struggle against National Socialism. However, with Nuncio Angelo Rotta and Primate Serédi in the lead, it subsequently did so decisively. It was due to the Hungarian episcopate and the Church that 10,000 Hungarian Jews could escape death during the German occupation (1944–45).

The military occupation of Hungary by the Red Army on 4 April 1945 also produced substantial changes in the relations of state and Church. Hungary gradually became a Socialist People's Republic in 1949, in which the Communist Party acquired absolute power. The employment of the ecclesiopolitical principles of the Communist Party also came to full flower in Hungary. As early as April 1945 Nuncio Rotta had to leave the country. By means of an abundance of administrative measures from 1945 to 1950 the Church was deprived of all its property, its societies, its schools, its institutions, the press, all religious orders, and its freedom of movement. In an effort to divide the clergy, there arose in 1950 the so-called Priests' Peace Movement, a clerical collaboration with the state authorities. Cardinal Primate József Mindszenty (1945–74) and the episcopate, with the help of religious institutions and inner renewal, unsuccessfully led a defensive struggle. The power of the Church was broken, and its leading personalities were condemned in show trials to long imprisonment: Mindszenty in 1949, Archbishop József Grösz in 1951. The Church was completely excluded from public life.

In 1950 an agreement between state and Church was forced on the episcopate; it completely surrendered the Church to the system in return for trivial concessions by the state. Even the popular uprising of 1956 was unable to halt this process. Meanwhile, the Vatican's Eastern policy, introduced under the auspices of the international policy of a relaxation of tensions, made possible in 1964 the concluding of a partial accord between Hungary and the Holy See. Since then, on four occasions (1969, 1972, 1974, 1975) appointments to the Hungarian episcopate could take place. However, neither the exiling of Mindszenty in 1971 nor his removal from office in 1974 nor the appointments of bishops and other efforts of the Holy See were able to impede or suspend the further consistent implementation of the Communist religious policy in Hungary.

Yugoslavia

The Kingdom of the Serbs, Croats, and Slovenes, called Yugoslavia since 3 October 1929, originated on 1 December 1918 through the union of the southern Slavic territories of the Austro-Hungarian Monarchy with Serbia and Montenegro. The formation of the state took place, because of the military occupation of southern Hungary, not without acts of violence against the Catholic Church, and Cardinal Secretary of State Pietro Gasparri protested to Belgrade against them. The new state included 248,987 square kilometers, with a population of 12 million, a variety of nations and religious communities, including 5.5 million Orthodox, 4.7 million Catholics, and 1.3 million Muslims. The predominance of the Orthodox Serbs, who were establishing their own state, in comparison to the Catholic Croats and the unclarified legal status of the Church organization required a reorganization of the Church and the prompt clarification of relations of state and Church, all the more since the previous concordats with individual countries had been annulled by the founding of the new kingdom.

The preference for Orthodox Serbs in the administration of the state and the military, on the occasion of land reform and colonization, and in the distributing of state finances for religious communities, even though according to the constitution of 28 June 1921 all recognized religious communities were made equal, led to serious tensions between Church and state. On 23 July 1919 the Serbian school law of 1904, which recognized no Church schools, was extended to all areas of the state. In this way the Church lost all its elementary and secondary schools. And twenty monasteries and 920 cadastral yokes (ca. 460 hectares) of Church property were transferred to the state. Various religious societies, such as the Marian Congregations, were dissolved, and the youth in school were compelled to join the antireligious youth organization, *Jugoslovenski Sokol.* The bishops protested in vain against these measures in a common pastoral letter in 1923 and 1933. They accomplished only the opposite — the sharpening of the suppression. Hence the episcopal conferences in 1924 and 1925 proposed the concluding of a concordat.

As early as 1920 the Holy See sent a nuncio to Belgrade and was ready to conduct discussions on the diplomatic level. As a token of its good will, it erected the apostolic administrations of Banat in 1922 and Bačka in 1923, established the archbishopric of Belgrade in 1924, and made Skopje an exempt see in 1924. The negotiations for the concordat were difficult. It was only on 25 July 1935 that an agreement was signed, after the state had already regulated its relations with the Orthodox in 1929, the Muslims in 1931, and the Protestants and Jews in 1933.

The concordat guaranteed the reestablishing of the Church organization, the free nomination of bishops by the Holy See, the free activity of the Church, Church property, state subsidies, ecclesiastical celebration of marriages without a previous civil marriage, Church associations and organizations, schools, and religious orders, in brief, the complete religious freedom of Catholics. For its part, the Holy See promised to elevate the apostolic administrations to bishoprics. Hence the concordat envisaged the equality of Catholics with the Orthodox. Precisely for this reason, however, Orthodoxy under the leadership of Patriarch Varnava led a relentless fight against the agreement. When the *Skupština* (House of Delegates) accepted the concordat on 23 July 1937, the Holy Synod of Yugoslavia excommunicated all Orthodox members of the government and of parliament who had voted for the acceptance. Hence Minister President Milan Stojadinovič did not submit the concordat to the Senate at all, but removed it from the agenda and informed the Synod that in new negotiations with the Vatican the patriarchate would first be consulted. In this way a concordat in Yugoslavia was made dependent on Orthodoxy, that is, forever excluded. However, as a consequence of the domestic and foreign policy situation, the spirit of the concordat could be realized. Church life flowered. Especially in the press, education, the societies, the care of souls, and the religious orders a rise was noticeable.

The Second World War was an especially severe blow to the Church. From 27 March 1941 Yugoslavia was occupied by German and Italian troops. Croatia declared itself an independent kingdom (1941–45), but in reality it was a satellite state dependent on the Axis Powers. There the government was very accommodating to the Catholic Church, but it often compelled it to collaborate and involved it in the bloody conflicts of the Croatian *Ustaza* and the Serbian partisan bands. These circumstances led at the war's end, on the occasion of the expulsion of the German population, to cruel acts of violence also against the Catholic Church. A pastoral letter of the bishops in 1945 bemoaned the murder of 243 priests and the plundering and destruction of many churches.

After the Second World War, Yugoslavia became a federated Peoples' Republic on 29 November 1945, with the old political and diocesan boundaries. Although the constitution of 31 January 1946, while separating state and Church, guaranteed liberty of conscience and religion, there soon occurred, as in the other neighboring Socialist states, a massive persecution of the Church. The Franciscan order alone had 139 victims. Catholic schools and organizations were liquidated, monasteries were for the most part dissolved, religious instruction and ecclesiastical activity were almost completely stopped, and a union of collaborating priests was founded to split the clergy. After a temporary relaxation following the break of President Josip Broz Tito with the Cominform in 1950 and after a new intensification of the situation by the elevation of Stepinac to the College of Cardinals in 1953, the papal nuncio was expelled. But the Church did not give in. On 23 September 1952 the bishops sent a letter of energetic protest to Tito and repeatedly told him that they were not empowered to conclude an agreement with the government.

After the death of Cardinal Stepinac in 1960, the situation gradually relaxed. On 26 June 1964 the Holy See made direct contact with Yugoslavia. The discussions led on 26 June 1966 to an agreement, which guaranteed the liberty of the Church but also affirmed the loyalty of the Church to Yugoslavia. Diplomatic relations were also restored between the Holy See and Yugoslavia. On 14 August 1970 an internuncio was sent to Belgrade. Indications of further relaxation were the raising of the apostolic administration of Bačka to a bishopric in 1968, the more extensive autonomy of the apostolic administration of Banat by the naming of a titular bishop in 1971, and in the same year Tito's visit to the Vatican. Despite some difficulties, the Church in Yugoslavia now enjoyed a relative freedom of religion. This appeared especially in the interior life of the Church.

C H A P T E R   9 9

The Church in the German-Speaking Countries

Germany

In the frenzy of national solidarity to which the peoples of Europe gave themselves as they moved against one another at the beginning of the First World War, the German Catholics were as much caught up as were other ideological groups. Just the forces which had stood sharply opposed, at least for a while, to the Empire's domestic policy overwhelmingly experienced the urge to show an undoubted profession to the German national state by the evidence of patriotic acceptance of sacrifices. This was true of the social democratic electorate no less than of the Catholic part of the population. And so there was a great attempt in the war effort to grasp at the opportunity to refute, once and for all, the accusation of a lack of loyalty to the Empire, hurled during the *Kulturkampf.* It was all the easier for the individual to accept the consequences of entering the war when the decision on war and peace was, according to Catholic political theory, so completely the responsibility of the rulers that its necessity or avoidability was not a subject of discussion for the simple citizen with his limited viewpoint. And while guiding principles of Catholic social doctrine in domestic policy caused distance and alternatives to political reality, the few general principles of the Church's ethics of war did not suffice in the field of foreign policy to give a critical judgment in the concrete case on the *ultima ratio* of the use of weapons.

Compared with the lines of communication, which led from all episcopal sees of the *orbis catholicus* to the Vatican central office, the interrelationships among the national Catholicisms of Europe were only meagerly developed. This explains why a committee composed of prominent French laymen and prelates perceived so few restraints in supporting the antagonism of the warring parties in the ecclesiastical sphere also. Especially venomous was the impact of the attempt, undertaken in a polemical work, to throw suspicion on the German Catholics of a diffused and global lack of loyalty to the faith. Naturally, those attacked defended themselves with a counterpublication.

By means of a questionable attack a little later, the Belgian Cardinal Mercier threatened to involve the hierarchy in the dispute over the war. Concentrating entirely on the miseries of Belgium, which, without any provocation, had become the first victim of hostilities through the German invasion, the archbishop of Mechelen appeared to his German brothers in office to cooperate in setting up an episcopal tribunal. He intended to free the Belgian civil population from the accusation of sniper warfare, hence from that accusation by which the German army command had sought to justify bloody reprisals in the first weeks of the war. Since Mercier at once publicized his project without any internal close contact, he caused the most serious embarrassment for those addressed. Only with difficulty was Cardinal Hartmann (1851–1919), since 1914 chairman of the Prussian episcopate, restrained from an equally public retort. Absolutely loyal to the Empire, even if without the political ambition of his predecessor Kopp, Hartmann hesitated between overcaution and inflexibility. In 1917–18 he displayed little foresightedness and sense of reality in his opposition to the elimination of the undemocratic three-class franchise in Prussia. The fact that the spokesman of the Prussian bishops, in contrast to the other bishops, opposed an overdue constitutional reform weakened the power of conviction of a common pastoral letter of All Saints Day 1917, which sought to exorcise the revolutionary unrest in the underground.

Presented with a fait accompli in November 1918 through the military defeat and the proclamation of the republic, the Center Party concentrated on giving full effect to its political weight in the national constituent assembly. What the party accomplished in the discussions on the constitution, both constructively and as preventive measures, considerably surpassed what could be expected from its numerical strength. If nevertheless the Fulda episcopal conference in November 1919 registered doubts, from the viewpoint of the Church's self-awareness, against individual items of the constitutional work, this concern for rights was a precaution for possible future controversies, but not a criticism of what had been achieved at Weimar by the delegates of the Center.

In May 1917 Benedict XV had entrusted the Munich nunciature to Eugenio Pacelli, one of the most capable curial diplomats. He came as precursor of the Pope's work for peace, directed to all the warring leaders, but a personal visit of the nuncio to the imperial headquarters was unable to secure from the Germans the concessions which a further discussion of the project that had prospects of success would have required. After the constitutions of the Reich and of the states had built political life on a republican plan, the nuncio faced a field of activity of vast extent. In the establishing of a nunciature for the Reich at Berlin, which Pacelli administered from Munich in a personal union from 1920 to 1925, and in the accreditation of the hitherto Prussian envoy von Bergen, as ambassador of the

Reich at the Holy See, there was reflected the importance which in Berlin was attributed to diplomatic relations with the Vatican.

The Foreign Office worked especially to have this developed in a concordat with the Reich in international law in the critical convulsions of the first postwar years, because it assured itself of a consolidation, with the moral power of the Church, of the German frontiers in dispute in the east (Upper Silesia) and west (the Saarland). But the desire for a concordat that would apply to all German dioceses flagged when at the end of 1923 the period of political weakness had been overcome. For his part, Pacelli did not lose sight of the long-range goal of a concordat with the Reich, but at first he had to make certain of the state concordat with Bavaria, planned as early as 1919. Well disposed to the Vatican's ideas of state and Church, but by no means uncritically opposing them, the cabinet posts held by the Bavarian Popular Party offered, from Pacelli's view, more favorable presuppositions for the creating of a "model concordat" than other state governments, in which the Catholic parties had a less strong position. If the nuncio hoped to gain from the Bavarian precedent a sort of norm, by which the readiness for concessions of future treaty partners would be measured, the agreeableness displayed by Bavaria in no sense acted as a stimulus, but rather consolidated the inclination against a concordat of the Socialist, liberal, and Protestant groups. Only after protracted preliminary discussions was the treaty signed at Munich on 29 March 1924 and approved by the *Landtag* at the beginning of 1925.

The collaboration of the bishops could not long evade the centralizing tendencies of the new state organization. The distinctly tribal consciousness of the Bavarian bishops opposed a merging of the conferences of Fulda and Freising, which had operated side by side, following an all-German prelude from 1867 to 1872, since the beginning of the *Kulturkampf*. Also, the autocratic rule which Cardinal Kopp had exercised over the Prussian episcopate was still vivid in memory. Thus in 1920 there first occurred a personal bridging of the episcopal main line, while each of the two conference chairmen was invited to the meetings of the sister conference. Without regard for regional preferences, the bishops in north and south were finally united in a single consultative community in 1933 by the Nazi totalitarianism that sought uniformity; within its framework, of course, the Freising conference continued to exist, and the West German episcopal conference was reorganized from 1934 in special meetings, mostly at Kevelaer.

The chairmen of the Bavarian episcopate, Michael von Faulhaber (1869–1952), since 1917 archbishop of Munich and Freising, had already acquired from Speyer, where he had worked as bishop from 1911, a reputation as a preacher of the faith and critic of the age of great stature. Of a princely appearance and from 1921 a cardinal, Faulhaber seemed destined by providence to step into the vacuum which the forced departure of the Wittelsbachs had created in the sensitivities of broad strata of the population.

From the baroque element in the appearance of the archbishop of Munich no connecting line led to the figure of Cardinal Adolf Bertram (1859–1945) of Breslau, a sober Lower Saxon. Bishop of Hildesheim in 1906, of Breslau in 1914, and cardinal in 1916, in 1920 he assumed the chairmanship of the Fulda episcopal conference. Conversant with law, world-wise, zealous, and extremely diligent, he proved to be the master of written memoranda to governmental officials on every level.

The Catholics in the south and west of the Reich expressed their assent to the Weimar state neither unanimously nor with equal decisiveness. How strongly their views diverged came to light in 1922 at the Munich *Katholikentag* in the sensational controversy between Cardinal Faulhaber and the president of the meeting, Adenauer. Neither spoke for himself alone but for a considerable following, the one as spokesman of a royal Bavarian, the other as representative of a Rhenish democratic Catholicism. True, Faulhaber's harsh judgment was directed first at the revolution as such, but all later interpretations did not soften the thrust at the present reality of the republic.

One of the most significant gains, which the Catholic Church, along with all religious bodies, owed to the republican constitution was the exclusion of state influences in the bestowal of ecclesiastical offices. To regard this as progress was denied to the bishops so long as the constitutional law remained a dead letter, because the ministerial officials of individual German state governments opposed a stubborn resistance to the transforming of this constitutional norm into administrative practice. Cardinal Bertram and Nuncio Pacelli reacted in notably different ways to the ever clearer obstructionist tactics of Prussia, by far the single most powerful state, with 60 percent of the population of the Reich. While the chairman of the Fulda episcopal conference first aimed to see the constitutional point of departure restored before the granting by treaty of possibilities of hearing agencies in the appointment to church offices could be discussed, the nuncio was bound to the prospect of being able to move on to talk of a concordat even before the overdue liquidation of the *Kulturkampf* laws.

Prussia's willingness for a treaty, however, only made itself felt after the Bavarian model had stirred in Berlin the desire likewise to move up to the "concordat state." In regard to content, the Prussian concordat of 14 June 1929 could only lag behind the Bavarian model because of differently arranged parliamentary circumstances, and with the renunciation of school regulations it became almost a torso, because it even lacked what from the Vatican's viewpoint only made a treaty with the Church really a concordat. Nevertheless, the positive yield was significant: the erecting of the see of Berlin, the elevation of Breslau and Paderborn to archiepiscopal status with a new distribution of the auxiliary sees, the participation of the Prussian cathedral chapter in the election of the bishop. The state of Baden followed with the concordat of 12 October 1932.

In regard to cultural policy the 1920s were under the auspices of the conflicts over the Reich's school law demanded by the Weimar Constitution. There had already been bitter struggles over the school article in the discussions of the constitution. They had the character of a compromise, and, despite several attempts, the Center Party did not succeed in putting through the equality of rank, prescribed by canon law for the denominational school, with the public school favored by the cultural and political Left.

The ideological oppositions broke out again over three drafts of laws submitted in the course of the years. Although the Catholic school organization sought to gather the advocates of the denominational school without regard for party boundaries, and in a campaign for signatures in 1922–23 some 75 percent of all Catholics qualified to vote opted for this type of school, this changed nothing in the majority situation in the *Reichstag*. Since the prospects for a Reich school law that would have partly corresponded to Catholic ideas thereby disappeared, the defenders of the denominational school finally turned entirely to the defensive under the slogan "Rather no Reich school law than a bad one."

In its beginnings an offshoot of the Popular Union for Catholic Germany, the Catholic school organization had experienced a steep ascent since 1913, while the Mönchen-Gladbach branch-enterprise fell into a crisis of existence. After a maximum membership of more than 800,000 in 1914, the social, economic, and political upheavals of the war and postwar periods had so obstructed the Popular Union that in 1928 it counted only 400,000 members. After the Catholic association system in Germany had displayed, up to the beginning of the war, an amazing breadth, dynamism, and diversity, now the dark sides of the differentiation became perceptible. For the most part liable to subscription in several societies, the members first economized in times of need in what was unnecessary. Moreover, the superorganization favored a certain weariness of association. In the Mönchen-Gladbach case a lack of economic decisions and the struggle against a crippling mountain of debts did more than was needed to cause the glorious "Union of Unions" to become one of the first victims of Hitler's liquidation policy in mid-1933. Once on its way down current, the Popular Union foundered on the inability of its leaders to shape it beyond the socioethical goals of the time of foundation to the general Catholic union, a plan which, in view of the distribution of functions in the association sector that had meanwhile occurred, apparently had little chance in any case.

Without ignoring the representation of legitimate church claims and interests among the Reich officials, and stressing the primacy of the pastoral in his understanding of his episcopal office, Cardinal Bertram respected the existing institutional distribution of competencies between the entire episcopate and the Catholic Center Party and Bavarian People's Party. He was thoroughly opposed to a competitive juxtaposition on the field of Church politics, before which his predecessor Kopp showed no dread at all. In any event, Bertram, by commission of his fellow bishops, internally occupied a position toward individual projects of laws to the extent that inner church interests were concerned, but for the rest the freedom of decision of the Catholic delegates was left intact, however much current ideas aspired to see in them mere agents of the executive power of the Church's leadership.

On the outside the Church's closeness to the Catholic parties was manifested in a number of clerical bearers of mandates, the not entirely uncritically so-called Center prelates, who mostly belonged to the distinctive, even if not leading, minds of their parties but had to thank not their clerical status but their professional achievements. Pope Pius XI had fundamental reservations about the conflict-laden double commitment of pastoral care and party politics without abruptly cutting off the connections that had grown historically. In Germany the problem of interfering professional fields in the life of the nuncio's adviser and leader of the Center, Ludwig Kaas, became as evident as in Austria in the activity of the prelate Ignaz Seipel, who had risen to be chancellor.

That the Weimar Constitution of 1919 was serious about the demand for equality, without distinction, of all citizens and thereby realized the points of the program to whose implementation the founders of the Center had earlier joined together, could not be without repercussions on the inner unity of the electoral body. For with the demolition of the last vestiges of the *Kulturkampf* the previously attractive long-range goals had become pointless. As the conviction among Catholics loyal to the Church, formerly self-evident, of the indispensability of the Center constantly waned, it could be gathered from election statistics in consequence of which the proportion going over to the Center and the BVP in the votes cast between 1919 and 1933 dropped from 18 percent to 14 percent. Between the loss in external recruiting power and the disappearance in inner cohesion existed a clear connection. Symptomatic of the strengthening of the centrifugal forces was the inability at the end of 1928 of the Center representatives to agree on a successor to Wilhelm Marx, who had resigned, as party chairman. For the first time in the history of the Center an ecclesiastic, the Trier prelate Ludwig Kaas (1881–1952), had to take the chairmanship in order to bridge the gulf between the wings.

Just as before, the Catholic parties could count on the indirect support of the episcopate in the form of electoral pastoral letters before critical votes. Not made use of sparingly enough, such episcopal appeals to Catholic cohesion concealed the danger of weakening the force of episcopal authority in case it needed to pronounce on ultimate ideological questions. The bishops felt themselves obliged to just this after the sudden increase of Hitler's National Socialist Party to a mass movement of millions in 1930. One after another they underlined the incompatibility of Christianity and National Socialism in the spring of 1931. The prohibition to join the Hitler movement was based on the racism and nationalism of his party, on the extravagance and malice of its agitation, on its violence against those who thought differently. In the daily papers the warnings of the German episcopate against National Socialism provoked an unusually more violent reaction than the directives issued in 1921 in regard to atheistic socialism and based on the same principles.

With their authoritative refusal the bishops could influence Catholics who might be thinking of changing their vote, and this was proved when on 5 March 1933 Hitler "clearly obtained the least votes in the parts of the Reich that had a Catholic majority" (R. Morsey), but they could not prevent other strata of the population from turning to the Nazi movement. Not by accident did there occur with the agony of the Weimar state the outbreak of an intellectual current within German Catholicism, which under the collective term *Reichsideologie* produced an immense number of publications between 1929 and 1934, but remained almost exclusively confined to intellectual circles in its influence. In the quest for a counterimage to the depressing political reality, authors of the most varied provenance came together in the attempt to revive the medieval notion of the Empire. In fact historically concealed illusionism, the concept was nonetheless in the process of exercising a considerable fascination on some contemporaries. It received religious impulses from the *consecratio mundi,* demanded at the same time by the liturgical movement. With the mutual institutional interpenetration of the original powers of state and Church the representatives of the *Reichsideologie* painted an image, the actualization of which had failed more than once in the history of Europe. This applies to the period before as well as after Hitler's accession to power on 30 January 1933.

Two decisions settled matters for the attitude of Catholics attached to the

Church toward this event: the agreement of the Center to the Enabling Law on 23 March and the proclamation of the German episcopate, indirectly dependent on it, five days later. Appealing to the assurances in Hitler's governmental declaration, the bishops conditionally withdrew their general prohibitions and warnings against the National Socialist Party. They took this step, not in an opportunist adaptation but with the purpose of sparing their flocks a worrisome test that was daily showing itself more sharply. This was done first in the conflict between loyalty to the Church and the obedience of the citizen, which became acute the moment when in Adolf Hitler a politician began to personify the authority of the government, who was at the same time leader of a party with an ideological appeal. In this dilemma the cautiously formulated position of the episcopate freed to that part of the German Catholics who wanted cooperation the way to collaboration, without however intending thereby to recommend Hitler's party.

In league with Vice-Chancellor von Papen (1879–1969), Hitler surprised the Vatican at the beginning of April 1933 with the offer of a concordat with the Reich. To the Church he promised the guaranteed by treaty of the denominational schools; for his part he demanded, on the model of the Italian concordat, a prohibition on the clergy taking part in party politics. For a short time he was fascinated by the idea of dealing the Catholic parties a mortal blow by forcing the Church to withdraw all clerical office-holders; in the long view the advantages of a comprehensive regulation of the relations of state and Church seemed to be in his grasp. Franz von Papen's motives were more multifaceted. As a Catholic he wanted for the Church what he regarded as best. As a politician he speculated on his reputation as a successful protector of the Church's interests in order thereby to underpin the claim to represent the Catholic part of the population in Hitler's cabinet.

Around the vice-chancellor gathered the alliance "Cross and Eagle," a group inspired by the *Reichsideologie,* which had as its goal to build a bridge between the Catholic Church and the Nazi state. Taken with as little seriousness by the Nazi side as by the Catholic people, within a short time the Papen establishment was as isolated as was its protector in the cabinet. After the change of name to "Workers' Community of Catholic Germans," it was taken in tow even in its organization by the Nazi Party in the fall of 1933. Numerically a tiny group, it disappeared from the scene a year later, after it had served its time as a pretense. In contrast to the Evangelical Church, in which the church organization broke into pieces over the opposition between Nazi "German Christians" and the denominational movement, the German Catholics avoided a self-destructive polarization, which enabled them to preserve their inner cohesion during the years of totalitarian oppression between 1933 and 1945.

In the summer of 1933 the revolutionary process of controlling everything in Germany outstripped the Roman negotiations for a concordat. When on 20 July the treaty was signed at the Vatican, there were no longer any Catholic parties which the article on depoliticization, demanded by Hitler, could have injured. They had not fallen victim to any rule of the concordat but had been liquidated as had been the entire parliamentary system.

All the greater exertions were made by the Vatican negotiators to create by the concordat protection for the no less threatened Catholic associations. Accordingly, in addition to the assurance of existence for the denominational school, the guaranteeing of the Church's association system gained urgent present significance. As can be gathered from the layers of the article on the protection of the associations (ARTICLE 31), the offensive to bring everything under the control of the Nazi organization was stopped by these regulations of the concordat at an extremely critical time for the afflicted Catholic societies. What was thought of as a peace treaty changed unexpectedly into an instrument of defense. After the defeat of the frontal attack, the war against the denominational societies was continued with more subtle methods — despite the concordat. Not to belong to the pertinent Nazi organizations meant for the future a severe handicap for professional promotion and in some places also for social repute. By the prohibition of double membership Nazi organizations excluded members of Catholic associations from admission and hence from their special rights in order thereby to move them to abandon the ecclesiastical associations. Not all societies showed the same spirit of resistance. While the Catholic Teachers' Association capitulated as early as August 1933, the association of Catholic German women teachers maintained itself in spite of all pressures until it was forcibly dissolved by the Gestapo in the autumn of 1937. From the summer of the same year on, the Catholic association of young men, especially annoying to the Nazi regime, was suppressed by the state police in one diocese after another.

After the crushing of domestic political (parliamentary opposition) and inner party counterforces (the "Röhmputsch") and the death of President von Hindenburg on 2 August 1934, Hitler saw in the Christian Churches the chief obstacle for a Nazi permeation of the entire population. With the help of a network of seemingly unconnected regulations the Nazi regime thus sought to drive every ecclesiastical influence out of public life. This became especially obvious in the gradual repression of Catholic journalism. The first victim was the Church-oriented daily press. After 1933 Catholic papers could no longer be designated as such in the title, and in 1935 they were transformed into mere acclamation agents by a legally concealed decree of the propaganda ministry. To muzzle the Church's periodical system Propaganda Minister Goebbels made use of different methods. They extended from warnings through temporary prohibitions to the complete suppression of a periodical. To this were added trivial prescriptions on the organization of the content in order to deprive the church publications of any attraction to readers and bring them into the odor of a musty religiosity. From 1936 pastoral letters could no longer be printed even in the diocesan newspapers protected in the concordat.

Especially malicious, because it aimed purposely to mislead, was the invention of the *Auflagenachricht.* Made obligatory by the propaganda ministry, it had to be accepted by Catholic papers without regard to its content and without its compulsory character being indicated or its being criticized. While all freedom was permitted to anticlerical agitation, gestures toward a counter-defense were answered with prompt sanctions. However, excess of power did not necessarily mean power of conviction. When in the summer of 1937 Goebbels made use of the morals trials of individual religious to mobilize his complete media potential for a week-long campaign against the Church, at the end it was not so much the credibility of the Catholic orders as that of the Nazi press that was in doubt. Economic difficulties because of the war finally supplied the pretext in mid-1941 completely to silence the Church press, still strong in circulation, except for a handful of theological professional journals.

The Nazi authorities laid greater value on camouflage in their school policy that directly contradicted the statements of the concordat of 1933. Decisive ministerial edicts were "not intended for publication." The certainly to be anticipated resistance of Catholic parents to the forcible introduction of the public school was neutralized by periodically staggered regional procedures, pseudovoting was interpreted for the result desired. Religious instruction had previously become an object of reform, its imparting was often removed from clerics and turned over to teaching personnel not authorized by the Church, who then reduced the number of hours provided for it. Schools of orders were compelled to close and entrusted to state or communal management.

On the government's part even the Reich Church Ministry, created in 1935, was unable to bring order into the chaos of competencies characteristic of the Hitler state. The reason was not because the church minister, Hanns Kerrl (1887–1941), was not powerful enough within the party to impose his will against more powerful rivals with ambitions in Church policy. His office lacked a directly subordinate executive agent, whereas the lesser ranking Police Chief Himmler possessed in the Gestapo an instrument which he used in its proper perfection of power, without much concern for the Church minister. Consequently it was not Kerrl who determined the course of the struggle for suppression of the Church, but his rivals, Himmler, Heydrich, Bormann, and Schirach, who for their part emulated one another in radical activity.

For the bishops the ideology, claims to power, and claims to domination of a totalitarian ideological state were as strange phenomena as for most contemporaries, so that they first had to find their way in the new reality. Against every encroachment of this political system in the Church's sphere Cardinal Bertram, as chairman of the entire episcopate, protested in writing with appeal to the legal situation, as he was accustomed to do and without letting himself be misled by the lack of results of his ideas. A chain of diplomatic notes from the Holy See aimed in the same direction. The Vatican's protest against the disregard of the concordat left nothing to be desired in clarity and sharpness. Since it was in vain, in fact for the most part remained even without at a reply, Pius XI finally broke his silence by denouncing the hostility of the Nazi regime before the whole world in the encyclical *Mit brennender Sorge* of March 1937.

Differing from the Pope, Cardinal Bertram could not then decide upon a departure from his policy of memoranda, when despite the best intentions its ineffectiveness could no longer be doubted. The bishop of Berlin, Preysing, demanded a revision of this defensive tactic as early as autumn 1937 but he could not put this over at Breslau. After Hitler's passing to an expansionist foreign policy, introduced with the annexation of Austria in March 1938, the agitating pressure in domestic politics lessened temporarily, it is true, but the goal of gradually confining and finally destroying the Church was unchanged. It was carried further, with still more brutal harshness, after the outbreak of war in the fall of 1939 under the pretense of alleged war requirements.

With the elimination of the Catholic kindergartens, unilaterally decreed by the state's edict, the last hindrance to the total grasp of the rising generation fell.

Unpopular priests were reprimanded by the party or were sent without trial to the concentration camp at Dachau, where many succumbed to hardships or mistreatment.

In 1940–41 the Gestapo undertook a raid in the grand manner when it arbitrarily confiscated by turns abbeys, religious houses, and seminaries and threw the occupants into the streets. At the same time the Nazi dictatorship, in the elimination of the emotionally ill, euphemistically called euthanasia, and in the deportation and murder of the European Jews pushed the perversion of the Reich to dimensions beyond the human power of conception. Nevertheless, Cardinal Bertram could not be moved from the policy of internal protest, which he unerringly continued. In his understanding of his office, determined by the experience of the *Kulturkampf,* the maintaining of the administration of the sacraments and of the parochial care of souls held absolute precedence over other episcopal duties, in the concrete case to publicly standing up for basic personal rights. The spokesmen of an energetic progressive defense did not intend the total break feared by the cardinal of Breslau with its devastating consequences. However, this was not the alternative to the policy of memoranda, disavowed by its total ineffectiveness. For the holders of power were by no means insensitive to the pressure of opinion of a great part of the population, which the exposure of the crimes of the regime would have had to produce. What they feared and the Church's members hoped from its bishops, the unique echo, appeared in the summer of 1941, which the three great sermons of Bishop Galen (1878–1946) of Münster against the violent domination of the Gestapo and the murdering of the emotionally ill elevated to an event of European rank.

Differently from the action on euthanasia, which could not be hidden despite all efforts at camouflage, there came into view for the observer inside Germany only the last but one act of the "final solution of the Jewish question," forcible deportation, and even this only in a local sector. As early as 1935 the Fulda Episcopal Conference had united the assistance efforts of the *Sankt Raphaelsverein* and the German Charity Association in the "Assistance Committee for Catholic non-Aryans," but the boundaries of its success were very narrowly drawn through the restriction on the admittance of people from overseas. A local center of gravity was constituted by the "Assistance Work in the Episcopal Ordinariate of Berlin," which Bishop Preysing had called into being. In the last common proclamation of the episcopate during the Nazi epoch, the Decalogue Pastoral Letter of August 1943, which stressed the indivisibility of the right to life in all clarity, there was also unmistakable thought of "men of foreign races and descent." Of course, matters did not proceed as far as a public protest of the bishops against the annihilation of the Jews.

What fate was destined for the Church in the event of a victorious outcome of the war was demonstrated by Hitler's representatives in the territories annexed to the Reich in the West and East. After the *Anschluss* in March 1938 Austria was declared a territory freed from its concordat and in its ecclesiastical institutions abandoned to the forcible rule of the party functionaries. Austria, Lorraine, and in extremely radical fashion the Warthegau supplied the negative proof for the protective influence which the concordat with the Reich, despite highly defective respect, produced to the end in the dioceses of the old Reich.

After the unconditional surrender on 8 May 1945, the victorious powers liquidated, with the rest of Hitler's rule, also the inner constitution of the German political system. In many places the Church was the single institution which was able to keep its personal identity beyond the zero hour. Its generally known spiritual opposition to National Socialism gave it, at least among the Western Allies and in the initial phase of the communal reorganization, a certain authority, but soon other influences gained the upper hand in the military governments of the four occupation zones.

In view of the unmistakable material misery the Church's efforts in the first postwar period were especially directed to charitable help. The wretchedness moved to its climax with the stream of millions of refugees from the East, who, robbed of all they had, were driven from their ancestral homes. Arbitrarily drawn zone frontiers disrupted dioceses and carried the German partition into the ecclesiastical sphere. After Cardinal Bertram's death on 6 July 1945, a German vicar capitular, Ferdinand Piontek, functioned in Breslau, but a month later he was induced to resign by the determined Cardinal Hlond. As primate of Poland, the latter himself assumed the diocesan administration, so that, provided by the Holy See with the title of apostolic administrator, he could immediately send auxiliary bishops to the eastern areas of Germany now placed under Polish administration.

Under the chairmanship of the archbishop of Cologne, Josef Frings (b. 1887, archbishop in 1942, cardinal in 1946), the German bishops met at Fulda in August 1945 for their first postwar meeting. As previously against the violations of rights by the Nazi regime, they now protested for a nation without a voice at the Allied Control Council, against anarchy and arbitrariness, against the automatic interning of merely nominal party members, against the expulsion of millions of East Germans from house and farm. During the war years Pope Pius XII had maintained an intensive correspondence with many German bishops. The Pope's voice was also the first which appealed on a world level for discretion and justice toward the defeated, while the wave of hatred released by Hitler turned back in full fury on the Germans in their totality.

After the closing of all diplomatic representations in Berlin by the victorious powers, not excepting the apostolic nunciature, Pius XII left nothing untried to remain present, advising and helping, through an informal representation at least. Thus there originated the Vatican Mission at Kronberg near Frankfurt in late autumn 1945. From 1946 it was splendidly occupied by Aloysius Muench (1889–1962), an American bishop of German ancestry, and became the germ cell of a revived representation of the Holy See in Germany, which was transferred to Bad Godesberg after the establishing of the Federal Republic in 1951 and was elevated to a nunciature.

Population displacements of unprecedented size, introduced by Nazi resettlements and flight before bombs, climaxed in the influx of over 11 million expelled from their homeland, who, apart from the humanitarian needs, also created completely new problems of pastoral care. In some regions confessional boundaries, which had been more or less fixed since the Reformation, were shifted without plan and order or became entirely outmoded by a fundamental mixing of Catholics and Protestants. That thereby a diaspora situation arose virtually everywhere was first made painfully known to many participants at the Mainz *Katholikentag* of 1948 in the brief formula "Germany — Mission Country."

As in all areas, also in the religious the reconstruction proceeded from the bottom up. There struck the great hour of the parish principle. Hence the bishops in no sense made a virtue of necessity when they sought to organize the care of souls according to the so-called natural states and energetically resisted the formation of superdiocesan central associations in the old style. Nevertheless, although these rose again from the ruins and the worn-out parish principle lost in brilliance, no renaissance of any length was allowed to the Catholic associations. The great period of the denominational mass organizations with their members amounting to the hundreds of thousands was apparently over. To the change of climate of a dread of every organizational connection there contributed not a little in the early postwar period the rigorism with which especially the American occupation power subjected the last member of the Nazi Party to the process of de-Nazification. But the definitive change was first introduced with the arrival of television in the 1950s, whereby a competitor entered the scene which damaged every form of sociability outside the home.

The war of annihilation of National Socialism against Christianity had simply forced churchmen and politicians of both denominations without question into one defensive front. From the start this removed all reservations which might have made it difficult for the Catholic bishops, after the founding of the Christian Social Union (CSU) in Bavaria and the Christian Democratic Union (CDU) in the rest of Germany, to agree to an integrated party of a basic Christian direction. Hence not without skepticism they saw how staunch adherents of the Center called it again into being on a purely denominational basis, as in North Rhine-Westphalia, and thereby split the Catholic electorate. The outcome was that the notion of union became fully productive in some regions only with a certain delay. The electoral pastoral letters of the postwar period became more blurred after the resumption of this tradition in the 1960s; they especially stressed the duty of voting and the necessity of voting for candidates of proved Christian outlook. Only in a very few individual cases was there an ecclesiastical representative. The postconciliar inclination of the younger theology professors to be active for so-called election initiatives was countered by the German episcopal conference in the fall of 1973 with the prohibition "for a priest to take a stand publicly within a party, for a party, and for the election of a party."

During the preliminaries for a constitution of the Federal Republic, which was established in 1949 in the territory of the three Western occupation zones, the episcopate exerted itself energetically for an anchoring of the rights of parents in the Bonn basic law, but the proponents could not carry the day in the parliamentary council. Also heavily fought was the continued validity of the concordat of 1933. What on this point was established in a more general way in ARTICLE 123 of the Federal Constitution was differently interpreted according to the viewpoint of each party. For obligatory clarification the second Adenauer cabinet appealed to the Federal Supreme Court at Karlsruhe, complaining in 1955 against the state of Lower Saxony because of its nonobservance of the school regulations of the concordat. The verdict of 26 March 1957 agreed on the one hand to the continued validity of the treaty, but denied to the Federation the power to enforce provisions of the treaty where these touched the cultural supremacy of the states. Unsatisfactory as the Karlsruhe verdict, seen as a whole, turned out to be for the ecclesiastical partner to the treaty, nevertheless it became the impetus for a bilateral agreement between the state of Lower Saxony and the Holy See, the concordat of 26 February 1965. The concordat concluded with Rhineland-Westphalia on 15 May 1973 took care of regulating the school question.

According to the norms established by the Second Vatican Council, the German Episcopal Conference, actually in existence for decades, gave itself its proper statute in 1967 and a legal structure in the union of the dioceses of Germany. At the end of 1965 its leadership had passed from Cardinal Frings, who remained archbishop of Cologne until 1969, to the Munich Cardinal Julius Döpfner (1913–76, bishop of Würzburg in 1948, bishop of Berlin in 1957, cardinal in 1958, and archbishop of Munich in 1961). Whether the auxiliary bishops, called by the council to participate in the conference and in some places increased rapidly, would be conducive to the function of the bishops' assemblies remained to be seen. In addition to the complete conference there also existed on the regional level the Bavarian and the West German Episcopal Conference and the East German conference of ordinaries, but participation by these last in the plenary meetings at Fulda had been forbidden since the erecting of the Berlin Wall in 1961 through the policy of demarcation.

In the tracks of the Eastern policy pursued by the SPD-FDP government coalition since 1969 and yielding to the stubborn pressure of Poland's episcopate and government, the Holy See at the end of June 1972 for its part recognized the Oder-Neisse Line as Poland's frontier and in the territories annexed to Poland created a new diocesan arrangement. The German Democratic Republic strove for an analogous concession from the Vatican in order to maintain through the merger of West German enclaves and its own jurisdictional areas a diocesan division whose circumscription would coincide with the state frontiers.

Austria

In Austria, where the proclamation of the republic in 1918 deprived the Catholic Church of its imperial protector, tension-filled cultural-political times dawned after the First World War. If in Germany social democracy suspiciously rejected the Church, so too the ideologically incomparably virulent Austrian Marxism fought it with an aggressive hostility. In Austria, 90 percent Catholic, the oppositions were polarized as regards party politics into the two great blocks of the Christian Socialists and the Socialists.

The latter went far beyond the atheistic or nonreligious basic attitude of the Socialist International in the sense that they imprinted on the ideological ingredients of the party program the stamp of exclusiveness. Socialism was called a counterreligion, and whoever wanted to profess it had to break with the Church. Only against this background can the at times fanatical agitation be understood with which the freethinking electors and members of the Socialist party, standing on the left, sought to separate from the Church. Occurring in two waves, the departures from the Church between 1918 and 1928 amounted in a total population of 6.1 million Catholics to 135,000, an alarming process for the Church. The fact that the leadership of the Christian Socialists and of the federal government rested for years in the hands of a priest produced an additional ingredient of tension in domestic politics. Monsignor Ignaz Seipel (1876–1932), chairman of the Christian Social Party from 1921 to 1930, acquired as federal chancellor from 1922 to 1924 and from 1926 to 1929 influence and esteem beyond Austria. The caliber of a statesman was attested to him even by his political opponents, but he also had to struggle with the vocation problem of the priest-politician. He was able to feel its specific vulnerability when he was denounced as a "prelate without leniency" because of his use of the police after the burning of the Palace of Justice at Vienna in 1927. In any event, from the episcopate's viewpoint the disadvantages of a commitment of clerics to party politics so clearly prevailed that the Austrian episcopal conference at the end of 1933, hence a year after Seipel's death and the elimination of parliament by Dollfuss, called upon all priests to give up the mandates exercised by them.

In as much as the archbishop of Vienna resided in the capital of Austria, he was affected much more strongly by governmental events as chairman of the episcopate than was Cardinal Bertram at Breslau. In 1918, during the period of transition from monarchy to republic, Gustav Piffl (1864–1932, archbishop in 1913, cardinal in 1914) maintained a soberly shrewd attitude. His successor, Theodor Innitzer (1875–1955, archbishop in 1932, cardinal in 1933), was a rain of charity, who, for example, stood up for the Jews in the period of persecution.

The bishops viewed, not without reservation, the experiment of a Christian corporate state, introduced by the Christian Socialist Federal Chancellor Dollfuss (1932–34) and continued by Schuschnigg (1934–38), but they did not intend, for their part, to create difficulties for the Catholics of the government, hard pressed by Hitler and his Austrian followers. For this reason it was also not unproblematic to withdraw from the government's course, because the planners of the corporate state appealed to a papal encyclical. Now, of course, the derivation of this project from *Quadragesimo anno* was controvertible, but this did not hinder critics from charging the Church with coresponsibility for the Austrian effort to implement it. In 1930 negotiations for a concordat were conducted with the Curia, in order especially to do away with the confusion over marriage which Socialist state officials had brought up when they sought to overcome the strictness of the state-Church marriage legislation of the monarchy by dubious acts of self-help. Only the government of Dollfuss brought the treaty to a conclusion on 5 June 1933, not without the expectation of thereby substantially consolidating its position in domestic and foreign policy.

In the days of the Anschluss euphoria in March 1938, Cardinal Innitzer temporarily succumbed to the deceptive maneuvers of the Nazi agents, but as early as October he was the butt of violent demonstrations of displeasure on the part of the Nazis. Meanwhile, the brutally instituted oppression of the Church had done away with all illusions. In order to create a free field of operations the Austrian concordat was declared not binding, while the validity of the concordat with Germany was restricted to the old Reich. This permitted the state and party officials more drastically to curtail the Church's sphere of influence in Austria within five months than they had been able to do in Germany in five years. By means of

unilateral decrees, associations were dissolved, Catholic schools and theological faculties — Innsbruck, Salzburg, Graz — were closed, religious property was
confiscated, religious instruction in accord with the school plan was abolished.

In contrast to Germany, which was not "freed," as was Austria, but was "conquered," an Austrian political government could be set up at Vienna in April 1945
before the end of the war, although for a decade it had to share its authority and
competence with the four occupation powers.

After 1945 the Austrian People's Party, as successor of the Christian Social Party,
and the Socialist Party of Austria worked together for more than two decades
in coalition cabinets, both overcoming the hostile attitude displayed during the
first republic.

Between the government parties the legal obligatory force of the concordat of
1933 was long disputed. Finally a compromise was reached in regard to Rome to
agree in principle to the continuing validity but at the same time to attach to it the
wish for a new treaty. However, Pius XII would have nothing to do with a sacrifice of
the content of the concordat. Only under his successor were discussions resumed
which led to a series of individual agreements.

These especially put the diocesan organization on a definitive basis by eliminating the provisional arrangements which had prevailed after 1919 as transitional
solutions. Thus the diocese of Eisenstadt was erected on 23 June 1960 in Burgenland, annexed to Austria after the First World War, and the dioceses of Innsbruck
on 7 July 1964 and Feldkirch on 7 October 1968 out of North Tyrol and Vorarlberg
parts of the see of Brixen. The regulation of problems of property law in the treaty
of 23 June 1960 also contributed to the relaxation of tension in state-Church relations. In return for an annual adjusting payment, thereafter the religious fund was
transferred, up to 90 percent, to the possession of the state. As early as 1945 the
bishops had spoken out for the maintenance of the system of Church contributions. Likewise in the treaty of 9 July 1962 a satisfactory compromise was worked
out for the financing of Catholic private schools.

The ground had first to be prepared for an understanding of the coalition
partners over partly highly controversial material in a gradual demolition of
cultural-political oppositions. Contributing not unsubstantially to this was the fact
that the last champions of anticlerical Austrian Marxism of the period between the
wars had moved increasingly into the background in the course of the generation
change since the mid-1950s.

Switzerland

Four linguistic communities, still partly separated from one another by transverse
denominational boundaries, make Switzerland not only in territorial politics a
common system of complex diversity. With five bishoprics directly subject to the
Holy See, which exist side by side without any connection and without constituting
an ecclesiastical province, it constitutes also a special case in Church organization.
From this again the Swiss Episcopal Conference developed an enclosing function
for supradiocesan unity, as belongs to the episcopal communities of no other
countries to the same degree.

Initial steps for a resumption of relations with the Holy See, broken off in the nineteenth century, developed during the First World War when a papal agent made a permanent stay in Switzerland with the assent of the Federal Council in order to promote the humanitarian assistance work of Benedict XV. It was then only a step to the accrediting of a nuncio in Berne in 1920. Because it was quite certain that there would be rejection from some Protestant groups, no Swiss diplomat was sent to the Vatican.

Although in their concrete coexistence the traditional denominational contrasts gradually lost their sharpness, there was not for decades a thought of eliminating from the Swiss constitution the anti-Catholic article forbidding monasteries and Jesuits. The actually liberal administration of the disputed stipulation was able to lessen its weight in practice, but it was ultimately neither in conformity with the constitution nor appropriate to remove the thorn of the legal inequality. A turn was first produced by the revision of the constitution on the basis of the popular vote of 20 May 1973. Of course, on reflection it is correct that only 55 percent of those voting were in favor of the removal, and no less than 44 percent for the retaining, of the undemocratic burden. To this extent the event was instructive for the severity with which a part of the Protestant Swiss themselves clung to deeply rooted denominational prejudices against the advice of their political and ecclesiastical leadership.

Politically, the greatest number of Swiss Catholics feel themselves bound to the Christian Democratic People's Party, which was founded in 1912 as the Swiss Conservative People's Party. In the parliamentary elections of 1975 it obtained 21 percent of the votes cast, because of which, beside the Social Democrats with ca. 2 5 percent and the Liberals with more than 22 percent, it ranks as an almost equally strong political force.

The Situation in the German-Speaking Area
after the Second Vatican Council

After the close of the Second Vatican Council the Catholic Church in the German-speaking area was confronted to a considerable degree with equally constituted developments and problems. Since the programmatic conciliar decrees coincided with a worldwide "culture revolution," their realization, beginning after 1965, was only partially identical with the intentions of the council fathers. As a consequence one must distinguish between what is expressed in the conciliar decrees and what came from them under the diverting influence of catalysts outside the Church. In the wake of partly radical movements of emancipation, which blindly identified the change with progress and despised objective justifications, the content of the decrees issued became secondary and had to yield to the appeal to an imaginary "spirit of the council." In place of a quiet, organic, and well planned translation of the conciliar ideas into the reality of the Church stepped the capricious impetus of the revolutionary spirit of the age; in place of a reliable organization, arbitrary experiment. More than other areas of church life, the liturgy was affected by this. The territorial episcopates displayed more continuity and decisiveness in the defense of basic ethical values, as, for example, in confrontations concerning the freedom from punishment of abortion, in connection with which their calls for protest demonstrations in the Federal Republic and the impetus to a collecting of signatures in Austria produced a noteworthy echo.

On the other hand, through the freeing of theological investigation from worn-out and discredited control mechanisms a situation was created which exposed the average believer to unaccustomed burdens. That a powerfully pursued questioning did not spare even the essential ingredient of the Catholic faith but raised it pluralistically to the same level as peripheral concerns made the question of what is characteristically Catholic ever more unanswerable. In view of the confusing talk of the theologians and the extraordinary reserve of the *magisterium,* insecurity and confusion spread among the faithful. To await calmly the resolution of theological differences of opinion became problematic for the holders of the teaching office not least because the mass media were interested in controversies within the Church because of their sensational value and essential imponderableness.

After the superabundantly distributed advance laurels for the postconciliar epoch, the disillusionment over the actual course of the development was inevitable. However, it explained only to a small degree why the union between the mass of the faithful and the institutional Church was so strikingly loosened. Even when the turning away did not go to a formal break, although the departures from the Church grew to an alarming degree, where faith activity is statistically capable of being determined, incontrovertible data indicate loss of authority and disappearance of trust. In the falling curve of regular Mass attendance and reception of the sacraments, especially in baptisms and weddings, can be read how the most deeply non-Catholic concept of the dispensability of the Church's ministry of salvation draws wider circles. An impetus to such ideas of relativeness was first given by the ecumenically conceived evaluation of the other Christian denominations, still more of course the crude propagating of a churchless "anonymous Christianity," by which the meaning of being a Catholic becomes entirely questionable to the average believer.

Even the liturgical reform, introduced with high expectations, made the churches not fuller but more empty. The universally accepted prelude, the permitting of the vernacular, was followed by a period of uncontrolled experimentation, which stood under the auspices of a subjectivism completely foreign to the Catholic notion of worship. The new Mass formularies, meanwhile definitively prescribed, have tried to check this, it is true, but in no sense to stop it.

The priest's idea of his office and self-awareness were hardest hit by the general crisis of the Church. This was expressed externally in an abrupt numerical decline, so that ever fewer parochial offices could be filled by a priest, an emergency which will nevertheless be worked out completely only in the future. This overturning of the age pyramid was caused by a drop in the number of recruits and by the turning of many active priests to other professions.

Offshoots of antiauthoritarian and antiinstitutional currents produced in some dioceses loose unions of priests of the middle and younger generations, which understood themselves as a critical pendant to the bishop's authority. Although there was no lack of journalistic support and echo to the various priests' solidarity groups during the foundation period, 1969–70, these disappeared again a little later from public discussion. That they were formed at all was an indication of the limiting of the episcopal freedom of decision.

After some preliminary deliberations and fumbling efforts to bring the impulses of the council into a practicable program on the parish level in diocesan synods at Hildesheim and Vienna, the trend toward synods on the national level established itself at the end of the 1960s. As the first, there was constituted in Würzburg at the beginning of January 1971 the Common Synod of the Dioceses of the German Federal Republic. This was followed, though with a partly differently constituted order of procedure, by the Austrian Synodal Process and the Swiss Synod '72. By way of the start to "Germanize" the council, the Würzburg meeting, with its catalogue of themes at first embracing more than fifty points, went considerably beyond the framework of the council. However, then in fact only eighteen proposals were enacted, many with impressive majorities, others, like the draft "Church and Workers," only after sharp controversy. To the Catholics of central Germany the road to Würzburg was closed by the restrictive policy of the German Democratic Republic. As in all areas of Communist domination, the Church of the German Democratic Republic was under strict state supervision and enjoyed only that freedom of movement which was officially allowed it, in the German Democratic Republic since 1957 by the Office for Church Questions. Left to themselves the Central German Catholics established their own church assembly, the "Pastoral Synod of the Jurisdictions in the German Democratic Republic," which held its meetings in the Dresden court church.

Ten years after the Second Vatican Council the Church as a whole has obviously not crossed the postconciliar valley of reform in all its breadth. In what form and with what authority it will come out of this process of change only the future can show.

CHAPTER 100

The Church in the Benelux Countries

Belgium

After the war of 1914–18, in which the patriotic bearing of Cardinal Mercier increased its reputation, the Church of Belgium found itself facing a new reality. The introduction of the general right to vote ended the dominance of the Catholic Party that had been in power since 1884. In order to maintain the religious influence on the still Christian parts of the population and to restore it in the areas where it had been lost, the bishops, under the sure leadership of Cardinal Van Roey (1925–61), exerted themselves to increase those institutions and organizations whose legal status the law of 1921 on nonprofit associations had finally regulated. Further, the bishops worked for the political unity of the Catholics, which seemed to be very necessary in order to defend these organizations and to promote a specific notion of society.

The Catholic educational system expanded further and was progressively organized until the founding in 1957 of the National Secretariat for Catholic Education. Thanks to the reconciliation of the parties, the law of 1914 on subsidies was applied after the war to elementary schools. From 1921 to 1969 the proportion of pupils who attended Catholic schools grew from ca. 46 to 51 percent. The long neglected professional training now became the preferred object of the clergy. The financial problems of the Catholic school system, already long present, led from 1950 to 1958 to a new school conflict. This was settled by a "school treaty," which the three great parties signed and the parliament ratified in 1959. In the same manner the state little by little assumed almost all the costs of university education. Except for the university area, religious instruction was imparted to a growing degree in almost all educational systems publicly operated.

The social organizations took root powerfully. The Christian unions which in 1925 included only one-fourth of the membership of Socialist unions, outstripped these in the 1950s and displayed a growing pugnacity. The professional groups were rich and numerous and variously organized. The assurances of reciprocity and the institutions of the health system and of the social sphere constituted a dense and ever more active network.

Among the apostolic works, Catholic Action experienced an upsurge especially among the youth. The *Action catholique de la jeunesse belge* was in principle intended for all groups, but the *Jeunesse ouvrière chrétienne* (JOC), established by Abbé Cardijn right after the war, finally brought it about that it was accepted as a specialized movement of Catholic Action. Its dynamism had as a consequence the transformation of the general Catholic Action into specialized movements, which at a given moment were aimed at students, middle class, and farmers. Alongside the traditional youth groups a Catholic branch of the Boy Scouts was also formed.

In order to take account of and accommodate the growth of the population from 7,423,784 inhabitants in 1910 to 9,650,944 by 1970 — 30 percent — the rhythm of which of course slowed down, the bishops created new parishes, especially in the developed areas of high population density. The number of dioceses grew, through the founding of the sees of Antwerp in 1961 and Hasselt in 1967, from six to eight.

This extraordinary growth of the ecclesiastical administrative organization was compensated by the fact that the diocesan clergy grew relatively faster up to 1960 than the population.

In an effort to assure the Catholics a maximum in organizational strength, the bishops stood for the retention of a strong and united Catholic party. For the sake of this goal, of course, the tensions which threatened to split the Catholics in two had to be relaxed: on the one hand, the conflict between the various social classes, on the other hand that between the Flemish and the Walloon factions. The effort was made to bring the Catholic forces together again with the aid of the Congress of Mechelen in 1936 and in 1937 to reform the party by creating a Catholic bloc, which embraced a Flemish and a Walloon wing.

After the Second World War, in which the episcopate played a very much more cautious role than in 1914–18, the attempt to overcome the split between Catholics and anticlericals by means of a *Union démocratique belge* soon collapsed. During the following decades the *Parti social chrétien,* which tended a little farther to the left than the former Catholic party and was easily de-confessionalized, gathered, especially in Flanders, the greatest part of the faithful around it. This party maintained its role as support for the Catholic organizations and especially for the Catholic instructional system. But as soon as the school treaty had been concluded, the linguistic tensions split the Catholics more and more and finally led to the separation of Louvain from the francophone university in 1966–68. Thereafter the party experienced a considerable decline in favor of the regional parties.

Attendance at Sunday Mass remained during the entire period on a low level: in 1950 ca. 50 percent of the population to whom the command applied were present at Sunday Mass. In 1964 the proportion had dropped to 45 percent, and from then on it went down quickly: in 1972 it was only 34 percent. A difference between particular regions is clearly discernible: Flanders with 48 percent, the Walloon areas with 31 percent — in regard to which, of course, there are enormous differences between the industrial areas and the Ardennes — and Brussels with 23 percent in 1967. In contrast to this, people maintained the essential practices, such as baptism, church weddings, and ecclesiastical burial. In 1972 there were still 90 percent of baptisms, 82 percent of weddings, and 84 percent of Church burials. Even in regions like Seraing and perhaps also Charleroi, which ca. 1900 were strongly influenced by anticlericalism, these religious practices again increased in the period 1914–20. In the period between the two world wars, Antoinism, a religious movement of adherents of a miracle-healing sect, acquired a certain expansion in specific regions with a Walloon population. Some even turned to Protestantism.

But these internal difficulties could not impair very powerful missionary efforts. These included the activity of Father Lebbe, the initiatives of Father Charles for teaching the faith, and the founding of societies for promoting new forms of missionary presence. The number of missionaries, monks and nuns, rose from 4,759 in 1940 to 10,070 in 1960. In the same way concern was manifested for the Universal Church by the founding of the college for Latin America in 1954. In a country in which the non-Catholic minorities have little importance, the ecumenical movement developed on a higher level. This is attested by the Malines Conversations with the Anglicans from 1921 to 1925 and the foundation in 1926 of the Priory of Amay by Dom Lambert Beauduin, which is dedicated to the work for reunion and in 1939 was transferred to Chevetogne.

In internal life several movements among a minority led to a deepening of faith. These were, as early as the period between the two World Wars, but especially after 1945, the liturgical movement and the biblical renewal movement, stimulated by the group of the Louvain teacher, L. Cerfaux, also the "Residential District Groups," and finally apostolic works like the Legion of Mary. Furthermore, a foreign office for the pastoral care of immigrant workers was organized.

Side by side with the pastoral activity, the Catholic University of Louvain constituted an important center of Christian self-realization: some of its professors played an important role at the Second Vatican Council. Soon the new currents stirred in the conciliar atmosphere caused confusion which, however, operated less spectacularly and less toward renewal than in the Netherlands.

Luxemburg

The Grand Duchy of Luxemburg, occupied by Germany from 1914 to 1918, had to turn to Belgium after the war. After the abdication of Marie Adeléaïde, whom Grand Duchess Charlotte succeeded, and after the introduction of the universal right to vote in 1919, the Catholic party founded in 1914 came to power; it has been able to stay in first place up to the present. In this party, the clergy played a powerful role.

In contrast to the other Benelux countries, the Church has almost no schools of its own. On the other hand, the Church dominates the most important daily paper in the country, and pastoral care can rely firmly on the traditions of a region which up to ca. 1950 preserved a rural mentality, although heavy industry had settled in the country even before 1914. Religious practice remained in a good state.

The Netherlands

Period of Flowering (1919–60)

The development of the Catholic Church in the Netherlands after the First World War ran in broad outline parallel to that in other European countries: thus, as elsewhere, the Dutch Catholics — ca. 30 percent in 1850, then increasing to ca. 40 percent by 1950 — came to the conviction that their faith would be jeopardized in living together with those thinking otherwise. The ideology whereby the others preserved their cultural, social, and political interests was to such a degree anti-Christian among liberals and Socialists and anti-Catholic among Protestants that the Catholics saw themselves forced to subordinate a series of life spheres, even those not of a strictly religious nature, to their own management. As regards the construction of entirely defined denominational associations for a community life and for cooperation, the Dutch Catholics went much farther than the Catholics in any other country. In this regard they also went much farther than the other ideologically marked groupings in their own country, namely, the Protestants (ca. 40 percent) the Socialists, and the liberals, the so-called "pillars," who likewise had their own "pillar" organizations. There thus arose the absolutely singular situation that the Dutch Catholics, although they lived together in a modern pluralist society with Protestants, humanists, Socialists, and so forth, nevertheless associated almost *exclusively* with other Catholics. In turn there were organized on a Catholic basis: the charitable institutions, the care of the sick and of the emotionally disturbed, the press — the supraregional dailies *De Tijd* and *De Maasbode,* both founded ca. 1850 — the educational system — from kindergartens to the Roman Catholic University of Nijmegen, founded in 1923, and the Catholic School of Economics in Tilburg, founded in 1927 — politics — Roman Catholic political party of 1898, since 1946 Catholic Popular Party (KVP) — social life in corporate organizations for the religious and moral interests of employees and economic life through unions, which more and more served economic interests — 1903, later under the name Dutch Catholic Union Alliance (NKV). And finally the entire field of entertainment — sports associations, and so forth. In 1926 a special Catholic broadcasting system, KRO, was founded.

This self-sufficient system, whereby the Catholics took secular activities into their own hands, developed further to about 1960. In this regard the Second World War was not much more than an interlude. The Catholics of the Netherlands remained at this time in a patient and unprovoking, consistently unselfish manner imperturbable under the courageous leadership of the archbishop of Utrecht, Monsignor Johannes de Jong, a cardinal in 1946. Many, even non-Catholics, saw in him a sort of personification of the spiritual resistance against National Socialism. In regard to the German occupation the bishops had recourse to the scorched-earth policy: as soon as the Germans extended their hand for one of the Catholic organizations, they gave the officers and members instructions to withdraw from all offices and to renounce their membership. The fact that the bishops were ready to destroy the monuments of the emancipation with their own hand is a proof of the deepest religious justification of the Catholic commitment in these secular fields. At the moment when the Catholic faith saw no more possibility of continuing to work in them, in their opinion these institutions had no more meaning. After the war the bishops passed a resolution to reestablish the earlier social and cultural organizations on a Catholic basis. Decisive for this was the pastoral argument: together with the great majority of Catholics they believed it was no longer possible to be responsible for withholding from the faithful the molding strength of their institutions, in any event not at this time in the moral disorder at the end of the war.

Around 1953 the Netherlands had overcome the consequences of the war and the loss of the colonies. In 1953 the Dutch Catholics celebrated in complete unity the centenary of the restoration of the hierarchy. Considered from without, it seemed that only a little changed in the situation of the Church in the Netherlands to 1960. External activity was astounding in all areas. The organization of the ecclesiastical province was further improved. Bishoprics were erected at Rotterdam and Groningen in 1955. Thereby the number of dioceses increased from five to seven. Catholic secondary schools were spread over the country: eight out of ten Catholics of higher schools attended a Catholic secondary school. In contrast to almost all other countries, Catholic parents needed to make no financial sacrifice for this, for the entire denominational school system was 100 percent supported by the state. Catholics had leading positions in all areas of national life. As the largest party — ca. 30 percent — in the government they were firm partners in the coalition with Socialists or with Protestants and liberals. Ninety percent of the Catholic electorate voted for the KVP, 79 percent were subscribers to a Catholic daily, 90 percent were subscribers to the KRO.

Also in the social and socioecclesiastical respect, Dutch Catholicism had special results: the workers did not leave the Church en masse. On the contrary: together with the middle class they formed precisely the supporting force of the Dutch believing community. From the social idealism of Catholics proceeded a transforming and adjusting strength to the whole Dutch society; it induced Pope Pius XI in 1931 on the occasion of an audience for a delegation of Dutch Catholic workers at Rome to declare that "there is no country in the world in which the doctrine of *Rerum novarum* is so well understood and is realized in fact." In this respect the Netherlands stood alone at the top.

The spiritual and ecclesiastical life in the stricter sense flowered here with "tropical" vitality. While in the century between 1855 and 1952 the number of Catholics trebled, the number of priests had become six times as large: from 624 to 3,695 per decade.

The expansion of its evangelizing activity was always the most eloquent sign of the vitality of Dutch Catholicism. In this regard the Netherlands was favored by the consequences of the anti-clerical developments in Germany and France. Many missionary congregations fled to the Netherlands. While the Dutch Catholics did not even constitute 2 percent of the total of Catholics in the world, in 1939 they accounted for 11 percent of all priest missionaries.

Disintegration (1960–70)

The 1960s were marked by a sudden increase of prosperity. The Netherlands moved into the circle of the ten richest countries in the world. The coalition cabinets of the postwar period, of Catholics with partners of the left and right, let this wealth benefit the weaker members of society with the aid of a broadly constructed system of social legislation. In 1967 expenses for social welfare amounted to 26.3 percent of the gross national product as contrasted with 22.1 percent in West Germany and 19.4 percent in Belgium.

More than other ideological groups, the Catholics profited from this increase in prosperity. Their persistent struggle for emancipation began to bear its choicest fruits at this time. Within the circle of Catholics the academically educated especially benefited from the good times. And precisely this group of people began to become very numerous in the 1960s. Young university-trained Catholics from the middle class rose in great numbers with their functions of leadership into the so-called upper middle-class. As often happens with the nouveaux riches, their rise went parallel with an assimilation to the hierarchy of values of this upper middle-class on the one hand and a loss of the feeling of union with the class and traditions in which they had gown up on the other hand. This social breakthrough acquired in them an ideological stamp and a corresponding justification in the so-called "breakthrough idea," which had already gained ground since the war, especially in the effort "to break out" of the special closed Catholic organizations to collaboration with others in neutral, supradenominational organizations. This breakthrough idea was at first restricted to a pretty small circle, but in the course of the postwar years exercised a growing power of attraction on the Catholics who were in process of emancipation, especially on the intellectuals, for whom this period was especially favorable in the social and economic respect. When the bishops determined that the process of alienation from the Church (between 1930 and 1947 an average of 10,000 Catholics annually left the Church) always won influence on those Catholics who did not belong to the "pillar" organizations, which acted as replacement for the traditional integrating factors that were becoming looser — village, neighborhood, family — in a pastoral letter of 1 May 1954 they came out against the breakthrough idea. In it they pleaded for "unity in an association of their own and from there for cooperation with others while reserving their independence" (no. 15). True, the Dutch Catholics received this pastoral letter — with threats of ecclesiastical penalties for listening to the Socialist radio, VARA, and for reading Socialist writings — in general without special comment; resistance was confined to a small group of intellectuals. In the 1960s these last obtained support from a large group of young academicians, priests, and laity, who together formed the advance guard of the Dutch movement of renewal.

Sociological investigations confirm that in the hierarchy of value of these nouveaux riches the free development of the personality and the "being able to be oneself" stood in high esteem. Authenticity, freedom, majority, pluralism, openness, rationality were the ideals favored by them. These obviously positive values were burdened with ideology by them so that they were appropriated with a certain exclusiveness, which the nouveaux rich cultivated. There was an allergic reaction to complementary values, such as the meaning of sacrifice and renunciation, rights of the community and the validity of authority, the transcendence of God, which were expressed, among other ways, in the creeds which were beyond reason, in mystic symbols and rites.

Of course, this hierarchy of values, accepted in all welfare states by the so-called social center and with the help of instruction, of the mass media, and of the entertainment industry, which were dominated by the new intellectual elite, was forced on the other classes. What was special, however, in the Dutch situation was that this new class knew how to force its power to a greater degree than elsewhere also than the average people of the Church. It could impose its image of people on all "ordinary" believers and on ecclesiastical developments. In its exercise of power the new elite obtained support from the same factors which originally constituted the power of the Dutch communities of believers: the strong and varied organizations and the high density of communication, now especially strengthened by television with its power of suggestion and its leveling presentation. As on the occasion of a dam bursting, through these channels a constant stream of criticism and doubts poured over the Dutch Catholics, who were much less prepared for it than the faithful elsewhere. This intensive, never diminished publicity set a process of fermentation in motion which made clear the magnitude and breadth of the Dutch movement of renewal. Mass expressions of it were, among others, the "Teilhard mode," the "Robinson mania" (40,000 copies *of Honest to God* were bought in four months), the unrest over the *New Catechism* (a half-million copies), the 15,000 dialogue groups after the council, the sudden, almost complete end of auricular confession, and the massive drop in the number of priests, brothers, and sisters. On the one hand there began in 1965 a massive departure of priests and religious almost three times as many as the world average. On the other hand, the number of priestly ordinations dropped. In neighboring countries, such as Germany and Belgium, the number of ordinations dropped to 50 and 40 percent respectively, in the Netherlands to less than 10 percent. And the faithful also remained apart from the Church in large numbers: attendance at Sunday Mass dropped from 70.75 percent in 1961 to 34 percent in 1976. The number of mixed marriages almost doubled between 1955 and 1972.

In the transition from one phase to the other it seemed as though the Dutch Catholics had found support in Monsignor W. Bekkers, bishop of the largest Dutch diocese, Den Bosch (1960–66), and a famed television speaker. A few months after

Bekkers's sudden death in May 1966 appeared *The New Catechism: Proclamation of the Faith for Adults,* a book with many merits but also with weaknesses of Dutch welfare Catholicism. These weaknesses were in connection with the one-sided incarnational theology, which focused on the downward-moving love of God for humans in Jesus Christ but less on the upward movement of the person to God in Jesus' sacrificial death and in the self-sacrifice of the person, in fact the latter was considered almost as a contradiction of the former. Corrections from Rome in 1968 in regard to original sin, the virginal birth, the sacrificial character of the Eucharist, and so forth were not accepted by the authors. Then the bishops let these corrections be published only in a special brochure.

Most extensive were the changes in connection with the education of priests. Within a few years all fifty minor seminaries had disappeared from the scene. Between 1963 and 1969 all thirty-two philosophical and thirty theological institutions were concentrated in five larger cities. Typical of the Dutch movement of renewal was the extent and compactness in this movement of concentration. The new project contained some positive points — openness, the corresponding instruments for work, selection of professors, better payment since the complete financing on the level of the university. But opposing these were negative points — the halving of the number of students — 1,000 instead of 2,000 — of whom only a small number sought a celibate priesthood. The episcopate had no great influence on the course of events relating to these institutions.

The Dutch Pastoral Council, which held six meetings at Noordwijkerhout from 1966 to 1970, seemed to be a sort of crowning of the work of the Dutch renewal movement. The meeting interpreted the enormous fluctuation of the last years entirely positively and irreversibly. The dramatic climax was the discussions on the abolition of obligatory celibacy. Despite the urging of the Pope not to treat this point, the meeting wanted by this very point to demonstrate its coming of age and freedom. The Pope made his protest clear by ordering the pronuncio, A. Felici, to stay away from the gathering. By an overwhelming majority the Council expressed itself for the so-called decoupling and for the reintroduction of married priests in the priestly ministry.

Since then the Dutch ecclesiastical province has given a clear example of the destiny which befalls a Church when it exchanges the direction of the legitimate holders of office for the power of persons who dominate opinion. Catholic faithful, who expressed the desire for the usual Catholic liturgy within the possibilities of the renewed official missal, parents who wanted to have their children given Catholic religious instruction, were characterized as "conservative," "unworldly," "intolerant," and the like, by the group which had power over the means of communication. Nowhere was the inner laceration of the Dutch believing community more visible than in the liturgy. In 1976 there was still no prospect that in the foreseeable future an official Dutch edition of the renewed missal would appear. People feared the normative impact of such an edition.

The desire for activity in the area of liturgy — 734 liturgical worker groups in 1975 — and the struggle against celibacy have burdened Dutch welfare Catholicism with the odium of being especially an inner Church movement.

In summary it can be said that, in comparison to the other ecclesiastical provinces, the crisis in the Netherlands began earlier and that the spirit of the enlightened bourgeoisie institutionalized itself in new Church structures, so that at first glance it is not to be expected that a movement more directed to the Universal Church could quickly make its influence prevail on minds. Unless, of course, Rome would let the suppressed voices of the "ordinary" Catholics have more support, as happened in the naming of Monsignor Dr. A. Simonis as bishop of Rotterdam on 30 December 1970.

The cadres of the dioceses — deaneries, administrative groups, councils, theology professors, and so forth — staged in newspapers, radio, and television a week-long campaign against this papal appointment. From this it became obvious how Dutch Catholicism was dominated by a small group of powerful persons, who exercised their domination through the mass media; the majority of the people of the diocese expressed themselves for the bishop.

At the naming of the bishop of Roermond, Dr. J. M. Gijsen, in February 1972 the same scene was repeated: protests in the press, on radio, and on television on the part of the cadres, agreement with this new bishop on the part of the great majority of his flock, who, however, could not assert themselves in the general communications happening. Throughout the entire country there appeared a growing movement of opposition, the "Open Church." A sociological analysis of this movement proves that the leaders and members belong to those categories which in our Western society exercise "a new priestly domination": the intellectuals and half-intellectuals from the "Third Sector" of the Relief State. Its considerable influence is the mightiest factor for the explanation of the crisis in the postconciliar Church in many Western countries. What is special about the Dutch church province seems to be only that this stratum has a firm grip on all key positions within the Church.

CHAPTER 1 0 1

Catholicism in Italy

In 1914 one could hardly speak of an Italian Church as of a homogeneous structure. The differences among the various regions were very great, and, because there was no episcopal conference, coordination was absent. The 279 dioceses were, also through the weight of tradition, not arranged in a rational way. Besides very large dioceses, such as Milan and Novara, there were, especially in the south, many very small dioceses.

The education of the clergy was in general defective, and for this there were chiefly two reasons: the consequences of the modernist crisis and the backwardness of the greatest part of the seminaries, to which a productive dialogue with secular culture was foreign. After the dissolution of the theological faculties at the state universities in 1872, academic degrees were earned either in the local faculties or at the Roman universities with mainly foreign teaching personnel and hence at a great distance from the problems of Italian reality. For its part the anti-modernist repression had removed qualified professors from the seminaries and at that time deprived the students of outstanding texts, as, for example, the church history books of F. X. Funk and F. X. Kraus and the patrology of G. Rauschen.

The fact that the clergy came predominantly from the country had, however, permitted the priests to keep in contact with social reality. While the students to some degree held themselves aloof, the tradition of the pastors close to the people proved to be very fruitful. For this, especially in the north, the parishes were the place where one could encounter the Christian experience: it was the place of religious instruction, of social and charitable education, and also of political orientation. In the south, on the other hand, the clergy was faced with a situation in which the emotional elements and the weight of folklore were much greater.

The religious life had a visible upsurge, and appeared especially in the sphere of charity with Don Orione, of aid for immigrants with Scalabrini and Cabrini, and of the press with Don Alberione. Eleven orders of men were founded after 1900. The number of orders of women founded after 1900 amounted to 120, of which 54 were in the north, 26 in the center, and 40 in the south and on the islands.

The First World War affected Italian Catholicism in a phase of transition after the dissolution of the *Opera dei Congressi* (1904), which the anti-modernist repression followed with the encyclical *Pascendi* of 1907. In the social sphere Pius X in July 1904 had dissolved the *Opera dei Congressi,* that organization of intransigence, which for thirty years had coordinated in its five sections almost all Catholic societies of the peninsula and had served as polemical mouthpiece for the protest of the Pope against the Italian government because of its "guilt" in the occupation of the Papal State and in an antiecclesiastical legislation which displayed little feeling of social needs. As soon as it had become clear that the opposition between the Old Guard represented by Ettore Paganuzzi and the new generation embodied by Romolo Murri was unbridgeable and that the democratically minded young people were at the helm, the Pope, by means of the letter of Cardinal Merry del Val, had declared the great central organization, whose president had been named by the Pope, to be dissolved and replaced it by three unions, one for the people, one for the economic-social area, and one for the electoral campaigns, which were now directly subject to the bishops. With this drastic measure, which Monsignore Radini Tedeschi regarded as a catastrophe, the Holy See was pursuing several purposes. It especially disapproved of Murri and his democracy of a Christian stamp, which was based on the autonomy of Catholics in the political sphere. Further, there was an accommodation to the efforts of individual church dignitaries, who wanted to exercise a decisive influence in the Catholic movement. Finally, the suppression of the *Opera dei Congressi* fitted into the plans of Pius X for a restoration of disciplinary unity and strict obedience, which not only the theological modernism of a Buonaiuti had jeopardized, but also the political modernism of a Murri with his demand for independence from the hierarchy.

In the area of the electoral campaigns the *non expedit* was weakened. The fear of a strong advance of the Socialists induced Pius X to undertake a dialogue with Giolitti and the moderate liberals, which led to the "Gentiloni Pact" of 1913. Gentiloni, president of the electoral union, promised the votes of the Catholics to those liberal candidates who obliged themselves in writing to respect a few conditions — rejection of divorce, defense of religious instruction in the schools, and so forth. In this way the moderate clerical influence, *clerico-moderatismo,* was strengthened. Italian Catholicism lived with this divided attitude — disciplinary rigidity on the one side, political opening to the moderate liberals on the other — until it was drawn into the First World War, which also for the Church marked a change in the peninsula.

The bishops at first stood for neutrality, except for a few prelates who subscribed to a nationalistic tendency. However, when on 24 May 1915 the Italian government began hostilities against the Central Powers, obedience to the secular authority caused bishops and people to uphold the war. Only a few isolated personalities, such as the Barnabite Alessandro Chignoni, remained loyal to the pacifist attitude.

The war evoked no substantial renewal of faith. The psychologist Father Agostino Gemelli proved that, after a momentary revival of an external piety as a consequence of the anguish at death, a return to indifference can be ascertained. Much more radical was *Coenobium,* the periodical of the Christian opposition, which branded it a scandal that the "theology of the sword" all too easily justified the war.

The reliable support of the Italian Church for the government and the active participation in the fatherland's war was for the Catholics the signal for the ending of the opposition to the state and their entry into politics. In an effort to sanction this new line, Don Luigi Sturzo (d. 1959) in 1919 created the *Partito Popolare Italiano,* and the Holy See abolished its *non expedit.* This new political formation, which had been preceded by the founding of the *Confederazione Italiana dei Lavoratori,* with a Christian outlook, warred against the liberal state; it denounced its excessive centralization and its slight respect for the freedom of teaching and for local autonomy.

Because its registered members were recruited especially from the rural classes, Sturzo's union took up the agrarian question, for which it advocated a bold reform program — partition of the *latifundia* with extensive cultivation, promoting of small ownership. It cultivated good-neighbor relations with the moderate trade unions, which were against indiscriminate strikes, especially the political, and occupation of factories. In coordination with the Socialists and at the same time with them it led a decisive fight for the eight-hour day and realized some social demands — ownership of stock and share in profits by workers, legal recognition and equality of rights for all union organizations. Although the Popular Party had originated in an openly declared social orientation, it fought the anarchist violence of the Socialist extremists, but could also not realize collaboration with Socialists in the government: attempts at this in 1921 failed not on social questions, but on the school problem and in 1924 because of the veto of the Holy See. In connection with Sturzo's initiative the political autonomy of Catholics vis-à-vis the hierarchy constituted the most important innovation. Although the Popular Party wanted to be the voice for the democratic appeal of the Catholics, it developed nondenominationally. Cardinal Gasparri repeatedly declared that the new union arose "without the intervention of the Holy See" from the consistent effort of the Catholic movement for adaptation to democratic society, in which each interest was promoted by the activity of the interest groups of the moment. Benedict XV had facilitated such a process, which surpassed the political-religious exaggeration of the *Opera dei Congressi* and its successor societies, by separating the field of politics from that of religion. While the new party organism did not present itself as the absolute final stage for the realization of political unity among Catholics, in reality, because of the special circumstances, it embraced almost the entire majority of Catholicism; the unanimous uniting of the Catholics on the political level had been caused by the necessity of reacting against the antipapal and anticlerical spirit of the other parties. Decidedly and incessantly Don Sturzo championed the autonomous role of the Catholic layman, who should act in the secular sphere freely and courageously with personal responsibility and not as the standing army of the hierarchy.

Although Socialists and liberals fought it, the Popular Party gained sympathy in the elections of 1919 and acquired 100 delegates' seats, whose number grew two years later to 107, when the threatening specter of Fascism had already appeared in the country. Don Sturzo was among the first to understand the incompatibility of the Gospel with the Fascist regime, that regime which embodied the pagan idolatry of the state, the antievangelical principle of power, and the Machiavellian spirit. In November 1922 the Popular Party sought cooperation with the Fascists in the government in an effort to guide it into a normal liberal channel. However, it was at once expelled by Mussolini when in April 1923 he had set foot on the crooked path of despotism, and, like all democratic formations, it was suppressed. Together with other like-minded persons, such as Ferrari, Donati, and others, Don Sturzo had to leave the country. De Gasperi was jailed. Only a very few former adherents of the Popular Party, so-called clerical Fascists, joined the dictatorship. The mass of Catholics was divided into two groups. Some participated actively, even though they remained in Italy, in the secret struggle of anti-Fascism, especially in the group of the Guelfs, led by Malvestiti at Milan and in several other cities, under Alcide De Gasperi and Igino Giordani in Rome, and under Guido Gonella and other leaders of the resistance. The majority belonged to Catholic Action, which, with considerable difficulty, was able to survive as the place for exclusively religious instruction and as a nursery for the future.

The founder of Fascism came from the Romagna and in 1919 had appeared on an election list together with Podrecca, the head of the most powerfully anticlerical-oriented newspaper, *Asino*. Perhaps he was favored by the fact that he was originally guided by no precisely defined doctrine. Fascism originated in 1919 under the auspices of change and demand for action. After Mussolini had in 1914 abandoned socialism, which represented neutrality, and was converted to interventionism, he more and more moved toward the right, where he found the assistance of the nationalists, of the middle class, and finally also of the upper middle-class strata and of the landed proprietors. He did not have the sympathy of the Catholics, who even energetically fought him with the aid of the Popular Party. He understood that he could not consolidate the power seized on 28 October 1922 by an extraparliamentary route without coming to an accommodation with the Church. At once, in 1923, although he at the same time expelled the Popular Party from his cabinet, he gained the hierarchy by some concessions in favor of denominational schools and other concessions. Many Catholics gradually put aside their mistrust and drew closer to the new regime, to which they attributed the merit of restoring order and the forcible suppression of Socialist violence. And the struggle against the Freemasons and liberalism was a good deed in the eyes of the Catholic public. Thus is to be explained why the Holy See abandoned the Popular Party completely and undertook direct discussions with Mussolini for the solution of the Roman Question. The Duce made use of the opportunity and was happy to show himself very generous with privileges in order to end the strife between Church and state, which neither Cavour in 1860 nor Crispi in 1887 nor Orlando in 1919 had been able to settle.

Almost all bishops welcomed the concluding of the Lateran Treaties on 11 February 1929 as an important event; Cardinal Ascalesi of Naples characterized Mussolini as the renewer of Italy. But not all Catholics agreed with this. De Gasperi, on the other hand, who had only recently emerged from Fascist prison, expressly distinguished between the treaty, which he evaluated positively because it put an end to any claims of the secular power, and the concordat, which he regarded as dangerous because of the possibility of a secret understanding between Church and dictatorship.

But the scruples of this elite did not prevent the Italian people in the plebiscite of March 1929 from sanctioning Fascism with 9 million votes in contrast to only 135,000 "no" votes. A further occasion for enthusiasm offered itself in 1936 when Italy occupied Ethiopia. A year earlier, on 28 October, Cardinal Schuster in a sermon in the Milan cathedral had sung a paean of praise to what seemed to him as a campaign of evangelization and a work of Christian civilization for the good of Ethiopian barbarians — the same cardinal who, three years later, attacked the regime because of the racial laws which crushed Christian universalism. It was not difficult for Mussolini to represent the enterprise in Spain as a holy crusade against atheistic Bolshevism.

There can be no question that Catholicism and Fascism existed side by side in the best understanding; it must rather be established that the Catholic consensus was of a passive rather than an active nature and was again and again interrupted by many acts of opposition. Catholic Action and especially Youth Action can be seen as controverted points. In ARTICLE 43 the concordat recognized the organizations belonging to Catholic Action insofar as their activities took place outside political parties and under direct dependence on the church hierarchy and for the realization of Catholic principles. What was then the real attitude of the Catholic movement in regard to the dictatorship? The evaluation of contemporaries is varied. Giuseppe della Torre, chief editor of *Osservatore Romano,* wrote that the meeting between Fascism and Catholic Action was a collision. On the other hand, De Gasperi spoke of the "pitiful spectacle" which some top leaders offered to their associations by their too broad compromises. In reality, the movement with its organizations in four divisions — male youth, female youth, men, women — with its registered members presented a power factor in regard to numbers which could not but arouse the suspicion of the regime. Open battle broke out in the spring of 1931. Mussolini was suspicious that Catholic Action wanted to take the place of the Popular Party and therefore dissolved 5,000 groups of male and 10,000 groups of female youth with a total of 800,000 members.

He had thereby severely hit those whom Pius XI had designated as his most loyal adherents. The attitude of the Italian episcopate hardened for several months. Pius XI let Mussolini know through Father Tacchi-Venturi that after long reflection and hesitation he was now convinced that he must censure Fascism, which he then branded in the encyclical *Non abbiamo bisogno* of 29 June 1931 as a pagan idolatry of the state. After a first phase of open opposition the desire not to destroy peaceful coexistence prevailed. On 2 September an agreement was signed which confirmed the right to life of Catholic Action in keeping with ART. 43 of the concordat, but at the same time laid down some restrictive measures: The organization had to limit its field of activity to the purely religious sphere; all associations on the diocesan level were placed under the bishop's responsibility, whereby they were cut off from the central direction.

After the crisis of 1931 Italian Catholicism experienced no further shocks. The majority of the episcopate had a benevolent attitude toward the regime, except for some basically anti-Fascist-minded bishops — Gaggia at Brescia, Elia della Costa at Padua and then at Florence, Endrici at Trent. But sympathy never passed to complete reconciliation. No Italian bishop made the Fascist ideology his own. If the bishops were accommodating to Mussolini in words, they could never be designated as "Fascist" in the sense that they had made compromises with the main ideological theses of Fascism; rather, one could speak of an a-Facist episcopate.

The episcopate was oriented extensively in the spirit of the concordat, which recognized the validity in civil law of religious weddings, introduced Catholic religious instruction in all schools, except the universities, and accepted some typical aspects of the Christian state. On this foundation there developed a pastoral practice which made harmony between civil and canon law its pivotal point — religion of the state, defense of morality, families of many children. The coexistence of the Church with Fascism had, however, only externally the appearance of an agreement; in reality, the basic dissent continued, and each tried to gain the greatest advantage in regard to the other side. In fact, no convinced Catholic occupied a leading position in the regime, just as no Fascist of the first hour was permitted greater responsibility in Catholic Action.

After years of a doubtful modus vivendi there occurred in 1938 the definitive break, when Mussolini, even though in moderate form, imitated Hitler in the persecution of Jews. Bishops such as Schuster or Nasalli-Rocca, who had sympathized with the activity of the dictatorial Italian regime, heartily concurred with Pius XI when on Christmas Eve he thanked the "most noble ruler" and his "incomparable" prime minister for the religious peace in Italy, but then immediately in his address complained of the bad handling of Catholic Action and the violation of the marriage regulations of the concordat by the racial laws.

Italy's participation in the war on Hitler's side contributed likewise to the cooling of relations between the Church and Fascism. The clergy became still more hostile to and distrustful of the Social Republic of Italy, which, under the protection of Hitler's arms, Mussolini established on 8 September 1943 and which the Holy See never recognized. When in the last phase of the Second World War the mass of Catholics held themselves aloof from Fascism, the active minority of anti-

Fascist Catholics, which hitherto had fought in secrecy, rose in armed resistance and then established the *Democrazia Cristiana.*

At the end of the Second World War there occurred in Italy a first phase of religious revival, which took place on the three levels of politics, organization, and piety. These levels were closely united and resulted from different factors: from a defensive attitude supported by concern in regard to the Communist Party and the laicized culture; from the idea that Italy must be defended as an officially Catholic country; finally, from an understanding of the Church with a hierarchical structure in the shape of a pyramid instead of a *communio.*

With the collapse of Fascism on 25 April 1945 there was presented the problem of the succession to the regime. De Gasperi united in himself the hope of the liberal and also of the social Catholics and wanted to avoid a return to the "historical railing," *storico steccato,* hence the frontal opposition between Catholics and laicists. And so he sought to direct the political experience of Italy in the democratic sense to a party which could be the guarantee of the value of freedom and of political pluralism. But the parties of the left objected to De Gasperi's line and complained that the *Democrazia Cristiana* had actually become a party of order and was not sufficiently committed in the social sphere.

The "Christian Democratic hegemony" served to defend civil and religious freedoms. The political unity of the Catholics was partly destroyed by the "Communist Catholics," a tiny minority, which opposed the fact that many Catholic workers opted for the extreme left. From the viewpoint of organization and numbers, Catholic Action represented an imposing power in the first postwar years. The number of members in the respective years rose from 884,992 to 1,215,977.

The religious upsurge was conditioned by the political struggle. Catholic Action seemed to become a reservoir of the leadership cadres for the *Democrazia Cristiana.* Besides initiatives of a social sort, in connection with which one thinks especially of Carlo Gnocchi (d. 1952), those with a more political character appeared, as, for example, the civic committees, *comitati civici.* The decisive points of spirituality in the parishes were the cult of the Eucharist and of the Mother of God — especially typical in the postwar period were Marian pilgrimages and marks of honor for the Pope. The traditional pilgrimages, whose centers had been at Loreto and Pompeii, were increased by new centers, as, for example, to San Giovanni Rotondo by Father Pio of Pietralcina (d. 1968) and to Syracuse. The apostolate of Father Riccardo Lombardi also found many collaborators; its goal was to proclaim Christianity in the "Crusade of Goodwill" and "Center of the Better World" as the sole alternative to the modern world.

But the cultural impetus was almost totally absent. There was a lack of centers for investigation and for general cultural initiatives. The book market itself preferred the production of edifying literature and the translating of foreign works. Italy encountered great difficulties with theological renewal. The series of biblical works directed by Salvatore Garofalo was begun in 1947 with outdated programs. Also typical was the aversion to Jacques Maritain's integral humanism. Nevertheless there occurred, even if only with severe efforts, a freeing of Italian theological culture from provincialism in the years after 1960, thanks to foreign influence. To be mentioned as especially vital centers are: Turin with Michele Pellegrino, Milan with Carlo Colombo, Brescia with the publishing house Morcelliana, Father Giulio

Bevilacqua (d. 1965), Mario Bendiscioli at Milan, Bologna with the Centro di Doc-
umentazione di Scienze Religiose founded by Giuseppe Dossetti, and Rome with
Giuseppe De Luca. Two "obedient prophets" especially played the most important roles in the process of fermentation in Italian Catholicism: Primo Mazzolari
and Lorenzo Milani.

In the first years after 1900 persons were of the opinion that a specially important role had to be attributed to a university for Italian Catholics. The long-desired
institution became a reality in 1921 and was the work of the converted Franciscan, Agostino Gemelli (d. 1959), assisted by Armida Barelli (d. 1952) and Vico
Necchi. The Catholic University of the Sacred Heart aimed in the sphere of higher
culture to emphasize the ideal of a free school and a Christian culture. The purpose of this institution was the founding of a center for the creating of an organic
culture, in a sense of a new *Summa* of knowledge, the educating of the leading
classes of the country, and the freeing of the new generation from the influence
of the laicized and unbelieving state school. Gemelli saw himself faced with the
choice between the French model of a university completely free from the state's
sphere of influence and the model of Louvain. Thanks to support by Benedetto
Croce and Giovanni Gentile, he obtained state approval in 1924, which, it is true,
meant a partial diminution of autonomy, but also a valuable official recognition.
Later, other decisions had to be made, such as were determined by the chronic
economic difficulties, and a choice had to be made between a university for the
masses or for an elite. Around 1931 the ideological pluralism was restricted. But
altogether the balance for the first half-century of existence was positive in regard
to the level of scholarly production, while the ideal of an all-embracing education
and not only one limited to the professions was only partly achieved. The reasons
for this were: the lack of a faculty of theological sciences — a department for religious sciences was only established in 1969 — the excessive number of students,
the effects of the struggle against modernists, the absence of qualified Catholics
in critical fields of scholarship.

Around 1960 Italian society underwent radical changes: a rapid industrialization, a doubling of the per capita income between 1950 and 1970, a decline of those
occupied in agriculture, a powerful and chaotic displacement of great masses of
people from the south to the north and from country to city. Now arose the mass
university. The number of students increased from 210,228 in 1955 to 886,894 in
1974–75. The considerable increase of votes for parties of the left proceeded along
with a noticeable loss to the *Democrazia Christiana* — from a majority in 1948 to
38.3 percent in 1963 — and so the "Opening to the left" had to take place, that
is, an alliance of the Catholic Party with the Socialists. At that time the political
power of the unions also grew.

The religious situation, of which one could have made a snapshot for the period
before 1962 at the traditionalist Roman Synod held by John XXIII, changed fundamentally. Of course, this was not true of the institutional sphere, which remained
for the most part unchanged.

The crisis of the postconciliar period had significant effects in Italy also. The
Catholic association system suffered an obvious setback at the end of the 1960s.
The crisis had already advertised itself when Carlo Caretto in 1952 and then Mario
Rossi (d. 1976) in 1954 withdrew because they were not in agreement with the

conservative political line followed by President General Luigi Gedda. After 1968 pressure to spontaneous actions reduced the maneuverability of the movement in the extreme.

The critical situation of the Catholic world was revealed also in the political sphere by the increase of votes for the Communist Party and by the turning of declared Catholic representatives such as Paolo Brezzi and Raniero La Valle to this party, which made questionable the very existence of a Catholic Party. The present situation was also made more difficult by the seething of ecclesiastical cases of conflict, such as the Isolotto Congregation and Abbot Franzoni. The referendum for the abolition of divorce ended with a victory of 59.26 percent for the advocates of divorce as opposed to 40.74 percent for its opponents, and placed before the Catholic world the much greater problem of how in a pluralistic society Christian ideals can be assured.

CHAPTER 102

The Catholic Church of France

The denunciation of the concordat in 1905 produced between Rome and the Church of France a more intimate relationship than ever before.

In addition, the accessions of Benedict XV and Pius XII roughly coincided with the outbreak of the two world wars, which had an impact on the interior life of the French Church. And so it is admissible to divide this latest sector in the life of French Catholicism according to the three pontificates of Benedict XV, Pius XI, and Pius XII.

Under Benedict XV

The state of war in which France was placed by the declaration of war of 3 August 1914 hastened considerably a development already begun in the ecclesiastical situation of France. The Dreyfus Affair had shown that the Catholics, whom patriotic republicans had long charged with placing the interests of the Church above those of the nation, stood in the front line of patriots, that is, of nationalists. At that time the radical left represented pacifist tendencies, and the relations of the Catholics with the government were thereby not better. The voting on the law for the introduction of a three-year period of military service in August 1913 had made it clear: this very republican government had understood that it had to do something better than devote itself to the excluding of clerical influence. The declaration of war strengthened this tendency: in view of the threat to the country's frontiers, clericalism ceased to be the chief enemy. This change was expressed on both sides in concrete actions: priests and seminarians submitted with enthusiasm to the general obligation to military service, and the expelled religious returned in order to comply with the mobilization order, pastors prevented by age preached from the pulpit the duty to obey the induction order and make the financial sacrifices caused by the war. For his part, Minister of the Interior Malvy suspended the implementation of the laws of 1905 against the property of religious communities that had not yet been liquidated.

Influential Catholics, including prelates such as Monsignore Baudrillart, established a Catholic committee for the support of French foreign propaganda with the aid of brochures and lectures. These were especially intended for Catholic countries such as Spain and Latin America, where the anticlerical policy of the government had greatly reduced French influence. Of course, anticlericalism did not entirely disappear. It continued during the war in connection with the diplomatic exertions of Benedict XV for ending the "unnecessary shedding of blood"; the Vatican was presented as a power which absolutely favored the Central Powers. The French Catholics now aimed to demonstrate that they kept themselves aloof from the papal policy. Thus the Dominican Father Sertillanges proclaimed in a sermon, whose text the cardinal archbishop of Paris had censured, from the pulpit of Notre-Dame in Paris: "Most Holy Father, we cannot comply with your words of peace to the present. We are sons who say 'no, no...'" But still more than through such sensational rhetoric, the Catholics and their clergy were freed from any doubt as to their patriotic devotion by the spectacle which 25,000 priests, religious, and seminarians called to military service offered, half of whom accepted misery in the trenches, and 4,608 of whom never returned.

The comradeship which had united pastor and teacher in the slime of the trenches and under the bombardment of cannon left lasting impressions. On the day of demobilization many participants in the war returned with the determination to preserve "the sanctified union." Clemenceau could still conduct the negotiations at Versailles in a spirit which was as hostile to the Holy See as to the Habsburg Monarchy. But the elections of 1919 produced a majority of moderates in the Chamber of Deputies, who were opponents of the sectarian laws from the beginning of the century. Of course, these laws could not be revised, for the Senate remained under the influence of the radical party; but when Clemenceau became a candidate for president of the republic in the elections, the nationalists made him atone for his obdurate anticlericalism: they preferred Deschanel, and Clemenceau left politics.

It was known that Clemenceau was against restoration of diplomatic relations with the Holy See; but the experience of the war had taught that it was a disadvantage for France to have no such connection as an embassy at the Vatican represented. Besides, the reversion to France of the provinces of Alsace and Lorraine, to which in 1871 Bismarck had allowed the status of the Napoleonic concordat, raised questions which demanded dialogue with the Holy See; for the generals and the first high commissioners had promised to the Alsatians and Lorrainers the maintenance of their religious status. In order to keep their word, people had to renounce the principles of centralizing Jacobinism and laicism and grant that the two provinces retain their regime in accord with the concordat, that priests there be paid by the state, and that the school remain denominational.

The government of the Republic had to begin conversations with Rome and resume from the break of 1905. The representative of the law of separation, Aristide Briand, was one of the first to express himself for the reestablishing of a French embassy at the Holy See, and many members of the former government shared his opinion. The Catholics worked for the realization of this project, and the Holy See showed itself to be very accommodating. However, the idea encountered the resistance of anticlerical opponents and also did not find the good will of the extreme right, who saw in it a sort of recognition of the hateful regime by the Holy See. Nevertheless, the project, which included the reestablishing of an embassy at the Holy See and the installing of a nuncio at Paris, was approved by the Chamber of Deputies, but rejected by the Senate. When Aristide Briand became president of the council, he nevertheless on 17 May 1921 named Jonnart as French ambassador to the Holy See, and the new president of the Republic, Deschanel, in July accepted the credentials of Nuncio Ceretti.

The resumption of diplomatic relations with the Vatican neither allowed the restoration of the concordat nor improved the material situation which the expropriations since 1905 had created. Nevertheless, Benedict XV conceded to the French government a right in regard to the naming of bishops: the Holy See would communicate to the Quai d'Orsay at the proper time the name of the newly chosen before publication in order to accommodate, if necessary, objections of a political sort that might occur. Only in the dioceses of Strasbourg and Metz did the concordat remain in force, whereby the French government had the right of nominating.

After these first agreements, discussions were resumed in order to create a basic juridical situation for the value of church property in France. The Church societies rejected by Pius X could be taken into consideration in so far as they were founded on the basis of the agreements which had been worked out between the Church and the state, and with the presupposition that the authority of the hierarchy was assured. Nevertheless, with all respect the French bishops opposed an agreement which seemed to contradict the rejection which Pius X had imposed on them little more than ten years earlier. The acceptance of new societies, named diocesan societies, was the act of Pius XI, the new Pope. In 1924 he declared that he agreed that in each diocese a society should be founded under the presidency of the bishop to administer church property and to accept foundations and legacies.

Under Pius XI

This regulation contained no compensation for the expropriations of 1905, it even left religious buildings in the ownership of political communities and contained assurance neither for the Christian school nor the religious orders. Hence it was unable to arouse any enthusiasm among the faithful, who declared "war against laicism and its principles even to the annulment of the unjust laws which proceeded from them."

People were already on the eve of an election in which an anticlerical left and a right allied with the Church opposed each other. The vote of May 1924 was in favor of the alliance concluded between the radicals and the Socialists and elevated Édouard Herriot to the position of president of the Council. For a moment people believed that the age of Combes had returned: the head of the government announced that he intended to abolish the embassy at the Holy See and would invoke the expulsion laws against religious, who had returned to France as a result of the mobilization; Herriot also promised that he would enforce the laicization laws in the provinces of Alsace and Lorraine. But he ran into an opposition which he had not foreseen. The *Fédération Nationale Catholique,* whose president was General de Castelnau, organized protest meetings, and the Freemasons were accused of having conspired at the same time against the Church and against French unity. The Alsatians and Lorrainers publicly expressed the desire that the promises in regard to worship and school should be kept. The religious threatened with expulsion loudly pointed out their character as war veterans and through the pen of Father Doncoeur cried out the eventually famous: "We will not go!" The succeeding financial crisis put an end to the left coalition and made it understood that in 1925 anticlericalism had lost its impetus in the election struggles.

Of course, this did not absolutely prove that France had again become Christian: in wide areas of the population indifference took the place of hostility to religion. True, religious events such as the pilgrimage to Lourdes, the celebrations at the canonization of Joan of Arc, and a little later the pilgrimages to Lisieux brought together passionately committed believers, as was also true of the rallies of the *Fédération Nationale Catholique.* Religious practice made progress in the middle class and especially among students and at the big schools. As forerunner of the *Jeunesse Étudiante Catholique* (JÉC) in 1929 the *Fédération Française des Étudiants Catholiques* from 1922 on founded local groups. But apart from this elite there were, as is well known, large groups in the population that had been educated outside the Church in the laicized schools. The *Association Catholique de la Jeunesse Française* continued its work in order to prepare its members for civic activity in the future. The *Semaines Sociales* carried their educational work further in order to inform the Catholics on the social doctrine of the Church and its effects. For the same end the *Action Populaire,* which had moved from Rheims to Paris in 1919, improved its publications. *The Confederation Française des Travailleurs Chrétiens* worked to unite all unions to which all wage earners in commerce and industry belonged, and in 1920 it already had 140,000 members.

Nevertheless, many Catholics saw in the removal of the Freemasonic and anticlerical Republic the basic assumption for the return of France to the faith of the Fathers. The alliance between nationalism and Catholicism, consolidated by the war, found embodiment in the movement of the *Action Française,* whose changing fate had serious consequences. There was a unique alliance between the leader *of Action Française,* Charles Maurras, who was a pupil of Auguste Comte, and the conservative Catholics who joined his movement. But Maurras declared all agents of de-Christianization, rationalists, Freemasons, and Protestants to be enemies of the French nation and extolled Roman Catholicism as the necessary foundation for the reconstruction of the monarchy. *Action Française* found in the Catholic area, in youth, in universities and seminaries, in the religious orders, and even in the body of bishops an assent which to a degree inclined to enthusiasm.

This influence of a movement which glorified nationalism, which made no secret of its aim to unite the Catholics against the Republic, met the resistance of democratic Catholics. It was also unable to obtain the assent of Pius XI, who was seeking a reconciliation with the Republic. Moreover, the personal attitude of Maurras and his slogan "Politics in First Place" urged caution. The first warning, which came from France at Rome's demand, was a letter of the archbishop of Bordeaux, Cardinal Andrieux, of 25 August 1926. The letter contained gross distortions, it is true, but nevertheless Pius XI gave it his general assent. But at the same time it became known that several books by Maurras had been put on the Index, a decision which was under way as early as 1911 but which had again and again been postponed by Pius X and Benedict XV. Immediate violent counterattacks of *Action Française* were answered by Rome with sanctions: On 29 December 1926 the reading of the newspaper *of Action Française* and membership in this union were entirely forbidden. The consequence of disobedience was refusal of the sacraments, and priests who absolved those not repentant became reserved cases *ratione sui.* The leaders of *Action Française* characterized these measures as the result of a plot which had been contrived for the advantage of democracy and Germany, and with their anticlericalism they competed with the radicals, who were otherwise attacked by them. Some Catholics appealed to the freedom of political opinion to disregard the Roman prohibitions. The directive for the refusal of the sacraments was often ignored but also often applied with a severity which exceeded the intentions of the instructing office. In the clergy and the religious orders the condemnation of *Action Française* not only involved the retirement of Cardinal Billot but also the withdrawal of a whole class of leaders and the election of new men, who were not prepared for the functions they had to assume.

In 1927 Father Lhande published his book, *Le Christ dans le Banlieu.* In it he revealed to the faithful and even to the clergy of the capital that in the immediate geographical neighborhood, namely, in the midst of their own parishes, existed masses of people to whom the Church was not only foreign but entirely unknown. The construction association, founded by the new archbishop, Cardinal Verdier, for the building of churches in the suburbs was not sufficient to alter the situation. At the same time Abbé Guérin, vicar in a workers' parish, obtained knowledge of the *Manuel du Jociste Belge* of Abbé Cardijn. He believed that he could find there the solution for the problem of the education of young workers, for that problem to which the *Action Catholique de la Jeunesse Française,* in his opinion, gave only an insufficient answer. The ACJF, which celebrated the fiftieth anniversary of its founding in 1936, invited young workers and young bourgeois to common meetings; but because it aimed chiefly at the formation of a leadership elite, it reached the young workers only with difficulty. Entirely in the meaning of Abbé Cardijn, who had in mind a movement restricted to the working class, young French workers held their first meeting at Clichy in October 1926. The newspaper edited by them, *Jeunesse Ouvrière,* appeared in January 1927 in its first issue. The movement (JOC) quickly stirred enthusiasm and spread to Lille, Lyon, and Marseille. The hierarchy, with Cardinal Dubois at Paris, assisted by Canon Gerlier as director of the associations, and with Cardinal Liénart at Lille supported The movement. When the "Popular Front" came to power in 1936 and began a movement of strikes and occupation of factories, great hopes were centered on the picked troops of militant adherents of the Christian Young Workers' Movement, *Jocists,* who defended their rights and those of their worker colleagues, but still always maintained loyalty to the faith and its moral demands. From this moment on, the union of Christian workers acquired a new upsurge; by 1938, 2,400 unions with 500,000 members existed. The celebration of the tenth anniversary of JOC from 16 to 21 July 1937 brought together at Paris ca. 80,000 *Jocists* and took on the features of a triumph.

The special character of these movements consisted in their apostolic orientation. The Scout Movement, on the other hand, basically had in view the training of youth, and so its pedagogical method was based on physical activity and a life in the group. In 1938 it had in France and overseas 78,000 young followers and became the nursery for vocations to the priesthood and the religious life. Many scout groups were recruited from the pupils of Catholic high schools, in which vocations found a favorable environment.

While in this period the élan of movements of Catholic Action was well known, still the goal of all zealous exertions of the hierarchy and of all financial sacrifices of the faithful remained the more traditional form of the education of young men in the Christian schools. The laws of 1905 had severely hurt the congregations active in schools but had not changed the legal bases which proclaimed the principle of free instruction, namely, the Falloux Law of 15 March 1850 for high school instruction, the law of 12 July 1875 for university instruction, the law of 30 October 1886 for elementary school instruction, and the law of 25 July 1919 for the training of technical experts. But apart from this last-named law, which expressly envisaged the granting of financial aid, this legislation refused any assistance to private education. Hence the faithful united in several associations to defend the existence of Christian schools and demand for them the granting of public assistance. Thus the *Alliance des maisons d'education chrétienne,* founded in 1872, from which came in 1925 the syndicate of *Directeurs et Directrices des maisons d'education chrétienne,* was involved in the publication of texts for instruction and published its own periodical, *L'Enseignement chrétienne.* The *Association de Chefs de Families de France* aimed to stress the rights of Christian families, loudly proclaimed war against a standardized elementary school, and demanded of candidates in election to the legislative bodies assurances of the intact freedom of instruction. Together with other unions it represented the viewpoint that freedom also presupposed school proportion, that is, the proportional dividing of the sums of money expended for education between the state and the private schools corresponding to the number of pupils.

A first demand in this sense, a projected law with the stipulation that pupils in possession of a scholarship could choose between the two kinds of school, was rejected by the Senate in 1920. The Catholics, encouraged to this by the FNC, insisted on their demand and were, in expectation of this regulation, ready to make considerable financial sacrifices for their schools. The growth of the high school stage between the two world wars achieved a degree that upset the radical left.

Despite the retaining of the laicist laws and official neutrality, the feeling of the threat from without, evoked by the remilitarizing of the Rhineland, the *Anschluss* of Austria to the German Reich, and the expectation of the annexation of Czechoslovakia by Hitler, produced a new rapprochement between the government of the Third Republic and of the Church. A journey of Pope Pius XI to France for the dedication of the basilica of Saint Thérèse de Lisieux was planned.

Cardinal Secretary of State Pacelli was received as the Pope's representative in 1937 at Paris and Lisieux with the same honors as were customary for a head of state. Without repudiating its official laicism, the Third Republic came closer to the Church on the brink of its collapse.

Under Pius XII

Two years later, when the diplomatic missions of Cardinal Pacelli to both secular and Catholic France were still remembered, Pacelli was elected as successor of Pius XI on 2 March 1939. This election was greeted in France with enduring satisfaction; for it was known that he would undertake all efforts to save the peace which daily became more fragile. It is true that his offers of mediation in May 1939 with a view to a peace conference were without prospects, but he was able to establish another peace through reconciliation with *Action Française.* In the course of years the leaders *of Action Française* had understood that they were making a mistake with the precipitate break in relations. On the other side were the penalties which had been imposed on the adherents *of Action Française,* in clear opposition to the concluding of concordats with the Fascist and Nazi government, which could be charged with more than mere verbal violence. Pius XI had accepted with kindness the attempts at a rapprochement by Maurras, which the Carmel of Lisieux had suggested, and on 20 October 1938 the committee director *of Action Française* wrote a letter which was submitted to the Holy Office. The accession of Pius XII was accompanied by no hesitation. George Bonnet, minister for foreign affairs, replied to the nuncio as a result of his inquiry, that this question should be treated exclusively in the religious sphere. Although some bishops expressed hesitations, on 10 July 1939 the *Osservatore Romano* published the decree of the Holy Office which lifted the excommunication imposed on *Action Française* at the same moment in which a letter of the periodical disavowed all theories that were contrary to the teachings of the Church. The Second World War was near and created new problems for the Church of France.

The declaration of war of 3 September 1939 proceeded this time from France and England and was the result of the German invasion of Poland, which for its part was a consequence of the Soviet-German nonaggression pact. The Catholics were in agreement with the government, and the declaration of war let them see in the war a new crusade against the powers of evil, which Pius XI had unmasked in his two encyclicals against National Socialism and communism. But the great mass of the population had for a long time lulled itself in the hope that the war of 1914 had been the last of all wars. And so it did not feel again the patriotic élan of August 1914. Priests, religious, and seminarians joined in the mobilization with members of all social strata and there encountered religious indifference and ignorance rather than hostility. The collapse of June 1940 could not be charged to the Church, which had lost all influence on political and even on public life. Rather it was the Catholics and the military leaders who were inclined to make the laicized school responsible because it had educated the new generations. The collapse again evoked feelings which had temporarily fallen into oblivion because of the harmony between the two powers. Thus preachers pointed out that the defect was God's punishment for the nation's official atheism. But on the other hand they strove to revive hope by indicating that Providence had always had pity on France. Once it had sent the country the eighteen-year-old Joan of Arc, and now it sent Pétain, the eighty-year-old venerable man. The hierarchy, in general very hesitant with its expressions, declared with a certain vigor in regard to the new regime the obligatory loyalty for the government, in which were many Catholics, also through the appeal which the regime directed to the spiritual values, and finally through measures such as the abolition of Freemasonry and especially through a new legislation which corrected the laws of the Third Republic in two essential points, namely, education and religious institutes. A law of April 1942 lifted the prohibition of the orders and provided for a legal recognition of religious communities. The new school laws reintroduced religious instruction in state lyceums and high schools and granted certain financial subsidies to the Christian schools.

Of course the devotion of the clergy to the Vichy regime was not unconditional. Tensions soon arose, and first of all in the education of youth. In a letter to the head of state the bishops protested that the state laid its hand on youth: "A uniform youth — no!" The anti-Semitic policy followed by the occupying power likewise met resistance, which found its formal expression in declarations or letters of the archbishops of Lyon and Toulouse, Gerlier and Saliège, and of Bishop Théas of Montauban. Thus encouraged, many priests, religious, and religious institutions could preserve Jews, especially their children, from deportation. The *Service du Travail Obligatoire* (STO), that is, the drafting of young French workers for German war industry, created new problems of conscience, for which the church authorities found various solutions. Meanwhile, the religious sentiment awakened by the defeat and the disadvantages of the war called forth mass movements such as that of the *Grand Retour:* countless faithful from 1943 to 1946 carried a statue of Mary from Boulogne through the whole of France. Millions of pictures and rosaries were distributed, and millions of signatures were collected under the text of the consecration to the Immaculate Heart of Mary.

When in 1944 the provisional government of General de Gaulle abolished the government of Marshal Pétain, the new power in the state aspired to purge the episcopate, which it accused of compliancy toward the Vichy regime. Together with the demand for the recall of Nuncio Valerio Valeri it demanded the resignation of some bishops. Pius XII agreed to replace his nuncio, because there was question of a measure which affected all envoys accredited to the Vichy regime, but he absolutely refused a purge of the episcopate. The new nuncio Angelo Roncalli brought it about that this decision was accepted and resignations were limited to three. From this time on, the French episcopate created for itself a common organization. Since 1919 the cardinals and archbishops had customarily met and on occasion published common statements. Immediately after the Second World War the permanent Secretariat of the Episcopate was established, and finally in 1951 there took place the first plenary meeting of all French bishops.

In public life it was a new phenomenon that declared Catholics participated in the provisional government of General de Gaulle and then in the government of the Fourth Republic, which succeeded it in 1946. Again and again people who came from the ACJF were to be found in ministerial offices in ever quicker succession. Only the Ministry for National Education remained closed to them. The constitution adopted by a bare majority of votes on 13 October 1946 decided anew that the republic was a laicized state and freedom of teaching was excluded from the constitutionally legal freedoms. Nevertheless, the hierarchy, unperturbed, continued the struggle for the free school. As early as 13 March 1946 a declaration of the French cardinals and archbishops affirmed: "The entire French episcopate is determined to maintain the freedom of instruction by all the means at its disposal." In the autumn of 1947 a public demonstration of the French Catholic educational system supplied the opportunity to recall "the complementary service which free instruction does for the country" and it was again emphasized that "justice, freedom, and equality" demand that the Christian school system receive its share in the financial expenditures which the state dispenses for the education of French youth. In the same year the treasury brought suits against the organizers of charity bazaars, which were held to cover school costs. In some cases this brought even bishops to court and thereby gave them the opportunity to call to mind the principles of justice. The politicians could not be entirely deaf to such appeals. In 1948 two decrees empowered state and local commissions to consult on a form of support for free schools. This again called forth the opposition of the entire left, and in some parts of the press were again heard the tones of the old anticlericalism. Despite this, the bishops in 1949 again insisted that "the Christian school is the concern of everyone who is called a Christian," and they admonished parents of their duty to care for a Christian education of their children. Finally a law of 28 September 1951, called *Loi Bérangé,* granted to free elementary schools a subsidy of thirty-nine francs per year and per pupil as a contribution to the teachers' salary. This law quite obviously did not claim to have solved the school question, but it aimed only to make a beginning.

The new development introduced by this law was the work of the new government, which General de Gaulle had formed on his return to power. A law of 31 December 1959 gave the free schools the choice among four solutions: full integration into the state school, full freedom of the status quo, a social treaty whereby the state would appoint the teachers and lay down the general plans of instruction while undertaking all the costs of instruction, and finally individual treaties according to which the teachers chosen by the school would be subject to the conditions of state examinations and controls and would be paid by the state.

These regulations did not silence all discussion of the free school. This type of school met objections from Catholics themselves, not only among those who advocated the state school system, from which they knew that it could give a testimony of great apostolic importance, but also in the clergy itself, where some asked what was to happen with the traditional institutions. These attitudes can be all the better understood when one considers that Catholics not only knew how to succeed in the cultural sphere but even also in the leadership strata of the state universities, which for a long time had with good reason been regarded as an instrument of de-Christianization. The intellectual and scholarly renewal of French Catholicism has since gone beyond the ecclesiastical frontiers.

Obviously, however, many works reached only a restricted elite. Only a few publications with a wider circulation, such as *Les Études* and *La Vie Intellectuelle,* could obtain a larger public for their investigations, but they caused difficulties and precautions which influenced the encyclical *Humani generis* of 1950. Other works, on the other hand, served direct practice. The presentation of a world which had been formed outside the Church and the problems which this world raised for the Church made a deep impression on Cardinal Suhard, archbishop of Paris from 1940 to 1959. He decided on the founding of a Mission de France together with his interdiocesan seminary at Lisieux. This mission included a program and a special regulation of the phases of education for work in the workers' world. In May 1949 the Mission de France was granted a temporary statute by Rome. Finally an apostolic constitution of 15 August 1954 gave it a clearly defined status: as a prelacy *nullius,* whose territory was the ancient Cistercian Abbey of Pontigny. In 1955 the mission counted 181 priests.

Cardinal Suhard had also undertaken by way of experiment to allow "worker priests." This initiative was based on various experiences, especially the setbacks in the apostolate in the proletarian environment, the positive experiences of the Dominican Father Loew, who had been a dockworker at Marseille, and of the priests and seminarians who had been drafted for compulsory work during the war. To become workers in order to understand the worker, to make oneself understandable to the worker and to bring him the message of Christ: this was the basic idea which led Cardinal Suhard to permit some priests to take up work in the factories. In 1946 there were six worker priests in Paris and a few others in Provence; in 1947 a group was established at Limoges, and others followed these. There were about ninety worker priests when in 1951 the Holy See ordered the suspension of recruiting. This undertaking had begun with obviously very high-minded priests, but without previously giving them the corresponding preparation, and so it incurred the most serious difficulties. The worker priests saw themselves confronted with a harshness of life they had not imagined; they frequently committed themselves to trade-union actions and in many cases let themselves be gained for the theory of class conflict, while others among them did not know how to maintain their priestly life and celibacy intact. In September 1953 the nuncio Marella informed the bishops that they must recall the priests subject to them, and religious superiors received a corresponding instruction from the Congregation of Religious. At the end of 1956 all religious had obeyed the command to leave, and about forty diocesan priests had likewise submitted, while a somewhat larger number proved by their resistance how urgently necessary Rome's intervention had been.

This was not the end of all efforts of the hierarchy in regard to the apostolate in the workers' world. As early as 1943 Cardinal Suhard established the *Mission de Paris,* and in the following October Father Epagneul founded the community of *Frères missionaires des campagnes* for the rural proletariat. The *Fils de la Charité,* founded by Father Anizan in 1913, likewise continued their work in this environment. One of them, Abbé Michoneau, in 1946 published the experiences he had had in the five years of his pastoral activity in the parish of Colombes in a book with the programmatic title *Paroisse communauté missionaire.* At Lyon the *Prêtres du Prado,* under the direction of Monsignor Ancel, united physical labor with the priestly and apostolic life in a parish association and a priestly community — in 1955 there were 514 priests. "Right in the heart of the masses," according to the rule of Father Voillaume, the *Petits Frères de Jésus* sought to unite existence in the world through manual labor and contemplation in the religious community.

These exertions of various types showed that the hopes placed in the specially oriented movements had not been fulfilled. These movements, as, for example, the JOC, had been able to train an elite of persons who had been loyal to their function to the point of heroism but who did not succeed in dealing with the difficulties of the milieu of the moment and the class-struggle mentality. In 1956 a crisis became visible between the ACJF, which claimed the entire religious schooling of all five movements (JOC, JEC, JAC, JIC, and JMC), and the JOC, which sought autonomy in this area. The resignation of its president led in practice to the dissolution of the old ACJF. The JAC, on the contrary, was less dependent on its social milieu. Hence it did not suffer as much as the JOC during the crisis of 1956 and was able to maintain its membership and strength of personality in agriculture (Rémond).

One can regard these movements which caused shocks in the French Church as signs of its vitality. The numbers of vocations to the priesthood and the religious life also testify to vitality in the postwar period.

Apostolic activity is dependent on the occupation of young priests together with older priests, many of whom have passed the age of sixty.

Even if France was not a Christian country in its entirety on the eve of the Second World War, still it presented the picture of a nation in which the Catholic Church possessed solid positions: a very thick network of rural parishes, a network of urban parishes and religious institutions at least in accord with the demands of the hour, an educational group active especially in the field of elementary schooling, and finally a prudent intellectual elite. The contrasts, like the gains from the beginning of the century, to some degree compensate, so that the Church of France seemed to be in a favorable starting position to regain the terrain lost in a century.

CHAPTER 103

The Church in Spain and Portugal

Spain

In 1914 there were sixty-one dioceses, including the two now independent vicariates of Fernando Póo and Morocco, and nine archiepiscopal sees, which increased to eleven.

The history of the Spanish Church in the last decades is divided into three parts: the Monarchy of Alphonso XIII (1914–31), the Second Spanish Republic and the Spanish Civil War (1931–39), and the postwar period after 1939.

The Monarchy of Alphonso XIII (1914–31)

The year 1914 did not play as decisive a role in the history of Spain as it did in the other European countries. But it produced a great shock, which operated like an avalanche in the course of the disquieting years of the twentieth century. The concern of contemporary Catholics was concentrated on a series of neuralgic points: the hotly discussed problem of the two Spains — the traditional and Catholic Spain and the liberal and reforming Spain — the tensions between religion and politics as concomitant symptoms of the liberalism of the nineteenth century, the question of education, the social problem, and so forth. All of them crossed the path of the Spanish Church.

The Problem of the Two Spains.   This theme represents the background of all other problems, and contains a concept of the national life by means of definite guidelines and principles. What is the historical background of Spain? What is its destiny as a nation? On the answer to these questions depends the idea of the present history of Spain and with it the function which the Church must exercise in it. The basic answers which have been given to solve the historical riddle of Spain and which constitute the origin of the problem of the so-called two Spains goes thus: "Progressivism and traditionalism are the true and decisive comrades-in-arms of our twentieth century from the Cortes of Cádiz to the Restauración de Sagunto," so says, quite rightly, Laín Entralgo. After the restoration of 1874 the two opposed tendencies basically remained, with the natural change of reforms and renewals the two chief representatives of the Spanish drama. This situation prevailed with more or less serious incidents until 1936. On both sides were outstanding representatives. In the first third of the twentieth century there prevailed the prototype of the Catholic wing, Marcelino Menéndez Pelayo (1856–1912), even after his death, like El Cid in the saga, an incomparable master, who united in his person and in his gigantic work all works of Spanish culture. As no other, he raised a song of praise to the Catholic unity of Spain in the epilogue of his *Historia de los Heterodoxos Españoles:* " . . . Spain, preacher of the gospel in half the world; Spain, terror of heretics, light of Trent, sword of Rome, cradle of Saint Ignatius . . . ; this is our greatness and unity: we have no other."

On this line lay the declarations of the Popes and of the Spanish episcopate in their encyclicals, briefs, speeches, or pastoral letters respecting the glorious traditions of the nation. This tradition was constantly the background and determined the manner of speaking of the Church's officials; national greatness and Catholic tradition were one.

Facing this traditionalist position of Catholic Spain stood the other Spain, which we find incarnate in one of the greatest representatives of modern Spanish thought: José Ortega y Gasset (1883–1955). On 23 March 1914 he said on the occasion of a lecture delivered by him in the Teatro de la Comedia at Madrid: "We are sure that a great number of Spaniards agree with us that the destiny of Spain is intimately connected with the progress of liberalism." In this connection he explained what he understood by liberalism: "that radical stimulation, always vital in history, which tries to exclude from the state every influence of extrahuman nature and which always expects from the new social measures a better result than from the old and traditional." Hence, an end to the influence of the Church, because it is subject to human influence, and an end to the old traditions. In still more definite words he confronted tradition and consolidated his ideas in his work on tradition, *Meditaciones del Quijote,* which appeared in 1914: "The traditional reality in Spain has consisted precisely in this, permanently to destroy the opportunities of Spain. No, we cannot follow tradition . . . just the opposite is commanded: We must proceed against tradition, beyond tradition." For Ortega y Gasset the Church was a permeating leaven. "Without doubt the Church is antisocial, religion is exclusive." In the same way he thought of religious education: "The denominational school is, in comparison with the nondenominational, the beginning of anarchy, because it represents a singular pedagogy." For him regeneration, that is, renewal, would bring Spain real political health, synonymous with Europeanization. "Spain was the problem, and Europe the solution." In this way European Spain should lift itself above the traditional, that is, the unholy, unchurchly Spain. Around these two Spains were assembled and organized the Spaniards, intellectuals, workers, and peasants. The life of the Church unfolded by constraint within this sociological environment which influenced all its national and international activities.

Christian Syndicalism. In his lecture at the Teatro de la Comedia in 1914 Ortega y Gasset declared that the two current modern tendencies in Spanish public life were the Socialist Party and the trade-union movements. Without intending to oppose this thesis, it is clear that the union movement and with it the so-called Social Question had won powerful importance in national events. What measures did the Spanish Church take, once it was faced with this serious problem?

Some historians and sociologists have sought, from the viewpoint of the second half of the twentieth century, to play down the countless initiatives which proceeded from the Church to render this problem harmless. The Church could be charged with neither passivity nor ignorance. Despite great difficulties, which had to be mastered, it laid for itself a road through the shaken social world. After the death of the Jesuit Antonio Vicent (1837–1912), "the patriarch of Spanish social Catholicism," as his famous pupil Severino Aznar called him, the Christian union movement began to gain in strength and extent. The ideal solution would have been at this moment the formation of workers' or peasants' unions without group ideologies. But considering the fact that the union acted in an antireligious manner and firmly attacked the Church, there was nothing else left except to organize the Christian union; in regard to this there occurred within the Catholic ranks a strong polemic, which partly absorbed the energies of the Catholic union. Nevertheless, successes was attained among the peasant unions, since the rural population adhered to the Church more than did the industrial workers. Hence it is incorrect to speak of a failure of Christian unions.

The Church unions, regardless of whether they were denominationally oriented or not, had to follow the Church's guidelines; hence they could not offer the worker the revolutionary stimulus of the *Union General de Trabajadores* (UGT) or of the *Confederación Nacional del Trabajo* (CNT), otherwise they would stand outside the Church's social doctrine and would not have been ecclesiastical unions.

Second Spanish Republic and Civil War (1931–39)

In an effort to end the social-political confusion which externally impaired Spanish life in the first third of the twentieth century, three political solutions were tried in succession: a concrete application of parliamentary government by Antonio Maura; the dictatorship of General Primo de Rivera, established on 13 September 1923; the Second Republic of 1931.

The first two efforts were unsuccessful. The result of the communal elections of 12 April 1931, which had favored the monarchy numerically, produced the abdication of Alphonso XIII and the proclamation of the republic on 14 April. Seen from the religious standpoint, this meant the official establishment of anticlericalism in Spain, which within six years drove the Spanish Church into a frightful catastrophe without comparison in the history of the Church. The burning of monasteries and churches on 11 May 1931 and the expulsion of the bishop of Vitoria and of the primate of Toledo from Spain were clear indications of the religious attitude of the most powerful agents of the new Spanish policy. The spirit of the constitution of the republic was stamped by *sectarismo* to such a degree that even the president of the republic, Niceto Alcalá Zamora, conceded that those measures were an invitation to civil war. Concerning ARTICLE 26 of the constitution, which dealt with the religious orders, José María Gil Robles, minister of that republic, says in his *Memorias:* "The enacting of ARTICLE 26 of the basic law was not only a remarkable injustice but represented a mistake with incalculable consequences. The religious problem was changed into a state of war with the danger of conflict between the two Spains." Nevertheless, the ecclesiastical dignitaries recommended to the Spanish Catholics "respect and obedience to the lawful authorities and cooperation in all those matters whose aim was the general welfare and social peace."

Even the members of the cabinet were surprised by the respect shown by the Church toward the republic. But they still did not feel induced to change their damaging attitude; on the contrary, the antireligious legislation went further. On 24 January 1932 a law was passed whose content was the abolition of the Society of Jesus; it had to seek its salvation in exile. The justification of the law was that the Jesuits paid obedience to a foreign power, the Pope. Some days later the divorce law was enacted; immediately thereafter there appeared in the *Gaceta* a decree on the secularization of cemeteries. Another decree prescribed that the cross be removed from the schools. All these measures injured in the keenest way the sensitivities of the overwhelmingly Christian families. In the face of this more or less open persecution nothing else was left to the Church than to issue a sharp protest. At first, on 25 May 1933, the Spanish episcopate published a "Declaración sobre la ley de Confesiones religiosas." A few days later, on 3 June, appeared Pius XI's encyclical *Dilectissima nobis,* in which he lamented the situation in Spain.

The Civil War (1936–39)

Out of the elections of 16 February 1936 there emerged as victor, with the aid of the prevailing election system, which provided a bonus for the majority, the Popular Front, that is, a union of all the leftist parties. This victory was fostered by the votes of the members of the CNT and the split of the right parties. The new government tried unsuccessfully to satisfy its electors. Then political disintegration overtook the broad public. The leader of the national bloc, José Calvo Sotelo, drew in the parliament a sad balance of the events within the Popular Front government of six weeks from 16 February to 2 April 1936: there occurred 199 attacks and burglaries, 36 of them on churches; 178 fires were counted, including 106 churches burned down and 56 destroyed; 74 dead and 345 wounded were to be lamented. A few months later Calvo Sotelo himself was murdered in the night of 13 July 1936 by Popular Front police. This deed was declared an expressly political crime and sharply condemned by the sensible population of the country. It occasioned the *Movimiento;* the only way out was civil war. The army and the right joined in the struggle against the Marxist revolution. The *Movimiento Nacional* rose on 18 July; the two Spains were divided into two battlefields: the Red and the National Zones.

The Red Zone. The Church did not take part in the *Alzamiento.* But through the bishop of Gerona, Dr. Castañía, it proclaimed "the gratitude that an innocent victim feels for its generous defender." One year after the outbreak of war the Spanish bishops on 1 July 1937 addressed all the Catholic bishops of the world. In their letter they expressed in their concern for religion, home, and humanity not an empty thesis but "the events which characterize our war and give it its special features." Spain was divided in two: on the one side the Communist revolution with its barbaric, antireligious, and anti-Spanish licentiousness, on the other side the National Movement with its respect for the religious and national order. In this situation the Church, always remaining within its pastoral sphere and without pawning its spiritual freedom, had no other way out than to place itself on that side which "took the field for the defense of order, social peace, traditional civilization and homeland, and not least the defense of religion" (A. Granados). The tone of the episcopal letter was moderate, of emotional balance and realistic attitude. Only two bishops did not sign it: the archbishop of Tarragona, Francisco Cardinal Vidal y Barraquer, and the bishop of Vitoria, Mateo Múgica. The former, because he believed secret written information to the bishops of the various nations would be more effective and joined with less danger of reprisal against those who still lived in the Red Zone than a public common letter; the latter, because he was outside his diocese. The rest of the episcopate, forty-three bishops and five vicars general, signed it. The echo of the common letter was loud. "All members of the episcopate [ca. 900 bishops] replied by recognizing the legitimacy of the war on the part of national Spain and its character as a crusade for the Christian religion and civilization," said the future Cardinal Pla y Deniel.

Meanwhile the real confrontation was carried out on the battlefield and beyond the fronts. It demanded of the Spanish Church a heavy tribute of blood and glorious martyrdoms. Twelve bishops of the dioceses of Sigüenza, Lérida, Cuenca, Barbastro, Segorbe, Jaén, Ciudad Real, Almería, Guadix, Barcelona, Teruel, and the auxiliary bishop of Tarragona died as martyrs. True to their evangelical task and with full knowledge of the danger to which they were exposed on the outbreak of war, they still remained at their posts. "I cannot leave out of fear; here is my duty, cost what it may," said the bishop of Cuenca to those who recommended flight. And for this reason the other shepherds remained with their flocks.

Because of their office, 4,184 priests had to die; they were hunted like game.

Some dioceses suffered very heavy losses, as, for example, that of Barbastro; there 123 of the 140 pastors died, at Lérida 270 out of 410, and at Toledo 286 out of 600. Of the religious 2,365 died, some of them between seventeen and eighteen years old. Worst hit were the following institutes: Claretians with 259 dead, Franciscans with 226 dead, Piarists with 204 dead, Marists with 176 dead, Brothers of the Christian Schools with 165 dead, Augustinians with 155 dead, Dominicans with 132 dead, and Jesuits with 114 dead. The number of murdered sisters amounted to 283; even as women they were not spared persecution and torment. Altogether 6,832 priests, sisters, and brothers sacrificed their lives for the faith: an unmistakable proof of the vitality of the Spanish Church. As regards the type of martyrdom, no method known in history was overlooked: mutilation, death by fire, or even crucifixion.

The National Zone. At the outbreak of the *Movimiento* a religious movement was to be noted among the Spanish people and the warriors. There was a genuine rebirth of the religious life in the entire country. Victories at the front were celebrated with Masses, Te Deums, and *Salve Reginas*. The new government began to draw up new laws with a Christian meaning. The cross was again hung in the schools, and religious instruction was again introduced. Important laws, such as the *Carta Magna del Fuero del Trabajo* of 1936 for the support of families, were oriented to the Church's social teaching. Great amounts of money were made available for the reconstruction of more than 20,000 destroyed churches. The corps of chaplains was reintroduced. All churches and chapels, the residences of bishops and priests with their grounds, and seminaries and monasteries were exempted from the land tax. In May 1938 the Society of Jesus was again permitted, with restoration of all rights and goods it had enjoyed before its dissolution. On 2 February 1939 the juridical status of all religious orders was restored. The republican legislation on divorce and civil marriage, the secularization of cemeteries, and the limitations on Catholic burials were repealed. In short, all those rights were again recognized in the Church which were contained in canon law. Respect for the Church and its institutions was again holy and removed from any discussion.

The chaplains at the front wrote a glorious chapter for the history of the Spanish Church.

Spain in the Postwar Period (Since 1939)

The thirty years between 1939 and 1970 can be divided into two parts, of fifteen years each, which were marked by two different sorts of generation: a traditional generation (1939–55) and a critical generation (after 1955). The two groups are the same in exterior structure but different in dynamism.

The Twofold Trend

Traditional Generation. The religious organization in the Spain of the postwar epoch had its origin in the Catholic tradition that was the ideal of the Spain which had once gained victory on the fields of battle. Hence one can speak of an amazing revival of the content of this tradition. Of this there were the following signs: strengthening of church authority and respect for Church offices; increase of ecclesiastical vocations; improvement of ecclesiastical institutions and refounding of institutions; the wide extension of charitable activities, as, for example, the missions; spiritual exercises and religious courses; jubilee years with pilgrimages to Santiago de Compostela and Holy Week processions; attendance at Sunday Mass and reception of Easter Communion; the strong movement of the lay apostolate with Catholic Action, the Marian congregations, and other institutions. Religious books obtained a dominant position on the national book market. Religious publishers spread the works of the great authors throughout the world. The climax of this period was the concordat of 1953 as the embodiment of the classical principles of the canon law then in force and of the traditional spirit of Catholic Spain. It would take us too far afield to evaluate all phenomena. The influence of the Spanish Church on Spanish society was enormous. Probably until then the Spanish Church never had so many possibilities of forming a society by means of Christian ideals. In 1940 the Church had charge of 60 percent of all high schools and hence could exercise its influence on youth in so critical a period of life; in 1955 it was still 42 percent. Furthermore, the Church gave religious instruction in public schools and universities and was able to exercise influence in this way also.

Critical Generation.   In the course of the years the number of members of a small group of Catholics with an outlook directed to Europe and the world grew. This movement let itself be guided by the political philosophy of Jacques Maritain in questions of relations between Church and state. It also caused the introduction of liturgical forms from beyond the Pyrenees and the dissemination of foreign points of view and unfamiliar morals in Spain. The more these trends gained in importance, the certainty was strengthened that the block of classical Spanish thought began to crumble and that the traditional concept of Spanish life incurred the danger of losing its vigor. The polemic on the theme, carried out on the national and international level, had reached its highest intensity when the Second Vatican Council began. Some of the most important, hitherto disputed points of the notion of Christian life were raised by it to postulates. This fact produced a deep crisis on several levels of Spanish Catholicism.

Institutions.   As outstanding representatives of the institutions within Spanish Catholicism must be mentioned: the episcopal conference, some institutes, Catholic Action, and the National Catholic Association of Propagandists.

Episcopal Conference.   Since its establishment after the Second Vatican Council, the episcopal conference took over the control and administration which were previously cared for by the conferences of metropolitans. The decisions of the conference theoretically have no binding force for each diocese, but they are observed as if they were obligatory. In general, today the Spanish Church reacts on the collegial plane in all common questions. What is there discussed and decided is therefore of great general importance. The guidelines issued by the episcopal conference are in practice observed in the entire country. One of the most important stands of the episcopal conference was the declaration of January 1973 on "The Church and the political community," which was passed by a vote of

fifty-nine for and twenty against, a situation in which is reflected the sociological structure of the episcopal conference. In this declaration the most important
themes were treated which concerned the relations of Church and society, of
Church and public order, the relations between Church and state with regard for
the Catholic religion as the state religion, the revision of the concordat of 1953,
and the renunciation of privileges and of the paying of ecclesiastics.

Religious Communities.   The improvement of the traditional institutes already in
existence and the founding of new institutes are consequences of the religious
revival of the postwar period. These institutes displayed a great activity in schools
and the press. Outstanding among the lay institutes is the Sociedad Sacerdotal
de la Santa Cruz, or, for short, Opus Dei, founded at Madrid in 1928 by Monsignor
José María Escrivá and recognized as an institute in 1947.

Catholic Action.   In 1926 Spanish Catholic Action was subjected to a profound
restructuring. Previously it had been rather a loose union of the personnel present
as a central organization; all Catholic personnel retained their own autonomy.
After 1939 a strict centralization of all activities of the lay apostolate was introduced; it led to confrontations among the current personnel and partly impaired
their work. From 1945 special institutions appeared with the founding of *Juven-
tud Obrera Católica* (JOC) and *Hermandad Obrera de Acción Católica* (HOAC).
On 5 December 1959 the conference of the Spanish metropolitans issued the
new "Statute of Catholic Action," which consolidated the already existing central
unity. This statute was replaced by a new statute issued on 1 February 1968 by
the episcopal conference.

Asociación Católica Nacional de Propagandistas.   Among the Catholic lay groups
that exercise great influence on Spanish public opinion must be mentioned the
Asociación Católica Nacional de Propagandistas. Founded at Madrid in 1908 by
the Jesuit Ángel Ayala with the aim of preparing a group of the Catholic Men's
Union of Saint Louis for Catholic propaganda, it had as president the future Cardinal Ángel Herrera Oria, who possessed an extraordinary gift for organizing. In
1911 it bought the Madrid newspaper *El Debate* and a year later Herrera founded
El Editorial Católica as economic and ideological support of the paper. The union
was concerned with all problems which preoccupied the Spanish Church in
this century. After the war *El Debate* was stopped and in its place appeared *Ya,*
which together with *ABC* are the two most important daily newspapers of the
country. After the war *La Editorial Católica* began the publication of the series
Biblioteco de Autores Cristianos, which today consists of more than three hundred volumes. The great activity of Catholic propaganda, without precedent in
the history of the Spanish Church, achieved its climax in 1947 with the founding
of the Centro de Estudios Universitarios (CEU); a division of the Centro is today
the Colegio Universitario de San Pablo at Madrid with 5,000 students and eight
faculties.

Portugal

The development of Portuguese history in this century went through three phases: the anticlerical revolution of the bourgeoisie of 1910 (1910–26); the new regime (1926–60); and the era of the Second Vatican Council from 1960.

The Anticlerical Revolution (1910–26)

After the overthrow of the monarchy by the republican forces, the latter proceeded against the Church. The bishops were sharply attacked because of their rejection of the divorce law of 20 April 1911 and in the course of 1912 driven from their dioceses, with one exception — the archbishop of Évora. Diplomatic relations with the Holy See were broken until 1918, and clerics were deprived of their property. The wearing of the cassock and the exercise of their activity as directors of committees named by the state in the sphere of the administration of the Church were forbidden to the clergy. Minor seminaries were closed by law, and of the major seminaries only five were spared from this measure, those of Braga, Pôrto, Coimbra, Lisbon, and Évora.

By recourse to the laws of Pombal and those of the liberal regime of 1834 the members of 164 houses of thirty-one orders were expelled. But from 1917 on some congregations were reorganized. The revolution also forbade religious instruction in elementary and high schools and closed the theological and ecclesiastical faculty of Coimbra. Nevertheless, in the First World War there were again field chaplains.

The lay apostolate awoke as a reaction to these measures. Thus in 1913 occurred the reactivation of the *Centro Académico de Democracia Cristá* (CADC), founded at Coimbra in 1903. At the same time was founded the *Centro Católica,* which from 1915 sent its representatives to the Chamber of Deputies and the Senate, even though only a small number.

The New Regime (1926–60)

With the movement of General Gomes da Costa and the presidency of General Carmona begins a new order of authoritarian character, whose most important representative became Oliveira Salazar. This movement led in the area of the relations between Church and state to the concordat of 1940. The position of the Church improved; it included seventeen dioceses and three archdioceses.

Religious instruction was reintroduced in the elementary and high schools. The number of schools with religious direction, especially schools for girls, increased, although they were attended mostly by the rich segment of the population and although there was no state aid. The education in these schools was primarily humanistically oriented and scarcely scientifically. Around 1930 a university institute for social assistance was founded at Lisbon.

Among the most important institutions for social communication are the newspaper *Novidades* and the Catholic Broadcasting Radio Renascença, which was silenced by the revolutionary forces in 1975 and was later given back by the government.

The number of traditions in worship was increased by the great crowds on pilgrimage to the national shrine of Fátima since 1931. In addition, catechesis and liturgy again grew in importance, especially due to the exertions of the Lisbon seminary and the Benedictines. The lay apostolate began to take new routes. After the prohibition of political parties it withdrew from political life, to which so far the *Centro Católico* had devoted itself, and strengthened its collaboration with the Church authorities. In 1932 the bishops founded the official *Acção Católica*, which in November 1933 obtained a juridical statute confirmed by Pope Pius XI. Portugal's missionary work produced in Angola up to 1940 as many as 500,000 Catholics with 174 missionaries, in Mozambique as many as 60,000 Catholics with 126 priests; but up to 1970 as many as 2.5 million in Angola and 1.25 million in Mozambique.

Under the Influence of the Second Vatican Council (from 1960)

The Portuguese Church appeared at the council with only its bishops, hence without *periti*. In other words, it was a preponderantly traditional and authoritarian Church. In 1968 it numbered 4,500 diocesan and 900 religious priests; a slight increase in comparison to 1947, but this was also caused by the growth of the population, everything else being equal. These relations also remained constant in regard to the rural or urban origin of vocations.

By 1960 the *Acção Catolica* achieved its zenith. In this regard the national meetings of the *Juventude Católica Universitária* from 1953 to 1963 represented the climax. Among the ranks of the lay apostolate movements were to be observed which tended to achieve a greater independence in regard to the episcopate. In the field of the university apostolate the founding of the Catholic University at Lisbon and of two other universities must not be forgotten. Still, the realities did not correspond to the structures. In the confrontation of the Church with the revolution of 1974 it was revealed that the former was poor, apolitical, without organized youth, with seminaries overtaken by crisis, and without adequate personnel. The present difficulties in the country have produced a concentration of Catholic forces, which allow one to hope for new initiatives.

CHAPTER 104

The Countries of the English-Speaking Area

Europe

Great Britain

Population. In 1966 the total population of England and Wales amounted to 48,075,000; the Catholic population had grown to 4,000,695, including 5,096 diocesan priests and 2,791 religious priests, with 3,446 public churches and chapels and 1,196 private devotional sites. The Catholics had spread equally in the large cities and suburbs, but not in the rural areas; Catholicism remained an urban phenomenon. At the same time the number of Catholics in Scotland rose to 809,680 in a total population of 5,191,000.

This growth was based partly on the natural increase of the population, on conversions, and on the immigration of refugees from the continent, especially Poles and Ukrainians, but chiefly on immigration from Ireland. In fact, about three-fourths of the Catholics in Great Britain were of Irish descent, insofar as they were not themselves born in Ireland. The heterogeneity proceeding from this was gradually broken down by the integration of the immigrants into British Catholicism. The annual number of adult converts — between 12,000 and 10,000 — remained almost unchanged from 1925 to the Second World War, in spite of growth of the total population. Many converts were the future or present husbands or wives of Catholics. Of the rest, more Catholics came from the middle class, who were better able to cope with the claims of the Church than the lower class, and in proportion there were more converts among the Nonconformists, whose organized religious life quickly dissolved, than among the Anglicans. Meanwhile, however, the Church suffered a constant "loss"; even a great part of the children who came from Catholic schools soon gave up their practice of religion. These factors prevented the percentage of Catholics in England from increasing notably. Partly as a consequence of the prejudices of their fellow citizens and partly because of their own cultural inferiority, the influence of the English Catholics in public life did not correspond to their numerical strength.

Organization. From 1911 there were in England and Wales three metropolitan sees — Westminster, Liverpool, Birmingham — and thirteen dioceses. In 1916 the archdiocese of Cardiff emerged from the diocese of Newport in Wales, with Menevia as its only auxiliary see. New episcopal sees were erected in 1917 at Brentwood and in 1924 at Lancaster. In 1965 the diocese of Southwark was raised to metropolitan status, and at the same time its auxiliary see of Arundel and Brighton was erected. There were then in England and Wales five provinces with five archdioceses and fourteen dioceses. In addition, in 1957 the archbishop of Westminster was named apostolic exarch for the Ukrainians of the Byzantine Rite, which numbered more than 20,000 adherents; in 1961 Augustine Eugene Hornyak, O.S.B.M., a Ukrainian priest, was made his auxiliary bishop, and six years later he himself became apostolic exarch for Great Britain.

In Scotland from 1878 the archdiocese of Saint Andrews and Edinburgh had existed as metropolitan see with four auxiliaries, and the archdiocese of Glasgow had belonged to no ecclesiastical province; in 1947 the last named became a metropolitan see with two auxiliary sees, which were newly erected at Motherwell and Paisley.

Furthermore, the archbishop of Westminster represented the episcopate in discussions with the government. The following occupied this post: 1903–35, Francis Bourne, a cardinal in 1910; 1935–43 Arthur Hinsley, cardinal in 1937; 1943–56 Bernard Griffin, cardinal in 1946; 1956–63 William Godfrey, cardinal in 1958; 1963–75 John Heenan, cardinal in 1965; and since 1976 Basil Hume, O.S.B., cardinal in the same year.

From the reign of Elizabeth I Great Britain had no diplomatic relations with the Holy See, but after the outbreak of the First World War the government sent Sir Henry Howard to convey the congratulations of the King to the newly elected Pope Benedict XV and to explain to him the reason for the entry into the war. The British representative stayed in Rome as extraordinary ambassador and minister plenipotentiary "on special mission." In 1920 the legation was made a regular and permanent institution. But the relations were never brought to reciprocity. No nunciature was established in London; in fact not until 1938 was an apostolic delegation opened in the British capital. The first apostolic delegate was an Englishman, William Godfrey, who took care of this post until he became archbishop of Liverpool in 1953.

Educational System.   In 1914 343,472 pupils were educated in 1,169 Catholic primary schools and 24,129 in 387 Catholic secondary schools. In conformity with the Education Act of 1902 denominational schools had to be erected and repaired by voluntary offerings, although the expenses of maintenance and the salaries of teachers were paid out of public funds. They were endangered by the inability of the faithful in an age of rising costs to care for adequate premises and equipment. Discussions conducted in a friendly atmosphere between representatives of the state and the Church produced the "Scottish solution." In accord with the Scotland Education Act of 1918, the directors of the already existing Church schools or those to be established in the future were authorized to sell their schools to the education authorities, to lease them, or to transfer them in other ways. But the education authorities could themselves also erect new denominational schools. The officials were from then on to exercise complete control over the schools, including the appointment and dismissal of teachers, but in this connection the teachers on hand were to retain their positions. In the future no teacher could be appointed before he or she had been accepted by the relevant denominational corporation, "in regard to religious faith and character." An unpaid supervisor, who had likewise to be accepted by the denomination, was to be appointed for every school. The supervisor had the right of access to all classes which were specified for religious instruction and worship, and he had to report to the Church authorities on the effectiveness of the religious instruction that was given. (In Catholic schools this supervisor was normally the parish priest, and diocesan inspectors had permission to give examinations in religion.) Thus was ended the administrative dualism, as the local authorities desired it, but the religious dualism was retained, because the bishops insisted on it in order to preserve the Catholic character of their schools. In spite of their security precautions and the fact that this agreement was to a great extent the work of William Francis Brown, whom the Pope had named as apostolic visitor for Scotland the previous year, the Scottish bishops and the Catholics in general were frightened by it. Finally, the Holy See with its only intervention in educational questions directed them to accept the agreement. This regulation functioned smoothly from the beginning and in the course of time was regarded from the Catholic standpoint as one of the best arrangements in the entire world. The Scottish Catholics opened many free schools for the primary and secondary grades and several colleges operated by religious orders, and all were supported by local and national public financing. (A few private Catholic schools which raised instructional fees likewise continued in existence.)

The situation of the Catholics in England and Wales differed from that of the Scots in many respects and in 1918 the bishops could not agree to give up the rights of ownership of their schools. Between 1914 and 1930 the Catholics built ninety-six schools with 60,000 places at a capital expenditure of £1,700,000. Meanwhile, construction costs steadily mounted and many of the older schools had to be replaced or expanded, and, especially in the cities, new schools had to be erected. The burden became intolerable. In order to draw public attention to the injustice of their situation, the Catholics organized great protest gatherings and called upon the members of parliament to give assistance. After the founding of the Irish Free State in 1921, English Catholics no longer had many friends in parliament, and the Labour Party had many members who by tradition were hostile to Catholicism, although it depended, especially in certain areas, also on the votes of the Catholic English workers. In 1931 the Catholic Educational Council decided to carry out a campaign for the adoption of the Scottish system in England and Wales, but the prospects of achieving this goal became less as each year passed, partly because the National Teachers' Association did not want to accept any system that would have meant the introduction of denominational instruction in a much larger number of schools under state ownership and religious examinations for specific teachers.

In 1936 the Catholics were forced to accept aid under conditions that were quite other than favorable. The Education Law of this year authorized the local authorities to contribute 50 to 75 percent of the costs for the erecting of voluntary schools. These schools had become necessary by the express intention of the state to raise the age of leaving school to fifteen years on 1 September 1939 and to "reorganize" the educational system. In order to correspond to the demands of the Free Churches and of the National Association of Teachers, this regulation had to be severely limited in time: applications had to be filed within three years; only the furnishing of the high schools was provided, although there was a greater need for the reorganization of the elementary schools; the teachers in those schools which obtained building subsidies had to be appointed by the local school officials, if even a small part of them — on which the directors of the schools and the officials had to agree — had to be "reserved" teachers, that is, such as were chosen in discussion with the school administration and were qualified to impart the relevant denominational instruction. In all voluntary schools there had to be given, in the event the parents wished it, a nondenominational religious instruction in keeping with the teaching plan prescribed for the local public schools. Finally, the aid was only permitted, but not prescribed as an obligation. Because the Catholics, under the leadership of the new archbishop of Westminster, Arthur Hinsley, feared that the Catholic high schools would lose their students to the better equipped public schools if they were not reorganized, they decided to make use of the offer and at the same time to work to retain their elementary schools.

The effects of these legal measures were not entirely satisfactory, although because of them a good by-product resulted: the setting up of diocesan school commissions in places where previously there had been none. The reorganization in rural areas, which included the erection of central schools, was delayed by the difficulties growing out of the great distances and the need of means of transportation, and it threatened to divide the life of the parish congregations. In the cities the development proceeded faster. Many offices, including London, were ready to grant the full financial subsidy, 75 percent, conceded by the law; others gave 50 percent.

When the Second World War broke out, only 44.8 percent of the Catholic school districts had been reorganized. Even in 1942 there were still no less than 399 dilapidated Catholic school buildings on the "Black List" of the education office — this list included schools with defective equipment. The continuation of the reorganization was prevented by the war, and the age of leaving school could not be raised at the intended time. Of the 289 Catholic applications, which were submitted in accord with the law of 1936, only the 9 approved were implemented. Although there was only one English community without a Catholic school — Morley near Leeds — almost 20 percent of the Catholic children in the country were not in Catholic schools. Nevertheless, the 1,200 Catholic schools made up 12 percent of the voluntary schools and instructed 8 percent of the total population of obligatory school age.

When the government began with the planning of a coherent system in the sphere of the primary grades, the secondary grades, and the higher school system, the Catholics began an active campaign of organized opposition to this project — the *Green Book* of 1941 — and emphatically demanded that in their schools the denominational character remain intact. The Catholic Parents' Associations, the first of which was founded in 1940 at Ilford in the diocese of Brentwood, were increased on the parish level and coordinated by diocesan councils, which for their part were represented in an interdiocesan Council of the Catholic Parents' and Electors' Association. Its chief concern consisted for several years in assuring and promoting Catholic interests in the educational system.

Before a law was introduced in parliament there were long discussions with the president of the Board of Education, R. A. Butler, and representatives of the Anglicans, the Catholics, the Free Churches, and the teachers. However, the Catholic speakers were isolated, for the Anglicans had acquiesced, and the Free Churches and the professional associations had the upper hand. Because the Catholics failed to obtain even the slightest concessions, they opposed the law until parliament had passed it. The result showed that people in England and Wales, who, differently from Scotland, were already strongly de-Christianized, could not appeal to an influential public opinion which was convinced that religion formed the heart of education; one could claim only "equality of opportunity," the right of parents to have their children educated in their own faith and at no greater cost than what their non-Catholic neighbor had to pay.

The Education Law of 1944, the "Butler Act," provided financial aid for three categories of denominational primary and secondary schools. In all these schools all costs for secular and religious education were to be defrayed from public sources, but the state retained the right to assure itself that the schools were needed and that new schools were erected only to the extent that the national finances permitted: (a) The "voluntary aided schools" should remain totally denominational. But the state was now ready to pay to the school administrators 50 percent for approved necessary repairs and improvements and up to 50 percent of the expenses for specific reconstructions. Normally the school administrators were helped by loans with favorable conditions, and auxiliary services — medical examinations, school meals — were paid for by the state. (b) The "special arrangement schools" were supported in accord with the provisions of the law of 1936; the applications filed within the prescribed time, which had not been approved or implemented, could now be revived with the necessary alterations in the previously determined conditions in regard to a limiting of the number of those teachers who were recognized because of their qualifications for imparting denominational instruction. Other regulations should be the same as for the first category. (c) "Controlled schools" were to be financed and supported exactly as if they were public schools, with the exception of some concessions, which were made as an accommodation for the cession of the buildings, for example, the right of the denominational officials to name one-third, instead of two-thirds, of the school administrators.

The Catholics completely rejected the "controlled" status. As a result, they faced the most difficult task of raising the funds needed for their "voluntary aided schools" — half the costs of modernizing, reconstruction in new places, and accommodation of "transferred" students — and also the means for their "special arrangement schools" — from one-fourth to one-half — and for new schools — the total costs of building sites and the buildings. The heaviest burden was for the Catholics, especially for male and female religious institutes, the secondary school system because of the higher age for obligatory schooling and because of the abolition of all fees in the state schools. The existing Catholic secondary schools for the most part accepted the status of elementary schools, and, except for those which were especially instituted for the higher classes, strove to be recognized by the education authorities as "effective" in their various categories. By 1948 the number of "recognized" schools had risen to 109, and the number of those which obtained state money to 73.

Two supplementary laws of 1946 and 1948 eased somewhat the burden laid on the Catholics, but the expenses mounted further. A pupil's place, which had cost ca. £60 in 1939, in 1949 required between 91 and £400, with variations from diocese to diocese. Meanwhile, the number of Catholic children who did not go to Catholic schools rose from one to four. In 1950 the hierarchy proposed some redress and set up an "Action Committee" to guide local deputations drawn from the parishes and lay organizations; they were to inculcate these proposals in the candidates for parliament during the general election of that year. Although the Catholic electors were informed of the positions of the candidates, this campaign did not succeed in obtaining noteworthy support from them, especially because no political party showed an inclination to take up this controversial matter.

Because the Catholics were not in a position to erect sufficient secondary schools, from 1956 they again made demands for state aid, but this time they did not have recourse to public agitation. Some 30 percent of the Catholic children of school age were at this time not in Catholic schools, although the Church had, between 1945 and 1959, raised the number of its schools by almost 25 percent, that is, by more than 300 schools, created 100,000 new school places, and projected a further 150,000. The education law of 1959 was accepted in part as answer to the demands of the Catholics and Anglicans. This law raised the aid due previously from 50 to 75 percent and granted subsidies of 75 percent for the erecting of new voluntary secondary schools, which were totally or very greatly necessary to take those children from the primary schools of the same denomination which had existed on 15 June 1959 or who came from such primary schools as had been erected to replace the schools existing at this same time. For the Catholics the limitation imposed by the date and the exclusion of aid for the building of primary schools was, of course, a disappointment.

The Catholics again presented their requests and demanded 85 percent of all building costs. Finally they were satisfied with the provisions of the education law of 1967, which was introduced by the Labour Government and accepted by parliament almost without opposition. The state raised not only the existing subsidies for all voluntary schools or those supported by special arrangement, so far as they were paid for approved repairs and improvements, to 80 percent, but it now also counted what was still more important 80 percent for the erecting of entirely new schools or for the expansion of existing schools, even if such aid had previously not been granted to these. The government was able to concede these increased subsidies in part because the Churches had established more harmony among themselves.

In order to be able to supply these schools with personnel, the existing teachers' training schools were improved and new ones were established. The erection of five new institutions for teacher training in the years after 1960 was the result of long discussions with the Ministry of Education and the Council of Catholic Education. In 1968 there were fourteen Catholic institutions for teacher training in England and Wales.

The attempt to found a Catholic university was not made in these years. However, in 1922 the University Catholic Federation of Great Britain had been founded to unite the Catholic associations at the English universities; it was attached to the *Pax Romana,* from which it had obtained the stimulus for its founding. It was reorganized in 1942, when the nongraduates founded the Union of Catholic Students and the graduates the Newman Association; the two organizations cooperated closely. The Union began with the publishing of a periodical and of an annual, in which in detail were presented the various methods by which it aspired to stress the Catholic influence in the life and works of the universities. The Newman Association attracted graduates from various professions and states of life; it set up a center in London and some active local branches. It also began the publishing of a monthly bulletin, *Unitas,* and displayed useful activities such as vacation courses, lecture series, and public university courses, some of which obtained recognition from the University of London Extension Board.

Social Movement.   The chief impulse for the social movement was the Catholic Social Guild. A group of priests and lay persons from the middle-class intellectuals had founded it in 1909 for the following ends: (1) to facilitate dialogue between Catholic students and workers; (2) for assistance in the achieving of applications of Catholic principles to actual social conditions; (3) to awaken in Catholic circles a greater interest in social questions and to assure their cooperation in the promotion of social reforms according to Catholic guidelines. With the encouragement of the hierarchy, this guild pursued these goals predominantly through study clubs or groups. Within the educational program for adults the guild introduced a correspondence course, for which it granted certificates and diplomas. In addition, it produced and disseminated literature which treated social questions; it planned and promoted instructional programs, some textbooks, and examinations for the various groups. Especially influential were its publications on international law after World War I and on the union system and employee-employer relations. Under the guidance of the guild days of recollection for workers were held. Finally, the guild trained lecturers and instituted lectures. In 1919 the headquarters of the administration was moved from London to Oxford.

In 1920 the guild arranged the first summer vacation course lasting one week. Its aim was to bring different classes together, to awaken understanding between employers and employees, and to make Catholic social doctrine known in broader circles. At the end of the 1950s the vacation courses were stopped.

In 1921 the guild founded the Catholic Workers' College at Oxford in order to educate men, and from 1923 women also, as leaders for their worker colleagues. This was a "monument" to Charles Plater (1875–1921), one of the founders of the guild. The college instituted courses on political and economic theory and history, likewise on social ethics and moral philosophy, but also on special themes, such as unions, community administration, and international relations. In 1925 it was recognized by the Education Office because of its provisions for adult education and empowered by the university to grant diplomas. All students received stipends from the financial means which came from varied sources, and from 1926 they could also receive a stipend of the Education Office. Most students came from England, Scotland, and Wales, but in later years there were also a few from abroad. In the first twenty-six years of its existence the college trained only 146 students. Nevertheless, some of its graduates were active in community politics and in the union movement.

When interest in the study groups slackened, obviously because study was regarded as an end in itself instead of a means to an end, action groups were founded. Likewise in 1954 the guild called the action group service into being, which from week to week supplied a system and a plan for study. This change could not entirely transform the trend to inflexibility. Finally, lay persons obtained the leading position, after the offices of the manager-secretary in 1958 and of the principal of the College of Workers in 1962 had been filled by them; they were merely advised by a priest, whom the bishops had named as moderator.

In the course of the years the guild took a stand for definite concerns. After

World War I it supported a guaranteed minimum wage and the family money plan. In 1926 it supported the general strike, until Cardinal Bourne condemned it. In the disturbed years after 1920 and 1930 the guild stood up for the unions and their rights. In its publications it explained the "corporate order" which Pius XI had recommended in *Quadragesimo Anno.* In the years after 1940 the guild found fault with the welfare state, but most Catholics gradually came to consider it with limited approval.

True, the Catholic Social Guild avoided detailed plans or programs and thereby was satisfied to promote a knowledge of general principles, which the individual Catholic could then apply to special situations; but some of its members from the very start favored a clearly articulated, concrete program that was based on a policy of social reform. Some of them, especially among the younger, devoted themselves to the doctrine of Distributism, which was represented by Hilaire Belloc, Gilbert Keith Chesterton, Eric Gill, and Father Vincent McNabb, O.P. The "Distributists" abhorred both industrial capitalism and socialism and recommended instead a wide distribution of property to private ownership. They presented their theory in numerous articles, which they published. The literary basis of the movement was strengthened by a social structure when in 1926 the Distributist League was founded in London. Within three months there arose affiliates in the large cities of England and Wales. At regular intervals the league organized public lectures and discussions on timely affairs; these events were attended by a relatively large number of auditors. But all their exertions led only to unimportant results, partly because of differences of opinion among the Distributists themselves. While a few called for action, Chesterton and his adherents were satisfied with propaganda — although Chesterton and Belloc submitted proposals and recommended their implementation to the government. The members of the league were also not in agreement on the right to property and the use of machines. Controversies left in the broad public the impression that they were utopian theoreticians and uncritical admirers of medieval civilization. The Birmingham Plan, proposed in 1928 by the affiliate in that city and later revised from time to time, was the most practicable, and *The Distributist Program,* which was published by the league in 1934, outlined the practical measures by which the ideal situation could be realized. But there were only a few persons willing to make the required renunciation of all those comforts and amenities which industrialization had contributed and again lead a simple handicraft life. Besides, other Catholics, especially members of the Catholic Social Guild, reviled the Distributists as unrealistic. From ca. 1939 every effective activity of the league ended, but individual Distributists continued in the years after 1950 their publications and proposals on their theory.

The recommendation of the Distributists for the gaining of the necessary livelihood by agriculture as a form of practical action was realized in the Back-to-the-Land Movement. In 1929 The Scottish Catholic Land Association was founded, and in 1931 and 1932 five regional Catholic agricultural societies were established in England. The six associations were represented by a standing joint committee, and *Land for the People,* begun by the Scots in 1930, was the common organ until 1934; in this year it returned to control by the Scots. At the same time the associations in England and Wales were reorganized as the Catholic Land Federation, which established a new official organ, *The Cross and the Plough*. Each local society had as its protector the local bishop or bishops, a priest as chairman, and a layman as secretary. The chief function of the associations consisted of establishing communities of small farmers with the secondary occupations united with them. In this way the natural right of man to private ownership would again be confirmed; unemployment would be mitigated, and Catholic life on the land would be renewed. Because the urbanized proletariat had first to be educated in agricultural methods, the societies instituted teaching farms, in which unmarried men should obtain a three-year teaching program in theory and practical instruction and also spiritual direction. However, these farms had only a brief life because of lack of money. For the same reason the societies could not set aside any land for settlement by independent farmers. The hierarchy entirely refused to approve and support a collection and thereby to give this movement official recognition, because it feared that this money would be diverted from the budget for the building of schools and churches in new localities, and because it doubted the financial practicability of the entire plan. Also the general indifference of the Catholics, doubts that the small holdings were a means against unemployment, and their distrust of the leading theoreticians in the movement, and also the lack of any support at all by the government — all this contributed to the dissolving of the associations and of the federation. However, The North of England Catholic Land Association, with corresponding subsidies from the government, until 1942 trained young men as farm workers — first for three months in a youth hostel or a home, then with a farmer — and *The Cross and the Plough* continued its issues until mid-1949.

During the great economic crisis, other Catholics, such as Father Paul Crane, S.J., John Fitzsimons, and other members of the Catholic Social Guild, saw in the work of Peter Maurin and Dorothy Day in the United States a model for action. In June 1935 they founded a new periodical, *The Catholic Worker,* whose first editor was John Ford. This newspaper was sold in all large cities on the streets, and the sellers formed discussion and action groups. In imitation of the American model they established Friendship Houses in some places. Among clergy and laity not everyone approved the aims of this movement, but *The Catholic Worker* continued until 1959. In that year its last editor, Robert P. Walsh, became organizational secretary of the Catholic Social Guild and editor of its monthly, *The Christian Democrat.*

Around 1935 *The Christian Democrat* had directed attention to the *Jeunesse Ouvrière Chrétienne* in Belgium and France, and, when the Young Christian Workers were officially founded in England in 1937, their directors were selected from a study group of the Catholic Social Guild, which consisted of sellers of the newspaper *The Catholic Worker.* Father Gerard Rimmer founded the first group, and one of its members was Patrick Keegan, the future president of the World Union of Christian Worker Movements. The movement of the Young Christian Workers spread quickly and reached a part of the population which the Catholic social movement had previously not affected, but before the outbreak of World War II their organization had still not acquired a solid basis. The YCW also began with the preparation of boys and girls, before they left school, and from this work emerged the Pre-YCW, which Keegan founded in 1949. Also in the postwar years former members of the YCW developed the Family Social Apostolate to put its religious principles into practice in married life.

The Catholic Social Guild, the Catholic Women's League, the Catholic Education Council, and other organizations appointed delegates to the Catholic Council for International Relations, which had been founded in 1924 as a sort of uniting committee. Its function was to establish unity of action among the Catholics of all nations in all matters which affected their faith and to foster the business of international peace. Its work was chiefly of the educational type and was carried out by public announcements and international conferences.

Between the two world wars there appeared still other organizations. A lay group, which had regularly visited the ships in the harbor of Glasgow, established the Apostleship of the Sea in 1920. In the following year the administrator of the archdiocese approved the temporary guidelines and statutes. In 1922 Archbishop Donald A. Mackintosh communicated the blessing and a letter of recognition from Pius XI and became the first president of the society. Its task was the spiritual care of seamen. The work soon spread in Great Britain and to other countries; in 1927 200 churches in numerous harbors of the world were designated as sailors' centers. The administrative headquarters was first transferred from Glasgow to London, and in 1952 Pius XII established the general secretariat at Rome.

While the beginnings of an organization of Catholic contractors had only slight success, the British Catholic workers belonged to the general unions and never tried to establish unions of their own. But they held an annual National Conference of Catholic Trades Unionists and later founded diocesan associations of Catholic unionists. After the war the local associations were united in a national corporation. It aimed at the organization of the opposition to Communist intrigues in the unions and worked to make its members better Catholics and better unionists. In both respects it achieved remarkable successes, but in the years after 1950 the energy and influence of the Catholic unionists slackened.

The apparently most impressive movement which was started by Catholics during these years was the Sword of the Spirit, founded in 1940 by Cardinal Hinsley, an ardent patriot, who made a deep impression on the English people especially by his moving radio talks in the first years of World War II. It was the goal of this movement to assert the principles of Christianity and of the natural law against National Socialism and other totalitarian doctrines, for this end to support the national interest in the war, to seek for the postwar period a regulation and reorientation of Europe on the basis of such principles, and to unite all citizens for these goals. The activities of this movement were under the keywords "Prayer" — including sermons, retreats, days of recollection, and spiritual reading — "Study" — including lectures and discussion groups, for whose leadership plans were handed down — and "Action," which should be undertaken not in the name of the movement itself but through individuals and groups, who acted according to its principles. The original stimulus to this movement came from Christopher Dawson, who was first named lay leader and later was vice-president. Also many other prominent lay persons, men and women, were active in it, and groups were established among the French, Belgians, Poles, and Czechs who had fled to Great Britain and were living there in exile. But the totality of Catholics in the nation was not prepared for this movement. And because the other bishops had not previously been consulted, many of them gave no effective support. Nevertheless, it was at first enthusiastically welcomed by the Protestants. One of its first results was in December 1940 a declaration, signed by Cardinal Hinsley, by the archbishops of Canterbury and York, and by the moderator of the Free Church Federal Council. In it all accepted the five points of Pius XII for peace and added to them five criteria of their own, according to which economic situations and proposals could be examined. Such a cooperation with Protestants caused some Catholics to conjure up the danger of a dogmatic compromise or of indifferentism. Therefore the movement of the Sword of the Spirit soon decided, although it had invited to membership all men of good will who were willing to recognize the Catholic leadership, that non-Catholics could be only associate members without voting right. In spite of the disappointment thereupon expressed in some Protestant publications, Christian charity could be preserved thanks to the good offices of the Anglican bishop of Chichester, G. K. Bell, and others. The high point of this movement was reached in June 1942, when representatives of the Sword of the Spirit and those of Religion and Life, a similar movement among Protestants, composed a declaration on their collaboration, in which they appealed to the total Christian population of the country to act together in order to assure a noticeable influence of Christian teaching and of Christian witness in the solving of social, economic, and civil law problems at this time and in the postwar period. Accordingly, community weeks and meetings were held in all England, and local Christian councils were set up, not only to plan these events and realize them, but to put pressure on all parties who had to do with religious problems common to all denominations. This sort of interdenominational cooperation ceased when, with the end of the war, its chief propelling power was eliminated. The death of Cardinal Hinsley in March 1943 had deprived the Sword of the Spirit of his dynamic leadership, and in the first postwar years its activity generally slackened. Because of double work and overlapping, a coordination of its goals and actions with those of other Catholic societies could not be completely achieved. Under the new archbishop of Westminster, Cardinal Griffin, the center of gravity moved to the international area, to the social and political actions of Catholics on the continent, to the work of the United Nations and the special organizations affiliated to it, and to aid for refugees in Great Britain. In this way the "Sword" movement corresponded to a need which no other Catholic organization fulfilled. By 1954 it had lost its character as a mass movement and had become a center for the spread of information on all concerns of the Church in the whole world; furthermore, it was supposed, when necessary, to summon Catholic public opinion to action.

Catholics had always been free to support any of the greater political parties. Cardinals Bourne, Hinsley, and Griffin and other bishops frequently gave this answer when questions arose in regard to the Labour Party and its alleged championing of socialism. Most Catholics belonging to the working class actually preferred the Labour Party by an overwhelming majority; such membership for its party helped to prevent the party from developing into socialism.

Catechetical and Apologetic Work. The organized catechetical and apologetic work of the Catholic Church in Great Britain was promoted in various ways. The Catholic Truth Society, founded in 1884, circulated small and inexpensive writings, including some with a devotional and pedagogical content for Catholics and others for the information of Protestants. The founder of the society, James Britten, worked zealously up to his death in 1924. When in 1921–22 the headquarters of the society was moved and enlarged in order to accommodate a circulating library, an expansion of the program was due to the leadership talent and professional knowledge of an American, William Reed-Lewis. The publications of the society and its lectures were often concerned with particular themes of current interest, such as social and political ideologies in the years after 1920 and 1930, and later with birth control; but such controversial writings were never so important to the society as those which were aimed at the instruction of Catholics. Branch offices were set up throughout England and also in Scotland, Australia, India, Hong Kong, and the United States.

Another method for the instruction of non-Catholics was street-preaching, which was directed to all who wished to stop and listen. This was the function of the Catholic Evidence Guild, which Vernon Redwood, a New Zealander, had founded in London, with the permission of Cardinal Bourne, in 1918 shortly after the end of the war. The first guild worked only in the archdiocese of Westminster, but eventually independent guilds were also founded in other English dioceses and in the United States and Australia. In the springtime of the first guild there was elaborated a training program which took care of teaching courses in theology, philosophy, and Scripture; it was brought to the candidates, as meetings were held in the open; they were examined by study directors and other chaplains whom the local bishop had appointed, and there was also present a lay person, who as *advocatus diaboli* represented the crowd of listeners. The Marble Arch in Hyde Park became the most popular spot for speaker platforms in London. This sort of presentation to the outside was limited to Catholic doctrine; controversial questions of a social and economic nature and all political questions were strictly excluded. The text of the guild, *Catholic Evidence Training Outline,* which first appeared in 1925 and thereafter in revision, had been composed by Frank Sheed and Maisie Ward, two of the best known lay members. Of course, the work of the guild was impaired by the war, but after that it was intensified. In 1949 there were eighteen guilds with a total of 638 members and 302 speakers ready to act in England.

Liturgical Movement.   In Great Britain the liturgical movement had a slow start and achieved no very great success before the Second Vatican Council. The Society of Saint Gregory was founded in 1929. It published the periodical *Music and Liturgy* and conducted summer vacation courses. After World War II it expanded its area of work by giving up its earlier preference for music and shortened the name of its periodical to *Liturgy.* But the movement only obtained real esteem after the encyclical *Mediator Dei* and some decrees had been issued from Rome.

Samuel Gosling, an English priest, came to the conviction that the retention of Latin as the only liturgical language of the Roman Rite was a serious impediment to pastoral work. In 1943 he founded the English Liturgy Society for clerics and lay persons, who "want to promote the use of the vernacular in public Mass in so far as this is in harmony with the teachings and traditions of the Church." In the next year he started a small periodical, *The English Liturgist,* which he published until his death in 1950. The society obtained only modest support and encountered bitter opposition, but it exercised a direct influence even in the United States, where the American Vernacular Society was established in 1946.

Journalism. After 1914 only a few new newspapers and periodicals of importance were begun, but many of the old ones were continued. In 1915 Wilfrid Ward resigned as editor of the *Dublin Review,* but his successors continued the tradition on the same high level and with the same broad view, especially Shane Leslie, Denis Gwynn, and Christopher Dawson, who also composed numerous books, especially historical and biographical works. The periodical remained in the possession of the archbishop of Westminster. In 1961 its name was changed to *Wiseman Review* — shortly before, Norman St. John-Stevas became editor — and four years later again back to the *Dublin Review.* In the winter of 1968–69 it stopped appearing. Among the periodicals published by religious orders, the *Month,* the organ of the Jesuits, was continued in its original intellectual style until 1949. From then on its editor, Philip Caraman, S.J., began a new series, which devoted as much attention to literature and the arts as to theology and philosophy; this policy, for its part, was again changed in 1964. The *Downside Review* reflected the scholarship of the Benedictines in that abbey. In 1920 Bede Jarrett, O.P. founded *Blackfriars* as the organ of the Oxford Dominicans.

The weekly *Tablet* was continued by John George Snead-Cox until 1920 according to conservative guidelines, with little sympathy for the political ambitions of the Irish; it was essentially the mouthpiece of the old Catholic families. Its defensive and hostile attitude toward Anglicans was retained by Ernest Oldmeadow, a converted Methodist minister, whom Cardinal Bourne had chosen as editor in 1923 chiefly for his polemical skill. As religious controversies lost ever more in power of attraction, the circulation of the paper dropped to less than 3,000, and in 1936 Cardinal Bourne's successor sold the *Tablet* to a group of laymen, among them Douglas Woodruff, who then replaced Oldmeadow as editor; by expanding the areas of interest for the paper he succeeded in again stabilizing its existence. Woodruff made it an outstanding source of news, especially on foreign affairs, and he employed a number of competent journalists.

Among the other old weekly papers the London *Universe* prospered because it used the techniques of modern journalism. After it had acquired the *Catholic Times* in 1962, it increased its circulation to more than 300,000 and in this way became the most widespread religious newspaper in the entire country. Although the *Catholic Times* had likewise been modernized, it had retained more of its original character and for the future remained the preferred paper of many Catholics of Irish birth or ancestry. The *Catholic Herald* addressed a growing number of Catholic students at the provincial universities. When in 1934 a group of lay persons had acquired it, they completely transformed it. From then on Count Michael de la Bédoyère, who occupied a middle position between the *Tablet* and the *Universe,* edited it until 1962 in a very capable manner. After his retirement Desmond Fisher became editor and directed the paper as a journal of opinion, which treated world news of all sorts from the Catholic standpoint. The *Glasgow Observer* remained the only Catholic weekly published in Scotland; it appeared in the eastern and northern areas of the country under the title of *Scottish Catholic Herald;* it became in reality an affiliated enterprise of the London *Catholic Herald.*

Some other English and Irish Catholic weekly papers also published Scottish editions. The *Catholic Times* ran for forty years as an appendage of the *Welsh Catholic Times,* which appeared at Cardiff and was stopped in 1962.

Ireland

Population.   In the twenty-six counties of the Republic of Ireland the number of Catholics in 1961 was 2,673,473 in a total of 2,818,341. After the acquiring of independence, the percentage of Catholics grew with each census, whereas the total population declined, because emigration was stronger than the natural growth. Thereby the republic became, in regard to religion, constantly more homogeneous. In addition, the great majority of these Catholics practiced their faith, and so Catholicism was more visible in Ireland than in any other English-speaking country. In the six counties of Northern Ireland, on the other hand, the total population grew to 1,425,462 in 1961, while the number of Catholics increased to 498,031.

Political Development.   At the outbreak of World War I there was still violent debate on the already long spiritedly discussed question of Home Rule for Ireland. The chief difficulty resulted from the refusal of the Protestants in Ulster to accept an arrangement whereby Catholics would constitute the majority and so be in the position to bring clericalism to power or introduce a theocratic state. The Catholics, for their part, feared that in a partition of the island the Catholics in Ulster would be oppressed by a Protestant majority and that in the granting of autonomy to these northern parts of the country the principle of denominational education would be replaced by that of mixed education.

In the first years of the war the episcopate and clergy generally supported the participation of the Irish in the mobilization and recruiting. But at the end of 1915 this original enthusiasm for the war exertions changed to apathy. Edward Thomas O'Dwyer, bishop of Limerick, declared that it was England's and not Ireland's war. Although the hierarchy had several times condemned the Irish Republican Brotherhood, which organized the uprising in 1916, it did not unanimously disavow the rising. The rebel leaders who took part in the Easter rebellion were at least nominally Catholics, and of those who were jailed and condemned to death all except one received the sacraments before their execution by the British. However, public opinion as a whole condemned the immoral means they had used to assert the claim of the Irish people to independence. Of course, then the cruel treatment by the British government brought the rebels the sympathy of the people. Bishop O'Dwyer expressed the general indignation at the harshness of the British suppression.

When the Irish Parliamentary Party had lost the confidence of the public, the bishops and especially the younger priests gradually gave preference to the Sinn Fein Movement and at the same time helped to keep it from recourse to physical force. In fact, between May 1916 and the beginning of 1919 no noteworthy acts of violence occurred in Ireland. In this period the participation of those who claimed the title Sinn Fein conferred on the usual operations of a political party of the new movement the aura of trustworthiness which it needed in order to find the approval of the clergy on a broader basis. The primate of All Ireland and archbishop of Armagh, Cardinal Michael Logue, however, expressed in a pastoral letter of November 1917 his opposition to the Sinn Fein, because he regarded its dream of establishing an Irish Republic as a utopia, which would likely end in disaster.

When the military service law was submitted to parliament, in order to give the government authority to apply the conscription of troops also to Ireland, which had hitherto been exempted from it, the permanent committee of the bishops and individual bishops warned the British government in the spring of 1918 against the effort to force through such a law. Later the entire hierarchy condemned compulsory conscription as an inhuman law of suppression. The Irish people, they said, had the right to resist this law by every means that was in accord with the law of God. The bishops instructed the clergy to use certain practical measures to avert this wrong. By the fact that they placed themselves at the head of the campaign against the draft, the bishops maintained their influence on the people and fostered in fact, especially in the west, a better cooperation between the clergy and the Sinn Fein.

After the *Dáil Éireann* had proclaimed the Irish Republic in 1919, the Anglo-Irish war erupted. The British government tried to induce the bishops to condemn the rebels, but they refused. Some bishops openly supported the loan of the *Dáil*. When in 1919 the *Dáil* instituted courts of arbitration, it took care that priests were *ex officio* judges in these courts for lesser legal cases. Thus through the lower clergy the Church acquired a voice in the national movement without the risks of a direct commitment of the bishops. The participation of the clergy in the courts also gave the republic at least a certain degree of legitimacy. When the Irish Republican Army (IRA) led its pitiless attacks on the British troops, and the latter exercised brutal retaliation, many bishops declared that the attacks of the IRA were deplorable but understandable in view of the suppression by the authorities. In October 1920 the hierarchy censured the furious reprisals of the government as cruelties and excesses. Many volunteers maintained with the assent of a few clerics that the killing of a policeman or of a British soldier was not murder but a war action. Nevertheless, many priests approved membership in the IRA. With the approval of the *Dáil,* its president, Eamon De Valera, proclaimed in March 1921 the formal acknowledgment of a state of war with England and responsibility for the actions of the IRA. But when in June De Valera personally asked the hierarchy for a formal recognition of the republic, the bishops merely emphasized the right of Ireland to choose its own form of government. The agreement of December 1921 between the British government and the Irish plenipotentiaries on the establishing of the Irish Free State was welcomed by the Church with a feeling of relief and joy. The hierarchy as such did not approve this agreement, but several bishops did so as individuals.

After the treaty had been ratified by the *Dáil Éireann* in 1922, De Valera and the IRA rejected it and the government created by it. At first the bishops hoped for a constitutional solution of the crisis; only when the obdurate Republicans led by De Valera began the civil war against the new government led by William T. Cosgrave as president did the hierarchy announce a general excommunication of all those against the treaty. In a common pastoral letter of 10 October 1922 the hierarchy declared that the government of the Free State possessed the legitimate authority, that it was a serious wrong to resist it by armed force, and that the guerrilla war continued by the Republicans was to be condemned. The Republicans, on the other hand, disdained this condemnation and continued the war until De Valera summoned his adherents the following spring to stop hostilities. Although some few among the Republicans were still resentful toward the Church for decades, De Valera did not become the rallying point for an anticlerical party.

Ecclesiastical Organization.   When Ireland was politically divided, this did not affect the territorial integrity of the Church. From then on the ecclesiastical and the political spheres of jurisdiction no longer coincided. The four provinces with twenty-eight dioceses retained their previous boundaries, and the hierarchy continued to act as a single body. Generally, the bishops met twice a year, and a permanent committee, consisting of the four archbishops, two bishops as secretaries, and one member elected from each province, met quarterly. National councils in which representatives of the lower clergy and the religious institutes took part were held at Maynooth in 1927 and 1956.

Relations with the State.   In 1929 the Irish Free State established full diplomatic relations with the Holy See. Thereafter, an apostolic nuncio resided at Dublin, and an Irish ambassador at Rome. The first nuncio was Paschal Robinson, who occupied this post until his death in 1948; he was born in Ireland and grew up in the United States. A concordat was never discussed.

In the absence of the Republican delegates, who declined to recognize the *Dáil* elected in 1922, a constitution for the Free State was decided by this body in the same year. In it the Catholic Church was not even mentioned; freedom of religion was merely guaranteed to every citizen, and all laws were declared null and void which would subsidize any religion or give preference to anyone because of his religious faith or his position. Nevertheless, from the start the Cosgrave governments, which consisted predominantly of Catholic ministers, and the *Dáil* dominated by him showed their readiness to employ the power of the state for the protection of Catholic moral values. Thus in 1923 they approved the law for film censorship, in 1924 and 1927 the laws against strong alcoholic drink, and in 1929 the law for the censorship of publications, provided by a censorship committee consisting of one Catholic priest as chairman, three Catholic laymen, and one Protestant.

In 1927 De Valera and a majority of the Republicans decided to enter the *Dáil* as the Fianna Fail Party. A minority of unreconciled Republicans, under the name of the Irish Republican Army, rejected the status quo for the future and strove for the forcible union of Northern Ireland with the twenty-six counties. The hierarchy formally condemned the IRA in a common pastoral letter of 1931. At the same time it also condemned as Communist the Saor Eire organization allied with it. The Saor Eire gradually disappeared, but the IRA remained active, and the Communist influence in it was furthermore strong. By 1935 the bishops in their Lenten pastoral letter frequently warned the faithful against communism. In January 1956 the hierarchy again condemned the IRA and declared it was a "mortal sin for a Catholic to become or to remain a member of an organization or society which claims the right to bear arms or to use them against its own or another state," and "likewise sinful for a Catholic to cooperate with such an organization or society, to applaud it, or to support it in other ways." Nevertheless, many pious Catholics still supported the IRA. These Irish accepted the authority of the Church in the sphere of religion but rejected it in the area of politics.

When De Valera became Prime Minister in 1932, he continued the policy of his predecessors with the upholding of Catholic values and even identified "Irish" with "Catholic." Thus the supplementary decree of 1935 to the penal law forbade the sale and the import of contraceptive means (Section 17), and the law against public dance establishments of the same year eliminated an evil against which bishops and priests had long taken the field.

The constitution of 1937 respected Catholic teaching in regard to the family, marriage, education, and private ownership. With special reference to religion it declared: "The state recognizes the special position of the Holy Roman Catholic and Apostolic Church as the custodian of the faith which the great majority of citizens profess" (ARTICLE 44). It also recognized the Protestant, the Jewish, and other religions existing in the nation. This article had been introduced on De Valera's personal initiative; the bishops had not asked such recognition. Afterwards the authorities never agreed whether the "special position" could have any juridical effect. Although this constitution championed Catholic values to a greater degree than that of 1922, the state still did not always concede to the Church the status of a person in public law and also no financial means or subsidies at all. The Church itself was not empowered to possess property or to undertake public-law activities; it always had to employ the trustee system and obtain its entire income from the voluntary gifts of the people. On the other hand, the state claimed no influence on the naming of bishops or on other internal affairs of the Church. The Supreme Court of the Irish Free State had declared in 1926 that the canon law of the Catholic Church was a foreign law in civil law and in civil courts, whose validity had to be proved by expert witnesses. The constitution of 1937 did not change the status of canon law and thereby did not exclude the difficulties which occurred in marriage-law cases from the differences between canon law and civil law, although the constitution also forbade divorce.

In the south no large political party ever assumed an anticlerical attitude. Even the Labour Party supported the upholding of Catholic value concepts.

Educational System. Nevertheless, the Irish Free State was helpful to the Church in the area of education and allowed it to exercise over the schools in the twenty-six counties more control than in any other country in the world. In the constitution of 1937 the state recognized the family as the proper and natural teacher of the child; it guaranteed respect for the unalterable right and duty of the parents to care, in accord with their means, for the religious and moral, intellectual, physical, and social education of their children. For primary education, up to the age of fourteen, the state also granted for the future subsidies to all school boards which complied with its instructions; these subsidies were to cover the salaries of teachers, specified maintenance expenses, and two-thirds of the construction costs for new schools — more than two-thirds in areas of poverty. The state did not establish a competing system of its own. The primary schools were in private ownership, and almost all were allied with one or another denomination. Each school was controlled by a school director, who appointed the teachers; in the case of the Catholic schools the pastor was usually also the school director. On the other hand the state prescribed the curriculum, inspected the schools, and gave the examinations. Some of the Catholic secondary schools were the property of lay persons, but most were in the possession of dioceses or religious institutes. On this basis, by a law of 1924 the Irish Free State introduced a system of per capita subsidies under the condition that definite rules were observed. These subsidies proved to be ever less adequate, but they were not raised until 1954.

Irish politicians were satisfied with the school system, which left control in the hands of clerics. The bishops reacted promptly to every proposal to reduce their influence. But from 1963 several important reforms in the educational system were prescribed by law with the consent or at least the approval of the hierarchy.

In the field of higher education the hierarchy had, long before the achieving of independence, asked for the erecting of a university which was acceptable to Catholics. In 1908 the British government agreed to this request with the founding of the National University of Ireland, with colleges at Dublin, Cork, and Galway. Although formally nondenominational, it was intended to assure a considerable influence to the Catholic hierarchy in its governing bodies. Nevertheless, the archbishop of Dublin considered it necessary in 1944 to forbid Catholics "to enter the Protestant university of Trinity College without the previous permission of the diocesan bishop," and he declared that disobedience to this prescription was a mortal sin, and perseverance in disobedience made one unworthy to receive the sacraments. The National Council of 1956 likewise forbade Catholic youth, under threat of mortal sin, to attend Trinity College and Catholic parents or guardians to send young men there. Only the archbishop of Dublin should be competent to decide under what circumstances and with what guarantees against the danger of apostasy attendance at this institution could be tolerated. In practice, however, dispensations were frequently granted.

Social Movement. In the first three decades of the twentieth century the social movement was relatively weak among Irish Catholics because they had to devote their energies chiefly to the political struggle and the work of church building and the religious organization. The social movement was delayed also by the intellectual backwardness of the Catholic population. Progress was speeded after the publication of the encyclical *Quadragesimo Anno* by Pius XI in 1931. In the same year Father John Hayes founded *Muintir na Tire* (People of the Land), a production association, which later held agricultural weekends and weeks and study congresses. It developed into a movement for the improvement of social life in the rural areas of Ireland, which was threatened with annihilation by the irresistible march of industrialization. Local societies were formed, which represented each sector of the community, and particular interests were subsumed under a higher group on the level of the parish, which represented the organizational unity. This movement was not formally Catholic, but Catholic priests and laity actively supported it. Prominent Protestants were also members of these local societies and took part in the meetings. The underlying ideology can be termed "occupational." *Muintir na Tire* became one of the most important intermediaries for the spread of Catholic social doctrine in Ireland.

Among the newspapers, the weekly *The Standard,* founded in 1928, was from 1938 on the most effective organ for propagating Catholic social teaching; its preference was the association system. Its editor-in-chief, Dr. Alfred O'Rahilly, professor and later president of the University College at Cork, wrote on economic and religious themes.

In the late 1930s the bishops proclaimed social doctrine ever more loudly in their pastoral letters. In 1941 McQuaid created the Catholic Social Service Conference for the coordination and spread of charitable work in view of the deficient situation, because of the war, in nourishment, clothing, and especially heating material as well as in the areas of dwellings, occupation, and care of mothers. The conference used voluntary cooperation and obtained aid from the state and local officials. In Dublin it changed the type and manner of social work.

The founding of the Christus Rex Society announced new progress of the social movement; it was approved by the Irish hierarchy in 1945 and held its first congress the next year. Its membership was restricted to diocesan priests, but members of religious institutes and lay persons often gave talks at the annual congresses. Its goals were: "to clarify public opinion on social questions and help in the forming of a public awareness that is sensitive to social grievances . . . ; to promote the study of Catholic social doctrine among the clergy and through them among the laity; to encourage Irish priests to common exertions with a view to abolishing social evils and realizing the principles of the social encyclicals in public life." In 1947 the society began the publication of the quarterly *Christus Rex,* which became the leading periodical for the discussion of social questions in Ireland.

One of the best known publicists and speakers on social questions in the postwar period was Cornelius Lucey, professor of ethics at Maynooth from 1921 to 1951, coadjutor bishop of Cork from 1951 to 1952, and from 1952 bishop of Cork. Bishop Brown also gave expression to his views on public affairs. Both bishops represented conservative ideas.

When the government proposed a law for the "Care for Mother and Child," the hierarchy unanimously decided in April 1951 that this plan was opposed to Catholic social doctrine. Then when the minister of health, Dr. Noel Browne, resigned for various reasons, there began in the press a controversy on the role of the hierarchy. The bishops were concerned about the dangers which resulted from the growth of the state's power and the possibility of an un-Christian sexual teaching. When in 1952 the government proposed a new health law, the hierarchy likewise intervened in order to put through a few supplements, as, for example, one which assured the free choice of a hospital for each individual. The chief reason for the efforts of the Irish hierarchy to exert influence on the precise prescriptions for social services in the country was that it was against the centralizing tendencies of the government and its bureaucratic forms. But still, on the whole relations between the hierarchy and the government were friendly from 1923 to 1970.

In contrast to other European countries with a large Catholic proportion in the population, in Ireland no workers' union was created which was fostered by or united with the Church. The political exertions and actions of the workers' movement were aimed at avoiding church objections, and the danger of Marxist infiltration declined after 1921. The example and the influence of the British unions and the desire to maintain unity with the numerous Protestant workers in the north constituted further factors, which saw to it that the workers' movement in Ireland remained totally secular.

Lay Apostolate.   In 1921 there was founded at Dublin that organization which was to become one of the largest organized movements of the lay apostolate in the whole world: the Legion of Mary. A group of lay persons, motivated by awareness of their Christian vocation to be witnesses and inspired by the teachings of the Popes, met in the church of Saint Nicholas of Myra in Francis Street with the curate, Father Michael Toher, to seek suitable methods with which they could transform their discussions on the mystical body of Christ and the writings of Saint Louis Marie Grignion de Montfort into concrete action for the service of their fellow men. The form of their organization was influenced also by the Saint Vincent De Paul Society, with which they were all connected. Originally the new society was called Association of Our Lady of Mercy; in 1925 the name was changed to the Legion of Mary, and the titles which were given to all parts of its organization were taken from the usage of the old Roman army. The work began with visiting the sick in the South Dublin Union Hospital. Soon the legion directed its attention to organized prostitution and opened at Dublin its first home for prostitutes. In 1927 it founded the Morning Star Home for destitute men and the Regina Coeli Home for women.

The legion decided that its membership should be open to men and women from all educational strata, so long as they were practicing Catholics and at least eighteen years old. It was expected of the members that they lead an exemplary life and possess the "spirit of the Legion" or desire to possess it. They had to take part in the weekly meeting of their group, in which they were formed and spiritually stimulated by legion prayers, spiritual reading, and guidance from the spiritual leader; also they had to devote a considerable part of their free time each week to an apostolic work allotted to them, at least two hours. It was required of each member as his personal responsibility to recruit new members, both active and auxiliary. Auxiliary members performed only a service of prayer. The leadership of the legion lies in a *concilium,* the headquarters of which has always remained at Dublin. It was to consist of representatives of all legionary societies which were in immediate relations with it, and of the members of the Dublin *curia* and of the spiritual director appointed by the Irish bishops. This strict supervision of the lesser units by the superior councils assured, together with the manual of guidelines, which was later translated into twenty-five languages and 125 dialects, the uniformity of the legion throughout the world. The legion declared its readiness to carry out any type of social service and Catholic Action, which the local ordinary or parish priest asked or approved. At the weekly meeting of the *praesidia,* the smallest units, an oral report had to be made on the work done and then the work for the coming week was assigned. Gradually the house visits of legionaries, who went in pairs, became their characteristic activity. Also, the legion took care of homes, clubs, and study groups, distributed pamphlets and Lenten books, and gave catechetical instruction. All these activities had to be directed to individuals, but the giving of material help was forbidden. In the forty years since the founding, more than 60,000 active groups were founded, which worked in more than 1,500 dioceses, vicariates, and prefectures on five continents. In 1964 there were more than 1 million active and more than 9 million auxiliary members. A legion was first established in the United States in 1931.

North America

The United States

Population. In 1964 the Catholic population had increased to 44,874,371 in a total population of 183,783,493. Although it continued to grow after that, the rate of growth had already declined, in that year it amounted to 1.7 percent in comparison to 2.4 percent in 1963. The downward trend in the number of baptisms began in 1962 and was doubtless an indication that the practice of artificial birth control had spread further and that the national birthrate was reflected in it.

The immigration from Europe, through which the Catholic population had grown so rapidly until 1914, first dropped because of World War I and thereafter because of restrictive laws. These laws were motivated in part by the fear on the part of Protestants that the country could be inundated by Catholics and Jews. The Emergency Quota Law of 1921 limited the number of immigrants from each country per year to 3 percent of the respective national group living in the United States in 1910. The Immigration Law of 1924 reduced this number to 2 percent. These measures greatly lessened the entrance of Catholics from eastern, central, and southern Europe, and in 1931 President Hoover lowered the quotas so strongly because of unemployment that the immigration of European Catholics almost stopped entirely for the rest of this decade. However, hundreds of thousands of Mexicans and French Canadians, who were exempted from the quota restrictions, moved across the southern and northern frontiers. There also came Catholics from American possessions, especially Puerto Ricans, who settled in New York and some other cities, and Filipinos, who went to California. After World War II Spanish-speaking Catholics poured into the northern cities, and many European Catholics came into the country in accord with the stipulations of the Displaced Persons Act of 1948. The principle of national origin, which favored the Nordic peoples, was again confirmed in the McCarran-Walter Law of 1952, despite the protests of Catholics and others.

The Church gradually lost its immigrant status and its opposition attitude and thereby gained more and more esteem among non-Catholics. Besides, after World War II more Americans than previously acknowledged their membership in a denomination. Many of them felt attracted to the Catholic Church, which constituted the largest individual body in the country and conducted respected institutions on the local and national level. By the fact that the Church exposed itself more to the glare of publicity, it brought the blind zealots to silence and gained more open ears for its demands. The apostolate for converts gained in esteem through the holding of hours of consultation in the parishes, through the free distribution of literature, for which advertisements in the secular newspapers solicited, and through individual talks with entirely individual instruction. In this way 146,212 converts were received into the Church in 1960; this was the highest number which was ever ascertained for a single year. In the following period the annual figures dropped again.

A constantly increasing percentage of Catholics lived in cities. Even in 1967 there were of the altogether 3,080 rural districts in the United States still 671 without a permanent priest. The fact that almost 40 million Americans did not live within reach of a priest was characteristic of the predominantly urban character of American Catholicism.

Organization. In 1914 there were in the United States fourteen ecclesiastical provinces and eighty-four dioceses; in addition, there was still one vicariate apostolic and one Ruthenian Greek diocese. Fifty years later there were 27 archdioceses, 114 dioceses, 1 Ukrainian Catholic archeparchy, 2 Ukrainian Catholic eparchies, and 2 eparchies of the Byzantine Rite. The archdiocese with the largest number of Catholics was Chicago.

Although the archbishops took care to hold annual meetings, the entire hierarchy was not organized until September 1919 when 92 of the existing 101 ordinaries took part in the first general meeting at the Catholic University of America in Washington, D.C. They decided by an overwhelming majority to establish the National Catholic Welfare Council, as the organization was originally called. It was a logical further development of the National Catholic War Council, which had been founded in August 1917 by the delegates of sixty-eight dioceses and twenty-seven national Catholic associations to coordinate the efforts of the popular Catholic groups in the contemporary emergency by six committees of priests and lay persons, which in turn were active under a controlling committee of bishops. The effectiveness of the war council in its various efforts made it seem desirable to have a permanent organization on the national level for the coordination and stimulation of actions in the period of peace. Pope Benedict XV had in a general way agreed that commissions for the handling of school and social problems should be set up and that they should hold annual general meetings. But because some bishops feared that the organization would interfere in the jurisdiction of the ordinary in their own dioceses, they transmitted their objections to the Holy See. Cardinal Gaetano De Lai, secretary of the Consistorial Congregation, and some other officials of the Roman Curia for their part were afraid that the NCWC would promote the beginnings of a "national" Church in the United States. They persuaded Benedict XV to revoke the approval granted by him provisionally and by way of experiment. He had already drafted a decree for the dissolution of the organization but was prevented by death from signing it. His successor, Pius XI, thereupon signed this decree and had it published. The administrative committee of the NCWC protested against this decision and delegated from its ranks the bishop of Cleveland, Joseph Schrembs, to explain the arguments of the NCWC at Rome. In protracted discussions he convinced De Lai and other cardinals. On 2 July 1922 a new decree was issued which approved the organization according to the original plan; only the name was easily changed by substituting the word "Conference" for "Council"; in this way the organization, which was erected on a voluntary basis and had only an advisory function, could not be misunderstood as a legislative body. However, it became the highest authority in the decisions of the Catholic Church on public affairs and on the implementing of commonly agreed-upon guidelines. In addition to the administrative council there were created right from the start five departments: for education, lay activity, press, social action, and the missions; three more, for immigration, legal questions, and youth, were later added. The first business manager or secretary general was John Burke, C.S.P., the former editor of the *Catholic World* and chairman of the meeting at which the war council had been founded and also chairman of the Committee for Special Actions in the period of the war. He served in this position until his death in 1936. The NCWC continued its function until it was reorganized in 1967 and thereafter, as the United States Catholic Conference, constituted a corporation in civil law. At the same time the National Conference of Catholic Bishops came into existence as a canon law corporation.

In these years the founding of parishes continued on the territorial and national level. When the world economic crisis began, the Poles alone had approximately one thousand parishes in the United States. When after World War II many Catholics began to move from the large cities to the suburbs, the number of national parishes declined.

Educational System. In 1914 there were 230 Catholic colleges or high schools for young men and 680 academies or high schools for girls; in addition, there were 5,403 parochial schools, attended by 1,429,859 children. In 1964 there were 1,557 high schools of the dioceses and parishes with 677,169 students and 901 private high schools, for the most part conducted by religious men and women, with 391,255 students. At the same time 4,471,415 pupils were registered in 10,452 elementary schools of the parishes and institutes, and 85,201 in 450 private elementary schools. After 1964 began a downward trend in proportion to the previous numbers of registrations, not only in the Catholic but also in the public schools.

During this period Catholic schools were affected by several state laws on which, one after the other, decisions were rendered by the Supreme Court of the United States. In 1922 the voters of Oregon approved a petition in which it was required that, with a few expressly named exceptions, all children from age 8 to age 16 had to attend public schools from September 1926, in connection with which parents or guardians who disobeyed this law were to be condemned to a fine or prison or — in each case according to the seriousness — to both. Two societies of Freemasons claimed the authorship of this law, and the Ku Klux Klan, along with other secret societies, supported it with the assertion that only in public schools could children be taught to respect and maintain the free institutions of the nation. Religious prejudice, patriotic zeal, and nationalistic mistrust were the chief motives for the advocates of this law. Both the already existing and the recently founded Catholic organizations resisted, and even several Protestant groups issued declarations in which the law was condemned. The Sisters of the Holy Names of Jesus and Mary, who operated several schools in Oregon, and the Mill Hill Academy filed motions for the issuance of a temporary injunction by which the state should be forbidden to put the law into effect. After the District Court of the United States had issued the injunction in 1924, the state attorney general of Oregon appealed to the Supreme Court. But in the meantime the legislature of Michigan had agreed that constitutional amendments on voting should be submitted to the voters whereby the parochial schools in this state should be abolished. But in 1924 these proposals were rejected by considerable majorities, after similar proposals there had already been rejected four years earlier. In 1925 the Supreme Court of the United States declared the Oregon law unconstitutional, confirmed the rights of parents, and set limits to state authority. This decision annulled all other attempts to do away with Catholic schools by way of legislation.

In the following period other states sought to assist in various ways children who attended nonpublic schools, but these were attacked in the courts. In 1930 the Supreme Court confirmed as constitutional a law of Louisiana which allowed the state to supply textbooks to children in all schools. This decision was based on the theory that not the schools themselves or their administrators, the churches, were the beneficiaries of such state grants, but the children. This theory of "child benefit" became the justification for the asking of state aid for children in private schools. In the celebrated case *Everson* vs. *Board of Education* the Supreme Court in 1947 recognized as constitutional a law of New Jersey, which approved the use of public funds to reimburse parents for expenses incurred by transporting their children to all schools, public or private. Nevertheless, only less than half of all states put buses at the disposal of children who attended private schools. In 1968 the Supreme Court of the United States decided that neither the individual state constitution nor the Constitution of the United States was violated by a law of the state of New York which demanded that the public schools lend nonreligious schoolbooks to pupils in private schools, including the parochial, in grades seven through twelve. In the same year the state of Pennsylvania granted direct payment of public money to private schools for services in nonreligious school subjects. But the Supreme Court of the United States later declared this law invalid because the concept of the "purchase of services" was incompatible with the First Amendment to the U.S. Constitution. The constitutions of thirty-three states forbade any use of public funds for the support of denominational schools.

Some bishops and other Catholics had, besides, not wanted any state aid for their schools, because they feared an interference, joined with it, of the state into the Church's control of the schools. In 1961 the administrative committee NCWC stated that the federal government, if it generally supported the school system, must also give to Catholic children the right to claim support, because they were otherwise victims of a discriminatory legislation. Nevertheless, Congress excluded nonpublic schools from the aid which it granted to the schools in specific districts, in which special burdens were laid on the local taxpayers by a federal institution. The 1965 Elementary and Secondary Education Act, also called the Johnson Education Act, included also the children of private schools by granting them a share in specific special programs, which were undertaken by a local educational office and implemented by a public school; thus, for example, courses for the physically handicapped or socially ill-adapted children, supplementary classes in reading and mathematics, library services, health and food services, books, and even clothing — of course, only for children from low income families. The constitutionality of this law was doubted by various groups, as by Protestants and other Americans United for the Separation of Church and State, by the American Jewish Congress, and by the American Civil Liberties Union, all of which constantly strove to prevent any public aid, even indirect, for Catholic schools.

The regulations for the imparting of religious instruction to Catholic children who attended public schools varied according to the laws of the particular states. There arose controversies over other stipulations according to which pupils were granted absence from the public schools for a specified time to enable them to take part in religious instruction. When in 1948 an objection was raised before the Supreme Court of the United States to a plan approved by the legislature of the state of Illinois, the Supreme Court forbade the imparting of religious instruction on the premises of public schools during school hours and declared such a practice a violation of the First Amendment. However, four years later the same court declared that "released time" programs were constitutional if the pupils left the public school during regular school hours in order to receive denominational religious instruction.

Responsibility for the assuring of religious instruction for these children in public schools was entrusted to the Confraternity of Christian Doctrine. Although the confraternity had been introduced in the United States as early as 1902, it had grown only slowly until Pius XI issued his motu proprio *Orbem Catholicum* in 1923. The best-known promoter of the Confraternity in the United States was Edwin V. O'Hara, first bishop of Great Falls, Montana (1930–39), then of Kansas City, Missouri (1939–56); he was also chairman of the Bishops' Commission from its founding in 1934 until his death in 1956. Under his leadership a Catholic center was erected in Washington, D.C., in 1933 to provide information and advice to the diocesan organizations. Besides the instruction of children who attended public schools, the confraternity organized in many places programs for religious vacation courses, discussion clubs for parents, teachers, and other adults, special religious courses for handicapped children, correspondence courses in religion, training centers for lay teachers of religion, university retreats, religious radio programs, and an apostolate of good will which was aimed at those outside the Church. In 1935 the first national Catechetical Congress was held in Rochester, New York, and this was then followed by yearly congresses until 1941, when a five-year cycle was introduced. The publications department of the national center published an information service, which was intended especially for diocesan directors, and also textbooks and other practical literature. In the early 1940s the confraternity subsidized revisions of the several editions of the Baltimore Catechism and a new translation of the Bible. It introduced the new catechetical methods and techniques developed in Europe and adapted them to American needs.

In the area of higher education there were in 1964 295 Catholic colleges and universities, in which 366,172 students were registered. The Catholic colleges had increased in this period. But the Catholic institutions of the higher educational system received, in contrast to the Catholic elementary and secondary schools, some state aid directly. Thus, for example, the veterans of World War II and of the Korean War obtained federal funds for instruction and livelihood, regardless of what educational institution they decided on, and the National Defense Education Act of 1958, which was intended to improve instruction in mathematics, natural science, engineering, and modern languages and in 1964 was extended also to English, geography, and other fields, made no distinction in regard to Catholic colleges and universities; it even granted loans for schools of the middle level which belonged to the Church. Federal officials made agreements with such schools for research projects or granted them subsidies for this purpose, and there were also federal funds at their disposal for the construction of buildings.

In the late 1950s nine Catholic universities had graduate schools, which could grant doctoral degrees, but half of them restricted their doctoral program to a few fields. The Catholic universities and colleges also instituted many professional school faculties. Many other Catholic colleges and universities had programs for some of these professional areas but they had not organized them as separate professional schools.

The Newman Movement was organized for the religious instruction and pastoral care of the ever growing number of Catholic students who attended secular universities and colleges. By 1925 a few bishops and priests, especially Jesuits, attacked the concept of such Catholic foundations as that which had begun in 1920 at the University of Illinois to offer religious courses recognized at the university; the opponents feared that a positive program of religious instruction would attract students to the secular universities who would otherwise have gone to Catholic colleges. The educational importance of the Newman apostolate was not officially recognized until 1962, when the College and University Division of the National Catholic Educational Association completed its regulations to the effect that it gave membership to Newman educational centers, even if not full membership.

The Federation of Catholic College Clubs was established in New York City in 1915; although it consisted officially only of student clubs, it was in reality directed by the faculties, alumni, and chaplains. In 1938 it became the Newman Club Federation. Due to the efforts of its chaplain general, John W. Keough, who watched over its growth from 1917 to 1935, it successfully resisted the persistent opposition. But in 1941 it obtained full membership in the College and University Division of the National Council of Catholic Youth, which had been instituted by the American hierarchy. Then it acquired a permanent headquarters with a managing secretary in the Youth Division of the NCWC. After World War II the number of full-time chaplains rapidly grew, and in 1950 the National Newman Chaplains Association was established as an organization. In addition to the meetings and institutes which it offered, in 1962 it opened an institution for the training of new chaplains. In order to gain Catholic teachers and administrators from secular institutions for these unions, the National Newman Association of Faculty and Staff was called into being in 1959. In 1962 the various national organizations were united and formally approved as constituents of the National Newman Apostolate, which for its part became a fully qualified section in the Youth Division of the NCWC. In the meantime religious sisters and brothers and educated laymen in ever greater numbers had been appointed to the staffs of the Catholic centers and parishes that were reproducing themselves at secular universities in order to support the chaplains with their teaching and pastoral tasks.

American Catholics were also concerned with creating special possibilities of education for blacks. The Sisters of the Blessed Sacrament for Indians and Colored People, established by Mother Katharine Drexel, erected many elementary and high schools for blacks in the South. With the financial support of the foundress, the sisters opened Xavier University of Louisiana, for which the arrangements were concluded in 1918; colleges for the humanities and natural sciences, for teachers and for pharmacy were opened at the beginning of the 1920s, and in 1937 a graduate school which offered the master's degree. This was the first and only Catholic university for blacks in the United States. After World War II blacks, including the Catholics, left the rural areas of the South in ever greater numbers for the large cities in the North and the far West, where they were closer to the Church's ministry. Most of the black beneficiaries of Catholic educational work were non-Catholics. The same was true also of the social services performed by

Catholics, as, for example, of the Friendship Houses of Catherine De Hueck, of which the first was founded in 1938 in Harlem, the black quarter of New York, and also of Fides House, erected in 1940 at Washington, D.C.

Social Movement. From the end of World War I the Catholic Church in the United States became actively involved in social justice. In 1919 the administrative committee of the National Catholic War Council published an announcement which in the future was called the "Bishops' Program for Social Reconstruction." Its author was Father John A. Ryan, professor of moral theology at the Catholic University of America, who especially by means of his writings on the ethical and economic aspects of the wage system had become the best known and most productive American representative of the social doctrine of Leo XIII. The Bishops' Program was to a great extent intended to counteract the Socialist influence on the program for social reconstruction of the British Labour Party; it aimed at improving the conditions of the workers partly by voluntary collaboration in industry and partly by legal measures on the level of the individual states. It was a progressive document, evoking opposition; it proposed concrete reforms, like minimum wages, insurance against unemployment, sickness, and age. Some Catholics and others regarded such reforms as too radical and they were not established in law until the 1930s. In November 1919 the plenary meeting of the bishops published a comprehensive pastoral letter which contained a section on industrial relations. With reference to Leo XIII they stressed the moral and intellectual aspect of the social question and its solution; they deplored unnecessary strikes, in regard to which only the claims of the mutually struggling parties were considered and the rights of the public were disregarded, and they recommended that a quarrel which could not be settled by discussions between the parties concerned should be submitted to arbitration. They stated that unions of workers or professionals were necessary, but "must be supplemented by societies or meetings which are composed of employers and employees," because they would maintain the common interests rather than the differing strivings of the two parties.

From 1920 the NCWC Department of Social Action was the chief agent for propagating the Church's social doctrine. It published some books and many praiseworthy brochures, it financed lectures in Catholic colleges and universities. In 1922 it founded the Catholic Conference on Industrial Problems, which up to 1940 held almost one hundred national and regional meetings in various places, for it had been proved that this was the most effective method to acquaint both non-Catholics and Catholics with the Church's position. The divisional director, Father Ryan, with his assistant, Father Raymond A. McGowan, developed a general program for industrial democracy, whereby the worker would be made an integrating element of this system. Pius XI's encyclical on the reconstruction of the social order, *Quadragesimo anno,* confirmed many of Ryan's proposals, especially the principle of the living wage, which should include the support of the worker's family.

With different stress, the American Catholics sought to apply the papal social teachings to the sufferings of their country during the Great Depression. Because Ryan based his economic analysis chiefly on the underconsumption theory of John A. Hobson, he was extremely critical of President Hoover's caution and cordially welcomed the policy of his successor. President Franklin D. Roosevelt invited Ryan to serve as policy adviser for the New Deal, and in 1934 he became a member of the industrial professional committee of the National Recovery Administration. He regarded as the climax of his life's work the Fair Labor Standards Act of 1938, the first law that prescribed a minimum wage and maximum weekly hours for the employees of firms which were involved in interstate commerce. But because Ryan trusted in the state as the only institution which could provide social justice, he was opposed by other Catholics, who feared that the centralizing of power in the federal government was dangerous for a religious minority and who were more uneasy than appeared to him to be justified by the threats from secularism, communism, war, and the welfare state.

Finally, Ryan came into open conflict with the so-called Radio Priest, Charles E. Coughlin, pastor of the Shrine of the Little Flower at Royal Oak, Michigan. The latter had achieved national fame because at the beginning of the depression he had boldly attacked the abuses in the American economic system and offered remedies inspired by *Rerum novarum* and later by *Quadragesimo anno.* His ordinary, Bishop Michael James Gallagher of Detroit, encouraged him to propagate the social teachings of the papal encyclicals and remained his confidant, adviser, supporter, and defender until his death in 1937. Although Coughlin always stressed the right to private property, he found fault with the old industrial capitalism or plutocracy; he blamed the "international bankers," questioned the possibility of democracy because of the corrupt and self-seeking nature of politicians, supported extensive measures of the government for the economy, protection of the small business people and farmers, and a just wage for workers. In 1936 he founded the weekly newspaper, *Social Justice,* which within one year achieved a circulation of 1 million copies. Cardinal William O'Connell, archbishop of Boston, then publicly criticized Coughlin, even though never using his name, as a hysterical demagogue, and finally other Catholic bishops and priests, newspapers and periodicals, even *Osservatore Romano,* reprimanded him for intolerance of differences of opinion and for mixing in politics. His opponents accused him of seeking the creation of a Fascist dictatorship and mocked his financial proposals. In his extremely popular radio talks on Sunday afternoons he showed a growing disillusionment with American political institutions at the end of the 1930s and championed the establishing of a corporate state for bringing about social justice. In 1938 his newspaper proclaimed and demanded the organization of the Christian Front as a general alliance of Catholics and Protestants against communism. He openly expressed his antipathy for Jews and suspected them of being Communists who had conspired for the destruction of Christian culture, but he rejected the inevitable reproach of anti-Semitism brought against him. Many Catholics were as ready as were Protestants likewise to regard Jewish "money changers" as responsible for the economic misery of the nation and the world. Cardinal George Mundelein, archbishop of Chicago, and other prominent Catholics from clergy and laity sought to keep the Church aloof from any incitement to racial prejudice and race hatred. Coughlin's newspaper appeared as the advocate of the Fascist regimes in Germany and Italy, because they opposed communism, but he himself professed to be anti-Nazi. He preached nationalism, isolationism, and hatred of England when international tensions were deteriorating into armed conflict. At the end of 1940 he was put off the radio because both the national networks and the local stations declined to renew his contracts for broadcasting. In 1942 the government obtained the suspension of the newspaper *Social Justice* by the threat of a suit because of the crime of insurrection, allegedly begun with its opposition to the war. The new archbishop of Detroit, Edward Mooney, commanded Coughlin to discontinue all public statements. Nonpartisan judgments admitted that this priest was sincerely disturbed by the misery of the poor and the Communist danger and denied that he was a Fascist, but they conceded that he understood nothing about the economy and that the eclectic solutions which he proposed were ineffectual because of his all too simplistic, unsystematic, and confused analysis of the situation.

Many of the better educated and wealthy Catholics who took no pleasure from Coughlin's proposals founded the league of Social Justice on the national level in 1932 in order to study and apply the economic teachings of Pius XI. The director of this movement was Michael O'Shaughnessy, an oil manager and industrial publicist, who also published the *Social Justice Bulletin* as a monthly for timely events in this area. Although the league never counted more than 10,000 members, it seems to have exercised a widespread influence through the press and various Catholic organizations. It promoted a reform of the capitalist social order through control of the seeking of profit and by industry's being forced to consider also the interests of the workers and the public as a whole.

Another search for a solution of the contemporary problems was undertaken by a group which aspired to alleviate the misery of individuals by direct contact and was not prepared to await clerical leadership or trust guidance by the hierarchy. Well known in this group was Dorothy Day, a recently converted journalist, who had previously been a radical activist and Communist. In 1932 she started the Catholic Worker movement. She took up the idea of a Christian synthesis, as Peter Maurin, an itinerant social thinker from France, proclaimed it; he longed to repair, with the aid of an integral Catholicism, the unity of modern society shattered by secularism. The program advocated by him contained three points: (1) Roundtable discussion by workers and intellectuals; (2) Friendship houses, in which Catholics could do justice to their personal responsibility toward the poor by doing works of mercy; (3) Farm communes, in which Catholic workers and students could learn to take care of themselves and build cells for a future Christian social order. Miss Day opened in Manhattan a House of Hospitality, which united the functions of a soup kitchen, a discussion club, and a reform center. Up to 1940 thirty such houses were erected in various cities. On 1 May 1933 she began the publication of the monthly *Catholic Worker,* which presented social doctrine in concrete guiding principles and in a brief time achieved a circulation of over 100,000. In order to supply an example for a really Catholic community and a model for the solution of the problem of unemployment, the Catholic Workers in 1936 established a farm commune in the neighborhood of Easton, Pennsylvania. It received great publicity but also harsh criticism as an example of romantic and utopian agrarianism. In addition to their assistance to the poor by their own voluntary poverty, by manual and intellectual work, and by the bestowing of personal attention, the Catholic Workers took part in strikes and demanded the forming of unions, although, according to their theory, they put little trust in unions or other centralized institutions. They sought by these practical methods to oppose Communist influences, to demonstrate Christian love, to inculcate spiritual values as a counterpole to materialism, and to promote personal sanctification. In addition, they fought anti-Semitism and discrimination against blacks. During the Spanish Civil War they came out for neutrality, and when the danger of America's involvement in World War II grew, many of them became pacifists and refused military service for reasons of conscience. These controversial positions caused internal decline and external repudiations. The strong emphasis on personalism prevented the Catholic Workers from solving the problems of society by an intelligent concept of the relation of the individual to the state and of his confidence in the capability of the government.

In 1937 a group of Catholic Workers founded the Association of Catholic Trade Unionists in New York with the aim of making known to their members a knowledge of Catholic social teaching in order that these could then apply its principles in their own unions. Hence it advocated also the spread of the union system and supported justified strikes. It opened an evening school for workers, held training sessions, and published a newspaper, the *Labor Leader.* Other workers' schools, in which the students were instructed in practical subjects, such as public speaking, parliamentary procedure, and Communist tactics, were under the direction of diocesan officials, Jesuits, fraternities, and colleges. In this way more than 7,000 persons were annually prepared to reform and democratize their unions. The Catholics, who were represented in great numbers in the unions and in some even had an overwhelming majority, contributed to the ending of the Communist influence which had threatened the independence of the whole worker movement. When this aim was achieved in the postwar years, the workers' schools and the ACTU turned their efforts to removing other abuses in the unions.

Not only the urban industrial workers and craftsmen but also the farmers constituted objects of special concern for the Church in the period between the two world wars. Edwin V. O'Hara had studied the problems of the rural population while he was still a priest of the archdiocese of Portland, Oregon; in 1920 he was invited to set up a bureau for agriculture in the NCWC Department of Social Action. He successfully proved the value of vacation schools for children, of religious correspondence courses for children and adults, and of associations. In 1923 he convened a meeting of Catholic agricultural leaders, at which the National Catholic Rural Life Conference was founded, and he was made its managing secretary. This society later counted thousands of laymen in its ranks, who were organized under diocesan directors and agricultural chairmen in some Catholic societies. In cooperation with the religious and secular organizations in the locality, they promoted committees for the development of communities, cooperative sales societies, credit unions, and educational institutions.

A further aspect of social justice which became consciously clearer to American Catholics in these years was the just treatment of members of the black race. Dr. Thomas W. Turner, a black Catholic teacher at the Hampton Institute in Virginia, in 1917 organized the Committee against the Extension of Race Prejudice in the Church, which made personal appeals to the bishops to do away with prejudice in churches, societies, schools, and seminaries. In order to enlarge the scope of this work there was founded in 1925 a militant organization called Federated

Colored Catholics of the United States. In the first five years its leaders were exclusively black. Interest in it grew among white clerics and lay persons, and in 1932 this change was reflected in the new title, then adopted, of National Catholic Federation for the Promotion of Better Race Relations.

However, the conscience of white Catholics was only gradually sharpened for the unhappy situation of blacks, and for a long time people were concerned only about local conditions. In 1927 Father John La Farge, S.J., founded the Catholic Laymen's Union, a group of blacks who were active in professional and business life. Seven years later the union convoked a mass meeting at New York, at which, with the approval of the archbishop, Cardinal Patrick Hayes, the first Catholic Interracial Council in the United States came into existence. In the succeeding thirty years more than sixty such associations were created in various places in the nation. Until 1962 Father La Farge was chaplain of the New York society and until 1960 his headquarters was a center of the movement for justice in race relations; he published the monthly *Interracial Review,* formed an exchange office for information, distributed educational materials, and performed advisory services for other societies. However, each society was autonomous, responsible only to the local ordinary, and each decided independently how to bring the influence of Catholic doctrine to bear in its special situation. The chief activity of the societies was of an educational sort. In second place was its aim of eliminating racial discrimination in Catholic churches, schools, hospitals, and other institutions and societies. Finally their efforts should be united with those of other organizations for racial equality and social actions and cooperate with these for the welfare of the community as a whole. In 1960 the Catholic Interracial Councils and similar organizations founded the National Catholic Conference for Interracial Justice, with the aim of assisting the local societies and other Catholic institutions in the development of full-time professional staffs and in their programs; besides, they were to represent the societies on the national level. Their central office in Chicago became the office of exchange of information and a source for publications and technical capabilities. It held national meetings which were attended by their members in great numbers.

After World War II some bishops in the country caused a stir by their decisions in regard to the racial question in their respective dioceses. In 1947 Archbishop Joseph E. Ritter instructed his priests to end racial segregation in the schools of the archdiocese of Saint Louis with the beginning of the school year, and when irritated parents threatened to obtain a temporary court injunction against his orders, he warned them against this, because in accord with Catholic law they would automatically incur excommunication for impeding a bishop in the exercise of his pastoral duties. In 1948 the archbishop of Washington, Patrick A. O'Boyle, began the integration of white and black pupils in the Catholic schools of this archdiocese. In June 1953 Bishop Vincent J. Waters of Raleigh opened all Catholic churches, schools, hospitals, and other institutions in North Carolina to all, regardless of their color, and he did not yield before the severe opposition of some Catholics and non-Catholics. All these courageous steps had been taken before the Supreme Court of the United States ended racial segregation in the public schools with its famed decision of 17 May 1954. Likewise in 1953 Archbishop Joseph F. Rummel excluded racial segregation also from the churches of the archdiocese of New Orleans after he had first achieved this in Catholic societies and associations. But not until 1962 did he venture to order the end of racial segregation also in the Catholic schools of his archdiocese, and even then he still encountered violent opposition from some lay persons.

Liturgical Movement.   The Liturgical Movement was introduced into the United States chiefly by persons who were also interested in social action. The reformers of the liturgy sought to overcome individualism, which both in the Church and in secular society isolated people from one another, and so they aspired to make Catholics more keenly conscious of their membership and solidarity in the mystical body of Christ. The leading representative of this movement, Virgil Michel, a Benedictine monk of Saint John's Abbey, Collegeville, Minnesota, was also a prominent interpreter of the social encyclicals. He had undertaken extensive study journeys to Europe and there consulted the leaders and experts, especially Lambert Beauduin. Michel brought the ideas of liturgical renewal back to the United States and spread them in the monthly *Orate Fratres,* which first appeared in Advent 1926; in 1951 the title was changed to *Worship.* He also founded the Liturgical Press, which publishes texts, books, and brochures. The first liturgical "meeting" was held at Saint John's Abbey in 1929, and since 1940 a national Liturgical Week is held annually with the support of the Benedictine abbeys of the United States. The Benedictine Liturgical Conference, which formed the organ for implementing the annual "weeks," decided to reorganize on a broader basis, and in 1944 it was transformed into an association as the Liturgical Conference. In the 1950s its membership increased, because the liturgical reforms proceeding from Rome drew attention to its activity; this activity was widened to satisfy the requirements of dioceses and parishes. In addition to Michel, who died in 1938, Gerald Ellard, S.J., professor at Saint Mary's College in Kansas, was likewise a pioneer; with his books and periodical articles, in connection with his teaching and lecturing, he promoted the movement in the United States. For a while it encountered the opposition of some conservative prelates, but it gradually put itself across. Lay persons procured hand missals in English in ever larger numbers, and the Dialogue Mass spread more and more. Gregorian chant became better known, after the Pius X School of Liturgical Music, founded at Manhattanville College in 1916, had fostered it. Nonliturgical forms of devotion, like novenas, accordingly lost some of their popularity. Nevertheless, American Catholics were hardly prepared for the fundamental reforms which resulted from the Second Vatican Council.

The Situation in American Society.   At least into the 1960s many fellow citizens regarded Catholics with secret distrust and open hostility. Anti-Catholicism was furthered, especially in the South, by periodicals such as *Tom Watson's Magazine,* published by the fanatical United States senator from Georgia, and *The Menace,* whose circulation reached its peak with 1.5 million in 1915. Even after Catholics had in World War I proved their undisputed loyalty, which was maliciously disputed by their enemies, they experienced in the early 1920s a new wave of attacks by the revived Ku Klux Klan, which also denounced and threatened Jews and blacks. The Klan expanded from the South to the Midwest and the far West, and at its peak counted 5 million members; but after 1925 it lost its reputation when the crimes and scandals of its leaders were exposed. When in 1928, for the first time in American history, the Democratic Party nominated a Catholic, Alfred E. Smith, governor of New York, as its presidential candidate, the anti-Catholic forces again stirred up religious hatred by attacking the candidate's Church and contributing to his defeat in the election. Catholics were not only effectively excluded from the highest office in the country, but between 1789 and 1933 only four Catholics held posts in the cabinets of the presidents.

For Catholics the election of Franklin D. Roosevelt signaled the beginning of a new era in American society. Al Smith had roused his fellow Catholics, especially in the big cities, to support the Democratic Party; Roosevelt obtained their devotion by the recognition which he gave them and the skillful treatment which he allotted to them. Many of the American bishops, including first of all Cardinal Mundelein, publicly proclaimed their approval of Roosevelt's policies, especially in the first terms of his administration. And the Catholic press took a generally positive attitude toward the New Deal. However, many Catholic leaders and newspapers deplored the president's decision to recognize the Soviet Union and to institute diplomatic relations with it, although they appreciated the efforts he made in the negotiations to secure guarantees of religious freedom. The Knights of Columbus and others also strongly criticized his silence and inaction in regard to the persecution of Catholics by the Mexican government. When Father Coughlin, who had supported Roosevelt at the beginning of his presidency, later attacked him both because of his economic policy, especially in regard to currency, credit, and banks, and also because of his alleged favoring of communism, Monsignor John A. Ryan defended the president in 1936 in a national radio address. In the previous year Coughlin had founded the National Union for Social Justice, which was intended to act as a lobby of the people or as a civic-minded nonpartisan force, to give emphasis to the demand for legal mooring of those reform principles which he extracted from the papal encyclicals and in keeping with this to work for the nomination and election of like-minded candidates to Congress in each party; it attained a membership of perhaps 5 million, especially among the workers of Irish and German descent in the East and Midwest, and it also achieved some of its goals. Later the radio priest created the Union Party and chose as its presidential candidate William Lemke, for whom he then conducted in 1936 an energetic but, as it finally turned out, useless election campaign.

Because of the well-known opposition of the Church to communism, anti-Catholic propaganda declined during the Cold War. Nevertheless, some loud opponents continued to find public attention. The most notorious among them was Paul Blanshard, who directed his diatribes against the Church's authoritarian and antiliberal principles and accused the hierarchy of undermining American values and the ideals of freedom and democracy. He was the chief spokesman for an organization which had been founded in 1947 and called itself Protestants and Other Americans United for the Separation of Church and State, later Americans United for the Separation of Church and State. It worked with a great display of votes to prevent any public aid to parochial schools, which it designated as divisive and un-American; it also denied to any Catholic the ability to hold a public office. The nomination of another Catholic by the Democratic Party in 1960, John F. Kennedy, evoked a new outburst of antireligious feeling, and the candidate deemed it necessary to deny beforehand that the Church could exercise any influence at all on his official decisions. Political scientists have stated that many people who normally belonged to the Democratic Party voted against Kennedy because of his religion. After he had been elected by a very slender majority, he consistently resisted all proposals to support at least those parents who had to bear extra expenses so that they could send their children to Catholic schools. His electoral victory, his nonpartisan administration of his office, and his unusual popularity among all classes of the population lessened anti-Catholicism as a force in American society, and two years after his tragic death the declaration of the Second Vatican Council on religious liberty confirmed this effect still more; the American bishops had especially insisted on it.

When on 23 December 1939 President Roosevelt named Myron C. Taylor, an Episcopalian, as his personal representative to Pope Pius XII with the rank of ambassador, an anti-Catholic outcry was raised. Taylor's job was to establish a connection between the two leading personalities in the promotion of peace and to coordinate the assistance of the Vatican and of the United States during and after the war. When Protestants protested strongly against the sending of an ambassador as a violation of the principle of the separation of state and Church, and demanded the ambassador's recall, Roosevelt insisted that this temporary mission did not involve the establishment of diplomatic relations. Although the opponents declared their opposition again at the end of the war, Taylor exercised his office until his recall in 1950. In October 1951 President Harry Truman nominated General Mark Clark as ambassador at the Vatican, but the Protestants raised such a storm of indignation that the president later withdrew the nomination at the general's request, before it was discussed in the Senate.

The Position of the Church in International Affairs. The unfriendly attitude of many of their fellow citizens did not deter the American Catholics from giving their opinion on international affairs. At the outbreak of World War I most writers in Catholic newspapers and periodicals advocated neutrality, and many, especially in the Midwest, even took the side of the Central Powers. Catholics of Irish birth or descent were of course against the British, and the German Catholic *Centralverein* pledged its total sympathy to Germany in 1914. Although a few bishops, such as Cardinal James Gibbons of Baltimore, praised President Woodrow Wilson for not intervening in the conflict in Europe, the majority of American Catholics opposed the foreign policy of the government, which favored the Allies, and, as it seems, the majority voted in the presidential election of 1916 for the Republican candidate. Some of the leading Catholics, however, admonished their coreligionists not to tread upon the sensitivities of other Americans by participating in German-American efforts for union or entering into partisan politics. But as soon as the United States had entered the war, a wave of patriotism drowned all pro-German inclinations.

After the war American Catholics generally opposed Wilson's peace policy, partly because he refused to work for the independence of Ireland. They brought forward many reasons against the anticipated entry of the United States into the League of Nations and, together with the majority of their fellow citizens, took refuge in isolationism. However, a few leaders, such as Father John A. Ryan, Judge

Martin T. Manton, and Professor Carlton J. H. Hayes founded in 1927 the Catholic Association for International Peace for the instruction "of all men of good will on their obligation" to bring about world peace by justice and charity. The association championed many measures which were later realized, as, for example, for technical support and foreign aid. From Wilson's first administration to Roosevelt's second, American Catholics urged the government incessantly but vainly to intervene in Mexico in favor of the persecuted Catholics.

Even before World War II the American bishops at the request of the German hierarchy had supported all who had to flee from persecution by the Nazis by means of the Catholic Committee for Refugees and Refugee Children, founded by them. In 1940 they founded the Bishops' War Emergency and Relief Committee and took up a special collection in all churches for its support. The next year began the annual collections on *Laetare* Sunday for support of victims of war among the people of fifteen nations and among those who had sought refuge in various places in Europe and the Middle East. In 1942 the bishops established the War Relief Services, and in the next year this obtained the certificate for admission to the National War Fund, from which they obtained financial support until 1947. Meanwhile, the bishops continued the *Laetare* Sunday collections to obtain money for purely religious tasks, to which belonged special applications for aid from the Holy See and from numerous bishops and Catholic organizations abroad. In 1947 they expanded their annual appeal for donations in order to support the comprehensive program for help overseas, for rehabilitation, and for resettlement, which the War Relief Services had carried out. Even before the ending of hostilities the War Relief Services began their operations in the countries freed from the Axis Powers in Europe, Africa, and Asia. Shortly after the war's end there began also comprehensive aid programs in the hitherto hostile countries: Germany, Austria, Hungary, and Japan. But the assistance actions which were under way in Poland, Hungary, Czechoslovakia, Rumania, and Yugoslavia were forbidden by the Communist governments of these countries. Although the War Relief Services originally were to be only an institution for a limited time, it was later understood that they were permanently needed; and so in 1955 their name was changed to Catholic Relief Services of the NCWC. Because of their connections with local agencies and their expanding network of aid programs, the Catholic Relief Services were in the position of making full use of the surplus food which the American government in the 1950s destined for overseas assistance. In addition, they distributed clothing which Catholics had donated in the yearly collection at Thanksgiving. At the end of 1963 the Catholic Relief Services had shipped overseas food, clothing, medicines, and other means of help with a total weight of 5.6 million tons and a total value of $1.25 billion and had distributed these to needy persons and institutions. They helped more than 400,000 refugees settle in the United States or in other havens. They extended their field of activity to more than seventy countries, especially to the newly arising nations of Africa and the underdeveloped countries of Latin America, in which connection they promoted with greater emphasis than before technical aid, such as projects of self-help, which was intended to end social injustices, economic situations of dearth, sickness, and ignorance. In this way from the Catholic Relief Services came the greatest voluntary private organization for providing aid of the United States overseas.

American Catholics displayed their feeling of responsibility for other countries also by encouraging the foreign missions with personnel and money. Before World War I only a few Americans had gone abroad to proclaim the message of faith. Although the first religious congregation which was established in the United States for this purpose, namely, the Catholic Foreign Mission Society of America, usually called Maryknoll Missioners, had been approved by the American bishops and allowed, as an experiment, by Pius X as early as 1911, the first group of missioners with South China as goal, did not leave until 1918. In the postwar years many other religious institutes, especially the Society of Jesus, also sent men and women to the foreign missions. In 1958 Cardinal Richard Cushing, archbishop of Boston, founded the Missionary Society of Saint James the Apostle for the restoring and preserving of the faith in Latin America; it was to consist of diocesan priests, who voluntarily obliged themselves for five years, and they were to develop among the poor a life in the parish community. Within five years there were ninety-three members from nineteen different dioceses in English-speaking countries. Earlier, in 1950, the Grail, an international lay movement of Catholic women, had begun a regular course of training for the missionary apostolate of the laity. A lay organization for men and women was approved under the title of Papal Volunteers for Latin America. Within three years 245 papal volunteers served without pay, usually for a period of three years, in twelve countries; they were invited by the local bishops and were active predominantly in the area of education, medicine, and social work.

In 1966 9,303 American priests, brothers, sisters, and men and women from the lay state worked in many countries of America, Asia, and Latin America. American Catholics supplied donations to the missionary institutes and the papal work for the propagation of the faith.

Lay Movements. In the decades following World War I laymen began to display a greater activity in the Church. The National Council of Catholic Men and the National Council of Catholic Women were established under the National Catholic Welfare Conference in 1920 as a merger of parochial, supraparochial, diocesan, individual state, and national organizations. Both parent organizations created a broadly conceived program for spirituality, information, civic and social action, family life, youth, and international affairs. They provided aid to the affiliated organizations in the planning and implementation of local programs. Of course, in most places they operated by means of diocesan societies of Catholic men and women. The national associations represented the Catholic laity in other national and international organizations and at meetings of both a religious and a secular sort, and also in committees of Congress. To the men's council was given the responsibility for all Catholic radio and television programs, which were regularly broadcast on the national networks. The best known program was the "Catholic Hour," which was broadcast from 1930 by the National Broadcasting Company. In 1971 the two associations united as the National Council of Catholic Laity.

Two specialized lay movements acquired national importance. The Cana Conference began as a series of retreats conducted in Saint Louis in 1944. Such meetings, which were more unstructured and relaxed than spiritual exercises in the strict sense, were intended to apply religious principles to the secular aspects of married life in a manner which was sensible to twentieth-century Americans. These meetings instilled community sense and led to the forming of Cana Clubs for regular study and prayer in the homes of participants together with a chaplain. A further result was participation in the social apostolate to a greater extent. In most dioceses directors of family life were appointed, and thousands of priests and lay persons were gained for the implementing and spreading of this movement. In addition, numerous Pre-Cana Conferences for engaged couples spread, and for widowed persons Naim Conferences, also called Post-Cana Clubs, were formed. The Bethany Conference was a further extension for single persons.

A similar function was performed by the Christian Family Movement, which had begun in Chicago as a Catholic Action group for men and in 1947 was transformed into an organization for married couples. The basic units consisted of from five to six couples, usually from the same parish, who met in their homes and carried out a program for discussions and actions in the area of the lay apostolate. These units rapidly increased; by 1963 more than 40,000 couples actively took part in the group meetings that occurred every two weeks in the United States and Canada; in other countries there was probably an equally large number. In 1949 a national coordinating committee with headquarters in Chicago was set up to exchange ideas and reports of experiences with the help of some publications and annual programs. The members of every group were to examine from time to time a special aspect of family, cultural, political, economic, or international life, come to a judgment on whether it was entirely humane and Christian, and then decide possible actions, which were to be undertaken by the couples, either individually or collectively. Most participants, however, were chiefly interested in family problems, as, for example, the rapidly increasing national divorce rate.

Other organizations of Catholic Action which had begun in the United States after World War II were the Young Christian Workers and the Young Christian Students, which had been founded on the European model. In the same period the Exercises Movement led to a deepening of the spiritual life of the laity in the midst of secular professional activity. Catholic professional societies likewise prospered.

Journalism. After World War I the Catholic press underwent a noteworthy development. The ownership of most newspapers was transferred by lay persons to the dioceses. But even then, when a diocesan weekly newspaper was designated as "official organ" or "the voice" of the local authorities, a distinction was made between authoritative views of the Church and the opinions of the publisher. There now also appeared Catholic newspaper chains. In 1929 the newspaper *Catholic Register,* which had begun five years earlier with the publication of a national edition, published at Denver its first edition for another diocese, and within nine years this system increased to nineteen editions, with a circulation of 400,000; in 1964 it had thirty-three editions with a total circulation of 778,196. The paper *Our Sunday Visitor,* which had been founded in 1912, chiefly for apologetic purposes as a reaction to anti-Catholic and pro-Socialist newspapers, began in 1937 the publication of an edition for another diocese; in 1964 it produced eleven diocesan editions, a Canadian national edition, and a national news edition, with a total circulation of 892,148. Other chains of smaller size were formed in Ohio and Wisconsin.

The first larger Catholic daily newspaper in English in the United States was the *Tribune,* founded in 1920 at Dubuque, Iowa, and two years later moved to Milwaukee, Wisconsin. It was strongly apologetic in tone. A lay group in 1964 began the *National Catholic Reporter.* This weekly became very familiar among liberal Catholics, because it gave religious news without restrictions and critically interpreted it; it even incurred censure from the bishop of Kansas City, but this was ineffective.

In order to supply Catholic newspapers with news on national and international affairs the NCWC News Service was established in 1920; it took over the work of a smaller agency which had previously been operated by the Catholic Press Association of the United States and Canada. It erected an overseas service, hired correspondents in almost every part of the world, obtained subscriptions in sixty-five countries, and finally supplied services for leading articles, pictures, radio, and eventually also for television and some other services. The Catholic Press Association, founded in 1911, also held annual meetings, published a monthly and a historical "annual," and promoted the increase of circulation and the advertising business; it likewise especially supported the Catholic press in Latin America and the mission press in general.

Catholic newspapers in foreign languages appeared and again disappeared during this period. In 1964 there were altogether thirteen foreign-language papers with a total circulation of 195,434.

Among Catholic magazines those prospered which were concerned with the home and foreign missions. The first magazine which promoted the foreign missions exclusively was published by the Maryknoll Missioners, first under the title *Field Afar* and later *Maryknoll.* In the 1960s it increased its circulation to more than 300,000.

Magazines which had been founded before World War I continued to exist side by side. The organ of the Third Order of Saint Francis, *St. Anthony Messenger,* had begun in 1893 and became a popular family magazine, which in 1960 had a circulation of 330,000. The oldest Catholic newspapers which appeared at this time were the *Catholic World* of the Paulists, in which the effort was made to bring the faith into relation with American society, and *Ave Maria* of the Congregation of the Holy Cross, which aspired to form family life in a Christian way. The two most important opinion-forming weeklies were *America,* begun in 1909 and published by Jesuits, and *Commonweal,* begun in 1924 and published by lay persons, both of which sought to treat contemporary problems and cultural themes from a Catholic standpoint. The total circulation of the Catholic press in the United States in 1969 amounted to 25,599,766.

By 1964 journalism was offered as an academic course in one form or another in about half the Catholic universities and colleges in the United States. The only College of Journalism was founded in 1915 at Marquette University in Milwaukee, but graduate study in the mass media was later likewise instituted in other Catholic institutions. In recent years ever more courses in radio and television were offered. In the academic programs both technical courses in theory and practice of the various communications media were contained, as well as theoretical courses on their role in society and their professional ethics.

Statistics prove that the connection of Catholics with their Church dropped considerably before 1968, when Pope Paul VI issued the encyclical *Humanae Vitae.* A famous sociologist of religion refers the decline of traditional forms of church practice, for example, attendance at Sunday Mass, to the strong repudiation on the part of many of the faithful to the teaching contained in this papal document on birth control. Other analysts are of the view that rather a whole complex of various factors played a role: the growing secularism, an exaggerated personalism, thorough permissiveness, libertinism, and antinomianism, an anti-"Establishment" attitude and religious indifferentism, as has been characteristic of the manner of thought in the United States and in many other countries of the free world since the beginning of the 1960s. The loss of respect for Pope and bishops is due in part to the fact that certain theologians publicly and at times loudly held themselves aloof from declarations of the *magisterium.* The most important Protestant Churches in the United States experienced a similar downward trend; only the smaller fundamentalist and Pentecostal sects, which appealed to special revelations or made lofty demands on their adherents, have grown disproportionately. Although the teachings and reforms of the Second Vatican Council were generally greeted by American Catholics, the hope and expectation of a new flowering of the Church in the United States have not been realized in the postconciliar period.

Canada

Population. Between 1911 and 1961 Canada's total population rose from 7,206,643 to 18,238,247 inhabitants. In this period the number of Catholics increased from 2,841,881 — 39.4 percent — to 8,342,826 — 45.7 percent. However, Catholics were not uniformly distributed: 56 percent lived in the province of Quebec.

Organization. In 1914 there were ten archdioceses, twenty-five dioceses, five vicariates apostolic, one Ruthenian bishop, and one prefecture apostolic. Fifty years later there were fifteen archdioceses of the Latin Rite — fourteen provinces plus Winnipeg — one province of the Ukrainian Byzantine Rite, forty dioceses, one abbey *nullius,* three eparchies, and eight vicariates apostolic.

Educational System. In each province the Catholic elementary and secondary schools stood in one or another relationship to the secular authorities. In the province of Quebec the schools were regarded as public institutions and were supported by general taxes, but supervised by Catholic and Protestant committees of the Council of Public Instruction. Hence the two systems developed pretty much in independence of each other: The Catholic system followed the French tradition in education, and the Protestant followed the English. Private or independent schools played a more important role in Quebec than in other provinces. The most important were the classical colleges; they offered an eight-year course which one entered upon completing elementary school and which led in two stages of four years each to the bachelor's degree.

Newfoundland also had a system of provincial denominational schools. Here the five large denominations operated their own schools under the supervision of a school superintendent, who was responsible to the deputy minister of education of the province. All schools followed the same curriculum.

In Ontario, Saskatchewan, and Alberta the first school which was erected with the support of taxes in one community had always to be a provincial school, open to all children. But the school law allowed Catholic or Protestant minorities to withdraw from the provincial school system and establish their own school-sponsoring bodies and schools, which were termed "separate" schools. The local inhabitants could choose which system they wanted to support with their taxes, and usually they made their choice according to their religion. Both the provincial and the separate schools were subject to the jurisdiction of the provincial Department of Education and both obtained provincial aid. In Saskatchewan and Alberta separate Catholic schools could be erected only in the large cities where Catholics were represented in sufficient number. In Ontario separate schools could offer only the eight elementary and two lower secondary grades; hence Catholics had to erect private schools for the three higher secondary grades.

The provinces on the Atlantic coast — New Brunswick, Nova Scotia, and Prince Edward Island — and Manitoba in accord with the law maintained only provincial schools, but on the basis of a "Gentlemen's Agreement" there were, within the provincial school system in areas where there were many English and French Catholics, also English-language and French-language Catholic schools. Outside the French-language areas of Manitoba, for example, Saint Boniface, the Catholics had also to finance at their own expense their private or parochial schools, in addition to the taxes which they had to pay for the support of the provincial schools.

British Columbia likewise provided only a provincial system, and such schools could under no circumstances be denominational; hence Catholics were forced to support their own schools in addition to the provincial schools. In the Yukon and Northwest, thanks to the collaboration of dominion and local authorities with the denominational bodies, systems had been developed in which Catholic elementary schools for the sparse population of Indians, Eskimos, and whites obtained full support through taxes from the government and the local authorities.

In western Canada there were no independent Catholic colleges or universities, because the legislators refused to grant to each province more than one academic degree-granting institution. But the Basilians and Jesuits founded colleges, which were united with the provincial universities in various ways or were affiliated to them. Thus, in the sphere of higher education these two orders experimented with new forms of merger with non-Catholic universities for the sake of the academic and economic advantages which they sought thereby.

Social Movement.   Various sources gave the theoretical impulse for the Canadian Catholic social movement. In addition to the papal encyclicals, the pastoral letters of the bishops also treated social questions, in which connection they passed from the problems predominantly connected with agriculture and rural life at the beginning of the twentieth century to problems of industrialization and the working class in the later decades. In 1950 the archbishops and bishops of the civil province of Quebec issued a common pastoral letter entitled "The Workers' Problem in the Light of the Church's Social Doctrine," in which they took a bold stand on some points, as, for example, in regard to the codetermination of the worker in the direction of an industry. Two private institutions provided further theoretical fuel: the École Sociale Populaire, founded in 1911, promoted social studies, issued publications, and from 1920 supported the annual *Semaines Sociales du Canada,* which brought together leading personalities of social doctrine and of social action in order to consult together on common concerns. And the École des Sciences Sociales of Laval University, founded in 1932, made noteworthy contributions.

The workers' union (local syndicates), organized on a formally Catholic basis by priests and laymen in various parts of the province of Quebec, merged in 1921 with the *Confédération des Travailleurs Catholiques du Canada.* At first non-Catholics could be members but not hold office. This restriction was gradually ended. Likewise, every union had a chaplain, a Catholic priest, who at first was authorized to inform the bishops of every decision which, in his opinion, was contrary to Catholic social doctrine; in practice, the chaplains rarely exercised this right and finally became merely moral advisers, who attended all meetings and could present their views but had no vote. In its original constitution the *confédération* expressly declared its loyalty to the social doctrine of the Catholic Church, but in 1960 the denominational ties were broken; the expression "Christian principles" was put in their place, and the name was changed to *Confédération des Syndi-cats Nationaux.* From the late 1930s the Catholic syndicates had about one-third of all members of unions of the province of Quebec in their ranks; the others belonged mainly to international (American) unions. However, the *confédération* exercised on the worker movement as a whole and on worker legislation an influence which was in no proportion to its size and presumably was based on its social and ideological concerns.

An expressly Catholic movement was also started for workers in agriculture. In 1924 2,400 farmers meeting in Quebec City founded the *Union Catholique des Cultivateurs.* This organization defended and fostered the general interests of the rural population, especially in regard to the educational system. In the 1950s it also established rural syndicates in order to deal collectively with the buyers of farm products. In 1965 there were almost 700 local syndicates with more than 50,000 members as opposed to a possible membership of 65,000 to 70,000. As in the workers' syndicates, the role of the chaplain developed from that of a participant exercising power to that of a moral adviser or attorney, but the word "Catholic" was not removed from the organization's name.

For Catholic manufacturers and employers there was no permanent organization until the *Association Professionnelle des Industriels* was founded in 1943. It was intended to protect the interests of management and promote a Christian social order. Despite its limitation it played a leading role and, it is true, by cooperation with other groups, in which regard it directed the attention of management to the working class and to the human problems in business life. It was also an active member of the *Union Internationale Chrétienne des Dirigeants d'Entreprise.*